GEOGRAPHICAL INFORMATION SYSTEMS

VOLUME 1 : PRINCIPLES

GEOGRAPHICAL INFORMATION SYSTEMS

PRINCIPLES AND APPLICATIONS

EDITED BY

DAVID J MAGUIRE,
MICHAEL F GOODCHILD
AND
DAVID W RHIND

Copublished in the United States and Canada with
John Wiley & Sons, Inc., New York

Longman Scientific and Technical,
Longman Group UK Ltd
Longman House, Burnt Mill, Harlow,
Essex CM20 2JE, England
and Associated Companies throughout the world.

copublished in the United States and Canada with
John Wiley & Sons, Inc., 605 Third Avenue, New York,
NY 10158

© Longman Group UK Limited 1991

All rights reserved; no part of this publication may be reproduced, stored in a retrieval system, or transmitted in any form or by any means, electronic, mechanical, photocopying, recording, or otherwise without either the prior written permission of the Publishers or a licence permitting restricted copying in the United Kingdom issued by the Copyright Licensing Agency Ltd, 90 Tottenham Court Road, London W1P 9HE.

Trademarks
Throughout this book trademarked names are used. Rather than put a trademark symbol in every occurrence of a trademarked name, we state that we are using the names only in an editorial fashion and to the benefit of the trademark owner with no intention of infringement of the trademark.

First published 1991
Reprinted 1992
Reprinted 1993

British Library Cataloguing in Publication Data
Maguire, David J.
 Geographical information systems: Principles and applications
 I. Title II. Goodchild, Michael F.
 III. Rhind, David W.
 910.901

 ISBN 0-582-05661-6

Library of Congress Cataloging-in-Publication Data
Maguire, D. J. (David J.)
 Geographical information systems / by D. J. Maguire, Michael F. Goodchild, and David W. Rhind.
  p. cm.
 Includes bibliographical references and index.
 Contents: v. 1. Principles – v. 2. Applications.
 ISBN 0-470-21789-8 (USA only)
 1. Geographical information systems.
 I. Goodchild, Michael F. II. Rhind,
 David. III. Title.
 G70.2.M354 1991
 910'.285–dc20   91-3724
                                  CIP

Set in Great Britain by Fakenham Photosetting Limited.

Printed and Bound in Great Britain at the Bath Press, Avon

Dedicated to the memory of

DAVID S SIMONETT

1926–90

David Simonett was born in Australia in 1926. After earning a Doctorate at the University of Sydney, he became a leading pioneer in the field of Remote Sensing, holding faculty positions at the University of Kansas, the University of Sydney and the University of California, Santa Barbara. He was director of land use applications at Earth Satellite Corp from 1972 to 1975.

As Chair at Santa Barbara from 1975, he was able to build one of the foremost Geography programs in the US, culminating in 1988 with the establishment of the National Center for Geographic Information and Analysis. The Santa Barbara site of the Center was renamed the David Simonett Center for Spatial Analysis in 1990 in recognition of his role in its creation. He received the Honours Award from the Association of American Geographers and the Victoria Medal from the Royal Geographical Society.

David Simonett lost a courageous fight against cancer on December 22, 1990 in the course of the preparation of his contribution to this book. The editors dedicate this book to his memory and to the outstanding role he has played in the development of the field of Geographical Information Systems.

VOLUME 1 : PRINCIPLES

Preface   *xiii*
List of contributors   *xvii*
Acknowledgements   *xxvii*

Section I Overview

Introduction   3–7
D J Maguire, M F Goodchild and D W Rhind

1. An overview and definition of GIS   9–20
   D J Maguire

2. The history of GIS   21–43
   J T Coppock and D W Rhind

3. The technological setting of GIS   45–54
   M F Goodchild

4. The commercial setting of GIS   55–65
   J Dangermond

5. The government setting of GIS in the United Kingdom   67–79
   R Chorley and R Buxton

6. The academic setting of GIS   81–90
   D J Unwin

7. The organizational home for GIS in the scientific professional community   91–100
   J L Morrison

8. A critique of GIS   101–7
   R T Aangeenbrug

Section II Principles

Introduction   111–17
M F Goodchild, D W Rhind and D J Maguire

VOLUME 1 : PRINCIPLES

(a) Nature of spatial data

9. Concepts of space and geographical data — **119–34**
   A C Gatrell

10. Coordinate systems and map projections for GIS — **135–46**
    D H Maling

11. Language issues for GIS — **147–63**
    A U Frank and D M Mark

12. The error component in spatial data — **165–74**
    N R Chrisman

13. Spatial data sources and data problems — **175–89**
    P F Fisher

14. GIS and remote sensing — **191–213**
    F W Davis and D S Simonett

(b) Digital representation

15. Computer systems and low-level data structures for GIS — **215–25**
    Wm R Franklin

16. High-level spatial data structures for GIS — **227–37**
    M J Egenhofer and J R Herring

17. GIS data capture hardware and software — **239–49**
    M J Jackson and P A Woodsford

VOLUME 1 : PRINCIPLES

18. Database management systems *R G Healey*	**251–67**
19. Digital terrain modelling *R Weibel and M Heller*	**269–97**
20. Three-dimensional GIS *J F Raper and B Kelk*	**299–317**

(c) Functional issues

21. The functionality of GIS *D J Maguire and J Dangermond*	**319–35**
22. Information integration and GIS *I D H Shepherd*	**337–60**
23. Cartographic modelling *C D Tomlin*	**361–74**
24. Spatial data integration *R Flowerdew*	**375–87**
25. Developing appropriate spatial analysis methods for GIS *S Openshaw*	**389–402**
26. Spatial decision support systems *P J Densham*	**403–12**
27. Knowledge-based approaches in GIS *T R Smith and Ye Jiang*	**413–25**

VOLUME 1 : PRINCIPLES

(d) Display issues

28. Visualization **427–43**
    B P Buttenfield and W A Mackaness

29. Computer name placement **445–56**
    H Freeman

30. Generalization of spatial databases **457–75**
    J-C Muller

(e) Operational issues

31. GIS specification, evaluation and implementation **477–88**
    A L Clarke

32. Legal aspects of GIS **489–502**
    E F Epstein

33. Managing an operational GIS: the UK National On-Line Manpower Information System (NOMIS) **503–13**
    M J Blakemore

34. Spatial data exchange and standardization **515–30**
    S C Guptill

Consolidated bibliography *531–591*
List of acronyms *593–598*
Author index *599–613*
Subject index *615–649*

VOLUME 2 : APPLICATIONS

Preface	*xiii*
List of contributors	*xvii*
Acknowledgements	*xxvii*

Section III Applications

Introduction D W Rhind, D J Maguire and M F Goodchild	**3–10**

(a) National and international GIS programmes

35. A USGS perspective on GIS *L E Starr and K E Anderson*	**11–22**
36. Development of GIS-related activities at the Ordnance Survey *M Sowton*	**23–38**
37. National GIS programmes in Sweden *L Ottoson and B Rystedt*	**39–46**
38. The development of GIS in Japan *S Kubo*	**47–56**
39. Land and Geographical Information Systems in Australia *J F O'Callaghan and B J Garner*	**57–70**
40. GIS and developing nations *D R F Taylor*	**71–84**

(b) Socio-economic applications

41. Land information systems *P F Dale*	**85–99**
42. GIS and utilities *R P Mahoney*	**101–14**
43. Car navigation systems *M White*	**115–25**
44. Counting the people: the role of GIS *D W Rhind*	**127–37**
45. GIS and market analysis *J R Beaumont*	**139–51**

VOLUME 2 : APPLICATIONS

(c) Environmental applications

46. Soil information systems 153–69
    P A Burrough

47. Integration of geoscientific data using GIS 171–84
    G F Bonham-Carter

48. Multisource, multinational environmental GIS: lessons learnt from CORINE 185–200
    H M Mounsey.

49. Environmental databases and GIS 201–16
    J R G Townshend

50. Global databases and their implications for GIS 217–31
    D M Clark, D A Hastings and J J Kineman

(d) Management applications

51. GIS and public policy 233–45
    H W Calkins

52. Urban GIS applications 247–60
    R Parrott and F P Stutz

53. Land resource information systems 261–73
    K C Siderelis

54. Land management applications of GIS in the state of Minnesota 275–83
    A Robinette

55. GIS in island resource planning: a case study in map analysis 285–95
    J K Berry

56. Integrated planning information systems 297–310
    D J Cowen and W L Shirley

Section IV Epilogue

Epilogue 313–27
D W Rhind, M F Goodchild and D J Maguire

Consolidated bibliography *329–389*
List of acronyms *391–396*
Author index *397–411*
Subject index *413–447*

PREFACE

The idea for a book on Geographical Information Systems (GIS) came shortly after the Portland Association of American Geographers conference in 1987. It was clear from the papers presented in Portland and at similar meetings in 1986 and 1987 that GIS, although still a rapidly developing field, had reached a level of maturity sufficient to make production of a large reference compendium a feasible task. In 1988, the editors were appointed and in late 1988 they began to recruit authors. Manuscripts were delivered, edited and revised in early 1990. Final editing took place in late spring and summer 1990 and *Geographical Information Systems: principles and applications* was finished at the end of 1990.

At the outset, the aim of the book was to assemble a team of international experts to write a major reference work on GIS. The book was designed to be a benchmark volume, that could be used as a reference against which trends in the field might be assessed. Indeed, it was suggested that the book should carry a 'health warning' to the effect that, after the early 1990s, it should only be read in conjunction with the proceedings of the latest AUTOCARTO, GIS/LIS or International Spatial Data Handling Symposium conferences; one would thus provide the general context and long term view, the other to contribute specific details of current developments. The authors were selected primarily because of their expertise, but the editors were also keen to choose a set of authors who reflected the geographical distribution of work effort and the sometimes disparate views of GIS. The North America/UK bias is an inevitable manifestation of these processes. This is not however in any way intended to decry the important work in Australasia, continental Europe and many other places.

Bearing in mind that the book was to be a reference volume, authors were asked to write around 5000 words (excluding references) on the fundamental enduring principles of their topic, rather than current trends which may lack substance and longevity. The variations in the length of the resulting chapters in part represent authors' views of their subject's perceived size and importance. Authors were asked to pitch their chapters at a level suitable for advanced undergraduates, postgraduates, professionals and research workers. Thus, each of the contributions is a mixture of overview, review and purview, with both a pedagogic and a research element.

The choice of topics was a difficult one. It proved impossible, even in 56 chapters, to cover the field of GIS comprehensively. The initial list of topics was refined several times by the editors and additional chapters were commissioned following initial editing, in an attempt to cover the main areas adequately. Inevitably however, the final list still has its limitations, reflecting the restrictions imposed by space, time and the differential development of GIS. Ideally, the geographical coverage might have been extended to include more on Africa, South America and planets other than Earth. The book only briefly touches on temporal GIS, the atmosphere and oceans. In Section III, **Applications**, it would also have been interesting to have more on economic and organizational issues, particularly some examples of where GIS has failed or been uneconomic. Nevertheless, the editors believe that the selection captures the main thrust of the spirit and purpose of GIS in the early 1990s.

The organization of the book has purposely been kept simple. Even so, in one or two cases the chapters contain material relevant to more than one section or subsection. Subjects such as data capture, error, the raster-vector dichotomy, generalization and visualization which pervade many aspects of GIS are discussed in a large number of chapters from a variety of perspectives and the authors present interesting comparisons of their role and importance.

The book has four main sections offering an **Overview** of GIS and covering the fundamental **Principles** and key **Applications**. In a final brief section the editors provide an **Epilogue** to the main work. Each of the four sections begins with an introduction by the editors which discusses the context of the work and shows how the chapters link together. In these introductions, the editors have also attempted to offer some critical remarks about the material and GIS in general. The material is split into two volumes. The first includes the preliminary material and the **Overview** and **Principles** sections; the second includes the **Applications** and **Epilogue** sections. Both volumes contain an author and subject index, a list of acronyms used and a consolidated bibliography.

Section I, **Overview**, contains eight chapters which provide the context of GIS. The section begins with discussion of the definition of GIS: other chapters discuss the main intellectual, technical and organizational forces which have had, and which continue to have, a profound impact on the development of GIS.

Section II, **Principles**, has five subsections: Nature of spatial data; Digital representation; Functional issues; Display issues; and Operational issues. The six chapters dealing with the nature of spatial data examine the characteristics, sources and problems of using and interacting with data. The six digital representation chapters deal with the way geographical data are captured, stored and structured. The seven chapters on functional issues show how data can be integrated, manipulated and analysed using GIS. The penultimate subsection contains three chapters that examine issues involved in the display of data. The final subsection, on operational issues, has four chapters that look at the economic, legal and managerial implications of using GIS. This is a crucially important yet often undervalued aspect of GIS. Together the chapters in this section constitute a major synthesis of important past and recent work on the principles of GIS.

Section III, **Applications**, has four subsections: National and international GIS programmes; Socio-economic applications; Environmental applications; and Management applications. The six chapters covering national and international programmes overview the current state of GIS development at national, continental and world scales. In the remaining three subsections of Section III, selected GIS applications are organized thematically. This list is clearly not comprehensive and never could be given the diversity of interests of GIS users. The application areas were chosen to represent the main broad application areas of GIS in the early 1990s. These applications are a mixture of general overviews of application areas and specific examples which highlight the everyday aspects of using GIS. Hopefully, readers will be able to generalize about the main advantages and disadvantages of the GIS approach from this material.

Section IV, **Epilogue** which concludes the volume has been written by the editors. It is an essay which examines the internal state of GIS and its wider context. Some predictions for the future are also presented in this final chapter.

This book has been written with a wide variety of users in mind. The list of people interested in GIS includes professionals in the commercial sector, government workers, specific application-oriented end-users, academics and students. Each of these groups has different interests and will find different parts of the book more relevant than others. It is tempting to try and summarize which areas of the book are relevant for each group. All the editors' experience shows, however, that in fact the differences between these groups is not as great as might at first be imagined. Successful professional organizations often prefer to hire people with a general education rather than specific training, academics are forced to try and make money by acting as system developers and consultants, and many users and students are not as narrow minded, naive and misguided as many imagine. Awareness, in its many forms, is relevant to us all.

A compendium such as this is to some extent the result of a democratic process, each author contributing an individual viewpoint and piece of a much larger puzzle. At the same time, the editors have been conscious of the need to provide a focus and direction, and to ensure that the whole is greater than the sum of the individual parts. The editors' invisible and visible hand has been used throughout to maintain consistency, avoid overlap and develop a coherent view. *Geographical Information Systems: principles and applications* is a statement about GIS in the early 1990s. The editors are responsible for the overall message, but we thank all the individual authors for providing the substance of what we wanted to say.

Many people have contributed a great deal of time, effort and forbearance to the production of this book. The editors would especially like to record their gratitude to the following key individuals. The diagrams were expertly and imaginatively drawn by Mrs Kate Moore of the Department of Geography at the University of Leicester. The author and subject indexes and list of acronyms were compiled by Mr Craig Wood of the Computers in Teaching Initiative Centre for Geography at the University of Leicester. Ms Vanessa Lawrence of Longman Scientific and Technical was responsible for commissioning the book and has been with the project over the 4 years from conception to delivery. She deserves great credit for her vision, persistence and considerable ability in coping with the editors. Finally, we thank our wives Heather, Fiona and Christine who sacrificed a lot, though they did discover the Green Parrot.

David J Maguire
Michael F Goodchild
David W Rhind

January 1991

LIST OF CONTRIBUTORS

THE EDITORS

David J Maguire
Formerly Lecturer in GIS, University of Leicester. Currently Technical Director, ESRI UK. Research interests include data integration, areal interpolation, database design and GIS education.

ESRI (UK)
Doric House
23 Woodford Road
Watford
WD1 1PB
UK

Michael F Goodchild
Professor of Geography at the University of California Santa Barbara and Co-Director of the National Center for Geographic Information and Analysis. Current research interests include the generic issues of GIS such as accuracy, spatial decision support systems and data structures for global GIS.

Department of Geography
University of California
Santa Barbara
California
93106
USA

David W Rhind
Formerly Professor of Geography, Birkbeck College, London. Currently Director General and Chief Executive of the Ordnance Survey of Great Britain. Author of over 100 papers on GIS and related topics. Current research interests include the generalization of spatial databases, environmental information systems, multimedia GIS and data charging and access issues.

Ordnance Survey
Romsey Road
Maybush
Southampton
SO9 4DH
UK

THE AUTHORS

Robert T Aangeenbrug
Professor of Geography and Chair at the University of South Florida, Tampa. Director of the Center for Spatial and Environmental Analysis. Research interests include urban and natural resource systems modelling and GIS education.

Department of Geography
University of South Florida
Tampa
Florida
33620–8100
USA

K Eric Anderson
Head of Eastern Mapping Division of the US National Mapping Agency, the US Geological Survey National Mapping Division, and Chairman of the International Cartographic Association's Commission on Advanced Technology.

Head of Eastern Mapping Division.
United States Geological Survey
Reston
Virginia
22092
USA

John R Beaumont
Professor in Management and Head of the School of Management at the University of Bath. Member

xvii

List of Contributors

of the Council of the Economic and Social Research Council and Chairman of their Research and Resources Advisory Group and Regional Research Laboratories Steering Committee.

School of Management
University of Bath
Claverton Down
Bath
BA2 7AY
UK

Joseph K Berry
Associate Professor in the Department of Forest and Wood Sciences, Colorado State University, and Principal in Berry and Associates, Consultants in GIS Technology. Board member, Spatial Information Systems Corporation. Interested in applications fully incorporating map analysis techniques into the decision-making process.

Department of Forestry & Wood Sciences
Colorado State University
Fort Collins
Colorado
80524
USA

Michael J Blakemore
Executive Director of NOMIS at the University of Durham. Research interests in data quality and the development of integrated access to national and international geographical information.

NOMIS
Unit 3P
Mountjoy Research Centre
University of Durham
DH1 3SW
UK

Graeme F Bonham-Carter
Research Scientist, Geological Survey of Canada and Adjunct Professor of Geology, University of Ottawa. Current research interests in the applications of GIS for modelling in geology.

Mineral Resources Division
Geological Survey of Canada
601 Booth Street
Ottawa
Ontario
K1A OE8
Canada

Peter A Burrough
Professor of Physical Geography and Geographical Information Systems at the University of Utrecht, the Netherlands. Chairman of the Netherlands Centre for Geographical Information Processing and the Steering Committee of EGIS (European GIS Congress Organization). Research interests include the development and application of GIS technology for environmental modelling with special attention to the use of non-exact techniques such as geostatistics and error propagation, fuzzy reasoning and fractals in groundwater and surface water models, soil, water and air pollution and land evaluation.

Department of Physical Geography
Faculty of Geographical Sciences
University of Utrecht
Heidelberglaan 2
PO Box 80115
Utrecht
The Netherlands

Barbara P Buttenfield
Assistant Professor in the Department of Geography, State University of New York at Buffalo. Researcher and member of the Scientific Policy Committee of the National Center for Geographic Information and Analysis. Research interests include map generalization and scale dependent geometry, and the use and design of GIS graphics for analysis and illustration.

NCGIA-Buffalo
301 Wilkeson Quad
State University of New York at Buffalo
Buffalo
New York
14261
USA

Richard Buxton
Principal Associate in the Government Services Division of Coopers & Lybrand Deloitte and manager of the government sector GIS consultancy practice. Special interests include GIS strategy in central and local government and the cost/benefit analysis of GIS investment in the public sector.

Coopers and Lybrand Deloitte
Plumtree Court
London
EC4A 4HT
UK

Hugh W Calkins

Associate Professor of Geography, State University of New York at Buffalo. Research Scientist at the National Center for Geographic Information and Analysis. Active in development and use of GIS for town planning and local government since the mid 1960s.

NCGIA-Buffalo
301 Wilkeson Quad
State University of New York at Buffalo
Buffalo
New York
14261
USA

Roger Chorley

Chairman of the Committee of Enquiry into the Handling of Geographic Information and member of the House of Lords Select Committee on Science and Technology. Past President of the Royal Geographical Society and President of the Association for Geographic Information and the National Trust. Former Senior Partner and currently advisor, Coopers & Lybrand Deloitte.

The National Trust
36 Queen Anne's Gate
London
SW1H 9AS
UK

Nicholas R Chrisman

Associate Professor of Geography at the University of Washington, Seattle. Previously spent ten years at the Harvard Laboratory for Computer Graphics and Spatial Analysis and five years at the University of Wisconsin, Madison.

Department of Geography
University of Washington
406 Smith Hall
Seattle
Washington
98195
USA

David M Clark

Scientific Assistant to the Director of the National Geophysical Data Center, part of the National Oceanographic and Atmospheric Administration. Research interests include GIS applications for the study of the Earth system and global change, and integrated vector/raster GIS.

NGDC/NOAA
325 Broadway
Boulder
Colorado
80303
USA

Andrew L Clarke

Marketing Manager, Australian Surveying and Land Information Group, Canberra. Experience in surveys for the Australian and Antarctic mapping programmes, development of national digital spatial databases, and acquisition and management of GIS.

Australian Surveying and Land Information Group
PO Box 2
Belconnen
ACT 2616
Australia

J Terry Coppock

Emeritus Professor of Geography at the University of Edinburgh. Currently Editor of the *International Journal of Geographical Information Systems*.

Department of Geography
University of Edinburgh
Drummond Street
Edinburgh
EH8 9XP
UK

David J Cowen

Professor of Geography and Director of the Humanities and Social Sciences Computing Laboratory at the University of South Carolina. US delegate to the IGU Commission on GIS and member of the National Research Council Mapping Sciences Committee.

Department of Geography
University of South Carolina
Columbia
South Carolina
29208
USA

Peter F Dale

Professor of Land Surveying at East London Polytechnic. Member of the AGI council. Past President of the Royal Institution of Chartered Surveyors Land Surveyors' Division. Research interests in Land Information Systems especially in developing countries.

List of Contributors

Department of Land Surveying
Polytechnic of East London
Longbridge Road
Dagenham
Essex
RM8 2AS
UK

Jack Dangermond
President of ESRI Inc., Redlands California, the developers of ARC/INFO. Author of many papers on GIS and influential in its development.

ESRI Inc
380 New York Street
Redlands
California
92373
USA

Frank W Davis
Associate Professor in the Department of Geography, University of California Santa Barbara. Research interests include biogeography, plant ecology, ecological modelling using remote sensing and GIS.

Department of Geography
University of California
Santa Barbara
California
93106
USA

Paul J Densham
Assistant Professor of Geography, State University of New York at Buffalo, and Research Scientist in the NCGIA. Research interests include spatial decision support systems, locational analysis and parallel algorithms.

Department of Geography
114 Wilkeson Quad
State University of New York at Buffalo
Buffalo
New York
14261
USA

Max J Egenhofer
Research Assistant Professor at the National Center for Geographic Information and Analysis. Research interests include the design of database management systems for GIS, spatial query languages and spatial reasoning.

NCGIA
Department of Surveying Engineering
University of Maine
Orono
Maine
04473
USA

Earl F Epstein
Professor of Natural Resources, Ohio State University. Trained as a scientist (PhD Physical Chemistry) and in Law (JD). Interests include legal, economic and institutional development of GIS and LIS.

School of Natural Resources
Ohio State University
2021 Coffey Road
Columbus
Ohio
43210–1085
USA

Peter F Fisher
Lecturer in GIS at the Department of Geography, Leicester University. Research interests include many aspects of error in geographical data, especially soils and remotely sensed data, and geographical applications of artificial intelligence.

Department of Geography
University of Leicester
University Road
Leicester
LE1 7RH
UK

Robin Flowerdew
Lecturer in Geography at the University of Lancaster and North West Regional Research Laboratory. Interested in statistical applications in geography, especially population and urban geography.

Department of Geography
University of Lancaster
Bailrigg
Lancaster
LA1 4YB
UK

Andrew U Frank
New England ACSM Professor in Land Information Studies and Associate Director of the National Center for Geographic Information and Analysis at

the University of Maine. Research interests include database management systems, methods to represent geometrical properties in a database, software engineering and user interfaces for GIS.

NCGIA
119 Boardman Hall
University of Maine
Orono
Maine
04473
USA

Wm. Randolph Franklin
Associate Professor in the Electrical, Computer, and Systems Engineering Department, Rensselaer Polytechnic Institute, Troy. Research interests include algorithms and data structures for efficient processing of large geometric databases on parallel machines.

Electrical, Computer & Systems Engineering Department
Rensselaer Polytechnic Institute
Troy
New York
12180
USA

Herbert Freeman
State of New Jersey Professor of Computer Engineering, Rutgers University, and Director, CAIP Machine Vision Laboratory. Research interests include computer image processing, machine vision, pattern recognition, computer graphics and computerized cartography.

CAIP Center
Rutgers University
PO Box 1390
Piscataway
New Jersey
08855–1390
USA

Barry J Garner
Professor and Head of the School of Geography at the University of New South Wales. Chairman of the National Committee for Geography, Australian Academy of Science and member of the Australian Survey and Mapping Industries Council. Research interests include the application of GIS techniques in urban and regional analysis and GIS education.

School of Geography
University of New South Wales
PO Box 1
Kensington
NSW
2033
Australia

Anthony C Gatrell
Senior Lecturer in the Department of Geography, Lancaster University and Co-Director of the ESRC-funded North West Regional Research Laboratory. Interested in the applications of GIS techniques in environmental and geographical epidemiology.

North West Regional Research Laboratory
Department of Geography
Lancaster University
Lancaster
LA1 4YB
UK

Stephen C Guptill
Scientific Advisor for Geography and Spatial Data Systems, National Mapping Division, US Geological Survey. Research studies concentrate on conceptual modelling of geographical and cartographical features, scale-independent databases, spatial accuracy, and the design of advanced GIS.

USGS National Mapping Division
Office of Research
519 National Center
Reston
Virginia
22092
USA

David A Hastings
Chief, Data Integration and Remote Sensing, National Geophysical Data Center, NOAA, USA. Current research uses GIS for combining disparate data layers into optimally integrated regional and global databases.

NGDC/NOAA
325 Boulder
Colorado
80303
USA

Richard G Healey
Lecturer in Geography at the University of Edinburgh. Research interests in parallel processing and database applications of GIS.

List of Contributors

Department of Geography
University of Edinburgh
Drummond Street
Edinburgh
EH8 9XP
UK

Martin Heller
Researcher at the Department of Geography, University of Zurich. Lectures in GIS architecture, computational geometry and computer graphics. Current research focuses on object design for adaptive terrain modelling.

Department of Geography
University of Zurich
Winterthurerstrasse 190
CH 8057
Zurich
Switzerland

John R Herring
Senior Systems Consultant in the GIS, Mapping and Energy Division of Intergraph Corporation. Responsible for supporting product development in GIS, mapping and related fields. Played a major role in Intergraphs's TIGRIS research project.

Intergraph Corporation
Mail Stop IW17A2
One Madison Industrial Park
Huntsville
Alabama
35807–2174
USA

Michael J Jackson
Managing Director of Laser-Scan Limited and formerly Head of the Natural Environment Research Council Thematic Information Services.

Laser-Scan Limited
Science Park
Milton Road
Cambridge
CB4 4FY
UK

Brian Kelk
Formerly Assistant Director responsible for Information and Marketing, now Head of Geosciences Information Technology, British Geological Survey.

British Geological Survey
Keyworth
Nottingham
NG12 5GG
UK

John J Kineman
Environmental scientist and ecologist, working for the National Geophysical Data Center, National Oceanic and Atmospheric Administration on global environment data projects for national and international global change programmes. Research interests include global ecological monitoring and analysis and developments in global applications.

NGDC/NOAA
325 Broadway
Boulder
Colorado
80303
USA

Sachio Kubo
Professor of Geography, Keio University. Research interests include 'intelligent GIS' and multimedia GIS.

Keio University
Faculty of Environmental Information
5322 Endo
Fujisawa
Kanagawa
Japan

William A Mackaness
Research Associate for the National Center for Geographic Information and Analysis, University of Maine. Research interests include human-computer interaction and automated map design.

NCGIA
University of Maine
348 Boardman Hall
Orono
Maine
04469–0110
USA

Robert P Mahoney
Director of Business Information Management, a company providing independent GIS consultancy services. Extensive experience in utility mapping as Project Manager for the British Gas South Eastern Digital Records Trial and British Gas corporate evaluation project. A major contributor to the Ordnance Survey Digitizing and Quality Assurance procedures.

Business Information Management
14 Kings Avenue
Denton
Newhaven
East Sussex
BN9 0NA
UK

Derek H Maling
Author of many papers and several influential books on map projections and cartography. Now retired and living in Wales.

Tredustan Hall
Defynnog
Brecon
Powys
LD3 8YH
UK

David M Mark
Professor of Geography at SUNY Buffalo and Chair of the Scientific Policy Committee of NCGIA. Current research interests include spatial cognition, human-computer interaction and geographical data structures.

NCGIA-Buffalo
Department of Geography
State University of New York at Buffalo
Buffalo
New York
14261
USA

Joel L Morrison
Assistant Division Chief for Research in the National Mapping Division of the USGS at Reston Virginia. Past President of the International Cartographic Association and the American Congress on Surveying and Mapping. Currently Secretary of AM/FM International (North American Division).

USGS
MS 519
National Center
Reston
Virginia
22092
USA

Helen M Mounsey
Senior Associate in GIS and related matters at one of the largest multi-national management consultants. Formerly a lecturer in GIS at Birkbeck College, University of London.

Coopers and Lybrand Deloitte
Plumtree Court
London
EC4A 4HT
UK

Jean-Claude Muller
Professor and Chairman of the Department of Cartography, International Institute for Aerospace Survey and Earth Science (ITC). Research interests include generalization of spatial databases, expert system guidance and decision support systems for geoinformation production, map design and modelling in GIS.

Department of Cartography
International Institute for Aerospace Surveys and Earth Sciences (ITC)
PO Box 6 7500 AA
Enschede
The Netherlands

John F O'Callaghan
Chief of the CSIRO Division of Information Technology, which contains the Centre for Spatial Information Systems, Canberra. Research interests include image processing, visualization, GIS and decision support systems.

Division of IT
CSIRO
PO Box 1599
Macquarie Centre
North Ryde
New South Wales
2113
Australia

Stan Openshaw
Professor of Geography, Technical Director of the North East Regional Research Laboratory and member of the Centre for Urban and Regional Studies. Author of several books and many papers on quantitative geography, particularly with respect to medical and urban geography and nuclear power.

Department of Geography
University of Newcastle
Daysh Building
Newcastle upon Tyne
NE1 7RU
UK

Lars Ottoson

Head of research and development department at the National Land Survey and member of its board of executive directors. Main GIS interest is the introduction of new techniques in production of maps and geographical databases. Swedish and Scandinavian representative on CERCO working groups and for many years secretary of the Swedish Cartographic Society.

National Land Survey
Lantmaterigatan 2
S-801 82
Gavle
Sweden

Robert Parrott

Director of Research and Information Systems, San Diego Association of Governments (SANDAG). Twenty years experience in conducting surveys and acquisitions for San Diego County and California Mapping Applications, the development of Regional Digital Spatial Databases and Management of Geographical Information Systems for growth management and land use and facility planning.

San Diego Association of Governments
401 B. St. Suite 800
San Diego
California 92101
USA

Jonathan F Raper

Lecturer in Geography at Birkbeck College and Director of the Apple Mapping Centre. Research interest in 3-D GIS spatial languages and interfaces.

Department of Geography
Birkbeck College
University of London
7–15 Gresse Street
London
W1P 1PA
UK

Alan Robinette

Assistant Commissioner for the Minnesota State Planning Agency with lead responsibility for the Land Management Information Center, a data clearing house and service centre for GIS in the State.

Minnesota State Planning Agency
300 Centennial Office Building
658 Cedar Street
St Paul
Minnesota
55155
USA

Bengt Rystedt

Head of the information systems division within the R&D department of the National Land Survey of Sweden. Main interests are design, specification and applications of national geographical databases. Chairman of the ICA Commission on National Atlases and the GIS section of the Swedish Cartographic Society.

National Land Survey
Lantmaterigatan 2
S-801 82
Gavle
Sweden

Ifan D H Shepherd

Principal lecturer in GIS and GIS Laboratory Director at Middlesex Polytechnic. Teaches computer cartography, remote sensing, GIS, computer applications and human-computer interfacing, and manages an authorized training centre for Autocad. Current research interests include the adaptation and integration of desktop software for GIS use, cartographic generalization, hypermedia, and alternative realities.

School of Geography and Planning
Middlesex Polytechnic
Queensway
Enfield
Middlesex
EN3 4SF
UK

W Lynn Shirley

Project Manager at the Humanities and Social Sciences Computer Laboratory at the University of South Carolina. More than 12 years experience in GIS.

Department of Geography
University of South Carolina
Columbia
South Carolina
29208
USA

Karen Siderelis
Head of Center for Geographic Information and Analysis which has provided GIS support and expertise to state agencies for more than a decade.

Center for Geographic Information and Analysis
NC Department of Environment, Health, and Natural Resources
512 North Salisbury Street
PO Box 27687
Raleigh
North Carolina
27611–7687
USA

David S Simonett*
Formerly Professor of Geography at the University of California Santa Barbara and Co-Director of the National Center for Geographic Information and Analysis.

Department of Geography
University of California
Santa Barbara
California
93106
USA
* Deceased

Terence R Smith
Professor of Computer Science and Professor of Geography, University of California Santa Barbara. His various research interests include the development of theoretical bases for logic-based and object-based spatial database systems, as well as implementation aspects of such systems and their application to the modelling of complex geographic phenomena.

Department of Computer Science
University of California
Santa Barbara
California
93106
USA

Michael (Sam) Sowton
Head of Research and Development in the Ordnance Survey since 1983. Chairman of the UK National Transfer Format (NTF) Steering Committee. Experience in surveying and mapping in Great Britain and overseas with Military Survey, the Ordnance Survey and the Directorate of Overseas Survey. Currently responsible for projects concerned with the development of digital mapping and topographic databases.

Ordnance Survey
Romsey Road
Maybush
Southampton
SO9 4DH
UK

Lowell E Starr
Chief of the National Mapping Division of the US National Mapping Division of the US Geological Survey until his retirement in February 1991. Since then he has been working in the private sector.

USGS National Mapping Division
521 National Center
Reston
Virginia
22092
USA

Frederick P Stutz
Professor of Geography, San Diego State University in San Diego, California. Experience in building information systems and conducting mapping for land use management and transportation problem solutions for the California Department of Recreation, California Department of Transportation and the City and County of San Diego. Federal research contracts were awarded by the US Department of State, Aid for International Development, US Department of Health and Human Services, US Department of Commerce, the National Oceanographic and Atmospheric Administration and the Environmental Protection Agency.

Department of Geography
San Diego State University
San Diego
California
92182
USA

D R Fraser Taylor
Professor of Geography and International Affairs, Carleton University, Ottawa, Canada, and Associate Dean (International) and Director of Carleton International. Research interests include the preparation and design of maps for computer screens, computer cartography in spatial planning processes in developing nations and the

development of the theory and practice of the 'New Cartography'.

Department of Geography
Carleton University
Ottawa
K1S 5B6
Canada

C Dana Tomlin
Formerly Associate Professor of Natural Resources, Director of the Natural Resources Information Laboratory and Assistant Director of the Center for Mapping at The Ohio State University and Associate of the Harvard Forest at Harvard University. Currently Associate Professor Department of Landscape Architecture, University of Pennsylvania. Interested in the development and application of digital cartographic modelling capabilities.

Department of Landscape Architecture
University of Pennsylvania
210 South 34th Street
Rm 119 Meyerson Hall
Philadelphia
19104–6311
USA

John R G Townshend
Professor and Chair, Department of Geography, University of Maryland College Park. Previously Director of the NERC Unit for Thematic Information Systems, Department of Geography, University of Reading UK. Research interests include applications of remote sensing and integration of remote sensing with other data sets.

Department of Geography
Room 1113 Lefrak Hall
University of Maryland
College Park
Maryland
20742
USA

David J Unwin
Senior Lecturer in Geography at the University of Leicester, Co-Director of the Midlands Regional Research Laboratory and Director of the Computers in Teaching Initiative Centre for Geography. Research interests in spatial analysis and GIS education.

Department of Geography
University of Leicester
University Road
Leicester
LE1 7RH
UK

Robert Weibel
Senior Software Engineer, Prime Wild GIS, Zurich. Also Lecturer in GIS at the Department of Geography, University of Zurich. Research interests include digital terrain modelling, automated map generalization, and computer graphics and cartographic visualization.

Prime Wild GIS AG
Hohlstrasse 192
CH-8040
Zurich
Switzerland

Marvin S White Jr
Vice-President, Research and Development at ETAK Inc, a company concerned with navigation and digital geography.

ETAK Inc
1430 O'Brien Drive
Menlo Park
California
94025
USA

Peter A Woodsford
Chairman of Laser-Scan Limited and Chairman for 1991 of the UK Association for Geographic Information.

Laser-Scan Limited
Science Park
Milton Road
Cambridge
CB4 4FY
UK

Ye Jiang
Doctorate candidate in Department of Computer Science, University of California Santa Barbara.

Department of Computer Science
University of California
Santa Barbara
California
93106
USA

ACKNOWLEDGEMENTS

Graeme Bonham-Carter acknowledges that much of the GIS computer work reviewed in his chapter was carried out by Danny Wright. Frits Agterberg played a major role in the study and reviewed the manuscript. Gordon Watson, Andy Rencz, Ramesh Reddy and Alan Goodacre are also thanked for their contributions. Graeme Bonham-Carter's chapter is Geological Survey of Canada Contribution Number 44789.

Peter Burrough acknowledges that sincere thanks are due to all colleagues who over the years have contributed to the successful introduction of quantitative methods and GIS in soil and land resource survey. Thanks are especially due to A. Mateos for permission to use the data in Figs 46.5 and 46.6, to Alfred Stein of the Department of Soil Science and Geology of the Agricultural University, Wageningen, The Netherlands for Figs 46.7, to R. A. MacMillan, Alberta Research Council, Canada for Plate 46.1, S. de Jong, V. Jetten and E. J. Henkens of the Department of Physical Geography, University of Utrecht for Plate 46.2 and Arnold Bregt of the Winand Staring Centre for Integrated Land, Soil and Water Research, Wageningen, The Netherlands for Plate 46.3.

Nicholas Chrisman acknowledges US National Science Foundation Grant SES 87–22084 which provided partial support for this contribution.

Terry Coppock and David Rhind owe a considerable debt to many people in writing about the history of GIS; the list is too long to enumerate. They have both gained immensely from discussions since the 1960s with fellow enthusiasts, often in the most unlikely of places. They trust that they have contributed to a useful result.

Frank Davis and David Simonett acknowledge that Mark Friedl and John Estes provided useful comments on the draft manuscript.

Max Egenhofer acknowledges the support from NSF for the NCGIA under grant number SES 88–10917, Digital Equipment Corporation under TP–765536 and Intergraph Corporation.

Andrew Frank and David Mark acknowledge that their chapter represents part of Research Initiative #2, 'Languages of Spatial Relations', of the National Center for Geographic Information and Analysis, supported by a grant from the National Science Foundation (SES 88–10917); support by NSF is also gratefully acknowledged. Valuable comments on an earlier draft were provided by Max Egenhofer, Michael Gould and Werner Kuhn.

Randolph Franklin acknowledges that his work was supported by NSF Presidential Young Investigator grant CCR–8351942. Partial support for this work was also provided by the Directorate for Computer and Information Science and Engineering, NSF grant CDA–8805910. Equipment at the Computer Science Department and Rensselaer Design Research Center at RPI was used for the work. Part of the work was conducted using the computational resources of the Northeast Parallel Architectures Center (NPAC) at Syracuse University, which is funded by and operates under contract to DARPA and the Air Force Systems Command, Rome Air Development Center (RADC), Griffiss Air Force Base, NY, under contract F306002–88-C-0031. Part of the research reported here was made possible through the support of the New Jersey Commission on Science and Technology and the Rutgers University CAIP Center's Industrial Members.

Acknowledgements

Herbert Freeman acknowledges that most of his chapter is based on the research activities of the author and two of his graduate students, John Ahn and Jeffrey Doerschler. Other graduate students who contributed to the research effort were Andy Heard, Vinciane Lacroix, John Nastelin and Bradford Nickerson. The work was supported by the National Science Foundation under grants ECS84–07900 and DMC–8518621; this support is gratefully acknowledged.

Anthony Gatrell is associated with the North West Regional Research Laboratory at Lancaster University, funded by the Economic and Social Research Council. The University and ESRC are thanked for their financial support of the RRL initiative. Colleagues at Lancaster have provided a stimulating intellectual environment, for which the author is most grateful. Michael Goodchild (Santa Barbara) and David Unwin (Leicester) helped improve an earlier version, though any remaining fuzzy thinking is his and not theirs!

Richard Healey acknowledges the support of the Economic and Social Research Council in funding the Regional Research Laboratory for Scotland and thanks are due to Anona Lyons for drawing the original versions of the diagrams.

Brian Kelk acknowledges that he publishes with the permission of the Director, British Geological Survey.

David Maguire and Jack Dangermond acknowledge the contribution of Jonathan Raper and Nicholas Green in formulating the GIS functionality classification.

David Rhind thanks David Pearce and Chris Denham at the Office of Population Censuses and Surveys in Britain and Bob Marx at the Bureau of Census who helped provide material and insight for the chapter. The UK Economic and Social Research Council funded part of the work of the South East Regional Research Laboratory and this review emanates from that work.

Karen Siderelis acknowledges first, and foremost, the superb CGIA staff; in particular her chapter could not have been written without the assistance of Scott Carr, Timothy R. Johnson, Zsolt Nagy and Thomas N. Tribble. Thanks are also due to the client organizations whose work is summarized including the Albemarle-Pamlico Estuarine Study, the UNC Sea Grant College Program, the NC Hazardous Waste Management Commission and the NC Board of Science and Technology. Finally, Dr. Walter Clark, Dr. Earl Mac Cormac, Dr. Bill Dunn, Darrell Hinnant, Dr. Robert Holman, Prof David Rhind and Tom Scheitlin have all been most helpful in ways which they should know!

John Townshend acknowledges that much of the material used in his chapter on the distinctive problems of environmental data sets arose through the activities of the NERC Working Group on Geographic Information, which the author chaired. The contributions of the members of the working group (G. Darwell, A. Laughton, B. Kelk, C. Milner, J. Plevin and D. Pugh) are gratefully acknowledged.

Several US authors are associated with the National Center for Geographic Information and Analysis sites at the University of California Santa Barbara; the State University of New York at Buffalo; and the University of Maine. Michael Goodchild acknowledges the role that the US National Science Foundation has played in establishing and funding the NCGIA through grant SES 88–10917, and in supporting the activities of himself, Andrew Frank, David Mark, Terence Smith, Frank Davis, David Simonett, Max Egenhofer, Paul Densham, Je Yiang, Barbara Buttenfield, William Mackaness, Hugh Calkins and many others.

We are grateful to the following for permission to reproduce copyright figures and tables:

American Congress on Surveying & Mapping for fig. 13.6 from fig. 1 (Beard & Chrisman, 1988); American Society for Photogrammetry & Remote Sensing for table 13.4 from table 1M (Merchant, 1987) copyright 1987 by the American Society for Photogrammetry & Remote Sensing; Butterworth & Co. (Publishers) Ltd. for fig. 13.3 from fig. 2.1, p. 8 (Parry & Perkins, 1987); the editor, *Cartographica* (University of Toronto Press) for fig. 13.1a from fig. 1 (Gardiner, 1982); Environmental Systems Research Institute, Inc. for figs 22.4 & 22.6 from figs 4 & 1 (ESRI, 1989 © 1991 Environmental Systems Research Institute, Inc.); the author, J

Hogg for fig. 9.5 from figs 2–5 (Gahegan & Hogg, 1986); London Regional Transport (L. T. Museum) for fig. 9.4; Longman Group UK Ltd. for figs 13.1b & 13.2 from figs 32, 126, 129, 165, pp. 46, 160, 161, 192 (Keates, 1989); the author, Dr. D H Maling for fig. 9.6 from fig. 14.4 (Maling, 1989); McGraw–Hill Inc. for fig. 45.5 from fig. 6, p. 24 (Rapp & Collins, 1987 copyright 1987 McGraw–Hill Inc.); National Joint Utility Group for fig. 42.3; Swiss Federal Office of Topography for figs 19.3, 19.9, 19.10, 19.12, 19.13, 19.15–17; Taylor & Francis Ltd. and the respective authors for figs 13.5 from fig. 7, p. 93 (Rhind & Clark, 1988), 13.8 from fig. 2, p. 245 (Flowerdew & Green, 1989) and table 13.1 from table on p. 132 (Tobler, 1988); the author, Prof. I P Williamson for figs 39.1 & 39.2 from figs 1 & 2 (Williamson & Blackburn, 1987).

While every effort has been made to trace the owners of copyright material, in a few cases this has proved impossible and we take this opportunity to offer our apologies to any copyright holders whose rights we may have unwittingly infringed.

We are grateful to the following for permission to reproduce copyright photographs:

Altek Corporation for plate 17.1; DATANET Plus Mapping and Land Management Information Center (LMIC) for plate 54.8; René L'Eplattenier for plates 19.4, 19.5; Intergraph (UK) Limited for plate 17.6; Laser–Scan Limited for plates 17.5, 17.7, 17.8, 17.9, 17.10; Land Management Information Center (LMIC) for plates 54.6, 54.10; E Meier, University of Zurich and ESA/Earthnet for plate 19.2; Minnesota Board of Water and Soil Resources and Land Management Information Center (LMIC) for plate 54.2; Minnesota Department of Natural Resources for plates 54.7, 54.11, 54.13; Minnesota Geological Survey for plate 54.14; Minnesota Pollution Control Agency and Land Management Information Center (LMIC) for plates 54.1, 54.5, 54.9; N Quarmby and the NERC Unit for Thematic Information Systems for plate 49.4; David A Reece, Knoxville Utilities Board for plate 42.1; Rochester–Olmstead County Planning and Land Management Information Center (LMIC) for plates 54.3, 54.4; Scan Graphics for plates 17.2, 17.3; SPOT Image Corporation © 1989 CNES for plates 56.8, 56.9; Tangent Engineering, Inc. for plate 17.4; G Wadge and the NERC Unit for plates 49.5, 49.6.

While every effort has been made to trace the owners of copyright material in a few cases this has proved impossible and we take this opportunity to offer our apologies to any copyright holders whose rights we may have unwittingly infringed.

SECTION I

OVERVIEW

Introduction *D J Maguire, M F Goodchild and D W Rhind*	**3–7**
1. An overview and definition of GIS *D J Maguire*	**9–20**
2. The history of GIS *J T Coppock and D W Rhind*	**21–43**
3. The technological setting of GIS *M F Goodchild*	**45–54**
4. The commercial setting of GIS *J Dangermond*	**55–65**
5. The government setting of GIS in the United Kingdom *R Chorley and R Buxton*	**67–79**
6. The academic setting of GIS *D J Unwin*	**81–90**
7. The organizational home for GIS in the scientific professional community *J L Morrison*	**91–100**
8. A critique of GIS *R T Aangeenbrug*	**101–107**

SECTION I

INTRODUCTION

D J MAGUIRE, M F GOODCHILD AND D W RHIND

The field of Geographical Information Systems (GIS) is relatively new and rapidly developing. People new to the field and even many who have been working in it for some time are unsure about its extent and content. The first section of this book, therefore, aims to overview the field of GIS, to examine its context and to introduce many of the themes discussed in later sections. Section I contains eight chapters by ten authors currently working in North America and Europe but with world wide experiences.

The section begins with a chapter by David Maguire which overviews and defines GIS. The text is a mixture of purview and review. It briefly introduces a number of the key themes taken up in later chapters and synthesizes many of the different views about GIS. A number of the principles on which GIS is founded are introduced. These are discussed in more detail on several occasions throughout this book and the subject is taken up again in the Epilogue. There are two key ideas discussed in this chapter. First, the term *GIS* can be applied to both technology and to a new discipline. Although the former use has been more common in the past, the latter is now more prevalent and is widely used in this book. Secondly, the term *GIS* has multiple meanings and three widely held views emphasize the importance of map processing, databases and spatial analysis.

The next six chapters have a common theme, namely, they discuss the contextual setting of GIS from historical, technological, commercial, government, academic and organizational perspectives. They offer insights into the origins and contemporary status of GIS.

The historical setting of GIS is considered in Chapter 2 by Terry Coppock and David Rhind. Their contribution is not a chronology of events; compiling such a list would be a very difficult task for any field, let alone GIS which has a paucity of accessible literature and a rapid rate of development. The authors offer a personal narrative of the key issues, individuals and organizations which have shaped GIS over the past 30 years or so. Their perspective discusses the important roles of the US Bureau of Census, the US Geological Survey, the Harvard Laboratory for Computer Graphics and Spatial Analysis, the Experimental Cartography Unit and Environmental Systems Research Institute. Latterly, the significant impact of government initiatives is also noted.

In Chapter 3 Michael Goodchild discusses the technological setting of GIS. Goodchild assesses the degree to which technology has constrained or driven GIS. It is clear that in the early days of GIS, developments were technology driven. More recently, however, computer hardware and software have declined in their perceived importance as the price : performance ratio of hardware has increased dramatically and good quality software is available in abundance. Attention in the early 1990s is now focused on the availability of well trained personnel, together with the institutional and management implications of implementing and using GIS. The technological foundation of GIS is further considered in Chapter 15 by Randolph Franklin.

One of the main reasons for the massive interest in GIS is their great commercial significance. In Chapter 1 Maguire sets out some global and European estimates for the size of the GIS market. Jack Dangermond discusses the commercial setting of GIS in Chapter 4. He takes a general view of the nature of commercial GIS business, from the perspective of both commercial organizations themselves and GIS users and researchers. He examines the main areas of business activity (hardware, software, application programming, database design etc.) and the types of firms currently operating in the GIS marketplace. The role of commercial companies in the development of GIS is discussed by Coppock and Rhind in Chapter 2. For the future, Dangermond is very optimistic about the commercial opportunities which GIS offers. He sees the continued development of new products and the application of the technology to substantive social and environmental problems.

In Chapter 5 Roger Chorley and Richard Buxton explore the impact of government on GIS. Because of the great differences in the way governments operate in different countries, it would be impossible to produce a comprehensive synthesis. Instead, they use the United Kingdom as an example to illustrate some general points. This allows Chorley to recount his experiences as chairman of the UK Government's committee of Enquiry into Handling Geographic Information. In the United Kingdom, the role of government has been expressed most significantly in the form of three government reports published in the past decade or so. Chorley and Buxton present some examples of the way government influences activities such as national mapping, land registration, health and defence. The activities of the UK national mapping agency, the Ordnance Survey, are considered in detail by Sam Sowton in Chapter 36 and in Chapter 7 Joel Morrison draws some parallels between the actions of UK and US governments.

In the early 'pioneer' (to use Coppock and Rhind's term) days of GIS, universities were at the forefront of research and development. Presently, universities and other academic institutions undertake important 'blue-sky' research and are primarily responsible for educating the GIS technicians, users and managers of tomorrow. In Chapter 6 David Unwin concentrates on the educational role of academia and explores the problems of introducing GIS programmes into higher education. Unwin's critical, pessimistic remarks are in sharp contrast to the optimistic tone of other chapters. He is concerned about the technological focus, content driven nature and slow rate of progress of much of what passes for GIS education. Unwin does, however, commend the efforts of the US National Center for Geographic Information and Analysis in producing a core curriculum and other materials for teaching GIS.

In Chapter 7 Joel Morrison looks at the organizational or institutional setting of GIS. He examines the impact of academia, government, industry and professional organizations on GIS. The list of international and national organizations with an interest is long and varied, and there is considerable overlap between many of these organizations. At the international level no single organization seems to have assumed dominance, although within individual countries there are signs of the formation of single united groups (e.g. the Association for Geographic Information in the United Kingdom). Morrison suggests that today the weak links in the development of GIS are the provision of trained professionals and the availability of accurate, accessible and compatible data sets. This is a view shared by many authors. In the early 1990s training for GIS professionals is carried out principally, but not exclusively, in academic departments of geography and this practice is probably best continued although a larger throughput is required. Governments, Morrison argues, will probably have to be responsible for addressing the data problems, although governments of capitalist, free market economies may have other ideas.

Chapter 8, the final chapter in Section I, is a critique of GIS by Robert Aangeenbrug. Any area of great commercial significance, rapid growth and relative immaturity is bound to suffer from problems of rhetoric, hyperbole and boosterism. GIS is no exception to this general rule. Aangeenbrug reviews the contradictions, false claims and great opportunities of GIS in a wide ranging critical essay. He concludes that GIS is exceedingly useful for solving many important social and environmental problems, in spite of the current tendency for overselling. The status of GIS and current problems and agenda are further considered in the Epilogue.

Two further important issues, which could have been included in Section I, are the legalistic setting and an introduction to the literature of GIS. On balance, it seemed more appropriate to put Earl Epstein's contribution on legal aspects of GIS in the operational issues subsection of Section II as Chapter 32. The literature of GIS does not warrant a chapter in its own right and is, therefore, included as part of this introduction.

THE LITERATURE OF GIS

The history, transactions and debates of any discipline are recorded in its literature. Literature is also a crucial resource for education and training. The literature on GIS is characterized by both its sparsity and inaccessibility, although this is rapidly changing. Four main factors account for this situation. First, the immaturity of the discipline means that in the early 1990s there are comparatively few substantial journals and textbooks devoted specifically to GIS. Secondly, historical accident has also played a part. No one could have foreseen the impact of the AUTOCARTO series of conferences and their proceedings when the series was initiated in 1973. For many years this outlet stifled development of more traditional publishing. Thirdly, the commercial nature of the field means that much research and development is considered to be proprietary and is kept secret. There is, not surprisingly, a reluctance by system developers to publish details of, for example, their polygon overlay, network and surface modelling algorithms and data structures. Lastly, the rapid rate of development and massive interest in GIS has led to a proliferation of conferences and a publishing culture based on little and often in conference proceedings, rather than substantial considered papers in refereed journals.

Thus, much of the useful material and many of the fundamental principles of GIS are recorded only in the relatively inaccessible grey literature of conference proceedings and ephemeral publication series. In the late 1980s and early 1990s, however, there has been a burgeoning of publications of all types. This is partly a direct consequence of the explosion of interest in GIS, but it also reflects the maturity of the discipline and attempts to set out the fundamental principles and agenda for future activity.

The literature of GIS has been examined on two recent occasions and this discussion, therefore, summarizes and updates these two comprehensive reviews. As part of a book on information sources in cartography edited by Perkins and Parry (1990), Monmonier (1990), Maguire (1990) and Mason (1990) review, respectively, the literature on GIS, computer cartography and satellite remote sensing. These offer comprehensive reviews of textbooks, periodicals and other grey literature. A bibliography of GIS was published by Bracken *et al.* (1989).

The literature on GIS may conveniently be broken down by type of publication into three groups: textbooks, periodicals, and conference and symposia proceedings. A small, currently specialist, but rapidly increasing, amount of material is being disseminated in magnetic or electronic form as videos, floppy disks, CD-ROMs and electronic mail. Much of this is reviewed in Perkins and Parry (1990). The chapters later in this book review the literature of specialist areas of GIS and so only general GIS literature will be considered here.

GIS Textbooks

Textbooks are for many people the only contact with a discipline. They also offer authors the opportunity to reflect at length on some more substantial and fundamental issues. The main textbooks relevant to GIS are set out in Table I.1. The first textbook to address GIS explicitly was published in 1986 by Peter Burrough and even that had a land resources and computer cartography orientation. It was not until the publication of Stan Aronoff's book in 1989 that the spirit and purpose of GIS was expressed in textbook form. The spate of texts in 1989 and 1990 seek to address both the generic aspects of GIS (Aronoff, Star and Estes) and specific aspects (Samet, Tomlin). The volume by Peuquet and Marble (1990) is a compendium of mostly previously published papers. DoE (1987) is an interesting addition to this list. Strictly speaking it is a government report, but it includes very useful introductions to various aspects of GIS and details about government uses of GIS.

Table I.1 GIS textbooks

Aronoff S (1989) *Geographic Information Systems: a management perspective*. WDL Publications, Ottawa Canada

Burrough P A (1986) *Principles of Geographical Information Systems for Land Resources Assessment*. Clarendon, Oxford

Calkins H W, Tomlinson R F (1977) *Geographic Information Systems: methods and requirements for land use planning*. IGU Commission on Geographical Data Sensing and Processing Resource and Land Investigations (RALI) Program, USGS Reston Virginia

Dale P F, McLaughlin J D (1988) *Land Information Management*. Clarendon, Oxford

DoE (1987) *Handling Geographic Information*. HMSO, London

Goodchild M F, Gopal S (1989) *Accuracy of Spatial Databases*. Taylor & Francis, London

Maguire D J (1989) *Computers in Geography*. Longman, London

Marble D F, Calkins H W, Peuquet D J (1984) *Basic Readings in Geographic Information Systems*. SPAD Systems Ltd, Williamsville New York

Mounsey H M (ed.) (1988) *Building Databases for Global Science*. Taylor & Francis, London

Peuquet D J, Marble D F (1990) *Introductory Readings in Geographic Information Systems*. Taylor & Francis, London

Samet H (1990) *The Design and Analysis of Spatial Data Structures*. Addison-Wesley, Reading Massachusetts

Star J, Estes J E (1990) *Geographic Information Systems an introduction*. Prentice Hall, Englewood Cliffs New Jersey

Tomlin C D (1990) *Geographic Information Systems and Cartographic Modelling*. Prentice Hall, Englewood Cliffs New Jersey

GIS Periodicals

Refereed journal articles are the primary source of information about most subjects and GIS is no exception. The main periodical devoted to GIS is the *International Journal of Geographical Information Systems* founded in 1987. There are three important features to be noted about the list of GIS periodicals presented as Table I.2. The first is the demise of *Geo-Processing* in 1987 which was for many years the only journal devoted (though not explicitly) to GIS. Had it been able to struggle on for only a few more years it might have been able to climb on board the GIS bandwagon. The second is the tendency for journals to become realigned to GIS by changing their name (e.g. *Cartography and Geographic Information Systems*) or including specific sections and theme issues on GIS (e.g. *Photogrammetric Engineering and Remote Sensing*). The third is the proliferation of new journals in the late 1980s (e.g. *International Journal of Geographical Information Systems, International Journal of Imaging, Remote Sensing and Integrated Geographical Systems* and *Journal of the Urban and Regional Information Systems Association*).

Table I.2   GIS periodicals (previous names in parentheses)

Cartographica (*The Canadian Cartographer and Cartographia Monographs*)

Cartography and Geographic Information Systems (*The American Cartographer*)

Computers & GeoSciences

Geo-Processing – now ceased publication

GISWorld

International Journal of Geographical Information Systems

International Journal of Imaging, Remote Sensing and Integrated Geographical Systems

Journal of the Urban and Regional Information Systems Association

Mapping Awareness

Photogrammetric Engineering and Remote Sensing

Surveying and Land Information Systems (*Survey and Mapping*)

GISWorld published in the United States and *Mapping Awareness* published in the United Kingdom are published more frequently, and adopt a more journalistic and less academic style than the others. Both are in great demand and they fulfil a valuable short-term information dissemination role.

GIS Conference and Symposia Proceedings

The large number of collections of published GIS conference and symposia proceedings has mixed blessings. On the positive side, it has undoubtedly led to production of more written material than might otherwise have been the case. On the negative side, such proceedings are often difficult to obtain and much of the material incorporated within them is of dubious quality. The best known collection of conference proceedings is the AUTOCARTO collection initiated in 1973. The European equivalent is the less well known EUROCARTO collection which began in Oxford in 1981. For several years the American Urban and Regional Information Systems Association has devoted a volume of the annual conference proceedings to GIS. More recently, a number of other series have been established including: the International Spatial Data Handling Symposia (started in 1984) sponsored by the IGU; GIS/LIS (started in 1988) sponsored by a consortium including the American Congress on Surveying and Mapping, the American Society for Photogrammetry and Remote Sensing, the Association of American Geographers and the Urban and Regional Information Systems Association; and the European GIS symposia (EGIS) was started in 1990. Many other one-off or short collections of conference and symposia proceedings have been published over the years in many countries.

Miscellaneous

In addition to the well-established collections of papers described above a number of less well known or more ephemeral sources of literature are worthy of mention here. The classic 18-volume Harvard Laboratory for Computer Graphics Mapping Collection is a very important source of information. Many government organizations, such as the USGS, have produced series of working papers over the years which contain important general material. More recently, the government-sponsored GIS research initiatives in, for example, the United States (National Center for Geographic Information and Analysis), the United Kingdom (Regional Research Laboratory) and the Netherlands (Nederlands Expertise Centruum voor Ruimtelijke Informatiererwerkig) have contributed a very large collection of working papers and research reports. Finally, the annual yearbooks published by the UK Association for Geographic Information (AGI) offer good summaries of national and international activity.

REFERENCES

Bracken I, Higgs G, Martin D, Webster C (1989) A classification of Geographical Information Systems literature and applications. *Concepts and Techniques in Modern Geography* **52**: Environmental Publications, Norwich

Maguire D J (1990) Computer cartography. In: Perkins C R, Parry R B (eds.) *Information Sources in Cartography*. Bowker-Saur, London, pp. 201–13

Mason K (1990) Cartographic applications of satellite remote sensing. In: Perkins C R, Parry R B (eds.) *Information Sources in Cartography*. Bowker-Saur, London, pp. 142–67

Monmonier M S (1990) Geographic Information Systems. In: Perkins C R, Parry R B (eds.) *Information Sources in Cartography*. Bowker-Saur, London, pp. 214–31

Perkins C R, Parry R B (eds.) (1990) *Information Sources in Cartography*. Bowker-Saur, London

AN OVERVIEW AND DEFINITION OF GIS

D J MAGUIRE

Geographical Information Systems (GIS) have been generating massive interest world wide. Their comparative recency, rapid rate of development, commercial orientation and diversity have not assisted in producing a clear and unambiguous definition of GIS. This chapter attempts to provide an overview of GIS, focusing on efforts to develop a satisfactory definition, the fundamental principles on which they are based and the evolution of applications. The term GIS can be applied to computer technology, integrated systems for use in substantive applications, as well as a new discipline. Estimates of the size and importance of the GIS market suggest that it is of national and global significance and that it is growing at a rapid rate. Three widely held views of GIS emphasize the importance of map processing, databases and spatial analysis. The evolution of GIS is described as a three stage process encompassing resource inventory, analysis and management activities.

INTRODUCTION

The term *Geographical Information System (GIS)* and its synonym *Geographic Information System* used in North America, is frequently applied to geographically oriented computer technology, integrated systems used in substantive applications and, more recently, a new discipline which is generating massive interest world wide. For a number of reasons, GIS is more difficult to define than might at first be imagined. Although there has been some debate about the origin of the term and the date of initiation of work in the field (see Coppock and Rhind 1991 in this volume), it is clear that GIS are a relatively recent phenomena. Throughout the last 30 years there has been a very rapid rate of theoretical, technological and organizational development in the GIS field, culminating in a period of intense activity in the last five years or so. The recent origin and rapid rate of progress has not been conducive to the analysis and definition of GIS.

The commercial orientation of much GIS activity has led to a great deal of hyperbole and rhetoric. There has been a mushrooming of new computer systems which purport to be GIS, many of which are existing systems re-badged and re-packaged in an attempt to exploit market opportunities. Associated with this has been a rise in the number of GIS consultants, many of whom appear to offer conflicting advice and information about GIS. Any subject or concept which is in widespread use by a heterogeneous group of users is almost certain to be difficult to define.

The GIS field is further characterized by a great diversity of applications. GIS are integrating systems which bring together ideas developed in many areas including the fields of agriculture, botany, computing, economics, mathematics, photogrammetry, surveying, zoology and, of course, geography, to name but a few. Inevitably, it is difficult to distinguish between the competing claims of different organizations and individuals all of whom wish to be represented in a vibrant and profitable field.

It is also difficult to define GIS because there are many different ways of defining and classifying objects and subjects. Not surprisingly, given the diversity of the field, many different methods have been applied to GIS. Classifications based on functionality have been particularly popular (Maguire and Raper 1990; see also Maguire and Dangermond 1991 in this volume) and others have tried to develop schemes based on genealogy, cost, size, platform, application area and data model (Clarke 1986a).

The final reason for definitional difficulties stems from genuine academic debate about the central focus of current GIS activity. As the discussion below demonstrates, some people believe that hardware and software are the central focus, others argue that the key element is information processing or even applications.

Together these factors have conspired to obfuscate an issue which has never really been satisfactorily discussed or analysed in any detail. The individuals and organizations working with GIS have instead employed themselves developing new methods and applying the systems to substantive problems. Given the current stage of evolution of GIS it seems appropriate to attempt to develop a considered view of exactly what they are and how they relate to other similar systems.

This chapter aims to provide an overview of GIS. It focuses on efforts to develop a satisfactory definition of GIS, the fundamental principles on which they are based and the evolution of GIS applications. The discussion is intended to act as an introduction to some of the main themes and key issues discussed later in this book. The chapter begins with a review of existing attempts to define GIS and the relationship between GIS and other information systems. These ideas are synthesized and presented as three views of GIS. Next the benefits and then the basic elements of GIS are considered. This is followed by a brief review of some of the major applications of GIS. Finally, some conclusions are presented.

TOWARDS A DEFINITION OF GIS

GIS are seen by many as special cases of information systems in general (de Man 1988; Carter 1989). Information is derived from the interpretation of data which are symbolic representations of features (Benyon 1990). The value of information depends upon many things including its timeliness, the context in which it is applied and the cost of collection, storage, manipulation and presentation. Information is now a valuable asset, a commodity which can be bought and sold for a high price (Openshaw and Goddard 1987). Information and its communication is one of the key development processes and characteristics of contemporary societies.

On the basis of the tasks performed, two types of information system can be identified: transaction processing systems and decision support systems. In transaction processing systems, emphasis is placed on recording and manipulating the occurrence of operations: banking and airline reservation systems are well known examples. Transaction processing systems, whether they operate in on-line or batch mode, can be update or retrieval oriented and are based on clearly defined procedures. In decision support systems the emphasis is on manipulation, analysis and, particularly, modelling for the purposes of supporting decision makers such as company managers, politicians and government officials. Decision support systems are used for applications such as tactical warfare and market analysis. They are normally retrieval oriented and need to be able to operate in a flexible manner.

Information systems have a number of important general attributes (de Man 1988; Carter 1989). The information in the system must be organized such that it will have utility when retrieved; access to information in the system must be managed and carefully regulated; there must be continued support and maintenance of the information and technology within the system over time; and staff and users need to be encouraged and educated.

Strictly speaking, GIS include both manual and computer-based information systems (Dickinson and Calkins 1988; Aronoff 1989; Starr and Estes 1990). In practice, however, all contemporary information systems are computer based. Some selected definitions of GIS are given in Table 1.1.

Table 1.1 Selected definitions of GIS

DoE (1987:132)
a system for capturing, storing, checking, manipulating, analysing and displaying data which are spatially referenced to the Earth.

Aronoff (1989:39)
any manual or computer based set of procedures used to store and manipulate geographically referenced data.

Carter (1989:3)
an institutional entity, reflecting an organizational structure that integrates technology with a database, expertise and continuing financial support over time.

Parker (1988:1547)
an information technology which stores, analyses, and displays both spatial and non-spatial data.

Dueker (1979:106)
a special case of information systems where the database consists of observations on spatially distributed features, activities, or events, which are definable in space as points, lines, or areas. A GIS manipulates data about these points, lines, and areas to retrieve data for ad hoc queries and analyses.

Smith *et al.* (1987:13)
a database system in which most of the data are spatially indexed, and upon which a set of procedures operated in order to answer queries about spatial entities in the database.

Ozemoy, Smith and Sicherman (1981:92)
an automated set of functions that provides professionals with advanced capabilities for the storage, retrieval, manipulation, and display of geographically located data.

Burrough (1986:6)
a powerful set of tools for collecting, storing, retrieving at will, transforming and displaying spatial data from the real world.

Cowen (1988:1554)
a decision support system involving the integration of spatially referenced data in a problem-solving environment.

Koshkariov, Tikunov and Trofimov (1989:259)
a system with advanced geo-modelling capabilities.

Devine and Field (1986:18)
a form of MIS [Management Information System] that allows map display of the general information.

There has also been some debate about whether GIS should be defined in narrow technological terms, or whether a wider organizational/institution perspective is more appropriate. DoE (1987) typifies the narrow focus and Carter (1989) is a proponent of the wider view. Dickinson and Calkins (1988) also argue that GIS comprise three key components: GIS technology (hardware and software), a GIS data base (geographical and related data) and GIS infrastructure (staff, facilities and supporting elements).

Cowen (1988) suggests that there are four basic approaches to defining and separating GIS from other types of information system: the process- or function-oriented, application, toolbox, and data base approaches. The process-oriented approach emphasizes the information handling capabilities of GIS and is typified by the DoE (1987) and Ozemoy, Smith and Sicherman (1981) definitions (Table 1.1). The application approach divides information systems on the basis of the problems they seek to address (e.g. welfare, banking and transport information systems). GIS themselves may also be subdivided on this basis as is shown in Table 1.2. The link between these apparently disparate intellectual areas is that they share common technology and methods. GIS vendors have recently started to use this as a sales ploy in an attempt to stimulate vertical niche markets. The toolbox approach emphasizes the generic aspects of GIS and is represented by the widely used definition of Burrough (1986). This approach is, not surprisingly, frequently used by GIS vendors who wish to maximize the size of their market. The database approach is probably the most widely used, because of the influence of database theory and practice on GIS. The definitions of Dueker (1979) and Smith *et al.* (1987) typify this approach. In addition to these four approaches many authors have also highlighted the importance of GIS as decision support systems (Cowen 1988; Parent and Church 1987; see also Densham 1991 in this volume) and management information systems (Devine and Field 1986). Other authors, however, (Densham and Goodchild 1989; Rhind 1988) have reservations about how well current GIS can be used in these ways.

Many of the definitions discussed above are relatively general and cover a wide range of subjects and activities. All of the definitions, however, have a single common feature, namely that GIS are systems which deal with geographical information. In GIS, reality is represented as a series of geographical features defined according to two data elements. The geographical (also called locational) data element is used to provide a reference for the attribute (also called statistical or non-locational) data element. For example, administrative boundaries, river networks and point locations of hill tops are all geographical features used to provide a reference for, respectively, census counts,

Table 1.2 Example types of GIS classified according to the application area addressed. It is also possible to consider these as alternative names for GIS.

Cadastral information system
Image based information system
Land data system
Land information system
Geographically referenced information system
Natural resource management information system
Market analysis information system
Multipurpose cadastre
Planning information system
Property information system
Soil information system
Spatial information systems
Spatial decision support system
Urban information system

river water flows or site elevations. In GIS, the geographical element is seen as more important than the attribute element and this is one of the key features which differentiates GIS from other information systems.

The terms 'spatial' and 'geographical' are often used interchangeably to describe geographical features. Strictly, the term spatial refers to any type of information about location and can include engineering and remote sensing, as well as cartographic information. On the other hand, geographical refers only to locational information about the surface or near surface of the earth at real-world scales and in real world space (Frank 1988). Similarly, the term 'aspatial data' is often used as a synonym for 'attribute data'.

GIS and other Information Systems

The relationship between GIS and computer-aided design, computer cartography, database management and remote sensing information systems is important in establishing a definition of GIS. It is sometimes argued that GIS are a subset or a superset of these systems (Fig. 1.1). Newell and Theriault (1990:42), for example, suggest 'almost any system that is capable of putting a map on the screen on a CRT these days calls itself a GIS' and Clarke (1986b) observes in the minds of many GIS is simply a catch-all for almost any type of automated geographic data processing.

Computer-aided design (CAD) systems were developed for designing and drafting new objects. They are graphic based and use symbols as primitives to represent features in the interactive design process. CAD systems have only rudimentary links to databases which typically might contain part listings or stock reference numbers. They use only simple topological relationships and, on the whole, deal with relatively small quantities of data (Newell and Theriault 1990). CAD systems do not usually allow users to assign symbology automatically on the basis of user-defined criteria (Cowen 1988) and have limited analytical capabilities.

Computer cartography systems focus on data retrieval, classification and automatic symbolization (Cowen 1988). They emphasize display rather than retrieval and analysis. Computer cartography systems utilize simple data structures which lack information on topology. They can be linked to a database management system but only simple retrieval operations are normally undertaken. Computer cartography systems usually have many facilities for designing maps and producing high quality output in vector format.

Database management systems (DBMS) are well-developed software systems optimized for storing and retrieving non-graphic attribute data. They have limited graphical retrieval and display capabilities. DBMS are designed for the short-term retrieval and update of relatively small quantities of data (Newell and Theriault 1990) and lack anything other than simple analytical functions. They have very limited capabilities for implementing spatial analytical operations. (The characteristics of DBMS for GIS are reviewed in Healey 1991 in this volume.)

Remote sensing systems are designed to collect, store, manipulate and display raster data typically derived from scanners mounted on aircraft or satellite platforms, although they can usually handle any data in raster format (Mather 1987). Most remote sensing systems have limited capabilities for handling vectors and, therefore, are unsuitable for operations like network analysis and producing high quality plots from coordinate geometry which are best carried out using data in vector format. They usually have only very limited capabilities for handling attribute data and only

An Overview and Definition of GIS

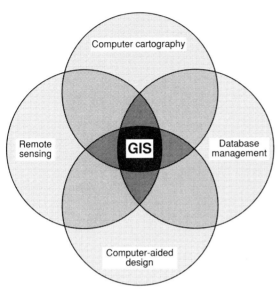

Fig. 1.1 The relationship between GIS, computer-aided design, computer cartography, database management and remote sensing information systems.

poor links to DBMS. Although they have quite sophisticated facilities for enhancing and classifying data, most have limited true spatial analytical capabilities. The relationship between remote sensing and GIS is discussed at length in Marble and Peuquet (1983) and in Davis and Simonett (1991 in this volume).

These systems all predate GIS which, because they have evolved from them, have many features in common. GIS, however, have a number of other features not available in other systems. The major characteristic of GIS is the emphasis placed on analytical operations. Goodchild (1988:67) states this point clearly suggesting that 'the ability of a Geographic Information System to analyse spatial data is frequently seen as a key element in its definition, and has often been used as a characteristic which distinguishes the GIS from systems whose primary objective is map production'. In functional terms, Cowen (1988) believes that spatial searching and overlay are the only operations unique to GIS (see Maguire and Dangermond 1991 in this volume for further discussion of these terms.)

Thus it appears that GIS are best viewed as a subset and not a superset of the other types of information system represented in Fig. 1.1 and discussed above. The emphasis on spatial analysis in GIS raises the question of the difference between GIS and statistical analysis systems. Goodchild (1988:68) again makes a useful contribution defining spatial analysis as 'that set of analytical methods which require access to both the attributes of the objects under study and to their locational information'. Conventional statistical analysis systems, such as SAS and Minitab, are oriented toward the analysis of aspatial data and lack appropriate capabilities for spatial analysis and modelling (Anselin 1989). These views of GIS as spatial analysis systems, must be tempered with caution, for as Rhind (1988:26) indicates 'virtually all GIS developments thus far have resulted in "data retrieval and sifting" engines; modelling work has not yet been brought together with this technically accomplished sub-structure'.

Three views of GIS

The various ideas about GIS can be synthesized and presented in the form of three distinct but overlapping views. These can be termed the map, database and spatial analysis views. Other views of GIS have been suggested, the most notable being the application view in which the idea of GIS as the technology to deal with global scientific problems is prominent. However, the disparate nature of these ideas and the lack of clear focus on GIS means that this view is not as well developed as the others and will, therefore, not be discussed here.

The map view focuses on cartographic aspects of GIS. This view has its origins in the work of McHarg (1969) and today is strongly represented by Berry (1987) and Tomlin (1990, 1991 in this volume). Supporters of this view see GIS as map processing or display systems. In map processing, each data set is represented as a map (also called a layer, theme or coverage). The maps are usually held in raster format and are manipulated by a function that might add, subtract or search for patterns. The output from these operations is another map. Topographic and thematic mapping agencies also support the map view and place great emphasis on the ability of GIS to produce high quality maps and charts usually in vector format.

The database view of GIS emphasizes the importance of a well-designed and implemented database (Frank 1988). A sophisticated database management system is seen as an integral part of a

GIS. This view predominates among members of the GIS community who have a computer science background. Applications which record transactions and require the frequent use of simple queries are particularly suited to this approach. Complex analytical operations which require the use of many types of geographical data can be incorporated into this view only with difficulty.

The third view of GIS emphasizes the importance of spatial analysis. This view focuses on analysis and modelling in which GIS is seen more as a spatial information science than a technology (Goodchild 1990; see also Openshaw 1991 in this volume). Although current proprietary systems have limited functionality for spatial analysis, it is clear that this is a major development area. This view looks likely to become the most widely accepted by the GIS community and already it can be used to differentiate between GIS and other information systems.

Although these views of GIS are widely held, few people see them as conflicting. A single system may be viewed in all three ways depending on the perspective of the user or the application in hand. Nevertheless, this classification serves a useful function in highlighting the ways in which GIS are used by the GIS community. It also illustrates once again the widespread applicability of GIS and the heterogeneity of the GIS community.

THE BENEFITS OF GIS

The reasons for the introduction and success of new ideas and technology are many and varied and they operate at a number of different scales. At the general level there are four main reasons why GIS has become so popular in the past decade or so.

There has without doubt been a massive proliferation of information about many aspects of the cultural and natural environment in the past few years. Remote sensing satellites, population and market surveys, topographic surveys, transaction loggers and the like are now being widely used to collect vast quantities of data in computer format. Many of these data have some type of explicit or implicit geographical reference associated with them. An explicit geographical reference might be a Cartesian or latitude/longitude coordinate and an implicit reference might be the name of an administrative unit, a town, or a physical feature, such as a mountain. In many cases it is possible to derive an explicit reference from an implicit reference. This geographical reference has proved to be an effective means of linking data sets together and this principle, perhaps more than any, is the reason for the success of GIS.

GIS have great commercial application. Recent estimates by Daratech, USA (a leading firm of marketing consultants) suggest that GIS 'may become one of the most dynamic computer systems-related businesses of the 1990s' (*Computer Graphics World* 1989:22). The Daratech study shows that GIS is already big business world wide (Table 1.3) and, more importantly, that it is rapidly expanding. The study predicts a 32 per cent annual growth in the GIS market through to 1993. Another report (Smallworld Systems 1990), produced by polling users on their actual or budgeted expenditure, argues that the European market alone was worth $322 million in 1989. Most of this spending was by utilities or government but some 9 per cent was being spent on environmental applications; this annual total was predicted to grow to $546 million by 1991. Figure 1.2 illustrates the trends. GIS have commercial application because they can be used to address many significant global, national and local social and scientific problems. Some of the major application areas are briefly examined below and there are many detailed examples in Section III of this book.

Table 1.3 GIS market estimates for 1988 in $ billion (*Computer Graphics World* November 1989:22).

Revenues of GIS software companies	$0.52
Hardware sales arising from GIS	$1.10
Market for GIS-related services	$2.40

A final factor of great significance in the expansion and continued success of GIS has been the rapid reduction in the price of computer hardware and software over the past few decades. The introduction of the microprocessor and especially the microcomputer in the late 1970s has been of particular significance in this process (see Goodchild 1991 in this volume). Early GIS software systems were almost all mounted on mainframes or minicomputers, but recently lower priced

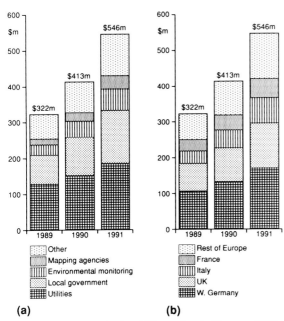

Fig. 1.2 Growth in the GIS market in Europe 1989 to 1991 (Smallworld Systems 1990).

microcomputers and workstations are being used (Dangermond and Morehouse 1987). Croswell and Clark (1988) estimate that the price : performance ratio of computer hardware increased 8 times in the period 1979–88, while at the same time the space required for computers decreased 5 times. With the continued development of smaller, faster and cheaper microchips in the 1990s this trend looks set to continue. It is not fanciful to suggest that by the end of the century GIS will be used every day by everyone in the developed world for routine operations.

THE ELEMENTS OF A GIS

GIS comprise four basic elements which operate in an institutional context: computer hardware, computer software, data and liveware. The hardware element can be almost any type of computer platform, including relatively modest personal computers, high performance workstations and minicomputers and mainframe computers (see Franklin 1991 in this volume; see also Goodchild 1991 in this volume). In the early 1990s the trend is very much towards workstations running the Unix operating system. In addition to the standard input, storage and output devices, specialist peripherals are required for data input (e.g. scanners, digitizers and tape drives), data output (e.g. plotters) and, sometimes, data storage and processing.

There is now a great deal of what claims to be GIS software. The annual surveys in *GISWorld* (*GISWorld* 1990) and other similar reviews show that much of this software has been developed to sophisticated levels. Major software packages have several hundred commands and a wide variety of functionality. Although there are variations in the organization and capabilities of GIS software, three basic designs have evolved (Aronoff 1989; Bracken and Webster 1989). These are called the file processing, hybrid and extended designs. In the file processing design, each data set and function is stored as a separate file and these are linked together during analytical operations. Examples of systems using this design are IDRISI (Eastman 1987) and MAP (Tomlin 1986). This is the approach adopted in map processing systems. In the hybrid design, attribute data are stored in a conventional DBMS and separate bespoke software is used for geographical data. ARC/INFO (Morehouse 1989) and Deltamap/Genamap (Reed 1986) are examples of hybrid designs. In situations where attribute data are stored in a relational DBMS these are sometimes referred to as geo-relational (Morehouse 1985). In the third design type, the extended DBMS, both the geographical and the attribute data are stored in a DBMS which is extended to provide appropriate geographical analytical functions. The best known examples using the extended design are SYSTEM9 (Ingram and Phillips 1987) which extends the EMPRESS DBMS and TIGRIS (Herring 1987) which uses a bespoke DBMS.

The third important element in a GIS is the data. In many respects data are a crucial resource. Geographical data are very expensive to collect, store and manipulate because large volumes are normally required to solve substantive geographical problems. Although estimates vary, it is not uncommon for the cost of data collection to exceed the cost of hardware and software by a factor of two (Rowley and Gilbert, 1989, suggest 70 per cent of the total cost of implementing a GIS). Until relatively recently there was a paucity of data for use in GIS, but the widespread use of remote sensing satellites, the ambitious national mapping programmes of many countries and the collaborative international ventures which aim to create global databases (Mounsey 1988; see also Clark, Hastings and Kineman 1991 in this volume) now mean that there are significant problems of data volumes.

The final and most significant GIS element is the liveware; the people responsible for designing, implementing and using GIS. Without properly trained personnel with the vision and commitment to a project little will be achieved. The lack of adequately trained personnel has been highlighted on a number of occasions (see for example DoE 1987) and although a number of education and training initiatives have been undertaken (see Unwin 1991 in this volume) much remains to be done before the skill shortage is alleviated. The significance of the people involved in GIS is, regrettably, all too often overlooked by those with a more technological focus.

APPLICATIONS

GIS can be applied to many types of problem. Rhind (1990) sets out a general classification of the types of generic questions which GIS are frequently used to investigate (Table 1.4). The location question involves querying a database to determine the types of features which occur at a given place (e.g. what is the population of a given census tract?). The condition question is really the converse, since it involves finding the location of sites which have certain characteristics (e.g. where is all the land within 200 metres of a road which is forest covered?). Where more than one type of data are involved this is sometimes referred to as the 'intersection' question since it necessitates finding the intersection of data sets (Maguire 1989). The trend question involves monitoring how things change over time (e.g. what is the change in the traffic flow along roads?). The other questions are more complex and involve some type of spatial analysis. The routing question requires calculation of the best (fastest, quickest, shortest, most scenic, etc.) route between places (e.g. which is the nearest doctors surgery?). The patterns question allows environmental and social scientists and planners to describe and compare the distribution of phenomena and to understand the processes which account for their distribution (e.g. is there some pattern in the distribution of diseases which are thought to be caused by exposure to radiation?). The final question allows different models of the world to be evaluated (for example, which areas of the earth will be affected by a 20 centimetre rise in sea level?).

Table 1.4 Basic questions that can be investigated using GIS (after Rhind 1990).

1	Location	What is at …?
2	Condition	Where is it …?
3	Trend	What has changed …?
4	Routing	Which is the best way …?
5	Pattern	What is the pattern …?
6	Modelling	What if …?

Crain and MacDonald (1984) have developed a threefold scheme describing the stages in the evolution of GIS (Fig. 1.3). They suggest that the initial reason for establishing most information systems and, therefore, the main activity in the initial development phase is assembling, organizing and undertaking an inventory of features of interest. In a GIS context this might mean an inventory of forest types, soils, utility pipe networks or schools. During this phase systems are used primarily to undertake simple data queries such as the location and condition questions identified by Rhind (1990).

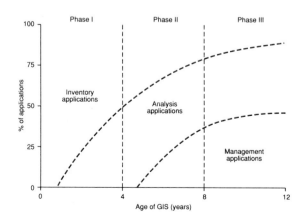

Fig. 1.3 Stages in the development of GIS applications (after Crain and MacDonald 1984).

The second phase in the evolution of information systems according to Crain and MacDonald (1984) arises from users' desires to undertake more complex analytical operations. Frequently these require access to data spread across several data layers and the use of statistical and spatial analytical techniques. GIS applications such as determining the suitability of land for locating, say, waste disposal sites or new retail stores, and monitoring changes in ice sheets are typical of this phase. More complex forms of Rhind's condition and trends questions fall into this category.

The third and most developed phase sees the evolution of an information system from a transaction processing system to a decision support system. In this management phase systems are used to support the activities of decision makers. There is considerable emphasis on sophisticated spatial analytical and modelling activities. During this phase a GIS might be used to determine which of a number of hospitals should close, or the optimum pattern of land use. Rhind's routing, patterns and modelling questions all fall into this category.

The Crain and MacDonald scheme was developed from their work in the Canada Land Data System (CLDS). This system contains the Canada Geographic Information System (CGIS) and is probably the best known and longest established GIS. For CLDS they suggest an inventory application phase from about 1971 to 1979, an analysis phase from about 1979 to 1987 and then a move to the management phase. Although systems initiated after CLDS have benefited considerably from the experience gained in the operation of this and other early systems and the software tools now available are more sophisticated, it is clear that there is still likely to be a 3–5 year lead time before current systems move beyond the inventory stage (Dickinson and Calkins 1988). It is also likely to be a further 3–5 years before they evolve into management information systems. Thus in the early 1990s, while there are many well developed GIS at the inventory stage, there is a much smaller number which are used for analytical purposes and only a select few which are employed in a management context. This is in part due to the state of maturity of systems, but it also reflects the lack of attention paid to spatial analysis until relatively recently. Given the statistical problems inherent in implementing spatial analytical techniques and the almost total lack of appropriate functionality in current proprietary GIS software (see Openshaw 1991 in this volume), the transition from inventory to analysis and then management information system may take longer than some expect.

CONCLUSIONS

GIS are clearly big news. They have enormous commercial importance and, more significantly, they are already being used to make valuable contributions to the understanding and solution of key socio-economic and environmental problems. Interest in GIS is currently expanding rapidly and it is reasonable to expect that over the next decade there will be a several fold increase in activity.

GIS are used by a heterogenous group of individuals and organizations for an incredibly wide variety of applications. Inevitably this means that there are many different ideas about the nature and scope of GIS. A Geographical Information System is best described as an integrated collection of hardware, software, data and liveware which operates in an institutional context. Although many terms have been proposed for the name of the new discipline, because of its widespread use Geographical Information Systems is preferred.

It appears that the only satisfactory way to develop an appropriate definition of GIS is to summarize the many disparate ideas in the form of a series of views of GIS. Three main views are evident, namely, the map, database and spatial analysis views. A central element of all these views is that GIS are a special case of information systems in general and that they share many features in common with other information systems. The key features which differentiate GIS from other information systems are the general focus on spatial entities and relationships, together with specific attention to spatial analytical and modelling operations. In a technical sense it is the ability to organize and integrate apparently disparate data sets together by geography which make GIS so powerful. The spatial searching and overlay operations are a key functional feature of GIS.

The evolution of GIS can be described as a three stage process. Systems in their early stages of development are oriented towards data collection and inventory operations. After about 3–5 years emphasis shifts to more analytical operations. Most systems reach maturity in a further 3–5 years when they evolve into true decision support systems. It is only in this last phase that spatial analytical and modelling operations are routinely employed. While there are many well-developed GIS in the inventory phase, only a small number have presently progressed into the analysis phase. This is due in part to the youthfulness of GIS as a discipline, but also it is due to the technical problems inherent in developing appropriate robust and widely applicable spatial analytical methods.

REFERENCES

Anselin L (1989) What is special about spatial data? Alternative perspectives on spatial data analysis. *NCGIA Technical Paper 89–4* NCGIA, Santa Barbara: 20pp.
Aronoff S (1989) *Geographic Information Systems: a management perspective*. WDL Publications, Ottawa Canada

Benyon D (1990) *Information and Data Modelling*. Blackwell Scientific Publications, Oxford
Berry J K (1987) Fundamental operations in computer-assisted map analysis. *International Journal of Geographical Information Systems* **1**: 119–36
Bracken I, Webster C (1989) Towards a typology of geographical information systems. *International Journal of Geographical Information Systems* **3**: 137–52
Burrough P A (1986) *Principles of Geographic Information Systems for Land Resources Assessment*. Clarendon, Oxford

Carter J R (1989) On defining the geographic information system. In: Ripple W J (ed.) *Fundamentals of Geographic Information Systems: a compendium*. ASPRS/ACSM, Falls Church Virginia, pp. 3–7
Clark D M, Hastings D A, Kineman J J (1991) Global databases and their implications for GIS. In: Maguire D J, Goodchild M F, Rhind D W (eds.) *Geographical Information Systems: principles and applications*. Longman, London, pp. 217–31, Vol 2
Clarke K C (1986a) Recent trends in geographic information systems. *Geo-Processing* **3**: 1–15
Clarke K C (1986b) Advances in Geographic Information Systems. *Computers, Environment and Urban Systems* **10**: 175–84
Computer Graphics World (1989) Daratech survey. *Computer Graphics World* November, p. 22
Coppock J T, Rhind D W (1991) The history of GIS. In: Maguire D J, Goodchild M F, Rhind D W (eds.) *Geographical Information Systems: principles and applications*. Longman, London, pp. 21–43, Vol 1
Cowen D J (1988) GIS versus CAD versus DBMS: what are the differences? *Photogrammetric Engineering and Remote Sensing* **54**: 1551–4
Crain I K, MacDonald C L (1984) From land inventory to land management. *Cartographica* **21**: 40–6
Croswell P L, Clark S R (1988) Trends in automated mapping and geographic information system hardware. *Photogrammetric Engineering and Remote Sensing* **54**: 1571–6

Dangermond J, Morehouse S (1987) Trends in computer hardware for geographic information systems. *Proceedings of AUTOCARTO 8*. ASPRS/ACSM, Falls Church: pp. 380–5
Davis F W, Simonett D S (1991) GIS and remote sensing. In: Maguire D J, Goodchild M F, Rhind D W (eds.) *Geographical Information Systems: principles and applications*. Longman, London, pp. 191–213, Vol 1
de Man E (1988) Establishing a geographical information system in relation to its use: a process of strategic choice. *International Journal of Geographical Information Systems* **2**: 245–61
Densham P J (1991) Spatial decision support systems. In: Maguire D J, Goodchild M F, Rhind D W (eds.) *Geographical Information Systems: principles and applications*. Longman, London, pp. 403–12, Vol 1
Densham P J, Goodchild M F (1989) Spatial Decision Support Systems: a research agenda. *Proceedings of GIS/LIS'89*. ACSM, ASPRS, AAG, URISA, AM/FM International, Falls Church, pp. 707–16
Devine H A, Field R C (1986) The gist of GIS. *Journal of Forestry* August, 17–22
Dickinson H, Calkins H W (1988) The economic evaluation of implementing a GIS. *International Journal of Geographical Information Systems* **2**: 307–27
Department of the Environment (DoE) (1987) *Handling Geographic Information*. HMSO, London
Dueker K J (1979) Land resource information systems: a review of fifteen years experience. *Geo-Processing* **1**: 105–28

Eastman J R (1987) *IDRISI: a grid-based geographic analysis system*. Graduate School of Geography, Clarke University, USA

Frank A U (1988) Requirements for a database management system for a GIS. *Photogrammetric Engineering and Remote Sensing* **54**: 1557–64
Franklin Wm R (1991) Computer systems and low-level data structures for GIS. In: Maguire D J, Goodchild M F, Rhind D W (eds.) *Geographical Information Systems: principles and applications*. Longman, London, pp. 215–25, Vol 1

GISWorld (1990) *GIS Technology '90: Results of the 1990 GISWorld geographic information systems survey*. GISWorld, Fort Collins, 16pp.
Goodchild M F (1987) A spatial analytical perspective on

GIS. *International Journal of Geographical Information Systems* **1**: 327–34

Goodchild M F (1988) Towards an enumeration and classification of GIS functions. In: Aangeenbrug R T, Schiffman Y M (eds.) *International Geographic Information Systems (IGIS) Symposium: The research agenda*. AAG, Falls Church Virginia: pp. 67–77

Goodchild M F (1990) Spatial information science. *Proceedings of the 4th International Spatial Data Handling Symposium*. International Geographical Union, Ohio. pp. 3–14

Goodchild M F (1991) The technological setting of GIS. In: Maguire D J, Goodchild M F, Rhind D W (eds.) *Geographical Information Systems: principles and applications*. Longman, London, pp. 45–54, Vol 1

Healey R G (1991) Database management systems. In: Maguire D J, Goodchild M F, Rhind D W (eds.) *Geographical Information Systems: principles and applications*. Longman, London, pp. 251–67, Vol 1

Herring J R (1987) TIGRIS: Topologically integrated geographic information system. *Proceedings of AUTOCARTO 8*. ASPRS/ACSM, Falls Church, pp. 282–91.

Ingram I K, Phillips W (1987) Geographic information processing using a SQL-based query language. *Proceedings of AUTOCARTO 8*. ASPRS/ACSM, Falls Church, pp. 326–35

Koshkariov A V, Tikunov V S, Trofimov A M (1989) The current state and the main trends in the development of geographical information systems in the USSR. *International Journal of Geographical Information Systems* **3** (3): 257–72

McHarg I L (1969) *Design with Nature*. Doubleday, New York

Maguire D J (1989) *Computers in Geography*. Longman, London

Maguire D J, Dangermond J (1991) The functionality of GIS. In: Maguire D J, Goodchild M F, Rhind D W (eds.) *Geographical Information Systems: principles and applications*. Longman, London, pp. 319–35, Vol 1

Maguire D J, Raper J F (1990) An overview of GIS functionality. *Proceedings of GIS Design Models and Functionality Conference*. Midlands Regional Research Laboratory, Leicester, 10pp

Marble D F, Peuquet D J (1983) Geographic information systems. In: Colwell R N (ed.) *Manual of Remote Sensing*, 2nd edn. American Society of Photogrammetry, Falls Church, pp. 923–58

Mather P M (1987) *Computer Processing of Remotely-sensed Images: an introduction*. Wiley, London

Morehouse S (1985) ARC/INFO: a Geo-relational model for spatial information. *Proceedings of AUTOCARTO 7*. ASPRS, Falls Church, pp. 388–97

Morehouse S (1989) The architecture of ARC/INFO. *Proceedings of AUTOCARTO 9*. ASPRS/ACSM, Falls Church, pp. 266–77

Mounsey H (ed.) (1988) *Building Databases for Global Science*. Taylor & Francis, London

Newell R G, Theriault D G (1990) Is GIS just a combination of CAD and DBMS? *Mapping Awareness* **4** (3): 42–45

Openshaw S (1991) Developing appropriate spatial analysis methods for GIS. In: Maguire D J, Goodchild M F, Rhind D W (eds.) *Geographical Information Systems: principles and applications*. Longman, London, pp. 389–402, Vol 1

Openshaw S, Goddard J (1987) Some implications of the commodification of information and the emerging information economy for applied geographical analysis in the United Kingdom. *Environment and Planning A* **19**: 1423–39

Ozemoy V M, Smith D R, Sicherman A (1981) Evaluating computerized geographic information systems using decision analysis. *Interfaces* **11**: 92–8

Parent P, Church R (1987) Evolution of geographic information systems as decision making tools. *Proceedings of GIS '87*. ASPRS/ACSM, Falls Church VA, pp. 63–71

Parker H D (1988) The unique qualities of a geographic information system: a commentary. *Photogrammetric Engineering and Remote Sensing* **54** (11): 1547–49

Reed C N (1986) DELTAMAP just another new GIS? *Proceedings of the 3rd International Symposium on Spatial Data Handling*. IGU Commission on Geographical Data Sensing and Processing, Williamsville NY, pp. 375–83

Rhind D W (1988) A GIS research agenda. *International Journal of Geographical Information Systems* **2**: 23–8

Rhind D W (1990) Global databases and GIS. In: Foster M J, Shand P J (eds.) *The Association for Geographic Information Yearbook 1990*. Taylor & Francis and Miles Arnold, London, pp. 218–23

Rowley J, Gilbert P (1989) The market for land information services, systems and support. In: Shand P J, Moore R V (eds.) *The Association for Geographic Information Yearbook 1989*. Taylor & Francis and Miles Arnold, London, pp. 85–91

Shand P J, Moore R V (eds.) *The Association for Geographic Information Yearbook 1989*. Taylor & Francis and Miles Arnold, London, pp. 85–91

Smallworld Systems (1990) GIS in Europe – summary report. *Geodetical Info Magazine* **4** (4): 28–9

Smith T R, Menon S, Starr J L, Estes J E (1987) Requirements and principles for the implementation and construction of large-scale geographic information systems. *International Journal of Geographical Information Systems* **1**: 13–31

Star J, Estes J E (1990) *Geographic Information Systems*. Prentice Hall, Englewood Cliffs New Jersey

Tomlin C D (1986) *The IBM Personal Computer version of the Map Analysis Package*. Harvard University Graduate

School of Design Laboratory for Computer Graphics and Spatial Analysis, Cambridge Massachusetts

Tomlin C D (1990) *Geographic Information Systems and Cartographic Modelling*. Prentice Hall, Englewood Cliffs New Jersey

Tomlin C D (1991) Cartographic modelling. In: Maguire D J, Goodchild M F, Rhind D W (eds.) *Geographical Information Systems: principles and applications*. Longman, London, pp. 361–74, Vol 1

Unwin D J (1991) The academic setting of GIS. In: Maguire D J, Goodchild M F, Rhind D W (eds.) *Geographical Information Systems: principles and applications*. Longman, London, pp. 81–90, Vol 1

THE HISTORY OF GIS

J T COPPOCK AND D W RHIND

Computer-based GIS have been used since at least the late 1960s: their manual predecessors were in use perhaps 100 years earlier. Acknowledging the paucity of well-documented evidence, this chapter describes the background to the development of such systems, stressing the context in which such development took place, the role of organizations and individuals where this can be ascertained, and the applications which the systems were intended to meet. A broad definition is taken of GIS so as not to exclude any significant developments; computer mapping systems of all types (including those with line-printer graphics, the forerunners of contemporary raster systems) are included.

It is demonstrated that most, but by no means all, of the early developments originated in North America. The roles of key organizations such as the US Bureau of the Census, the US Geological Survey, the Harvard Laboratory for Computer Graphics and the Experimental Cartography Unit are described and the activities of the commercial sector are exemplified by a case study of Environmental Systems Research Institute. Reasons are suggested for significant international differences in the development of GIS, such as the attitudes to ownership of data and the perceived role of the state. It is concluded that several stages of evolution of GIS can be defined. These overlap in time and occur at different moments in different parts of the world. The first, or pioneering age, extended from the early 1960s to about 1975; in this, individual personalities were of critical importance in determining what was achieved. The second phase, approximately from 1973 until the early 1980s, saw a regularization of experiment and practice within and fostered by national agencies; local experiment and action continued untrammelled and duplication of effort was common. The third phase, running from about 1982 until the late 1980s, was that of commercial dominance. The fourth (and current) phase is one of user dominance, facilitated by competition among vendors, embryonic standardization on open systems and increasing agreement on the user's perception of what a GIS should do and look like.

INTRODUCTION

A variety of information indicates that the field of GIS has expanded rapidly in recent years (see Maguire 1991 in this volume). From where did all this business and the resulting jobs arise? Unhappily, we scarcely know. GIS is a field in which history is little more than anecdotal. To rectify this, a search through the archives of government departments and agencies would certainly help. As yet, however, few organizations have given any thought to formalizing the history of their involvement in GIS and at least one major player (Ordnance Survey; see Finch 1987) has refused to let its detailed records be examined by external researchers. Less certainly, the records of computer hardware and software companies could also be a source of relevant information but no such material has been uncovered. Unfortunately for those writing the history of GIS, neither staff of commercial companies nor government officials have a tradition of writing books or papers on their experience of an emerging technology. Research staff in government or private sector research organizations are exceptions to this rule but, even for them, writing papers for the benefit of the scientific community at large has a relatively low priority. As far as is known, the only official attempt anywhere to provide a broad overview of the field as a whole is that given by the Report of the Committee of Inquiry into the Handling of Geographic Information (Department of the Environment 1987; Rhind and Mounsey 1989).

The main source of information, with all the risks of partisan bias, remains researchers in the academic community. In reality, however, even the numbers of academics working in this field were quite small until the expansion of the last decade. Moreover, as Chrisman (1988) and Rhind (1988) both testify, those active in universities in this field in the early stages of the development of GIS were often outside the formal academic career structure and were so heavily involved in project work that they had little time or inclination to write papers. In any case, at the beginning there were no obvious outlets for publication in a topic that was seen as marginal to a large number of interests; Rhind's (1976) report, for instance, may well be the first example of a record of GIS conference papers which were described as such in a mainstream academic publication. While the advent of specialist GIS conferences (often disguised by use of other titles such as AUTOCARTO) provided one publishing mechanism from 1974 onwards, the early conference proceedings were intermittent and were not easily accessible to those who had not attended the gatherings. We do not believe this postulated paucity of recorded history represents incompetence on our part: a correspondence prompted by the editor of *Photogrammetric Engineering and Remote Sensing*, for example (Marble 1989; Tomlinson 1989), generated great controversy and revealed a lack of documentation on the first use of GIS in the refereed literature.

Finally and most crucially, the content of any history of GIS depends in large measure on the definition adopted. A strict definition, as a computer-based system for *analysing* spatially referenced data, would greatly restrict the field because, with the major exception of the Canada Geographic Information System (Tomlinson 1967), this was not a common feature until the 1980s. A more general interpretation, as any system for handling geographical data, would greatly widen the field and hence enlarge the number of contributors. Such a definition would embrace, not only the whole field of automation in cartography (which was often the precursor to any involvement in GIS and provided, in terms of computer-generated graphics, the most common form of output for most early systems), but also many general-purpose statistical and database packages capable of handling x,y,z point data. Formal definitions of GIS are not, therefore, of much help and relatively little reliance is placed on them in this book as a whole. In any event, the field evolved not from some *ex cathedra* definition of the subject but through sets of interactions. The main backgrounds of those involved have been cartography, computer science, geography, surveying, remote sensing, commercial data processing, mathematics and statistics. The purposes to which the systems have been put include environmental protection, urban and regional planning, land management, property ownership and taxation, resource management, the management of utilities, site location, military intelligence and tactics, and many others – as later chapters in this volume testify. The field has developed, then, from a melting pot of concepts, ideas, practice, terminology and prejudice brought together by people from many different backgrounds, interacting with each other often on a chance and bilateral basis in the early days and normally proceeding in blissful ignorance of what was going on elsewhere. The essence of GIS is thus its multidisciplinary character, with some at least of those involved in developing this technology having little previous involvement, or even interest, in the handling of geographical data as such (see Maguire, 1991 in this volume for further discussion of the definition of GIS).

This review of the history of GIS is inevitably a consequence of the authors' accidental exposure to early developments and their own set of value-judgements; different views certainly exist, such as that manifested in Cooke's portrayal of the genealogical structure of geoprocessing systems in general (Fig. 2.1). In particular, it is suspected that the role of those who did not contribute to the formal literature has been underplayed, especially those working in the military. While regrettable, this is probably unavoidable: history very often consists solely of what has been written down.

THE GRASS ROOTS EVOLUTION OF GIS

What seems clear is that there were many initiatives, usually occurring independently and often in ignorance of each other, concerned with different facets of the field and frequently originating in the interests, often disparate, of particular individuals. Like the reality (as opposed to the reporting) of scientific research, there was no strictly logical progression towards the development and implementation of GIS, but rather a mixture of failures, set-backs, diversions and successes. Inevitably, more is known about the successes than about the failures which, according to both Dangermond and Smith (1988) and Tomlinson (1988), have been numerous and often attributable to bad advice, ignorance and a determination to go it alone. This is unfortunate because failures are often as illuminating as successes, if not more so (Giles 1987). What also seems clear is that particular individuals and institutions played key roles, acting as examples or as sources of expertise, advice and often skilled personnel; since these contributions are now better recorded than is the generality of progress, this account will tend to emphasize them, particularly those of Howard Fisher in the Harvard Laboratory for Computer Graphics (LCG), Roger Tomlinson in the Canada Geographic Information System (CGIS) and Jack Dangermond in the Environmental Systems Research Institute (ESRI) in North America, and David P. Bickmore at the Experimental Cartography Unit (ECU) in the United Kingdom. Many others played significant parts (e.g. Tobler 1959; Nordbeck 1962; Cook 1966; Hagerstrand 1967; Diello, Kirk and Callander 1969 and Boyle (see Rhind 1988)), but these four have been the subject of particular articles in a special and invaluable issue of *The American Cartographer* (Tomlinson and Petchenik 1988). Fortunately, these individuals seem to typify the interests, attitudes and commitments of those working in the vintage era of GIS from the late 1950s to the end of the 1970s.

The motivations for developing GIS or components of such systems have varied very widely. They have ranged from academic curiosity or challenge when faced with the possibility of using new sources of data or techniques, through the desire for greater speed or efficiency in the conduct of operations on spatially referenced data, to the realization that desirable tasks could be undertaken in no other way. The last was undoubtedly a powerful motive in two key developments which are discussed in more detail below – the Oxford System of Automated Cartography and the Canada Geographic Information System. It was the experience of publishing the *Atlas of Great Britain and Northern Ireland* (Bickmore and Shaw 1963) and the criticisms this attracted of being out of date and unwieldy that convinced D. P. Bickmore, probably in 1958 but certainly no later than 1960, that only the computer could provide a cost-effective mechanism to check, edit and classify data, to model situations and to facilitate experiments in graphic display (Rhind 1988). Similarly, it was the impossibility of analysing maps of East Africa at an acceptable cost that first led R. Tomlinson (1988) to think of a digital approach. A calculation made in 1965 indicated the need for some $Can 8 million in 1965 prices and a requirement for 556 technicians for three years in order to overlay the 1 : 50 000 scale maps of the Canada Land Inventory; this unacceptable level of resources acted as an incentive to develop a more automated approach.

It was, of course, the advent of the digital computer and the order-of-magnitude decrease in computing costs every six years over a 30-year period (Simonett 1988) that made such alternative digitally based approaches viable. It is interesting to note, however, that not all early work used the digital computer. Thus perhaps the earliest attempt to automate map production, the preparation of the *Atlas of the British Flora*, employed a modified punch card tabulator to produce maps on pre-printed paper from cards on which had been punched the grid references of recorded occurrences (Perring and Walters 1962). Although this approach was not repeated and Perring (1964) later recognized that the analysis of voluminous data could more easily be undertaken by computer, it anticipated the widespread mapping in the late 1960s by line printer. It is also interesting to note that Perring was a botanist, with no training in cartography, who was faced with the task of providing 2000 maps from data that had been

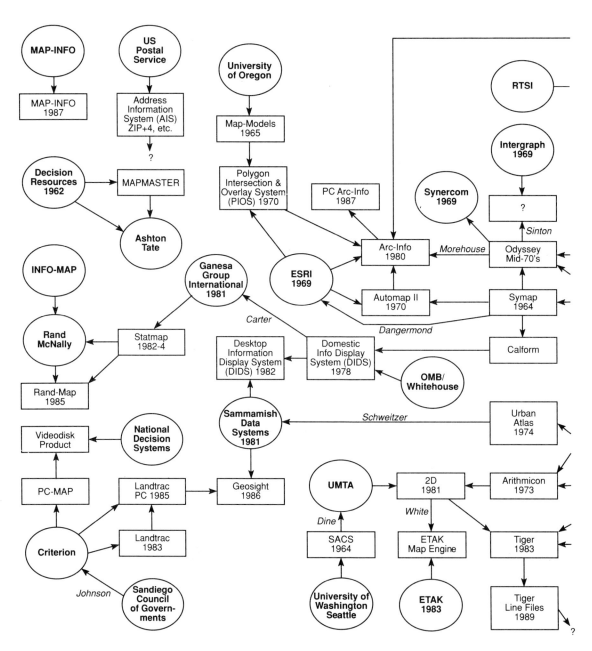

Fig. 2.1 An individual perception of the genealogy of geoprocessing in the United States (Pers. Comm. Don Cooke, 1990). Circles are 'places', i.e. companies, government agencies, universities, etc.; rectangles are ideas or concepts, often embodied in a software package or database; directed lines show direct or indirect migration or influence in a number of different ways. Examples of flows or lack of expected ones include:

The History of GIS

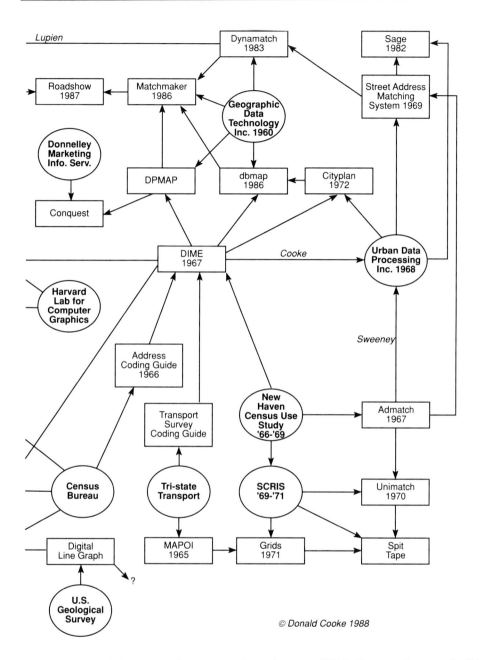

© Donald Cooke 1988

- Harvard Labs influence on GIS vendors (Morehouse to ESRI, Sinton to Intergraph; Odyssey to Synercom)
- DIME was independent from the SACS (Small Area Census Studies)
- the diagram suggests that the USGS and the US Postal Service had very little influence on most developments.

recorded on punch cards. His initiative also illustrates an aspect to be repeated in many later projects where the application of technology was driven by an urgent need of the users, that such a task would have to take advantage of the best available technology – whatever its limitations – rather than await the ideal solution; it was also similar to many later applications in that it was a 'one-off' development which, having served its purpose, was not taken any further. Slightly later work (around 1967) by Bertin in Paris involved the modification of IBM 'golfball' typewriters driven directly by punch card readers to produce proportional symbol maps.

It is also clear that it was in North America that most of the significant early developments in, and applications of, GIS and related technology were made. By the early 1980s, Tomlinson (1985) estimated that there were probably more than 1000 systems in North America, a figure that must have represented a very high proportion of the systems then existing in the world as a whole. The bulk of this account will accordingly focus on North America, with later references to the United Kingdom and other European countries and to developments elsewhere in the developed world. It is only in the late 1980s that any significant developments have occurred in developing countries and then often through the aid and encouragement of developed countries (see Taylor 1991 in this volume).

THE NORTH AMERICAN SCENE

Aangeenbrug (pers. comm. 1990) has argued that the earliest antecedents of GIS in the United States can be traced back to the University of Washington. In the 1950s, both geographers (notably Garrison) and transportation engineers (notably Horwood) developed quantitative methods in transportation studies. Garrison's colleagues and students included Berry, Tobler and Marble; Horwood's included Barb and Dueker (see Dueker's important 1974 paper). Much of the original leadership of the Urban and Regional Information Systems Association (founded in 1963) and that of other key bodies was derived from or directly influenced by this group.

By the early 1960s, at least in North America, large mainframe computers were becoming widely available. In 1964, IBM introduced its 360/65 computer, with a processing speed 400 times faster and a memory 32 times as great as its predecessor, the IBM 1401 (Tomlinson 1985). These machines were employed primarily for one of two very different purposes: for routine administrative and data management tasks in business and government (such as pay-roll, stock control and record keeping of various kinds) and for scientific applications involving extensive computations, notably in chemistry, mathematics and physics. There was inevitably a good deal of discussion in government departments and agencies about the possibility of applying computer technology to handle numerical data, especially where these were already in machine-readable form, as with many censuses, where punch-card technology was widely used. In 1965 the US Bureau of the Budget compiled an inventory of automatic data processing in the Federal Government, in which it noted the significant use of computers to handle land use and land title data (Cook and Kennedy 1966). The following year, a conference on a comprehensive unified land system at the University of Cincinnati was advised that a system must be designed such that it obtained the maximum benefit from electronic data processing equipment (Cook 1966). The conference also heard that the District of Columbia already had a property data bank, which could be searched, updated and retrieved, and that Nassau County in New York would be the first to provide fully-automated access to records of land ownership.

The significance of the developments at the US Bureau of the Census, stemming directly from its need for automated address matching, is difficult to overemphasize. This need arose from the predominantly mail out/mail back nature of the US census and the requirement to produce area based tabulations from records whose only geographical reference was the postal address. An early advisory committee on small area data included Garrison (see above), who urged a development project to test automated data linkage procedures. A director hired to run the test, Caby Smith, recruited a team which included Corbett, Cooke, Maxfield, White, Farnsworth, Jaro, Broome and others who appear elsewhere in these pages. The first demonstrations of address matching, computer mapping and small area data analysis were provided through the 1967

New Haven Census Use Study (USBC 1969–73). Subsequent studies elsewhere in the United States, the launch of the DIME workshops in 1970 and the development and widespread distribution of ADMATCH (address matching software) all had major impacts upon government and academia in the United States. Indeed, the Census Use Study also sponsored the First International DIME Colloquium in 1972, leading to the creation of the Segment (later re-named as the Spatially) Orientated Referencing Systems Association (or SORSA), an organization which still holds international conferences.

Increasing availability of computers in universities was undoubtedly instrumental in the development of the quantitative revolution in academic geography in the early 1960s (James and Martin 1978; Hudson 1979), particularly in the field of spatial analysis (a term which was in general use by the late 1960s – see Berry and Marble 1968), with its emphasis on the statistical treatment of geographical data and on modelling. However, these applications, despite their potential relevance to handling geographical data, had little interaction with computer mapping, primarily because the statistical methodology was largely aspatial. One exception is a paper in an edited collection on computers in geography which related modelling to a crude cartography using the line printer (Rushton 1969). It is only in the middle and late 1980s that successful attempts have been made to develop closely coupled spatial statistics and 'geographical' displays.

Computers in the 1960s had, in general, no explicitly graphical facilities, usually operated in batch mode and were very expensive by today's standards. Despite this, Tobler (1959) had early recognized their potential for automating cartography, as had Nordbeck (1962) in Sweden. There were, indeed, developments in automating cartography in several national agencies concerned with mapping and in military establishments which could afford equipment that was prohibitively expensive to others. The US National Ocean Survey was creating charts on a Gerber plotter for the production of 'figure fields' or matrices of depth values and such organizations as the Aeronautical Charting and Information Center at St Louis, the Rome Air Development Center and the Central Intelligence Agency were active in aspects of this field (Diello, Kirk and Callender 1968; Tomlinson 1972). By the end of the 1960s, map production assisted by computer appears to have become widespread; for example, the Canadian Hydrographic Survey had automated display facilities in operation and Surveys and Mapping had embarked on a programme to apply automated cartography to the 1 : 50 000 series in Canada. In the main, however, the aim in computer applications in national mapping agencies was to mimic manual methods of production and so to produce maps that were virtually indistinguishable from their manual counterparts. Little information appears to be available on the extent to which these methods were cost effective, although Tomlinson (1985) suggests that the high cost of hardware placed them at a disadvantage in competition with manual systems: continuing evaluations of costs by the Ordnance Survey in Britain, for example, did not find automated approaches to map production as a whole to be cost effective until the 1980s. Unlike the situation in Britain, where a digitizing production line was in operation from 1973, the Topographic Division of the United States Geological Survey did not implement plans to automate the production of topographic maps until the start of the 1980s – a severe handicap to the development of many geographically-based information systems in the United States.

An entirely different approach to the automation of cartography was adopted elsewhere, notably in the universities, using the standard line printer as a mapping device. In cartographic terms, the results were crude, but this was not the point; the aim was to produce maps quickly and cheaply so as to display the characteristics of the data (especially statistical data for census tracts and the like) and to undertake simple analyses of such data by relating different parameters. It was here that Howard Fisher made a significant contribution and this approach found ready applications in landscape design, in urban and regional planning and, to a lesser extent, in resource management.

The Harvard Laboratory for Computer Graphics

Fisher was not a cartographer but trained and practised as an architect. He had begun work on a computer mapping system in 1963 while at the North Western Technical Institute (Schmidt and

Zafft 1975). On his retirement, he succeeded in obtaining a grant from the Ford Foundation to develop this work and, after making unsuccessful approaches to Chicago and Northwestern Universities (both strongholds of non-spatial computer applications to the analysis of geographical data), established the Laboratory for Computer Graphics (a title subsequently lengthened by the addition of 'and Spatial Analysis') in 1965 in the Graduate School of Design at Harvard University – from which he himself had graduated. There he built up a team of programmers and others to create a mapping package (SYMAP) which used the line printer as a mapping device and was capable of producing isoline, choropleth and proximal (Thiessen polygon or Dirichlet tessellation) maps. The package was easy to use by the standards of the day, particularly in relation to data for census tracts, incorporated default options when nothing was specified by users and was widely distributed. In addition to many pirated copies, over 500 institutions acquired SYMAP (Schmidt and Zafft 1975; Chrisman 1988); half of these were in universities, with the remainder equally divided between government agencies and private institutions. Copies were acquired not only in North America but also in Europe and elsewhere and the manual was translated into several languages, including Japanese. A subsequent program, CALFORM, which produced higher quality choropleth maps by pen plotter and reflected the increasing (if still sparse) availability of these plotters, seems to have had less success although it too was a pioneering effort. SYMAP was important as the first widely distributed computer package for handling geographical data. It introduced large numbers of users to the possibilities of computer mapping; it was the precursor, and possibly the progenitor, of a large number of other programs using the line printer; and it found a wide range of applications particularly through the connection between the Harvard Laboratory and landscape architects in the Graduate School of Design, notably C. Steinitz and his associates – one of whom, D. Sinton, produced a cell-based program (GRID) which permitted multiple overlays of data. Somewhat surprisingly, the appointment of a theoretical geographer, W. Warntz, to succeed Fisher as Professor of Theoretical Geography and Planning and head of the Laboratory in 1969, had little effect on the work and apparently stimulated little interaction between quantitative geography and computer mapping.

The Laboratory generated a wide range of contracts which, after the expiry of its grant from the Ford Foundation, became the main source of finance, along with income generated by the sale of mapping packages. It never developed a teaching programme (which might have prolonged its life) and thus only directly added a few new professionals to the field, although it did organize a highly significant symposium on topological data structures in 1977 and hosted influential Harvard Computer Graphics Weeks between 1978 and 1981. It also attracted at various times talented individuals who contributed in many ways to the development of computer mapping and, by extension, to geographical information systems. Among these are N. Chrisman, J. Dangermond, G. Dutton, S. Morehouse, T. Peucker and D. Sinton, several of whom contributed to the design and construction of ODYSSEY, arguably the prototype of contemporary vector GIS (Chrisman 1988). Unhappily, the subsequent history of this system was characterized by a series of unsuccessful marriages between the Laboratory and commercial enterprises and the departure of key staff from Harvard. As a consequence, numbers of staff declined and the Laboratory finally closed in the late 1980s. Overall, probably its most important contributions were in sparking creative thinking on GIS, creating a widespread awareness of the possibilities of handling and (to a lesser extent) analysing spatial data, and in stimulating programmes elsewhere which have contributed to the longer term development of GIS.

The Canada Geographic Information System

At about the same time as Fisher was developing his ideas on computer mapping at Harvard, R. Tomlinson (Tomlinson 1988) was involved in creating possibly the first true GIS – and certainly the first to be so entitled. Tomlinson can be thought of as the father of GIS through his role in persuading the Canadian Government that the creation of the Canada Geographic Information System (or CGIS, as it became known) in 1966, was a worthwhile investment. The origins of this, however, go back to 1960 when he was working for an air survey company, Spartan Air Services, which was undertaking a forest survey in East Africa. The firm had been asked to analyse all available map sources to identify locations for new plantations and for a new mill. The estimated costs of doing this manually were so high that the proposal was rejected. Tomlinson had argued that such analyses could be undertaken by computer and was given the opportunity to develop a digital methodology. None of the computer companies he approached was interested, although a subsequent chance encounter led to an expression of interest by IBM, which was already involved in digitizing air photographs. Another chance encounter on an internal flight found him sitting next to Lee Pratt, an administrator in the Department of Agriculture, which was then planning a Canada Land Inventory (CLI) involving the production of many maps of land capability for the whole of settled Canada; the analysis of these maps was expected to throw light on the agricultural rehabilitation of marginal farms. Tomlinson again expressed his belief that computer-based techniques would perform such analyses both faster and more cheaply. He clearly succeeded in impressing Pratt, whose subsequent support was critical to the development of the system. A contract was awarded to Spartan Air Services to undertake a feasibility study of a computer mapping system for the CLI. With the help of computer expertise from the staff of IBM, Tomlinson compiled a report which was accepted by the Department of Agriculture and he was then invited to direct its development within the Canadian Agricultural Rehabilitation and Development Administration (ARDA).

This development involved a large number of people both within ARDA and in IBM, and led to several significant developments for the future of GIS – among them, the creation of a drum scanner for the rapid digitization of maps (based on earlier IBM work of digitizing aerial photographs), of a data indexing scheme (the Morton Index 1966, which was subsequently widely emulated) and of a topological coding of boundaries involving the first known use of the link/node concept of encoding lines. The drum scanner, together with digitizing tables, provided the input to the system which was then based on an IBM 360/65 mainframe computer; output could be by line printer for numerical results and by ponderous Gerber plotter if a graphical output was required. It is interesting to note that there was minimal contact between CGIS and other bodies engaged in automated cartography and quantitative geography.

Tomlinson left the CGIS project in 1969, by which time Pratt had also left the Department of Agriculture. Although the various capabilities of the CGIS had been successfully demonstrated by this time, it was not until 1971 that the system was fully operational and subsequently it was reorganized and simplified. It now contains a digital archive of some 10 000 maps on more than 100 different topics. From the outside, it is difficult to evaluate the success of CGIS. Excluding those systems based on remote sensing data and the much more recent TIGER system (see Rhind 1991 in this volume), it may still be the largest GIS in operation and the only one to cover an area of continental extent in such detail; but its use seems to have been limited, in part no doubt because it took much time to build up the database as maps became available and because it came successively under four different departments, being given a different remit on each occasion. No doubt the facts that 'land' is a provincial responsibility in Canada and that CGIS was, for most of its existence, a passive organization, administered by technicians waiting for users to seek its services were also contributory factors. Its location in Ottawa, the lack of computer networking at the time and the prior availability of easily distributed printed maps of land capability – which users elsewhere in Canada may have regarded as more accessible – were other possible factors in its limited operational (as opposed to technical) success.

Early government activities in the United States

Tomlinson departed in 1969 to become a private consultant within the GIS field, one of an initially rare but increasingly necessary breed as proprietary systems multiplied and salespeople sought to persuade clients of the desirability of their systems. In addition, he continued to play an important role as Chairman, for the first 12 years of its existence, of the International Geographical Union's Commission on Geographical Data Sensing and Processing, which had been established in 1968 and which sponsored two major international conferences in Ottawa in 1970 and 1972, the first such conferences to be specifically identified with GIS. This emphasis helped to give currency to the name which the CGIS had pioneered, to promote contacts between delegates from a wide range of disciplines and locations, and to provide an overview of developments in the early 1970s (Tomlinson 1970, 1972). Subsequently, the Commission undertook an evaluation of the handling of digital spatial data within the US Geological Survey which, in 1976, had more than 15 information system activities concerned with the gathering and handling of spatial information in the fields of geology, geography, topography and water resources. The Commission also published, under the auspices of the UNESCO Natural Resources Research Series, a major monograph on the computer handling of geographical data (Tomlinson, Calkins and Marble, 1976).

These investigations also revealed that by 1976 there were at least 285 items of computer software handling spatial data which had been developed outside the USGS; by 1980, when a revision of the findings of this project was published, the number had risen to over 500 (Marble 1980). These figures are one measure of the rapid progress in this field in the late 1960s and the 1970s. They also illustrate one feature of that development which the CGIS had earlier demonstrated, that there was relatively little contact between the developers of such software. As a result, there was also considerable duplication, with programs being developed independently by different agencies to perform the same function. In part this was a consequence of a growing awareness of the possibilities provided by computers for handling spatial data and for displaying results of analyses through automated cartography. Within the universities, too, individuals were writing programs, often to fulfil a contractual obligation with a locally based agency that lacked the expertise to do so itself.

Tomlinson (1988) described the 1970s as a period of lateral diffusion rather than of innovation and there is considerable piecemeal evidence to show an increasing interest among a variety of agencies at all levels of government – federal, state, county and city. These include military and security establishments (such as the Central Intelligence Agency, which developed a world data bank for its own purposes and then made it available in the public domain (see Anderson, Angel and Gurney 1978); land management agencies such as the US Forest Service (Shumway 1986); conservation bodies such as the Fish and Wildlife Service (Christianson 1986); the Department of Housing and Urban Development (Goldstein, Wertz and Sweet 1969); the Bureau of the Census (see earlier description and USBC 1969–73)) and others at federal level; states such as California, Maryland, Minnesota, New York and Oregon; counties such as Fairfax in Virginia (Lay 1975) and cities such as Kansas City and Oakland. Some took existing software, as in the application of SYMAP in the Oakland Planning Information System (Goldstein, Wertz and Sweet 1969); others developed their own software in-house.

No comprehensive record exists of these various, local approaches but those adopted in the Bureau of the Census and in the USGS may be taken to represent the federal level. Initially, they developed quite separately, but have partially come together in the late 1980s to link digital cover from the USGS 1 : 100 000 topographic map series with census tracts for the 1990 population census, developments that will provide the basis for a variety of GIS initiatives throughout the United States (Callahan and Broome 1984).

As already indicated, the Bureau's substantial involvement in geographical data processing began with the New Haven Census Use Study in 1967 (USBC 1969–73) which led to the Dual Independent Map Encoding (DIME) scheme as the standard method for encoding data for census areas and (later) the preparation of experimental computer-generated maps of census data (Schweitzer 1973). The essence of DIME was a method of describing the urban structure through recording the topological relationships of streets; the earliest DIME files contained no coordinates. The advantage of proceeding thus was to provide an automated method of checking the completeness of areas built up from street boundaries – of particular importance since the US Census is substantially a mail out/mail back operation and the descriptions of the geography were assembled in many Census offices across the country (Dewdney and Rhind 1986). During 1972, the Bureau decided to embark on the creation of atlases for the major metropolitan areas (Schweitzer 1973), a task with which the Harvard Laboratory became involved in 1975 (Chrisman 1988). The Urban Atlas Project required the digitizing of maps of some 35 000 census tracts in the metropolitan areas and demonstrated the cost effectiveness of such an approach. It also required the development of software for handling this large quantity of data. Particularly significant in all these developments in the Bureau was a small group of mathematicians led by James P. Corbett and including Marvin White. Although it appeared subsequent to the Loomis (1965) paper, Corbett's definitive paper on the topological principles underlying cartography and GIS appeared in 1975 and a readily obtainable version of it was later published by the Bureau itself (Corbett 1979); it is clear that much of the credit for defining how topology theory is applied in the field of GIS is due to this group and to others working in applications areas in the Census at the time, such as Don Cooke. From this beginning came the subsequent extensions to DIME, the development of ARITHMICON and, ultimately, the creation of TIGER (see Rhind 1991 in this volume), possibly the largest and most all-embracing civilian GIS project yet and on which the success of the 1990 US Census critically hinged.

The practical involvement of the USGS in the GIS field is exemplified by the development of a system to handle and analyse land resource data, the Geographical Information Retrieval and Analysis System (GIRAS), developed from 1973 onwards to handle the increasingly large data sets becoming available (Mitchell *et al.* 1977). This was developed specifically to handle information on land use and land cover, held on manually produced maps at a scale of 1 : 250 000 derived from aerial photography, although these are subsequently derived/updated directly from imagery without manual intervention, using data from the Landsat series of satellites. Such maps had first to be digitized in polygon format to provide the input to the system which had been designed to store, manipulate and analyse these data, together with others on political and administrative subdivisions and public land ownership. GIRAS was developed initially as a batch processing system (GIRAS 1) but an interactive version was subsequently developed (GIRAS 2), with access via remote terminals. Output could be produced either in statistical or graphical form, the latter through display on a CRT screen or as a plot from a Calcomp drum plotter. The system also had a capacity to convert polygonal data into gridded data, an attribute of increasing importance with the use of remotely sensed data. The USGS has since made a myriad of other contributions to the development of GIS, not least in converting many data from paper map or stereo photo to digital form. Starr and Anderson (1991 in this volume) have summarized its recent activities and future plans.

State systems may be exemplified by the Minnesota Land Management Information System (MLMIS) which appears to be one of the more successful of such systems and illustrates the transition from a university research facility to an operational system within a state agency. It is described in more detail by Robinette (1991 in this volume) but it illustrates the difficulty of finding a secure financial base for such a system and the weaknesses deriving from an early decision to collect data on a rather coarse grid. MLMIS was started in 1976 as a research project located in the Center for Urban and Regional Analysis in the University of Minnesota, where the emphasis was on pilot projects but where some limited production work was carried out (which proved to be unsuited to a university environment). The system was based upon a digital land use map of the state, prepared from aerial photography. It was subsequently taken over by the state and established as a service bureau within the state planning agency, where it operated on a 'fee for service' basis, an approach which nevertheless required that the system operation and management be subsidized. It appears that very few users were at that time willing to pay for database development and the service found that it had to take on an increasing number of projects that were marginal to its main purpose in order to remain viable. This requirement to pay its way also led to raised fees and a consequent reduction in use. Nevertheless, it has undertaken several hundred successful GIS projects during its lifetime.

The commercial sector: the example of ESRI

MLMIS is interesting as one of the systems that had a continuing existence. Many others came into being, often created by university groups under contract to local or national agencies, and subsequently disappeared for lack of funding or because a key member of the team left. Little is known of the many equivalent developments in the commercial sector although the later history of the Harvard Laboratory provides one illustration of a commercial system that failed to get off the ground. After reaching a low point in the 1970s, following the exhaustion of the original Ford grant and the withdrawal of support by the Harvard landscape architects, the Laboratory had grown again, developing software and applications. One of its central activities was the development of the vector-based GIS system, ODYSSEY. A working version of this system was in operation by 1979 and a 'hazy deal' was struck with ISSCO, a software firm involved in computer graphics, to market it. The firm advertised the software but then withdrew, leaving the Laboratory with heavy debts which left it unable to recover as a major innovator in this field.

A happier example, also with roots in the Laboratory, is represented by the success of the Environmental Systems Research Institute (ESRI), founded in 1969 by J. Dangermond, a landscape architect who had gone to Harvard in 1968 to complete a master's degree and had then returned to his native California. ESRI was not, of course, the only firm operating in this field. Intergraph (again involving a product of the Harvard Laboratory, D. Sinton, and led by James Meadlock), ComputerVision and Synercom were other major players even in the 1970s. Most of these – apart from ESRI – came into GIS from the CAD/CAM area. But, in the light of published knowledge and because it is a highly successful enterprise, ESRI must serve as an exemplar for them all.

ESRI began as a non-profit organization engaged in the field of environment consultancy, although a brochure published in 1970 identified computer graphics as one of the professional services provided (Dangermond and Smith 1988). It used and developed the cell-based package GRID as its main applications package until the launch of ARC/INFO in 1982, and also developed a three-dimensional version called GRID TOPO; in the mid/late 1970s, it developed and sold a vector-based system, the Planning Information Overlay System (PIOS). A few years after its launch, it became clear that ESRI would not succeed in raising the necessary finance for growth as a non-profit organization and it consequently became a with-profit enterprise. The firm initially used the University of California mainframe computer but, with falling costs of hardware and increasing computer use, found it more convenient and cost effective to acquire its own minicomputer. By the mid-1970s it was also advertising its competence in GIS and by the early 1980s was providing a turnkey GIS. This proved very popular and a large and growing number of such systems has been installed. ESRI's ability to make its ARC/INFO system function across computer platforms ranging from personal computers, through workstations and minicomputers up to the largest mainframes has clearly been beneficial to the company.

Initially, most of ESRI's project work was on relatively small applications, relating to site or location analyses, but it became increasingly involved in environmental questions, reflecting the growing recognition of environmental problems in the United States. In 1973, it began work on its first state-wide system designed for mapping environmental suitability, the Maryland Automatic Geographic Information (MAGI) system, which became a model for other state systems. It had earlier participated in several applications in town planning in the United States, Australia, Canada, France, Japan and Venezuela. Other projects were undertaken in wastewater management, biological conservation, land reclamation, floodplain management, recreational planning and other topics.

Throughout the 1970s and early 1980s, staff of ESRI undertook a great deal of the project work themselves in the absence of appropriate expertise in commissioning agencies. It is unclear how far this widening range and increasing number of applications was due to a growing awareness of ESRI's capabilities and its own efforts to make these known, and how far it was due to an increasing need by potential clients to find efficient ways of handling large quantities of data. Dangermond and Smith (1988) have suggested that, in the 1970s and early 1980s, it was a matter of pressing GIS solutions on unaware and unwilling potential users, involving constant selling and subsequent support. Nevertheless, the fact that ESRI staff were heavily involved in the projects meant that they identified any flaws in their own software at an early stage and had a strong project-oriented approach, a fact that helped to build confidence in the firm. In contrast to the 'selling job' of the 1970s, the 1980s were characterized by an increasing and accelerating trend towards acceptance of GIS, with increasing numbers of requests for information and advice (Dangermond and Smith 1988). In the circumstances where this has been the case for over a decade, users can undertake projects with little outside advice or help although ESRI seeks, through its ARCNEWS and user conferences in different parts of the world, to provide continuing support. Of all GIS vendors, ESRI has probably been the most successful in the 1980s: much of its success can be attributed to ARC/INFO. Many other factors played a role, including the personality of the ESRI founder and the forging of close links with users in education and other sectors. By the end of the 1980s, more than 2000 systems of GIS software for use on personal computers were being sold each year and ESRI had expanded from a staff of 15 in the early 1970s (though already operating throughout the United States and overseas) to one with over 350 staff and operating in a global market.

Spreading the word

Two other aspects are worthy of note, the development of teaching (initially in computer cartography and then, in the 1980s, in GIS itself) and the growing communication between workers in these fields. Many of those who had attended the early SYMAP conferences at Harvard began to develop teaching applications and, as early as 1972, a monograph on computer cartography (on which a whole chapter was devoted to SYMAP) was available in the Association of American Geographers' Resource Papers Series (Peucker 1972). Among those developing competence in this field were the University of New York at Buffalo, Simon Fraser University and the University of Saskatchewan in Canada, although Tomlinson (1988) has argued that in the 1970s there was probably more on-the-job training in commercial and government agencies than in universities.

The roles of conferences and publications in this field have already been noted. One of the first groups to publish a newsletter was the Urban and Regional Information Systems Association (URISA), founded in 1963 and holding annual meetings thereafter. Like many maturing organizations, it has eventually found the need to create its own journal and the founding issue in 1989 was largely devoted to GIS. The roles of the Harvard Graphics Weeks and the two Ottawa conferences under the auspices of the IGU Commission have already been noted. The most significant other development was the AUTOCARTO series begun (although not under that name initially) in 1974 as an International Symposium on Computer-Assisted Cartography held at Reston, Virginia (Chrisman 1988). It is interesting to note that, whereas some 40 people attended the first Ottawa conference in 1970, 300 attended the second and some 500 the first AUTOCARTO meeting (Tomlinson 1970, 1974; Chrisman 1988). Such meetings have been held at biennial or shorter intervals since that time. Such conferences became a fruitful outlet for publications by those involved in this field, although other papers were being prepared in a wide variety of professional journals (notably in the *International Journal of Geographical Information Systems*, co-edited in the United Kingdom and United States). Of course, developments in related fields must not be forgotten. Relevant papers appeared in the conferences of the Association for Computer Machinery, in publications devoted to computer-aided design, and in computing and engineering journals, especially those of the latter related to the utility companies.

By the late 1980s, then, GIS can be said to have become widely accepted in North America. The numbers of systems, courses, conferences, projects and facilities continue to multiply. Central, regional, state and local governments are increasingly involved, as are those in retailing and service delivery (see Beaumont 1991 in this volume) and in asset management (see Mahoney 1991 in this volume). The field has also acquired a degree of scientific recognition in the establishment of a National Center for Geographic Information and Analysis (NCGIA), funded by the National Science Foundation, as a cooperative venture between the Universities of California, Maine and New York (Abler 1987; see also Morrison 1991 in this volume). What is particularly interesting to an outsider is the speed with which acceptance of GIS has accelerated, to a stage where GIS is now a 'buzz word', and the extent to which the development has largely happened outside the political process, at least at a federal level. There seems, at a national level, to have been no official declaration of policy that this is a desirable path to follow. Initiatives and investments seem largely to have been effected through the bureaucratic system, although the USGS has been recognized by other federal agencies as having a coordinating role in this field at the federal level. As far as can be seen, the decision of the USGS and the US Bureau of the Census to develop what became the TIGER files and the associated line graphs for the whole of the United States was largely an internal, inter-agency agreement, unprompted by wider political considerations.

THE BRITISH EXPERIENCE

The British experience in the GIS field is in marked contrast in this regard, although there are some similarities – notably in the influential role of key personalities at an early stage in the development of GIS. Perhaps because there is little publicly owned land in the United Kingdom (and hence little direct responsibility for land management) and because the small size of the country and the highly centralized government have made for limited appreciation of spatial contrasts, the official pressures to develop computer-based methods of handling spatial data have been more limited. Moreover, local government, where such systems might usefully be applied, has experienced increasing financial constraints and a reduction in several of its key functions throughout the late 1970s and 1980s. These differences, have, however, been turned to advantage.

As in North America, the first beginnings can be seen in the 1960s in a number of areas, in the national mapping agency, in local planning and in the universities and polytechnics. A proto-GIS was proposed to the short-lived Natural Resources Advisory Committee in 1964 but, with the demise of that body, no further action was taken (Coppock 1988). A growing perception that computers provided a potential aid to land-use planning led in the late 1960s to the formation of joint working parties of officials from both central and local government and to the publication in 1972 of a report entitled General Information Systems for Planning (or GISP). This report (DoE 1972) outlined an approach that local authorities might follow, although there was never much encouragement by central government to do so nor any indication that it would adopt such an approach in its own agencies.

Bickmore, the ECU and the Ordnance Survey

Again, as in North America, a driving force in the automation of cartography was a research group, established almost entirely through the persistence and persuasiveness of one individual, D. P. Bickmore (Rhind 1988). He had been the cartographic editor of the Clarendon Press and one of the two editors of what was in effect a national atlas (Bickmore and Shaw 1963). This experience led him to the conclusion that the computer offered the only possibility of undertaking such a project reasonably expeditiously with up-to-date data. In collaboration with R. Boyle, later to be a major player in the development of automated cartography in North America, he secured funds from the Press to develop the Oxford System of Automated Cartography and, although this led to the manufacture of the world's first free-cursor digitizer and possibly the first map-making using a photohead on a high precision plotting table, no complete system was ever produced. However, Bickmore was successful in persuading the newly formed Natural Environmental Research Council (NERC) to fund a research unit in automated cartography. The Experimental Cartography Unit (ECU) became fully operational in 1967–68 at the Royal College of Art in London and focused its attention initially on the computer-assisted production of high-quality printed maps (see, for instance, Experimental Cartography Unit 1971; Rhind 1971). From 1973 onwards, it largely concerned itself with GIS issues. In 1975, the ECU was absorbed into the Natural Environment Research Council headquarters at Swindon and later became the NERC Unit for Thematic Information Systems at Reading University.

Like the Harvard Laboratory in its later years, the work of the Unit was highly project based, in collaboration with the Ordnance Survey (the national mapping agency), national agencies for geology, soils and oceanography, and planning agencies. Software was developed for changing projections, editing, data compression, automated contouring and so on, and experimental maps produced for the cooperating agencies. No marketable software analogous to SYMAP or other Harvard Laboratory programs was developed although plans were laid in 1971–72 to market the Unit's interactive editing software which ran on a DEC PDP 15 computer. But like the Laboratory, it exercised an important influence on thinking about automation and Rhind (1988) has argued that, without the Unit, the Ordnance Survey (OS) would not have begun its investigations into digital mapping or the production of digital maps until several years later at least.

The path initially followed by the ECU was not directly concerned with GIS. Nor, indeed, did the OS involvement in automated map making at first have any direct bearing on GIS. The approach adopted by the OS from 1971 onwards (see Sowton 1991 in this volume; Finch 1987) was to simulate manual production of its maps as closely as possible, an approach which facilitated map production but made it impossible to use the resulting digital data in an information system because they are unstructured. By 1973, the OS had established a production line to digitize and plot automatically versions of its large-scale plans as they came up for revision, a process that was necessarily random in its spatial occurrence. This approach did not become cost effective until the late 1980s, but it gradually came to be appreciated (both within the OS and outside) that a digital map framework could provide the base through which digital records of soil, geology, vegetation, assets and plant and the like could be related. An attempt was, therefore, made as early as 1974–75 to restructure the digital data through the development of appropriate software. The approach to preparing such a digital base through the process of map revision was not only random but also slow and the OS has come under increasing pressure to accelerate production of digital maps, at least for the bulk of the populated areas (which now seems likely to be completed not later than 1995). If this is achieved, OS will have well in excess of 200 000 maps in computer form – a total unmatched anywhere else in the world. In the British situation, where a consistent and large-scale series of maps exists, compiled to a common standard and datum and updated continuously, this coverage provides a highly valuable spatial framework on which other data can be assembled and linked (see Sowton 1991 in this volume).

Finally, it may not be appreciated by readers outside the United Kingdom that there are two Ordnance Survey departments within the nation state: one for Great Britain and the other for Northern Ireland. The latter became committed to a database approach rather than a map reproduction one earlier than did the former (see, for instance, Brand 1986). The Northern Ireland OS operates in a quite different – and generally more favourable – government and financial environment from that responsible for mapping the rest of the United Kingdom, but its task is much smaller and less onerous.

Other British developments of GIS

A variety of other historical developments has influenced the current GIS scene in the United Kingdom. For example, research staff in the Department of the Environment (DoE) had developed a mapping system for use in the Department and in central government as early as 1969 (Gaits 1969), but it seems to have had only limited application there, presumably because its usefulness was not recognized by administrators and planners. The Scottish Development Department, the planning ministry in Scotland, did fund a pilot rural information system, the Rural Land Use Information System (RLUIS), involving a large number of national agencies and two local authority districts in Fife, but this work was discontinued when the originating body, the Standing Committee on Rural Land Use, was abolished (Lyall 1980). Probably the greatest interest in GIS was expressed by the agencies concerned with environmental matters but these were small, with limited budgets, and were largely dependent on data collected by others, so that until the 1980s only limited progress was made. In Scotland, however, a consortium of three agencies (the Countryside Commission for Scotland, the Forestry Commission and the Scottish Tourist Board) did commission a university research unit, the Tourism and Recreation Research Unit, to construct and operate a simple GIS, the Tourism and Recreation Information Package (TRIP), to assist them in planning and policy making (Duffield and Coppock 1975).

Initiatives taken within planning authorities in local government to establish information systems following the 1972 GISP Report varied greatly, although in total they can only be described as disappointing until the late 1980s (Rhind 1987). The National Gazetteer Pilot Study in the Metropolitan County of Tyne and Wear was the first of a number of property-based systems, probably taken furthest in the now-abolished Greater London Council and the Merseyside Metropolitan County. The experience of several such systems, with particular reference to Berkshire, Nottinghamshire and Warwickshire, has been reviewed by Grimshaw (1988), who suggests that, probably for a variety of institutional reasons, the use of such systems has declined. Certainly the encouragement offered by the GISP Report led to only limited development, in part because of the determination and ability of central government to restrain expenditure by local authorities. There appears to have been an increasing interest in the use of automated map production in planning departments, initially by line printer maps using programs such as SYMAP; a study sponsored by the DoE and the Scottish Development Department to develop a proto-information system for planning in Scotland led instead to guidance through workshops and consultancies on the ways in which such mapping could assist the planning process (Coppock and Barritt 1978). There was, too, an increasing attention to management information systems in local government, as exemplified by the innovative Local Authority Management Information System (LAMIS) developed by International Computers Ltd (Rhind and Hudson 1980), but this appears to have had relatively little impact on GIS. The potential significance of applications of computer-based handling of data was, however, increasingly recognized. The Royal Town Planning Institute established a committee on the topic in the early 1970s, a British equivalent of the Urban and Regional Information Systems Association (BURISA) was established in 1970 and the National Computing Centre attempted to promote interest in this field. Nevertheless, the practical results of such interests were small, although these developments no doubt assisted the explosion of interest which occurred in the late 1980s.

As in North America, initiatives by central and local government were sometimes undertaken through the agency of university researchers, with the Universities of Durham, Edinburgh and London among the main foci of such work. The staff of such universities were also involved in a number of initiatives in computer mapping; in particular, T. C. Waugh (1980) developed his widely used GIMMS package at Edinburgh from 1970 onwards. Other initiatives were undertaken by researchers in the Institute of Terrestrial Ecology (ITE), where national databases of environmental and land use data were developed (Brown and Norris 1988).

Despite the late start, the single most important influence on GIS in the United Kingdom in recent years has probably been the growth in use by utilities of digital mapping data in conjunction with records of their own plant. Indeed, they are now the main driving force behind the acceleration of the digitizing of the coverage of OS digital maps. Since this is very recent, currently involves no major methodological advance in GIS and is described by Sowton (1991) and by Mahoney (1991) in this volume, no more will be said here except to stress its importance in providing data which are also useful for other purposes.

Official inquiries relating to GIS

A distinguishing characteristic of the United Kingdom in the decade between 1978 and 1987 is the series of inquiries carried out by the British Government or Parliament into geographical data and its use (see Chorley and Buxton 1991 in this volume). These demonstrate a shift in emphasis in successive inquiries. The first of these was the Ordnance Survey Review Committee, appointed in 1978 to advise on long-term policy for the OS. It paid considerable attention to the adoption of digital mapping, recommending that – if it was proved (as the Committee expected it would be) that digital mapping was cost effective – the OS should accelerate conversion from manual methods to provide digital coverage at the 1 : 50 000 scale by 1982–83 and at the basic (i.e. primary mapping) scales (of 1 : 1250, 1 : 2500 and 1 : 10 000) by 1992–93; it made no reference to GIS as such. This report, then, considered OS very much in terms of its role as a traditional map producer, but producing the paper maps in future by digital means.

The Report of the House of Lords Select Committee on Science and Technology (House of Lords 1984; see also Rhind 1986) investigated both digital mapping and remote sensing. It was much more appreciative of the potential benefits of digital data as such and, among its many recommendations were several on the need to accelerate the OS digitizing programme and the manner in which this should be done. In addition, it recognized the pervasive nature of geographical data and the many interrelationships and dependencies being built up, principally with regard to OS data. Therefore, it recommended the establishment of a Committee of Enquiry into the handling of geographical data. Such a Committee was established under the chairmanship of Lord Chorley and found widespread interest in such data; a large part of its

Report (DoE 1987; Rhind and Mounsey 1989; Chorley and Buxton 1991 in this volume) was devoted to the role of the OS in providing a digital map framework. In addition, however, it strongly emphasized the role of GIS, examined the value of standards for spatial referencing, noted that the lack of 'awareness' of what is possible and what is already going on in other areas was a major impediment to the widespread use of GIS, and recommended the establishment of a centre for coordination and advice on the handling of geographic data. Some of the recommendations were acted upon speedily: thus considerable resources have since been put into GIS research in the United Kingdom by the Natural Environment and the Economic and Social Research Councils (Goodchild and Rhind 1990). More significantly, there has been a move away from maps as products in themselves towards the view that they are only one of many sources providing geographical data for use in GIS. In essence, a database approach is now firmly established in British government thinking and, because of the highly centralized nature of the state in comparison to that of the United States and the existence of a ubiquitously used and country wide spatial referencing framework (the National Grid), this approach may be expected to permeate most organizations quite quickly.

Yet, despite this initiative to study what should be done in the national interest, the commitment by government departments to making geographical data generally available has been less than had been hoped. This is significant because data are not 'in the public domain' in the United Kingdom; government sees itself as entirely justified in charging for its data and, indeed, OS receives over one-third of its budget from cost recovery – a figure which will certainly rise (Rhind 1990). The military have marketed (through OS) Digital Elevation Models at 50 m resolution derived from the OS 1 : 50 000 scale contours and the Census offices have agreed to code each 1991 Census household response with a postcode (1.3 million of which exist for the country, so a multiplicity of small area data sets could be constructed for particular purposes). A significant factor is that income generated by sales of data by government departments does not generally accrue to them but reverts to the Treasury; since no part of their budget is provided for making data available and since to do so demands resources, little incentive exists for data to be provided. However, recent relaxations in rules as some departments are converted into executive agencies may alter the situation.

If activity in the United Kingdom in GIS was disappointingly small in the 1970s and early 1980s after the pioneer work of the ECU and OS, it expanded greatly in the late 1980s, stimulated by the publication of the Chorley Report. As already pointed out, much of the funding to stimulate action has come from the utilities, which need large-scale digital databases for the efficient management of the networks they control (NJUG 1987); their pressure has been influential in simplifying the specification for digitizing OS maps and in accelerating that programme. Local authorities, too, are showing a keener interest and, along with the utilities, have been major actors in the establishment in 1989 of the Association for Geographic Information (AGI), a national umbrella organization which involves vendors, chartered surveyors, geographers, educationalists, users in commerce and industry, software houses, learned societies and many others: its primary roles are to ensure the dissemination of knowledge, promote standards and advance the field. Commercial interest, which had been notably lacking in the 1970s, also rapidly developed, particularly in relation to market research (see Beaumont 1991 in this volume), plant location, local planning and traffic guidance systems, and is exemplified by the formation of Pinpoint Analysis Ltd which, in collaboration with the OS, has prepared a national database of centroid references of all properties in Britain (Rhind 1988). Finally, an exceptional contribution has been the creation of GIS demonstrators (Green 1987) and tutors (Raper and Green 1989) which have served to instruct and inform a world-wide audience.

DEVELOPMENTS ELSEWHERE IN THE WORLD

It is obvious that developments elsewhere cannot be covered in the same detail as for North America and the United Kingdom. None the less, several important distinctions need to be made. Developments elsewhere in Europe appear, apart from any military interest, to be associated primarily with national mapping agencies and with the maintenance of cadastral records of property. In respect of the latter, one of the most interesting developments has been that of the Swedish Land Databank System (SLDS), initiated in the early 1970s by a decision of the Swedish Parliament to replace the earlier manual system of property and land registration by an electronic system. An agency, the Central Bureau for Real Estate Data (CBRED), was created to establish and maintain this system. A pilot system was introduced in Uppsala County and operated under legal authority from 1976, and the system was progressively implemented, half the country having been covered by 1986 (Andersson 1987). It had a much wider application than solely in the field of property (see Dale 1991 in this volume; also Ottoson and Rystedt 1991 in this volume) and is being combined with statistics on housing and population (routinely available in Sweden on the basis of individual properties) as an input to urban and regional planning and to throw light on policy issues of various kinds, such as nuclear emergencies, civil defence and second homes.

Many applications elsewhere in the world are more recent than those in the United States. In Australia, initiatives have come primarily from two sources, cadastral mapping (a state responsibility) and applied scientific research (O'Callaghan and Garner 1991 in this volume). The handling of land records is now well established in all Australian states, having begun very early in South Australia, and is indeed internationally regarded as a major Australian success. GIS in the science area has been developed mostly through the Commonwealth Scientific and Industrial Research Organization (Cocks, Walker and Parvey 1988), where a continental-scale GIS, the Australia Resources Information System (ARIS), was begun in the late 1970s. It arose from an initial need seen in the mid-1970s for the production of maps of local government data and was stimulated by the availability of digital files of local government boundaries from the Division of National Mapping. By 1982, a wide variety of natural and socio-economic data were available. This system is essentially a research tool which has been used in a number of applications, from the location of new cities, through the identification of areas that should be withdrawn from pastoral use and of other ungrazed areas that might be devoted to this purpose, to the representativeness of National Parks. It remains a prototype, produced on a limited budget, which might serve as a model for an operational system at some future date.

Despite its immense commitment to the electronics industry, Japan showed little interest in the 1960s and 1970s in GIS, although here too interest in GIS developed very rapidly in the 1980s (Kubo 1987; see also Kubo 1991 in this volume). The only related activity in the 1970s appears to have been the production of digital land data by the Geographical Survey Institute using a 1 km grid; but no indigenous software was available to process the data and their use was accordingly very limited. The recent surge of interest has apparently been encouraged by the commercial survey and computing industries, which are very keen to acquire new business, and by central government agencies wishing to extend their control.

It is unclear from the account by Koshkariov, Tikunov and Trofimov (1989) at what stage interest in GIS occurred in the Soviet Union, although the immense challenges which that country faces in the management of natural resources throughout its vast territory seem to cry out for use of such systems; the impression is that not much had happened before 1980. By 1983, the Institute of Geography in the USSR Academy of Sciences was holding a conference on the problems of GIS science and, in the same year, the first of a series of schools and seminars for young scientists was held in the Far Eastern Research Centre on cartographic modelling and GIS. The main emphasis generally seems to have been on developing systems of automated mapping and on the preparation of cartographic databases, rather than in GIS *per se*. In this regard, the Soviets seem to be following the same path undertaken by the United States and the United Kingdom a decade or more earlier.

The history of GIS in developing countries is, in the main, similarly restricted to the 1980s when, partly through the initiatives of aid groups, a number of systems was established (see Taylor 1991 in this volume). For example, the Jamaica GIS (JAMGIS) was begun in 1981, funded by the US Agency for International Development using Michigan State University's Comprehensive Resource Inventory and Evaluation System (CRIES) as the basis (Eyre 1989), and a Land Titling Project was begun in Thailand in 1985 through a World Bank loan and technical assistance from the

Australian International Development Assistance Bureau (Angus-Leppan 1989). The latter has highlighted the importance of the staff of the host country being intimately involved in the work, of using familiar concepts and terms wherever possible, of providing comprehensive training and education, and of the role of persuasion by adequately briefed advisers.

Not all developments in such countries, however, are dependent on outside support. In the People's Republic of China, where work on digital mapping had begun in 1972 and tapes of satellite imagery had been acquired by 1975, a conference at the Academia Sinica in 1980 led to the establishment of a working group on GIS and to a number of regional initiatives. Chen Shupeng (1987) has summarized the numerous developments since then, mostly related to environmental hazard prediction and management, and carried out on microcomputers.

For completeness, reference should be made to the attempts at multinational and global GIS. Of course, the problems of developing and implementing GIS across national boundaries reflect, in exaggerated form, experiences within each country (notoriously those within the United States) of a lack of correspondence between mapping systems, data collection and the like. The European Commission (EC) has sought to develop a coordinated system of environmental mapping for the whole community. The main emphasis to date has been on the collation and evaluation of comparable data for the constituent countries and on software to handle them (Wiggins *et al.* 1987). At a global level, the availability of data from satellites, an increasing concern for the global environment and experience with such cartographic databases as World DataBank II have led to increasing interest in the possibility of world wide systems, a view that has led to initiatives to develop a topographic framework for such databases, initially through the activities of D. P. Bickmore, Chairman of a Commission of the International Cartographic Association (ICA) on a World Digital Database for Environmental Science from 1987 until 1990. Mounsey and Tomlinson (1988) have chronicled the progress of GIS in managing and exploiting global databases; it is clear from their book that such developments are still embryonic but are developing rapidly (see Clark, Hastings and Kinneman 1991 in this volume; also Townshend 1991 in this volume).

CONCLUSIONS

A history of GIS is necessarily piecemeal and partial. Inevitably, events are duplicated in different countries at different times. But, despite the unsatisfactory nature of the evidence and the fact that such conclusions are necessarily approximations to reality, four overlapping phases may be distinguished in the development of GIS in the more advanced countries. The first is the pioneer or 'research frontier' period, from the 1950s to about 1975 in the United States and the United Kingdom. This was characterized by individual – even idiosyncratic – developments, limited international contacts, little data in machine-readable form and ambitions which far out-ran the computing resources of the day. Individual personalities greatly influenced events. The second phase was that in which formal experiment and government-funded research was the norm, stretching from about 1973 to the early 1980s; the role of individuals was diminished somewhat in the international and national arenas except for strong-minded heads of national mapping agencies, but at the local level the effect of individuals persisted strongly. Rapidly replacing this phase was the commercial phase commencing *circa* 1982 which, in the light of strong competition among vendors, is now giving way to a phase of user dominance. The last two phases can also be characterized as ones in which systems handling individual data sets on isolated machines (latterly workstations) gave way to those dealing with corporate and distributed databases, accessed across networks and increasingly integrated into the other non-spatial databases of the organization. A vital characteristic of both the latter phases is that these activities became routine: in earlier phases, skilled 'fixers' were required to be on hand to cope with problems in the software, data or hardware.

What particularly emerges from this chapter is the dominant contribution of North America to the development and implementation of GIS up to the mid- and late-1980s, a function of the persuasive power of key individual pioneers, the size of the internal market, the leading role of the United States in the development of computer hardware and software and – above all – an increasing appreciation by many North American users of the need for efficient, speedy and cost-effective means of handling large quantities of geographical data. It is that perception of need which led potential users to seek GIS solutions and has encouraged commercial providers to develop and offer turnkey systems to convert that perceived need into a reality. What is not clear from the piecemeal evidence, however, is the ratio of failures to successes or how many operational systems are fully used and living up to their promises. A federal system of government, where large bureaucracies have considerable powers to take initiatives on their own account and where states are often as large as many independent countries, are no doubt important features, as is the large area of public land to be managed directly by federal and state agencies. Being continental in scale faces both Canada and the United States with particular problems, but it also helps to create an awareness of the importance of GIS to policy. Even so, CGIS remains unique in its scale, comprehensiveness and ambition at a time of inadequate technology.

Developments elsewhere in GIS were more limited until late in the 1980s, although those in Japan, the United Kingdom and several other countries in mainland Europe seem in rapid evolution. Land registration promises to make GIS a globally used technology from the 'bottom up' while earth monitoring from satellites promises to achieve global use 'top down'. It is a reasonable expectation that routine (and often boring, if valuable) use of GIS will be nearly ubiquitous over the next 20 years. This is the end of the beginning of GIS.

REFERENCES

Abler R F (1987) The National Science Foundation National Center for Geographic Information and Analysis. *International Journal of Geographical Information Systems* **1** (4): 303–26

Anderson D E, Angel J C, Gurney A J (1978) World Data Bank II. In: Dutton G (ed.) *Harvard Papers on Geographical Information Systems 2*. Laboratory for Computer Graphics and Spatial Analysis, Harvard University, Cambridge Massachusetts

Andersson S (1987) The Swedish Land Data Bank. *International Journal of Geographical Information Systems* **1** (3): 253–63

Angus-Leppan P (1989) The Thailand Land Titling Project: first steps in a parcel-based LIS. *International Journal of Geographical Information Systems* **3** (1): 59–68

Beaumont J R (1991) GIS and market analysis. In: Maguire D J, Goodchild M F, Rhind D W (eds.) *Geographical Information Systems*. Longman, London, pp. 139–51, Vol 2

Berry J L, Marble D F (1968) *Spatial Analysis: a reader in statistical geography*. Prentice Hall, Englewood Cliffs New Jersey

Bickmore D P, Shaw M A (1963) *Atlas of Great Britain and Northern Ireland*. Clarendon Press, Oxford

Brand M J D (1986) The foundation of a geographical information system for Northern Ireland. In: Blakemore M J (ed.) *Proceedings of AUTOCARTO London*. Royal Institution of Chartered Surveyors, London, pp. 4–9

Brown M J, Norris D A (1988) Early applications of geographical information systems at the Institute of Terrestrial Ecology. *International Journal of Geographical Information Systems* **2** (2): 153–60

Callahan M, Broome F R (1984) The joint development of a national 1 : 100 000 scale digital cartographic database. *Proceedings of the Annual Conference of the American Congress on Surveying and Mapping*, Washington DC, pp. 246–53

Chen Shupeng (1987) Geographical data handling and GIS in China. *International Journal of Geographical Information Systems* **1** (3): 219–28

Chorley R, Buxton R (1991) The government setting of GIS in the United Kingdom. In: Maguire D J, Goodchild M F, Rhind D W (eds.) *Geographical Information Systems: principles and applications*. Longman, London, pp. 67–79, Vol 1

Chrisman N (1988) The risks of software innovation: a case study of the Harvard Lab. *The American Cartographer* **15** (3): 291–300

Christianson C J (1986) Geoprocessing activities in the Fish and Wildlife Survey. *Proceedings of a Geographical Information Systems Workshop*, American Society of Photogrammetry and Remote Sensing, Falls Church Virginia, pp. 43–6

Clark D M, Hastings D A, Kineman J J (1991) Global databases and their implications for GIS. In: Maguire D J, Goodchild M F, Rhind D W (eds.) *Geographical Information Systems: principles and applications*. Longman, London, pp. 217–31, Vol 2

Cocks K D, Walker P A, Parvey C A (1988) Evolution of a continental-scale geographic information system. *International Journal of Geographical Information Systems* **2** (3): 263–80

Commission on Geographical Data Sensing and Processing (1976) *Second interim report on digital spatial data handling in the US Geological Survey*. International Geographical Union, Ottawa

Cook R N (1966) The CULDATA system. In: Cook R N, Kennedy J L (eds.) *Proceedings of a Tri-State Conference on a Comprehensive Unified Land Data System (CULDATA)*. College of Law, University of Cincinnati, pp. 53–7

Cook R N, Kennedy J L (1966) (eds.) *Proceedings of a Tri-State Conference on a Comprehensive Unified Land Data*

System (CULDATA). College of Law, University of Cincinatti

Coppock J T (1988) The analogue to digital revolution: a view from an unreconstructed geographer. *The American Cartographer* **15** (3): 263–75

Coppock J T, Barritt M (1978) *Application of digital techniques to information systems for planning.* Consultants' report to the Scottish Development Department, Edinburgh

Corbett J P (1979) Topological principles in cartography. Technical Paper 48, US Bureau of the Census, Suitland (also published in *Proceedings of AUTOCARTO 4* 1975, pp. 22–33. American Congress on Survey and Mapping/American Society for Photogrammetry, Washington DC)

Dale P F (1991) Land information systems. In: Maguire D J, Goodchild M F, Rhind D W (eds.) *Geographical Information Systems: principles and applications.* Longman, London, pp. 85–99, Vol 2

Dangermond J, Smith K L (1988) Geographic Information Systems and the revolution in cartography: the nature of the role played by a commercial organization. *The American Cartographer* **15** (3): 301–10

Diello J, Kirk K, Callender J (1968) The development of an automatic cartographic system. *Cartographic Journal* **6** (1): 9–17

Department of the Environment (DoE) (1972) *General Information Systems for Planning*, Department of the Environment, London

Department of the Environment (DoE) (1987) *Handling geographic information: the report of the Committee of Inquiry.* Her Majesty's Stationery Office, London

Dewdney J C, Rhind D W (1986) The British and United States Censuses of Population. In: Pacione M (ed.) *Population Geography: progress and prospects.* Croom Helm, London, pp. 35–57

Diello J, Kirk K, Callander J (1969) The development of an automated cartographic system. *Cartographic Journal* **6**: 9–17

Dueker K (1974) Urban geocoding. *Annals of the Association of American Geographers* **64**: 318–25

Duffield B S, Coppock J T (1975) The delineation of recreational landscapes: the role of computer-based information systems. *Transactions of the Institute of British Geographers* **66**: 141–8

Experimental Cartography Unit (1971) *Automatic Cartography and Planning.* Architectural Press, London

Eyre L A (1989) JAMGIS, the first Jamaican Government comprehensive multi-data geographical information system: achievements and problems. *International Journal of Geographical Information Systems* **3** (4): 363–71

Finch S (1987) *Towards a national digital topographic data base.* Unpublished PhD thesis, University of London.

Gaits G M (1969) Thematic mapping by computer. *Cartographic Journal* **6**: 50–68

Giles R H (1987) The creation, uses and demise of a Virginia USA Geographical Information System.

Proceedings of the International Geographical Union GIS Workshop, Beijing, China: pp. 507–24

Goldstein H, Wertz J, Sweet D (1969) *Computer Mapping: a tool for urban planners.* Battelle Memorial Institute, Cleveland

Goodchild M F, Rhind D W (1990) The US National Center for Geographic Information and Analysis: some comparisons with the Regional Research Laboratories. In: Foster M J, Shand P J (eds.) *The Association for Geographic Information Yearbook 1990.* Taylor & Francis, London, pp. 226–32

Green N P A (1987) Teach yourself geographical information systems: the design, creation and use of demonstrators and tutors. *International Journal of Geographical Information Systems* **1** (3): 279–90

Grimshaw D J (1988) Land and property information systems. *International Journal of Geographical Information Systems* **2** (1): 67–79

Hagerstrand T (1967) The computer and the geographer. *Transactions of the Institute of British Geographers* **42**: 1–20

House of Lords (1984) *Remote sensing and digital mapping.* Report 98 of the House of Lords Select Committee on Science and Technology, Her Majesty's Stationery Office, London

Hudson J C (1979) (ed.) Seventy-five years of American geography. *Annals of the Association of American Geographers* **69** (1): 185pp.

James P E, Martin G J (1978) *The Association of American Geographers: the first seventy-five years 1904–1979.* Association of American Geographers, Washington DC

Koshkariov A V, Tikunov V S, Trofimov A M (1989) The current state and main trends in the development of geographical information systems in the USSR. *International Journal of Geographical Information Systems* **3** (3): 257–72

Kubo S (1987) The development of geographical information systems in Japan. *International Journal of Geographical Information Systems* **1** (3): 243–52

Kubo S (1991) The development of GIS in Japan. In: Maguire D J, Goodchild M F, Rhind D W (eds.) *Geographical Information Systems: principles and applications.* Longman, London, pp. 47–56, Vol 2

Lay J C (1975) Mapping services in Fairfax County, Va. *Proceedings of AUTOCARTO 4.* American Congress on Survey and Mapping/American Society for Photogrammetry, Washington DC, pp. 143–7

Loomis R G (1965) Boundary networks. *Communications, Association for Computing Machinery* **8**: 44–8

Lyall G A (1980) Planning and land assessment in Scotland – the role of the Rural Land Use Information Systems Working Party. In: Thomas M F, Coppock J T (eds.) *Land Assessment in Scotland.* Aberdeen University Press, Aberdeen, pp. 107–17

Maguire D J (1991) An overview and definition of GIS. In:

Maguire D J, Goodchild M F, Rhind D W (eds.) *Geographical Information Systems: principles and applications*. Longman, London, pp. 9–20, Vol 1

Mahoney R P (1991) GIS and utilities. In: Maguire D J, Goodchild M F, Rhind D W (eds.) *Geographical Information Systems: principles and applications*. Longman, London, pp. 101–14, Vol 2

Marble D F (1980) (ed.) *Computer Software for Spatial Data Handling*, 3 volumes. Commission on Geographical Data Sensing and Processing/International Geographical Union, Ottawa Canada

Marble D F (1989) Letter to PERS. *Photogrammetric Engineering and Remote Sensing* **55** (4): 434–5

Mitchell W B, Guptill S C, Anderson E A, Fegeas R G, Hallam C A (1977) GIRAS – a Geographic Information Retrieval and Analysis System for handling land use and land cover data. *Professional Paper 1059*, USGS Reston Virginia

Morrison J L (1991) The organizational home for GIS in the scientific professional community. In: Maguire D J, Goodchild M F, Rhind D W (eds.) *Geographical Information Systems: principles and applications*. Longman, London, pp. 91–100, Vol 1

Morton G M (1966) *A Computer Oriented Geodetic Data Base and New Technique in File Sequencing*. IBN Ltd, Ottawa Canada

Morton Index (1966) In: Tomlinson R F (1972) (ed.) *Geographic Data Handling*. Commission on Geographical Data Sensing and Processing. International Geographical Union, Ottawa Canada

Mounsey H M (1988) (ed.) *Building Databases for Global Science*. Taylor & Francis, London

National Joint Utilities Group (NJUG) (1987) *The NJUG specification for digital map data*. Working Note 12, NJUG, c/o Electricity Council, London

Nordbeck S (1962) Location of areal data for computer processing. *Lund Studies in Geography, Series C, General, Mathematical and Regional Geography No. 2*, Lund University Sweden

O'Callaghan J F, Garner B J (1991) Land and Geographical Information Systems in Australia. In: Maguire D J, Goodchild M F, Rhind D W (eds.) *Geographical Information Systems: principles and applications*. Longman. London, pp. 57–70, Vol 2

Ottoson L, Rystedt B (1991) GIS in Sweden. In: Maguire D J, Goodchild M F, Rhind D (eds.) *Geographical Information Systems: principles and applications*. Longman, London, pp. 39–46, Vol 2

Perring F H (1964) Contribution to Session 6, The mapping of vegetation flora and fauna. In: Bickmore D P (ed.) *Experimental Cartography – Report of the Oxford Symposium*. Oxford University Press, Oxford

Perring F H, Walters S M (1962) *Atlas of the British Flora*. Nelson, London

Peucker T K (1972) Computer cartography. *Commission on College Geography, Resource Paper No.17*. Association of American Geographers, Washington DC

Raper J F, Green N P A (1989) Development of a hypertext-based tutor for geographical information systems. *British Journal of Educational Technology* **3**: 164–72

Rhind D W (1971) The production of a multi-colour geological map by automated means. *Nachr. aus den Karten und Vermessungswesen* Heft Nr. **52**: 47–51

Rhind D W (1976) Geographical Information Systems. *Area* **8** (1): 46

Rhind D W (1986) Remote sensing, digital mapping and Geographical Information Systems: the creation of government policy in the UK. *Environment and Planning C: Government and Policy* **4**: 91–102

Rhind D W (1987) Recent developments in geographic information systems in the UK. *International Journal of Geographical Information Systems* **1** (3): 229–41

Rhind D W (1988) Personality as a factor in the development of a new discipline: the case of computer-assisted cartography. *The American Cartographer* **15** (3): 277–89

Rhind D W (1990) Topographic databases derived from small scale maps and the future of Ordnance Survey. In: Foster M J, Shand P J (eds.) *The Association for Geographic Information Yearbook 1990*. Taylor & Francis, London, pp. 87–96

Rhind D W (1991) Counting the people: the role of GIS. In: Maguire D J, Goodchild M F, Rhind D W (eds.) *Geographical Information Systems: principles and applications*. Longman, London, pp. 127–37, Vol 2

Rhind D W, Hudson R (1980) *Land Use*. Methuen, London

Rhind D W, Mounsey H M (1989) The Chorley Committee and 'Handling Geographic Information'. *Environment and Planning A* **21**: 571–85

Robinette A (1991) Land management applications of GIS in the State of Minnesota. In: Maguire D J, Goodchild M F, Rhind D W (eds.) *Geographical Information Systems: principles and applications*. Longman, London, pp. 275–83, Vol 2

Rushton G (1969) A comprehensive model for the study of agricultural land use patterns. *Computer Assisted Instruction in Geography. Commission on College Geography, Technical Paper No. 2*. Association of American Geographers, Washington DC, pp. 141–50

Schmidt A H, Zafft W A (1975) Progress of the Harvard University Laboratory for Computer Graphics and Spatial Analysis. In: Davis J C, McCullagh M J (eds.) *Display and analysis of spatial data*. Wiley, London, pp. 231–43

Schweitzer R H (1973) *Mapping Urban America with Automated Cartography*. Bureau of the Census US Department of Commerce, Suitland Maryland

Shumway C (1986) Summary of the US Forest Service Geographical Information Systems activities. *Proceedings of Geographical Information Systems Workshop*. American Society for Photogrammetry and Remote Sensing, Falls Church, pp. 49–52

Simonett D S (1988) Considerations on integrating remote sensing and Geographic Information Systems. In:

Mounsey H M, Tomlinson R F (eds.) *Building Databases for Global Science*. Taylor & Francis, London pp. 105–28

Sowton M. (1991) Development of GIS-related activities at the Ordnance Survey. In: Maguire D J, Goodchild M F, Rhind D W (eds.) *Geographical Information Systems: principles and applications*. Longman, London pp. 23–38, Vol 2

Starr L E, Anderson K E (1991) A USGS perspective on GIS. In: Maguire D J, Goodchild M F, Rhind D W (eds.) *Geographical Information Systems: principles and applications*. Longman, London, pp. 11–22, Vol 2

Taylor D R F (1991) GIS and developing nations. In: Maguire D J, Goodchild M F, Rhind D W (eds.) *Geographical Information Systems: principles and applications*. Longman, London, pp. 71–84, Vol 2

Tobler W R (1959) Automation and cartography. *Geographical Review* **49**: 526–34

Tomlinson R F (1967) *An Introduction to the Geographic Information System of the Canada Land Inventory*. Department of Forestry and Rural Development, Ottawa Canada

Tomlinson R F (1970) (ed.) *Environment Information Systems*. Commission on Geographical Data Sensing and Processing. International Geographical Union, Ottawa Canada

Tomlinson R F (1972) (ed.) *Geographic Data Handling*. Commission on Geographical Data Sensing and Processing. International Geographical Union, Ottawa Canada

Tomlinson R F (1974) *The application of electronic computing methods to the storage, compilation and assessment of mapped data*. Unpublished PhD thesis, University of London

Tomlinson R F (1985) Geographic Information Systems – the new frontier. *The Operational Geographer* **5**: 31–6

Tomlinson R F (1988) The impact of the transition from analogue to digital cartographic representation. *The American Cartographer* **15** (3): 249–62

Tomlinson R F (1989) Letter to PERS. *Photogrammetric Engineering and Remote Sensing* **55** (4): 434–5

Tomlinson R F, Calkins H W, Marble D F (1976) *Computer Handling of Geographical Data*. Natural Resources Research Series XIII, UNESCO Press, Paris

Tomlinson R F, Petchenik B B (1988) (eds.) Reflections on the revolution: the transition from analogue to digital representations of space, 1958–1988. *The American Cartographer* **15** (3): 243–334

Townshend J R G (1991) Environmental databases and GIS. In: Maguire D J, Goodchild M F, Rhind D W (eds.) *Geographical Information Systems: principles and applications*. Longman, London, pp. 201–16, Vol 2

USBC (1969–73) *Census Use Study Reports 1 to 12*. US Bureau of Census, Washington DC

Waugh T C (1980) The development of the GIMMS computer mapping system. In: Taylor D R F (ed.) *The Computer in Contemporary Cartography*. Wiley, London, pp. 219–34

Wiggins J C, Hartley R P, Higgins M J, Whittaker R J (1987) Computing aspects of a large geographical information system for the European Community. *International Journal of Geographical Information Systems* **1** (1): 77–87

3

THE TECHNOLOGICAL SETTING OF GIS

M F GOODCHILD

The development of GIS has been driven at least in part by technology, particularly the specific technology required to support spatial and graphic applications in computing. This chapter reviews the degree to which technology has constrained or driven GIS, and looks at prospects for the future given likely trends in the computing industry. GIS is becoming less dependent on technology as factors such as data volumes and the need for trained staff become more critical.

INTRODUCTION

GIS is a late bloomer among applications of computing technology in part because it is so demanding, and simply could not be supported in any useful fashion by the resources available in the typical computer system of, say, 1960. In addition, the spatial nature of geographical data is not easily accommodated within the essentially linear structure of conventional computers, and early input and output devices lacked the spatial resolution necessary to deal with these kinds of data. Indeed, it is often noted that the human eye and mind are still superior to the best digital technology in such spatial tasks as pattern recognition. The previous chapter (Coppock and Rhind 1991) has already argued that the history of GIS development can be linked to more general advances in hardware and software, although other factors such as education and awareness and the actions of key individuals have also been important. The purpose of the present chapter is to review the technological setting of GIS in the early 1990s, to identify the key technologies on which GIS depends, and to discuss certain significant trends that will likely influence this technological setting in the coming decade. The chapter is divided into two major sections: the four parts of the first section discuss the current setting from the perspectives of input, storage, manipulation and output; and the second section looks at the state of the GIS industry in the early 1990s in the context of several key issues.

Looking back over the past three decades of GIS development, it seems that the application imposes certain specific requirements, each of which had to be met before GIS could really blossom. Although developments such as CGIS (the Canada Geographic Information System; Tomlinson, Calkins and Marble 1976) took place when many of these were not available, or available only at high cost, their primitive technological environments certainly presented their developers with enormous problems. The following list is undoubtedly far from complete, but serves to emphasize the demanding nature of the GIS application (see also Maguire, 1989, for an overview of computers and geography):

- *Interactive.* The user must be able to interact with the computing system, continually issuing instructions and receiving responses. Widespread availability of interactive computing dates from the late 1960s, and has now largely replaced the earlier batch mode.
- *Multiuser.* Many users must be able to access the geographical database simultaneously. Multiuser operating systems date from the late 1960s. More recently, technology has become available to support distributed databases, avoiding the need to concentrate all data in one central location.

- *Graphic.* The system must be able to input and output data graphically, as it is otherwise very difficult for the user to work with geographical information. Primitive graphic output devices date from the mid-1960s, while the first digitizer for map input became available in the early years of the same decade.

- *Volume and speed.* Geographical data sets are often large and complex, and therefore require large digital storage devices. At the same time the system must be capable of processing large volumes quickly, and providing immediate answers to queries. Magnetic tape, which was the primary storage medium for computing until the mid-1960s, is too slow for interactive use.

- *Virtual memory.* Until recently the central, random access memory of computing systems was very expensive. The development of virtual operating systems (e.g. DEC's VMS) in the late 1970s allowed applications to process large volumes of data using comparatively small central memories.

- *Database management systems.* Contemporary GIS are enormously complex software systems. The GIS itself must be supported by an operating system, and will likely also depend on the presence of a graphics package for input and output, routines supplied by the programming language in which the GIS is written, and numerous other software products. Many of the more powerful contemporary GIS are designed to rely on a data base management system (DBMS), relieving the GIS developer of many of the common data housekeeping functions. DBMSs were adopted widely in the computing industry in the 1970s (Tsichritzis and Lochovsky 1977). At the same time the marriage between GIS and DBMS which began to emerge in the software products of the 1980s is not perfect. GIS require the rapid display of large quantities of data, and access to information through location as well as attributes, and it has proven difficult to accommodate the multidimensional nature of geographical data (two or three dimensions of location plus attributes) within the framework of many DBMSs.

- *Cost.* GIS is a minor application compared to the needs of accounting, mathematical modelling, word processing, etc. A resource management agency or utility company is willing to adopt GIS only when its perceived benefits exceed its costs (Dickinson and Calkins 1988). The explosion of interest in GIS in the 1980s is due at least in part to the steady and spectacular drop in the costs of computing technology over the past three decades.

THE CURRENT SETTING

Input

Most of the contents of geographical databases continue to be derived from paper maps, and the technology of the early 1990s offers two main methods of input: digitizing and scanning. Digitizing requires a human operator to position a map on a table, and move a cursor over it, thus capturing the positions of points, and building up digital representations of line and area features. Digitizing is error prone, tedious, time consuming and expensive – issues that are dealt with in more detail by Fisher (1991 in this volume). Estimates of the current cost of successfully inserting a single area, such as a land parcel, into a data base range from $1 to $40 (Goodchild and Rizzo 1987; Goodchild 1987). In essence, digitizing technology remains at a stalemate. Map-size digitizers were developed in the 1960s, and there have been few if any advances in the past two decades (see Jackson and Woodsford 1991 in this volume). Software for intelligent management of the digitizing process and interactive editing of the results was developed in the late 1970s. These functions require a small, dedicated workstation with simple graphics capabilities, and can be readily provided by the current generation of personal computers and workstations.

Scanning captures the entire contents of the document automatically. However, the process of interpreting features from the scanned image of the map is error prone, requiring frequent human intervention, and it is often necessary to redraw the document to provide a sufficiently clean image. Map-size scanners are large and expensive, and unlikely to become much cheaper. The most important factor in the development of scanning technology is the software for feature detection. Simple problems such as the recognition of characters in feature labels, or the interruption of contours by elevation annotation remain major challenges for software developers. If they can be overcome, or removed through the appropriate redesign of map formats (Shiryaev 1987) then scanning will inevitably win in the cost effectiveness battle with digitizing, but in the early 1990s the contest is still even. Jackson and Woodsford (1991 in this volume) present a detailed discussion of the current state of data capture technology.

Maps are a form of analogue geographical database in their own right, and a very important source of digital geographical data, but they are certainly not the only source. Maps are often designed for purposes that have little to do with geographical databases, a primary purpose of map design being the communication of information to the reader through visual perception (Robinson 1953). For example, the purpose of a set of elevation data in a GIS is likely to be to provide accurate estimates of the elevation of any point on the earth's surface in the area covered by the data set; the purpose of a map showing contours of elevation is likely to be to provide the reader with an impression of the general form of the surface (Imhoff 1982). Maps use methods of representing geographical variation, such as contours, that may be far from optimal for digital representation.

Thus an increasing amount of GIS data is now being provided by non-map sources. Davis and Simonett (1991 in this volume) review the current state of technology in remote sensing (see Ehlers, Edwards and Bedard, 1989 for a review of GIS/remote sensing integration), and explain the tension that exists between two paradigms: remote sensing as a method of collecting and compiling information on geography through image interpretation; and remote sensing as a source of data to support studies of environmental processes and earth system science. For map data, the key problem is the high cost of conversion to digital form, but for remote sensing, the problem is just the opposite. The Landsat technology of the 1970s created an avalanche of images from space that greatly exceeded the capacity of the data analysis technology of the time. Despite the enormous advances in image processing and GIS since then, the technology of remote sensing instruments is moving rapidly. The Eos systems proposed for the 1990s will include much higher spatial and spectral resolution than the current generation (10 m and 256 bands are proposed, respectively, leading to estimates of 1 Tb or 10^{12} bytes of information per day) and it is likely that storage and analysis capabilities will lag far behind.

A major advance in data capture technology is occurring with the development of GPS (Global Positioning System: the magazine *GPS World* is a useful source of information on this technology). Hand-held GPS receivers will soon be able to determine position anywhere on the earth's surface in latitude/longitude coordinates to an accuracy of fractions of a second of arc (1 second of arc latitude is approximately 30 m). As well as being an accurate source of raw geographical information, GPS has potential in such applications as tracking vehicles and shipments, emergency response and resource management. Its accuracy is already greater than that of the best base mapping commonly available in most countries, including the United States.

The accuracy of GPS has interesting implications for the future of mapping. For a relatively small investment (around $100 000), it is already possible to equip a vehicle to make accurate surveys of road or railway alignments. Since the vehicle can travel at speeds of up to 100 km/h and still maintain adequate accuracy (defined as the accuracy of currently available topographic mapping, e.g. 1 : 25 000), the costs of this method of map making may be an order of magnitude less than conventional methods based on photogrammetry. GPS is likely to play a major role in the creation and updating of future road and street network databases. In addition, there is strong interest in the merging of GPS-surveyed road and rail alignments with images, for instance, of road surface quality or road signs. This will require multimedia technology, where the GIS is capable of handling both structured network data, to represent the road alignment, and unstructured video images.

GPS and remote sensing are useful illustrations of the difference between data and information, as neither provides any intelligent interpretation of the data they capture. Just as the retina provides limited interpretation of images rather than send them uninterpreted through the optic nerve to the brain, the proposed data rates of Eos are so high that some sort of intelligent filtering will be almost inevitable before the data are transmitted or stored. Digitizing and scanning technologies both concentrate on capturing the contents of a map accurately and completely, leaving the more demanding tasks of data interpretation and compilation to the cartographer. Only recently has it been possible to begin developing more intelligent data capture systems, using digital representations of knowledge about geography. The recent developments in scanning systems described by Jackson and Woodsford (1991 in this volume) fall into this category, and research is currently under way in a number of organizations to apply digital technology to the task of compiling and interpreting geographical information, as distinct from capturing geographical data. Hutchinson (1988), for example, has developed improved methods of building elevation databases using knowledge about hydrology.

Storage

Modern GIS store data using a variety of technologies, some of which are generic and some of which are almost uniquely appropriate to this application. In general, geographical databases demand large amounts of storage, and have only become feasible with the decline of storage costs and dramatic improvements in storage technology of the past three decades. Paradoxically, the paper map is a highly efficient store of data, and the problem of converting its contents to a manageable digital representation has been at least partly responsible for the comparatively slow pace of GIS development.

The primary storage medium is currently the fixed magnetic disk, or 'hard disk', with capacities ranging from tens of megabytes (1 Mb $\approx 10^6$ bytes) to tens of gigabytes (1 Gb $\approx 10^9$ bytes). For comparison, a megabyte is sufficient to store the contents of a book of roughly 200 000 words. The contents of maps are so variable that it is difficult to give meaningful estimates of their storage requirements in digital form, but experience in agencies such as the US Geological Survey and the Defense Mapping Agency suggests that a typical topographic map's contents can be stored with acceptable precision in roughly 10 Mb, to within an order of magnitude, which is also the approximate volume of one band of a Landsat scene; and the US Bureau of the Census TIGER database which includes digital representations of most streets in the United States, occupies roughly 10 Gb. Any item of data on a hard disk is accessible within milliseconds.

Magnetic tape (capacity roughly 100 Mb) remains a useful storage medium for geographical data and the primary method of back-up for fixed disk. However, long times are required to 'seek' data by winding through tape serially. Optical disks, such as the CD-ROM (Compact Disk–Read Only Memory) and WORM (Write Once Read Many) with capacities from 250 Mb to 2 Gb can seek in fractions of a second, and are particularly suitable for archives because of their long-term stability, which matches the nature of much geographical data. Once a master CD-ROM has been manufactured, it is possible to print and distribute copies at very low cost, so this medium is becoming increasingly popular for such data sets as TIGER. But against the advantages of long-term stability of the medium, it must be added that this technology is in a state of rapid flux.

Despite their high capacity, none of these media offers solutions to the problems of storing geographical data sets of terabyte size (1 Tb $\approx 10^{12}$ bytes), such as the US Geological Survey's Digital Cartographic Database, or the databases of many major utilities or cities (For a discussion of very large spatial databases see Crain 1990.) A number of automated magnetic tape stores have been built, capable of mounting tapes from a library of perhaps 10^4 volumes in minutes, but these are cumbersome and expensive. Optical platters can be mounted in 'jukeboxes' offering seek times of tens of seconds, but it is difficult to build stores using fixed disks for more than about 10^{11} bytes.

Because of these constraints, which effectively limit the amount of data available for interactive use at any one time, most large geographical databases are partitioned in one way or another. The term 'tile' is commonly used to refer to geographical partitions, often on the basis of map sheets or political units; although the database may be partitioned internally, the user may nevertheless see it as 'seamless'. Partitions by subject matter are referred to as 'layers', 'themes' or 'coverages', and the system may impose constraints on the different classes of features that can be stored in any one such partition. In addition, many GIS databases are partitioned temporally, maintaining maps of an area at different points in time.

Within any one partition, it is desirable that the user be able to retrieve any feature as rapidly as possible. Rather than search sequentially through the features in the partition in response to a request, many systems use some form of index for more rapid access. Indexes may be based on the characteristics of features, or on their locations, and used to support queries based on characteristics and locations respectively. Buchmann *et al.* (1989) include several papers on recent developments in indexing large spatial databases, and Samet (1989) gives a comprehensive review.

The most critical form of memory for a computer system is 'core', 'central' memory or RAM (Random Access Memory), which is the fast access memory used by the central processor (see Maguire, 1989, for an excellent general review of the architecture of computers in the context of geographical enquiry). As recently as the late 1970s, the high cost of RAM was reflected in the small amount available even in large mainframe computers. MS-DOS, still the dominant operating system of the IBM PC, is limited to 640 Kb (1 Kb ≈ 10^3 bytes). But more recent multitasking operating systems such as OS/2 and Unix have been able to take advantage of improvements in manufacturing technology that have reduced the cost of RAM in 1990 to roughly $100/Mb. Cheap RAM means that computers can perform many tasks simultaneously, and analyse large data sets more efficiently.

Manipulation and analysis

Until the late 1970s the dominant configuration for GIS consisted of a mainframe computer serving a number of connected users, each operating a 'terminal'. All information, graphic or text, passed through a communication line and was constrained by the line's capacity, which might be no more than 30 characters/second. Coding systems, such as Hewlett Packard's HPGL (Hewlett Packard Graphic Language), or Tektronix's 4010 code, were used to express graphic information in the form of sequences of text characters. A terminal capable of displaying colour graphic information might cost over $10 000.

By 1990 the functions of mainframe computing and graphic display had been combined into powerful personal 'workstations', and the previously clear lines of distinction between personal computing and mainframes had become hopelessly blurred. The concept of a workstation emerged in the late 1980s as a specialized desktop system for scientific and engineering applications, offering a characteristic computing environment with little resemblance to that of the PC or Apple Macintosh, and dominated by the Unix operating system. The typical workstation of the early 1990s, costing no more than the graphic display terminal of 1980, has the computing power, storage capacity and display capabilities to support a powerful GIS in a single, integrated desktop 'platform'. It may have a central processor speed of over 10 MIPS (Million Instructions Per Second), 10 Mb of RAM, and 1 Gb of hard disk. Workstations are commonly networked, and can share distributed databases (the 'diskless' workstation has no local storage, obtaining all of its data over a network). The workstation's graphic display resolution is normally expressed in terms of rows and columns of picture elements (pixels), and the number of colours simultaneously displayable on the screen. For GIS applications, minimal requirements are typified by 480 rows by 640 columns, 16 colours displayable (the EGA standard of the IBM PC); high quality is typified by 1024 rows by 1280 columns, 256 colours displayable (10^6 pixels = 1 'megapel').

Although the contents of GIS databases continue to be dominated by structured geographical information, including well-defined objects with coded attributes, other forms are increasingly important in some applications. In digitizing, for example, it may be useful to display an unstructured image of a map or an air photograph on the screen, allowing the user to input the locations of features directly. This is a commonly used approach in digitizing utility installations such as underground pipes. In emergency management applications it may be useful to allow pictures of buildings to be retrieved and displayed on the screen. Sound may also be important. The GIS community is increasingly recognizing that structured geographical data are only one form of spatial information, and that other forms can be exploited very effectively using appropriately designed platforms. (For a discussion of multimedia databases see Shepherd 1991 in this volume.) The power of the eye (and ear) to interpret and recognize pattern is so great that the high degree of interpretation present in a structured GIS database may not always be necessary.

Because of its reliance on map input, GIS has been seen as a two-dimensional technology.

Surfaces, such as that of the earth, can be handled only if they are single-valued functions of the two spatial dimensions (see Weibel and Heller 1991 in this volume), and the earth's curvature must be dealt with by use of map projections (see Maling 1991 in this volume). Raper and Kelk (1991 in this volume) and Raper (1989) deal with current developments in 3-D GIS, which are occurring in a rapidly changing technological setting. In the context of display, Tektronix introduced a device in the mid 1980s that allows objects on the screen to be seen in stereo vision using polarizing filters. The screen displays alternately the left and right images using twice the normal refresh rate. These are then polarized in opposite directions by a filter installed in the front of the screen. The user wears eyeglasses containing polarizing filters, but otherwise interfering very little with normal vision.

Several of the 1990 generation of workstations, typified by the IBM RS/6000, include graphics processors (or 'adaptors') with 3-D display functions, capable of computing, displaying and texturing 3-D solid objects on the screen at high rates. With specifications of 10^5 3-D vectors per second, these systems are able to offer real-time display and manipulation of scenes containing illuminated solid objects in a desktop computing environment for investments of the order of $10 000. For GIS, this means the ability to simulate oblique views of terrain with superimposed geographical distributions; to replace abstract cartographic symbols and classes with 'artists' impressions' of real physical appearance; to animate displays; to work with geographical distributions over the curved surface of the globe; and to build and manipulate true 3-D databases in applications such as oceanography, geology and subsurface hydrology.

The workstation has replaced the old centralized view of computing as a mainframe with connected users, as modified by the independent personal computer, with a network of distributed computing power and distributed databases, communicating through common standards and protocols. Unix has emerged as the standard operating system of choice in this environment, replacing both the proprietary operating systems of the mainframes, and the simple environments of the PCs. Unix has been enormously successful at offering a uniform computing environment over a variety of vendor products, and at integrating systems from the simplest to the most powerful. At the same time, the conventional form of user interaction has moved strongly away from the old, text command format to the graphic user interface (GUI) pioneered by Xerox and Apple, among others, in which the user communicates largely by pointing at objects on the screen. Frank and Mark (1991 in this volume) discuss the implications of the move to GUI and visual metaphors for GIS and spatial databases. As yet, none of the competing GUI standards has emerged as dominant in the GIS field.

Output

Numerous devices can be used to create an output image in the form of a map. In the early days of automated cartography, the line printer was even used, by overprinting characters to create various shades of grey, despite the limitations of a picture element measuring 1/6 inch by 1/10. Early plotters offered enormous improvement by allowing the user to direct the movement of a pen, but required a substantially different software design to create an image by random pen movements ('vector') rather than by sequentially printed picture elements ('raster'). As computer processors have become cheaper, it has been possible to offer devices with substantial internal computing power for conversion between raster and vector, blurring the distinction between plotter and printer. Thus the electrostatic plotter, probably the most popular GIS map output device of 1990, generates images by assembling uniform-size picture elements sequentially (with typical resolutions of hundreds of dots per inch) but can be driven as a plotter by sending information in the format of pen movements. The distinction between 'plotter' and 'printer' has become largely meaningless as the relatively unreliable technology of moving pens has given way to various forms of electrostatic printing.

THE GIS MARKETPLACE

GIS is a complex and diverse field, more a loose consortium of interests than a mature industry. Its products reflect this, and it is possible to speculate endlessly about whether the future holds greater uniformity or greater diversity. Numerous surveys of GIS products have been published; those in the *AGI Yearbook* (an annual publication assembled by the Association for Geographic Information in the United Kingdom and published by Taylor and Francis) and the *GIS Sourcebook* (published annually by GISWorld, Fort Collins, Colorado) are comparatively accessible and updated regularly. Estimates of the total number of GIS products on offer range up to 1000. The purpose of this section is to provide an organizing framework in terms of several key issues, as a means of describing the technological setting of this volume.

Arguably the most fundamental means of distinguishing between GIS products is through an understanding of each system's data model. Since geographical reality is infinitely complex, it is necessary to generalize, approximate or abstract in order to create a representation in the finite, discrete space of a digital store. A data model is defined here in the sense of Peuquet (1984) as 'an abstraction of the real world which incorporates only those properties thought to be relevant to the application or applications at hand, usually a human conceptualization of reality'. Tsichritzis and Lochovsky (1977: 21) also offer a useful definition: 'a data model is a set of guidelines for the representation of the logical organization of the data in a data base. It is a pattern according to which the data, and the relationships among the data, can be logically organized. It consists of named logical units of data and the relationships among them.' (See also Guptill, 1991 in this volume, and Maguire and Dangermond 1991 in this volume.)

Although numerous data models have been devised, no one system offers all of them. Moreover some data models are better able to represent a given geographical phenomenon than others, so the choice of data model(s) offered by a given system is driven by, and in turn constrains, that system's applications.

The second way of differentiating current systems is through the supporting platform, and its associated operating system, database management system, and so on. While some vendors offer similar products over the full range of platforms from personal computers through workstations to mainframes, others are limited to one or perhaps two operating systems, and, therefore, to the platforms that support them.

Finally, it is possible to differentiate current systems according to their areas of application. Although some vendors attempt to market their products across the entire range of GIS applications, others have specialized into particular market niches.

The following discussion does not attempt to provide a comprehensive list of products, or detailed information on their availability. For these, the reader is referred to current lists and reviews, such as those cited earlier.

Data models

Perhaps the strongest cleavage in the marketplace is between systems dominated by raster and vector data models, although the distinction is rather blurred (see below). A raster database models each layer or theme as an assemblage of cells or pixels, specified in some standard order. No coordinates are stored, as they are implied by the position of each cell in the sequence. Raster systems differ in the constraints imposed on the number and types of values allowed in each cell of a layer. Arbitrarily shaped features on the earth's surface, such as lakes or roads, must be represented by giving appropriate values to cells. For example, a lake may be represented by giving the value 'L' to cells whose centre points lie in the lake, and a 'Lake' layer can be constructed by giving '0' to all cells not classified as 'L'. In this form the existence of a named lake, for example Lake Superior, is implicit, and its dimensions can only be found by searching for a contiguous block of 'L' cells. The various forms of the MAP package originally developed by Tomlin (1983) are examples of this approach. Some raster systems, for example TYDAC's SPANS, support the notion of a feature more explicitly by coding all of the Lake Superior cells with a unique feature number, and associating these with a table identifying the characteristics of each feature.

Vector systems, on the other hand, employ a dominant data model that describes features as points, lines or areas through sets of coordinate pairs. ESRI's ARC/INFO, for example, allows a point, line or area coverage to contain the respective class of feature, with an associated table of attributes. Rasters can be handled in a number of ways in several parts of the system, just as vectors can be used as a convenient method of input in raster systems such as IDRISI, but in both cases the data model must be transformed to take full advantage of the system's capabilities.

The functions offered by each system depend closely on the data model. Transformation of coordinate systems, and use of map projections are common features of coordinate-based vector systems, but less well represented in raster systems. Most raster systems include the ability to generate an oblique view of an elevation data set, but this is rare in vector systems. Although raster systems offer comparatively consistent functionality, there is an enormous range of variability both of data models and functionality within the vector domain. A utility company installing IBM's GFIS, for example, would take an entirely different approach from one using ESRI's ARC/INFO. In part this is because a collection of features, for example areas, can have a much wider range of meanings than a layer of raster cells. Some systems, such as ESRI's ARC/INFO, require that the areas in a coverage be 'planar enforced', meaning that they may not overlap, and must exhaust the plane, so that every place lies inside exactly one area. Other systems, such as Intergraph's TIGRIS, allow coverages to contain any mixture of points, lines and areas with or without overlap. Planar enforced systems often 'store topology', meaning that they store adjacency relationships between areas. Others such as TIGRIS may have 'integrated topology', meaning that all intersections, containments and adjacencies between the arbitrary collection of features in a coverage are stored. Some systems, such as Prime's SYSTEM/9, allow the user to define complex objects as collections of simple objects, and to give them their own graphic symbols on output. Data models are an important key to understanding the design of a GIS product, and its functionality, and are much less predictable in the vector domain. (See Maguire and Dangermond, 1991 in this volume, for discussion of the link between functionality and GIS.)

Platforms

From a historical perspective, it is possible to identify three classes of computing: mainframes, consisting of large multiuser processors connected to interactive terminals; personal computers, which are small independent computing systems; and workstations – larger and more powerful than personal computers, with multitasking operating systems and networking capabilities. The distinction between the three classes is not precise. A fourth class, the 'minicomputer', was important in the 1970s and early 1980s but is now largely absorbed by the workstation and mainframe categories. Each class has had its dominant operating systems: proprietary systems such as DEC VMS, IBM VM/CMS or PRIME Primos for mainframes, Microsoft MS-DOS for PCs and various forms of Unix for workstations. Each has also had its associated market, with PCs dominant in small business and home applications and workstations oriented to science and engineering.

A few GIS vendors have attempted to offer similar products across the entire range of platforms, and ESRI's ARC/INFO, which started as a mainframe product, is the clearest example. Others, such as Intergraph, have historically provided software for customized hardware environments. TYDAC is an example of a vendor that began in the PC marketplace under MS-DOS, and has migrated to OS/2 on the same platform, and to workstation Unix. As the networking advantages of Unix become clearer, and this operating system is increasingly available on mainframes and PCs, it will likely come to dominate the GIS field as a platform-independent environment. Nevertheless MS-DOS has a powerful hold on the small computer marketplace, and the Macintosh GUI environment is also popular.

Applications

In this last section the differentiation of the GIS marketplace by application is examined. The chapters in Section III of this volume provide additional comments on GIS products in various application contexts. In municipal and utility applications, where GIS is used as a means of gaining geographically based access to large inventories of facilities, parcels and records, the sheer size of the application dictates the use of a large mainframe. Small workstations and PCs may be integrated as platforms for editing or intensive analysis, but the GIS of choice is likely to be one that runs under a mainframe operating system, or increasingly Unix (e.g. ARC/INFO, Genasys and GeoVision).

In market research, planning and emergency applications data volumes are much smaller, and the need for personal input and management of data much higher. Vector-based systems such as Strategic Mapping's Atlas GIS, Generation 5's Geo/SQL, MapInfo and Caliper's GIS Plus have been able to penetrate this market, using small MS-DOS platforms, and several Macintosh products are significant also. In resource management applications, where remote sensing input is significant and the concept of continuous geographical variation is more acceptable, raster-based PC systems, such as MAP, IDRISI and EPPL7 have been successful. Finally, TYDAC's SPANS has been able to provide a limited degree of integration of raster and vector models on the PC platform.

Although many GIS products are moving to the workstation platform, among the earliest were systems designed for scientific and modelling applications, such as GRASS. Because of their intermediate status between PCs and mainframes, and the integrating power of Unix and networking, workstations are now the platform of choice for many GIS, and this trend can only accelerate as the distinction between the three types of platforms becomes less distinct.

CONCLUDING REMARKS

The technological setting of GIS is changing rapidly, as workstation computing power increases by a factor of roughly two every year, as hardware of all types continues to become cheaper, and as networking protocols and standards become more widespread. Among the very few constants in this dynamic field are those involving humans – the high cost of digitizing, and the constant demand for faster computing, larger and more accurate databases, and better and more friendly user interfaces. There seems to be no limit to the potential complexity of software systems, as the technology has already gone far beyond the point where any one individual can understand every detail of the design of an operating system or a GIS. Storage and computing power will continue to fall in price over the next decade, 3-D and animated graphics will become cheaper, more widespread and easier to use. Unix will strengthen its grip as the universal operating system for the new distributed style of computing. GIS vendors will also continue to offer a wide variety of products adapted to the needs of particular applications.

In this environment of continuous change it is difficult sometimes to see the more fundamental longer term changes. For a long time the controlling factor in GIS applications was hardware cost, but now software cost is at least as important. Communication speed was critical in the early 1970s when GIS relied on terminal–mainframe interaction. Now that these challenges have diminished, new ones have become important – for example, there is no reasonable way of processing the enormous volumes of data about to come from Eos, and current GIS offer a very limited view of the rich world of geographical data modelling. Databases are still largely map based, and filled with structured geographical information.

In the coming decade the technological problems which plagued earlier generations of GIS products will be far less important than the human ones – lack of trained staff, the high personnel costs of digitizing, poor planning and management, resistance to technological change within institutions, and so on. At the same time expectations will continue to rise in step with the technology, and to demand ever more precise data, in ever larger volumes. Although many of the simpler technical problems have been solved, and costs have fallen dramatically, the technological environment of GIS will continue to constrain the expectations of its users.

REFERENCES

Buchmann A, Günther O, Smith T R, Wang Y-F (1989) *Design and Implementation of Large Spatial Databases. Lecture Notes in Computer Science 409.* Springer-Verlag, New York

Coppock T, Rhind D W (1991) The history of GIS. In: Maguire D J, Goodchild M F, Rhind D W (eds.) *Geographical Information Systems: principles and applications.* Longman, London, pp. 21–43, Vol 1

Crain I K (1990) Extremely large spatial information systems: a quantitative perspective. *Proceedings of the 4th International Symposium on Spatial Data Handling* International Geographical Union, Columbus Ohio, pp. 632–41

Davis F W, Simonett D S (1991) GIS and remote sensing. In Maguire D J, Goodchild M F, Rhind D W (eds.) *Geographical Information Systems: principles and applications*. Longman, London, pp. 191–213, Vol 1

Dickinson H J, Calkins H W (1988) The economic evaluation of implementing a GIS. *International Journal of Geographical Information Systems* **2** (4): 307–28

Ehlers M, Edwards G, Bedard Y (1989) Integration of remote sensing with GIS: a necessary evolution. *Photogrammetric Engineering and Remote Sensing* **55** (11): 1619–27

Fisher P F (1991) Spatial data sources and data problems. In: Maguire D J, Goodchild M F, Rhind D W (eds.) *Geographical Information Systems: principles and applications*. Longman, London, pp. 175–89, Vol 1

Frank A U, Mark D M (1991) Language issues for GIS. In: Maguire D J, Goodchild M F, Rhind D W (eds.) *Geographical Information Systems: principles and applications*. Longman, London, pp. 147–63, Vol 1

Goodchild M F (1987) Application of a GIS benchmarking and workload estimation model. *Papers and Proceedings of Applied Geography Conferences* **10**: 1–6

Goodchild M F, Rizzo B R (1987) Performance evaluation and workload estimation for geographic information systems. *International Journal of Geographical Information Systems* **1**: 67–76

Guptill S C (1991) Spatial data exchange and standardization. In: Maguire D J, Goodchild M F, Rhind D W (eds.) *Geographical Information Systems: principles and applications*. Longman, London, pp. 515–30, Vol 1

Hutchinson M F (1988) Calculation of hydrologically sound digital elevation models. *Proceedings of the 3rd International Symposium on Spatial Data Handling*. International Geographical Union, Columbus Ohio, pp. 117–33

Imhoff E (1982) *Cartographic Relief Presentation*. de Gruyter, Berlin

Jackson M J, Woodsford P A (1991) GIS data capture hardware and software. In: Maguire D J, Goodchild M F, Rhind D W (eds.) *Geographical Information Systems: principles and applications*. Longman, London, pp. 239–49

Maguire D J (1989) *Computers in Geography*. Longman, London

Maguire D J, Dangermond J (1991) The functionality of GIS. In: Maguire D J, Goodchild M F, Rhind D W (eds.) *Geographical Information Systems: principles and applications*. Longman, London, pp. 319–35, Vol 1

Maling D H (1991) Coordinate systems and projections for GIS. In: Maguire D J, Goodchild M F, Rhind D W (eds.) *Geographical Information Systems: principles and applications*. Longman, London, pp. 135–46, Vol 1

Peuquet D J (1984) A conceptual framework and comparison of spatial data models. *Cartographica* **21** (4): 66–113

Raper J F (1989) *Three Dimensional Applications in GIS*. Taylor & Francis, London

Raper J F, Kelk B (1991) Three-dimensional GIS. In: Maguire D J, Goodchild M F, Rhind D W (eds.) *Geographical Information Systems: principles and applications*. Longman, London, pp. 299–319, Vol 1

Robinson A H (1953) *Elements of Cartography*. Wiley, New York

Samet H (1989) *The Design and Analysis of Spatial Data Structures*. Addison-Wesley, Reading Massachusetts

Shepherd I D H (1991) Information integration and GIS. In: Maguire D J, Goodchild M F, Rhind D W (eds.) *Geographical Information Systems: principles and applications*. Longman, London, pp. 337–60, Vol 1

Shiryaev E E (1987) *Computers and the Representation of Geographical Data*. Wiley, New York

Tomlin C D (1983) *Digital cartographic modelling techniques in environmental planning*. Unpublished PhD Thesis, Yale University.

Tomlinson R F, Calkins H W, Marble D F (1976) *Computer Handling of Geographical Data*. UNESCO, Paris

Tsichritzis D C, Lochovsky F H (1977) *Data Base Management Systems*. Academic Press, New York

Weibel R, Heller M (1991) Digital terrain modelling. In: Maguire D J, Goodchild M F, Rhind D W (eds.) *Geographical Information Systems: principles and applications*. Longman, London, pp. 269–97, Vol 1

4

THE COMMERCIAL SETTING OF GIS

J DANGERMOND

This chapter deals with the commercial setting of GIS, in contrast with historical, technological, government or academic settings. After an introduction and a brief indication of the present scope of the GIS business, GIS firms are distinguished from those in closely related technologies, and a typical commercial GIS is briefly described. Then, in the chapter's major section, the wide variety of commercial GIS firms are categorized, and each category briefly described; a related section describes how commercial firms support the GIS systems cycle. Then the contribution of commercial firms to the field, their problems, some of their frustrations, the GIS trends of which they are a part, and the future of the commercial sector are each discussed in turn. Finally, some brief concluding remarks are provided.

INTRODUCTION

GIS technology provides a framework for all forms of spatial data storage, retrieval, analysis, display and modelling. It provides the 'front end' technology for multimedia spatial databases including video, CD-ROM, tabular, and other forms of data.

Market forces and healthy commercial competition are a primary driving force causing thinkers to forge ahead with new ideas, concepts and techniques in any technological field. It was apparent, 20 years ago, that the GIS field would grow rapidly only if large commercial organizations could be enticed to enter it.

Development in the GIS field demanded many elements: hardware, to provide the fundamental enabling capabilities required; construction of a sound theoretical basis for geographical relationships and a model of how geographical reality could be abstracted for data processing; engineered software products which would encapsulate the scientific notions of spatial analysis and geographical data processing; creation of demand for spatial information in order to address complex problems about geography; creation of an industry which could manufacture and distribute GIS technology; and creation of a research environment with all its competitive mechanisms, for ensuring advances in methods and techniques. Each of these elements required appropriate institutional settings and the development of people who would create and drive these institutions.

Over the last two decades, these elements have come into being. The GIS field is now coming of age with: the founding of the US National Center for Geographic Information and Analysis (NCGIA) and its equivalent in other countries; the selection by IBM of GIS as one of its five strategic markets for the 1990s; the adoption of GIS by virtually all US national agencies; the massive emerging general interest in cartography and geography; environmental crises at local, national and global levels; resource shortages; the decay as well as rapid growth of cities; and the need to manage natural resources better.

This chapter describes what GIS in the commercial sector presently supplies, how it goes about its business, what problems it faces, and where present trends are leading. The chapter concentrates on those aspects of commercial operations which are influenced directly by doing business in the GIS field. The perspective is that of a major firm in the field, which now supplies a broad range of GIS technology, but which recalls vividly what a 'start-up mode' of operation was like.

is now approaching 1 000. Annual gross sales are difficult to determine, in part because of varying definitions of what the GIS business includes (e.g. including or excluding sales of general-purpose computing machinery which is used for GIS applications). Using a broad definition, annual sales of GIS technology are probably about 500 million US dollars at the present time. Software sales may represent a quarter of that amount.

THE LITERATURE

In comparison with the literature of the computer field, the literature of the GIS field is still in a rather undeveloped state; this is especially so with regard to the strictly commercial aspects of the field. Nevertheless, there are a few sources which identify vendors of GIS hardware, software, and services. Often company profiles are also provided.

Surveys of the commercial sector in the United Kingdom are included in the AGI Yearbooks (Shand and Moore 1989; Foster and Shand 1990). The most thorough survey of the US industry is that by Walker and Miller (1990). An annually updated sourcebook for the United States (*GISWorld* 1990) also provides useful up-to-date information.

A number of privately prepared (and quite costly) survey reports aim to describe the commercial GIS field. These provide dollar estimates of total revenues, market share, sales by sector, estimates of growth rates by sector and similar kinds of data. Some also include company profiles and technical accounts of recent developments. These include, for example, those of Dataquest, Inc. (San Jose, California, a subsidiary of Dun & Bradstreet) and Daratech, Inc. (Cambridge, Massachusetts).

Commercial GIS and closely related technologies

Commercial GIS are commonly based on both vector and raster computer technologies; however, the commercial GIS field is also related to a number of other spatial information technologies, usually because of interchanging data with them, or using them in managing or displaying data. Many commercial firms supply these other technologies along with GIS-related products. Many commercial organizations which perform photointerpretation, remote sensing, photogrammetry, or image processing now offer some GIS-related products, such as creating automated geographical databases which include the products of their work; many organizations which supply computer aided drafting or cartographic services also offer GIS-related products. A number of computer hardware manufacturers have begun to offer GIS software as well. A large number of firms which have specialized in services to a particular industry (e.g. forestry, engineering) have begun to offer GIS services and consulting in support of their project work. General purpose computer software suppliers are now creating some software (such as DBMS software) useful in GIS.

SCOPE OF COMMERCIAL GIS BUSINESS

The GIS business began about 20 to 25 years ago, was relatively small for the first decade of its existence, and has been growing very rapidly in the last decade. While estimates vary, growth rates around 25–35 per cent per year over the next five years seem reasonable (see Maguire 1991 in this volume). The number of firms which claim to provide at least some GIS-related goods or services

'TYPICAL' COMMERCIAL GIS

A minimal GIS might consist of a computer with accompanying memory, some sort of GIS software, geographical data, a person to operate the system, and a set of procedures which are to be followed in its use. More complete GIS commonly include digitizing tablets, colour graphics terminals, and hardcopy devices such as plotters, electrostatic printer/plotters, or the like. Larger GIS can be created by adding more components; using larger capacity or more sophisticated devices; connecting components together; and increasing staffing, data and organizational complexity. Because GIS often perform compute-intensive operations (such as overlaying), many user organizations have found it best to dedicate a computer system entirely to GIS operations rather than running GIS as one of several applications. Even then, graphic displays are often slow unless a very powerful graphics processor is included in the system. Because large databases are usually involved, GIS often require very large memory resources. At present, commercial GIS can be based on mainframe computers, minicomputers, workstations, or personal computers, and GIS and their component hardware can be networked together in various ways. The accompanying figures (Figs. 4.1–4.5) show several such GIS configurations and their approximate costs (in US dollars). At present, sales of workstation and personal computer based systems are growing more rapidly than those of other configurations.

CATEGORIES OF COMMERCIAL GIS

Primary GIS businesses

Hardware technology

Hardware development continues to be a major driving force in the development of GIS. The major trend in this area is towards less expensive, faster and smaller computers; in the early 1990s these are workstations of the 20–50 MIPS variety. By the mid-1990s, these are expected to become 50–250 MIPS workstations at a cost affordable for personal computing. These computers, together with file servers and very large capacity storage devices, are rapidly being networked and, in the future, they will operate as nodes within a vast computer and data management environment (for more discussion of the technological setting of GIS see Goodchild 1991 in this volume).

Most hardware development is of general-purpose computing machinery, which is then applied to GIS. Only a few hardware devices are completely GIS specific, but some devices, such as digitizers, plotters and scanners, find especially important applications in the GIS field. The marketing of computer hardware for GIS use has become increasingly oriented to an 'open system' approach in which buyers are purchasing a variety of independent system devices and avoiding the overhead costs of solutions in which a single vendor supplies all the hardware for a complete GIS.

A discussion of the diversity of the commercial hardware business, even as it applies to GIS, is far beyond the scope of this chapter.

Software technology

Software used in GIS may be GIS specific, although some software, such as DBMS software, may be a general purpose product applied to GIS. The development of GIS-specific software may represent the 'purest' primary GIS business, since the product has no other application than GIS and is essential to the existence of a GIS.

Because of intense competition and rapid technical developments, the most critical factor in a firm's commercial success in GIS software development is probably a programme of continuous research and development, together with the creation of popular user applications. Reputation among users, the number of installed systems, the quality of software documentation and user training, and the firm's ability to deal with its customers/users are also quite critical to commercial success. To meet these demands, a successful GIS software developer probably requires staff trained in computer science, geography, cartography and a range of related disciplines. As the software becomes more sophisticated, staff specializing in the particular fields to which the GIS software is to be applied also become valuable.

Some commercial GIS software systems are hardware specific, others run on a variety of hardware systems. Similarly, some systems interface with a variety of DBMS, graphics software, and so on, while others offer less flexibility. A variety of strategies are used in coping with the problems which portability, or lack of it, presents.

The organization and functions of a commercial firm supplying GIS software are similar to firms supplying other kinds of software. These include functions like software development, quality assurance, documentation, installation, training, field support, marketing, and the like. Sales of software for major GIS often involve considerable consulting, often by third parties. Sales and distribution seem to be most effective when potential users receive actual demonstrations of the

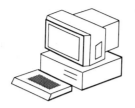

Fig. 4.1 Personal computer ($5 000–$25 000)

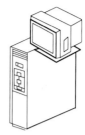

Fig. 4.2 Single user workstation ($10 000–$50 000)

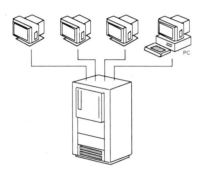

Fig. 4.3 Minicomputer using VMS, AOS/VS, X-OS, or similar operating systems ($80 000–$1 million)

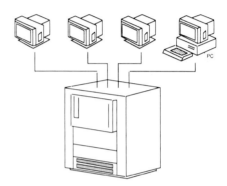

Fig. 4.4 Mainframe using VM/CMS, MVS, or similar operating systems ($2 million–$15 million)

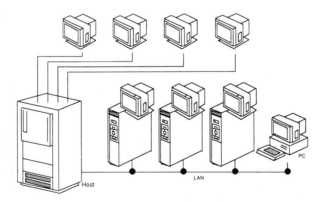

Fig. 4.5 Network with server(s) using UNIX and mainframe or minicomputer operating systems ($100 000–virtually unlimited)

Five different hardware platform approaches to supporting geographical information systems and ranges of typical hardware cost. (Cost ranges assume purchase of new equipment) capabilities of the software, although with the wider distribution of GIS, more potential buyers are familiar with GIS capabilities before they contact software vendors. Programming support and hotline support are important in the GIS field because the technology is relatively new, because it is just beginning to be taught extensively in colleges and universities, and because the applications of the technology are rapidly diversifying. User groups are still useful because of these same factors, but they are already specializing by application type, hastened by the rapid increase in the number of GIS users in the world.

Sales of GIS software for personal computers is already a much simpler process than that for GIS software on other computer platforms: following receipt of a written or phone request, and subsequent payment for the product, the user receives the user installable software, written documentation and a training package (perhaps including videotaped instruction and a training database). As personal computers continue their evolution into higher performance workstations, these lower end focused application products will play the valuable role of attracting new users into the GIS field.

Applications programming

General purpose GIS software must often be adapted to particular applications (urban planning, forestry, etc.; see also the chapters in Section III of this volume). This application may be accomplished by the user, by the original software vendor who offers prepackaged applications, by using 'macro' languages (which make it easier for users to write their own applications programs), or by a custom programming service. A major trend in recent years has been the development of third party organizations which provide application assistance to users. Many persons who gained experience in the GIS field in the late 1970s and early 1980s are now providing such 'value added' services to clients who have GIS systems. Some of these firms are also becoming GIS software distributors for the major GIS software vendors. They then add value by providing either their applications software packages or custom programming support.

Database development

The largest cost in most GIS continues to be the database. For the last 20 years automation of geographical data has been performed chiefly by digitizing and key entry. In recent years, scanning and conversion from existing automated files have also become important. Nevertheless, no present technology permits easy and inexpensive capture of previously mapped data, let alone spatial data in other non-digital forms.

For this and other reasons, there is an enormous backlog of geographical data which various organizations would like to put into digital form. A growing number of firms is providing complete assistance in the processes of database design, data capture, data conversion, data automation, data editing, database creation and related services. Many of these firms specialize, some working chiefly with natural resource data, others with urban data, and so on.

Database creation is an exceedingly complex task (see, for example, Dangermond and Harnden 1990), involves many steps, and requires great care, skill and experience if the result is to be satisfactory. Some of the firms perform their work parameter by parameter, perhaps integrating the data after automation; others integrate and standardize data before they are automated.

Some GIS are old enough that one or more cycles of complete updating by commercial firms have now been undertaken (as in rapidly growing urban areas).

Many GIS are now being designed for continuous updating through transactions, presenting problems in GIS administration which are now under intense study.

Commercial organizations applying GIS technology

The growth in the number of commercial firms which apply GIS technology in particular fields has been explosive in the last few years. Such organizations work in the fields of surveying, photointerpretation and photogrammetry, image processing, urban and regional planning, real estate, vehicle navigation, utilities, energy, mining and minerals, market research, landscape architecture, architecture, development, forestry, coastal planning, ecology, environmental planning and regulation, parks and recreation, land management, agriculture, military/defence, cartography and national mapping, water resources, flood control, civil engineering, transportation engineering, sanitary engineering, transportation planning, communications, and many others. (In part because of the employment opportunities being created in such firms, a growing number of colleges and universities are acquiring GIS for use in teaching.)

Consulting

A significant number of organizations and individuals now offer consulting on various aspects of GIS. The services offered include assessment of possible applications of GIS, GIS feasibility studies, system and database design, project design, assistance in designing specifications and Requests for Proposals (RFPs), project supervision, benchmark testing, advice on special problems in GIS, and so on. Some of the consultants also offer the capability to execute the plans they devise, including complete implementation of a system; others are third-party providers of services only.

General-purpose GIS technology firms

A few firms offer to provide a very wide range of GIS-related goods and services. These are often firms which have been in the field for more than a decade, are relatively large in size, and have accumulated a good deal of experience. These firms typically offer a wide range of consulting services, turnkey GIS, database creation, custom software programming, and complete project support services, from concept to final working system. Another approach is for a firm to offer organizational management and financing for the GIS, and then contract for all the required elements of the final GIS.

GIS-related businesses

Training/education

As contrasted with colleges and universities which may deal with education, these firms usually offer highly specific training about GIS and its applications. Some of these firms offer a broad range of related services as well. A few concentrate on seminars and courses which introduce GIS in a more academic setting. A number of commercial organizations now offer services in organizing GIS-related meetings, conferences, symposia and the like. These seem to function in ways somewhat similar to professional societies.

Publishing

A number of commercial organizations are now heavily involved in providing GIS-related journals, newsletters, market reports, research reports, and the like. A much larger number of such organizations deal with the field more peripherally by running occasional GIS-related advertisements, articles, reviews, application descriptions and similar materials. As well as potential sources of revenue, these offer a useful means of information dissemination and advertising.

Database publishers

A few commercial firms exist which might be said to be 'database publishers'. These firms provide previously created digital databases of various kinds of geographical information in some exchange format. An example is the firms providing road centreline files, initially driven by the requirements of road navigation systems. As rights in data are clarified, arrangements for data sharing with governmental agencies are worked out, and the demand for quick availability of geographical data increases, these firms may find an important niche in the GIS field, much like national government's publication of digital files.

Others

In addition to the firms mentioned above with involvement in photogrammetry, image processing, there are other firms, in a wide range of data capture and data processing areas, which simply supply their products to others for automation. These firms, nevertheless, play an absolutely essential role in the creation and support of GIS technology: their development in the last 20 years, along with developments in computer hardware technology, are probably the two major driving forces in the growth of the GIS field itself.

SYSTEM CYCLE SUPPORT

While some experienced GIS user organizations continue to buy selected GIS goods and services, the rapid growth of GIS use has meant that a growing number of customers want complete support for their GIS, from initial concept to a complete functioning system. The complete GIS development cycle, as it is supported by some commercial organizations, will be sketched out in this section. The basic steps in the development cycle are indicated in Figure 4.6 (see also Clarke 1991 in this volume).

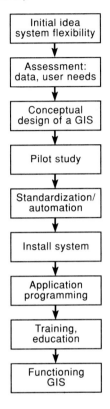

Fig. 4.6 A simplified view of the GIS system cycle

The process (described here only in skeleton outline) begins with formulation of needs and a concept; this is best done under a single director, using hard working, highly motivated 'teams of two' persons (one technically oriented, the other management oriented). Then a thorough study is made of user needs, of existing data resources, and of how the GIS will affect decision making. A cost/benefit or feasibility analysis of the proposed GIS may be performed at this point. The hardware, software, database, staff, organization, and other resources required are identified and then a design for the system and an implementation plan are created and reviewed with the user organization. If approved, the system implementation is begun. Vendors are contacted, site visits made, necessary consultants employed, applications identified, alternatives considered. A request for proposal may be drafted, including specifications, performance criteria, requirements for a technology selection test, and other requirements. Vendor selection follows. The data to be used are gathered, organized, reclassified as necessary, standardized for the new database, updated as necessary, integrated, prepared for automation, automated, edited, displayed for comparison with the source data, prepared for storage, and included in the growing database. Hardware is acquired, installed and tested, and systems software installed. Software is acquired and installed. Users are trained, and then their training reinforced by work on a pilot project which tests the entire GIS.

For a specific project, the system is used to prepare atlas maps of the project site, models are prepared for analysing the project data, outputs of various kinds are obtained, and, based on these, a plan, recommendations, decisions, or similar outputs are provided.

For a GIS providing continuing support to an organization's decision-making process, the initial database is gradually expanded, updated and enhanced, perhaps through the transaction process. Over the years the system cycle may have to be repeated, providing for updated, enlarged, or additional capabilities. Reorganizations, changes in mission or mandate, and other changes, may affect this process. Experience suggests that many GIS will have to be expanded as soon as users discover what they are capable of doing. Upgrading of skills, introduction to new techniques and methods, and similar ongoing education and training are required throughout the system's life.

Commercial organizations may also assist in integration of a GIS with an existing information system, GIS technology transfer, software conversion to new hardware platforms, creation of specific GIS products (such as atlases, special maps, etc.), and other, more specialized, services.

COMMERCIAL FIRMS' CONTRIBUTIONS TO THE GIS FIELD

The commercial sector makes a variety of contributions to the GIS field as a whole. A good deal of research and development is undertaken, in order to bring new products to the market; pilot studies of actual applications are often an important part of the process. Commercial firms are often the first actually to provide delivery of new technology to users in the form of hardware, software, methods and techniques, applications, training and so on. Having made it available, commercial firms continue its support through hotlines, technical consulting, technical literature, user groups and the like. Commercial firms may provide partial or complete subsidies of the development of new technology by other sectors, especially educational institutions and individual researchers; they may also make the technology (e.g. hardware, software, project support) available at low cost or no cost to educational institutions and special classes of users, such as non-profit organizations, international organizations dealing with the underdeveloped world, or the like. Donations of new and used equipment may be made to institutions which could not otherwise afford to acquire it. Commercial organizations usually provide major sponsorship of technical meetings and conferences, technical journals and technical research. Advertising by such firms performs an educational function for potential users, making them more aware of the technology and what it can do; advertising revenues are a major source of funds supporting the existence of professional journals. Representatives of individual firms or industry groups often take the lead in organizing industry committees and working groups or joint committees involving all the sectors of the GIS field, such as those dealing with standards; industry representatives often provide certain kinds of public policy advice to government agencies at nominal cost. Industry is a major employer of persons who practise GIS, probably exceeded by government, but, today, ahead of academia in this regard. Commercial firms often conduct extensive education and training efforts for their own employees, either formally or informally, and create a major reservoir of trained and experienced professionals and technicians which eventually enriches all sectors of the GIS field.

PROBLEMS OF COMMERCIAL GIS BUSINESS

While its success has been remarkable in recent years, the commercial sector of the GIS field must work hard to solve various problems if it is to continue to flourish; a few of these problems are mentioned below.

Problems of perception and understanding of the technology

The vast majority of people who could usefully employ GIS technology still know little or nothing about it. The message about its usefulness is still not being heard in the places where the technology is most needed, such as in the Third World, in the vast majority of municipal governments throughout the world, on the farms of the world, and by average citizens, whose access to the technology (often paid for by public funds) is difficult or impossible. Present educational efforts in colleges and universities, and even the expanding use of the technology, will only improve this situation over a period measured in decades (see Unwin 1991 in this volume for further details).

Potential buyers and users of GIS technology continue to be confused and, in some cases, turned away from GIS use by various advertising and sales practices of some commercial GIS firms. The number of commercial firms claiming to have GIS is rapidly expanding, but the vast majority of these software systems have only rudimentary GIS capabilities.

Companies continue to announce GIS software long in advance of the earliest possible delivery dates, and many such programs are never delivered to users at all. Many GIS continue to perform so badly that users, and those who listen to them, are convinced that the 'promise' of GIS technology is no more than a deception.

Many of these problems would be eliminated if potential users were far better informed and educated about the technology, if professional standards of practice were observed, and if more users would make use of objective tests, such as benchmarks, to evaluate the competing claims of vendors. But beyond this, all sectors of the GIS field need to work harder at explaining what GIS technology is, what it can do, and how it can be most effectively and inexpensively employed.

Problems with GIS technology

There are numerous technical problems to resolve at the present time, but, perhaps paradoxically, these are likely to be resolved much sooner than the problems mentioned above. These technical problems, discussed elsewhere in this volume, include the difficulties in connecting hardware and software from different vendors; the difficulties in interconverting data created in different ways; the data automation problem; and so on.

Problems between the sectors of the GIS field

Finally, commercial organizations continue to find themselves in competition with government and sometimes academia in providing goods and services to users. As in other technical fields, this is a source of concern for all parties; it may also be a source of creative tension which benefits all.

SOME FRUSTRATIONS OF THE COMMERCIAL SECTOR

Some problems are so intractable and persistent that they colour every aspect of commercial operations in the GIS field. While opinions will differ as to what these intractable problems are, here is one short list:

- Given the speed with which the field is developing, and the difficulty commercial organizations are having in keeping up with that growth, it may seem paradoxical to suggest that the slowness with which the technology has been accepted is frustrating; but, given what the technology is capable of, and the rapid march of the global problems which it could help to alleviate, the relative snail's pace of its development is extremely frustrating.

- Though costs are falling rapidly, the continuing high cost of the technology is also frustrating.

- It is frustrating to GIS professionals to deliver such an effective and powerful technology and then see it either underused, misused, or abandoned by users, for reasons which have nothing to do with the technology itself. A related frustration is commercial firms' inability, thus far, to deliver GIS technology to those who need it most in the world, the people in underdeveloped countries. Both these frustrations may be related to a third, the difficulty in transferring this technology to users who lack a rather rich educational and, perhaps, cultural background (this issue is explored further in Taylor 1991 in this volume).

- Of the GIS technical problems, the most frustrating continues to be the collection and automation of data, still probably the chief technical barrier to wider use of GIS (see Jackson and Woodsford 1991 in this volume).

TRENDS OF THE COMMERCIAL SECTOR

Many changes have occurred in the business of GIS in the 25 or so years of its existence. Only a few can be mentioned here. Figure 4.7 also indicates some of these.

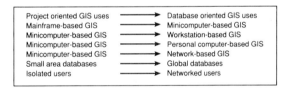

Fig. 4.7 Some of the trends in the commercial sector

The dominant trend in the commercial sector is unquestionably the rapid growth in the sales of GIS. This certainly reflects, in turn, steeply rising user acceptance of, and user demand for, the technology.

An underlying trend, which has probably fuelled these rapid increases, has been the rapid increase in the performance/cost ratio of general-purpose computer hardware over the entire history of GIS. This permitted commercial firms to break into the GIS turnkey system business in the 1970s by being able to support GIS on minicomputers instead of just on mainframes; in the 1980s, GIS could be based on personal computers. Now performance is being enhanced through the use of workstations and by networking hardware components.

One reflection of these changes has been a clear trend from GIS being used to perform the work of single, isolated projects, to the sale of the technology to users who create databases and systems which they intend to use continuously, over a long period, for a series of applications. This trend has made the industry what it is today. A decade ago the largest part of the business was in services, usually performance of complete projects for users. Now the largest part is sales of hardware, software, training and support, to users.

As users have become increasingly responsible for their own systems, and the cost for entry-level GIS has fallen, the diversity of users (Fig. 4.8) has increased; so also has the number of systems serving many different purposes.

	Computer-aided drafting	Remote sensing	Raster GIS	Vector GIS	Network analysis	Coordinate geometry	3-D modelling	Laser disk storage
National development		▨	▨					
Urban planning	▨			▨				
Renewable resources		▨	▨		▨			
Utilities	▨			▨	▨	▨		
Transportation	▨			▨	▨			
Environment		▨	▨				▨	
Agriculture		▨	▨					

Fig. 4.8 Spatial data technology and applications

The practical upper limit in the size and complexity of GIS databases is growing rapidly; the first true global GIS have only been around for a few years (see Clark, Hastings and Kineman 1991 in this volume). As database size has expanded, increased efforts have been devoted to data capture and automation. As the field has aged, increasing efforts have been devoted to database maintenance and updating.

If present trends in falling cost, increasing ease of use, and rising user interest continue, GIS may become as commonly used as computer graphics.

FUTURE COMMERCIAL DEVELOPMENT OF NEW TECHNOLOGIES

Many factors influence whether and when a particular development in GIS technology becomes 'commercial'. These include cost, potentially useful applications, ease of use or 'user friendliness', concept demonstration through suitable pilot applications, the willingness of one or more firms to invest in bringing the technology to market, availability of necessary supporting technologies, and so on. Sometimes what is most necessary, or most lacking, is a 'champion': a person or an organization to push the technology until it is accepted.

An example of a technology which seems to offer considerable promise, but which is not presently significant in GIS-related sales, is artificial intelligence/expert systems (see Smith and Ye Jiang 1991 in this volume). Some GIS applications have been made, but have not yet been widely accepted by users.

Scanning is finding increasing acceptance for data capture, although it continues to have major technical limitations in dealing with many kinds of mapped data.

CONCLUSIONS

The commercial sector of the GIS field is just beginning its period of most rapid growth. Like the rest of the field, the commercial sector is just emerging from its 'pioneering' phase. As information technology improves and diversifies, users will increasingly be able to mix freely GIS, CADD (computer-aided design and drafting), image processing, and other spatial information technologies. On the one hand, the decade or two just ahead may see commercial GIS further emerge as a recognizable industry; on the other hand, the technology may become so pervasive that it 'disappears', becoming transparent to users in the same way as that of the telephone, the computer and computer graphics. At present, the former course seems the more likely.

The commercial sector of the GIS field is increasingly recognized as a major player in the field as a whole. It provides competitive and market mechanisms and creative forces that can be channelled to make great progress, if parochialism, protectionism, nationalism, and unfair forms of competition can be avoided, and open, global markets for GIS technology can be created.

REFERENCES

Clark D M, Hastings D A, Kineman J J (1991) Global databases and their implication for GIS. In: Maguire D J, Goodchild M F, Rhind D W (eds.) *Geographical Information Systems: principles and applications*. Longman, London, pp. 217–31, Vol 2

Clarke A L (1991) GIS specification, evaluation and implementation. In: Maguire D J, Goodchild M F, Rhind D W (eds.) *Geographical Information Systems: principles and applications*. Longman, London, pp. 477–88, Vol 1

Dangermond J, Harnden E (1990) *Map Data Standardization*. Environmental Systems Research Institute, Redlands California

Foster M J, Shand P J (eds.) (1990) *The Association for Geographic Information Yearbook 1990*. Taylor & Francis and Miles Arnold, London

GISWorld (1990) *GIS Technology '90: results of the 1990 GISWorld geographic information systems survey*. GISWorld, Fort Collins Colorado, 16 pp.

Goodchild M F (1991) The technological setting of GIS. In: Maguire D J, Goodchild M F, Rhind D W (eds.) *Geographical Information Systems: principles and applications*. Longman, London, pp. 45–54, Vol 1

Jackson M J, Woodsford P A (1991) GIS data capture hardware and software. In: Maguire D J, Goodchild M F, Rhind D W (eds.) *Geographical Information Systems: principles and applications*. Longman, London, pp. 239–49, Vol 1

Maguire D J (1991) An overview and definition of GIS. In: Maguire D J, Goodchild M F, Rhind D W (eds.) *Geographical Information Systems: principles and applications*. Longman, London, pp. 9–20, Vol 1

Shand P, Moore R (1989) *The Association for Geographic Information Yearbook 1989*. Taylor & Francis and Miles Arnold, London

Smith T R, Ye Jiang (1991) Knowledge-based approaches in GIS. In: Maguire D J, Goodchild M F, Rhind D W (eds.) *Geographical Information Systems: principles and applications*. Longman, London, pp. 413–25, Vol 1

Taylor D R F (1991) GIS and developing nations. In: Maguire D J, Goodchild M F, Rhind D W (eds.) *Geographical Information Systems: principles and applications*. Longman, London, pp. 71–84, Vol 2

Unwin D J (1991) The academic setting of GIS. In: Maguire D J, Goodchild M F, Rhind D W (eds.) *Geographical Information Systems: principles and applications*. Longman, London, pp. 81–90, Vol 1

Walker T C, Miller R K (1990) *Geographic Information Systems – an assessment of technology, applications, and products*. SEAI Technical Publications, Madison Georgia USA

THE GOVERNMENT SETTING OF GIS IN THE UNITED KINGDOM

R CHORLEY AND R BUXTON

No one would doubt the enormous significance of central and local government in the development of GIS. In many countries their supporting role continues to be crucial and the United Kingdom is no exception. This chapter examines the role of the Government in the historical and contemporary development of GIS in the United Kingdom. In the first part, the importance of three government committees, the Ordnance Survey Review in 1979, the House of Lords Select Committee on Science and Technology in 1984 and the Committee of Enquiry into the Handling of Geographic Information in 1987, is examined alongside developments elsewhere in the country. In the second part, the present role of government is examined through a series of short case studies which include the activities of the Ordnance Survey, the Land Registry, the Health Service and defence.

INTRODUCTION

This chapter examines the impact of central and local government on the development of GIS. Because of the enormous differences in the way governments in different countries operate, the United Kingdom is chosen as a case study to illustrate some more general points. Other chapters in this book offer contrasting views of the situation in other countries, for example, the United States (Starr and Anderson 1991 in this volume), Sweden (Ottoson and Rystedt 1991 in this volume), Japan (Kubo 1991 in this volume), Australia (O'Callaghan and Garner 1991 in this volume) and developing countries (Taylor 1991 in this volume). The chapter by Morrison (1991 in this volume) compares the UK and US situations in particular.

The constitution of the United Kingdom is not contained in any single document. Rather it has been formed over a long period of time, partly by common law, partly by statute and partly by convention. Within this framework, the legislature, Parliament, is the supreme authority. The executive consists of: (1) the Government – Cabinet and other ministers who are responsible for initiating and directing national policy; (2) government departments, which are responsible for national administration; (3) local authorities, which administer and manage many local services; and (4) public corporations responsible for operating particular nationalized industries or, for example, a social or cultural service, subject to ministerial control in varying degrees. The judiciary determines common law and interprets statutes and is independent of both legislature and executive (Central Office of Information 1988).

Any attempt at a full description of the government setting for GIS in the United Kingdom is, therefore, necessarily complex. Such a description must take into account the extent to which the executive role of government extends into society. In the context of geographical information, the UK Government cannot be regarded as a single entity, with one clearly defined set of policies. Instead, it is necessary to consider the UK Government as a network of independent units operating within a broad framework of policy and financial accountability.

These independent units may be the central functions of government ministries, such as Defence, Transport, Environment and Agriculture; they may be departments such as the Office of

Population Census and Surveys (OPCS) or executive agencies, with fewer financial restrictions, such as the Ordnance Survey (OS) and Her Majesty's Land Registry (HMLR); they would also, until the latter half of the 1980s have covered the public utilities such as gas, water, electricity and telecommunications, although by the beginning of the 1990s these had largely moved into the private sector; and there are the Research Councils who are responsible for the distribution of funds for the full range of academic research, including issues relating to geographical information. In the United Kingdom, central government is responsible for the funding of Regional and District Health authorities, and over half the income of local government is in the form of grants from central government.

All the organizations identified above are linked by being significant collectors, users and purveyors of geographical information. Each organization has its own needs and priorities and these may conflict with the needs and priorities of others. At various stages in the course of the last two decades, successive governments have sought to provide some form of overall policy framework. Three major committees, established by the Government, have considered and reported on issues relating to the use of computer systems for handling geographical information. The extent to which these committees have had an impact on government policy and the interaction between policy and practice within the diverse web of the machinery of government will be explored in this chapter.

HISTORICAL BACKGROUND: 1791–1985

Although this chapter is primarily concerned with the government setting for GIS in the United Kingdom as it stands at the beginning of the 1990s, that setting is itself a result of an evolutionary process that can be traced back over many years. The formal involvement of the UK Government in issues relating to the handling of geographical information could be said to extend back some 200 years to the original Trigonometrical Survey of 1791 and the formation of the Ordnance Survey of Great Britain (Ordnance Survey Review Committee 1979).

The current work of the Ordnance Survey will be considered in more detail by one of the other contributors to this volume (Sowton 1991). The institutional role of the Ordnance Survey must, however, be considered within the overall context of the more general framework of UK Government involvement in issues relating to geographical information.

Through the work of the Ordnance Survey, Britain has been fortunate to have a single national series of maps based on a country-wide National Grid (a metric grid on a Transverse Mercator Projection; see Maling 1991 in this volume). These currently comprise more than 220 000 separate maps at seven principal scales. Of these, 97 per cent are accounted for by the basic scales (1 : 1250, 1 : 2500 and 1 : 10 000), the largest available for any given area. Complete national coverage is provided at the smaller scales of 1 : 25 000, 1 : 50 000, 1 : 250 000 and 1 : 625 000, which are derived from the basic scale maps.

Although the Ordnance Survey had been the subject of some 20 Parliamentary or other committees during the course of 150 years, it was the report of the Ordnance Survey Review Committee (1979) which first drew widespread attention to the potential use of computers for mapping purposes.

This theme was followed up in 1984, when a House of Lords Select Committee on Science and Technology, chaired by Lord Shackleton, reported on satellite remote sensing and digital mapping (House of Lords 1984). This Committee was able to take account of the rapid improvement in computer technology since the 1979 Ordnance Survey Review Committee. In its examination of remote sensing and digital mapping, the Shackleton Committee recognized that the computer provided the potential for an enormous range of disparate information types (or data sets) to be collated, spatially related and processed as an aid in decision making and recommended that a further committee of enquiry be set up specifically to look at these issues. The Government accepted this recommendation and the Committee of Enquiry into the Handling of Geographic Information, chaired by Lord Chorley, was established in 1985. The influence of this Committee will be considered in the next section of this chapter.

The Chorley Committee played a very important role in publicizing the potential contribution that GIS could make to both public and private sectors. Major users of geographical information in the United Kingdom had, however, already begun to implement computer-based systems for handling geographical information as far back as the early 1970s.

The Ordnance Survey first made digital maps available to users in 1975 and in 1982 an important study was started by the utility companies, through their national organization NJUG (National Joint Utilities Group). This project was based on the provision by the OS of 246 maps at 1:1250 scale covering 50 square kilometres. All these maps were held on a single minicomputer and acted as a common background for the digitized mains records of the participating utilities. One of the results of this information sharing was to reduce by half the amount of underground plant damage (Guinn 1990; see also Mahoney 1991 in this volume).

A further project was established in 1983 by the Taunton Joint Utilities Group (TJUG) with the objective of investigating methods for the exchange of records among local utility companies, including gas, electricity, water and telecommunications. Subsequently, the relevant local government authority was also included. The initial trial was based on a 1 square kilometre area, later expanded to 6 square kilometres, using OS digitized maps. The utility records for the trial area were digitized, with each utility company holding its own copy of the records either in digital form or on hard copy. The importance of this trial was its demonstration of the need for guidelines on the format for the exchange of data, in terms of transportability across a range of manufacturers' systems and also efficiency, in view of the large volumes of data involved.

At the same time as these early moves into computer-based mapping technology, initiatives were underway in relation to the complex problems of locational references. The Coordinating Committee on Locational References was set up in 1971 to advise central government departments on the policies they should adopt towards locational referencing. In 1972, the Department of the Environment published a report (General Information Systems for Planning) on the collection and recording of information to help meet the new information needs of the 1968 Town and Country Planning Act. The GISP proposals turned out to be far too ambitious and unnecessarily complex (DoE 1987) and many of the issues of locational referencing remain unresolved today.

COMMITTEE OF ENQUIRY INTO HANDLING GEOGRAPHIC INFORMATION

In 1985, in response to the recommendation of the House of Lords Select Committee on Science and Technology, the Government set up a Committee of Enquiry into the Handling of Geographic Information, referred to as the Chorley Committee after its chairman (DoE 1987). The terms of reference of the Committee were:

> To advise the Secretary of State for the Environment within two years on the future handling of geographic information in the UK, taking account of modern developments in information technology and of market needs.
> (DoE 1987)

Although the Ordnance Survey had started the experimental digitizing of the national map series in 1973, the Chorley Committee found that the OS was still forecasting completion dates for the major urban areas of 1995 and for other parts of the country, where there was a demand for digital maps, the forecast completion date was the year 2005. This situation was clearly unsatisfactory and this was reflected in the conclusions reached by the Committee, which included the following main areas of recommendation:

> *digital topographic mapping* – the Committee recommended a more rapid programme for the conversion of Ordnance Survey basic scale mapping into digital form. This more rapid conversion was to be based on a revised specification and increased funds being provided by the main users of the maps;

> *availability and linking of data* – spatial information held by the Government and other public sector organizations should be made more widely available, with national grid references, addresses and unit postcodes as the base for spatial referencing;

> *coordination and the role of government* – a

central body independent of Government should be set up to provide a focus and forum for common interest groups in the geographical information area, undertake promotional activities and review progress and submit proposals for developing national policy. Its members should be from all interested groups and it should maintain strong links with the Government.

The report of the Chorley Committee contained relatively little new information as much of the Report had already been published in scientific, technical or management literature (Rhind and Mounsey 1989). The particular importance of the report lay in its generation of widespread awareness in the potential offered by GIS. The Committee also played a further important role in encouraging constructive discussions between organizations such as the Ordnance Survey and NJUG which were to set the framework for progress in increasing the availability of digital mapping. This process of discussion helped to ensure that there was a general framework of agreement for the recommendations of the Committee. According to Rhind and Mounsey (1989) 'for many, the report was an anticlimax – but also an acceptable one for which they were already prepared. It is important, however, not to underestimate the wider impact of the report beyond the previously narrow GIS community.

The Government's response to the Report of the Chorley Committee was published in a formal document released in March 1988 (DoE 1988). This response was essentially positive, with the Government appearing to recognize the potential benefits of GIS:

> The Government are grateful to the Committee for the thorough consideration given to this wide ranging subject. They share the Committee's view that the potential exists for a rapid spread of applications of information technology in the handling of geographical information and that these offer the prospect of very considerable benefits. The publication of the Committee's report has itself been a major step in drawing attention to this potential and in making prospective users aware of the opportunities.

In responding to the specific recommendations in the Chorley Report, the Government was able to draw attention to a number of factors that had changed since the publication of the Report. The completion dates forecast by the OS for the digitizing programme had been substantially brought forward, with the forecast completion date for the major urban areas advanced to 1992, with the 1:2500 series scheduled for completion well before the original date of 2005.

The reasons for this radical change were twofold. Firstly, the Ordnance Survey has been able to come to agreement with the major potential digital map users, primarily utility companies, for those major map users to themselves let digitizing contracts. Where these digitized maps met the Ordnance Survey quality standards, they would form part of the Ordnance Survey digital map stock with income from sales shared between the Ordnance Survey and the organization letting the digitizing contract. New quality control standards based on a statistical sample surveying technique were also introduced, known as NJUG 13 (National Joint Utilities Group Publication No 13, 1988).

At the same time, agreement was also reached on a map specification. This agreement, known as OS 1988, was much simpler than that previously in use. The Ordnance Survey had originally considered that data for map production needed about 160 feature codes – with OS 1988 that figure was reduced to just 35. The effect of this reduction on the cost of map production was dramatic, as it enabled maps to be produced for about £150 each rather than the previous £600–£800 (Rhind and Mounsey 1989). This progress in the digitization programme has continued and Sowton (1991 in this volume) provides a review of its status. As the number of maps available has increased, so have sales. Looking back, in 1983–84 total sales of digital maps amounted to just 1300 sheets. By 1986–87 sales had reached 14 200 with sales for 1989–90 almost 38 000.

On the issue of the availability and linking of data, the Government accepted that the National Grid and the Irish Grid should be the fundamental locational referencing systems for data relating to the land area of the United Kingdom. In addition, the postal address and postcode systems were accepted as the preferred referencing systems for address based data. The Government was also able to point to the Tradeable Information Initiative, which it had already established to encourage wider use of government data, although the practical impact of this initiative was constrained by the additional cost of making data available and confidentiality. The Government also accepted the Chorley Committee's recommendations on open access to details of land ownership held by HM Land Registry and this will be considered in more detail below.

The Government supported the view of the Committee that there should be an organization independent of Government to provide a forum for users and suppliers, to promote awareness and to provide impartial and informed advice, although the Government took the view that this should be through a development of existing organizations.

The real test of the Government's attitude towards GIS cannot, however, be assessed simply from the words of response to the findings of the Chorley Committee. It is now several years since the publication of the Chorley Report and it is possible to review the actions that have actually been taken and the policies implemented. The remaining sections of this chapter will concentrate on that review.

THE PRESENT POSITION

It has already been noted in the introduction to this chapter that the UK Government cannot be regarded as a single entity, with one clearly defined set of policies relating to geographical information. It has also been noted that the organizations within government are users as well as collectors and purveyors of geographical information.

The Ordnance Survey retains a key role as a supplier of geographical information, but it is necessary to address the issue of the extent to which the current governmental framework within which it operates allows it to meet the needs of the market. HM Land Registry, transferred to Executive Agency status from July 1990, is another potential key provider of geographical information, but will the new status allow it to invest in the provision of new information services? The Tradeable Information Initiative was claimed by the Government, in its response to the Chorley Report, to be encouraging the use of government data, but to what extent has this been achieved in reality?

Other issues to be considered will be the growing use of spatial information in the National Health Service, in defence and in local government. Much of the future of GIS in the United Kingdom will depend on research and education and the extent of government involvement in these key fields will be reviewed. Finally, the role of the Government in the formation and subsequent operation of the Association for Geographic Information (AGI) will be evaluated.

Spatial referencing in the United Kingdom

Before turning to the current role of the Ordnance Survey, it is useful to give brief attention to the current position concerning the issue of locational referencing. Of particular relevance to the government setting for GIS in the United Kingdom is the postcode. In the United Kingdom there are 1.5 million unit postcodes, each covering an average of 14 addresses (DoE 1987). These unit postcodes were recognized by the Committee of Enquiry as an important spatial unit and the Committee's report recommended that socio-economic data and the 1991 Census of Population should be made available on a unit postcode basis.

There is, however, a number of problems with the postcode as a spatial unit for data collection and analysis. The postcode system was designed to meet the specific needs of the Post Office in sorting and delivering mail. The postcodes do not, therefore, take into account administrative boundaries or topographic features. With the Post Office under increasing commercial pressures, it has little incentive to undertake modifications to the postcode system unless they are to its direct advantage. In addition, there are some 18 000 changes made each year to unit postcode boundaries. A further issue relating to unit postcodes is that of confidentiality. With an average of only 14 addresses to each unit postcode, there would generally be a requirement for aggregation where sensitive information was involved to ensure that individuals could not be identified.

For both of the above reasons, the debate on the postcoding of the 1991 Census has moved from initially favouring a fully postcoded Census to a much more restricted approach, where postcodes will be collected but not necessarily used for the presentation of data. This limited approach adopted by the Department of the Environment has been criticized (Openshaw 1990), particularly as the government response to the Chorley Report had appeared to accept the recommendations on spatial referencing. In Scotland, however, the 1991 Census is based on unit postcodes, as indeed was the 1981 Census.

The introduction of government legislation in the autumn of 1989 to regulate works on the public highway, has served to highlight the issue of the spatial referencing of the highway network. This legislation is likely to include provision for a computerized street works register, which will allow information on all road works to be shared across all the agencies who carry out such works.

At present, no standard specification exists for a street gazetteer, with each utility company and local authority operating its own street register. The recognition that this absence of any standard specification for a street gazetteer could pose problems for the easy exchange of street-related data has led to the formation of a working party by the local government organization GISG (Geographic Information Steering Group, see below), supported by the Department of Transport, to develop a standard specification. The requirement to use a street gazetteer to this standard specification may be included in the forthcoming legislation for the computerized street works register.

The Ordnance Survey

In many ways, the Ordnance Survey of Great Britain remains today much as it has been for years past. The origins of the Ordnance Survey in map production continue to dominate its perspective and its position as a near monopoly supplier of large-scale mapping, with extensive copyright protection, has provided little incentive for rapid innovation. According to Rhind (1990), although the Ordnance Survey has a massive asset base (the topographic archive), it also has many constraints of history such as staffing levels, union agreements, politically imposed direction and user and staff expectations of perfection in products whatever the price.

Yet despite these constraints of history, the Ordnance Survey has begun to change. Pressure from the user community, particularly the utility companies, has led to the progress already noted in this chapter on the digitization programme. At the same time, the Ordnance Survey has started to develop a new range of products based on structured data, rather than the unstructured lines that sufficed for purely mapping purposes.

The ability of the Ordnance Survey to respond to the demands of the market for these new products is, at least in part, constrained by the financial regime under which it operates. Although the Ordnance Survey made the formal transition from government department to executive agency in May 1990, this has not led to a major change in its financial position. The Ordnance Survey remains restricted by the imposition of strict financial and manpower constraints. Investment in new product development cannot generally be undertaken where this would involve significant short-term increases in staffing or other costs, even where a long term prospect exists for generating new business. This has been a major factor in the limited progress on the provision of small-scale digital mapping (Rhind 1990).

These problems were recognized by the Chorley Committee, which recommended that the current restrictions on OS staff numbers and gross running costs should be lifted; a restriction on net costs and a recovery rate target being all that are required. The response of the Government to this recommendation was not positive, with government plans for the overall size of the civil service and the continuing need for government subsidy of large-scale mapping cited as reasons for maintaining the restrictions imposed on the Ordnance Survey. At the same time, the Government has been increasing the proportion of turnover that the Ordnance Survey must raise from its sales and royalty payments, although some potential users of OS large-scale mapping are already being dissuaded by the price of a map sheet (£110 in 1990 for an area covering only 0.25 km^2).

A combination of all the above factors has led to some questioning of the future of the Ordnance Survey. Openshaw (1990) has argued that new technology could lead to increasing competition for the Ordnance Survey: 'A monopoly exists because of inertia and the OS role as a *status quo de facto* standard. However, the cost of starting again and developing a new non-OS large-scale digital map database is falling and it is not implausible that the necessary technology will become within reach of large users during the 1990s.'

Although the Ordnance Survey has started the development of new products based on the structured database approach which is increasingly required by GIS users, this process has been slow. According to Openshaw (1990), this slow progress will encourage the search for viable alternatives to OS large scale mapping, with the eventual outcome proving to be 'disastrous to the OS'.

The Ordnance Survey of Northern Ireland

The Ordnance Survey of Northern Ireland (OSNI) is entirely separate from the Ordnance Survey organization which covers the rest of the United Kingdom. The OSNI Topographic Database (COMTOD) project has the aim of creating a single, integrated GIS for Northern Ireland through which all major public utility and local authority type functions will be integrated (Brand and Gray 1989). The project was initiated in 1981, with data conversion to a fully structured topographic database still on schedule for completion by the mid 1990s. A number of exploratory studies have taken place with various potential users of the system, including the Northern Ireland Land Registry, the Water Service and the Roads Services.

OSNI is also in the process of developing in parallel a further digital database derived from the 1:50 000 mapping of Northern Ireland.

The Land Registry

On 2 July 1990, Her Majesty's Land Registry made the transition from government department to executive agency. HM Land Registry has been in existence since 1862. Its function is to provide a safe, simple and economic system of land transfer in England and Wales. The Registry was not founded to create a general-purpose land information system for the public at large, rather a system whereby the interests of individual or corporate bodies owning land or legal interests in land are protected (Smith 1989).

Geographical information is at the heart of all Land Registry operations. The primary official records created and maintained by HMLR are the register, the filed plan and the public index map. For each registered title there is held a register in the form of a card or cards, identified by a unique title number, which provides an official description of the land, the name of the owner and details of any legal interests which adversely affect the land, such as mortgages or restrictive covenants.

Under existing legislation, land does not become registered until it is sold or granted on long lease, within a designated area of compulsory registration. For this reason, the pattern of registration is spasmodic and indeed, under this legislation, a property which is not bought or sold will never actually get registered at all. Nevertheless, in areas where compulsory registration has been in operation for a long period, more than 98 per cent of the land may be registered. About 11.5 million titles are registered at the present time and this figure is increasing by about 660 000 titles each year. It is estimated that the total number of registered titles could rise to about 22 million in the long term, given appropriate changes in statutory provisions relating to compulsory registration.

Traditionally, access to the information held by the Land Registry has been restricted to formal enquiries in connection with a land purchase transaction. No legal right existed which allowed open access to the details of land ownership held by the Land Registry. One of the recommendations contained in the Chorley Report (DoE 1987) was for legislation to lift the restrictions on access then in place. This recommendation was accepted by the Government and the Land Registration Act 1988 included a provision allowing any person to inspect the entries on the register itself and any documents referred to in the register. The actual date for this legislation to come into operation is expected to be 1991.

The Land Registry first introduced interactive computer graphics in 1983 for a technical feasibility study. This study resulted in an internal report produced in 1985 which indicated that the use of digital mapping technology for land registry purposes was technically feasible and would produce a range of benefits, although these were not quantified. In order to establish the likely costs and benefits in an operational environment, it was decided to carry out a pilot project using one of the district land registries and this pilot project has been in live operation since May 1986.

The pilot project has provided a major input into a formal study into the justification for introducing digital mapping on a significant scale into the operation of the Land Registry. That formal study has effectively been completed and the initial pilot project is now continuing as a fully operational system with plans to extend the system to further areas, although this is likely to take many years to complete.

In the medium term, the more important project is the computerization of the register and the replacement of the card based system. Without this computerization, it would be difficult to provide a high level of service in response to the demand which is likely to follow the implementation of the open access provisions of the Land Registration Act 1988.

The recent transition from government department to executive agency has provided the Land Registry with a greater degree of freedom to determine its investment strategy. The ability of the Registry to exploit the vast information resources at its disposal remains restricted by cost reduction targets and staffing limitations. The Registry remains unable to generate net additional income through new services, where these would require additional staff. In order to obtain this freedom, it would be necessary for the Registry to be granted 'trading fund' status, where the targets set for the Registry would relate to overall profitability, rather than the more restrictive targets currently in force.

Tradeable Information Initiative

One of the recommendations in the Chorley Report (DoE 1987) was that 'unaggregated spatial data held by Government Departments should be made available to other users provided that the costs of doing so are borne by the users and that there are no overriding security, privacy or commercial considerations'. In its response to the Chorley Report, the Government was able to point to the Tradeable Information Initiative, which had been launched by the Department of Trade and Industry in 1986. The Government (DoE 1988) was able to 'accept the spirit of this recommendation although in addition to the considerations mentioned, availability is also dependent on statutory requirements and on the undertakings given when the data was collected. The Tradeable Information Initiative was set up to assist in making appropriate Government data holdings accessible to private sector information providers and a new sub-group will be formed to consider locationally referenced data.'

Tradeable information is not restricted to either information with a spatial content, or computer based information. Instead, it covers any information held by government which has commercial value.

The Inter-Departmental Working Group on the Tradeable Information Initiative (TIIWG) was established following the Government's response to the Chorley Report, and is managed by the Department of the Environment in conjunction with the Department of Trade and Industry. The TIIWG is concerned with facilitating the wider availability of spatially referenced data held by central government through the provision of information about holdings of spatial data in a consistent and up-to-date format (Garnsworthy 1990).

The aim of the TIIWG in this exercise is that this 'information-about-information' should lend itself to easy presentation through registers and other means, although the form of the release of the data has not yet been decided. The practical impact of the Initiative as a whole has therefore to date been very limited.

National Health Service

Service delivery in the National Health Service is provided through the mechanism of Regional and District Health Authorities, Health Boards and Family Practitioner Committees. Whereas many of the GIS applications in the Ministry of Defence relate to topographical mapping, the applications within the Health Service tend to involve spatial analysis linking health and population data with other information.

In recent years, there has been increasing interest in linking the incidence of disease and other conditions in local populations to factors such as environmental hazards and social deprivation. The establishment of the Small Area Health Statistics Unit (SAHSU), for example, resulted from the recommendations of the Black Inquiry (1984) into the incidence of childhood leukaemia around the nuclear reprocessing plant at Sellafield. Recommendation 5 of the Inquiry concluded (Black Report 1984) '... that encouragement should be given to an organization ... to coordinate centrally the monitoring of small area statistics around major installations producing discharges that might present a carcinogenic or mutagenic hazard to the public. In this way early warning of the untoward health effect could be obtained.'

A further use of GIS concerns the allocation of resources, where a GIS can be used to analyse the distribution and characteristics of patients and health facilities. The Resource Allocation Working Party (RAWP) provides an illustration of this, where the distribution of central funds to Regional Health Authorities has been determined by a RAWP formula which takes into account information such as population estimates, standardized mortality rates and service usage in resident populations.

Although there is now widespread use of GIS techniques within the various components of the National Health Services in the United Kingdom, there is as yet no central policy towards GIS. Nevertheless, the potential importance of GIS has been reinforced by proposed government legislation (Department of Health and Social Security 1989). Under these proposals, the separation of the NHS purchaser and provider roles within the internal market would demand the accurate evaluation of health needs by Regional and District Health Authorities to ensure that the contracts for services were appropriate to the health needs of their inhabitants.

Finally, requirements for health authorities to manage all their assets with a value in excess of £1000 are likely to stimulate further demand for GIS, with managers facing the complex task of locating and compiling information on large numbers of assets across vast hospital sites.

GIS applications in defence

Defence is one of the major areas of government where applications for GIS are expanding rapidly with a wide diversity of potential uses. Some of the application areas such as those concerned with improving the command and control operations are similar, in principle, to those being developed for the civil emergency services, although much more comprehensive in scope.

In addition, there are also major developments in navigation; in line-of-sight assessment for applications such as communications planning and weapons sighting; in terrain analysis; and in the visualization and simulation for training. For all of these, geographical information is a vital component.

The defence organizations particularly concerned with mapping, which in the United Kingdom are under the control of the Hydrographer of the Navy for all aspects below the high water mark and of the Director General of Military Survey for everything above that line, have also been making extensive use of digital methods for some time in their production of traditional charts and maps. These capabilities will be integrated into an overall GIS as the systems mature.

The sophisticated and integrated nature of the user systems currently under development and the complex ways in which the terrain-related information is to be analysed, have made it essential to adopt fully topologically structured vector data for most applications. The sheer size of the data collection task, as well as the need to achieve inter-operability between the forces of different allied nations, has made it important to develop the defence GIS on an international basis. Within the NATO countries this has been tackled by the Digital Geographic Information Working Group (DGIWG) which is developing exchange and product standards. These standards are freely available and have generated considerable interest in the wider civilian community in several countries.

Although most defence requirements will need data in topologically structured vectors, there are two major exceptions. One of these is elevation data, with matrix format Digital Terrain Elevation Data (DTED) well established as a defence standard. The other exception concerns information in raster form, which is proving extremely valuable for map background displays in, for example, command and control and aircraft cockpit applications. Matrix and raster data are also covered by the DGIWG standardization.

Overall, defence GIS is a growth area and, because of the variety and level of the requirements, it tends to provide many particularly demanding applications. This is true at all levels, from the support to decision making in battle, through the effective management of communications and the defence estate, to support to aircraft simulators which reduce the need for low level flying in peacetime. New applications continue to emerge and there remains a substantial challenge, both in planning the systems and in preparing the data for operation.

Local government and geographical information

Local government in Britain is provided through the mechanism of just over 500 local authorities. The major functions covered by local government include: education; personal social services; planning and development control; most highway functions; public health (street cleansing, refuse collection, some pollution control functions); public sector housing; some leisure services; and a range of other specialist services. The fire service, and to some extent the police service, can also be considered as part of local government.

In the large urban areas, these services are largely provided by a single local government authority. Outside these areas, the service is divided between District Councils with populations ranging from 25 000 to almost 400 000 and County Councils covering a number of Districts, typically four to six. Local government is funded through a locally determined uniform charge on each resident, a business property tax and central government grants. Almost all of the work of local government involves spatial information, with the following specifically identified in the Chorley Report (DoE 1987):

Monitoring changes in resources (land and building, equipment and infrastructure) and conditions (economic, social, demographic, environmental, etc.).

Forecasting changes in housing requirements, in school roles, in travel patterns, in the economy and in the demand for land, leisure and community services.

Service planning through identifying and forecasting changes in patterns of need for services and investments as a basis for the delivery of services and deployment of resources. This will determine both the scale of provision and its location; it will also highlight areas of social deprivation.

Resource management of, for example, building maintenance, refuse collection, grass cutting, route scheduling of supplies vehicles, mobile libraries, social service ambulances.

Transport network management including provision and maintenance of highways, public transport schedules, school transport, street cleaning.

Public protection and security systems including police command and control systems, definition of police beats, location of fire hydrants, patterns of crime and incidents of fire.

Property development and investment including the preparation of development plans; assessing land potential and preparing property registers; promoting industrial development; rural resource management.

Education use of a wide range of data for teaching purposes, including the use of demonstration software packages.

With all these and other potential uses of geographical information in local government, many local authorities have started to take an active interest in the application of GIS technology. To ensure that the specific requirements of local government in relation to geographical information were taken into account at a national level, the local authorities, through their four national Associations, formed in 1988 the Geographic Information Steering Group (GISG).

GISG receives an annual grant of just under £200 000 as part of the overall central government financial support for local government and these resources have been used to fund practical GIS-related research. In particular, two studies have been carried out on the GIS requirements covering both County Council and District Council levels. Local government also actively participates in a range of joint central and local government working parties on matters relating to spatial information, including the 1991 Census (Caulfield 1989).

GIS research and education

In the United Kingdom, five Research Councils, funded by Government, provide the major source of funding for civil research and development. Of these, two have taken an active interest in GIS: the Natural and Environmental Research Council (NERC); and the Economic and Social Research Council (ESRC).

In 1988, joint ESRC/NERC funding was approved for GIS research. The focus of this research was to be the handling of geographical information and the exploration of the potential of GIS and related tools in application areas. Funding of just over £1 million was made available for a three year period beginning in 1989.

In addition to specific individual projects, the ESRC has funded the development of the Regional Research Laboratories (RRLs). The trial phase for the RRLs began in 1987 and was followed by the main phase from 1988 to 1991. The eventual sum allocated for this main phase was over £2 million and 8 RRLs were created covering the whole of the United Kingdom (Masser 1988).

The RRLs are concerned with building up an integrated data resources strategy to meet the needs of social science research in the 1990s. It is planned that each RRL should be able to develop links with regionally based client communities, providing training and advisory services for users in both academic institutions and private and public sector agencies. The target is that each RRL should become self-financing within three years, by means of research contracts for specialized work, contracts from government departments, local authorities and the private sector.

Both the ESRC and NERC have also played a role in GIS education through their provision of grants for those wishing to study GIS at a master's degree level at the Universities of Edinburgh and Leicester. The first undergraduate course in GIS, funded through the normal central government grant mechanism for higher education, was introduced in 1989 at Kingston Polytechnic and a number of universities in the United Kingdom are now offering short courses in GIS (see Unwin 1991 in this volume).

The Association for Geographic Information

One of the recommendations of the Committee of Enquiry into Handling Geographic Information was that there should be a central body, independent of government, set up to provide a focus and forum for common interest groups in the field of geographical information. It has already been noted that the Government initially took the view that this central body should be based on the work of existing organizations, with the European Division of AM/FM and the Regional Research Laboratories specifically mentioned.

The AM/FM TODAY Conference held in the United Kingdom in March 1988 served as a forum for debating the various issues associated with the recommendations of the Committee of Enquiry concerning the centre for geographical information and the Government's response. Part of this debate concerned the use of the term 'AM/FM'. These discussions gave rise to the formation of the Association for Geographic Information (AGI). This body, which is associated with, although not part of, AM/FM Europe, is a non-profit-making organization which undertakes activities initially in five main areas:

- The promotion of GIS technology, its applications and benefits.
- The coordination and organization of related interest groups.
- The collection and dissemination of information about GIS.
- The development of policy advice and lobbying of government.
- The encouragement of research into the technology and its uses.

The Government's support for the formation of the AGI was expressed by the presence of the Parliamentary Under Secretary of State for the Environment at the formal launch of the AGI in January 1989. The view expressed on behalf of the Government was that the AGI would fulfil the role identified by the Chorley Committee, as the centre of geographical information in the United Kingdom, although the AGI did not fully meet the specification that the Committee had envisaged.

Since its formation, the AGI has been particularly active in the areas of awareness and training. In addition, the AGI has become active in the issue of standards and has taken on responsibility from the Ordnance Survey for the National Transfer Format. National Transfer Standards were initially developed by a working party of representatives from a number of agencies concerned with the interchange of digital mapping data and were first published in January 1987. The published Standards Manual included the National Transfer Format (NTF) and supporting documents about data quality and data classification and a second release of NTF was published in 1989. Its main strength is in its ability to cater for the different transfer requirements of a digitized map, comprehensive attribute coding and topologically structured data within a standardized environment. Work is currently underway to make a user definable format compatible with ISO 8211 Specification for a Data Descriptive File for Information Interchange so that NTF will become acceptable for European use. Responsibility for achieving this will rest with the AGI.

While the AGI has been able to carry out the work in relation to NTF, some concern has been expressed about its ability to fulfil all the functions envisaged in the Chorley Report for the Centre for Geographic Information. Rowley (1990) has argued that while the AGI is capable of handling procedural aspects, it is not in a position to carry out much of the other work that is required, including coordination of GIS research. The AGI exists essentially as a voluntary organization representing a range of interests in GIS which are always diverse and sometimes competing and this may serve to be both its strength and weakness.

CONCLUSION

Over the course of the last ten years, the UK Government has played, at least in one respect, a positive role in generating awareness of GIS and its potential. The decision to commission the Committee of Enquiry into the Handling of Geographic Information and its subsequent report, gave considerable impetus to GIS in the United Kingdom. In addition, the Government has provided some funding for a series of GIS research initiatives and supported the formation of the Association for Geographic Information.

At the same time, however, some aspects of government policy appear to be severely limiting the potential offered by the more widespread and sophisticated use of geographical information. The constraints on both the Ordnance Survey and HM Land Registry, even as executive agencies, are limiting the supply of key information and, at least in the case of the Ordnance Survey, this could threaten its long term survival. The Tradeable Information Initiative appears to have delivered few practical results as far as spatially referenced information is concerned and the AGI is not able to fulfil entirely the role envisaged for the Centre for Geographic Information.

Perhaps it is that geographical information is not perceived as central to the core policy making objectives of government. Rather, geographical information exists at an operational level, where the potential for its more widespread use and exploitation are increasingly becoming recognized. The fragmented and complex nature of the operational government framework has tended to ensure that these issues have not been addressed seriously at a policy level. For this to change, it is likely that external pressure will have to be applied, with the AGI as the obvious mechanism. Whether the AGI can succeed in that role, remains to be seen.

REFERENCES

Black Report (1984) *Investigation of the Possible Incidence of Cancer in West Cumbria. Report of the Independent Advisory Group.* HMSO, London
Brand M J, Gray S (1989) From concept to reality. *Proceedings of AGI89* 5.2.1–5.2.7

Caulfield I (1989) The role of GISG and LAMSAC in local government. *Proceedings of the National Mapping Awareness Conference.* Miles Arnold, London
Central Office of Information (1988) *Britain 1988.* HMSO, London

Department of the Environment (DoE) (1987) *Handling Geographic Information.* HMSO, London
Department of the Environment (DoE) (1988) *Handling Geographic Information. The Government's response to the report of the Committee of Inquiry.* HMSO, London
Department of Health and Social Security (1989) *Working for Patients.* HMSO, London

Garnsworthy J (1990) The Tradeable Information Initiative. In: Foster M J, Shand P J (eds.) *The Association for Geographic Information Yearbook 1990.* Taylor & Francis, London, pp. 106–8
Guinn R (1990) The NJUG Perspective. In: Foster M J, Shand P J (eds.) *The Association for Geographic Information Yearbook 1990.* Taylor & Francis, London

House of Lords (1984) *Remote sensing and digital*

mapping. Report 98 of the House of Lords Select Committee on Science and Technology, Her Majesty's Stationery Office, London

Kubo S (1991) The development of GIS in Japan. In: Maguire D J, Goodchild M F, Rhind D W (eds.) *Geographical Information Systems: principles and applications*. Longman, London, pp. 47–56, Vol 2

Mahoney R P (1991) GIS and utilities. In: Maguire D J, Goodchild M F, Rhind D W (eds.) *Geographical Information Systems: principles and applications*. Longman, London, pp. 101–14, Vol 2

Maling D H (1991) Coordinate systems and map projections for GIS. In: Maguire D J, Goodchild M F, Rhind D W (eds.) *Geographical Information Systems: principles and applications*. Longman, London, pp. 135–46, Vol 1

Masser I (1988) The Regional Research Laboratory Initiative: a progress report. *International Journal of Geographical Information Systems* **2**: 11–22

Morrison J L (1991) An organizational home for GIS in the scientific professional community. In: Maguire D J, Goodchild M F, Rhind D W (eds.) *Geographical Information Systems: principles and applications*. Longman, London, pp. 91–100, Vol 1

National Joint Utilities Group (1988) *The quality control procedure for large scale Ordnance Survey maps digitized to OS 1988. Publication Number 13* NJUG, London

O'Callaghan J F, Garner B J (1991) Land and Geographical Information Systems in Australia. In: Maguire D J, Goodchild M F, Rhind D W (eds.) *Geographical Information Systems: principles and applications*. Longman. London, pp. 57–70, Vol 2

Openshaw S (1990) Spatial referencing for the user in the 1990s *Mapping Awareness* **4** (2): 24–9

Ordnance Survey Review Committee (1979) *Report of the Ordnance Survey Review Committee*. HMSO, London

Ottoson L, Rystedt B (1991) National GIS programmes in Sweden. In: Maguire D J, Goodchild M F, Rhind D W (eds.) *Geographical Information Systems: principles and applications*. Longman, London, pp. 39–46, Vol 2

Rhind D W (1990) Topographic databases derived from small scale maps and the future of Ordnance Survey. In: Foster M J, Shand P J (eds.) *The Association for Geographic Information Yearbook 1990*. Taylor & Francis, London, pp. 87–96

Rhind D W, Mounsey H (1989) GIS/LIS in Britain in 1988. In: Shand P J, Moore R V (eds.) *The Association for Geographic Information Yearbook 1989*. Taylor & Francis, London, pp. 267–71

Rowley J (1990) Land Information Systems. In: Foster M J, Shand P J (eds.) *The Association for Geographic Information Yearbook 1990*. Taylor & Francis, London, pp. 278–84

Smith P (1989) Tomorrow's open land registry and the dawn of a national information system. *Proceedings of National Mapping Awareness Conference*. Miles Arnold, Oxford

Sowton M. (1991) Development of GIS-related activities at the Ordnance Survey. In: Maguire D J, Goodchild M F, Rhind D W (eds.) *Geographical Information Systems: principles and applications*. Longman, London, pp. 23–38, Vol 2

Starr L E, Anderson K E (1991) A USGS perspective on GIS. In: Maguire D J, Goodchild M F, Rhind D W (eds.) *Geographical Information Systems: principles and applications*. Longman, London, pp. 11–22, Vol 2

Taylor D R F (1991) GIS and developing nations. In: Maguire D J, Goodchild M F, Rhind D W (eds.) *Geographical Information Systems: principles and applications*. Longman, London, pp. 71–84, Vol 2

Unwin D J (1991) The academic setting of GIS. In: Maguire D J, Goodchild M F, Rhind D W (eds.) *Geographical Information Systems: principles and applications*. Longman, London, pp. 81–90, Vol 1

THE ACADEMIC SETTING OF GIS

D J UNWIN

Because of their technological, integrative and rapidly changing nature, GIS pose major challenges to the education system which it is ill equipped to meet. In higher education a number of initiatives have been taken to provide education about, and training with, GIS. These include courses, model curricula and software to assist student learning. There are dangers that these responses will prove to be too little, too late; will fail to address important issues in GIS management; and will lead to GIS becoming a marginal concern within the education system.

INTRODUCTION: A PERSONAL NOTE

I am by profession a geographer who has worked in higher education for the past 25 years, teaching an uneasy combination of environmental science and spatial analysis. Currently, I teach bits of undergraduate courses in so-called 'quantitative geography' and a substantial part of a graduate degree programme in GIS. Unlike many, I can remember the exact moment, though not the precise date, when I first heard the term 'geographical information system'. The year was 1974. At the time I was secretary of the Quantitative Methods Study Group of the Institute of British Geographers and I was looking for a topic and organizer for the Group's next conference. Help came in the form of a telephone call from a (then) young lecturer at Durham University in which he volunteered to organize a meeting on GIS. I had a rough idea of what this might entail and in due course the meeting was held in May of 1975. An organizer's account can be found in Rhind (1976); it may well have been the first meeting of academics concerned with GIS to be held in the United Kingdom.

Three impressions of that conference, which concern content, attendance and education, remain with me. First, the term GIS was used fairly loosely for any integrated software dealing with geographical data and the meeting's content reflected this. Secondly, the attendance was so low that it was possible to meet at a small public house on the outskirts of Durham City. Thirdly, although 'the conviction that geographical research and *teaching* could be carried out using machines in ways which are very much more efficient than those common at present' (Rhind 1976: 46, emphasis added) was well illustrated for research, I have no memory of any teaching implications actually being discussed. At the time the education system was expanding, but, with the possible exception of a short-lived Master's degree in 'Spatial Data Handling' at Durham University, nobody was able to report any kind of formal educational programmes in GIS or anything like it.

Fifteen years on, things have changed. GIS is big business, substantial research funds have been allocated to initiatives such as the NCGIA, NEXPRI and the ESRC RRLs, and conferences about it attract attendances in hundreds, if not thousands. What is perhaps unusual about the current activity is the realization by almost all concerned that it is necessary not only to undertake research in GIS but also to teach about it, and there have been a number of academic initiatives in the field.

This chapter reports some of the problems in the introduction of GIS programmes into higher education. After a review of the various educational difficulties GIS pose for educators, it records a number of responses from the educational system, concluding with some rather pessimistic observations on the entire enterprise.

THE EDUCATIONAL CHALLENGE OF GIS

The introduction of any new technology can create problems for educators and the general nature of these problems in industry is well documented (see, for example, Bentley 1981), but GIS has proved especially difficult. From the point of view of the education system, GIS has not yet been put in its place. This failure has been to do with the characteristics of both GIS and the education system into which it has been introduced. First, GIS is an enabling technology so that it is possible to teach both with it and about it. At the time of writing, almost all the reported educational effort has been directed into teaching about GIS with very little work reported in which it is used to assist learning in some other area. Some notable forward-looking exceptions to this generalization are the BBC 'Domesday' system for which a number of teaching initiatives have been described (see Maguire 1989a), the urban planning simulation 'SimCity' (Joffe and Wright 1989), and some observations by Thompson (1990).

Secondly, almost by definition GIS integrate concepts and methods from a variety of formerly distinct disciplines such as land survey, spatial analysis, computer cartography, remote sensing and database management. This interdisciplinary nature of GIS means that responsibility for providing education and training in it is not unequivocally within the province of any specific, traditional discipline in higher education (see Morrison 1991 in this volume). In practice, however, the use of the adjective 'geographical' has tended to locate most of this responsibility within departments of geography. This interdisciplinary nature also means that there is a variety of possible viewpoints as to what an education in GIS should include, making any kind of specification of course content extremely difficult (see, for example, Tyrie 1986; Tucker and Devine 1988; Dale 1990; Toppen 1990; Unwin et al. 1990). A particular difficulty relates to the apparent conflict between a need to teach in depth about the underlying concepts in GIS while at the same time covering sufficient breadth to enable students to appreciate GIS applications (Goodchild 1985).

Thirdly, it is possible to consider GIS as either a technology, for which the major educational requirement is that of training in its use, or as a group of concepts, for which the requirement is education in its underpinnings. This leads to very different specifications of the aims and objectives of any teaching and allows a variety of formats for delivery from short 'hands on' training in system specifics (such as might be provided by system vendors) to extended, largely theoretical, courses at the Master's degree level (see, for example, Gittings 1989; Heywood and Petch 1990). It follows that more than one problem is involved in GIS education and training, with different kinds of GIS knowledge being required by managers, users and system developers, and the evident tension between a 'training' view and 'education' remains unresolved.

Fourthly, with the exception of some degree of association between the design model adopted and GIS functionality (Maguire and Raper 1990), the technology is neutral with respect to its applicability. It can be used for spatial data over a very large range of scales, with widely differing data contents and required functions. As Rhind (1987) points out, considerable variations already exist in the way GIS has developed internationally so that the balance of applications differs very considerably. This in turn means that the 'market' for GIS education is very diverse and the balance of what is taught, and how that information is passed on, may well vary substantially. An additional difficulty for educators is that, to date, it is not at all clear what the demand is for GIS personnel not only in terms of their quantity but also in respect of their qualitative characteristics.

Finally, GIS is a very rapidly expanding and changing technology which also happens to be fairly expensive to deliver. For the education system, this creates major problems of resource provision. Although there are a number of excellent low cost GIS available and it is possible to teach basic ideas without access to any proprietary production system, there is a widespread perception within education that GIS is expensive to provide and maintain. The rapidity with which the demand for GIS education and training has arisen has meant that there are very few academics competent to teach it, and this is a problem exacerbated by a steady loss of competent academics to the private sector. Usually in education course developers have access to a wide range of texts and other library materials, have models of relevant curricula derived from their own student days, and, most probably, also have research experience in the field. With the exception of a handful of GIS pioneers, virtually all instructors currently teaching programmes in GIS have none of this background and have been forced to teach themselves from whatever materials happened to have been available. Because of the rapidity of change, the academic publishing industry has generally been unable to keep pace with developments so that much of the relevant literature needed to support teaching is either systems documentation that is not in the public domain, or is in the form of voluminous conference proceedings of varying quality, or is otherwise hard to acquire. For educators working in the United Kingdom or the United States this problem of access to materials is nowhere near as difficult as it is for those working in other parts of the world where good access to materials is often lacking. Very few general textbooks are yet available, the exceptions being the well-known, but dated, account by Burrough (1986), Aronoff (1989), and an introductory text from Santa Barbara (Star and Estes 1990). For a fuller review of the literature of GIS see Maguire, Goodchild and Rhind (1991 in this volume).

In addition to these characteristics of GIS, several characteristics of the education system have created major challenges to would-be GIS educators. First and foremost, GIS technology has been developed and introduced during a period in which the education system over most of the so-called 'First World' has been either static or in steady decline as societies have adapted to different economic and demographic circumstances. There have been two reactions to the problem of introducing new developments into a contracting system. At some educational establishments GIS has been seen as a major new 'investment opportunity', affording the possibility of marketing academic skills on the open commercial market. Although this strategy has been an evident short-term success at some institutions, it remains to be seen whether or not the investment will be worth while in the medium to long term and it is clearly not practicable for every institution (for a commendably honest account of one institution's response see Heywood and Petch 1990). At other establishments GIS has been seen as yet another demand on a rapidly diminishing budget, to be serviced as cheaply as possible consistent with appearing to offer some form of programme in it.

Secondly, the location of responsibility for education in GIS within departments of geography (Morgan 1987) has been both a strength and a weakness. Although some of the antecedents to GIS (such as remote sensing, computer-assisted cartography, and spatial analysis) were firmly located within geography departments, many of its technical underpinnings (such as basic geometry, algorithms, and database management) are difficult to teach solely within the same context. On academic grounds, GIS should not be the preserve of geographers, since potential benefits exist for virtually every science that has a spatial content. It may well be that it is more difficult to offer a complete programme in GIS in the highly compartmentalized academic structures prevalent in Europe, where departmental autonomy is a much-prized 'asset', than it is in North America where such autonomy is often lacking. It is also possible that an anti-quantitative, almost anti-science, reaction within some parts of academic geography has meant that developments in GIS education have been less rapid than might have been the case had they been introduced a decade or so earlier (for evidence of this reaction see Hart 1982, 1983; Golledge *et al* 1982; Healey 1983).

THE EDUCATIONAL RESPONSE

In spite of these evident difficulties, the education system has responded to the need to provide education and training in GIS in a number of ways, notably in the provision of courses and useful computing resources.

Courses and curricula

Perhaps it is a reflection of the difficulties faced by educators wishing to provide programmes in GIS, but there is no doubt that there has been a general willingness to share experiences by publication of detailed course structures and curricula. The autonomy of institutions, departments and individuals to determine, deliver and examine whatever they see fit has meant that very few accounts of these individual initiatives have been published in more traditional areas of the curriculum. Despite these subjects having been taught for decades, the author doubts that there have been more than a handful of published accounts of curriculum development projects in political geography, geomorphology, or even cartography, and similar comments could be made about curricula in related disciplines such as planning and environmental science. Yet, within the five years from 1985 to 1990, several authors have published accounts of their GIS curricula.

In 1985 the academic journal *The Operational Geographer* published a special issue containing essentially preliminary thoughts on what should be taught about GIS and how this teaching should take place (see Goodchild 1985; Maher and Wightman 1985; Poiker 1985) and virtually every major GIS-related conference since then has had at least one session devoted to educational issues. Examples from North America include Banting (1988), Kuennucke (1988), Tucker and Devine (1988), Hamilton (1989), Nyerges (1989) and Nyerges and Chrisman (1989). Essentially similar contributions have been made in the United Kingdom by Tyrie (1986), Gittings and Mounsey (1989) and Green and McEwen (1989) and Toppen (1990) has surveyed developments in the Netherlands. In addition, during the late 1980s and continuing through into the 1990s, there has been a succession of academic conferences (notably those held each June at Ohio State University under the benevolent organization of Duane Marble and an International Geographical Union Commission) concerned solely with the problems of teaching GIS.

These contributions have their value, but they are isolated reports of uncoordinated activities which may, or may not, have wider significance. What is even more unusual about GIS within the education system is that they have already produced two collaborative course development projects of a type that are hardly ever seen within higher education. The more modest of these, the 'AUTOCARTO' syllabus, took the form of a two-day symposium held at the University of Leicester in 1988. This brought together nine participants representing a range of interests in GIS and its result was a proposal for a syllabus of 37 sessions covering the context of GIS, the spatial and analytical underpinnings, the realization of these in a computing environment, operational considerations, applications and 'institutional' issues (Unwin *et al.* 1990). An outline of this curriculum is given in Fig. 6.1.

This 'AUTOCARTO' syllabus merely lists a framework of titles for what might be included in a GIS programme, but the other project, from the US National Center for Geographic Information and Analysis (NCGIA) goes two steps further. First, it provides outline lecture notes for each suggested topic in the syllabus and, secondly, it includes other curriculum material in the form of laboratory classes and handouts (Goodchild and Kemp 1990). Figure 6.2 gives a summary of its content and structure. This 'core curriculum', is one of the most forward looking curriculum development projects ever to be undertaken in higher education and is unusual in a number of respects.

First, it is unusual by the mere fact of its existence! Given the general goal of the entire National Science Foundation's original initiative (Abler 1987) which was to reduce impediments to GIS use, most funding agencies would have directed resources towards research rather than teaching. The Economic and Social Research Council's 'Regional Research Laboratory' initiative (Masser 1988), which is the nearest UK equivalent to the NCGIA, would seem to have very little room for educational initiatives and, in practice, responsibility for guiding the development of GIS education in the United Kingdom seems to have been left in the hands of a number of *ad hoc* bodies.

Secondly, given the academic level at which the NCGIA curriculum was directed and the nature of its potential users, traditional curriculum development strategies using the formal specification of aims and objectives were not followed. Instead, after specifying the major areas of course content, a 75 lecture outline was produced and draft lecture notes collated with the assistance of some 60 GIS professionals from all over the world. The result is very much a core curriculum resource of lecture notes and accompanying laboratory classes from which educators can draw as they see fit to fill a specific need. The reported demand for the draft form of the curriculum during 1989 (Goodchild and Kemp 1990), and the reactions from at least one institution (Coulson and Waters 1990), make it clear that this approach was both realistic and sensible.

Fig. 6.1 Basic units within the AUTOCARTO GIS Syllabus (from Unwin 1990).

Section 1: Introduction – the context for GIS.
Three lectures on definitions and history, data and information as a commodity, and an 'advance organizer' real world example to illustrate GIS potential.

Section 2: Cartographic and spatial analytical concepts in GIS.
Eleven lectures on types of spatial data, georeferencing, map projections, coordinate transformations, fundamental spatial concepts, and basic operations on points, lines, areas and surfaces.

Section 3: Realization in a computing environment.
Eight lectures on digital representation of information at low and high level, data models (raster, vector, object oriented), errors, the vector/raster debate, and relevant advances in computing.

Section 4: Operational considerations.
Five lectures on hardware, data storage media, processors and processing environments, displays and an example study of at least one production system.

Section 5: Applications of GIS.
Five lectures on applications fields, global scale use, decision making using GIS, project management and cost-benefit analysis.

Section 6: Institutional issues.
Five lectures on access to data, quality assurance and standards, legal implications, GIS and management and education and training.

(There are 37 lectures in all)

Fig. 6.2 The structure of the NCGIA draft 'Core Curriculum' in GIS (from Goodchild and Kemp 1990).

---

a) Introduction to GIS
Introduction, hardware/system software, raster-based GIS, data acquisition, nature of spatial data, spatial objects and relationships, GIS functionality, raster/vector contrasts and issues.

b) Technical issues in GIS
Coordinate systems and geocoding, data structures and algorithms (vector), raster data storage, data structures and algorithms for surfaces, volumes and time, databases, error modelling and data uncertainty, visualization.

c) Applications issues in GIS
GIS applications areas, decision making in a GIS context, system planning, system implementation, new directions in GIS.

(There are 25 lectures in each course, 75 in all)

Thirdly, the initiative is unusual in that it has attempted to evaluate its effectiveness by a series of reviews directed at both the teachers and the taught and by user group meetings. These review materials were used to direct the production of the second version of the curriculum.

It seems certain that these projects will have a lasting effect on the content of GIS education in both the United States and the United Kingdom, but it remains to be seen whether or not this effect will be good or bad. The author has taught one of the NCGIA's 25 lecture units, on 'Technical Issues in GIS', at the Master's degree level and used the AUTOCARTO syllabus as a basis for an introductory overview at the undergraduate level. Although the NCGIA notes are themselves sufficient to act as an *aide mémoire*, they could not easily be used by students as self-instructional material, or, for that matter, by teachers who do not also have a reasonable first-hand knowledge of the field. Yet there is a danger that these materials, and the attitudes towards the field that they represent, will be passed on uncritically to students for many years to come. Almost inevitably they concentrate on issues and concepts thought to be relevant in 1989 and the availability of specific GIS software, yet, if the pace of change in the past decade is any guide, much of this content may rapidly become redundant. Fortunately, both curricula are alike in that they assert that a primary need is for *education* in the basic theories and concepts of the discipline. Familiarity with today's production systems, and the way the current technology implements these theories and concepts, while important to some potential GIS users, is seen by both projects to be a secondary consideration.

Software

The AUTOCARTO syllabus and the NCGIA curriculum are also alike in that both assert that any education and training in GIS must also contain some practical hands on experience in its use. In part this reflects a training objective to provide students with some familiarity with the sort of software tools that they might have to use later in their careers. However, it also reflects a conviction that direct, student centred activities using GIS are a very good route towards learning that have all sorts of educational advantages (Brown and Atkins 1988; Unwin 1980). At first sight it might be thought that standard production GIS can, and should, be used to support this laboratory work. There are a number of reasons to suggest that this is not the case. By their very nature, production systems include as much functionality as they can and are often command, rather than menu, driven. This means that students must learn a command language and a great deal about other system specifics before they are able to do any useful analysis. Alternatively, faced with an enormous list of possible GIS functions, they succumb to a 'desire to try out as many types of analyses as possible even when they were inappropriate' (Coulson and Waters 1990: 3). Certainly, whatever the instructor's stated objectives, experience with complete production systems for computer cartography and image processing suggests that such teaching tends to degenerate into user familiarization and little else. Rather than concentrating on what they are using them for, students tend to struggle with the details of the hardware and software and this is not what higher education should be about. As Coulson and Waters (1990: 4) also observe, teaching the use of one specific product would for them have been 'a full time job which will of necessity need to start on day one of the course and will continue right up to the last day'. Whatever the individual's views about the merits of any specific system, most would agree that it is dishonest to pretend that the particular set of GIS terminology, concepts and functions it contains somehow constitutes the entire field, yet using a production system as a basis for all laboratory work carries with it a danger of creating this impression. One solution to this problem lies in the provision of practical guides to GIS illustrated using a specific system, and the training manuals produced by at least one vendor in conjunction with educators at Birkbeck College London (ESRI 1990) are a good example of this approach.

Production systems are also expensive to provide. Not only is there the direct cost of the software, there are also costs in providing and maintaining a sufficient number of hardware platforms. Even if 'state of the art' when purchased, for educational use it is almost inevitable that for a substantial proportion of their active life such systems will seem old fashioned. In the United Kingdom, standard computer software for use in the universities has often been provided through centrally negotiated arrangements with suppliers so that the capital cost of the software for at least one GIS production system can be avoided by individual users (Wise and Burnhill 1990). This is a luxury that is unlikely to be available to educators in other countries and the problems in its use, outlined above, remain. In summary, the idea that in order to have a convincing education in GIS students must have access to 'state of the art' production systems is both a snare and a delusion.

It is clear that what is needed are systems that are relatively cheap to install and maintain while at the same time allowing most of the standard GIS analyses to be illustrated using realistic case study data. Fortunately educators have responded by providing some very good basic GIS and support materials. Those available in 1989 are reviewed in Fisher (1989).

One step away from the use of a full or 'cut down' GIS is the use of software designed specifically for computer-assisted learning (for a review of work in geography, see Shepherd 1985). Several years ago, the realization that GIS concepts and potential could be illustrated using the computer led to the development at Birkbeck College London of ARCDEMO (Green 1987). This was written specifically for the VMS operating system using Tektronix displays for output and was made available over the UK academic computer network called JANET. Its success led Raper and Green (1989) to use a different computing platform and newly available software tools to create the tutor called GIST which uses the Macintosh Hypercard system. GIST enables its user to move freely through a series of screens of information which illustrate GIS concepts in much the same way as one might browse through a conventional textbook, but with the advantages of some animation, improved indexing, and a careful attention to sequencing of the material. It is undoubtedly a useful resource for a simple, self-paced introduction to GIS functions without any need to access and use proprietary GIS software.

Finally, an alternative CAL approach reported by Maguire (1989b) is to use a production system to create a series of linked screens of information that can be viewed as a sequence to demonstrate a typical application using a limited number of GIS functions. His DEMOGIS system takes its user through what is essentially a sieve map operation to suggest sites for the location of further mining and quarrying activity in the Charnwood district of Leicestershire. This carefully controlled demonstration of GIS capabilities is obviously a useful adjunct to the usual applications material given out in lecture classes and the general approach of learning though concrete examples has a lot to commend it.

CONCLUSIONS AND CONCERNS

It can be seen that there have been several educational developments relating to GIS and that the education system has attempted to respond to the needs both of science and of industry by providing appropriate programmes of study. Rather than playing a leading role in developments, education has, by and large, been placed in a reactive position and there are at least three areas of concern about this role.

First, and for what in the past have always been seen to be very good reasons, most of higher education has a relatively long response time to any change. From the acceptance of the need for change to the delivery of graduates can take (in the United Kingdom) at least three, and often as many as five, years. Even if the will and the resources existed, to produce graduates who have been thoroughly exposed to GIS is likely to take many more years than the industry would like or is prepared to accept.

Secondly, higher education has only a limited range of tools available to it. Despite numerous developments in some institutions these remain the traditional content-obsessed lecture course and the practical class or laboratory. In consequence, most of the developments outlined above have been concerned with curriculum content, with an emphasis on what students ought to be taught rather than what they should end up knowing. *It cannot be stressed too highly that this content will date very rapidly and that there is a lot of good educational evidence to show that content, as specified by the teacher, is not what in the long term students acquire from their education.* Alternative methods of delivery, such as student self-pacing, resource-based courses, short modular courses, internship programmes, and various forms of distance learning, which might well be appropriate for education and training in GIS, remain relatively unexplored. Moreover, as Dale (1990) points out, the culture of the university is such that, until recently, project management has not been taught, or has been treated simply as a series of rather trivial skills that almost anyone can acquire after the real business of 'getting a degree'. Yet if GIS is not to become yet another technology looking for an application, it is essential that its teaching includes education about, and for, management (Aronoff 1989).

Finally, in the more specific context of degree programmes in geography there are signs that the incorporation of GIS into curricula is following a trajectory that is very similar to that of quantitative methods during the 1960s after the so-called 'quantitative revolution' in the discipline (Burton 1963). The sociological interpretation of this by Taylor (1976) should be essential reading for all those who are currently promoting GIS within the subject. After an initially rapid spread into research, geographers throughout education enthusiastically incorporated instruction about statistical methods into teaching at virtually all levels. However, this was almost always as an addition to pre-existing curricula, often in the form of a self-contained practical (laboratory) class that had little or no relevance to the rest of the course. Interestingly, and somewhat amusingly for those who now work in GIS, any material removed from the curriculum to make way for these 'new' methods would almost certainly have been the 'old fashioned' practical geography of map projections, cartography and land survey. In the late 1960s and throughout the 1970s, all of this was thought to be irrelevant to the brave new world of quantitative geography yet almost all of it is now reappearing as parts of these new GIS curricula! Certainly, the diet of practical geography the author was fed as a student in the pre-revolutionary London University of the early 1960s has far more relevance to what he now teaches as GIS than almost all the statistical analysis which replaced it.

The evident failure to use quantitative analysis in any real geography also led to a concentration on technique divorced from both underlying theory and possible applications. Graduates from these programmes may well have been able to go through the mechanics of a particular statistical operation but were frequently totally unable to relate what they were doing to any meaningful geographical application or idea and the entire quantitative revolution ended in the 1970s as an essentially marginal, and marginalized, activity within the discipline. It may well be that GIS contains elements that make such a process less likely, but the danger is still very real (see Unwin and Dale 1990) that it will follow the same trajectory. In order for it to become fully incorporated into the education system, it is essential that GIS is taught in contexts other than as a simple technology without much reference to its applications. This will only happen if educators harness its power to help students learn about real, substantive issues within their disciplines. At the moment most educators seem to be asking what they can do to teach people about GIS; perhaps the real question they should be asking is what GIS can do for their teaching.

REFERENCES

Abler R F (1987) The National Science Foundation National Center for Geographic Information and Analysis. *International Journal of Geographical Information Systems* 1: 303–26

Aronoff S (1989) *Geographic Information Systems: a management perspective*. WDL Publications, Ottawa

Banting D (1988) Using GFIS for teaching GIS concepts. *Proceedings of GIS/LIS '88*. American Society for Photogrammetry and Remote Sensing, Falls Church, pp. 678–84

Bentley T J (1981) *Making Information Systems Work*. The Macmillan Press, London

Brown G, Atkins M (1988) *Effective Teaching in Higher Education*. Methuen, London

Burrough P A (1986) *Principles of Geographical Information Systems for Land Resources Assessment*. Clarendon Press, Oxford

Burton I (1963) The quantitative revolution and theoretical geography. *Canadian Geographer* 7: 151–62

Coulson M R, Waters N (1990) Teaching the NCGIA curriculum in practice. In: Unwin D J (ed.) *GIS Education and Training, Collected Papers of a Conference, University of Leicester 20–21 March 1990*. Midlands Regional Research Laboratory, Leicester

Dale P (1990) Education in land information management. In: Unwin D J (ed.) *GIS Education and Training, Collected Papers of a Conference, University of Leicester 20–21 March 1990*. Midlands Regional Research Laboratory, Leicester, 6 pp.

ESRI (1990) *Understanding GIS – the ARC/INFO Method*. Environmental Systems Research Institute, Redlands California

Fisher P F (1989) Geographical information system software for university education and research. *Journal of Geography in Higher Education* 13: 69–78

Gittings B (1989) Education and training – the missing link. In: Shand P, Moore R (eds.) *The Association for Geographic Information Yearbook*. Taylor & Francis and Miles Arnold, London, pp. 323–4

Gittings B, Mounsey H M (1989) GIS and LIS training in Britain: the present situation. *Proceedings of the First National Conference of the Association for Geographic*

Information, *'GIS as a Corporate Resource'*. AGI, Birmingham England, pp. 4.4.1–4.4.4

Golledge R G et al. (1982) Commentary on 'The highest form of the geographer's art'. *Annals of the Association of American Geographers* **72**: 557–8

Goodchild M F (1985) Geographic Information Systems in undergraduate geography: a contemporary dilemma. *The Operational Geographer* **8**: 34–8

Goodchild M F, Kemp K (1990) Developing a curriculum in GIS: the NCGIA Core Curriculum Project. In: Unwin D J (ed.) *GIS Education and Training, Collected Papers of a Conference, University of Leicester 20–21 March 1990*. Midlands Regional Research Laboratory, Leicester

Green D, McEwen L J (1989) GIS as a component of information technology courses in higher education. Meeting the requirements of employers. In: *Proceedings of the First National Conference of the Association for Geographic Information, 'GIS as a Corporate Resource'*. AGI, Birmingham England, pp. c1.1–c1.6

Green N P A (1987) Teach yourself geographical information systems. The design, creation and use of demonstrators and tutors. *International Journal of Geographical Information Systems* **11**: 279–90

Hamilton W L (1989) Concurrent development of academic geo- computing facilities and curricula for undergraduate education: a case study. *Proceedings of GIS/LIS '89*. ASPRS/ACSM, Bethesda Maryland, pp. 495–505

Hart J F (1982) The highest form of the geographer's art. *Annals of the Association of American Geographers* **72**: 1–29

Hart J F (1983) More gnashing of false teeth. *Annals of the Association of American Geographers* **73**: 441–3

Healey R G (1983) Regional geography in the computer age: a further commentary on 'The highest form of the geographer's art'. *Annals of the Association of American Geographers* **73**: 439–41

Heywood D I, Petch J R (1990) GIS education: a business perspective. In: Unwin D J (ed.) *GIS Education and Training, Collected Papers of a Conference, University of Leicester 20–21 March 1990*. Midlands Regional Research Laboratory, Leicester, 11 pp.

Joffe B A, Wright W (1989) SimCity: thematic mapping + city management simulation = an entertaining, interactive gaming tool. *Proceedings of GIS/LIS '89*. ASPRS/ACSM, Vol 2, Bethesda Maryland pp. 591–600

Kuennucke B H (1988) Experiments with teaching a GIS course within an undergraduate geography curriculum. *Proceedings of GIS/LIS '88*. ASPRS, Falls Church, pp. 302–07

Maguire D J (1989a) The Domesday interactive video system in geography teaching. *Journal of Geography in Higher Education* **13**: 55–68

Maguire D J (1989b) DEMOGIS Mark 1: an ERDAS based GIS tutor. *Proceedings of AUTOCARTO 9*. ASPRS/ACSM, Falls Church Virginia, pp. 620–30

Maguire D J, Raper J F (1990) Design models and functionality in GIS. *Proceedings of the GIS Design Models and Functionality Conference*. Midlands Regional Research Laboratory, Leicester, 10 pp.

Maguire D J, Goodchild M F, Rhind D W (1991) Section I. Introduction. In: Maguire D J, Goodchild M F, Rhind D W (eds.) *Geographical Information Systems: principles and applications*. Longman, London, pp. 3–7, Vol 1

Maher R V, Wightman J F (1985) A design for geographic information systems training. *The Operational Geographer* **8**: 43–6

Masser I (1988) The Regional Research Laboratory initiative: a progress report. *International Journal of Geographical Information Systems* **2**: 11–22

Morgan J M (1987) Academic geographic information systems education: a commentary. *Photogrammetric Engineering and Remote Sensing* **53**: 1443–5

Morrison J L (1991) The organizational home for GIS in the scientific professional community In: Maguire D J, Goodchild M F, Rhind D W (eds.) *Geographical Information Systems: principles and applications*. Longman, London, pp. 91–100, Vol 1

Nyerges T L (1989) Components of model curricula development for GIS in university education. *Proceedings of AUTOCARTO9*. ASPRS/ACSM, Bethesda Maryland, pp. 199–204

Nyerges T L, Chrisman N R (1989) A framework for model curricula development in cartography and geographic information systems. *Professional Geographer* **41**: 283–93

Poiker T K (1985) Geographic information systems in the geographic curriculum. *The Operational Geographer* **8**: 38–41

Raper J F, Green N P A (1989) Development of a hypertext based tutor for geographical information systems. *British Journal of Educational Technology* **9**: 3–23

Rhind D W (1976) Geographical Information Systems. *Area* **8**: 46

Rhind D W (1987) Recent developments in geographical information systems in the UK. *International Journal of Geographical Information Systems* **1**: 229–41

Shepherd I D H (1985) Teaching geography with the computer: possibilities and problems. *Journal of Geography in Higher Education* **9**: 3–23

Star J, Estes J (1990) *Geographic Information Systems: an introduction*. Prentice Hall, Englewood Cliffs New Jersey

Taylor P J (1976) An interpretation of the quantification debate in British geography. *Transactions of the Institute of British Geographers* New Series **1**: 129–42

Thompson D (1990) GIS – a view from the other (dark?) side: the perspective of an instructor of introductory geography courses at University level. In: Unwin D J (ed.) *GIS Education and Training, Collected Papers of a Conference, University of Leicester 20–21 March 1990*.

Midlands Regional Research Laboratory, Leicester, 16 pp.

Toppen F (1990) GIS education in the Netherlands: a bit of everything and everything about a bit? In: Unwin D J (ed.) *GIS Education and Training, Collected Papers of a Conference, University of Leicester 20–21 March 1990.* Midlands Regional Research Laboratory, Leicester, 10 pp.

Tucker D F, Devine H A (1988) GIS education – eclectic, integrated and evolving *Proceedings GIS/LIS '88.* ASPRS, Falls Church, pp. 528–40

Tyrie A (1986) LIS education versus training: a surveying perspective. In: Blakemore M J (ed.) *Proceedings of AUTOCARTO London*, Vol. 2. London, Royal Institution of Chartered Surveyors: 340–50

Unwin D J (1980) Make your practicals open-ended. *Journal of Geography in Higher Education* **4**: 37–42

Unwin D J, Dale P (1989) An educationalist's view of GIS. In: Foster M J, Shand P (eds.) *AGI Yearbook 1990.* Taylor & Francis and Miles Arnold, London, pp. 304–12

Unwin D J *et al.* (1990) A syllabus for teaching geographical information systems. *International Journal of Geographical Information Systems* **4** (4): 457–65

Wise S, Burnhill P (1990) GIS: models of use and implications for service delivery on higher education computing campuses. In: Unwin D J (ed.) *GIS Education and Training, Collected Papers of a Conference, University of Leicester 20–21 March 1990.* Midlands Regional Research Laboratory, Leicester

THE ORGANIZATIONAL HOME FOR GIS IN THE SCIENTIFIC PROFESSIONAL COMMUNITY

J L MORRISON

The rapid rise in interest in GIS fostered by rapid developments in technology has occurred faster than existing professional organizations and academic departments have been able to react. Only now is it possible to begin to talk about bringing the institutional home for the GIS professional in synchronization with developments in the technology. Training for GIS professionals appears to be in academic departments of geography. Technological developments in the computer industry continue to occur at a rapid rate. Today GIS hardware, and for the most part GIS software, is sufficient. Trained professional users and accurate, accessible, compatible data sets are the weak links in the current GIS environment. Universities must provide the training and because of data's tremendous cost and frequent change, governments will probably have to pay the data cost. The home for GIS appears to depend largely upon the future cooperation of academia, government and industry.

INTRODUCTION

Because of its rapid rise in popularity, it should not be surprising that one of the more interesting speculations at the beginning of the 1990s revolves around where the professional organizational *home* of GIS should reside. Clearly, as is the case whenever a bandwagon begins to roll, many spurious characters try to jump on board and ride it for its benefits. The GIS bandwagon is rolling and there is jockeying for ownership and leadership by several professional organizations. This chapter examines the contribution and claims of professional organizations in several countries to the past and future development of GIS. International organizations are examined first, followed by national organizations.

It is useful to break the term GIS into two constituent parts for the purposes of this paper.

GIS = Geographical + Information System

On the surface, geography would appear to be the natural disciplinary home for GIS. After all, the word geographical or geographic is the first word in GIS. Geography, the mother of sciences, has been equated with the study of space (spatial) in the sense of position and relationships among positions on the surface of the planet earth. Clearly it is this spatial (= geographical) notion that is important in GIS (as opposed to one-dimensional or simpler information systems). Within geography two aspects of space have competed for attention during the past three decades (since the onset of the quantitative revolution in the discipline): visualization and parameterization.

Cartography, as a discipline, has mainly concerned itself with visualization while spatial data experts, a small group of professionals within the geography discipline, have mainly been concerned with parameterization of space and spatial relationships. Authors have recognized three levels of interest in space: existence, location and structure (Robinson and Petchenik 1976). Existence and location, or 'here is' information, have been the traditional province of general cartography, that is topographic maps and reference atlases. On the other hand, structure is concerned with spatial relationships. These have been investigated, specified and calculated by statisticians, spatial data specialists and cartographers in the form of thematic maps. Precise location and distances are not sought on thematic maps. Users are concerned instead with examining spatial relationships and patterns, that is, structure.

A third discipline, the cadre of remote sensing specialists, has concerned itself with both visualization and parameterization but has limited itself to what is known as the raster format for data (see Egenhofer and Herring 1991 in this volume). All three sets: geographers, cartographers and remote sensing specialists, have some ties to the discipline of geography.

The second part of GIS, Information System, has appealed to a much wider variety of professionals. There are many information systems: some deal with text, for example a telephone directory; others with sound, for example recorded phone messages; and others with visual information, for example a book of photographs. GIS are a further subset of information systems. Information about space is important and ranges from large-scale concerns expressed by surveyors, geodesists, utility companies and highway engineers, and planners, to small-scale concerns expressed by global modellers from a variety of systematic disciplines such as climatology, geology, meteorology, botany and zoology.

Those professionals in need of large-scale information primarily want information about space, that is existence and location. Those in need of small-scale information primarily want visualization and parameterization about structure. The net effect is that a myriad of traditional professional groups contain subgroups that are interested in GIS and are aboard the GIS bandwagon. These groups are competing with one another for the right to steer the direction of GIS and the perceived right of ownership.

Within the English speaking nations of the world, geographers and computer scientists, supported by major vendors of hardware and software have united to drive developments in GIS. The decade of the 1980s saw a tremendous development that has made GIS readily affordable and thus available to a wide variety of users. User groups have formed around many GIS software packages and the feedback from such groups is vital to the continued progress of GIS developments. These developments have allowed GIS to become a useful tool to professionals in medicine, chemistry and all the social sciences. But fundamentally GIS is a tool, if not the major tool, of the discipline of geography.

The quandary thus created is simple: where does GIS belong in the traditional professional society/academic department framework? Does GIS force a redistribution of traditional professional memberships or does it require a new professional organization and/or academic departments? Surveyors, planners, utility engineers, cartographers, remote sensing specialists, spatial data specialists, and geographers all want a piece of the action. Computer scientists may yet try to claim part as well. What is the professional organizational home of GIS, what should it be, or what will it be? Will it differ from country to country? These questions are investigated in the next section.

International organizations

There is a large number of international organizations with interests in GIS. The most prestigious, the International Council of Scientific Unions, ICSU, is a complex organization consisting of 20 international scientific unions, 75 national members, associates and observers and 26 scientific associates (International Council of Scientific Unions 1989). ICSU, along with many of its constituent members, is interested in GIS. The Union has initiated the International Geosphere Biosphere Program, IGBP. This programme has four research themes:

1. documenting and predicting global change;

2. observing and improving our understanding of dominant forcing functions;

3. improving our understanding of interactive phenomena in the total Earth system; and

4. assessing the effects of global change that will cause large-scale and important modifications in the availability of renewable and non-renewable resources (International Council of Scientific Unions 1989).

A GIS can be an important tool in each of these four themes as it can provide the visualization and parameterization about spatially associated existence or structure. IGBP is just one of ICSU's programmes.

The International Geographical Union, IGU, a member of ICSU, established a Commission on GIS at its 1988 General Assembly in Sydney, Australia. The Commission is under the leadership of M. Lyew of Costa Rica. This Commission is a direct outgrowth of previous IGU commissions headed by R. Tomlinson and D. Marble. This group of international scientists has been concerned with spatial data handling for over 20 years and possesses a wealth of information about working with spatial data (Tomlinson 1972; Marble 1980). Publications and conferences convened by the former commissions have presented the leading edge of this work to the world. From 1984 until 1990 a series of four international symposia on spatial data handling have been held. These symposia have been events of primary importance to the development of GIS as their proceedings attest.

CODATA, Committee on Data for Science and Technology, is an interdisciplinary scientific committee of ICSU which seeks to improve the quality, reliability, processing, management, and accessibility of data of importance to science and technology. In particular, CODATA seeks to promote the production and distribution of databases for the disciplines of physics, chemistry, engineering, bioscience and geoscience. CODATA Task Groups adopt sets of standard reference data to encourage on an international basis the appropriate use of data and the uniformity of data reporting (National Research Council 1989). GIS is becoming of increasing concern to CODATA and sessions at its July 1990 International Conference included 'Geoscience numerical information processing'. It is early yet in the history of GIS, but CODATA principles applied to data reporting may well be the necessary and most efficient way to foster the IGBP.

Other international professional organizations, not members of ICSU, who have an interest in GIS include the International Cartographic Association, ICA, the International Society of Photogrammetry and Remote Sensing, ISPRS, and the Fédération International de Géomètres, FIG. Several international trade fairs, often concentrating on hardware and software rather than theoretical or analytical problem solving, are being held annually, including those sponsored by the National Computer Graphics Association, NCGA, Autofact, Micad and A/E/C systems.

NATIONAL ORGANIZATIONS

Different approaches to the unification of professionals interested in GIS are evident in many countries and the situations in the United States and the United Kingdom offer perhaps the most striking contrast. In the United States a combination of an *ad hoc* grouping of professional organizations and a centrally funded scientific initiative have led the way from the bottom up. In the United Kingdom a top down approach led by central government has been largely responsible for formation of a single coordinating body. A third approach is perhaps at work in Japan where private industry is taking the lead role in trying to organize GIS activities. These approaches and developments in other countries are reviewed below.

The United States

Within the United States, several large and established professional organizations make at least some claim to GIS. In 1987 the American Congress on Surveying and Mapping, ACSM, joined with the American Society of Photogrammetry and Remote Sensing, ASPRS, to host a GIS conference in San Francisco. The idea actually began as a regional conference, but the interest and enthusiasm exhibited in the conference from beyond that region quickly elevated it to national prominence.

The success of GIS/LIS'87 in San Francisco led to an agreement between the Association of American Geographers, AAG, and the Urban and Regional Information Systems Association, URISA, to join with ACSM and ASPRS and sponsor GIS/LIS'88 in San Antonio. GIS/LIS'88 was hugely successful, attracting over 3000 attenders and sporting an overflowing exhibition hall. AM/FM (Automated Mapping/Facilities Management) International, a fifth professional organization, with a motto of 'AM/FM is GIS' agreed to join the other four organizations in sponsoring GIS/LIS'89 in Orlando.

As a result of these activities, serious discussions within each of the sponsoring organizations were encouraged or forced (depending on your point of view). During 1989 both ACSM and ASPRS voted to discontinue their joint autumn conferences in favour of promoting the GIS/LIS series. The 1989 joint autumn conference in Cleveland ended the series sponsored by these two societies for over 25 years. Meanwhile GIS/LIS'89 held in Orlando was another success for the five sponsoring organizations. Due to the current strengths of the five sponsoring professional organizations and to the current spirit of cooperation it would appear that it is not immediately likely that a separate society devoted to GIS will emerge in the United States. A closer look at each professional organization and its changing activities is given below. Changes forced by the increased prominence of GIS are noted.

The Association of American Geographers, AAG, is primarily a professional organization of academics, most of whose members teach in departments of geography at the colleges and universities within North America. Over 50 per cent of the members hold a PhD degree and college/university employment plus active student status account for two-thirds of the total membership (5803 in 1988). The AAG has approximately 40 specialty groups of which the Geographic Information Systems Specialty Group is the largest with over 800 members.

The American Society of Photogrammetry and Remote Sensing, ASPRS, is a professional society of over 8000 members in 1988. ASPRS membership is varied; federal, state and local government employees make up 35 per cent of the membership while 30 per cent consists of engineering and consulting firm employees. Until November 1988 there were four divisions, but a fifth GIS division was announced at that time. The ASPRS established the GIS division due to a 'tremendous ground swell of interest in GIS' (Hoffer 1989: 1031). The GIS division's stated purpose is to provide members with a forum for discussing and disseminating information relating to techniques for applications of, and the system technology associated with, the design, development, applications and maintenance of GIS (Parker 1989). It is too early to determine how effective this new ASPRS division will be.

Beginning with the September 1987 issue, the monthly ASPRS publication *Photogrammetric Engineering and Remote Sensing*, began a column entitled GIS News. This section has grown and includes information on events, developments and people involved in GIS. Clearly ASPRS has established a home for GIS professionals if they choose to reside there.

The American Congress on Surveying and Mapping, ACSM, is a congress of three organizations: the National Society of Professional Surveyors (7400 members in 1988); the American Cartographic Association (2150 members in 1988), and the American Association for Geodetic Surveying (1700 members in 1988). During the 1980s ACSM served as the conduit for the establishment of the National Committee on Digital Cartographic Data Standards which created the forerunner of the Spatial Data Transfer Standard, SDTS, which is a basic standard for the interchange of digital data and of major utility to the GIS industry. Within ACSM the American Cartographic Association has taken the lead in the GIS arena and the National Society of Professional Surveyors has been concerned with a subset of GIS namely Land Information Systems, LIS. Some changes to date include a decision to rename the publication of the American Cartographic Association from *The American Cartographer* to *Cartography and Geographic Information Systems*, and to rename the publication of the National Society of Professional Surveyors from *Surveying and Mapping* to *Surveying and Land Information Systems*, with effect from 1990.

There is a rather large overlap in membership between the American Cartographic Association and the AAG. Most cartographers, remote sensing specialists and some GIS experts belong to both organizations. The American Cartographic Association, in addition to changing the name of its publication, has suggested 11 changes to its by-laws to include additional emphasis on GIS.

The Urban and Regional Information Systems Association, URISA, is a professional/educational organization for individuals concerned with the effective use of information systems by local/

regional/state/province governments. URISA strives to bridge gaps among information producers, users, and system/service vendors – to bring about a better understanding of ways in which timely and meaningful information is or can be available for decision and policy making. There are currently 2800 members which represent a multidisciplinary cross-section of government, private industry, and academic professionals. Most members are in management positions with county or municipal governments.

URISA sponsors an annual conference and produces multi-volume annual conference proceedings. Because of the increased interest in GIS one volume of the multi-volume set of proceedings has been devoted to GIS for each of the last few years.

AM/FM International, AM/FM, is the youngest of the five professional associations in the United States claiming interest in GIS. The organization has 1400 individual members but has the strong support of the vendors of GIS hardware and software, particularly the major vendors. The majority of AM/FM members work in private industry, most for a utility. The membership is young and well educated. More than half the membership is under 40 and more than half has formal education beyond the bachelor's degree.

Catering to large-scale GIS databases, AM/FM International is often most closely associated with utility and urban infrastructure building and management. The organization has adopted a motto of 'AM/FM is GIS' and includes discussions at its annual meetings of GIS versus AM/FM. The results from the discussions should be obvious from the adopted motto. AM/FM has actively supported standards for data inputs into GIS systems. It is the first professional organization to provide financial support for standards testing and development that will assist the GIS industry.

The National Center for Geographic Information and Analysis, NCGIA, was a concept advanced by professional geographers and brought to fruition by NSF. In the summer of 1987 the NSF issued a 'Request for Proposals' for NCGIA. Five areas in need of research were identified for consideration:

1. Improved methods of spatial analysis and advances in spatial statistics.

2. A general theory of spatial relationships and database structures.

3. Artificial intelligence and expert systems relevant to the development of GIS.

4. Visualization research pertaining to the display and use of spatial data.

5. Social, economic, and institutional issues arising from the use of GIS technology (Abler 1987).

The solicitation explicitly called for NCGIA to meet four goals:

1. To advance the theory, methods, and techniques of geographic analysis based on GIS.

2. To augment the United States' supply of experts in GIS and geographical analysis.

3. To promote the diffusion of analysis based on GIS through the scientific community.

4. To act as a clearinghouse for the dissemination of information about GIS research, teaching, and applications (Baerwald 1989).

A consortium of universities led by the University of California at Santa Barbara, UCSB, won the competition. UCSB along with the State University of New York at Buffalo, and the University of Maine at Orono, established the NCGIA in December 1988. NSF funding consists of $1.1 million per year for a period of up to eight years. The innovative proposal by this triad of universities initially called for 12 research initiatives. Five were initiated in 1989: Accuracy of Spatial Databases; Languages of Spatial Relations; Multiple Representations; Use and Value of Geographic Information; and Architecture of Very Large GIS Databases (NCGIA 1989).

The NCGIA competition had many side benefits for professionals of GIS in the United States. Positions were established at a number of major universities for the study of GIS and several top academics were enticed to move to form clusters of strength in GIS.

A sub-field of GIS, Land Information Systems, LIS, has also been active and the Institute for Land Information, ILI, has established centres of excellence in LIS at several universities and a regional centre in New England and eastern Canada called the Atlantic Institute. The University of Maine at Orono is an active participant in both the NCGIA and the ILI's centre of excellence programme. Such activity coupled with the continuing NSF support for NCGIA assures the United States of a cadre of well-trained university graduates who will be the future leaders of GIS. NCGIA and the LIS centres of excellence personnel are active participants in the GIS/LIS series of conferences as well as in all five of the professional organizations listed above.

Clearly GIS professionals in the United States can select a home from among several professional organizations. So long as the five major professional organizations already sponsoring the GIS/LIS conferences cooperate, it is probably unnecessary for a new organization to form in the United States. This annual conference is probably a sufficient forum to allow interested professionals to introduce their work to the world and to discuss current and future developments and needs.

United Kingdom

The concept of the Association for Geographic Information, AGI, was voiced in 1987 and a provisional council was established in March 1988 which led to the formal launch of the AGI in January 1989. The AGI is a multidisciplinary organization dedicated to the advancement of the use of geographically related information (Shand and Moore 1989). AGI is defined to cover all interest groups including local and national government, utilities, academia, system and service vendors, consultants and industry. Two overriding aims are to increase the awareness of the benefits brought by the new technology of GIS and to assist practitioners in the attainment and use of these technologies (*AGI* 1988).

The concept of AGI follows a recommendation made by a committee of the UK Government headed by Lord Chorley (DoE 1987; Chorley and Buxton 1991 in this volume). One of the Chorley Committee's principal findings was a lack of awareness of developments in information technology which had important implications to users of spatial data. The committee was convinced that firms, organizations and nations who most successfully tackled this problem would gain important competitive advantages. The Committee emphasized a need for a central body to provide a focus and a forum for the great diversity of users of geographical information (*AGI* 1988). AGI was the result.

AGI functions as a National Centre for Geographic Information and provides an 'umbrella' organization for professional bodies and individuals interested in this technology (Wellings 1989). AGI's first national conference was held in Birmingham in October 1989 and over 600 delegates attended. The theme 'GIS a Corporate Resource' emphasized managerial issues and implementation. The Association publishes a quarterly newsletter (*AGI NEWS*) and annual yearbooks.

The United Kingdom is not without organizations similar to the five professional organizations in the United States (e.g. the British Cartographic Society, the Institute of British Geographers and the Royal Geographical Society), yet probably due to the leading role played by the Chorley Committee a new association was formed prior to the establishment of big annual meetings. Many of the individuals prominent in AGI are also leaders in other professional organization activities within the United Kingdom.

The Regional Research Laboratory, RRL, Initiative which commenced in February 1987 (Goodchild and Rhind 1990), is the United Kingdom's equivalent to the NCGIA in the United States. Initially four centres, later expanded to a network of eight centres, were funded by the Economic and Social Research Council, ESRC. The objectives are:

1. To establish a resource base for research and policy analysis.

2. To examine methodological issues arising from the management of large scale databases.

3. To develop centres of expertise within the United Kingdom (Masser 1988).

The research projects within the centres show a similarity to those being conducted by NCGIA. A core group of newly well trained experts in GIS appears to be forthcoming within the United Kingdom. In 1990 it was announced that ESRI, the vendor of ARC/INFO agreed with the Combined Higher Education Software Team, CHEST, to provide the GIS software system ARC/INFO to all of the United Kingdom's 192 higher education establishments (ESRI 1990). This will undoubtedly produce a significant number of graduates versed in GIS skills.

Whether this early top down organizational focus in the United Kingdom will result in fostering developments and educational opportunities in GIS faster or more efficiently than similar developments in the United States remains to be seen. Certainly the leaders of AGI are not unaware of GIS activities in the United States and vice versa.

Japan

A 'caretaker's group' has been established to lead establishment of an organization primarily interested in GIS in Japan. The group consists of corporate, utility, government and research institute members. A meeting was held at the annual meeting of the Japan Surveyors Association in 1990 and the group is in contact with organizations in the United States. Exactly in what manner the organization will form remains to be seen. Clearly there is a need, and whether a new organization forms or an amalgam of older organizations takes the leadership role, Japan will respond to the current interest in GIS. The financial strength of corporations in Japan and their abilities to form loose organizations and to work together to attain an agreed upon goal spells success for future GIS activities in Japan (see Kubo 1991 in this volume).

Netherlands

NEXPRI, the Nederlands Expertise Centruum voor Ruimtelijke Informatiererwerkig, (Dutch Expertise Centre for Spatial Data Analysis) is jointly funded by the Dutch National Science Foundation and computer firms and environmental consultancy agencies (NEXPRI 1989). The universities at Amsterdam, Delft, Utrecht, Wageningen and the International Institute for Aerospace Survey and Earth Science, ITC, in Enschede jointly cooperate in NEXPRI which began in 1989. The goals are:

1. Research into the development and applications of GIS and spatial analysis.

2. Coordination of GIS research and training in the Netherlands.

3. Collaboration with similar research programmes elsewhere.

Four major research initiatives were undertaken in pursuit of these goals:

1. Theory of spatial analysis.

2. Quantitative land evaluation.

3. Transport of materials and pollution studies.

4. Development of GIS methods and techniques.

Canada

GIS developments in Canada often are included and reported along with the activities of professional organizations in the United States. The close connection between professionals in Canada and the United States is indicated by the fact that two of the five professional organizations mentioned under the United States above, AAG and URISA, held their 1990 annual meetings in Canada, Toronto and Edmonton respectively, and AM/FM held an informational meeting in Etobicoke, Ontario. Nevertheless, Canadian professionals interested in GIS have organized conferences on GIS and Canadian entrepreneurs and firms have made significant contributions to GIS developments.

The Department of Energy, Mines and Resources Canada, EMR, and the Canadian Institute of Surveying and Mapping, CISM, jointly sponsored the first of a series of national conferences in early 1989 in Ottawa. This national conference was entitled 'Challenge for the 1990s GIS' and brought together professionals interested in GIS from many nations. A volume of presented papers, exceeding 1400 pages in length, was an impressive result (Grant 1989). Canadian societies paralleling those in the United States are interested in GIS and the GIS professional activity in Canada focuses on this newly established series of GIS conferences much like similar attention focuses on the GIS/LIS series of conferences in the United States.

Republic of South Africa

Thanks to the advent of *NAGIS News* in June 1989 by an energetic group of GIS experts in Pietermaritzburg and the SAGIS89 Conference in 1989, the Republic of South Africa, RSA, has jumped aboard the GIS bandwagon (Natal/ KwaZulu Association for Geographic Information Systems 1989). *NAGIS News* reports a modest amount of undergraduate GIS education within the RSA in 1989 at eight universities. While GIS education at RSA universities is only beginning perhaps the greatest need, according to *NAGIS News*, is for a self-standing GIS course for those individuals already established in professional careers. Equally important are short courses for decision makers/managers. A shortage of skills in GIS is evident in RSA and this fact could potentially foster the establishment of a GIS centre of excellence which would help to concentrate the current efforts. It appears to be agreed that the success of GIS in RSA will depend on the training of potential users by universities and vendors. The energetic group in Natal has started this process and was responsible for the EDIS87, Earth Data Information Systems, conference, held in Pretoria in September 1987 (South African Society for Photogrammetry, Remote Sensing and Cartography 1987).

Other Nations

The Utvecklingsradet for Landskapsinformation, ULI, in Sweden is in operation. This organization encouraged and sponsored in part by the Lantmateriverket in Gävle is led by a full-time professional. It serves as a professional forum for GIS activities in Sweden, holding regular meetings, workshops, education tours and publishing useful literature (Cederholm 1989; see also Ottoson and Rystedt 1991 in this volume).

The AFI3G in France has sponsored several successful conferences and would appear to be one organization fostering interest and interchange between French corporations and individuals interested in GIS in France.

GIS is being introduced into the People's Republic of China at a rather rapid rate. Systems are working at the National Bureau of Surveying and Mapping in Beijing, Wuhan Technical University, and Nanjing University to name but three sites. Interest is very keen and Chinese professionals are attending international GIS conferences in large numbers.

Within Eastern Europe and the Soviet Union the introduction of GIS has been much slower. Recent political events should tend to hasten its introduction but the lack of foreign exchange may keep GIS from widespread use in the near future. Most large GIS systems already being utilized in this region are closely controlled by the governments. Open systems are often very small and run on rather dated hardware and hence the more sophisticated GIS software perhaps cannot be accommodated.

DISCUSSION AND CONCLUSIONS

GIS is an enabling computer-based technology which allows its practitioners to collect, analyse and display spatial data. Those capabilities will lead to needs for vast spatial databases which will form one part of an information infrastructure which all levels of government, private enterprise and individual citizens will profit from utilizing in the future. The potential for use of GIS as a tool for bettering mankind is staggering. Not surprisingly, professionals leading the developments in this technology seek the opportunities to meet and discuss the major challenges, to compare their research results and to chart future directions for the creation, maintenance and use of these databases and the invention and extension of analytical procedures useful when applied to these data. Usually professional membership organizations, through annual conventions and publications, provide these opportunities, and university departments provide the basic education for a cadre of new professionals in the technology. Private industry, sometimes supported by governmental development dollars, provides the technology itself.

The rapid rise in interest in GIS fostered by rapid developments in technology has occurred faster than existing professional organizations and academic departments have been able to react. Only now is it possible to begin to talk about bringing the institutional homes for the GIS professional into synchrony with developments in the technology. The situation in North America is following a 'bottom-up' path where professionals from a number of existing organizations have sponsored a series of meetings in an attempt to accommodate this GIS interest.

In contrast, the situation in the United Kingdom has followed a 'top-down' approach. Resulting directly from a government study, the AGI was established and GIS professionals in the United Kingdom have their own separate membership organization.

Training for GIS professionals for the moment appears to be in academic departments of geography. The NCGIA is closely associated with departments of geography in the United States and the AGI is hopeful that its influence will promote GIS education at selected UK institutions of higher education. For a technologically dependent tool it is appropriate that one scientific discipline assumes the leadership role. Geography appears to have done so and it is to be hoped that it will continue to rise to the occasion and satisfy national needs for GIS professionals in all nations.

Technological developments in the computer industry for the moment continue to occur at a rapid rate. Because of this a spirit of cooperation among GIS professionals enables individuals to maximize the accessibility to the latest technological advances. If technology advancement slows this spirit of cooperation may not continue. It is not absolutely necessary for a technologically driven tool to have its own society or association. With the current spirit of cooperation among the professional associations in the United States, it is possible to accommodate the needs of GIS professionals in the existing societies. If the UK model results in more focused developments at a faster pace an association similar to AGI may be created within North America. Barring the above and assuming the continued cooperation in North America, GIS will find its professional home wherever it finds an open door and a comfortable couch.

Today GIS hardware, and for the most part GIS software, is sufficient. Trained professional users and accurate, accessible, compatible data sets are the weak links in the current GIS environment. Universities must provide the training and it has been proven to be to the manufacturer's advantage to donate hardware and software to established university curricula. The collection of validated data is the most expensive part of the equation. Because of data's tremendous cost and because useful data change so rapidly, the huge data costs will probably have to be paid by government and/or distributed among governmental agencies and some private firms. The GIS environment cannot afford restricted or copyrighted data sets. Current basic data must be made available on an 'as needed' basis to all potential users. Continuing education to keep professionals abreast of technological developments is also important. The potential operation and contribution of GIS in a national information infrastructure may in fact prove to be too large for a single professional organization to handle. In the interim it is important to ensure the continued development of GIS and its full utilization. If development proceeds the professional home for GIS will become self-evident in the future.

REFERENCES

Abler R F (1987) The National Science Foundation National Center for Geographic Information and Analysis. *International Journal of Geographic Information Systems* **1** (4): 303–26

Association for Geographic Information (1988) *AGI NEWS* **1** (1): 1–8

Baerwald T J (1989) Fostering cooperation among academia, industry, and government – the establishment of the National Center for Geographic Information and Analysis in the USA. In: Grant N G (ed.) *Proceedings of National Conference Challenge for the 1990s GIS*. Canadian Institute of Surveying and Mapping, Ottawa, pp. 4–10

Cederholm T (ed.) (1989) *Utvecklingsradet for Landskapsinformation Geografiska Informationssystem*. Landmateriverket, Gävle Sweden

Chorley R, Buxton R (1991) The government setting of GIS in the United Kingdom. In: Maguire D J, Goodchild M F, Rhind D W (eds.) *Geographical Information Systems: principles and applications*. Longman, London, pp. 67–79, Vol 1

Department of the Environment (DoE) (1987) *Handling Geographic Information*. HMSO, London

Egenhofer M J, Herring J R (1991) High-level spatial data structures for GIS. In: Maguire D J, Goodchild M F, Rhind D W (eds.) *Geographical Information Systems: principles and applications*. Longman, London, pp. 227–37, Vol 1

ESRI (1990) *ARC News* Spring. ESRI, Redlands California

Goodchild M F, Rhind D W (1990) The US National

Center for Geographic Information and Analysis: some comparisons with the Regional Research Laboratories. In: Foster M J, Shand P J (eds.) *The Association for Geographic Information Yearbook 1990* Taylor & Francis and Miles Arnold, London, pp. 226–31

Grant N G (ed.) (1989) *Proceedings of National Conference Challenge for the 1990s GIS*. Canadian Institute of Surveying and Mapping, Ottawa

Hoffer R M (1989) President's Inaugural Address. *Photogrammetric Engineering and Remote Sensing* **55** (7): 1031–2

International Council of Scientific Unions (1989) *Yearbook 1989* ICSU Press, Paris

Kubo S (1991) The development of GIS in Japan. In: Maguire D J, Goodchild M F, Rhind D W (eds.) *Geographical Information Systems: principles and applications*. Longman, London, pp. 47–56, Vol 2

Marble D F (ed.) (1980) *Computer Software for Spatial Data Handling* 3 volumes. IGU Commission on Geographical Data Sensing and Processing for the US Department of the Interior Geological Survey, Ottawa

Masser I (1988) The Regional Research Laboratory Initiative: a progress report. *International Journal of Geographical Information Systems* **2**: 11–22

Natal/KwaZulu Association for Geographic Information Systems (1989) *NAGIS NEWS* June. Institute of Natural Resources, Pietermaritzburg 3200 Natal South Africa

National Research Council (1989) *Numerical Data Advisory Board Annual Report 1988–1989*. National Academy Press, Washington DC

NCGIA (1989) The research plan of the National Center for Geographic Information and Analysis. *International Journal of Geographical Information Systems* **3**: 117–36

NEXPRI (1989) *Geographical Information Systems for Landscape Analysis Research Programme*. NEXPRI, University of Utrecht

Ottoson L, Rystedt B (1991) National GIS programmes in Sweden. In: Maguire D J, Goodchild M F, Rhind D W (eds.) *Geographical Information Systems: principles and applications*. Longman, London, pp. 39–46, Vol 2

Parker H D (1989) *The GIS Sourcebook*. GIS World Inc., Fort Collins Colorado

Robinson A H, Petchenik B B (1976) *The Nature of Maps: essays toward understanding maps and mapping*. University of Chicago Press, Chicago

Shand P, Moore R (eds.) (1989) *The Association for Geographic Information Yearbook*. Taylor & Francis and Miles Arnold, London

South African Society for Photogrammetry, Remote Sensing and Cartography (1987) *Proceedings of Earth Data Information Systems, EDIS 87*. South African Society for Photogrammetry, Remote Sensing and Cartography, Pretoria

Tomlinson R F (ed.) (1972) *Geographical Data Handling* 2 volumes. IGU Commission on Geographical Data Sensing and Processing for UNESCO/IGU Second Symposium on Geographical Information Systems, Ottawa

Unwin D J (1991) The academic setting of GIS. In: Maguire D J, Goodchild M F, Rhind D W (eds.) *Geographical Information Systems: principles and applications*. Longman, London, pp. 81–90, Vol 1

Wellings C (1989) A review of the Association for Geographic Information Yearbook 1989. *Mapping Awareness* **3** (4): 51

A CRITIQUE OF GIS

R T AANGEENBRUG

The rapid introduction of GIS has created a booster type atmosphere where critics have been scarce. The size of investments made and the urge to declare success before delivery have not been sufficiently tempered by a willingness to admit that GIS is a young, somewhat poorly defined and difficult technology. The buzz words and rhetoric surrounding GIS can divert GIS researchers from their twin tasks of attempting to solve substantive social and environmental problems, and addressing unresolved problems in, for example, interfaces, handling time data and resolving the lack of organizational acceptance of GIS.

INTRODUCTION

This chapter reviews the contradictions, false claims and great opportunities in GIS. The rapid development of GIS in academia, the private sector and all levels of government has created a booster type atmosphere where critics have been scarce or dismissed as anti-progress. In the rush to join the GIS bandwagon taking stock of basic problems and defining limits has been rare. In fact the proceedings of most GIS meetings reflect the urge to promise newer and better systems, while documented case studies of numerous GIS failures and false starts are rare. The size of the investment made, the urge to declare successes before delivery have not been sufficiently tempered by a willingness to admit this is a young, somewhat poorly defined and difficult technology. GIS goals and objectives are worth while, progress is undeniable, but GIS experiences in dealing with local and global complexity are new.

This chapter begins by describing the way in which some disciplines have attempted to join the new GIS club and claim a share of the GIS pie at the probable expense of supporting its own rich research agenda. This process is illustrated using movements in cartography as an example. Next, the confusion of terms and claims in GIS is exemplified by reference to object-oriented systems. Considerable confusion arises here because terminology from computer science is blended with a tradition of less precise objects (regions, plans, priorities, choices, etc.) which are highly variable in spatial terms. The chapter continues with a reminder that spatial analysis, the scientific objective of earlier GIS development, has not progressed at the same rate as hardware, software and information systems. The discussion then considers problems with GIS interfaces and the incorporation of temporal data. The last major section deals with the technical issues and organizational problems yet to be successfully addressed by GIS practitioners. Finally, some brief conclusions are presented.

GIS is proclaimed to be a new discipline (Congalton 1986; Parent 1988; Goodchild 1990). Although this claim is not as easily documented as others, it is persistent. Both the scope and breadth of the problems addressed in GIS are often beyond the capacity and willingness of current academic disciplinary practices, including cartography, computer aided design and remote sensing (see Maguire 1991 in this volume).

Abler (1987) has noted that GIS is a new technology with great impact; it is very much akin to the introduction of the microscope, telescope and systems analysis in other disciplines. The difficulty lies in a desire, especially in the United States and Europe, for results, or, at least, progress in better geographical description and analysis. This often leads to implementation of the technology without reviewing the need for analysis.

The key forces which drive GIS include global, national and local questions of human survival in this earthly environment. Often the forces which contribute to solutions are from mission (real world) -oriented agencies or operations. The sense of survival depends on the best available solutions. Two examples can be used to illustrate this point. First, few models except the escape mode will be of use in attempts to develop protection schemes for 24-hour storm surge warnings in coastal areas. Secondly, prevention of lowland flooding can only be attempted with a long lead time and within an information system analysis cycle of considerable length. GIS generate an opportunity to improve systems analysis and to design better solutions. However, at present, knowledge of such activities is limited to conceptualizing about major features (or foci) of the environment.

Kates (1987) argued that the great questions of human occupance are interdisciplinary. Morrill (1987) noted that combining environmental and spatial variables in a broad location theory will be needed in order to understand the complex interplay between the framing influence of space and the space-defining power of individuals, groups, and social institutions. Golledge (1982) notes that perhaps much of the confusion that lies at the heart of geography (GIS) today results from an awareness that there are simply many geographies and many possible worlds.

GIS is the description tool which it is hoped will include an analytical modelling capacity suited to the transdisciplinary community of users. That means that the complexity critique levied against systems' vendors may be specious. They deliver open-ended systems in order to let users fine-tune their systems.

CARTOGRAPHY WILL BE SUPERSEDED BY GIS

It has been suggested in some quarters (for example, Marble 1979; Carter 1985, 1987; Goodchild 1985, 1988) that GIS will supersede cartography. This view is expressed in several ways including: cartography is obsolete; paper maps are tedious, expensive and slow to produce and too costly to update and maintain; map reproduction will be automated and the products will be primarily digital. Some argue that cartography has handicapped itself and does not contribute to the debate generated by the needs of modern spatial analysis. Although many of these observations are true, the need for cartographic research is greater than ever. The questions raised by the need for improved knowledge are automatic placement of text, symbolization, generalization and the design of maps for automated map making from remotely sensed images. These questions generate a substantive research agenda. In addition, a serious inability to compare two-dimensional images, let alone complex surfaces, requires analyses and procedures to live with the output generated by GIS. In fact, a large issue, that of visualization, will generate an interest in, and research questions on, the analysis of both dynamic and imagined complex views of maps (see Buttenfield and Mackaness 1991 in this volume for further discussion of visualization).

In cartography, new confusion has been introduced from the outside, that is, the use of the term 'cartographic modelling' which involves models (or representations) expressed in cartographic form (Tomlin 1990; see also Tomlin 1991 in this volume). As the term suggests, cartographic modelling is oriented more towards process than product. Its major concern is not the way in which data are gathered, maintained or conveyed, but the way they are used. Traditional use of this approach, which goes back to the work of McHarg (1969), has been called overlay mapping and it has become very popular in recent years. Its roots, especially in landscape planning, are persuasive and effective, especially where there is a mix of different kinds of geometric phenomena, for example, points, lines, and areas (roads, wells and regions). This simplistic joint description is powerful and effective. However, it fails to incorporate the ancient foes of spatial analysis: unique distribution, spatial autocorrelation, and the lack of general spatial statistics for multivariate relationships (Anselin 1989). The best way to summarize the potential problem is to use an example. If for Plot 1 the coverage status for vegetation type is accurate at the 0.8 level and if the coverage status for wetlands is accurate at the 0.8 level, the probability that the relation of soil and vegetation is $0.8 \times 0.8 = 0.64$. If a layer of, say, wildlife species with an accuracy of 0.7 is added it would be possible to argue that the combined layer could depict with a probability of 0.448 (0.7×0.64). The lack of attention to error propagation during overlay has been bemoaned by Goodchild and Gopal (1989). Although cartographic modelling will undoubtedly improve descriptive and prescriptive views of reality, the statistical and analytical basis is not clear. The power of the cartographic modelling process is obvious and effective. There is a need to guard against its use without supporting the quality control and the interdisciplinary nature of the process. Also, the term is not yet part of the academic cartographic lexicon nor is it widely accepted in geographical analysis. For example, the term does not appear in either Monmonier (1985) or Star and Estes (1990).

The need for models of map making and map analysis is the result of output and input requirements of GIS users and producers. As Clarke (1990) recently noted, the characteristics of geographical data (location, high volume, dimensionality and continuity), as well as the fundamental properties (size, distribution, pattern, neighbourhood property, contiguity, shape and scale) affect how and what is encoded, errors detected and storage optimized. Thus far, studies on the relationship of the phenomenology of the size and distribution of polygons of certain phenomena are poorly understood. Hence, editing, quality control, and analysis of, for example, soil or vegetation maps, are rather primitive.

OBJECT-ORIENTED SYSTEMS – SAY WHAT?

Object-oriented systems are appealing to salespeople and meaningful to computer scientists. To physical and social scientists the term may be more confusing than comforting. Considerable debate about the term can be documented in the computer science and, increasingly, in the GIS literature (Egenhofer and Frank 1987; Worboys, Maguire and Hearnshaw 1990). There is little doubt that the utility of object-oriented database models can aid in collecting, manipulating and understanding complex spatial data collections as well as geographical analytical needs. The advantages of the models include their high semantic modelling capability and their ability to handle fundamental needs of inheritance (specialization), aggregations and association (groupings). Eagerness to push the technology forwards leads to incorporation of the arsenal of new constructs with limited analysis and critique of the constraints of object encoding or for that matter object-oriented database structure. Three limits have been noted recently: many geographical constructs are implicitly uncertain, spatial objects are often the products of interpretation or generalization, and it is, therefore, difficult to form the world into the mould of rigidly bounded objects (Goodchild 1990).

In their enthusiasm for marketing and their need for explicit instructions, the salespeople and the computer specialists overlook the constraints of spatial analysis. One of the oldest problems in geography is how to define an object – the region. Although cultural geographers (Jordan and Rowntree 1982) suggested a Gestalt approach (i.e. you will know it when you see it), the variable definition, use and interpretation of spatial objects is well known.

The open-ended aspect of spatial ordering and representation is often more intuitively obvious than anticipated with clear encoding. Even if a database organized on spatial objects is developed, the analysis of non-spatial features will be compromised. It is necessary to recognize the difficulty and be aware that spatial ordering, analysis, and representation have exacting requirements not always met in a non-spatial object ordered system. Moreover, theory is not sufficiently advanced to develop a spatial object environment which will be explicit for a large set of users.

GIS LEADS TO IMPROVED SPATIAL ANALYSIS

Surely the presence of more data will lead to better analysis – so saith the naive scientist. Information overload is common in today's rapidly evolving technological society. It has been suggested (Roe 1989; Waldrop 1990) that a sinister facet of this overload appears to be surfacing, one that carries serious economic and social implications. This is the time-lag between data and information gathering, storage and retrieval, as well as what proportion of such data and information can be analysed, interpreted and used. Not only can new data sets often not be absorbed, but also there is a general inability to recognize the need to cope with the overload of data and to adapt, recognize and redefine what is seen, needed and absorbed.

It is possible to document many successful applications of GIS in local and state and national government. The best examples have provided an improvement in base mapping and drafting, and analysis of land use and related phenomena. It is easy to point to improved capacity in description of much of the natural environment. What is lacking, however, is a capacity to analyse relationships, for example, between point pollution and mensuration of the effect. Worse yet, the models to analyse much of what can be seen are also lacking.

There is a need to pay more attention to spatial analysis and, especially, to spatial models of the environment. This is not only a task for geographers, planners and foresters but also one for most disciplines and public policy analysts. GIS may lead to improved spatial analysis, but only if the need is recognized and more segments of society can be involved in absorbing the data and information generated. A good example which illustrates this is the difficulty faced in universities when the demand for GIS education and training began to outstrip the capacity to respond.

In an academic setting five approaches to GIS education can be cited. First, and yet to be developed, the use of GIS as an introduction to science in the liberal arts curriculum; secondly, the use of GIS as an introduction to spatial analysis in undergraduate geography; thirdly, GIS as an advanced undergraduate course in geographical methods; fourthly, GIS as an introduction to geography methods at the graduate level; and fifthly, GIS as an advanced spatial analysis course in the graduate programme. Given the lack of a consensus on which approach to teach, combined with the lack of materials (software, equipment, space, case studies) and a shortage of instructors, it is not surprising that no single approach has yet emerged in most countries. The first approach seems to be the most challenging and will have the greatest impact. Demystifying GIS and documenting their potential is important. It is crucial to educate citizens, potential policy makers, scientists and users. There is also a need to develop case studies to underscore the utility of GIS as well as the dangers of misinterpretation of maps. This dual need in education is sometimes lost as new tools are eagerly introduced.

GIS INTERFACE – THUS FAR LIMITED!

It is possible to identify at least eight distinct types of GIS: mental, natural resource, urban planning, AM/FM (urban housekeeping), global systems, intelligence (international policy and military), emergency response and citizen-scientist (Aangeenbrug 1982; Carter 1989; Maguire 1991 in this volume). Each has different object sets, variable or fixed scale and dynamic or static inputs. Hence it is difficult to prepare a common interface to all user communities. This has been recognized by Raper and Rhind (1990) as at least a twofold problem: first, the knowledge of the command lexicon required to use a system is complex and mistakes are easily made; second, many GIS require a broad knowledge of spatial analysis and theory to utilize the command structure and sequence of operations used in standard tasks. The perception of space, and the visualization of objects, in reality, versus what can be manipulated in a GIS are not clearly understood. Here the contributions from cartographers, psychologists and artists will be crucial in defining and designing better interfaces. Not only is this important for current training and education requirements, but also the user communities' expectations may be guided to realistic paths of what is possible. Perhaps the need to develop bounded explicit rationales with clear purposes and operational objectives will be required for many GIS. The notion that a GIS is a 'do-all' basic to any organization is false. The difficulties which often occur are rooted in handling multi-source, non-standard, heterogeneous data; these can also include inadequate standards and, in some cases, variable expectations after the fact. For example, after users see the output, they may ask about, for example, the relations between variable x and y. This is difficult, especially if y is not available, at the same scale, or the same time period. In view of the incomplete literature and few textbooks, and lack of clear models of GIS none of the current interfaces is yet sufficient for users with limited GIS expertise.

TEMPORAL GIS – CURRENT LIMITS

An increasing demand for time series analysis of environmental phenomena, or observation and monitoring of key indicators (e.g. land use, forest canopy damage and nuclear waste status) is driving developers to consider adding temporal data to GIS. Current systems are poorly equipped to handle temporal data and models of spatial succession are too general if they exist at all. There are computer systems that monitor traffic flow, meteorological data, and hydrologic phenomena, but they mostly lack important functionality and cannot, therefore, be considered true GIS. This limits their scope for scientific experiments in the spatial domain. Three factors come to mind as demand to deliver the capacity for space–time modelling increases: first, it will be important to document data quality in terms of time; secondly, historical series need to be incorporated to review rates of change in natural resource systems; thirdly, scenarios about the state of the environment will need to be developed. Constraints on this work are serious: first, historical data are difficult to obtain, often collected at varied intervals and varied scales; secondly, the ability to view the seamless database is limited. When a time gradient is added perceptual skills may limit users' ability to comprehend the subtle changes of spatial time series; current knowledge of the proper interval of data collection, or planned changes is primitive.

There have been some dramatic examples of how useful a time series can be. The collection of models of Mount St Helens, before and after its recent eruption, provides a useful example of rapid assessment of environmental change. Simulation of constraints for proposed land use are similarly effective (e.g. transmission line right of ways, airport noise zones and viewsheds).

The ability to perceive, evaluate and model spatial and temporal data effectively is in its early stages. Interactive spatial display with backward and forward time projections is more dream than reality. It represents a difficult challenge to GIS experts, users and students alike.

GIS: A THREAT TO ORGANIZATIONS

At the increasingly frequent GIS meetings, many presentations focus on what will be (or may be), little follow-up on what happened is ever reported. Documented failures are rare and documented successes not too numerous (Vevany 1987; Danziger, Dutton and Kraemer 1982). It is argued that this new, expensive and promising technology needs a sponsor, nurturer and protector in every organization. Competing claims for expenditure in government organizations are the norm, yet there is no model for installation of a GIS in local government. In the United States, for example, the wide array of city functions and operations is reflected in a wide set of organizations. State laws limit the authority of local governments differently in many states. The size and complexity of each local authority will also vary the likely 'home' for GIS. In addition, the experience (success or failure) with prior innovations may favour certain administrative units in different locations.

In a classic review of urban data systems, Downs (1967) warned that the uncertainties connected with the technical payoff from urban data systems loom large in the minds of those who must decide whether such systems will actually be built or installed. Four technical payoffs may be recognized for GIS. First, GIS tend to transmit data directly from events themselves to top-level officials. As a result, lower- and intermediate-level officials have little or no opportunity for 'screening' important data before they reach top-level officials. 'Screening' can mean either distorting information by altering or leaving out parts of it, or adding personal interpretation to it, or both. Secondly, GIS inevitably shift some emphasis in decision making towards more easily quantifiable factors and away from immeasurable ones. Thirdly, such systems free lower-level officials from many routine reporting and recording chores. It is often perceived that this results in changes of job or elimination of responsibility. Fourthly, GIS provide officials capable of understanding and using them with much better information about many aspects of environmental assessment.

The technical impacts of GIS tend to produce specific power shifts among the various 'actors' in the government decision-making process. Downs (1967), for example, cites: lower- and intermediate-level officials tend to lose power to higher-level officials and politicians; legislators tend to lose power to administrators and operating officials; while technically educated officials within governments gain power at the expense of old-style political advisers.

Downs concludes that a new advisory role will appear for those who possess both technical sophistication and wisdom. For example, the evolution of PCs which access optical disks containing geographical data may arm citizen activists in a manner not seen before. This may be the equivalent of photo-essays and photo-journalism which brought urban slums to the public attention in the late 1890s. It remains to be seen how effective these efforts will be and if governments continue to limit access to public information.

In any case, the current GIS literature barely focuses on organizational issues. The lack of acceptance of GIS in many agencies is due to at least three factors. First, the technical design and hype of GIS is not always understood or appreciated by officials preoccupied with other more pressing issues. They are often intuitively resistant to the all-purpose claims by GIS 'pushers'. Secondly, few, if any, independent analyses of the cost benefit of GIS have been documented outside the GIS vendor/consultant community (see Calkins 1991 in this volume). As the industry matures, the emergence of firms seen as reasonably independent judges of the value of GIS is expected to rise. Yet it should be noted that most GIS are sold, at least at the local level, for specific projects rather than a broad base application technology for all departments. Thirdly, social scientists have not been actively engaged in documenting the value of GIS in state and local governments.

The limited acceptance and effective use of GIS by various government organizations is affected not only by the high cost of getting started, the difficulty of training and keeping technical personnel, and the fear of organizational change. It is also constrained by the limited documentation of successful implementation. In the United States over half the states have one or more agencies utilizing GIS and nearly 400 local governments have installed GIS. If cost-effective systems, reasonably trained staff and better documentation can be delivered, this trend is bound to accelerate.

CONCLUSIONS

It is clear that GIS, although exceedingly useful for solving many types of environmental and social problems, have been oversold in recent years. There is a need for practitioners to develop a more considered view of the applicability of GIS for solving substantive problems. Successful and, perhaps more importantly, unsuccessful GIS projects must be examined and reported to the GIS community in order to develop the discipline further. Vendors and researchers must also avoid the use of jargon and avoid hype if GIS are to be taken up and applied successfully.

The complexity of the earth surface is such that in order to understand it a holistic view is essential. There is a need to use every available view and approach to study this complexity. GIS reflect our quest to combine all in order to see and predict better. GIS also allow, in fact demand, detailed analysis of a complex set of subjects of the environment. A clear understanding of the earth is still a long way off, but already scientists are better able to reflect on its complexity. It will require an enormous team effort of specialists, integrators, poets, politicians, and constant debate on how to do it better. The earth and its occupants demand it.

REFERENCES

Aangeenbrug R T (1982) The future of Geographic Information Systems. *Computer Graphics News* **2** (2): 4

Abler R F (1987) The National Science Foundation National Center for Geographic Information and Analysis. *International Journal of Geographical Information Systems* **1** (4): 303–26

Anselin L (1989) What is special about spatial data? Alternative perspectives on spatial data analysis. *NCGIA Technical Paper 89–4*, 20 pp.

Buttenfield B P, Mackaness W A (1991) Visualization. In: Maguire D J, Goodchild M F, Rhind D W (eds.) *Geographical Information Systems: principles and applications*. Longman, London, pp. 427–43, Vol 1

Calkins H W (1991) GIS and public policy. In: Maguire D J, Goodchild M F, Rhind D W (eds.) *Geographical Information Systems: principles and applications*. Longman, London, pp. 233–45, Vol 2

Carter J R (1985) Curricula standards, certification, and other possibilities in cartographic education. *Technical Papers of the 45th Annual Meeting of the American Congress on Surveying and Mapping*. ACSM, Falls Church, pp. 2–7

Carter J R (1987) Defining cartography as a profession. *ACSM Bulletin* August, 23–6

Carter J R (1989) On defining the geographic information system. In: Ripple W J (ed.) *Fundamentals of Geographic Information Systems: a compendium*. ASPRS/ACSM, Falls Church Virginia: pp. 3–7

Clarke K C (1990) *Analytical and Computer Cartography*. Prentice Hall, Englewood Cliffs New Jersey

Congalton R G (1986) Geographic information systems specialists. *Proceedings of Geographic Information Systems Workshop*. ASPRS, Falls Church, pp. 37–42

Danziger J N, Dulton W H, Kraemer K L (1982) *Computers and Politics: high technology in American local government*. Columbia University Press, New York

Downs A (1967) A realistic look at the final payoffs from urban data systems. *Public Administrations Review* **27** (3): 204–10

Egenhofer M J, Frank A U (1987) Object oriented databases: database requirements for GIS. In: Aangeenbrug R T, Schiffman Y M (eds.) *International Geographic Information Systems (IGIS) Symposium, Arlington, Virginia II*. ASPRS, Falls Church Virginia, pp. 189–211

Egenhofer M J, Herring J R (1991) High-level spatial data structures for GIS. In: Maguire D J, Goodchild M F, Rhind D W (eds.) *Geographical Information Systems: principles and applications*. Longman, London, pp. 227–37, Vol 1

Golledge R G (1982) Fundamental conflicts and the search for geographical knowledge. In: Gould P R, Olssen G (ed.) *A Search for Common Ground*. Pios, London: 11–21

Goodchild M F (1985) Geographic Information Systems in undergraduate geography: a contemporary dilemma. *The Operational Geographer* **8**: 34–8

Goodchild M F (1988) Stepping over the line: technological constraints and the new cartography. *The American Cartographer* **15** (3): 311–19

Goodchild M F (1990) Spatial information science. *Proceedings of 4th International Symposium on Spatial Data Handling*, Vol. 1. International Geographical Union, Columbus Ohio, pp. 3–12

Goodchild M F, Gopal S (1989) *Accuracy of Spatial Databases*. Taylor & Francis, London

Jordan T G, Rowntree L (1982) *The Human Mosaic: a thematic introduction to cultural geography*, 3rd edn. Harper and Row, New York

Kates R W (1987) The human environment: the road not taken, the road beckoning. *Annals of the Association of American Geographers* **77** (4): 525–34

Maguire D J (1991) An overview and definition of GIS. In: Maguire D J, Goodchild M F, Rhind D W (eds.) *Geographical Information Systems: principles and applications*. Longman, London, pp. 9–20, Vol 1

McHarg I L (1969) *Design with Nature*. Doubleday, New York

Marble D F (1979) Integrating Cartographic and Geographic Information Systems education. *Technical Papers of the 39th Annual Meeting of the American Congress on Surveying and Mapping*. ACSM, Falls Church, pp. 493–9

Monmonier M S (1985) *Technological Transitions in Cartography*. The University of Wisconsin Press, Madison

Morrill R L (1987) A theoretical imperative. *Annals of the Association of American Geographers* **77** (4): 535–41

Parent P (1988) Universities and Geographical Information Systems: background, constraints and prospects. *Proceedings of Mapping the Future*. URISA, Washington, pp. 1–12

Raper J F, Rhind D W (1990) UGIX (A): the designs of a spatial language interface for a topological vector GIS. *Proceedings of the Fourth International Symposium on Spatial Data Handling*, Vol. 1. International Geographical Union, Zurich, pp. 405–412

Roe K (1989) Information overload. *Science* **356** (11): 563

Star J, Estes J E (1990) *Geographic Information Systems: an introduction*. Prentice-Hall, Englewood Cliffs New Jersey

Stroutstrop B (1988) What is object-oriented programming. *IEEE Software* **5** (3): 10–20

Tomlin C D (1990) *Geographic Information Systems and Cartographic Modeling*. Prentice-Hall, Englewood Cliffs New Jersey

Tomlin C D (1991) Cartographic modelling. In: Maguire D J, Goodchild M F and Rhind D W (eds.) *Geographical Information Systems: principles and applications*. Longman, London, pp. 361–74, Vol 1

Vevany M J (1987) A critical evaluation of the proliferation of automated mapping systems in local governments. In: Aangeenbrug R T, Schiffman Y M (eds.) *International Geographic Information Symposiums: The Research Agenda*, Vol 3. Association of American Geographers, Washington, pp. 165–77

Waldrop M M (1990) Learning to drink from a fire hose. *Science* **248** (11): 674–5

Worboys M F, Hearnshaw, H M, Maguire D J (1990) Object-oriented data modelling for spatial databases. *International Journal of Geographical Information Systems* **4**: 369–83

SECTION II

PRINCIPLES

Introduction — 111–17
M F Goodchild, D W Rhind and D J Maguire

(a) Nature of spatial data

9. Concepts of space and geographical data — 119–34
   A C Gatrell
10. Coordinate systems and map projections for GIS — 135–46
    D H Maling
11. Language issues for GIS — 147–63
    A U Frank and D M Mark
12. The error component in spatial data — 165–74
    N R Chrisman
13. Spatial data sources and data problems — 175–89
    P F Fisher
14. GIS and remote sensing — 191–213
    F W Davis and D S Simonett

(b) Digital representation

15. Computer systems and low-level data structures for GIS — 215–25
    Wm R Franklin
16. High-level spatial data structures for GIS — 227–37
    M J Egenhofer and J R Herring
17. GIS data capture hardware and software — 239–49
    M J Jackson and P A Woodsford
18. Database management systems — 251–67
    R G Healey
19. Digital terrain modelling — 269–97
    R Weibel and M Heller
20. Three-dimensional GIS — 299–317
    J F Raper and B Kelk

(c) Functional issues

21. The functionality of GIS — 319–35
    D J Maguire and J Dangermond
22. Information integration and GIS — 337–60
    I D H Shepherd
23. Cartographic modelling — 361–74
    C D Tomlin
24. Spatial data integration — 375–87
    R Flowerdew
25. Developing appropriate spatial analysis methods for GIS — 389–402
    S Openshaw
26. Spatial decision support systems — 403–12
    P J Densham
27. Knowledge-based approaches in GIS — 413–25
    T R Smith and Ye Jiang

(d) Display issues

28. Visualization — 427–43
    B P Buttenfield and W A Mackaness
29. Computer name placement — 445–56
    H Freeman
30. Generalization of spatial databases — 457–75
    J-C Muller

(e) Operational issues

31. GIS specification, evaluation and implementation — 477–88
    A L Clarke
32. Legal aspects of GIS — 489–502
    E F Epstein
33. Managing and operational GIS: the UK National On-line Manpower Information System (NOMIS) — 503–13
    M J Blakemore
34. Spatial data exchange and standardization — 515–30
    S C Guptill

INTRODUCTION

M F GOODCHILD, D W RHIND AND D J MAGUIRE

The term GIS was coined twice in the 1960s, in two very different settings. Roger Tomlinson used the term to describe a system which would allow the Canadian Government to process and analyse the vast amounts of geographical data being collected for the Canada Land Inventory. The system would provide a cost-effective solution to the problem of overlaying maps of different themes, and measuring areas, both of which are difficult and expensive to do by hand. In addition it would support a range of user-defined queries, such as requests for tabulations of land classes within irregular polygons. Duane Marble, on the other hand, used the term to describe a complex of software and data built to support large-scale urban transportation studies. Both made use of rapidly developing digital technology to respond to particular, practical problems.

In the years since, the term GIS has continued to be defined more by its applications and technology than by any clear principles, or any strong sense of an intellectual or conceptual core. There are several alternative ways of defining the term GIS – by its capabilities, its applications, or the contents of its databases – and each of the many disciplines involved in the field brings a somewhat different perspective (see Maguire 1991 in this volume for further discussion).

After almost three decades GIS are now changing: vendor products are stabilizing, texts are appearing and the field is becoming increasingly respectable as a subject for support by funding agencies (see Coppock and Rhind 1991 in this volume). In the United States, the National Science Foundation has established a National Center for Geographic Information and Analysis, and one of the NCGIA's first tasks has been the production of a Core Curriculum as a first attempt to define the intellectual and scientific core of the field at the undergraduate level (see Morrison 1991 in this volume; see also Unwin 1991 in this volume). A small number of organizing principles have emerged from the mass of GIS experience: raster versus vector; query versus product; and spatial analysis versus spatial information.

This section on GIS principles is organized by identifying key scientific questions of GIS. To some extent these overlap with the key technological issues which GIS have had to solve over the past 25 years in creating a viable software product. But GIS are much more than software, as the effective use of the technology raises a host of issues, many of which have little to do with computing, but which are at least as important to the user. Many of these wider issues are much harder to solve, and will be significant research questions for many years to come. In its research plan, the NCGIA (1989) identified what it called 'impediments', in other words problems which prevented the full exploitation of the capabilities of GIS software. Many of these have to do with the level of understanding of the nature of spatial data itself, and the ways in which humans reason with spatial data, learn about them, and make decisions based on them.

The key scientific questions of GIS are grouped into five sets which form subsections of Section II, although this is largely for convenience and there is clearly substantial overlap between them. Generalization, for example, is often thought of as an issue of data display, but actually pervades much of the debate over the nature of spatial data, database design and analysis. The five groupings are as follows: nature of spatial data; digital representation; functional issues; display issues; and operational issues.

NATURE OF SPATIAL DATA

The purpose of digital spatial data handling is to give the user a cost-effective method of querying and analysing geographical variation. In that sense, its success is determined by the extent to which it can provide the user with an accurate view of the world. But geography is infinitely complex and must be generalized, approximated or abstracted in order to be represented within the finite dimensions of a discrete computing device. Thus GIS present a host of problems which can only be addressed through a high level of understanding of the nature of spatial data. How can geographical variation be sampled and measured? How can its uncertainty and error be described?

This subsection begins with Chapter 9 by Gatrell on the nature of space itself. Geography as seen through a GIS database is like a container occupied by objects, but as Gatrell points out, space is better defined through the relationships between places. Various spaces can be visualized, depending on the nature of those relationships. Couclelis (1991) makes the point that space defined through relationships is more consistent with the role of geography in many forms of planning than is space defined through its contents. In this sense the applications of the current generation of GIS to planning can be seen as somewhat limited.

Maling's Chapter 10 on map projections provides a much needed view of coordinate systems and their transformations. Since the area covered by many GIS projects is small, the earth's curvature has rarely been seen as a major issue in GIS and associated functionality is often missing entirely. Yet GIS concepts of data integration and spatial analysis will clearly have a major role to play in the rapidly developing field of global science, particularly in studying the relationships between human and physical systems.

Frank and Mark provide the connection in Chapter 11 between the abstract design of digital spatial databases and human processes of spatial cognition. If GIS technology is to support such activities as navigation, for example, then it will be necessary to provide natural language interfaces and to deal with the complex mapping which exists between abstract geometrical operations and terms like 'in' and 'on'. Is it possible, for example, to design a portable GIS to allow blind people to answer the simple question 'where am I?' from readily available perceptual evidence?

Many of the problems associated with the use of GIS derive from the ability of GIS to subject uncertain, imprecise geographical data to rigorous, precise analysis. The makers of maps may never have anticipated that their products would be digitized to the nearest fraction of a millimetre and accurately superimposed on other maps. Horror stories of the results of this sort of analysis abound in the GIS applications literature. Chrisman, in Chapter 12, looks at accuracy as a fundamental attribute of geographical data, as well as some of the problems of describing and modelling it. Fisher, in Chapter 13, reviews the issues surrounding the accuracy problem and looks at some of the indicators of accuracy which can be used to provide the basis for better and more appropriate use. He also discusses some of the main sources of data for GIS.

This first subsection ends with Chapter 14 by Davis and Simonett which discusses the relationship between remote sensing and GIS. From a limited, technological perspective, this is an issue of data transfer and of the different formats and data structures used by the two technologies. In practice, however, the problem is much broader, as it raises questions of how best to learn about geography through space images, how ancillary geographical data from a GIS can inform the interpretation of remotely sensed scenes and how remote sensing can be used to overcome some of the problems of currency which pervade map-based geographical databases. Davis and Simonett look at the remote sensing view of the nature of spatial data which stands in sharp contrast to the earlier chapters: remote sensing encourages a view of the world as continuous, rather than occupied by discrete objects and its error models are correspondingly different.

DIGITAL REPRESENTATION

Debate over the nature of spatial data leads to a set of conceptual models, each of which may be more or less appropriate to a given class of phenomena.

For example, numerous ways have been devised to model the continuous variation of the earth's topographic elevation, and they vary in efficiency depending on the type of terrain. Once a conceptual model is chosen, it is necessary to find an efficient form of digital representation, or data structure, and GIS provide a number of options. But to make matters confusing, one data structure may provide an efficient representation for several conceptual models, and one conceptual model may have many associated data structures. This m : n mapping between conceptual data models and data structures is characteristic of GIS, and presents enormous difficulties to users who may not be fully aware of its subtleties. In the long run, users might look for vendor products which support all conceptual data models with appropriate data structures, but at this time each vendor product supports its own limited set of data structures and provides little help in mapping these to conceptual data models.

Examples of the intellectual questions presented by the need to find efficient digital representations of conceptual data models might include the following. What is the set of possible data structures for each conceptual data model? What measures can be used to rate their relative efficiencies for retrieval, storage and processing? What systems of spatial indexing are most efficient in each case? To what extent is the choice of data structure generic and to what extent does it depend on the nature of the phenomena being represented? What measures of the phenomena are most effective in choosing data structures and indices?

The subsection begins with Chapter 15 by Franklin on the hardware environment for GIS and associated issues from a largely computer science point of view. Egenhofer and Herring build on this in Chapter 16 with a review of data structures and spatial indexing schemes. If geographical space is continuous and location can potentially be measured with infinite precision, then how is it possible to build a consistent system of processing in a machine which is fundamentally discrete? Egenhofer and Herring discuss a number of approaches to this very fundamental problem.

Chapter 17 by Jackson and Woodsford looks at the digital representation domain from the perspective of data entry, reviewing the current state of the art in digitizing and scanning. Despite the intellectual challenges of data modelling and representation, data entry remains a substantial practical bottleneck to GIS, particularly in application areas which must deal with project-specific data. Only a very substantial increase in the effectiveness of scanning can offer any significant hope for improvement in the future.

Spatial data present unique problems for digital representation. As noted above, geographical reality is infinitely complex and an infinite number of items of spatial information can be generated from a single variable such as topographic elevation, by measuring elevation at an infinity of distinct geographical locations. Because it must involve some loss of information, geographical data modelling is distinct in offering a number of choices to the user, with associated advantages and disadvantages. Geographical data are also distinct in the enormous potential richness of geographical relationships.

Because of this distinctiveness, it is perhaps not surprising that geographical data fit none of the standard database models particularly well. Of the three classical models – hierarchical, network and relational – GIS designers have had the greatest success with the relational because of its flexibility, and because its basic constructs of tuples, tables and linkages fit our notions of spatial objects reasonably well. Despite this, many designers have chosen to represent only the non-locational component of spatial data within the relational model, and to build their own specific managers for the locational component (e.g. ESRI's ARC/INFO). Healey, in Chapter 18, reviews the classical models, and presents the detailed case for the relational model. Recently, the GIS literature has contained numerous references to the potential of object-oriented databases (OODB), which seem to offer advantages over the relational model, but it will be some time before there is much consensus over the precise contribution of OODB.

The last two chapters in this subsection address major spatial data modelling problems which fall outside the conventional two-dimensional view of the world and present their own representation issues. In Chapter 19 Weibel and Heller provide an extensive review of terrain modelling and the associated data models: contours, triangles and grids. Of these, triangles are perhaps the most exciting, as they have no equivalent in traditional ways of mapping and representing topography and yet they appear to offer very significant advantages in storage and processing. Contours are used as the primary method of terrain representation on maps, as they are very effective in providing the eye with a general perception of the shape of the land surface. But in a spatial database, terrain representations are used for all sorts of additional purposes, such as modelling runoff and determining intervisibility between points. So it is not surprising that the issues of terrain modelling are much richer in the digital environment.

To end this subsection, in Chapter 20 Raper and Kelk look at recent work in three-dimensional GIS, with applications to geology, subsurface hydrology, oceanography and atmospheric science. For three-dimensional data, the digital environment provides not only the means for analysis, but also a method of visualizing variation which would otherwise be very hard to display or perceive. Recent software, coupled with developments in 3-D display technology, allow the user to explore three-dimensional solids in ways which have no precedent in the non-digital world. At the same time they provide a host of challenging issues. How does a geologist wish to explore the subsurface? What metaphors should guide the development of the user interface – the pick hammer, a knife, peeling layers? How can the digital environment aid the geologist in building a model of subsurface variation from limited evidence?

FUNCTIONAL ISSUES

All GIS share the same core set of common functions, including the ability to retrieve objects based on location or attributes, compute areas, overlay maps and build buffers around objects. It is the last two which most clearly differentiate GIS from other computer systems. But beyond these very primitive operations, there is little consensus about the set of processes which a GIS should provide, or about how primitive capabilities must be combined to satisfy requirements for complex forms of spatial analysis. Spatial analysis itself is poorly structured, consisting more of an unorganized mass of techniques.

Key questions in this area of GIS functionality include the following. What is the set of GIS primitives, and how are these best expressed in query languages which go beyond the confines of standards like SQL? How can complex spatial analyses be best represented as combinations of primitives? Is there a natural taxonomy of GIS operations and spatial analysis techniques? How do errors and uncertainties in a database propagate through each GIS process? What effects do inaccuracies have on the outcome of complex analysis and modelling? How can GIS functionality best serve the needs of spatial decision making?

In addition to the chapters in this subsection, which are explicitly about functionality, a number of others also touch on this important issue. The first chapter in this subsection, Chapter 21 by Maguire and Dangermond, reviews the functional capabilities of GIS and provides a framework for evaluating vendor products. It seems that the set of possible GIS functions is virtually unlimited, but that certain primitive operations can be enumerated and more complex operations expressed as combinations of them. Maguire and Dangermond organize their classification by data structure and point out that this is only one of many possible organizing principles. Following this, in Chapter 22 Shepherd examines the various possibilities for combining computer software to deal with typical everyday practical GIS applications. In Chapter 23 Tomlin presents a formalization of functionality, specifically in the raster domain, as an organizing framework for thinking about GIS capabilities, and for structuring GIS query and command languages.

The remaining four chapters discuss various extensions of current functionality, particularly with regard to higher level structures and tools which can be built on a base of simple primitives. Each approach leads closer to a full exploitation of the potential of GIS, but at the same time requires a much higher level of integration of software capabilities and a higher conceptual plane. In the first of these, Chapter 24, Flowerdew looks at the problem of analysing data from different sources where the spatial basis varies from one source to another. For example, it is common to encounter applications in which each set of data has been obtained for different (possibly unique) sets of reporting units. These may be zones or points, and may or may not share boundaries and locations. Simple primitive GIS operations, like overlay and area measurement, can be used to transfer or interpolate data from one set of units to another and to evaluate the potential errors introduced by doing so. Much research, however, remains to be done on this technology before it can be used extensively and reliably.

Openshaw's work on novel methods of spatial analysis, which more fully exploit the capabilities of GIS, will be known to many readers. He has argued in a number of papers that GIS environments create the potential for a whole new range of methods of analysis, which make use of GIS abilities for massive processing, exploration of data, visualization, and the continuous analysis of data as they are acquired. Not surprisingly, in Chapter 25 he questions many of the more traditional assumptions of spatial analysis, and argues that there is still a long way to go in exploiting the potential of the new technology for acquiring insight and finding explanations, particularly for social and economic processes.

The last two chapters in this subsection approach analysis from the perspective of decision making, arguing that GIS are ultimately a technology for supporting spatial decisions, and that their potential will not be realized until they can be harnessed more successfully to this type of application. In Chapter 26 Densham describes the concept of a Spatial Decision Support System (SDSS), together with the components and tools needed to provide an SDSS shell. An SDSS would allow the user to solve poorly structured problems by providing access to a set of well-structured models, along with a variety of tools for preparing input and displaying results. By contrast, Smith and Ye Jiang describe knowledge-based techniques in Chapter 27 in which the user surrenders much decision-making responsibility to the system, in return for some degree of automated intelligence.

DISPLAY ISSUES

Depending on the type of analysis or query, the results of a GIS operation might be graphical, textual or numerical, in the form of maps, graphs or tables. Numbers are unequivocal, as are words if expressed in formally defined terms. Graphic output, however, will always be open to interpretation and cartography has developed many principles of map design to assist the process of communicating spatial information to the user. At the same time, the capabilities of the electronic display media used for GIS output are far greater technically than those of the cartographer's pen, as they include potential for animation, continuous gradation of tone or colour, display of data uncertainty, and so on. Visualization, and particularly the effective design of visual displays, is an unfortunately neglected aspect of much GIS work, which often falls victim to such cartographic outrages as the arbitrary assignment of colour to classes in choropleth mapping.

The issues involved in effectively displaying geographical data can easily be posed as a set of scientific questions. What, for example, is the relationship between methods of display and human perception? In what ways can the enhanced capabilities of electronic display be exploited to improve communication? How can the rules of cartographic design be expressed in terms sufficiently procedural to be implementable in a GIS? What are the roles of multiple media – sound, digital versus analogue video and touch – in data display? Is it possible to express the cartographic techniques of generalization as procedural rules?

This subsection begins with Chapter 28 by Buttenfield and Mackaness. Their review of visualization issues and current research touches on cartographic design principles, the increasing role of visualization techniques in science generally, and specialized problems associated with human–computer interaction. By contrast, in Chapter 29, Freeman provides a discussion of recent research in a very specific GIS problem, that of finding positions for labels for objects, particularly polygons. This has proven to be one of the more challenging of the GIS primitives, as it turns out to be remarkably difficult to express the rules which a cartographer would use in procedural terms, despite the apparent simplicity of the problem statement.

Generalization is a pervasive issue which extends over a much broader area than simply data display. Narrowly, generalization can be defined as a process of simplification or smoothing, such as occurs when scale is reduced and detail is no longer important. In fact generalization is a much more significant process which is much less clearly tied to scale change. Broadly, generalization may be defined as a process of fitting geographical form according to some model and thus of identifying a specific form as an instance of some more general class. In this sense it has much in common with interpretation. For example, a bump on a contour might be identified as an instance of a ravine. While the volume of data might be reduced in the process of generalization, the information content might actually increase, as more would probably be known about ravines than about bumps on contours. In this more general sense, Muller's Chapter 30 might equally well fit in the first subsection, on the nature of spatial data.

OPERATIONAL ISSUES

However attractive the technology itself might be, the value of GIS is ultimately determined by the uses to which GIS are put, and the costs involved in doing so. A technology which performs, but is nevertheless rejected on grounds of cost or management problems, is effectively useless. As a new technology, GIS have had to be content with their share of organizational problems, including resistance to innovation and change. In fact many have argued that the management and organizational issues of GIS are far more important in the long term than the technical ones (Rhind 1988). On the other hand, many of these issues may not be unique to GIS and many may be fundamentally intractable or insoluble. For example, the benefits of GIS information are every bit as hard to quantify as the benefits of any other type of information. But the difficulties in doing so may be no different in the spatial case. It seems unlikely that research on many of these generic issues would produce results in the GIS case when it has failed to do so in other areas. 'Poor management' may be a scapegoat, a cause of last resort for problems which are actually more fundamental. The failure of a GIS to recommend a course of action may be due to a more basic inability to model the objectives and constraints of a problem, but may appear instead as a failure of management.

The chapters in this last subsection on principles address some of the operational issues which are undoubtedly unique to GIS and the spatial context. Unlike the topics covered in earlier subsections, there is still a paucity of good, detailed, published work on this crucially important topic. This subsection begins with Chapter 31 by Clarke, which reviews the process of GIS acquisition by an agency, from the initial definition of functional requirements through to benchmarking and final installation. Formal methods for doing this exist in consulting companies operating in the GIS field, but it is rare to find the process described in the open literature. Epstein, in Chapter 32, discusses legal issues and touches on some of the ways in which GIS are being used to support legal arguments and in which GIS users are being called on to defend themselves in litigation. Some of these are to be expected, but some are surprising and illustrate the misuses of data which pervade the GIS field. Since GIS are becoming more and more common as a method for supporting spatial decision making, it is to be expected that demands for quality control will increase, not only in data but also in the operation of the system itself and in the coding of software.

Blakemore, Chapter 33, uses the example of the UK on-line GIS NOMIS to make a number of points about the impact of GIS on organizations. As local governments and resource management agencies move towards GIS solutions to their spatial data handling problems, few realize the potentially substantial effects on the organization itself. A GIS treats data as a common resource, in sharp distinction to the data ownership patterns common in multi-department agencies. It creates pressure for effective data planning and for reorganization around the provision of data.

The final chapter in Section II, Chapter 34 by Guptill, deals with the development of data standards. In the early days of GIS each system developed independently, and the question of data sharing rarely arose. More recently standards have become important as more and more common digital data have become available from data-gathering agencies. But the vast majority of data used in most applications is still digitized locally, in formats and structures determined by the local software. The current world of GIS is thus dominated by two sets of standards, each containing several alternatives. One is the set established by data-gathering agencies, designed for the specific purpose of promulgating their particular data products. The other is the set of internal standards established by the vendors and subject to assorted pressures of marketplace competition. There should be a dramatic change in this situation in the next few years. On the one hand, it is becoming increasingly impossible for any one vendor to dominate the entire range of GIS functionality and applications, and vendor products will likely become increasingly specialized. To survive in such a market, the vendor community will of necessity develop standards, which will allow A's products to talk to B's. At the same time the diversity of products being offered by the data-gathering agencies will require more comprehensive standards, not only of format and structure but also of quality and interpretation. So the need for standards will undoubtedly increase. Unfortunately it is difficult to see how comprehensive standards can be put together in the current complex of vendors, organizations, agencies and users. No one agency, company or organization is sufficiently powerful to take the lead, or sufficiently representative of the range of applications in the entire field.

Section II, on GIS principles, includes a wide range of material. The treatment is not comprehensive of course; no book could ever be in a field as wide and rapidly developing as GIS. Nevertheless, the key issues important for an understanding of the basis of GIS are incorporated in the discussion. In Section III, the discussion turns from abstract, conceptual and theoretical considerations, to the practical applications of GIS.

REFERENCES

Coppock J T, Rhind D W (1991) The history of GIS. In: Maguire D J, Goodchild M F, Rhind D W (eds.) *Geographical Information Systems: principles and applications*. Longman, London, pp. 21–43, Vol 1

Counclelis H (1991) Requirements for a planning-relevant GIS: a spatial perspective. *Papers of the Regional Science Association*

Maguire D J (1991) An overview and definition of GIS. In: Maguire D J, Goodchild M F, Rhind D W (eds.) *Geographical Information Systems: principles and applications*. Longman, London, pp. 9–20, Vol 1

Morrison J L (1991) The organizational home for GIS in the scientific professional community. In: Maguire D J, Goodchild M F, Rhind D W (eds.) *Geographical Information Systems: principles and applications*. Longman, London, pp. 91–100, Vol 1

NCGIA (1989) The research plan of the National Center for Geographic Information and Analysis. *International Journal of Geographical Information Systems* **3**: 117–36

Rhind D W (1988) Recent developments in geographical information systems in the UK. *International Journal of Geographical Information Systems* **1** (3): 229–42

Unwin D J (1991) The academic setting of GIS. In: Maguire D J, Goodchild M F, Rhind D W (eds.) *Geographical Information Systems: principles and applications*. Longman, London, 81–90, Vol 1

CONCEPTS OF SPACE AND GEOGRAPHICAL DATA

A C GATRELL

Space is defined here as a relation on a set of objects. Different types of space may be created, depending upon how this relation is defined; Euclidean distance is perhaps the simplest example. This chapter begins by reviewing such concepts of space and then considering what is meant by the term 'spatial object'. Different categories of such objects are discussed and the varying types of attributes or data that can be associated with those objects are examined. Having looked at standard concepts of distance some consideration is given to other measures of spatial proximity, such as time distance. The need to visualize spaces defined by different types of relation is addressed and examples are presented of map transformations (such as cartograms).

INTRODUCTION

The true potential value of Geographical Information Systems lies in their ability to analyse spatial data using the techniques of spatial analysis. (Goodchild 1988: 76)

Although something of an over-simplification, it is worth making a distinction between two ways in which GIS can be used. The first is to use GIS to ask descriptive questions, such as spatial queries of the form: 'locate and display all settlements with a population greater than 5000'. These are questions of the 'what' or 'where' type and are, of course, genuinely important in planning and resource management. Embodied in the quotation, however, is a second category of use: the need to ask analytical questions, perhaps to construct models and perform predictions. These may involve questions prefixed with 'why' or 'what if'. It is essential, therefore, that we endow a GIS with capabilities for spatial analysis (see Openshaw 1991 in this volume), 'that set of analytical methods which requires access both to the attributes of the objects under study and to their locational information' (Goodchild 1988: 68).

Given that spatial analysis and GIS are thus inextricably linked there is a need to investigate more fully what concepts of space are appropriate and what types of spatial objects and data must be handled. This is undertaken here by first seeking a general, and very powerful, definition of 'space' and then constructing a typology of 'spaces'. Different types of spatial object are then considered before examination of different types of spatial relationship. Examples of visual representations that arise from such spatial relationships are offered later.

THE WORLD IS FULL OF SPACES

Space is taken to mean 'a relation defined on a set of objects'. This immediately requires definition of what is meant by 'relation' and 'object': much of this chapter is concerned with uncovering the meanings of these words. To be more concrete, consider an example (Fig. 9.1), where the objects of primary interest are landmarks in Manhattan and the relation that binds these landmarks together is the 'distance' between them. (It will soon become clear why there are quotation marks around the word distance.)

It may be assumed that the objects are of interest (otherwise they would never have become

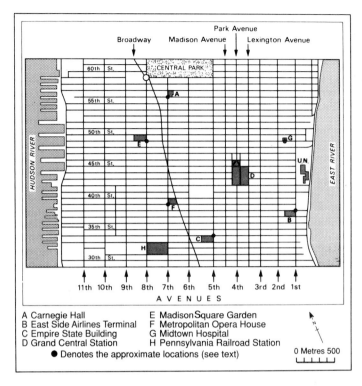

Fig. 9.1 A set of landmarks in Manhattan, New York City, USA.

part of a GIS!) and, therefore, that they have attributes or properties associated with them; numbers of people employed, or rateable value, for instance. Indeed, spatial objects such as these may be defined as a set of spatial locations together with a set of properties characterizing those locations (Smith *et al.* 1987). The term 'object' has a different meaning in the field of object orientation where it simply means any feature of interest (including spatial features, as defined above, non-spatial features and attribute data; see Maguire, Worboys and Hearnshaw 1990).

Thus, 'space' embraces the following: a 'set' of objects (what Peuquet, 1988, prefers to call 'entities' and others refer to as 'features'), to which may be attached associated attributes ('properties' in Peuquet's terminology), together with a relation, or relations, defined on that set. A straight line drawn between pairs of objects is one such relation. As is made clear below, however, this is only one way of conceptualizing 'distance', and there are in turn several other ways of looking at spatial relationships.

Metric spaces

The concept of metric space can be illustrated by examining the landmarks in Manhattan a little more closely and assuming, for the sake of argument, that they occupy point locations rather than physical areas. Thus there is a set of locations whose coordinates can be denoted as $\{x_i, y_i\}$ and distance can be measured conventionally between members of this set as:

$$d(i,j) = \sqrt{[(x_i - x_j)^2 + (y_i - y_j)^2]} \qquad [9.1]$$

This is a formal definition of Euclidean distance learnt at school as part of Pythagoras' theorem. At the scale considered here (embracing a relatively small part of New York City) complications due to the curvature of the earth's surface can reasonably be ignored, but at wider spatial scales they would need to be taken into account (see Maling 1991 in this volume).

Euclidean distance is an example of what mathematicians call a 'metric'. A formal definition of this is offered elsewhere (Gatrell 1983: 25–6) but, briefly, two properties are important; first, such distances are symmetric: d(i,j) = d(j,i); second, they obey the so-called triangle inequality:

$$d(i,k) \leq d(i,j) + d(j,k) \qquad [9.2]$$

For example, the distance from the Empire State Building to East Side Airline Terminal is no greater than the sum of the distances from the Empire State Building to the Metropolitan Opera House and East Side Airline Terminal to the Metropolitan Opera House.

This Euclidean view of the world is firmly embedded in most of what happens under the name of GIS. It is, of course, entirely appropriate in land management applications, in survey work and in the kind of large-scale digital mapping undertaken by the utilities (see Mahoney 1991 in this volume). In other words, for most descriptive applications of GIS it will suffice, as indeed it will for much spatial analysis. However, it is quite clear that Manhattan is not a flat, featureless plain but that space there is structured by the road network. A Euclidean view of Manhattan is inappropriate because 'real' distances are not, in most cases, as the crow flies. Instead, city blocks are traversed. This is familiar to anyone giving or receiving directions in a 'grid-based' urban environment; 'go two blocks north and three blocks east'.

An alternative method of measuring distance, which takes this into account is called 'Manhattan' or 'taxicab' distance:

$$d(i,j) = |x_i - x_j| + |y_i - y_j| \qquad [9.3]$$

Three points can be made about this measure of distance. First, as with Euclidean distance, it too has the properties of a metric; distances are still symmetric and the triangle inequality still holds. Secondly, if questions are asked about spatial proximity, the results obtained in terms of the relative orderings of distances may well differ from those given by the Euclidean metric (Gatrell 1983: 25–9). Thirdly, Manhattan distances are not coordinate invariant; if the axes are reoriented, different measurements of distance between pairs of points can be obtained. This suggests that the Manhattan metric may only be of real value in grid-like cities in which the axes follow the street pattern.

The differences between Euclidean and Manhattan metrics are not purely of academic interest. Different results will be obtained from GIS functions depending on which of these two metrics is used. The following two examples illustrate this. First, if Thiessen polygons are constructed around points (which might be a first simple attempt to define catchment or trade areas) in Euclidean terms this can be done by finding bisectors of straight lines joining pairs of points (Fig. 9.2). This is a common function in GIS. However, if this is carried out in Manhattan space then quite irregular boundaries are obtained (von Hohenbalken and West 1984). Within each polygon are all locations lying closer to the central point than to any other, but this 'closeness' is defined in an unconventional way (Fig. 9.2).

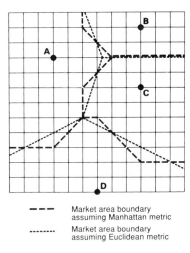

– – – Market area boundary assuming Manhattan metric
········ Market area boundary assuming Euclidean metric

Fig. 9.2 Thiessen polygons using Euclidean and Manhattan metrics.

As a second example, suppose it is important to find an optimal location for a new supermarket or public facility. Using a very simple example, suppose that the 'demand nodes' at which the service is required are equally weighted and exist at only a handful of point locations in Manhattan space (Fig. 9.3). It is easily verified that, if there is an odd number of demand nodes (Fig. 9.3a), then there is a unique optimal location (that which minimizes the sum of distances to demand nodes); this may be located, as here, at one of those nodes. However, if there is an even number of demand nodes (Fig. 9.3b) there is no unique optimum; rather, there is a region, within which any location is equally optimal. In Manhattan space, therefore, it is possible to detect some 'uncertainty' in location and this is simply a property of space itself.

121

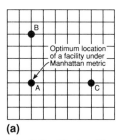 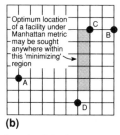

Fig. 9.3 Optimal locations using the Manhattan metric.

Armstrong (1988) has looked empirically at how different definitions of distance influence the results of such location (and location-allocation) models, using an example from the southeastern United States. Having defined a set of 26 demand nodes and 10 facilities to be allocated he then computes distances along the road network, where this is digitized at different scales. He compares these estimates with Euclidean and Manhattan distances and demonstrates how the results change quite dramatically as different measures of spatial separation are adopted. There needs to be wider recognition of this variation among users of location-allocation models within a GIS framework.

Non-metric spaces

So far, only metric spaces have been considered. Yet non-metric spaces will be encountered frequently in some applications of GIS, even if the formal properties of such spaces are unlikely ever to be defined. For instance, some GIS permit weights or impedances to be attached to the route links in transport networks. These might be used to model one-way streets, for instance, or to restrict movement along narrow roads and encourage use of major roads as is done in sophisticated shortest path algorithms (Dunn and Newton 1989). One of the implications of such work is that a new model of space is defined, one which is unlikely to be metric. In general, distances will not be symmetric, nor will the triangle inequality hold.

Thus far it has been assumed that spaces in which objects have locations are characterized by a pair of coordinates $\{x_i, y_i\}$. There are two remarks to be made about this, one of which requires an extended discussion. The first comment is that, because of inherent uncertainty, the locations of spatial objects may be endowed with a spurious accuracy. For instance, soil or land use boundaries may be represented by strings of locational coordinates but these lines are inherently fuzzy (see Chrisman 1991 in this volume). While some attempts have been made to introduce notions from the theory of fuzzy sets (Robinson, Miller and Klesh 1988; Burrough 1989), no work has been done on how fuzzy spaces may be incorporated within a proprietary GIS. This is an important area of research since our everyday spatial concepts (for example, 'near', 'far', 'close to'), which may be used to phrase spatial queries, are inherently vague and uncertain (Mark, Svorou and Zubin 1988; see also Frank and Mark 1991 in this volume).

The second remark to be made about locational referencing is that it is not always necessary to have accurate coordinate information. In the case of how to use a GIS to navigate from one node to another on a road network (see White 1991 in this volume), is it really essential to know all the locational coordinates of the links on the network to perform this task adequately? Consider the well-known example of the London underground map (Fig. 9.4). This contains all the useful information needed to get from i to j on the network. Yet the locations are, to some extent, arbitrary and the relation that defines this non-metric space is simply one of connectedness; whether stations are adjacent on the network. The visual representation allows us to make spatial deductions about the ease of travel between stations which are not adjacent.

Many will be familiar with this map and with the fact that it is commonly used in textbooks to introduce the concept of topology (e.g. see Abler, Adams and Gould 1971). The map is a visual representation of a topological space. Note, as an aside, that even in fully vector-based GIS, with all locations represented by $\{x_i, y_i\}$ pairs, people speak of the topology of the link–node structure. This refers to the ability of the GIS to store (among other things) what lies to the left and right of a line segment. Thus it is possible to refer to the topology of a Euclidean representation of space. To repeat, a topological space is one in which there is some arbitrariness in the positioning of locations and arcs and where the only relation that matters is contiguity.

Some GIS adopt a data structure that is a hybrid of Euclidean and topological space. A good example is the TIGER system (Topologically Integrated Geographic Encoding Referencing) used by the US Census agency (Broome 1986). Here, a

Concepts of Space and Geographical Data

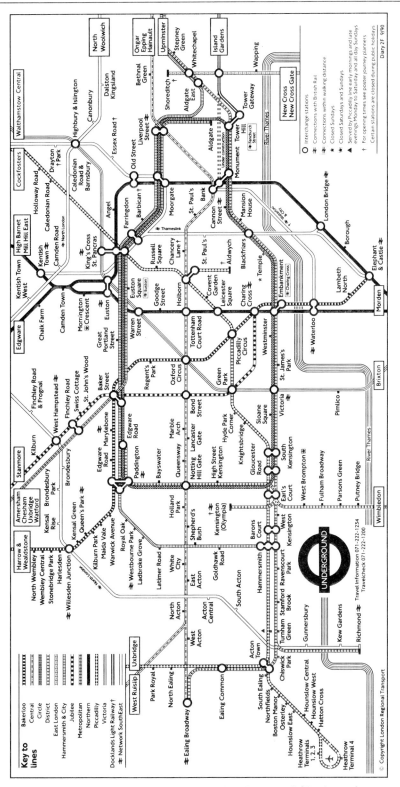

Fig. 9.4 A topological map of the London, England underground (Registered user no. 91/1341).

street name is stored, together with locational coordinates for the start and end nodes of that street. The blocks to the left and right are also stored, in the form of property identifiers for the first and last dwellings in those blocks. This is in contrast to structures adopted elsewhere, notably by Pinpoint Analysis Ltd in Britain. In the late 1980s this company started the task of digitizing all properties in Britain and attaching full Ordnance Survey grid references to them.

Carving up space

When digitizing a map in vector mode it is possible to capture a locational coordinate anywhere on that map if necessary. To any point on the earth's surface may be attached a locational reference of some form, be it a pair of Cartesian coordinates at large scales or latitude and longitude at smaller scales (see Maling 1991 in this volume). In essence, therefore, a continuous view of space can be adopted. Some attributes, notably physical ones such as air temperature and pressure, are, in principle, observable at any location. However, in many applications of GIS, data are collected for areal units and this gives a discrete representation of space. It is necessary to say something about different ways of producing this discretization.

Remote sensing deals with discrete space, the units typically comprising squares or 'pixels' whose dimensions depend upon the available satellite technology. This 'raster' view of the world has been mimicked by some GIS, particularly those which are targeted at microcomputers; IDRISI (Eastman 1988) and pMAP (Berry 1988) are examples. Much has been written about the merits and disadvantages of such raster-based systems, about algorithms for converting from raster to vector and vice versa, about storage of raster data, and so on (see Egenhofer and Herring 1991 in this volume). Suffice it to say here that while a raster-based view of the world hardly matches our daily experience, such systems do offer computational advantages. For instance, apart from grid squares lying at the edge of the map each cell has a fixed number of neighbours and all cells are of constant size and shape. These properties do make many types of spatial analysis much easier. The overlay of maps and the use of various logical operators is very simple, compared with the substantial amounts of processing required in the vector overlay of polygons. Irregular polygonal zones, as used widely for administrative (notably, census) purposes, create numerous problems because of the varying sizes, shapes and neighbours (see Flowerdew 1991 in this volume).

Problems of storing raster data have been much researched. If blocks of pixels cover large areas of homogeneous territory (e.g. 'forest') then, rather than storing data about that property for each pixel it can be stored for the first element and then the number of pixels that follow can be counted, given some ordering scheme for the pixels. This compressed storage is known as 'run-length encoding' (Goodchild and Grandfield 1983). Other researchers have examined different schemes for producing one-dimensional ordering of two-dimensional rasters; some of these are reviewed and illustrated in Goodchild and Mark (1987).

An alternative to such raster schemes is provided by the 'quadtree' (and its equivalent in three dimensions, the 'octree'). Here, a map is divided into four quadrants. Each is then further subdivided until the minimum pixel size is reached (Fig. 9.5). As the illustration makes clear, large areas of contiguous and identical pixels do not require subdivision and may be stored at a higher level of the hierarchical tree. Samet (1984, 1990) has provided a full review of such storage methods. They are not merely of academic interest, since some GIS, notably SPANS, are built around just such data structures.

TYPOLOGY OF SPATIAL OBJECTS

'One of the classic characterizations of data in this field is as 'points, lines and areas. I think that's a pretty primitive model' (Tobler 1988: 51).

Having reviewed different types of space and space-dividing strategies, it is now appropriate to unravel further the definition of space ('a relation defined on a set of objects') and say something about those objects. The discussion has, inevitably, already touched on this subject.

Tobler's stricture addresses the conventional wisdom of classifying spatial objects, as set out in Robinson *et al.* (1984) and Haggett (1965), and used in spatial analysis for many years (Unwin 1981; see also Maguire and Dangermond 1991 in this volume). Points are objects represented by a single pair of locational coordinates. Lines are sets of

Concepts of Space and Geographical Data

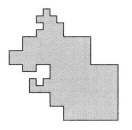
(a) A region such as a field or a forest

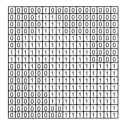
(b) A binary image of the region

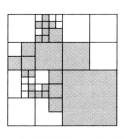
(d) Block decomposition of the region showing the maximal blocks

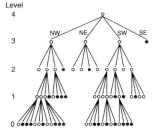
(c) Quadtree representation of the blocks with black nodes shown by solid dots

Fig. 9.5 The quadtree data structure (*Source*: Gahegan M, Hogg J (1986) *A pilot GIS based on linear quadtrees and a relational database for regional analysis*. Working Paper 464, Uni. of Leeds, p. 19).

ordered and connected points; they may represent inherently linear features such as roads or streams, or they might denote boundaries. Areas (zones or polygons) are collections of line segments that close to form discrete units. Classically, these objects are thought of as having a length dimension of 0, 1 and 2, respectively (see DCDSTF, 1988, for further definition of such objects). For reasons that will become clear shortly, these are referred to as 'topological dimensions'.

This trilogy covers the set of objects embedded in a space of two dimensions. However, points can exist in three-dimensional space (a small ore-body in a large geological structure, for instance). In three dimensions, lines will no longer necessarily exist in a plane but might trace convoluted paths through volumes. The implication of this is that it is necessary to distinguish between two types of 'dimension': the topological dimension of the object, and the dimension of the space within which it is embedded.

Surfaces have also been considered as a class of spatial object (Unwin 1981), but they are rather different features in that they are defined by data; terrain or temperature surfaces cannot exist without height or temperature data. Within a GIS, surfaces can be represented in a variety of ways. Commonly, their cartographic representation is as a set of contours (1-D objects embedded in a 2-D space). Alternatively, input data used to create a surface after interpolation may be spot-heights (0-D objects in a 2-D space). Finally, a surface may be represented as a Triangulated Irregular Network (TIN), wherein 2-D objects (triangles) are, strictly speaking, embedded in a 3-D space.

Fractals

Until about 20 years ago definitions of the 'topological dimensionality' of objects were not considered problematic. In 1967, however, the French mathematician Mandelbrot published an article that drew upon earlier work by Lewis Richardson and which popularized the concept of a line of fractional dimension (Mandelbrot 1967). Richardson had demonstrated empirically that the measured length of an irregular line depends upon the scale at which it is measured; specifically, its length increases as the scale increases, since more detail is revealed. This can be verified readily by walking a pair of dividers along the line and then repeating this with the dividers set to a narrower width. In contrast, a perfectly straight line has a constant length regardless of scale. If the logarithm of length is plotted against the logarithm of the sampling interval, an approximately linear relationship is observed (Fig. 9.6). For a measured straight line this relationship will appear as a horizontal line. The slope of the line may be denoted as (1-D), suggesting that for a perfectly smooth line on the map $D = 1$. The more irregular the line on the map (and hence the steeper the slope of the line on the graph) the higher the value of D. At the limit, a line can be imagined so irregular that it in effect 'fills' a piece of paper; such lines have the property $D = 2$. Since D can take on values between 1 and 2 Mandelbrot referred to it as a measure of fractional dimensionality and gave the name 'fractal' to an irregular line.

The same principles hold for surfaces. A perfectly flat, featureless plain has $D = 2$ while a solid cube has $D = 3$. Surfaces of varying

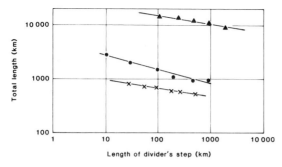

Fig. 9.6 Relationship between length of a line and sampling interval (*Source*: Modified from Maling D (1989) *Measurements from Maps*. Pergamon Press, Cambridge, p. 286).

irregularity have fractional dimension between 2 and 3. It is possible to simulate surfaces of various degrees of roughness (see Goodchild and Mark 1987) and it has been argued that they provide 'norms for the interpretation of geomorphological observations' (Goodchild and Mark 1987: 271).

One of the key properties of fractals is that they are 'self-similar'. This means that any part of the object, when enlarged, is indistinguishable from the object as a whole. Practically, what this means is that an entire coastline, for instance, has the same 'look', and is generated by the same process, as any small part of that coastline. Needless to say, geomorphologists find this hard to believe, since different coastal processes operate at different spatial scales. Despite this caveat, cartographers have found fractals useful, especially in studies of line generalization and line enhancement (see Muller 1991 in this volume).

More broadly, scale determines how to characterize the topological, as much as the fractional, dimensionality of spatial objects. For instance, at a small scale, dealing with data for an entire region or country, settlements can be stored as point objects, with whatever attributes are appropriate. However, at larger scales, of course, such objects must be defined as area objects, the boundaries of which are those of the built-up area. At a yet more detailed scale these area objects are, in fact, collections of buildings (stored at that scale as point objects), while at scales of perhaps 1 : 1500 or greater those buildings are areal objects and the perimeters and areas are stored as attribute fields.

The dimensionality of objects is not as simple as might first be supposed!

Transforming objects

One of the functions that a GIS should support is the ability to create new objects from quite simple or primitive ones. An obvious example is where one area map (e.g. land use) is overlaid with another (e.g. geology) to create, via 'polygon overlay', new areal objects. Several further examples of this are discussed below.

First, the discussion of Euclidean and Manhattan spaces has shown how to create a Thiessen polygon. Thiessen polygons are simply areal objects defined on a set of point objects. All locations within such a polygon lie closer to the point used to define that polygon than to any other such point. Thiessen polygons (also called Voronoi polygons) are useful in the geometric analysis of point patterns (Boots and Getis 1988) and are particularly useful in creating artificial polygons when true boundaries have not been digitized. For example, the primary data collection units in the British Population Census are Enumeration Districts (EDs) and these are not generally available in digital form. However, the census does provide point references for each ED and these may be used to define 'pseudo-EDs' (Fig. 9.7).

This procedure can be examined in reverse. Given a set of areal boundaries is it possible to replace the area definition by a point? This is trivial, in that any point 'seed' can be placed anywhere within an areal unit. However, a GIS is frequently required to define a geographical centre or 'centroid' of such an areal unit (see Monmonier 1982: 116–18 for algorithms) and this is useful if there is a need to measure distances between areas, as is required in location-allocation decisions. One well-known problem is that the centroid can lie outside the areal unit if the latter has a very convoluted shape. In such cases, interactive map editing is required to re-position it.

Surfaces can be regarded as transformations of lower dimensional objects. For instance, a set of spot-heights can be defined and interpolation methods used to create a Digital Terrain Model (DTM); the kind of representation depends upon the density and spacing of sample points. Alternatively, a set of point locations can be used to construct a TIN; algorithms may be used to 'thread'

Concepts of Space and Geographical Data

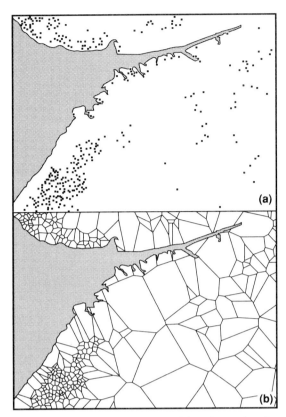

Fig. 9.7 A set of point objects (a) and associated Thiessen polygons (b) for Enumeration Districts in part of Lancashire, England.

contours through the facets of such a network. (Research on DTMs within GIS is discussed by Weibel and Heller 1991 in this volume.)

The creation of complex objects from simple points, lines and areas is an important area of research. It is particularly important in the translation of digital maps into a GIS framework. National mapping agencies such as the Ordnance Survey in Britain (see Sowton 1991 in this volume) and USGS in the United States (see Starr 1991 in this volume) are heavily involved in digital mapping, attaching feature codes to objects such as fences, edges of buildings, and so on. Yet, if there is a need to define land parcels for planning enquiries, methods are required to allow definition of these 'higher order' objects. For example, in the case of the object 'university', at a large scale the digital representation would code buildings, squares, playing fields, car parking areas, and so on, as separate features. There is a need to structure the data in such a way as to collect these objects together to define 'university'. It is to this problem that contemporary research on 'object-oriented' databases is addressed (see Healey 1991 in this volume).

A GIS must, therefore, allow the user to create complex objects from basic building blocks. The above examples show how objects of different dimension are created, but a GIS must also permit the definition of more complex objects of the same dimension. For instance, in the case of a set of line segments representing a street network, a shortest path through that network is not itself a primitive object but may need to be defined as a new object, to which attributes (such as traffic flows) should be attached.

Objects for spatial analysis

The preceding discussion demonstrated that spatial objects have locations and properties (attributes). It is now necessary to say something about the ways in which GIS can assist in analysing the geometry of the locational patterns and in analysing the attribute data. There is no need to dwell on this at length since the subject of spatial analysis is covered elsewhere (see Openshaw 1991 in this volume).

Attribute data may be analysed by statistical methods and models that do not necessarily require reference to location. To compute simple descriptive statistics (e.g. means and variances) does not require knowledge of locations. The methods used for such analysis depend on the level of measurement of the data, be this nominal (categorical), ordinal (ranked) or interval/ratio (continuous). Full discussion of such methods and data types are available in introductory texts (e.g. see Ebdon 1985). Relatively few GIS permit much in the way of statistical analysis and modelling. Efforts to devise transparent links between such systems and conventional statistical packages such as MINITAB, SPSS(X) and GLIM are, therefore, to be encouraged (Kehris 1989).

Equally, the vast battery of techniques used by geographers for many years to describe map pattern have yet to find wide adoption within GIS. For instance, while all GIS handle point objects and some allow the construction of Thiessen polygons, it is hard to find many proprietary systems that allow quantitative analysis and modelling of point data; for instance, the analysis of order neighbour relations or the second-order analysis of point patterns (Diggle 1983).

One important tool in spatial analysis that serves to fuse the geometric and attribute properties of spatial objects is that of spatial autocorrelation. Excellent introductions to this topic are available elsewhere (Goodchild 1986; Odland 1988). Suffice it to say here that spatial autocorrelation refers to the patterning of objects and attributes on the map. For instance, if a variable is measured over a set of areal units and it is observed that high values tend to cluster in one region and low values elsewhere the map is said to exhibit positive spatial autocorrelation. The absence of autocorrelation suggests that attributes are arranged randomly across the map. If high and low values tend to alternate in periodic fashion this is referred to as negative spatial autocorrelation. Thus if there is autocorrelation on the map there is a clear relationship between 'spatial similarity' (i.e. proximity) and attribute similarity (Hubert, Golledge and Costanzo 1981).

Measures of autocorrelation have been devised for point and area objects (and can be adapted for line features also). Measures are available for nominal, ordinal and interval/ratio data. Goodchild (1986) has provided simple program listings to allow implementation of such statistics, while Griffith (1987) shows how to implement them within MINITAB. However, these very useful descriptions of map pattern are still not widely available within proprietary GIS. They should be, since they offer a powerful summary description of the map and a quantitative assessment of whether what is displayed there is any more than would be expected on a chance basis.

Reference has already been made to the concept of 'fuzziness' in spatial data. As has already been mentioned, uncertainty often exists about both location and attribute(s). The attachment of coordinate values to spatial objects often gives a false sense of precision, while there will also frequently be uncertainty associated with attribute data. For example, population data attached to areal units are derived usually from national censuses. There is uncertainty associated with such headcounts, not to mention the fact that, were the data wholly error-free at the time of collection, they are error-laden soon after they are released, since demographic change occurs continuously. There is still a need for research on map and attribute error and how to attach 'uncertainty scores' (however these might be defined!) to such data.

TYPOLOGY OF SPATIAL RELATIONS

Having examined different concepts of space and said something about different types of spatial object and spatial data the discussion now examines more closely some alternative definitions of spatial relationship. To date, emphasis has been on spatial relations, defined largely in terms of some measure of physical distance, although this assumption was relaxed in the brief examination of non-metric spaces. Here, other ways of conceiving spatial proximity are investigated.

Before doing so, recall that space is defined as a relation on a set of objects. This may be a relation existing between one set and another set of objects. (To give a simple example, this might be a 'preference relation' between a set of GIS users and a set of software products!) This is potentially a very powerful way of conceptualizing GIS functions. Figure 9.8 shows in schematic form how some operations in GIS (only a handful are illustrated) can be regarded as relations between different sets of spatial object (Unwin 1981; Goodchild 1985). For instance, 'point-in-polygon' operations relate points to areas. A study of rail routes transporting hazardous cargoes across particular areal units uses a line–area relation. Polygon overlay is an area–area relation, and so on. For simplicity, only half of this table is shown suggesting that it is symmetrical. As a generalization this is an adequate representation, although detailed examination shows that there are differences between some relations. For example, determining if a point is in an area (area-point) is different from creating a set of areas (Thiessen polygons) from a set of points (point-areas).

	Points	Lines	Areas
Points	• is a neighbour of • is allocated to	• is near to • lies on	• is a centroid of • is within
Lines		• crosses • joins	• intersects • is a boundary of
Areas			• is overlain by • is adjacent to

Fig. 9.8 Relations between classes of spatial object.

It is clear, then, that there is a whole variety of 'spatial relations'. In this section, however, attention is restricted to point–point relations: Euclidean and Manhattan distances were two earlier examples.

In our everyday worlds, rather than the artificial worlds constructed in GIS, spatial separation is experienced less in terms of physical distance and more in terms of time, cost, or 'perception' (Gatrell 1983). What use has been made of these other ways of regarding proximity or separation within a GIS framework? The simple answer is – not much!

Time-distance

Spatial separation, in terms of travel time, can be examined at a variety of spatial scales: global, national or local. A set of spatial objects may be defined, typically point locations such as towns at a national scale or nodes on a road network at a local scale, and a matrix of travel times between all pairs of places constructed. It is possible to look at either a single row or column of the matrix, or to analyse the structure of the entire matrix. But before carrying this out it should be made clear that there is no single relation defined on any such set of places. While physical distances remain constant, travel times themselves are time dependent, varying on an hourly basis within urban areas and perhaps over longer time scales globally (as improvements in transport technology work their way through the system). Moreover, the relation certainly does not define a metric space; time–distances will not, in general, be symmetrical, nor will the triangle inequality necessarily hold.

Notwithstanding these problems there is still scope for exploring the usefulness of such relations in GIS. Consider an application in which there is a requirement to describe and display the travel times from one centre or node on a network to all other locations in a spatial database. There is a need for GIS that will interpolate between such locations to produce an 'isochrone map', comprising contours which represent lines of equal travel time (Fig. 9.9a). The scale of such a map is still in physical distance units, however, and there should be the ability within GIS to transform or distort the underlying base map so that the isochrones become concentric circles (Fig. 9.9b) and the geometry of the transport network (and other spatial objects on the map) is modified (Muller 1978; Clark 1977). Some software systems currently available do indeed offer the option of defining catchment or trade areas based on travel time. For purposes of visualization it would be useful, however, to have more capabilities for producing distorted maps (what Muehrcke, 1978, has called 'linear cartograms').

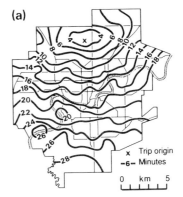

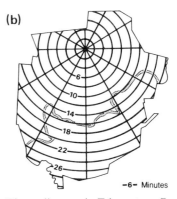

Fig. 9.9 Time–distance in Edmonton, Canada: (a) isochrones in geographical space; (b) isochrones in time–space.

It is very difficult to use all the information contained in the travel time matrix, rather than only one row or column, because the relation is not metric. (Given a matrix of physical distances between a set of places, it is quite feasible, using trilateration methods from surveying, to produce a map of correct locations; e.g. see Tobler 1982.) Fortunately, methods are available for producing a metric space from non-metric data; such procedures go under the general name of 'multi-dimensional scaling' (MDS).

There is insufficient space here to deal at length with such map transformation methods; a full treatment is available in Gatrell (1983). Suffice it to say that MDS seeks to provide a spatial configuration of a set of objects such that the distances between objects in that configuration match as closely as possible the input data (such as travel times). In principle, this configuration or 'map' might have three or more dimensions; in practice, two will often suffice for the kinds of application geographers deal with. Many algorithms are available to perform MDS, the most widely known being ALSCAL, part of the SPSS(X) package. However, no attempt has been made to marry this method with GIS software.

Given the importance of travel time in human behaviour, in assessing planning needs, and so on, it seems worth contemplating such a marriage, particularly in view of the importance attached to visualization. As an example, consider planning proposals for a bypass in the town of State College, Pennsylvania (Fig. 9.10a). In this study (Weir 1975), 42 nodes on the road network were defined and peak-hour travel times estimated among all pairs. MDS was then used to generate from this matrix a configuration of nodes in 'time–space' (Fig. 9.10b). Various options for the bypass were considered, each producing a different travel time matrix. One such option, for a northern bypass, generated a configuration that may be compared with the *status quo* (using rigorous methods for performing overlays of point patterns). The visual evidence for the impact of such a proposal is striking, revealing how locations in the north-west are pulled east, while those in the south-east are pulled north. This kind of approach allows transport planners to see the potential impacts of alternative proposals. There is really no reason why such methods could not be adopted within GIS, with other contextual map information being added if required.

Other measures of spatial proximity

Muller (1982, 1984) has modified the MDS approach to map transformations. He seeks configurations of points such that the distances in the configuration match the input data (travel time, cost, etc.), but depart from the MDS model by allowing more general definitions of distance in the transformed space. His algorithm fits models to the input data of the form:

$$d(i,j) = (a|dx|^p + b|dy|^p)^r \qquad [9.4]$$

where dx and dy are differences in the x and y directions and a, b, p and r are parameters to be estimated. (Compare this with the formula for Euclidean distance, where a and b are 1, $p = 2$ and $r = 1/2$). For example, looking at the costs of sending parcels among a set of 14 Canadian cities, he obtains:

$$d(i,j) = (4.33dx^{0.56} + 3.62dy^{0.56})^{0.39} \qquad [9.5]$$

Note that as $p < 1$ the space is a non-metric one. Muller shows how to represent such functions graphically, along with the resulting configurations. Such transformed maps do offer the possibilities of new visual perspectives, though whether they will ever become standard in proprietary GIS products is debatable.

All this work can be regarded as 'vector based', inasmuch as (x,y) locations of places are sought, albeit in transformed spaces. In the case of raster-based approaches, the obvious measure of spatial separation is based on Pythagorean distance. However, Berry (1988) has shown how to generalize this to incorporate, within a PC-based GIS (pMAP), more sophisticated measures of separation. For example, weights can be assigned to particular grid squares, according to how easy it is to traverse particular types of terrain (woodland versus open land, for instance). These weights can be based on notional time or cost estimates. Berry also shows how barriers can be placed between grid cells, either restricting movement or denying it altogether. Indeed, any GIS should be capable of allowing the user to attach weights or 'impedances' on to particular links. These might reflect different classes or capacities of road, the existence of one-way streets, and so on. Such facilities greatly enhance the usefulness of such systems in network modelling.

One important aspect of such network modelling is, of course, to deal with flows through the network. There is a vast literature on spatial interaction modelling (see Senior 1979 for an introduction), which does not, as yet, seem to have found its way into many proprietary GIS. There is insufficient space to deal with such models here, but they are mentioned because there is a very real sense in which the volume of such interaction serves as a measure of 'proximity'. Two places, between which considerable movement of traffic takes place, are 'closer' in an 'interaction space' than are places between which little interaction occurs.

Concepts of Space and Geographical Data

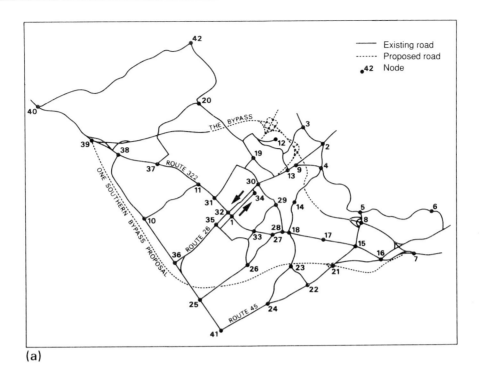

Fig. 9.10 State College, Pennsylvania, USA in (a) geographical space and (b) time-space.

Cartograms

Reference has been made earlier to the importance of visualization in GIS. Using MDS, it is possible to manipulate data on spatial relationships to produce transformed maps. Production of such transformations using area objects with associated map attributes is now considered. The maps that are produced are known as 'area cartograms' (Muehrcke 1978) or 'cartograms' for short.

Consider a map of local government administrative units ('wards') in Lancaster, England (Fig. 9.11a), the boundaries of which are in digital form in a GIS. Given data for each areal unit on total population, it is possible to re-draw the map so that the new areas are in proportion to population size and contiguity and adjacency maintained. It is possible, though tedious, to produce a graphical solution (in effect, numerous possible solutions) by hand, using nothing more than graph paper (e.g. see Monmonier 1977). However, efforts have been made over many years to automate such map production (Tobler 1973; Dougenik, Chrisman and Niemeyer 1985; Selvin, Merrill and Sacks 1988).

Dougenik *et al.* have suggested one method, which was employed to produce a transformed map of Lancaster (Fig. 9.11b). Their method operates on all points comprising the boundaries of areas, computing a vector displacement for each point and then checking to see if the new areal units correspond better to the 'target' data (such as the population count for each area). The displacement is a function of the difference between actual and 'desired' area, together with the distance from that point to the centroid of the polygon. The procedure is then repeated in an iterative fashion. However, the method can give rise to topological problems and checks for these must be built in.

One issue that has not been given sufficient attention in cartogram production has been the need to devise ways of associating point objects with the transformed map. For instance, data on the locations of disease cases may be available for display on a population cartogram. Selvin *et al.* (1988) have offered a solution to this problem, by devising an alternative algorithm for cartogram generation.

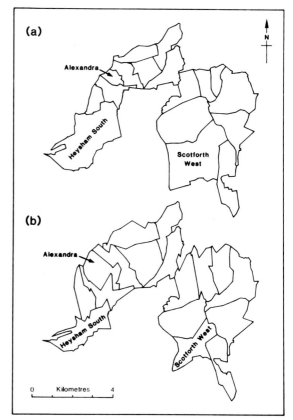

Fig. 9.11 Electoral wards in Lancaster, England urban area in (a) geographical space and (b) as a cartogram.

CONCLUSIONS

It should be clear from the above that space is not as simple as might first be imagined. Different 'spaces' arise as the definition of the relation on a set of objects changes. While Euclidean distance has, quite properly, long been accorded a primary place within GIS, there is scope for encouraging more imaginative and flexible approaches, whereby other measures of spatial separation are incorporated. Of particular value is likely to be the greater use of travel time, both as a source of data for analysis and modelling, and as a means of visualizing spatial relationships. Visualization in GIS would also profit from the wider incorporation of options to produce cartograms. These are particularly valuable in epidemiological work.

These new ways of looking at space and spatial relations within a GIS context are unlikely to prove of value to those more interested in land management and in digital mapping, in which a Euclidean perspective rightly reigns supreme. For those interested in the analytical side of GIS, or for those seeking novel descriptions, however, such views may be appealing and offer fresh insights into geographical patterns; this should be the ultimate aim of research that uses GIS technology.

REFERENCES

Abler R, Adams J, Gould P R (1971) *Spatial Organization: the geographer's view of the world*. Prentice-Hall, Englewood Cliffs New Jersey

Armstrong M P (1988) Distance imprecision and error in spatial decision support systems. In: Aangeenbrug R T, Schiffman Y M (eds.) *International Geographic Information Systems (IGIS) Symposium, Arlington, Virginia*, Vol 2. NASA, Washington DC, pp. 23–34

Berry J K (1988) Computer-based map analysis: characterizing proximity and connectivity. In: Aangeenbrug R T, Schiffman Y M (eds.) *International Geographic Information Systems (IGIS) Symposium, Arlington, Virginia*, Vol 2. NASA, Washington DC, pp. 11–22

Boots B, Getis A (1988) Point pattern analysis. *Sage Scientific Geography Series, Number 8*. Sage Publications, London

Broome F (1986) Mapping from a topologically encoded database: the US Bureau of the Census example. In: Blakemore M J (ed.) *Proceedings of AUTOCARTO London*. Royal Institution of Chartered Surveyors, London, pp. 402–11

Burrough P A (1989) Fuzzy mathematical methods for soil survey and land evaluation. *Journal of Soil Science* **40**: 477–92

Chrisman N R (1991) The error component in spatial data. In: Maguire D J, Goodchild M F, Rhind D W (eds.) *Geographical Information Systems: principles and applications*. Longman, London, pp. 165–74, Vol 1

Clark J W (1977) Time–distance transformations of transportation networks. *Geographical Analysis* **9**: 195–205

DCDSTF (Digital Cartographic Data Standards Task Force) (1988) The proposed standard for digital cartographic data. Volume 1. *The American Cartographer* **15**: 9–140

Diggle P J (1983) *Statistical Analysis of Spatial Point Patterns*. Academic Press, London

Dougenik J A, Chrisman N R, Niemeyer D R (1985) An algorithm to construct continuous area cartograms. *Professional Geographer* **37**: 75–81

Dunn C, Newton D (1989) Notes on shortest path algorithms for GIS. *North West Regional Research Laboratory Research Report 3*. North West Regional Research Laboratory, Lancaster

Eastman R (1988) *IDRISI: a grid-based geographic analysis system*. Graduate School of Geography Clark University, Massachusetts

Ebdon D (1985) *Statistics in Geography: a practical approach*, 2nd edn. Basil Blackwell, Oxford

Egenhofer M J, Herring J R (1991) High-level spatial data structures for GIS. In: Maguire D J, Goodchild M F, Rhind D W (eds.) *Geographical Information Systems: principles and applications*. Longman, London, pp. 227–37, Vol 1

Flowerdew R (1991) Spatial data integration In: Maguire D J, Goodchild M F, Rhind D W (eds.) *Geographical Information Systems: principles and applications*. Longman, London, pp. 375–87, Vol 1

Frank A U, Mark D M (1991) Language issues for GIS. In: Maguire D J, Goodchild M F, Rhind D W (eds.) *Geographical Information Systems: principles and applications*. Longman, London, pp. 147–63, Vol 1

Gatrell A C (1983) *Distance and Space: a geographical perspective*. Oxford University Press, Oxford

Goodchild M F (1985) Geographical information systems in undergraduate geography: a contemporary dilemma. *The Operational Geographer* **8**: 34–8

Goodchild M F (1986) Spatial autocorrelation. *CATMOG 47* GeoAbstracts, Norwich

Goodchild M F (1988) Towards an enumeration and classification of GIS functions. In: Aangeenbrug R T, Schiffman Y M (eds.) *International Geographic Information Systems (IGIS) Symposium, Arlington, Virginia*, Vol 2. NASA, Washington DC, pp. 65–77

Goodchild M F, Grandfield A W (1983) Optimizing raster storage: an evaluation of four alternatives. In: *Proceedings of AUTOCARTO6 (2)*. ASPRS, Falls Church, pp. 400–7

Goodchild M F, Mark D M (1987) The fractal nature of geographic phenomena. *Annals of the Association of American Geographers* **77**: 265–78

Griffith D A (1987) Spatial autocorrelation: a primer. *Association of American Geographers, Resource Publications in Geography*. Association of American Geographers, Washington

Haggett P (1965) *Lotational Analysis in Human Geology*. Edward Arnold, London

Healey R G (1991) Database management systems. In: Maguire D J, Goodchild M F, Rhind D W (eds.) *Geographical Information Systems: principles and applications*. Longman, London, pp. 251–67, Vol 1

Hubert L, Golledge R G, Costanzo C M (1981) Generalized procedures for evaluating spatial autocorrelation. *Geographical Analysis* **13**: 224–33

Kehris E (1989) Interfacing ARC/INFO with GLIM: a progress report. *North West Regional Research Laboratory Research Report 5*. North West Regional Research Laboratory, Lancaster

Maguire D J, Dangermond J (1991) The functionality of GIS. In: Maguire D J, Goodchild M F, Rhind D W (eds.) *Geographical Information Systems: principles and applications*. Longman, London, pp. 319–35, Vol 1

Maguire D J, Worboys M F, Hearnshaw H M (1990) An introduction to object-oriented Geographical Information Systems. *Mapping Awareness* **4** (2): 36–9

Mahoney R P (1991) GIS and utilities. In: Maguire D J, Goodchild M F, Rhind D W (eds.) *Geographical Information Systems: principles and applications*. Longman, London, pp. 101–14, Vol 2

Maling D H (1991) Coordinate systems and map projections for GIS. In: Maguire D J, Goodchild M F, Rhind D W (eds.) *Geographical Information Systems: principles and applications*. Longman, London, pp. 135–46, Vol 1

Mandelbrot B (1967) How long is the coast of Britain? Statistical self-similarity and fractional dimension. *Science* **156**: 636–8

Mark D M, Svorou S, Zubin D (1988) Spatial terms and spatial concepts: geographic, cognitive, and linguistic perspectives. In: Aangeenbrug R T, Schiffman Y M (eds.) *International Geographic Information Systems (IGIS) Symposium, Arlington, Virginia*. NASA, Washington DC, pp. 101–12

Monmonier M S (1977) Maps, distortion and meaning. *Association of American Geographers Resource Paper in Geography*, **75–4**. Association of American Geographers, Washington

Monmonier M S (1982) *Computer-Assisted Cartography: principles and prospects*. Prentice-Hall, Englewood Cliffs New Jersey

Muehrcke P (1978) *Map Use: reading, analysis and interpretation*. J P Publications, Madison Wisconsin

Muller J-C (1978) The mapping of travel time in Edmonton, Alberta. *Canadian Geographer* **22**: 195–210

Muller J-C (1982) Non-Euclidean geographic spaces: mapping functional distances. *Geographical Analysis* **14**: 189–203

Muller J-C (1984) Canada's elastic space: a portrayal of route and cost distances. *Canadian Geographer* **28**: 46–62

Muller J-C (1991) Generalization of spatial databases. In: Maguire D J, Goodchild M F, Rhind D W (eds.) *Geographical Information Systems: principles and applications*. Longman, London, pp. 457–75, Vol 1

Odland J (1988) Spatial autocorrelation. *Sage Scientific Geography Series Number 9*. Sage Publications, London

Openshaw S (1991) Developing appropriate spatial analysis methods for GIS. In: Maguire D J, Goodchild M F, Rhind D W (eds.) *Geographical Information Systems: principles and applications*. Longman, London, pp. 389–402, Vol 1

Peuquet D J (1988) Representations of geographic space: toward a conceptual synthesis. *Annals of the Association of American Geographers* **78**: 375–94

Robinson A H, Sale R D, Morrison J L, Muehrcke P C (1984) *Elements of Cartography*, 2nd edn. John Wiley, Chichester

Robinson V B, Miller R, Klesh L (1988) Issues in the use of expert systems to manage uncertainty in geographic information systems. In: Aangeenbrug R T, Schiffman Y M (eds.) *International Geographic Information Systems (IGIS) Symposium, Arlington, Virginia*, Vol 2. NASA, Washington DC, pp. 89–100

Samet H (1984) The quadtree and related hierarchical data structures. *ACM Computing Surveys* **16**: 187–260

Samet H (1990) *The Design and Analysis of Spatial Data Structures*. Addison-Wesley, Reading Massachusetts

Selvin S, Merrill D W, Sacks S (1988) Transformations of maps to investigate clusters of disease. *Social Science and Medicine* **26**: 215–21

Senior M L (1979) From gravity modelling to entropy maximizing: a pedagogic guide. *Progress in Human Geography* **3**: 179–210

Smith T R, Menon S, Star J L, Estes J E (1987) Requirements and principles for the implementation and construction of large-scale geographical information systems. *International Journal of Geographical Information Systems* **1**: 13–32

Sowton M (1991) Development of GIS-related activities at the Ordnance Survey. In: Maguire D J, Goodchild M F, Rhind D W (eds.) *Geographical Information Systems: principles and applications*. Longman, London, pp. 23–38, Vol 2

Starr L E, Anderson K E (1991) A USGS perspective on GIS. In: Maguire D J, Goodchild M F, Rhind D W (eds.) *Geographical Information Systems: principles and applications*. Longman, London, pp. 11–22, Vol 2

Tobler W R (1973) A continuous transformation useful for redistricting. *Annals of the New York Academy of Sciences* **219**: 215–20

Tobler W R (1982) Surveying multidimensional measurement. In: Golledge R G, Rayner J N (eds.) *Proximity and Preference: problems in the multidimensional analysis of large data sets*. University of Minnesota Press, Minneapolis, pp. 3–4

Tobler W R (1988) Geographic information systems research agenda: the scientific community perspective. In: Aangeenbrug R T, Schiffman Y M (eds.) *International Geographic Information Systems (IGIS) Symposium, Arlington, Virginia*, Vol 1. NASA, Washington DC, pp. 49–52

Unwin D J (1981) *Introductory Spatial Analysis*. Methuen, London

von Hohenbalken B and West D S (1984) Manhattan versus Euclid: market areas computed and compared. *Regional Science and Urban Economics* **14**: 19–35

Weibel R, Heller M (1991) Digital terrain modelling. In: Maguire D J, Goodchild M F, Rhind D W (eds.) *Geographical Information Systems: principles and applications*. Longman, London, pp. 269–97, Vol 1

Weir S (1975) *Getting around town: modifications in a local travel time space caused by expressway construction*. Unpublished MSc thesis. Department of Geography, Pennsylvania State University

White M (1991) Car navigation systems. In: Maguire D J, Goodchild M F, Rhind D W (eds.) *Geographical Information Systems: principles and applications*. Longman, London, pp. 115–25, Vol 2

10

COORDINATE SYSTEMS AND MAP PROJECTIONS FOR GIS

D H MALING

The subjects of coordinate systems and map projections are treated under three major headings. First, it is necessary to emphasize the need for economical methods of handling GIS data and to describe some of the ways in which economies may be introduced to the transformation processes. Secondly, there is a short account of some of the methods of transformation which may be used in GIS. Thirdly, there is a description of a method of choosing suitable projections for particular GIS applications.

INTRODUCTION

This chapter is concerned with a review of the principal methods which may be used to transform positional data so that they may be registered with other positional data and so that the results of analyses can be output as maps. The terminology relating to map projections is that used by Maling (1968, 1973), Royal Society (1966) and ICA (1973); the appropriate theoretical background is to be found in Richardus and Adler (1972) and Maling (1973). Because this chapter is wholly concerned with geometric transformations applied to positional data, unqualified use of the word data in this chapter refers to the positions of points on a map, photograph, remotely sensed image, or in a file.

Figure 10.1 illustrates the various types of coordinate system which are used in this chapter. The discussion proceeds from the initial assumption that the primary sources for GIS positional data are printed maps which have been converted by digitizing into machine readable form. This information may be converted into either three-dimensional terrestrial coordinates or two-dimensional plane coordinates. In the first form these are either geographical coordinates of latitude and longitude, (φ, λ) or three-dimensional Cartesian coordinates (X, Y, Z). In the second form the stored data are referred to a plane coordinate system. This may be simple plane Cartesian, polar coordinates, a raster grid or a map projection. At first sight it seems sensible to use terrestrial coordinates as the preferred method of storing data. However, the objection to relying upon this procedure is the sheer volume of data which needs to be handled and stored. A file representing a vector digitized map may comprise many tens of thousands of points. For example, Cocks, Walker and Parvey (1988) have described the contents of the GIS of Australia (AIS) in which each map base comprises 20 000 coordinate pairs for the low resolution outline and 300 000 coordinate pairs for high resolution use. A Landsat Multi-spectral Scanner (MSS) image for only one waveband comprises more than 7 million pixels; a complete Landsat Thematic Mapper (TM) image (seven bands each comprising 5700 lines of 6900 pixels) occupies 262 Mb of storage. From the point of view of handling these data economically in the transformation from geographical position through the formation and registration of layers, it is desirable to transform the raw data extracted from map sources into a uniform system of positional referencing within the system itself. This removes the need for preliminary processing of each layer every time it is registered to another layer. This is especially important if there is a mixture of vector and raster data to be standardized.

One of the commonest solutions is that of the

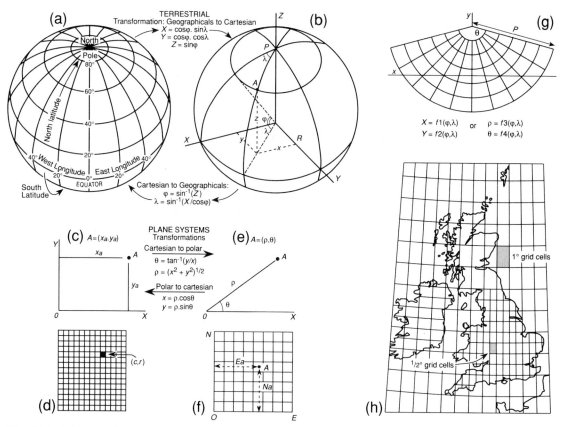

Fig. 10.1 The coordinate systems used in this chapter. (a) and (b) Terrestial systems: (a) Geographical coordinates of latitude (φ) and longitude (λ). (b) Three-dimensional Cartesian coordinates (X, Y, Z). (c) – (h) Plane systems: (c) Plane Cartesian (x, y) coordinates. (d) Raster (c, r) coordinates in which position is determined by counting cells rather than by analogue measurement. (e) Plane polar (ρ, θ) coordinates. (f) A map grid is another example of a plane grid expressed in linear measurement (E, N), which are usually metres on the ground. (g) Graticule in which φ and λ are expressed in either (x, y) or (ρ, θ) coordinates.

At the output stage, map projections are defined either in Cartesian or in polar coordinates vis:

$x = f_1(\varphi,\lambda),$
$y = f_2(\varphi,\lambda),$
$\rho = f_3(\varphi,\lambda),$
$\theta = f_4(\varphi,\lambda),$

(h) Grid cells are a compromise between geographical coordinates and a grid. They are created by subdividing the graticule into quadrangles of suitable dimensions. In this example, quadrangles of size 1° × 1° and ½° × ½° are illustrated.

grid cell, comprising a fairly close pattern of spherical quadrilateral cells which are derived from subdivision of the graticule into one-degree or half-degree units. They are, therefore, much larger than a typical raster cell. The Australian AIS makes use of both of these dimensions, together with even larger units (Cocks, Walker and Parvey 1988; see also O'Callaghan and Garner 1991 in this volume). Grid cells are neither square nor rectangular because their sides are formed from two meridians and two parallels. The convergence of the meridians towards the poles means that the grid cells have a pair of sides of different length (Fig. 10.1h). Since great use is made of this unit by the United States Geological Survey (USGS) as the basis for the sheet lines of its maps, the word 'quadrangle' is frequently used to describe it.

GIS FRAMEWORK

The next development from using grid cells to hold data is to use a map projection at this intermediate stage. The concept is so important that it is here called the 'GIS framework' to distinguish it from the methods already considered and any other projection which may be used for purposes of illustration of the same data. This device is obviously of increasing importance the greater the area to be covered by a GIS, for two reasons. First, the database for the whole of a large country or a continent will be large and storage of data in terrestrial coordinates is impractical. Secondly, the area covered will be far too large for any convenient approximations that the earth is flat so a plane grid will not suffice. The GIS framework is most likely to be that used for national surveys, usually the Universal Transverse Mercator (UTM), the Soviet equivalent to UTM, or the Lambert Conformal Conical projection. However, in many instances the coverage of the GIS extends beyond the single state so that the different origins and projections used by different states must be reconciled. Also, the projections used for some thematic maps to be incorporated into the GIS may differ from those of the topographical base. Maps of maritime distributions are almost invariably on different projections to those used for land maps.

Briggs and Mounsey (1989) and Mounsey (1991 in this volume) have emphasized the difficulties which arise in handling numerous and disparate sources in creating CORINE, the environmental database for the European Community. They have cogently argued the need for a common projection framework to relate all the component layers. For a continental GIS it may even be necessary to use more than one type of projection as the framework. In the design of the environmental GIS for Antarctica, Sievers and Bennat (1989) describe the design of a set of Lambert conformal conical and stereographic projections created as raster grids to serve as the mathematical framework for the system.

Economy of data handling

A fundamental principle of conventional cartography is that there is a limit to the smallest size of object which can be shown legibly on a map. This is usually taken to be a map distance of about 0.15 mm and it is often called the zero dimension. It has the important effect of placing a limit upon the degree of complexity which is needed in the design and production of a map (see Fisher 1991 in this volume). If a particular computation or cartographic technique affects the plotted position of a point by less than this amount, a simpler procedure may suffice. Thus the zero dimension permits a series of assumptions to be made about the way in which original surveys are computed and plotted and how much credence should be put on measurements (including digitizing) made from maps. It is also important in making a choice about the suitability of a certain projection for a particular job, even if this is often used in the negative sense of deciding whether the projection of the existing map, though incorrect, will suffice. Since maps are the primary source of data for a GIS, the limit created by the zero dimension and any other imperfections (see Maling 1989) revealed during measurement from it, are transferred to the GIS, irrespective of the degree of sophistication of the methods of data capture used to digitize the maps. This is just reiteration of the fundamental truth that no data are better than their sources.

Assumptions about the shape and size of the earth

Short cuts may be made to computations involving the shape and size of the earth by assuming that its shape is geometrically simpler than it actually is. The first of these assumptions made in surveying and mapping, as described in varying detail in books on geodesy, surveying and map projections (e.g. Richardus and Adler 1972; Maling 1973; Jackson 1980), is that the rather complicated surface of the geoid may be replaced by a reference figure or spheroid. There is considerable temptation to write programs which apply transformations with geodetic precision so that distances and directions between points on the curved surface and plane coordinates for the principal projections used for topographical and cadastral mapping are all referred to a particular spheroid. Although such practices are appropriate to field surveys and simulated maps, they do not necessarily apply to handling those GIS layers whose sources were paper maps. It follows that the spherical assumption is still justified in transforming most map data. For example, Snyder (1985, 1987b), Shmutter (1981) and Doytsher and Shmutter (1981) have all presented formulae for transforming data to and from various projections, all of which have been derived for a spherical earth. Thus the spherical assumption is still as valid as it was in the days before computers made it so easy to refer all calculations to the spheroid.

The simplest assumption of all is, of course, that the earth is flat, so that a satisfactory map can be made by plane surveying. For many local surveys carried out for municipal, civil and mining engineering purposes, the extent of the survey and, therefore, the influence of earth curvature is so small that the plane assumption will suffice. Vincenty (1989) has reconsidered this subject in the light of modern survey practice. Extending the flat-earth argument to photogrammetry, an analogue plotter has a plane datum surface which is simulated by its base carriage. Therefore, the pair of aerial photographs placed within the plotter are referred to a plane datum.

Economy in the design of formulae

The actual formulae used in the transformations may be redesigned for more economical processing. Those which have been taken straight from the literature of geodesy and map projections were originally designed for ease of computation using tables and logarithms. Vincenty (1971), Williams (1982), Snyder (1985) and King (1988) have all demonstrated how the well-known geodetic and projection formulae may be improved for digital processing by a little reorganization. An example of such an improvement is given in eqn [10.24].

An apparent complication of the geodetic and projection formulae used before digital computing is the frequent appearance of the term sin 1″, used to convert from an angle expressed in radians into seconds of arc or vice versa. For an explanation of this computing trick see Maling (1973). The conversion was necessary in the days when tables of trigonometric functions were used and the argument was in degree measure. With digital computers came the subroutines for calculating trigonometric functions which had to be accessed using the angles expressed in radians as the argument. Consequently, the need for making the majority of the conversions disappeared. Nevertheless, many early programs written to compute Transverse Mercator coordinates of the spheroid were copied straight from the literature of the pre-digital era,

including all the sin 1″ terms, so that CPU time was wasted in making unnecessary conversions of angles from seconds of arc into radians and back again for no reason. Some of these economies which have so far been described appear to offer a negligible saving when used to transform only a few points, but the cumulative effect of applying them to each point in turn can result in considerable savings in both storage space and CPU time when a whole map is transformed. A number of other economies which have greater impact upon the design of GIS are discussed below.

Economies in map use

Most national topographical maps are based upon conformal projections and, consequently, this has become the commonest base for the GIS framework. However, an equal-area projection would theoretically be a more suitable base for many distribution maps. Therefore, it is appropriate to question whether the difference matters.

In using topographical maps as a source for distribution mapping in a country the size of Britain, the influence of the projection can usually be ignored without any serious consequences. Ordnance Survey maps of Britain are based upon a particular version of the Transverse Mercator projection so that there is a certain amount of area distortion on these maps. However, for maps of mainland Britain the area scale nowhere exceeds the range 0.999 08–1.000 92; in other words it varies from the constant area scale of an equal area projection by less than 0.1 per cent. Since this is likely to be smaller than the errors which arise from the imperfections of the source map, it follows that judgements about density of distribution or measurement of area occupied by different categories of land use, for example, are unaffected by the fact that the map projection used is theoretically incorrect.

Economies through independence from artificial boundaries

Nearly all spatial data collected for administrative and cadastral purposes are recorded in parcels (or polygons) which are parts of the earth enclosed by political, administrative or property boundaries (see Dale 1991 in this volume). This is how they are entered in data files, simply because there is no other way of handling the data initially. However, the polygons thus defined do not usually correspond to other kinds of boundary, such as those of geology, vegetation or land use. Moreover, the artificial boundaries of administrative units are often frequently changed so that much time may be spent in revising and updating these files. Cocks, Walker and Parvey (1988) argue that the difficulties of revising such files are an important objection to using them and that this is sufficient reason for converting, wherever possible, to holding the data in grid cells.

Economies through interpolation algorithms

Alternative methods may be used to eliminate particularly slow computations by introducing interpolation methods. Thus the detail shown in a small square or quadrangle on a map may be transformed to another projection by carrying out the full transformation for the corner points of the figure only and then using interpolation formulae to change the internal detail. This is the digital equivalent of using proportional dividers; it has been particularly well exploited in mapping from remotely sensed imagery. Since the algorithms are described elsewhere (e.g. see Mather 1987), they need not be described here.

THE TRANSFORMATION METHODS

The Cartesian coordinates (x, y) of a point on a map are functionally related to position on the earth's surface expressed in geographical coordinates (φ, λ)

$$\left. \begin{array}{l} x = f_1(\varphi, \lambda) \\ y = f_2(\varphi, \lambda) \end{array} \right\} \quad [10.1]$$

There are three basic methods of relating (x, y) to (φ, λ) or various forms of plane coordinates used on other maps, aerial photographs or scanned imagery. These are referred to here as:

- Analytical transformation;
- Direct or grid-on-grid transformation;
- Polynomial transformation.

Analytical transformation

Analytical transformation is the most obvious and straightforward solution to the problem of relating Cartesian coordinates on a map to geographical coordinates on the earth's surface. This is because it approximates to the methods of classical cartography, that is, locating and plotting points from their geographical coordinates. In the automated applications, the objective is to convert the (x', y') coordinates of points digitized on a source map into their geographical coordinates. These, in turn, are used to determine the (x, y) coordinates for the GIS framework or to create a new map.

The conversion from geographical coordinates into plane coordinates is the normal practice of constructing a map projection and is regarded as the *forward solution*. The preliminary conversion required to find the geographical coordinates from the (x', y') system of digitized coordinates is correspondingly called the *inverse solution*. Thus the transformation model is:

$$(x', y') \rightarrow (\varphi, \lambda) \rightarrow (x, y) \quad [10.2]$$
<Inverse solution><Forward solution>

Most of the standard works on map projections only provide the equations for the forward solution. This is because in the days before digital mapping became a practical possibility, only the forward equations were needed to construct a graticule; all subsequent transfer of detail was manual. It was only in the field of topographic mapping, using the Transverse Mercator and Lambert Conformal Conical projections in particular, that the two conversions 'geographicals to grid' and 'grid to geographicals' were likely to be employed and both were provided for by the projection tables. The only comprehensive source for both the forward and inverse equations for the commonly used map projections is Snyder (1987a). This manual also includes worked examples of both computations for spherical and spheroidal assumptions.

The analytical transformation equations for Mercator's projection

The relationship between the forward and inverse coordinate expressions may be exemplified by the sets of equations used to define the normal aspect of Mercator's projection which is the basis of virtually all nautical charts. For the projection of the sphere, eqn [10.3] for the forward solution is to be found in most of the standard works on map projections:

$$x = R.\lambda$$

$$y = R.\ln\tan(\pi/4 + \varphi/2) \quad [10.3]$$

where ln is the natural logarithm (to base ϵ), the longitude, λ, is expressed in radians and the radius of the earth, R, is expressed in millimetres at the scale of the proposed map. In order to express (φ,λ) in terms of (x, y), which is the inverse solution, it is necessary to write

$$\varphi = \pi/2 - 2\tan^{-1}(\epsilon^{-y/R})$$
$$\lambda = x/R + \lambda_0 \quad [10.4]$$

where λ_0 is the datum meridian from which longitudes are measured. Here ϵ is the base of natural logarithms ($= 2.718\,281\,8...$). It is written as the Greek epsilon to avoid confusion with the eccentricity of the spheroid, e, in the next three equations.

The first complication which needs to be considered is the corresponding relationships for the projection of the spheroid, having semi-axes a and b with eccentricity e derived from

$$e^2 = (a^2 - b^2)/a^2 \approx 0.0067... \quad [10.5]$$

For the forward solution of Mercator's projection of the spheroid, eqn [10.3] has to be modified to the corresponding equations

$$x = a.\lambda$$
$$y = a.\ln\tan(\pi/4 + \varphi/2)[(1 - e.\sin\varphi)/(1 + e.\sin\varphi)]^{e/2}$$
$$[10.6]$$

For the inverse calculation the equation to find latitude is transcendental, needing an iterative solution

$$\varphi = \pi/2 - 2\tan^{-1}\{t[(1 - e.\sin\varphi)/(1 + e.\sin\varphi)]^{e/2}\} \quad [10.7]$$

and $t = \epsilon^{-y/a}$ The first trial solution is to find

$$\varphi = \pi/2 - 2\tan^{-1}(t) \quad [10.8]$$

The result is inserted as φ in the right hand side of eqn [10.7] to calculate a new value for φ on the left-hand side. The process is repeated until the results have converged to a difference between the two values for φ which the user considers to be insignificant and the final value for φ may be accepted. Longitude, is obtained from a simple modification for the λ expression in eqn [10.6], namely

$$\lambda = x/a + \lambda_0 \quad [10.9]$$

Further transformations

The number of stages in the inverse solution may have to be extended for various other reasons. Because most digitizing is done in Cartesian coordinates and it is sometimes appropriate to deal with a map projection which is best derived in polar coordinates, it may be necessary to change plane rectangular coordinates (x',y') into plane polar coordinates (ρ,δ) before determining the geographical coordinates. Thus the transformation model contains an additional stage, as follows:

$$(x',y') \rightarrow (\rho,\delta) \rightarrow (\varphi,\lambda) \rightarrow (x,y) \quad [10.10]$$
$$<\text{Inverse solution}><\text{Forward solution}>$$

Similarly a change in aspect, for example to a transverse or oblique projection, involves yet another stage in the succession of transformations. Change in aspect is commonly effected through the system of (z,α) bearing and distance coordinates (Maling 1973), using spherical trigonometry to convert from (φ,λ) into (z,α). Thus:

$$(x',y') \rightarrow (\rho,\delta) \rightarrow (\varphi,\lambda) \rightarrow (z,\alpha) \rightarrow (x,y)$$
$$<\text{Inverse solution}><\text{Change in aspect}><\text{Forward solution}>$$
$$[10.11]$$

An alternative to this method of changing aspect is to use a three-dimensional Cartesian system (X, Y, Z) instead of geographical coordinates to relate positions on the spherical surface. Following the work of Wray (1974), Barton (1976) and Arthur (1978) the change in aspect may also be obtained by rotating these axes through the three Eulerian angles at the centre of the sphere. This time the transformations are:

$$(x',y') \rightarrow (\varphi,\lambda) \rightarrow (X,Y,Z) \rightarrow (X',Y',Z') \rightarrow (\varphi',\lambda') \rightarrow (x,y)$$
$$<\text{Inverse solution}><\text{Change in aspect}><\text{Forward solution}>$$
$$[10.12]$$

where (X',Y',Z') are the rotated coordinates of the point (X, Y, Z).

The advantages and disadvantages of the analytical method

The analytical method is rigorous and it is independent of the size of the area to be mapped. However, it can be inconveniently slow. It seems at first sight that this is no longer a problem; that modern high-speed computers have reduced these considerations to insignificance. However, the clumsiness of the analytical method becomes apparent when applied to large data files. This is well demonstrated by eqn [10.11] relating to change in aspect, where each additional transformation stage may involve either the solution of a separate spherical triangle or, in eqn [10.12], the determination of three-dimensional coordinates and rotation of them for every point on the map.

A further problem, highlighted by Snyder (1985, 1987c), is that the naming of projections on existing maps leaves much to be desired and that even when the correct name has been used, important information such as the positions of the standard parallels in a conical projection or the central meridian of the particular version of the Transverse Mercator projection in use has not been stated. Snyder (1985) has written a program which attempts recognition of the projection in use, based upon the digitized coordinates of nine points (on three parallels and three meridians) of the map, but even this can only distinguish between fairly simple examples.

Direct transformation by the Grid-on-Grid Method

This method does not require inverse solution of the geographical coordinates (φ, λ) of the original map, but is based upon the relation between the rectangular coordinates of the same points on the two projections. This technique was used in traditional cartography for such purposes as regridding or plotting a second grid on a military topographical map – hence the name 'grid-on-grid'. This method is also important in mapping from remote sensing and is the method adopted in modern analytical plotters for use with conventional aerial photography. Practically all the methods of applying geometrical corrections to remote sensing imagery, including that derived from Landsat MSS, Landsat TM and SPOT sensors, utilize such techniques employing ground control points of known position to determine the transformation parameters.

The simplest transformation model is, of course:

$$(x', y') \rightarrow (x, y) \qquad [10.13]$$

Two relatively simple numerical procedures which are commonly employed in the mapping sciences are the linear transformations from one plane Cartesian coordinate system into another. There are two major kinds of transformation: the *linear conformal, similarity* or *Helmert* transformation; and the *affine* transformation. The former is expressed in the general form:

$$x = A + Cx' + Dy'$$
$$y = B - Dx' + Cy' \qquad [10.14]$$

The affine transformation is as follows:

$$x = A + Cx' + Dy'$$
$$y = B - Ex' + Fy' \qquad [10.15]$$

In these equations, the known (or digitized) (x', y') coordinates of a point in one system are transformed into the (x, y) coordinates of the second system, through the use of four or six coefficients A–F. In the Helmert transformation the C and D coefficients are common to both the equations for x and y, but in affine transformation it is necessary to introduce separate corrections for each direction. Both transformations may be resolved into three components:

- Translation of the axes or change of origin, corresponding to the coefficients A and B in both eqns [10.14] and [10.15].
- A change in scale from one grid system to the other.
- The rotation of the axes of one grid system with respect to their directions in the other. These are illustrated in Fig. 10.2.

Helmert transformation

For the Helmert transformation the effects of all three displacements are combined to produce the pair of equations

$$x = (m \cdot x' \cdot \cos \alpha + m \cdot y' \cdot \sin \alpha) + A \qquad [10.16]$$
$$y = (-m \cdot x' \cdot \sin \alpha + m \cdot y' \cdot \cos \alpha) + B \qquad [10.17]$$

where A and B are the coefficients in eqn [10.14] which correspond to the shift in the origin of the coordinates parallel with the x and y axes, the angle α is the rotation of the axes required to make these axes parallel and m is a scale factor. Thus if two points, j and k in the first system correspond to J and K in the second, the ratio of the distances jk/JK must be applied to the first system to bring it to the same scale as the second.

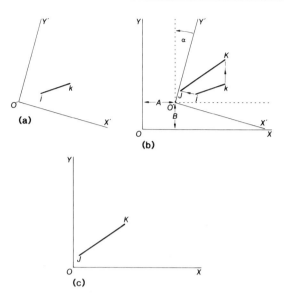

Fig. 10.2 The geometry of Helmert transformation. (a) Initial conditions: showing two points j and k referred to Cartesian axes $O'X'$ and $O'Y'$ which are orthogonal. (b) The three stages in transformation superimposed upon one another. These are, first the scale change by which the line jk is transformed into the line JK. Secondly, the rotation of the X' and Y' axes through the angle α about the point O' to make the axes parallel to the final OX and OY system. Third is the translation of the origin O' through the distances A and B respectively to refer J and K to the (X, Y) system. (c) Final conditions: indicating the positions of J and K within the (X, Y) system.

The complete transformation may be expressed in matrix form as

$$\begin{pmatrix} x \\ y \end{pmatrix} = \begin{pmatrix} C & D \\ -D & C \end{pmatrix} \cdot \begin{pmatrix} x' \\ y' \end{pmatrix} + \begin{pmatrix} A \\ B \end{pmatrix} \qquad [10.18]$$

where $D = m' \sin \alpha$ and $C = m' \cos \alpha$. The inverse transformation is that of determining the (x', y') coordinates of points whose (x, y) coordinates are already known. Thus

$$\begin{pmatrix} x' \\ y' \end{pmatrix} = \begin{pmatrix} C' & -D' \\ D' & C' \end{pmatrix} \cdot \begin{pmatrix} x \\ y \end{pmatrix} - \begin{pmatrix} A \\ B \end{pmatrix} \qquad [10.19]$$

where $C' = \cos \alpha / m$ and $D' = \sin \alpha / m$.

If there are only two points (x'_1, y'_1) and (x'_2, y'_2) on the first surface corresponding to (x_1, y_1) and (x_2, y_2) on the second surface whose coordinates are known or have been measured, the method of finding C and D is through eqns [10.20] and [10.21].

$$C = [\delta x \cdot \delta y' - \delta y \cdot \delta x']/[\delta x'^2 + \delta y'^2] \qquad [10.20]$$

$$D = [\delta y \cdot \delta y' + \delta x \cdot \delta x']/[\delta x'^2 + \delta y'^2] \qquad [10.21]$$

where

$\delta x = (x_1 - x_2), \delta x' = (x'_1 - x'_2), \delta y = (y_1 - y_2)$

and

$\delta y' = (y'_1 - y'_2)$

If there are more than two common points, such as occurs in vector digitizing, the adjustment of aerial triangulation or fitting a remotely sensed image to many ground control points, the determination of the coefficients from only two or three of them is inadequate because the coordinates of any of those points may contain small errors, which, in turn, introduces errors into the transformation of all other points. Therefore, all of the data available for the determination of C and D ought to be taken into consideration. This involves a solution of the coefficients by the method of least squares which is described under the determination of polynomial coefficients.

Affine transformation

The assumption which is made in the Helmert transformation is that the scalar, m, is a single unique value. In other words the ratio jk/JK is the same whatever the directions of these lines. This is a reasonable assumption for some purposes but it may not always be justifiable. For example, in photogrammetry the location of image points on a film may be affected by deformation of the film base by stretching and shrinking and this is not usually the same in all directions. In the extraction of positional information by digitizing a paper map, the influence of differential stretching or shrinking of the paper is even more erratic. For these applications it is desirable to use the affine transformation or even a higher order polynomial because this allows for different scales in the directions of the two axes, m_x and m_y. This may also be combined with small departures of the coordinate axes from the perpendicular, as illustrated in Fig. 10.3. Here it can be seen that the (x, y) axes intersect at an angle $\gamma \neq 90°$. The solution is described in greater detail by Mikhail (1976) and Sprinsky (1987).

Numerical transformation methods

The third method of relating Cartesian coordinates on a map to geographical coordinates on the earth's

Coordinate Systems and Map Projections for GIS

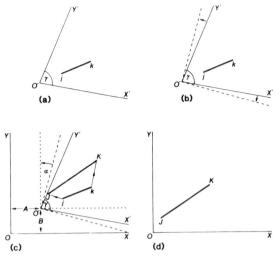

Fig. 10.3 The geometry of affine transformation.
(a) Initial condition: showing two points j and k referred to Cartesian axes $O'X'$ and $O'Y'$ which are not orthogonal but intersect at some angle γ. The same effect is produced by differential scales in the directions of the two axes. (b) Creation of the orthogonal axes. here shown by the broken line. This is also equivalent to making the linear scale in the X' direction equal to that in the Y' direction (c) All transformation stages are superimposed. The third, fourth and fifth stages comprise those in the Helmert transformation, i.e. the uniform scale change to represent jk by JK; the rotation of the axes through the angle α and, finally, the translation through A and B to refer the points J and K to the OX and OY axes. (d) Final transformation illustrates this stage, where J and K are shown within the OXY system.

surface is to construct polynomial expressions to fit the data and use the resulting coefficients to transform the coordinates of the remaining points of map detail. This method is, of course, important in numerical analysis and has many different applications. In the narrower field of transforming positional data for GIS applications this method may be used with equal efficiency for transformation from geographical into grid coordinates (eqn [10.22]) as for making the grid-to-grid transformations (eqn [10.23]).The required number of common points needed to determine the coefficients and the amount of computation needed vary according to the order or degree of the polynomial. For example, a third-order polynomial, containing terms in φ and λ up to φ^3 and λ^3 requires ten coefficients denoted a_{ij}, and the ten in b_{ij} as in

eqn [10.22] determined by solving ten or more equations.

The third-order polynomial expression relating grid to geographical coordinates may be written in the form:

$$x = a_{00} + a_{10}\lambda a_{01}\varphi + a_{20}\lambda^2 + a_{11}\lambda\varphi + a_{02}\varphi^2 + a_{30}\lambda^3 \\ + a_{21}\lambda^2\varphi + a_{12}\lambda\varphi^2 + a_{03}\varphi^3$$
$$y = b_{00} + b_{10}\lambda + b_{01}\varphi + b_{20}\lambda^2 + b_{11}\lambda\varphi + b_{02}\varphi^2 + \\ b_{30}\lambda^3 + b_{21}\lambda^2\varphi + b_{12}\lambda\varphi^2 + b_{03}\varphi^3 \quad [10.22]$$

Similarly the polynomial equations used to transform from grid to grid are:

$$x = c_{00} + c_{10}x' + c_{01}y' + c_{20}x'^2 + c_{11}x'y' + c_{02}y'^2 + \\ c_{30}x'^3 + c_{21}x'^2y' + c_{12}x'y'^2 + c_{03}y'^3$$
$$y = d_{00} + d_{10}x' + d_{01}y' + d_{20}x'^2 + d_{11}x'y' + d_{02}y'^2 \\ + d_{30}x'^3 + d_{21}x'^2y' + d_{12}x'y'^2 + d_{03}y'^3 \quad [10.23]$$

In pre-computer days polynomial expressions were usually left in this form because it was generally easier to compute each term individually. However, in view of what has already been said about economy in the design of equations, a nested form of each equation may be obtained from a little algebraic rearrangement. For example, the expression for x in eqn [10.22] may also be written (Snyder 1985) as:

$$x = a_{00} + \varphi(a_{01} + a_{02}\varphi) + \lambda(a_{10} + \varphi(a_{11} + a_{12}\varphi)) + \\ \lambda^2(a_{20} + a_{21}\varphi + a_{30}\lambda)\ldots \quad [10.24]$$

This example is particularly instructive. Snyder (1985) has reported that the savings which result from using eqn [10.24] rather than the expression for x in eqn [10.22] are between 20 and 30 per cent in the solution of a fifth-order polynomial.

Snyder has also shown that conformal projections of the spheroid may be transformed more accurately (therefore requiring a lower-order polynomial) by using the isometric latitude ψ, in place of geodetic latitude in eqns [10.22]. For an explanation of the purpose and use of isometric, and other auxiliary latitudes, the reader is referred to Snyder (1987a) and Richardus and Adler (1972).

Determination of the polynomial coefficients

In order to find the 20 coefficients a_{ij}, b_{ij} in the third-order polynomials above, it is necessary to know the plane rectangular coordinates of 10 corresponding points x_i, y_i and φ_i, λ_i to form the linear equations from which the coefficients can be solved. The amount of data needed to determine the coefficients of a polynomial depends upon the order of the polynomial, which, in turn, depends upon the highest powers of the independent variables used in the terms. For example, first, second, third, fourth and fifth degree polynomials require a minimum of 3, 6, 10, 15 and 21 corresponding points respectively. The common solution is to use even more than these minimum numbers, to obtain the required coefficients by the method of least squares. This is the condition that the sum of squares of differences between the measured and the theoretical coordinates in the new projection should be minimized. Modern textbooks on survey adjustments and computations, for example, Cooper (1974), Mikhail (1976) and Methley (1986) all deal with this subject. The following ($m \times n$) matrix solution is applicable for any number of coefficients, n, and common points, m, but a practical limit is usually created by the capacity of the computer. It is well known in numerical analysis that although a polynomial may be extended to include higher powered terms in $\varphi^4, \lambda^4, \varphi^5, \lambda^5$, etc., the labour of determining the coefficients will hardly justify the extra computing time. Snyder (1985) provides the example of the solution of eqns [10.22] which shows that increasing the degree of the polynomial from third order to fourth order barely justifies the greater accuracy obtained for any purpose other than geodetic work.

In eqns [10.25] and [10.26], the individual coefficients form the column matrix on the left hand side and the control, or common point coordinates are the column matrix on the right hand side.

$$\begin{pmatrix} a_{00} \\ a_{01} \\ \ldots \\ \ldots \\ a_m \end{pmatrix} = \mathbf{D} \cdot \begin{pmatrix} x_1 \\ x_2 \\ \ldots \\ \ldots \\ x_m \end{pmatrix} \quad [10.25]$$

$$\begin{pmatrix} b_{00} \\ b_{01} \\ \ldots \\ \ldots \\ b_m \end{pmatrix} = \mathbf{D} \cdot \begin{pmatrix} y_1 \\ y_2 \\ \ldots \\ \ldots \\ y_m \end{pmatrix} \quad [10.26]$$

The matrix $\mathbf{D}$ is calculated from

$$\mathbf{D} = [\mathbf{A}^T . \mathbf{A}]^{-1} . \mathbf{A}^T \quad [10.27]$$

where the ($m \times n$) matrix $\mathbf{A}$ is formed from the geographical (or grid) coordinates of the corresponding points. Thus for the third degree polynomial requiring ten terms per line, $n = 10$

$$\mathbf{A} = \begin{pmatrix} 1 & \lambda_1 & \varphi_1 & \lambda_1^2 & \lambda_1\varphi_1 & \varphi_1^2 & \lambda_1^3 & \lambda_1^2\varphi_1 & \lambda_1\varphi_1^2 & \varphi_1^3 \\ 1 & \lambda_2 & \varphi_2 & \lambda_2^2 & \lambda_2\varphi_2 & \varphi_2^2 & \lambda_2^3 & \lambda_2^2\varphi_2 & \lambda_2\varphi_2^2 & \varphi_2^3 \\ \ldots & & & & & & & & & \ldots \\ \ldots & & & & & & & & & \ldots \\ 1 & \lambda_m & \varphi_m & \lambda_m^2 & \lambda_m\varphi_m & \varphi_m^2 & \lambda_m^3 & \lambda_m^2\varphi_m & \lambda_m\varphi_m^2 & \varphi_m^3 \end{pmatrix}$$

[10.28]

This solution is due to Wu and Yang (1981) with a fuller derivation by Snyder (1985). The method depends for its accuracy upon the size of the area mapped. This is because a polynomial transformation works well enough with homogeneous data, but a file comprising data digitized from a paper map may not be homogeneous because different parts of it have been affected differently by paper deformation. Just as it is necessary to treat separately the panels of a map which has at some time been folded, it may be necessary to divide the whole map into blocks and transform each block separately.

SOME FACTORS INFLUENCING THE CHOICE OF A SUITABLE PROJECTION

The principles and methods of transformation which have been described are applicable to maps of any scale. However, application of a GIS to a large country or even a continent necessitates choice of a projection, first to serve as the GIS framework and possibly as a suitable projection for displaying the results. It is a fundamental principle of distortion theory that the particular scales and, therefore, exaggeration of areas and angles increase from the origin of the projection towards its edges. Therefore, it is desirable to choose a projection in which either the average or the extreme distortions are small. The amount of distortion on a map depends upon the location, size and shape of the area to be mapped. Distortion is least in the representation of a small, compact country and greatest in maps of the whole world. The three variables – location, size and shape – usually determine the choice of origin, aspect and class of a suitable projection. These may be chosen by the graphical and analytical methods described by Maling (1973). These are based upon the principle that the distortion pattern, its fundamental property, remains constant within a particular projection even when the aspect of the projection is changed. Therefore, the plotted pattern of distortion isograms may be regarded as a frame which can be used to imagine how the distortion will occur, just as an artist may compose a picture by looking at objects through a small rectangular cardboard frame or a photographer uses the rectangular ground glass screen of the camera viewfinder.

In the pre-computer period when the methods were evolving, this was carried out using transparent overlays which were placed singly or in groups over a rough outline sketch map of the country or continent drawn at the same scale. By shifting the position and orientation of the overlay it is possible to estimate any advantage to be gained from a change in origin or change in orientation of the lines of zero distortion. The actual choice of projection depends upon comparison of the patterns of distortion isograms for different projections. When two or more overlays for different projections are superimposed, the extreme values for area scale or maximum angular deformation may be estimated from the isograms. Fig. 10.4 illustrates such a comparison.

It must be realized that the outlines shown on the underlying map are only a rough guide, for the detailed relationship between these and the isograms is only true for that aspect and projection upon which the map was compiled. The purpose of the outline is to indicate approximately the extent of the country or continent; it is the comparison between the distortion isograms which is important.

TOWARDS AN AUTOMATIC METHOD OF CHOICE OF MAP PROJECTION

Although the method just described was developed using sheets of transparent plastic to represent the overlays, this method of choice is obviously well suited to GIS applications. However, the author has no knowledge whether this particular application has yet been attempted so that there is plenty of scope for further research here.

The only example of the development of an interactive program intended to choose a suitable projection appears to be that by Jankowski and Nyerges (1989) who have tackled the problem in a

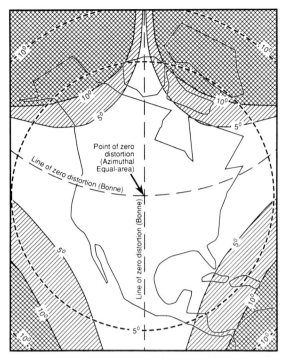

Fig. 10.4 The comparison of the relative merits of Bonne's projection and the Azimuthal Equal-area projection for a map of the North American continent. Both of these are equal-area projections so that the best way of comparing them is through maximum angular deformation, ω. The origin of both projections is the point with latitude 45° North, 100° West. Isograms for maximum angular deformation are shown for both projections at intervals of $\omega = 5°$ and 10°. The shaded patterns refer to the isograms for Bonne's projection. Note that the coastlines are drawn roughly to indicate their approximate location. They do not coincide with their positions on either of these projections accurately and are only an approximate guide to the extent of the area to be mapped. Although this example is for maps and systems of continental dimensions, the same method may be employed for comparison of maps for individual countries. In such cases the isograms would be for values of ω for every degree or even every half degree.

(*Source*: Maling 1973)

wholly different fashion. They have proceeded through the medium of existing software packages resulting in the series of programs which they have called the 'Map Projection Knowledge-Based System'. Among the many questions asked in the interactive development of a choice of projection, the user must specify a preference for special property which only distinguishes between conformality, equidistance and equivalence. The default is equivalence and there seems to be, at present, no way of selecting a projection which does not possess one of these special properties. At the stage when Jankowski and Nyerges published their paper, work on the system was still in progress.

REFERENCES

Arthur D W G (1978) Orthogonal transformations. *The American Cartographer* **5**: 72–4

Barton B A (1976) A note on the transformation of spherical coordinates. *The American Cartographer* **3**: 161–8

Briggs D, Mounsey H M (1989) Integrating land resource data into a European geographical information system: practicalities and problems. *Applied Geography* **9**: 5–20

Cocks K D, Walker P A, Parvey C A (1988) Evolution of a continental-scale geographical information system. *International Journal of Geographical Information Systems* **2**: 263–80

Cooper M A R (1974) *Fundamentals of Survey Measurement and Analysis*. Crosby Lockwood Staples, London

Dale P F (1991) Land information systems. In: Maguire D J, Goodchild M F, Rhind D W (eds.) *Geographical Information Systems: principles and applications*. Longman, London, pp. 85–99, Vol 2

Doytsher Y, Shmutter B (1981) Transformation of conformal projections for graphical purposes. *Canadian Surveyor* **35**: 395–404

Fisher P F (1991) Spatial data sources and data problems. In: Maguire D J, Goodchild M F, Rhind D W (eds.) *Geographical Information Systems: principles and applications*. Longman, London, pp. 175–89, Vol 1

ICA (International Cartographic Association) (1973) *Multilingual Dictionary of Technical Terms in Cartography*. ICA, Wiesbaden

Jackson J E (1980) *Sphere, Spheroid and Projections*. Granada, London

Jankowski P, Nyerges T (1989) Design considerations for MaPKBS-map projection knowledge-based system. *The American Cartographer* **16**: 85–95

King C W B (1988) Computational formulae for the Lambert conformal projection. *Survey Review* **29**: 229, 230, 323–37, 387–93

Maling D H (1968) The terminology of map projections. *International Yearbook of Cartography* **8**: 11–65

Maling D H (1973) *Coordinate Systems and Map Projections*. Philip, London

Maling D H (1989) *Measurements from Maps*. Pergamon Press, Oxford

Mather P M (1987) *Computer Processing of Remotely-sensed Images: an introduction*. Wiley, Chichester

Methley B D F (1986) *Computational Models in Surveying and Photogrammetry*. Blackie, Glasgow

Mikhail E M (1976) *Observations and Least Squares*. IEP-Dun-Donnelly Harper & Row, New York

Mounsey H M (1991) Multisource multinational environmental GIS: lessons learnt from CORINE. In: Maguire D J, Goodchild M F, Rhind D W (eds.) *Geographical Information Systems: principles and applications*. Longman, London, pp. 185–200, Vol 2

O'Callaghan J F, Garner B J (1991) Land and geographical information systems in Australia. In: Maguire D J, Goodchild M F, Rhind D W (eds.) *Geographical Information Systems: principles and applications*. Longman, London, pp. 57–70, Vol 2

Richardus P, Adler R K (1972) *Map Projections for Geodesists, Cartographers and Geographers*. North-Holland, Amsterdam

Royal Society (1966) *Glossary of Technical Terms in Cartography*. Royal Society, London

Shmutter B (1981) Transforming conic conformal to TM coordinates. *Survey Review* **26**: 130–6, 201

Sievers J, Bennat H (1989) Reference systems for maps and digital information systems of Antarctica. *Antarctic Science* **1**: 351–62

Snyder J P (1985) Computer-assisted map projection research. *US Geological Survey Bulletin* **1629**. US Government Printing Office, Washington

Snyder J P (1987a) Map projections – a working manual. *US Geological Survey Professional Paper* **1395**. US Government Printing Office, Washington

Snyder J P (1987b) Differences due to projection for the same USGS quadrangle. *Surveying and Mapping* **47**: 199–206

Snyder J P (1987c) Labeling projections on published maps. *The American Cartographer* **14**: 21–7

Sprinsky W H (1987) Transformation of positional geographic data from paper-based map products. *The American Cartographer* **14**: 359–66

Vincenty T (1971) The meridional distance problem for desk computers. *Survey Review* **21**: 136–40, 161

Vincenty T (1989) The flat earth concept in local surveys. *Surveying and Mapping* **49**: 101–2

Williams W B P (1982) The Transverse Mercator Projection – simple but accurate formulae for small computers. *Survey Review* **26**: 205, 307–20

Wray T (1974) The seven aspects of a general map projection. *Cartographica Monograph* **11**, 72 pp.

Wu, Zhong-xing, Yang, Qi-he (1981) A research on the transformation of map projections in computer-aided cartography, *Paper presented at the 10th International Cartographic Conference Tokyo*, 22 pp.

11

LANGUAGE ISSUES FOR GIS

A U FRANK AND D M MARK

Interaction with computing systems can take place in formal or natural language. This chapter reviews the role of language in GIS, with particular emphasis on the design of user interfaces. Formal languages have their roots in the models used to conceptualize and represent geographical data, and here there are strong parallels between language, and its implications for patterns of human reasoning, and the models adopted by GIS. Natural language has subtle and mostly unrecognized effects on the structuring of space, and these become particularly important in a cross-linguistic context. Later sections of the chapter review the significance of natural language interfaces in GIS, particularly in such applications as vehicle navigation systems, and the problems presented by linguistic boundaries.

INTRODUCTION: DEFINITION OF TERMS

Users must be able to interact with GIS. For this reason, it is important to study how communication between users and GIS can be made most effective. In the past, for GIS, as for other information systems, most of the effort in this area has been centred on constructing appropriate query and command languages. The approaches proposed have been to use natural language or to construct formal languages. This chapter reviews and discusses why language issues in a broad sense, including cognitive issues, are crucial for the further development of GIS.

Natural languages comprise the 'everyday languages' that people use – English, French, German, Chinese, Spanish, and so on – with all their rules, exceptions and 'idiomatic' expressions. In principle, natural languages have three components: a vocabulary (lexicon), listing words (terms) that are used; a syntax and grammar, which describe how valid sentences can be formed from these words; and semantics, indicating what the sentences mean. None of these can be fully formalized (at least not today). The language that native speakers actually use is much richer and of more interest to GIS than the 'prescriptive' view of the language defined by dictionaries, academics and grammarians.

Formal languages, on the other hand, are artificially constructed languages, following formally defined rules. These too have vocabulary, syntax and semantics, and often are modelled on natural languages, but in these cases all of the components are fully described in a rigorous format.

The use of either natural or formal language to query a GIS may result in problems such as how to describe the information needs of a user. If natural language is used, the program must 'translate' the question into an unambiguous form which can be processed. This can be difficult, given the complex structure of natural languages. On the other hand, if users are made to express a query in a formal language format, they are forced to learn this language and to translate their information needs into this format. This has the potential to limit a user's ability to interact with systems, and also limit system access itself to specialized and trained individuals.

In the past, designers of formal query languages have not paid much direct attention to the linguistic aspects of the problem. Instead, they have selected formal structures following well-known models, probably inadvertently introducing structural elements of their own natural language. The tendency for the formal language to mimic the structure of the designer's natural language will make such systems easier to use for speakers of the same language, but perhaps more difficult for other users.

The terminology used formally has not always been based on concepts that people would use naturally; this applies to all information systems. In geographical systems, discussions on design have mostly been centred on the formulation of GIS queries, and have not considered the visualization and interaction necessary to inform the user of the result.

In this chapter a comprehensive approach is advocated. People use a finite set of concepts to organize their perception of space. These concepts should be respected when designing systems to communicate regarding spatial situations, both when users formulate queries and when responses are presented to them. On the other hand, computers require formal definition of terms in order to retrieve the necessary information. Thus the communication process can be seen as a translation between human spatial concepts and the formal spatial concepts in a computer program.

The discussion in this chapter is on a conceptual, logical level, and does not attempt to explain how these methods should be implemented. It seems very important that the GIS literature separates the concepts involved in a program from the mechanics of its implementation as a program. Such a separation has been advocated in a database design standard (Tsichritzis and Klug 1975), separating the conceptual database schema from the physical storage arrangement (internal schema). The standard also defines a third, external schema, namely 'user views', which describes subsets of the conceptual view, as appropriate for a specific task and which may be different from the 'corporate' view (Fig. 11.1).

The confusion in GIS literature between concepts and implementation is a severe impediment to progress in the field. Discussion is needed to determine what a system does independently from how it is achieved, especially in light of the extremely rapid development of the computer tools, where the 'how' might change overnight. The discussion of the 'what' is intrinsically linked to cognitive and linguistic issues,

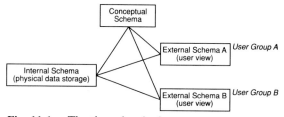

Fig. 11.1. The three-level schema.

and this chapter discusses the 'conceptual' and 'user view' (in terms of the standard mentioned above) and their relations.

MATHEMATICAL FORMALISMS FOR GEOGRAPHICAL INFORMATION

A computer is a machine whose chief function is to execute a set of instructions which manipulate symbols. These symbols are selected and structured to represent some situation in the real world, as it is perceived by people. The critical problem is that an individual's cognitive methods are informal and fluid, and allow ambiguities or contradictions to exist. The data processing in a computer is formal and follows strict rules of logic; even when computers are used to mimic 'fuzzy' human reasoning, a strict formalism is used to explain the fuzziness (e.g. Zadeh 1974).

In GIS a structure to represent spatial situations (as perceived by people) must be formally defined. Once defined, the appropriate operations and their outcome must also be defined. This is a language issue, as the objects and the operations applicable to them are defined in terms of the GIS user's chosen spatial language (Woodcock and Loomes 1989).

Despite the fact that space is a fundamental, everyday notion, its formalization is not simple. People sometimes look to the objects that fill space, thus treating space as an attribute of the objects (this follows a Kantian viewpoint). Or, it is possible to look at space and the properties of objects that are encountered at each point, and thus attributes and objects become properties of the location (following a more Descartian viewpoint). People use both these methods interchangeably, depending on what is more suitable for the task at hand.

The well-known concepts of Euclidean geometry (see Gatrell 1991 in this volume), which seem to be fully consistent with an appropriate concept of space, in fact help to obscure the problem. In fact, Euclidean geometry captures only limited and highly abstracted aspects of geometry and space. One aspect of the abstraction is the concept of a continuum of possible coordinates, positions and lengths. This may be fully consistent with the view held by scientists, engineers and many other GIS users, but does not apply strictly to all human experience and inference. Perhaps more critical, the real numbers and continuity they apply cannot formally and perfectly be implemented on finite computer systems, and this technical misspecification may occasionally influence results. For example, in a Euclidean, real-numbered world, a precise polygon overlay procedure (no tolerances or 'snapping') could combine three coverages in a way that would not be order dependent; however, when all coordinates are represented on a computer, order dependency may result.

The conceptual implications of these two major geometrical data models (feature based or location based) are discussed in this chapter. Computer scientists generally use the term 'data model' for the tools or methods that are available to describe the conceptual structure of the data, that is, the language available to describe reality or our perception of reality; this is different from some uses in the GIS literature. The consequences of the internal representation and the data structures necessary to implement these two views, often referred to as 'vector' and 'raster', are treated elsewhere in this volume (Egenhofer and Herring 1991 in this volume). Here, the discussion concentrates only on how people interact with the data stored in the GIS. This is parallel to the discussion regarding data models, primarily the network and the relational model (Codd 1982), in computer science. The discussion of user interfaces here is thus, in principle, on a purely conceptual level and in theory, completely independent from implementation; in practical terms, however, it is not known how to translate between the two major geometrical data models without small but observable differences.

The extension of these concepts to three-dimensional GIS problems will not be trivial; because 3-D GIS is a fairly new and as yet small subfield, such problems will not be discussed here (Raper 1989; Turner 1990; see also Raper and Kelk 1991 in this volume).

Regular tessellation models

A system with a square regular tessellation geometrical data model (a raster) is built on the notion of a subdivision of space into cells of regular size and shape (Fig. 11.2). Methods other than subdivision in squares have been studied (Diaz and Bell 1986) but are not widely used (Fig. 11.3). For implementation in a data structure, regular subdivisions of space, which allow a hierarchical structuring of areas of varying size are very convenient (Fig. 11.4). An example of this is the very popular quadtree structure (Samet 1984). This, however, does not alter the conceptual data model and the behaviour of the operations at the user interface. Everything a raster system can do a quadtree system can do, and vice versa – the only noticeable difference would be the execution speed and other computer resource requirements.

Fig. 11.2. Example raster.

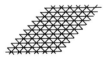

Fig. 11.3. An alternative tessellation.

Fig. 11.4. A hierarchical square raster.

For each raster cell, values for all attributes can be made available to the user. The concept can be thought of as an array with integer indices, where each array cell contains a value for each attribute of interest. This can also be visualized as a superposition of similar arrays, which each contain the attribute values for one property.

map : property $\times i_x \times i_y$ *-->> value*

Based on this geometric data model, a 'map algebra' can be built (Tomlin 1983a, 1983b, 1989). Operations are defined such that they have one or two maps as input and produce a new map according to a specific rule. This output map has exactly the same spatial structure as the input map (but a different content) and can thus be used as input in further operations.

Irregular tessellation model

The alternative is an irregular subdivision of space, an 'irregular tessellation' geometric data model (Fig. 11.5). This model is based on the concept of cells as defined by algebraic topology (Alexandroff 1961; Giblin 1977; Spanier 1966). Each cell has a specific dimension; terminology varies:

0-cell = point, node, vertex;
1-cell = line, arc, edge;
2-cell = area, region, cell.

Each cell is bounded by cells of lower dimension, for example, a line is bounded by two points at each end and each cell is the boundary for some cells of higher dimension, for example, a line is the boundary between two areas. For all points, coordinate values are given that determine their location. Also in some systems, the lines between nodes can have arbitrary shape, in others they are restricted to straight lines. In order to simplify implementation it has been argued that only triangular cells – or generally simplices – should be allowed and other cells subdivided accordingly (Frank and Kuhn 1986).

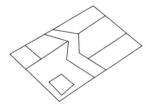

Fig. 11.5. Example of an irregular tessellation.

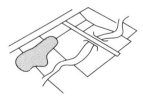

Fig. 11.6. The integrated data model.

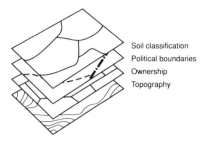

Fig. 11.7. The layered model.

Using an irregular tessellation as a geometrical foundation, three views are possible:

- An 'integrated geometry' concept, where all the layers are integrated at once and the cells are the largest areas for which all attribute values are homogeneous (Fig. 11.6). Nevertheless a 'layer view' can be established as a 'user view' utilizing the operations of the map algebra.

- A 'layer' concept (Fig. 11.7), where each layer represents a single property and the cells in this layer show the largest spatial units that have a common attribute value for this property (e.g. a layer for 'soil classification' and another one for 'ownership'). The user can then overlay, or combine, these layers and produce new layers. The operations are similar to the map algebra mentioned previously.

- An 'object' concept, where attention concentrates on the individual objects, each having geometrical and non geometrical properties. In this view, the fact that all objects fill the space (or even create the space) is not stressed.

Properly built software should allow these three viewpoints to coexist on top of a single data collection. Each of these viewpoints, however, is sufficiently different from the others to require its own language for a user to think about, to formulate queries with, and to understand the responses from the system.

Earlier, GIS were built as collections of points and lines – sometimes referred to as 'spaghetti' (Fig. 11.8). The lines were just lines and all intersections had to be deduced from coordinates. The points represented either point features or areas (centroids) whose boundaries had to be sought in the collection of lines using operations from analytical geometry. Again, this is essentially an 'irregular tessellation' data model as all equivalent properties can be deduced. These deductions are not only costly in terms of computer operations, but also they cannot be executed reliably (i.e. without leading to internal contradictions) on a finite computer. Thus users can observe artefacts which are due to the limitations of the specific implementation.

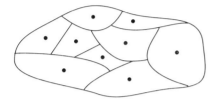

Fig. 11.8. An example of spaghetti: note the undershoots and overshoots at junctions.

In the irregular tessellation data model, topological relations are included (it is thus a 'full topology' model). The neighbours of each cell are known. The topology in the model is very often also used to verify that the actual data are a valid representation of a topologically correct situation (Corbett 1975, 1979). Of course, in a 'regular tessellation' model, topology is also included, although it is implicit in the tessellation pattern and tile numbering system.

The regular tessellation and earlier, line-based representations should in principle be equivalent. In practice, however, they are not – the limitations of computers as finite machines affect the exact behaviour of the operations. It is a reasonable assumption that the spatial resolution of a regular tessellation model (i.e. the fineness of the grid of cells) is much coarser than the spatial resolution of an irregular tessellation model (i.e. how many bits are used for point coordinates); typical examples are 100 m cells for the one and coordinate values with centimetre precision, which results in a 10^4 ratio of resolutions. This results in observable differences between corresponding operations executed in one or the other system.

Other geometric data models

The two models discussed present methods to deal with situations where space is subdivided in mutually exclusive and collectively exhaustive cells.

There are phenomena for which these models are not appropriate. In this subsection two additional models are briefly mentioned.

Feature based models

If only isolated features are of interest, like roads, rivers, lakes or settlements, localized in space but without concern for the areas between them, using an irregular tessellation model may be inappropriate. Instead, a number of GIS have been built around a geometrical data model that includes:

- point features,
- linear features,
- areal features,

each defined by sets of coordinates. Details of individual models differ (Burton 1979; Cox, Rhind and Aldred 1980). A number of alternatives are discussed in the proposed US cartographic data exchange standard (Digital Cartographic Data Standards Task Force (DCDSTF) 1988).

Continuous field

Other phenomena, like temperature, magnetic fields, and so on, are thought of as continuous, that is, for every point in space there is a value and the values change gradually. The phenomenon is organized, mathematically speaking, as a function of the location in space $f(x,y)$. If there is a single value (not a vector) associated with each point, the field may be visualized as a continuous surface. The mapping from a point in space to a value can be determined by a mathematical formula or interpolated from measured values. Current GIS are not designed to handle such phenomena directly.

COGNITIVE SCIENCE, NATURAL LANGUAGE AND GEOGRAPHICAL SPACE

What is cognitive science?

The conceptual basis for this treatment of models of geographical space comes primarily from the field of cognitive science. George Lakoff offered the following definition:

> 'Cognitive science is a new field that brings together what is known about the mind from many academic disciplines: psychology, linguistics, anthropology, philosophy, and computer science. It seeks answers to such questions as:
>
> - What is reason?
> - How do we make sense of our experiences?
> - What is a conceptual system and how is it organized?
> - Do all people use the same conceptual system?
> - If so, what is that system?
> - If not, exactly what is there that is common to the way all human beings think?
>
> The questions aren't new, but some recent answers are'. (Lakoff 1987: xi)

Why is such a field introduced here? A fundamental premise of this work is that a main objective of GIS is to allow the user of the system to interact vicariously with actual or possible phenomena of the world (Mark 1989). From this, it follows that models of the human mind, and in particular how our minds deal with concepts and objects of geographical space, are a strict prerequisite to designing effective GIS. This is a bold claim and the need for explicit cognitively based data models as a basis for GIS data structures can be questioned. However, there is little question that effective user interfaces must be based at least in part on such models.

The Rosch–Lakoff–Johnson model of cognitive categories

The mathematical concepts that are typically used to provide data models and structures for GIS include classical set theory and, in particular, the idea of geographical concepts, regions and areal objects as sets. In the classical model, every member of a set is an equally good example of it, and furthermore there is some necessary and sufficient set of properties for determining whether some object is or is not a member of a set. The first part of this model would predict, for example, that every familiar bird would be an equally good example of the class of all birds. However, it is known that, when people are asked to give an example of a bird, they tend to give 'robin' or 'sparrow' or 'canary' far more often than they give 'ostrich' or 'penguin' or 'duck'; this is the concept of prototypes.

The second part of the model (necessary and sufficient observable properties to define set membership) also breaks down when applied to cognitive concepts. The repeated and largely unsatisfying attempts by quantitative and statistical geographers to use techniques such as discriminant analysis to define classic geographical regions such as the American 'corn belt', or 'Appalachia' are an indication that such regions are not equivalent to classical sets.

Whereas such problems with set theory were noted early on, it was the research and writings of Eleanor Rosch (1973, 1978) that provided a clear statement of the problem and summary for the evidence. Several solutions have been proposed, including the 'fuzzy set theory' of Zadeh (1974). Smith and Medin (1981) also treat the problem in great detail. They propose two groups of solutions. One group is probabilistic and is related to fuzzy set theory. While many of the problems of classical set theory are solved, solutions in this group still contain fundamental flaws, especially in the way they treat conjunctions of classes. The other approach discussed by Smith and Medin involves the concept of exemplars. Classes are defined by exemplars and by rules for establishing similarity to these exemplars. The image-schema model of cognition (Johnson 1987) and the broader philosophical position termed experiential realism (Lakoff 1987), appear to provide an even more appropriate basis for concept modelling. Rather than using actual instances as exemplars, classes have idealized or generalized prototypes. These prototypes for classes can in turn be based largely on a small number of schemata that embody properties and transmit them, through prototypes, to class members:

> 'A schema is that portion of the entire perceptual cycle which is internal to the perceiver, modifiable by experience, and

somehow specific to what is being perceived. The schema accepts information as it becomes available at sensory surfaces and is changed by that information; it directs movements and exploratory activities that make more information available, by which it is further modified.' (Neiser 1976: 54)

Johnson (1987) follows Neiser in claiming that mental activities such as perception and cognition are heavily influenced by what Johnson calls image-schemata, which he defines as follows: 'A schema consists of a small number of parts and relations, by virtue of which it can structure indefinitely many perceptions, images, and events. In sum, image-schemata operate at a level of mental organization that falls between abstract propositional structure, on the one side, and particular concrete images on the other' (Johnson 1987: 29). He goes on to add: '... much of the structure, value, and purposiveness we take for granted as built into our world consists chiefly of interwoven and superimposed schemata...' (Johnson 1987: 126). Recently, Mark (1989) has discussed how an image-schematic model of geographical categories and concepts might operate, and how it could relate to concepts of 'user views' of a geographical database.

Sapir–Wharf hypothesis about language and thought extends this logically to the idea that speakers of different languages may think differently, at least about some topics (Lakoff 1987: 304–37).

A central issue involves the concepts of 'language universals' and 'language primitives'. A universal would be a property that applies to all natural languages. Explicit universals may be non-existent, but it is possible to turn to look for primitives, building blocks that may themselves be universal, and from which linguistic expressions can be built. Obviously, identifying such items would be essential to the design of a multilingual, natural language understanding system. Some of the primitives for the language of geographical space seem to be exactly the topological relations used in graph theory and in GIS, as discussed above. The image-schemata of Johnson (1987) form another set of primitives (Mark 1989). The search for still more conceptual primitives for geographical space, and the study of how they combine in particular languages, is an open research question, and a critical part of the research agenda. There is little doubt that geographers and others in the GIS community will make substantial contributions to cognitive science in this area.

How language structures space

In the introduction to an earlier section, the term 'data model' was used for the tools or methods that are available to describe the conceptual structure of the data, that is, the language available to describe reality or perception of it. If 'cognitive/linguistic model' is substituted for 'data model', this is almost exactly the thesis of Leonard Talmy in his seminal paper, 'How language structures space' (Talmy 1983). The basic idea that Talmy presents in that paper is that human natural languages provide individual speakers with a set of terms that are linked to cognitive concepts. Then, consistent with the ideas of schemata discussed above, these mental concepts constrain the way people think, reason, and talk about both perceptual spaces, which can be seen from one viewpoint, and geographical spaces, which must be integrated over repeated experiences of parts of space. The somewhat controversial

Fundamental spatial relations

Freeman (1975) produced an important and early review paper on formal representation of spatial relations. He proposed that the following form a complete set of primitive spatial relations for elements in a (2-D) picture, a view of everyday (3-D) object space:

1. left of;
2. right of;
3. beside (alongside, next to);
4. above (over, higher than, on to);
5. below (under, underneath, lower than);
6. behind (in back of);
7. in front of;
8. near (close to, next to);
9. far;
10. touching;

11. between;
12. inside (within); and
13. outside.

Note that this is not a minimal set of relations, since some can be defined as combinations of others.

Freeman's list is very similar to the list of terms presented by Abler (1987: 306) in his discussion of the research agenda for 'Geographical Information and Analysis'. The cardinal directions can be added to Freeman's list through the addition of one more axiom. If 'north' is associated with 'up', then by deduction, 'south = down', 'west = left', and 'east = right' can follow. Peuquet and Zhan (1987) extended Freeman's relation set in exactly this way, including the cardinal directions as spatial relations without comment, and substituting 'north' for 'above' and 'south' for 'below' in the example they drew from Freeman's paper (Peuquet and Zhan 1987: 66). Note that the 'north = up' axiom is quite arbitrary. Indeed, the etymology of the Indo-European root for the word 'north' is based on 'left' (Svorou 1988); this relation results from an earlier 'east = forward' convention, and world maps in Medieval times were presented with an east up orientation.

Some cultural and linguistic groups, including the Hawaiians, use a radial coordinate system for referencing in geographical space (see Mark, Svorou and Zubin 1987). This uses the 'inside–outside' dichotomy of the Container image-schemata (see Mark 1989) for one spatial dimension, and 'toward some landmark' (spatial action, rather than relation) as the other. Other island peoples use similar spatial reference frames (see Haugen, 1957, for a discussion of this for Iceland).

Herskovits (1985, 1987) has discussed formal and computational models for locative expressions in English. In particular, she discusses about 30 'use types' for the English prepositions 'in', 'on' and 'at'. Recently, Mark (1989) has proposed a link between the image-schemata model of Johnson (1987) and the models of Herskovits. For example, conceptualizing something as a Container means that an English speaker is likely to use the preposition 'in'. The use of 'in' would, in turn, cause the listener or reader to use a similar Container schema in interpreting the meaning of the expression.

SPATIAL QUERY LANGUAGES AND DATABASE INTERFACES

Requirements for a query language

A query language is the tool a user needs in order to extract data from a database and present the result in a useful format. The query is expressed in a language understandable by the query execution program. Thus the query processor must fulfil two important functions:

- Select the subset of the data the user needs.
- Render the selected data in a format that is meaningful to the user.

This section concentrates on the expressive power, that is, what can be specified with a given language, and does not discuss the specific syntax or implementation issue. The discussion is restricted to properties in which spatial query languages differ from ordinary query languages, as they are commonly used for administrative data processing. Eight requirements for a spatial query language are listed, which deal with the selection of data and with its representation (Egenhofer 1989c).

Spatial selection criteria

The user will need to select data to be retrieved, not only based on predicates over attribute values (e.g. the standard question 'select all employees with salary > 50 000') but also based on spatial properties (e.g. 'select all parcels owned by Smith and on or within 100 metres of a lake or pond'). The query language must be extended with predicates to select data based on 'neighbour', 'connected to', 'inside', and so on. Such an extension should be systematic, that is, the set of predicates covers all cases and the predicates have meaningful relations to each other. The predicates must then be given a formal meaning in terms of one of the geometrical data models explained before. An arbitrary set of terms from, say, the English language is not a good starting point. For a subset of spatial relations, namely the topological ones, a systematic set has been established (Egenhofer 1989a). From these proposed base relationships, the user can construct more complex ones, with specific meaning appropriate to the application.

Selection based on pointing

Users of a GIS will naturally ask questions like 'what is this?', or 'who owns this building?'. The query syntax must, therefore, be extended to accept as values objects visible on the screen to which the user points. Integration of pointing gestures with queries is one of the central concepts of the CUBRICON interface (Neal and Shapiro 1990; Neal *et al.* 1989).

These requirements deal primarily with the selection of data for retrieval. The following group of requirements deal with rendering of the result on the screen. The standard query languages, as used in administrative data processing, assume automatically that the result of the query can be displayed in the form of a table; this is obviously not true for a GIS, where many outputs will be in map form.

Combination of query results

The visual integration of the result from more than one query is an important feature of a GIS. It must be possible to specify that the result of a new query is added to (superimposed on) the already displayed map, that it is removed from it, or that the objects selected are highlighted to make them easier to find.

Spatial context

The result of a spatial query cannot always be interpreted by itself, for example, the query 'show the town of Orono' would result in a point with a label on an otherwise empty screen as shown in Fig. 11.9 – this is hardly useful (Egenhofer and Frank 1988; Frank 1982). The query language must, therefore, include a means for the users to specify the necessary context needed to understand the result as in Fig. 11.10 (e.g. 'show AS TOPO SHEET ....', directing the system to use the standard content of a topographic map). It should also include default rules, such as how a query is expanded to include a minimal context, if the user opted not to specify one. This is necessary, because although context is ubiquitous in human interaction, people are not used to thinking about the context explicitly, and thus it is especially onerous for users to deal with context explicitly.

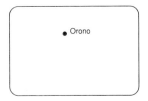

Fig. 11.9. The town of Orono, showing no context.

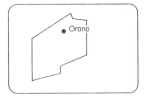

Fig. 11.10. As Fig. 11.9 but with some context (outline of the containing state).

Selection of query window

Access to data in a spatial database is usually explicitly or implicitly restricted by an 'area of interest', for example, 'show all school buildings' means 'show all school buildings in the Orono school administration district'. Again, the query language must include methods to describe the area of interest and contain rules for how a default is selected if the user does not specify one (e.g. use the value of the previous query).

Description of scale

In some instances a display must have a certain scale to be specified by the user.

Description of map legend

The map legend describes a mapping between the data objects in the database and their graphical rendering. The user must be able to select a map legend and change it when necessary.

Differentiate representation based on attribute values

Users often need to observe how an attribute value is spatially distributed (e.g. which houses in a city were built in which year). It is customary in manual cartography to build classes for objects with similar values and assign specific graphical values to them (e.g. colour, raster) (Bertin 1983). Thus the query language for a GIS must essentially include everything that is necessary to specify choropleth and similar maps.

SQL extensions

A number of research projects (Egenhofer 1984; Egenhofer 1989b; Egenhofer and Frank 1988; Frank 1982) and some GIS manufacturers (Herring, Larsen and Shivakumar 1988; Ingram and Phillips 1987) have addressed the problem of constructing a GIS query language by selecting a standard database query language and exploring what extensions would be necessary. Most often the SQL language, based on the relational data model, is used as a starting point (ANSI X3H2 1985; Chamberlin and Boyce 1974; Chamberlin et al. 1976). It is very obvious that a language that contains commands to deal with all these problems must be quite extensive and hence may become difficult to learn. Most of the extensions which have been studied fulfil only some of the requirements and are limited to the most important extensions using default methods for other parameters (for an overview see Egenhofer 1989c).

The conclusions drawn from these efforts to extend SQL are:

- Extending SQL with spatial relations and operators is straightforward once the semantics of the relations are formally defined (Pullar and Egenhofer 1988).

- SQL is not as easy to use for complex queries as is often claimed [it is much better than the previous proposals (Reisner, Boyce and Chamberlin 1975), but it was designed in the early 1970's and is considered dated]. GIS queries tend to include complex conditions, which require careful planning for translation into SQL.

- Extending SQL to include pointing as input is feasible, but no syntax or flow of actions that have been found are compatible with natural language/human cognitive patterns. A new keyword PICK (Frank 1982) or MOUSE (Ingram and Phillips 1987) has been created which can be used anywhere an object is required. During query execution the user is then asked to point to the appropriate object.

- It is advisable to build a separate SQL styled command language to deal with the graphical output issues, and not include these commands into the SQL select-from-where clause. This language will become quite complex.

GIS query languages based on direct manipulation

The SQL language which is most often extended for GIS query languages is a typed language with traditional syntax and keywords. Since its design, a new paradigm for constructing user interfaces, based on direct manipulation, has been developed and applied successfully (e.g. the Apple Macintosh personal computer) (Shneiderman 1983, 1987; Smith et al. 1983). Some attempts to apply these concepts to query languages in general (Jackson 1990; Kuhn 1991) and to GIS in particular have been studied (Egenhofer and Frank 1988).

It has been found that the construction of a direct manipulation-based interface for a raster-based system is feasible and a number of implementations are known (Intergraph 1989; Pazner, Kirby and Thies 1989; Jackson 1990). The regular conceptual structure of the data model can be translated to visual objects and their manipulations. This could be extended to an 'irregular tessellation' data model, when the 'layer' structure is stressed. This type of interface is based on processes which combine or otherwise manipulate the 'layers'. It is procedural and the user is responsible for combining the processes in the correct order to achieve the desired result.

On the other hand, constructing non-procedural, purely descriptive spatial query languages for GIS with an object oriented user view is more difficult. Translating a keyword based language more or less literally to a screen-based input reduces some of the complexity of the interface – the user need not remember the keywords and is prompted for the parameters – and thus makes the interface more versatile and usable. However, it does not reduce the cognitive complexity of the object and operations.

More promising is the selection of appropriate metaphors and their correct visualization for a GIS query facility. The authors have explored metaphors for the 'pan' and 'zoom' operation which is very powerful in selecting the area of interest and will be expanding it to other suitable tasks, e.g. the selection of content (Jackson 1990; Kuhn 1991).

NATURAL LANGUAGE PROCESSING FOR GIS

Beyond being a basis for design of formal languages and associated data structures, natural language studies are themselves important issues for the designers of GIS for several distinct reasons. The most difficult problem in dealing with natural language in a computational sense is to understand its meaning. People understand each other based on both the formal and conventional structure of their language, and on a large collection of perceptual and cognitive experiences discussed. For a computer, the 'understanding' of natural language is taken to mean that the computer acts on commands, queries and other linguistic input with a response similar to the one that would be given by a person in a similar situation. Similarly, ideal natural language output by a computer will evoke in a human reader reactions that are similar to those which would be given to words and sentences generated by a person. Of course, this is more or less a restatement of the 'Turing test' of artificial intelligence fame, and a general solution is not expected immediately. However, for a limited domain such as GIS, or particularly for some GIS application area, success, or at least substantial progress, seems to be a reasonable expectation.

One important application of natural language processing in GIS involves the potential for the input of queries and commands in natural language; whereas natural language queries in typed form may be of only limited utility, natural language commands and queries will become a common form of system interaction when real-time interpretation of normal speech becomes practical. Next, increasing need for input of geographical data and information in text form is foreseen, ranging from text on biological specimen labels to interpretation of newspaper articles, explorers' journals, or tape-recorded field notes. Natural language production for limited domains, such as generation of verbal descriptions of routes for drivers is already possible, and currently is being extended to other, relatively simple cases and domains, such as the production of legal boundary descriptions for parcels of land.

More general natural language text generation is further away, but production of grammatically correct descriptive paragraphs for direct inclusion in reports would be a desirable feature of future GIS.

Natural language input for queries and commands to GIS

In general terms, natural language understanding is still very difficult to implement. The problem of 'understanding' natural language in this sense can be restated as a problem of 'translating' between natural languages and formal languages within a very limited domain. For such a translation, among other things, a better, more formal understanding of spatial terms in natural language is needed, as well as more complete, formal geometrical data models, and, last but not least, translation methods between them. It is apparent that people may use several concepts of geometry and of geographical space, depending on the task, and a single, unified geometrical data model that satisfies all expectations has not yet been found. Therefore, translations between partial formal systems of geometrical reasoning may be necessary. Such translations are, mathematically speaking, mappings between algebraic systems (i.e. morphism) (see Egenhofer and Herring 1991 in this volume).

There are generally three advantages seen in natural languages query and command input:

- The system user needs less training ('everybody knows natural language').

- The user can better represent demands ('natural language is the best representation of human thought').

- Commands can be issued faster ('we speak faster than we type').

It is not clear whether the argument that natural language reduces training requirements applies to the GIS situation: it is based on the assumption that users are conversing with the system about objects of their daily experience for which they possess an adequate vocabulary. This is not necessarily the case. The current systems are still quite restricted in their representation of space and spatial situations. Thus users have to learn how to translate their concepts into the concepts of the system; therefore, training is required to convey to the user the concepts the system uses. It is possible to argue that training the user in the system's formal command language is an effective method to convey to the user the concepts that are utilized in the system. However, these arguments are not yet based on experience, given the lack of natural language systems. Thus the examples in training sessions show not only how commands are used, but also what they achieve and when they can be used – this is in the best of all possible worlds, where training is effectively organized and delivered.

It is further doubtful that the second argument, that natural language is the best expression for ideas, holds. It is not evident that there is a natural language expression for all spatial concepts that well-versed professionals use (e.g. experienced planners). Professional jargon is rife with artificially constructed words or ordinary words that are used with a different meaning. Again training in a formal language would establish a coherent vocabulary. Finally, understanding the natural language input is not sufficient for a system to be usable. If users have to detail every explanation in the most intricate manner and cannot rely on the 'common sense' and general understanding of goals, the circumstances of the task, they will not experience the natural language dialogue as natural.

Thus, natural language may become a very important input in the future for certain GIS applications. Natural language in itself does not solve many of the problems of GIS query languages and most of the problems discussed above in the section on formal query languages apply at least in part to natural language interfaces.

Natural language queries and commands

The process of natural language understanding should deal with the understanding of spoken language. Equipment is currently available to understand a limited vocabulary of spoken natural language, as issued by arbitrary speakers, or to understand a larger (but still limited) vocabulary by a speaker for whom the system has been trained. Typically, such equipment can only recognize words spoken with clean breaks between them (so-called discrete speech), and cannot cope with the continuous speech that people usually utter. Systems should also understand unrestricted vocabulary. Programs to analyse typed natural language sentences with a limited domain vocabulary and somewhat limited syntactical structure are available; users of these systems must either rephrase statements or be able to train the system to understand new terms.

For effective natural language interaction with GIS, systems will need to understand dialogue and not just isolated sentences. Research in dialogue understanding is underway, and has been applied to GIS situations. Such research should lead to usable systems within a few years. It also will be necessary to understand gestures and other non-verbal input, integrated with speech, since discussion of spatial situations between people typically involves substantial amounts of non-verbal gestures, sketches, and so on (Neal and Shapiro 1990). Despite some interesting results in advanced research the routine use of such tools is still a few years away.

Input of textual geographical data to GIS

Considerable amounts of geographical data are collected not in the form of maps and diagrams but in textual form. In perhaps the most prominent current example, there are many millions of biological specimens in museums and herbaria; current efforts to computerize such collections are similar to the production of computerized catalogues for libraries, but also include a desire to geocode the data to allow for mapping and for entry into GIS (McGranaghan and Wester 1988). But, although these specimens have labels on which the locality data and collecting date are indicated, the location is hardly ever in the form of coordinates or a map – rather, it is in the form of natural language (McGranaghan 1989). For the small labels on birds and insects, the location may be just a place name. For plant specimens, which usually are mounted on paper, providing more room for description, the place name often is supplemented by a verbal description, roughly equivalent to instructions for relocating the site (McGranaghan 1989). If such data can be automatically analysed and translated to spatial locations in a GIS, they could be subject to both mapping and advanced forms of spatial analysis, and thus become far more valuable, especially for endangered species, which are often more common as museum specimens than as living examples.

Another current practical problem is understanding boundary descriptions of properties in deeds, and the translations among coordinate, graphic and verbal representations. In most jurisdictions, the contract for selling (or otherwise conveying) a parcel of land must include a description of the land, that is, its boundary. This description is often in verbal form and in many parts of the world the verbal description is the chief legal document. Most counties in the United States collect large amounts of such data, which are legally relevant, in their registry of deeds, but such data are not easily accessible for GIS. These data are needed in map form, such as the maps used by tax assessors. Descriptions of the boundaries of the ranges of biological populations are similar and often are found in reference volumes and checklists.

The input of other forms of geographical information in verbal form becomes more speculative and futuristic. It is conceivable that systems of the future might be able to assimilate and analyse explorers' journals, such as Columbus's logs or the journals of Lewis and Clark. They could be checked for consistency and perhaps new inferences could be made about the itineraries of their travels. Field workers of the future might be able to speak their notes into tape-recorders and later have the tapes not only transcribed but also analysed and integrated directly into GIS. A number of agencies and companies would be interested in devices which would accept spoken descriptions of locations from their field personnel and integrate their observations with map data. As appealing as these ideas may be, the development of such applications may be many years away.

Natural language production for GIS

Generation of verbal descriptions of routes for drivers already is possible, and indeed is an option of at least one current commercial GIS: the ARC/INFO 'Directions' command produces a verbal description of a route through a street network (ESRI 1989: Chapter 4: 9). Also, there are commercially available real-time, computer-based navigation aid systems for vehicles (ETAK 1988; Zavoli 1989) which produce in-car maps for use in route planning. There is considerable evidence, however, suggesting that driving instructions in verbal form may be more effective than maps (see McGranaghan, Mark and Gould, 1987, for a review). Davis (Davis 1986; Davis and Schmandt 1989) has described a system to provide driving directions over cellular phone systems. Experimental work also has investigated the idea of using complexity of verbal description as a cost heuristic for route selection itself, finding 'simplest-to-describe' paths rather than 'shortest' paths (Ma 1987; Mark 1985). This is a fertile area for further research.

Again drawing on speculation, the GIS of the future might produce grammatically correct paragraphs for direct inclusion in reports. One example is to go from a discrete set of observation points for some species of animal or plant, to a polygon representing the range of that organism, to a clear verbal description of where the organism can (or could) be found. Verbal descriptions of patterns, shapes and spatial relations are important parts of environmental impact reports, and again their generation by GIS would probably be desirable.

CROSS-LINGUISTIC ISSUES FOR GIS

In designing the GIS user interface, the GIS community should also pay attention to differences among various natural languages as to how they represent and express concepts, relations and objects of geographical space. It is most likely that currently favoured query languages are influenced by the natural language of their designers, commonly English or occasionally German. Without conscious choice, designers tend to select terminology and concepts based not only on their own everyday use of natural language, but also on word order and other major structural elements of that language.

Unless underlying concepts are explicitly and conscientiously used, compared and translated, the use of GIS in non-English speaking areas may be severely impeded. Any user–computer interface bridges the user's cognitive structure and the representation in the computer system. Obviously, constructing an interface must take into account both components. If a GIS is moved from one linguistic culture (say North American English) to another (say South American Spanish), some form of 'translation' of the interface is highly desirable, if not essential. In fact, many professionals and technicians in the non-English-speaking world have some working knowledge of English, and thus are able to use English-language software; but this is far from desirable, and restricts access to the technology to a very small subset of the population.

The 'translation' of an interface would include the actual translation of the words used in the interface, including commands, menus and help texts, but such translations are not always straightforward, since the concepts underlying the interface may not match those of the target language. Cross linguistic transfer of computer technology certainly calls for more than the translation of the manuals. Customarily that is the most that is done, but the GIS industry has not yet touched on the deeper issues. Computer science and the computer industry have studied systems supporting languages which are not based on the roman alphabet, and how such differences affect database query language (see King 1989 and other papers in the same volume).

Observations of adaptations of cultures to new languages often show a facility to adopt a new vocabulary, but to persist in using elements of the underlying structures of previous language. By analogy, it is suggested that the translation of a user interface's 'surface' vocabulary addresses the less urgent part of the problem, since using new words for old concepts may be fairly easy for users to adapt to in any case.

The first reaction to issues such as these is, almost invariably, to build more 'flexibility' into the GIS, and to make the interface more adaptable by the user. If this flexibility is well designed, it can indeed be used to adapt to individual differences. Ideally, the base structure of the programs – the geometrical data model and its operations – is available, and furthermore completely devoid of artefacts of the cognitive structure and linguistic traditions of the designer(s). However, in practice it is doubtful that this is ever the case. Otherwise, the construction of the interface has to translate the data model into a structure akin to the cognitive structure of the class of users. This is clearly no simple task and it will be desirable to identify parts which are useful everywhere, and others which depend on certain categories and which vary between target languages. The exploration of 'language universals', discussed briefly above, thus becomes very important, as it would allow the separation of what is generally applicable from what needs to be adapted to a local language, culture, or subculture. These cross linguistic issues for GIS have been addressed in more detail by Mark, Gould and Nunes (1989).

CONCLUSION

Observing natural language usage to describe spatial situations is very important for the designers of GIS to achieve a system which is compatible with the way users conceptualize their problem domains. Since current GIS structures are based largely on maps and mathematics, and since maps and mathematics represent previously formalized representations of naive concepts of geographical space, adoption of a cognitively based concept structure for GIS will not necessarily involve radical changes.

The most important issue is to understand the separation between the conceptual view of GIS, which explains how the system operates to the user community, and the implementation, which should be of interest only to programmers and systems maintenance personnel. The GIS literature continues to mix the two sets of issues, beginning even before the famous 'First International Study Symposium on Topological Data Structures for Geographical Information Systems' (Dutton 1979) hosted by Harvard University in 1977, and continuing to the present. The conceptual design, the geometrical and attribute data models, the user interface style – all of these have fundamental ties to cognitive and linguistic research, whereas the implementation of the GIS software connects to computer science.

To the extent that they have been recognized at all, linguistic issues in GIS have in the past been seen primarily as issues for user interface design, especially in spatial query languages. However, recent research in these areas has shown that a GIS needs an approach based on a 'dialogue' model, and that the standard 'question and answer' model is insufficient (Mark *et al*. 1989a; Neal *et al*. 1989). The debate concerning whether natural language interfaces are more appropriate than formal system interaction 'languages' is ongoing (Shneiderman 1981) and definite results cannot be expected before some of the technical limitations of understanding naturally spoken language (continuous speech) have been removed.

The cognitive and linguistic issues in GIS span a much wider set of issues, and touch on the general problem of how to translate users' concepts into executable operations. The current model, which is to train users in translating their task into a procedural, formal geometrical problem (which is then submitted to the GIS) severely limits GIS technology to trained users. The relative merits of the tendency of technology designed in this way to promote and maintain a specialized class of 'gurus' to act as 'gate-keepers' to the technology is beyond the scope of this chapter, and has been discussed in detail by Winograd and Flores (1986). To go beyond this approach needs a more profound understanding of how people in general think and reason about space and things spatial.

Last, but not least, the structure of GIS interfaces, as available today, is, essentially, the product of an Anglo Saxon (or at least, Germanic) cognitive and linguistic culture. In order to make GIS useful in other language groups and cultures, it may not be sufficient to translate the 'surface structure' of the systems, such as the command language, or menu contents, or manuals. Instead, attention must be given to the deeper syntactic and cognitive structures that underlie other languages. It is clearly desirable to build alternatives to the 'verb-oriented' languages currently used for commands and queries. A metaphor-based, direct manipulation interface is clearly an attractive alternative, but such interfaces have their own problems. Unfortunately, the most appropriate metaphors and associated visualizable image-schemata are not known for geographical information for any natural language, let alone across many languages. Also, building such a visual interface will not resolve the cross-linguistic problems of GIS technology transfer and use, since the use of visual symbols often is as much culturally and linguistically determined as are the languages themselves.

It is to be expected that these issues will increase greatly in importance and recognition within the GIS community world wide.

REFERENCES

Abler R (1987) The National Science Foundation National Center for Geographic Information and Analysis. *International Journal of Geographical Information Systems* **1** (4): 303–26

Alexandroff P (1961) *Elementary Concepts of Topology*. Dover, New York

ANSI X3H2 (1985) *American National Standard Database Language SQL*. American National Standards Institute, Washington DC

Bertin J (1983) *Semiology of Graphics*. University of Wisconsin Press, Madison, Wisconsin

Burton W (1979) Logical and physical data types in geographic information systems. *Geo-Processing* **1** (4): 167–81

Chamberlin D D, Boyce R F (1974) Sequel: a structured English query language. In: Rustin R (ed.) *Workshop on Data Description, Access and Control*. ACM SIGMOD, Ann Arbor, Michigan, 249–64

Chamberlin D D, Astrahan M M, Eswaran K P, Lorie R A, Mehl J W, Reisner P, Wade B W (1976) SEQUEL 2: a unified approach to data definition, manipulation, and control. *IBM Journal of Research and Development* **20**: 560–75

Codd E F (1982) Relational database: a practical foundation for productivity. *Communications of the ACM* **25** (2): 109–17

Corbett J P (1975) Topological principles in cartography. *Proceedings, International Symposium on Computer-Assisted Cartography, AUTOCARTO2*. Reston, Virginia, US Department of Commerce

Corbett J P (1979) Topological principles of cartography. *Technical Report 48*. Bureau of the Census, US Department of Commerce, Washington DC

Cox N J, Rhind D W, Aldred B K (1980) A relational database system and a proposal for a geographic data type. *Geo-Processing* **1**: 217

Davis J R (1986) Giving directions: a voice interface to a direction giving program. *Proceedings, 1986 Conference, American Voice I/O Society*. September, pp. 77–84

Davis J R, Schmandt C M (1989) The back seat driver: real time spoken driving directions. *Proceedings, First Vehicle Navigation & Information Systems Conference (VNIS '89)*. IEEE, New York, pp. 146–50

Diaz B M, Bell S B M (eds.) (1986) *Spatial Data Processing using Tesseral Methods (collected papers from Tesseral Workshops 1 and 2)*. NERC Unit for Thematic Information Systems, Natural Environment Research Council, Swindon

Digital Cartographic Data Standards Task Force (1988) The proposed standard for digital cartographic data. *The American Cartographer* **15** (1): 9–140

Dutton G (ed.) (1979) *First International Study Symposium on Topological Data Structures for Geographic Information Systems*. Addison-Wesley, Reading, Massachusetts

Egenhofer M J (1984) Implementation of MAPQUERY, a query language for land information systems (in German).

Report 79. Institute for Geodesy and Photogrammetry, Swiss Federal Institute of Technology (ETH), Zurich

Egenhofer M J (1989a) A formal definition of binary topological relationships. In: Schek W L, Schek H-J (eds.) *Proceedings, Third International Conference on Foundations of Data Organization and Algorithms (FODO), Paris*. Springer-Verlag, New York, pp. 457–72

Egenhofer M J (1989b) *Spatial Query Languages*. Unpublished PhD dissertation, University of Maine

Egenhofer M J (1989c) Spatial SQL: a spatial query language. *Report 103*. Department of Surveying Engineering, Orono Maine

Egenhofer M J, Frank A U (1988) Towards a spatial query language: user interface considerations. *Proceedings, 14th International Conference on Very Large Data Bases, Los Angeles*. Morgan Kaufmann, Los Altos, California, pp. 124–33

Egenhofer M J, Herring J R (1991) High-level spatial data structures for GIS. In Maguire D J, Goodchild M F, Rhind D W (eds.) *Geographical Information Systems: principles and applications*. Longman, London, pp. 227–37, Vol 1

ESRI (1989) *Network Users Guide*. Environmental Systems Research Institute, Redlands California

ETAK (1988) *ETAK MapEngine, Programmers Guide*. ETAK, Menlo Park California

Frank A U (1982) MAPQUERY – database query language for retrieval of geometric data and its graphical representation. *ACM SIGGRAPH* **16** (3): 199–207

Frank A U, Kuhn W (1986) Cell graph: a provable correct method for the storage of geometry. *Proceedings of the 2nd International Symposium on Spatial Data Handling, Seattle*. International Geographical Union, Williamsville New York, pp. 411–36

Freeman J (1975) The modelling of spatial relations. *Computer Graphics and Image Processing* **4**: 156–71

Gatrell A C (1991) Concepts of space and geographical data. In: Maguire D J, Goodchild M F, Rhind D W (eds.) *Geographical Information Systems: principles and applications*. Longman, London, pp. 119–34, Vol 1

Giblin P (1977) *Graphs, Surfaces and Homology*. Chapman and Hall, London

Haugen E (1957) The semantics of Icelandic orientation. *Word* **13**: 447–60

Herring J R, Larsen R, Shivakumar J (1988) Extensions to the SQL language to support spatial analysis in a topological data base. *Proceedings of GIS/LIS '88*. ASPRS/ACSM, Falls Church, pp. 551–60

Herskovits A (1985) Semantics and pragmatics of locative expressions. *Cognitive Science* **9**: 341–78

Herskovits A (1987) *Spatial Prepositions in English*. Cambridge University Press, Cambridge Massachusetts

Ingram K J, Phillips W W (1987) Geographic information processing using a SQL-based query language. *Proceedings of the Eighth International Symposium on Computer-Assisted Cartography, Baltimore*. ASPRS/ACSM, Falls Church, pp. 326–35

Intergraph Corp (1989) *Tigris Imager Reference Manual*. Intergraph Corporation, Huntsville

Jackson J (1990) Developing an effective human interface for geographical information systems using metaphors. *ACSM/ASPRS Annual Convention* **3** (1): 117–25

Johnson M (1987) *The Body in the Mind: the bodily basis of meaning, imagination and reason*. University of Chicago Press, Chicago

King R (1989) Introduction to the special issue on non-English interfaces to databases. *IEEE Transactions on Database Engineering* **12** (4): 1–7

Kuhn W (1991) Are displays maps or views? *Proceedings of AUTOCARTO10*. ACSM/ASPRS, Bethesda Maryland

Lakoff G (1987) *Women, Fire, and Dangerous Things: what categories reveal about the mind*. University of Chicago Press, Chicago

Ma P (1987) An algorithm to generate verbal instructions for vehicle navigation using a geographic database. *East Lakes Geographer* **22**: 44–60

Mark D M (1985) Finding simple routes: 'ease of description' as an objective function in automated route selection. *Proceedings, Second Symposium on Artificial Intelligence Applications, Miami Beach*

Mark D M (1989) Cognitive image-schemata for geographic information: relations to user views and GIS interfaces. *Proceedings of GIS/LIS '89*, Vol. 2. ASPRS/ACSM, Falls Church, pp. 551–60

Mark D M, Gould M D, Nunes J (1989) Spatial language and geographic information systems: cross-linguistic issues. *Proceedings, II Conferencia Latinoamericana sobre el (Technologia de los Sistemas de Informacion Graficos (SIG)*. Universidad de Los Andes, Merida, Venezuela, pp. 105–30

Mark D M, Svorou S, Zubin D (1987) Spatial terms and spatial concepts: geographic, cognitive, and linguistic perspectives. *Proceedings, International Symposium on Geographic Information Systems: The Research Agenda*, Vol. II. National Aeronautics and Space Administration, Washington DC, pp 101–12

Mark D M, Frank A U, Egenhofer M J, Freundschuh S M, McGranaghan M, White R M (1989a) Languages of spatial relations: Initiative Two specialist meeting report. *Technical Report 89–2*. National Center for Geographic Information and Analysis, Santa Barbara California

McGranaghan M (1989) Context-free recursive-descent parsing of location-description text. *Proceedings, Ninth International Symposium on Computer-Assisted Cartography*. ACSM/ASPRS, Falls Church, pp. 580–7

McGranaghan M, Mark D M, Gould M D (1987) Automated provision of navigation assistance to drivers. *The American Cartographer* **14**: 121–38

McGranaghan M, Wester L (1988) Prototyping an herbarium collection mapping system. *Proceedings 1988 ACSM-ASPRS Annual Convention*. ACSM/ASPRS, Falls Church, pp. 232–8

Neal J G, Shapiro S C (1990) Intelligent multi-media

interface technology. In: Sullivan J W, Tyler S W (eds.) *Architectures for Intelligent Interfaces: elements and prototypes*. Addison-Wesley, Reading Massachusetts

Neal J G, Thielman C Y, Dobes Z, Haller S M, Shapiro S C (1989) Natural language with integrated deictic and graphic gestures. *Proceedings, DARPA Speech and Natural Language Workshop*. Morgan Kaufmann, Los Altos CA

Neiser U (1976) *Cognition and Reality: principles and implications of cognitive psychology*. Freeman, San Francisco

Pazner M, Kirby K C, Thies N (1989) *MAP II Map Processor*. Wiley, New York

Peuquet D, Zhan C-X (1987) An algorithm to determine the directional relationship between arbitrarily-shaped polygons in a plane. *Pattern Recognition* **20**: 65–74

Pullar D, Egenhofer M J (1988) Towards formal definitions of topological relations among spatial objects. *Proceedings of the 3rd International Symposium on Spatial Data Handling, Sydney*. International Geographical Union, Columbus OH, pp. 225–41

Raper J F (1989) *Three Dimensional Applications in GIS*. Taylor and Francis, London

Raper J F, Kelk B (1991) Three-dimensional GIS. In: Maguire D J, Goodchild M F, Rhind D W (eds.) *Geographical Information Systems: principles and applications*. Longman, London, pp. 299–317, Vol 1

Reisner P, Boyce R F, Chamberlin D D (1975) Human factors evaluation of two database query languages – Square and Sequel. *Proceedings, National Computer Conference (AFIPS)*, pp. 447–52

Rosch E (1973) On the internal structure of perceptual and semantic categories. In: Moore T E (ed.) *Cognitive Development and the Acquisition of Language*. Academic Press, New York, pp. 111–44

Rosch E (1978) Principles of categorization. In: Rosch E, Lloyd B B (eds.) *Cognition and Categorization*. Erlbaum, Hillsdale New Jersey, 27–48

Samet H (1984) The Quadtree and related hierarchical data structures. *ACM Computing Surveys* **16**: 187–260

Shneiderman B (1981) A note on human factors issues of natural language interaction with database systems. *Information Systems* **6** (2): 125–9

Shneiderman B (1983) Direct manipulation: a step beyond programming languages. *Computer* **16**: 57–69

Shneiderman B (1987) *Designing the User Interface: strategies for effective human-computer interaction*. Addison Wesley, Reading Massachusetts

Smith D C, Harslem E, Irby C, Kimball R, Verplank W (1983) Designing the Star user interface. *Proceedings, European Conference on Integrated Interactive Computing Systems: Stresa, Italy*. North-Holland, Amsterdam

Smith E E, Medin D L (1981) *Categories and Concepts*. Harvard University Press, Cambridge Massachusetts

Spanier E (1966) *Algebraic Topology*. McGraw-Hill, New York

Svorou S (1988) *The Experiential Basis of the Grammar of Space: evidence from the languages of the world*. Unpublished PhD dissertation, Department of Linguistics, State University of New York at Buffalo

Talmy L (1983) How language structures space. In: Pick H, Acredolo L (eds.) *Spatial Orientation: theory, research, and application*. Plenum, New York, pp. 225–82

Tomlin C D (1983a) *Digital Cartographic Modeling Techniques in Environmental Planning*. Unpublished PhD dissertation, Yale University

Tomlin C D (1983b) A map algebra. *Proceedings, Harvard Computer Graphics Conference*. Cambridge, Massachusetts

Tomlin C D (1989) *Geographic Information Systems and Cartographic Modeling*. Prentice Hall, Englewood Cliffs New Jersey

Tsichritzis D, Klug A (eds.) (1975) *The ANSI/X3/SPARC DBMS Framework Report of the Study Group on Database Management Systems*. AFIPS Press, Montvale, New Jersey

Turner A K (1990) *Three-Dimensional Modeling with Geoscientific Information Systems*. NATO Advanced Research Workshop

Winograd T, Flores F (1986) *Understanding Computers and Cognition: a new foundation for design*. Addison-Wesley, Reading Massachusetts

Woodcock J, Loomes M (1989) *Software Engineering Mathematics*. Addison-Wesley, Reading Massachusetts

Zadeh L A (1974) *Fuzzy Logic and its Application to Approximate Reasoning, Information Processing*. North-Holland, Amsterdam

Zavoli W B (1989) Navigation and digital maps interface for fleet management and driver information systems. *Proceedings, First Vehicle Navigation & Information Systems Conference (VNIS '89)*. IEEE, New York, pp. A9–A14

12

THE ERROR COMPONENT IN SPATIAL DATA

N R CHRISMAN

Although most data gathering disciplines treat error as an embarrassing issue to be expunged, the error inherent in spatial data deserves closer attention and public understanding. This chapter presents a review of the components of error in spatial data, based on Sinton's scheme of roles in the measurement process and also on the categories in the US Proposed Standard for Digital Cartographic Data Quality.

BACKGROUND: ERROR AND DATA QUALITY DEFINITIONS

No map can be picked apart into completely independent pellets of information. There is something collective and comprehensive about the spatial representation. First, the map is spatially continuous and connected. There is also a deeper reason. Individual facts become more useful information through an interaction with a structure of theory that provides a context to interpret the individual facts. In common usage, the main distinction between data and information arises from meaning, but meaning is context dependent. To be more concrete, the process of converting a particular fact into information must comprehend the fitness of that fact for some particular purpose. This line of argument provides an important introduction to the role of data quality in an information system.

Quality has various definitions in industrial engineering (Hayes and Romig 1977), but one accepted definition is 'fitness for use' (Chrisman 1983). Recently, the US National Committee Digital Cartographic Data Standards Task Force (DCDSTF 1988) has adopted this definition formally for inclusion in a US national standard for exchange of spatial data. The standard requires a quality report that provides the basis for a user to make the final judgement – the conversion to information by interpretation for a particular use.

This particular element of the US proposal has also been adopted, at least in spirit, by a British proposal (Haywood 1986), and the French (Salgé and Sclafer 1989), among others.

Quality is a neutral term, fitting for a national standard, but the tough issues of quality are best evoked by the loaded word 'error'. In common usage, error is a bad thing, and many professions related to spatial data share this attitude. For instance, geodesists, surveyors and photogrammetrists go to great lengths to reduce the error in their measurement products. For these disciplines the full attention focuses on the reduction of deviation between positional measurements and 'ground truth'. Cartographers, perhaps because they often cannot remove all error, have two incompatible approaches, both designed to avoid the issue. One tendency is to generate authoritative maps, through their official status or some other form of paternalism. The traditional approach to standards places little emphasis on a user's determination of a particular need. The other tendency, more common in academic circles, adopts the communication paradigm and expects the cartographer to use all means to communicate the message (Robinson *et al.* 1984). The communication paradigm, like a paternalist agency, assumes that the map maker controls the process, particularly the judgement of fitness for use. In summary, the disciplines of mapping technology are bent on reducing error or minimizing its importance. While this may be a reasonable approach to foster the current divisions of labour, it does not lead to the full exploitation of spatial information.

Error is not a problem unique to spatial evidence. Other disciplines have created other solutions which are worth considering. Most physical, biological and social sciences integrate data collectors and data analysts into the same discipline, while mapping places them in distinct guilds. Perhaps as a result, error bars or some other estimates appear on the display of most physical measurements. Also, even the popular press presents a standard error of estimate for opinion poll results. Reporting error is not a sign of weakness in these other disciplines, because the error estimate provides crucial information which must be preserved for correct interpretation. The most developed scientific approach to error is the body of statistical procedures which have developed over the past century. However, many of the advanced techniques in statistics are not attuned to the problems inherent in geographical information.

For some attempts to understand the statistical basis of errors in spatial databases see White (1978), Goodchild and Dubuc (1987) and Goodchild and Gopal (1989).

Basic terms for error

Before delving deeper, it is useful to present some fundamental terms to discuss error. Under the general intent of describing data quality the goal is to describe fitness for some particular use. Many numerically oriented disciplines have developed a concept of error as a deviation (or distance) between a measurement and the 'true' value. Different disciplines use different terms to refer to this concept, and some of these terms conflict. This chapter will follow the general practice of the mapping sciences (see DCDSTF 1988: 28) and use the term accuracy to refer to the closeness of an observation to a true value (or one accepted as true). This definition of accuracy implies an independent, objective external reality and sets the highest standard for the concept of accuracy. In some contexts, a measurement system may produce inaccurate results that preserve local relationships. Statistically, such a condition arises from 'systematic' error (as opposed to random error). Systematic error involves a uniform shift of values, hence the term 'bias' which is applied in some

measurement sciences. Such systems are described by cartographers as having 'relative accuracy', but this property is usually a sign that the process of data preparation (compilation) has not been completed. In the spirit of 'fitness for use', relative accuracy may be perfectly viable for some applications, while unfit for others which depend on geodetic registration.

The concept of accuracy is essentially independent of the issue of resolution although both contribute to overall data quality. The resolution of a measurement system is the minimum distance which can be recorded. Clearly, resolution sets a lower bound on accuracy. It is considered good practice to make this minimum difference smaller than the accuracy of the whole system, but a user should not confuse the two. Both resolution and accuracy can be applied to the various components of spatial information, both attributes (Dueker 1979) and positions (Tobler 1988; see also Fisher 1991 in this volume).

This chapter argues that error is an integral part of spatial information processing. The goal is to cover the full range of error in geographical databases as a fundamental introduction to the nature of spatial data. The chapter first describes the conceptual role of error in the nature of spatial data with particular attention to the question 'How many dimensions?' This is followed by a review of spatial error models in a variety of disciplines, structured by the categories proposed for the Quality Report mandated by the US National Committee for Digital Cartographic Data Standards. From this review, a comprehensive view of error should emerge.

DEALING WITH SPATIAL DATA: HOW MANY 'DIMENSIONS'?

It is relatively commonplace, particularly for those schooled in thematic cartography, to consider spatial data to consist of two major ingredients: position and attribute (see, e.g. Peucker 1972: 23). However, the concept of information in GIS cannot be restricted to recording attribute and position; more 'dimensions' are required. Any measurement of these components has an inherent uncertainty. In general, error must not be treated as a potentially embarrassing inconvenience, because error provides a critical component in judging fitness for use. Understanding the error in spatial databases is necessary to ensure appropriate application of GIS and to ensure progress in theory and tool development.

Basic dimensions

It does not take a complex philosophical effort to observe that we inhabit a three-dimensional world. Distances of length, breadth and height serve to construct human artefacts and place them on the landscape. Thus, it is to be expected that a spatial database (a GIS) be embedded in the basic dimensions of the earth.

But are these physical dimensions the only ones? This question must be answered in order to understand the complete nature of spatial data. A scientific investigation must occur in the full dimensionality of the problem or critical issues become confused. Discovering the complete dimensionality of a geographical investigation is a crucial step, although it is not commonly approached in these terms. The design phase of an information system, often conducted as a 'needs analysis', attempts to define all the information required. In many of the routine applications of this technology, the demands for information can be reasonably easily predicted. However, a major advantage of a GIS lies exactly in its ability to accommodate unanticipated needs. Fundamental dimensions may be distinct from the details seen in a typical needs study.

The design of GIS must understand the complete scope of the components of spatial information. The basic questions behind the 'nature of spatial data' are: 'What do we need to know and how should we structure that knowledge?'. An answer to these questions must address how we know what we know, because not all information is equally reliable or useful.

The initial answer to the full dimensionality of geographical information can be given using the long-standing conventions of cartography. The development of thematic cartography has fostered the recognition of space, attribute and time as the basic components of mapping. This list seems complete for describing the surface of the earth. However, the requirements for a geographical information system cannot be simply contained by a description of the surface of the earth. There is an important distinction between the real world and the symbolic representations that can be manipulated. To take Korzybski's (1948) dictum perhaps more literally than he did: 'the map is not the territory'. In the early enthusiasm of GIS, users treated their data as a perfect model of the world too often. On slight reflection, it should be apparent that no representation captures a perfect replica of something as complex as the earth. These forcible deviations between a representation and actual circumstances constitute error.

Because error is inescapable, it should be recognized as a fundamental dimension of data. A scheme for representation should be extended to include the amount of deviation in each component (space, attribute and time). Only when error is included into the representation is it possible to answer some probing questions about the limitations of current knowledge.

Of course, one goal of any information specialist is to avoid needless error. By directly recognizing error, it may be possible to confine it to acceptable limits. Still, error cannot always be avoided cheaply or easily.

Beyond dimensions: the changing roles of position, attribute and error

In 1977, David Sinton (1978) presented a fundamental analysis of the information contained in a GIS. His three basic components (he used the terms location, theme and time) were widely accepted long before then in thematic cartography [Robinson (1960: 11–12) makes the distinction between 'base data' and 'subject matter']. Before thematic cartography emerged, map information was not viewed in as analytical terms. The development of thematic cartography led to the recognition that the geometrical framework of a map (the base layer) could be used to portray multiple 'themes', essentially attributes of the objects represented in the base layer. In doing so, there is at least a tacit recognition of time as well.

The critical development in Sinton's paper was the recognition of three distinct roles that location, theme and time play in a particular information context. While the goal is to obtain a measurement, measurement of one component can only be made inside explicit constraints on the other components.

The roles Sinton described are termed fixed, controlled and measured. Most spatial information sources fix one of the three components; in the case of maps, it is time which is normally fixed. Of course it is possible to graph the amount of rainfall at a specific weather station over time, but this information is usually robbed of its temporal depth when placed into the spatial framework. Whichever it is, the fixed component does not exhibit any variation, by definition. In order to make a measurement, a second component is usually controlled, meaning that its variation is limited and predicted. A common form of spatial control is to summarize (total, average, etc.) a spatial distribution (attribute) for a collection zone or administrative region. These units provide the spatial control for the measurement of the thematic attribute. Once the fixed and controlled elements are established, it is possible to make a measurement.

Map sources nearly universally fix time, leaving space and attribute – the two components recognized by thematic cartographers. Time is a rich area for further research into the nature of spatial information (Langran and Chrisman 1988). However, to build a theory of error, it is important to scrutinize Sinton's distinction between controlled and measured.

Sinton's scheme was proposed largely to organize the difference between methods that control space compared with those that control attributes. Sinton's own work during that period had concentrated on grid cell databases which impose a lattice of cells as a control framework for a series of diverse maps. Each theme (attribute) was measured inside each cell. While Sinton's grid inventories were typically performed by armies of students, most remote sensing sources also fall into this general approach using nearly regular cells as control. These remote sensing sources include satellite platforms along with photogrammetric equipment used to create digital elevation matrices. Although some of these sources attempt to acquire only a categorical measurement (e.g. of land use), the inherent method permits a measurement on a continuous scale (as, e.g. reflectance or elevation). Not all forms of spatial control use a uniform tessellation of cells. Census tabulations and administrative data such as school attendance are usually summarized for irregular spatial units, often as a means to understand an unmeasurable continuous surface (such as population density). While these varieties of data are not usually handled together, the nature of spatial control creates some similarities discussed below.

The opposite case arises by using attributes as control in order to obtain spatial measurements. Sinton was particularly focused on types of maps such as vegetation, geology and soils. While these look like choropleth maps made with administrative zones, they are conceptually distinct, particularly when considering the error ramifications. No term has received universal approval for this form of map: Chrisman (1982a) suggested 'categorical coverage', ESRI adopted the term 'coverage' for a more general use in ARC/INFO, Mark and Csillag (1989) used 'area-class map' (citing Bunge 1966: 14–23) and Muehrcke (1986) used 'mosaic surface'. All these terms communicate the difference much better than Burrough's (1986a) use of the 'choropleth map' to cover both cases.

Beyond the categorical coverage, many other circumstances require attributes as control to obtain positional measurement. Much of the traditional cartography on topographic maps and nautical charts portrays discrete 'features'. Recognition of a feature's existence is the control, then the spatial footprint is recorded. To some extent, a 'feature' database is fairly similar to a coverage database without the concern for exhaustive, comprehensive and exclusive classification. Whereas a coverage forces all places to have one and only one category present, a particular feature may have a number of distinct characteristics, while much of the study area is simply a void. Still, these two are unified to the extent that the attribute classification provides control to the geometric measurement. Without cataloguing all of the differences, it should be apparent that these diverse cases deserve consideration in understanding the nature of spatial data and its inherent error.

A TAXONOMY OF ERROR IN GIS DATA

Understanding error in GIS must take account of Sinton's framework, although an alternative approach is suggested by Veregin (1989). This section will take up the testable components specified in the US Proposed Standard, connecting them to Sinton's framework. After this review, the different views of disciplines will be placed in some sort of perspective.

Positional accuracy

The best established issue of accuracy in the mapping sciences has been lumped into the testable component of 'positional accuracy' by the US Proposed Standard (DCDSTF 1988: 132–3). The geometrical accuracy of maps has been a topic of concern long before computerization. The earlier US National Map Accuracy Standard (Bureau of the Budget 1947) considered the accuracy of 'well-defined points' as the sole measure of a map. The well-defined point means that there is no attribute ambiguity; it can act as control for the positional measurement. Because it is a point, there is no dimensional ambiguity either. The focus on the most identifiable cartographic features persists in the revised procedures for testing large-scale line maps adopted recently by the American Society for Photogrammetry and Remote Sensing (ASPRS) (1989). The disciplines of geodesy, surveying and photogrammetry define map accuracy as absolute positional accuracy. There was an attempt in the earlier drafts of the ASPRS standard to separate the components of bias (mean deviation) in a test, leaving the relative accuracy as an identifiable quantity (standard deviation from the mean). However, there was well-placed opposition, and the standard reverted to a single measure of absolute accuracy (root-mean-square deviation from zero). The fact that certain government agencies wish to have a simple standard does not mean that the problem is simple. A test for positional accuracy will generate a set of displacements between the observed and 'true' values. These numbers should be reported so that a user can extract the particular measure for the particular use. In a GIS setting, bias can often be eliminated through some form of best fit. In fact, many geometrical measures like polygon area are immune to such systematic ('relative') errors (Chrisman and Yandell 1988), although the fundamental tool of polygon overlay relies upon absolute positioning between layers.

In testing a GIS layer, the source of 'truth' may be relatively easy to determine. There are often external sources of higher accuracy for a few features in a database (such as monuments used as control for topographic maps which are also located in street intersections). Still, it may be necessary to obtain the higher accuracy data directly, causing a potential recursion. The ASPRS standard specifies that a check survey to determine true locations must have a positional accuracy of one-third the amount expected for the product to be tested. Any such survey must ultimately tie back to the geodetic reference network. Indeed, the geodetic reference network cannot be checked in this manner, since it is constructed from relative measurements to create the absolute framework for everything else. The arcane nature of geodesy will become more relevant to the average GIS user as Global Positioning System (GPS) surveys become more prevalent.

Although the positional accuracy of maps is well accepted, few actual tests are published (one test of USGS DLG data appeared in Vonderohe and Chrisman 1985). The National Map Accuracy Standard is written like the text of a nuclear weapons treaty because it places each producer in charge of the decision of whether to test or not. Users of positional information, even if it claims to comply with the National Map Accuracy Standard, should be aware that the particular product was probably not tested. Most US agencies infer that the particular sheet would have passed the test based on compliance with certain specified procedures and equipment. This inference should be calibrated with a testing programme, but even that may be less frequent than most users imagine. As the new standards come into force, and the technology for direct field measurement (e.g. with GPS technology) becomes available, perhaps the prevalence of testing will change.

Many of the data in a GIS do not fit the restrictive definition of well-defined points. There are two approaches to resolve this. The standard approach assumes that all features on a map can be characterized by the error in the position of the well-defined points. This is an unwritten assumption behind many efforts in cartography. However, this assumption can only be used as a lower threshold. The uncertainty in positioning an 'ill-defined' object must be added on to the error in the well-defined points. But where would the lack of definition come from? The fact that an object does not have a sharp location to test may come from certain geometrical constraints. For example, the standards expect to test right-angle road intersections, so that the linear feature can be confined to a specific point. This geometrical characteristic goes beyond Sinton's framework. However, many of the features in a GIS do not fit purely geometrical constraints. The object may not really have the sharp attribute definition required to rely on the attribute for control. A number of research workers (e.g. Burrough 1989) have recognized that fuzzy sets often are a better description of certain layers. In this case, it would be impossible to test for positional accuracy without converting the fuzzy classification into a sharp system of control. These cases are better handled by including the attribute alongside the position in the test, a concept developed below.

Attribute accuracy

Testing attribute accuracy falls into two broad groups, depending on the level of measurement of the attribute. Position has a built-in metric, that is, the conversion between coordinates and distance makes sense. The measurement of error is quite direct with such a metric. Some attributes use continuous scales whose values can be treated in much the same manner as position. The clearest example is the surface of relief or elevation, encoded in digital terrain models of various descriptions. In fact, the ASPRS standard includes specific treatment of the positional accuracy of contours, treated as a three-dimensional position. The horizontal allowance for the contour under the map accuracy standard is widened by the horizontal equivalent of half the contour interval vertically. This works because elevation is measured in the same metric as horizontal position. In practice, the photogrammetric treatment is accepting that horizontal accuracy and vertical accuracy cannot be separated in the contour presentation.

More generally, a surface can be tested by measuring the deviation between the 'true' height and the observed height reported by classical descriptive statistics as with positions. When a surface is expected to be essentially continuous, an impressive array of mathematical tools is available to analyse the spatial variation. A field of geostatistics has arisen around an approach to interpolation called 'Kriging' which creates models of spatial dependence and lag (Burgess and Webster 1980; Burrough 1983, 1986a, 1991 in this volume). These models of spatial variation offer important tools to the GIS user, but they are restricted to the particular form of spatial data where the attribute is continuous and measured at locations controlled by specific sampling sites (e.g. wells) or controlled to a regular grid. Kriging has developed in the natural sciences, often to treat interpolation between sparse sampling sites. There is a related mathematics developed from the spatial adaptation of time series analysis in the social sciences under the general title 'spatial autocorrelation'. Sometimes spatial autocorrelation deals with continuous measures of distance between points. However, in geography it is more often targeted to removing the effects of spatial collection zones on spatially aggregated attributes (Cliff and Ord 1981; Goodchild 1988). There are significant differences between the area basis of this 'modifiable areal unit problem' (Arbia 1989) and the point basis of Kriging, but both use a form of spatial control, with attributes measured. For this combination, there are many analytical procedures which have been developed, but these procedures are not as widely used as they should be (Burrough 1986b).

The other group of attributes are categories, usually nominal classes as used in land use, soils and vegetation inventories. Polygon coverages of such maps have formed a critical core of early GIS operations because they could benefit from simple analytical tools such as polygon overlay (Goodchild 1978). Some commentators on GIS follow the pattern in most sciences and consider categorical data to be of lower standing. These authors are often correct in their criticism of the blind adoption of sharp set theory for much more complex environments (e.g. Burrough 1989). However, the role of control in spatial data cannot be taken by a continuous measure. In the pure form, categorical coverages are constructed by setting the attribute as control and measuring the location of the boundaries between classes. In practice, of course, there is significant error in identifying the categories on such maps. Certain disciplines, particularly remote sensing interpretation, place central importance on testing the accuracy of classification. With categorical attributes, there is no such thing as a close value or a metric of deviations. A class is either right or wrong (some wrong answers might be ordered by degree of dissimilarity, but that nuance will be ignored here). So, there is no easy summary of performance to compare with the summary statistics of deviations reported in the ASPRS positional test. A test involves determining the classification from two sources, and ideally one should be a source of higher accuracy. The results of a test will create a square misclassification matrix, cross-tabulating the observed category with the true result. In reading this matrix, it is possible to proceed by rows or columns. A row consists of all the observations which should have been classified in a particular category. A column consists of all the observations which were so classified. The diagonal of the matrix will fit both, and captures the agreement of the two sources. Errors along rows are errors of omission with respect to that category. Errors along columns are errors of commission. In medicine these are called false negatives and false positives respectively.

It is common to summarize this matrix by the percentage correct, the total of the diagonal. This measure, unfortunately, is not a reliable index of success across projects with differing frequencies in the various categories (Rosenfield and Melley 1980; Chrisman 1982b). A number of alternative measures of success have been suggested, notably Cohen's Kappa, a measure which deflates the percentage correct by the amount which could be expected to fall into the diagonal under an independent rule of joint probability. Still the raw matrix offers the most complete information to assess fitness for use.

The misclassification matrix is typically obtained through a process of point sampling (Berry and Baker 1968; Fitzpatrick-Lins 1981). A set of points is selected from some spatial sampling scheme, and the classification obtained from each source. Despite its widespread use, there are some difficulties associated with such a point-based approach. The classifications on a coverage map are not always a pure fit to the sharp set theory required to make it work. Often a classification system has some implicit (or explicit) scale involved. If a point happens to fall in a convenience store (in US context; in UK a newsagent) parking lot, does that mean that a residential land use code is invalid? The residential category involves a bit less homogeneity than the mathematical purity would suggest. A few neighbourhood commercial enterprises are a part of residential character, such businesses would not locate in purely commercial surroundings anyway. Hence, the point sampling method cannot really test simply one point, it involves an area and it can become confused when it is near an edge. In some tests, the points are deliberately positioned away from edges, but that may introduce a whole new set of difficulties. One alternative, not much practised yet, is to produce the misclassification matrix by overlaying a complete second coverage (e.g. see Ventura, Sullivan and Chrisman 1986). The second coverage can be chosen deliberately to use a similar scale and resolution in its categories or a more refined set of categories and more detailed scale (see for example Beard 1987). In either case, the result of the overlay will give a raw measure of area in the misclassification matrix. Furthermore, the nature of the overlaid objects will give some clues to the origin of the error. Chrisman (1989) has presented a taxonomy of the results obtained. He creates a basic distinction between error caused by misclassifying whole objects (identification error) and error in positioning boundaries (discrimination error). The former is a purely attribute error, but the latter includes some of the 'fuzzy' effects discussed by many authors. These two tendencies create specific forms in the overlay test. Identification errors will have lines mainly from one source, while discrimination errors will tend to have lines in roughly equal amounts from the two sources. In addition, this taxonomy is modified by the effects of scale. Smaller and larger objects may clearly arise from different sources. Considering all the possible ramifications of error, it seems unlikely that a single number can compress all the information available from such a test.

In Sinton's framework, a test for attribute accuracy fits the opposite cases compared to positional accuracy. The classical test of a well-defined point (attribute controlled, position measured) depends critically on identification of the proper points to test. If the wrong point is tested, error estimation procedures based on Gaussian error will misbehave dramatically. There is significant literature in the fields of geodesy (e.g. Crossilla 1986) and photogrammetry (e.g. Kubik, Lyons and Merchant, 1988, and Shyue 1989) on detecting such 'blunders'. Outlier handling procedures are not designed as tests of attribute accuracy; their mathematics make them more like the tests of logical consistency discussed below. However, the fundamental cause for such blunders may be in the identification of the point to test.

B. Logical consistency

The traditional approach to map accuracy never makes explicit mention of a category of testing which has become quite important in the computer age. Actually, a large amount of the manual practice of cartography involved testing the logical consistency of the product with the highly sophisticated visual processor of the human cartographer. The human eye–mind combination can detect slight gaps in linework and other patterns, but it is difficult to discipline employees to spend all day scrutinizing a complex map. In some agencies, it was common to test the consistency of a coverage of polygons by colouring them in with coloured pencils. This process would point out missing lines by finding that colours (keyed by the soil labels) would not have an intervening boundary. The process would also detect any polygon without a label to start the colouring. It might take the employee all day to check a polygon network which could be checked in a minute or less using a computer algorithm for topological testing (Chrisman 1986, 1987).

The use of the topological model in modern GIS provides one example of logical consistency checking. The redundant nature of the topological encoding can detect a number of flaws in the data structure (White 1984; Chrisman 1987), such as missing boundaries or unlabelled polygons. Use of logical consistency checks can avoid errors which would be interpreted as routine errors in position or attribute.

The topological model is not the only means to check logical consistency. Whenever there is some external mathematical or logical relationship which must be maintained, a consistency test should be administered. Some database management systems implement valid ranges on attribute fields, but the spatial nature of a GIS, with the ability to relate layers, offers a much richer set of consistency checks. A simple computation of point-in-polygon could avoid placing buoys on dry land or rivers outside their floodplain. Although these seem ridiculous, a GIS database will contain such errors until the full analytical power of the tool is turned back against its own database. Once an error is detected by a logical consistency check, it may be resolved through a panoply of procedures, approximating the manual process of compilation which resolves conflicting sources.

Completeness

The last component of testing in the US Proposed Standard is completeness. In some circumstances, usually in creating a base layer of named objects such as parcels, census tracts or whatever, there is an externally known list of objects which should appear in the database. A coverage of parcel polygons could be tested polygon by polygon as a verification of attribute accuracy. A simpler, less complete check could be performed by checking whether the database included all the parcels in the master list. All differences could be immediately flagged as errors. Such a test falls somewhere near a logical consistency check and an attribute accuracy test. For convenience, it can be termed completeness.

Another aspect of completeness deals with the mapping rules associated with many cartographic presentations. Some categorical coverages will set a threshold of minimum areas or widths to include on the map. Often these are prescribed in the manual, but never explicitly tested. This aspect of the quality report deals with the scale effects discussed in the context of the polygon overlay testing procedure.

ERROR: A DISCIPLINARY MOSAIC

Investigations of geographical information have been an amalgamation pasted together from a variety of different disciplines. The list of different forms of error presented above naturally connects to the divergent problems of specific disciplines. Each discipline constitutes a group faced with a particular circumstance – a particular set of tools and purposes. Any combined view depends on understanding the diversity and mobilizing the different perspectives to a redefined purpose. Disciplinary divergences are relatively common, but particularly notable in the treatment of spatial error.

Error reduction is a primary goal in the earth measurement disciplines of surveying, photogrammetry and geodesy. These disciplines have developed procedures to obtain reliable positional measurements through the use of repeated measurement and a specialized version of least-squares estimation (Mikhail 1976). Much of the mathematics for surveying adjustments has been developed inside the discipline without substantial borrowing from other disciplines, because it is tailored to the specific form of error expected from each type of equipment. By contrast, social scientists (including geographers) tended to develop quantitative methods by borrowing statistical tools from others. The approach to error is thus imported as well. Standard statistical procedures deal most directly with errors from sampling, although there has been substantial development of spatial autocorrelation. Cartographers have developed two distinct tracks, an analytical school and a communication school. The first fits in with quantitative geography, while the second treats the psychophysical process of map reading and the divergence between the message intended and received. Out of these utterly incompatible disciplines, the field of GIS must try to forge a unified understanding of the errors that occur and how they must be treated.

LIVING WITH ERROR

Once a model of error is developed, what good does it do? In the traditional view, say of a surveyor, a measure of error helps to eradicate error. Under such a regime, a data producer (map maker) attempts to keep all maps accurate to a specified tolerance. Many agencies embarking on an automation campaign do so inside the guidelines of their disciplinary perspective. It is only natural to carry along the attitudes towards error.

As GIS develops, databases will become more and more pivotal to a diverse range of users, and the ability to determine a blanket tolerance will become less certain. Measures of data quality will provide a key to suitability for a specific task (fitness for use). With this transition, any disciplinary narrowness will not survive.

The field of GIS should also put significant effort into the development of methods to report and visualize the error in databases. A reporting scheme would permit statements, such as those permissible using standard statistical tests, except that they would adjust for the particularly spatial form of the error. A few such tools, mentioned above, exist, but most do not. Even fewer are implemented in production GIS.

REFERENCES

American Society for Photogrammetry and Remote Sensing (1989) Interim accuracy standards for large scale line maps. *Photogrammetric Engineering and Remote Sensing* **55**: 1038–40

Arbia G (1989) Statistical effect of spatial data transformations: a proposed general framework. In: Goodchild M F, Gopal S (eds.) *Accuracy of Spatial Databases*. Taylor & Francis, London, pp. 249–60

Beard M K (1987) How to survive on a single detailed database. *Proceedings of AUTOCARTO8*. ASPRS/ACSM, Falls Church, pp. 211–20

Berry B J L, Baker A M (1968) Geographic sampling. In: Berry B J L, Marble D F (eds.) *Spatial Analysis*. Prentice Hall, Englewood Cliffs New Jersey, pp. 91–100

Bunge W (1966) *Theoretical Geography*. Gleerup, Lund Sweden

Bureau of the Budget (1947) *National Map Accuracy Standards*. US Government Printing Office, Washington DC

Burgess T M, Webster R (1980) Optimal interpolation and isarithmic mapping of soil properties. I. The semivariogram and punctual Kriging. *Journal of Soil Science* **31**: 315–31

Burrough P A (1983) Multiscale sources of spatial variation in soil. I. The application of fractal concepts to nested levels. *Journal of Soil Science* **34**: 577–97

Burrough P A (1986a) *Principles of Geographical Information Systems for Land Resources Assessment*. Clarendon Press, Oxford

Burrough P A (1986b) Five reasons why geographical information systems are not being used efficiently for land resources assessment. In: Blakemore M J (ed.) *Proceedings of AUTOCARTO London*, Vol. 2. Royal Institution of Chartered Surveyors, London, pp. 139–48

Burrough P A (1989) Fuzzy mathematical models for soil survey and land evaluation. *Journal of Soil Science* **40**: 477–92

Burrough P A (1991) Soil information systems. In: Maguire D J, Goodchild M F, Rhind D W (eds.) *Geographical Information Systems: principles and applications*. Longman, London, pp. 153–69, Vol 2

Chrisman N R (1982a) A theory of cartographic error and its measurement in digital databases. *Proceedings of AUTOCARTO5*. ASPRS, Falls Church, pp. 159–68

Chrisman N R (1982b) Beyond accuracy assessment: correction of misclassification. *Proceedings International Society of Photogrammetry and Remote Sensing Commission IV*, 24-IV, pp. 123–32

Chrisman N R (1983) The role of quality information in the long-term functioning of a GIS. *Proceedings of AUTOCARTO6*, Vol. 2. ASPRS, Falls Church, pp. 303–21

Chrisman N R (1986) Quality report for Dane County soil survey digital files. In: Moellering H (ed.) *Report 7, National Committee for Digital Cartographic Data Standards*, pp. 78–88

Chrisman N R (1987) Efficient digitizing through the combination of appropriate hardware and software for error detection and correction. *International Journal of Geographical Information Systems* **1**: 265–77

Chrisman N R (1989) Modeling error in overlaid categorical maps. In: Goodchild M F, Gopal S (eds.) *Accuracy of Spatial Databases*. Taylor & Francis, London, pp. 21–34

Chrisman N R, Yandell B (1988) Effects of point error on area calculations. *Surveying and Mapping* **48**: 241–6

Cliff A D, Ord J K (1981) *Spatial Processes: models and applications*. Pion, London

Crossilla F (1986) Improving the outlier separability in geodetic networks according to the generalized orthomax criterion. *Manuscripta Geodaetica* **11**: 38–47

DCDSTF (1988) The proposed standard for digital cartographic data. *The American Cartographer* **15**: 9–140

Dueker K J (1979) Land resource information systems: spatial and attribute resolution issues. *Proceedings of AUTOCARTO4* Vol. 2. ASPRS, Falls Church, pp. 328–36

Fisher P F (1991) Spatial data sources and data problems. In: Maguire D J, Goodchild M F, Rhind D W (eds.) *Geographical Information Systems: principles and applications*. Longman, London, pp. 175–89, Vol 1

Fitzpatrick-Lins K (1981) Comparison of sampling procedures and data analysis for a land use and land cover map. *Photogrammetric Engineering and Remote Sensing* **47**: 343–51

Goodchild M F (1978) Statistical aspects of the polygon overlay problem. In: Dutton G (ed.) *Harvard Papers on Geographic Information Systems,* Vol 6. Addison-Wesley, Reading Massachusetts

Goodchild M F (1988) *Spatial Autocorrelation*. CATMOG (Concepts and Techniques in Modern Geography), Vol. 47. GeoBooks, Norwich

Goodchild M F, Dubuc O (1987) A model of error for choropleth maps with applications to geographic information systems. *Proceedings of AUTOCARTO8*. ASPRS/ACSM, Falls Church, pp. 165–74

Goodchild M F, Gopal S (eds.) (1989) *Accuracy of Spatial Databases*. Taylor & Francis, London

Hayes G E, Romig H G (1977) *Modern Quality Control*. Bruce, Encino California

Haywood P E (ed.) (1986) *Final Draft Papers of the Working Party to Produce National Standards for the Transfer of Digital Map Data*. Ordnance Survey, Southampton

Korzybski A (1948) *Science and Sanity: an introduction to non-Aristotelean systems and general semantics*, 3rd edn. The International Non-Aristotelean Library Publishing Co., Lakeville CT

Kubik K, Lyons K, Merchant D (1988) Photogrammetric work without blunders. *Photogrammetric Engineering and Remote Sensing* **54**: 51–4

Langran G, Chrisman N R (1988) A framework for temporal geographic information. *Cartographica* **25** (3): 1–14

Mark D M, Csillag F (1989) The nature of boundaries in 'area-class maps'. *Cartographica* **26** (1): 65–78

Mikhail E H (1976) *Observations and Least Squares*. IEP, New York

Muehrcke P C (1986) *Map Use*, 2nd edn. JP Publications, Madison Wisconsin

Peucker T K (1972) *Computer Cartography,* Resource Paper 17. Association of American Geographers, Washington DC

Robinson A H (1960) *Elements of Cartography*, 2nd edn. Wiley, New York

Robinson A H, Sale R D, Morrison J L, Muehrcke P C (1984) *Elements of Cartography*, 5th edn. Wiley, New York

Rosenfield G, Melley M (1980) Applications of statistics to thematic mapping. *Photogrammetric Engineering and Remote Sensing* **46**: 1287–94

Salgé F, Sclafer M N (1989) A geographic data model based on HBDS concepts: the IGN cartographic database model. *Proceedings of AUTOCARTO9*. ACSM/ASPRS, Falls Church, pp. 110–17

Shyue S W (1989) *High Breakdown Point Robust Estimation for Outlier Detection in Photogrammetry*. Unpublished PhD dissertation, University of Washington

Sinton D (1978) The inherent structure of information as a constraint to analysis: mapped thematic data as a case study. In: Dutton G (ed.) *Harvard Papers on Geographic Information Systems*, Vol. 6. Addison-Wesley, Reading MA

Tobler W (1988) Resolution, resampling and all that. In: Mounsey H (ed.) *Building Databases for Global Science*. Taylor & Francis, London, pp. 129–37

Ventura S, Sullivan J G, Chrisman N R (1986) Vectorization of Landsat TM land cover classification data. *Proceedings URISA* **1**: 129–40

Veregin H (1989) A taxonomy of error in spatial databases. *Technical Paper 89–12*. National Center for Geographic Information and Analysis University of California, Santa Barbara California

Vonderohe A P, Chrisman N R (1985) Tests to establish the quality of digital cartographic data: some examples from the Dane County Land Records Project. *Proceedings of AUTOCARTO7*. ASPRS, Falls Church, pp. 552–9

White M (1978) A geometric model for error detection and correction. *Proceedings of AUTOCARTO3*. ASPRS, Falls Church, pp. 439–56

White M (1984) Technical requirements and standards for a multipurpose geographic data system. *The American Cartographer* **11**: 15–26

SPATIAL DATA SOURCES AND DATA PROBLEMS

P F FISHER

Data used in GIS are derived from many different sources, both analogue and digital. The primary source is still undoubtedly the hardcopy map and this chapter starts by reviewing factors which determine the information content and usefulness of maps. Aspects of analogue attribute data are then discussed. The major step in actually generating GIS data is, however, the analogue to digital conversion process, and some of the small amount of research that has been done on this process is outlined. Data sources originally in digital form are then mentioned and, finally, the pros and cons of purchasing library digital data as against original digitizing are discussed.

INTRODUCTION

Many of the data that are incorporated into GIS are initially in analogue form, most commonly as hardcopy maps. To be used in GIS, however, map data must undergo a conversion process known as digitizing, a labour-intensive task which is time consuming and prone to error. Fortunately, increasing amounts of data are now obtainable directly in digital form. The problems associated with each approach and their advantages and disadvantages are the subject of this chapter. The chapter begins with a discussion of analogue and digital data sources for GIS organized under the headings of scale, audience, currency, coverage, accuracy, and sheets and series. Next attribute data for GIS are considered with socio-economic attributes introduced first followed by natural resource attributes. Data conversion methods are then briefly introduced. The final major section before some brief conclusions discusses digital data sources.

ANALOGUE DATA SOURCES

The most important source of analogue spatial data is the map. Since prehistory, maps have been produced with the specific purpose of recording the spatial relationships observed and measured by the map's compiler. Maps are used to convey spatial knowledge to others and to store knowledge for the compiler's future use (Robinson *et al.* 1984). The set of maps in existence form a significant resource which is not without problems, largely because maps are no more than an abstraction or generalization of reality.

Many of the problems encountered in developing geographical databases from maps have not been hindrances to the use of maps in the past, because conventional uses place less stringent demands on the analogue medium. But users of digital geographical databases are often unaware of the limitations of conventional maps and, consequently, may make unreasonable or inappropriate assumptions about the data derived from them. The following discussion about the potential limitations of analogue maps is based mainly on Rhind and Clark (1988).

Map scale

Scale determines the smallest area that can be drawn and recognized on a paper map (Table 13.1). On a topographic map at a scale of 1:50 000, it is not possible to represent accurately any object of dimensions less than one line width, or less than about 25 m across. However, small features can be important, so cartographers have devised methods for selecting and symbolizing small but significant features, even though their physical dimensions on the ground may be less than one line width (Robinson *et al.* 1984; Tobler 1988; see also Muller 1991 in this volume). Thus many roads and rivers which are less than 25 m across are nevertheless shown on 1 : 50 000 maps. Scale may determine which rivers are shown in a drainage network (Gardiner 1982), or which roads in a road network (Fig. 13.1; Keates 1989). Similarly, scale may determine whether the various features in a class, such as roads, are shown as a single feature class or differentiated (e.g. highway, motorway, main road, minor road, etc.).

Scale influences the material included on thematic maps as well as on general topographic maps. On a vegetation map, for example, a minimum area or 'minimum mapping unit' is established based on the map scale. Areas which would be below this size are merged with neighbouring areas, despite having distinctly different vegetation. Thus, the class of vegetation assigned to an area is merely the dominant class in the area and it is accepted that there may be significant inclusions of other classes present. For example, the classification of a map unit as hemlock forest rarely means that only hemlock is present, but rather that it is the dominant species. If the area was mapped at another scale and so with another minimum mapping area in use, the original area might either be broken up into more specific units, or agglomerated with others to yield a more general unit, depending on the direction of the scale change. Similarly, in the case of soil maps different scales are characterized by different mapping units reflecting different degrees of map unit purity (Fisher 1987).

By contrast, a digital database appears, initially, to be independent of scale because it may be portrayed at any scale. If the data were originally collected from a map or maps, then the map scale is important because it determines the size of the minimum mapping area (Table 13.1) and the material included and excluded. As a piece of information with respect to the digital data, however, it is only an identifier of the original map series. In the database, it is more appropriate to

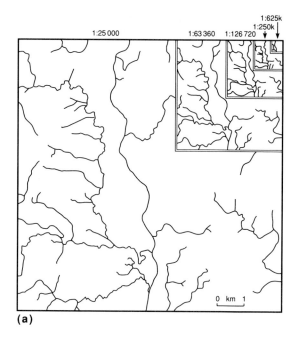

Fig. 13.1 Presentation of the same information about the same area requires cartographic generalization, where some features become exaggerated and others obscured. The progressive elimination of information with changing scale is shown on (a) a stream network (*Source*: Gardiner 1982), and (b) the interaction of road network and urban area (*Source*: Keates 1989).

Table 13.1 Minimum discernible mark on a map assuming a minimum spot of 0.5 mm

Map scale	Resolution (m)	Detection (m)
1 : 10 000	5	10
1 : 50 000	25	50
1 : 100 000	50	100
1 : 250 000	125	250
1 : 500 000	250	500
1 : 1 000 000	500	1000

Source: Tobler 1988.

identify the map series exactly, and then give the accuracy of the database as a representation of the map. Indeed, this is exactly the approach used by various agencies in producing digital databases for general use (USGS 1987; SCS 1984b).

Scale is misused all too often as a measure of accuracy. In a recent edited volume on the development of global databases, for instance, many authors refer to the database they are generating as, for example, a 1 : 1 million database (Mounsey 1988). This tells the reader that the data are being collected from maps of that scale, but nothing of the actual properties of the database. This reflects a deplorable confusion over the nature of the digital database and the conceptual evolution from analogue maps to digital database. A few contributors do refer to a 1 km resolution cell, for example, which gives the data user a property of the digital data, but still it is not a really useful statement of accuracy.

This confusion over the role of scale in digital data is not uncommon. The US Geological Survey (USGS) distributes a number of digital databases of the United States. The most detailed of these is digitized from 1 : 24 000 source maps, and the USGS database manuals refer to these as being, for example, 'from 1 : 24 000 maps' and the manuals specify how accuracy should be reported (USGS 1986a, 1987). In the GIS community and within the documents themselves, however, the data set is referred to as 'the 1 : 24 000' Digital Line Graph (DLG) or Digital Elevation Model (DEM) (USGS 1986a, 1987). Similarly, Land Use and Land Cover data sets for the United States, derived from 1 : 100 000 and 1 : 250 000 maps, tend to be referred to by the map scales (USGS 1986b). The supporting documentation of these USGS products does give many further details and it is to be hoped that other products will also be backed by such statements.

In contrast, the US Department of Agriculture (USDA) Soil Conservation Service (SCS) is generating three nation-wide soil spatial databases from source maps at different scales. These databases have been given scale-independent names (Table 13.2), which shows clearer separation

Table 13.2 Soil Conservation Service National Soil Databases

Database name	Source map scale
SSURGO	1 : 15 840 to 1 : 31 680
STATSGO	1 : 250 000
NATSGO	1 : 7 500 000

Source: Reybold and TeSelle 1989.

between the digital data and the original maps. As with the USGS products, these SCS databases are supported by precise technical specifications (e.g. SCS 1984a, 1984b).

Map audience

Assumptions about the map's audience determine the intensity of information included, and the need for additional reference material. A map designed for a technical audience will probably have a higher information density compared to one designed for the public or one designed for a 'wide user community'. Those in the latter category may contain more by way of contextual information such as roads, buildings and towns, at the expense of accurate representation of feature position (Fig. 13.2: Keates 1989). The cartographer must juggle the conflicting needs of audience and scale. Similarly, the compiler of a database formed by digitizing maps may need to consider the purposes for which those maps were created.

Currency

A map is a representation of features in space as they existed at the time they were surveyed. The real world of geographical information changes continuously, but many maps remains static. Thus maps become increasingly inaccurate as a representation of the world over time. The long

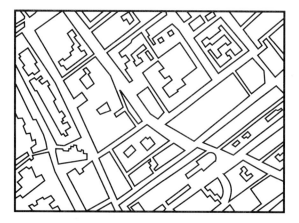

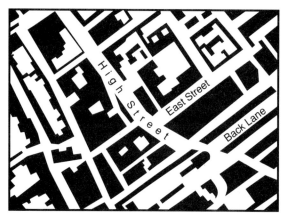

Fig. 13.2 The purpose for which a map is designed affects map content and precision of that content. Here the actual line plan is compared with the same area, at the same scale, but in a street atlas. Many roads have exaggerated widths, to accommodate road names and enhance visibility, while many building and block outlines are simplified (*Source*: Keates 1989).

time delay between mapping and publishing often means that most maps are not true records of spatial relations when they are used. Most human users expect this, and compensate for it, although many road-map users still may not understand exactly why some roads are not shown on their maps. Map sheets are revised periodically, of course, and all national mapping agencies maintain a revision programme, but features continue to change.

Vegetation and land use maps require constant revision. Although soils and geology are less subject to change, even these classes of maps must be updated regularly to accommodate new field work and general improvements in the level of human understanding of soils and geology.

In generating a digital database, it may not be possible to find a truly current map of an area, but before digitizing every effort should be made to acquire the most up-to-date information. Care should be taken to ensure that the information used was derived by survey. Stories abound of, for example, maps derived from construction plans in which there are significant deviations between planned routes of roads and actual routes.

Once the data are in digital form, data accuracy and completeness are still time dependent (Langran and Chrisman 1988), but the capability exists to edit or update the database on a regular and frequent basis, which is not possible for a hardcopy map. The data may still be out of date soon after collection, however.

Map coverage

The actual geographical area for which a geographical database might be constructed is variable, from less than one to thousands of square kilometres. Therefore, the source-map coverage must be chosen as appropriate to the task in hand. Scales and completeness of map coverage of different geographical areas are, however, highly variable. This point can be illustrated by reference to mapping in two of the world's most advanced countries: the United States and Britain. In the United States the most detailed complete coverage scale of topographic maps is 1 : 24 000, whereas in Britain it is a combination 1 : 1250, 1 : 2500 and 1 : 10 000 (see Starr and Anderson 1991 and Sowton 1991 in this volume).

Thematic map coverages are even more patchy, and, although there are some global scale map coverages of some environmental themes, such as soil and geology (Rhind and Clark 1988; see also Clark, Hastings and Kineman 1991 in this volume), the extent is much more irregular at larger scales. In the United States, for example, soil mapping at the county level at scales of 1 : 15 840 or 1 : 31 680 is nearly completed, although much remains unpublished. In the United Kingdom, although there is now full coverage at 1 : 250 000 as a result of an EEC initiative, larger scale soil maps are relatively uncommon, covering a small fraction of the country. By contrast geological mapping of the United Kingdom at 1 : 63 360 is complete and being extensively revised, while less than 50 per cent of the United States has been mapped at scales of 1 : 250 000 or larger (Thompson 1988).

In contrast to these two developed nations, many countries in the world have neither topographic nor thematic maps at any detailed scale (Parry and Perkins 1987; Brandenberger and Ghosh 1985; Fig. 13.3). National agencies and aid agencies from developed countries are often working to improve this situation.

Map accuracy

As noted above, maps are an abstraction of reality, and so map makers have been concerned to give concise statements of the accuracy of their products. The US National Map Accuracy Standard, issued by the Bureau of the Budget in 1947 and still in force, is perhaps the best known example of these (see Thompson 1988). Some of the major points included are summarized in Table 13.3, and the standard has recently been revised by a committee of the American Society of Photogrammetry and Remote Sensing (Merchant 1987) which specifies acceptable root-mean-square error terms for horizontal locations for various maps (Table 13.4).

Names and attribute information on maps are

Table 13.3 Summary of important parts of the US National Map Accuracy Standard US Bureau of the Budget

1. On scales smaller than 1 : 20 000, not more than 10 per cent of points tested should be more than 1/50 inch in horizontal error, where points refer only to points which can be well defined on the ground.
2. On maps with scales larger than 1 : 20 000 the corresponding error term is 1/30 inch.
3. At no more than 10 per cent of the elevations tested will contours be in error by more than one half the contour interval.
4. Accuracy should be tested by comparison of actual map data with survey data of higher accuracy (not necessarily with ground truth).
5. If maps have been tested and do meet these standards, a statement should be made to that effect in the legend.
6. Maps that have been tested but fail to meet the requirements should omit all mention of the standards on the legend.

Source: Thompson 1988.

Table 13.4 Planimetric coordinate accuracy requirement of well-defined points, expressed as the square root of the sum of mean deviations from the true positions (root-mean-square (rms) error)

Map scale	Limiting rms error (m)
1 : 50	0.0125
1 : 100	0.025
1 : 200	0.05
1 : 500	0.125
1 : 1000	0.25
1 : 2000	0.5
1 : 4000	1.0
1 : 5000	1.25
1 : 10 000	2.5
1 : 20 000	5.0

Source: Merchant 1987.

not subject to a specific standard. There is no statement to the effect that all, or even any roads shown as major roads are not dirt tracks, or that 90 per cent of the place names given on the map are those currently in use locally.

By contrast, in mapping land attributes as part of the Land Use and Land Cover mapping programme of the USGS, standards have been set which are summarized in Table 13.5. Similarly, the USDA SCS states that within an area delimited on a soil map the conditions of attribute purity summarized in Table 13.6 should be met. This

Table 13.5 Accuracy specifications for USGS Land Use and Land Cover maps

1. 85 per cent is the minimum level of accuracy in identifying land use and land cover categories.
2. The several categories shown should have about the same accuracy.
3. Accuracy should be maintained between interpreters and times of sensing.

Source: Anderson *et al*. 1976.

information is supported in soil survey reports by a statement of the nature of included soil types and even the percentage of the area they occupy, sometimes based on statistical assessment.

For these standard statements to have any usefulness, they should be subject to rigorous

Table 13.6 Accuracy specifications for USDA SCS soil maps

1. Up to 25 per cent of pedons may be of other soil types than that named if they do not present a major hindrance to land management.
2. Up to only 10 per cent of pedons may be of other soil types than that named if they do present a major hindrance to land management.
3. No single included soil type may occupy more than 10 per cent of the area of the map unit.

Source: SCS 1984b.

implementation and subsequent testing. Even when they are implemented, as in the case of the National Map Accuracy Standard, very little testing is published in the literature, and important questions remain. For example, it would be useful to know the actual rate of errors on maps which have been tested and found to fall within the accuracy standards. On contour maps, it would be useful to know the accuracy of elevations at points not on contours, as well as accuracy levels for the contours themselves (Vonderohe and Chrisman 1985). Actual testing of attribute accuracy standards is also unusual. For example, the accuracy requirements noted above for the USGS Land Use and Land Cover maps (Anderson *et al*. 1976) were stated in the original document that established the classification scheme used in constructing such maps, but seem rarely to have been achieved (Fitzpatrick-Lins 1978), and often no other error statement is given for a map. Soil surveyors have been among the most self critical of mapping unit purity, but many published examples show that the stated standard has not been maintained in practice (reviewed by Fisher 1989; Thomas, Baker and Simpson 1989).

The US Proposed Standard for Digital Cartographic Data (OCDSTF 1988) requires a test for locational accuracy similar to the National Map Accuracy Standard. This is partly implemented in the USGS DEM *Data User's Guide* (USGS 1987), but only in relation to the source map data from which the DEM was derived. Unfortunately these data are already one step removed from reality. The Proposed Standard goes on to recommend a

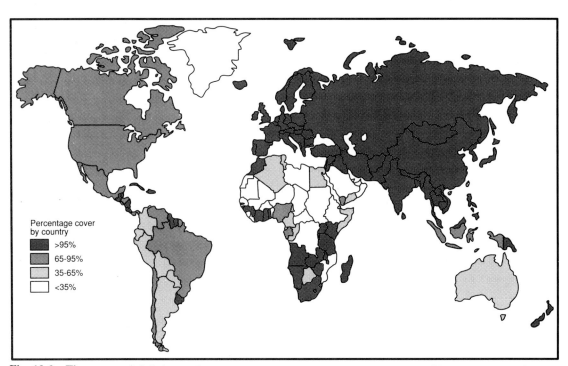

Fig. 13.3 The extent of global mapping as of 1986, at scales of 1 : 100 000 or larger (*Source*: Parry and Perkins 1987).

statement of attribute accuracy measured or estimated by one of a number of methods, including deductive estimation, or misclassification matrices based on independent point samples or polygon overlay (American Cartographer 1988). The main factors preventing implementation of accuracy standards are time and cost. All mapping programmes are subject to deadlines and cost limits, and coverage and timeliness will always be given more weight than accuracy in allocating scarce resources.

On the other hand, conventions have been developed to show qualitative uncertainty in various maps. For example, on topographic maps, streams can be coded to show their permanence, as can lakes (Fig. 13.4a, b; Keates, 1989), and the position of sand dunes may be indicated by a dashed line to imply the possibility of movement. Similarly, the geological community distinguishes various levels of positional accuracy of a geological contact (Fig. 13.4c).

It is rather surprising that among the least accurate of data sources are the records of legal property boundaries, or cadastre, where high detail and accuracy might be expected (Dale and McLaughlin 1988). Dale and McLaughlin document a number of examples of developing countries where until recently maps of titles, and even legal deeds did not exist (e.g. Uganda, Kenya and Thailand). In the United Kingdom they note that one in eight land transactions still contains an error in delimiting the land plot, and that this must be rectified by the Land Registry. In the United States the uncertainty of property boundaries is such that a small industry of surveyors is involved day to day in identifying boundaries and re-registering them. In some areas, the original deed is a written description given in metes and bounds, which record the boundary by measured distances and directions. Often the description is very hard to match precisely with modern landmarks, because the named landmarks may have been removed, or the distances and directions only poorly specified (Brown, Landgraf and Uzes 1969).

Map sheets and series

The traditional paper map series is sometimes designed, drafted and published as a collection of individual map sheets, because each separate map sheet or quadrangle is intended to stand alone as a

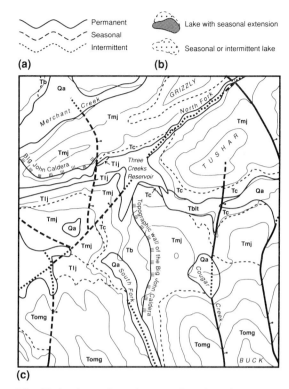

Fig. 13.4 A number of conventions have been developed to indicate areas of imprecision on standard topographic maps. Three examples are shown: (a) three symbols show depiction of permanent, seasonal and intermittent streams (*Source*: Keates 1989); (b) the illustration of lakes as permanent, seasonal and ephemeral is again shown by varying the intensity of the symbolization (*Source*: Keates 1989); and (c) the precision of geological rock contacts and fault lines is shown by a combination of solid (observed), dashed (not observed, but fairly certain) and dotted (inferred) lines. Other lines are contours (*Source*: Anderson *et al*. 1980).

single entity. This gives the individual paper map an internal coherence and a pleasing appearance. If the reader is interested in an area beyond that covered by the current map, it must be filed and another extracted from the library. There is no guarantee of conformity across the seam of the maps, however. Many researchers and other users have found to their cost that edge-matching between map sheets can be a major problem. In map series with overlap between contiguous sheets (e.g. 1 : 50 000 OS maps of Britain) large features in the zone of overlap may not conform between sheets (Fig. 13.5). This can be even worse in the case of maps prepared on poorly rectified orthophotomaps such as those included with county soil reports by USDA SCS.

In the digital environment, the integrity of the map sheet is removed, because digital data users are unlikely to be constrained by the edge of the map sheet and increasingly expect so-called 'seamless' databases. This cannot, however, be achieved without either re-surveying features in the vicinity of the sheet boundaries, or making mathematical assumptions in order to automate feature matching over the boundary (Beard and Chrisman 1988; Fig. 13.6).

At the joins between map sheets in one series it is often possible to find features that do not cross over because of different dates of publication. For example, soil type boundaries may be different on either side of the sheet boundary, and even where the soil boundaries may be traced across the sheet join, the map units may differ on the two maps, because of the different publication dates. For the

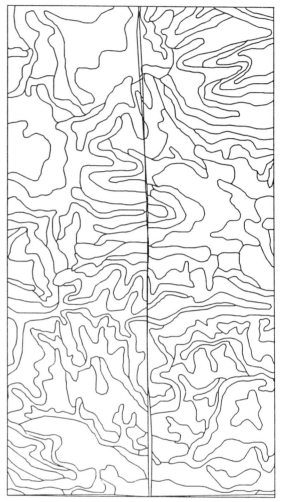

Fig. 13.6 Matching edges between different map sheets is often very complex. This digital representation shows many boundary lines which fail to continue across at the map join (*Source*: Beard and Chrisman 1988).

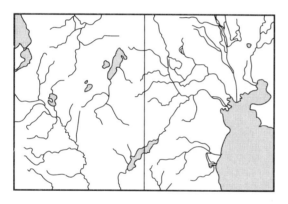

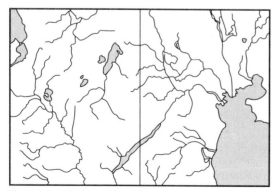

Fig. 13.5 The variation of representation of a single lake in the zone of overlap in two neighbouring operational navigation charts of the US Defense Mapping Agency (*Source*: Rhind and Clark 1988).

same reason, a road may appear to end abruptly at the join of two maps.

Map users may also experience difficulties when they attempt to compare different map attributes because of variations in scale and projection. In Britain, for example, the use of 1:63 360 base maps for both soil and geology has allowed these attribute themes to be compared, but lack of conformity with the topographic map series of that scale has meant that comparison with topographic information is not necessarily reliable. In the United States, geology is mapped at the various scales of the standard topographic map series, but soils are commonly mapped by county on orthophotomaps at a scale of 1 : 15 840, almost precluding precise comparison with either topography or geology. The ability to analyse and overlay maps with different attribute data types is, however, integral to GIS. Software has been developed to force data into common scales and projections, either through mathematical transformations or 'rubber-sheet' approximations (Campbell 1987; Tobler 1988; see also Maling 1991 in this volume).

ATTRIBUTE DATA

Attribute data are complementary to locational data and describe what is at a point, along a line, or within a polygon. All spatial features have some immediately associated attribute or attributes, such as building type, soil type, etc. Some, such as low level census divisions, are no more than a code value to enable association with other attribute information.

Socio-economic attributes

Some of the most widely used sets of longitudinal (time series) attribute data are derived from national census offices. Census data are essential to planning by many government agencies. Most census offices prepare a number of different censuses (Bureau of the Census 1982, 1984a, 1984b), but the most common and important is the census of population. All population censuses collect a myriad of social variables wherever people occur and operatives can reach (see Rhind 1991 in this volume).

Census results are reported at a number of spatial resolutions (see, for example, Fig. 13.7) and using a variety of media. The results of the 1990 US Census are available in computer readable form for all 7.5 million census blocks (basic enumeration areas), as well as in printed form for the sub-state local government units, and for the smaller block numbering areas (Fulton and Ingold 1989). Data are available as printed tabulations and in computer-readable form on both tape and CD-ROM (Fulton and Ingold 1989). As in most census reporting, some data are published as absolute counts within geographical areas, while others are based on only a sample of households (Denham and

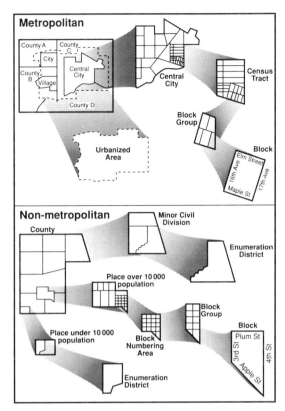

Fig. 13.7 The hierarchy of census divisions in US metropolitan and non-metropolitan areas (*Source*: Bureau of the Census 1982).

Rhind 1983; Bureau of the Census 1982; also see Rhind 1991 in this volume).

Reported census data are, however, subject to numerous problems of accuracy and reliability. The foremost of these is that individuals are counted in the United States by their 'usual place of residence', which may be different from their legal residence, their voting residence or their domicile (Bureau of the Census 1982). Undercounting is a perennial problem, due to illiteracy, illegal immigration, homelessness and simple unwillingness to complete census returns despite legal inducements (Bureau of the Census 1982). Overcounting is also a problem. In some countries a more systematic bias may be introduced because census takers fail to penetrate particularly inaccessible regions, or have trouble counting all the inhabitants of a village. Furthermore, it is usual in a census to count people by their night time location and, although location of workplace may be included in the census (Bureau of the Census 1982), only a poor representation of day time and working place population distributions may be recorded.

In some cases the counts for certain geographical areas may be so small that statistical representation is uncertain (Kennedy 1989). This introduces a considerable problem of confidentiality since if too few individuals are in a sample it may be possible to identify the individuals concerned. Indeed, in the United Kingdom the data are specifically modified by randomly assigning values of +1, 0 and -1 to low counts (Dewdney 1983), while in the United States low counts are simply suppressed (Bureau of the Census 1982).

Once collected and published, census data are not without further problems. The term 'ecological fallacy' (Robinson 1950) describes the drawing of false inferences about individuals from aggregate data (Norris 1983), and often limits the applicability of statistical methods that might otherwise project values on to individuals from census data (Openshaw 1983). Census data are published and analysed for specific geographical areas, but the effects of changing those reporting areas is poorly understood. The Modifiable Areal Unit Problem (MAUP), discussed in detail by Openshaw (1984), demonstrates that the number of different ways in which a set of small areal units may be agglomerated is substantial and the statistics that result from different agglomerations may vary considerably. Analysis of data collected under alternate regionalizations forms another aspect of the MAUP, since census reporting zones rarely coincide with voting districts, postal code areas, natural watersheds, or even divisions in previous censuses (Fig. 13.8). Various statistical methods exist for inferring values in the target areal units from the census divisions, but produce somewhat unpredictable results when tested (Flowerdew and Green 1989; see also Flowerdew 1991 in this volume).

The most acute problem with census data is temporal; by the time they reach the user community they are out of date. Someone will have received a pay rise, someone will have moved, someone married, etc. The assumption is that in the short term such changes are not important, because publicizing attributes of individual citizens is not a purpose of census data and reporting zones have an averaging effect (Fig. 13.7). As the time since the day of the census increases, however, it may become progressively less appropriate to use fine geographical divisions for analysis.

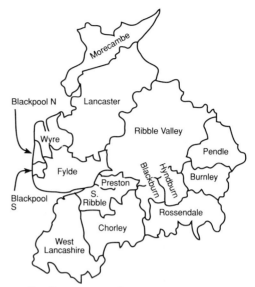

Parliamentary Constituencies

Districts

Fig. 13.8 An area may be divided into any number of areal units for analysis, and this diagram shows the difference between two such divisions, namely the parliamentary constituencies and local government districts in north-west England. This is an aspect of the Modifiable Areal Unit Problem, and the challenge here is to map the data from one regionalization on to the other (*Source*: Flowerdew and Green 1989).

Natural resource attributes

Natural resource attribute information can also be of count data type (e.g. animal censuses). These data are subject to all the problems of data from human censuses, compounded by the inherent mobility of animals: random and systematic, annual and diurnal.

More commonly, however, natural resource data (such as soil, geology, vegetation and land use) are comparatively static and categorical. Each area has its own primary attribute, such as land use, but may have any number of associated or interpretive attributes. Thus soil reports typically contain numerous interpretations of the soil mapping units for land capability and land suitability.

Interval and ratio data such as slope, erodibility and land productivity (in currency units) can also be attached to each mapping unit. Methods for handling such data are varied, but include sophisticated geostatistical methods designed specifically to minimize statistical variability in the interpolated data (Burrough 1986).

ANALOGUE TO DIGITAL DATA CONVERSION

Two primary methods of analogue to digital data conversion exist, namely automated scanning or manual digitizing. The technical aspects of the hardware and the challenge of developing the software associated with these are reviewed in this volume by Jackson and Woodsford (1991). Chrisman (1987) reviews the merits of the two technologies.

Manual digitizing requires the operator to generate a caricature of the line, not a precise representation (Douglas and Peucker 1973). This may lead to various complications which will be summarized here very briefly. Chrisman and Yandell (1988) and Prisley, Gregoire and Smith (1989) discuss the consequences of operator error on polygon area calculations, while Blakemore (1984) shows how analytical procedures may go wrong, and in particular how point locations may be assigned to incorrect polygons due to over-simplification of boundaries. The role of the digitizer operator in introducing error and the form of that error is, however, under-researched. Keefer, Smith and Gregoire (1988) present a statistical treatment of digitizer operator error, using an autoregressive model. Maffini, Arno and Bitterlich (1989) develop a digitizing error model and discuss how it may be applied in spatial analysis.

Computer-controlled photogrammetric devices are another means of transferring analogue data (stereo pairs) into digital data. Contour lines, spot-heights and planimetrically rectified locational data are now as easily delivered in digital form as in the traditional map form (Lillesand and Kiefer 1987). Such systems are usually still under the control of human operators, but research is advancing to remove this bottleneck in data collection (Dowman and Muller 1986).

DIGITAL DATA SOURCES

Two major sources of direct digital data collection exist, largely based on satellite technology. Remote sensing on a variety of platforms, both within and without the atmosphere, is perhaps the single most important source of digital data. Data gathered from satellite sensors, particularly the Landsat and SPOT sensor systems, have been widely shown to be of value in providing a means of updating natural resource and topographic maps (Campbell 1987). Currently, the multi-spectral data of Landsat TM and MSS and of the SPOT HRV are best for vegetation and land cover mapping (Campbell 1987), while the high resolution panchromatic mode of the SPOT HRV shows most promise for updating topographic maps (Konecny et al. 1987).

Vegetation and land cover mapping from remote sensing is not without problems of accuracy, however. Classification of imagery is typically achieved by various multivariate strategies which rely on the numeric values of spectral reflectance in each of the electromagnetic bands recorded. Some classification strategies use a textural approach which incorporates information on pixels neighbouring the area currently under consideration. Others are relying more and more on approaches from artificial intelligence and vision research (such as region growing; Mason et al. 1988). These numerical methods will only work satisfactorily if the reflectances are pure. However, the large size of resolution cells of the sensors ensures that there is a high probability of more than one cover type contributing to reflectance values, which means a continuing unreliability in the classifications produced. This is reflected in reported classification accuracies, which show that it is often difficult to do as well as the 85 per cent accuracy required for the USGS Land Use and Land Cover mapping (Table 13.6, Anderson *et al.* 1976; Campbell 1987; Fitzpatrick-Lins 1978). Continuing algorithm research and the use of ancillary geographical information do show promise of delivering more acceptable and usable land cover maps (Fisher and Pathirana 1989; Mason *et al.* 1988), as may the still higher resolution (both spectral and spatial) of the next generation of sensors (see Davis and Simonett 1991 in this volume).

In the field of surveying, Global Positioning Systems based on navigation satellites also are capable of delivering digital location data (Leick 1987). If these are combined with dataloggers and programmable field computers (Fisher *et al.* 1987) the combination may provide a full location and attribute gathering station in the future.

DECIDING ON THE SOURCE OF DATA

Whatever the original source of the locational data used in a spatial database, a number of different options exist for acquisition. A two-way division of the alternatives is recognized here: extraction from digital data collections, or digitizing.

Existing data collections

Currently, the main source of spatial data is archived records of government agencies. Organizations in many countries are heavily involved in generation of digital spatial data; most notable are countries of the developed world. In the United States, for example, the USGS is digitizing and distributing topographic, land cover and other thematic maps; the Bureau of the Census developed and distributes a spatial database (TIGER), for mapping and analysis of the 1990 decennial census; the USDA SCS is digitizing soil maps; the US Fish and Wildlife Service is generating a digital version of the National Wetland Inventory; and the Environmental Protection Agency (EPA), National Aeronautics and Space Administration (NASA) and National Oceanographic and Atmospheric Administration (NOAA) all have large holdings of digital data. All of these agencies have been responsible for developing spatial databases which are now available to the public, usually at a moderate cost, based on the ethic of public access to information as required by US law (Epstein 1988).

In the United Kingdom, a partially similar position exists with the Ordnance Survey, the British Geological Survey, the Soil Survey, and the Institute of Terrestrial Ecology, to mention just a few agencies involved in data collection. Availability of information is, however, very different from the United States since all is controlled by Crown copyright and the current political paradigm of cost recovery by government agencies (Department of the Environment 1987). In both the United States and the United Kingdom privacy and confidentiality are also of concern in instances where data may reveal the identity of, or information about, individuals (Epstein 1988).

Databases derived from government agencies do have a number of advantages over other options. They will probably have been generated by experienced operators to a specific set of published standards (e.g. American Cartographer 1988; SCS 1984b; USGS 1986b), although accuracy statements are sometimes based on no more than visual examination and internal consistency checking (USGS 1986a, 1987). Databases are increasingly being generated and distributed by private publishing companies and these may have less certain specifications. Originally such data are often derived from digital data distributed by government agencies, due to the lack of copyright and royalty payments on such products, or through cooperative agreements. The extent of changes to the data is, however, usually undocumented.

The would-be acquirer of this governmental information may find problems in identifying whether data exist and from where they can be acquired. In the United States, the National Cartographic Information Center is a clearinghouse of governmental data sources, giving access to data from all the US data collection agencies mentioned above (Thompson 1988). It would appear that the British Library is planning to provide such a service in the United Kingdom (Finch and Rhind 1986). Discovering geographical data sources is a problem in many countries, but in some a centralized GIS makes an obvious point of contact (e.g. Jamaica: Eyre 1989; Sweden: Andresson 1987).

Original database generation

Although data are increasingly available from the types of governmental agencies discussed above, it is often the case that the data do not meet the accuracy requirements of the user, are out of date, were digitized from source maps at the wrong scale, or have other problems. Under these circumstances GIS developers have two options available. They may either set up a digitizing program within the organization, or contract database preparation to a third party.

Developing a database internally can be a costly and undesirable alternative. The disadvantages of this approach are that staff will need to be trained in software and hardware use, that the organization may be left at the end of the process with a number of highly skilled digitizing technicians with no digitizing to do, and that the actual cost may be excessive due to the considerable time it takes to learn how to use much digitizing software. The advantages are that the organization has day-to-day control of data entry and can rapidly respond to requests for fresh information or to altered circumstances. The contracting company option has exactly opposite characteristics. The company should have a pool of highly experienced technical staff who are totally familiar with the existing software and hardware (in fact this may not always be the case), and data conversion and transfer problems will be addressed by the contractor (again drawing on experience). On the other hand, the GIS operation may be left with no one skilled in the database structure or data editing which will undoubtedly be necessary in the long run to enable updating of spatial data, and will not be able to respond to rapid changes in database requirements. Probably the most desirable alternative is for a combination of both, with the mass digitizing being contracted, and a small in-house group training to be able to edit and update the data.

CONCLUSION

Almost all analogue or digital data that are available for input to GIS may have limitations in their usefulness for a particular purpose. Considering some of the factors discussed here, however, should assist the developer in preparing the best database at an acceptable cost, with data at an achievable accuracy. Ignoring these factors will in the long run almost inevitably cause the developer problems which may be sufficient to endanger the phenomenon the system is designed to help manage, be it a nature reserve, a city, or a country

REFERENCES

Anderson J J, Sigmund J M, Cunningham C G, Steven T A, Lanigan J C, Rowley P D (1980) Geologic map of the Delano Peak SW Quadrangle, Beaver County, Utah. *Miscellaneous Field Studies Map, MF-1225*. USGS, Reston

Anderson J R, Hardy E E, Roach J T, Witmer R E (1976) A land use and land cover classification system for use with remote sensor data. *Professional Paper 964*. USGS, Reston

Andresson S (1987) The Swedish Land Data Bank. *International Journal of Geographical Information Systems* **1**(3): 253–63

Beard M K, Chrisman N R (1988) Zipping: a localized approach to edgematching. *The American Cartographer* **15** (2): 163–72

Blakemore M J (1984) Generalization and error in spatial databases. *Cartographica* **21**: 131–9

Brandenberger A J, Ghosh S K (1985) The world's topographic and cadastral mapping operation. *Photogrammetric Engineering and Remote Sensing* **51** (4): 437–44

Brown C W, Landgraf H F, Uzes F D (1969) *Boundary Control and Legal Principles*, 2nd edn. Wiley, London

Bureau of the Census (1982) *Guide to the 1980 Census of Population and Housing*. US Department of Commerce, Washington DC

Bureau of the Census (1984a) *Guide to the 1982 Economic Census and Related Statistics*. US Department of Commerce, Washington DC

Bureau of the Census (1984b) *Guide to the 1982 Census of Agriculture and Related Statistics*. US Department of Commerce, Washington DC

Burrough P A (1986) *Principles of Geographical Information Systems for Land Resources Assessment*. Clarendon Press, Oxford

Campbell J B (1987) *Introduction to Remote Sensing*. Guildford Press, New York

Campbell W G, Church M R, Bishop G D, Mortenson D C, Pierson S M (1989) The role for a geographical information system in a large environmental project. *International Journal of Geographical Information Systems* **3** (4): 349–62

Chrisman N R (1987) Efficient digitizing through the combination of appropriate hardware and software for error detection and editing. *International Journal of Geographical Information Systems* **1** (3): 265–77

Chrisman N, Yandell B S (1988) Effects of point error on area calculations: a statistical model. *Surveying and Mapping* **48** (4): 241–6

Clark D M, Hastings D A, Kineman J J (1991) Global databases and their implications for GIS. In: Maguire D J, Goodchild M F, Rhind D W (eds.) *Geographical Information Systems: principles and applications*. Longman, London, pp. 217–31

Dale P F, McLaughlin J D (1988) *Land Information Management: An Introduction with Special Reference to*

Cadastral Problems in Third World Countries. University Press, Oxford

Davis F W, Simonett D S (1991) GIS and remote sensing. In: Maguire D J, Goodchild M F, Rhind D W (eds.) *Geographical Information Systems: principles and applications.* Longman, London, pp. 191–213, Vol 1

DCDSTF (Digital Cartographic Standards Task Force) (1988) The proposed standard for digital cartographic data. *The American Geographer* **15**: 7–140

Denham C, Rhind D W (1983) The 1981 Census and its results. In: Rhind D W (ed.) *A Census User's Handbook.* Methuen, London, pp. 17–88

Department of the Environment (DoE) (1987) *Handling Geographic Information: Report of the Committee of Enquiry Chaired by Lord Chorley.* Her Majesty's Stationery Office, London

Dewdney J C (1983) Censuses past and present. In: Rhind D W (Ed.) *A Census User's Handbook.* Methuen, London, pp. 1–15

Douglas, D H, Peucker T K (1973) Algorithms for the reduction of the number of points required to represent a digitized line or its caricature. *Canadian Cartographer* **10**: 112–22

Dowman I, Muller J P (1986) Real-time photogrammetric input versus digitized maps: accuracy, timeliness and cost. In: Blakemore M J (ed.) *Proceedings of AUTOCARTO LONDON*, Vol. 1. Royal Institution of Chartered Surveyors, London, pp. 538–43

Epstein E F (1988) Legal and institutional aspects of global databases. In: Mounsey H M (ed.) *Building Databases for Global Science.* Taylor & Francis, London, pp. 10–30

Eyre L A (1989) JAMGIS, the first Jamaican Government comprehensive multi-data geographical information system: achievements and problems. *International Journal of Geographical Information Systems* **3** (4): 363–71

Finch S, Rhind D W (1986) Cartographic and remote sensing digital databases in the UK. *British Library Information Guide 6.* British Library, London

Fisher P F (1987) The nature of soil data in GIS: error or uncertainty. In: Aangeenbrug R T, Schiffman Y M (eds.) *Proceedings of International Geographic Information Systems (IGIS) Symposium: the research agenda*, Vol. 3. NASA, Washington DC, pp. 307–18.

Fisher P F (1989) Knowledge-based approaches to determining and correcting areas of unreliability in geographic databases. In: Goodchild M, Gopal S (eds.) *Accuracy of Spatial Databases.* Taylor & Francis, London, pp. 45–54

Fisher P F, Pathirana S (1989) Evaluation of fuzzy membership of land cover classes in suburban areas of north-east Ohio. *ASPRS Technical Papers, 1989 ASPRS/ACSM Fall Convention.* ASPRS, Falls Church VA, pp. 125–32

Fisher P F, Pearson M P, Clarke S R, Ragg J M (1987) Computer program to assist the automation of soil description. *Soil Use and Management* **3**: 26–31

Fitzpatrick-Lins K (1978) Accuracy and consistency comparisons of land use and land cover maps from high-altitude photographs and Landsat multispectral imagery. *Journal of Research, US Geological Survey* **6** (1): 23–40

Flowerdew R (1991) Spatial data integration. In: Maguire D J, Goodchild M F, Rhind D W (eds.) *Geographical Information Systems: principles and applications.* Longman, London, pp. 375–87, Vol 1

Flowerdew R, Green M (1989) Statistical methods for inference between incompatible zonal systems. In: Goodchild M F, Gopal S (eds.) *Accuracy of Spatial Databases.* Taylor & Francis, London, pp. 239–47

Fulton P N, Ingold J H (1989) Highlights of geographic coverage and content for the 1990 census data products program. In: Frazier J W, Epstein B J, Schoolmaster F A (eds.) *Papers and Proceedings of Applied Geography Conferences*, Vol. 12. pp. 215–17

Gardiner V (1982) Stream networks and digital cartography. *Cartographica* **19** (2): 38–44

Jackson M J, Woodsford P A (1991) GIS data capture hardware and software. In: Maguire D J, Goodchild M F, Rhind D W (eds.) *Geographical Information Systems: principles and applications.* Longman, London, pp. 239–49, Vol 1

Keates J S (1989) *Cartographic Design and Production*, 2nd edn. Longman, London

Keefer B J, Smith J L, Gregoire T G (1988) Simulating manual digitizing error with statistical models. *Proceedings of GIS/LIS '88.* ACSM, Falls Church, pp. 475–83

Kennedy S (1989) The small number problem and the accuracy of spatial databases. In: Goodchild M F, Gopal S (eds.) *Accuracy of Spatial Databases.* Taylor & Francis, London, pp. 187–96

Konecny G, Lohmann P, Engel H, Kruck E (1987) Evaluation of SPOT imagery on analytical photogrammetric instruments. *Photogrammetric Engineering and Remote Sensing* **53** (9): 1223–30

Langran G, Chrisman N R (1988) A framework for temporal geographic information. *Cartographica* **25** (1): 1–14

Leick A (1987) GIS point referencing by satellite and gravity. In: Aangeenbrug R T, Schiffman Y M (eds.) *Proceedings of International Geographic Information Systems (IGIS) Symposium: the research agenda*, Vol. 2. NASA, Washington DC, pp. 305–17

Lillesand T M, Kiefer R W (1987) *Remote Sensing and Image Interpretation*, 2nd edn. Wiley, New York

Maffini G, Arno M, Bitterlich W (1989) Observations and comments on the generation and treatment of error in digital GIS data. In: Goodchild M F, Gopal S (eds.) *Accuracy of Spatial Databases.* Taylor & Francis, London, pp. 55–67

Maling D H (1991) Coordinate systems and map projections for GIS. In: Maguire D J, Goodchild M F, Rhind D W (eds.) *Geographical Information Systems: principles and applications.* Longman, London, pp. 135–46, Vol 1

Mason D C, Corr D G, Cross A, Hogg D C, Lawrence D H,

Petrou M, Tailor A M (1988) The use of digital map data in the segmentation and classification of remotely-sensed images. *International Journal of Geographical Information Systems* **2** (3): 195–215

Merchant D C (1987) Spatial accuracy specification for large scale topographic maps. *Photogrammetric Engineering and Remote Sensing* **53** (7): 958–61

Mounsey H M (ed.) (1988) *Building Databases for Global Science.* Taylor & Francis, London

Muller J-C (1991) Generalization of spatial databases. In: Maguire D J, Goodchild M F, Rhind D W (eds.) *Geographical Information Systems: principles and applications.* Longman, London, pp. 457–75, Vol 1

Norris P (1983) Microdata from the British census. In: Rhind D W (ed.) *A Census User's Handbook.* Methuen, London, pp. 301–19

Openshaw S (1983) Multivariate analysis of census data: the classification of areas. In: Rhind D W (ed.) *A Census User's Handbook.* Methuen, London, pp. 243–64

Openshaw S (1984) The modifiable areal unit problem. *CATMOG 38.* GeoBooks, Norwich

Parry R B, Perkins C R (1987) *World Mapping Today.* Butterworths, London

Prisley S P, Gregoire T G, Smith J L (1989) The mean and variance of area estimates computed in an arc-node geographic information system. *Photogrammetric Engineering and Remote Sensing* **55** (11): 1601–12

Reybold W, TeSelle G W (1989) Soil geographic databases. *Journal of Soil and Water Conservation* **44** (1): 28–9

Rhind D W (1991) Counting the people: the role of GIS. In: Maguire D J, Goodchild M F, Rhind D W (eds.) *Geographical Information Systems: principles and applications.* Longman, London, pp. 127–37, Vol 2

Rhind D W, Clark P (1988) Cartographic data inputs to global databases. In: Mounsey H M (ed.) *Building Databases for Global Science.* Taylor & Francis, London, pp. 79–104

Robinson A, Sale R, Morrison J, Muehrcke P C (1984) *Elements of Cartography*, 5th edn. Wiley, New York

Robinson G K (1950) Ecological correlation and the behaviour of individuals. *American Sociological Review* **15**: 351–7

SCS (1984a) *Soil Survey Manual.* Government Printing Office, Washington DC

SCS (1984b) *Technical Specifications for Line Segment Digitizing of Detailed Soil Survey Maps.* Government Printing Office, Washington DC

Sowton M (1991) Development of GIS-related activities at the Ordnance Survey. In: Maguire D J, Goodchild M F, Rhind D W (eds.) *Geographical Information Systems: principles and applications.* Longman, London, pp. 23–38, Vol 2

Starr L E, Anderson K E (1991) A USGS perspective on GIS. In: Maguire D J, Goodchild M F, Rhind D W (eds.) *Geographical Information Systems: principles and applications.* Longman, London, pp. 11–22, Vol 2

Thomas P J, Baker J C, Simpson T W (1989) Variability of the Cecil map unit in Appomattox County, Virginia. *Soil Science Society of America, Journal* **53** (5): 1470–4

Thompson M M (1988) *Maps for America*, 3rd edn. US Geological Survey, Reston

Tobler W R (1988) Resolution, resampling and all that. In: Mounsey H M (ed.) *Building Databases for Global Science.* Taylor & Francis, London, pp. 129–37

USGS (1986a) Digital line graphs from 1:24 000-scale maps. *Data User's Guide*, Vol. 1. US Department of the Interior, Reston

USGS (1986b) Land use and land cover digital data from 1:250 000- and 1:100 000-scale maps. *Data User's Guide*, Vol. 4. US Department of the Interior, Reston

USGS (1987) Digital elevation models. *Data User's Guide* Vol. 5. US Department of the Interior, Reston

Vonderohe A P, Chrisman N R (1985) Tests to establish the quality of digital cartographic data: some examples from the Dane County Land Records Project. *Proceedings of AUTOCARTO7.* ASPRS/ACSM, Falls Church, pp. 552–9

GIS AND REMOTE SENSING

F W DAVIS AND D S SIMONETT

This chapter briefly reviews remote sensing as both a data collection technology providing data for GIS and a user of spatially referenced data for scientific analysis. The discussion focuses on the importance of linking raster remote sensing systems with vector GIS to create Integrated GIS (IGIS). The use of IGIS is examined in applications such as image classification, calibration and environmental modelling. There is clearly great complementarity between remote sensing and GIS. Both areas developed independently to some extent, especially in the early days. By linking the technology, concepts and theories of both in IGIS, information systems considerably richer and more sophisticated can be created for use in substantive applications. Almost all projects currently employing satellite data or dealing with environmental data could potentially benefit from the development of truly integrated GIS.

INTRODUCTION

This chapter discusses the integration of digital remotely sensed data and cartographic information for GIS. Synergisms between remote sensing and GIS for land surface analysis are emphasized, specifically for surface classification, sensor calibration and physical modelling of earth surface processes.

There is a need to distinguish at the outset the difference between *measurements*, such as radiances obtained by a remote scanner system, and *geographical information*, that is knowledge of geographical phenomena obtained by the analysis of surface measurements or other geographical data. *Cartographic information* is geographical information obtained from maps. *Data* refers to measurements or information input to a geographical analysis. These distinctions are important in discussing the integration of remote sensing and GIS. Unquestionably, a large proportion of measurements of the earth's surface are now obtained from satellites and these provide an opportunity for greatly expanding and revising understanding of earth systems. To serve as input to GIS, satellite data must be well calibrated and in a suitable format and data structure. Also in the context of GIS, it is of paramount importance to know how best to use existing (and imperfect) geographical information to maximize the information potential of satellite measurements.

Early discussions of the relationship between digital remote sensing and GIS focused on the benefits of incorporating classified satellite imagery into land information systems for GIS-based analysis (e.g. Peplies and Keuper 1975). Treating the output of a remote sensing analysis as input to GIS tended to isolate the respective analysts and hindered the integration of remote sensing and GIS (Marble *et al.* 1983). The separation grew increasingly artificial as remote sensing analysts relied on ancillary geographical information to improve image classification (e.g. Hoffer *et al.* 1979; Strahler 1981; Mason *et al.* 1988) and as GIS analysts relied on satellite data for purposes such as cartographic rectification and map update (e.g. Hill and Kelly 1987).

Several recent papers have treated remote sensing and GIS in the more general framework of integrated spatial analysis, considering remotely sensed imagery as one element of a GIS for earth surface modelling (e.g. Marble *et al.* 1983; Jackson and Mason 1986; Ehlers, Edwards and Bedard 1989; Parker 1988; Star and Estes 1990). This has expanded the discussion of remote sensing and GIS from methods for improving image classification accuracy and data structure conversion, towards the more general problem of jointly representing and analysing disparate geographical data that can vary in structure, acquisition date, resolution, and level of pre-processing or human interpretation (e.g. Zhou 1989; Logan and Bryant 1987). The objective of this chapter is to extend this discussion in the light of recent advances in remote sensing theory and application. For a general review of remote sensing principles, the reader is referred to the *Manual of Remote Sensing* (Colwell 1983) and recent texts by Richards (1986), Elachi (1987) and Asrar (1989). The discussion focuses on the following issues:

- spatial resolution of digital satellite measurements, and the regularization of surface spatial variation by remote sensing systems;

- temporal resolution of satellite measurements and remote monitoring of earth surface dynamics;

- data structures for handling remotely sensed data and integrated geographical analysis;

- integrated GIS analysis for land surface classification, sensor calibration and physical modelling of surface properties.

There are other important aspects of the integration of remote sensing and GIS that will not be addressed because of space restrictions. The close links between aerial photointerpretation, existing map products and GIS will not be discussed explicitly. For example, since 1957 all operational maps produced by the US Government have used some form of remote sensing data as a base. Advances in production of digital orthophotography are especially significant in accelerating the integration of non-satellite remote sensing and GIS. The practical problems that hinder the integration of digital satellite data into existing land information systems for local planning are also not addressed, although many of the issues raised are germane to this important subject area.

Similarly, the significant fiscal and institutional impediments to integrating remote sensing and GIS technologies (Ehlers *et al.* 1989) are not considered. These issues are addressed in part by other authors in this volume. The discussion instead concentrates on some scientific issues that need to be considered in order to take fullest advantage of integrated GIS for research, resource analysis and management.

REMOTE SENSING AS A SOURCE OF GEOGRAPHICAL DATA

Remote sensing is defined narrowly here as measurement of the electromagnetic properties of a surface or object without being in contact with it. The discussion here is limited to digital data collected by aircraft or satellite. While most local environmental surveys still depend on manual interpretation of aerial photography, the use of digital imagery for regional analysis is now commonplace and will undoubtedly increase in the future. As a source of geographical information, digital remote sensing represents more than a simple extension of conventional aerial photography, requiring fundamentally different approaches to the analysis of earth surfaces (Everett and Simonett 1976).

Spatial characteristics of remotely sensed data

Remote sensing systems range from active microwave systems, which measure how a signal is scattered by the surface, to passive systems, which measure surface reflectance or emission. In a GIS context, especially important features of remotely sensed data are their sampling characteristics in the space and time domains.

The basic properties of a remote sensor can be summarized as:

- spectral coverage (spectral band locations);

- spectral resolution (spectral band width);

- spectral dimensionality (number of bands);

- radiometric resolution (quantization);

- instantaneous field of view (IFOV);

- angular field of view;

- point spread function (PSF);

- temporal response function (Strahler, Woodcock and Smith 1986).

Sensor *spatial resolution* has deliberately not been listed, as this term can be defined in several ways that give quite different values (Forshaw *et al.* 1983). Image resolution is the ground area covered by picture elements (pixels), which are themselves a function of the sensor IFOV, scene characteristics and data pre-processing. Even estimates of sensor IFOV can vary depending on the criteria that are used, and can change through time depending on the satellite orbital altitude. For example, estimates of the IFOV for the Landsat MSS have ranged from 73.4 to 81 metres (Simonett *et al.* 1983).

From a practical point of view, spatial resolution is defined by the size of the smallest object that can be reliably detected against a spectrally contrasting background, referred to as the effective resolution element (ERE). ERE is image specific, depending not only on the sensor IFOV, but on a host of other factors including the sensor PSF, surface–sensor geometry, atmospheric conditions, scene properties such as spectral contrast and object geometry, and data processing such as image rectification or enhancement (Billingsley *et al.* 1983; Duggin 1985; Strahler *et al.* 1986). Image dependencies become crucial as pixel size approaches the Nyquist limit for scene elements of interest (see below).

In a broader sense, the spatial resolution of a remote sensor varies with the task to which the data are applied, specifically: (1) *detection*, determining the presence of an object; (2) *identification* or labelling of an object; or (3) *analysis*, where information is obtained about an object beyond its initial detection and identification. Simonett *et al.* (1983) suggest that for low contrast targets the effective resolution of sensors required for analysis may be as much as 10 times less than that for identification and 30 times less than that for detection.

Autocorrelation and regularization in satellite imagery

Spatial variation in a satellite image is produced by the convolution of intrinsic variation in surface electromagnetic properties with the sampling field of the sensor. Surface variation can be categorized as *continuous* (gradients), *discrete* (mosaics), *linear* or *localized* (e.g. intermittent extreme events, point processes and disc processes) (see also Getis and Boots 1978). It is also important to recognize whether the surface process being investigated is *stationary*, so that its statistical properties do not depend on absolute spatial location (Cliff and Ord 1981), and whether the pattern of surface variation is random, contagious or regular.

Statistical properties of environmental processes are typically highly *scale dependent*. Scale is the interval of space or time over which a measurement is made, so that *scale dependence* refers to the relationship between the magnitude or variability of a spatial process and the scale of measurement. Most natural surfaces are non-stationary over large areas, manifesting many different types of variation within and between different measurement scales. This renders satellite measurements highly sensitive to sensor IFOV, scan angle effects (e.g. National Oceanographic and Atmospheric Administration (NOAA) Advanced Very High Resolution Radiometer (AVHRR) pixels range from 1.1 x 1.1 km at nadir to 4 x 1.1 km at 55.4° off-nadir) and pre-processing involving pixel resampling and interpolation. Multiple scales of surface variation also make it unreliable to calibrate sensors using ground measurements made over sample areas that depart significantly from sensor resolution.

Much research is needed on spatial variability of earth surfaces to utilize satellite data fully. Some recent studies have examined scale-dependent variation in terrain variables such as topography and radiation (e.g. Mark and Aronson 1984; Mulla 1988; Dubayah, Dozier and Davis 1990), and soils (Burrough 1983; Oliver and Webster 1986). Digital satellite data have been analysed to study scale dependence in vegetation patterns (e.g. Woodcock and Strahler 1987; Davis, Dubayah and Dozier 1989; Townshend and Justice 1990). Inferring surface variation from spatial variation in satellite data is not straightforward, however, because satellite radiances are affected by non-surface factors such as sun–earth–satellite geometry and atmospheric characteristics. Furthermore, as mentioned earlier, surface variation is filtered by the sensor in the process known as scene *regularization*. This is an important feature of satellite data that distinguishes them from most other sources of geographical information (Star and

Estes 1990). Recent work by Jupp, Walker and Penridge (1986) and Jupp, Strahler and Woodcock (1989) provides useful insight into how surface variability is regularized by satellites. Some of their results are summarized below.

The reflected radiance of a surface at location x at time t can be summarized as (Moik 1980):

$$f(x,\lambda,t,p) = r(x,\lambda,t,p)\, i(x,\lambda,t) \qquad [14.1]$$

where $r(x,\lambda,t,p)$ is the reflectance of the surface as a function of position (x), wavelength (λ), time (t) and polarization (p), and $i(x,\lambda,t)$ is the incident illumination. For simplicity, consider only the variation in reflectance with spatial position, $f(x)$. One important property of this variation is its *spatial autocorrelation* or *autocovariance*, which measures how $f(x)$ varies as a function of the distance and orientation between observations. Ignoring directional effects, spatial autocovariance in reflectance of a surface at points separated by distance h, denoted by $cov(h)$, can be described using the *isotropic variogram*, where

$$V(h) = cov(0) - cov(h) = 1/2\, E(f(x) - f(x+h))^2 \qquad [14.2]$$

In remote sensing, surface spatial variation is 'regularized' through the convolution of $f(x)$ with the sampling field of the sensor, $\mathbf{Z}$. For intermittent surfaces, the regularization of $f(x)$ by $\mathbf{Z}$ leads to a new spatial function

$$f_Z(y) = 1/Mes(\mathbf{Z}) \int_{\mathbf{Z}_y} f(x)\, d|x| \qquad [14.3]$$

where $\mathbf{Z}_y$ is the sampling field (e.g. square pixel) centred at location y and $Mes(\mathbf{Z})$ is the sample area. The variogram for the regularized image then becomes:

$$V_Z = (T*V)_h - (T*V)_0 \qquad [14.4]$$

where T is the overlap function for $\mathbf{Z}$,

$$T = I_Z * I_Z^* / Mes^2(\mathbf{Z}) \qquad [14.5]$$

where $*$ is convolution and I_Z is the indicator function ($I_Z(x) = 1$ for $\mathbf{x} \in \mathbf{Z}$, 0 else, and $I_Z^*(t) = I_Z(-t)$). Equation [14.4] states that the variogram that results from the regularization of a surface by a satellite sensor is related to the variogram of the surface convolved with the covariance function of the pixel.

The variograms that result as a surface is regularized to different pixel sizes can be predicted from the *point* variogram of the unregularized surface (Jupp et al. 1986). However, the unregularized variogram of natural surfaces is usually not known. Simulations based on the regularization of different surface types has proven useful. For example, Jupp et al. (1986) analyse binary surfaces covered by discs of different size and pattern, a simple analogy to scattered trees on uniform terrain, to relate image regularization to image texture, fractal behaviour and estimated cover (see also Goodchild 1980).

The semi-variogram of an image is closely related to image local variance, which is the average standard deviation of image brightness in a moving three-by-three window:

$$T_{i,j} = \left[1/8 \sum_{k=i-1}^{i+1} \sum_{l=j-1}^{j+1} (x_{k,l} - \bar{x}_{i,j})^2 \right]^{1/2} \qquad [14.6]$$

This measure, which is often used for edge detection and for image segmentation and classification, is the regularized value of the semi-variogram at a step size equal to or slightly greater than (for diagonals) image resolution or pixel size (Jupp et al. 1989).

Strahler et al. (1986) distinguish two fundamentally different models, the H-resolution model, in which scene elements are large compared to image resolution, and the L-resolution model, in which elements are smaller than the image resolution area and are not individually detectable. Image texture increases as image resolution approaches the dimensions of scene elements. Large local variance can be problematic in image classification using high resolution sensors such as Landsat Thematic Mapper (TM) and SPOT to map land cover types such as urban areas or woody vegetation, where sensor resolution approaches the size of individual buildings or clearings. Scene elements are often organized into larger features (e.g. buildings into blocks and trees into stands) that are manifested as additional peaks in image texture at larger pixel sizes. To the degree that different surface processes have characteristic scale dependencies, multi-resolution imagery (*image pyramids*) ranging from H- to L-resolution may be effective in surface recognition and classification (e.g. Wharton 1989).

The *regularization* of surface spatial variation by imaging systems means that information derived from analysis of satellite data differs fundamentally from most cartographic information, which usually derives from *generalization* of perceived spatial variation (e.g. in producing soils maps) or *interpolation* of point measurements of the surface (e.g. mapping of surface topography or climate data). The intermixing of regularized, generalized and interpolated surfaces in GIS convolves intrinsic surface variation with the effects of resolution and processing of the satellite data, map scale and generalization procedures, data structure and data conversion, modelling procedures, etc. The theory of GIS is still a long way from a formal decomposition of these effects. Special attention must be paid to non-linear scale dependencies of some surface types, because these surfaces will be highly sensitive to source image resolution (e.g. Lovejoy and Shertzer 1985).

Temporal characteristics of remotely sensed data

Satellite sensors provide the opportunity for consistent multi-temporal measurements of large areas over time periods of days to decades. Sensor coverage and repeat interval are determined by platform altitude, angular velocity, orbital inclination relative to the Equator and orbital orientation relative to the vernal equinox (Elachi 1987). Many optical sensors are placed in sun-synchronous near-polar orbits to achieve global coverage and consistent illumination geometry (e.g. Landsat, AVHRR). The repeat interval varies among these sensors depending on their altitude and velocity. Others are placed in geosynchronous orbits to provide high frequency coverage of the same region (e.g. the GOES meteorological satellites).

The ability to detect changes in a surface imaged over time depends on the spatial (geometrical registration and resolution), spectral (band location and width), radiometric and temporal (imaging frequency) properties of the sensor system (Townshend and Justice 1988). The comparison of images acquired by the same sensor on different dates is complicated by any changes in instrument gain and offset as well as differences in atmospheric properties, notably in sub-pixel cloud cover. Change detection is considerably more complicated when more than one sensor system is used because of differences in sensor IFOV, PSF, bandwidths and spectral response properties (Duggin 1985).

Many techniques have been developed for atmospheric correction and radiometric calibration of satellite imagery for multi-temporal analysis (e.g. Holben and Fraser 1984; Hall and Badhwar 1987; Singh and Saull 1988; Schott, Salvaggio and Volchok 1988; Suits, Malila and Weller 1988). Less easily accounted for are changes in surface reflectance properties caused by illumination geometry. These are especially problematic because they can greatly affect the relationship between satellite radiances and surface properties (Deering 1989). Thus extracting detailed quantitative information from multi-date imagery requires sophisticated algorithms to correct for scene-specific illumination geometry, atmospheric effects and sensor characteristics.

Much of the previous discussion about spatial environmental variation applies to temporal variation as well. A process operating through time can be described as continuous, discrete or intermittent, as *stationary* or *non-stationary*, and as random, autocorrelated or regular (Jenkins and Watts 1968). For many applications, remote sensing can be treated as point sampling in the time domain (i.e. the time interval over which the image is acquired can be assumed negligibly short).

Equation [14.1] can be rewritten as a function of time:

$$f(t) = r(t)\, i(t) \qquad [14.7]$$

If T is the time interval between successive samples, then a series of repeated satellite observations of a location can be considered the convolution of continuous spectral change in the environment by the temporal sampling filter $i(t)$, which can be modelled as a series of delta functions:

$$i(t) = \sum_{n=-\infty}^{\infty} \delta(t - n\mathbf{T}) \qquad [14.8]$$

Thus

$$f_T(t) = f(t) i(t) \qquad [14.9]$$

$f(t)$ can be recovered from $f_T(t)$ for temporal changes manifested over periods of $\geq 2\mathbf{T}$, or less than the Nyquist frequency of $1/2\mathbf{T}$. Processes that change at higher frequencies (shorter periods) will be aliased into $f_T(t)$.

Surface electromagnetic properties change over

time scales from fractions of seconds to years. For example, vegetated surfaces change within seconds as a result of physiological adjustments of plant canopies and wind-driven changes in leaf orientation, whereas successional processes can operate over decades to centuries. The high frequency variation contributes unavoidable noise in multi-temporal imagery. Rapid atmospheric changes and surface reflectance changes with illumination also contribute noise, but it may be possible to remove these effects.

Despite considerable high frequency 'noise', satellite data have been used effectively to monitor surface processes that are continuous or persist over more than a few days and that can manifest detectable change within a few years. Detection of intermittent high magnitude events such as fires and floods is feasible but their short duration means that they can only be described probabilistically over large areas (Robinson 1987). Systems undergoing gradual directional change (e.g. expansion of urban areas) or more rapid but non-directional change (e.g. shifting cultivation of tropical forest lands where the proportions in different stages of use or recovery remain unchanged) are also problematic because the information about such surfaces is especially sensitive to both spatial and temporal sampling properties of the sensor system. Unfortunately, there is scant quantitative information on scale-dependent spatio-temporal variation of earth surfaces, though such analyses are now feasible over large areas using satellite data.

Townshend and Justice (1988) provide a useful example of space–time interactions in remote sensing in the context of monitoring changes in land cover over large regions. They note that most landscapes undergo a wide variety of changes through space and time at many different characteristic scales. The ability of sensor systems to monitor such state changes in a surface depends on the radiometric contrast between states and on how temporal change in states is distributed in space (e.g. uniform area changes uniformly through time, sharp extensive boundary between two states moves progressively, a state expands radially from a point through time). They conclude that high spatial resolution is especially critical for land surface monitoring. Presumably, an opposite conclusion would apply to ocean surface monitoring, where high temporal resolution is much more important than spatial resolution (Table 14.1).

Operational and planned satellite remote sensors

The civilian satellite remote sensing programme in the United States has operated since the mid-1960s, providing global coverage by the Landsat series since 1972 and by the NOAA AVHRR series since 1978. Landsat 1,2 and 3 alone acquired more than 1 million images (Lauer 1990). Many other sensors have been launched subsequently, and a wide array of research instruments are expected to be launched over the next decade (Eos Science Steering Committee 1987).

In summarizing the information needs for a satellite-based Earth Observing System, Goddard Space Flight Center (1984) listed 30 major environmental parameters that could be measured with operational or planned sensors over time scales of $10^{-4}-10^1$ years and spatial scales of $10^{-4}-10^3$ km^2. Some surface parameters are listed in Table 14.1. Existing and planned sensor systems capable of providing such information are summarized in Table 14.2. Some examples of future research sensors, such as HIRIS and MODIS, have been included to show the remarkable capabilities expected from the next generation of research sensors, and to indicate the probable direction of future operational systems.

INTEGRATING REMOTE SENSING AND GIS

Previous sections described the general features of remotely sensed data and alluded to some of the issues that must be addressed in integrating these data with other information sources for geographical analysis. In this section some technical and analytical concerns related to data integration and spatial modelling are considered. Three points are particularly emphasized:

1. Satellite data differ from nearly all other geographical data in their consistency, high positional accuracy, high spatial and temporal resolution, and low level of human abstraction or interpretation. GIS require raster capabilities to store and analyse large volumes of these data with minimum loss of resolution or radiometric precision.

Table 14.1 Some important earth surface parameters that can be measured remotely, and required spatial and temporal sampling frequencies for various applications (modified and simplified Table 2 from Goddard Space Flight Center 1984). Spatial frequencies are expressed in terms of maximum pixel dimension germane to the application.

Parameter	Application	Spatial frequency	Temporal frequency
Soil			
types	Geochemistry, agriculture, forestry	30 m	Annual
moisture	Hydrology, geochemistry	30 m–10 km	Weekly
erosion	Agriculture, geochemistry	30 m	Annual
carbon, nitrogen	Geochemistry	30 m	Monthly
permafrost	Bioclimatology	30 m	Annual
Surface temperature			
land	Bioclimatology	1 km	12 h
inland waters	Pollution, climatology	30 m	12 h
ocean	Climatology	1–4 km	12 h
ice	Climatology	1 km	Daily
Vegetation			
types	Resource analysis	30 m	Annual
	Geochemistry, bioclimatology	1 km	Weekly
composition	Resource analysis	30 m	Weekly
condition	Geochemistry, bioclimatology	1 km	Weekly
Land use	Demography, planning, Resource analysis	10–30 m	Annual
Snow	Hydrology	1 km	Weekly
Radiation (SW, LW)	Climatology, hydrology	1 km	Daily
Precipitation	Climatology, hydrology	1 km	Daily
Phytoplankton	Fisheries, biogeochemistry	1–4 km	2 days
Turbidity	Pollution, erosion, geochemistry	30 m–1 km	2 days
Surface elevation			
land	Geomorphology, hydrology, ecology	10–30 m	10 years
ocean	Oceanography	25 km	2 days
Rock mineralogy	Geology, pedology	30 m	10 years

2. Maps use points and lines to portray selected features of reality in a highly abstracted and generalized form. This information establishes a conceptual spatial context for the analysis of remotely sensed data. GIS require vector capabilities to store such information in a feature-oriented data model that minimizes feature distortion and loss of topological information.

3. Integrated geographical analysis will require multiple data structures and software that support a wide range of spatial queries and promote statistical and deterministic modelling. No existing GIS has all of these capabilities.

Spatial data structures

Spatial data structure refers to the form in which geo-referenced data are represented and stored in a computer. Frank and Barrera (1990) list four major ways that spatial data structures can differ from one another:

1. Type of geometrical data (point versus region)

Table 14.2 Some operational and research satellites for earth surface analysis (Goddard Space Flight Center 1984; Ehlers, Edwards and Bedard 1989).

Platform	Sensor	Year	Bands	Spectral	IFOV	Repeat Cover	Country
Landsat	MSS	1972–	4	VIS/NIR	80 m	16 d	USA
	TM4, 5	1982–	7	VIS/NIR/TIR	30/120 m	16 d	USA
	TM6	1992–	8	VIS/NIR/TIR	20/30/120 m	16 d	USA
NOAA	AVHRR	1978–	5	VIS/NIR/TIR	1–4 km	12 h	USA
GOES	VISSR	1975–	2	VIS/TIR	0.9/8 km	12 h	USA
NIMBUS-7	CZCS	1978–	1	VIS	10 km	27 d	USA
HCMM	HCMR	1978–1980	2	VIS/TIR	500 m/600 m	16 d	USA
Shuttle	LFC	1984		Film	VIS/NIR	10–20 m	USA
	SIR-A, B	1981–	1	Radar		17–58 m	USA
	SIR-C	1991–	2	Radar		10–60 m	USA
EOS-A	HIRIS	1998–	192	VIS/TIR	30 m	4 d	USA
	MODIS-N	1998–	35+	VIS/TIR	250–1000 m	2 d	
	MODIS-T	1998–	64	VIS/TIR	1 km	2 d	
SPOT	HRV-P	1986–	1	VIS	10 m	2.5 d	France
	HRV-XS	1986–	3	VIS/NIR	20 m	2.5 d	
MOS/LOS	MESSR	1987–	4	VIS/NIR	50 m	17 d	Japan
	VTIR	1987–	4	VIS/TIR	1–3 km	17 d	
	MSR	1987–	1	Radar	25 m	17 d	
ERS-1	AMI	1990–	1	Radar	30 m	3 d	EEC
	ASTR	1990–	3	TIR	1 km	3 d	
RADARSAT	SAR	1990–	1	Radar	30 m	3 d	Canada

2. Object handling (non-fragmenting versus fragmenting)

3. Retrieval (direct versus hierarchical)

4. Subdivision of space (regular versus data determined).

Data are most commonly represented in GIS in either *grid raster* (region, fragmenting, direct, regular) or *vector* (region, non-fragmenting, direct, data determined) form. Satellite measurements are acquired in raster format, whereas much existing GIS software and many widely available databases are in vector format. The incompatibility of these data structures and the need for reconciling the raster/vector dichotomy is a pervasive theme in the literature on the integration of remote sensing and GIS (e.g. Logan and Bryant 1987; Archibald 1987; Smith *et al.* 1987a; Barker 1988; Peuquet 1988; Ehlers *et al.* 1989; Zhou 1989). The discussion here focuses on the use of one or both data structures for handling and analysing remotely sensed data and for integrated geographical analysis. (Technical features and relative merits of raster and vector representations are discussed in detail by Egenhofer and Herring 1991 in this volume and are only briefly discussed here.)

Raster data structures

Raster data structures tessellate space and assign each spatial element a unique value, thus providing *explicit* information for each location (Burrough 1986). Raster structures include *regular* versus *irregular* tessellations, and *hierarchical* versus *non-hierarchical* models. They have been described as *field-based* (Ehlers *et al.* 1989), as opposed to *object-based* representations provided by vector structures, referring to the fact that fields are assigned object attributes in a raster model whereas objects are given locations and attributes in the latter model.

The most common raster structure is a square lattice whose values are stored as two-dimensional arrays in the computer. This structure is convenient for imaging systems such as satellite sensors or other digital scanning devices, and has many additional advantages including (Burrough 1986):

- simplicity;
- ease of image display and processing;
- ease of data aggregation and data overlay;
- uniform cell size and shape for multidimensional spatial analysis and spatial simulation modelling.

Also, the square grid is the only practical structure for maintaining full radiometric precision and spatial resolution of satellite data. This is because the advantages of other data structures such as hierarchical or vector structures depend on the presence of large fields of pixels with identical values. Such fields are uncommon in satellite data acquired over land, where much of the variation occurs at high spatial frequencies (e.g. Davis *et al.* 1989).

Although well suited to satellite data, the raster structure has many limitations:

1. Gridding of point and line features entails loss of locational precision.

2. Griding of uniform polygons leads to misclassification of perimeter areas and to areal estimation error, both of which depend on grid resolution and polygon shape (e.g. Switzer 1975; Muller 1977; Goodchild 1980; Crapper 1980; Crapper, Walker and Nanninga 1986).

3. Many surfaces are more naturally fitted with alternative shapes such as irregular triangles (see Weibel and Heller 1991 in this volume).

4. Local interactions are not easily modelled on a square lattice because of differences in the distance and degree of connectedness among vertical and horizontal versus diagonal neighbours. This is especially awkward in modelling contagious diffusion processes such as fire spread, which are better described using a hexagonal lattice.

5. Analyses requiring metric or topological information (e.g. the length of a linear feature, the size and shape of a patch, network relationships, degree of connectedness among patches) cannot be performed on raster data without first reassembling those objects.

The regular lattice can impose large data volumes because lattice resolution is generally selected to capture the smallest feature of interest. Raster data structures are often chosen specifically because of the desire to incorporate satellite data, and all other cartographic information is gridded to the resolution of those data. In practice, such databases rapidly grow very large because of the analyst's desire to use the highest resolution satellite data that can be obtained.

Hierarchical raster data structures

Several methods of data compaction have been developed to store raster data more efficiently, including different coding schemes (e.g. run-length or block coding) and hierarchical representations such as quadtrees, hextrees, R-trees and field trees (Samet 1984; Frank and Barrera 1990). Hierarchical data structures require tessellations that can be recursively decomposed into similar patterns of smaller size (Smith *et al.* 1987a). The square tessellation is used most commonly in constructing a hierarchy in which a cell at each level in the tree can be subdivided into four cells at the next sublevel, down to the level of individual pixels (Bell *et al.* 1983). Smith *et al.* (1987a) distinguish *image pyramids*, in which information for all levels is retained, from quadtree regionalizations in which information is stored to the level of a homogeneous subregion and no further. Similar hierarchies have been constructed for point and line data (Samet 1984).

Hierarchical data structures offer several advantages over raster structures for integrated analysis of satellite and map data (Jackson and Mason 1986). Data volume and processing time can be greatly reduced depending on image or map complexity. Spatial overlay and proximity analyses are facilitated by the more *object-like* representation of surface variation. Similarly, this representation makes it easier to incorporate information on size, shape and scale dependence into algorithms for pattern recognition and image classification, thus lending itself to knowledge-based GIS analyses (Chen 1987; Smith *et al.* 1987b; Menon 1989). Despite these substantial advantages, hierarchical data structures are still field based and can provide only limited and geometrically artificial information about objects. Similarly, although quadtrees may allow more precise representation of points and lines, their raster structure still imposes some loss of locational precision, and they are not easily adapted to handling network phenomena.

Vector data structures

Vector data structures represent spatial variation using lines located in continuous coordinate space. Lines in the original analogue map are stored as strings of coordinates, and the spatial relationships among map entities are stored explicitly or are computed when needed (Peuquet 1988). Vector representations may be *unlinked*, in which object boundaries are encoded without reference to neighbours, or *topologically linked*, in which sections of boundary lines (arcs) are referenced by their endpoints, orientation and the attributes of adjoining regions (Peucker and Chrisman 1975). The identity of map entities is preserved by this data structure, which can thus to some extent be considered *object oriented*.

The vector data structure has some serious disadvantages for spatial analysis. Information is lost during data encoding due to line generalization and digitizing errors (see Veregin 1989 for review; Prisley, Gregoire and Smith 1989). The high data volume per element in a vector model makes storage costs prohibitive for dense maps or unprocessed satellite data. The data structure is more complex than raster or hierarchical structures, and operations such as overlay and display are more difficult (Burrough 1986). Spatial analyses involving spatial statistics or simulation are much less straightforward because each polygon has a unique size, shape and orientation.

The evolution of vector-based GIS software has been driven largely by the desire to encode and analyse existing mapped information. The vector model of points, lines and polygons in *continuous coordinate space* permits the closest approximation to the original map. Furthermore, implicit topological relationships in the original maps such as network linkages can be retained as attributes in vector data structures.

The distinction between the *map-oriented* vector structure and the *data-oriented* raster structure calls attention once more to the differences among cartographic *information*, remotely sensed *measurements* and information derived from those data (Maffini 1987). Maps represent surface variation in a highly generalized, selective and abstracted form (Ehlers *et al.* 1989), and the processes and data used to generate the cartographic information are usually unknown or irretrievable. For instance, boundary placement on a soils map can be driven as much by the analyst's purposes and underlying model of reality as by observed or measured patterns in surface variation. Conversely, satellite measurements involve little or no human interpretation other than for registration and calibration.

Conversion of satellite data to vector format generally requires classification (i.e. interpretation) of low-level information at the expense of measurement precision and spatial detail, whereas rasterizing a map to be conformal with satellite data means disaggregating and degrading high-level cartographic information. These are fundamental trade-offs that must be confronted in the integration of satellite and cartographic data into a single data structure.

Integration of disparate data structures

There are case-dependent technical and analytical advantages and disadvantages to raster, hierarchical and vector data structures, and recent literature has tended to emphasize the use of more than one data model in geographical analyses (e.g. Haralick 1980; Logan and Bryant 1987; Rhind and Green 1988; Peuquet 1988; Simonett 1988; Ehlers *et al.* 1989; Zhou 1989). A recent survey noted that nearly half of all GIS packages now support both vector and raster structures, suggesting that the advantages of flexibility in choice of data structure outweigh the burden of additional processing software and analysis time (Parker 1989).

The term *Integrated Geographical Information Systems* (IGIS) has been coined to describe systems capable of processing both vector and raster data. The simplest kind of integrated system, what Ehlers *et al.* (1989) term the separate but equal strategy, provides for data conversion, data transfer between vector GIS and image processing software, and simultaneous display of raster and vector data. Examples of such systems are provided by Logan and Bryant (1987) and Goodenough (1988). Relational GIS have also been developed in which raster and vector data are linked through a relational database management system (RDBMS) (Zhou 1989). Cartographic information can be digitized in vector format but is converted and processed with satellite data in a raster environment. However, feature attributes that were encoded during vector processing are retained in non-spatial relational data structures and can be linked to the raster data for analysis. Such systems are useful, but it should be recognized that multiple conversions of vector and raster data carry with them the cost of data degradation through loss of precision and accuracy.

A somewhat fuller integration would allow tandem raster and vector processing, hierarchical representation and object-oriented handling of remote sensing data. Some quadtree-based GIS such as the Knowledge Based Geographical Information System (KBGIS) have many of these capabilities, including heuristic search procedures and learning capacities (Smith et al. 1987b). Ideally, a fully integrated GIS should be *seamless* in maintaining both object-oriented and field-oriented representations of geographical data, and should facilitate a wide range of spatial queries and analyses that would promote both statistical and deterministic modelling of earth surfaces (Ehlers et al. 1989). Much of the impetus for developing such a GIS has come from resource analysts trying to incorporate satellite data into land information systems, and from the scientific community concerned with modelling physical and biological systems at regional to global scales (e.g. Archibald 1987; Goodenough 1988; Estes and Bredekamp 1988). The remainder of this chapter is devoted to a fuller discussion of some model types that are specially suited to IGIS analysis, some of the issues that need to be addressed in applying such models, and some recent examples of IGIS analysis for modelling terrestrial ecosystems.

INTEGRATED GIS MODELLING OF EARTH SURFACES

Remote sensing models

Strahler et al. (1986) distinguish three basic model types in remote sensing: *sensor*, *atmosphere* and *scene*. In practice, the analysis of satellite imagery may incorporate one or more of these. Models are further divided into *empirical* versus *deterministic* and *invertible* versus *non-invertible*. Empirical models rely on the statistical association of sensor measurements and surface characteristics, whereas deterministic models rely on radiative and heat transfer theory. Invertible models are those in which unknown properties of the scene can be inferred from remote sensing measurements. Strahler et al. (1986) point out that these dichotomies are really endpoints in continua of model types. For example, deterministic models often have empirical components, and non-invertible models can sometimes be inverted under restricted conditions. Classification and calibration of satellite imagery both exemplify the empirical invertible modelling approach, while physical scene modelling represents the other extreme of deterministic (and often non-invertible) models. Each is discussed below in the context of IGIS analysis.

Classification

Classification is the grouping of objects into classes based on their similarity with respect to one or more variables, whereas discrimination is the assigning of objects to pre-defined classes based on object properties. The objective of most remote sensing applications is to discriminate and map pre-determined ground information classes, usually with the aid of statistical clustering or discrimination methods. The literature on remote sensing often refers to cluster analysis as unsupervised classification and to discrimination as supervised classification or pattern recognition. This enormous literature cannot be reviewed here. Readers are referred to works by Moik (1980), Haralick and Fu (1983) and Richards (1986).

Unsupervised classification involves clustering individual pixels into spectral classes based on measured reflectance values in the original channels or transformations of those channels. The spectral classes are then assigned to ground information classes (e.g. land use/land cover categories) by an analyst based on field observations or interpretation of air photos.

In supervised classification, pixels are assigned to ground information classes through a discriminant function based on observed spectral properties of the information classes in a set of preselected training sites. Statistical discriminant functions include *maximum likelihood estimators*, where the spectral mean vector and covariance matrix of the training sites are taken to be those of the information class, and *Bayesian estimators*, where the Probability Density Function (PDF) of the information class is assumed to be known *a priori* and training samples are used to refine the PDF to obtain an *a posteriori* discriminant function. Another form of discrimination is *syntactic* pattern recognition, which uses hierarchical decision structures and grammar rules to recognize information classes based on a set of primitive features characteristic of each class (Haralick and Fu 1983).

Some classification approaches combine supervised and unsupervised methods, using unsupervised classification to generate training classes with multivariate normal probability density functions that are subsequently used in a supervised classification procedure (see Richards 1986). Another hybrid approach is *guided* clustering, which involves initial seeding of spectral clusters or pooling of spectral clusters based on training class statistics (Peterson and Running 1989).

Problems in the statistical classification of satellite imagery

In statistical classification and discrimination, objects are usually classified based on measurement variables relevant to the information classes. For example, plant species abundance data are used to classify vegetation samples into vegetation types. In remote sensing, however, surface electromagnetic properties are surrogates for relevant properties of the information classes such as land use, timber type, and so on (Robinove 1981). The strength of this surrogate relationship is strongly scene dependent because the information classes do not possess unique electromagnetic signals (Hoffer 1978). Usually the information class pertains to one feature of the environment, for example crop type. The spectral signature for that type will vary with changes in soil characteristics, stage of crop development, illumination, atmosphere and so forth. Atmospheric corrections and radiometric rectification to account for illumination changes reduce some of the unwanted signature variation. Band ratios and spectral transformations such as the Kauth–Thomas Tassled Cap Transformation help to isolate the reflectance variation related to plants (Kauth and Thomas 1976). Classification accuracy can also be improved by using multi-temporal imagery. For example, multi-temporal profiles have been used to improve crop recognition based on crop-specific phenology (Hall and Badhwar 1987). In the final analysis, however, local and regional variation in physical and biological processes and scene-specific radiative transfer conditions mean that there is always a strong local, empirical element to statistical classification of satellite imagery.

A second concern in satellite-based classification of earth surfaces relates to the earlier discussion of object-oriented versus data-oriented analysis. Classification systems evolve through the interaction of human needs and human capabilities to structure available information. Environmental classification systems in use today (e.g. Anderson, Hardy and Roach 1976) describe entities that have been abstracted by humans from ground observations and, more recently, from air photo data. Humans recognize these environmental entities in remotely sensed imagery based in part on local tone and colour, but principally on complex spatial attributes of pattern, size, shape, texture and context that are not involved in per-pixel classification or discrimination procedures (Estes, Hajic and Tinney 1983).

A number of digital processing procedures have been implemented that utilize local textural or temporal data in addition to per-pixel spectral data, image segmentation or expert system approaches to generate more object-like image classes (Haralick and Fu 1983; Wang *et al.* 1983; Goodenough *et al.* 1987; Wharton 1989; Bryant 1990). These methods tend to produce better results than per-pixel classifiers, and, because they rely on other information beyond absolute spectral reflectances, reduce reliance on scene-specific optimization of statistical classification parameters (Wharton 1989). Furthermore, because these procedures produce image classes with spatial properties closer to those of idealized ground information classes, they render satellite-based maps that are more compatible with the traditional needs of local and regional land planners and managers and are more readily incorporated into vector GIS.

Errors in the classification of remotely sensed imagery

Classification accuracies are now routinely reported for satellite classifications of land surfaces.

Misclassification of satellite imagery is usually measured using a *confusion matrix* or *contingency table* that compares image class to actual class for a sample of pixels from the image (Dozier and Strahler 1983). Actual class is determined by ground survey or from more reliable image or map data. The simplest statistic that can be derived from the table is the per cent correctly classified, although additional measures can be derived (Card 1982; Congalton, Oderwald and Mead 1983; see Veregin 1989 for a review). Image class and ground class may disagree for a variety of reasons, notably:

- misregistration of satellite data to cartographic coordinate system;
- misregistration of ground data to cartographic coordinate system;
- inadequate spectral separation of information classes;
- inappropriate statistical or contextual classifier;
- analyst misclassification of actual information class in test data;
- spatial disaggregation of a ground feature into several spectral classes;
- mixed pixel or boundary effects.

It should be noted that it is difficult to obtain a sufficiently large and unbiased sample of test sites to measure confidently thematic map accuracy (Congalton 1988a). Also, in many applications the classification bias (class-specific errors of omission versus commission) and spatial distribution of errors may be as important as overall accuracy. Experience shows that image classifications are often biased, that error rates nearly always differ systematically among information classes, and that errors are rarely (if ever) randomly distributed (e.g. Campbell 1981; Walsh, Lightfoot and Butler 1987; Congalton 1988b). Such error distributions may be difficult to model analytically and can have serious consequences in a decision or spatial modelling framework (Anselin 1989).

IGIS-based land surface classification

Integration of cartographic and satellite data has proven an effective partial solution to many of the problems of satellite image classification, and the use of both data sources for land surface classification is now commonplace. Many different GIS variables and approaches have been used, for example:

- Use of digital elevation data to account for illumination effects in pixel radiance values (e.g. Hutchinson 1982; Franklin *et al.* 1986; Jones, Settle and Wyatt 1988).
- Use of digital elevation data to account for elevational zonation of environmental factors, plant species and vegetation types (e.g. Hoffer *et al.* 1979; Strahler 1981; Satterwhite, Rice and Shipman 1984; Cibula and Nyquist 1987).
- Use of map information to stratify a satellite scene into more homogeneous and statistically stationary subregions in which to apply statistical pattern recognition methods (e.g. Gaydos and Newland 1978; Hutchinson 1982).
- Use of map information as an aid to labelling spectral clusters in unsupervised classification (Hutchinson 1982; Ustin *et al.* 1986).
- Spectral/geomorphometric mapping of terrain features (Franklin, Peddle and Moulton 1989).
- Selection of training sites for supervised classification.
- Selection of scene-invariant targets for atmospheric correction.
- Location of field sites for map accuracy assessment.
- Aid in visual interpretation of image features (e.g. Harding and Forrest 1989).
- Knowledge-based image segmentation and classification (Estes, Sailer and Tinney 1986; Goodenough *et al.* 1987; Tong, Richards and Swain 1987; McKeown 1986; Mason *et al.* 1988).

In several of the applications listed above, map information provides a basis for segmenting the scene into regions that are physically, ecologically or spectrally more homogeneous. In this way, map data are used to constrain the classification of satellite reflectance measurements, to improve the surrogate relationship between satellite measurements and information classes, and to make the spatial attributes of spectral classes more consistent with those of other geographical data.

Integration of satellite and cartographic data for land surface classification introduces new sources of error into the classification product because of inaccuracies in the GIS data as well as imperfect specification of the relationship between ground information classes and GIS variables. GIS errors are treated by Chrisman (1991 in this volume), so only a few examples are cited here:

- GIS data may contain measurement or estimation errors that will lead to incorrect image segmentation or use of inappropriate prior classification probabilities. For instance, digital elevation data are prone to non-randomly distributed errors, and derivatives of elevation such as slope angle and aspect can be unreliable (Walsh *et al.* 1987; Weibel and Heller 1991 in this volume).

- Maps of hydrology, land use or land cover are rapidly outdated.

- Misregistration of satellite and GIS data can be problematic unless map features are much larger than pixel size [satellite data may often have higher positional accuracy than the base maps used for their rectification (Welch and Usery 1984)].

- Maps may be too generalized to be of much value for image segmentation (Rhind and Clark 1988).

- Use of geographical data to develop and apply weights or prior probabilities to image classification depends on a correctly specified statistical model as well as on accurate maps for applying the model.

In general, the gains in classification accuracy obtained by incorporating GIS data more than offset misclassification due to GIS errors. Because errors in image classification are often associated with changes in illumination and background, including information on these variables reduces map bias and non-random spatial pattern in classification errors. This underscores the notion that classification products produced by IGIS are not classified satellite imagery, as they are often called, but are a qualitatively different amalgam combining features of both satellite and cartographic data.

Calibration models

As opposed to classification models, the term *calibration models* is used to refer to statistical models that relate satellite radiances or their derivatives to measured physical or biological surface properties. As pointed out by Deering (1989), calibration studies that compare surface properties to ground-based radiometers can be the first stage in the development of deterministic remote sensing models. Here the concern is with the calibration of satellite data using ground measurements. Such modelling is increasing as scientists attempt to take advantage of the spatial coverage and temporal resolution of satellite data to parameterize physically based ecological and climatological models (Hall, Strebel and Sellers 1988). Examples include the use of radiances or derived indices to predict surface radiation (Tarpley 1979), canopy leaf area index (LAI), photosynthesis or respiration (Sellers 1985), soil properties such as organic matter or moisture content (see Irons, Weismuller and Petersen, 1989, for review), snowpack condition (Dozier 1989) or surface mineralogy (Goetz 1989).

A basic problem in calibration modelling is obtaining sufficiently accurate and representative satellite and surface measurements (Curran and Hay 1986). Measurement accuracy can be reduced by errors in:

- measurement of remotely sensed variables;

- measurement of ground variables;

- physical correlation of ground variables and remotely sensed variables caused by spatial and temporal misregistration.

Error sources in remotely sensed variables were discussed earlier and can be summarized as variation in irradiance over the time interval of scene acquisition, sensor miscalibration, sensor radiometric resolution signal digitization, atmospheric attenuation and atmospheric path radiance (Curran and Hay 1986). These errors are non-trivial, but methods to minimize them continue to be refined. Ground measurement errors, on the other hand, can be substantial for the many biophysical variables that cannot be measured over the full IFOV of a sensor, but must instead be estimated by sub-sampling (Curran and Williamson 1986).

Curran and Hay (1986) discuss the problem of measurement error in the context of regression analysis, where remotely sensed radiance or reflectance data (y) are predicted by ground measurements of a surface variable (x) using the linear model:

$$y = \beta x + \alpha + \varepsilon \qquad [14.10]$$

α and β are regression coefficients and ε is an error term due to uncontrolled exogenous variables and errors in the measurement of y. If there are measurement errors in x, the estimate of β will be biased, such that:

$$\hat{\beta}^* = \beta/(1 + \sigma^x_v/\sigma^2_x) \qquad [14.11]$$

where $\hat{\beta}^*$ is the estimate of β, σ^x_v is variance from measurement errors in x and σ^2_x is variance due to 'true' variance in x. Thus large measurement errors in x can result in substantially underestimating β.

A larger problem in calibration models could be described as *specification errors* that occur from using an inappropriate model form, incorrect variables or parameter values (Anselin 1989). Models fitted to a narrow region and/or time period may be mis-specified for other conditions. For example, Weiser *et al.* (1986) needed different regression coefficients to relate NDVI to LAI for burned versus unburned grasslands, and for the same grasslands in different years. Box, Holben and Kalb (1989) showed that the relationship between NDVI and variables such as annual evapotranspiration or net primary productivity depended on topographic conditions and varied systematically between different major vegetation types.

Careful field measurements of a wide variety of environments will be needed to calibrate remotely sensed measurements (Deering 1989). IGIS analysis of cartographic data and satellite data offers a means of reducing ground measurement errors during model development and minimizing mis-specification errors when applying these models over large heterogeneous surfaces. The applications of IGIS are similar to those listed in the previous section, and involve the delineation of homogeneous regions for stratified ground sampling and for model application. At present, the merits of different data types for scene segmentation are poorly understood. There are trade-offs between: depending solely on ground measurements and satellite data; combining ground, map and satellite data; and perhaps combining ground and satellite data with lower resolution satellite data.

An example of the use of IGIS capabilities for reducing errors in ground measurements is provided by FIFE, the First ISLSCP Field Experiment. The ISLSCP experiments are designed to study regional land surface climatology and to develop methods for deriving quantitative information about surface climate variables from satellite observations (Sellers *et al.* 1988). The experiment was conducted between 1987 and 1989 over a 16 x 16 km^2 region near Manhattan, Kansas. FIFE's sampling approach was to acquire simultaneously ground measurements and remotely sensed data spanning a range of spatial scales throughout the growing season.

A major challenge in FIFE has been integrating local ground measurements of surface climate parameters such as leaf area, biomass and soil moisture to obtain statistically reliable estimates of these parameters over 1 km^2 or larger areas resolved by meteorological satellites. In an effort to reduce errors in ground-based estimates, a stratified sampling design was used based on topographic and land management characteristics. Digital maps of these variables are being used to derive site-wide estimates of variables such as biomass and soil moisture based on point measurements within the different strata.

A problem encountered in FIFE and likely to be encountered in all similar experiments was selecting a site stratification scheme that was appropriate for many different meteorological and biophysical variables. The stratification used in FIFE was based on previous research, but the criteria for determining the number and characteristics of strata were necessarily somewhat *ad hoc*. Davis *et al.* (1990) subsequently showed that an improved *a priori* stratification could be obtained based on the correspondence of digital terrain variables with TM imagery. Plate 14.1 shows their results for the Konza Long Term Ecological Research (LTER) Area, which occupies the northwestern portion of the FIFE site. The new stratification, which was based on regression tree analysis of the image and map database, performed better that the initial stratification for integrating ground measurements of both soil moisture and total biomass. Davis and Dozier (1990) used a similar approach to develop a land classification system for a region in coastal California based on the association of vegetation patterns with maps of geology and seasonal insolation. In both studies, hierarchical land classifications were derived from joint analysis of satellite and digital terrain data. This is comparable to the production of index maps from GIS weighting and overlay maps (Burrough 1986), but here variable weights and nested combinations are constrained to have maximum correspondence with satellite measurements.

Much of the current effort to calibrate satellite measurements is directed towards coupling those measurements with physical and ecological process models for regional and global forecasting. This coupling, which has been made possible by the evolution of IGIS and by increasingly powerful computers, represents a significant departure from the early applications of remote sensing for classification and inventory. It is also a different application of many process models that were originally developed to improve understanding about the temporal dynamics of spatially homogeneous systems (Costanza, Sklar and White 1990). Implementing these models over large areas requires their re-formulation to account for spatial heterogeneity, spatial interactions and stochastic uncertainty.

Considerable progress has been made in spatial simulation modelling and in incorporating satellite data to parameterize models of processes such as crop growth (Kanemasu, Asrar and Fuchs 1985), forest photosynthesis and transpiration (Running *et al*. 1989), and surface mass and energy fluxes (Smith *et al*. 1990). GIS-based regionalizations have only recently been used to account for spatial heterogeneity in applying process models. Examples include drainage basin partitioning for modelling runoff (Band and Wood 1988), evapotranspiration and photosynthesis (Running *et al*. 1989). Davis and Dozier (1990) demonstrated the potential impact of cartographic errors on the information value of GIS-based regionalization, but to date there has been little progress in formally accounting for cartographic errors and their propagation in the development and application of physical and ecological models. Heuvelink, Burrough and Stein (1989) have developed a method for predicting error propagation that may

occur when using continuously distributed random variables in the quantitative analysis of gridded data in a raster GIS. The method, which depends on approximating errors by Taylor expansion, can be applied to regression-type models. The authors applied the method to surfaces derived by semi-variogram analysis and Kriging of point measurements, but note that simpler surfaces may also be analysed. A great deal more research and technical development is needed to support process modelling efforts. Simonett (1988) suggests the following areas require attention:

- Research on space–time dynamics and scale dependence of surface processes.

- Additional investigations such as FIFE to determine the best mix of ground measurements, satellite measurements and existing cartographic information for parameterizing process models.

- Studies on the effects of satellite data preprocessing on model outputs.

- Theoretical and empirical studies on effects of data resolution and quality on error propagation in process modelling.

- Tests of the model sensitivities to missing data.

- Identification of appropriate spatial statistical models for calibration and verification.

- Development of fully integrated GIS; such an IGIS must provide for flexible handling of multiple data structures and multi-scale data, and must support complex spatial queries and spatio-temporal statistical analyses (Ehlers *et al*. 1989).

Deterministic models

Physical scene models are deterministic models that use theories of radiative transfer or energy balance to derive quantitative estimates of surface reflectance or emission. This brief discussion is restricted to physical models that have been developed to describe the reflectance properties of plant canopies. A good review of current modelling approaches to other surface variables can be obtained in Asrar (1989).

Physical models are often not intended for

application to satellite data, but are formulated to improve understanding of processes that contribute to the signal received by satellite sensors. Many of the models cannot be inverted, while inversion of others requires that they be coupled to atmospheric and sensor models and calibrated with detailed ground and atmospheric data. All models must make simplifying assumptions to account for spectral heterogeneity of the medium at practically all scales of measurement due to variations in composition, spatial arrangement and non-Lambertian bidirectional reflectance of constituent elements.

Among plant canopy models, for example, one model class (*geometrical models*; Goel 1989) treats individual plants as solid objects with prescribed shape and reflectance characteristics that are distributed in some statistical fashion across a ground surface possessing specified reflectance properties (Li and Strahler 1985; Richards, Sun and Simonett 1987). Another class of models (*turbid medium models*) treats plant canopies as homogeneous clouds of small particles with specified orientation, absorption and reflectance characteristics (Verhoef 1984; Norman 1979). Still another class of *hybrid* models has been developed that considers both the geometrical arrangement of plants and multiple scattering by plant canopy elements (Goel 1989).

Some canopy models are sufficiently simplified that they can be parameterized with field reflectance measurements to invert satellite data. These might be considered semi-empirical models, in that physical calculations are combined with statistical spectral mixture models to invert reflectance data (Pech, Graetz and Davis 1986; Jupp *et al.* 1986; Jasinski and Eagleson 1989).

Inversion of physically based canopy models over actual land surfaces is still in an early stage of development. To be made operational, these models need to be coupled to atmosphere and sensor models, parameterized for a representative set of conditions and validated empirically. In complex environments, the number of parameters needed to model the system accurately exceeds the dimensionality of satellite measurements (Goel 1989). Use of spatial measures such as local image variance, as well as multi-temporal and multi-view imagery, can provide additional dimensions (Kimes 1981; Li and Strahler 1985). Also, cartographic information can be used to segment the scene or add other variables so that the model inversion provides more realistic results. For example, Woodcock, Strahler and Jupp (1989) have used digital elevation data and forest stand maps to segment TM imagery into stand types before applying the Li–Strahler geometrical–optical canopy model to map timber volume in the Stanislaus National Forest in California.

For those models that cannot be implemented due to their complexity or to the lack of appropriate data, IGIS offer a powerful tool for conducting simulation and model sensitivity studies over realistic surfaces. For example, Generic Scene Simulation Software (GENESSIS) has been developed that combines physically based atmosphere and scene models to simulate spatially and radiometrically accurate visible and infrared imagery (Acquista 1986; Reeves, Anding and Mertz 1987). Model inputs include illumination geometry, atmospheric properties, surface topography and surface reflectance and emittance. Sub-pixel electromagnetic variation can also be specified. Scene simulation is performed by aggregating point-by-point ray calculations to produce apparent radiances for each pixel of specified spatial resolution. The model has performed well across a wide range of sensor and environmental parameters, and appears to offer many opportunities to investigate IGIS-based physical modelling of terrestrial phenomena. Computing demands are a practical concern in applying GENESSIS or many other spatial simulation models to realistically large and heterogeneous data sets, and may well require additional IGIS capabilities such as parallel processing (Costanza *et al.* 1990; Ehlers 1989).

RESEARCH CHALLENGES IN THE INTEGRATION OF REMOTE SENSING AND GIS

This chapter has highlighted some of the technical and scientific challenges to fuller utilization of remote sensing and GIS. The coupling of satellite measurements with other spatial data has tremendous potential for characterization and analysis of earth surfaces, but the relationship between these hybrid products and the surfaces that they represent is still poorly understood on both physical and statistical grounds. Some of the recent research cited here has just begun to address the difficult issues of 'artifacting, indeterminacy, improper extrapolation between scales, and environmental modulation of spatial error budgets' (Simonett 1988:124) that were identified 15 years ago by Everett and Simonett (1976). However, such studies are few in number and have been nearly exclusively at local to regional scales.

In closing, the following list of general research topics, some repeated from earlier sections is offered. These must be given high priority in integrated analysis of geographical data:

- Characterize space-time interactions and scaling properties of terrain variables.

- Compile/create high quality, representative real and simulated data sets for IGIS model testing and validation.

- Develop appropriate sampling, measurement and modelling strategies for different environment types, including identification of the best mix of ground, satellite and map data for classification, calibration and process models.

- Improve methods for display and visualization of IGIS products.

- Determine the error properties of IGIS products and error propagation in modelling using those products.

- Identify appropriate methods to calibrate and test the performance of spatial models implemented over large regions (e.g. Turner, Costanza and Sklar 1989).

- Develop parallel processing capabilities to operate complex spatial models on large data sets.

- Improve software and hardware interfaces among existing data handling and analysis systems, notably image processing, GIS, database management, expert systems, and statistical packages.

- Identify appropriate data structures and data management strategies for processing large quantities of satellite data, including the use of GIS data to guide the timing and location of image acquisition (e.g. areas of change) and the choice of suitable image resolution, and spatial and non-spatial statistical packages.

- Develop specific technical and scientific guidelines and data standards for future IGIS hardware and software development.

REFERENCES

Acquista C (1986) GENESSIS computer code reference manual. *Photon Research Associates Report R-135–86*. PRA Inc, La Jolla California

Anderson J E, Hardy E E, Roach J T (1976) A land use and land cover system for use with remote-sensor data. *US Geological Survey Professional Paper 964*: 28

Anselin L (1989) What is special about spatial data? Alternative perspectives on spatial data analysis. *Technical Paper 89–4*. National Center for Geographic Information and Analysis, Santa Barbara California

Archibald P D (1987) GIS and remote sensing data integration. *Geocarto International* **3**: 67–73

Asrar G (ed.) (1989) *Theory and Applications of Optical Remote Sensing*. Wiley, New York

Band L E, Wood E F (1988) Strategies for large-scale distributed hydrologic simulation. *Applied Mathematics and Computation* **27**: 23–37

Barker G R (1988) Remote sensing: the unheralded component of geographic information systems. *Photogrammetric Engineering and Remote Sensing* **54**: 195–9

Bell S B M, Diaz B M, Holroyd F, Jackson M J (1983) Spatially referenced methods of processing raster and vector data. *Image and Vision Computing* **1**: 211–20

Billingsley F C, Anuta P E, Carr J L, McGillem C D, Smith D M, Strand T C (1983) Data processing and reprocessing. In: Colwell R N (ed.) *Manual of Remote Sensing*. American Society of Photogrammetry, Falls Church Virginia, pp. 719–88

Box E O, Holben B N, Kalb V (1989) Accuracy of the AVHRR Vegetation Index as a predictor of biomass, primary productivity and net CO_2 flux. *Vegetatio* **80**: 71–89

Bryant J (1990) AMOEBA clustering revisited. *Photogrammetric Engineering and Remote Sensing* **56**: 41–7

Burrough P A (1983) Multiscale sources of spatial variation in soil. I. The application of fractal concepts to nested levels of soil variation. *Journal of Soil Science* **34**: 577–97

Burrough P A (1986) *Principles of Geographical Information Systems for Land Resource Assessment*. Clarendon Press, Oxford

Campbell J B (1981) Spatial correlation effects upon accuracy of supervised classification of land cover.

Photogrammetric Engineering and Remote Sensing **47**: 355–63

Card D H (1982) Using known map category marginal frequencies to improve estimates of thematic map accuracy. *Photogrammetric Engineering and Remote Sensing* **48**: 431–9

Chen Z (1987) *Quadtree and Quadtree Spatial Spectra in Large Geographic Information Systems: the hierarchical handling of spatial data.* Unpublished PhD dissertation, University of California, Santa Barbara California

Chrisman N R (1991) The error component in spatial data. In: Maguire D J, Goodchild M F, Rhind D W (eds.) *Geographical Information Systems: principles and applications.* Longman, London, pp. 165–74, Vol 1

Cibula W G, Nyquist M O (1987) Use of topographic and climatological models in a geographic database to improve Landsat MSS classification for Olympic National Park. *Photogrammetric Engineering and Remote Sensing* **53**: 67–75

Cliff A D, Ord J K (1981) *Spatial Processes: models and applications.* Pion, London

Colwell R N (1983) *Manual of Remote Sensing.* American Society of Photogrammetry, Falls Church Virginia

Congalton R G (1988a) A comparison of sampling schemes used in generating error matrices for assessing the accuracy of maps generated from remotely sensed data. *Photogrammetric Engineering and Remote Sensing* **54**: 593–600

Congalton R G (1988b) Using spatial autocorrelation analysis to explore the errors in maps generated from remotely sensed data. *Photogrammetric Engineering and Remote Sensing* **54**: 587–92

Congalton R G, Odervwald R, Mead R (1983) Assessing Landsat classification accuracy using discrete multivariate analysis statistical techniques. *Photogrammetric Engineering and Remote Sensing* **6**: 169–73

Costanza R, Sklar F H, White M L (1990) Modeling coastal landscape dynamics. *Bioscience* **40**: 91–107

Crapper P F (1980) Errors incurred in estimating an area of uniform land cover using Landsat. *Photogrammetric Engineering and Remote Sensing* **10**: 1295–301

Crapper P F, Walker P A, Nanninga P M (1986) Theoretical prediction of the effect of aggregation on grid cell data sets. *Geo-processing* **3**: 155–66

Curran P J, Hay A M (1986) The importance of measurement error for certain procedures in remote sensing at optical wavelengths. *Photogrammetric Engineering and Remote Sensing* **52**: 229–41

Curran P J, Williamson H D (1986) Sample size for ground and remotely sensed data. *Remote Sensing of Environment* **20**: 31–41

Davis F W, Dozier J (1990) Information analysis of a spatial database for ecological land classification. *Photogrammetric Engineering and Remote Sensing* **56** (5): 605–13

Davis F W, Dubayah R, Dozier J (1989) Covariance of greenness and terrain variables over the Konza Prairie. *Proceedings of IGARRS 89*, pp. 1322–5

Davis F W, Michaelsen J, Dubayah R, Dozier J (1990). Optimal terrain stratification for integrating ground data from FIFE. *Proceedings of the AMS Symposium on the First ISLSCP Field Experiment (FIFE).* American Meteorological Society, Boston Massachusetts, pp. 11–15

Deering D (1989) Field measurements of bidirectional reflectance. In: Asrar G (ed.) *Theory and Applications of Optical Remote Sensing.* Wiley, New York, pp. 14–65

Dozier J (1989) Spectral signature of alpine snow cover from the Landsat Thematic Mapper. *Remote Sensing of Environment* **28**: 9–22

Dozier J, Strahler A H (1983) Ground investigations in support of remote sensing. In: Colwell R N (ed.) *Manual of Remote Sensing.* American Society of Photogrammetry, Falls Church Virginia, pp. 959–86

Dubayah R, Dozier J, Davis F W (1990) Topographic distribution of clear-sky radiation over the Konza Prairie, Kansas. *Water Resources Research* **26** (4): 679–90

Duggin M J (1985) Factors limiting the discrimination and quantification of terrestrial features using remotely sensed radiance. *International Journal of Remote Sensing* **6**: 3–27

Egenhofer M J, Herring J R (1991) High-level spatial data structures for GIS. In: Maguire D J, Goodchild M F, Rhind D W (eds.) *Geographical Information Systems: principles and applications.* Longman, London, pp. 227–37, Vol 1

Ehlers M (1989) Remote sensing and geographic information systems: towards integrated spatial information processing. *Proceedings of IGARRS 89*, pp. 63–6

Ehlers M, Edwards G, Bedard Y (1989) Integration of remote sensing with geographic information systems: a necessary evolution. *Photogrammetric Engineering and Remote Sensing* **55**: 1619–27

Elachi C (1987) *Introduction to the Physics and Techniques of Remote Sensing.* Wiley, New York

Eos Science Steering Committee (1987) *Earth Observing System Volume II. From pattern to process: the strategy of the Earth Observing System.* National Aeronautics and Space Administration, Washington DC

Estes J E, Bredekamp J H (1988) Activities associated with global databases in the National Aeronautics and Space Administration. In: Mounsey H M (ed.) *Building Databases for Global Science.* Taylor & Francis, London, pp. 251–69

Estes J E, Hajic E J, Tinney L R (1983) Manual and digital analysis in the visible and infrared regions. In: Simonett D S, Ulaby F T (eds.) *Manual of Remote Sensing*, 2nd edn. Vol. 1. American Society of Photogrammetry, Falls Church Virginia, 987–1123

Estes J E, Sailer C, Tinney L R (1986) Applications of artificial intelligence techniques to remote sensing. *Professional Geographer* **38**: 133–41

Everett J, Simonett D S (1976) Principles, concepts and philosophical problems. In: Lintz J L, Simonett D S (eds.) *Remote Sensing of Environment.* Addison-Wesley, Reading Massachusetts, pp. 85–127

Forshaw M R B, Haskell A, Miller P F, Stanley D J,

Townshend J R G (1983) Spatial resolution of remotely sensed imagery: a review paper. *International Journal of Remote Sensing* **4**: 497–520

Frank A U, Barrera R (1990) The fieldtree: a data structure for geographic information systems. In: Buchmann A, Gunther O, Smith T R, Wang Y-F (eds.) *Design and Implementation of Large Spatial Databases.* Springer-Verlag, New York, pp. 29–44

Franklin J, Logan T L, Woodcock C E, Strahler A H (1986) Coniferous forest classification and inventory using Landsat and digital terrain data. *IEEE Transactions on Geoscience and Remote Sensing* **GE-24**: 139–46

Franklin S E, Peddle D R, Moulton J R (1989) Spectral/geomorphometric discrimination and mapping of terrain: a study in Gros Morne National Park. *Canadian Journal of Remote Sensing* **15**: 28–42

Gaydos L, Newland W L (1978) Inventory of land use and land cover of the Puget Sound region using Landsat digital data. *US Geological Survey Journal of Research* **6**: 807–14

Getis A, Boots B (1978) *Models of Spatial Processes* University Press, Cambridge

Goddard Space Flight Center (1984) Earth Observing System: Science and Mission Requirements, Working Group Report, Volume H 1. *NASA Goddard Space Flight Center Technical Memorandum 86129.* National Aeronautics and Space Administration, Greenbelt Maryland

Goel N S (1989) Inversion of canopy reflectance models for estimation of biophysical parameters from reflectance data. In: Asrar G (ed.) *Theory and Applications of Optical Remote Sensing.* Wiley, New York, pp. 205–51

Goetz A F H (1989) Spectral remote sensing in geology. In: Asrar G (ed.) *Theory and Applications of Optical Remote Sensing.* Wiley, New York, pp. 491–526

Goodchild M F (1980) The effects of generalization in geographical data encoding. In: Freeman H, Pieroni G (eds.) *Map Data Processing.* Academic Press, New York, pp. 191–205

Goodenough D G (1988) Thematic Mapper and SPOT integration with a geographic information system. *Photogrammetric Engineering and Remote Sensing* **54**: 167–76

Goodenough D G, Goldberg M, Plunkett G, Zelek J (1987) An expert system for remote sensing. *IEEE Transactions on Geoscience and Remote Sensing* **GE-25**: 349–59

Hall F G, Badhwar G D (1987) Signature-extendable technology: global space-based crop recognition. *IEEE Transactions on Geoscience and Remote Sensing* **GE-25**: 93–103

Hall F G, Strebel D E, Sellers P J (1988) Linking knowledge among spatial and temporal scales: vegetation, atmosphere, climate and remote sensing. *Landscape Ecology* **2**: 3–22

Haralick R M (1980) Edge and region analysis for digital image data. *Computer Graphics and Image Processing* **12**: 60–73

Haralick R M, Fu K (1983) Pattern recognition and classification. In: Colwell R N (ed.) *Manual of Remote Sensing*, 2nd edn. American Society of Photogrammetry, Falls Church Virginia, pp. 793–805

Harding A E, Forrest M D (1989) Analysis of multiple geological data sets from the English Lake District. *IEEE Transactions on Geoscience and Remote Sensing* **27**: 732–9

Heuvelink G B M, Burrough P A, Stein A (1989) Propagation of errors in spatial modelling with GIS. *International Journal of Geographical Information Systems* **3**: 303–22

Hill G J E, Kelly G D (1987) A comparison of existing map products and Landsat for land cover mapping. *Cartography* **16**: 51–7

Hoffer R M (1978) Biological and physical considerations in applying computer-aided analysis techniques to remote-sensor data. In: Swain P H, Davis S M (eds.) *Remote Sensing: the quantitative approach.* McGraw-Hill, New York, pp. 227–87

Hoffer R M, Fleming M D, Bartolucci L A, Davis S M, Nelson R F (1979) Digital processing of Landsat MSS and topographic data to improve capabilities for computerized mapping of forest cover types. *LARS Technical Report 011579*, p. 159

Holben B N, Fraser R S (1984) Red and near-infrared sensor response to off-nadir viewing. *International Journal of Remote Sensing* **5**: 145–60

Hutchinson C F (1982) Techniques for combining Landsat and ancillary data for digital classification improvement. *Photogrammetric Engineering and Remote Sensing* **48**: 123–30

Irons J R, Weismuller R A, Petersen G W (1989) Soil reflectance. In: Asrar G (ed.) *Theory and Applications of Optical Remote Sensing.* Wiley, New York, pp. 66–106

Jackson M J, Mason D C (1986) The development of integrated geo-information systems. *International Journal of Remote Sensing* **7**: 723–40

Jasinski M F, Eagleson P S (1989) The structure of red-infrared scattergrams of semivegetated landscapes. *IEEE Transactions on Geoscience and Remote Sensing* **27**: 441–51

Jenkins G M, Watts D G (1968) *Spectral Analysis and Its Applications.* Holden-Day, Oakland California

Jones A R, Settle J J, Wyatt B K (1988) Use of digital terrain data in interpretation of SPOT HRV-1 multispectral imagery. *International Journal of Remote Sensing* **9**: 669–76

Jupp D L B, Strahler A H, Woodcock C E (1989) Autocorrelation and regularization in digital images: II. Simple image models. *IEEE Transactions on Geoscience and Remote Sensing* **27**: 247–56

Jupp D L B, Walker J, Penridge L K (1986) Interpretation of vegetation structure in Landsat MSS imagery: a case study in disturbed semi-arid Eucalypt woodlands. Part 2. Model-based analysis. *Journal of Environmental Management* **23**: 35–57

Kanemasu E T, Asrar G, Fuchs M (1985) Application of remotely sensed data in wheat growth modeling. In: Day

D W, Atkin R K (eds.) *Wheat Growth and Modelling.* Plenum, New York, pp. 407–25

Kauth R J, Thomas G S (1976) The tasselled cap: a graphic description of the spectral-temporal development of crops as seen by Landsat. *Proceedings of the 3rd Symposium on Machine Processing of Remotely Sensed Data*, Vol. 4B. Purdue University, West Lafayette Indiana, pp. 41–51

Kimes D S (1981) Remote sensing of temperature profiles in vegetation canopies using multiple view angles and inversion techniques. *IEEE Transactions on Geoscience and Remote Sensing* **GE-19**: 85–90

Lauer D (1990) *An Evaluation of National Policies Governing the United States Civilian Satellite Land Remote Sensing Program.* Unpublished PhD dissertation, Department of Geography, University of California, Santa Barbara California

Li X, Strahler A H (1985) Geometric-optical modeling of a conifer forest canopy. *IEEE Transactions on Geoscience and Remote Sensing* **GE-23**: 705–21

Logan T L, Bryant N A (1987) Spatial data software integration: merging CAD/CAM/mapping with GIS and image processing. *Photogrammetric Engineering and Remote Sensing* **53** (10): 1391–5

Lovejoy S, Schertzer D (1985) Generalised scale invariance in the atmosphere and fractal models of rain. *Water Resources Research* **21**: 1233–50

Maffini G (1987) Raster versus vector encoding and handling: a commentary. *Photogrammetric Engineering and Remote Sensing* **53**: 1397–8

Marble D F, Peuquet D J, Boyle A R, Bryant N, Calkins H W, Johnson T (1983) Geographic information systems and remote sensing. In: Colwell R N (ed.) *Manual of Remote Sensing.* American Society of Photogrammetry, Falls Church Virginia, pp. 923–57

Mark D M, Aronson P B (1984) Scale-dependent fractal dimensions of topographic surfaces: an empirical investigation, with applications in geomorphology and computer mapping. *Mathematical Geology* **16**: 671–83

Mason D C, Corr D G, Cross A, Hoggs D C, Lawrence D H, Petrou M, Tailor A M (1988) The use of digital map data in the segmentation and classification of remotely-sensed images. *International Journal of Geographical Information Systems* **2**: 195–215

McKeown D M (1986) The role of artificial intelligence in the integration of remotely sensed data with Geographic Information Systems. *Report CMU-CS-86-174.* Department of Computer Science, Carnegie-Mellon University, Pittsburgh Pennsylvania

Menon S (1989) *Spatial Search for Multi-component Objects in a Geographic Information System Using Symbolic Models and Hierarchical Data Structures.* Unpublished PhD dissertation, University of California, Santa Barbara California

Moik J G (1980) Digital processing of remotely sensed images. *NASA SP-431.* Scientific and Technical Information Branch National Aeronautics and Space Administration, Washington DC

Mulla D M (1988) Using geostatistics and spectral analysis to study spatial patterns in the topography of southeastern Washington State, USA. *Earth Surface Processes and Landforms* **13**: 389–405

Muller J-C (1977) Map griding and cartographic errors: a recurrent argument. *The Canadian Cartographer* **14**: 152–67

Norman J (1979) Modeling of complete crop canopy. In: Barfield B G, Gerber J F (eds.) *Modification of the Aerial Environment of Plants.* American Society of Agricultural Engineers, St Joseph Mississippi, pp. 249–77

Oliver M A, Webster R (1986) Semi-variograms for modelling the spatial pattern of landform and soil properties. *Earth Surface Processes and Landforms* **11**: 491–504

Parker H D (1988) The unique qualities of a geographic information system: a commentary. *Photogrammetric Engineering and Remote Sensing* **54**: 1547–9

Parker H D (1989) GIS software 1989: a survey and commentary. *Photogrammetric Engineering and Remote Sensing* **55**: 1589–91

Pech R P, Graetz R D, Davis A W (1986) Reflectance modelling and the derivation of vegetation indices for an Australian semi-arid shrubland. *International Journal of Remote Sensing* **7**: 389–403

Peplies R W, Keuper H F (1975) Regional analysis. In: Reeves R G, Anson A, Landen D (eds.) *Manual of Remote Sensing*, Vol. 2. American Society of Photogrammetry, Falls Church Virginia, pp. 1947–98

Peterson D L, Running S W (1989) Applications in forest science and management. In: Asrar G (ed.) *Theory and Applications of Optical Remote Sensing.* Wiley, New York, pp. 429–73

Peucker T K, Chrisman N R (1975) Cartographic data structures. *The American Cartographer* **2**: 55–69

Peuquet D J (1988) Issues involved in selecting appropriate data models for global databases. In: Mounsey H M (ed.) *Building Databases for Global Science.* Taylor & Francis, London, pp. 66–78

Prisley S P, Gregoire T G, Smith J L (1989) The mean and variance of area estimates computed in an arc-node Geographic Information System. *Photogrammetric Engineering and Remote Sensing* **55**: 1601–12

Reeves R, Anding D, Mertz F (1987) First principles deterministic simulation of IR and visible imagery. *Photon Research Associates Report R-024-88.* PRA Inc., La Jolla California

Rhind D, Clark P (1988) Cartographic data inputs to global databases. In: Mounsey H (ed.) *Building Databases for Global Science.* Taylor & Francis, London, pp. 79–104

Rhind D W, Green N P A (1988) Design of a geographical information system for a heterogeneous scientific community. *International Journal of Geographical Information Systems* **2**: 171–89

Richards J A (1986) *Remote Sensing Digital Image Analysis: an introduction.* Springer-Verlag, New York

Richards J A, Sun G Q, Simonett D S (1987) L-band radar

backscatter modeling of forest stands. *IEEE Transactions on Geoscience and Remote Sensing* **GE-25**: 487–98

Robinove C J (1981) The logic of multispectral classification and mapping of land. *Remote Sensing of Environment* **11**: 231–44

Robinson J (1987) The role of fire on earth: a review of the state of knowledge and a systems framework for satellite and ground based observations. *NCAR Cooperative Thesis 112*. National Center for Atmospheric Research, Boulder Colorado

Running S W, Nemani R R, Peterson D L, Band L E, Potts D F, Pierce L L, Spanner M A (1989) Mapping regional forest evapotranspiration and photosynthesis by coupling satellite data with ecosystem simulation. *Ecology* **70**: 1090–101

Samet H (1984) The quadtree and related hierarchical data structures. *ACM Computing Surveys* **16**: 187–260

Satterwhite M, Rice W, Shipman J (1984) Using landform and vegetation factors to improve the interpretation of LANDSAT imagery. *Photogrammetric Engineering and Remote Sensing* **50**: 83–91

Schott J R, Salvaggio C, Volchok W J (1988) Radiometric scene normalization using pseudoinvariant features. *Remote Sensing of Environment* **26**: 1–16

Sellers P J (1985) Canopy reflectance, photosynthesis, and transpiration. *International Journal of Remote Sensing* **6**: 1335–72

Sellers P J, Hall F G, Asrar G, Strebel D E, Murphy R E (1988) The first ISLSCP field experiment (FIFE). *Bulletin of the American Meteorological Society* **69**: 22–7

Simonett D S (1988) Considerations on integrating remote sensing and Geographic Information Systems. In: Mounsey H (ed.) *Building Databases for Global Science*. Taylor & Francis, London, pp. 105–28

Simonett D S, Reeves R G, Estes J E, Bertke S E, Sailer C T (1983) The development and principles of remote sensing. In: Colwell R N (ed.) *Manual of Remote Sensing*. American Society of Photogrammetry, Falls Church Virginia, pp. 1–32

Singh S M, Saull R J (1988) The effect of atmospheric correction on the interpretation of multitemporal AVHRR-derived vegetation index dynamics. *International Journal of Remote Sensing* **25**: 37–51

Smith E A, Crosson W L, Cooper H J, Weng H (1990) Heat and moisture flux modeling of the FIFE grassland canopy aided by satellite derived canopy variables. *Proceedings of the Symposium on FIFE*. American Meteorological Society, Boston Massachusettes, pp. 154–62

Smith T R, Menon S, Star J L, Estes J E (1987a) Requirements and principles for the implementation and construction of large-scale geographic information systems. *International Journal of Geographical Information Systems* **1**: 13–31

Smith T R, Peuquet D, Menon S, Agarwal P (1987b) KBGIS-II. A knowledge-based geographical information system. *International Journal of Geographical Information Systems* **1**: 149–72

Star J, Estes J E (1990) *Geographic Information Systems: an introduction*. Prentice Hall, Englewood Cliffs New Jersey

Strahler A H (1981) Stratification of natural vegetation for forest and rangeland inventory using Landsat digital imagery and collateral data. *International Journal of Remote Sensing* **2**: 15–41

Strahler A H, Woodcock C E, Smith J A (1986) On the nature of models in remote sensing. *Remote Sensing of Environment* **20**: 121–39

Suits G, Malila W, Weller T (1988) Procedures for using signals from one sensor as substitutes for signals of another. *Remote Sensing of Environment* **25**: 395–408

Switzer P (1975) Estimation of the accuracy of qualitative maps. In: Davis J C, McCullagh M J (eds.) *Display and Analysis of Spatial Data*. Wiley, New York, pp. 1–13

Tarpley J D (1979) Estimating incident solar radiation at the earth's surface from geostationary satellite data. *Journal of Applied Meteorology* **18**: 1172–81

Tong L, Richards J A, Swain P H (1987) Probabilistic and evidential approaches for multisource data analysis. *IEEE Transactions on Geoscience and Remote Sensing* **GE-25**: 283–93

Townshend J R G, Justice C O (1988) Selecting the spatial resolution of satellite sensors required for global monitoring of land transformations. *International Journal of Remote Sensing* **9**: 187–236

Townshend J R G, Justice C O (1990) The spatial variation of vegetation at very coarse scales. *International Journal of Remote Sensing* **11**: 149–57

Turner M G, Costanza R, Sklar F H (1989) Methods to evaluate the performance of spatial simulation models. *Ecological Modelling* **48**: 1–18

Ustin S L, Adams J B, Elvidge C D, Rejmanek M, Rock B N, Smith M O, Thomas R W, Woodward R A (1986) Thematic Mapper studies of semiarid shrub communities. *Bioscience* **36**: 446–52

Veregin H (1989) A taxonomy of error in spatial databases. *Technical Paper 89–12*. National Center for Geographic Information and Analysis, Santa Barbara California

Verhoef W (1984) Light scattering by leaf layers with application to canopy reflectance modeling: the Sail model. *Remote Sensing of Environment* **16**: 125–41

Walsh S J, Lightfoot D R, Butler D R (1987) Recognition and assessment of error in geographic information systems. *Photogrammetric Engineering and Remote Sensing* **53**: 1423–30

Wang S, Elliott D B, Campbell J B, Erich R W, Haralick R M (1983) Spatial reasoning in remotely sensed data. *IEEE Transactions on Geoscience and Remote Sensing* **GE-21**: 94–101

Weibel R, Heller M (1991) Digital terrain modelling. In: Maguire D J, Goodchild M F, Rhind D W (eds.)

Geographical Information Systems: principles and applications. Longman, London, pp. 269–97, Vol 1

Weiser R L, Asrar G, Miller G P, Kanemasu E T (1986) Assessing grassland biophysical characteristics from spectral measurements. *Remote Sensing of Environment* **20**: 141–52

Welch R, Usery E L (1984) Cartographic accuracy of Landsat-4 MSS and TM image data. *IEEE Transactions on Geoscience and Remote Sensing* **GE-22**: 281–8

Wharton S W (1989) Knowledge-based spectral classification of remotely sensed image data. In: Asrar G (ed.) *Theory and Applications of Optical Remote Sensing.* Wiley, New York, pp. 548–77

Woodcock C E, Strahler A H (1987) The factor of scale in remote sensing. *Remote Sensing of Environment* **21**: 311–32

Woodcock C E, Strahler A H, Jupp D L B (1988) The use of variograms in remote sensing: I. Scene models and simulated images. *Remote Sensing of Environment* **25**: 323–48

Woodcock C E, Strahler A H, Jupp D L B (1989) Autocorrelation and regularization in digital images: II. Simple image models. *IEEE Transactions on Geoscience and Remote Sensing* **27**: 247–56

Zhou Q (1989) A method for integrating remote sensing and geographic information systems. *Photogrammetric Engineering and Remote Sensing* **55**: 591–6

COMPUTER SYSTEMS AND LOW-LEVEL DATA STRUCTURES FOR GIS

WM. R FRANKLIN

This chapter is an introduction to several aspects of computer science that are applicable to Geographical Information Systems. First, some of the choices in computer systems and the likely coming advances in hardware and software are discussed. Then some of the general properties of low-level data structures, with principles like abstract data structures versus their implementations, and examples like hash tables, extendible arrays, uniform grids and Voronoi diagrams are considered. Next there is an introduction to algorithms analysis, its limitations when applied to practical problems, new trends such as randomized algorithms and implementation considerations. This is followed by an introduction to software engineering, including the traditional waterfall model, the newer rapid prototyping technique and the importance of profiling the program to improve it.

COMPUTER SYSTEMS

Classification of systems

Computer systems may be partitioned by their memory size and I/O (input/output) speed into personal computers, workstations, minicomputers, mainframes and supercomputers. In general, within a class the larger machines may be more cost efficient, but between classes of machines, the smaller classes are more cost efficient. That is, it is most economical to run a computation on the smallest class of machine that will support it. A workstation in the early 1990s typically has the following features:

- 16 megabytes (i.e. about 16 million bytes) of real memory;
- three times as much virtual memory;
- a 500 megabyte hard disk;
- a bit mapped display with 1 million pixels;
- a 10 MIPS (10 million instructions executed per second) processor. However, note that MIPS is only a rough measure of speed, and differences of under 50 per cent can probably be ignored. Floating point performance is also important;
- a 32 bit wide I/O bus to carry data between the processor, memory, and the input/output devices;
- a timesharing operating system, such as Unix (AT&T Bell Laboratories 1978, 1984; Quarterman, Silberschatz and Peterson 1985);
- high level languages, such as C, Modula, or Fortran-77.

Optional, but increasingly common features include the following:

- colour and grey-scale displays;
- CD-ROMs (compact disk-read only memory) and optical disks (laser disks) to store large, fixed databases up to about 1 gigabyte (10^9 bytes);

- database tools, or 'fourth generation languages', such as Oracle, object-oriented languages such as C++, artificial intelligence aids such as expert systems, and numerical libraries such as IMSL or NAG (Numerical Algorithm Group).

A personal computer, in contrast, would have each measure of capacity, such as memory and disk space, several times smaller. Each of these capacities and speeds is increasing at 20–100 per cent per year. The contrast in cost between disk and main memory is notable since while disk is 10 000 times slower to access, it is only 10 times cheaper.

All this means that a 100 megabyte database can now be processed easily on a workstation. For larger databases, the workstation can be supplemented by access to a supercomputer. Extremely large databases, such as those obtained from earth observation satellites and now stored on magnetic tape, can be over 50 Tb (terabytes, 10^{12} bytes) and are still growing. Mel *et al.* (1988) give a view of the personal computer in the year 2000.

For most GIS researchers, the workstation is probably the relevant machine. The personal computer currently has too little memory for processing large databases and, unlike workstations, often does not have virtual memory or a timesharing environment. In addition, after peripherals are added, personal computers are almost as expensive as workstations. Current workstations have as much memory and are as fast as the mainframes of a few years ago. Because of their much better price performance, workstations have made minicomputers and mainframes obsolete for many purposes.

Hardware advances

Trends that will affect computer systems in the next few years include hardware advances like parallel processing, practical storage of audio and video, and more efficient communication. Although massively parallel machines such as Thinking Machines Corp's 64 000 processor CM-2 exist, they are not yet recommended for production use because of their cost, scarcity, and lack of software. Operating systems are still rudimentary; for example, there may not even be code to buffer or efficiently route messages between processors. In the future, a generally useful parallel machine will probably involve dozens of powerful processors, such as might be used alone in a workstation, and each processor will have a considerable amount of memory. At the present time, the best method actually to compute something is to use a fast serial machine. The best reason for a parallel implementation is to learn the techniques for the time when parallel machines become useful. This must happen sometime since the speed of a single processor is limited by physical laws such as the speed of light, some machines already being so fast that an electrical signal can travel only 10 centimetres during one cycle of the central processing unit.

Parallel machines may be classified by whether the multiple processors execute the same instruction – SIMD (single instruction multiple data), or whether each processor may execute a different instruction – MIMD (multiple instruction multiple data). SIMD machines, such as the CM-2, are simpler since the same instruction is decoded and then broadcast to all the processors which have separate memories. To implement an if–then–else, processors may also be selectively disabled from executing instructions. In the following code:

if (test) then true-code else false-code

each processor executes *test* to compute a bit. Then those processors whose bit is 0 disable themselves and the remainder execute *true-code*. Finally, those processors whose bit was 1 disable themselves, while the others enable themselves and execute *false-code*.

A MIMD machine is like a Hypercube or Sequent, or like a roomful of workstations. Each processor executes a different program, and communicates with other processors by some network. This is more powerful, but also more expensive per processor than a SIMD machine.

Practical storage and processing of audio and video data will arrive in the next few years, assisted both by larger mass storage, and by sufficient processing power to compress and expand the data in real time. This will be assisted by faster networks – several hundred megabit per second local area networks and megabit per second wide area networks built on telecommunication standards such as ISDN (integrated services digital network), a standard for future communications.

Computers typically have large flat address

spaces of main memory, which means that a programmer can address any one of eight or more Mb equally easily. However, since the processors are faster than the I/O bus, the processors also have on-chip caches of typically 8 Kb to contain the most recently used data. Therefore, programs whose data references hit the cache more often will be more efficient. Even if memory were free, programs would still need to conserve it. Indeed, there is a cost associated with retrieving data over the bus and larger data sets mean fewer cache hits.

Software advances

The term 'software engineering' was coined some years ago in an attempt to imbue the software production process with some of the rigour associated with traditional engineering. That has been a limited success. The goal has been to devise more and more powerful stratagems so that software production becomes more and more automatic. The continued failure to achieve this has led Brooks (1987) to suggest that automated software production is not possible because the problem is inherently difficult.

Whatever software advances occur in computer systems in the future are likely to be less spectacular than in the past. Artificial intelligence is not having the impact predicted a few years ago and formal methods of program design are still being extended (Hoare 1987). Cohen (1988) describes logic programming techniques that look promising for the future. Some applications to geometry and the map overlay problem are described by Franklin and Wu (1987) and Franklin et al. (1986). The most important advance would be the more widespread availability of tools that have existed for many years, such as code management and debugging tools, WYSIWYG (what you see is what you get) text processors, database managers, fourth generation languages, and so on (Boehm 1987; Rich and Waters 1988). Many universities have no access to such tools as already exist.

The other significant software advance is the spread of standards, such as the Unix operating system and X Windows. Standards allow portability not only of the program to other machines and projects, but also of the programmer to other projects. Frequently a standard is not quite state-of-the-art, such as vendors' proprietary versions of Fortran that each contain a few features unique to that vendor that are not in the standard. A programmer must consider whether the extra advantages of these features compensate for being locked in to that vendor.

LOW-LEVEL DATA STRUCTURES

Abstract data structures versus their physical realizations

When designing a data structure, it is important to separate the abstract data structure from its physical realization (Aho, Hopcroft and Ullman 1983). This separation is assisted by newer languages with information hiding, such as Ada (Pyle 1985), or object-oriented languages, such as C++ (Stroustrup 1987) and Smalltalk (Goldberg 1984). However, these newer languages are usually not universal enough, or are too inefficient, to use in GIS systems. Programmers must, therefore, enforce this separation themselves.

The abstract data structure is defined by the set of elements that are to be stored, the operations to be performed on them and, perhaps, the possible error conditions. For example, consider the problem of choosing a data structure for representing a map, or planar graph.

1. *Elements*: Polygons representing states or other regions.
2. *Operations*:
    (a) Draw the whole map or any polygon.
    (b) Verify the internal consistency of a map.
    (c) Calculate any property of a polygon, such as area.
    (d) Find the adjacent polygons to a polygon.
    (e) Scale a map or transform it to another coordinate system.
    (f) Overlay two maps.
3. *Design criteria*:
    (a) Amount of storage used.
    (b) Likelihood of errors.

(c) Ease of implementation.
(d) Efficiency of execution.

The physical realization of the data structure covers how it is actually implemented. There are two major choices here, depending on the major element of the database.

- *Polygon based*: The polygons are stored explicitly, as a sequence of points. Thus each point on an interior edge is stored twice, once for each of the adjacent polygons. With this method, it is easy to operate on individual polygons. However, more storage is used, and inconsistencies can arise if the two versions of each point are not identical down to the last bit.

- *Edge based*: Here the edges or chains separating the polygons are stored. The polygons exist only in the ID numbers used to refer to them. Each edge contains the numbers of its two adjacent polygons. This method is more compact than the previous one. However, operating on one polygon requires finding all the edges on it.

With the edge-based method there are two choices, whether to store a complete chain of points, or to store each edge separately. The former is more compact but has variable length data elements that are more complicated to work with.

A clean implementation of the logical map data structure would not allow most of the program direct access to the data. Instead the desired operations would be decomposed into the primitive operations like the following:

- Return the total number of polygons.
- Return the external name of the polygon that is internally i.
- Return the number of points in polygon i.
- Return point j of polygon i.

Then a user-callable procedure would be made available for each primitive operation.

The advantage of this separation of logical from physical realization is that the implementation may be changed as the system evolves, as experience with the data structure's actual use is obtained by performance monitoring. The prime disadvantage is that in a low level language, such as one without macros, the clean implementation of this concept requires many subroutine calls, which is clumsy and slow.

Examples of data structures

Some examples of generally useful data structures are presented in this section. For a broader guide to the field consult any standard text, such as Knuth (1973) or Aho, Hopcroft and Ullman (1983).

Hashing

In abstract terms, a hash table is a mapping from a key, such as a character string or a number, to an entry in the table. Unlike an array where the elements are addressed 1,2,3,..., in a hash table, a list of 10 countries can be accessed by their names, or information about 100 people can be stored and accessed by their 9 digit social security number. The following is a brief description that conveys the flavour of hashing while omitting complexities and options.

Suppose the key K is an integer in the range $1...B$]. If there are N records to store, a table of size $M = 3N/2$ or so is allocated. The problem is to reduce a key ranging up to B to a table location L ranging up to M. The simplest method is to use $L = (K \text{ modulo } M) + 1$, where modulo is the remainder function (e.g. 10 modulo 3 = 1 because dividing 10 by 3 leaves a remainder of 1). The + 1 occurs because modulo returns numbers in the range $0...M - 1$] whereas the table is assumed to be indexed from 1 to M.

The collision of two different records that hash to the same location can be solved in two ways. All the colliding records may be chained together with a linked list. Alternatively, the colliding record may be placed in the next available location, which means that when retrieving a record its hash location must be computed and successive locations checked until a free location is seen. If the table is nearly full, then runs of consecutive used table locations can grow surprisingly. If the load factor, or fraction of table slots occupied, is α, then the average number of slots that must be examined in an unsuccessful search for a key is $(1 + 1/(1-\alpha)^2)/2$. In our example, with $\alpha = 2/3$, this is 4–5 slots. If $\alpha = 0.9$, this would be 50, which is totally unacceptable.

On the other hand, if the overflow records are chained together, then the pointers occupy storage.

If the key is a character string, such as *Switzerland*, then each 4 bytes can be considered as an integer. In this case, the three integers which have bit codes corresponding to *Swit*, *zerl*, and *and* must be combined into one integer, perhaps by multiplying the ith integer by i, ignoring overflows, adding them, and taking the absolute value. Then the above modulo process can be used.

Hash tables are very efficient for inserting and retrieving records when the total number is known in advance. They are less efficient for deleting records and for growing tables dynamically to an initially unknown size, since the whole table must be recomputed in a larger area whenever it overflows. It is impossible to retrieve the records in order from a hash table without sorting them. If these operations are necessary, a more complicated data structure, such as a B-tree, is preferable.

Extendible arrays

Often there is a requirement to use a logical array, where read and write elements are keyed by the subscripts which are small integers from 1 up, but where there is no *a priori* idea of how large the array will grow. None of the conventional choices for implementation are appealing. A binary tree carries a large time overhead of $\theta(\log(N))$ to access an element, if there are already N elements (the notation $\theta(\log(N))$ means that time rises with the logarithm of the number of elements. It also carries a coding overhead in that unless the tree is kept balanced by rotation, that access time may deteriorate to $\theta(N)$ (rising more steeply, in proportion to N). A hash table has the earlier mentioned problems. A simple array requires advance estimation of the maximum likely N, and the array must be copied over if this is exceeded. Therefore, this last choice is not often used.

However, the extendible array, where the array is reallocated and recopied when it overflows, is actually quite efficient. Assume that each such time, a new array is allocated that is bigger by a factor of α. Then if the array grows from a size of 1 up to a very large size, the average element is copied only $1/(\alpha-1)$ times. If the array is doubled each time, then the average element is copied only once. Indeed, the last half of the elements are never copied after being first inserted. The previous quarter are copied once, the previous eighth are copied twice, and so on. In a language such as C, the array can be grown and copied with one procedure call, to *realloc*. If there is a restricted language with only static storage allocation at compile time, then special dynamic allocation routines must be implemented to suballocate storage from a large static array. However, this must be undertaken for any of the methods.

Thus extendible arrays are an efficient method for implementing arrays when the initial size is unknown.

Uniform grids

A fundamental low-level operation in overlaying maps and testing for interference is that of finding all the intersections among a large set of small edges. The theoretically optimal method is by Chazelle and Edelsbrunner (1988), which finds all K intersections of N edges in time $\theta((K + N)\log N)$. It has been implemented, but is complicated and is not obviously parallelizable. A simpler method using a scan line is by Bentley and Ottmann (1979), with slightly larger time. Note that if $K = N^2/2$ then this is worse than the naive time of $\theta(N^2)$.

The uniform grid of Franklin *et al.* (1988, 1989, 1990) is an alternative method. It is simple to program, parallelizable, and has expected execution time $\theta(K + N)$. The worst case time is $\theta(N^2)$, but this has not been observed in practice. The uniform grid is a flat, non-hierarchical grid overlaid on the edges to be intersected. The grid size is a function of the number and length of the edges. The actual size is not critical; a factor of three variation either way from the optimum tends to increase the execution time less than 50 per cent. The method is fast even for unevenly spaced data; hierarchical methods such as quadtrees are not necessary here. When implemented on a 16 processor Sequent Balance 21000, the program runs 10 times as fast as when one processor is used. When implemented on a 32 processor hypercube, the communication costs are only one-third of the total time, and the slowest processor to finish is only twice as slow as the average time. On a Sun 4/280 serial machine, finding all 144 666 intersections of the 116 896 edges of the US Geological Survey's Digital Line Graph sampler tape (of Chicamauga, Tennessee) takes only 37 CPU seconds.

The technique also extends to higher level operations, such as finding the areas of the intersection polygons resulting from overlaying two maps (Franklin 1990). When applied to two maps, the conterminous states of the United States, with 1081 vertices, 892 edges, and 49 polygons, and July isotherms at 10°F intervals, with 920 vertices, 892 edges, and 6 polygons, calculating the areas of all the output polygons, once the data had been read in, took only 7.2 CPU seconds on a Sun 3/60.

Voronoi diagrams

How should a set of N (one-dimensional) numbers be stored so that the closest existing number to a new one can be located? The obvious data structure is a sorted array. Sorting the array to build the structure takes $T_{preprocessing}(N) = \theta(N\log N)$, while determining the closest old number to some new one takes $T_{query}(N) = \theta(\log N)$ with a binary search.

A Voronoi diagram (Preparata and Shamos 1985; Sedgewick 1983) allows N 2-D points to be stored so that it is possible to insert a new point, delete a point, determine the closest old point to a new point, and perform many other location problems in time $T_{query}(N) = \theta(\log N)$. The Voronoi diagram, which can be built in $T_{preprocessing}(N) = \theta(N\log N)$, partitions the plane into a set of polygons, also called Thiessen polygons, one around each input point. The dual of this diagram, called a Delaunay triangulation, has an edge joining a pair of original points whenever their polygons are adjacent. This is useful for interpolation of a value at any point given the values of some function only at the set of N randomly located input points. To calculate the function value at the new point, interpolate the values at the vertices of the Delaunay triangle containing it.

Generalized Voronoi diagrams allow other objects than just points (Drysdale 1979). A scene with points, edges, circles, and so on, can be pre-processed so that when a new point is presented, the closest old object can be determined quickly. However, generalized Voronoi diagrams are much more complicated to implement.

Large databases

Many data structure textbooks are not completely appropriate for the size of data structures that are reasonable to use today, where a workstation may have several megabytes of memory and many megabytes of disk. For example, consider that perennial favourite the binary tree, if used to organize 1 million 4-byte integers. If the pointer to each integer also requires 4 bytes, then this tree would occupy 8 megabytes of memory. Why would this tree be the wrong solution?

If the tree were perfectly balanced, it would be 20 levels deep, so that accessing any element would require following 20 pointers, probably to 20 widely separated locations in memory. This would activate 20 pages in the cache or virtual memory handler. Worse, the tree could not be perfectly balanced if it were being modified. A practical tree here would be an AVL tree (Aho, Hopcroft and Ullman 1983), which allows the left and right sub-trees of each node to differ in height by up to one. An AVL tree with 1 million elements would be perhaps 35 levels deep, which is even worse. Basically a binary tree is obsolete for large databases.

A B-tree, where each node can have from M to $2M-1$ sons for some fixed M, such as 100, would be much more efficient, and in this case would result in a tree about six levels deep. The B-tree can also be used to organize data on a disk. If M is made so large that one node is the size of one track of the disk, or whatever the most efficient quantity of data is to read, and if the first two levels or so of the tree are stored in main memory, then any element of a 10^9 byte tree can be read in one or two disk accesses.

For smaller data sets, the best version of a binary tree is the splay tree (Tarjan 1987). Here the tree is readjusted during every query to move that record to the root. This is not so bad as it sounds since locating the record requires $\theta(\log N)$ work and moving the record to the root requires only additional work proportional to that. This causes the average access time to be minimized even when some elements are retrieved more often than others.

ALGORITHMS

Theoretical analysis

Deep theoretical analysis of algorithms and data structures is desirable when possible. Some standard books dealing with this include Aho, Hopcroft and Ullman (1983) and Knuth (1973). Tarjan's Turing Award lecture (Tarjan 1987) is also excellent. Unfortunately, this analysis is subject to error. Even highly selective theoretical computer science conferences and monographs have published repeated errors. A more serious limitation, at the moment, is that what is theoretically analysable is not always what is most needed. Cartography needs expected time analysis as much as worst case analysis; however, expected time analysis is still almost impossible for sophisticated data structures.

Some useful notation for theoretical analysis follows. $T(N) = \theta(f(N))$ means that the worst-case execution time of an algorithm for all problems of size N grows proportional to $f(N)$ as $N \to \infty$. $T(N) = \theta(f(N))$ means that the execution time grows at most as fast as $f(N)$, and $T(N) = \Omega(f(N))$ means that it grows at least as fast as $f(N)$. Thus since it is known how to multiply two $N \times N$ matrices in cubic time, and that it takes at least quadratic time, therefore, here $T_{matrix-mult}(N) = \theta(N^2)$ and $T_{matrix-mult}(N) = \Omega(N^3)$. The actual minimum time is not known. This notation, which was devised to hide dependencies of the time on particular machines, can hide too much. If one algorithm's time is N^3, while another's is $1\,000\,000 N^2$, then the latter is asymptotically faster, but practically slower for $N < 1\,000\,000$. Finally, it is necessary to distinguish between a particular problem and the various algorithms to solve it. The problem of matrix multiplication has several algorithms, from the naive, with $T_{naive}(N) = \theta(N^3)$, to the Schönhage–Strassen (Schönhage and Strassen 1971), with $T_{SS}(N) = \theta(N^{2.81})$, to even (asymptotically) faster ones.

Expected time analysis is difficult in cartography because the statistical distribution of the input data is not well characterized. However, it is known that cartographic data can be distributed much worse than if it were independent and uniform. Consider, for example, the edges of a map of a city such as Chicago, where each edge is one block of a street. Along each street there will be dozens of correlated, collinear, edges, which could not happen if the edges were random. This severe degeneracy can cause problems for a scan line algorithm.

The US Geological Survey's Digital Line Graph sampler tape illustrates how statistically unusual GIS data can be. If the 116 896 piecewise straight edges are scaled to fall in a 1000 × 1000 square, then the mean edge length is 2, but with a standard deviation of 8, which is a very skewed distribution (since there are no negative lengths). Another unusual feature is that 34 edges have zero length, to six significant digits. This non-randomness, which is typical of cartographic databases, can destroy an algorithm that makes uniformity or normality assumptions.

Randomized algorithms

A powerful recent concept in algorithm design is randomization, that is, the algorithm 'flips a coin' and alters its actions depending on the outcome. A simple example of this is when running a scan line up a database of city streets, where there is one edge per block. For each position there might be a requirement to process the active edges, or those which cross that scan line. If both the scan line and the streets are horizontal, when the scan line coincides with a long street then there will be many horizontal active edges. If the program is comparing all active edges against each other, perhaps to build up chains, then this can be a serious problem. The solution is to rotate the map by a random angle before processing.

Another example occurs in the operation of sorting N numbers by a quicksort. Here it is possible to proceed by divide-and-conquer, a common method of algorithm design. A pivot number is chosen from the set and the set is partitioned into those numbers smaller than, those equal to, and those larger than the pivot. The first and last subsets are then recursively quicksorted. If all inputs are equally likely then the average time is $E(T(N)) = \theta(N\log N)$, which is quite good. The problem occurs if the pivot element is the smallest number in the set, which will happen if the set is already sorted, which is not so unusual, and the first element is chosen as the pivot. Now $T(N) = \theta(N^2)$, which is totally unacceptable. However, if the pivot element is selected randomly, there are now no bad inputs. Even if the set is already sorted, $E(T(N)) = \theta(N\log N)$, where there is averaging over different outputs of the random number generator. Every time the algorithm is run on some fixed input, it will take a different time. However, the average of all those times for the same input is fast.

The virtue of simplicity

For many low-level data structures and algorithms, it has been determined after extensive analysis that the best choice is the simplest. For example, in random number generation, a linear congruential generator:

$$x_{i+1} = (7^5 x_i) \bmod (2^{31} - 1)$$

is better than many more complicated methods, including those used in many packages and textbooks (Park and Miller 1988). The coefficients in the above equation were chosen with great care to achieve this.

In hashing, a simple modulo operation for the key to bucket transformation is excellent, and for handling overflows, similar simple methods are adequate. A second example may be used to illustrate this point. In virtual memory paging, an important question is which current page is to be paged out so that a new page may come in to satisfy a page fault. The simple concept of writing out the LRU (least recently used) page is quite adequate. Finally, there are many problems, called NP (non-deterministic polynomial time), for which the best known (deterministic) algorithm requires exponential time (Garey and Johnson 1979). However, many of them, such as the travelling salesperson problem, have obvious heuristics with which an almost optimal solution can be found in linear time.

Finally, when locating a number in a long sorted list, guessing where the number should be usually beats a binary search (Perl, Itai and Avni 1978). For example, when trying to locate the number 73 in a list of 100 independent numbers ranging from 1 to 1000, the first probe should be at the seventh number, not at the fiftieth. With this interpolation searching, if the numbers are independently and uniformly distributed, then the average number of probes to find a number in a sorted list of N numbers is $E(T_{query}) = \log_2(\log_2 N)$, although the worst case is $T_{query} \leq N$. This can be compared to the average and maximum in a binary search, which are both $T_{query} = \log_2 N$. For example, if $N = 1$ million, then binary search takes 20 probes, while interpolation search may take about five.

Of course heuristics do fail at times. In addition, simple concepts may not be simple to implement in practice; as Einstein said, 'A theory should be as simple as possible but no simpler'. When attempting to wring the last bit of performance out of a system, a design might get quite complicated. However, if machine speeds are doubling each year, then a 40 per cent increase in speed can be achieved by waiting six months for a new machine, which is better than spending more than six months getting that same degree of improvement from the software.

Implementability

A major advantage of simplicity is that the system is then more implementable. Instead of programmers spending all their time getting the system just to compile correctly, there is time to profile and improve the working system. In addition, the largest feasible system is determined by the point at which details are forgotten and new bugs are created as fast as system details are remembered and old bugs fixed. Simpler systems mean that the largest feasible system will have greater functionality.

Size–time trade-offs

Many data structures and algorithms have different possible versions depending on the relative costs of memory versus CPU cycles. For instance, consider allocating memory to a routine whose needs will gradually increase, as in the extendible array described above. When the block that has been allocated is full, a bigger region must be allocated, the complete old block copied over into the new region and any pointers updated. If bigger blocks are allocated then more memory is used but reallocations will be fewer. Another example occurs in storing and transmitting digital images. It is possible to compress typical 8 bit per pixel black and white images by a factor of ten with little visible degradation of the image quality. A video image such as a TV transmission can be compressed by a factor of 100 by the expenditure of considerable, and so far impracticable, processing. In the design of hardware, such as multipliers, there is also a continuum of trade-offs between multiplication time and cost.

Nevertheless, sometimes smaller is also faster. Many small computers are limited by the speeds of the I/O bus and memory since those technologies are advancing more slowly than processor technology. If some very big, often accessed, data structure can use, say, 2 byte integers instead of 4 byte integers, then I/O requirements are halved, and twice as many data elements will fit in the cache, raising the cache hit percentage. The disadvantage is that the program will hit a hard limit when 2 bytes becomes insufficient. Hard limits such as this are the most common reason for the death of a type of hardware. Consider, for example, the enormous problems caused for users of IBM PCs by Intel's decision to use first 16 and then 20 bit addressing for the CPU in the PC. This restricts the system to 2^{20}, or 1 megabyte of memory. After the operating system's requirements, the user is left with only 640 Kilobytes of memory. Thankfully, the processors in the IBM PS/2s have removed this restriction.

Given relative costs of memory, disk space and processing power, it is possible to calculate how often a word in memory must be referenced before it is better to swap it out to disk, and the trade-offs between storing and recalculating intermediate results. A good summary of data compression techniques, useful for implementing the tradeoff, is Lelewer and Hirschberg (1987).

SOFTWARE DEVELOPMENT STRATEGY

Waterfall model

The traditional software development strategy is the waterfall model, named from a popular method of diagramming the process, which has several stages. This can be illustrated with the problem of determining the area of New York State above 1000 metres elevation.

1. *Requirements analysis*:   Global analysis of the problem, deciding whether to use satellite photographs, US Geological Survey databases, or even renting a plane, flying around the state and estimating by eye. This step is about 5 per cent of total life-cycle system cost.

2. *Specification*:   Deciding the user-visible parts of the program, such as commands and database formats – 5 per cent.

3. *Design*:   Designing the internal details of the system, such as data structures and subroutine interfaces – 10 per cent.

4. *Coding*:   Actually writing the programs – 5 per cent.

5. *Debugging and testing*:   Getting the code to work, and, if verification and validation are involved, proving its correctness. The system is released to the customer at the conclusion of this step – 25 per cent.

6. *Maintenance*:   Modifying the released system to account for new hardware or users' needs, or to fix newly discovered bugs – 50 per cent.

This model is best when it is possible to predict in advance the system requirements. It is now being partly replaced by rapid prototyping.

Rapid prototyping

Here a small prototype with stubs of the major components is readied for the user's comments. Then new functions are gradually added. This has the advantage of better feedback from users, who may be unable to specify the requirements in advance, but will know what they want when they see it. However, the evolutionary development may allow major irreversible decisions to be taken before all the implications are known, and this can lock the designer into a bad choice.

For example, suppose a mapping display system is being designed. It might be pointless to specify everything, such as legend format, in detail in advance, if it is necessary to see some finished maps to know whether the total effect was appropriate. On the other hand, through lack of planning ahead, a data structure might be picked that does not allow later program porting from a low resolution colour display device to a high resolution black and white one. This might happen if certain special, unused, values were used for the colour pixels to code for properties such as the pixels used for the legend. A higher resolution device, with only 1 bit per pixel, would have no unused pixel values and allocating extra bits per pixel might not be possible because of the total number of pixels.

Another case of an innocent early decision causing later problems appears when porting a system written for European users into Japanese. The idea that message characters are chosen from a small possible set, such as ASCII, each character representable in 7 or 8 bits, is so thoroughly embedded in most program libraries that converting to Kanji is a major task. Even the appropriate data structures are totally different. Dispatch tables, which are used to parse input text by branching on each character, are more suited to 128 entries than to 2000 entries.

Profiling and improvement

It is impossible to predict in advance how most systems will be used and which parts will consume the most resources. Thus it is important to profile the system in actual use to determine which parts should be improved. Then the data structures and algorithms that are too simple can be selectively upgraded to more complicated but faster versions. This is how Unix was originally developed. It was all written in C, then profiled and about 10 per cent recoded in machine language.

In Unix, typical profiling tools include *lint* to detect most syntax errors and to perform an elementary static flow analysis to detect unused variables, *prof* to profile the CPU time used in each procedure, and *tcov* to count the number of times each statement is executed (Sun Microsystems 1985). With these tools the critical parts of the system can selectively be improved.

Profiling a system, perhaps by adding extra counters and timers, is also critical in understanding how a complicated program is actually behaving inside. For example, how full does a hash table get? How many collisions occur during insertion, or during retrieval? When splitting edges with a uniform grid, how many segments does the average edge get split into, or the worst edge? How many edges does the average cell contain, or the worst cell? Most people have not the faintest idea. The process of software development does not end when the program compiles correctly, or even when it can process a small test case. To produce a work of art, cleanly designed and coded, and efficient, requires following systematic design steps and then watching how the program performs in actual use.

CONCLUSION

If computer science has any meaning other than as a sterile intellectual exercise, it is to help other disciplines use the computer more effectively. GIS practitioners need not recapitulate computer scientists' painful process of learning if they can learn from their experience, as described above in this chapter. It is not sufficient to design GIS to use current computer systems; they must be planned for the computer systems that will be available when the new GIS is ready.

REFERENCES

Aho A V, Hopcroft J E, Ullman J D (1983) *Data Structures and Algorithms*. Addison-Wesley, Reading Massachusetts

AT&T Bell Laboratories (1978) *Bell System Technical Journal* 57 (6)

AT&T Bell Laboratories (1984) *Bell System Technical Journal* 63 (8)

Bentley J L, Ottmann T A (1979) Algorithms for reporting and counting geometric intersections. *IEEE Transactions on Computing* C-28 (9): 643–7

Boehm B W (1987) Improving software productivity. *Computer (IEEE)* 20 (9): 43–57

Brooks F P (1987) No silver bullet – essence and accidents of software engineering. *Computer (IEEE)* 20 (4): 10–19

Chazelle B, Edelsbrunner H (1988) An optimal algorithm for intersecting line segments in the plane. *Proceedings, 29th Annual Symposium on Foundations of Computer Science, White Plains*

Cohen J (1988) A view of the origins and development of prolog. *Communications ACM* 31 (1): 26–36

Drysdale R L (1979) *Generalized Voronoi Diagrams and Geometric Searching*. Unpublished PhD dissertation, Department of Computer Science, Stanford University

Franklin W R (1990) Calculating map overlay polygon areas without explicitly calculating the polygons – implementation. *Proceedings of the 4th International Symposium on Spatial Data Handling*. Zurich International Geographical Union, Ohio, pp. 151–60

Franklin W R, Wu P Y F (1987) A polygon overlay system in prolog. *Proceedings of AUTOCARTO8*. ASPRS/ACSM, Falls Church Virginia, pp. 97–106

Franklin W R, Wu P Y F, Samaddar S, Nichols M (1986) Geometry in prolog. In: Kunii T (ed.) *Advanced Computer Graphics, Proceedings of Computer Graphics Tokyo '86*, pp. 71–8

Franklin W R, Chandrasekhar N, Kankanhalli M, Seshan M, Akman V (1988) Efficiency of uniform grids for intersection detection on serial and parallel machines. In: Magnenat-Thalmann N, Thalmann D (eds.) *New Trends in Computer Graphics (Proceedings, Computer Graphics International '88)*. Springer-Verlag, New York

Franklin W R, Chandrasekhar N, Kankanhalli M, Sun D,

Zhou M-C, Wu P Y F (1989) Uniform grids: a technique for intersection detection on serial and parallel machines. *Proceedings of AUTOCARTO9*. ASPRS/ACSM, Bethesda Maryland, pp. 100–9

Franklin W R, Chandrasekhar N, Kankanhalli M, Akman V, Wu P Y F (1990) Efficient geometric operations for CAD. In Wozny M J, Turner J U, Preiss K (eds.) *Geometric Modeling for Product Engineering*. Elsevier, Amsterdam, pp. 485–98

Garey M R, Johnson D S (1979) *Computers and Intractibility: a guide to the theory of incompleteness*. Freeman, San Francisco

Goldberg A (1984) *Smalltalk-80: the interactive programming environment*. Addison-Wesley, Reading Massachusetts

Hoare C A R (1987) An overview of some formal methods for program design. *Computer (IEEE)* **20** (9): 85–91

Knuth D E (1973) *The Art of Computer Programming*. Addison-Wesley, Reading Massachusetts

Lelewer D A, Hirschberg D S (1987) Data compression. *ACM Computing Surveys* **19** (3): 261–96

Mel B W, Omohundro S M, Robinson A D, Skiena S S, Thearling K H, Young L T, Wolfram S (1988) Tablet: personal computer in the year 2000. *Communications ACM* **31** (6): 639–46

Park S E, Miller K W (1988) Random number generators: good ones are hard to find. *Communications ACM* **31** (10): 1192–201

Perl Y, Itai A, Avni H (1978) Interpolation search – a log log n search. *Communications ACM* **21** (7): 550–3

Preparata F P, Shamos M I (1985) *Computational Geometry: an introduction*. Springer-Verlag, New York

Pyle I C (1985) *The Ada Programming Language: a guide for programmers*. Prentice-Hall, Englewood Cliffs New Jersey

Quarterman J S, Silberschatz A, Peterson J L (1985) 4.2bsd and 4.3bsd as examples of the Unix system. *ACM Computing Surveys* **17** (4): 379–418

Rich C, Waters R C (1988) The programmer's apprentice: a research overview. *Computer (IEEE)* **21** (11): 10–25

Schönhage S, Strassen V (1971) Schnelle multiplikation grosser zahlen. *Computing* **7**: 281–92

Sedgewick R (1983) *Algorithms*. Addison-Wesley, Reading Massachusetts

Stroustrup B (1987) *The C++ Programming Language*. Addison-Wesley, Reading Massachusetts

Sun Microsystems (1985) *Programming Utilities for the Sun Workstation*. Sun Microsystems

Tarjan R E (1987) Algorithm design. *Communications ACM* **30** (3): 205–12

Plate 14.1(a) 15 August 1987 TM-derived Greenness Vegetation Index (GVI) for the Konza LTER. Image brightness is proportional to GVI. Image is oriented to UTM north, 6.3 km west to east and 5.7 km north to south. Black areas are outside the LTER or masked cropland. Brightest areas are riparian forest and woodland (e.g. northeast corner) and upland prairie burned in spring (e.g. southwest corner).

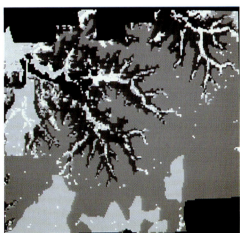

Plate 14.1(b) IGIS-derived stratification for the Konza LTER based on regression tree analysis of GVI data and digital terrain variables. Stratification variables include vegetation type (wooded *vs* non-wooded), burned *vs* unburned prairie and elevation (three zones). Image brightness is proportional to mean GVI for each of seven strata. Image size, orientation and masking are identical to Plate 14.1(a).

Plate 17.1 An Altek 36 inch × 48 inch digitizing table, backlit and with fully adjustable height and tilt and lightweight cursor (courtesy of Altek Corporation).

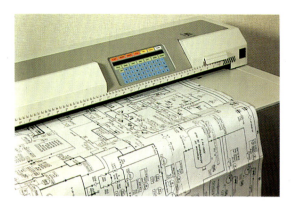

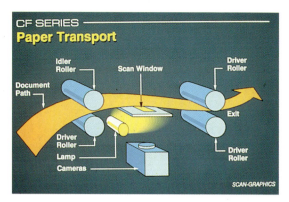

Plate 17.2 A large format continuous feed scanner: the document is digitized as it is fed through the scanner (courtesy of Scan-Graphics Inc.).

Plate 17.3 A continuous feed scanner in diagrammatic form, showing the paper transport mechanism and the CCD cameras (courtesy of Scan-Graphics Inc.).

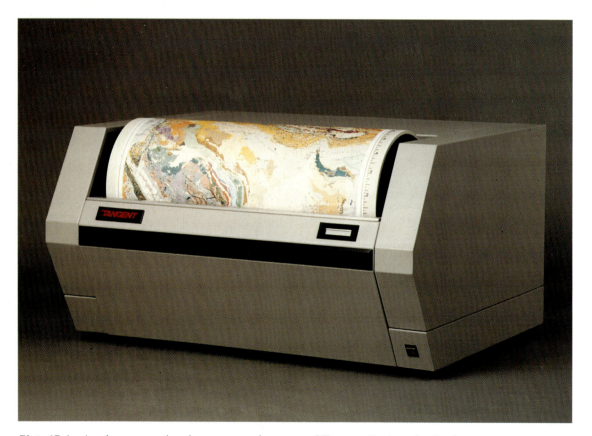

Plate 17.4 A colour separation drum scanner (courtesy of Tangent Engineering Inc.).

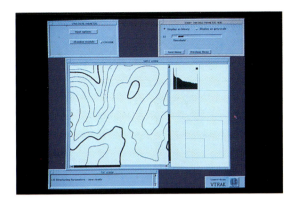

Plate 17.5 Use of a histogram of grey levels to set a binary threshold interactively (courtesy of Laser-Scan Ltd).

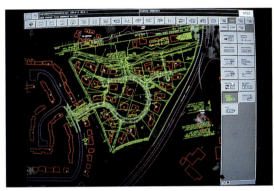

Plate 17.6 Overlay or 'heads-up' digitizing (courtesy of Intergraph (UK) Ltd).

Plate 17.7 Vector representation of contour lines superimposed on a raster source. Note that features in green remain to be captured; 'painted-out' features in red have been captured (courtesy of Laser-Scan Ltd).

Plate 17.8 Results of vertex extraction and building squaring. The window display shows the vector data points representing the building features (courtesy of Laser-Scan Ltd).

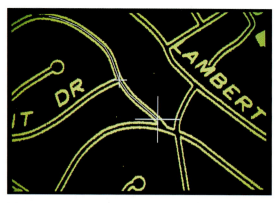

Plate 17.9 Extraction of road centre lines from cased road. Road junctions are represented by nodes in the resulting topological structure (courtesy of Laser-Scan Ltd).

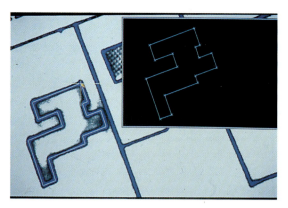

Plate 17.10 Illustration of the creation of clean vector data (in the window display) extracted from a greyscale raster source by variable thresholding (courtesy of Laser-Scan Ltd).

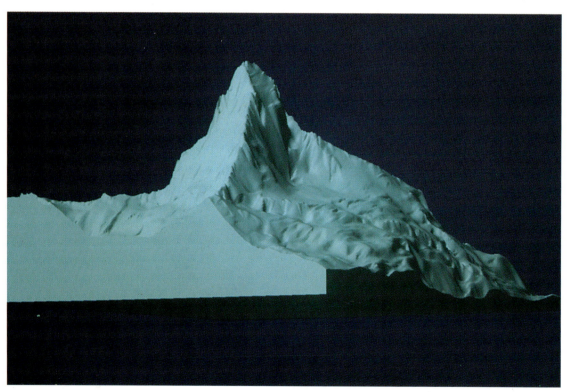

Plate 19.1 Perspective block diagram (Matterhorn, Switzerland) using simple shading (DTM data courtesy of Swiss Federal Office of Topography).

Plate 19.2 Perspective visualization of Landsat TM satellite data (Mt Pilatus, Lake Lucerne in central Switzerland): (a) satellite image intensities are used to shade DTM facets; (b) free 'camera' orientation is necessary for flight simulation; using ray tracing algorithms, atmospheric effects such as haze can be visualized. (courtesy of E Meier, University of Zurich; true colour rendition by K Seidel, ETHZ; image data provided by ESA/Earthnet).

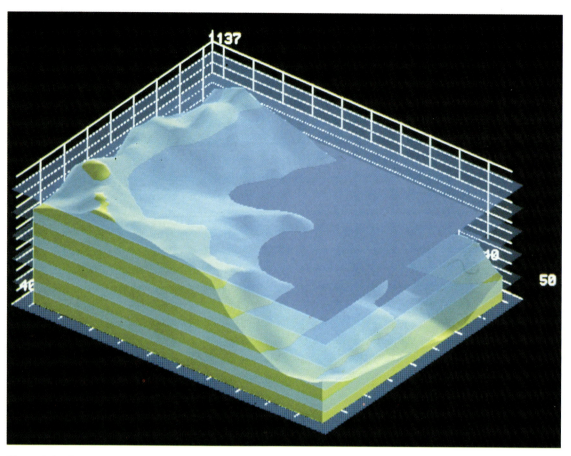

Plate 19.3 Interactive perspective visualization and interpretation. Semi-transparent planes may be used to indicate altitudes, for example for planning of reservoirs. (courtesy of R L'Eplattenier, University of Zurich.)

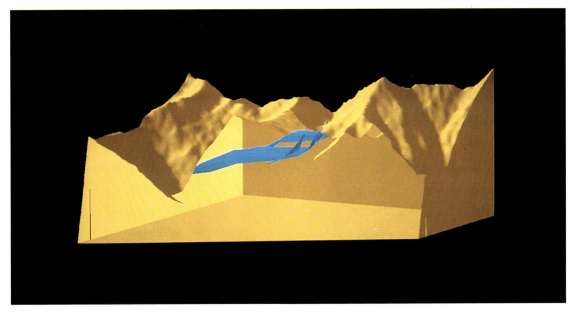

Plate 19.4 Interactive perspective visualization and interpretation. Use of model clipping and semi-transparent surfaces to display subsurface structures. (courtesy of R L'Eplattenier, University of Zurich.)

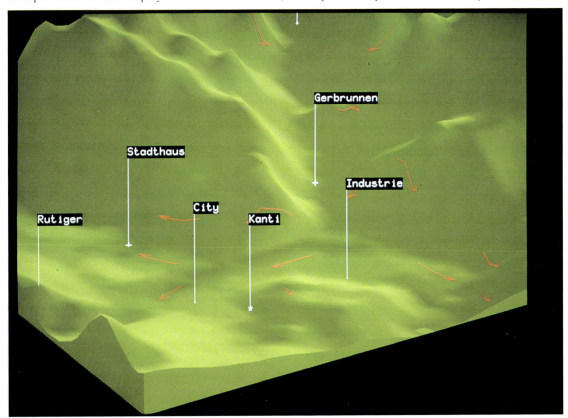

Plate 19.5 Interactive perspective visualization and interpretation. Name labels are used to indicate place locations; arrows (in red) visualize the flow of air masses in relation to topography. (courtesy of R L'Eplattenier, University of Zurich.)

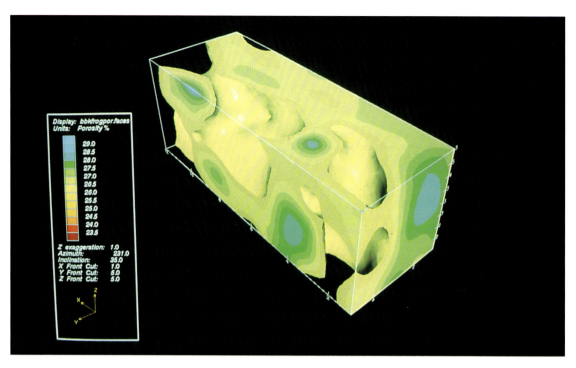

Plate 20.1 Solid model of a limestone block showing complex 3-D variability of porosity.

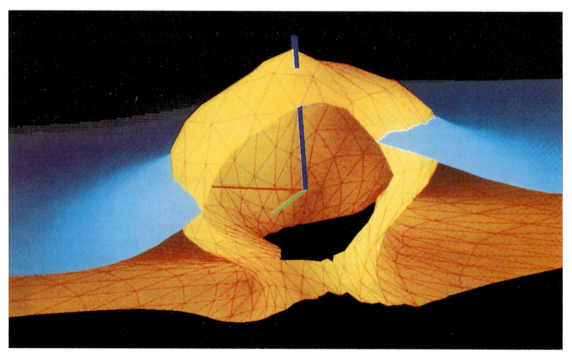

Plate 20.2 Solid 3-D model of a salt dome from GOCAD.

HIGH-LEVEL SPATIAL DATA STRUCTURES FOR GIS

M J EGENHOFER AND J R HERRING

The chapter focuses on the semantics of spatial concepts and their formalizations. A framework is proposed consisting of spatial concepts, spatial data models (or high-level spatial data structures) and (low-level) spatial data structures. Examples of spatial data models include spaghetti, regular and irregular tessellations. The implementation of each of these in (low-level) data structures is discussed.

INTRODUCTION

The organization of spatial data in a computer system has drawn much attention in the field of GIS. Since its early beginnings, designers and developers of GIS have been looking for appropriate representations of geometrical objects. Peucker and Chrisman (1975), Nagy and Wagle (1979), Peuquet (1984), Burrough (1986) and, most recently, Samet (1989) have published comprehensive compilations of these previous studies. The most popular abstractions organize spatial data as points, lines and areas. These elements have also been incorporated as fundamental components of the cartographic data exchange standard (DCDSTF 1988). The goals of methods for organizing spatial data, often called spatial data structures, are: (1) to process geometrical user queries and other geometrical operations for application programs; and (2) to implement these operations so that they are consistently, robustly, and efficiently executed in a computer system. The latter is frequently associated with computational geometry (Preparata and Shamos 1985; Edelsbrunner 1987), while spatial query processing is of particular interest to spatial database management systems (Frank 1988; Egenhofer 1989b).

The selection of a specific spatial data structure may considerably influence the processing of spatial queries. For instance, in the case of a collection of records of house ownership deeds, a user may enquire about the owners of the parcels adjacent to the house lot '461 Ocean Boulevard'. Depending on the organization of parcels, the query may be processed in different ways:

1. Each parcel in the database could be checked to determine whether its bounding nodes have the same geodetic coordinates as one of the nodes of parcel '461 Ocean Boulevard' and the corresponding owner found. Of course, this sequential comparison will be quite inefficient as the number of parcels stored in the database increases because each parcel has to be retrieved and all its nodes need to be checked against all the nodes of the target parcel.

2. The performance of this operation improves if spatial objects can be accessed based on their spatial location. Such an access method allows for searching parcels within a given region, for example a rectangle, so that the set of objects to be tested against the target is relatively small. Then the actual neighbours can be found with the same type of checking as above, based on a much smaller number of parcels.

3. Another way to organize parcels is to record explicitly the neighbours for each parcel. The neighbourhood query is then reduced to accessing the related parcels based on the stored adjacency information.

The semantics of spatial concepts common to multiple implementations of spatial data structures and their formalizations are the focus of this chapter. The former specifies what operations can be performed on spatial objects, while the latter defines how these operations are implemented so that they can actually be executed in a computer. A similar separation has been proposed for the schema design of database management systems, distinguishing physical, conceptual, and user schemata or views (ANSI 1975). This distinction advocates data independence so that the implementation of a specific model of a mini-world may be updated without affecting the remaining software system (Codd 1982). Since the remainder of the software system relies upon the concepts implemented behind well-defined interfaces, changes in the physical schemata will be hidden from users at the logical level – except for performance or storage requirements. Likewise, in the realms of programming and query languages, there is often a differentiation between procedural languages – to describe how a function should be performed – and descriptive languages – to explain the goal without specifying how it should be achieved. Essentially, the same difference exists between data structures and data models – even if sometimes data models are explained in an exemplary fashion by describing how operations should be performed.

This chapter defines the terms 'data model' and 'data structure' which in the past have sometimes been thought of as high-level and low-level data structures. It proceeds with the definition of a framework to distinguish spatial data models from high-level and low-level spatial data structures. The next sections discuss formalizations of spatial concepts known from mathematics and examples of spatial data models and spatial data structures. The conclusion focuses on the integration of different data models under a common user interface.

A CONCEPTUAL FRAMEWORK FOR SPATIAL DATA MODELS AND STRUCTURES

Solutions for geometrical problems may appear to be trivial when determined using principles of Euclidean geometry, the popular school model for solving geometrical problems (see Gatrell 1991 in this volume). Euclidean geometry is based on a continuous space consisting of an infinite number of points. Analytical geometry is a convenient mapping to the coordinate space and relies on real numbers where between any two numbers another one exists. This is necessary to represent the property of Euclidean geometry in which between any two points another one can be inserted. Unfortunately, finite computers and their number systems cannot guarantee this assumption and the immediate use of floating point or integer arithmetic for Euclidean geometry frequently leads to undesired effects, thus contradicting our common sense of geometrical properties and violating some laws of geometry. Examples of such counter-intuitive effects of implementations of Euclidean coordinate geometry in computer systems are:

- the scaling of coordinates may change topology by moving points, initially close to a line, from one side to another (Franklin 1984);

- the intersection of two lines does not necessarily lie on both lines (Nievergelt and Schorn 1988); and

- the application of two inverse geometrical operations may generate a geometry which differs from the original geometry (Dobkin and Silver 1988; Hoffmann 1989).

Euclidean coordinate geometry is but one concept humans employ when dealing with space and geometry. Point-sets, for example, are another concept for dealing with spatial objects. A framework for the organization of spatial data proposed here consists of (1) spatial concepts, (2) spatial data models (or high-level spatial data structures), and (3) (low-level) spatial data structures.

Spatial concepts

Humans employ spatial concepts to organize and structure their perception of (geographical) space. For this purpose, they use different concepts depending on the observers' different experiences and the context in which a person views some situation. Humans have the particular ability to handle multiple concepts simultaneously, to select the most appropriate for solving a specific task, and to switch between them whenever necessary or appropriate (Mark *et al.* 1989). For example, people may use an essentially Euclidean geometry when operating and reasoning in their immediate neighbourhood, for instance, on a desktop. On the other hand, they employ the spatial concept of a network when navigating a car.

Although these spatial concepts are frequently employed in everyday life, they are only informally defined. A few formalized spatial concepts, (e.g. Euclidean geometry) are based on assumptions, such as an infinitely precise numbering system, which restrict them from being correctly implemented on finite computer machines. Image schemata, for example, play an important role in humans' perception and understanding of space (Lakoff and Johnson 1980); however, they are defined in linguistic terms (Talmy 1983; Herskovits 1986) which lack formalism and mathematical rigour.

This topic is the focus of Frank and Mark (1991 in this volume) and, therefore, needs no further elaboration here.

Spatial data models

The semantics of spatial concepts are defined and formalized by spatial data models. Spatial data models are formalizations of the concepts humans use to conceptualize space. Such formalizations of spatial concepts are necessary, because computer systems are essentially formal systems that manipulate symbols according to formal rules. They do not understand – in the sense of human beings' understanding – the meanings of symbols or what they stand for; instead, they follow the instructions of their programs blindingly fast, but without any 'common sense'. The formalization of geometrical concepts employs well-understood mathematical findings to describe the meanings of the operations to be performed on spatial objects (Egenhofer and Frank 1990).

The common use of abstraction from concepts by humans helps to make these concepts implementable on computer systems, without the need to describe actual implementation details. The view of geometry in a spatial data model is, therefore, independent of implementation aspects. The role of a spatial data model is similar to the conceptual schema in the three-schema view: concepts get separated from the actual implementations, thus implementations of certain parts of the large GIS software system become more independent and may be updated without affecting the remaining software parts. Finally, the formalisms may serve as a means for users to verify that implementations of operations concur with their expectations.

A commonly employed approach in modelling with spatial properties is to separate them into geometrical and non-geometrical classes. Abstractions similar to these formalizations can be found in areas other than geometrical data handling as well. Probably best known is the formalization of the concept of a table in the relational data model (Codd 1970). Humans frequently employ the organization of data in the form of tables in business. The relational data model formally describes the operations on tables and their semantics. This formalization leads to a possible implementation of how humans deal with tables, but it does not yet describe the actual implementation of these operations in a computer system.

Low-level spatial data structures

Spatial data structures, also called low-level data structures, are the implementations of spatial concepts. In order to be a valid implementation of a spatial concept, a spatial data structure must follow the properties defined in the corresponding spatial data model. Several spatial data structures may be implemented for the same spatial data model. It should, therefore, be possible to exchange different spatial data structures for the same data model with only implementation changes and no observable effects for the user. Spatial data structures are concerned with the efficiency of the implementation, namely: (1) minimizing storage requirements to reduce the amount of space to hold the data; and (2) maximizing performance to improve the processing speed of geometrical operations. For these reasons, the representation of data internal to a computer system and its architecture are crucial factors to be considered in the design of spatial data structures. Spatial data structures are then built from standard data structures as developed in computer science (Knuth

1973), such as stacks, queues, lists, and trees, and specific index structures to provide fast access to spatial data based on a spatial location (Samet 1989; see also Franklin 1991 in this volume).

An example of different levels in the framework

The following example demonstrates the roles of the different levels in this framework:

- When dealing with land parcels, humans may employ the concept of a discrete 2-dimensional space in which the parcels form an ideal partition of the space.

- One formalization of a discrete space is the spatial data model of a raster of squares of equal size. Within a raster, adjacent cells can be determined and distances between points can be calculated in terms of raster units.

- A raster may then be implemented in various low-level spatial data structures, e.g. as quadtree (Samet 1984), linear quadtree (Gargantini 1982), run-length encoded (Burrough 1986), and so on. These implementations have the same behaviour, but they may have varying efficiency with respect to the data storage requirements and performance of operations.

Formalizations of spatial concepts

Spatial data models formally describe the semantics of concepts present in the geometrical data model. With the help of the mathematical concepts of topology, metric and order, various types of geometrical questions may be answered which are particularly important for GIS (Kainz 1989). Examples of such questions include 'How far is it from Bangor to Boston on Interstate I-95?', 'Which provinces in Canada share a common boundary with the state of Maine?', and 'What county contains Bangor?' These concepts are not completely unrelated since every metric space has a topology – and some different distance functions describe even the same topology. Likewise, the concept of inclusion/containment is a property which can be expressed in both topology and order.

Order

The concept of order allows for the comparison of two or more elements from a set. A relation R over a set X is a strict order relation if for all x, y, z elements of X, R is

asymmetric: $x\,R\,y \rightarrow \text{NOT}\,(y\,R\,x)$ [16.1]
transitive: $x\,R\,y$ AND $y\,R\,z \rightarrow x\,R\,z$ [16.2]

Within strictly ordered sets, any two elements can be compared with each other, that is for all x, y elements of S: $x\,R\,y$ AND $y\,R\,x$; therefore, a strict order relation establishes a hierarchy.

Strict order relations are different from order relations. To distinguish the two, the structure defined by an order relation is called a partially ordered set or poset. A relation R over a set X is an order relation if, for all x, y, z elements of X, R has the following three properties (Gill 1976):

reflexivity: $x\,R\,x$ [16.3]
anti-symmetry: $x\,R\,y$ AND $y\,R\,x \rightarrow x = y$ [16.4]
transitivity: $x\,R\,y$ AND $y\,R\,z \rightarrow x\,R\,z$ [16.5]

Order, both strict and partial, can be applied to GIS, for instance, to determine whether one spatial object is inside another – and its inverse operation whether a spatial object contains another one (Saalfeld 1985; Greasley 1988) – as well as for perspectives, such as left/right, in front/behind (Freeman 1975; Pullar and Egenhofer 1988). For example, the relation inside between cities and counties is an order relation, indicating that each city belongs to exactly one county, and that a county can have several cities. On the other hand, the relation between school districts and voting districts is a partial order: while some school districts may be completely included within a voting district, not all boundaries of the voting districts coincide with school district boundaries.

The application of order to sort non-geometrical property values derived from the geometry of spatial objects, such as the areas of regions or the lengths of lines, is the same as for conventional data, for example, integers or strings, and, therefore, does not introduce any new challenges due to handling geometrical data.

Topology

Topology is the study of the characteristics of geometrical objects that are independent of the underlying coordinate system. Topology treats those properties that are preserved under topological transformations, characterized by a group of bijective (a function $f: A \rightarrow B$ is bijective if there exists another function $g: B \rightarrow A$ such that $g(f(A)) = A$ and $f(g(B)) = B$) and continuous (a function $f: A \rightarrow B$ is continuous if for each element a of A every open set V in B is mapped on to an open set U in A containing a such that $f(U)$ is a subset of V) transformations which have also continuous inverses. Properties that are preserved under topological transformations are called topological invariants. Examples of topological transformations are translation, rotation, and scaling.

The major purpose of using topologically structured data is to improve the spatial analysis capability of GIS (Herring 1987; Pullar and Egenhofer 1988; Herring 1989b; Egenhofer 1989a). This is achieved using the techniques of problem translation and symbolic manipulation as used in algebraic topology (Alexandroff 1961) and results in the following:

- The intersection of two points or lines becomes the search for common nodes.
- The coincidence of two linear objects becomes the search for their common edges.
- The adjacency of a linear object to a region is the search for common edges (or nodes depending on the definition of adjacency) in the line and the boundary of the region.
- The adjacency of regions is reduced to determining the common edges or nodes in the boundaries of the regions, probably from opposite sides.
- Polygon overlay is the analysis of common faces.

Metric

A metric space is defined by a function $d(p,p) \rightarrow R$ calculating the distance between two points p. This distance function must obey the following four axioms:

1. The distance from a point to itself is zero (eqn [16.6]).

2. If the two points are not identical then the distance between two points is greater than zero (eqn [16.7]).

3. The distance is symmetrical (eqn [16.8]).

4. The sum of the lengths of two legs of a triangle is greater than or equal to the length of the third leg (eqn [16,9]).

$$d(p,p) = 0 \qquad [16.6]$$

$$d(p1,p2) > 0 \text{ if } p1 \neq p2 \qquad [16.7]$$

$$d(p1,p2) = d(p2,p1) \qquad [16.8]$$

$$d(p1,p3) \leq d(p1,p2) + d(p2,p3) \qquad [16.9]$$

A common metric space is the Euclidean space described by the Pythagorean distance. The metric of an n-dimensional Euclidean space is defined by the following distance function between two points $p1(x_1,\ldots,x_n)$, $p2(x'_1,\ldots,x'_n)$:

$$d(p1,p2) = ((x_1 - x'_1)^2 + \ldots + (x_n - x'_n)^2)^{1/2} \quad [16.10]$$

Two other distance functions are sometimes used describing the taxicab metric and the max metric (Croom 1989; see also Gatrell 1991 in this volume). In the plane, the taxicab metric, also called the Manhattan or city block distance, is defined by a function d calculating the distance from point $p1$ to $p2$ as the sum of the lengths of a horizontal segment and a vertical segment joining $p1$ to $p2$ (eqn [16.11]). The max metric is defined by the chessboard distance as the largest of the absolute values of the coordinate differences between $p1$ and $p2$ (eqn [16.12]):

$$d(p1,p2) = \sum_{i=1}^{n} |x_i - x'_i| \qquad [16.11]$$

$$d(p_1,p_2) = \max \{|x_i, x'_i|\}_{i=1}^{n} \qquad [16.12]$$

Each of these functions is a different implementation which has the properties defined by the axioms of a distance function. Metrics are used in GIS applications to determine distances between objects, to find shortest paths, and to identify nearest neighbours.

EXAMPLES OF SPATIAL DATA MODELS

Various models have been developed to represent geometrical properties. These models differ in their powers and capabilities to guarantee the formalizations of spatial concepts. Their deficiencies become apparent when users try to modify the geometry or want to verify its consistency. Some structures are quite primitive so that without the help of Euclidean coordinate geometry certain operations cannot be performed. Whenever an operation, such as the intersection of two lines, the test for the inclusion of a point within a region, or the coincidence of a point with a line, requires coordinate calculations, the imprecisions of the underlying number systems affect the results and consistency cannot be guaranteed.

Spaghetti data structure

Maps, as a basic data type, hold all their information in the form of graphical representations. Roads are red, rivers are blue, and so on. This simple view of geographical data formed the basis for many of the earlier GIS, but was designed for the purpose of mapping rather than geographical analysis. The process of digitizing spatial data from maps was mimicked directly in the digital domain, and thus initiated what is sometimes called the spaghetti data structure, by analogy with a plate of disconnected, but intertwined and intertangled pasta. In such structures geometry is represented as sequences of straight edges, essentially imitating the manual or stream digitizing process. Thus, a line-string is represented as a sequence of n connected edges with two end points and $n-1$ breakpoints. This data structure is sufficient for graphical purposes, such as redrawing the digitized map. However, it provides insufficient information for most non-geometrical and all complex geometrical operations.

Spaghetti structures have their greatest usage in situations involving a large number of simple geometrical edits through a graphics interface. They are especially well suited for data capture scenarios in which connectivity is of prime importance. The simplistic nature of the data leads to simple and robust system designs and, consequently, this structure is popular in GIS.

To extend the usefulness of spaghetti structures, some simple steps are usually taken to annotate the geometry. These include feature type association by symbology (line colour, style, level if provided), or data segregation into separate files (one for roads, one for parcels, etc.). This need to separate data into different files, layers, or overlays is very similar to the manner in which the map colour lithographic process requires the separation of symbols by the colour of ink required.

Another option for spaghetti data is the association of external database linkages via a 'user-data' segment in the graphical record, which acts as a foreign key to an external attribute database. This is preferable in an environment in which the data held or the analysis needed goes beyond the manual, graphics-oriented environment.

While spaghetti data structures are useful in recording connectivity between points, they show major deficiencies for dealing with neighbourhood and inclusion (Frank 1984). Given these problems, most GIS systems take either another approach or an additional, parallel, approach to geometrical storage and analysis.

Regular tessellations

Regular tessellations come close to the perception of spatial objects when data are captured with remote sensing or scanning devices. Such regular tessellations, also called rasters, are based on aggregates of picture cells, called pixels, representing regions. A pixel is characterized by: (1) the area it covers and (2) one or several values describing nonspatial properties of the entire pixel. The simplest pixel value is a Boolean-type representation in which a pixel can have two values, 'on' or 'off'. Pixels assigned with the value 'on' represent parts of an object, while 'off' pixels stand for the empty embedding space. The most common shapes of pixels are squares, but equilateral triangles and hexagons are also occasionally used (Diaz and Bell 1986). A raster image is a collection of pixels which together form a contiguous, non-overlapping image or partition.

A first step toward a data model for regular tessellations has been accomplished with a semi-formal description of the associated operations, the MAP algebra (Tomlin 1990; see also Tomlin 1991 in this volume). By applying more rigid, mathematical methods, such as algebraic specifications (Guttag,

Horowitz and Musser 1978; Zilles 1984), a geometrical data model for regular tessellations can be fully formalized. An algebraic specification defines the finite set of objects, called SORTs, to be treated and characterizes the behaviour of the model in terms of the effects of related operations (OPNS) to change and observe instances within this model. For example, the spatial relationship 'inside' (Egenhofer 1989a) can be formally defined for a region, a finite set of pixels, as follows (the specifications of the sort set of pixels and the operations 'interior' and 'boundary' are omitted for the sake of clarity):

```
SORT    region
OPNS    create: set of pixels -> region
        intersection: region x region ->
                region
        interior: region -> region
        boundary: region -> region
        inside: region x region -> boolean
VARS    r1, r2: region
EQNS    inside (r1, r2) IF intersection
        (r1,interior (r2)) = r1 and
        intersection (r1, boundary (r2)) = {}
```

Irregular tessellations

During the nineteenth and twentieth centuries, topologists developed a theoretical tool to study the invariance of properties under groups of transformations by decomposing the geometrical objects, called manifolds, into relatively simple geometrical shapes, called cells, which were joined along their common borders much like a biological organism is a collection of living cells. By decomposing the manifold into simple cells, topologists reduced complex geometrical problems into equivalent combinatorial problems, based upon intercellular relationships, attackable through algebraic methods (Alexandroff 1961; Munkres 1966; Spanier 1966; Artin and Brown 1969; Lefschetz 1975; Switzer 1975).

In geographical terms, such a decomposition results in an organization of space based upon irregularly shaped polygons for surface modelling or polyhedra for solids modelling. The storage of polygons is generally vector, although, topologically, it does not matter whether the polygons are composed of line-strings or of curvilinear function segments, such as spline curves, but much of their manipulation is raster-like. For example, given two topologically structured overlays or map coverages, a finer topological coverage can be produced that divides the cells of each of the input coverages into finer cells in the output coverage. The attributes of these subdivisions can be combined in any manner analogous to the combinations of values or attributes in raster overlays. Thus a topological data structure can support the same type of map algebra supported by classical grid-based GIS systems (Tomlin 1990).

EXAMPLES OF (LOW-LEVEL) SPATIAL DATA STRUCTURES

(Low-level) spatial data structures are the implementations of geometrical concepts. In contrast to spatial data models, spatial data structures focus on efficiency, for both storage and performance. Several spatial data structures may be the implementation of the same data model. For example, the raster data structure may be implemented as a matrix, run-length encoded, as a quadtree, as a linear quadtree, and so on. Each of these data structures follows the formally defined data model of a regular tessellation and is distinguished only by its storage requirements and its speed when processing raster operations.

Spatial data structures are supported by spatial index structures to provide fast access to spatial data stored in primary and secondary memory. In order to reduce the bottleneck in fast processing of large amounts of spatial data, they cluster spatial data according to their neighbourhood (Frank 1981) and organize the storage of spatial data such that the number of disk accesses is minimized. A large number of storage and index structures for spatial data have been proposed, such as the popular grid file (Nievergelt, Hinterberger and Sevcik 1984) and R-tree (Guttman 1984). For an overview over other structures and performance evaluations, see Samet (1989) and Kriegel *et al.* (1989), respectively.

Implementations of regular tessellations

Raster data structures implement the regular tessellation data model. Generally, their implementations are simple and versatile and some of them reduce storage requirements and increase performance considerably. Most popular are implementations of data structures for tessellations with square pixel shape.

Two-dimensional matrices

Rasters can be simply stored as two-dimensional matrices in which each pixel occupies a specific position (column and row) according to its spatial location. By convention, 'true' is used to represent filled elements, while 'false' describes empty elements. Variations of these binary representations distinguish multiple values for the representation of objects.

Matrices are convenient because they are: mathematically well defined and simple to comprehend; generally usable because for each pixel the same operation can be applied; simple to implement because two-dimensional arrays are immediately supported by most high-level programming languages; and easy to use because operators to loop over matrices are immediately available in programming languages. The disadvantages of using matrices for raster representation include:

- detail – the whole image is represented in the same way and no advantage is taken from the existence of larger areas covered by the same type of pixel;
- abstraction – in order to get less detailed representations, all the data have to be considered and no different levels of abstraction can be achieved without checking all details;
- storage capacity – potential waste of storage space;
- size of data sets – transmission of raster data is limited by the bandwidth of the transmission channel and matrix representation is an impediment when transferring collections of rasters at a high rate; and
- inefficiency – the whole image has to be kept in main memory which can be critical for very large images.

The storage of raster images in matrix form is space consuming and introduces considerable overheads. The storage space required depends on the extension of the area to be represented and the resolution, but is independent of the actual objects contained. Particularly, for regions with a low 'population' matrices are an inefficient data structure. Besides the argument for less storage space, there is also the need for increased processing speed of raster operations. Matrix operations are inherently dependent on the size of the matrix, that is, the area of the space modelled, and make no use of any information about the objects in this space. More efficient storage techniques are necessary, especially for sparse distributions of pixels. These processes are frequently referred to as data compression and their goal is to reduce the amount of space required to store a raster without losing information. Two structures have become popular, less in GIS than in image processing and robotics: run-length encoding and quadtrees.

Run-length encoding

Run-length encoding is a technique that makes use of the fact that objects frequently extend over areas larger than a single pixel. Instead of recording the values of each pixel, run length encoding groups the rows of a raster into blocks with an identical value. A binary image, for instance, may be horizontally segmented into black and white intervals whose lengths are recorded.

Quadtrees

The most common hierarchical organization of a raster is the quadtree. The quadtree is a maximal block representation in which the blocks have standard sizes and positions, that is, powers of two (Samet 1989; see also Gatrell 1991 in this volume). Its principle is divide and conquer, the successive subdivision of an image array into quadrants, each of which in turn can be subdivided into another four quadrants, and so on. This structure forms a tree with nodes representing heterogeneous areas and leaves for homogeneous areas with a single value. A quadtree in general reduces considerably the space needed to represent a raster image, because it makes use of aggregates of neighbouring pixels of the same kind.

Implementations of irregular tessellations

The data structures above share one common overriding attribute: they all divide space into a collection of essentially regular geometrical shapes. In topological data structures this is not necessarily the case. There are two basic types of topological decomposition techniques depending on the prototypical cell type. The algebraically and logically simpler one is based on cells homeomorphic to the convex hulls of $(n+1)$ independent points in a Euclidean n-space, called a simplex, giving a simplicial decomposition. An equivalent, but algebraically more complex approach, uses cells homeomorphic to the unit disc and unit sphere in the same Euclidean n-space, called simply a cell, giving a cellular decomposition.

Simplicial topology

The simplest of the basic tools of topology is the simplex (Alexandroff 1961; Frank and Kuhn 1986; Egenhofer, Frank and Jackson 1989). In the most general of terms, an n-dimensional simplex, or n-simplex, is the convex hull of $n+1$ points, in general position, embedded in a space of dimension n or greater. Thus, for the modelling of real three-dimensional space a 0-simplex is a single point, a 1-simplex is a line joining two distinct points, a 2-simplex is a filled triangle joining three non-collinear points, and a 3-simplex is a solid tetrahedron joining four non-coplanar points. The boundary of an n-simplex contains $n+1$ $(n-1)$-dimensional simplices. For example, a 2-simplex has three 1-simplex faces. An n-dimensional simplicial complex is a collection of n-simplices sharing common boundaries. Most geographers are familiar with two-dimensional simplicial complexes in the form of the triangulated irregular network (TIN) used in terrain modelling (Peucker and Chrisman 1975; Frank, Palmer and Robinson 1986; see also Weibel and Heller 1991 in this volume), and with one-dimensional simplicial complexes in the form of path–node graph models used in network analysis.

In terms of implementation, the simplicial complex approach has the advantage of consistency throughout dimensions, making software development much easier, especially if linear interpolation is used between the vertices in a simplex.

Cellular topology

A more complicated notion in topology which is logically equivalent to the simplicial complex is the cellular complex. A homeomorphism between two geometrical objects is an invertible function from one to the other such that both the function and its inverse are continuous. The two objects are said to be homeomorphic (from Greek *homoiómorphos*, meaning 'of similar form'). An n-disc is the set of points in Euclidean n-space with distance from the origin less than or equal to 1. An n-cell is any object homeomorphic to an n-disc. The surface of the $(n+1)$-disc, that is, all points at a distance exactly 1.0, is called the n-sphere. The boundary of an n-cell is that portion of the n-cell mapped on to the $(n-1)$-sphere by any homeomorphism. An n-dimensional cellular complex, or n-complex, is a collection of n-cells, such that portions of their boundary, homeomorphic to $(n-1)$-cells, have been identified with one another.

Comparison

The fundamental approach to using these topological structures within a GIS to describe space is to view the underlying coordinate space as a union of disjoint, fundamental topological entities. In a two-dimensional simplicial implementation, there would be points, open lines, and the interior of triangles. In a two-dimensional cellular implementation, there would be points, simple curves, and connected areas possible with holes – in some implementations, phantom lines (1-cells) are used to remove holes from the areas and make them 2-cells.

The critical decision is over which method of storage is most appropriate to an automated GIS environment. The simplicial approach has the advantage of simplicity and easy generalization of code to higher and higher dimensions. It is appropriate for models with a great deal of microstructure, such as models of surface and subsurface geology. The cellular approach, as used in vector GIS such as ARC/INFO and TIGRIS, and exchange structures, such as DLG, has the advantage of reduced data set sizes – fewer entities, more coordinates per entity.

CONCLUSIONS

Current commercial systems implement only a single data model; however, a modern GIS should integrate several spatial concepts and provide the corresponding geometrical data models. The properties of the different data models are quite different.

The extension to multiple concurrent data models requires not only their coexistence, but also the interconnections between data. Like humans switching between different spatial concepts, a GIS should select the representations which are most appropriate to solve a specific task. A framework for such a system has been proposed with the category model (Herring 1989a; Herring, Egenhofer and Frank 1990) as a unifying theory integrating multiple spatial paradigms.

REFERENCES

Alexandroff P (1961) *Elementary Concepts of Topology*. Dover Publications, New York
ANSI Study Group on Database Management Systems (1975) Interim report. *SIGMOD* 7
Artin E, Brown H (1969) *Introduction to Algebraic Topology*. Charles E Merrill Publishing Company, Columbus

Burrough P A (1986) *Principles of Geographical Information Systems for Land Resources Assessment*. Oxford University Press, Oxford

Codd E F (1970) A relational model for large shared data banks. *Communications of the ACM* **13** (6): 377–87
Codd E F (1982) Relational database: a practical foundation for productivity. *Communications of the ACM* **25** (2): 109–17
Croom F (1989) *Principles of Topology*. Saunders College Publishing, Philadelphia

Diaz B, Bell S (eds.) (1986) *Spatial Data Processing using Tesseral Methods*. Natural Environment Research Council, Reading UK
DCDSTF (Digital Cartographic Data Standards Task Force) (1988) The proposed standard for digital cartographic data. *The American Cartographer* **15** (1): 9–140
Dobkin D, Silver D (1988) Recipes for geometry and numerical analysis, part 1: an empirical study. *Proceedings of Fourth ACM Symposium on Computer Geometry*, pp. 93–105

Edelsbrunner H (1987) *Algorithms in Combinatorial Geometry*. Springer-Verlag, New York
Egenhofer M J (1989a) A formal definition of binary topological relationships. In: Litwin W, Schek H-J (eds.) *Third International Conference on Foundations of Data Organization and Algorithms (FODO), Paris* (Lecture Notes in Computer Science, Volume 367). Springer-Verlag, New York, pp. 457–72
Egenhofer M J (1989b) *Spatial query languages*. Unpublished PhD Thesis, University of Maine, Orono
Egenhofer M J, Frank A U (1990) Lobster: combining AI and database techniques for GIS. *Photogrammetric Engineering and Remote Sensing* **56** (6): 919–26
Egenhofer M J, Frank A U, Jackson J (1989) A topological data model for spatial databases. In: Buchmann A, Gunther O, Smith T, Wang Y (eds.) *Symposium on the Design and Implementation of Large Spatial Databases* (Lecture Notes in Computer Science, Volume 409). Springer-Verlag, New York, pp. 271–86

Frank A U (1981) Applications of DBMS to land information systems. In: Zaniolo C, Delobel C (eds.) *Proceedings of Seventh International Conference on Very Large Data Bases, Cannes, France*. Morgan Kaufmann Publishers, Los Altos, pp. 448–53
Frank A U (1984) Computer assisted cartography – graphics or geometry. *Journal of Surveying Engineering* **110** (2): 159–68
Frank A U (1988) Requirements for a database management system for a GIS. *Photogrammetric Engineering and Remote Sensing* **54** (11): 1557–64
Frank A U, Kuhn W (1986) Cell graph: a provable correct method for the storage of geometry. *Proceedings of the 2nd International Symposium on Spatial Data Handling, Seattle*. International Geographical Union, Columbus Ohio, pp. 411–36
Frank A U, Mark D M (1991) Language issues for GIS. In: Maguire D J, Goodchild M F, Rhind D W (eds.) *Geographical Information Systems: principles and applications*. Longman, London, pp. 147–63, Vol 1
Frank A U, Palmer B, Robinson V (1986) Formal methods for the accurate definition of some fundamental terms in physical geography. In: Marble D (ed.) *Proceedings of Second International Symposium on Spatial Data Handling, Seattle*. International Geographical Union, Ohio, pp. 583–99
Franklin W R (1984) Cartographic errors symptomatic of underlying algebra problems. In: *Proceedings of International Symposium on Spatial Data Handling, Zurich*. International Geographical Union, Zurich Irchel, pp. 190–208
Franklin Wm R (1991) Computer systems and low-level data structures for GIS. In: Maguire D J, Goodchild M F, Rhind D W (eds.) *Geographical Information Systems: principles and applications*. Longman, London, pp. 215–25, Vol 1
Freeman J (1975) The modelling of spatial relations. *Computer Graphics and Image Processing* **4**: 156–71

Gargantini I (1982) An effective way to represent quadtrees. *Communications of the ACM* **25** (12): 905–10
Gatrell A C (1991) Concepts of space and geographical data. In: Maguire D J, Goodchild M F, Rhind D W (eds.) *Geographical Information Systems: principles and applications*. Longman, London, pp. 119–34, Vol 1

Gill A (1976) *Applied Algebra for the Computer Sciences.* Prentice-Hall, Englewood Cliffs New Jersey

Greasley I (1988) Data structures to organize spatial subdivisions. *Proceedings of ACSM-ASPRS Annual Convention, St. Louis*, pp. 139–48

Guttag J, Horowitz E, Musser D (1978) Abstract data types and software validation. *Communications of the ACM* **21** (12): 1048–64

Guttman A (1984) R-trees: a dynamic index structure for spatial searching. *Proceedings of the Annual Meeting ACM SIGMOD, Boston*, pp. 47–57

Herring J R (1987) TIGRIS: topologically integrated geographic information systems. *Proceedings of AUTOCARTO8.* ASPRS, Falls Church, pp. 282–91

Herring J R (1989a) The category model of spatial paradigms. In: Mark D M, Frank A U, Egenhofer M J, Freundschuh S, McGranaghan M, White R M (eds.) *Languages of Spatial Relations: Report on the Specialist Meeting for NCGIA Research Initiative 2.* National Center for Geographic Information and Analysis, Santa Barbara, pp. 47–51

Herring J R (1989b) A fully integrated geographic information system. *Proceedings of AUTOCARTO9.* ASPRS, Falls Church, pp. 828–37

Herring J R, Egenhofer M J, Frank A U (1990) Using category theory to model GIS applications. *Proceedings of the 4th International Symposium on Spatial Data Handling, Zurich.* International Geographical Union, Columbus Ohio, pp. 820–9

Herskovits A (1986) *Language and Spatial Cognition: an interdisciplinary study of the prepositions in English.* Cambridge University Press, Cambridge

Hoffmann C (1989) The problems of accuracy and robustness in geometric computation. *IEEE Computer* **22** (3): 31–42

Kainz W (1989) Order, topology, and metric in GIS. *Proceedings of ASPRS-ACSM Annual Convention, Baltimore.* ASPRS/ACSM, Falls Church, pp. 154–60

Knuth D (1973) *The Art of Computer Programming.* Addison-Wesley Publishing Company, Reading Massachusetts

Kriegel H-P, Schiwietz M, Schneider R, Seeger B (1989) Performance comparison of point and spatial access methods. In: Buchmann A, Gunther O, Smith T, Wang Y (eds.) *Symposium on the Design and Implementation of Large Spatial Databases* (Lecture Notes in Computer Science, Volume 409). Springer-Verlag, New York, pp. 89–114

Lakoff G, Johnson M (1980) *Metaphors We Live By.* University of Chicago Press, Chicago

Lefschetz S (1975) *Applications of Algebraic Topology.* Springer-Verlag, New York

Mark D M, Frank A U, Egenhofer M J, Freundschuh S, McGranaghan M, White R M (1989) Languages of spatial relations: report on the specialist meeting for NCGIA Research Initiative 2. *Technical Report 89–2*, National Center for Geographic Information and Analysis, Santa Barbara

Munkres J (1966) *Elementary Differential Topology.* Princeton University Press, Princeton,

Nagy G, Wagle S (1979) Geographic data processing. *ACM Computing Surveys* **11** (2)

Nievergelt J, Hinterberger H, Sevcik K (1984) The grid file: an adaptable, symmetric multi-key file structure. *ACM Transactions on Database Systems* **9** (1): 38–71

Nievergelt J, Schorn P (1988) Line problems with supralinear growth (in German). *Informatik Spektrum* **11** (4)

Peucker T, Chrisman N (1975) Cartographic data structures. *The American Cartographer* **2** (2): 55–69

Peuquet D J (1984) A conceptual framework and comparison of spatial data models. *Cartographica* **21**: 66–113

Preparata F, Shamos M (1985) *Computational Geometry.* Springer-Verlag, New York

Pullar D, Egenhofer M J (1988) Towards formal definitions of topological relations among spatial objects. *Proceedings of the 3rd International Symposium on Spatial Data Handling.* International Geographical Union, Columbus Ohio, pp. 225–42

Saalfeld A (1985) Lattice structure in geography. *Proceedings of AUTOCARTO7.* ASPRS, Falls Church, pp. 482–97

Samet H (1984) The quadtree and related hierarchical data structures. *ACM Computing Surveys* **16** (2): 187–260

Samet H (1989) *The Design and Analysis of Spatial Data Structures.* Addison-Wesley Publishing Company, Reading Massachusetts

Spanier E (1966) *Algebraic Topology.* McGraw-Hill Book Company, New York,

Switzer R (1975) *Algebraic Topology-Homotopy and Homology.* Springer-Verlag, New York

Talmy L (1983) How language structures space. In: Pick H, Acredolo L (eds.) *Spatial Orientation: Theory, research, and application.* Plenum Press, New York

Tomlin C D (1990) *Geographic Information Systems and Cartographic Modeling.* Prentice-Hall, Englewood Cliffs

Tomlin C D (1991) Cartographic modelling. In: Maguire D J, Goodchild M F, Rhind D W (eds.) *Geographical Information Systems: principles and applications.* Longman, London, pp. 361–74, Vol 1

Weibel R, Heller M (1991) Digital terrain modelling. In: Maguire D J, Goodchild M F, Rhind D W (eds.) *Geographical Information Systems: principles and applications.* Longman, London, pp. 269–97, Vol 1

Zilles S (1984) Types, algebras, and modelling. In: Brodie M, Mylopoulos J, Schmidt J (eds.) *On Conceptual Modelling.* Springer-Verlag, New York, pp. 441–50

17

GIS DATA CAPTURE HARDWARE AND SOFTWARE

M J JACKSON AND P A WOODSFORD

The strong trend that exists towards hybrid raster/vector technology to support GIS applications is equally beneficial to the issues of data capture and the population of GIS databases. Techniques range from the fully automatic, through automated aids to interactive processes and manual data capture. Flowlines must be designed to incorporate the optimum mix of techniques to suit the constraints of the available source documents and the requirements of the target data formats. There is also a need to ensure that the necessary level of quality assurance is built into the data capture processes and that it can be simply and independently verified. Slowly the balance of attention will shift from the issue of populating GIS databases to the issue of ensuring that they are maintained and updated.

INTRODUCTION

Progress in the commercial application of GIS technology is in practice more likely to be limited in the foreseeable future by the rate at which GIS databases can be populated rather than by shortcomings in the applications software. It is now widely accepted in the literature, and has been apparent for some time to the practitioners, that the cost of data collection (or data capture) is by far the dominant component of overall GIS project costs. For example, Prof. G. Konecny in his Keynote Paper to the fourth European AM/FM Conference in 1988 (Konecny 1988) analysed a range of mature Land Information System projects and concluded that acquisition of the data for the database constituted the single largest expenditure element, between 38 and 84 per cent of total cost. The larger the project, the less the hardware and software costs mattered.

Certain GIS applications can be supported entirely by data in raster form, but for many GIS purposes data have to be available in the feature-coded, vector form. Increasingly there is a requirement for structured data, either in a link and node form or in some object-oriented form. In practice, with the growth of hybrid raster/vector GIS capabilities, both forms of data are required. This chapter describes hardware and software techniques for raster and vector data capture, and the associated issues of data structuring and attribute tagging.

The data capture process can be split into two different operations:

- Primary data collection, for example from aerial photography or from remote sensed imagery.

- Secondary data collection, for example from conventional cartographic sources.

Data capture from secondary sources typically raises many problems associated with the analytical use of GIS. Where map data are merely to be captured for use as a visual backdrop to other geographical data sets these problems may remain largely hidden. Once the data are integrated into the database for analysis many issues are raised, for example:

- What was the source of information for the map and what are the characteristics of this source?

- Were there multiple sources?
- What was the inherent precision of the source materials?
- What interpretation was applied in the mapping process?
- Is the categorization of data defined, for example what constitutes the difference between urban open space on the periphery of an urban area and non-urban land use?
- Is the categorization applicable to the current GIS application?

These and further aspects of secondary data (see Fisher 1991 in this volume) have given many scientists and end applications users an instinctive preference towards primary data capture where greater control and specificity can be applied. While tailored survey is possible in some instances, it is frequently ruled out on the grounds of cost and the elapsed time necessary to undertake the work. This has particularly been the case where comprehensive, large area coverage is required of topography and recourse is made to national generalized map series information. In practice both forms of data are essential to GIS and for practical reasons secondary data dominate. Both approaches are discussed below.

PRIMARY DATA CAPTURE

The introduction of remote sensing, particularly from the early 1970s with the Landsat series of land resource satellites, produced a climate of expectation that generalized access to primary data sources would be available together with automated techniques of land use and feature extraction. Unduly optimistic attempts at totally automated classification of imagery led to a period of scientifically interesting, but ultimately unsuccessful, research into ever more sophisticated attempts to use remotely sensed data in an isolated image processing environment. Papers tracking this development identify a sequence (see Davis and Simonett 1991 in this volume) whereby unsupervised classification of single images is followed by supervised per-pixel classifications of single images and later developments which add textural and contextual algorithms to both multi-temporal and multi-sensor imagery. Although higher resolution and multi-channel data are now available from a range of satellites and stereoscopic capabilities have been introduced, the lesson which, despite some early prophets, was finally learnt only in the last few years is that remotely sensed data are rarely sufficient in isolation.

The learning of this lesson can be seen in the evolution of developments in the associated data interpretation hardware and software. The early approaches to using digital remotely sensed data were preoccupied by the issues of handling and real-time processing of large raster data sets and the desirable full colour display capability needed for visualization. These systems employed dedicated and often specialized pipeline or parallel processing hardware. The software was focused on raster data manipulations and classification of the image data. The image processing environments which emerged were very different from the typically vector graphics-based cartographic and mapping systems. The hardware, the software and even the user communities were largely separate and distinct, and there was little of the cross-fertilization or synergy so necessary for effective GIS application.

The evolution of hardware and software for primary data collection has, however, been more rapid in the late 1980s. Direct surveying techniques employing in-the-field digital recording, GPS technology for precision positioning and vehicle location tracking are becoming routine tools (see Goodchild 1991 in this volume). The use of remotely sensed data is gradually offering the theoretical benefits identified in the early 1970s. These benefits are only being achieved, however, by introducing a radical change of thinking in the user community.

While remote sensing was isolated by its specialized computing environment, it was almost inevitable that the community remained inward looking seeking progression through ever improving spatial, temporal and radiometric resolution, as well as more and more sophisticated and computationally intensive algorithms. The lateral move towards seeing remotely sensed data as just one set of data among many, and image-processing techniques as but one of a family of techniques, has instead opened up many new possibilities. The new environment required, however, is one where all forms of data can be handled and used together. Existing map or GIS database information will be supplemented by field survey and intelligence (knowledge) and the combined information will help to guide the classification of newly arrived remotely sensed data, the outcome of which will in turn update the GIS database. The resulting synergy is likely to bring the use of remotely sensed techniques into mainstream GIS applications development and in turn provide the necessary justification, to date largely lacking, for continued investment in earth resources satellites.

The new hardware and software resulting from this trend reflect the need for an open architecture and powerful integrated data processing environment with good visualization. This is met in hardware terms by the current and emerging generation of desktop workstations. These offer an easily networkable environment for local or wide area processing yet provide locally to a single user a dedicated fast processor (e.g. more than 20 MIPS), large memory (e.g. more than 24 Mb) and substantial disk storage capacity (e.g. over 1 Gb) in a desktop, office environment machine and at a cost of less than $60 000 (see Goodchild 1991 in this volume).

The corresponding evolution of software has required a much greater consideration to be given to the overall design of GIS. This has been necessary to ensure access to multiple data structures, to allow greater attention to be given to quality assurance and error train analysis, and to provide a user interface that gives a consistent view of all data and facilities available rather than one specific to a single type of data. Much has been achieved in the interim by developing more efficient links between remote sensing packages and mapping systems, as in the ARC/INFO-ERDAS 'live-link'. This approach is now being replaced, however, by new 'integrated GIS' packages which incorporate the fundamental redesign necessary (Fig. 17.1).

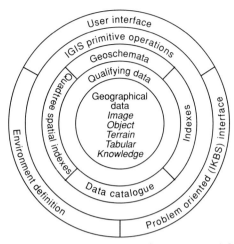

Fig. 17.1 Conceptual design of an Integrated GIS.

considerable, with near term targets of substantial or complete coverage at certain scales. For example the Annual Report of the UK Ordnance Survey (1990) indicates progress as shown in Table 17.1 for the three scales of basic national mapping cover (for a review of digital programs in the Ordnance Survey see Sowton 1991 in this volume).

Table 17.1 Status of the three scales of basic mapping for the United Kingdom (1990)

Scale	Total No. of Maps in Series	Digital Maps Available
1 : 1250	57 395	49 736
1 : 2500	163 357	31 326
1 : 10 000	1709*	43

*Number of sheets not covered at larger scales.

This programme has roots going back to the early 1970s. At the present time the annual running roots of digitizing is approximately 20 000 sheets.

The range of cartographic source materials has already been discussed in Chapter 13 (Fisher 1991). It is worth, however, summarizing the distinctive characteristics of maps from the data capture standpoint, and the factors that distinguish them from other mass conversion sources such as engineering drawings. Factors which affect the capture techniques that can be used include the following:

SECONDARY DATA CAPTURE

Despite the perceived benefits of primary data, for the immediate future the largest source for GIS data will continue to be existing maps. In some countries, the scale of map digitizing programmes is

• Maps are accurate and to scale. The scanner or

digitizer, and the processing algorithms, must deliver a high and consistent planimetric accuracy.

- Maps are high resolution and contain fine detail. Line weights of 0.004 in (0.1 mm) are commonplace.

- Maps contain a wide variety of symbolization and linestyle, and different map series differ widely in these respects.

- Maps, in particular small-scale maps, are multi-coloured documents.

- Map sheets represent parts of a large continuum and edge matching is generally required.

- Maps are multi-purpose documents and, in consequence, map data formats and quality standards have to support a range of users and applications. The possibilities for redesign of maps in order to improve data capture have been discussed at length by Shiryaev (1987) but generally the needs of data capture have had little impact on map design.

- Maps, like all other documents come in variable qualities. The paper map is subject to substantial distortion when folded, or when affected by varying humidity.

Where vector data are required for GIS applications, a range of data formats can be identified, as follows:

- *Vector data in layers*. Lineal information is partitioned into a small number of 'layers'. The layers may be physically distinguishable (by line weight, linestyle, or colour, or by text characteristics), or the distinction may be only logical.

- *Vector data in feature coded form*. Graphical information is partitioned into 'features' according to some schema. Each feature has a distinguishing code, and optionally some associated attribute information or a link to a relational database. In general the feature coding schema is not sufficiently well defined for algorithmic implementation.

- *Structured data*. There is increasing demand for data in link and node form or in an object-oriented form. A major concern in these cases is the completeness and integrity of the structure.

In addition to the definition of the format and structure of the digital data required, the following factors have to be defined to arrive at an adequate specification of the data capture task:

- *Accuracy*. A traditional specification is to require that the digital data represent the source to within one line width (or a half line width). It is important that any automated conversion process provides an inbuilt accuracy check to the required tolerance. If data are being used, *inter alia*, to support cartographic production, contention may arise over the cartographic acceptability of data which nevertheless meet the formal accuracy specification.

- *Representation*. Data volumes should be minimized, for example a rectangle should be represented by four points. Different classes of features require different representations.

- *Abstraction*. For some classes of features the task is not to reproduce the geometry on the map, but an abstraction, for example cased roads by centre lines, broken lines by coordinate strings with appropriate codes, point symbols by coordinate pairs with symbol code text by ASCII codes.

- *Selection/completeness*. In many cases, not all the information recorded on the source map is required in the GIS database. None of the required data may be omitted or repeated.

The specification is not complete until the external Quality Assurance procedure is also defined. The detection and rectification of errors in digital map data are both expensive affairs. Any automated process should give the confidence to permit validation on a limited sample basis. It will only meet this criterion if Quality Assurance checks are built in. Finally, top of the agenda for any conversion process is the bottom line cost, including all phases. This must be containable and acceptable, and the results produced must be timely and fit for the purpose.

After this somewhat lengthy, but very necessary treatment of the definition of the data capture task, the hardware and software technologies that are available will now be examined. Since this is a very dynamic field and the subject of much current research, this review will soon become dated; nevertheless some key trends are identifiable.

HARDWARE

Manual digitizers

The most commonly used equipment for graphical data capture is the manual digitizing table or tablet. The key elements of the technology are the digitizing surface and the puck or cursor used by the operator to record coordinates. The whole may be regarded conceptually as a 'reverse drawing board'. The surface may be translucent, providing a backlit capability which is very useful for film, as opposed to paper, source documents. In the most widely used technologies, the surface contains a precise grid of current-carrying fine wires. The precision of this grid determines the basic accuracy of the table. Accuracy specifications are typically expressed as root-mean-square (RMS) deviations from a true and square grid over the active area of the table. The cursor used by the operator to record coordinate measurements consists of a target (usually cross-hairs), possibly viewed under magnification, embedded in a conveniently held puck. This incorporates buttons used to trigger coordinate measurement and to communicate with the controlling software. Sometimes 'stream digitizing' is used to control the frequency of coordinate measurement, on a time or distance basis. Typically the electrical interface to the receiving computer system is a serial line and the data format is coordinate strings in ASCII format.

Operator fatigue is the major issue in manual digitizing, and table ergonomics are of crucial importance. A good modern design such as the Altek table illustrated in Plate 17.1 incorporates fully adjustable height and tilt, variable backlighting and a lightweight cursor with four control buttons and 16 feature coding buttons. Accuracies typically range from 0.003 inch (0.075 mm) to 0.010 inch (0.25 mm). Digitizing tablets are similar in concept to digitizing tables, offering reduced accuracy at lower cost.

Scanners

A scanner is a piece of hardware for converting an analogue source document into digital raster form. The most commonly encountered scanner in everyday life is the FAX machine, and the requirements of this marketplace, *inter alia*, are steadily reducing the costs of scanner technologies to the benefit of niche market applications such as GIS.

The key characteristics of a scanner reflect the documents it can handle (size, accuracy and speed) and the nature of the data it produces (resolution, greyscale and colour). All scanning involves systematic sampling of the source document, by either transmitted or reflected light. The fundamental technology used in many scanners is the charge-coupled device (CCD) array. CCD arrays are available as one- or two-dimensional regular rectangular structures of light-sensitive elements. Two-dimensional arrays are not at present economically available at resolutions useful for map source documents. A single linear CCD array typically has a resolution of 5000 elements. The key decision in utilizing this in a scanner design is whether to move the document or the scanning element. A low cost arrangement involves scanning a single linear CCD array over a magnified image of the source document – the so-called 'digital camera'. These are extremely rapid in operation (a whole image in a matter of seconds) but are currently restricted in resolution to about 5000 by 6000 elements.

For most GIS applications, a larger information content (resolution) is required than can be provided by digital cameras and scanners based on multiple linear CCD arrays are necessary. A commonly used arrangement is the 'continuous feed' scanner illustrated in Plate 17.2, in which the document is passed rapidly by a set of, say, five or ten concatenated linear arrays, or CCD cameras. The key elements are the pinch roller document handler (accuracy in the direction of document motion is determined entirely by this component) and the alignment optics (see Plate 17.3). The hardware design must manage the overlap between the individual CCD cameras in a mechanically stable manner, in addition to compensating for differences in sensitivity between them. Continuous feed scanners provide high throughput rates [an A0 sheet at a resolution of 500 dots per inch (dpi.) or 20 dots per millimetre in a few minutes] at reasonable cost, with accuracies of the order of 0.02 inches (0.5 mm). Input widths up to 60 inches (150 cm) are available and document length is theoretically unlimited. Documents can be paper, film, vellums, sepias, linen or cardboard.

Several forms of flatbed scanners are available, including 'pushbroom' designs where the linear array is systematically translated over the document bed. This approach can be implemented at very low incremental cost by employing a scanning head as an attachment to be a conventional pen plotter, as described by Drummond and Bosma (1989) in their review of low-cost scanners. The dominant technology to obtain very high precision scanning, as for example to meet the colour separation requirement, is the drum scanner (Plate 17.4). The document is mounted on the exterior (sometimes the interior) of a precision drum which rotates at high speed, while the sensor is very precisely translated parallel to the axis of the drum by a lead screw arrangement. Most drum scanners, particularly for colour work, use single sensors (typically based on photomultiplier tube technology) to avoid the problems of matching different sensors. Such an arrangement can scan and colour process a map sheet in times of the order of 20 minutes.

The performance outlined above can be expected to improve steadily with CCD technology, although it will be some time before two-dimensional CCD arrays (as used in portable video cameras) are available at resolutions of relevance to GIS applications.

Raster images may be required for GIS applications in binary, greyscale or colour formats [specified as red, green and blue components (RGB) or as indexed colours]. For binary data, some form of thresholding is essential (typically each element of the CCD array returns an 8-bit greyscale level, determined by the amount of light falling on it). The threshold for binary data may be set by operator control, experimentally or more conveniently in conjunction with a preview display of the data and/or of a histogram of the distribution of levels (Plate 17.5). Some scanners incorporate dynamic thresholding, using a local averaging technique to take out effects of background variation. Sophisticated colour separation systems allow the operator to set up indexed colours by reference to areas of colour on the scanned image.

All scanners based on CCD technology have an inherent sampling resolution. Lower resolution data are available by averaging (usually provided by the scanner hardware) and higher resolution data are sometimes provided by interpolation. Resolution in terms of the source document (e.g. dots per inch dpi.) is determined by the magnification of the optical system. Accuracy is determined by a combination of the inherent accuracy of the CCD array, together with the amount of distortion in the optical system and in the translation stage. Reproducibility is such that accuracy can be enhanced by calibration. Registration of source documents is in practice achieved by registration marks on the documents.

The dominant factor in scanner and system performance is data volume. A 20 inch by 20 inch (50 cm by 50 cm) map sheet scanned at 500 d.p.i. or 20 dots per mm (for display purposes, say) results in 100 million pixels. For binary data, uncompacted, this amounts to 12.5 Mb; for greyscale, 100 Mb and for colour 400 Mb. At 1000 d.p.i., as may be required for automatic vectorization, volumes are increased by a factor of four. In practice, a high performance scanner needs a PC or workstation server, both to deal with the bandwidths of data transfer involved while scanning, and to implement and/or manage data compaction (see below).

In the past a variety of ingenious devices have been developed for analogue scanning and for optical line following. However, the ubiquity of raster technology and the availability of workstations and personal computers with appropriate power and storage capacity has concentrated developments in data capture on digital techniques.

Workstations and data compaction

The pace of advances in workstation technology is such that the availability of computing power is rapidly ceasing to be a limiting factor in GIS data capture applications, particularly in distributed systems using local area network (LAN) or cluster technology. Standard platforms with open system architectures and windowing environments need little or no augmentation. Special purpose parallel hardware may have some place, but it is at least arguable that the same results will be achieved by tomorrow's conventional processors. Despite the advances in optical storage technology, the widespread use of raster data is likely to pose a continuing requirement for data compaction implemented in hardware or by software. Since this requirement is particularly associated with GIS applications, it is appropriate to outline some of the principles involved.

The simplest forms of raster data compaction use run length encoding (RLE), based on the observation that it takes fewer bits to say '123 blank pixels' – namely 7 bits for 123 and 1 control bit – than 123 bits each zero (see discussion in Egenhofer and Herring 1991 in this volume and Blakemore 1991 in this volume). PackBits (Aldus Corporation 1988) is a byte-oriented run length scheme modified to handle literal data for areas that do not compress well.

Where space efficiency is paramount, the CCITT-3 and -4 standards established by the International Telecommunications Union (ITU) for facsimile transmission have become *de facto* standards (CCITT 1985). Both 1-D (modified Huffman RLE) and 2-D forms exist. The main characteristic of the 2-D formats is that each scan line is described in terms of changes from the previous scan line. Hardware for compression and decompression of large raster data sets is not yet readily available, but tiling techniques can be used to overcome this. LZW (Lempel-Zif and Welch) is an encoding scheme (Welch 1984) which can handle all kinds of data from binary to full RGB colour (colour defined by its red, green and blue components) at good compression factors, while being fully reversible. Originally designed to be implemented in hardware, it has proved challenging to implement efficiently (Welch 1984).

All the above data compaction schemes are encompassed in TIFF – the Tag Image File Format devised by Aldus/Microsoft for transfer of image data between desktop publishing systems (Aldus Corporation 1988). This is now seeing increased use for map image data and is becoming a *de facto* standard for scanner output formats. Extensions are also under way to encompass tiled raster images. TIFF defines a standard housekeeping header around the various encodings. It is an example of a standard arising in the wider information technology context, but having relevance to geographical information systems.

SOFTWARE

Manual data capture

The reader will have already observed incursions across the hardware/software divide, if such can be said to exist. Software for manual data capture using digitizing tables is sufficiently well established not to need detailed description and in any case it is reviewed in Rhind (1974), Marble, Lauzon and McGranaghan (1984) and Yeung and Lo (1985). Efficiency is determined at least as much by operator procedures and flowline design as by software functionality. A macro command language is highly desirable to enable flowlines to be efficiently tailored and most systems now incorporate on-line digitizing with immediate graphical feedback, including colour display of feature coding. Some protagonists still argue, however, that off-line digitizer operation is more efficient, because of the constant operator distraction caused by viewing the graphics display. Despite the use of pop-up or pull-down menus, complex feature coding schemata are an unavoidable burden on the operator. Some users have reported success in using voice input to alleviate the feature coding burden, but this technique is by no means well established. Further improvements in the cost of voice recognition technology remain to be exploited.

Overlay digitizing

The widespread availability of hybrid vector/raster GIS software, or at least, of vector editing/drafting software supporting raster image data as backdrop, has led to new methods of manual data capture. Such systems were originally developed as 'interim solutions' which allowed many GIS applications, for which map data are required only as a passive background frame of reference, to proceed in the absence of vector map data. They depend on establishing a means of registration between the vector data and the raster image, and of providing fast zoom and pan capabilities. These capabilities also provide the means of 'heads-up' or screen digitizing from raster images of map sources. Vector data, created either by manual point input using a screen cursor or by use of higher level drafting functions, is immediately displayed, superimposed on the raster source image (Plate 17.6). Accuracy is still dependent on manual positioning, augmented, albeit clumsily, by the ability to work at high magnification. The content of the available display window is also a significant limitation. Nevertheless, many protagonists have reported significant gains over the use of digitizing tables, particularly for large-scale maps and plans. As raster storage of source documents becomes more the norm, the small footprint and other advantages of this technique make it increasingly attractive. It is worthy of note that if greyscale backgrounds are supported the technique can be applied to the creation of vector data from remote sensing images or scanned aerial photographs. Also, if interactive thresholding of the greyscale background is available, useful data can be captured from poor quality source documents. A recent advance has been the use of 'raster-snapping' to improve accuracy.

Interactive automatic systems

An important alternative to fully automatic raster-to-vector conversion techniques is exemplified by the Laser-Scan VTRAK system (Waters 1989) and the Hitachi CAD-Core Tracer system (Sakashita and Tanaka 1989). These systems involve the extraction of vector data from the raster source on a feature-by-feature basis, with real-time display of the results to operators, who control the overall sequence of data capture, provide the interpretation necessary for feature coding prior to feature capture, and intervene in the case of ambiguity or error. This approach also provides for selective data capture in the frequently occurring case where only some of the features present in the source documents are required in the GIS database.

Coding of features prior to capture provides an invaluable aid to automatic feature extraction in that the extraction algorithm used can be matched to the class of feature. In an ideal system, feature recognition would be automatic, but in practice when working with cartographic sources this goal is rarely achievable. Since coding has to be done at some stage it is a system advantage to do it early, so that the appropriate automatic feature extraction algorithms can be invoked, and the appropriate data representations created. Thus, using the VTRAK system as an example, for contours and other curvilinear features, a centre-line extraction algorithm and a data point reduction algorithm (based on the Douglas–Peucker algorithm described below) which preserves shape to within prescribed tolerances is appropriate (Plate 17.7). Rectilinear features on the other hand require vertex extraction algorithms and, in the case of buildings, optionally a squaring algorithm (Plate 17.8). Broken lines, the edges of solid areas and the centre lines of cased roads can all be followed and the appropriate vector representation produced. The data produced can be either vector spaghetti or, if junction recognition is invoked, a link-and-node structure. Thus in Plate 17.9 a network of road centre lines is being created from cased roads. Nodes and intermediate data points are differentiated in the data (by colour on the screen). In this mode, nodes and links are measured once only, are given unique values and a topological structure is created for further processing. Symbol measurement is also provided, for example for buildings and cadastral symbols.

The key elements of such systems are: the ability to zoom and pan rapidly across the combined raster source and vector overlay; appropriate local feature extraction algorithms using all the available raster information; and a 'paintout' facility as a visible and logical progress check. As features are captured, their representation in the raster source is changed, so that they are displayed to the operator in a different colour (as 'done'), and so that they are no longer 'visible' to the feature extraction algorithms. This avoids duplication, and also simplifies the data capture task as the whole process is subtractive. In cases where the source document is of variable quality, the source raster image can be held as greyscale. This increases the size of working files (e.g. by a factor of four). However, the ability to vary the threshold according to the context is very powerful and enables clean vector data to be produced from unpromising material (Plate 17.10).

In practice, if separations are available or if the source contains features of only one class, operator interaction is not necessary and features can be extracted as a batch process in an 'autopass' mode. This works well for contour or drainage separations and for polygon networks, particularly as there is provision for indicating 'no-go' areas. The interactive automatic system software can be installed on a standard workstation platform, together with editing and post-processing software. A typical flowline is a combination of autopass, interactive feature extraction and overlay editing. At all stages there is a continuous visual assessment of the resulting vector data against the raster source, building in data quality checks as the data are created.

An interesting alternative technique for the creation of structured and attributed vector data is exemplified by the SysScan GEOREC system (Egger 1990). In this, the startpoint is the set of vectors created by an automatic raster-to-vector conversion process. Features are recognized and extracted from this set of vectors by the application of a 'production line' which can utilize combinations of more than 150 algorithms held in a 'method bank'. Algorithms include vector geometry enhancements, methods which handle neighbourhood relationships, a statistical recognition package for text and methods for replacing vectorized geometry with symbol references. Geometrical elements are classed as nodes, symbols, lines, areas and texts. Topological information between these elements is maintained via a set of suitable forward and backward pointers, and groups of geometrical elements which form a logical entity can be combined in sets. Recognition and structuring proceeds by sequences of operations under the generic descriptions of 'select', 'grow' and 'apply'. A 'production line' is usually set up interactively, but is controlled by a programming language (GPL), so that once the control structures have been created for the classes of features in a given map series, the whole process of feature extraction can be invoked automatically, with only exceptions needing subsequent manual editing. Knowledge and experience of manual digitizing flowlines are invaluable in the development of GPL programs. Good quality, cost effective results are reported in some instances from good quality, well-behaved source maps.

Data capture and processing algorithms

The resolution of the source raster image must be adequate for the geometry to be accurately extracted by the vectorization algorithms. Typically, there needs to be at least 2–3 pixels in the finest lines in order to establish a cartographically acceptable vector representation. On the other hand it is important that the vector representation contains an optimal number of points, approximately the same as would result from an experienced manual digitizer. Superfluous points will clutter up GIS databases for a long time! Data point reduction is therefore an important requirement, and the Douglas–Peucker algorithm (Douglas and Peucker 1973), originally devised in the context of cartographic generalization, is widely used for this purpose. The principle is illustrated in Fig. 17.2.

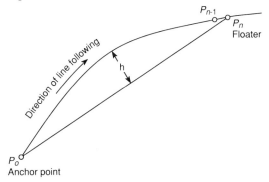

Fig. 17.2 Use of the Douglas–Peucker algorithm to reduce the number of data points required to represent curvilinear features.

The following description is adapted for thinning data points from a dense set representing a line, as they emerge from a line-following algorithm applied to a raster source. The first point on the line is used as an 'anchor' point and the last point of the line segment currently under consideration as a 'floater'. The point with the greatest perpendicular distance from the line joining the anchor to the floater is examined. If this distance is less than the prescribed tolerance, the next point along the line as extracted from the raster image becomes the floater and the process is repeated. If the tolerance is exceeded, the point preceding the floater is passed through to the vector representation and becomes the new anchor point, and the whole process recommences. Intermediate points from the raster image are discarded. If the tolerance is chosen to be half the line width, say, an acceptable representation of the shape is obtained with an optimal number of data points.

Vertex extraction algorithms hinge on the

recognition of changes of direction, and on the fitting of straight line segments to the data points on either side of the putative vertex. Special cases arise when vertices are separated by distance comparable to the line thickness. Squaring algorithms abound, differing in the sophistication of the control parameters they provide.

Software for dealing with source document distortion and with changes of geographical projection (Snyder 1987; see also Maling 1991 in this volume) is well established. It is good practice to ensure before any correction is applied that the vector data are totally congruent with the raster source, except where discrepancies are deliberate. Such checking can be performed on screen, by vector-on-raster overlay, or by the traditional checkplot. Such quality assurance procedures are treated in more detail in the next section. Distortion is typically removed by least-squares fitting to an appropriate number of control points, over and above the corner points required to register the coordinate system. In some instances it may be appropriate to use any orthophoto sources to improve or correct the control on the cartographic sources. Coordinate transformations for projection changes can then be applied before output in the required GIS data format.

The problems of creating a seamless continuous map from a set of not necessarily homogeneous map sheets is peculiar to GIS applications. Quasi-automatic edge-matching software is available, but in practice the prevalence of anomalies can dictate a considerable human input to the process if fully edge-matched data are a requirement. Techniques for organizing sheet-based source data to present effectively continuous or 'seamless' cover are now well established. The practical problems arise from source data overlap or inconsistency (see Fisher 1991 in this volume).

The automatic creation of link-and-node structured data greatly facilitates the creation of correct polygon or parcel data, although software is also available to create such data from unstructured 'spaghetti'. Again the issue is considerably complicated by issues of matching across sheet boundaries.

Quality assurance

The key to the reduction of the burden of data capture costs on a project is data sharing. The most important aspect of data sharing is validation that the data are of a quality acceptable to the needs of a wide community of users. Validation needs to be based on objective tests that can be externally applied however the digital data are captured. Considerable effort by interested parties in the United Kingdom led to the establishment of agreed criteria between the Ordnance Survey and the National Joint Utilities Group (NJUG 1988). Although these criteria are drawn up in terms of large scale (1 : 1250 and 1 : 2500) plans, the principles are of general applicability. Eight tests are applied:

1. Data format – readability
2. Number of data points – no more than 25 per cent excess
3. Coding accuracy – colour code, visual check
4. Positional accuracy – remeasure random samples; mean and standard deviation criteria
5. Squareness of buildings – tested on a sample basis
6. Line junction fitting – by visual inspection on a workstation screen
7. Text – by random sampling in each category
8. Completeness – using an overlaid check plot

Given a specification and an appropriate validation procedure, how are valid data to be captured in a cost-effective and timely manner? Whether manual or automatic techniques are used, checks and feedback mechanisms must be built in throughout the process, as it is not sufficient to check quality only at the end. Automatic techniques, properly applied and controlled, can produce consistent and reliable data quality much more rapidly and cheaply than manual techniques, but flowlines must be designed so that automatic processes fail safe rather than producing copious errors that are then expensive to correct. Whenever possible, structure inherent in the data (e.g. a link and node structure) should be used to ensure that data are correct.

REFERENCES

Aldus Corporation (1988) *TIFF – Tag Image File Format Specification Revision 5.0 (Final)*

Blakemore M J (1991) Managing an operational GIS: the UK National On-line Manpower Information System (NOMIS). In: Maguire D J, Goodchild M F, Rhind D W (eds.) *Geographical Information Systems: principles and applications*. Longman, London, pp. 503–13, Vol 1

CCITT, The International Telegraph and Telephone Consultative Committee of the International Telecommunications Union (1985) *CCITT-3 and CCITT-4 – Terminal Equipment and Protocols for Telematic Services. Series T Recommendations Geneva.* CCITT Volume VII, Fascicle VII.3

Davis F W, Simonett D S (1991) GIS and Remote sensing. In: Maguire D J, Goodchild M F, Rhind D W (eds.) *Geographical Information Systems: principles and applications*. Longman, London, pp. 191–213, Vol 1

Douglas D H, Peucker T K (1973) Algorithms for the reduction of the number of points required to represent a digitized line or its caricature. *The Canadian Cartographer* **10**: 112–22

Drummond J, Bosma M (1989) A review of low-cost scanners. *International Journal of Geographical Information Systems* **3** (1): 83–95

Egenhofer M J, Herring J R (1991) High-level spatial data structures for GIS. In: Maguire D J, Goodchild M F, Rhind D W (eds.) *Geographical Information Systems: principles and applications*. Longman, London, pp. 227–37, Vol 1

Egger G (1990) Cost-effective automated data conversion using SysScan's (A)DC and GEOREC. *Proceedings of FIG 90*

Fisher P F (1991) Spatial data sources and data problems. In: Maguire D J, Goodchild M F, Rhind D W (eds.) *Geographical Information Systems: principles and applications*. Longman, London, pp. 175–89, Vol 1

Goodchild M F (1991) The technological setting of GIS. In: Maguire D J, Goodchild M F, Rhind D W (eds.) *Geographical Information Systems: principles and applications*. Longman, London, pp. 45–54, Vol 1

Konecny G (1988) Keynote address: current status of geographic and land information systems. *Proceedings of AM/FM European Conference IV, Montreux*

Maling D H (1991) Coordinate systems and map projections for GIS. In: Maguire D J, Goodchild M F, Rhind D W (eds.) *Geographical Information Systems: principles and applications*. Longman, London, pp. 135–46, Vol 1

Marble D F, Lauzon J P, McGranaghan M (1984) Development of a conceptual model of the manual digitising process. *Proceedings of the 1st International symposium on Spatial Data Handling*. Universität Zurich-Irchel, Zurich, pp. 146–71

National Joint Utilities Group (1988) *Quality Control Procedures for Large Scale Ordnance Survey Maps Digitised to OS 1988*

Ordnance Survey (1990) *Annual Report*, HMSO, London

Rhind D W (1974) An introduction to the digitising and editing of mapped data. In: Dale P F (ed.) *Automation in Cartography. British Cartographic Society Special Publication* **1**: 50–68

Sakashita S, Tanaka Y (1989) Computer-aided drawing conversion (an interactive approach to digitize maps). *Proceedings of GIS/LIS '89, Orlando*. Vol. 2. ASPRS/ACSM, Bethesda Maryland, pp. 578–90

Shiryaev E E (1987) *Computers and the Representation of Geographical Data*. Wiley, New York

Snyder J P (1987) Map projections – a working manual. *US Geological Survey Professional Paper 1395*. Government Printing Office, Washington

Sowton M (1991) Development of GIS-related activities at the Ordnance Survey. In: Maguire D J, Goodchild M F, Rhind D W (eds.) *Geographical Information Systems: principles and applications*. Longman, London, pp. 23–38, Vol 2

Waters R S (1989) Data capture for the Nineties: VTRAK. *Proceedings of AUTOCARTO9*. ACSM/ASPRS, Bethesda, Maryland, pp. 377–83

Welch T A (1984) A technique for high performance data compression. *IEEE Computer* **17** (6)

Yeung A K W, Lo C P (1985) Cartographic digitizing for geographical application: some hardware and software considerations. *Asian Geographer* **4**: 9–22

DATABASE MANAGEMENT SYSTEMS

R G HEALEY

Database Management Systems (DBMS) are an integrated and crucial component of most successful GIS. DBMS are used to store, manipulate and retrieve data from a database. A key element in creating a spatial database is database design using a variety of data modelling techniques. Although the range of DBMS structures used in GIS includes inverted list, hierarchical, network and relational designs, it is the latter which has come to dominate the field. Two main approaches have been used in the design of GIS software systems: the hybrid and integrated models. Both have advantages and disadvantages for specific applications. Looking to the future, the main issues facing the spatial database world are the likely impact of the ideas of the object-oriented community and the need to develop distributed systems capable of handling temporal data in an efficient manner.

INTRODUCTION

Among the different threads that can be observed in the development of GIS methodology, one major one has been the progressive realization of the importance of database management systems (DBMS), initially for handling map attribute data, but increasingly for handling digital cartographic data also. While many of the operations required for data manipulation in GIS are now seen to be specific instances of more general classes of database problem, standard database tools have also been shown to have a number of limitations when applied to GIS processing.

This chapter examines the principles of database management, as they apply to GIS, and the strengths and weaknesses of alternative approaches to the use of database tools. The first section examines the fundamental characteristics of DBMS. This is followed by sections on data modelling, database design, database structures and alternative methods of utilizing a DBMS within GIS. The final section examines future developments and the ways in which they may contribute to the solution of outstanding technical and methodological problems in database management for GIS.

FUNDAMENTAL CHARACTERISTICS OF DBMS

To clarify definitions at the outset, the term 'database management system (DBMS)' will be used to refer to a software package for the storage, manipulation and retrieval of data from a database. A database is a collection of one or more data files or tables stored in a structured manner, such that interrelationships which exist between different items or sets of data can be utilized by the DBMS software for manipulation and retrieval purposes. The database will, in general, serve the data requirements of a variety of users rather than a single individual. If the restriction is enforced that the DBMS software provides the only means of access to the database, there are a number of important implications (Martin 1976):

- The method of data storage can be considered independently of the programs that access the database.

- A controlled and standardized approach to data input and update can be enforced, with appropriate validation checks to ensure data integrity and consistency between data files.

- Security restrictions on access to specific data subsets can be applied.

- A consistent approach can be adopted for managing simultaneous multi-user read and update operations on specific files or tables.

It is these factors, coupled with the elimination of unnecessary redundancy in data storage because multiple users can share data, that gives the combination of DBMS software and database its greatly enhanced efficiency and productivity in data management, as compared to individuals working with their own programs and file structures.

DBMS software components

The central component of a DBMS is the kernel software, usually written in C or FORTRAN, which controls the processing of queries, access paths to data, storage management, indexing and multi-user read/update operations. Linked to the kernel are a variety of interfaces to the user. These include query language interfaces, bulk data loaders, screen forms management systems, menu handlers, report writers and programming language interfaces. Query language interfaces allow the user to issue *ad hoc* queries against the database which result in data from one or several linked tables or files being retrieved. These queries are expressed in high level languages, which formerly were often system specific (Collins 1982; Martin 1983). Now there is convergence in the commercial marketplace on SQL, the ANSI standard for DBMS query languages. If the query language contains additional procedural functionality, which SQL itself does not, it can be called a 'fourth generation language'. Since these languages operate with query language commands, which may individually cause large amounts of program code in the database kernel to be executed, they are at once very powerful and potentially CPU intensive.

Programming language interfaces perform a different function. They enable users to embed query language statements within programs written in standard general purpose 'third generation' languages such as FORTRAN or C. Data can be retrieved from the database directly into variables or data structures accessible to the program, where they can be further processed. This approach is more flexible and efficient in the use of computing resources than employing a fourth generation language, but it is considerably more costly in terms of users' time! Interface programs such as screen handling systems, referred to above, are generally implemented as stand-alone utility programs which use these programming language interfaces to pass requests for data from the users through to the database kernel. A simplified diagram of the relationships between the host processor, the DBMS software and application programs is given in Fig. 18.1.

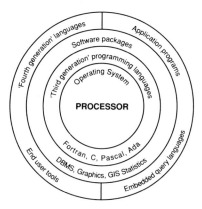

Fig. 18.1 The DBMS as part of a layered software model.

DATABASE DESIGN

Physical and logical database design

As a database is likely to be a shared resource which as it develops will come to represent a major investment by any given organization, it is most important that this investment is protected by careful database design. An initial distinction should be made between physical and logical design. Physical design is concerned with the location of different parts of the database within the file system of the computer. This may include considerations such as spreading the database across multiple disk drives to balance input/output load or for security in the event of disk media failure. Physical design is the responsibility of the database administrator and should be quite distinct from logical design, which represents the user's view of the interrelationships between data sets stored in the database. If physical and logical design are kept separate, users can access their data sets without having to concern themselves with details about where and how those data sets are physically stored (Martin 1976).

Data analysis

The first stage in logical database design is the use of data analysis techniques to develop a clearly defined conceptual model of the relationships between different data sets. These relationships may be specific to a small number of data sets required for a single user, or they may extend to all the components of a large corporate database. Regardless of the size of system, if this conceptual model is not built correctly, the likely outcome will be an inefficient database structure with unnecessary redundancy in data storage and a poor match to users' requirements for data access and retrieval.

There are a variety of data analysis or data modelling techniques that can be used (Howe 1985; Worboys, Hearnshaw and Maguire 1990a), but the entity–relationship model approach (Chen 1976) has met with the widest acceptance. Chen's approach is based on a number of fundamental concepts including entity sets, attributes, domains, relationship sets and mappings.

Entity sets represent the generic structure of phenomena which are relevant to the specific database being designed. They might be towns, census districts, hotels or national parks, for example. Each entity belonging to a particular entity set will have a number of characteristics or attributes. In the case of census districts these might include an identification number, X,Y coordinates of a centroid and a list of census variables. Each attribute will have a range of possible values which constitutes its domain or value-set. For example, identification numbers may range between 0001 and 9999 or hotels may have tourist guide quality ratings between 1 and 5. Relationship sets are formally defined as subsets of the cross product of two or more entity sets (Tsichritzis and Lochovsky 1982). The specific relationship between individual members of the respective entity sets provides the subsetting mechanism, for example the fact that certain members of the hotel set are located in a particular town. Specific relationships or mappings between entity sets may take a variety of forms. One-to-one mappings refer to the situation where, for example, each town has one and only one set of municipal offices, while a one-to-many mapping would be where a town had a number of hotels. Many-to-many mappings deal with cases such as that of wholesalers distributing goods to different shopping centres. Each centre will be served by multiple wholesalers and each wholesaler will distribute goods to several centres. A number of refinements in the specification of relationships are possible (Ellis 1985) depending, for instance, on whether or not they are defined to be mandatory (every hotel must be located in one and only one town).

Using these fundamental concepts, it is possible to develop sophisticated models of data interrelationships. The availability of diagramming methods linked to the concepts allows graphical representations of models to be drawn. These are powerful aids to model articulation and as a means of communication. A simple example involving national parks, scenic trails and landscape features is given in Fig. 18.2.

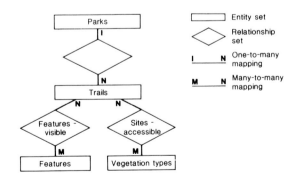

Fig. 18.2 An example entity–relationship model for a national parks database.

While the use of data analysis techniques is much less prevalent in the GIS literature than is desirable, important examples of the application of these methods to the structuring of relationships between types of digital cartographic data can be found in van Roessel and Fosnight (1984) Tuori and Moon (1984) and Hearnshaw, Maguire and Worboys (1989).

TYPES OF DBMS STRUCTURE

Once the data analysis is complete, the resulting data model must be implemented using suitable DBMS software. This might be developed in-house, but unless the organization is large and the programming resources considerable, it is unlikely it would have the required facilities. More likely, the software will be one of the large number of systems currently available commercially. These systems can be broadly categorized into four main types:

- inverted list systems;
- hierarchical systems;
- network systems;
- relational systems.

Important new approaches, which have not yet established a major presence in the commercial marketplace, are discussed in a later section. While some software packages may have characteristics drawn from more than one of the above types, in general the category into which any given package falls gives a clear indication of the way in which it structures data sets and their interrelationships at the level of logical database design. It should be noted also that the first two categories developed from refinement and improvement of commercial approaches to data management and are largely represented by older systems (Date 1986), while the last two are in turn both more recent in origin and more soundly based on theoretical, rather than pragmatic considerations. Choosing any one of these different types of system will have a major impact on the way in which the data model for a particular application problem maps onto the underlying database structure.

Inverted list systems

The basic storage mechanism for data in this DBMS structure is by means of tables/files containing rows (records) and columns (fields). The specific ordering of rows within tables has importance for the ways in which the data can be accessed. Further means of retrieving data are provided by search keys which index the occurrence of values for a specific field. If the field occurs in more than one table, this information will also be incorporated in the index (Date 1986). The index takes the form of an inverted list with a pointer from each row in the list to the actual disk location where the relevant data may be found.

The inverted list structure can be illustrated using the national parks example. Assume that there is a Trails entity set that has four attributes (Table 18.1(a)): an identification number (Trail#), Name, Category (easy E or difficult D for walking) and an identification number for the Park in which it is located (Park#). Similarly a Landscape Features entity set has attributes of Feature#, Type and Origin. The last of these describes the type of process responsible for its formation. The Features-visible relationship set has attributes Trail#, Feature# and two attributes for the latitude (Lat) and longitude (Long) in decimal degrees of the point on the trail from which the feature is visible. Directly translated into the format of data tables these might appear as indicated in Table 18.1(a).

A simple inverted list representation of the contents of the Features-visible table, if Feature# were defined to be a search key, can be seen in Table 18.1(b). More probably a number of search keys would be defined, including Trail# and Feature#, both of which appear in more than one table, and a combined key Trail#/Feature#. The overall sequence of index entries for the multiple search keys might appear as in Table 18.1(c).

In this way a single index structure can be created across all the tables in the database. Index entries for the same data value in the corresponding field in two different tables (cf. the first two lines of the index in Table 18.1(c)) are found adjacent to each other. This facilitates searches which require information to be retrieved on both the attributes of one parent and indeed any entity set can be linked to any other (Martin 1976).

Each entity set with its attributes is considered to be a node in the network. Relationship sets are represented as linkages in the form of pointers between individual entities in different entity sets. As a result, all the different forms of mapping – one-to-many, many-to-many, etc. – can be handled directly with large numbers of pointers. An example of how the parks database might be structured as a network database is given in Fig. 18.4, with the pointers represented as solid or dashed arrows.

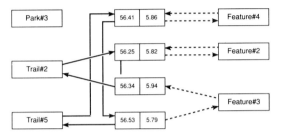

Fig. 18.4 Part of the national parks database in a network structure.

The network approach is powerful and flexible. For many applications it is also very fast and efficient in terms of CPU resources. From the implementation viewpoint, however, it may be comparatively difficult to set up the database correctly and, although the query language is comprehensive, it may also be complex and confusing for less expert users. Major restructuring of the database may be time consuming because of the extensive pointer structures that have to be rebuilt.

It might reasonably be thought that network databases would have found ready application in certain areas, such as work involving both GIS and locational analysis, where problems may fit quite naturally into the network structure. While important examples of this can be found (Armstrong, Densham and Rushton 1986; Densham and Armstrong 1987), it appears that the disadvantages of network systems from the user's viewpoint continue to militate against their widespread use in GIS.

Relational systems

The concepts of the relational approach were first set out by Codd (1970, 1979), as a means of describing data with their 'natural' structure only and ensuring independence of user-written application programs from the detailed storage formats of data within a database. In comparison to the previous approaches, relational systems are characterized by simplicity, in that all the data are represented in tables (relations) of rows and columns.

From the database design viewpoint, entity–relationship modelling fits very closely with relational systems. Each entity set is represented by a table, while each row or 'tuple' in the table represents the data for an individual entity. Each column holds data on one of the attributes of the entity set. Unlike other types of database, relationship sets describing many-to-many relationships between entity sets are also represented by a table of data values. The tables contain columns which reference the entity sets being related, together with further columns for any attributes of the relationship itself. Referring back to Table 18.1(a), the 'Features-visible' table is a good example of a relationship table, containing two columns, each of which references an entity set (the Trails and Features tables). A further pair of columns contain locational data which are attributes of the relationship set itself, as the coordinates are determined by the relative location of a particular feature with respect to viewpoints along a particular trail. Since relationships between entities are directly represented as tables, there is no requirement for pointers or linkages between data records to be set up, as was the case with hierarchical or network systems. The principal features of relational databases, the primary key, relational joins and normal forms, are now discussed in turn.

The primary key

The relational approach is firmly grounded in the mathematical theory of relational algebra (Ullman 1982). This has important implications for the design of database tables. Firstly, a set, as mathematically defined, cannot have duplicate values. Since each table or relation represents a set, it cannot, therefore, have any rows whose entire contents are duplicated. Secondly, as each row must be different to every other, it follows that a value in a single column, or a combination of values in multiple columns, can be used to define a primary key for the table, which allows each row to be uniquely identified. Irrespective of whether the primary key is restricted to one column or spans several, no column that forms part of a key can be null, that is can contain a row location without a value, because this would have the potential for permitting duplicate rows to be stored. The uniqueness property allows the primary key to serve as the sole row level addressing mechanism in the relational database model (Date 1986).

Relational joins

The mechanism for linking data in different tables is called a relational join. Values in a column or columns in one table are matched to corresponding values in a column or columns in a second table. From the second table a further match to a third table can be made, and so on until the necessary data from the requisite number of tables have been retrieved. Matching is frequently based on a primary key in one table linked to a column in the second which is termed a foreign key. An example of the join mechanism is shown in Fig. 18.5. It should be noticed that in the relationship set table for 'Features-visible' the primary key spans the two columns containing id-numbers, because both are required to identify the row uniquely. Each of the two also acts as a foreign key to match to the id-numbers in the entity set tables.

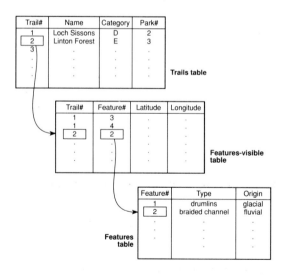

Fig. 18.5 Part of the national parks database in relational form as relational tables and with relational joins (see also Table 18.1).

Normal forms

A certain amount of necessary data redundancy is implicit in the relational model because the join mechanism matches column values between tables. Without careful table design it is all too easy to introduce further unnecessary redundancy into the database. To prevent this, table design should follow Codd's (1970) theory of normal forms, which specifies what types of values columns may contain and how columns in a table are to be dependent on the primary key.

The first requirement of the theory is that all the tables must contain rows and columns as already noted, and column values must be atomic, that is they do not contain repeating groups of data, such as multiple values of a census variable for different years. The second requirement or normal form is that every column, which is not part of the primary key, must be fully dependent on the primary key. This can be understood most readily by considering the example in Fig. 18.6 of a table which is not in second normal form. In this case the feature name is dependent on Feature#, but not Trail#, because feature Type is not an attribute of the 'Features-visible' relationship set, but of the Features entity set. The effect of not meeting the requirement can be seen by the introduction of unnecessary redundancy into the table in rows 1 and 4. If the feature Type was changed in the first row and the corresponding change in the fourth row was overlooked, the database would be left in an inconsistent state.

Primary key				
trail#	feature#	type	latitude	longitude
1	3	Delta		
1	4	Corrie		
2	2	Braided channel		
2	3	Delta		

Fig. 18.6 An example of a national parks database table not in second normal form.

The third normal form requires that every non-primary key column must be non-transitively dependent on the primary key. Again, an example which is not in third normal form will be used for illustration (Fig. 18.7(a)). At first sight this may appear to be a convenient way of finding out which vegetation types can be seen in which parks, but the unnecessary redundancy in rows 1 and 3 highlights the error. The Park# is related to the Veg-type#

via the Trail#, that is two distinct relationship sets have been conflated. This transitive dependence is to be avoided (Fig. 18.7(b)). Instead, the relationship set tables should be kept distinct, thereby avoiding the transitive dependence problem (Figs. 18.7(c) and 18.7(d)). This eliminates the redundancy while making it very easy to add new Veg-type/Trail or Trail/Park combinations to the database. Further refinements of the basic normal forms to deal with a variety of design requirements, have led to the identification of Boyce-Codd, fourth and fifth normal forms (Fagin 1979). Nevertheless, the fundamental working rule for most circumstances has been summarized by Kent (1983) as ensuring that each attribute of a table represents a fact about the primary key, the whole primary key and nothing but the primary key. While this is entirely valid from the design viewpoint, it must also be said that practical implementation requirements may, on occasion, override theoretical considerations and lead to tables being merged and de-normalized, usually for performance reasons.

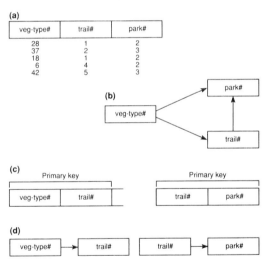

Fig. 18.7 The national parks database in relational form: (a) a table not in third normal form; (b) an illustration of transitive dependence; (c) normalizing the table structure; (d) avoidance of transitive dependence.

Advantages and disadvantages of relational systems

The advantages can be summarized as follows:

- Rigorous design methodology based on sound theoretical foundations.

- All the other database structures can be reduced to a set of relational tables, so they are the most general form of data representation.

- Ease of use and implementation compared to other types of system.

- Modifiability, which allows new tables and new rows of data within tables to be added without difficulty.

- Flexibility in *ad hoc* data retrieval because of the relational join mechanism and powerful query language facilities.

Disadvantages include:

- A greater requirement for processing resources with increasing numbers of users on a given system than with the other types of database.

- On heavily loaded systems, queries involving multiple relational joins may give slower response times than are desirable. This problem can largely be mitigated by effective use of indexing and other optimization strategies, together with the continued improvement in price performance in computing hardware from mainframes to PCs.

The important advantages of the relational approach and the availability of good proprietary software systems such as ORACLE, INGRES and DB2 have contributed greatly to the rapid adoption of this technology, both in the GIS field and automated data processing operations of all other kinds, since the beginning of the 1980s. Relational systems now dominate the market for DBMS in the GIS sector and this will continue for the foreseeable future.

Hybrid and Integrated Approaches to GIS Database Management

With continued developments in database design, storage methods and retrieval performance, it is now quite feasible to hold tens of gigabytes of digital cartographic data, map attribute data or both, using proprietary software and the more powerful hardware platforms available from a variety of vendors. Some examples of large spatial databases are shown in Table 18.2. Sheer data volume, therefore, may no longer be a severe problem other than for the most demanding requirements of the military or national mapping agencies. Yet, if digital cartographic data, in particular, are to be retrieved from a commercial database for display mapping purposes at the user's screen, it may be necessary to retrieve thousands of rows of data in a small number of seconds, for effective graphical interaction to be possible (Frank 1984, 1988). This remains a problem even for fast workstations, because of the overheads of query language processing, index access and data unpacking that accompany the use of database software. Use of the computer file system directly, rather than through the intermediate step of the DBMS will generally yield faster response times. On the other hand, the DBMS provides a wide range of ready made data manipulation tools so programming effort can be concentrated on algorithms for spatial analysis and user interface requirements.

Table 18.2 Some large spatial databases.

Database	Object types	No. of co-ordinates ($\times 10^6$)	Nature of data
WDDES	polygons, lines	300	contours, rivers, boundaries
SOTER	polygons	150	soil polygons
CORINE	polygons, lines	50	natural resource and political
CGIS-CLI	polygons	90	land use potential
Alberta LRIS	polygons, lines	140	land tenure
Edmonton City	polygons, lines, points	4	urban infrastructure

WDDES = World Digital Data for the Environmental Sciences; SOTER = Soil and Terrain Database; CORINE = Coordinated Information on the European Environment; CGIS = Canada Geographic Information System; LRIS = Land Resources Information System.

The differing emphasis placed by GIS system designers on the advantages of the file system approach versus the database approach for storage of digital map coordinates, has led to the development of two different approaches to implementation, based on either a hybrid or an integrated data model (Bracken and Webster 1989). These will now be examined in greater detail.

The hybrid data model

The starting point for this approach is that data storage mechanisms which are optimal for locational information are not optimal for attribute/thematic information (Morehouse 1985; Aronson 1985). On this basis, digital cartographic data are stored in a set of direct access operating system files for speed of input/output, while attribute data are usually stored in a standard commercial relational type DBMS such as INFO, ORACLE, INGRES or INFORMIX (Fig. 18.8). The GIS software manages linkages between the cartographic files and the DBMS during different map processing operations such as overlay. While a number of different approaches to the storage of the cartographic data are used, the linking mechanism to the database is essentially the same, based on unique identifiers stored in a database table of attributes that allow them to be tied to individual map elements.

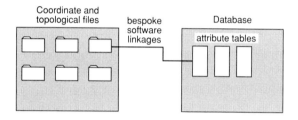

Fig. 18.8 The hybrid GIS model.

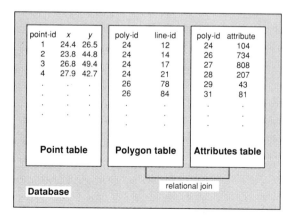

Fig. 18.9 The integrated GIS model with a normalized structure.

Since most hybrid systems use relational databases, any classification of hybrid types must rely largely on differences in the cartographic data storage mechanism. Several types can be identified, including CAD-based, vector–topological and quadtree-based systems. In CAD-based systems, map features are held as graphics elements, but without any topological information, so it is legitimate to enquire as to whether they really fall into the category of GIS rather than digital mapping systems, because spatial analysis cannot readily be performed. Examples of this type would include INTERGRAPH IGDS/DMRS and MICROSTATION-32. The former, it should be noted, uses a network rather than a relational DBMS. Smaller systems that provide links between graphics software such as AUTOCAD and PC DBMS would also fit into this category (cf. Cowen *et al.* 1986). Vector–topological systems may hold the topological map information in a set of linked files very similar to the structure that might be expected if the data were inside, rather than outside, the relational DBMS (Morehouse 1989). Alternatively, a more compact file structure may be used. The ESRI ARC/INFO, GEOVISION and INTERGRAPH MICROSTATION GIS systems are examples of this approach. The last of these provides software to convert graphics-based design files into topologically structured files (Intergraph Corporation 1989a). Quadtree-based systems do not have the same level of representation in the commercial marketplace, at the time of writing, as the previous types, but research using such systems shows considerable promise (Gahegan and Hogg 1986; Gahegan and Roberts 1988). It is also expected that commercial quadtree-based systems such as SPANS will provide linkages to relational databases in the future.

From an initial situation where each GIS supported only one DBMS, a clear trend is now being established to provide access to multiple DBMS systems (McLaren 1990), with vendors such as ESRI, INTERGRAPH and others developing generic relational DBMS interfaces (ESRI 1989; Intergraph Corporation 1989b). Since these DBMS systems are also actively developing a distributed capability, to allow data to be stored transparently on different computer nodes, but accessed and updated as though they were held locally (Date 1985), the potential number of issues raised in relation to system configuration, performance and management is very large indeed. Some of these have been examined by Webster (1988) and Seaborn (1988).

The integrated data model

The integrated data model approach is also described as the spatial database management system approach, with the GIS serving as the query processor sitting on top of the database itself (Guptill 1987; Morehouse 1989). Most implementations to date are of the vector–topological kind, with relational tables holding map coordinate data for points/nodes and line segments, together with other tables containing topological information, in a manner partly similar to that described by van Roessel (1987). Attributes may be stored in the same tables as the map feature database or in separate tables accessible via relational joins (Fig. 18.9).

The integrated data model has a number of implications in terms of the special characteristics of spatial data. From the database viewpoint, it is perfectly possible to store both the coordinates and the topological information required to characterize digital cartographic elements using a design based on Codd's Normal Forms, as van Roessel's detailed analysis has shown. Using this approach, X,Y coordinate pairs for individual vertices along line segments are stored as different rows in a database table. However, from the GIS viewpoint, these data often need only to be accessed as 'bundles', each one comprising all the pairs of coordinates for a given line, or all the line identifiers for the lines forming the bounding edges of polygons. This is the case when the data are being retrieved for display purposes and little or no analysis is being performed on individual coordinate values.

Under these circumstances, storage of individual coordinate pairs in different rows of a database table creates substantial performance overheads, if large amounts of data have to be retrieved quickly for graphics purposes. To achieve satisfactory retrieval performance it has been found necessary to store coordinate strings in long or 'bulk data' columns in tables. This means, however, that the table is strictly no longer in first Normal Form, because each column value is not atomic (Fig. 18.10). This point has been emphasized by independent developments on several different integrated data model systems (Lorie and Meier 1984; Bundock 1987; Charlwood, Moon and Tulip

1987; Waugh and Healey 1987). Empirical evidence of the performance differential is given in Lewis (1987). It has also been shown that retrieving batches of rows containing coordinates using an 'array fetch' mechanism (Dimmick 1985), can reduce the performance overhead while avoiding the use of non-normalized tables (Sinha and Waugh 1988).

```
Line-id   Coordinates
   1      24.4 26.5 23.8 44.8 26.8 49.4 27.9 42.7 . . .
   2      36.3 41.5 38.4 56.8 38.8 59.2 40.2 58.8 . . .
   3      78.4 50.2 81.5 45.5 82.6 47.4 889.5 34.6 . . .
   .      . . . .
   .      . . . .
   .      . . . .
                                              Line table

Poly-id   Linelist
   24     12 14 17 21 . . . .
   26     78 84 93 95 . . . .
   27     43 45 67 56 . . . .
    .     . . . .
    .     . . . .
    .     . . . .
                                           Polygon table
```

Fig. 18.10 The integrated GIS model using long data types.

The performance issue must also be addressed in respect of very large digital cartographic data banks, since both the US Geological Survey (Guptill 1986; Starr and Anderson 1991 in this volume) and the Ordnance Survey (Smith 1987; Sowton 1991 in this volume) have developed integrated data models for national mapping applications, suitable for implementation in a relational database framework. The Ordnance Survey solution has been to implement its system using a Britton-Lee IDM dedicated database computer. Machines of this kind have hardware support to accelerate standard operations such as relational joins and can support a much larger number of concurrent data accesses by multiple users than a software only database system (Su 1988).

A further aspect of handling large spatial databases is the need to convert 2-D coordinate information into 1-D spatial keys that can be stored as database table columns. These can then be indexed in the normal way and used for fast retrieval of map elements contained within or overlapping a specified geographical search area (Abel and Smith 1986; Waugh and Healey 1987; Abel 1988).

Comparison of hybrid and integrated data model approaches

From the commercial viewpoint, the success of hybrid systems cannot be denied, while integrated systems such as Prime's SYSTEM9, although developed later, have yet to make a comparable impact on the market. In the past, the problem for integrated systems may have been a function of the powerful hardware required to achieve good performance and the correspondingly high cost of entry. With the rapid growth of the graphics workstation market and technological improvements this factor is rapidly declining in importance. Much more significant for the future, when comparing hybrid and integrated approaches, will be the rapid expansion of networked and distributed computing. This increases the problems of multi-user data access, data security, data integrity and overall database management (Bundock 1987) for which the DBMS vendors, as opposed to GIS vendors, are well advanced in attempting to provide solutions. In hybrid systems, special purpose programming is currently used to link the digital cartographic and attribute data, instead of the standard relational join mechanism used in an integrated system. Extending the argument, there is a danger that a great deal of further specialist programming will have to be done, for a distributed hybrid GIS to attain the functionality that can already be provided by the leading DBMS packages. The performance advantage of hybrid systems remains, but it can be expected that integrated systems will progressively close the gap by the use of memory caching techniques, bulk data types and array fetching mechanisms, to minimize database input/output. Further improvements in determining optimal search paths for database queries, particularly when distributed processing is involved, can also be anticipated.

Both hybrid and integrated approaches can, therefore, be expected to coexist for the foreseeable future, but with a growing appreciation of the advantages of the integrated model, as the price–performance of hardware continues to improve.

SPATIAL QUERY LANGUAGES

Implicit in the spatial database approach is a requirement to query and interrelate different data sets in a manner that is meaningful in the GIS context. Unfortunately, standard query languages like the Structured Query Language, SQL, are restricted to supporting queries based on relational joins, sub-queries, grouping functions and query combination operators. Some types of GIS function, such as retrieving map elements that fall within or overlap a rectangular window, can be performed using standard, albeit complex SQL queries. Others, such as data layer intersection (overlay), cannot, because they require operations to be applied to the data which are beyond the scope of the available query language functions. A summary of the range of operators required for spatial query languages is given by Guptill (1986). There are now several systems where the query language has been extended to incorporate such operators (Charlwood, Moon and Tulip 1987; Ingram and Phillips 1987; Herring, Larsen and Shivakumar 1988). With relational DBMS systems there are different ways in which such facilities can be implemented. One approach is to pre-process non-standard SQL and convert, if possible, the spatial operators into more complex but standard SQL, which is then passed to the database kernel. A second approach, at the pre-processing stage, is to convert the query into a component that can be used to retrieve data from the DBMS. These data are then further processed by calls to user-supplied code which perform the GIS operations. A third approach is to link the user-supplied code directly to the database kernel, which will render the developer unpopular with the vendor, but will enable the spatial operators to become fully part of the query language!

OBJECT-ORIENTED DBMS: THE FUTURE FOR GIS DATABASE MANAGEMENT?

Extensions of the integrated model to incorporate spatial query language functions are a tacit recognition that, in the final analysis, it is not sufficient merely to hold data on map elements in the database. For GIS purposes it must also be possible to access the operations to be performed on these elements. This brings the conceptualization of the problem very close to that provided by the object-oriented approach (Aronson 1987).

As the most recent of the models for data handling and processing discussed here, care needs to be taken with the term 'object oriented' (Maguire, Worboys and Hearnshaw 1990). Even some of the main proponents are reluctant to use it too widely, since 'few people agree on exactly what it means' (Rowe and Stonebraker 1987). Following Somerville (1989) and Rowe (1986) an object can be defined as an entity that has a state represented by the values of local variables (instance variables) and a set of operations or methods (instance methods) that operate on the object. Individual objects belong to a class that defines the type of object. Classes may have variables that describe characteristics of the class as a whole. Each class has a superclass from which it can inherit both instance variables and methods. For example, an object class called polygon may be defined which is also the superclass for another class called land parcel. The object definitions might, therefore, appear as indicated in Table 18.3(a) and 18.3(b). By convention, the superclass (object) is at the top of the object hierarchy, which might be structured as in Fig. 18.11. All the instance methods and variables of the polygon superclass are inherited by the land parcel class, unless they are re-defined at the land parcel level.

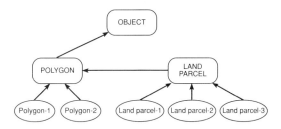

Fig. 18.11 A hierarchy of object classes.

The designers of POSTGRES, an object-oriented DBMS designed to be the successor to INGRES, the relational DBMS, have developed a variety of techniques to facilitate object management within a database environment. These include storage of the structure of object hierarchies in relational tables, inheritance of instance variables and methods, storage of query language or programming language procedures representing instance methods, as special fields in relational tables, and support for abstract/user defined data types and the operations supported on them. It should be noted that the POSTGRES designers

Table 18.3(a) Polygon object definition.

Superclasses (object)

Class variables

    Number_of_polygons

Instance variables

    List_of_nodes
    List_of_arcs
    Area

Instance methods

    Calculate_centroid
    Draw
    Overlay

Table 18.3(b) Land parcel object definition.

Superclasses (polygon)

Class variables

Instance variables

    Value
    Owner

Instance methods

    Transfer_ownership
    Re_zone

regard an evolutionary approach as the best way forward, that is adding object-oriented facilities to an existing relational database framework. This is in contrast to some of the proponents of object-oriented programming, who wish to achieve the same kind of functionality, but without the perceived constraints of the relational model (Cox 1986; Wells 1988; Stroustrup 1988). Other authorities expect to see convergence of the programming and database viewpoints in future (Tsichritzis and Nierstrasz 1988).

The major example of the object-oriented approach in the GIS field is the INTERGRAPH TIGRIS system (Herring 1987) which utilizes object-oriented programming, rather than object-oriented DBMS techniques or an object-oriented interface. Further work in this area has been reported, in terms of user interface aspects (Egenhofer and Frank 1988), data modelling (Kemp 1990; Orenstein 1990; Worboys, Hearnshaw and Maguire 1990a) and query modelling (Worboys, Hearnshaw and Maguire 1990b). It is clear, however, that a fuller exploration of the potential of object-oriented DBMS systems, as the organizing framework for spatial databases, may have to wait until they move further from the 'proof-of-concept' stage (Thatte 1988) towards widespread availability.

CONCLUSIONS

Evolving trends in the design and implementation of general purpose database management systems have been examined, with regard to their significance for the handling of both digital cartographic and attribute data. The leading role of relational methods has been identified. The fact that their widespread adoption in the data processing world at large coincided with the rapid upsurge of interest in GIS in the 1980s, has undoubtedly contributed to their success. Extensions to the relational model and query languages to handle both spatial operators and object orientation are already well advanced. Further developments in the handling of temporal attributes in spatial databases will assume greater importance in future, as data volumes grow and database update in mature systems takes over from database creation (Snodgrass 1987; Rowe and Stonebraker 1987; Langran 1988, 1989; Price 1989).

Finally, across the entire spectrum of database applications there is the possibility of using methods from knowledge-based systems and natural language processing; but these are discussed by Smith and Ye Jiang (1991 in this volume). In an analogous manner to object-oriented methods, however, it remains uncertain as to whether an extended relational or other type of DBMS should act as the repository for the knowledge base (Tsichritzis and Nierstrasz 1988). Past history suggests that while in the research phase a variety of approaches will vie for position, subsequently market pressures will enforce a concentration on standardized solutions, characterized by maintainability and simplicity of structure.

REFERENCES

Abel D J (1988) Relational data management facilities for spatial information systems. *Proceedings of the 3rd*

International Symposium on Spatial Data Handling. International Geographical Union, Columbus Ohio, pp. 9–18

Abel D J, Smith J L (1986) A relational GIS database accommodating independent partitionings of the region. *Proceedings of the 2nd International Symposium on Spatial Data Handling.* International Geographical Union, Columbus Ohio, pp. 213–24

Armstrong M P, Densham P J, Rushton G (1986) Architecture for a microcomputer based spatial decision support system. *Proceedings of the 2nd International Symposium on Spatial Data Handling.* International Geographical Union, Columbus Ohio, pp. 120–31

Aronson P (1985) Applying software engineering to a general purpose geographic information system. *Proceedings of AUTOCARTO 7.* ASPRS, Falls Church Virginia, pp. 23–31

Aronson P (1987) Attribute handling for geographic information systems. *Proceedings of AUTOCARTO 8.* ASRPS, Falls Church Virginia, pp. 346–55

Bracken I, Webster C (1989) Towards a typology of geographical information systems. *International Journal of Geographical Information Systems* 3: 137–52

Bundock M (1987) An integrated DBMS approach for geographic information systems. *Proceedings of AUTOCARTO 8.* ASRPS, Falls Church Virginia, pp. 292–301

Charlwood G, Moon G, Tulip J (1987) Developing a DBMS for geographic information: a review. *Proceedings of AUTOCARTO 8.* ASPRS, Falls Church Virginia, pp. 302–15

Chen P (1976) The Entity–Relationship Model – towards a unified view of data. *Association for Computing Machinery Transactions on Database Systems* 1 (1): 9–36

Clark D M, Hastings D A, Kineman J J (1991) Global databases and their implications for GIS. In: Maguire D J, Goodchild M F, Rhind D W (eds.) *Geographical Information Systems: principles and applications.* Longman, London, pp. 217–31, Vol 2

Codd E F (1970) A relational model of data for large shared data banks. *Communications of the Association for Computing Machinery* 13 (6): 377–87

Codd E F (1979) Extending the database relational model to capture more meaning. *Association for Computing Machinery Transactions on Database Systems* 4 (4): 397–434

Collins J (1982) *Review of Competitive Database Software.* Savant, Carnforth

Cowen D J, Hodgson M, Santure L, White T (1986) Adding topological structure to PC-based CAD databases. *Proceedings of the 2nd International Symposium on Spatial Data Handling.* International Geographical Union, Columbus Ohio, pp. 132–41

Cox B J (1986) *Object-Oriented Programming: An evolutionary approach.* Addison-Wesley, Reading. Massachusetts. 274pp.

Crain I K (1990) Extremely large spatial information systems: a quantitative perspective. *Proceedings of the 4th International Symposium on Spatial Data Handling*, Volume 2. International Geographical Union, Columbus Ohio, pp. 632–41

Date C J (1985) *An Introduction to Database Systems.* Volume II. Addison-Wesley, Reading Massachusetts

Date C J (1986) *An Introduction to Database Systems.* 2nd edn. Addison-Wesley, Reading Massachusetts

Densham P J, Armstrong M (1987) A spatial decision support system for locational planning: design, implementation and operation. *Proceedings of AUTOCARTO 8.* ASPRS, Falls Church Virginia, pp. 112–21

Dimmick S (1985) *Pro-Fortran User Guide.* Oracle Corporation, Menlo Park California

ESRI (1989) *ARC/INFO V5.0 Users Guide*, Volumes I and II. ESRI Inc., Redlands California

Egenhofer M J, Frank A U (1988) Designing object-oriented query languages for GIS: human interface aspects. *Proceedings of the 3rd International Symposium on Spatial Data Handling.* International Geographical Union, Columbus Ohio, pp. 79–96

Ellis H (1985) Twenty years of data analysis. In: Holloway S (ed.) *Data Analysis in Practice.* Database Specialist Group, The British Computer Society, London, pp. 99–120

Fagin R (1979) Normal forms and relational database operations. *Proceedings of the ACM SIG-MOD International Conference on Management of Data*, pp. 153–60

Frank A U (1984) Requirements for database systems suitable to manage large spatial databases. *Proceedings of the 1st International Symposium on Spatial Data Handling*, Volume 1. International Geographical Union, Columbus Ohio, pp. 38–60

Frank A U (1988) Requirements for a database management system for a GIS. *Photogrammetric Engineering and Remote Sensing* 54 (11): 1557–64

Gahegan M N, Hogg J (1986) A pilot geographical information system based on linear quadtrees and a relational database for regional analysis. In: Diaz B M, Bell S B M (eds.) *Spatial Data Processing Using Tesseral Methods.* Natural Environment Research Council, Swindon, p. 213–32

Gahegan M N, Roberts S A (1988) An intelligent, object-oriented geographical information system. *International Journal of Geographical Information Systems* 2: 101–10

Guptill S C (1986) A new design for the US Geological Survey's National Digital Cartographic Database. In: Blakemore M J (ed.) *Proceedings of AUTOCARTO LONDON*, Volume 2. Royal Institution of Chartered Surveyors, London, pp. 10–18

Guptill S C (1987) Desirable characteristics of a spatial database management system. *Proceedings of AUTOCARTO 8.* ASPRS, Falls Church Virginia, pp. 278–281

Hearnshaw H M, Maguire D J, Worboys M F (1989) An introduction to area-based spatial units: a case study of Leicestershire. *Midlands Regional Research Laboratory Research Report 1*. MRRL, Leicester

Herring J R (1987) TIGRIS: topologically integrated geographic information system. *Proceedings of AUTOCARTO 8*. ASPRS, Falls Church Virginia, pp. 282–91

Herring J R, Larsen R C, Shivakumar J (1988) Extensions to the SQL query language to support spatial analysis in a topological database. *Proceedings of GIS/LIS '88*, Volume 2, ASPRS/ACSM, Falls Church Virginia, pp. 741–50

Howe D R (1985) *Data Analysis for Data Base Design*. Edward Arnold, London

Ingram K, Phillips W (1987) Geographic information processing using a SQL-based query language. *Proceedings of AUTOCARTO 8*. ASPRS, Falls Church Virginia, pp. 326–35

Intergraph Corporation (1989a) *Microstation Analyst (MGA) Reference Manual*. Intergraph Corporation, Huntsville Alabama

Intergraph Corporation (1989b) *Relational Interface (RIS) User Reference Manual*. Intergraph Corporation, Huntsville Alabama

Kemp Z (1990) An object-oriented data model for spatial data. *Proceedings of the 4th International Symposium on Spatial Data Handling*, Volume 2. International Geographical Union, Columbus Ohio, pp. 659–68

Kent W (1983) A simple guide to five normal forms in relational database theory. *Communications of the Association for Computing Machinery* **26** (2): 120–25

Langran G (1988) Temporal GIS design tradeoffs. *Proceedings of GIS/LIS '88*, Volume 2. ASPRS/ACSM, Falls Church Virginia, pp. 890–99

Langran G (1989) A review of temporal database research and its use in GIS applications. *International Journal of Geographical Information Systems* **3**: 215–32

Lewis P (1987) Spatial data handling using relational databases. Unpublished MSc thesis, Department of Geography, University of Edinburgh, Scotland.

Lorie R A, Meier A (1984) Using a relational DBMS for geographical databases. *Geo-Processing* **2**: 243

Maguire D J, Worboys M F, Hearnshaw H M (1990) An introduction to object-oriented geographical information systems. *Mapping Awareness* **4** (2): 36–9

Martin J (1976) *Principles of Database Management*. Prentice-Hall, Englewood Cliffs New Jersey

Martin J (1983) *4th Generation Languages*, Volume 1. Savant, Carnforth Lancashire

McLaren R A (1990) Establishing a corporate GIS from component data sets – the database issues. *Mapping Awareness* **4** (2): 52–8

Morehouse S (1985) ARC/INFO: a geo-relational model for spatial information. *Proceedings of AUTOCARTO 8*. ASPRS, Falls Church Virginia, pp. 388–97

Morehouse S (1989) The architecture of ARC/INFO. *Proceedings of AUTOCARTO 9*. ASPRS, Falls Church Virginia, pp. 266–77

Olle T W (1978) *The Codasyl Approach to Database Management*. Wiley, Chichester. 287pp.

Orenstein J A (1990) An object-oriented approach to spatial data processing. *Proceedings of the 4th International Symposium on Spatial Data Handling*, Volume 2. International Geographical Union, Columbus Ohio, pp. 669–78

Price S (1989) Modelling the temporal element in land information systems. *International Journal of Geographical Information Systems* **3**: 233–44

Rowe L A (1986) A shared object hierarchy. In: Stonebraker M R, Rowe L A (eds.) *The POSTGRES Papers. Memorandum No. UCB/ERL M86/85*. College of Engineering, University of California, Berkeley

Rowe L A, Stonebraker M R (1987) The progres data model. *Proceedings of the 13th Conference on very large databases*, Brighton, England, pp. 83–96

Seaborn D W (1988) Distributed processing and distributed databases in GIS – separating hype from reality. *Proceedings of GIS/LIS '88*, Volume 1. ASPRS/ACSM, Falls Church Virginia, pp. 141–4

Sinha A K, Waugh T C (1988) Aspects of the implementation of the GEOVIEW design. *International Journal of Geographical Information Systems* **2**: 91–100

Smith N S (1987) Data models and data structures for Ordnance Survey. *Proceedings of the Ordnance Survey/SORSA Symposium, Durham, May 1987*.

Smith T R, Ye Jiang (1991) Knowledge-based approaches in GIS. In: Maguire D J, Goodchild M F, Rhind D W (eds.) *Geographical Information Systems: principles and applications*. Longman, London, pp. 413–25, Vol 1

Snodgrass R (1987) The temporal query language TQUEL. *Association for Computing Machinery Transactions on Database Systems* **12**: 247

Somerville I (1989) *Software Engineering*, 3rd edn. Addison-Wesley, Reading Massachusetts, 653pp.

Sowton M (1991) Development of GIS-related activities at the Ordnance Survey. In: Maguire D J, Goodchild M F, Rhind D W (eds.) *Geographical Information Systems: principles and applications*. Longman, London, pp. 23–38, Vol 2

Starr L E, Anderson K E (1991) A USGS perspective on GIS. In: Maguire D J, Goodchild M F, Rhind D W (eds.) *Geographical Information Systems: principles and applications*. Longman, London, pp. 11–22, Vol 2

Stroustrup B (1988) What is Object-Oriented Programming? *IEEE Software* **5** (3): 10–20

Su S (1988) *Database Computers: principles, architectures and techniques*. McGraw-Hill, New York, 497pp.

Thatte S (1988) Report on the object-oriented database workshop: implementation aspects. In: Power L, Weiss Z (eds.) *OOPSLA '87 Addendum to the Proceedings. Special Issue of SIGPLAN Notices* **23** (5): 87

Tsichritzis D C, Lochovsky L C (1982) *Data Models.* Prentice-Hall, Englewood Cliffs New Jersey

Tsichritzis D C, Nierstrasz O M (1988) Fitting round objects into square databases. In: Gjessing S, Nygaard K (eds.) *Proceedings of ECOOP '88, the European Conference on Object-Oriented Programming.* Springer-Verlag, Berlin, pp. 283–99

Tuori M, Moon G C (1984) A topographic map conceptual data model. *Proceedings of the 1st International Symposium on Spatial Data Handling*, Volume 1, International Geographical Union, Columbus Ohio, pp. 28–37

Ullman J D (1982) *Principles of Database Systems.* Computer Science Press, Rockville Maryland

van Roessel J W (1987) Design of a spatial data structure using the relational normal forms. *International Journal of Geographical Information Systems* **1**: 33–50

van Roessel J W, Fosnight E A (1984) A relational approach to vector data structure conversion. *Proceedings of the 1st International Symposium on Spatial Data Handling*, Volume 1. International Geographical Union, Columbus Ohio, pp. 78–95

Waugh T C, Healey R G (1987) The GEOVIEW design. A relational database approach to geographical data handling. *International Journal of Geographical Information Systems* **1**: 101–18

Webster C (1988) Disaggregated GIS architecture. Lessons from recent developments in multi-site database management systems. *International Journal of Geographical Information Systems* **2**: 67–80

Wells D (1988) How object-oriented databases are different from relational databases. In: Power L, Weiss Z (eds.) *OOPSLA '87 Addendum to the Proceedings. Special Issue of SIGPLAN Notices* **23** (5): 81

Wiederhold G (1983) *Database Design.* 2nd edn. McGraw-Hill, London, 751pp.

Worboys M F, Hearnshaw H, Maguire D J (1990a) Object-oriented data modelling for spatial databases. *International Journal of Geographical Information Systems*. 369–83

Worboys M F, Hearnshaw H, Maguire D J (1990b) Object-oriented data and query modelling for geographical information systems. *Proceedings of the 4th International Symposium on Spatial Data Handling.* International Geographical Union, Columbus Ohio, pp. 679–88

19

DIGITAL TERRAIN MODELLING

R WEIBEL AND M HELLER

Digital terrain models (DTMs) are a major constituent of geographical information processing. DTMs help to model, analyse and display phenomena related to topography or similar surfaces. This chapter is an attempt at a comprehensive review of relevant techniques and applications of DTMs. The individual elements of digital terrain modelling – techniques for the generation, manipulation, interpretation (analysis) and visualization of DTMs – are outlined. Application domains that use DTMs and their specific functional requirements are identified. Due to the complexity of the topic this chapter should be considered primarily as an annotated guide to the rich literature on digital terrain modelling.

INTRODUCTION

Digital terrain models (DTMs) have been used in geoscience applications since the 1950s (Miller and Laflamme 1958). Since then they have become a major constituent of geographical information processing. They provide a basis for a great number of applications in the earth and the engineering sciences. In GIS, DTMs provide an opportunity to model, analyse and display phenomena related to topography or other surfaces.

A DTM may be understood as a digital representation of a portion of the earth's surface. Since overhanging cliffs and faults are relatively rare in nature, topographic surfaces are most often represented as 'fields' (i.e. simply connected surface models, having unique z-values over x and y). In this sense a DTM is a '2.5-D' rather than a 3-D model. Extensions to model cliffs and faults are commonly provided by application-specific systems, where they may be crucially important, such as those used in modelling geological surfaces (see, for instance, McCullagh 1988; Raper and Kelk 1991 in this volume). Some authors argue that the term 'Digital Elevation Model' (DEM) should be used instead of 'Digital Terrain Model' when merely relief is represented, 'because the term "terrain" often implies attributes of a landscape other than the altitude of the landsurface' (Burrough 1986:39). Although this point is well taken, here the term 'digital terrain model' is intentionally used since it allows the possibility of including landscape attributes other than topography, as a means of improving the digital representation of a section of terrain. In a more general sense, a DTM may be used as a digital model of any single-valued surface (e.g. geological horizons and even air temperature or population density). Here, however, attention is focused on digital models of terrain since many aspects of the digital modelling of other surface phenomena are functionally related to terrain modelling.

As will be shown in the course of this chapter, the input data, data models and algorithms required by digital models of terrain or other surfaces are quite different from those used in representing planimetric (i.e. two-dimensional) data. The activity of modelling and processing digital terrain data may thus be regarded a system component of GIS that is functionally disparate from modelling 2-D data, yet needs to be closely linked to other processing functions of GIS (e.g., polygon, network and raster processing). Digital terrain modelling encompasses the following general tasks (cf. Weibel and Heller 1990):

- *DTM generation*: sampling of original terrain data, formation of relations among the diverse observations (model construction);
- *DTM manipulation*: modification and refinement of DTMs, derivation of intermediate models;
- *DTM interpretation*: DTM analysis, information extraction from DTMs;
- *DTM visualization*: graphical rendering of DTMs and derived information;
- *DTM application*: development of appropriate application models for specific disciplines. DTM application forms the context for digital terrain modelling: each particular application has its specific functional requirements relative to the other terrain modelling tasks.

Flexibility and adaptability to given problems are fundamental objectives of a digital terrain modelling system. Thus, as Fig. 19.1 shows, deriving products from a DTM should not be viewed as a one-way process, but rather as the result of various interrelated stages in modelling. For example, a DTM may be modified by model manipulation procedures. It might then be displayed by visualization procedures, or analysed through interpretation functions. Visualization and/or interpretation in turn may require or support further modification or adaptation of the original DTM. Thus, results of individual modelling steps may feed back into previously run procedures.

In the course of this chapter the individual constituents of a comprehensive DTM system are gradually introduced. The text is structured according to the tasks of digital terrain modelling listed above. Given the restrictions in space, the discussion concentrates on a comprehensive overview of relevant techniques and applications. The functional interdependencies between the various processing tasks are identified and references are provided to further reading material and information about sources of current research. One of the objectives is that this text may be used as an annotated directory to the key literature on DTMs.

DTM GENERATION: TERRAIN DATA CAPTURE AND CONSTRUCTION OF DIGITAL TERRAIN MODELS

Data sources and data capture for digital terrain models

The choice of data sources and terrain data sampling techniques is critical for the quality of the resulting DTM. Data for a DTM should consist of observations about terrain elevations and, whenever possible, additional information about phenomena that significantly influence the shape of the terrain surface (i.e. structural features such as drainage channels, ridges and other surface discontinuities). There may be other criteria apart from DTM quality requirements, which will guide the selection of a particular sampling technique and scheme for any given application (e.g. efficiency, cost and technological maturity).

At present, most DTM data are derived from three alternative sources: ground surveys, photogrammetric data capture (in manual, semi-automated, or automatic mode), or from digitized cartographic data sources. Other methods occasionally used include radar or laser altimetry, and sonar (for subaquatic terrain). Data for geological models are obtained from either borehole records or seismic surveys.

As a further alternative, models of artificial

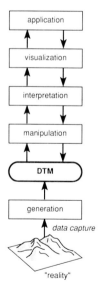

Fig. 19.1 The main tasks of a digital terrain modelling system.

terrain may be created through digital simulation, as noted by McLaren and Kennie (1989). Fournier, Fussel and Carpenter (1982) have proposed a method which is frequently used to generate quasi-realistic images of terrain. However, this technique is based solely on modelling stochastic processes. Other authors (Griffin 1987; Clarke 1988; Kelley, Malin and Nielson 1988; Musgrave, Kolb and Mace 1989; Szelinski and Terzopoulos 1989) have also tried to incorporate geomorphological simulation into their models.

Ground surveys

Survey data may be input directly into computer systems through data recorders which may be coupled to field instruments. Since ground survey data tend to be very accurate, and surveyors tend to adapt the survey to the character of the terrain (i.e. they measure significant terrain points), the accuracy of the resulting DTM is very high. However, as this particular data collection technique is relatively time consuming, its use is limited to small areas. Thus, ground surveys are commonly applied to specific projects (e.g. site planning of small areas) or used to complement photogrammetric data capture (e.g. to provide data for wooded areas).

Photogrammetric data capture

Photogrammetric data capture is based on the stereoscopic interpretation of aerial photographs or satellite imagery (e.g. from the French SPOT satellites), using suitable photogrammetric equipment (i.e. manual or analytical stereoplotters). It is possible to distinguish a number of different photogrammetric sampling techniques: regular sampling patterns, progressive sampling, selective sampling, composite sampling, and digital stereo image correlation for automatic DTM extraction. Each of these methods attempts to minimize the data collection effort (i.e. the number of elevation samples to be taken), while at the same time maximizing the accuracy of the resulting DTM. Depending on the sampling method and imagery that are used, the resulting DTM accuracy will be medium to high. Since remote sensing is used instead of field work, large areas may be handled in a relatively short amount of time. Photogrammetric data capture is used in large engineering projects (e.g. dams, open-cast mines and roads) as well as nationwide data collection.

The simplest photogrammetric sampling technique is that of regular sampling patterns. Regular patterns may be arranged as profiles or grids (Fig. 19.2(a) and (b)). Since a fixed sampling distance is used, it is important to consider the determination of the optimal sampling interval. Blais, Chapman and Lam (1986) discuss several strategies for this problem, including techniques based on spectral analysis, linear interpolation and variogram estimation. The advantage of regular sampling patterns is that they may be applied in a semi-automated or even automatic mode (if correlators are used). However, due to the fixed sampling distance, the usefulness of this technique is restricted to fairly low and homogeneous terrain. An excessive number of points tends to be sampled in regions of low relief, whereas too few points are captured in rugged terrain.

In 'progressive sampling', developed by Makarovic (1973), the density of sample points is adapted to the complexity of the terrain surface. The sampling process is initiated by measuring a

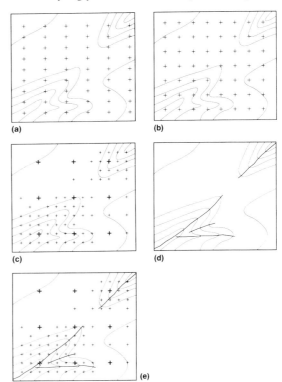

Fig. 19.2 Photogrammetric sampling techniques: (a) regular sampling pattern (profiles); (b) regular pattern (grid); (c) progressive sampling; (d) selective sampling; (e) composite sampling.

low density grid. The accuracy of the sampled data is then analysed. Wherever necessary, the sampling grid is recursively densified until the required accuracy level is reached. This results in a hierarchical sampling pattern (Fig. 19.2(c)). The method of progressive sampling may also be automated. Due to the adaptivity of the progressive sampling process, fewer points are needed to produce DTMs of higher accuracy than for regular sampling patterns. However, since a regular densification pattern is used, it still requires too many points to represent terrain breaks accurately.

In regions of sharp terrain discontinuities, it is sometimes necessary to capture topographic breaks selectively (Fig. 19.2(d)). This sampling method is termed 'selective sampling' (Makarovic 1984). If selective sampling of structural features is combined with progressive sampling, the technique is called 'composite sampling' (Makarovic 1977, 1979), in which selective sampling is used to capture abrupt topographic changes while progressive sampling yields the data for the rest of the terrain (Fig. 19.2(e)). Thus, the recursive refinement of progressive sampling can be kept to a minimum and terrain discontinuities are represented accurately. Composite sampling yields terrain data of high quality. However, since the selective sampling of structural features requires human intervention, this method may only be partially automated.

There has been an increased tendency during the past decade towards the fully automated extraction of terrain models through correlation of digital stereo images. This correlation can be achieved either by using correlation devices, or 'off-line', that is fully computationally without involvement of any photogrammetric equipment (Konecny and Pape 1981; Barnard and Fischler 1982; Day and Muller 1988; Lemmens 1988). In digital stereo correlation, corresponding picture elements or features are matched through cross correlation in order to obtain parallaxes and derive elevations. Although this technique is fast and seems suitable for large data collection projects, data quality is generally not very high since errors may be easily introduced (e.g. through pattern mismatches or through noisy digital data). Consequently, procedures for automated error detection and correction have to be devised to increase the data quality.

Cartographic data sources

It is also possible to derive DTMs from cartographic documents, such as contour maps and profiles. These analogue data may be digitized through manual digitization, semi-automated line-following, or by means of automatic raster scanning and vectorization. Due to the relatively high costs of direct methods for terrain data capture (i.e. surveying and photogrammetry) and the large volume of existing paper maps, this indirect method is predominant for large data collection projects. This is particularly true for national or military mapping agencies. Figure 19.3 shows a sample of scan-digitized contour lines generated for a project of this type. Despite their widespread use as a basis for DTMs, contour data present some problems. Contours are mainly a form of terrain visualization and are not particularly useful as a scheme for numerical surface representation. An excessive number of points is sampled along contours (oversampling), and no data across contours (undersampling). Furthermore, errors may be introduced (in drawing, line generalization, reproduction, etc.) and a lot of the original information is lost in the mapmaking process. Consequently, contour data yield DTMs of only limited accuracy. However, since large area coverage is achieved relatively cost effectively, digitized cartographic documents provide a compromise method of obtaining DTMs for use at medium or small scales.

Model construction

The process of terrain data capture generates a set of relatively unordered data elements (the 'original observations'). In order to construct a comprehensive DTM it is necessary to establish the topological relations between the data elements, as well as an interpolation model to approximate the surface behaviour.

Data structures for digital terrain models

The original data must be structured to enable handling by subsequent terrain modelling operations. A variety of data structures for DTMs has been in use over time (Peucker 1978; Mark 1979). Today, however, the overwhelming majority of DTMs conform to one or other of two data

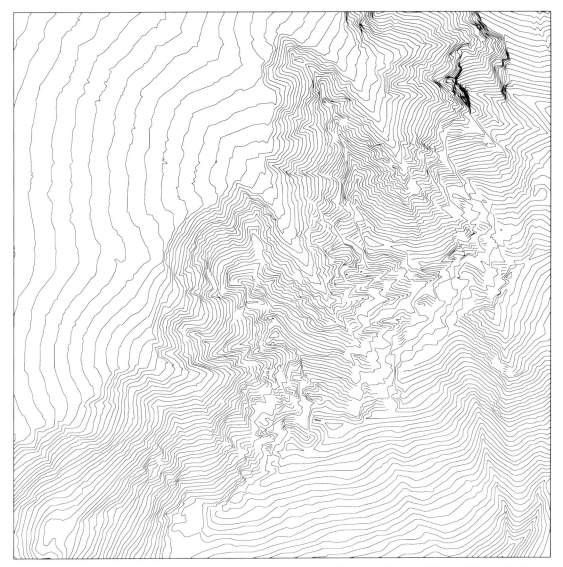

Fig. 19.3 Sample of scan-digitized and vectorized contour lines from the National Map of Switzerland at 1 : 25 000 scale. (Courtesy of Swiss Federal Office of Topography, 22.12.89)

structures: rectangular grid (or elevation matrix), or TIN (Triangulated Irregular Network; Peucker et al. 1978).

Grids present a matrix structure that records topological relations between data points implicitly (Fig. 19.4(a)). Since this data structure reflects the storage structure of digital computers (i.e. a grid can be stored as a two-dimensional array of elevations), the handling of elevation matrices is simple, and grid-based terrain modelling algorithms thus tend to be relatively straightforward. On the other hand, the point density of regular grids cannot be adapted to the complexity of the relief. Thus, an excessive number of data points is needed to represent the terrain to a required level of accuracy. Also, rectangular grids cannot describe structural features as topographic features; extensions to the basic model have to be added for this purpose (cf. Köstli and Sigle 1986; Ebner, Reinhardt and Hössler 1988).

TIN structures, on the other hand, are based on triangular elements, with vertices at the sample

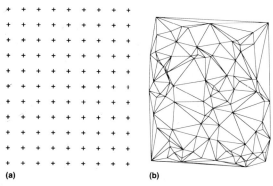

Fig. 19.4 The two most commonly used data structures for DTMs: (a) rectangular grid (or elevation matrix, gridded DTM); (b) Triangulated Irregular Network (TIN).

points (Fig. 19.4(b)). Structural features can easily be incorporated into the data structure. Consequently, TINs are able to reflect adequately the variable density of data points and the roughness of terrain. Fewer points are needed for a DTM of a certain accuracy. However, topological relations have to be computed or recorded explicitly. Thus, TINs become more complex and also more difficult to handle. Not all grid-based algorithms today have an efficient counterpart in TIN structures.

Both Peucker (1978) and Mark (1979) discuss additional advantages and disadvantages of rectangular grids, TINs and other DTM data structures so there is no need to dwell further on this subject here. It is more important to note that no data structure is clearly superior for all tasks of digital terrain modelling. Thus, the ability to switch between different data structures, as well as modify and refine the DTM become prime objectives of any flexible DTM system. To facilitate these processes, the system should be based on a data model that is general enough to accommodate a variety of uses: the original observations act as the basis for this model, and specific representations (such as TINs, grids, etc.) are derived from these and act as interfaces to DTM procedures (Weibel *et al*. 1987; Weibel and Heller 1990). These intermediate models only hold that particular subset of the basic DTM which is necessary for solving a given problem. The framework for such a system is described in more detail in Weibel and Heller (1990).

Interpolation

In digital terrain modelling, interpolation serves the purpose of estimating elevations in regions where no data exist. Interpolation is mainly used for the following operations:

- computation of elevations (z) at single point locations;
- computation of elevations (z) of a rectangular grid from original sampling points;
- computation of locations (x,y) of points along contours (in contour interpolation);
- densification/coarsening of rectangular grids (so-called resampling).

Abundant literature exists on methods for interpolation of DTMs. A number of articles may be used as an entry point to the exploration of different interpolation models (e.g. Schut 1976; Schumaker 1976; Lam 1983; Heller 1986; McCullagh 1988). Lam (1983) groups point interpolation into exact and approximate methods. The former preserve the values at the data points, while the latter smooth out the data. Another popular way to classify interpolation models is by the range of influence of the data points involved. Global methods, in which all sample points are used for interpolation may be distinguished from local, piecewise methods, in which only data points nearby are considered. Because topographic surfaces are non-stationary and non-periodic the use of overly distant points may deform the interpolated surface. For DTMs with sample points of sufficient quality and density, a local and exact interpolation method on surface patches is widely considered satisfactory.

There is insufficient space here to discuss individual interpolation models, rather it seems appropriate to refer to the rich literature and just briefly mention the characteristics and peculiarities of DTM interpolation from topographic samples:

- There is no 'best' interpolation algorithm that is clearly superior to all others and appropriate for all applications (e.g. see Lam 1983);
- The quality of the resulting DTM is determined by the distribution and accuracy of the original data points (i.e. the sampling process), and the adequacy of the underlying interpolation model

(a hypothesis about the behaviour of the terrain surface);

- The most important criteria for selecting a DTM interpolation method are the degree to which (1) structural features can be taken into account, and (2) the interpolation function can be adapted to the varying terrain character;

- Suitable interpolation algorithms must adapt to the character of data elements (type, accuracy, importance, etc.) as well as the context (i.e. the distribution of data elements). Satisfactory solutions exist for the interpolation of relatively well-selected and dense topographic samples (e.g. photogrammetric data). There are, however, a number of critical cases that still pose problems for current procedures (see Figure 19.5);

- Other criteria that may influence the selection of a particular method are the degree of accuracy desired and the computational effort involved.

The above considerations only partially apply to the interpolation of non-terrain surfaces. However, some of the review articles mentioned earlier (e.g. Lam 1983; Schumaker 1976) also discuss the interpolation of these surfaces.

Triangulation

Some of the more widely used local interpolation procedures are based on triangulation: interpolation is achieved by locally fitting polynomials to triangles (the simplest case being

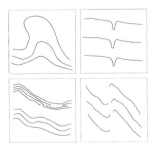

Fig. 19.5 Some critical cases for interpolation. For instance, interpolation procedures have to be able to interpret the fine structure of neighbouring contour lines and extend it across the area between lines. Note that such situations are not uncommon in real data (cf. Fig. 19.3).

linear interpolation within triangles). Furthermore, triangulation is used to construct TIN DTMs, as discussed earlier. Triangulation thus serves two purposes in terrain modelling: as a basis for TIN data structures, and as a basis for interpolation (e.g. of gridded DTMs or contours). However, TIN-based interpolation (in conjunction with the interpolation of gridded DTMs) is probably more common than TINs used as DTM data structures. TIN-based interpolation is essentially a two-step procedure: in the first step a TIN is constructed; it is then used for interpolation in the second step.

Of the many possibilities available to triangulate a set of points, the so-called 'Delaunay triangulation' has received particular attention. An example of such a triangulation is shown in Fig. 19.6(a). A triangulation of a set of points is a Delaunay triangulation if, and only if, the circumcircle of any of its triangles does not contain any other point in its interior. The Delaunay triangulation is bounded by the convex hull. The dual of the Delaunay triangulation is called a Voronoi diagram (or Thiessen polygons, or Dirichlet tessellation). Nodes of a Voronoi polygon are coincident with the circumcentres of Delaunay triangles (Fig. 19.6(b)). The perpendicular bisectors of Delaunay edges form the edges of Voronoi polygons. Since they are dual, the Delaunay triangulation may be constructed from its Voronoi diagram and vice versa. A more mathematical and profound treatment of Delaunay triangulation may be found in Preparata and Shamos (1985), or Edelsbrunner (1987). It is interesting to note that because of their specific properties, Delaunay triangulation and the Voronoi diagram have found widespread use in many fields other than surface modelling (e.g. computational geometry, physics, meteorology, economic geography, etc.). A number of efficient algorithms for constructing a Delaunay triangulation (or Voronoi diagrams) have been described (e.g. Guibas and Stolfi 1985; Preparata and Shamos 1985; Edelsbrunner 1987; Heller 1990). Heller (1986) provides further annotated references. Figure 19.7 shows a triangulated set of terrain spot heights.

It is important to observe that any product which is derived from a TIN – whether it is a perspective display, a set of slope values, or an interpolated grid DTM – will be heavily dependent upon the quality of the TIN. Since a TIN is

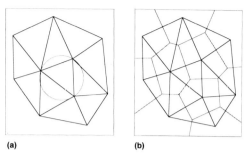

Fig. 19.6 The concept of Delaunay triangulation: (a) Delaunay triangulation with circumcircle of one of the triangles; (b) Delaunay triangulation and its dual, the Voronoi diagram (or Dirichlet tessellation or Thiessen polygons).

primarily a topological structure, quality also relates to the logical consistency of the TIN, that is whether or not the formation of the triangles complies with the geomorphological facts of the terrain surface being modelled. Obviously, several of the critical cases illustrated in Figs. 19.3 and 19.5 cannot be adequately handled by pure Delaunay triangulation (Fig. 19.8(a), and 19.8(c)). Thus, the Delaunay criterion has to be relaxed. The triangulation must be constrained so that segments

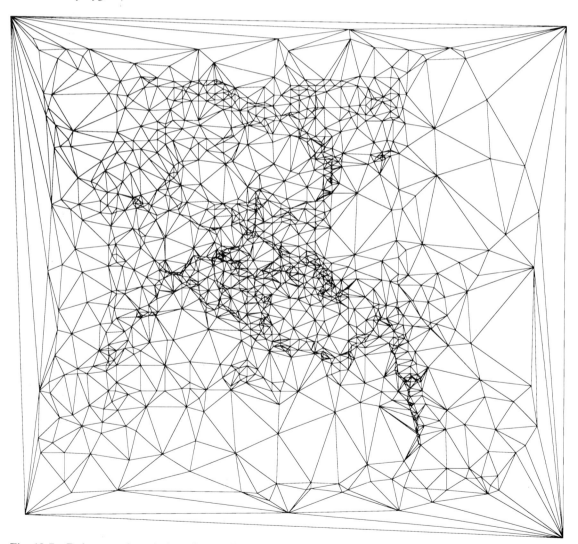

Fig. 19.7 Delaunay triangulation of a set of terrain spot heights.

of discontinuities or other features of spatial coherence form edges of triangles (Fig. 19.8(b)). The triangulation must also be adjusted for interpolation from contour data (Fig. 19.8(d)). Although several computer programs exist today that construct constrained triangulations, only a few authors have actually reported on their solution (e.g. McCullagh 1982; Christensen 1987; McCullagh 1988; Heller 1990).

Once the TIN has been constructed in the triangulation process, it can either be used directly as a TIN DTM, or else as a basis for interpolation. In TIN-based interpolation, the (interpolated) z-value of a point depends on the heights of the nodes of the triangle that contains it. The z-value is interpolated by substituting the x,y values of the point to a polynomial function that is fitted to the relevant triangle. If linear interpolation is used, the z-value can be computed directly from the heights of the nodes of the triangle. If a higher order function is applied (e.g. Birkhoff and Mansfield 1974; Akima 1978), coefficients of that function are estimated based on the heights of the triangle nodes, as well as their first and second order derivatives. The derivatives at a node depend on the heights of all its neighbours (i.e. nodes with which it shares a common edge). If discontinuities are included in the triangulation, no heights of nodes across a discontinuity are included in the computation of the derivatives. McCullagh (1982, 1988) demonstrates his approach to TIN-based interpolation in detail.

One of the main advantages of TIN-based interpolation is that it is very efficient. The first phase is independent of the second one. Once the TIN has been constructed, gridded DTMs or contours may be efficiently computed since the TIN provides a convenient means of locating the relevant nodes for interpolation. Further advantages of TIN-based interpolation are that it is a local method which allows discontinuities to be incorporated easily, and that it may be used to transform any TIN into a gridded DTM (i.e. data structure conversion).

Because of its local scheme and efficiency, TIN-based interpolation is one of the few methods that may be considered practicable even for very large point sets. To date, developments of TIN-based interpolation algorithms have focused on memory-resident methods. To manage very large data sets, disk-based algorithms should be used which divide the plane into regions (tiling), triangulate each region separately, and eventually patch the triangulated sub-areas together (joining).

A special case of interpolation: interpolation from contour data

As mentioned earlier, digitized contours are not a particularly useful digital representation of terrain, yet they remain a popular data source for DTMs. Furthermore, many of the special cases of Fig. 19.5 may be found in real contour data such as those displayed in Fig. 19.3. Interpolation from contours thus seems to be especially complex and certainly

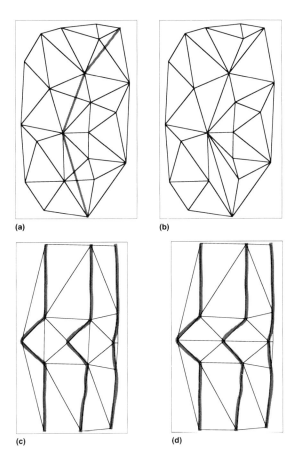

Fig. 19.8 Pure Delaunay triangulation may conflict with linear constraints: (a) Delaunay edges cross linear discontinuity; (b) constrained triangulation; triangle edges are coincident with linear constraints; (c) triangles have been formed of points on the same contour line; (d) adjusted triangulation.

deserves special attention. Several contour-specific interpolation algorithms have been developed. Most algorithms for interpolating regular grid DTMs (e.g. Clarke, Grün and Loon 1982; Oswald and Raetzsch 1984) use linear or cubic interpolation along straight lines (either along predefined directions or in the direction of steepest slope), 'in an attempt to extend across the areas between the contour lines at least some of the fine structure contained in the data contours' (Hutchinson 1988:126). Clarke, Grün and Loon (1982) present a thorough review and evaluation of this class of contour-to-grid algorithms. However, these methods are still not capable of resolving some of the critical cases illustrated in Fig. 19.5.

A more sophisticated procedure has been presented by Hutchinson (1988, 1989). His method includes a drainage enforcement algorithm, which automatically removes spurious sinks or pits in the fitted elevation grid, and an algorithm which automatically calculates ridge and stream lines from points of maximum local curvature on contour lines. These two techniques allow a more reliable interpolation of the fine structure in contours across the area between data contour lines. A partly similar approach that first computes aspect vectors from the contour data to enhance the interpolation model has been reported by Inaba, Aumann and Ebner (1988).

Apart from enhancing contour-to-grid interpolation methods, there has also been recent and growing interest in improving triangulation-based interpolation. The method of Christensen (1987), using the medial axis of contour polygons for triangulation, shows considerable improvement over Delaunay triangulation. However, it results in an overkill, as normally only few cases would actually require departure from the Delaunay criterion. Consequently, this procedure is not very efficient. Other approaches that attempt to recognize critical cases in contour data and locally relax the Delaunay criterion, are currently still under research.

DTM MANIPULATION: MODIFICATION AND REFINEMENT OF DTMS

Along with DTM generation procedures, the DTM manipulation processes are of fundamental importance for the performance and flexibility of a DTM system. They are needed for the modification and refinement of existing models. DTM manipulation consists of processes for DTM editing, filtering and merging, and for the conversion between different data structures.

DTM editing

DTM editing involves updating and error correction. An editor is required for interactive, selective modification of the properties of individual elements of a DTM. Edit operations for DTM elements should include: query, delete, add, move, change height, change attribute, etc. For gridded DTMs, however, editing is essentially restricted to modifying elevations at grid points. If TINs are edited, algorithms are required for local adjustment of the network topology after points have been inserted or deleted (Preparata and Shamos 1985; Heller 1990). Furthermore, it is helpful if an effective user interface is used. Interaction by direct manipulation supported by visual feedback (e.g. Apple 1987) will greatly simplify the editing task.

DTM filtering

DTM filtering may serve two purposes: smoothing or enhancement of DTMs, as well as data reduction.

Smoothing and enhancement filters for DTMs are equivalent to lowpass and highpass filters as they are known in other fields, such as image processing (e.g. see Gonzalez and Wintz 1987). They may be applied both in the spatial domain (by moving average operations) or in the frequency domain (by convolution of Fourier transforms). They are best applied to gridded terrain models. The effect of smoothing (i.e. applying lowpass filters) is to remove details, and make the DTM surface smoother. Enhancement (i.e. highpass filtering) has the opposite effect: surface discontinuities are emphasized, while smooth shapes are suppressed. Smoothing filters have been used to eliminate blunders (e.g. in photogrammetric data); they may also be used to some extent for cartographic generalization of DTMs (Zoraster, Davis and Hugus 1984; Weibel 1989; Muller 1991 in this volume). Enhancing (or highpass) filters have only rarely been applied to DTMs.

DTM filtering procedures are also used to

Fig. 19.9 Examples of adaptive triangular mesh (ATM) filtering for data reduction and grid-to-TIN conversion: (a) original gridded DTM (311 × 221 = 68 731 points); (b) remaining points (11 450 or 16.7 per cent) after TIN filtering has been applied using a tolerance of 5 m; (c) hillshading of corresponding TIN DTM; (d) remaining points (5732 or 8.3 per cent) after ATM filtering using a tolerance of 10 m; (e) corresponding TIN. (DTM data courtesy of Swiss Federal Office of Topography, 22.12.89)

(a)

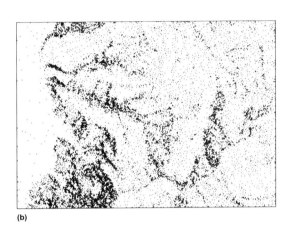
(b)

(c)

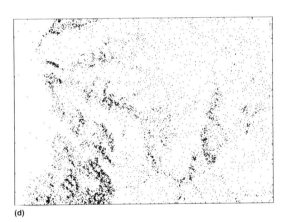
(d)

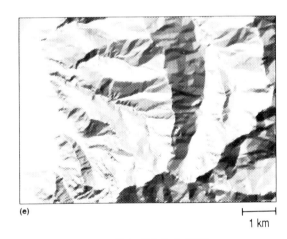
(e)

1 km

reduce the data volume of DTMs. A data reduction process of this kind may be desirable to eliminate redundant data points (e.g., within the digitizing tolerance), to save storage space and processing time, or to reduce a DTM's resolution (e.g., for comparison with other models). It may also be used as a pre-processing step in cartographic generalization of DTMs (Weibel 1989), or to convert a gridded DTM into a TIN (see below).

This problem has been addressed by Gottschalk (1972). As his method uses a global interpolation scheme, it is only practical for small data sets. An efficient approach – called adaptive triangular mesh (ATM) filtering – has been developed by Heller (1990). A given triangulation is fitted to a specified local height tolerance. The procedure is based on an algorithm that repeatedly adds the most significant point to the triangulation, until no additional points are needed to describe the surface within the specified tolerance. The importance of a point is given by the vertical distance (i.e. elevation difference) between the point and the retriangulated model without that point. The procedure builds a distance queue, adds the point with the largest distance, retriangulates its neighbourhood, updates the queue, and continues to insert points until the largest distance is smaller than the specified tolerance.

This algorithm may be used to reduce data volumes of both TINs and gridded DTMs. A grid may be considered as a special case of a TIN, with nodes arranged in a rectangular grid. Thus, grids may be triangulated and filtered in the same way other TINs would be processed. However, as some points will be deleted through the filtering process, grids will be transformed into TINs. An example of ATM filtering is shown in Fig. 19.9: starting from a gridded DTM (68 731 points), a TIN DTM with a tolerance of 5 m (with 11 450 remaining points or 16.7 per cent), and a TIN DTM with a tolerance of 10 m (5732 points or 8.3 per cent) were obtained.

DTM joining and merging

DTMs may be combined either by joining adjacent models or by merging overlapping models.

For gridded DTMs, joining is only straightforward if the grids correspond in grid resolution, orientation, etc. Otherwise, a resampling process (for coarsening, densification, and/or reorientation) has to be used to establish continuity. The joining of TINs requires algorithms for connection and readjustment of the TINs along their borders (zipping) to patch the models together (Guibas and Stolfi 1985; Preparata and Shamos 1985; Heller 1990).

Merging DTMs poses problems at two levels. The first task consists of inserting all elements of one model into the other model (e.g. by incremental triangulation versus full re-triangulation). The second problem domain involves combining data sets with conflicting attributes (elevation and gradients) and varying degrees of accuracy. It is complex and represents a fundamental methodical problem.

Data structure conversion

The task of converting a DTM of a certain representation (e.g. TIN) into another structure (e.g. grid) can be handled by a combination of DTM generation and manipulation procedures.

As has been shown earlier, grid-to-TIN conversion may be handled by the same procedure used for data reduction of TINs (i.e. ATM filtering). In order to be able to exploit the benefits of a TIN data structure (i.e. adapt the point density to the terrain complexity to save storage space), insignificant points must be discarded in the conversion process. As Fig. 19.9 shows, a grid can be successfully converted to a TIN of substantially reduced data volume using ATM filtering. There are also strong indications that this algorithm is more suitable for handling grid-to-TIN conversion than other approaches (e.g. Chen and Guevara 1987).

Other conversions are essentially equivalent to interpolation processes discussed in the preceding section. TIN-to-grid conversion is equivalent to TIN-based interpolation of a gridded DTM. Contour-to-grid and contour-to-TIN conversion are special variants of interpolation tasks. Grid-to-contour and TIN-to-contour processes are solved by contour interpolation (covered in the section on visualization below).

Miscellaneous DTM manipulation functions

A number of further manipulation operations may be included in a DTM system, such as densification or coarsening of gridded DTMs (i.e. grid resampling by interpolation), or interpolation of z-values for 2-D features (e.g. drainage features and roads). These functions can be satisfied by a combination of basic functions of DTM generation and manipulation as discussed above.

DTM INTERPRETATION: AUTOMATED TERRAIN ANALYSIS TO SUPPORT GIS MODELLING

Within a GIS, digital terrain models are most valuable as a basis for the extraction of terrain-related attributes and features. Information may be extracted in two ways: by visual analysis of graphic representations (i.e. through visualization) or by

Digital Terrain Modelling

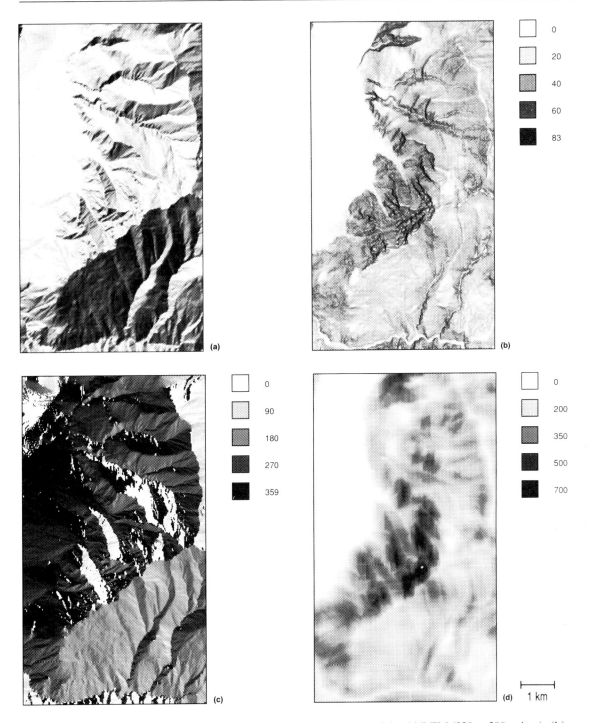

Fig. 19.10 Derivation of geomorphometric parameters from DTMs: (a) grid DTM (220 × 390 points); (b) corresponding map of gradient (in degrees); (c) map of aspect (in degrees); (d) map of local relief (range of altitude) within a 13 × 13 moving window. (DTM data courtesy of Swiss Federal Office of Topography, 22.12.89)

quantitative analysis of digital terrain data (i.e. through interpretation). Interpretation procedures, along with visualization functions, thus represent an important objective of GIS-related terrain modelling. The results of interpretation can be used as input to environmental impact studies, soil erosion potential models, hydrological runoff simulations, and many more applications.

Interpretation for geomorphometric analysis

A first objective of DTM interpretation is the derivation of geomorphometric parameters. According to Evans (1972:18), geomorphometric analysis may take two forms: general geomorphometry, 'the measurement and analysis of those characteristics of landform which are applicable to any continuous rough surface'; and specific geomorphometry, 'the measurement and analysis of specific landforms such as cirques, drumlins and stream channels, which can be separated from adjacent parts of the land surface according to clear criteria of delimitation'.

General geomorphometry

The most frequent use of general geomorphometry is the derivation of slope values from DTMs. Slope is defined by a plane tangent to the DTM surface at any given point, and comprises two components: gradient (maximum rate of change in altitude), and aspect (the compass direction of this maximum). This terminology has been used by Evans (1980); other terms frequently used include 'slope' to mean 'gradient' as just defined, and 'exposure' for 'aspect'. Examples of maps of gradient and aspect are shown in Figs. 19.10(b) and 19.10(c), respectively. Apart from being displayed as slope maps, gradient and aspect are often used as numerical input to GIS models, for example in trafficability studies or soil erosion modelling (e.g. Roo and Hazelhoff 1988). Besides gradient and aspect (i.e. the first derivatives of the altitude surface), the second derivative (or rate of change of slope) – convexity (or curvature) – is often used for geomorphological analysis. Convexity also has two components: profile convexity, i.e. the rate of change of gradient; and plan convexity, the convexity of contours (Evans 1980).

Although both slope and convexity are defined at a point, they are commonly assigned to DTM facets (i.e. triangles of TINs or rectangular cells of gridded DTMs) in slope analysis. Evans (1979) gives equations for the computation of gradient and aspect, and profile and plane convexity for points of a gridded DTM – by locally fitting a quadratic surface to a 3×3 submatrix. In an alternative approach, gradient and aspect may be determined using vector analysis. The z-component of the unit vector surface normal (in a given point) equals the cosine of gradient. Likewise, aspect is determined from the x- and y-components of the surface normal. The main task is to compute the surface normals of individual facets of the DTM. For triangles of a TIN, the surface normals are a by-product of the interpolation method (e.g. the cross-product of two vectors of the triangle in the linear case). For gridded DTMs, rectangular facets are formed from four adjacent grid points. Since rectangles are rarely plane, vectors have to be averaged according to one of the alternatives illustrated in Fig. 19.11. Computation of gradient and aspect is directly related to the procedure for

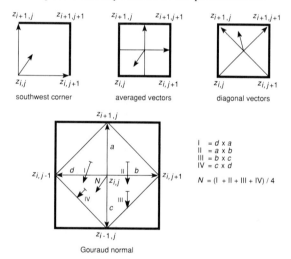

Fig. 19.11 Several alternatives to obtain averaged surface normals for square patches of either four or nine adjacent grid points.

obtaining shading intensities for automatic hillshading of DTMs.

A number of further parameters may be extracted from digital terrain data for geomorphological analysis. Mark (1975), Pike and Rozema (1975), Evans (1979), and Pike (1988) review various geomorphometric parameters and methods for their estimation: local relief (i.e. the range of altitude); hypsometric integral; drainage density; statistics of slope and convexity; parameters of the power spectrum; and others. The computation of these parameters is mainly based on gridded terrain data (Pike 1988; Weibel and DeLotto 1988). Parameter values are determined within a moving window of specified size (e.g. 11 × 11 grid points) with a technique comparable to that used in textural analysis in image processing (Haralick, Shanmugam and Dinstein 1973). Figure 19.10(d)) shows a map of the range of altitude for a moving window of 13 × 13. If this procedure is used, other parameters describing surface variation may be computed for the submatrix within the moving window, such as fractal dimension (Mandelbrot 1986; Roy, Gravel and Gauthier 1987) or entropy.

The above geomorphometric parameters may serve as input for multivariate classification of landforms (Pike 1988; Weibel and DeLotto 1988; Dikau 1989). DTMs may thus be used for applications such as landform analysis (Dikau 1989), classification of landslide hazards (Pike 1988), trafficability analysis, or as a means of supporting DTM generalization (Weibel 1989). Figure 19.12 shows the result of a multivariate classification of a DTM into regions of disparate terrain characteristics.

Specific geomorphometry

Techniques for specific geomorphometry have to date mainly focused on the delineation of terrain features related to surface hydrology. A range of features may be extracted from DTMs: surface-specific points (pits, peaks, passes, etc.); linear features (drainage channels and ridges); and areal features (drainage basins and hills). Definitions of these terms can be found for example in Douglas (1986). The objective of the analytical extraction process is to delineate the geometry of hydrological features, topologically connect them into contiguous networks, and obtain descriptive attributes for individual elements. This wealth of information may be used in applications such as hydrological runoff simulation (Band and Wood 1988; Band 1989), geomorphological modelling, support of interpolation procedures (Hutchinson 1988, 1989), or in cartographic generalization of DTMs (Weibel 1989).

Surface-specific point features may be identified by comparison of elevation differences in

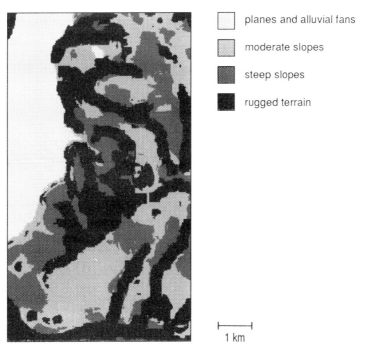

Fig. 19.12 Example of classification of a DTM (Fig. 19.10(a)) into regions of homogeneous terrain characteristics based on multivariate classification and subsequent region merging. (DTM data courtesy of Swiss Federal Office of Topography, 22.12.89)

a local neighbourhood (e.g. Peucker and Douglas 1975); peaks, for instance, are local elevation extremes. Algorithms for the extraction of linear hydrological features (channels and ridges) depend on the DTM data structure that is used. For gridded DTMs the so-called 'hydrological approach' (Mark 1984) is currently favoured by many authors (e.g. Marks, Dozier and Frew 1984; O'Callaghan and Mark 1984; Band 1989; Mark 1987). For a review and evaluation of other algorithms see Douglas (1986). In the hydrological approach, the drainage area of each grid point (i.e. the number of DTM points draining into that point) is first determined by climbing recursively through the DTM. The result of this operation is the so-called 'drainage area transform' (Band 1989), a matrix that contains the drainage area for all grid points. This information can subsequently be used to trace the channel pixels (i.e. those pixels with large drainage areas). Channels are recursively followed upstream until no further point can be found that exceeds a minimum drainage area threshold. The topology of

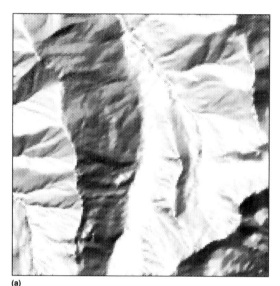

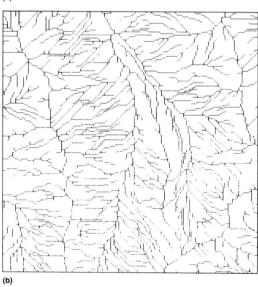
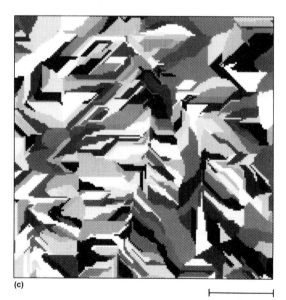

Fig. 19.13 Extraction of drainage features: (a) enlarged portion of the DTM of Fig. 19.9; (b) drainage channels and ridges for that portion; (c) drainage sub-basins for drainage channel links, shaded with random greytones. (DTM data courtesy of Swiss Federal Office of Topography, 22.12.89)

1 km

the channel network is formed concurrently with this trace operation. Ridges may be extracted by greyscale thinning of all non-stream pixels (Band 1986) or by delineating the boundaries of drainage basins. Figure 19.13(b) shows the complementary networks of channels and ridges that were identified by the above procedure.

The extraction of channels and ridges from TINs may be performed by vector analysis operations. For each triangle edge this may be determined from the direction of the surface normals of the two adjacent triangles. In a second more complex pass, channel and ridge edges are connected to contiguous topologically structured networks. A robust procedure should be able to enforce network connectivity even through artificial pits (caused by inadequate interpolation) or intermediate flat areas (e.g. lakes). Although most authors today use gridded DTMs for drainage feature extraction and apply the hydrological approach, it has to be noted that this method poses some obvious problems. Grids are a rigid sampling structure and cannot accurately represent discontinuities. The channels and ridges are forced to the locations of grid points although they would rarely pass through them in reality. Furthermore, some rather arbitrary operations (i.e. thresholding, greyscale thinning, etc.) are involved with that procedure.

Areal hydrological features (basins and hills) may be delineated using variants of the recursive DTM climbing or descending algorithms to find those grid points (or TIN facets, respectively) belonging to a specific channel or ridge link and thus constituting its sub-basin (Marks *et al.* 1984; Band 1989). Figure 19.13(c) shows the drainage sub-basins that relate to the stream channels of Fig. 19.13(b).

A number of topological attributes (e.g. link magnitude and topological order) and geomorphometric attributes (e.g. link length, mean slope and basin area) may be computed for individual links and their related sub-basins. Based on network topology, those attributes may also be aggregated for higher order links (e.g. for the root of a drainage basin). Topological models for tree-like networks are reviewed by Jarvis (1984). A useful model that combines channels and ridges into two interlocking networks has been presented by Werner (1988).

Interpretation for DTM quality assessment

Error detection and correction

Errors – blunders and constant, systematic and random errors – may occur in any sampling process (see Chrisman 1991 in this volume). Apart from geometrical errors, classification errors may occur (e.g. an edge in a DTM may be classified as part of a breakline when it is not). Procedures for detection and correction of errors are thus important.

The method most often used is visual inspection and interactive editing of the incorrect elements. Some display techniques are particularly useful for highlighting errors: on perspective displays, errors are detectable since they project out of the surface, whereas on hillshadings or maps of slope (or of other geomorphometric parameters) errors become obvious due to gradient anomalies. Apart from gradients, special error indices may be computed and visualized (Hannah 1981).

In conjunction with automated DTM extraction (by correlation of stereo images), there is a growing need for procedures for automated detection and correction of errors. Studies on reducing the amount of abnormal elevations at the time of DTM extraction have been reported by Nagao *et al.* (1988). A possible procedure for removing blunders in a post-processing step has been presented by Hannah (1981). In a first step, indicators of correctness are computed for individual DTM elevations (based on gradient differences around each DTM point). In a second step, an iterative procedure is employed to constrain errors to the elevation of adjacent points (based on correctness indicators).

DTM quality control

Quality control of a DTM may be performed by comparison with reference data (i.e. control points or another DTM). Parameters commonly used to evaluate the quality of a surface fit to reference points (e.g. Root Mean Square Error, RMSE), are reviewed by Willmott (1984). Other techniques are used for comparing two DTMs of the same area: statistical analysis of residual surfaces, comparative analysis of semi-variograms or frequency spectra. Procedures for DTM quality control may also be used to help detect systematic or constant errors. Day and Muller (1988) present a sample empirical study in which they assess the quality of DTMs produced by automatic stereo matchers.

Interpretation for planning and engineering applications

In addition to the tasks of geomorphometric analysis (mainly gradient and aspect mapping), planning and civil engineering applications require more specialized interpretation functions. One category of procedures is used for visibility analysis and for relief shadow analysis. The basic visibility algorithm for gridded DTMs determines the visibility of each point according to the schematic illustration of Fig. 19.14; an example of a visibility map is shown in Fig. 19.15. A more detailed description of this approach is given by Yoeli (1985a). A more efficient, recursive algorithm that obtains an approximate solution to the intervisibility problem has been proposed by Mark (1987). An algorithm to determine intervisibility within a TIN has been presented by De Floriani et al. (1986). Intervisibility may also be computed for multiple viewing points, by applying the visibility procedure for all viewing points and adding the results. The computation of relief shadows (Fig. 19.16) is closely related to visibility analysis (cf. Rogers 1985).

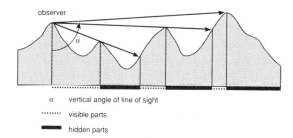

Fig. 19.14 Determining the visibility of a DTM point.

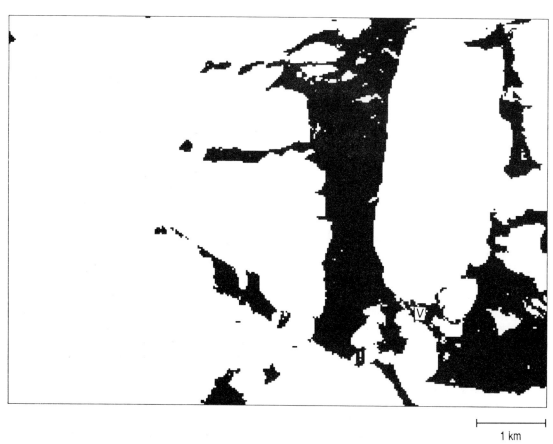

Fig. 19.15 Binary visibility map for the DTM of Fig. 19.9. Observer's location is at point V (same location as in Fig. 19.9). Visible parts are shown in black.

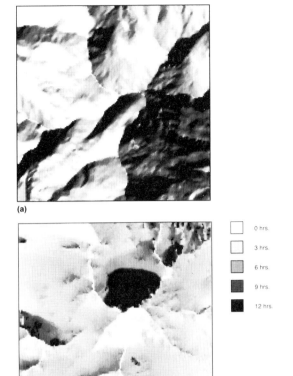

Fig. 19.16 Relief shadow analysis: (a) grid DTM (160 × 160 points); (b) shadow analysis shows how many hours each part of the DTM is in shadow; for 21 March, 6:00–18:00 MET (with V Antunes, FHS Karlsruhe). (DTM data courtesy of Swiss Federal Office of Topography, 22.12.89)

Instead of identifying the areas invisible from a given viewing location, the task is to determine the DTM elements that are obscured from a particular position of the sun (i.e. they lie in the shadow of other parts of the DTM).

Profile computation (cross-sections), and volumetric calculations (also called cut-and-fill) represent a second class of interpretation procedures for engineering and planning. These functions are used in applications such as road or reservoir design. Profiles are obtained by interpolating terrain heights at the intersection points of the profiles with the DTM. Volumetric computations are performed most easily on gridded DTMs. More accurate results can be achieved using TINs.

DTM VISUALIZATION: DISPLAYING DIGITAL TERRAIN MODELS AND RELATED DATA

Results of DTM (or GIS) modelling operations are most often communicated to users in graphical form (Buttenfield and Mackaness 1991 in this volume). Visualization thus plays a vital role in a DTM system. It is closely linked to interpretation: results of interpretation steps need to be displayed, and interpretation operations may in turn lead to improvements in visualization. Moreover, graphics themselves may directly support decision making (through visual interpretation) without involving any quantitative analysis.

Visualization commonly pursues two goals: interactive visualization, which helps the researcher to explore models and refine hypotheses; and static visualization (in the traditional form of paper maps), which is used to communicate results and concepts. The usefulness of visualization products mainly depends on their communicational effectiveness and their ability to support interpretation. In this light, utmost realism is not a primary objective.

Orthographic display techniques

Conventional forms of relief depiction (e.g. contours and hillshading) represent vast abstractions of reality, yet they are highly effective in solving many of the tasks related to the presentation and interpretation of terrain.

Contours

Contour lines (isolines) are probably still the most widely used technique for displaying relief. Contours represent a method for quantitative visualization of the third dimension. They are used to satisfy the requirement for extracting quantitative information from relief displays (e.g. in geology, topographic mapping and civil engineering). The major drawback of contours is that they give no immediate impression of the topographic forms.

The construction of contours (contouring) is closely related to DTM interpolation. A rich literature about contouring is available: many computer programs have been implemented for this task, and some of these developments have been documented in detail. Technical aspects of contouring TINs are for instance discussed by McCullagh (1981, 1988), and Gold and Cormack (1987); corresponding techniques for gridded DTMs are described by McCullagh (1981, 1988), Zyda (1988), among others. The best results are produced by methods that incorporate surface discontinuities into their contouring algorithm. Smooth contours may be generated by subdividing triangles or rectangular cells to yield a finer mesh for contour interpolation (e.g. McCullagh 1981, 1988). Alternative (more adaptive) methods produce smooth contours through contour following by successive solution of non-linear equations (e.g. Preusser 1984). Basic contouring may be further refined: index contours may be highlighted by special symbolization, contour labels added for index contours, and contour drawing may be suppressed in areas of steep gradient (i.e. where contours are too densely cluttered, only index contours are drawn).

A number of alternative methods exist for contour line display. Elevation data may simply be classified into equidistant altitude classes to produce a hypsometric tint display. Alternatively, gridded DTMs may be contoured by a technique called 'raster contouring': instead of threading contour lines through the grid, contours are determined on the basis of individual grid cells (Eyton 1984). Finally, two methods – called 'inclined contours' and 'relief or shaded contours' – may be used (Peucker 1972; Peucker and Cochrane 1974; Yoeli 1983). Both techniques attempt to extend contouring to give a better three-dimensional impression of relief. The first method represents intersections of the surface with parallel inclined planes that are orthogonal to the direction of the light source (i.e. inclined contour lines). The latter method draws contours by varying their width according to illumination brightness.

Hillshading

Analytical or automatic hillshading (Figs. 19.9, 19.10, 19.13 and 19.16) provides a convenient way of qualitative cartographic relief depiction. Landforms may be readily perceived from shaded relief displays. No clues are, however, provided about absolute terrain elevations. Hillshading for cartographic purposes was first automated by Yoeli (1965, 1967), and has become a standard terrain display technique since then.

The method is based on a model of illumination. Light intensities are computed for individual DTM facets, and facets are shaded accordingly. Shading values for DTM facets (i.e. light intensities) are computed in two steps. First, surface normals have to be determined for the individual facets (this sub-problem has already been discussed for slope analysis). Once the surface normal of a facet has been determined the illumination model is applied. The simplest model – Lambertian shading – assumes diffuse reflection of the illuminated object. The intensity of diffusely reflected light is proportional to the cosine of the angle between the surface normal and the illumination vector (i.e. the direction of the light source). And the cosine of that angle equals the dot product of the normalized illumination vector and the surface normal vector.

More sophisticated illumination models may be used. One technique, called Gouraud shading, interpolates smooth transitions of shadings between individual facets (this method has been applied to the block diagrams of Plates 19.3 to 19.4). Other advanced models (e.g. Phong shading and ray tracing) include further elements of illumination such as specular reflection, ambient light, transparency, or haze (cf. Plate 19.2(b)). A detailed discussion of illumination models may be found in Rogers (1985), or Foley et al.(1990). For the purpose of hillshading, however, it is most often sufficient to use a simple shading method.

Basic analytical hillshading may be further enhanced for cartographic purposes. Brassel (1974) has developed a model for automatic hillshading that attempts to emulate conventional cartographic principles. Vertical and horizontal adjustments of the light source are performed locally in order to enhance the depiction of landforms that run in the direction of the light source, and the general impression is improved by contrast enhancements. Yoeli (1985b) has attempted to automate relief depiction by hachures. However, although this traditional cartographic technique is quite artistic, it is probably not a very useful method for visualizing relief.

Combination with 2-D data, orthophotos

Contour displays as well as hillshading may be overlayed with other elements such as the results of interpretation procedures (e.g. visibility, slope and drainage networks); components of the DTM (e.g.

Digital Terrain Modelling

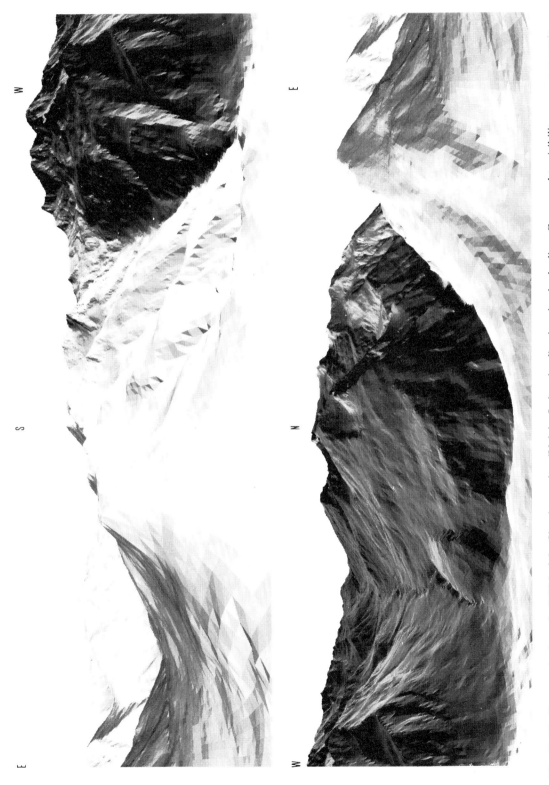

Fig. 19.17 Panoramic view of a DTM of the Simplon region (Valais, Switzerland) using simple shading. Compared to visibility maps panoramic views visualize the intervisibility situation in a more obvious way. (DTM data courtesy of Swiss Federal Office of Topography, 22.12.89)

data points, structural features and TIN triangles); or other 2-D data (e.g. roads, land use and geological maps). To combine areal data (e.g. land use) with hillshadings, the colour or intensity values of the areal data have to be modulated with the shading intensity at the corresponding location (for a description of this technique, see e.g. White 1985).

Orthophotos are a further orthographic display technique. They are generated from overlapping conventional aerial photos in a process called differential rectification (using DTMs) to eliminate image distortions due to topography (Slama, Theurer and Henriksen 1980). Orthophotos are commonly used in planning applications or topographic mapping.

Perspective display techniques

The advantage of orthographic displays is that all parts of the terrain surface are visible and relatively undistorted. Perspective displays, on the other hand, provide much more convincing visualization results (Plate 19.1). Two of the main problems that have to be solved for perspective display are the projection of the 3-D surface on to a 2-D medium, and the elimination of hidden elements from the display. The 3-D and perspective transformations (including 3-D clipping) necessary for perspective projection are described in standard textbooks on computer graphics (e.g. Newman and Sproull 1979; Foley et al. 1990).

As raster graphics devices (screens and plotters) have become predominant today, algorithms for hidden element removal are focusing on so-called image–space algorithms (i.e. the algorithm determines what is visible within each pixel of the raster display device). Algorithms may be further simplified for single-valued DTMs. Since no overlaps of DTM facets may occur in the depth dimension, this depth coherence may be exploited. For instance, a perspective block diagram may be generated by a series of vertical profiles. The corresponding procedure for removing hidden parts of profiles is the floating horizon algorithm (e.g. Rogers 1985). Instead of using line symbolization, the DTM may be displayed as shaded surface facets. Facets may either be shaded by applying a shading model as discussed for hillshading (Plate 19.1) or by using additional data such as land cover data or remote sensing images (Plates 19.2(a) and 19.2(b)).

Algorithms for hidden surface removal are needed to generate displays of this kind. Backface elimination (Newman and Sproull 1979) may be used as a pre-processing step. This typically halves the number of facets that need consideration during hidden surface computation. Descriptions of the basic hidden surface algorithms (e.g. the painter's or the z-buffer algorithm, including related techniques such as anti-aliasing) can be found in standard textbooks (e.g. Newman and Sproull 1979; Foley et al. 1990; Rogers 1985). More sophisticated algorithms are discussed in relevant periodicals (e.g. those published by ACM SIGGRAPH, or IEEE).

Many of today's graphics workstations provide hardware implementations for perspective projection, as well as hidden element removal (mostly z-buffer), and object rendering. These functions greatly simplify the task of building highly interactive display and analysis systems that are capable of handling surface models of considerable size.

Panoramic views are a special variant of perspective displays: the observer is located on or near the surface, and most often the view extends over a full circle. This visualization technique provides a useful extension to visibility maps for planning applications (Fig. 19.17). The transformations for panoramic displays and their construction have been described by Herzog et al. (1987) and Weibel and Herzog (1988).

Advanced visualization techniques and issues

The basic forms of perspective block diagrams may be extended in a number of ways to support interactive visual interpretation and analysis of surface data. Cartographic features (point, line or areal data) may be overlaid on the DTM surface, place name labels added, or transparent surfaces used to indicate elevations (e.g. of a planned reservoir). Additionally, 3-D objects (e.g. houses, subsurface structures) may be displayed in conjunction with the block diagram. Sample visualizations from a system for interactive display and analysis of DTMs (cf. L'Eplattenier 1987; Herzog et al. 1987) are shown in Plates 19.3, 19.4 and 19.5). A more general system for the visualization of geoscientific data (including meteorological space–time data) has been presented by Hibbard and Santek (1989).

The evolution of terrain display is gradually

Digital Terrain Modelling

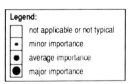

Fig. 19.18 Some DTM application domains and their functional requirements relative to digital terrain modelling.

moving towards more realistic renderings of DTMs. Examples of photorealistic scene rendering may be found in Musgrave, Kolb and Mace (1989); Kaneda *et al.* (1989) or Upstill (1990). Musgrave, Kolb and Mace (1989) present an efficient algorithm for ray tracing height fields such as elevation matrices. Ray tracing is a rendering technique that allows the modelling of illumination effects such as reflections, refraction, transparency and shadows. Kaneda *et al.* (1989) discuss a method of terrain visualization for environmental assessment: digitized aerial photographs are mapped onto the DTM, and planned objects (e.g. power stations) may be added into the perspective display for a montage.

Displays of terrain surfaces may also be animated (e.g. for flight simulation or computer-generated films). In animation, sequences of scene renderings are produced that correspond to frames of a film (by moving the viewing point). In flight simulation, abstraction of the terrain surface may be quite dramatic (to speed up computation for real-time display), while other animations provide more realism (e.g. Muller *et al.* 1988).

Visualization combines two processes: modelling and selecting relevant elements for representation (scene description); and displaying them effectively (scene rendering). For the second task, it is possible to profit from the steady progress in computer graphics: standardized rendering interfaces such as 'RenderMan' (Upstill 1990) will increasingly allow scene descriptions to be passed to a turn-key rendering system. Research in the GIS area thus will mainly have to focus on methods for generating appropriate scene descriptions, while rendering systems will take care of the actual display.

One of the issues related to scene description is that of cartographic generalization (Muller 1991 in this volume). As more and larger data sets are being handled it is becoming more urgent to be able to automate adaptation of the detail of DTM visualizations to the display scale. Generalization requires complex tasks such as feature recognition, simplification, and visualization. Its automation can be considered one of the most demanding problems of geoprocessing. A review of some approaches to surface generalization (as well as for generalization of 2-D elements) is given by Brassel and Weibel (1988); specific research is reported in Weibel (1989).

DTM APPLICATION: USING DIGITAL TERRAIN DATA

Due to the recent technological advances, terrain modelling systems of increasing complexity are being implemented which offer powerful solutions to applications. It is becoming feasible to create specific applications based on this core functionality. Practical use will then provide feedback for further enhancements of DTM concepts and techniques.

This final section summarizes the particular functional requirements of various application domains. Figure 19.18 represents an attempt to estimate the importance of individual DTM functions to some fields. Weights that have been assigned are intended to reflect relative importance and general traits rather than absolute and indisputable figures. Also, it should be mentioned that functional requirements are likely to change over time, as research and development proceeds and new applications emerge.

Many of the applications in spatial data handling do not require (or only rarely require) the use of digital terrain models. This is notably the case for cadastral mapping and utilities management (an area often termed 'automated mapping/facilities management' = AM/FM). On the other hand, a great number of applications do have a need for digital terrain modelling, most importantly those related to the management of natural resources. Five main application domains of DTMs may be distinguished: (1) surveying and photogrammetry; (2) civil engineering; (3) planning and resource management; (4) earth sciences; and (5) military applications. These fields differ in scope and importance, and they are not always clearly discernable. However, they all show particular characteristics in terms of functional requirements, professional background, and organizational structure. About one-third of all applications in these domains make use of digital terrain models or derived products at some point.

Surveying and photogrammetry

Surveying and photogrammetry is a relatively limited field with quite narrow functional requirements. The main purpose is to produce

DTMs for applications in other areas such as civil engineering or planning. Emphasis is on functions to generate high fidelity DTMs, evaluate their accuracy (numerically and visually), and generate high quality cartographic contours. Little analytical functionality is required. Typical applications include: survey or photogrammetric terrain data capture; data quality assessment; terrain data editing; orthophoto production; and topographic mapping.

Civil engineering

DTMs are used in civil engineering for applications such as road design, airfield design and earthwork calculations in site planning (e.g. dams, reservoirs and open-cast mining). Civil engineering is an important user of terrain modelling. Functional requirements, however, differ from those of other GIS applications: emphasis is on volumetric calculations and design functions, and data volumes are typically much smaller (i.e. often only a few thousand data elements).

Planning and resource management

Planning and resource management is one of the major application domains of DTMs. The field combines applications from a number of relatively diverse disciplines, such as environmental and urban planning, remote sensing, soil science, agriculture, forestry, meteorology and climatology – all disciplines that are centred around the management of natural resources. Typical applications include environmental impact studies; industrial site location; the geometric and radiometric correction of remote sensing images; support of image classification in remote sensing by DTM derivatives; soil erosion potential models; crop suitability studies; development of harvesting strategies; wind flow and pollution dispersion models; and many more. The diversity of applications within this domain necessitates a wide range of functionality: powerful tools for interpretation, flexible visualization procedures, functions for data capture and verification, and support of TIN as well as raster data structures are needed. Another characteristic of planning and resource management applications is that they require a close link between the terrain modelling system and the 2-D functions of the GIS software used – especially with respect to polygon, network, and raster data processing.

Earth sciences

Applications in the earth sciences – geology, geomorphology, hydrology, and glaciology – are treated as a separate group, although they share many similarities with other applications in natural resources management. They require specific functions for modelling and interpretation of terrain discontinuities (most importantly the drainage and divide network). Many of the uses of DTMs within this application domain need a concise representation of fluvial terrain discontinuities. Sample applications include: drainage basin monitoring (e.g. for flood and pollution control); hydrological runoff modelling; geomorphological simulation and classification (e.g. simulation of drainage basin development); geological interpretation and mapping.

Military applications

Military applications combine aspects of all the other application domains. Terrain is one of the most important components of the military environment at the local or regional scale. Military agencies are significant producers of DTMs, and thus put considerable weight on functions for terrain data capture (including stereo correlation of DTMs and automatic scan digitizing of contours). Military uses of DTMs include site planning operations similar to those in civil engineering. Terrain analysis for battlefield management involves tasks such as intervisibility analysis and vehicle trafficability analysis. Missile guidance and planning of communication networks (through intervisibility analysis) are other typical military uses of DTMs. Military applications also require advanced visualization functions such as photorealistic scene display and animation for flight simulation.

CONCLUSION

This chapter has sought to demonstrate the importance of Digital Terrain Models (DTMs) in many GIS applications. The discussion has outlined the scope of digital terrain modelling which encompasses the tasks of DTM generation; manipulation; interpretation; visualization; and application. Each of these processes has been examined with the discussion focusing on the relevant approaches adopted and algorithms used. At all stages, the need to combine mathematical and algorithmic approaches with environmental and, especially, geomorphological understanding has been highlighted.

In the early 1990s digital terrain modelling has reached the stage that some of its requirements have been satisfied. The agenda for the next few years includes the need for refinement of current techniques as well as the enlargement of their scope in order to handle increasingly complex DTMs. Developments in digital terrain modelling will be accelerated by general technological and scientific advances, and likely by synergy effects with parallel disciplines.

REFERENCES

Akima H (1978) A method of bivariate interpolation and smooth surface fitting for irregularly distributed data points. *ACM Transactions on Mathematical Software* **4** (2): 148–59

Apple Computer, Inc. (1987) *Human Interface Guidelines: the Apple Desktop Interface.* Addison-Wesley, Reading Massachusetts

Band L E (1986) Topographic partition of watersheds with digital elevation models. *Water Resources Research* **22** (1): 15–24

Band L E (1989) A terrain-based watershed information system. *Hydrological Processes* **3**: 151–62

Band L E, Wood E F (1988) Strategies for large-scale, distributed hydrologic simulation. *Applied Mathematics and Computation* **27**: 23–37

Barnard S T, Fischler M A (1982) Computational stereo. *ACM Computing Surveys* **14** (4): 553–72

Birkhoff G, Mansfield L (1974) Compatible triangular finite elements. *Journal of Mathematical Analysis and Applications* **47** (3): 531–53

Blais, J A R, Chapman M A, Lam W K (1986) Optimal interval sampling in theory and practice. *Proceedings of the 2nd International Symposium on Spatial Data Handling*. International Geographical Union, Columbus Ohio, pp. 185–92

Brassel K E (1974) A model for automatic hill-shading. *The American Cartographer* **1** (1): 15–27

Brassel K E, Weibel R (1988) A review and framework of automated map generalization. *International Journal of Geographical Information Systems* **2** (3): 229–44

Burrough P A (1986) *Principles of Geographical Information Systems for Land Resources Assessment.* Clarendon Press, Oxford

Buttenfield B P, Mackaness W A (1991) Visualization. In: Maguire D J, Goodchild M F, Rhind D W (eds.) *Geographical Information Systems; principles and applications.* Longman, London, pp. 427–43, Vol 1

Chen Z-T, Guevara J A (1987) Systematic selection of very important points (VIP) from digital terrain models for constructing triangular irregular networks. *Proceedings of AUTOCARTO 8.* ASPRS, Falls Church Virginia, pp. 50–6

Chrisman N R (1991) The error component in spatial data. In: Maguire D J, Goodchild M F, Rhind D W (eds.) *Geographical Information Systems: principles and applications.* Longman, London, pp. 165–74, Vol 1

Christensen A H J (1987) Fitting a triangulation to contour lines. *Proceedings of AUTOCARTO 8.* ASPRS, Falls Church Virginia, pp. 57–67

Clarke A L, Grün A, Loon J C (1982) The application of contour data for generating high fidelity grid digital elevation models. *Proceedings of AUTOCARTO 5.* ASPRS, Falls Church Virginia, pp. 213–22

Clarke K C (1988) Scale-based simulation of topographic relief. *The American Cartographer* **15** (2): 171–81

Day T, Muller J-P (1988) Quality assessment of digital elevation models produced by automatic stereo matchers from SPOT image pairs. *International Archives of Photogrammetry and Remote Sensing* **27** (B3): 148–59

De Floriani L, Falcidieno B, Pienovi C, Allen D, Nagy G (1986) A visibility-based model for terrain features. *Proceedings of the 2nd International Symposium on Spatial Data Handling.* International Geographical Union, Columbus Ohio, pp. 600–10

Dikau R (1989) The application of a digital relief model to landform analysis in geomorphology. In: Raper J F (ed.) *Three Dimensional Applications in Geographical Information Systems.* Taylor & Francis, London, pp. 51–77

Douglas D H (1986) Experiments to locate ridges and channels to create a new type of digital elevation model. *Cartographica* **23** (4): 29–61

Ebner H, Reinhardt W, Hössler R (1988) Generation, management and utilization of high fidelity digital terrain models. *International Archives of Photogrammetry and Remote Sensing* **27** (B11): III556–65

Edelsbrunner H (1987) *Algorithms for Computational Geometry.* Springer-Verlag, Heidelberg

Evans I S (1972) General geomorphometry, derivatives of altitude, and descriptive statistics. In: Chorley R J (ed.) *Spatial Analysis in Geomorphology.* Methuen, London, pp. 17–90

Evans I S (1979) *An integrated system of terrain analysis and slope mapping. Final report on DA-ERO-591-73-G0040: Statistical characterisation of altitude matrices by*

computer. Department of Geography, University of Durham

Evans I S (1980) An integrated system of terrain analysis and slope mapping. *Zeitschrift fur Geomorphologie (supplements)* **36**: 274–95

Eyton J R (1984) Raster contouring. *Geo-Processing* **2**: 221–42

Foley J D, van Dam A, Feiner S K, Hughes J F (1990) *Computer Graphics: Principles and Practice*, 2nd edn. Addison-Wesley, Reading Massachusetts

Fournier A, Fussel D, Carpenter L (1982) Computer rendering of stochastic models. *Communications of the ACM* **25** (6): 371–84

Gold C, Cormack S (1987) Spatially ordered networks and topographic reconstructions. *International Journal of Geographical Information Systems* **1** (2): 137–48

Gonzalez R C, Wintz P A (1987) *Digital Image Processing* 2nd edn. Addison-Wesley, Reading Massachusetts

Gottschalk H-J (1972) Die Generalisierung von Isolinien als Ergebnis der Generalisierung von Flèchen. *Zeitschrift für Vermessungswesen* **97** (11): 489–94

Griffin M W (1987) A rapid method for simulating three dimensional fluvial terrain. *Earth Surface Processes and Landforms* **12**: 31–8

Guibas L, Stolfi J (1985) Primitives for the manipulation of general subdivisions and the computation of Voronoi diagrams. *ACM Transactions on Graphics* **4** (2): 74–123

Hannah M J (1981) Error detection and correction in digital terrain models. *Photogrammetric Engineering and Remote Sensing* **47** (1): 63–9

Haralick R M, Shanmugam K, Dinstein I (1973) Textural features for image classification. *IEEE Transactions on Systems, Man, and Cybernetics* **SMC-3** (6): 610–21

Heller M (1986) Triangulation and interpolation of surfaces. In: Sieber R, Brassel K E (eds.) *A Selected Bibliography on Spatial Data Handling: data structures, generalization and three-dimensional mapping. Geoprocessing Series 6*. Department of Geography, University of Zurich, Zurich, pp. 36–45

Heller M (1990) Triangulation algorithms for adaptive terrain modeling. *Proceedings of the 4th International Symposium on Spatial Data Handling*. International Geographical Union, Columbus Ohio, pp. 163–74

Herzog A, L'Eplattenier R, Weibel R, Brassel K (1987) Experimental spatial data displays. *Proceedings of the 13th Conference of the International Cartographic Association*, Volume IV. ICA, Morelia, pp. 375–89

Hibbard W, Santek D (1989) Visualizing large data sets in the earth sciences. *IEEE Computer* **22** (8): 53–7

Hutchinson M F (1988) Calculation of hydrologically sound digital elevation models. *Proceedings of the 3rd International Symposium on Spatial Data Handling*. International Geographical Union, Columbus Ohio, pp. 117–33

Hutchinson M F (1989) A new procedure for gridding elevation and stream line data with automatic removal of spurious pits. *Journal of Hydrology* **106** (1/2): 211–32

Inaba K, Aumann G, Ebner H (1988) DTM generation from digital contour data using aspect information. *International Archives of Photogrammetry and Remote Sensing* **27** (B8): III101–10

Jarvis R S (1984) Topology of tree-like networks. In: Gaile G L, Willmott C J (eds.) *Spatial Statistics and Models*. D. Reidel, Dordrecht, pp. 271–91

Kaneda K, Kato F, Nakamae E, Nishita T (1989) Three dimensional terrain modeling and display for environmental assessment. *Computer Graphics (SIGGRAPH '89 Proceedings)* **23** (3): 207–14

Kelley A D, Malin M C, Nielson G M (1988) Terrain simulation using a model of stream erosion. *Computer Graphics (SIGGRAPH '88 Proceedings)* **22** (4): 263–8

Konecny G, Pape D (1981) Correlation techniques and devices. *Photogrammetric Engineering and Remote Sensing* **47** (3): 323–33

Köstli A, Sigle M (1986) The random access data structure of the DTM program SCOP. *International Archives of Photogrammetry and Remote Sensing* **26** (B4): 128–37

Lam S-N (1983) Spatial interpolation methods: a review. *The American Cartographer* **10** (2): 129–49

Lemmens M J P M (1988) A survey on stereo matching techniques. *International Archives of Photogrammetry and Remote Sensing* **27** (B8): V11–V23

L'Eplattenier R (1987) An interactive system for display and analysis of block diagrams. Unpublished MSc Thesis (in German). Department of Geography, University of Zurich, Zurich

Makarovic B (1973) Progressive sampling for digital terrain models. *ITC Journal* **1973** (3): 397–416

Makarovic, B (1977) Composite sampling for digital terrain models. *ITC Journal* **1977** (3): 406–33.

Makarovic B (1979) From progressive to composite sampling for digital terrain models. *Geo-Processing* **1**: 145–66

Makarovic B (1984) Structures for geo-information and their application in selective sampling for digital terrain models. *ITC Journal* **1984** (4): 285–95

Mandelbrot B B (1986) Self-affine fractal sets; parts I, II, and III. In: Pietronero L, Tosati E (eds.) *Fractals in Physics*. Elsevier North-Holland, Amsterdam, pp. 3–28

Mark D M (1975) Geomorphometric parameters: a review and evaluation. *Geografiska Annaler* **57A** (3–4): 165–77

Mark D M (1979) Phenomenon-based data structuring and digital terrain modeling. *Geo-Processing* **1**: 27–36

Mark D M (1984) Automated detection of drainage networks from digital elevation models. *Cartographica* **21**: 168–78

Mark D M (1987) Recursive algorithms for the analysis and display of digital elevation data. *Proceedings First Latin American Conference on Computers in Cartography, San José, Costa Rica*, pp. 375–97

Marks D, Dozier J, Frew J (1984) Automated basin delineation from digital elevation data. *Geo-Processing* **2**: 299–311

McCullagh M J (1981) Creation of smooth contours over irregularly distributed data using local surface patches. *Geographical Analysis* **13** (1): 52–63

McCullagh M J (1982) Mini/micro display of surface mapping and analysis techniques. *Cartographica* **19** (2): 136–44

McCullagh M J (1988) Terrain and surface modelling systems: theory and practice. *Photogrammetric Record* **12** (72): 747–79

McLaren R A, Kennie T J M (1989) Visualisation of digital terrain models: techniques and applications. In: Raper J F (ed.) *Three Dimensional Applications in Geographical Information Systems*. Taylor & Francis, London, pp. 79–98

Miller C L, Laflamme R A (1958) The digital terrain model – theory and application. *Photogrammetric Engineering* **24** (3): 433–42

Muller J-C (1991) Generalization of spatial databases. In: Maguire D J, Goodchild M F, Rhind D W (eds.) *Geographical Information Systems: principles and applications*. Longman, London, pp. 457–75, Vol 1

Muller J-P, Day T, Kolbusz J, Dalton M, Richards S, Pearson J C (1988) Visualization of topographic data using video animation. *International Archives of Photogrammetry and Remote Sensing* **27** (B4): 602–14

Musgrave F K, Kolb C E, Mace R S (1989) The synthesis and rendering of eroded fractal terrains. *Computer Graphics (SIGGRAPH '89 Proceedings)* **23** (3): 41–50

Nagao M, Mukai Y, Sugimura T, Ayabe K, Arai K, Nakazawa T (1988) A study of reducing abnormal elevations in automatic computation of elevations from satellite data. *International Archives of Photogrammetry and Remote Sensing* **27** (B4): 280–8

Newman W M, Sproull R F (1979) *Principles of Interactive Computer Graphics*, 2nd edn. McGraw-Hill, New York

O'Callaghan J F, Mark D M (1984) The extraction of drainage networks from digital elevation data. *Computer Vision, Graphics, and Image Processing* **28**: 323–44

Oswald H, Raetzsch H (1984) A system for generation and display of digital elevation models. *Geo-Processing* **2**: 197–218

Peucker T K (1972) Computer cartography. *Commission on College Geography Resource Paper 17*. Association of American Geographers, Washington DC

Peucker T K (1978) Data structures for digital terrain models: discussion and comparison. *Harvard Papers on Geographic Information Systems 5 (Proceedings First International Advanced Study Symposium on Topological Data Structures for Geographic Information Systems, held in 1977)*. 1–15

Peucker T K, Cochrane D (1974) Die Automation der Reliefdarstellung – Theorie und Praxis. *International Yearbook of Cartography* **XIV**: 128–39

Peucker T K, Douglas D H (1975) Detection of surface specific points by local parallel processing of discrete terrain elevation data. *Computer Graphics and Image Processing* **4**: 375–387

Peucker T K, Fowler R J, Little J J, Mark D M (1978) The triangulated irregular network. *Proceedings of the ASP Digital Terrain Models (DTM) Symposium*. American Society of Photogrammetry, Falls Church Virginia, pp. 516–40

Pike R J (1988) The geometric signature: quantifying landslide terrain types from digital elevation models. *Mathematical Geology* **20** (5): 491–510

Pike R J, Rozema W J (1975) Spectral analysis of landforms. *Annals of the Association of American Geographers* **65** (4): 499–516

Preparata F P, Shamos M I (1985) *Computational Geometry: an introduction*. Springer-Verlag, New York

Preusser A (1984) Computing contours by successive solution of quintic polynomial equations. *ACM Transactions on Mathematical Software* **10** (4): 463–72

Raper J F, Kelk B (1991) Three-dimensional GIS. In: Maguire D J, Goodchild M F, Rhind D W (eds.) *Geographical Information Systems: principles and applications*. Longman, London, pp. 299–317, Vol 1

Rogers D F (1985) *Procedural Elements for Computer Graphics*. McGraw-Hill, New York

Roo A P J de, Hazelhoff L (1988) Assessing surface runoff and soil erosion in watersheds using GIS technology. *Proceedings EUROCARTO 7, ITC Publication 8*. ITC, Enschede, pp. 172–83

Roy A G, Gravel G, Gauthier C (1987) Measuring the dimension of surfaces: a review and appraisal of different methods. *Proceedings of AUTOCARTO 8*. ASPRS, Falls Church Virginia, pp. 68–77

Schumaker L L (1976) Fitting surfaces to scattered data. In: Lorentz G G et al. (eds.) *Approximation Theory II*. Academic Press, New York, pp. 203–68

Schut G H (1976) Review of interpolation methods for digital terrain models. *The Canadian Surveyor* **30** (5): 389–412

Slama C C, Theurer C, Henriksen S W (1980) (eds.) *Manual of Photogrammetry*, 4th edn. American Society of Photogrammetry, Falls Church Virginia

Szelinski R, Terzopoulos D (1989) From splines to fractals. *Computer Graphics (SIGGRAPH '89 Proceedings)* **23** (3): 51–60

Upstill S (1990) *The RenderMan Companion: a programmer's guide to realistic computer graphics*. Addison-Wesley, Reading Massachusetts

Weibel R (1989) Concepts and experiments for the automation of relief generalisation. Unpublished PhD dissertation (in German). *Geoprocessing Series 15*, Zurich, Department of Geography, University of Zurich.

Weibel R, DeLotto J L (1988) Automated terrain classification for GIS modeling. *Proceedings of GIS/LIS '88*, Volume 2: ASPRS/ACSM, Falls Church Virginia, pp. 618–27

Weibel R, Heller M (1990) A framework for digital terrain modelling. *Proceedings of the 4th International Symposium on Spatial Data Handling.* International Geographical Union, Columbus Ohio, pp. 219–29

Weibel R, Herzog A (1988) Automatische Konstruktion panoramischer Ansichten aus digitalen Geländemodellen. *Nachrichten aus dem Karten- und Vermessungswesen Series* **I/100**: 49–84

Weibel R, Heller M, Herzog A, Brassel K (1987) Approaches to digital surface modeling. *Proceedings First Latin American Conference on Computers in Cartography, San José, Costa Rica*, pp. 143–63

Werner C (1988) Formal analysis of ridge and channel patterns in maturely eroded terrain. *Annals of the Association of American Geographers* **78** (2): 253–70

White D (1985) Relief modulated thematic mapping by computer. *The American Cartographer* **12** (1): 62–7

Willmott C J (1984) On the evaluation of model performance in physical geography. In: Gaile G L, Willmott C J (eds.) *Spatial Statistics and Models.* D. Reidel, Dordrecht, pp. 443–60

Yoeli P (1965) Analytical hill shading. *Surveying and Mapping* **25**: 573–9

Yoeli P (1967) Mechanisation in analytical hill-shading. *Cartographic Journal* **4**: 82–8

Yoeli P (1983) Shadowed contours with computer and plotter. *The American Cartographer* **10** (2): 101–10

Yoeli P (1985a) The making of intervisibility maps with computer and plotter. *Cartographica* **22** (3): 88–103

Yoeli P (1985b) Topographic relief depiction by hachures with computer and plotter. *Cartographic Journal* **22** (2): 111–24

Zoraster S, Davis D, Hugus M (1984) *Manual and Automated Line Generalization and Feature Displacement, ETL-Report ETL-0359 (plus ETL-0359–1).* US Army Engineer Topographic Laboratories, Fort Belvoir Virginia

Zyda M J (1988) A decomposable algorithm for contour surface display generation. *ACM Transactions on Graphics* **7** (2): 129–48

THREE-DIMENSIONAL GIS

J F RAPER AND B KELK

This chapter introduces and profiles three-dimensional (3-D) GIS which are differentiated from computer-aided design systems by the ability to represent complex geoscientific objects and apply volumetric spatial functions. Such 3-D GIS have grown rapidly to suit the needs of earth, atmospheric and ocean sciences, and are capable of using 2-D and 3-D spatially referenced data in a heterogeneous representation scheme. New forms of representation have emerged, based on 3-D vector and raster data structures, which can index spatial form and process, and support complex 3-D queries. In the future, the success of this new form of modelling depends on the quality of the model on which it is based, and the availability of 3-D data.

INTRODUCTION

For many GIS applications, a key assumption is that all spatial data handled are referenced to a 2-D Cartesian coordinate system. This convention restricts the scope for mapping the 'vertical' dimension over terrains or within the earth, oceans or atmosphere, since this third dimension must be converted to an attribute and expressed in 2-D as a line or zone with a constant value. Hence, following the considerable growth in GIS to meet the needs of digital mapping and of spatial database development (GIS World 1990), attention is now focusing on the design and implementation of 3-D GIS in a range of geoscientific application areas. Recent developments have been reported in the fields of oil exploration (Youngmann 1989), mining (Bak and Mill 1989), meteorology (Slingerland and Keen 1990), hydrogeology (Turner 1989), geological modelling (Kelk 1991), environmental monitoring (Smith and Paradis 1989), civil engineering (Petrie and Kennie 1990) and landscape architecture (Batten 1989).

Many of the recent developments referred to above have pioneered the use of new data structures to overcome the limitations of earlier (generally non-geoscientific) approaches to 3-D modelling.

While many 3-D modelling systems have been developed for high quality computer-aided design (CAD) (Requicha 1980) and graphic rendering of solid objects (Pixar 1988), these systems have limitations for geoscientific applications. Many such graphic modelling systems can only generate high quality visualizations of the features under study (Salmon and Slater 1987), which cannot be analysed or interrogated, while CAD systems have limited facilities for the management of complex geo-objects. However, with the simultaneous improvement in the price/performance ratio for hardware, the rapid development of software for realistic graphic display, and recent developments in the theory of 3-D spatial data structuring, many geoscientific modelling problems have become increasingly tractable using these systems.

The primary impetus behind the rapid improvement of hardware performance has been the development of new processor architectures (Goodchild 1991 in this volume; Franklin 1991 in this volume), in particular the Reduced Instruction Set Chip (RISC). This has brought compute performance to a point where the very large number of individual elements in a 3-D model can be analysed. For example, Bak and Mill (1989) showed the development of a mine model with more than

800 000 nodes which, following the construction of an index to the model, could easily be interactively manipulated on a workstation.

In addition to the developments of general purpose hardware, graphics accelerator chips have been developed to boost the performance of colour rendition and the floating point operations required to carry out interactive transformations in 3-D space. Since hundreds of thousands of 3-D transformations per second are used in 3-D applications (Flynn 1990), each involving hundreds of floating point calculations, the performance required is equal to tens of MFlops (millions of floating point operations per second). General purpose hardware must be augmented with special graphics processors to make this procedure interactive. Flynn (1990) estimates that the computational requirements for fully realistic 3-D graphic animation are 200 000 times more demanding than 2-D static graphics. Other hardware developments include immediate mode graphics to avoid the limitations of display list techniques, additional device buffers to allow refreshment of the buffer as the screen is built, and fast screen clears. Parallel hardware architectures also offer substantial performance improvements, although this hardware has more specific applications and requires associated software engineering.

Software developments have also helped to create the conditions for an expansion in 3-D modelling. Firstly, the movement towards UNIX as an operating system for high performance workstations has helped the process of standardization and reinforced the market development of fast hardware. Secondly, the creation of high quality computer graphics systems has been a key development (Salmon and Slater 1987). The growth of computer graphics led initially to 2-D graphics standards such as the Graphical Kernal System (GKS). This 2-D system (which is accepted as an ISO standard – ISO 7942) provides a library of machine-independent operations on screen representations. The X-Windows system developed at MIT is also widely used as a window management system on workstations, but is currently limited to 2-D. Basic 3-D modelling systems have developed through the definitions of standards such as the Programmers Hierarchical Integrated Graphics System (PHIGS); while PHIGS and PHIGS+ support the management of 3-D objects, they are based on (slower) display list graphics. However, PHIGS and X-Windows may be merged to form the PHIGS-Extended-to-X or PEX standard by the early 1990s. Currently, the state-of-the-art 3-D modelling systems are based on standards defined by commercially led consortia such as Renderman (Pixar 1988) and Silicon Graphics/IBM (Flynn 1990).

Other key developments in the field of graphic display include the routines for the visualization of 3-D models using perspective, hidden surface removal and depth cueing (see Fig. 20.1), along with the transformations needed for model manipulation through interactive viewpoint change (McLaren and Kennie 1989). Software for the realistic rendering of colour and shading also now permits the use of 24-bit colour schemes with a palette of 16.8 million colours as well as anti-aliasing techniques and lighting effects.

Fig. 20.1 Surface model for terrain in the Telford area, England.

Finally, it is important to note that the methodology of 3-D modelling has developed separately in a variety of different fields. A significant role has been played by the development of CAD applications, such as the EMS software from Intergraph (Kelk and Challen 1989), but solid modelling has also been pioneered in cinematic animation, using systems such as Renderman (Pixar 1988). Other developments have originated in 'scientific visualization' within crystallography, high energy physics, medicine (Gargantine 1991) and fluid dynamics (Harig 1990) where images of objects such as body organs have been built using the well known characteristics of these objects. Solid modelling has also become strongly developed in architectural planning and landscape design (Turnbull, McAulay and McLaren 1990).

However, typical algorithms for the visualization of solids assume valid, spatially unique and unambiguous solids. This kind of representation is ideal for visualizing molecular structures, engineering parts or architecture since establishing the primitives, solid geometry or bounding edges is usually straightforward. However, the geometrical, structural and resolution complexity of geoscientific data sets usually makes this approach difficult to apply in the modelling of geology, geomorphology, ocean or atmosphere (see Plate 20.1). These data are not easily modelled using simple primitives or algorithms and have required extensions to spatial theory (Raper 1990; Frank & Buyong 1991).

This chapter is composed of four main sections following this introduction. The next section discusses the dimensionality of spatial data and this is followed by sections discussing the role of surfaces in 3-D modelling, solid modelling in the geosciences, and the process of 3-D model development.

DIMENSIONALITY OF SPATIAL DATA

Geoscientific spatial data can be represented in two clearly distinct Euclidean dimensional contexts:

- 2-D: a spatial object or region which is defined in 2-D space by measurements on axes x, y;
- 3-D: a spatial object or domain extending through 3-D space defined by axes x, y, z.

The use of a 2-D representation has generally been to delineate 'objects in the plane' or 'fields of observations' (Goodchild 1990), specifically the mapping of spatial pattern and extent. Types of 2-D spatial objects or fields and the operations which can be carried out on them are considered at length in texts such as Burrough (1986) and Aronoff (1989) and need no elaboration here. Typical examples of such spatial objects would be land parcels, coastlines or fire hydrants which are readily handled in a GIS with an x,y coordinate system. It should be noted that most commercially available GIS are only designed to handle 2-D spatial data: some systems achieve limited 3-D capabilities for surface modelling by assigning an attribute for z values (such as elevation) to a set of x,y locations. Here only the x,y locations are stored within the spatial indexing system and the z value is defined as a pseudo-attribute. This involves making the assumption that it is only necessary to store a single z value for each x,y location, that is, the surface defined is not overfolded (Weibel and Heller 1991 in this volume). In practice this has been an acceptable limitation on the representation of surfaces.

However, many forms of geoscientific analysis seek to collect data about spatial objects and domains such as features of the solid earth (e.g. aquifers), oceans (e.g. currents) or atmosphere (e.g. weather fronts), which fill or enclose 3-D space. A complete representation of these phenomena requires the definition of each location known within an x,y,z coordinate system. This fully 3-D system allows a direct analogy between the real space and a simulated space to be established in the model. However, it also requires 3-D forms of spatial indexing which are much more difficult to create and manage than the existing 2-D systems (Raper 1989a).

Note that such spatial objects or domains can be described by any number of attributes. However, these are always expressed as descriptions of x,y,z locations, since these are the cardinal spatial dimensions. Time can be considered a further dimension, but must be considered qualitatively different, as Hazelton, Leahy and Williamson (1990) show, since time is not generally measured in the same units. Typically, therefore, evolving systems are represented by a sequence of 3-D models, although Hazelton, Leaky and Williamson (1990) show how a 4-D representation of space-time can be constructed where all units are light-seconds. In general, 3-D geoscientific models are also based on precise (though not necessarily accurate) representations rather than fuzzy ones. Due to the difficulty of visualizing fuzzy 3-D models (x-ish, y-ish, z-ish coordinates), a series of models reflecting different estimates is usually constructed, although some fuzziness can be displayed by the use of transparency to blur the edges of geo-objects (Flynn 1990).

However, these two classes of spatial data *representation* (2-D, 3-D) are also associated with sets of operations which can be carried out on each set of data types supported. For example, volume cannot be established in all situations where solid objects are represented in 2-D, due to the inability of the representation to handle multiple z values for a single x,y location in the plane. At present 3-D spatial operations are poorly understood, as there are few implemented systems which work with 3-D representations, although considerable research into appropriate algorithms is presently under way. Hence, at present many applications are being moved to 3-D representations in order to exploit the availability of these new 3-D operations.

One of the major problems for the development of true 3-D models is that generally they must still be imaged on semi-flat cathode ray tube screens. Although Welch (1990) reports the use of a 3-D stereo visualization system based on 120 Hz circularly polarized images, the majority of 3-D models are still portrayed in 2-D. This has given rise to a variety of forms of *visualization* for 2-D and 3-D representations which are discussed below.

2-D visualization

A 2-D visualization is a graph or raster where the z-value defining a surface is projected on to a 2-D plane and 0-D, 1-D and 2-D objects can be displayed (Fig. 20.2). Since z is usually a continuously varying value on the ratio scale, the value of z is usually grouped into a class and the class boundaries shown. This can be achieved by shading z-value classes or labelling the isolines which divide them. This is the preferred technique for the display of a 3-D spatial object such as a terrain on a 2-D map. Multiple z-values for a given location cannot be handled: if this situation occurs in some locations the isolines are often simply omitted.

2.5-D visualization

A 2.5-D visualization is an isometric model where the z attribute associated with an x,y location is

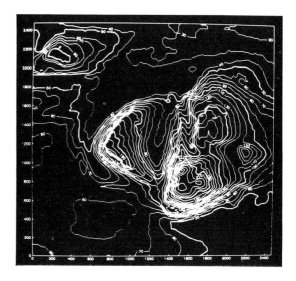

Fig. 20.2 A 2-D isoline map of Arthur's Seat, Edinburgh, Scotland.

projected onto an x,y,z coordinate reference system and all three axes displayed (Fig. 20.3). This operation transforms the map of z attributes for an x,y position, so that each z attribute defines a position on the z axis, creating a surface with no thickness visualized within 3-D space. This approach simulates the view that would be seen by a human observer from a point within the 3-D space. However, note that a 2.5-D *visualization* of a 2-D *representation* is only the display of a single-valued surface: multiple z-values cannot be handled for a single x,y point except by stacking a number of surfaces in the same 3-D space. This kind of visualization only contains information about the described surface, the state of a 3-D spatial object at a plane or interface or for a single observation cycle. Hence, a 2.5-D visualization is still limited by the basis of a 2-D representation.

3-D visualization

A true 3-D visualization is a full 3-D solid model where many x,y,z observations are structured into a solid structure and visualized in perspective view, complete with multiple occurrences of z. This kind of view is a precise analogue for the physical space inhabited by human observers, and allows the full specification of 3-D operations on the observed

Fig. 20.3 A 2.5-D isometric model of Arthur's Seat, Edinburgh, Scotland.

phenomena within the limits of the geometrical model employed (Plate 20.2).

Within contemporary geoscientific analysis only 2-D and 2.5-D *visualizations* of 3-D *representations* of reality are in common use, specifically, surfaces visualized in 3-D space. For such visualizations, 2.5-D techniques offer the opportunity to view the model, and are popular since they are calculated easily and match certain application requirements well. For example, surfaces can often be considered to be approximate analogues for sedimentary strata, since they frequently have a high area to thickness ratio, and the compression of the third dimension to zero may not cause the loss of significant information. Display of surfaces in 2.5-D may also be the appropriate visualization for interfaces such as water tables. However, these objects can only be handled where there are no multiple occurrences of z-values for any given x,y: in practice, therefore, 2.5-D visualization is limited to spatial objects with a planar continuity, although this assumption holds true for almost all terrains. It is also conventional for the z axis to be parallel to the action of gravitational forces, although this axis may be arbitrarily defined.

Note, however, that although several adjacent surfaces can be used to show multiple values of z for given locations in 2.5-D visualizations, this situation has several shortcomings for analysis. In particular, if the surfaces intersect they must be topologically connected, and it is still difficult to extract the true 3-D properties of solid spatial objects. Thus, to overcome these problems and to handle solid 3-D objects will require a 3-D visualization and a true 3-D representation scheme. This is particularly appropriate for the visualization of complex geo-objects where solid thresholding of internal property variance may be required, and where 3-D spatial operations are needed to characterize 3-D spatial objects.

SURFACE MODELLING IN 3-D

The creation of surfaces is a widespread form of modelling in the geosciences, and a wide range of application software is available to create 2.5-D visualizations. As discussed in the previous section the 2.5-D surface display can only be used to visualize a 3-D representation of reality within certain limits. For example, multiple z-values cannot be displayed. However, geometrically, surfaces may be thought of as complex spatial objects whose spatial configuration is not limited by the constraints of a 2.5-D visualization. Surfaces are developed by spatially structuring point- or line-based z-value data using raster (grid based) or vector (triangulated) techniques: therefore, surfaces can be used in a 3-D representation as a means of bounding 3-D space. This can be achieved by using limited 2.5-D visualization data or by developing new ways to represent surfaces in 3-D space. In this chapter the study of surfaces is confined to their use in 3-D modelling: the generation of 2.5-D surfaces and the storage of digital elevation models (DEMs) is considered extensively in Weibel and Heller (1991 in this volume).

While 2.5-D surface visualizations cannot handle multiple z-values, and can only partition space and not enclose it, they fulfil a useful role as basic building blocks or constraints in solid models. These links can be implied as in the case of plotting together multiple surfaces within a common spatial frame: this can allow the computation of simple solid characteristics such as the volume vertically between any two surfaces. These links can also be made by the geometrical connection of surfaces (Fig. 20.4): Christiansen and Sederberg (1978) described an algorithm for connecting isolines describing a surface together to form a solid.

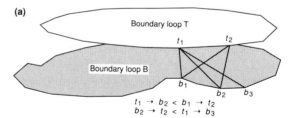

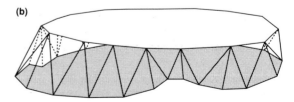

Fig. 20.4 An example of two planar, parallel isoline loops connected to form a triangulated solid: (a) the shortest span method of surface triangulation; (b) surface triangulation of two boundary layers.

However, the development of new forms of representation for surfaces has produced new approaches unconstrained by 2.5-D limitations. Such an approach described by Fisher and Wales (1991) has been the use of non-uniform rational B-splines (NURBS) to generate surfaces in hydrocarbon exploration. NURBS are piecewise parametric polynomial functions which can be used to model complex surfaces. These functions fit the data exactly, but create a smooth surface form, subject to local control by the manipulation of the poles associated with each segment of the surface (Fig. 20.5). NURBS can handle overfolds in a surface: however, solids must still be assembled from constituent surfaces. The procedure to model a geological surface described by Fisher and Wales involved picking the tops of geological formations (identified by the geologist) and interpolating 2-D isoline maps honouring all the data points using NURBS techniques. These isoline maps were then converted into a set of surface planes incorporating structural information such as faults, which were then connected to form a solid.

Kelk and Challen (1989) describe an application of the NURBS technique using Intergraph's EMS package to connect two limbs of an overfold in South Wales Coal Measures. In this case the use of NURBS allowed them to model the form of the fold connection from knowledge of the regional structure. The process was interactive allowing them to view four screen windows, one each for x, y and z perspectives and one 2.5-D view. Much of the work in this case was eased by rotating the surfaces to look along the strike of the folds when making the actual connection. Once connected, the complete new surface was incorporated into the structure of the two original folds (Fig. 20.6).

The value of surfaces in 3-D models is also demonstrated when they are used as estimators of general spatial process behaviour. Surfaces can be used to filter or transmit spatial processes: thus, one set of surface characteristics such as terrain, can be used to characterize other process surfaces such as runoff characteristics. 'Soft' data (indicative of behaviour) expressed in surface z_1 can be used as a template or predictor of specific local behaviour in surface z_2: surface z_1 can then be discarded. A more sophisticated procedure capable of relating complex behaviour of one surface to another is co-kriging (Leenaers, Burrough and Okx 1989; Burrough 1991

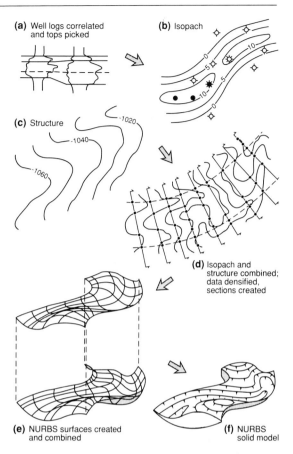

Fig. 20.5 The procedure for the creation of a NURBS solid model.

in this volume). When one variable is spatially dependent on another they are described as co-regionalized. By describing the form of the relationship and its variance it is possible to predict more accurately the value of the spatially dependent property at locations where it has not been measured. Leenaers, Burrough and Okx (1989) applied this technique to the modelling of lead deposition across a floodplain where the lead concentrations were expensive to sample but the floodplain elevations were easily surveyed. The co-regionalization of these two variables was found to be dependent on floodplain inundation frequency.

The development of surfaces can also be made completely interactive as described by Schaeben (1989) and Auerbach and Schaeben (1990). In this study, scattered points are triangulated under controlled conditions with the user placing the initial vertices of a Delaunay triangulation and inserting polylines which define the axis of any

Fig. 20.6 A view of the two original limbs of the fold structure now connected by the overfold.

geological features influencing the structure of the study area. The surface is then constructed using bivariate quadratic simplicial B-splines to create a smooth surface, although directional constraints can be defined. In order to make the surface representation modifiable the coefficients of the splines are visualized as geometrical points which can be manipulated to control the shape of the surface. This procedure can be used to create multiple surfaces which are then fastened together to create a full solid model.

Interactive surface design is also available within the GOCAD system (Mallet 1991) which uses a triangulated irregular network (TIN) to model a surface. GOCAD allows the creation of triangles interactively in a CAD system or algorithmically by conversion of surfaces interpolated from a grid into a triangulated form. The GOCAD TIN model can handle overfolds since the triangulation is constructed by iteratively examining a 3-D grid of cells for the entrance and exit points of triangular facets defining the boundary conditions for the surface. GOCAD can also incorporate fuzzy constraints into the specification of nodes and vectors in the TIN. The user interface to the GOCAD system is based on the use of 'cameras' which view the 3-D domain from any angle: transformation of the bounding surfaces can take place within these windows.

One particular characteristic of geological surfaces is the likely presence of faults which may lead to 'steps' in surfaces. The steps may be associated with vertical and lateral movement which may juxtapose different materials across the fault. Hence when creating surfaces to model solid geology it is necessary to prevent interpolation across a fault and to control interpolation around the ends of faults where they may plunge below the surface. Rüber (1989) has developed a surface interpolation system to support such constraints based on a series of modules: BILDED to support data capture from digitizers and grid files; SEISCO to convert depth to seismic travel time for heterogeneous seismic and geological data sets; DFAULT to allow the interactive definition of fault patterns and plane angles; FLINT to interpolate the fault-constrained surface; and INSECT to calculate intersections between interpolated surfaces and fault planes.

Finally, it should be noted that surfaces can also be generated as the result of a spatial query on a solid when defined either in terms of form, orientation or position in the model. Extractions of surfaces from solids can be useful when attempting to locate an interface which is important as a boundary of some kind. Hence surfaces can be seen to be important geometrical constructs whether 2.5-D or full 3-D techniques are used.

SOLID MODELLING IN 3-D GIS

Much of the early experience of solid modelling has been gained in the computer-aided drawing (CAD) field as described by Requicha (1980) and Meier (1986) who identified several distinct groups of 3-D representation techniques:

1. *Sweep representation* (*SR*): the sweep technique represents an object by sweeping a defined area or volume along a defined trajectory.

2. *Primitive instancing* (*PI*): this represents an object by a set of pre-defined shapes, or mathematical primitives, which are positioned in 3-D space without intersection. An instance of a primitive is defined by a set of numeric values where each value is a parameter in the mathematical equation describing the primitive shape.

3. *Constructive solid geometry* (*CSG*): this technique represents an object by combining primitive point sets using Boolean operations (union, intersection and difference).

4. *Boundary representation* (*BR*): this technique defines an object by its bounding surface. The latter can be represented as a set of coordinates and their connectivity.

5. *Spatial occupancy enumeration* (*SOE*): this represents an object by the union of a set of cells where the cell is a primitive shape which can be either regular or irregular. Cells are adjacent, connected and do not intersect.

These representations form a set of techniques to create 3-D models: Fig. 20.7 shows a typology of the representations commonly used in the geosciences. The suitability of one or other of these representations depends on the characteristics of the data set, the operations which it is desirable to carry out and the specific form of spatial indexing employed.

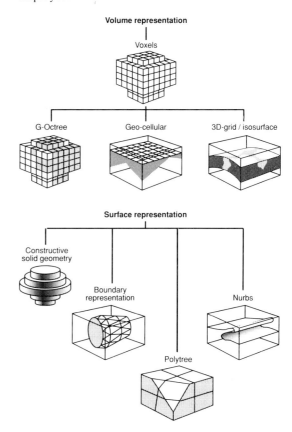

Fig. 20.7 3-D representations used in the geosciences.

Sampling

The first step in the solid modelling process is collection of appropriate measurements in the study domain consisting of attribute data for x,y,z locations which meet a specified set of criteria. The collection of these measurements is, however, a sampling exercise and in the subsequent modelling these measurements should be considered as the spatial representation of the probability that geo-object(s) exist in a particular location and configuration. Since many geo-objects have poorly known characteristics, the correct sampling frame (random or structured) and the sampling density can often not be determined in advance.

Often the type of sampling adopted is governed by economic or project-related, rather than geoscientific, criteria. For example, the sampling of ground conditions for a new road is often constrained to the centreline of the carriageway, and the automated estimation of surface heights in a photogrammetric survey generates a regular grid of values. Typical methods of obtaining geoscientific samples are seismic profiling, overflights, weather balloons, probes, systematic survey and boreholes. However, there are several drawbacks associated with point sampling of a geo-object using vertical sampling lines through a domain. First, it can be very difficult to distinguish between the multiple occurrence of a similar feature down a line and the repeated occurrence of a single object through folding or faulting. Secondly, the continuity between any two occurrences of the boundary of a geo-object taken from two neighbouring point samples cannot be assumed to be simple or predictable.

Another sampling difficulty associated with 3-D geo-objects arises in the case of dynamic phenomena, such as water movement in aquifers (Turner 1989) and oil flow through hydrocarbon reservoirs, or in evolutionary systems such as coastal sedimentary environments. It may be necessary to sample these data sets repeatedly over time which will generate multiple values of attributes for an x,y,z position. Burns (1988, 1990) described a system of 'structured vector fields' to manage x,y,z,t data (where t is time), and reported an application of the technique in the development of a geothermal production field northeast of San Francisco, California. The values of attributes in an x,y,z,t framework may also change over time according to positive process feedback. For example, the greater accumulations on a coastal salt marsh near a major creek (French 1989), or the drawdown of a piezometric surface near a well, may provide further sampling difficulties.

The results of the sampling process are crucial determinants of the forms of representation which are available. If the sampling procedure produced a regular grid of x,y,z point values or series of parallel lines, then using a regular tessellation of volume elements (voxels) involves no further operations. If the sampling has produced non-regular patterns of x,y,z points or polylines then some form of connection must be made among these elements, and a form of structuring must be selected. In this case objects must be formed from the points and are usually constructed using lines and polygons (to create volygons).

Representation and structuring

The approaches to 3-D representation and structuring of geo-objects can be categorized as raster, vector and function based: Jones (1989) gives a good summary of the main data structures available. The raster solutions to 3-D data representation are mostly based around the voxel as a basic unit. Optimization of this form of representation for complex geo-objects requires the use of spatial indexing systems to eliminate redundant storage when necessary. The simplest form of indexing for such data is a complete 3-D layer- and row-ordered raster, with each voxel stored explicitly and associated with attribute values. These models have been built by many oil exploration and reservoir management companies, for example by Shell (the MONARCH system) and by Exxon (the GEOSET system: Jones (1988)). These models can be displayed for any range of attribute values and offer high quality visualizations. However, their performance in queries and spatial analysis, such as connectivity tracing, can be poor.

These 3-D sets of voxels can be indexed effectively in a variety of ways, including 3-D run encoding (Mark and Cebrian 1986) where all the voxels are visited by, for example the Morton Order, although this technique can develop huge demands for storage. A more sophisticated technique is the 3-D equivalent of the quadtree called the octree (Kavouras and Masry 1987; Bak and Mill 1989) which recursively divides space into eight until any part of the subdivision is empty (outside the object) or full (inside the object), with the process continuing to a pre-determined level of resolution. The advantage of this form of indexing is the very efficient conduct of Boolean operations on geo-objects.

A modified version of the octree called the polytree has been proposed by Carlbom (1987) which identifies the logical content of each voxel, that is whether full or empty, or a vertex, edge or surface cell of the geo-object. This scheme has the advantage of a solid representation amenable to rapid Boolean operations for 3-D spatial operations, while also identifying the nature of the individual voxel, giving a pseudo object representation.

Various hybrid forms of representation utilizing both raster and vector concepts have recently been proposed which use or convert observations in x,y,z coordinate space to a 3-D raster and then form a vector-type representation from it. Smith and Paradis (1989) outlined an approach which uses a minimum tension interpolation algorithm to calculate the values of a 3-D phenomenon (sampled non-regularly) at the intersections of a gridded bounding block. The system then forms 'iso-surfaces' using a triangulated vector data structure (see Fig. 20.10), which are used to partition the 3-D grid by attribute value. Other design elements such as faulting and structural features with a known form (such as a salt dome) can also be added to the model. This design incorporates elements of both raster- and vector-based structuring, and the system can choose whichever structuring is most appropriate for a particular spatial query operation. This system forms the basis for the commercially available Interactive Volume Modelling (IVM) system from Dynamic Graphics.

Denver and Phillips (1990) show how known geological structure can be used to define bedding planes and faults, which can each be represented by 2.5-D grid mesh surfaces, where the cells in the mesh are shaded for geological composition. Composition shaded cells on the surface can then be used to define solid voxels which may fill each geological unit if desired. This system is the basis of the commercially available Stratamodel system. The advantage of these two hybrid systems is that they offer the facility to convert between space-bounding vector techniques and space-filling raster methods.

In the field of vector data structuring for geo-objects the systems used most commonly employ 3-D boundary representations ('B-reps') for the indexing of geometrical data. Attribute data can then be linked to this structure using an appropriate geo-relational system, although the processing overheads can be high (Molenaar 1990; Fritsch 1990). This kind of structure also requires the acceptance of planar enforcement as an organizing principle, that is, no domains or objects can overlap.

The simplest 3-D B-rep is a triangulated irregular network (TIN). Carlson (1987) described the theoretical basis for a 3-D TIN system based on simplicial complexes: a 0-simplex is equivalent to a point, 1-simplex to a line, 2-simplex to an area and 3-simplex to a volume. This structure is relatively easy to transform and visualize, but is very difficult to create. This is because 3-D geometry is poorly understood, and if the problem is reduced to the connection of 2-D nodes by projecting the points on to a plane, multiple values are likely. Assumptions necessary for 3-D triangulations include the need to ensure that volumes do not intersect except at edges, and that all the objects defined are tetrahedrons which are mutually disjunct.

Few, if any, systems using this full 3-D form of representation have been implemented. Most implemented systems fasten together surfaces defined in x,y or x,z space to avoid the problems of 3-D polygon structuring. The Lynx mine modelling system uses this technique to build 3-D objects by connecting geological sections to make volumetric 'components'. In order to define the 'components' each section is projected to a mid-plane, where the geological transitions are resolved. Note that Lynx also allows the creation of a voxel model for all the 3-D components identified oriented at any angle appropriate to the 3-D structure of the ore body (Clark, Houlding and Stoakes 1990).

Another 3-D system which uses a constructive framework for 3-D vector modelling is IREX (Lasseter 1990). IREX allows the display and interconnection of boreholes and their lithological characteristics within a visualization composed of a 3-D cuboid. The system can also show segments of 2.5-D surface and associated faults along with seismic sections available within the study area. IREX offers an environment where geoscientists can assemble structures from diverse forms of data using CAD-like tools: however, the tools embrace many of the complex data types which the geoscientist uses.

Function-based representations are generally based on piecewise parametric polynomial functions, such as NURBS (Fisher and Wales 1991), which have robust properties. These functions can structure points or primitive geometrical forms into a single exact 3-D model by assembly of surface components. Transformations and analysis of this representation are rapid and efficient, however, as a representation it enforces a continuity of curvature between known points: this is an acceptable assumption for many, but not all, geoscientific applications.

The choice of data structures will constrain the scope of the modelling by defining the 3-D functionality available. It is common for the coordinates of a geo-object of interest to be determined and the visualization created each time a model is made, since true 3-D representation of geoscience data has not hitherto been possible. However, now that 3-D spatial structuring is becoming more common, the alternatives of re-computing a new model or storing a 3-D representation will arise. As processing power becomes cheaper per unit, the choice between the alternatives of re-computing and full 3-D representation and structuring of the data will be determined by the application involved and the storage space available. Thus, representation is likely to become the rule when the resources consumed in the model creation process justify the retention of the model and its addition to a 3-D database.

Spatial functions

The keys to efficient access and use of 3-D geoscientific data, however structured, are the spatial functions or queries supported. It is possible to define sets of 3-D spatial functions in relation to several different systems of user conceptualization and system representation. Previous work on the definition of spatial functions has originated in diverse fields. Work in cognitive science by Johnson (1987), discussed by Mark (1989), has led to the definition of a class of spatial functions based around human metaphors for space known as 'image schemata'. Other work in linguistics (such as Talmy 1988) has emphasized the role of spatial prepositions, topology, viewpoint and distribution of attention as expressed through the structure of language used in spatial description. These approaches have confirmed the role of perception and understanding in the conceptualization of spatial relations in 2-D and 3-D, and hence the framing of spatial queries by the user of the system.

Work on spatial representation in 2-D has generated a more formal range of spatial functions, such as simple visualization properties (Freeman 1975), and complete sets of topological relationships between objects (Pullar and Egenhofer 1988). A set of functions for 3-D modelling of geoscientific data was proposed by Raper (1990) to formalize spatial functions without defining representation. Figure 20.8 shows a series of simple illustrations of the operation of these functions on a single object, and Table 20.1 gives an indication of the relative performance of raster and vector data structures across all these functions.

Table 20.1 shows in outline terms how raster and vector spatial structuring affects the speed of operation of the 3-D spatial functions. The relative merits of integral structuring and re-computation of the model also vary according to the type of data structure used. Note also that the accuracy of the representation must not exceed the real world determinacy of the data set. It is, therefore, suggested that a complete analysis of the available data and expected queries is the optimum way to decide on the type of representation which is appropriate for each model. The functionality of existing commercial systems can also be evaluated using this approach. Few if any of these 'solid' functions have yet been fully implemented for real geoscience data sets with all their inherent complexity, and so only the theoretical performance of these queries is considered in the establishment of Table 20.1 (although see Bak and Mill 1989 for some estimates of octree performance in spatial functions).

MODEL DEVELOPMENT IN 3-D

The application of these techniques of representation is crucially dependent on the identification or identity of the geo-objects of interest. While in many modelling environments the data and their spatial configuration are defined by external factors or customary practice, the process of conceptualization which precedes the representation of a model is a crucial stage in 3-D model development (Goodchild 1991). Raper (1990) suggested that the process of discretization of the perceived reality leads to the creation of a 'conceptual set' in 3-D: the structuring of the set of tuples x,y,z,p (where p is an attribute at time t)

Three-dimensional GIS

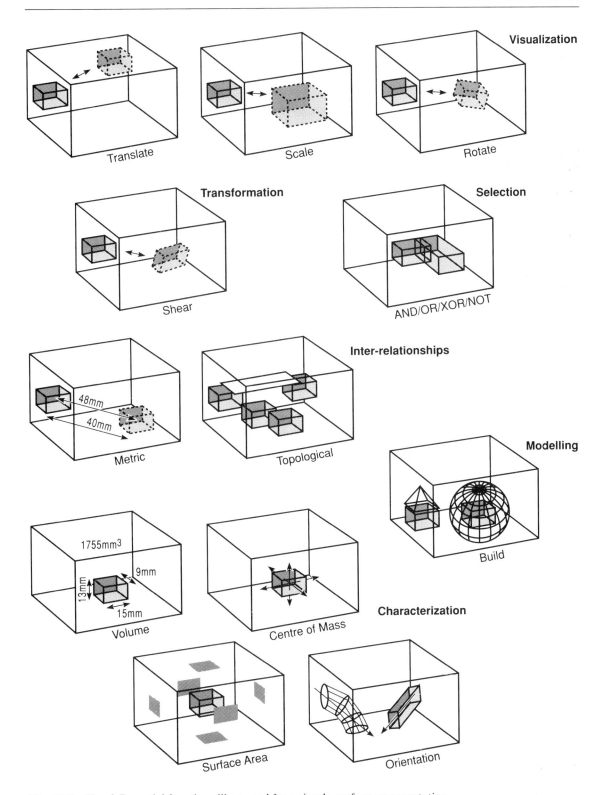

Fig. 20.8 Key 3-D spatial functions illustrated for a simple surface representation.

Table 20.1 Generic spatial functions in 3-D spatial modelling and their effectiveness under different 3-D data structures.

Spatial Function	Raster	Vector
Visualization		
Translate	slower	fast
Rotate	slower	fast
Scale	slower	fast
Reflect	slower	fast
Transformation		
Shear	slower	fast
Characterization		
Volume	fast	slower
Surface area	fast	fast
Centre of mass	fast	slower
Orientation	slow	fast
Selection		
AND	fast	slower
OR	fast	slower
XOR	fast	slower
NOT	fast	slower
Topological relations		
Separation	fast	fast
Adjacency	fast	fast
Modelling		
Build (axial or bounding)	fast	slow

associated with the conceptual set has a vital role in the representation choices made later.

The process of discretization (or data modelling) begins with the identification of structure in reality and is deeply embedded in practice and 'experience'. This step is normally followed by measurement of a number of parameters associated with the 'structure'. The observations on the 'suggestive' parameters are usually made with reference to a 3-D coordinate system which acts as a geometrical frame for the located tuples x,y,z,p. Perhaps two main kinds of approaches can be identified:

1. *Device exploratory*: in this case the measurement technology defines the geometrical arrangement of the observed tuples, and there is no search for an *a priori* object. Thus, boreholes impose a linear structure on the measurements, characterizing a regular sequence of points downhole, and a photogrammetric survey of a terrain or section will usually generate a grid of measurements over the visual field. However, a survey of the positions of tracer pebbles over a channel bar will be governed by hydraulic processes and recovery factors, and will generate a spatially non-regular set of observed tuples. In this process the tuples recorded only need have the means of collection or selection in common.

2. *Object exploratory*: in this case the search for an *a priori* object defines the geometrical arrangement of the observed tuples. The located tuples identified by the combination of 'suggestive' parameters form a spatial cluster of arbitrary configuration. In this process the tuples recorded may have a distinct spatial structure.

When the 'object' can be identified by a single key parameter and is known to exist in a discrete form from knowledge of the domain (e.g. mine access, destructive examination) then the spatial object can be termed 'sampling limited' (Raper 1989b). In this case the discretization proceeds by using the sampling theorem to create a parsimonious description of the object from selective observations. An example would be a perched aquifer, or a salt dome or a fault-limited block (Fig. 20.9).

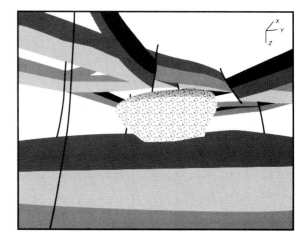

Fig. 20.9 A sampling limited geo-object: a salt dome and associated faulting modelled with IREX.

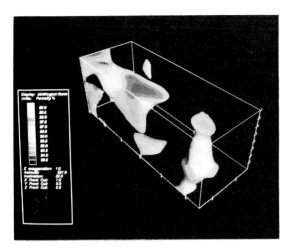

Fig. 20.10 Definition-limited objects: an IVM model of high porosity zones in a destructively tested limestone block.

When the object is transient or part of a continuum (e.g. a temperature field), or exists only as a spatially clustered set of observed tuples defined by a group of 'suggestive' parameters, then the spatial object can be described as 'definition limited (Raper 1989b). In this case the discretization proceeds by assembling a set of 'suggestive' parameters and searching for locations matching this *a priori* description. An example of a definition-limited object would be a plume of pollutants in the atmosphere or ocean defined by a physical threshold, or a sedimentary facies. Often the boundaries or conditions for selection of objects are 'picks' made on the basis of an interpretation of raw data (Fig. 20.10).

Although the set of tuples selected during the data collection stage can be structured in a variety of ways, there are probably only two major strategies:

1. *Domain partition*: use of the selected tuples to subdivide the whole 3-D domain into regular or non-regular constituent units.
2. *Entity construction*: use of the selected tuples to define entities within 3-D space using basic geometrical elements.

These two structuring strategies control the set of spatial functions available for the analysis of a model: they do not necessarily define the form of representation that should be chosen. In the main, however, domain partition leads to a raster type representation and entity construction leads to the use of vector or function type representations.

With the relative paucity of information often available to carry out such definition limited 3-D spatial modelling, the importance of the conceptual data model used in the analysis increases. This is because the geo-object itself is usually defined by the sampling or selection of parameters established by the data model. This data modelling process ought to be supported by knowledge about the geoscientific domain and associated processes (Raper 1988). For example, Kelk (1991) identified a number of characteristic geological data constraints which provided support for this exercise:

- Geological discontinuities (e.g. fault types)
- Regional structure (e.g. dip/strike and fold patterns)
- Sedimentation (e.g. fan systems)
- Volcanic (e.g. plutonic history)
- Process environment (e.g. glacial weathering).

The use of vertical profile models in sedimentary geology by such workers as Bouma and Allen has demonstrated that there is significant information content within sedimentary sequences (Turner 1989). This may include Markovian models of succession and cycling which reflect the behaviour of the physical system. This knowledge can be used to establish a data model for a sparse data set by providing guidance on the spatial dimensions or nature of a particular geo-object: one example would be the Bridge and Leeder (1979) model of meander belt migration behaviour. Conversely, by the use of simulation using Markov techniques, definition-limited models can be created under known conditions. This procedure can be used to form comparisons with other geo-objects which are established by the structuring of sparse data.

Specifically, the data model for a stratum believed to exist in the subsurface may be defined by lithological and structural parameters in a specific combination. The 3-D spatial identity of the geo-object is then established by searching the population of selected characteristics for the boundaries of the defining conditions and recording the x,y,z coordinates. Note, therefore, that by altering the contents of the data model and iterating the search process, a new set of x,y,z coordinates defining the object can be created. In the case of a study attempting to establish the overall architecture of a sedimentary sequence, the basic spatial arrangement of geo-objects can often be defined in different ways (and may overlap), depending on the contents of the data model for each element of the sequence defined (Raper 1988). Reconstruction of the structural development of basins, or dynamic behaviour of current systems or fluid flow regimes illustrates other evolutionary systems where the data model will change rapidly.

It is clear, therefore, that establishing the spatial identity of definition limited geo-objects in the subsurface is highly sensitive to the contents of the data model. The essential point is that the errors or bias inherent in the process of defining this data model can be as great as, or even greater than, those introduced in the spatial sampling of the parameters defining the geo-object or in the process of its visualization. Finally, it may be necessary to edit the data to select the values to be used in the 3-D spatial modelling. For example, it may be necessary to parse or validate the raw data, and subsequently to parameterize or regionalize the values before further analysis. These operations may impose their own indeterminacy on the identity of the geo-object under consideration.

Using the techniques and approaches described above it is possible to generate complex and realistic 3-D models visualized in 3-D. However, a key component in the modelling process is the spatial database and its design at the level of data types permitted. Any modelling process must also operate within the constraints of a database environment (see Fig. 20.11). Few specific database designs for the 3-D environment have been developed: Molenaar (1990), Fritsch (1990) and Hazelton, Leahy and Williams (1990) are the most complete attempts to date, all using relational concepts. One particular problem in a 3-D environment is the lineage of the model development, and the management of model versions (Newell, Theriault and Easterfield 1990). In a modelling environment it is also important to be able to incorporate data from different database sources (Turner, Kolm and Downey 1990), although few prospects for structured data transfer exist at present.

One well developed strategy for creating a 3-D model database involves spatial clustering of the elements defining the geo-object by a geometrical

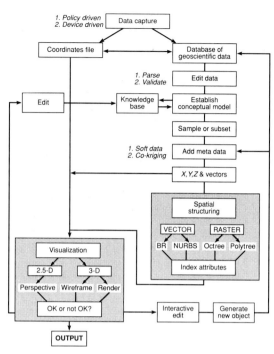

Fig. 20.11 A strategy for handling geoscience data and database input/output.

attribute in a geoscience database. Work by Schek and Waterfeld (1986) and Horn *et al.* (1989) has led to the establishment of a prototype database (the 'Geokernel'). This implements the storage of 3-D vector data items which are fully integrated with the associated attribute data. The storage structure used is based on hierarchical subdivision of the primary data attributes into sub-objects. The 3-D geometry is represented within this structure as a set of points, polylines or cuboids. These are spatially clustered by a regular or hierarchical subdivision of the 3-D space enclosing the objects. The usual mode of access would be by specifying (in system terminology) a 'clip' or 'compose' spatial query followed by a 'test' for the relevant non-spatial attributes. The chief advantage of this system is that it binds together the spatial and non-spatial components in a form of object orientation. It also allows the database to be set up for any data configuration. There are two main disadvantages. First, it requires a complex database operation to set up and bind each new data description to the database. Secondly, it does not use an explicit data structure to store 3-D geometry, but subdivides space around the objects identified in each project.

Three-dimensional visualizations cannot often be interactively interrogated. Hence, one ultimate design objective in the development of a 3-D modelling system is the production of high quality images which can also be interrogated by graphic interaction with the model on the screen, perhaps using a 3-D cursor such as the 'Dataglove' demonstrated by the Media Lab at MIT (Aldersey-Williams 1989). The rapid development of 'virtual reality' may also provide tools for interactive experiential manipulations of the model.

Dynamic 3-D models are also becoming a reality within the geoscience field. Tetzlaff and Harbaugh (1989) have recently described how clastic sedimentation can be simulated for a variety of processes, including river channel, deltaic and alluvial fan environments. These models are made in the SEDSIM environment which simulates clastic transport and sedimentation on a grain-by-grain basis. SEDSIM produces 3-D fence diagrams, shaded for grain size, which illustrate the geometrical outcome for a specific sedimentological model.

Experience with 3-D modelling also opens a new opportunity to accumulate knowledge of 3-D object metrics and behaviour which can be placed in knowledge bases. Dawson (1989) describes the development and structure of such a knowledge base at BP referred to as SEDMAC. Although this knowledge base is non-spatial in form, the potential to link to 3-D models exists. Finally, it should be noted that 3-D data can also be input into process driven models of 3-D behaviour, such as those used in hydrogeology (Turner 1989). The scope for this type of application is increasing as more systems are developed.

many existing geoscience questions can be more effectively answered in a 3-D modelling domain and since completely new questions can be posed, this form of analysis will be continuously extended.

However, the key control over the long-term development and refinement of tools for 3-D GIS will undoubtedly be the ability of the geoscientist to respond to the challenge to produce more *complete* models of geoscientific processes and their physical expression. This response is called for since these new modelling techniques require a greater quantification of assumptions and more complete data to establish geometrical form. In this respect, 3-D GIS has the potential to fuel a revolution in geoscientific data handling which will increase the speed at which models can be made and improved. These developments also form part of the revolution in scientific visualization whose developments will greatly improve the geoscientists' ability to communicate with their peers and the public.

One final consideration for 3-D GIS is the issue of how to manage the output of these new modelling processes, that is how to organize the database of models. Past and present practice in the geosciences has been to enshrine the results of a particular study or model in a paper map, perhaps as part of a definitive series. However, within a 3-D GIS database, models can be continuously replaced by new models, each of which may be capable of many visualizations. This suggests that a major challenge for the management of this powerful new technology is how to store and make available for future use the new insights which will emerge, in particular, how to ensure that the data and their interpretation are archived together.

CONCLUSIONS

This chapter has reviewed and interpreted the developments within the field of 3-D GIS at a time of particularly rapid development in theory and applications. This rapid growth indicates that the development of 2-D GIS has not provided the techniques of spatial data handling required by geoscientists. As a consequence, further developments in this field can be anticipated. The great advantages of the new 3-D modelling techniques are clear for all geoscientists to see:

REFERENCES

Aldersey-Williams H (1989) A Bauhaus for the media age. *New Scientist* **1655**: 54–60
Aronoff S (1989) *Geographic Information Systems: a management perspective*. WDL Publications, Ottawa
Auerbach S, Schaeben H (1990) Computer-aided geometric design of geologic surfaces and bodies. *Mathematical Geology* **22**: 723–42

Bak P, Mill A (1989) Three dimensional representation in a Geoscientific Resource Management System for the minerals industry. In: Raper J F (ed.) *Three Dimensional*

Applications in Geographical Information Systems. Taylor & Francis, London
Batten L G (1989) National capital urban planning project: development of a 3-D GIS. *Proceedings of GIS/LIS '89*. ACSM/ASPRS, Falls Church Virginia, pp. 781–6
Bridge J S, Leeder M R (1979) A simulation model of alluvial stratigraphy. *Sedimentology* 26: 617–44
Burns K L (1988) Lithologic topology and structural vector fields applied to subsurface prediction in geology. *Proceedings of GIS/LIS '88*. ACSM/ASPRS, Falls Church Virginia, pp. 26–34
Burns K L (1990) Three dimensional modelling and geothermal process simulation. *Proceedings of Symposium on Three Dimensional Computer Graphics in Modelling Geologic Structures and Simulating Processes*. Freiburger Geowissenschafliche Beitrage 2: 10–12
Burrough P A (1986) *Principles of Geographical Information Systems for Land Resources Assessment*. Clarendon, Oxford
Burrough P A (1991) Soil information systems. In: Maguire D J, Goodchild M F, Rhind D W (eds.) *Geographical Information Systems: principles and applications*. Longman, London, pp. 153–69, Vol 2
Carlbom I (1987) An algorithm for geometric set operations using cellular subdivision techniques. *IEEE Computer Graphics and Applications*. May: 45–55
Carlson E (1987) Three dimensional conceptual modelling of subsurface structures. *Proceedings of AUTOCARTO 8*. ACSM/ASPRS, Falls Church Virginia, pp. 336–45
Christiansen H N, Sederberg T W (1978) Conversion of complex contour line definitions into polygonal element mosaics. *ACM Computer Graphics* 12 (3): 187–92
Clark I, Houlding S, Stoakes M (1990) Direct geostatistical estimation of irregular 3-D volumes. *Proceedings of Symposium on Three Dimensional Computer Graphics in Modelling Geologic Structures and Simulating Processes*. Freiburger Geowissenschafliche Beitrage 2: 13–15
Dawson, M (1989) Developing a sedimentological database on an Apple Macintosh II. *BP International Information Systems Services paper*
Denver L E, Phillips D C (1990) Stratigraphic geocellular modelling. *Geobyte* February: 45–7
Fisher T, Wales R Q (1991) 3-D solid modelling of geo-objects using non-uniform rational B-splines (NURBS). In: Turner A K (ed.) *Three Dimensional Modelling with Geoscientific Information Systems*. Kluwer, Dordrecht
Flynn J J (1990) 3-D computing geosciences update. *Geobyte* February: 33–5
Frank A U, Buyong T B (1991) Geometry for 3D GIS in geoscientific applications. In: Turner A K (ed.) *Three Dimensional Modelling with Geoscientific Information Systems*. Kluver, Dordrecht
Franklin Wm R (1991) Computer systems and low-level data structures for GIS. In: Maguire D J, Goodchild M F, Rhind D W (eds.) *Geographical Information Systems: principles and applications*. Longman, London, pp. 215–25, Vol 1
Freeman J (1975) The modelling of spatial relations. *Computer Graphics and Image Processing* 4: 156–71
French J R (1989) Hydrodynamics and sedimentation in a macrotidal salt marsh, north Norfolk, England. Unpublished PhD Thesis, University of Cambridge, England
Fritsch D (1990) Towards three dimensional data structures in geographic information systems. *Proceedings of the EGIS '90*, pp. 335–45

Gargantini I (1991) Modelling natural objects via octrees. In: Turner A K (ed.) *Three Dimensional Modelling with Geoscientific Information Systems*. Kluwer, Dortrecht
GIS World (1990) *GIS Software Survey 1990*. GIS World Inc., Fort Collins Colorado
Goodchild M F (1991) Geographical data modelling. *Computers and Geosciences* 17
Goodchild M F (1991) The technological setting of GIS. In: Maguire D J, Goodchild M F, Rhind D W (eds.) *Geographical Information Systems: principles and applications*. Longman, London, pp. 45–54, Vol 1

Harig J (1990) Visualisation of 3-D finite element solutions of Navier–Stokes equations. *Proceedings of Symposium on Three Dimensional Computer Graphics in Modelling Geologic Structures and Simulating Processes*. Freiburger Geowissenschafliche Beitrage 2: 36–8
Hazelton N W J, Leahy F J, Williamson I P (1990) On the design of a temporally-referenced, 3-D Geographical Information System: development of a four dimensional GIS. *Proceedings of GIS/LIS '90*. AAG/ACSM/AMFM/ASPRS/URISA, Bethesda Maryland, pp. 357–372
Horn D et al. (1989) Spatial access paths and physical clustering in a low level geo-database system. *Geologisches Jahrbuch* **A 104** (Construction and display of geoscientific maps derived from databases)

Johnson M (1987) *The Body in the Mind: the bodily basis of meaning and reason*. University of Chicago Press, Chicago
Jones C B (1989) Data structures for 3-D spatial information systems. *International Journal of Geographical Information Systems* 3: 15–32
Jones T A (1988) Modeling geology in 3 dimensions. *Geobyte* February: 14–20

Kavouras M, Masry S (1987) An information system for geosciences: design considerations. *Proceedings of AUTOCARTO 8*. ACSM/ASPRS, Falls Church Virginia, pp. 336–45
Kelk B (1991) 3-D GIS for the geosciences. *Computers and Geosciences* 17
Kelk B, Challen K (1989) Experiments with a CAD package for spatial modelling of geoscientific data. *International Colloquium on 'Digital maps in the Geosciences', Würzburg Germany*

Lasseter T (1990) An interactive 3-D modelling system for integrated interpretation in hydrocarbon reservoir exploration and production. *Proceedings of Symposium on Three Dimensional Computer Graphics in Modelling Geologic Structures and Simulating Processes*. Freiburger Geowissenschafliche Beitrage 2: 45–6
Leenaers H, Burrough P A, Okx J (1989) Efficient mapping of heavy metal pollution on floodplains by co-kriging from elevation data. In: Raper J F (ed.) *Three

Dimensional Applications in Geographical Information Systems. Taylor & Francis, London, pp. 37–50

Mallet J-L (1991) GOCAD: a computer-aided design program for geological applications. In: Turner A K (ed.) *Three Dimensional Modelling with Geoscientific Information.* Kluwer, Dortrecht

McLaren R A, Kennie T (1989) Visualisation of digital terrain models: techniques and applications. In: Raper J F (ed.) *Three Dimensional Applications in Geographical Information Systems.* Taylor & Francis, London, pp. 79–98

Mark D M (1989) Cognitive image schemata for geographic information: relations to user views and GIS interfaces. *Proceedings of GIS/LIS '89.* ACSM/ASPRS, Falls Church Virginia, pp. 551–60

Mark D M, Cebrian J A (1986) Octrees: a useful method for the processing of topographic and subsurface data. *Proceedings of ACSM–ASPRS Annual Convention*, Volume 1. ACSM/ASPRS, Falls Church Virginia, pp. 104–113

Meier A (1986) Applying relational database techniques to solid modelling. *Computer Aided Design* **18**: 319–26

Molenaar M (1990) A formal data structure for three dimensional vector maps. *Proceedings of EGIS '90*, pp. 770–81

Newell R, Theriault D, Easterfield M (1990) Temporal GIS – modelling the evolution of spatial data in time. *Proceedings of GIS Design Models Conference.* Midlands Regional Research Laboratory, Leicester

Petrie G, Kennie T (eds.) (1990) *Terrain Modelling in Surveying and Civil Engineering.* Whittles, Latheronwheel

Pixar Inc. (1988) *Renderman Interface.* Pixar, San Rafael California

Pullar D, Egenhofer M J (1988) Towards formal definitions of topological relations amongst spatial objects. *Proceedings of the 3rd International Symposium on Spatial Data Handling.* International Geographical Union, Columbus Ohio, pp. 225–42

Raper J F (1988) A methodology for the investigation of landform-sediment relationships in British glaciated valleys. Unpublished PhD Thesis Queen Mary College, University of London

Raper J F (ed.) (1989a) *Three Dimensional Applications in Geographical Information Systems.* Taylor & Francis, London

Raper J F (1989b) The geoscientific mapping and modelling system: a conceptual design. In: Raper J F (ed.) *Three Dimensional Applications in Geographical Information Systems.* Taylor & Francis, London, pp. 11–20

Raper J F (1990) An atlas of 3-D functions. *Proceedings of Symposium on Three Dimensional Computer Graphics in Modelling Geologic Structures and Simulating Processes.* Freiburger Geowissenschafliche Beitrage **2**: 74–5

Requicha A A G (1980) Representations for rigid solids: theory, methods, and systems. *ACM Computing Surveys* **12** (4): 437–64

Rüber O (1989) Interactive design of faulted geological surfaces. *Geologisches Jahrbuch* **A 104** (Construction and display of geoscientific maps derived from databases)

Salmon R, Slater M (1987) *Computer Graphics.* Addison-Wesley, Reading Massachusetts

Schaeben H (1989) Improving the geological significance of computed surfaces by CADG methods, *Geologisches Jahrbuch* **A 104** (Construction and display of geoscientific maps derived from databases)

Schek H-J, Waterfeld W (1986) A database kernel system for geoscientific applications. *Proceedings of the 2nd International Symposium on Spatial Data Handling.* International Geographical Union, Columbus Ohio, pp. 273–88

Slingerland R, Keen T R (1990) A numerical study of storm driven circulation and 'event bed' genesis. *Proceedings of Symposium on Three Dimensional Computer Graphics in Modelling Geologic Structures and Simulating Processes.* Freiburger Geowissenschafliche Beitrage **2**: 97–9

Smith D R, Paradis A R (1989) Three-dimensional GIS for the earth sciences. In: Raper J F (ed.) *Three Dimensional Applications in Geographical Information Systems.* Taylor & Francis, London, pp. 149–54

Talmy L (1988) How language structures space. In: Mark D M (ed.) *Cognitive and linguistic aspects of geographical space.* National Center for Geographic Information and Analysis Publication. NCGIA, Santa Barbara California

Tetzloff D M, Harbaugh J W (1989) *Simulating Plastic Sedimentation.* Van Nostrand Reinhold, New York

Turnbull M, McAulay I, McLaren R A (1990) The role of terrain modelling in computer aided landscape design. In: Petrie G, Kennie T (eds.) *Terrain Modelling in Surveying and Civil Engineering.* Whittles, Latheronwheel, pp. 262–75

Turner A K (1989) The role of 3-D GIS in subsurface characterisation for hydrogeological applications. In: Raper J F (ed.) *Three Dimensional Applications in Geographical Information Systems.* Taylor & Francis, London, pp. 115–28

Turner A K, Kolm K, Downey J (1990) Potential applications of geoscientific information systems (GSIS) for regional ground water flow systems. *Proceedings of Symposium on Three Dimensional Computer Graphics in Modelling Geologic Structures and Simulating Processes.* Freiburger Geowissenschafliche Beitrage **2**: 108–10

Weibel R, Heller M (1991) Digital terrain modelling. In: Maguire D J, Goodchild M F, Rhind D W (eds.) *Geographical Information Systems: principles and applications.* Longman, London, 269–97, Vol 1

Welch R A (1990) 3-D terrain modelling for GIS applications. *GIS World*, October/November: 26–30

Youngmann C (1989) Spatial data structures for modelling subsurface features. In: Raper J F (ed.) *Three Dimensional Applications in Geographical Information Systems.* Taylor & Francis, London, pp. 129–36

21

THE FUNCTIONALITY OF GIS

D J MAGUIRE AND J DANGERMOND

The functionality of GIS is an important topic both academically and practically. This chapter presents an introduction to the generic functionality of GIS and explores the relationship between functionality and application. The basic principles of geographical database design and the main geographical models and structures are discussed along with the types of geographical features. The main body of the chapter is devoted to discussion of a functional classification of GIS. This is a convenient organizing framework for introducing the functionality of GIS. An important theme of this classification is the influence of the data model on functionality. The functional classification follows the logical progression of a GIS project from data capture, transfer and edit, through store and structure, on to restructure, generalize and transform, then query and analyse and, finally, present. The link between GIS functionality and application is then explored. The chapter concludes with some brief comments about the areas of GIS functionality requiring future attention.

INTRODUCTION

This chapter aims to provide a basic introduction to the generic functionality of GIS. In the context of this book, it is something of a link chapter which draws together many concepts discussed briefly elsewhere, although a number of new concepts are introduced. Functionality is defined as all the data collection, storage, manipulation, analysis and presentation operations carried out by GIS. The functionality of GIS has been widely discussed in recent years because of its importance in system comparison and classification. Functionality has been used to compare GIS mainly for the purposes of evaluating systems for purchase (Guptill 1988, 1989). Potential purchasers frequently ask software vendors to complete checklists of functions which they use to compare systems. GIS have been classified according to functionality for the purposes of developing a basic understanding and theory of the GIS discipline (GIS World 1990; Maguire and Raper 1990). The idea behind this is that a satisfactory classification of GIS will enable systems to be organized in a common framework using standard terminology. This will greatly facilitate information exchange and will have benefits for all people working in GIS. System comparisons, education and training, and the development of core GIS theory will all benefit from a better understanding of the relationship between systems and the use of standard terminology.

This chapter is based heavily on the work of Dangermond (1983) and Maguire and Raper (1990), although their ideas about GIS functionality are updated and extended to take into consideration new developments in the discipline. At the outset it must be acknowledged that it is very difficult to produce a clear and comprehensive description of GIS functionality for two main reasons: (1) GIS is a relatively youthful and rapidly evolving discipline and any models of the discipline are bound to date rapidly; (2) the applications of GIS are many and varied and any scheme will have to satisfy a very heterogeneous group of individuals. As a consequence of these two factors GIS is beset by problems of lack of standard terminology. The scheme presented here is, therefore, of necessity relatively general. It does not relate to any one system in particular, rather the attempt is to develop a generic high level scheme with widespread applicability.

This chapter is arranged in five sections. The first two introduce the ideas of geographical data models, data structures and geographical features which are central elements of the discussion. The third section is the most substantial and describes the generic functionality of GIS. The relationship between functionality and application is examined in the next section using four different application areas. Finally, some conclusions are drawn about the current status of GIS functionality.

GEOGRAPHICAL DATA MODELS AND STRUCTURES

In order to appreciate the reasons for including certain types of functions in GIS it is necessary to understand the basic principles of geographical database design and data models. Like many areas of GIS, there is some confusion over terminology here. The simple and unambiguous conceptual description of geographical databases expounded by Peuquet (1984) is a useful reference which will be used in this discussion (see also Goodchild 1991 in this volume; Guptill 1991 in this volume). Peuquet suggests four levels of abstraction are relevant to geographical databases (Fig. 21.1): reality – the phenomena as they actually exist, including all aspects which may or may not be perceived by individuals; data model (sometimes called a conceptual model) – an abstraction of the real world which incorporates only those properties thought to be relevant to the application in hand, usually a human conceptualization of reality; data structure (or logical model) – a representation of the data model which reflects implementation issues and is often expressed in terms of diagrams, lists and arrays designed to reflect the recording of the data in computer code; file structure (or physical model) – the representation of the data in storage hardware.

In a geographical data model, reality (the real world) is represented as a series of geographical

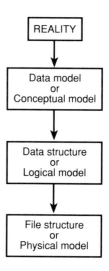

Fig. 21.1 Levels of abstraction relevant to geographical databases (after Peuquet 1984).

features (sometimes called entities or objects, but the term 'features' is preferred here to avoid confusion with other uses of these terms). The nature of geographical features is examined in the next section.

Creating a data model involves sampling the continuous or analogue space of reality and representing it in a discrete form (Fig. 21.2). Two fundamental geographical data models are used in designing geographical databases. These are referred to as the vector and tessellation (also called raster) models (Peuquet 1984; Egenhofer and Herring 1991 in this volume). There has been much debate over the past decade or so about the relative merits of both these systems, because the type of data model employed has a profound impact on the conventions and procedures of GIS. The selection of data model is influenced by many factors including the software available, the nature of the application, the training of the individual and historical precedent (Burrough 1986; Aronoff 1989; Star and Estes 1990).

Although the terms raster and tessellation are often used synonymously, strictly speaking a raster is a geographical data structure and only one method of implementing the tessellation geographical data model. In the tessellation model, geographical features are described as polygonal units of space in a matrix (also called a mesh, lattice or array). Usually, the polygonal units are regular squares referred to as pixels (derived from the term

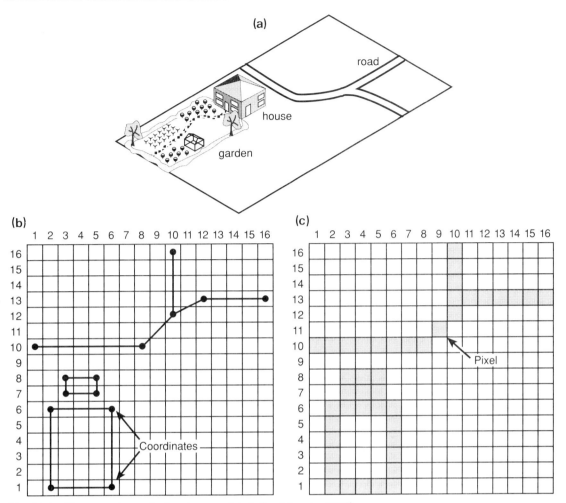

Fig. 21.2 Vector and tessellation data models (after Maguire 1989).

'picture element'), but regular and irregular triangles and hexagons have also been used (Peuquet 1984). Where the cells are organized such that they are stored in line scan order, the term *raster* can properly be used, but it is frequently applied to any unstructured tessellation model and it is in this more common general form that it is used here. At a general level, the tessellation model is conceptually simple, it is readily implemented on inexpensive microcomputers and it offers a relatively quick method of developing GIS analytical operations. The data model is area oriented in that greater emphasis is placed on the contents of areas rather than the boundaries between them. Boolean operations are easily incorporated into this model, as are many types of simulation (e.g. the impact of acid precipitation on woodlands, variations in groundwater caused by water extraction from aquifers or the impact of freight transport costs on factory location). It is difficult to represent boundary or line operations using the tessellation model and many socio-economic applications, which place great emphasis on these types of geographical feature, are not easily accommodated. The tessellation model tends to be favoured by researchers interested in environmental applications.

In the vector model, geographical features are represented as a series of x,y or x,y,z coordinates (Fig. 21.2). The vector model is much more complex than the tessellation model and is less readily adaptable to cheap microcomputer technology. Data collection and structuring using this model are on the whole more time consuming.

The boundary-oriented nature of the model has led to its use in a variety of socio-economic applications, especially those involving variable density phenomena (e.g. population characteristics), networks, coordinate geometry and high quality cartographic operations. The complex organization means that many analytical operations, such as polygon overlay and buffering, are conceptually complex and computationally intensive.

GEOGRAPHICAL FEATURES

In GIS, geographical features are usually defined according to their two data elements. The geographical (also called locational) data element is used to provide a reference for the attribute (also called statistical or non-locational) data element. For example, administrative boundaries, river networks and point locations of sites are all geographical features used to provide a reference for, respectively, census counts, river water flows or site elevations. In GIS the geographical element is more important than the attribute element and this is one of the key features which differentiates GIS from other information systems.

Four generic geographical features are normally recognized on the basis of Euclidean dimensionality: points, lines, areas and surfaces (Unwin 1981; DCDSTF 1988; Maguire 1989; Gatrell 1991 in this volume). In this scheme, points have no length dimension and are said to have a dimensionality of zero. Lines have a single length dimension and dimensionality of one. Areas have two length dimensions and dimensionality of two. Finally, surfaces have three length dimensions and are given a dimensionality of three. All these features can be represented in either the tessellation or vector models.

Each of these generic geographical features may be further subdivided according to the characteristics of the associated attribute data (Table 21.1). For example, points might be subdivided into houses, telephone boxes and soil pits; areas might be sub-divided into those with a population density of, say, 0–5000, 5001–10 000 and greater than 10 000 persons per square kilometre; and surfaces might be subdivided into those which are flat, steeply sloping and very steeply sloping.

There are various ways in which attribute data can be classified, the most widely used being the level of measurement (Stevens 1946). Stevens proposed the fourfold classification of Nominal, Ordinal, Interval and Ratio. Nominal data have only sufficient information associated with them to classify them into categories. For example, rocks can be classified as granite, limestone and schist, etc. Ordinal data contain sufficient information so that they can be ranked in ascending or descending order. For example, some social classifications seek to classify households by the occupation of the household head. People in professional occupations are usually placed in class 1, semi-professional in class 2, manual in 3, etc. Interval data have the property that distances between categories are defined as fixed equal size units. Thermometers, for example, measure temperature on an interval scale, ensuring that the difference between, say, 20 °C and 25 °C, is the same as that between 0 °C and 5 °C. However, because the scheme lacks a fixed zero only differences and not absolute values can be measured. Ratio data have in addition an absolute zero. A value of 0 mm of rainfall indicates no rainfall, whereas 0 °C does not indicate no temperature! It is possible to calculate ratios from data measured at the highest level. For example, 1000 mm of rainfall is twice as much as 500 mm, but it is not sensible to say that 50 °C is twice as warm as 25 °C. For most practical purposes in GIS the interval and ratio categories can be treated as one.

The dimensionality and levels of measurement classifications are usually linked together to give a two-dimensional table showing the basic types of

Table 21.1 A classification of geographical data (after Robinson *et al.* 1984; Unwin 1981). The maps are described according to the type of symbolism which can be used.

	Point	Line	Area	Surface
Nominal	Dot	Network	Colour class	Freely coloured
Ordinal	Ordered symbol	Ordered network	Ordered colour	Ordered colour
Interval /ratio	Graduated symbol	Flow line	Choropleth	Contour

data used in GIS (Robinson *et al.* 1984; Unwin 1981) as shown in Table 21.1.

Unfortunately, there are several problems in applying this simple classification. The dimensionality component fails to incorporate four important ideas. First, there is no provision for networks which are more than a collection of lines and, therefore, require a richer means of representation. Secondly, some geographical features can only be defined by reference to a pair of features (Goodchild 1988). For example, the exact position of many underground streams in limestone regions is unknown: the streams can be defined only in terms of the points at which the streams disappear (sinks) and reappear (springs). Thirdly, the definition of features as points, lines and areas is scale dependent. A city, for example, might be represented as a point on a small-scale map, or an area on a large-scale map. Fourthly, this view of features comprising points, lines, areas and surfaces is at variance with our everyday experience where geographical features are viewed as complete units. A forest, for example, is often not considered a collection of points, lines and areas, or even a collection of trees, but in many cases a single atomic feature. Object-oriented data modelling, although still in its early stages, offers some interesting possibilities for assisting in representing features in geographical databases (Egenhofer and Frank 1987; Worboys, Hearnshaw and Maguire 1990). Fifthly, this classification fails to incorporate the temporal dimension. Many of the processes which people wish to encapsulate in GIS can best be represented using some type of space–time model or geographical data matrix (Berry 1964; Dangermond 1983). Time can be considered a fourth dimension and in some instances it can be more important than the geographical component (Fig. 21.3). To date, there have been few attempts to incorporate time into GIS (Langran and Chrisman 1988), though it is certain to increase in importance. Chrisman (1991 in this volume), drawing principally on the work of Sinton (1978), shows how geographical phenomena can be modelled from their geographical (or locational), attribute (or thematic) and temporal components. In geographical modelling, one of these components must be fixed, the second allowed to vary and the third measured. For example, in a study of the socio-economic characteristics of a city using population census data, the year is normally fixed, the location allowed to vary (population is

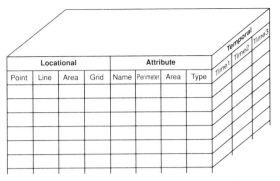

Fig. 21.3 The geographical data matrix used as the basis for much geographical enquiry (after Dangermond 1983).

usually reported for census tracts) and the socio-economic characteristics of the population are measured. This simple but powerful model offers a very useful organizing framework for geographical enquiry. Finally, a new challenge for GIS software developers and data modellers is how to represent sound and pictures as well as conventional data types in what might be termed multi-media GIS (Shepherd 1991 in this volume).

There are also two problems associated with the level of measurement classification. First, the simple Nominal, Ordinal, Interval and Ratio scheme gives no explicit provision for incorporating a count data type, such as the number of people in a census area with a particular disease. This is important because in some statistical modelling procedures count data must be considered quite differently from other data types (Flowerdew and Green 1989; Flowerdew 1991 in this volume). Secondly, in the case of areas it is important to distinguish between density measures (e.g. population density) and absolute measures (e.g. the number of people). These have an important bearing on the type of analyses that can be conducted (Unwin 1981; Flowerdew and Openshaw 1987) and, again, these ideas cannot easily be incorporated into the level of measurement classification.

In spite of these problems, which in some cases may be very significant, in the absence of any real alternative the dimensionality/levels of measurement typology remains the principal method of classifying geographical data.

This mode of thinking is predicated on the view that the part of reality designated as the study area for database purposes can be conveniently subdivided into discrete atomic features and that these features do not overlap. This process is termed *planar enforcement*. It is assumed that geographical features can be easily defined and classified. In some cases, mainly features created by humans, this assumption is valid, but in others it can only be applied with difficulty. It is, for example, very difficult to define the edge of an urban area or the boundary between soil types, because they do not occur sharply. This problem has long been recognized in geography and is not new to GIS. The field of fuzzy logic, which has received only scant attention from GIS workers, offers a potential alternative to the strict use of planar enforcement (Robinson, Miller and Klesh 1988; Burrough 1989). A further problem with this view of GIS is that it is fundamentally reductionist since it focuses attention on the differences rather than the similarities between individual elements. Given the nature of the problems which GIS are often used to tackle, a holistic approach might be more appropriate, but no one as yet has investigated how this might be achieved.

In summary, geographical features are represented in geographical databases as collections of geographical and attribute data. The present classification of geographical features, according to the dimensionality of the geographical data and the level of measurement of the attribute data, is universally used in the absence of any real alternative and despite some significant problems.

THE FUNCTIONALITY OF GIS

This scheme of GIS functionality is primarily based on the work of Maguire and Raper (1990) which in turn draws on Dangermond (1983) among other sources. The scheme is intended as a top-down hierarchical classification of the major types of functions which characterize GIS. It therefore embodies only the most important and widely used generic functions. Further details about these and other lower level functions may be found in publications such as Guptill (1988) or GIS World (1990). Specific details of how individual functions are implemented in GIS software can be obtained from appropriate system manuals.

In the proposed scheme ten major categories are identified (Fig. 21.4). These follow the logical progression of data in a GIS project: (i) capture; (ii) transfer; (iii) validate and edit; (iv) store and structure; (v) restructure; (vi) generalize; (vii) transform; (viii) query; (ix) analyse; and (x) present. Some of these major categories are subdivided on the basis of whether the functions deal with geographical or attribute data. A further level of subdivision uses the data structure employed. The vector and tessellation models (and their implementation as data structures) exert a fundamental conceptual and practical influence on the designers and users of GIS and so it is appropriate that they are given prominence in functional GIS classifications. It is, of course, impossible to develop a scheme of GIS functionality which is completely comprehensive. The heterogeneous nature of GIS means that systems have been developed and adapted to perform many different functions. There are also considerable problems of defining exactly what is meant by terms such as 'overlay', 'object orientation' and 'search'. While the functionality classification scheme follows the progression of data in a GIS project from capture to present, in any GIS project not all of the GIS functions, or even all of the major categories need be employed. It is also likely that a number of functions will be applied to the same data set several times. For example, during data integration a data set may be edited, generalized and transformed several times before it has satisfactory characteristics.

Capture, transfer, validate and edit

Capture, transfer, validate and edit are used to acquire and load error-free digital data into GIS. These functions are crucial to GIS since data capture is often one of the biggest bottle necks and most expensive GIS tasks. Many different techniques and devices are available for both geographical and attribute data (Rhind 1974; Marble, Lauzon and MaGranaghan 1984; Chrisman 1987; Maguire 1989; Jackson and Woodsford 1991 in this volume). Primary geographical data collection, using raster remote sensing systems (such as scanners and radars) and vector Global Positioning Systems (GPS) and field surveying, is employed in areas which have yet to be mapped and for updating existing digital databases. Since most of the world has now been mapped (Parry and Perkins 1987), secondary geographical data collection devices are now used more frequently for collecting digital data. However, given the comparatively low cost of data collection using GPS, this primary data collection method may replace secondary digitizing in the future. Secondary geographical data collection devices include raster scanners and vector semi-automatic table digitizers for 2-D data, and stereoplotters for 3-D data. Attribute data are collected using a plethora of different devices. These include automatic and semi-automatic data loggers, as well as keyboards and, increasingly, Optical Character Readers (OCR) and voice-recognition systems.

Transfer involves moving previously captured data into GIS, using electronic networks or magnetic media. A number of system-dependent and system-independent formats exist for both geographical and attribute data. For geographical data, system-dependent formats include ARC/INFO export format, INTERGRAPH Standard Interchange Format (SIF) and AUTOCAD DXF (see Guptill 1991 in this volume for further details of data transfer). System-independent formats for geographical data include the United States Geological Survey (USGS) Digital Line Graph (DLG), the US Bureau of the Census TIGER (Topological Integrated Geographic Encoding Referencing) format and the UK National Transfer Format (NTF). For attribute data, system-dependent formats are used infrequently. Instead there is a preference for the principal system-independent format, the American Standard Code for Information Interchange (ASCII). The choice of whether capture or transfer should be used to obtain digital data depends upon the cost and availability of data from other agencies relative to in-house collection. As the digital mapping programmes of national mapping agencies and the global monitoring satellite programmes progress (see Clark, Hastings and Kineman 1991 in this volume), data transfer is likely to increase in importance as the costs of map and document digitizing and scanning decrease.

Whether the data have been captured or transferred, they must be validated and, if necessary, edited to remove errors and inconsistencies. All good GIS software systems have routines for validating and editing geographical features. Database Management Systems and standard computer system editors are usually employed to validate and edit attribute data. In order to validate data it is necessary to check the data against an original and look for unusual values. This might involve producing a test plot or some statistics describing the data using some of the plotting and summary functions described later.

Store and structure

Data storage and structuring is a crucial stage in creating a geographical database using GIS. In the main, structuring is undertaken because structured data can usually be stored more efficiently and can support high levels of analytical operations more easily. As Maguire and Raper (1990) demonstrate, the type of data structure employed determines the range of functions which can be used for manipulation and analysis. Furthermore, transfer between structures (restructuring) is time consuming, expensive and error prone. A simple classification of the main schemes for structuring geographical and attribute data in GIS is presented in Fig. 21.4. Space does not permit a detailed review of each of them and in any case they are discussed extensively in Peuquet (1984), Aronoff (1989), Maguire and Raper (1990), Samet (1990) and Egenhofer and Herring (1991 in this volume). The raster-vector dichotomy is examined by Davis and Simonett (1991 in this volume) and Egenhofer and Herring (1991 in this volume). This aspect of the classification of GIS functionality is probably least well developed in the literature, principally because of the variety of structures available and terminology problems.

The major subdivision of geographical structures is into tessellation, vector and hybrid types. The tessellation structures are further subdivided into regular and irregular. Regular geographical tessellation structures include: unstructured schemes such as bitmaps and grids; simple structures such as rasters which are ordered by line scan, run length encoding methods, Morton ordering, etc.; and a whole host of hierarchical methods such as quadtrees, KDB-trees, octrees, etc. The main irregular method is the Triangulated Irregular Network (TIN) which is used to represent surfaces using triangles (Weibel and Heller 1991 in this volume).

Vector structuring techniques can be divided

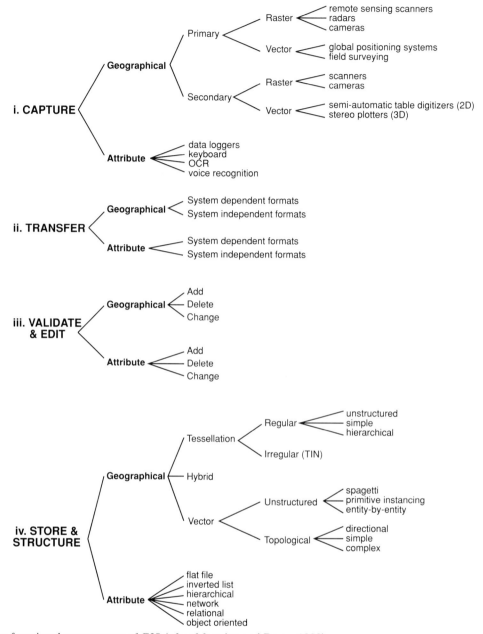

Fig. 21.4 The functional components of GIS (after Maguire and Raper 1990).

into unstructured and topological types. The former can be subdivided into the 'spaghetti', primitive instancing and entity-by-entity structures. The spaghetti structure is so called because the geographical features are represented as a simple collection of points and lines (also called links and nodes), analogous to a plate of spaghetti. Primitive instancing was developed primarily in Computer Aided Design (CAD) systems. In the database the basic elements are symbols representing buildings, roads, traffic lights, etc., which can be moved interactively and positioned at any appropriate location on a map. The entity-by-entity structure codifies geographical features as complete units, for

The Functionality of GIS

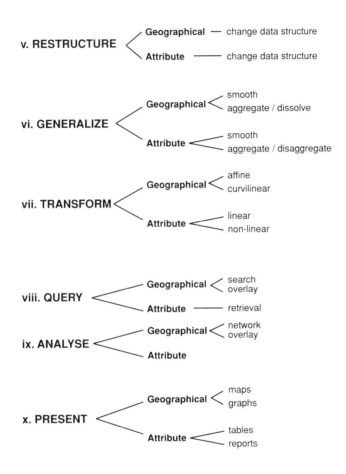

Fig. 21.4 (continued) The functional components of GIS (after Maguire and Raper 1990).

example as closed polygons, but no topological information is included. Such unstructured approaches are very useful for drawing simple maps and diagrams, but the absence of any structure within the data severely limits analysis. Topological data structures facilitate many types of geographical query and analysis such as retrieving adjacent areas and undertaking network analysis. Three types of topological structure are frequently identified. Directional topological systems, such as the US Bureau of the Census DIME system (Corbett 1979), record topology along with the direction of a line segment. Simple topological relationships are present in systems such as POLYVRT developed at the Harvard Laboratory for Computer Graphics and Spatial Analysis and incorporated in the ODYSSEY GIS and later systems. More recent systems such as ESRI's ARC/INFO and GeoVision's GIS use a fully topological structure.

The vaster structure was the first hybrid structure developed to make use of the advantages of both the vector and tessellation models (Peuquet 1984). In this model the basic unit is the swath which corresponds to a series of contiguous scan lines in a raster scheme. Each swath has a raster and a vector component allowing the logic of both systems to be used during processing. Although the vaster has found little favour with software developers, a number of other hybrid data structures have now been implemented. In large geographical databases it is quite common for quadtree indexing to be used to organize vector topological data. There have also been attempts to use vector indexing to store tessellation data.

Five main data structures have been used to organize attribute data in GIS: flat file, inverted list, hierarchical, network and relational (Healey 1991 in this volume). Flat files have a very simple 'card box' like structure and files cannot easily be related to each other. Because of this, flat files are seldom used in anything other than simple GIS. In the inverted list structure the row ordering of records has significance for retrieval. Key search fields are identified and these are used to create an inverted list (a secondary index) to data storage locations on a disk. Although not widely used in GIS, largely due to their restriction to large IBM mainframe computers, they have the advantage of being relatively fast at data retrieval. The hierarchical structure is a type of tree in which each feature can have several links to lower elements in a hierarchy, but only one link to a higher record. This system is useful for implementing one-to-many relationships, but it cannot adequately deal with many-to-many relationships. This lack of flexibility has restricted its use in GIS. The network structure overcomes the main limitation of the hierarchical structure by including a capability for many-to-many relationships at all levels. This model is comparatively efficient, but its complex structure has restricted its use in creating geographical databases. The relational model has a comparatively simple structure. Data are organized into a series of tables which are linked together by common key fields. Relational databases are generally thought to be easy to understand and set up. As a result of their widespread adoption in many application areas, relational database management systems have been used extensively in GIS.

The data structures discussed above have a number of inherent problems which limit their use for geographical database design. They do not easily allow incorporation of both simple and complex geographical features (e.g. points, lines, polygons, sets of polygons and rasters). Current systems do not have facilities for supporting multiple versions of the same feature, as would be necessary to create a database covering different time periods. The machine-oriented nature of existing systems also makes it difficult to model complex problems. The slow speed of systems based on proprietary DBMS is a further disadvantage. Object-oriented database design already discussed above is one possible approach which may alleviate some of these problems.

All the main structuring methods are used by at least one proprietary GIS software system. The ways in which geographical and attribute models are linked together in proprietary GIS systems is described elsewhere in this book (Healey 1991; Maguire 1991).

The process of storing and structuring geographical and attribute data in GIS may be achieved in several different ways. In some systems the data are structured at the time of digitizing by requesting the necessary information from the person digitizing. Other systems can structure data in a batch process from unstructured or partly structured data. A number of the automatic data collection devices, such as scanners, have associated software which also structure data as they are collected. Because it is so time consuming to structure data by hand, it is preferable to automate the operation as far as possible.

Restructure, generalize and transform

Data manipulation is a key area of GIS functionality since it allows data from disparate sources to be converted to a common format for analysis. This process is sometimes termed data integration (Flowerdew 1991 in this volume). The most important operations are restructure, generalize and transform.

Restructure involves changing the data structure used for the geographical and/or attribute data. In the case of geographical data, this usually means converting data between one of the vector and one of the tessellation structures. Peuquet (1981a, 1981b) reviews the principal approaches to restructuring geographical data and points out that vector–raster restructuring is considerably simpler and faster that raster–vector restructuring. All restructuring is time consuming, computationally intensive and, potentially, error prone and thus should be avoided, if at all possible. Unfortunately, there are still no truly integrated GIS which can analyse both vector and tessellation data simultaneously. Current systems employ the technique of restructuring either the vector or tessellation data to make them compatible.

Generalize includes both smoothing and aggregating features and their inverses (Muller 1991 in this volume). Several different functions exist for tessellation and vector data. They include line and grid smoothing, dissolving the boundary between two adjoining polygons to create a single larger polygon, and replacing attribute values by their mean. Generalization is still poorly developed in GIS and it will be a considerable time before automatic one-pass generalization of geographical data from, say, a scale of 1 : 10 000 to a scale of, say, 1 : 1 000 000 is possible. Current GIS only provide functions for operations such as weeding coordinates from lines or aggregating pixels with similar values.

Transformation of geographical data involves affine transformations of scale, rotation, translation and inversion, and curvilinear transformation of the type used to change between map projections. Map projection transformations tend to be most important in large countries, particulary those in high latitudes, and also in applications which use a wide variety of data types. They may be applied equally to both tessellation and vector data, although the mathematics and algorithms are quite different (Maling 1991 in this volume). Transformation of attribute data includes the application of linear and non-linear functions and constants, such as might be found in most basic statistical analysis packages (e.g. Minitab, SPSS and GLIM).

Query and analyse

To many it is query and, more especially, analysis that are at the heart of GIS. It is the ability to analyse geographical patterns and relationships which differentiates GIS from other computer systems, such as those used for computer cartography, computer-aided design, remote sensing and database management (Maguire 1991 in this volume). The classification of functions into the two groups, query and analyse, is somewhat simplistic since individual functions often overlap one or more groups. The difference between the two is really one of emphasis. Query functions are concerned with inventory questions such as 'Where is...?' Analysis functions deal with questions such as 'What if...?' Nevertheless, this binary classification is a useful organizing principle.

Spatial query and analysis necessitate distance and direction operations on spatial data. Query involves the retrieval of attribute data about spatial features. At its simplest it involves pointing at a feature and retrieving its name, but it can also involve retrieving all the attribute information about features within a certain distance of a feature or within a study area which has a complex shape. These operations use such functions as spatial searching and overlay. Spatial searching (also called buffering or proximity analysis) can be used to highlight a zone of interest around a point, line, area or cell feature which can then be used to retrieve attribute data or generate a new spatial feature. Overlay is the process of comparing spatial features in two or more map layers. For example, information about land suitability for housing development may involve comparing information on land ownership, land prices, building restrictions, geology, etc., all of which could be stored in separate data layers. When search and overlay are combined with query and comparison operations on attribute data, complex analysis can be undertaken. Examples include network routing, location allocation modelling, terrain intervisibility calculation and surface flow modelling. Certain types of operations are best carried out on data structured in different ways. For example, overlay and buffer calculation are most easily carried out using data structured as a grid or raster (Berry 1987, 1991 in this volume; Tomlin 1991 in this volume), whereas network analysis and high quality map production are best carried out on data structured using the vector system.

The process of relating geographical features on different data layers is often referred to as map algebra or map processing (Tomlin 1983, 1991 in this volume; Berry 1987) and its origin lies in the work of McHarg (1969) who first described its manual implementation. At its simplest, map processing involves the interaction of a single geographical feature and a single operator (also called a function). More often it involves relating at least two geographical features by overlay, on more than one map layer and using one or more operator(s). Berry (1987) suggests that overlay map processing encompasses point, neighbourhood and region operations. Point processors consider each geographical feature independently and can be conceptualized as 'vertically spearing' a series of features from a stack of co-registered data layers. Regional processors associate each location with a set of other locations having a similar characteristic. The features within the boundaries of each template become available for processing. Neighbourhood processors identify features for processing in terms of their spatial proximity (e.g. all features within 100 metres of a road). The map processing concept was developed for, and is still typically applied to, raster databases, but there seems no reason why the same concept cannot also be applied to vector databases. The results of map processing are usually output in the form of another map.

Defining the operators, particularly the minimum set, used in GIS analysis has been the subject of much debate. Freeman (1975) defined a set of 13 operators: left of, right of, beside, above, below, behind, in front of, near, far from, touching, between, inside and outside. Feuchtwanger (1989) listed only six: adjacency, proximity, subdivision, overlap, nearest neighbour and sub-region. Egenhofer and Frank (1987) used just four: neighbour, inclusion, distance and direction. The minimum set of spatial operators for defining topological relationships between spatial objects has been suggested by Peuquet (1984) as: distance, direction and the Boolean set operators of intersection, union and complement. In his examination of the logical principles of GIS, Robinove (1986) argues that GIS analytical operations can be described using the relationships of classes (types of geographical features) based upon the calculus of propositional functions (traditional rules of symbolic logic). He explains the logical relations of spatial position in terms of adjacency, proximity or connectedness, superposition and containment, together with the Boolean and statistical and mathematical operators.

Specific details of the action of geographical operators are given in Dangermond (1983), Burrough (1986), Berry (1987), Guptill (1988) and Tomlin (1990, 1991 in this volume).

The degree of integration of geographical and attribute data describing geographical features exerts an important influence on the way query and analysis operations are carried out and the results that are obtained. In simple systems, where the geographical and attribute data are not closely integrated and only a single attribute is associated with a geographical feature description, it is only possible to combine either the geographical or the attribute components. In more sophisticated systems where the two components are closely integrated and multiple attributes can be associated with a geographical feature description, an operation on one component results in a corresponding operation which updates the other component and thus maintains their referential integrity. For example, in closely integrated vector systems it is possible to join points, lines and areas on two coverages together by overlay, as well as some, or all, of their associated attributes. To date, only vector systems closely integrate geographical and attribute data components, but there is no theoretical reason restricting raster systems.

Present

The final stage in any GIS project is the presentation of the results. Geographical data can be presented in many forms, including maps, graphs, statistical summaries and reports, tables and lists. All of these methods of output should ideally be provided by a GIS. Though presentation is a vital part of any substantive application and one which can require access to a wide range of commands, technically it is much less sophisticated than some of the other functions discussed earlier. At the presentation stage, GIS are acting much like DBMS report generators and computer cartography systems. The emphasis is on formatting output and flexibility of display in, for example, a range of different colours, symbol types, high quality fonts and shading schemes. The best GIS offer users an interactive environment within which to experiment with the appearance and content of maps and graphs.

FUNCTIONALITY AND APPLICATION

It is not uncommon for GIS software systems to have several hundred functions because of their general purpose nature. Specific applications, not surprisingly, often use only a small selection of the overall functions. In this section four applications, which are representative of the overall spectrum, are used to illustrate the relative importance of different functions in certain contexts. For the purposes of this discussion it is assumed that all the applications are being carried out in an area with similar geographical characteristics. The relationship between functionality and application for a few example applications is summarized in Table 21.2.

Hazardous vehicle routing

The routing of vehicles carrying hazardous waste along the national road network is undertaken in many countries. In GIS terms there is an obvious need for a geographical database containing a description of the national road network. Even in relatively large well developed countries this is likely to constitute only a relatively small amount of data and so data capture, transfer, validate and edit are unlikely to be of critical importance. Network routing is best carried out on a database with the geographical data structured using the topological vector model, but since small quantities of attribute data are utilized the choice of structure for the attribute data is less important. It is unlikely that restructure, generalize and transform will be required in hazardous vehicle routing. Some limited query functions may be needed to locate the name of a road, junction or low bridge for example. The most important functions are likely to be those concerned with analysis and, in particular, network routing. This will involve the use of shortest path algorithms where impedances to movement are attached to the roads or road junctions. Output from the results of analytical operations is likely to be simple maps and reports giving directions and warning of obstructions.

Land ownership monitoring

Land ownership is a fundamental component of civilized societies (Dale 1991 in this volume). In

Table 21.2 The relationship between functionality and selected applications expressed on a scale of 1 (insignificant) to 5 (very significant).

	Hazardous vehicle routing	Land ownership monitoring	Forest resource management	Census map production
1. Capture	2	5	3	4
2. Transfer	2	4	2	2
3. Validate and edit	2	4	3	3
4. Store and structure	Topological vector	Entity-by-entity vector	Tessellation grid	Spaghetti or entity-by-entity vector
5. Restructure	1	1	5	1
6. Generalize	2	1	5	4
7. Transform	1	1	3	1
8. Query	3	5	4	3
9. Analyse	5	1	3	1
10. Present	2	2	3	5

highly populated countries, creating an inventory and monitoring ownership are significant problems for which GIS are frequently used. A land ownership or cadastral information system basically requires a database containing an accurate description of the boundary of a large number of land parcels, together with fast access to a relatively small quantity of attribute data about the owner. The system must be capable of logging large numbers of transactions as land is bought and sold. The geographical data must be held in vector format, but nothing more complex than the entity-by-entity structure is really needed. The need for rapid retrieval and update of relatively small quantities of attribute data means that an inverted list or hierarchical structure may be preferable. Because land parcels tend to be small, there is likely to be a very large number of them, and so data capture, transfer, validate and edit are usually seen as important. There is unlikely to be much call for restructure, generalize and transform. The key operation in land ownership monitoring is query. This might involve searching the database by parcel coordinates, size, parcel name, owner's name, etc. The functions for presenting such simple data need not be sophisticated.

Forest resource management

The management of forests and similar natural resources poses a number of different questions for the developers and operators of GIS. Natural resource management applications tend to require many types of different data which are reported on disparate spatial bases and which are easily definable. For example, identifying suitable land for planting sitka spruce trees involves the integration of data on climate, soils, existing vegetation, water, slopes, etc. Many of these data can be obtained by classifying satellite data. The need to compare data from many sources and to incorporate raster format satellite data means that most natural resource management applications utilize the raster or grid data structure for database design. Requirements for data capture, transfer and validate/edit are likely to be relatively modest, but costly because of the large number of data layers required for analysis and because of the expense of purchasing satellite data. Restructure and generalize, and to a lesser extent transform, are likely to be very important

because of their role in integrating disparate data. Query and analyse are the key operations, their relative importance depending on the use of the system for resource inventory, monitoring and management. Present is of average significance and although sophisticated maps are rarely required, the level of detail on such maps often necessitates advanced functions and technology for display.

Census map production

Many GIS are basically used for map production, be it in a national mapping agency concerned with topographic maps or a private company concerned with producing thematic maps of population census data (Rhind 1991 in this volume). Census mapping places emphasis on the presentation rather than the query and analysis of information. Because of the limited analytical requirements and the need for high quality output, a simple vector format is preferred such as the spaghetti or entity-by-entity structure. The small size of the basic census areas and the large amount of attribute data mean that capture, transfer and validate/edit are often of considerable significance. While there is little need to restructure and transform the data, the large data volumes and requirement for both large- and small-scale maps mean that generalize is important. There is limited application for query and, especially, analyse, but present is of primary importance.

CONCLUSIONS

This chapter has presented a brief overview of the generic functionality of GIS. Many specific examples of the use of GIS functions are given in other chapters in this book, especially those in Section III. The classification of GIS functions is important because it facilitates the comparison of systems and should assist in developing a set of standard terminology.

It is clear that there is an important link between the way in which data are structured in a geographical database and the type of functions that can best be employed. The database design stage of a GIS project is especially important because none of the current proprietary GIS software systems can satisfactorily handle both vector and tessellation data analysis simultaneously. Furthermore, restructuring geographical data is time consuming and error prone.

There are many different application areas which can benefit from using GIS and each requires a different set of functions. However, for commercial reasons the majority of GIS software vendors have attempted to develop systems with a wide range of sophisticated functionality. In some cases this leads to over-complex data structures and functions being used for certain applications. This problem is further compounded because the expense of data capture and the fact that departments in large organizations often share the same database, means there is a tendency to collect all possible types of data and to structure them in the most sophisticated way.

Although most current GIS projects are constrained by data collection and staffing difficulties, it would be wrong to assume that there are no gaps in the functionality of current systems. Maguire (1990) sets out a research agenda for GIS for the 1990s. Three key areas requiring attention are concerned with spatial analysis, integrated GIS and network processing. Incorporation of spatial analysis in GIS would allow probabilistic statements to be made about the outcome of GIS operations and, in particular, the magnitude of errors to be estimated (Openshaw 1991 in this volume). The development of truly integrated GIS would allow simultaneous query and analysis of both tessellation and vector data rather than restructuring. The development of network processing would allow more sophisticated utility and transport networks to be modelled.

REFERENCES

Aronoff S (1989) *Geographic Information Systems: a management perspective*. WDL Publications, Ottawa Canada

Berry B J L (1964) Approaches to regional analysis: a synthesis. *Annals of the Association of American Geographers* **54**: 2–11

Berry J K (1987) Fundamental operations in computer-assisted map analysis *International Journal of Geographical Information Systems* **1**: 119–36

Berry J K (1991) GIS in island resource planning: a case study in map analysis. In: Maguire D J, Goodchild M F, Rhind D W (eds.) *Geographical Information Systems: principles and applications*. Longman, London, pp. 285–95, Vol 2

Burrough P A (1986) *Principles of Geographic Information Systems for Land Resources Assessment*. Clarendon, Oxford

Burrough P A (1989) Fuzzy mathematical methods for soil survey and land evaluation *Journal of Soil Science* **40**: 477–92

Chrisman N R (1987) Efficient digitizing through a combination of appropriate hardware and software for error detection and editing *International Journal of Geographical Information Systems* **1**: 265–77

Chrisman N R (1991) The error component in spatial data. In: Maguire D J, Goodchild M F, Rhind D W (eds.) *Geographical Information Systems: principles and applications*. Longman, London, pp. 165–74, Vol 1

Clark D M, Hastings D A, Kineman J J (1991) Global databases and their implications for GIS. In: Maguire D J, Goodchild M F, Rhind D W (eds.) *Geographical Information Systems: principles and applications*. Longman, London, pp. 217–31, Vol 2

Corbett J P (1979) Topological principles in cartography. *Technical Paper 48*, US Bureau of Census, Suitland (also published in *Proceedings of AUTOCARTO 4* (1975), pp. 22–33 American Congress on Survey and Mapping/American Society for Photogrammetry, Washington DC)

Dale P F (1991) Land information systems. In: Maguire D J, Goodchild M F, Rhind D W (eds.) *Geographical Information Systems: principles and applications*. Longman, London, pp. 85–99, Vol 2

Dangermond J (1983) A classification of software components commonly used in geographic information systems. In: Peuquet D J, O'Callaghan J (eds.) *Design and Implementation of Computer Based Geographic Information Systems*. IGU Commission on Geographical Data Sensing and Data Processing, Amherst New York

Davis F W, Simonett D S (1991) GIS and remote sensing. In: Maguire D J, Goodchild M F, Rhind D W (eds.) *Geographical Information Systems: principles and applications*. Longman, London, pp. 191–213, Vol 1

DCDSTF (Digital Cartographic Data Standards Task Force) (1988) The proposed standard for digital cartographic data. Vol I. *The American Cartographer* **15**: 24–8

Egenhofer M J, Frank A U (1987) Object oriented databases: database requirements for GIS. In: Aangeenbrug R T, Schiffman Y M (Eds.) *International Geographic Information Systems (IGIS) Symposium, Arlington, Virginia*, Volume II. NASA, Washington DC, pp. 189–211

Egenhofer M J, Herring J R (1991) High-level spatial data structures for GIS. In: Maguire D J, Goodchild M F, Rhind D W (eds.) *Geographical Information Systems: principles and applications*. Longman, London, pp. 227–37, Vol 1

Feuchtwanger M (1989) Geographic logical database model requirements. *Proceedings of AUTOCARTO 9.* ACSM/ASPRS, Falls Church Virginia, pp. 599–609.

Flowerdew R (1991) Spatial data integration In: Maguire D J, Goodchild M F, Rhind D W (eds.) *Geographical Information Systems: principles and applications.* Longman, London, pp. 375–87, Vol 1

Flowerdew R, Green M (1989) Statistical methods for inference between incompatible zonal systems. In: Goodchild M F, Gopal S (eds.) *Accuracy of Spatial Databases.* Taylor & Francis, London and New York, pp. 239–59

Flowerdew R, Openshaw S (1987) A review of the problems of transferring data from one set of areal units to another incompatible set. *Research Report* Volume 4. Lancaster and Newcastle, Northern Regional Research Laboratory

Freeman J (1975) The modelling of spatial relations. *Computer Graphics and Image Processing* **4**: 156–71

Gatrell A C (1991) Concepts of space and geographical data. In: Maguire D J, Goodchild M F, Rhind D W (eds.) *Geographical Information Systems: principles and applications.* Longman, London, pp. 119–34, Vol 1

GIS World (1990) *GIS Technology '90: results of the 1990 GIS World geographic information systems survey.* GIS World, Fort Collins, 16pp.

Goodchild M F (1988) Towards an enumeration and classification of GIS functions. In: Aangeenbrug R T, Schiffman Y M (eds.) *International Geographic Information Systems (IGIS) Symposium, Arlington, Virginia.* ASPRS, Falls Church, pp. 67–78

Goodchild M F (1991) The technological setting of GIS. In: Maguire D J, Goodchild M F, Rhind D W (eds.) *Geographical Information Systems: principles and applications.* Longman, London, pp. 45–54, Vol 1

Guptill S C (1988) A process for evaluating geographic information systems. Technology Exchange Working Group – Technical Report 1. Federal Interagency Coordinating Committee on Digital Cartography. *US Geological Survey Open-File Report 88–105.* USGS, Reston

Guptill S C (1989) Evaluating geographic information systems technology. *Photogrammetric Engineering and Remote Sensing* **55** (11): 1583–7

Guptill S C (1991) Spatial data exchange and standardization. In: Maguire D J, Goodchild M F, Rhind D W (eds.) *Geographical Information Systems: principles and applications.* Longman, London, pp. 515–30, Vol 1

Healey R G (1991) Database management systems. In: Maguire D J, Goodchild M F, Rhind D W (eds.) *Geographical Information Systems: principles and applications.* Longman, London, pp. 251–67, Vol 1

Jackson M J, Woodsford P A (1991) GIS data capture hardware and software. In: Maguire D J, Goodchild M F, Rhind D W (eds.) *Geographical Information Systems: principles and applications.* Longman, London, pp. 239–49, Vol 1

Langran G, Chrisman N R (1988) A framework for temporal geographic information. *Cartographica* **25** (3): 1–14

McHarg I L (1969) *Design with Nature.* Doubleday, New York

Maguire D J (1989) *Computers in Geography* Longman, London

Maguire D J (1990) A research plan for GIS in the 1990s. In: Foster M J, Shand P J (eds.) *The Association for Geographic Information Yearbook 1990* Taylor & Francis, London, pp. 267–77

Maguire D J, Raper J F (1990) An overview of GIS functionality *Proceedings of the Design Models and Functionality Conference.* Midlands Regional Research Laboratory, Leicester, 10pp

Maguire D J (1991) An overview and definition of GIS. In: Maguire D J, Goodchild M F, Rhind D W (eds.) *Geographical Information Systems: principles and applications.* Longman, London, pp. 9–20, Vol 1

Maling D H (1991) Coordinate systems and map projections for GIS. In: Maguire D J, Goodchild M F, Rhind D W (eds.) *Geographical Information Systems: principles and applications.* Longman, London, pp. 135–46, Vol 1

Marble D F, Lauzon J P, MaGranaghan M (1984) Development of a conceptual model of the digitising process In: Marble D F, Brassel D J, Peuquet D J (eds.) *Proceedings of the 1st International Symposium on Spatial Data Handling.* Universitat Zurich-Irchel, Zurich, pp. 146–71

Muller J-C (1991) Generalization of spatial databases. In: Maguire D J, Goodchild M F, Rhind D W (eds.) *Geographical Information Systems: principles and applications.* Longman, London, pp. 457–75, Vol 1

Openshaw S (1991) Developing appropriate spatial analysis methods for GIS. In: Maguire D J, Goodchild M F, Rhind D W (eds.) *Geographical Information Systems: principles and applications.* Longman, London, pp. 389–402, Vol 1

Parry R B, Perkins C R (1987) *World Mapping Today.* Butterworths, London

Peuquet D J (1981a) An examination of the techniques for reformatting digital cartographic data Part 1: the raster-to-vector process. *Cartographica* **18** (1): 34–48

Peuquet D J (1981b) An examination of the techniques for reformatting digital cartographic data Part 2: the vector-to-raster process. *Cartographica* **18** (3): 21–33

Peuquet D J (1984) A conceptual framework and comparison of spatial data models. *Cartographica* **21**: 66–113

Rhind D W (1974) An introduction to the digitising and editing of mapped data. In: Dale P F (ed.) *Automation and Cartography.* British Cartographic Society Special Publication, Volume 1, pp. 50–68

Rhind D W (1991) Counting the people: the role of GIS. In: Maguire D J, Goodchild M F, Rhind D W (eds.)

Geographical Information Systems: principles and applications. Longman, London, pp. 127–37, Vol 2

Robinove C J (1986) Principles of logic and the use of digital geographic information systems. *US Geological Survey Circular 977*. USGS, Reston Virginia

Robinson A H, Sale, R D, Morrison J L, Muehrcke P C (1984) *Elements of Cartography*, 5th edn. Wiley, New York

Robinson V B, Miller, R, Klesh L (1988) Issues in the use of expert systems to manage uncertainty in geographic information systems. In: Aangeenbrug R T, Schiffman, Y M (eds.) *International Geographic Information Systems (IGIS) Symposium, Arlington, Virginia*, NASA, Washington DC, pp. 89–100

Samet H (1990) *The Design and Analysis of Spatial Data Structures*. Addison-Wesley, Reading Massachusetts

Shepherd I D H (1991) Information integration and GIS. In: Maguire D J, Goodchild M F, Rhind D W (eds.) *Geographical Information Systems: principles and applications*. Longman, London, pp. 337–60, Vol 1

Sinton D (1978) The inherent structure of information as a constraint to analysis: mapped thematic data as a case study. In: Dutton G (ed.) *Harvard Papers on Geographic Information Systems*, Volume 6. Addison-Wesley, Reading Massachusetts

Star J, Estes J E (1990) *An Introduction to Geographic Information Systems*. Prentice Hall, Englewood Cliffs New Jersey

Stevens S S (1946) On the theory of scales of measurement. *Science* **103**: 677–80

Tomlin C D (1983) A map algebra. *Harvard Computer Graphics Conference 1983*. Harvard University Graduate School of Design Laboratory for Computer Graphics and Spatial Analysis, Cambridge Massachusetts

Tomlin C D (1990) *Geographic Information Systems and Cartographic Modelling*. Prentice-Hall, Englewood Cliffs New Jersey

Tomlin C D (1991) Cartographic modelling. In: Maguire D J, Goodchild M F, Rhind D W (eds.) *Geographical Information Systems: principles and applications*. Longman, London, pp. 361–74, Vol 1

Unwin D J (1981) *Introductory Spatial Analysis*. Methuen, London

Weibel R, Heller M (1991) Digital terrain modelling. In: Maguire D J, Goodchild M F, Rhind D W (eds.) *Geographical Information Systems: principles and applications*. Longman, London, pp. 269–97, Vol 1

Worboys M F, Hearnshaw, H M, Maguire D J (1990) Object-oriented data modelling for spatial databases *International Journal of Geographical Information Systems* **4**: 369–83

22

INFORMATION INTEGRATION AND GIS

I D H SHEPHERD

The role of the GIS as an 'information integrator' is examined, and the various approaches taken in current systems to achieve information integration are described. It is shown that considerable effort must be expended to create a consistent geographical database before GIS can successfully integrate diverse information. Alternative approaches to information integration found in information technology are also discussed, in order to identify more effective approaches to integration within a GIS framework.

INFORMATION INTEGRATION AND GIS

'The benefits of a geographical information system depend on linking different data sets together.'   (DoE 1987: 2).

'A GIS brings information together, it unifies and integrates that information. It makes available information to which no one had access before, and places old information in a new context. It often brings together information which either was not or could not be brought together previously.'
(Dangermond 1989: 25).

GIS as an integrating technology

One of the most persistent and pervasive buzzwords in the field of GIS is 'integration'. Indeed, the ability of GIS to integrate diverse information is frequently cited as its major defining attribute, and as its major source of power and flexibility in meeting user needs (Maguire 1991 in this volume).

There are strong similarities in the way that GIS and the discipline of geography have been promoted as 'integrating' mechanisms. Geography, it is argued, is an integrating discipline because it unites the study of society with that of the physical environment. GIS, it is claimed, is an integrating technology because of the way in which it links together diverse types of information drawn from a variety of sources. By integrating information, users can take a unified view of their data and large organizations can establish a single, coherent, corporate information system.

The benefits of information integration

The benefits that follow from the integration of diverse information within a GIS are widely recognised:

- A broader range of operations can be performed on integrated information than on disparate sets of data.

- By linking data sets together, spatial consistency is imposed on them. This adds value to existing data, making them both a more effective and a more marketable commodity.

- Through the integration of data which were previously the domain of individual disciplinary specialists, an interdisciplinary perspective to geographical problem solving is encouraged.

- Users benefit from the perception that they have access to a seamless information environment, uncomplicated by the need to consider differences in data sources, information types, storage devices, computer platforms, etc.

Further advantages accrue if several organizations pool their individual data into a single integrated database (Bracken and Higgs 1990):

- Data acquisition costs are reduced, because of the elimination of duplicate data collection and conversion activities.
- Organizations can draw on a broader base of information than hitherto, and are thus able to address issues that were previously beyond their individual data resources.
- Organizations can cooperate with one another within the context of shared information, and thereby make more effective management decisions.

What is 'Information Integration'?

What is meant by 'information integration', and how is it achieved? The dictionary definition of integration, 'the combination of separate parts into a whole', provides a poor starting point for a discussion of this concept. The GIS literature can be equally unhelpful, for integration is frequently ascribed several distinct meanings, including:

- The bringing together of spatial data from a number of sources, including maps, field survey equipment, photogrammetry, and remote sensors, within a single system (e.g. Aybet 1990).
- The creation of a geometrical description of the earth's surface within a consistent topological framework (e.g. Marx 1986).
- The inter-conversion of raster (i.e. image) and vector (i.e. map) models of the world within a single software environment (e.g. Jackson and Mason 1986).
- The provision of a comprehensive set of geographical information handling functions within a unified software framework (e.g. Dangermond 1986).
- The interlinking of both spatial and attribute data within a single, coherent representation or model (e.g. ESRI 1990a).
- The synthesis of diverse spatial information by means of fundamental geographical operations such as spatial search and overlay (e.g. Cowen 1988).

It is also perhaps worth noting that over and above these multiple meanings of integration, there is further terminological confusion in the use of terms such as 'integrate', 'link', 'relate', 'combine' and 'match'. These are sometimes used interchangeably, but are sometimes given distinct meanings (e.g. in Rhind *et al.* 1984).

It may be useful, therefore, to provide a working definition that clarifies these issues, and which serves as a framework for subsequent discussion. In this review, *information integration* is seen as the synthesis of geographical information in a computer system which depends for its effectiveness on *information linkage* (i.e. of spatial and attribute data) within a coherent data model. This involves bringing together diverse information from a variety of sources (*information interchange*), requires the effective *matching* of supposedly similar entities in these sources, and demands *information consistency* across the source data sets.

THE CLASSIC APPROACH TO INFORMATION INTEGRATION IN GIS

The integration of spatial and attribute data

In commercial information systems, non-spatial data are typically integrated by storing them non-redundantly in a single database engine. In computer mapping systems, spatial data of various kinds are frequently integrated within a single graphical database, in either vector or raster format. Within each of these systems, the relationship between items of consistently recorded data can be used to answer a variety of questions. However, the range of questions that can be asked must be of a spatial or non-spatial nature.

Within GIS, information integration goes one step further, involving the linkage of non-spatial or attribute data to spatial information describing real world features. By performing operations across the two sets of information in tandem, a far richer set of questions may be asked, and a far broader range of problems can be solved than in those systems that handle just attribute or spatial data alone. For example:

1. Users can interrogate geographical features displayed on a computer map and retrieve associated attribute information, for display or further analysis.

2. Maps can be constructed by querying or analysing attribute information in a database.

3. New sets of information can be generated by performing spatial operations (such as polygon overlay) on the integrated database.

4. Different items of attribute data can be associated with one another through a shared locational code.

Two approaches, or models, have been widely adopted for achieving the linkage between spatial and attribute information within GIS: the composite map model and the geo-relational model (Aronson 1987; Bracken and Webster 1989; Healey 1991 in this volume). Each of these approaches to data integration is based on a particular type of spatial data model: the composite map model is usually based on a tessellated representation of space (typically the grid-cell tessellation), while the geo-relational model is usually associated with a vector representation of space (and particularly the arc/node topological model). For a fuller discussion of the relative merits of these and other spatial data models, see Peuquet (1984), Burrough (1986), Davis and Simonett (1991 in this volume) and Egenhofer and Herring (1991 in this volume).

The key element in both of these models is that links are established between attribute information and spatial features. The precise techniques used to create these links vary from GIS to GIS but, in general, involve establishing a pointer between each spatial feature in the database and its associated attribute information. In the composite map model, the links are implicit in the way that specific attributes are assigned to individual map layers, and in the process of assigning specific attribute values to the spatial entities (i.e. cells) on each layer. In the geo-relational model, by contrast, the links are established by arranging for each spatial feature's unique identifier (or ID) to be recorded in a key field of the appropriate database table(s) that store its attribute information.

For each data model, an appropriate set of operations is available that integrates across (or synthesizes) the two kinds of data in response to user queries. In the composite map model, the principal integration mechanism is a 'map modelling' capability that relates together two or more grid cell layers to produce new layers, on which further modelling operations may be performed (Berry 1985, 1987; Tomlin 1990, 1991 in this volume). In the geo-relational model, integration is accomplished by undertaking operations such as spatial search and overlay (ESRI 1990b).

The composite map model

The first method of linking spatial and attribute information is by means of a multi-layered map (Berry 1985; Tomlin 1990). This model is essentially a computerized version of the technique of filter or sieve mapping developed for landscape planning and resource management (Steinitz, Parker and Jordan 1976), but it is also closely associated with more recent developments in image processing.

In the composite map model, attribute information is referenced to artificial units of space (typically square grid cells) that form a regular grid. These units are usually constant in size, shape and orientation, and rarely have intrinsic meaning. Grids of cells are usually 'sliced' horizontally into a number of layers or planes, with information about specific variables or attributes stored on individual layers (see Fig. 22.1).

Within the context of this model, information integration proceeds by combining attribute values for cells that lie above or below one another in a 'stack' of superimposed layers. A quantitative model is generally used to derive secondary values from the source attribute values. This can be done in one of two ways: either the model is applied to each cell independently, or else the model operates on cell values within a layer that are within a given range or window. These are sometimes termed Type 1 and Type 2 operations (Heuvelink, Burrough and Stein 1990), and are illustrated in Fig. 22.1.

The grid-cell model is a relatively simple approach to data integration, both conceptually and operationally, and it has therefore been popular

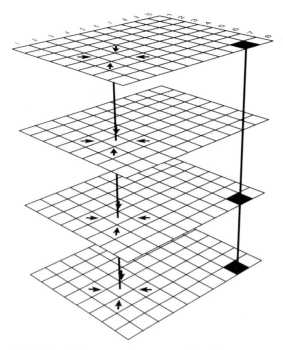

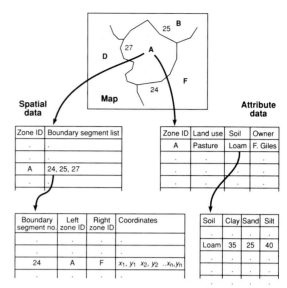

Fig. 22.1 The composite map model of information integration in which both spatial and attribute data are combined in the same layer.

Fig. 22.2 The geo-relational model of information integration in which spatial and attribute data are stored separately.

since the earliest days of GIS development. The model is currently implemented in a large number of 'cartographic modelling' and raster-based image processing systems.

The Geo-relational Model

In the second, and more recently developed, approach to information integration, attribute information is associated with point, line, zonal or other spatial entities that describe features occurring in the real world. Thus, for example, a point located feature such as a house may have associated with it such items of information as its local tax rate, its current market price, its owner, its occupants, and so on. Similarly, a linear feature such as a river might have associated with it such information as mean discharge, pollution levels, fishing rights, etc. In like manner, a zonal feature such as a field might be linked to information describing its owner, its current land use, its soil type, and so forth.

In this approach to data integration, spatial entities are usually linked with their associated attribute data by means of a common spatial key (commonly a unique identifier or ID assigned to each spatial feature). Different sets of attribute information are stored in different attribute tables, and the relevant information for a given set of spatial features is accumulated by relating (or joining) two or more tables of information (see Fig. 22.2). The collation of information from the attribute tables may be carried out in several ways: by exact matching, by hierarchical matching, or by fuzzy matching (ESRI 1990b; Flowerdew 1991 in this volume).

The geo-relational model has two important characteristics. The first is that the join works both ways; thus, attribute information can be found by selecting spatial features, and spatial features can be found by querying attribute information. Secondly, all attribute information within the model is associated with one or more spatial features, even though it may require a chain of joins between numerous tables in order to establish this relationship. Attribute information that is not linked (either directly or indirectly) to a spatial feature is normally not included in the attribute tables.

Most contemporary, vector-oriented GIS adopt the geo-relational model to conceptualize the links between spatial and attribute data. In addition, most usually adopt a dual or hybrid data storage strategy to implement the model, with spatial data held separately from the attribute data, and the system maintaining links between the software modules that handle each information type (Duecker 1985; Morehouse 1985). Locational data are typically represented using a topological (or arc–node) spatial data model, and thematic data are usually stored in the tables of a standard relational database. Thus, for example, in the case of ARC/INFO, the archetypical example of this approach, the spatial model is implemented in the ARC program, and the attribute data model is implemented in INFO, a fourth generation database system. Users of the system are able to address each software component separately, by means of the ARC macro language and INFO commands respectively. However, the tight coupling between ARC and INFO ensures the integrity of the relationships between spatial entities and their attributes.

Similarly, the GDS/AMS system consists of a graphics database (containing land feature data) and a textual database (containing assigned data) which are connected by an interface consisting of a lookup table. SICAD, too, combines a geographical database for storing topologically structured spatial information with a relational database for storing textual information (Wagner 1990). Many other operational GIS (including TerraSoft, Strings, and ILWIS) adopt this hybrid approach.

Because of the relative simplicity of this hybrid approach to implementing the geo-relational model, many LIS and AM/FM systems have been developed by end users linking together a CAD system (to store the spatial data) and a database program (to hold the attribute data) (Cowen 1986; Shepherd 1990a, 1990b, 1990c). In contrast to commercial GIS that adopt the hybrid data model, the component items of software in such 'do-it-yourself' GIS are usually loosely coupled, with intermediate files being used to exchange data about the links between the two types of information.

Limitations of current integration models

GIS do not (and maybe cannot) always provide an entirely satisfactory approach to the integration of geographical information. In particular, the overlay mechanism at the heart of most GIS software is not able of itself to guarantee error-free integration of spatial and attribute data. Errors introduced by data capture and conversion, together with residual errors not resolved by data consistency analysis, can combine with errors generated by the overlay process itself to provide output maps that have a probabilistically uncertain level of error.

In vector GIS, for example, where the accuracy of points, lines and areas stored in the geographical database is subject to small margins of error, the overlay process will propagate these errors when producing resultant maps (Rhind *et al.* 1984). Experiments in geographical sensitivity analysis clearly reveal how perturbations or errors in input maps can change the appearance of output maps (Lodwick, Monson and Svoboda 1990). The integration process can itself also generate errors, a well-known effect being the appearance of spurious sliver polygons as a result of vector overlay operations (Goodchild 1976). Chrisman (1984, 1991 in this volume) argues that earlier assessments of the errors associated with the overlay process need to be revised in the light of modern software, but acknowledges that the lack of appropriately accurate base map sources remains a prime source of integration errors.

Similar problems arise with integration operations in grid-cell GIS. For example, the validity of the layer combination process may be compromised if attribute information has been erroneously allocated to cells by the process of cell aggregation used in creating a consistent spatial base (Walker and Hutton 1986). Additionally, where uncertainties associated with coefficients used in the map combination model are unknown, then the relative contribution of the model to the total error in the output map will also be unknown (Heuvelink *et al.* 1990). Finally, where spatial units and/or data attributes are fuzzy rather than discrete, the standard set theoretic approach implicit in the overlay process may break down entirely (Wang, Hall and Subaryono 1990; Burrough 1989). For a fuller discussion of these issues, see Chrisman (1991 in this volume) and Tomlin (1991 in this volume).

Preparing for information integration

Organizations that are new to geographical information handling frequently make the mistake of assuming that the GIS is some kind of magical data integrator, an automatic 'information melting pot'. In reality, the rewards that may be reaped by adopting a GIS to perform integrated information analysis (as outlined above) are contingent upon the amount of effort expended in creating a consistent database in the first instance. The adoption of one or other of the currently fashionable models of information integration does not automatically create harmony among previously incompatible data sets. Information integration is in fact a two-step process: the first step involves the removal of inconsistencies between disparate data sets, to ensure their compatibility; the second involves the use of GIS software to interrelate consistent data in ways that meet the needs of particular applications (see Flowerdew 1991 in this volume).

The following sections examine the causes of inconsistent data, and the various methods available for, and some of the broad approaches taken in, creating consistent geographical databases.

The data inconsistency problem

Geographical data sets are difficult to integrate where there are inconsistencies between them. These inconsistencies may affect the spatial and attribute characteristics of data, and necessitate the use of various corrective measures. Inconsistencies result from a variety of causes:

- differences in recording or measurement techniques (e.g. observation times or periods, data gathering equipment, data categories, human observers/interviewers);

- errors in measurement or survey methods (e.g. malfunctioning data loggers, data recording errors by human observers);

- variations in the resolution (spatial, temporal or attribute) of the data gathered;

- vagueness or imprecision in definitions (spatial or attribute);

- fuzziness in spatial objects (e.g. soil boundaries);

- variations in the use of terminology and nomenclature.

Inconsistencies tend to be greater where:

- the study area involves several administrative or governmental data units, and/or where several organizations are responsible for gathering information;

- the information is drawn from multiple sources, at several scales;

- the information consists of several types (map, image, text, numeric, sound, etc.);

- the information is available at several points in time;

- the information is stored on diverse media, and on more than one computer system.

Problems of inconsistent data are frequently greater in developing countries than in the developed nations of the world (Casley and Lury 1981; Robinson et al. 1989). However, considerable problems arise even in developed countries when attempts are made to integrate information across national boundaries. An example is provided by the CORINE project, which sought to demonstrate the viability and utility of an integrated (vector) GIS for soil and land use planning in the European Community (Mounsey 1991 in this volume). This project revealed that problems of data inconsistency are frequently far more significant than those of data availability, accuracy, geographical coverage, large data volumes, or lack of adequate data structuring. Moreover, despite the use of a variety of techniques for overcoming problems of spatial inconsistency, it was nevertheless concluded that where a GIS involves a large surface area (in this case, 2.26 million km^2), and a number of political entities (in this case 12 nation states), 'the problem of data inconsistency is not easy to tackle and cannot wholly be resolved' (Briggs and Mounsey 1989: 16).

Techniques for removing inconsistencies in data

The creation of a consistent geographical database requires effort at a number of distinct levels: the resolution of differences in the meaning and significance ascribed to data by cooperating organizations; the integration of incompatible database schemata (Frank 1986; Nyerges 1989b); and the conversion of information between contrasting data models, data structures, and data media. Ideally, the removal of inconsistencies should proceed in a top-down manner, dealing first with differences in the meanings of data, before addressing issues of data representation and structure (Nyerges 1989b).

The specific techniques that may be used to create consistent data can be classified on the basis of the information being handled (see Table 22.1). Fuller accounts of these techniques are provided elsewhere (e.g. Rhind and Tannenbaum 1983; Rhind et al. 1984; Flowerdew 1991 in this volume).

Table 22.1 Methods for creating consistent databases (see Flowerdew 1991 in this volume for further details).

Spatial data

Map projection standardization, rectification of local geometrical distortions, coordinate registration, coordinate density equalization, feature generalization, edge matching, scale conversion, image-to-image registration, co-registration of maps and images, conversion between vector and raster data models, creation of multi-image mosaics, allocation of one set of zones to another, etc.

Attribute data

Aggregation of data classes, reclassification of raw data, reduction in numerical precision of data, reduction of levels of measurement to a common level, address matching, nominal record linkage, schema integration analysis, conversion from network or hierarchical database to relational database, greyscale normalization, etc.

In some cases, the task of ensuring consistency in spatial data can be undertaken separately from that of ensuring consistency in attribute data. Considerable benefits accrue, however, if these efforts proceed in tandem (an example is address/location matching). In particular, there are many occasions when the removal of inconsistencies in spatial data sets should follow their removal in attribute data. This is because a consistent attribute data set can often provide valuable guidance to the process of removing inconsistencies in spatial data (Nyerges 1989b). Similarly, the creation of a topologically consistent map base is a valuable precursor to ensuring geometrical consistency in a spatial database.

Sometimes, as is the case with map conflation (Saalfeld 1988), incompatibilities are best resolved by handling items of source information one pair at a time. In other operations, such as database schema integration (Nyerges 1989b), several sources of information are considered together.

A number of broad strategies may be adopted in creating consistency among disparate data sets. One approach is to permit inconsistent data to coexist, with explicit information being provided on the nature of the inconsistencies (Briggs and Mounsey 1989). Another approach is to convert all source data sets into a single target version, as in the integration of multiple database schemata (Nyerges 1989b). A third approach is to convert data stored in one data model to another data model, as is the case in preparing data for vector-only or raster-only GIS (see Peuquet 1981a, 1981b; Piwowar, LeDrew and Dudycha 1990). In many applications, data consistency is often achieved by reducing diverse spatial or attribute data to some lowest common denominator representation. For example, all attribute data may be reduced to nominal scale measurements, or all spatial data may be reduced to a relatively coarse grid-cell representation.

These approaches are also found in many mainstream commercial systems. Some integrated office packages, for example, store different types of data in separate files, and/or maintain different data models for each of the individual functions provided. Information is exchanged between the various components by automatic or manual file swapping. By contrast, some data handling packages use a single data model (e.g. the spreadsheet), and provide the necessary internal functions to store and structure the various types of user information within this single model.

The 'single model' approach is perhaps taken to its extreme in Document Image Processing (DIP) systems, in which various source materials (e.g. text, drawings, maps, photographs) are reduced to a single form: the Digital Image Document (DID). This is a standard scanned image, and large collections of such images may be indexed, stored, managed, accessed and displayed using tools available in a DIP system. As in raster GIS, the availability of optical storage devices (such as CD-ROMs and WORMs) with huge storage capacities has greatly accelerated the adoption of this approach.

Typically, a variety of techniques is applied in a given application to ensure consistent data. In the

CORINE project, for example, several techniques were adopted to remove or reduce spatial incompatibilities between source data incorporated into a geo-relational GIS (Briggs and Mounsey 1989). These included: conversion of data to a single reference map projection; removal of local geometrical distortions by rubber sheeting; adoption of two standard scales (1 : 1 million and 1 : 3 million) at which to store data; and generalization of larger scale data down to these standard scales.

The creation of a consistent database is still essentially a manual operation. It is frequently labour intensive, and usually requires the participation of those who are knowledgeable both in the characteristics of the source data and also in the application area for which the data are being assembled. More recently, however, many of the tasks undertaken to create consistent databases have been supported by software tools. These are available either as modules in a general-purpose GIS, or as special-purpose utility programs. Examples of the latter include software for rubber sheeting (Bedell 1988), zipping (Beard and Chrisman 1986), map conflation (Saalfeld 1988), and vector-to-raster conversion (Steneker and Bonham-Carter 1988).

Unfortunately, not all data inconsistencies are resolvable simply by using the battery of tools available. For example, the use of an interactive graphics editor to displace polygon boundary coordinates (what Dangermond (1988) calls 'graphic fudging') may be constrained or prevented by legal definitions of one of the boundaries in question. Similarly, the use of distance-based or point-in-polygon techniques to allocate one set of zones to another may lead to unacceptably high error rates. In other cases, it may not be possible or acceptable to reduce the variability in source information by creating or adopting a single, 'clean' data set. In some applications, it may be desirable to let mutually inconsistent versions of data to coexist in a controlled fashion within a GIS (Newell, Theriault and Easterfield 1990). Finally, many inconsistencies may be 'hidden' in apparently consistent data, and these may have to be flagged rather than corrected (Briggs and Mounsey 1989).

The operations needed to create a consistent geographical database can be implemented at various stages in the data conversion process (Dangermond 1988):

- Before data conversion: use of standard base maps (e.g. Integrated Terrain Units) to record field information, etc.

- During data conversion: templating, on-line transformation, automatic text annotation, automatic snapping, on-the-fly topological construction, etc.

- After data conversion: manual interactive editing, rubber sheeting, conflation, line snapping, schema integration analysis, attribute consistency checking, etc.

The amount of effort needed to ensure data consistency tends to increase at each stage of the conversion process. The dictum 'prevention is better than cure' applies just as much to the creation of a consistent database as it does in matters of personal health and safety. It is far cheaper to 'design out' possible inconsistency at an early stage in the development of a geographical database. Unfortunately, many geographical databases are created by merging existing digital data sets, and incompatibilities have, therefore, to be removed after data conversion has taken place.

Integrating contrasting spatial data models

One of the long-standing problems of operational GIS has been the separation of information derived from maps and information derived from images. The former has typically been the preserve of vector-oriented GIS, the latter has been the preserve of image processing systems.

Recently, however, major efforts have been made to integrate remote sensing data with cartographic data (e.g. Zobrist 1983; Jackson 1987; Logan and Bryant 1988; Goodenough 1988; Annoni et al. 1990). Designers of remote sensing systems have attempted to bridge the gap either by adding mapping capabilities to existing image processing functions (e.g. the drawing of vector ground reference features such as coastlines, rivers, and national boundaries), or by providing users with on-line access to GIS information (e.g. to assist with the process of image classification). Some raster GIS provide vector tracing or annotation functions for raster images (e.g. ERDAS and SPANS).

For their part, developers of vector GIS have tried to add a variety of raster/image processing

Information Integration and GIS

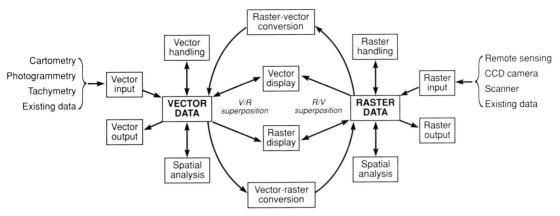

Fig. 22.3 The integration of vector and raster data in a GIS.

capabilities: displaying raster backgrounds beneath vector maps, vectorizing scanned images, and linking images to vector coordinate systems (Pevsner 1989; Annoni et al. 1990). A prime example of this trend is ARC/INFO, which enables vector information to be overlaid on raster images by means of its Image Integrator module. An increasing number of systems provide utilities to convert spatial data from the alternative model into its own native model, or to convert between the vector and raster data models.

Figure 22.3 illustrates the internal structure of a fully integrated GIS which attempts to combine both vector and raster information. (This figure is derived from a system diagram of the SICAD–HYGRIS system, and from Laser-Scan's idealized view of an integrated GIS architecture.) Several systems are now available that claim to be able to combine vector data and functionality with raster data and functionality, and these are sometimes labelled 'Integrated GIS' (or IGIS) to distinguish them from those that are limited to a single spatial data model (Jackson and Mason 1986; Gorte, Liem and Wind 1988).

Resolving inconsistent data formats and media

Beyond inconsistencies in the content of geographical data lie incompatibilities in the format or medium used to record the data. Format and media incompatibilities can arise wherever data are gathered by different methods or equipment, where data are stored on two or more computer systems, or where data are handled by two or more computer programs. Such incompatibilities require a further set of operations to enable successful data integration within a GIS (Aybet 1990).

The most common solution to this problem lies in the use of data translators to inter-convert a wide variety of cartographic, image and attribute data (numeric as well as text). Most translators are special purpose, working only with specific data formats, but general purpose data translation tools, driven by relational database technology, are also available (Waugh and Healey 1986; Pascoe and Penny 1990; Guptill 1991 in this volume). Once again, these translators are available either as stand-alone utility programs, or as modules within general-purpose GIS. By way of example, the data conversions available within the ARC/INFO system are illustrated in Fig. 22.4. In mainstream computer applications, utility programs are widely available for converting between text, database, spreadsheet and graphics data formats.

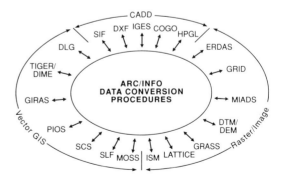

Fig. 22.4 Data conversion facilities in ARC/INFO. Reprinted courtesy of Environmental Systems Research Institute, Inc. Copyright © 1991 Environmental Systems Research Institute, Inc.

Two approaches are generally taken to the inter-conversion of incompatible data formats and media: one-to-one conversion using direct translators (necessitating n^2n-n translators for n different formats); and translation to and from a universal intermediate format (requiring 2_n translators for n different formats). Clearly, any strategy that reduces the number of data formats in general use simplifies this conversion problem. In the wider world of data processing, a number of *de facto* standards has emerged that simplify the exchange of attribute and spatial data (Table 22.2). The emergence of national and international standards for cartographic data (e.g. Haywood 1986; Zarzycki and Jiwani 1986; DCDSTF 1988) is an equally welcome step in reducing the problems associated with data exchange.

For the future, data exchange mechanisms other than the commonly used external file are likely to assume greater importance. One such mechanism is the 'live link', which enables items of information in separate application programs to be inter-connected. (In the personal computer environment, this facility is currently available in the form of the Dynamic Data Exchange (DDE) protocol, and the Inter-Application Communications (IAC) mechanism.)

By linking information directly together, some of the problems of data loss associated with conventional transfer may be avoided. In addition, the 'live link' approach makes possible several forms of data interchange: data snapshots may be passed automatically from one program to another; changes in the data held in one program (e.g. a spreadsheet) may be reflected in automatic changes to information held in another program (e.g. a desktop mapping program); real-time data (e.g. from data loggers) may be accessed automatically by data analysis and display software; and data queries may be made across multiple linked documents (Vose 1990). In addition, live data links may be established among programs running on a single multitasking computer, or on several different computers connected across a network.

Table 22.2 Standard formats for data exchange.

Structured data

Database formats: dBASE (DBF).

Spreadsheet formats: DIF, WK1 and WKS, SYLK.

ASCII (the lowest common denominator; this contains the data and, perhaps, data definition information, but none of the internal data structuring information specific to a particular data handling program) – common formats are CDF and SDF.

Text

Word processing formats: Word Perfect, Word, Wordstar, DCA/RFT.

ASCII (the lowest common denominator; this contains the text but none of the display and formatting characters found in standard word processing files).

Line Drawings

Line art and business graphics program formats: HPGL, CGM, Lotus PIC, Windows Metafile, General Parametric Videoshow, Postscript.

CAD program formats: DXF, IGES, SIF, Set, Step/PDES.

Maps

DIGEST, VPT, NTF, DLG, etc.

Painted pictures

Painting program formats: PCX, GEM, IMG, TGA.

Raster images

Scanned image format: TIFF, GIF.

FAX format: CCITT Group 3 and 4.

Presentation

NAPLPS, EPS.

Documents

ODA, CDA, DCA, DDIF, SGML, Edifact.

Linking existing databases

A major problem in establishing an integrated spatial database is that many organizations already have a massive installed base of computer-readable, geo-referenced data. In many cases, this information is handled by application-specific software; in others, it is handled by a standard database management system. Increasingly, the component data sets of a potential geographical database are distributed over several computers, often with incompatible operating systems. Frequently, attribute data are stored in one place and spatial data in another.

The ability to integrate data sets across several items of software and several computer systems is, therefore, a key factor in the success or failure of GIS technology within modern organizations. McLaren (1990) sees four approaches to the integration of existing information in such circumstances, each providing a different level of effectiveness:

1. *Data absorption*: information is copied from existing data handling software, either on a temporary or a permanent basis, into a GIS for analysis.

2. *Querying of external data sets*: features in a GIS are linked to sets of information held in external databases. The links are usually *ad hoc*, and the items of software are only loosely coupled.

3. *DBMS interfacing*: spatial objects modelled in a GIS are linked through a generic interface to attribute data held in an external DBMS.

4. *Full integration*: information on spatial objects is managed by a single, heterogeneous, distributed DBMS (or DDBMS).

The first three approaches are now commonplace, frequently being adopted where it is economically or operationally infeasible to transfer existing information to an entirely new system.

Several authors (e.g. Webster 1988; McLaren 1990) argue that the full potential of GIS will only be realized if a corporate approach is taken to information management, and particularly one that addresses the issue of distributed data. They also argue that conventional approaches to data integration which do not use mainstream DBMS technology to handle *both* spatial and attribute data are unlikely to allow the creation of integrated corporate databases. In this scenario, it is the coherent management of geographically distributed data, by means of a DDBMS, and not just the interlinkage of data items in diverse software systems, that is crucial to the success of an integrated geographical information system. Thus far, there have been only a few implementations of this approach (e.g. Green 1990; Nicholson 1990).

Organizational factors in data integration

The significance of organizational factors in the creation of fully integrated geographical databases cannot be overemphasized. For example, because different organizations collect data for different purposes, they may ascribe contrasting meanings to their data. These purposes, therefore, need to be taken into account when decoding the meanings of specific data items. This conclusion emerges clearly from work undertaken to create multipurpose land information systems in North America (Liley 1985; Nyerges 1989a).

Organizational factors are also critically important when establishing operational data exchange arrangements. This is illustrated by the development of a prototype GIS for inter-organizational decision making in mid-Wales (Bracken and Higgs 1990). A major conclusion derived from this exercise was that the benefits of an integrated database will only accrue if there is consensus among the participants (individuals, departments or organizations) involved in creating it, and that this consensus will only emerge if the data users see a clear value in the integrated database. An important contributory factor in achieving success is that the database users should have a tradition of information sharing.

ALTERNATIVE APPROACHES TO INFORMATION INTEGRATION

Limitations of current approaches to information integration in GIS

Several assumptions, both explicit and implicit, are made by current GIS vendors in their approach to information integration. For example, the range of information types currently integrated in most GIS is largely dictated by the *data models* they implement. In particular, the information they accept is limited to that which easily fits the database model of attribute space (i.e. numeric data and structured alphanumeric strings), and that which fits the map or image model of geographical space (i.e. vector or raster representations of space). Similar restrictions are imposed on the ability to integrate data available on different media.

Similarly, the way that information is integrated, and therefore the uses to which it can be put, are imposed by the *integration model* adopted by a particular GIS. This has two major implications, one concerning the use of precise locational referencing, the other concerning the cognitive model adopted for the integration process.

The traditional mechanism for integrating data within most GIS is the overlay process. This implies the use of some form of locational reference or geocode to link attribute data to their respective spatial features. The assignment of a unique spatial key to all data entities enables the software to store, retrieve, analyse and display diverse data in a precisely coordinated fashion, and ensures that all information for a given location can be brought together as required.

However, one of the dangers of using an unambiguous and precise location code as the principal data key or linkage mechanism is that information which cannot be explicitly or precisely tied into a particular locational referencing scheme runs the risk of being ignored, or relegated to an ancillary role. This has occurred with several types of information in the past, including: non-vertical aerial imagery (ground-based and low oblique aerial photographs); free text which describes broad geographical areas; environmental sounds; moving images; etc. However, it is just such information, with its richness, ambiguity, fuzziness and subtlety that many users want to be able to access in their information systems. Although steps have been taken during the past few years to accommodate such information within GIS (Dangermond 1988), this has typically been accomplished within the framework of an existing model of data integration.

Current thinking and research in GIS tends to ignore the information richness of the real world. In a recent volume on the design of databases for global science (Mounsey 1988), for example, it was assumed by most contributors that the structure of world-wide databases would depend primarily on just two major types/sources of information: the cartographic and the remotely sensed. Elsewhere, too, the discussion of geographical data in GIS is dominated by consideration of those models (notably the vector and the raster) which are best able to accommodate these two types of information.

A number of GIS workers do recognize that 'research is needed on ... techniques for integrating heterogeneous data' (Abler 1987: 308). However, the alternatives that are proposed are often conditioned by the prevailing view of geographical information (i.e. consisting of highly structured data), and by existing models of data integration (i.e. those based on precise locational referencing of spatial objects). These views are also heavily conditioned by an analytic form of thinking among geoscientists, and lead to the continued development of GIS which concentrate on the computer processing of precisely coordinated spatial data sets. However, in its overemphasis of the role of the GIS as a machine for data handling and analysis, this approach de-emphasizes the role of the end-user as an information integrator, interpreter and analyst.

It is clear from the use made of multiple window displays on modern workstations, for example, that users can benefit from being able to perform their own visual integrations of diverse information displayed on screen. Users also frequently integrate multiple sources of information in a relatively loose way outside a GIS. The use of desktop publishing software to produce environmental reports by merging information of many kinds is an example. In certain applications, therefore, user-centred methods of information integration complement the machine's algorithmic approach.

For these reasons, three alternative approaches to the integration of multiple types of information that have emerged from other fields in recent years will be considered further here. Each represents an alternative, even competitive, model of data integration to that provided by current GIS technology. They merit attention, because they suggest directions in which GIS might move in order to integrate information about the real world more effectively.

Multimedia databases

Recent developments in computer technology have led to a rapid expansion in the number of information types that can be routinely handled by computers. Most notable have been developments in optical storage technology, hardware for combining images from digital and video sources, digital sound sampling, and hi-fi sound output. Of greater importance in the present context, is the convergence of previously separate information handling technologies (e.g. video and audio, digital and analogue, and television and computing) (Press 1990), and the development of desktop 'multi media' computer systems that permit users to access many types of information (e.g. text, graphics, animation, sound and motion video) from a number of complementary sources (e.g. videodisk, CD-ROM, scanner, video camera, audio tape, digital sound sampler and data logger). Figure 22.5 illustrates a typical PC-based multimedia system.

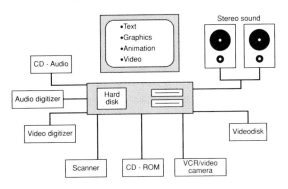

Fig. 22.5 The components of a desktop multimedia workstation.

This section considers how non-conventional information has been embraced by conventional database technology, and what implications this might have for GIS. Some DBMS have addressed the problem of non-standard data items by introducing the 'long record' or the 'binary large object' (BLOB). BLOBs consist of large volume data items (e.g. documents, software, faxes, graphs, images and voice information) that do not fit neatly into the standard database management system framework. One system that has embraced this approach is Informix, a standard RDBMS whose derivative product, Informix-OnLine, can handle not only the usual structured information, but also large-volume items with little or no standard structure (Shetler 1990). In this system, the two kinds of BLOB (text and byte) are stored separately from the regular data, perhaps on separate storage devices, but they are handled entirely by the standard database mechanisms. BLOBs can be selected, updated and inserted using standard SQL commands, and displayed to the database user on request. (How information is presented to the user depends on the output devices and device drivers available.) However, searching for BLOBs, or relating BLOBs to one another, on the basis of their content, would require extensions to standard SQL.

A number of multimedia database systems are also available in the PC environment. These usually involve relatively simple extensions to a standard database or information retrieval program so that database records can be linked to scanned or drawn images.

The multimedia database appears to be the current development route for several GIS. ESRI, for example, has identified eight related geographical data technologies which need to be interlinked in a GIS framework (ESRI 1989) (Fig. 22.6). Two of these, the vector GIS and the DBMS, are at the core of ARC/INFO operations, and are commonly found in many other GIS. The other technologies may be connected to the system by one or more of the following generic integration techniques:

1. *Image overlay*: Superposition of vector data on a raster image (e.g. network lines drawn on a scanned base map), and/or superposition of a raster image on a vector display (e.g. a satellite image draped over a DTM). In either case, no logical connection is made between the two data sets.

2. *Data conversion*: Conversion between vector and raster data representations, including data exchange between mapping and CAD systems with differing data formats.

3. *DBMS interfacing*: Linking cartographic feature data with attribute data managed by an external DBMS.

4. *Feature and attribute association*: Creation of an index link between a GIS feature and a displayable item (e.g. a raster document, a video image, an environmental sound, an animation sequence, an engineering drawing). These items may be stored on a separate storage medium (e.g. optical disk).

Each of these techniques is now increasingly used in commercial GIS. The last mentioned has

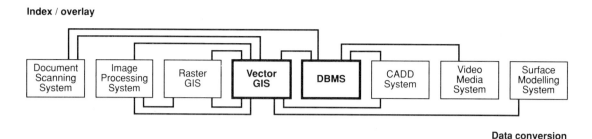

Fig. 22.6 Linkages between different information types in ARC/INFO. Reprinted courtesy of Environmental Systems Research Institute, Inc. Copyright © 1991 Environmental Systems Research Institute, Inc.

become particularly popular with the advent of optical mass-storage devices. For example, in a system that is used by Paris police to monitor events in the city as they happen, the operator can zoom down to street level on a vector map, and bring up a video image of key buildings from an optical disk system (Anon 1990).

However, several issues remain to be resolved before multimedia databases achieve their full potential in a GIS context. Among these are: how to handle spatial as well as linear multimedia objects (e.g. images and sound); how to handle the transfer of multimedia objects from the database, when some may require 'persistent' presentation and others 'non-persistent' presentation; how to control the capture and/or presentation of multimedia data once the data transfer has begun; and how to ensure efficient storage and transfer of multimedia information (Woelk and Kim 1987).

Some idea of the complexities involved in integrating non-conventional information in a GIS can be provided by briefly considering visual images. In GIS that associate images with database records, the link is usually made by assigning a field in the appropriate attribute data table in which to store a pointer (such as a file name) to an image stored elsewhere. The problem lies in deciding which spatial feature(s) in the database are to be associated with which image(s).

The simplest approach is to link an image to a point-located feature. Thus, for example, in a road network GIS, the user might point to a road intersection marker and bring up on screen a photograph of that intersection; or in a property database, clicking on a property symbol might bring up a photograph of a house. However, a single image may be linked to several types of feature (point, line or zone), in which case the spatial extent of the photograph will not match the geometry of one or more of these features.

This type of linkage provides only a weak form of integration of the spatial extent and content of an image with that of the other (conventional) information in the database. In order to associate the image with other spatial data in the database fully, some attempt needs to be made to rectify its geometry, perhaps using appropriate photogrammetric techniques. However, the space covered by a single image may be geo-referenced in several different ways, each appropriate for specific applications. It may, therefore, be necessary to store additional geometrical parameters in the database to suit these (Table 22.3).

Table 22.3 Geometrical parameters which can be added to databases to assist rectification.

Geometrical parameter	Application
Centre point	Retrieval
Viewer's eyepoint	Retrieval
Camera location, etc.	Photomontage
View direction	Environmental impact analysis, etc.
View envelope	Environmental impact analysis, etc.

If a particular geographical database is to serve multiple applications, then individual images will have to be described in each of these different ways. Moreover, different types of image (vertical, oblique, ground level, etc.), may require particular types of spatial referencing, and image sets and moving images will require yet more complex approaches to ensure effective linkage between the images and the database (see, for example, Baker 1990).

Another aspect of the image integration problem concerns the most appropriate means of representing the non-spatial content of images. One approach that holds promise for the future is the automatic scene interpretation techniques developed for industrial robots and autonomous vehicles. For the moment, however, manual methods of extracting and encoding the thematic content of images are more commonly used, if they are used at all.

The Community Disk of the BBC Domesday interactive video system provides an example of the way in which both systematic spatial referencing and a looser form of geographical association can coexist (Openshaw and Mounsey 1987; Rhind and Openshaw 1987; Maguire 1989). Users are able to search for a location by 'map walking' (i.e. zooming and panning visually across a seamless map of the United Kingdom), or by entering a place name which is checked against a gazetteer of some 250 000 place names. When an appropriate map is found, the user may then display photographs and pages of text associated with some part of the area covered by that map. Alternatively, users can search for textual material by entering appropriate keywords, and the associated photographs and map are retrieved and displayed by the system. Photographs may also be searched in this way, and the associated text and maps recovered for inspection (see Fig. 22.7).

The system is able to perform this linkage by means of a thesaurus of terms describing the contents of the text and photographs stored on the disk. By means of this mechanism, users can move rapidly from one type of information to the other.

This three-way cross-indexing of contrasting information is extremely powerful, and suggests a model for multimedia indexing of geographically locatable information. However, the Domesday model needs to be generalized, to provide n-way cross-indexing between a larger number of information types, to permit an arbitrary number of photographs to be linked to a map and text, and also to ensure that information about the links is not 'hard-wired' into the system.

One example of the direction this research is taking is the attempt by Ruggles (1990) to construct a generic solution to the problem of describing the

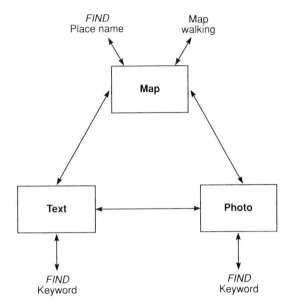

Fig. 22.7 Three-way information linkages in the BBC Domesday system.

links between images, so that standard query methods can be used to access them, and move from one to another. The problem is a complex one, because of the need to accommodate images with different geometries (vertical, oblique, ground level), individual images as well as sets of images, whole images as well as parts of images, single images as well as hierarchical collections of images, and tiled images as well as overlapping images. Nevertheless, systems such as Domesday demonstrate that highly effective multimedia GIS can be developed even where the locational links connecting items of information may not be precise, and where the geographical content of much of the information may be relatively low.

The Domesday approach to information integration also needs to be extended in other directions if it is to be more widely used as a basis for multimedia GIS. For example, the methods adopted for indexing the content of text and photographs need to be considerably more sophisticated, perhaps making use of artificial intelligence techniques that are being incorporated into commercial information retrieval systems. The indexing and linking of other types of real world information present additional problems. For this reason, the design of multimedia GIS will remain a fertile area for further research in the 1990s.

Interactive hypermedia systems

Another response to the emergence of multimedia technology that appeared during the 1980s is interactive multimedia (IMM). IMM is based on a combination of a personal computer and a mass digital storage device (commonly an optical disk such as a CD-ROM or WORM drive). The system captures, stores and displays any type of information that can be represented in digital form: sound, images, text, video, speech, maps, film, etc. (Ambron and Hooper 1988). As with earlier interactive video systems from which they derive many of their characteristics (Bayard-White 1985; Duke 1983; Parsloe 1983; Laurillard 1989), a major feature of IMM systems is that they handle large volumes of data. A critical factor in their success has, therefore, been the availability of an appropriate software environment which enables non-expert users to browse interactively through these data.

The currently preferred browsing model for multimedia information in such systems is represented by hypertext software (Conklin 1987; McAleese 1989; Nielsen 1990b; Hall and Papadopoulos 1990). Initially suggested by Bush in the 1940s (Bush 1945), and developed by Ted Nelson in his Xanadu project in the 1970s (Nelson 1981, 1987), hypertext was popularized by the HyperCard software distributed free with Apple Macintosh computers from the mid 1980s. Hypertext software enables users to follow chains of linked items of information, by pointing on screen to such graphical devices as 'buttons' and 'hot spots'. What hypertext does with items of text, hypermedia does with multimedia information: graphics, animation, sound, video, etc.

The key notion underlying hypertext and hypermedia is that all information and knowledge is inter-connected, and that users should therefore be able to wander freely through a universe of stored information in order to create 'islands of meaning' by making the appropriate associations. The user, rather than the computer, 'integrates' the various units of information in a hypertext or hypermedia system, by mentally linking together information retrieved on a particular theme. In many hypermedia systems, the user need not follow the links provided by the system designer; tools are provided for the user to modify existing links and to forge entirely new links between 'chunks' of information. In this way, the user can create personal pathways or networks in the stored database. This is sometimes referred to as the 'reader as author' approach to information browsing.

There are several major differences in the way information is handled in conventional GIS and hypermedia systems:

- Any type of information may be handled in hypermedia systems, drawn from a variety of media.

- Hypermedia treats any suitable 'chunk' of information as a basic data unit, whether it be a single word, an image, a multi-layered table of numeric data, a sequence of sounds, or a motion video extract. This contrasts strongly with the database model commonly used in conventional GIS, which demands highly structured attribute data, arranged in standard tables, and typically uses pointers to refer to non-standard information.

- The content of individual items of information (i.e. the nodes) is usually fixed in hypermedia systems. This is in contrast to GIS which can reconstitute information on the basis of (say) data aggregation or spatial overlay.

- In hypermedia systems, there is no explicit model of what the stored information means. In a database schema, some attempt is made to encode the meaning of data stored in the database.

- In a conventional GIS, the various sets of attribute data are systematically tied to a spatial data model using a common geo-referencing system. In a hypermedia system, such precise spatial referencing is less commonly found. Although IMM systems have been developed which permit point-located features (such as banks, shops or properties) to be displayed on a map, a more relaxed form of spatial referencing is more typically adopted. Thus, for example, a photograph may be related to a map because they both show a particular street; a recording of a bird's call may be linked to a map of a large expanse of salt marsh which forms that bird's habitat; or a computer simulation of the hydrological cycle may be linked to a map of an entire drainage basin.

- Hypermedia systems permit data units to be linked together in any way felt appropriate by the system designer and/or the system user. For example, the links between units of information in multimedia systems are often arbitrary, subjective and/or tenuous, and mostly serve a non-analytical purpose. (This idea goes far beyond the notion of multiple schemata in database technology.)

- In a hypermedia system, the user plays a major role in making sense of stored information, by switching rapidly from one unit of information to another, following any number of associative links to piece together a collage of information that serves a particular purpose, and by re-configuring links between data units as needs dictate (see Fig. 22.8). Essentially, therefore, hypermedia provides a browsing model for GIS (Marchionini and Schneiderman 1988). This contrasts with conventional GIS in which the software provides a toolbox of ready-made analytical techniques, most of which are designed to store, retrieve, link and compare spatially coordinated data in a systematic way.

Typical geographical applications for hypermedia technology include education and training, technical documentation, information browsing, and product catalogues (e.g. a 'browser' catalogue of GIS software or data sets). A training example is the GIST system (Raper and Green 1989), which was designed as an interactive demonstrator for basic GIS concepts. An educational example is provided by Ecodisk (McCormick and Bratt 1988), an optical disk which

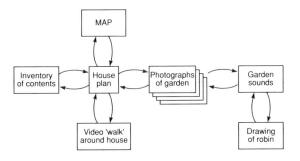

Fig. 22.8 Browsing through a multimedia GIS.

contains a wealth of information on a nature reserve in southern England. Finally, the use of hypermedia technology to provide flexible user navigation facilities for a distributed environmental database is provided by the Whole Earth Decision Support System (WEDSS) prototype (Davis and Deter 1990).

The challenge ahead is to combine the hypermedia approach to handling multi-source information with mainstream GIS. The rudimentary hypermedia ideas embedded in the Domesday system have already been described. Another approach, which aims to combine hypermedia techniques with the more traditional map-based approach of the GIS, is the 'geomatic hypermap' (Laurini and Milleret-Raffort 1989) in which a map is used as a graphical point-of-entry or front-end to information organized as hyperdocuments. A similar approach is taken by Wallin (1990), who suggests that the map might take the role of the 'home hyperdocument' in a hypermedia GIS.

Virtual reality systems

During the first two decades or so of GIS development, the user has been presented with (confronted by?) a highly unnatural representation of the real world involving a number of stylizations or abstractions. There is a strong emphasis on the two-dimensional, on a vertical or bird's eye view, highly symbolized feature representation, well structured data, and static time slices. Moreover, tight rules are usually imposed on how the user can interact with the computer model, and on the methods that are available to browse, navigate, query and manipulate the stored information.

Modern techniques of information gathering, particularly in the field of remote sensing, have greatly expanded the range of human sensory perception. It is ironic, therefore, that this sensory amplification has been accompanied by a corresponding sensory deprivation within GIS. In the GIS model, the direct human experience of the world, involving all of the senses, is replaced by an experience that involves the use of only a limited range of the senses – frequently, only the sense of sight.

Moreover, the informational richness of the real world is shoe-horned into a small number of information types within GIS, most notably numeric, textual and visual. Thus, for example, sounds are not heard, but are measured as point-located decibel readings and displayed as contours; colours are conventionalized or falsified; gradual change in the environment is replaced by widely spaced time slices; living conditions in an inner-city slum are summarized in numerical indexes of multiple deprivation; and the surrogate map walker expends no physical effort, and feels no physical strain, when following a footpath up hill and down dale on a computer screen. This is clearly not the fault of GIS alone, but it is perhaps a reflection of the way in which GIS have tended to reflect the approaches to information and information handling adopted in contemporary science.

Because of the limited sensory bandwidth of current GIS representations of the world, only a limited number of user responses are invoked, with a bias towards the cognitive rather than the affective and, more particularly, a bias towards visual information processing of a relatively abstract kind. This raises two questions: first, whether it is possible to provide users with a fuller sensory experience of the world, from their own desktop; and secondly, whether it is appropriate and useful to do so.

On the technical front, several developments have occurred during the 1980s, in a range of different fields, which suggest that it will soon be technically feasible to provide users with a multi-sensory representation of the world, involving a far wider range of information than hitherto. Most of these developments have been aimed at producing realistic computer graphic displays of real-world objects (e.g. Schacter 1983; Magnenat-Thalman and Thalman 1987; Muller *et al.* 1988). Others have focused on the development of multi-sensory interfaces to computer models (e.g. Foley 1987; Brooks 1987; Ware 1990; Ware and Osborne 1990). Among the relevant emerging technologies and their major application areas are: data visualization (scientific analysis), computer photomontage (civil engineering), building 'walk throughs' (architecture), environmental 'fly overs' (flight and battlefield training), surrogate walks (travel, education and training), hypertext/media (education), and multisensory simulations (arcade games and flight simulation).

Not only do many of these technologies integrate a far richer set of information than hitherto, and generate photo-realistic images, but some also permit users to interact directly with the computer representation of the world, using a fuller range of senses and faculties to do so. In the recently developed technologies associated with 'cyberspace' and 'alternative realities' (Gibson 1984; CADalyst 1989), prosthetic devices such as data gloves and head-mounted visors are used to manipulate the virtual world directly, and users (or 'participants') receive feedback in the form of continuous motion stereoscopic display, tactile response, and even whole body motion. This takes the concept of the 'direct manipulation interface', previously coined in the context of graphical user interfaces (Shneiderman 1983), to its logical conclusion.

The emerging technologies make it possible, perhaps for the first time, for GIS developers to consider integrating a complete range of information about the world in their systems and, moreover, to provide this information in a form that addresses the same senses that would be used by the observer or analyst when confronting the real world at first hand. Unlike current GIS, the emerging technologies integrate information in a more comprehensive manner, and attempt to present an environment for action that is fully three dimensional, is represented naturalistically, and in which changes occur in real time. Moreover, the user's role is considerably extended: users may interact directly with the environment, modify the environment, and receive multisensory information on the state of the environment, as well as multisensory feedback as a result of taking certain actions.

Of course, a considerable amount of research and development is needed before such facilities can be successfully provided for the purpose of geographical problem solving. Little work has been done, for example, on how to involve the human senses of touch, taste or smell within computer information systems. A wide-ranging discussion is also needed on the advisability of adopting such technologies for real world problem solving, as opposed to game playing in a simulated environment.

This is not the place to argue the relative merits of naturalistic representations of the world and more abstract and symbolized models. Nor is it appropriate to launch a discussion on the ethical or moral issues involved in providing users with surrogate multisensory experiences of the kind anticipated by Aldous Huxley's 'feelies'.

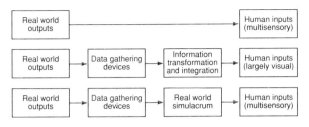

Fig. 22.9 Information flows between the real world and the geoscientist.

Nevertheless, it is important to consider in what circumstances, and for which applications, the heavily stylized model of the world provided by contemporary GIS should be retained, and those for which the more naturalistic, multisensory representation would be more appropriate. The alternatives are summarized in Fig. 22.9. Evidence is already available that in applications such as travel previews, estate agency demonstrations and emergency training, the provision of surrogate walks on an interactive video system, with their more naturalistic representation of space, is preferable to (and, more importantly, more useful than) the more abstract representation provided by the map. In work carried out on vehicle navigation (Mark 1987), it has been similarly found that a map-based display is not the most effective means of communicating information about tasks such as way finding.

Perhaps GIS developers should sidestep this decision altogether, and leave it to the user to decide. If both types of representation are made available in GIS, together with a simple means of switching from one to the other, then users can judge for themselves when it is most appropriate to use each model of the world.

Towards the 'omni-informational' GIS

It is possible that none of the alternative approaches discussed earlier will provide an appropriate model for information integration within GIS. Critics of hypermedia, for example, point to the fact that many users of hypertext and hypermedia systems become 'lost in hyperspace' when they begin to explore vast quantities of information. Much recent research has been aimed at refining this browsing model, either by constraining the freedom of users to ramble aimlessly through stored information, or else by providing orientation and structuring aids such as indexes, 'maps', tours, and quizzes (Weyer and Borning 1985; Hammond 1989; Hammond and Allinson 1987, 1989; Nielsen 1990a).

In the meantime, other developments may yet provide the impetus for more effective information integration in GIS. For example, a greater degree of integration than that afforded by the RDBMS environment may be provided by object-oriented database management systems (OODBMS). In one such system, for example, not only are multimedia objects (images, audio messages, etc.) defined as a hierarchy of classes, but so too are the devices (microphone, camera, screen, etc.) which capture, store and present those objects (Woelk and Kim 1987). In this system, a message-passing protocol is also established for interaction between these classes, and both the class hierarchies and the message protocol may be modified and/or extended by the user. In the 1990s, the hypermedia systems may well converge with GIS that adopt the object-oriented approach.

Alternatively, it may be necessary to look to developments in the field of electronic messaging and document handling, which have led to the creation of a number of standards that define the structure of multimedia messages and documents. The office document architecture (ODA), for example, is an ISO standard that defines the information content and structure of documents (IOS 1986). This currently permits a document to contain text, and geometrical and raster images, but an extension to the standard also allows colour, spreadsheets and sound. Yeorgaroudakis (1990) argues that future GIS software will need to adapt more effectively to office environments where information sharing is the norm, and this might imply adoption of emerging office information standards such as ODA, and the embracing of a far broader range of non-geographical information than hitherto.

Finally, although it is now generally accepted that information integration is best ensured by adopting a single, unifying data model, McKeown and Lai (1987) suggest that multiple data representations should be adopted by all spatial information systems. They argue that several internal representations should be adopted for spatial databases, each applied where it is most appropriate, and that a coordinating item of software should be developed to provide users with a uniform interface to these internal representations.

CONCLUSIONS

Over the past 25 years or so, considerable progress has been made in enabling GIS to integrate diverse information from a variety of sources. Currently, integration is usually achieved by adopting a coherent data model (typically the composite map model or the geo-relational model), which ensures that both spatial and attribute information are synthesized in any problem-solving or decision-making operation carried out by users.

This approach to integration provides major rewards to the user, but it is not without its problems. For example, it is clear that integration is not a magical by-product of pouring diverse data into a GIS; it is usually the result of considerable effort in overcoming the mutual intransigence of data drawn from various sources. Before a GIS can be used to interrelate diverse information, that information has first to be made comparable, compatible and consistent, and this usually involves considerable human effort.

There are also limitations on the extent to which current GIS can integrate information. Most current GIS betray their cartographic origins, and are consequently myopic in respect of the information they are able to integrate. In particular, most GIS are poor at integrating information through the three dimensions of the real world, across time, and for information about the world (such as environmental sounds) that have not been easy to handle using traditional computer facilities. Other systems reflect their underlying database technology, and are therefore highly selective in the types of information they handle. Most are designed to handle highly structured information, and link information by means of unambiguous locational references. Few are designed to handle unconventional information, that is only loosely geo-referenced, and is associated with other information by non-spatial links.

There are several alternative ways in which diverse information can be integrated in a computer-based information system. The traditional GIS approach has been to use a spatial location code as the primary key to relate all data. However, other methods which involve a looser, non-locational approach to information cross-referencing are also proving to be effective. It has also been shown how alternative user interfaces can considerably broaden the scope for user-centred information integration. Whether these approaches will lead to the appearance of several distinct types of GIS (e.g. the multimedia GIS, the hypermedia GIS and the multisensory GIS) is an open question.

It is certainly the case, however, that different approaches to data integration will be found to be more appropriate for specific applications and users. Thus, for example, spatial analysts might require a consistent spatial data representation, or facilities for converting between alternative spatial representations; those engaged in environmental monitoring, by contrast, might value facilities for the automatic update of linked information in real time; while environmental management trainees and the general public might be better served by interactive facilities for information navigation and browsing, and by tools that enable the arbitrary association of loosely connected information.

In the final analysis, information integration is not simply a function of smart algorithms, standard locational referencing schemes, unifying data models, powerful computers and multimedia storage devices. It is, perhaps above all else, the result of empowering users to explore alternative ways of linking the previously unlinked, and of enabling them to do this by a process of conjecture and refutation. Successful information integration is thus an essentially human activity, which may be carried out in private by the lone analyst, or across networks by communities of decision makers. Effective information integration thus hinges crucially on the ability of spatial analysts and decision makers to interact with one another, through the medium of computer-based information systems, as part of the process of making sense of the world about them.

REFERENCES

Abler R F (1987) The National Science Foundation Center for Geographic Information and Analysis. *International Journal of Geographical Information Systems* **1** (4): 303–26

Ambron S, Hooper C (1988) *Interactive Multi-media*. Microsoft Press, Redmond, WA

Anon (1990) The French Revolution of 1989. *Mapping Awareness* **4** (9): 48–9

Annoni A, Ventura A D, Mozzi E, Schettini R (1990) Towards the integration of remote sensing images within a cartographic system. *Computer Aided Design* **22** (3): 160–6

Aronson P (1987) Attribute handling for geographic information systems. *Proceedings of AUTOCARTO 8*. ASPRS/ACSM, Falls Church Virginia, pp. 346–55

Aybet J (1990) Integrated mapping systems – data conversion and integration. *Mapping Awareness* **4** (6): 18–23

Baker H H (1990) Scene structure from a moving camera. In: Blake A, Troscianko T (eds.) *AI and the Eye*. John Wiley, Chichester England, pp. 229–60

Bayard-White C (1985) *An Introduction to Interactive Video*. National Interactive Video Centre, and Council for Educational Technology, London

Beard M K, Chrisman N R (1986) Zipping: new software for merging map sheets. *Proceedings ACSM (vol 1)* ACSM, Falls Church Virginia **1**: 153

Bedell R (1988) *WARP: a program to warp computer drawings, maps and plans*. Terra Investigations and Imaging Ltd, Guildford Surrey

Berry J K (1985) Computer-assisted map analysis: fundamental techniques. *Proceedings of the 6th Annual NCGA Conference*, Volume 2, pp. 369–86

Berry J K (1987) Fundamental operations in computer-assisted map analysis. *International Journal of Geographical Information Systems* **1** (2): 119–36

Bracken I, Higgs G (1990) The role of GIS in data integration for rural environments. *Mapping Awareness* **4** (8): 51–6

Bracken I, Webster C (1989) Towards a typology of geographical information systems. *International Journal of Geographical Information Systems* **3** (2): 137–51

Briggs D J, Mounsey H M (1989) Integrating land resource data into a European geographical information system. *Applied Geography* **9** (1): 5–20

Brooks F P (1987) Grasping reality through illusion: interactive graphics serving science. CHI '90. *SIGCHI Bulletin* (special issue): 1–11

Burrough P A (1986) *Principles of Geographical Information Systems for Land Resources Assessment*. Clarendon Press, Oxford

Burrough P A (1989) Fuzzy mathematical methods for soil survey and land classification. *Journal of Soil Science* **40**: 477–92

Bush V (1945) As we may think. *Atlantic Monthly* **176**: 101–8

CADalyst (1989) When reality is not enough. *CADalyst* December: 40–53

Casley D J, Lury D A (1981) *Data Collection in Developing Countries*. Clarendon Press, Oxford

Chrisman N R (1984) The role of quality information in the long-term functioning of a geographical information system. *Cartographica* **21**: 79–87

Chrisman N R (1991) The error component in spatial data. In: Maguire D J, Goodchild M F, Rhind D W (eds.) *Geographical Information Systems: principles and applications*. Longman, London, pp. 165–74, Vol 1

Conklin J (1987) Hypertext: an introduction and survey. *IEEE Computer* **20**: 17–41

Cowen D J (1986) PC-CAD manages geographical data. *Computer Graphics World* **9** (7): 38–41

Cowen D J (1988) GIS versus CAD versus DBMS: what are the differences? *Photogrammetric Engineering and Remote Sensing* **54**: 1551–5

Dangermond J (1986) The software toolbox approach to meeting the user's needs for GIS analysis. *Proceedings of the GIS Workshop, Atlanta, Georgia, 1–4 April 1986*, pp. 66–75

Dangermond J (1988) A review of digital data commonly available and some of the practical problems of entering them into a GIS. *Proceedings of ACSM–ASPRS St Louis*. ACSM/ASPRS, Falls Church Virginia

Dangermond J (1989) The organizational impact of GIS technology. *ARC News* Summer: 25–6

Davis F W, Simonett D S (1991) GIS and remote sensing. In: Maguire D J, Goodchild M F, Rhind D W (eds.) *Geographical Information Systems: principles and applications*. Longman, London, pp. 191–213, Vol 1

Davis J S, Deter R S (1990) Hypermedia application: Whole Earth Decision Support System. *Information and Software Technology* **32** (7): 491–6

Digital Cartographic Data Standards Task Force (DCDSTF) (1988) The proposed standard for digital cartographic data. *The American Cartographer* **15**: 24–8

DoE (Department of the Environment) (1987) *Handling Geographic Information. Report of the Committee of Enquiry chaired by Lord Chorley*. HMSO, London

Duecker K J (1985) Geographic information systems: towards a georelational structure. *Proceedings of AUTOCARTO 7*. ASPRS/ACSM, Falls Church, Virginia, 172–75

Duke J (1983) Interactive video: implications for education and training. *CET Working Paper 22*. Council for Educational Technology, London

Egenhofer M J, Herring J R (1991) High-level spatial data structures for GIS. In: Maguire D J, Goodchild M F, Rhind D W (eds.) *Geographical Information Systems: principles and applications*. Longman, London, pp. 227–37, Vol 1

ESRI (1989) Integration of geographic information technologies. *ARC News* Winter: 24–5

ESRI (1990a) ESRI, IBM, and HTE develop interactive link between ARC/INFO and IBM AS/400 Parcel Management System. *ARC News* Winter: 30

ESRI (1990b) *Understanding GIS: the ARC/INFO method.* ESRI Inc, Redlands California

Flowerdew R (1991) Spatial data integration. In: Maguire D J, Goodchild M F, Rhind D W (eds.) *Geographical Information Systems: principles and applications.* Longman, London, pp. 375–87, Vol 1

Foley J D (1987) Interfaces for advanced computing. *Scientific American* **257** (4): 83–90

Frank A U (1986) Integrating mechanisms for storage and retrieval of land data. *Surveying and Mapping* **46**: 107–21

Gibson W (1984) *Neuromancer* Ace Science Fiction.

Goodchild M F (1976) Statistical aspects of the polygon overlay problem. In: Dutton G (ed.) *Harvard Papers on Geographical Information Systems*, Volume 6. Addison-Wesley, Reading Massachusetts, pp. 1–22

Goodenough D G (1988) The integration of remote sensing and geographic information systems. In: Damen M C J, Smit, G S, Verstappen (eds.) *Symposium on Remote Sensing for Resource Development and Environmental Management,* Balkema, Rotterdam, pp. 1015–28

Gorte B, Liem R, Wind J (1988) The ILWIS software kernel. *ITC Journal* **19**: 15–22

Green N P (1990) Towards truly distributed GIS. *Proceedings of the GIS Design Models and Functionality Conference.* Midlands Regional Research Laboratory, University of Leicester, 8pp.

Guptill S C (1991) Spatial data exchange and standardization. In: Maguire D J, Goodchild M F, Rhind D W (eds.) *Geographical Information Systems: principles and applications.* Longman, London, pp. 515–30, Vol 1

Hall P A V, Papadopoulos S (1990) Hypertext systems and applications. *Information and Software Technology* **32** (7): 477–90

Hammond N (1989) Hypermedia and learning: who guides whom? In: Maurer H (ed.) *Computer Assisted Learning.* Springer-Verlag, Berlin

Hammond N, Allinson L (1987) The travel metaphor as design principle and training aid for navigating around complex systems. In: Diaper D, Winder R (eds.) *People and Computers III.* Cambridge University Press, Cambridge, pp. 75–90

Hammond N, Allinson L (1989) Extending hypertext for learning: an investigation of access and guidance tools. In: Sutcliffe A, Macaulay L (eds.) *People and Computers V.* Cambridge University Press, Cambridge, pp. 293–304

Haywood P (1986) National transfer standards for Great Britain. *Land and Minerals Surveying* **4** (11): 569–78

Healey R G (1991) Database management systems. In: Maguire D J, Goodchild M F, Rhind D W (eds.) *Geographical Information Systems: principles and applications.* Longman, London, pp. 251–67, Vol 1

Heuvelink G B M, Burrough P A, Stein A (1990) Propagation of errors in spatial modelling with GIS. *International Journal of Geographical Information Systems* **3** (4): 303–22

IOS (International Organisation for Standardisation) (1986) *Office Document Architecture (ODA).* ISO 8613. ISO, Geneva

Jackson M J (1987) Digital cartography, image analysis, and remote sensing: towards an integrated approach. *Interdisciplinary Science Reviews* **12**: 33–44

Jackson M J, Mason D C (1986) The development of integrated geo-information systems. *International Journal of Remote Sensing* **7**: 723–40

Laurillard D (ed.) (1989) *Interactive Media: working methods and practical applications.* Ellis Horwood, Chichester England

Laurini R, Milleret-Raffort F (1989) Principles of geomatic hypermaps *Ekistics* **56** (338–39): 312–17

Liley R (1985) Integration – the big pay-off for geobased municipal systems. *Papers of the Urban and Regional Information Systems Association – URISA '85.* URISA, Ottawa, Canada **2**: 11–27

Lodwick W A, Monson W, Svoboda L (1990) Attribute error and sensitivity analysis of map operations in geographical information systems suitability analysis. *International Journal of Geographical Information Systems* **4** (4): 413–28

Logan T L, Bryant N A (1987) Spatial data software integration: merging CAD/CAM mapping with GIS and image processing. *Photogrammetric Engineering and Remote Sensing* **53** (10): 1391–5

McAleese R (ed.) (1989) *Hypertext: theory into practice.* Intellect Books, Oxford

McCormick S, Bratt P (1988) Some issues relating to the design and development of an interactive video disc. *Computers in Education* **12** (1): 257–60

McKeown D M, Lai R C T (1987) Integrating multiple data representations for spatial databases. *Proceedings of AUTOCARTO 8.* ACSM/ASPRS, Falls Church Virginia, pp. 754–63

McLaren R (1990) Establishing a corporate GIS from component data sets – the database issues. *Mapping Awareness* **4** (2): 52–8

Magnenat-Thalman N, Thalman D (1987) An indexed bibliography on image synthesis. *IEEE Computer Graphics and Applications* **7** (8): 27–37

Maguire D J (1989) The Domesday interactive videodisc system in geography teaching. *Journal of Geography in Higher Education* **13** (1): 55–68

Maguire D J (1991) An overview and definition of GIS. In: Maguire D J, Goodchild M F, Rhind D W (eds.) *Geographical Information Systems: principles and applications.* Longman, London, pp. 9–20, Vol 1

Marchionini G, Schneiderman B (1988) Finding facts versus browsing knowledge in hypertext systems. *Computer* **3** (1): 70–80

Mark D M (1987) On giving and receiving directions: cartographic and cognitive issues. *Proceedings of AUTOCARTO 8.* ACSM/ASPRS, Falls Church Virginia, pp. 562–71

Marx R W (1986) The TIGER system: automating the

geographic structure of the United States census. *Government Publications Review* **13**: 181–201

Morehouse S (1985) ARC/INFO: a geo-relational model for spatial information. *Proceedings of AUTOCARTO 7.* ACSM/ASPRS, Falls Church Virginia, pp. 388–97

Mounsey H M (ed.) (1988) *Building Databases for Global Science*. Taylor & Francis, London

Mounsey H M (1991) Multisource, multinational environmental GIS: lessons learnt from CORINE. In: Maguire D J, Goodchild M F, Rhind D W (eds.) *Geographical Information Systems: principles and applications*. Longman, London, pp. 185–200, Vol 2

Muller J-C (1977) Map gridding and cartographic errors: a recurrent argument. *Canadian Cartographer* **14**: 152–67

Muller J-P, Day T, Kolbusz J, Dalton M, Richards S, Pearson J (1988) Visualisation of topographic data using video animation. In: Muller, J-P (ed.) *Digital Image Processing in Remote Sensing*. Taylor & Francis, London, pp. 21–38

Nelson T (1981) *Literary Machines*. (2nd edn) Theodore Holm Nelson, Swarthmore

Nelson T (1987) *Computer Lib*. Microsoft Press, Redmond, WA

Newell R G, Theriault D, Easterfield M (1990) Temporal GIS – modelling the evolution of spatial data. *Proceedings of the GIS Design Models and Functionality Conference*. Midlands Regional Research Laboratory, Leicester, 10pp.

Nicholson R (1990) Public access to spatial information: the use of value added networks in the UK. *Proceedings of EGIS '90*, Volume 2. EGIS Foundation, Utrecht, pp. 782–8

Nielsen J (1990a) The art of navigating through hypertext. *Communications of the Association of Computing Machinery* **33** (3): 296–310

Nielsen J (1990b) *Hypertext and Hypermedia*. Academic Press, San Diego California

Nyerges T L (1989a) Information integration for multipurpose land information systems. *URISA Journal* **1** (1): 27–38

Nyerges T L (1989b) Schema integration analysis for the development of GIS databases. *International Journal of Geographical Information Systems* **3** (2): 153–83

Openshaw S, Mounsey H M (1987) Geographic information systems and the BBC's Domesday interactive videodisk. *International Journal of Geographical Information Systems* **1** (2): 173–9

Parsloe E (ed.) (1983) *Interactive Video*. John Wiley, Chichester England

Pascoe R T, Penny J P (1990) Construction of interfaces for the exchange of geographic data. *International Journal of Geographical Information Systems* **4** (2): 147–56

Peuquet D J (1981a) An examination of techniques for reformatting digital cartographic data. Part 1: The raster-to-vector process. *Cartographica* **18**: 34–48

Peuquet D J (1981b) An examination of techniques for reformatting digital cartographic data. Part 2: The vector-to-raster process. *Cartographica* **18**: 21–33

Peuquet D J (1984) A conceptual framework and comparison of spatial data models. *Cartographica* **21**: 66–113

Pevsner S (1989) Image processing in a GIS environment. In: Barrett E C, Brown K A (eds.) *Remote Sensing for Operational Applications*. The Remote Sensing Society, Nottingham England, pp. 323–30

Piwowar J M, Le Drew E F, Dudycha D J (1990) Integration of spatial data in vector and raster formats in a geographic information system. *International Journal of Geographical Information Systems* **4** (4): 429–44

Press L (1990) Compuvision or teleputer? *Communications of the Association for Computing Machinery* **33** (9): 29–36

Raper J R, Green N P A (1989) GIST: an object-oriented approach to a GIS tutor. *Proceedings of AUTOCARTO 9.* ACSM/ASPRS, Falls Church Virginia, pp. 610–19

Rhind D W, Openshaw S (1987) The BBC Domesday system: a nation-wide GIS for $4448. *Proceedings of AUTOCARTO 8.* ACSM/ASPRS, Falls Church Virginia, pp. 595–603

Rhind D W, Tannenbaum E (1983) Linking census and other data. In: Rhind D W (ed.) *A Census User's Handbook*. Methuen, London, pp. 287–300

Rhind D W, Green N P, Mounsey H M, Wiggins J S (1984) The integration of geographical data. *Proceedings of Austra Carto Perth*, Volume 1. Australian Institute of Cartographers, Perth, pp. 237–53

Robinson G M, Gray D A, Healey R G, Furley P A (1989) Developing a geographical information system (GIS) for agricultural development in Belize, Central America. *International Journal of Geographical Information Systems* **9** (2): 81–94

Ruggles C L N (1990) An abstract model for the structuring of a spatially indexed set of images. *Proceedings of EGIS '90*, Volume 2. EGIS Foundation, Utrecht, pp. 948–57

Saalfeld A (1988) Conflation: automated map compilation. *International Journal of Geographical Information Systems* **2** (3): 217–28

Schacter B J (1983) (ed.) *Computer Image Generation*. John Wiley, New York

Shepherd I D H (1990a) Mapping with desktop CAD: a critical review. *Computer Aided Design* **22** (3): 136–50

Shepherd I D H (1990b) Computer mapping: 21 roles for AutoCAD. *Bulletin of the Society of University Cartographers* **23** (2): 1–15

Shepherd I D H (1990c) Build your own desktop GIS? *Land and Minerals Surveying* **8** (4): 176–83

Shetler T (1990) Birth of the BLOB. *BYTE* **15** (2): 221–6

Steinitz C F, Parker P, Jordan L (1976) Hand-drawn overlays: their history and prospective uses. *Landscape Architecture* **66**: 444–55

Steneker M, Bonham-Carter G F (1988) *Computer Program for Converting Arc-Node Vector Data to Raster Format*. Geological Survey of Canada, K1Z 8R7, 300pp.

Tomlin C D (1990) *GIS and Cartographic Modelling.* Prentice-Hall, Englewood Cliffs New Jersey

Tomlin C D (1991) Cartographic modelling. In: Maguire D J, Goodchild M F, Rhind D W (eds.) *Geographical Information Systems: principles and applications.* Longman, London, pp. 361–74, Vol 1

Vose M (1990) Hot links to go. *BYTE* **15** (12): 373–7

Wagner G (1990) SICAD: profile of a raster indexed topological vector GIS. *Proceedings of the Conference on GIS Models and Functionality.* Midlands Regional Research Laboratory, University of Leicester

Walker P A, Hutton P G (1986) Grid cell representation of soil maps: an Australian example. *Australian Geographical Studies* **24** (2): 210–21

Wallin E (1990) The map as hypertext: on knowledge support systems for the territorial concern. *Proceedings of EGIS '90*, Volume 2. EGIS Foundation, Utrecht, pp. 1125–34

Wang F, Hall G B, Subaryono (1990) Fuzzy information representation and processing in conventional GIS software: database design and application. *International Journal of Geographical Information Systems* **4** (3): 261–83

Ware C (1990) Using hand position for virtual object placement. *The Visual Computer* **6** (5): 245–53

Ware C, Osborne S (1990) Exploration and virtual camera control in virtual three dimensional environments. *1990 Symposium on Interactive 3D Graphics: Computer Control* (special issue): in press

Waugh T C, Healey R G (1986) The GEOLINK system, interfacing large systems. In: Blakemore M J (ed.) *Proceedings of AUTOCARTO London*, Volume 1. Royal Institution of Chartered Surveyors, London, 76–85

Webster C (1988) Disaggregated GIS architecture: lessons from recent developments in multi-site database management systems. *International Journal of Geographical Information Systems* **2** (1): 67–79

Weyer S A, Borning A H (1985) A prototype electronic encyclopedia. *ACM Transactions on Office Information Systems* **31** (1): 63–88

Woelk D, Kim W (1987) Multimedia information management in an object oriented database system. In: Stocker P M, Kent W (eds.) *Proceedings of the 13th Very Large Databases Conference, Brighton*, pp. 319–29

Yeorgaroudakis Y (1990) The GIS of the future. *Proceedings of EGIS '90*, Volume 2. EGIS Foundation, Utrecht, pp. 1188–99

Zarzycki J M, Jiwani Z (1986) Canadian standards for exchange of digital topographic data. *Proceedings of the XVIII FIG Congress, Commission V*: 171–181

Zobrist A L (1983) Integration of Landsat image data with geographic databases. In: Peuquet D J, O'Callaghan J (eds.) *Proceedings of the United States/Australia Workshop on Design and Implementation of Computer-based Geographic Information Systems*. IGU Commission on Geographical Data Sensing and Processing, Amherst New York, pp. 51–63

23

CARTOGRAPHIC MODELLING

C D TOMLIN

Cartographic modelling is a general methodology for the analysis and synthesis of geographical data. It employs what amounts to an algebra in which single-factor maps are treated as variables that can be flexibly manipulated using a small but highly integrated set of cartographic functions. This chapter offers a brief introduction to the major conventions, capabilities and techniques of this methodology.

INTRODUCTION

To describe cartographic modelling as muddling may be a bit too harsh: in cartographic muddling, however, there lies an ounce of truth. Cartographic modelling does indeed represent an attempt to change the way things are done. It is not so much a set of new ideas as a collection of old ideas that have been organized, augmented and expressed in terms amenable to digital processing.

Cartographic modelling is a geographical data-processing methodology that purports to address diverse applications in a clear and consistent manner. It does so by decomposing data sets, data-processing capabilities and data-processing control specifications into elementary components that can then be recombined with relative ease and great flexibility. The result is what amounts to a map algebra in which maps of individual characteristics such as soil type, land value, or population density are treated as variables that can be transformed or combined into new variables by way of specified functions. It is this function-oriented (as opposed to object-oriented or relation-oriented) structure that distinguishes the cartographic modelling approach from other methodologies.

This chapter offers a first introduction to cartographic modelling methods. It presents a synoptic view that tends to proceed inductively from specific instances to more general concepts and broader implications. A more comprehensive and deductive treatment is available in textbook form (Tomlin 1990).

The chapter begins with a contrived but illustrative example (a second example of cartographic modelling is presented in Berry 1991 in this volume). Consider the cartographic image shown in Fig. 23.1. Here, each location within a certain geographical area is represented by a symbol indicating its elevation above sea level. Now consider a question. How is it possible to get to the biggest hill that lies within this area? It is a reasonable question and one that could certainly be answered by eye (given an eye of some skill and a great deal of patience) with the data presented in Fig. 23.1. It is also a question that can be answered (at considerably lower degrees of both skill and patience) by employing cartographic modelling techniques in a GIS.

To do so, however, the question must be interpreted in unambiguous terms. What is a hill? What defines the biggest hill within a given area? What are the factors that might determine a preferred access route to that hill? These questions can be addressed through a series of data-transforming steps.

In the first of these steps, the layer of elevation values shown in Fig. 23.1 is used to generate the layer shown in Fig. 23.2. There, each location has been set to a new value computed by averaging the initial elevations of all locations within a specified radius. The result is what amounts to a smoothed version of the original topographic surface. The averaging process has effectively lowered the hills and raised the valleys.

Suppose another new value is computed for

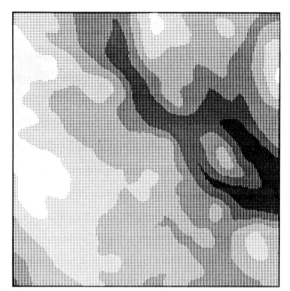

Fig. 23.1 A topographic surface. Varying shades of grey indicate ranges in height above sea level for locations throughout a geographical area. Here, the lighter shades of grey represent higher elevations.

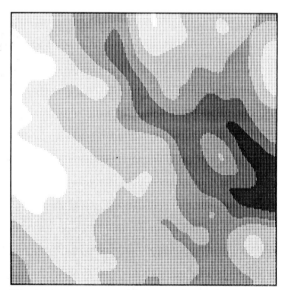

Fig. 23.2 A smoothed topographic surface. Varying shades of grey indicate ranges in average height above sea level for the neighbourhood surrounding each location throughout the area depicted in Fig. 23.1. Higher values are represented by lighter shades of grey.

each location by subtracting its value in Fig. 23.2 from its value in Fig. 23.1. This will generate the layer shown in Fig. 23.3. Here, each location's value indicates the degree to which its own elevation is greater or less than those of its neighbours. The higher values on this layer occur at locations that rise above the surrounding landscape (i.e. hills), while the lower values occur at locations that fall below their surrounding terrain (i.e. valleys).

Figure 23.4 is a layer that expresses this distinction explicitly. Here, each location has been placed into one of two categories according to whether or not its Fig. 23.3 value is above a specified level. If so, that location is deemed part of a hill.

A quick glance at Fig. 23.4 clearly indicates that the study area includes a number of hills, the biggest of which (in terms of its planimetric 'footprint') is apparent. What may be apparent to the human eye, however, must still be explicitly measured and recorded for processing by machine. It is necessary to generate a layer on which only that biggest hill (the one to the right of centre with the two lobes) is distinguished from the rest of the area. To do so, the layer shown in Fig. 23.4 is transformed into one on which each hill is uniquely identified. The areal size of each hill is then measured to determine the biggest and eliminate all others.

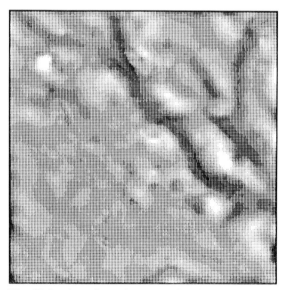

Fig. 23.3 A surface of topographic deviations. Varying shades of grey indicate each location's deviation from the mean topographic elevation within its vicinity. Positive and negative deviations are respectively represented by lighter and darker shades of grey.

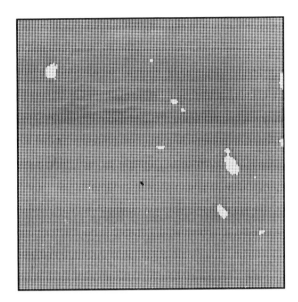

Fig. 23.4 A map layer depicting hills. By aggregating all locations where surface deviation values (as shown in Fig. 23.3) are above a specified level, distinct areas can be characterized as hills. Here, these areas appear in light grey.

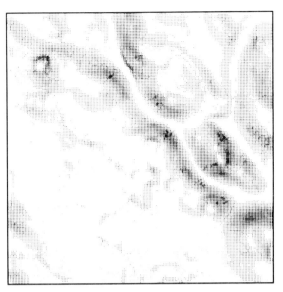

Fig. 23.5 A layer indicating topographic slope. The steepness at each location on the topographic surface shown in Fig. 23.1 is indicated by varying shades of grey, with darker shades representing steeper slopes.

Once that big hill has been isolated, how should it be accessed? Suppose accessibility is expressed in terms of hiking time. Suppose, furthermore, that the amount of time required to hike a given distance varies as a function of topographic slope. The more steeply a topographic incline ascends or descends (regardless of direction), the more it slows a hiker's pace. To measure steepness at each location, its elevation value (as shown in Fig. 23.1) must be compared to those of its adjacent neighbours. Results can then be expressed in the form of a layer like that shown in Fig. 23.5.

If topographic slope is regarded as the only factor affecting a hiker's pace, the information presented in Fig. 23.5 can be used to estimate the increment of time required to hike across any given location. By accumulating these increments in concentric 'waves' around the big hill shown in Fig. 23.4, each location's minimum travel time to that hill can be computed. A layer depicting these travel times is shown in Fig. 23.6.

So how is it possible to get to the hill? That question still remains. With the information presented in Fig. 23.6, however, it is possible to

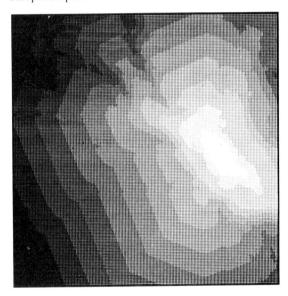

Fig. 23.6 A layer of travel times. The big hill shown in Fig. 23.4 is surrounded by concentric zones of proximity represented by varying shades of grey. Proximity is measured not in terms of straight-line distance, however, but in terms of travel time. This travel-time metric is defined such that more time is consumed traversing locations where topographic slopes (as shown in Fig. 23.5) are steeper.

formulate an answer. Imagine standing at a given location on the travel time surface shown in Fig. 23.6. Suppose you are at a travel time of T minutes away from the big hill. Suppose, furthermore, that your adjacent neighbours are at travel times T, $T + 1$, $T - 1$, $T + 3$, $T + 4$, $T - 9$, $T - 2$, and $T + 1$, respectively. To which of these neighbours should you step in order to get to that hill most quickly (assuming, for simplicity, that all of the neighbours are at the same distance from you)? If you step to the T neighbour, you will have made no progress. If you step to the neighbour at $T + 1$, you will have stepped in the wrong direction. It is only that neighbour at $T - 9$ who can offer the greatest reduction in travel time for this particular step.

A similar decision will have to be made for the next step and each subsequent step over the travel time surface shown in Fig. 23.6 until the big hill is encountered. Each of these steps will be in a direction of steepest descent over that surface of travel times. If this path of steps is traced for every location and then the number of paths traversing any given location is determined, the resulting pattern of 'traffic' will be shown to be dendritic. Lower volume branches will feed into higher volume trunk lines. Figure 23.7 depicts the major trunk lines of minimum access time to the hill and it thereby responds to the question initially posed.

As indicated earlier, this particular example has been contrived to illustrate certain aspects of the cartographic modelling approach. A fuller description of this approach is expressed below in terms of basic conventions, essential capabilities and variety of applied techniques.

CARTOGRAPHIC MODELLING CONVENTIONS

The fundamental conventions of cartographic modelling are not those of any particular GIS. On the contrary, they are generalized conventions intended to relate to as many systems as possible. They do not dictate specific hardware or software configurations but merely establish a construct by which to express them in unified terms. These terms relate to data, the way in which those data are processed and the manner in which that processing is controlled.

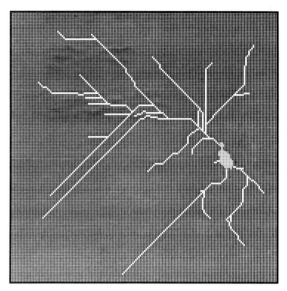

Fig. 23.7 A layer depicting the major routes of quickest access to the big hill. If a hiker at each location on the travel time layer shown in Fig. 23.6 were to use that travel time information to follow a minimum-time path, the resulting paths of greatest volume would be as shown in white.

Data conventions

From a cartographic modelling perspective, all data are organized as shown in Fig. 23.8. The complete body of data for a given geographical *study area* exists as a *cartographic model* comprised of *map layers*. Each layer is a two-dimensional image on which every location is associated with exactly one characteristic. Layers are represented by *titles* (character strings), numerical parameters indicating *orientation* (angular deviation from north) and *resolution* (geographical size of the smallest addressable cartographic location), and a set of one or more *zones*. A zone is a geographical condition associated with a recorded characteristic that distinguishes it from other such conditions. It is represented by a *label* (a character string), a *value* (a numerical quantity) and a set of one or more *locations*. Each of these locations is an elemental unit of cartographic space defined by a pair of Cartesian *coordinates*. In a raster-based system, each location would correspond to an individual grid cell or pixel. In a vector-based system, it would correspond to the area uniquely associated with a single point or node.

In the big hill example presented earlier, the

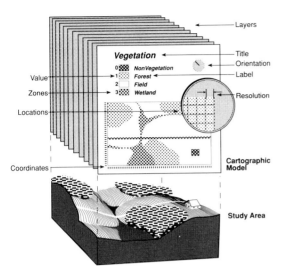

Fig. 23.8 Cartographic modelling data. The organization of data in a cartographic modelling system can be expressed as a hierarchy of familiar elements.

cartographic model initially included only the topographic layer shown in Fig. 23.1. This layer, entitled *Altitude*, depicts a study area in the northeastern United States oriented such that north is to the upper left. It is a layer of 32 640 locations, each representing a geographical area of 20 × 20 metres and associated with a zone whose value and label indicate a height above sea level. This particular cartographic model is atypically small in terms of both layers and locations. A more typical model might also include layers depicting geological formations, groundwater characteristics, soil types, landforms, surface water, vegetation, roads, structures, land use patterns, ownerships, political boundaries and so on. Furthermore, each of these layers might well encompass hundreds of thousands or millions of locations.

A cartographic model may also contain additional information relating to its geodetic position, its cartographic projection, its size, its origin, its format and so on. While this information may well be significant, it need not conform to any particular cartographic modelling conventions.

Data processing conventions

A cartographic model has so far been defined as a set of geographical data. The map layers shown in Figs. 23.1–23.7 comprise one example. Note, however, that a cartographic model may also include a set of specified data transformations. The model represented by the seven layers shown in Figs. 23.1–23.7, for example, could be expressed equally well as one layer (*Altitude*) and a set of six transformations. In fact, some cartographic models may be comprised of nothing more than a set of transformations, referring to generic types of data without ever specifying any particular geographical area.

Figure 23.9 is a diagram of the big hill accessibility model. Here, layers are shown as rectangles and layer-transforming functions as arrows. Each layer is identified by its title and each function by its name. Note that the structure of this model is not unlike that of an algebraic equation. In conventional algebra, variables exist as numerical quantities that are processed by way of *operations* such as addition, subtraction, multiplication and division. In the map algebra associated with cartographic modelling, variables exist as map layers that are processed by way of operations that are cartographic in nature. Among these are operations to reclassify zones, to combine layers, to calculate distances and directions, to measure sizes, to characterize shapes, to determine lines-of-sight, to simulate dispersion, and so on.

Each of these map algebraic operations accepts one or more existing map layers as its input and generates a new layer as its output. Thus, the output from any one operation can be used as input to any other. Sequences of these primitive operations are called *procedures*. Just as conventional algebraic operations can be combined to form complex systems of simultaneous equations, cartographic procedures can be constructed to model complex phenomena such as soil erosion or land development potential. While these procedures can sometimes become quite involved, their step-by-step structure and simple components make it possible to express even very complex models in a clear and consistent manner.

In addition to its data-transforming abilities, a viable cartographic modelling system must also provide capabilities relating to:

- data preparation (e.g. line digitizing, video scanning, aerial image enhancement and classification, cartographic reprojection, or reformatting of files);

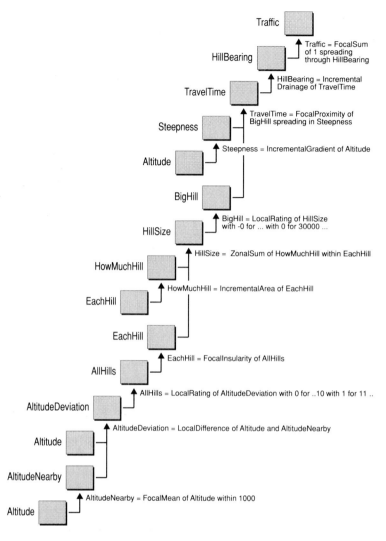

Fig. 23.9 An interpretive cartographic model. The sequence of data transformations shown in Figs. 23.1–23.7 exhibits a logical structure similar to that of an algebraic expression.

- data presentation (e.g. report generation, map drawing, or visual simulation); and
- programming (e.g. error handling, device control, or conditional execution).

For purposes of cartographic modelling, however, these capabilities need not conform to a particular set of conventions.

Data-processing control conventions

The control of a cartographic modelling system is a matter of specifying particular operations, identifying the map layers to which they apply and indicating the order in which they are performed. This may be done by way of typed commands, graphic gestures, spoken words, or other forms of communication depending on the particular GIS involved.

In order to refer to these various forms of communication in common terms, it is useful to adopt a standard set of notational conventions. These conventions can be expressed in the form of a high-level programming language in which each operation is represented by a *statement* in the following generic form:

NEWLAYER = FUNCTION of OLDLAYER HOW

Here, *NEWLAYER* is the title to be assigned to a new map layer generated by applying an operation called *FUNCTION* to an existing layer entitled *OLDLAYER*. The statement may also include additional modifying phrases, here represented by *HOW*. The following, for example, is a *program* comprised of the statements used in the big hill model.

AltitudeNearby	=	*FocalMean of Altitude within 1000*
AltitudeDeviation	=	*LocalDifference of Altitude and AltitudeNearby*
AllHills	=	*LocalRating of AltitudeDeviation with 0 for ... 10 with 1 for 11 ...*
EachHill	=	*FocalInsularity of AllHills*
HowMuchHill	=	*IncrementalArea of EachHill*
HillSize	=	*ZonalSum of HowMuchHill within EachHill*
BigHill	=	*LocalRating of HillSize with -0 for ... with 0 for 30000 ...*
Steepness	=	*IncrementalGradient of Altitude*
TravelTime	=	*FocalProximity of BigHill spreading in Steepness*
HillBearing	=	*IncrementalDrainage of TravelTime*
Traffic	=	*FocalSum of 1 spreading through HillBearing*

CARTOGRAPHIC MODELLING CAPABILITIES

Given these conventions, it is possible to begin to define a set of data-processing capabilities. The essential capabilities of a cartographic modelling system are those that facilitate the interpretation of cartographic data. Data interpretation is a process in which recorded facts of potential utility in a general context (i.e. data) are translated into recorded facts of actual utility in a more specific context (i.e. information). This ability to convert data into information is, in fact, the major distinguishing characteristic of a GIS.

The data interpretation process is generally one in which relationships and/or meanings that are implicit in a set of recorded facts are extracted and expressed in explicit form. Note, for example, that all of the information expressed in Figs. 23.2–23.7 is implicitly also there in Fig. 23.1. The big hill model merely serves to extract and present that information in the form of new map layers.

The interpretative capabilities of a cartographic modelling system ultimately arise from the functions associated with individual data-transforming operations and the ways in which these operations are combined. This transformation of data is facilitated by the fact that map layer zones are represented not by lines or symbols but by numerical values. It is also facilitated by the fact that these values are directly associated with individual locations. The use of numbers here makes it possible to transform geographical characteristics with mathematical functions. The fact that those numbers are associated with individual locations makes it possible to express each of these operations in terms of its effect on a single, typical location.

From this location-specific or *worm's eye* perspective (as opposed to the bird's eye perspective from which traditional cartographic products are normally viewed), the data-transforming functions of a cartographic modelling system can be classified into four major types. The four are respectively associated with local, zonal, incremental and focal operations.

Local operations

Local operations are those that compute a new value for every location as a function of one or more existing values associated with that location. Most do so by applying a familiar mathematical function to each location's value(s) on one or more existing map layers. These local operations and their functions are as follows:

LocalArcCosine	computes the arc cosine of each location's value on a specified layer;
LocalArcSine	computes the arc sine of each location's value on a specified layer;
LocalArcTangent	computes the arc tangent of each location's value on a specified layer (or ratio of values from two specified layers);
LocalCombination	computes a value that uniquely identifies the particular combination of

LocalCosine	computes the cosine of each location's value on a specified layer;
LocalDifference	subtracts from each location's value on one specified layer its value(s) on one or more additional layers;
LocalMajority	computes the most frequent of each location's values on two or more specified layers;
LocalMaximum	computes the maximum of each location's values on two or more specified layers;
LocalMean	computes the average of each location's values on two or more specified layers;
LocalMinimum	computes the minimum of each location's values on two or more specified layers;
LocalMinority	computes the least frequent of each location's values on two or more specified layers;
LocalProduct	multiplies each location's value on one specified layer by its value(s) on one or more additional layers;
LocalRating	translates the value of each location on an existing layer (or combination of values from two or more layers) into a new value that is either given as a constant or drawn from the same location on another specified layer;
LocalRatio	divides each location's value on one specified layer by its value(s) on one or more additional layers;
LocalRoot	raises each location's value on one specified layer to the power represented by the reciprocal of its value(s) on one or more additional layers;
LocalSine	computes the sine of each location's value on a specified layer;
LocalSum	adds each location's value on one specified layer to its value(s) on one or more additional layers;
LocalTangent	computes the tangent of each location's value on a specified layer; and
LocalVariety	computes the number of dissimilar values associated with each location on two or more specified layers.

The big hill model offers three examples of these local operations. First, the *AltitudeDeviation* layer shown in Fig. 23.3 is generated from the *Altitude* layer shown in Fig. 23.1 and the *AltitudeNearby* layer shown in Fig. 23.2 with an operation given as

AltitudeDeviation = LocalDifference of Altitude and AltitudeNearby

The range of values on *AltitudeDeviation* is then reclassified into two groups with

AllHills = LocalRating of AltitudeDeviation with 0 for ... 10 with 1 for 11 ...

to generate the *AllHills* layer shown in Fig. 23.4. A similar instance of *LocalRating*, given as

BigHill = LocalRating of HillSize with -0 for ... with 0 for 30000 ...

is later used to distinguish locations with *HillSize* values of 30 000 or more.

A number of additional functions (e.g. absolute values, logarithms, exponential products, modular differences, medians, factorials) can also be applied to local values. The decision as to whether or not these should be included in a tool box of cartographic modelling operations is largely a matter of anticipated utility and the degree to which such functions can be replicated by combining others. The same is true of the zonal, incremental and focal operations.

Zonal Operations

Zonal operations compute a new value for each location as a function of the existing values from a specified layer that are associated not (just) with that location itself but with all locations that occur within its zone on another specified layer. One example of this appears in the big-hill model, where an operation given as

HillSize = ZonalSum of HowMuchHill within EachHill

is used to add *HowMuchHill* values (indicating the inferred amount of each individual location that is part of a designated hill) within each *EachHill* zone (identifying a particular hill) and then assign that sum to all of that zone's locations on new layer entitled *HillSize*.

Expressed in terms of existing map layers that are generically entitled *ThisLayer* and *ThatLayer*, respectively, the zonal operations and their functions are as follows:

ZonalCombination	computes a value that uniquely

	identifies the particular combination of *ThisLayer* values in each *ThatLayer* zone;	*IncrementalAspect*	computes the compass direction of steepest descent at each location on a three-dimensional surface;
ZonalMajority	computes the most frequently occurring *ThisLayer* value in each *ThatLayer* zone;	*IncrementalDrainage*	computes the direction(s) from which surficial drainage would enter each location on a three-dimensional surface;
ZonalMaximum	computes the maximum *ThisLayer* value in each *ThatLayer* zone;		
ZonalMean	computes the average of all *ThisLayer* values in each *ThatLayer* zone;	*IncrementalFrontage*	computes the amount of boundary associated with each location as part of a two-dimensional pattern on a three-dimensional surface;
ZonalMinimum	computes the minimum *ThisLayer* value in each *ThatLayer* zone;	*IncrementalGradient*	computes the slope at each location on a three-dimensional surface;
ZonalMinority	computes the least frequently occurring *ThisLayer* value in each *ThatLayer* zone;	*IncrementalLength*	computes the total length associated with each location as part of a one-dimensional network on a three-dimensional surface;
ZonalPercentage	computes the percentage of each *ThatLayer* zone that shares its *ThisLayer* value;		
ZonalPercentile	computes the percentage of each *ThatLayer* zone that is of lower *ThisLayer* value;	*IncrementalLinkage*	classifies the form of each location as part of a one-dimensional network;
		IncrementalPartition	classifies the form of each location as part of a two-dimensional pattern; and
ZonalProduct	multiplies all of the *ThisLayer* values in each *ThatLayer* zone;		
ZonalRanking	computes the ordinal magnitude of *ThisLayer* values in each *ThatLayer* zone;	*IncrementalVolume*	computes the subsurface volume beneath each location as part of a two-dimensional pattern on a three-dimensional surface.
ZonalRating	translates a specified combination of *ThisLayer* values in each *ThatLayer* zone into a new value that is either given as a constant or drawn from the same location on another specified layer;		
ZonalSum	adds all of the *ThisLayer* values in each *ThatLayer* zone; and		
ZonalVariety	computes the number of dissimilar *ThisLayer* values in each *ThatLayer* zone.		

Incremental operations

The incremental operations characterize each location as an increment of one-, two-, or three-dimensional cartographic form. The size and shape of these increments are inferred from the value(s) of each location relative to those of its adjacent neighbours on one or more specified layers. The functions performed by these incremental operations are as follows:

IncrementalArea	computes the surface area of each location as part of a two-dimensional pattern on a three-dimensional surface;

Three examples of incremental operations appear in the big hill model. The first, given as

HowMuchHill = *IncrementalArea* of *EachHill*

transforms the *EachHill* layer of individual hills into a layer on which each location that is part of a hill is set to a value indicating its area. Locations toward the interior of each hill are set to a value of 400 (since each location corresponds to a grid square of 20 x 20 metres), while those along each hill's perimeter are set to a lower value reflecting an inferred smoothing of that perimeter. In the second example, an *IncrementalGradient* operation is used to transform the *Altitude* layer shown in Fig. 23.1 into the *Steepness* layer shown in Fig. 23.5. And in the third example, an *IncrementalDrainage* operation is applied not to a topographic surface like that of *Altitude* but to the abstract surface of *TravelTime* values shown in Fig. 23.6. The result is a layer entitled *HillBearing* on which each location's value indicates the direction(s) from which time-conscious hikers approaching the big hill would 'drain' into that location.

Focal operations

Focal operations are those that compute each location's new value as a function of the existing values, distances, and/or directions of neighbouring (but not necessarily adjacent) locations on a specified map layer. The distance relationship that establishes each location's neighbourhood may be defined in terms of physical separation, travel costs, or inter-visibility. The focal operations and their functions are as follows:

Focal Bearing	computes the compass direction from each location to the nearest of a set of locations defined on a specified layer;
Focal Combination	computes a value that uniquely identifies the particular combination of values within each location's neighbourhood on a specified map layer;
Focal Gravitation	computes the inverse-square-distance-weighted average of all values within each location's neighbourhood on a specified map layer;
Focal Insularity	computes a new value for each location that uniquely matches the new value computed for all other locations within its neighbourhood that share its original value on a specified map layer;
Focal Majority	computes the most frequent value within each location's neighbourhood on a specified map layer;
Focal Maximum	computes the maximum value within each location's neighbourhood on a specified map layer;
Focal Mean	computes the area-weighted average of all values within each location's neighbourhood on a specified map layer;
Focal Minimum	computes the minimum value within each location's neighbourhood on a specified map layer;
Focal Minority	computes the least frequent value within each location's neighbourhood on a specified map layer;
Focal Neighbour	sets each location to the value of the nearest of a set of locations defined on a specified layer;
Focal Percentage	computes the percentage of each location's neighbourhood that shares its value on a specified map layer;
Focal Percentile	computes the percentage of each location's neighbourhood that is of lower value on a specified map layer;
Focal Product	multiplies the values of all locations within each location's neighbourhood on a specified map layer;
Focal Proximity	computes the distance between each location and the nearest of a set of locations defined on a specified layer;
Focal Ranking	computes the number of zones within each location's neighbourhood that are of lower value on a specified map layer;
Focal Rating	translates a specified combination of zones within each location's neighbourhood on a specified layer into a new value that is either given as a constant or drawn from the same location on another specified layer;
Focal Sum	adds the values of all locations within each location's neighbourhood on a specified map layer; and
Focal Variety	computes the number of dissimilar values within each location's neighbourhood on a specified map layer.

The big hill model includes four examples of these focal operations. In the first step of that model, a *FocalMean* operation is used to transform the *Altitude* layer shown in Fig. 23.1 into the smoothed *AltitudeNearby* surface shown in Fig. 23.2. Later, a *FocalInsularity* operation is used to transform the *AllHills* layer shown in Fig. 23.4 into one on which each hill (i.e. each insular cluster of locations that are designated as part of a hill) is set to a different value. Next, an operation specified as

TravelTime = Focal Proximity of *BigHill* spreading in *Steepness*

is used to generate the *TravelTime* layer shown in Fig. 23.6 from a *BigHill* layer depicting just one of those hills (the biggest) and the *Steepness* layer shown in Fig. 23.5. And finally,

Traffic = Focal Sum of 1 spreading through *HillBearing*

generates the layer shown in Fig. 23.7 by counting the number of hikers (assuming one per location) within each location's 'upstream' neighbourhood. Note that upstream directions in this last case are defined not in reference to a topographic surface but to a surface of accumulated travel times (the *TravelTime* layer from which *HillBearing* was generated). None the less, the same kind of operations that might be used to simulate and monitor a flow of runoff over the surface of the earth (a *FocalSum spreading through* the results of an *IncrementalDrainage*) are here used to simulate and monitor a flow of impatient hikers. It is this kind of generality in the definition of elementary cartographic modelling functions that makes it possible to address diverse applications with only a small set of tools.

CARTOGRAPHIC MODELLING TECHNIQUES

Among the variety of more complex modelling techniques which can be implemented using these primitive tools, a broad distinction can be drawn between those concerned with what is or 'what could be' and those concerned with 'what should be'. This distinction can be expressed in terms of descriptive and prescriptive models.

Descriptive modelling techniques

Among those cartographic modelling techniques whose purpose is to describe, a further distinction can also be drawn between those that analyse and those that synthesize cartographic data. The former tend to decompose data into finer levels of meaning, while the latter tend to recompose data for use in particular contexts.

Techniques for the analysis of cartographic data generally involve the characterization of either position or form. In the big hill model there are examples of both.

The *TravelTime* layer shown in Fig. 23.6 characterizes each location's position in relation to a certain hill, where the positional relationship is expressed in terms of minutes. Other techniques for the analysis of position may involve rotation, translation, scaling and other forms of cartographic projection as well as measurements of proximity and bearing.

The *Steepness* layer shown in Fig. 23.5 characterizes each location not in terms of position but of form. In this case, it is the form of a three-dimensional surface. The same is true of the *AltitudeNearby* layer shown in Fig. 23.2 and the *AltitudeDeviation* layer shown in Fig. 23.3. It is also true of the *Traffic* layer shown in Fig. 23.7. Here, the surficial form involved is that of *TravelTime* and the characteristic measured at each location is upstream area. On the *AllHills* layer shown in Fig. 23.4 (and the *EachHill, HowMuchHill, HillSize* and *BigHill* layers derived from it), locations are also characterized in terms of their cartographic form. Here, however, that form is in two dimensions. Other techniques for analysis of cartographic form might address one-dimensional characteristics such as length or network configuration; other two-dimensional characteristics such as perimeter, roundness, narrowness, or topological genus; and other three-dimensional characteristics such as surface inflection or relief shading.

These analytic modelling techniques tend to be associated with applications that are oriented towards the acquisition of objective knowledge. The synthetic modelling techniques, on the other hand, tend to be associated with applications involving the exercise of subjective judgement. Most often, these techniques will call for the use of an operation such as *LocalCombination* or *LocalMean* to combine map layers that represent the major factors affecting a question or decision in a way that specifies the relative importance of those factors. Each factor layer, in turn, will typically be one that was generated by using an operation such as *LocalRating* to indicate the relative importance of each of the zones on a layer of observable site conditions. Each of those layers will be one that was either encoded as part of an original database or derived using the kind of analytic modelling techniques mentioned above.

In any case, the formulation of a descriptive cartographic model is a task that can generally be accomplished best not by proceeding inductively from existing data to envisioned results but by proceeding deductively from envisioned results to the data from which they will ultimately be derived. In this way, complex issues can be iteratively decomposed into a hierarchy of simpler components and subcomponents that ultimately arise from field data.

Prescriptive modelling techniques

As the application of cartographic modelling techniques moves from relatively passive forms of enquiry to more active and deliberate forms of decision making and problem solving, the techniques involved tend to be more prescriptive than merely descriptive in nature. These prescriptive techniques are generally associated with some form of cartographic allocation: the process of selecting locations in order to satisfy stated objectives. This is a process that generally involves three major steps: the statement of a problem; the generation of solutions to that problem; and the evaluation of those solutions.

The statement of a cartographic allocation problem is essentially a descriptive task. It will usually begin with an explicit description of how some geographical quality to be achieved arises from geographical conditions that either exist or could be made to exist in a given study area. In the big hill model, for example, the quality to be achieved is timely access to the hill. This quality is expressed in terms of the *Steepness* layer shown in Fig. 23.5 with the understanding that each location's *Steepness* value defines the 'cost' of one step along a path whose overall cost must be minimized.

To generate a solution for this problem, the statement of path-siting criteria must be transformed into a set of locations (i.e. a path or paths) that satisfy those criteria. The process is analogous to that of inverting an algebraic equation such as

$$Q = f(E, P)$$

(where Q is the geographical quality to be achieved, E is an indicator of existing site conditions, and P represents potential site modifications) into an equation such as

$$P = g(E, Q)$$

(where g is a function identifying those potential site modifications P that best achieve quality Q given existing conditions E). In the map algebraic case, however, inversion of the descriptive model into prescriptive form requires techniques that are spatial in nature. In this particular case, the inversion process must also contend with the holistic (rather than atomistic) nature of the quality to be achieved. It is not just a matter of selecting those individual locations that exhibit the lowest costs. It is a matter of selecting those sets of locations that constitute lowest cost paths. This is done by way of the technique embodied in the following operations.

TravelTime	=	*FocalProximity of BigHill* spreading in *Steepness*
HillBearing	=	*IncrementalDrainage of TravelTime*
Traffic	=	*FocalSum of 1* spreading through *HillBearing*

Once solutions to an allocation problem have been generated (regardless of their origin), cartographic modelling procedures can also be used to evaluate these results. This can be done not only in terms of the pre-defined criteria, but in terms of issues beyond the initial problem statement as well.

DISCUSSION AND CONCLUSION

This chapter has outlined the major conventions, capabilities and techniques associated with one approach to the use of GIS. To place this approach in a broader context, it remains to mention where this thing comes from, where it stands and where it may go from here.

The origins of cartographic modelling can be traced to those of manual overlay mapping techniques that have been in use since the early 1900s (Steinitz, Parker and Jordan 1976), but not widely recognized until the 1960s (McHarg 1969). Shortly thereafter, the idea of organizing and processing geographical data on a layer-by-layer basis was incorporated into a lineage of raster-based GIS software packages extending from SYMAP to GRID, IMGRID and MAP (the Map Analysis Package) among others. The cartographic modelling capabilities embodied in MAP were also advanced in a number of new renditions (e.g. IBM-PC-MAP, MacGIS, MAPS, MAP2, MAPII, OSU-MAP, pMAP, SAC and SCMAP), and the replication of selected functions in several other systems (e.g. ERDAS, GRASS, IDRISI, MOSS, PANACEA and SAGIS). Meanwhile the more fundamental concepts of cartographic modelling continued to evolve on paper, as can be seen in works by Tomlin (1975, 1983, 1985), Tomlin and Berry (1979), Tomlin and Tomlin (1981), Berry (1987) and Tomlin (1990).

As a methodology for organizing data, the cartographic modelling idiom shares objectives with the work of Dacey (1970), Youngman (1978), Shapiro and Haralick (1980), Cox, Aldred and Rhind (1980), Nyerges (1980), van Roessel (1987) and others who have sought to establish a uniform language for spatial representation. As a methodology for interpreting geographic data, it shares objectives that are reflected in the work of Tobler (1979), White (1985), Claire (1982), Chan (1988) and others who have attempted to characterize spatial relations and/or operations in reference to a unified construct.

The cartographic modelling methodology currently stands as one of several distinct approaches to the representation of geographical phenomena. Among the most prominent alternatives are one approach based on relational database management techniques and another based on feature- or object-oriented programming. In the relational idiom, geographical 'entities' (such as lines or areas) are explicitly characterized in terms of 'attributes' (such as names or numbers) and are explicitly associated with one another by way of 'relations' (such as adjacency or inclusion). These relations can also be characterized in terms of their own attributes and they too can be associated with one another by way of additional relations. The same is true in the feature- or object-oriented idiom. Here, however, primitive entities can be associated with one another not only in terms or relations but in terms of more complex entities as well. The cartographic modelling approach differs from these in its representation of spatial entities and associations between them.

The fundamental spatial entity in cartographic modelling is the location. Unlike the units of data in most relational and object-oriented systems, locations are not units of 'what' but of 'where'. Although locations can be aggregated into sets of lines, areas and surface features, they remain the elemental units for which attributes are recorded.

The cartographic modelling approach associates locations with one another not with declarative statements specifying selected relations but with the new entities that are generated by applying selected functions. To interrelate entities that are comprised of multiple locations, each is first disaggregated into a set of individual locations. A function is then applied to those locations to generate new attributes, which will ultimately be reaggregated to characterize the original entities or to form entirely new ones.

From this perspective, a question such as 'How far is this area from that area?', for example, would be expressed as 'What is the minimum distance between any location within this area and any location within that area?' or 'What is the distance between the centroid of this area and the centroid of that area?' The fact that there are two reasonable interpretations of that initial question from the worm's eye perspective reflects the utility of this point of view. It is a view that becomes particularly useful in dealing with more complex spatial relationships such as narrowness, enclosure, spottiness, interspersion, striation, and so on.

Perhaps the major advantage of the cartographic modelling approach is the clarity of its data and data-processing constructs from the perspective of a typical user. Its major disadvantage, on the other hand, may be that these constructs express both data and data processing in terms of discrete units. The result is a medium that tends to foster an analytic and atomistic rather than synthetic and holistic view of the phenomena it is used to represent.

The near future of cartographic modelling will likely be one of both refinement and extension. This is true not only in terms of new software (e.g. the MapBox system), but also in terms of new techniques in areas such as three-dimensional modelling, spatial statistics, interpolation, error tracking, feature extraction, temporal dynamics, flow simulation, and so on. If the cartographic modelling approach is truly successful, these new techniques will also involve high-level models that are specific to particular fields of application. Ideally, such techniques will come not from those who design these tools in the world of high technology, but from those who must ultimately put them to use in that other world just outside.

REFERENCES

Berry J K (1987) Fundamental operations in computer-assisted map analysis. *International Journal of Geographical Information Systems* **1**: 119–36.
Berry J K (1991) GIS in island resource planning: a case study in map analysis. In: Maguire D J, Goodchild M F, Rhind D W (eds.) *Geographical Information Systems: principles and applications.* Longman, London, pp. 285–95, Vol 2

Chan K (1988) *Evaluating Descriptive Models for Prescriptive Inference.* Unpublished PhD thesis, Harvard University
Claire R W (1982) Algorithm development for spatial operators. *Proceedings of PECORA9*, pp. 213–21
Cox N J, Aldred B K, Rhind D W (1980) A relational

database system and a proposal for a geographical data type. *Geo-Processing* **1**: 217–29

Dacey M F (1970) Linguistic aspects of maps and geographic information. *Ontario Geography* **5**: 71–80

McHarg I L (1969) *Design with Nature*. Natural History Press, New York

Nyerges T L (1980) *Modelling the Structure of Cartographic Information for Query Processing*. Unpublished PhD thesis, Ohio State University

Shapiro L G, Haralick R M (1980) A spatial data structure. *Geo-Processing* **1**: 313–37

Steinitz C F, Parker P, Jordan L (1976) Hand-drawn overlays: their history and prospective uses. *Landscape Architecture* **66** (8): 444–55

Tobler W R (1979) Cellular geography. In: Gale S, Olsson G (eds.) *Philosophy in Geography*. D. Reidel Publishing Company, Dordrecht Holland, pp. 379–86

Tomlin C D (1975) *The Tomlin Subsystem of IMGRID*. Unpublished Master's thesis, Harvard University

Tomlin C D (1983) *Digital Cartographic Modelling Techniques in Environmental Planning*. Unpublished PhD thesis, Harvard University

Tomlin C D (1985) The IBM Personal Computer Version of the Map Analysis Package. Laboratory for Computer Graphics and Spatial Analysis, Graduate School of Design, Harvard University

Tomlin C D (1990) *Geographic Information Systems and Cartographic Modelling*. Prentice-Hall, Englewood Cliffs New Jersey

Tomlin C D, Berry J K (1979) A mathematical structure for cartographic modelling in environmental analysis. *Proceedings of the 39th Symposium of the American Conference on Surveying and Mapping*, pp. 269–83

Tomlin C D, Tomlin S M (1981) An overlay mapping language. *Regional Landscape Planning: Proceedings of Three Educational Systems*. American Society of Landscape Architects: 155–64

van Roessel J W (1987) Design of a spatial data structure using the relational normal form. *International Journal of Geographical Information Systems* **1** (1): 33–50

White D (1985) A taxonomy of space–time relations. *Proceedings of the Princeton Conference on Computer Graphics and Transportation Planning*. American Society of Landscape Architects

Youngman C (1978) A linguistic approach to map description. In Dutton G (ed.) *Spatial Semantics: understanding and interacting with map data*. Laboratory for Computer Graphics and Spatial Analysis, Graduate School of Design, Harvard University

24

SPATIAL DATA INTEGRATION

R FLOWERDEW

Data integration is the process by which different sets of data within a GIS are made compatible with each other. These data sets may or may not be defined in terms of the same geographical referencing system. Different data sets have different spatial coverage; many data collecting agencies have their own system of regions, and these regional systems are subject to boundary changes over time. Data for different regions may be collected in incompatible ways, may vary in reliability or may be missing or undefined. The larger the number of different data sources needing to be integrated, the more such problems will be encountered.

Other problems in data integration relate to incompatibilities between the spatial entities for which data are recorded. Sometimes these are a result of differences in dimension; often data exist for a set of points but are needed for a continuous area, and the appropriate process is interpolation. Sometimes data are available only for a set of zones, and are needed for a different set of zones, or for point locations. Methods exist based on the assumption that such data reflect an underlying smooth surface, and other methods are being developed which take account of other variables in transforming data between zonal systems.

INTRODUCTION

Data integration is the process of making different data sets compatible with each other, so that they can reasonably be displayed on the same map and so that their relationships can sensibly be analysed (Rhind *et al.* 1984). As such, it is one of the most important topics in the whole field of GIS. It is often an essential preliminary to the use of GIS for investigation of substantive questions. It is a problem which recurs in almost all applications of GIS; the more ambitious the application and the more data sets that are needed, the more likely it is that data integration will be a problem. This may be particularly so when both environmental and socio-economic data are involved. This chapter reviews the main issues involved, although some are considered in more detail in other chapters. Most of the examples are taken from socio-economic applications of GIS, because this is where the author's main experience lies.

Data integration has several different aspects.

These can be summarized in terms of a number of straightforward questions (whose implications may be far from straightforward!):

- What type of data?
- Where do the data refer to?
- When do the data refer to?
- How accurate are the data?

It is assumed that the data are geographical, in other words that each observation to be included has two aspects – what was observed, and where it was observed. In many cases, it is also relevant to consider when it was observed. The first question can be regarded as being about the measurement scale of the data: does the observation refer to the presence or absence of something, to the category that something has been assigned to, or to some more quantitative measure of the size or intensity of whatever is being studied? The second question has two main aspects: does an observation refer to a point, a line or an area (each will be treated differently in a GIS), and how is the location of the observation represented (in other words, what reference system is used to record the data)? The third question may refer to a specific point of time or period of time. The fourth can refer to error of several kinds, both measurement and locational, including mistakes, imprecision and estimation. All of these issues will be referred to in the following sections. For further discussion of the nature of geographical data see Unwin (1981), Fisher (1991 in this volume) and Gatrell (1991 in this volume).

WHAT TYPE OF DATA?

- *Dichotomous or presence/absence.* This measurement scale is obviously relevant when considering the presence or absence of a plant or animal species in an area; it also applies where places are classified into one of two categories – a country may or may not be a member of NATO, a road may or may not be a dual carriageway (divided highway), a city may or may not have a convention centre.

- *Categorical.* This measurement scale is used when a place can be classified into one of several categories – rock type, vegetation cover and system of government are examples.

- *Ranked.* There are two types of ranked data; ranked (or ordered) categories are used where a set of categories has a natural ranking associated with it – for example, grades of agricultural land; alternatively a set of places may be ranked from first to last according to some criterion, such as the rankings of urban residential desirability fashionable in the United States (Cutter 1985).

- *Count.* Data consisting of the number of items or the number of times something has happened in a place – population, the number of species, the number of television channels, the traffic count or the number of customers.

- *Continuous.* A measurement on a continuous scale, such as wheat production, average annual rainfall, height above sea level or the unemployment rate. Sometimes this may be reducible to the ratio or the sum of count variables, sometimes not.

WHERE DO THE DATA REFER TO?

- *Points.* Data may relate to sample points, either selected randomly (as in some soil or vegetation surveys) or for convenience (spot heights; rain gauges); they may also relate to real entities, like trees, factories or cities (which can be considered as points at some scales).

- *Lines.* Line data may also be obtained for sample lines, like transects, or for real linear phenomena, like rivers, railways or geological faults.

- *Areas.* Some areas used in GIS may be thought of as natural units in Unwin's (1981) terminology, that is, areas whose boundaries are defined by the value of the variable under consideration, such as rock outcrops, islands or marshes; others may be imposed units, where data have been collected for some artificially defined unit, such as a local government area.

- *Surfaces* (interpolated points). Many phenomena are defined everywhere but can only be measured at discrete points – height above sea level, annual rainfall and vegetation cover are in this category. Within a GIS, interpolation methods can be used to estimate values for other points and to construct a surface. The TIN (Triangulated Irregular Network) surface representation is an example of how a surface can be stored and displayed within a GIS (see Weibel and Heller 1991 in this volume).

Reference systems

One way in which data from two maps of the same region may be integrated is through relating the location of map features to a reference system. This is typically a pair of numbers defining the distance east and the distance north from a fixed point (see Maling 1991 in this volume). In the vector representation system (the most common used in cartographic applications), a line is represented as a set of these number pairs defining the coordinates of points along the line. These numbers may be table coordinates, based simply on how the digitizing table was set up when points and lines were digitized with no other significance. Alternatively they may be unique to a particular map; commercially produced street maps may refer to locations in terms of their own specially designed grid.

It is more common, however, for map feature representations to be linked to one of a few standard referencing systems. The most general of these is the network of lines of latitude and longitude. Others include the Universal Transverse Mercator (UTM) system in common use in North America and the Ordnance Survey National Grid used in Great Britain. The fact that the world is (approximately) spherical and not flat, however, means that no two-dimensional coordinate system, and hence no two-dimensional GIS, can represent the earth's surface without distortion. Figure 24.1 illustrates the lack of conformity between latitude and longitude and the National Grid. This distortion increases in seriousness with the size of the area represented.

Maps based on latitude and longitude will not necessarily be compatible with each other because of the many different projections available for mapping. Even within the same map, problems arise because the length of a degree of longitude is not constant, changing quite dramatically approaching the poles. It is also the case that most projections do not represent lines of longitude as straight (often this is true of lines of latitude too). Although the US Geological Survey produces 7.5 minute quad sheets, defined by latitude and longitude boundaries, their curvature makes latitude and longitude unsuitable coordinates for a GIS (Aanstoos and Weitzel 1988). Digitizing a map can only be done with the aid of two orthogonal coordinate axes and points located with reference to curved lines cannot simply be integrated with data using an orthogonal system. Even those projections with straight-line graticules (of which Mercator is the best known), because of the distortions of shape and/or area involved, cannot easily be integrated with other data sources. Some fundamental GIS operations, like calculations of polygon areas, will of course be wrong if data have not been input from a map with an equal-area projection.

The British National Grid is only satisfactory

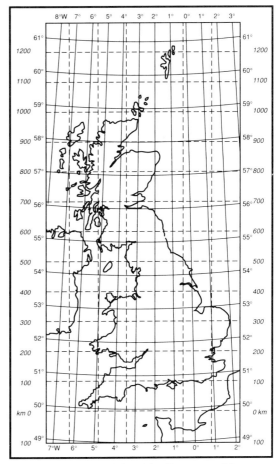

Fig. 24.1 Relationship of the Transverse Mercator graticule (solid) to the National Grid system (pecked) of the Ordnance Survey.

for use in GIS because Great Britain is small enough for distortion to be relatively minor; attempts to extend it, even if only as far as Ireland, rapidly become unacceptable. Other systems based on standard meridians or parallels are also subject to error increasing with distance from the centre of the map, leading to obvious errors when maps based on different standard lines are to be integrated. Mapping the state of Texas, for example, on the State Plane system (based on the Lambert Conformal Conic projection) would have necessitated using five separate coordinate systems, a problem which Aanstoos and Weitzel (1988) overcame by defining their own Lambert projection with parameters optimal for the entire state. Where a large area is mapped on a UTM system, integration problems arise for places equidistant from two of the standard meridians used to define the system. In Canada, for example, mapping the area around Calgary on a UTM system is problematic, since the metropolitan area is split between coordinate systems defined around two different meridians (a second example is illustrated in Fig. 24.2).

Fig. 24.2 Map of the Iberian peninsula showing divergence of UTM grids around zone boundaries.

A further type of reference problem occurs when photographic imagery is being input into GIS. If air photography is oblique, projection problems arise as a result of varying scale over the image. Even for vertical photographs, scale is not constant and distortions occur with increasing distance from the centre of the photograph (Maling 1989: 247–76). Such problems are particularly acute for satellite photography because the greater the altitude the greater the effect of the earth's curvature on image distortion.

Most of these projection problems are well known to surveyors and cartographers, and for many of them solutions exist and can be operationalized. Any GIS system should allow the conversion of table coordinates to a user-defined set (see Bracken and Webster 1990: 211–22), and many include routines for conversion between different projections. Algorithms exist for conversion between latitude and longitude and UTM, although they are complicated. It is not a simple matter, however, to combine within GIS, two maps drawn on different projections. Maling (1973) provides a good guide to problems of this nature.

Data set coverage

A very common problem in data integration is the difference in the area for which data are available for two different variables. The ideal would be for each variable needed in the GIS to be mapped separately at the same scale and for the same areal extent. In practice, map sheets will overlap and data may not be available for all the areas required.

If two or more map sheets are being input into the same GIS, problems may occur at the edges of map sheets, even if they are based on a common referencing system. Such problems are likely to be associated with linking up line or area phenomena which cross the boundary between the map sheets. A fundamental operation in any vector-based GIS system is polygon creation, in which the GIS operates on a set of line segments to produce a set of well-formed polygons. If two points (such as the western end of a line on one map and the eastern end on another) are intended to be the same but are actually digitized as being at slightly different locations, the system has major problems in deciding whether or not to treat the points as the same or different (Fig. 24.3).

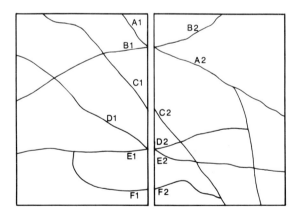

Fig. 24.3 Edge matching during data integration.

Both mapping agencies and data collection agencies organize their operations spatially. This might mean, first, that information must be acquired for a larger area than is actually needed because of the way map sheets, or data collection units, have been divided up. The English city of Oxford, for example, is in the South East Standard Region, the Central television area, the Western Post Office region and has its own Regional Health Authority. These are all different sizes and shapes and, therefore, only partially overlap. Hearnshaw, Maguire and Worboys (1989) provide a systematic treatment of the range of data units relevant to the English county of Leicestershire. Integrating data from all these sources may mean that the GIS is confined to a very narrow area, where all these regions overlap, or that much information must be collected that will never be used (Fig. 24.4). Most map users have experienced the frustration of having to acquire and handle large map sheets of which only one small corner is actually relevant to their needs (Fig. 24.5).

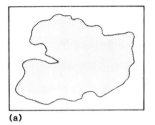

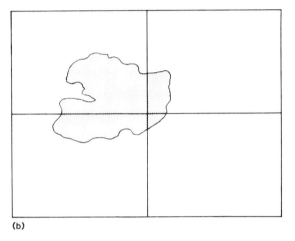

Fig. 24.5 (a) Ideal map sheet boundaries; (b) Actual map sheet boundaries.

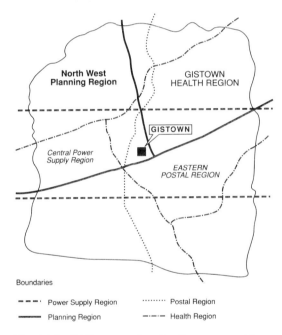

Fig. 24.4 Different regionalizations as a problem in data integration.

It may be that information is depicted or symbolized differently for different parts of the area being studied. A related problem may be that more detail is available for some parts than others. Little difficulty is caused if the phenomena mapped are equivalent but the symbolization is different – for example, if roads are drawn in red on one map and blue on another. Some digitizing problems may exist if they are depicted as a pair of parallel lines on one map and just as a centre line on another. If a different classification is used, the problem is greater – for example, one map (to give a British example) may distinguish between class A and class B roads, while another may distinguish between dual carriageways and undivided highways. A simpler example is that different maps may use different contour intervals – and hence a hill or depression of moderate size may be marked on one map and an exact equivalent omitted from another (Fig. 24.6). Integration is a still greater problem if the method of depiction is totally different. For example, a contour system for showing altitude cannot easily be compared with one reliant solely on spot heights; these systems can only be integrated by transforming one set of data. More realistically, a map showing cities as circles whose type depends on city size is not fully compatible with one showing the boundaries of their built-up area.

Data may not only be symbolized differently but also may actually have been collected differently. Regional offices of a national agency may have freedom to decide on how they collect

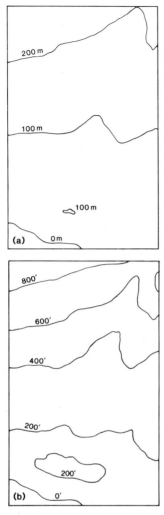

Fig. 24.6 The same landscape with (a) 100 metre contours; (b) 200 foot contours.

information, and may well make different decisions, perhaps for very good reasons. Even basic data sources like the British census include minor differences in the data collected between England and Wales, and Scotland (the definition of a room), while such differences are magnified where there is scope for subjectivity, as in geomorphological or soils maps.

Some of these problems are annoying rather than crucial, for example the overlapping regional data sets that must be assembled. Others are virtually insuperable, but may be tackled to some extent by trying to reconcile the data differences: usually this involves making intelligent guesses about what the data really needed would be like if they were available. Problems of this type can often be regarded as examples of missing data problems. Sometimes the obvious solution is to use only the lower quality or less detailed data if those are all that are available for the entire region of interest. However, if more detail is needed or data are absent altogether, then interpolation methods of various types may be used to try to guess what is going on. These methods are of two main types according to what information is used to guide the guesses. If information is available for variables related to the one required, an appropriate form of statistical estimation may be used to predict a likely value; for example regression or categorical data analysis (Williams 1984, 1986; Wrigley 1985). If the variable required is likely to show systematic spatial variation, spatial interpolation techniques may be appropriate. These methods are reviewed by Weibel and Heller (1991 in this volume) and, in different contexts, by Lam (1983), Schut (1976) and Tobler and Kennedy (1985).

WHEN DO THE DATA REFER TO?

Data for different places may be collected (or mapped) at different times; indeed, this is naturally to be expected where the process is expensive in time or resources. One map sheet may have been revised last year while its neighbour has long been out of date (Fig. 24.7). Changes in methods of symbolization may have occurred in the mean time as well as changes in the phenomenon concerned. More drastically, data may not yet have been produced for some areas. It may be that production is a time-consuming process and the agency concerned has not yet reached the areas in question. Alternatively the data may never be produced – it may not be cost effective to do so, people in the region may object to its collection or release, or there may just have been an oversight by the person responsible.

Comparison between places on the map may of course be made more difficult as a result of the data referring to different times. This problem is particularly acute for those producing an international atlas or statistical compendium. Sometimes maps may be available for one place for two dates and for another place at an intermediate

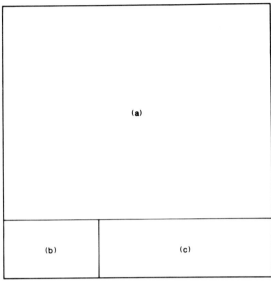

Fig. 24.7 Survey dates for revision for an imaginary topographic map (a) 1962–63; (b) 1963–64; (c) 1959. Revised for major roads and other significant changes 1974.

date; the best comparison may perhaps be based on estimating data for the first place at the intermediate date. To do this, however, requires some assumptions about the trajectory of change.

Another potential problem relates to shorter time scales. Many phenomena fluctuate on an annual or daily cycle, or perhaps more haphazardly. Comparisons may be distorted if observations for different places relate to different times in such cycles. It may be inappropriate to compare a vegetation survey of one place in July with one of another place in September. Even if surveys were done at the same time in different years, climatic fluctuations may distort the comparison.

Data may also represent accumulations of observations or averages over time. For example, the number of times relatively rare events (such as floods, earthquakes, power failures or mortgage defaults) have occurred may be of interest, but the figures are obviously sensitive to the period over which observations have been made. In addition, external events may affect such occurrences and, for example, mortgage defaults may look very different if they are observed over a period including a national or local economic recession than over a period of the same length characterized by boom conditions. Figures for average values of some fluctuating variable, such as rainfall, crop yields or disease occurrence, will also depend on the length of time (and the precise time period) for which data are collected. A 50-year rainfall average is likely to be more reliable than a 10-year average, and as usual the GIS user has the responsibility of deciding what to do if only the 10-year average is available.

ERROR AND ACCURACY

Data integration may also be affected by error in one or more of the maps incorporated into the GIS. This topic is discussed by Chrisman (1991 in this volume) and, with the related subject of accuracy in GIS, was the theme of the first of the major initiatives launched by the US National Center for Geographic Information and Analysis (NCGIA). The initiative's volume of position papers (Goodchild and Gopal 1989) is a goldmine of informed discussion and analysis of different aspects of these problems.

Veregin (1989) distinguishes between different types of error in two important respects. First, there is a distinction between 'cartographic' error, error in the positions of map features such as points, lines and areas, and 'thematic' error, error in the values of an attribute of map features. Second, he differentiates between 'measurement' error, or imprecision in the location or attributes of features, and 'conceptual' error, error associated with the process of translating real-world features into map objects. He also considers how these types of error are combined when two maps are overlaid (i.e. when data are integrated).

There is now a good deal of literature on the treatment of cartographic measurement error, which is usually thought of as arising from digitizing error, although error of this sort can also be generated during the original map production process. Burrough (1986), for example, discusses early work on this topic, while Maffini, Arno and Bitterlich (1989) provide one recent treatment of the issue. One problem arises simply from the level of precision possible on a paper map. As Goodchild and Gopal (1989: xii–xiii) point out, the precision with which map features are recorded on paper maps is generally less than that with which they are recorded in a vector-based GIS. The problem is accentuated because maps at different scales may be included in the same GIS; a reasonable level of precision in recording data from a large-scale plan may be totally spurious if they are to be integrated with other data taken from a smaller-scale map. The spurious precision with which data may be recorded in a GIS makes it impossible for the best digitizing technician to digitize the same line twice in exactly the same way; and human error and inaccuracy magnify the problem. The results of this imprecision may not matter for a map of a single phenomenon, but problems arise when data integration takes place. Overlaying two zonal systems, for example, may result in the creation of a host of 'sliver polygons' and 'dangling chains', geometrical entities arising in the topological structuring procedure of a vector GIS if points do not lie exactly on the lines they should be on (Fig. 24.8).

consistent between different digitizing sessions. Second, there must be consistency in the level of map generalization, as reflected in the degree of detail in line boundaries and the inclusion and exclusion of point and areal features. An important point may be whether topological relationships are preserved between two sets of phenomena digitized separately. For example, it may be important that a set of points is in one-to-one correspondence with a set of polygons (if they are to be used as 'label points'); a very small error in the position of either object can be a major problem if it results in a point being outside its polygon, while a much larger error may be unimportant if topological relationships are preserved. In Fig. 24.9, for example, a small error in locating point A might leave it in the wrong polygon, whereas a much greater error in locating B would be relatively harmless. Blakemore (1984) reviews these problems and suggests a technique based on the concept of 'epsilon' distance.

Most vector-based GIS have facilities for

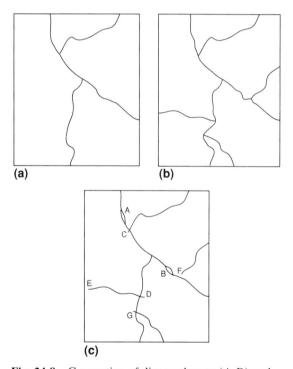

Fig. 24.8 Generation of sliver polygons (A,B) and dangling chains (C,D,E,F,G) from adding a new set of lines to an existing coverage. (a) Limited coverage; (b) New lines added; (c) result of adding (b) to (a).

Here it may be relevant to consider how digitizing can be done in a consistent manner. First, registration, the position of the map with respect to reference points with known coordinates, must be

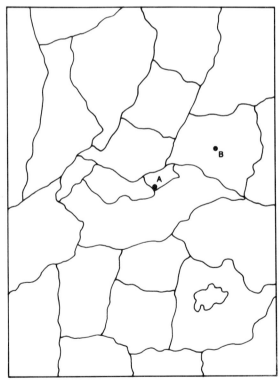

Fig. 24.9 The importance of topology when working with label points.

dealing with these problems usually based on the concept of 'tolerance', a critical distance within which two points are regarded as being identical. In theory, choice of a suitable tolerance level should remove the spurious lines and polygons and produce a correct map. In practice, at least in this author's experience, the process invariably leads to headaches. Either the tolerance is set too small and the mistakes are not removed, or it is set too large and distinct points are amalgamated; perhaps an isthmus or river meander is cut through, leading to the formation of new spurious polygons of a different type (Fig. 24.10). Flowerdew and Banting (1989) discuss problems of this type encountered when attempting to update a previously digitized map.

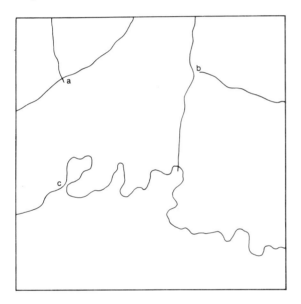

Fig. 24.10 Problems in setting tolerance levels when building topology. If the tolerance level is set large enough to correct the errors at a and b, the loop at c will also (incorrectly) be closed.

Thematic measurement error can itself be subdivided according to the scale at which the attribute is measured. If it is measured on a continuous scale, as with elevation or rainfall, for example, it can only be recorded to some specified level of accuracy. If it is a count or a categorical variable, exact recording is possible. However, whatever the scale of measurement, the map (or other data source) may not display the attribute to the level of accuracy possible. A point or line attribute (such as city size or pipeline diameter), for example, may be shown as one of a set of graduated symbols, and an area attribute (such as population density) may be depicted according to which of a set of class intervals it falls into. Of course, an important advantage of a GIS over a map is that attribute data can be stored accurately without having to tackle the problems of mapping them clearly, but accuracy in a GIS may not always be possible if it is not present in the component data sets.

Particular problems occur for data (such as the elevation and rainfall examples mentioned above) which are defined everywhere. Frequently these are mapped as isopleths or contours – even if these lines were totally reliable, a point between two lines could have any value within the range the lines define. An additional source of error here (perhaps better regarded as attribute conceptual error) is that the value for any point is likely to be based on an interpolation procedure and may be wildly out if the assumptions of the procedure do not hold.

Another important special case of thematic measurement error occurs with categorical attributes. The assignment of points, lines or areas to a category is based on a classification of some type, and many such classifications can be drawn up with differing degrees of detail. Zoning or land use maps are cases in point. Sometimes the categories apply to points in space rather than to pre-defined areal units – to categorical coverages in Chrisman's terminology (1989). Examples include geology, soils and vegetation maps. Such attributes raise particularly major measurement problems because of the varying level of detail to which classification is possible.

Cartographic conceptual error raises further difficulties in integrating data sets. There may be uncertainty about where to place a point symbol intended to represent a large city, but it is with line and area phenomena that the problem is greatest. The location of a coastline involves far from obvious decisions about high, low or median water levels, about generalization, and about historical change (Fig. 24.11). For a single map, this may not matter much but, when two data sets are overlaid, differences in the coastline can generate many sliver polygons and other incompatibilities. Decisions about the placement of property and other areal unit boundaries may raise similar difficulties. In addition to error of this type, perhaps attributable to conceptual fuzziness, other errors due to incompetence, incorrect guesswork, low standards of accuracy or intention to mislead should not be ignored. As an example of the third of these, attempts to integrate Canadian census and postal zone coverages ran up against the inadequacy of postal zone maps, which were not true to scale (unimportant for post office purposes provided that the zone boundaries were clearly marked, but fatal for data integration purposes). Demko and Hezlep (1989) illustrate the fourth point with their illustration of how Soviet maps were purposefully distorted until recently.

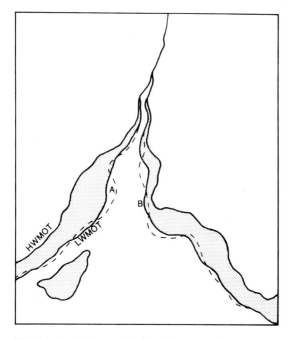

Fig. 24.11 Problems in digitizing coastlines. A, coastline in 1960; B, Coastline in 1969. HWMOT = High Water Mark, Ordinary Tides; LWMOT = Low Water Mark, Ordinary Tides.

Thematic conceptual error can likewise be a matter of incompetence, guesswork, inaccuracy or deliberate distortion. In addition it may arise from conceptual fuzziness. In the case of categorical coverages, like vegetation or soils, there may be difficult decisions to make about whether a small area, which differs from the surrounding region, should be picked out as constituting a separate patch. The concept of a transition zone also creates problems. Over space there may be a gradual change from a dominantly forest area to a dominantly grassland area, for example; constructing a categorical coverage forces the GIS user to split this transition zone into two distinct categories. Even if 'forest/grassland transition' is allowed as a separate category, the problem is not solved, because the user must then make a sharp boundary between the transition zone and each of the original categories.

Errors of all these types in individual maps create difficulties in GIS use, but what happens when several different maps are to be integrated? It might be claimed that the error involved in using any GIS is the sum of the errors in all the component data sets. A less stringent view would be that the error is at least as great as the error involved in the worst of the component data sets. A still more optimistic view is that errors in some data sets may cancel out, or that it may be possible to correct an error in one data set on the basis of the information contained in the others. In practice, of course, the effects depend on what the error is and how the maps are to be combined. Goodchild and Gopal (1989) and many of the contributors to their volume argue that one of the greatest research challenges in the GIS field is to track the effects of different types of error in GIS. They also argue (1989: xiv) that 'the objective should be a measure of uncertainty on every GIS product'.

Measuring the effects of error in the context of data integration is a major problem, and it is one tackled by Veregin (1989), Chrisman (1989), Maffini *et al.* (1989) and Lodwick (1989) among others. Openshaw (1989), in recognition of the fact that error in GIS databases is here to stay, advocates that there is a need to live with error. He suggests a general strategy based on Monte Carlo simulation to produce estimates of the likely extent and importance of error.

INCOMPATIBLE AREAL UNITS

Social, economic and demographic data are frequently collected for pre-defined zones of various types. Unfortunately for GIS users, however, the zonal systems used are not the same for different data sets, and may also be subject to change over time (see Flowerdew and Openshaw 1987 for a review of the problem). If one zonal system nests within another, the problem can be overcome by aggregation, although it should be remembered that the results of geographical data analysis may depend on the areal units used (Openshaw 1984). More generally, however, zonal systems overlap: either attempts at comparison must be forgone, or a method of estimating the values for one set of zones on the basis of another must be devised.

One method of transforming data from one set of areal units to another is to assume that the data can in principle be represented as a smooth surface, and that the values for any areal unit can be calculated by integrating the surface for the zone defined by the areal unit boundaries. This approach was put forward by Tobler (1979) under the name 'pycnophylactic interpolation'. It appears to have merit to the extent that the surface being represented can reasonably be expected to be smooth. Much zonal data, however, like population, may vary abruptly, for example at the boundary between urban and rural areas. A somewhat similar approach has been developed by Martin (1989) for a related problem. British small-area population data are released for Enumeration Districts, whose centroids are generally available although the boundaries are not. Martin fits a surface to the centroid values in order to construct maps of the underlying distributions.

An alternative approach is to apportion the known data for a zone in one system (the source zone) so as to construct estimates for a zone in another system (the target zone). The obvious way of doing this is to assume that the data are distributed evenly within the source zone, and hence that a target zone constituting a certain proportion of the source zone should contain that same proportion of the data for the source zone. This areal weighting or areal interpolation method has been described by Goodchild and Lam (1980).

The problem with this method is that many kinds of data are most unlikely to be distributed evenly within source zones. Often a GIS user will have information for the target zones, or for other units which Goodchild, Anselin and Deichmann (1989) refer to as control zones, that makes it highly improbable that the distribution of target zone data will be even. Flowerdew and Green (1989) have investigated ways in which such information can be used to improve areal interpolation estimates; they suggest the use of the EM algorithm, originally devised to allow statistical analysis where some observations are missing, to derive these estimates.

Langford, Maguire and Unwin (1991) illustrate the same approach with an application to population estimation from remote sensing data. Kehris (1990) has developed methods of linking a GIS to the statistical package GLIM to enable these methods to be operationalized.

CONCLUSION

This chapter has reviewed a number of considerations relevant to integrating different data sets within a GIS. There are several aspects of data integration that have not been treated. In particular, there is a large literature on the integration of cartographic and remote sensing databases (Bracken *et al.* 1989: 45–9; see also Davis and Simonett 1991 in this volume) and the related problem of integrating spatial data stored in raster and vector format (Devereux 1986). There have also been studies of the practical problems encountered in creating large integrated databases, for example in the CORINE project (Briggs and Mounsey 1989; see also Mounsey 1991 in this volume), in Belize (Robinson *et al.* 1989) and in the production of the BBC's Domesday videodisk (Openshaw, Wymer and Charlton 1986).

Two points should be made in conclusion. First, data integration is not a trivial or straightforward process; as with so many aspects of GIS use, the apparent ease and flexibility observable in a software demonstration obscures the necessity for a great deal of painstaking work. Further, the accuracy and tolerance levels of GIS may draw attention to problems that can be overlooked if cartographic comparison is all that is attempted. The process of data integration in a GIS may be salutary in that it forces GIS users to think explicitly about the comparability and accuracy of the different data sets they hold.

Second, and most important of all, data integration is at the very heart of GIS. The ability to combine together data of many different types and to display them in any combination is the main factor differentiating a GIS from mere database management systems on one hand and computer mapping systems on the other. The potential problems in data integration are many and fearsome, but it is well worth facing them, for that is the only way to get the full potential from GIS.

REFERENCES

Aanstoos R, Weitzel L (1988) Tracking oil and gas wells in Texas. *Proceedings of the Ninth Annual IASU Conference. Harnessing the hidden power of your system: maximizing your return-on-investment.* International Association of Synercom Users, Houston

Blakemore M J (1984) Generalisation and error in spatial data bases. *Cartographica* **21**: 131–9

Bracken I, Webster C (1990) *Information Technology in Geography and Planning: including principles of GIS.* Routledge, London

Bracken I, Higgs G, Martin D, Webster C (1989) A classification of geographical information systems literature and applications. *Concepts and Techniques in Modern Geography*, Vol. 52. Environmental Publications, Norwich

Briggs D, Mounsey H M (1989) Integrating land resource data into a European geographical information system: practicalities and problems. *Applied Geography* **9**: 5–20

Burrough P A (1986) *Principles of Geographical Information Systems for Land Resources Assessment.* Clarendon, Oxford

Chrisman N R (1989) Modeling error in overlaid categorical maps. In: Goodchild M F, Gopal S (eds.) *Accuracy of Spatial Databases.* Taylor & Francis, London, pp. 21–34

Chrisman N R (1991) The error component in spatial data. In: Maguire D J, Goodchild M F, Rhind D W (eds.) *Geographical Information Systems: principles and applications.* Longman, London, pp. 165–74, Vol 1

Cutter S L (1985) Rating places: a geographer's view on quality of life. *Resource Publications in Geography.* Association of American Geographers, Washington DC

Davis F W, Simonett D S (1991) GIS and remote sensing. In: Maguire D J, Goodchild M F, Rhind D W (eds.) *Geographical Information Systems: principles and applications.* Longman, London, pp. 191–213, Vol 1

Demko G J, Hezlep W (1989) USSR: mapping the blank spots. *Focus* **39** (1): 20–1

Devereux B J (1986) The integration of cartographic data stored in raster and vector formats. In: Blakemore M J (ed.) *Proceedings of AUTOCARTO London 1.* Royal Institution of Chartered Surveyors, London pp. 257–66

Fisher P F (1991) Spatial data sources and data problems. In: Maguire D J, Goodchild M F, Rhind D W (eds.) *Geographical Information Systems: principles and applications.* Longman, London, pp. 175–89, Vol 1

Flowerdew R, Banting D (1989) Evaluating the potential role of GIS for a market analysis company. *North West Regional Research Laboratory, Research Report 2.* NWRRL, Lancaster

Flowerdew R, Green M (1989) Statistical methods for inference between incompatible zonal systems. In: Goodchild M F, Gopal S (eds.) *Accuracy of Spatial Databases.* Taylor & Francis, London, pp. 239–47

Flowerdew R, Openshaw S (1987) A review of the problems of transferring data from one set of areal units to another incompatible set. *Northern Regional Research Laboratory, Research Report 4.* NRRL, Lancaster and Newcastle-upon-Tyne

Gatrell A C (1991) Concepts of space and geographical data. In: Maguire D J, Goodchild M F, Rhind D W (eds.) *Geographical Information Systems: principles and applications.* Longman, London, pp. 119–34, Vol 1

Goodchild M F, Anselin L, Deichmann U (1989) A general framework for the spatial interpolation of socio-economic data. Paper presented at the Regional Science Association meeting, Santa Barbara California

Goodchild M F, Gopal S (1989) (eds.) *Accuracy of Spatial Databases.* Taylor & Francis, London

Goodchild M F, Lam N S-N (1980) Areal interpolation: a variant of the traditional spatial problem. *Geo-Processing* **1**: 297–312

Hearnshaw H M, Maguire D J, Worboys M F (1989) An introduction to area-based spatial units: a case study of Leicestershire *Midlands Regional Research Laboratory Research Report 1.* MRRL, Leicester

Kehris E (1990) Interfacing ARC/INFO with GLIM. *North West Regional Research Laboratory Research Report 5* NWRRL, Lancaster

Lam N S-N (1983) Spatial interpolation methods: a review. *The American Cartographer* **10**: 129–49

Langford M, Maguire D J, Unwin D J (1991) The area transform problem: estimating population using satellite imagery in a GIS framework. In: Masser I, Blakemore M J (eds.) *Geographic Information Management: methodology and applications.* Longman, London

Lodwick W A (1989) Developing confidence limits on errors of suitability analyses in geographical information systems. In: Goodchild M F, Gopal S (eds.) *Accuracy of Spatial Databases.* Taylor & Francis, London, pp. 69–78

Maffini G, Arno M, Bitterlich W (1989) Observations and comments on the generation and treatment of error in digital GIS data. In: Goodchild M F, Gopal S (eds.) *Accuracy of Spatial Databases.* Taylor & Francis, London, pp. 55–67

Maling D H (1973) *Coordinate Systems and Map Projections.* George Philip, London

Maling D H (1989) *Measurements from Maps: principles and methods of cartometry.* Pergamon, Oxford

Maling D H (1991) Coordinate systems and map projections for GIS. In: Maguire D J, Goodchild M F, Rhind D W (eds.) *Geographical Information Systems: principles and applications.* Longman, London, pp. 135–46, Vol 1

Martin D (1989) Mapping population data from zone centroid locations. *Transactions of the Institute of British Geographers.* NS **14** (1): 90–7

Mounsey H M (1991) Multisource, multinational environmental GIS: lessons learnt from CORINE. In: Maguire D J, Goodchild M F, Rhind D W (eds.)

Geographical Information Systems: principles and applications. Longman, London, pp. 185–200, Vol 2

Openshaw S (1984) The modifiable areal unit problem. *Concepts and Techniques in Modern Geography.* Vol. 38. Geo Abstracts, Norwich

Openshaw S (1989) Learning to live with errors in spatial databases. In: Goodchild M F, Gopal S (eds.) *The Accuracy of Spatial Databases.* Taylor & Francis, London, pp. 263–76

Openshaw S, Wymer C, Charlton M (1986) A geographical information and mapping system for the BBC Domesday optical disks. *Transactions of the Institute of British Geographers* NS **11**: 296–304

Rhind D W, Green N P A, Mounsey H M, Wiggins J C (1984) The integration of geographical data. *Proceedings of Austra Carto Perth.* Australian Cartographic Association, Perth, pp. 273–93

Robinson G M, Gray D A, Healey R G, Furley P A (1989) Developing a geographical information system (GIS) for agricultural development in Belize, Central America. *Applied Geography* **9**: 81–94

Schut G (1976) Review of interpolation methods for digital terrain models. *Canadian Surveyor* **30**: 389–412

Tobler W R (1979) Smooth pycnophylactic interpolation for geographical regions. *Journal of the American Statistical Association* **74**: 519–30

Tobler W R, Kennedy S (1985) Smooth multidimensional interpolation. *Geographical Analysis* **17** (3): 251–7

Unwin D J (1981) *Introductory Spatial Analysis.* Methuen, London

Veregin H (1989) Error modeling for the map overlay operation. In: Goodchild M F, Gopal S (eds.) *Accuracy of Spatial Databases.* Taylor & Francis, London, pp. 3–18

Weibel R, Heller M (1991) Digital terrain modelling. In: Maguire D J, Goodchild M F, Rhind D W (eds.) *Geographical Information Systems: principles and applications.* Longman, London, pp. 269–97, Vol 1

Williams R B G (1984) *Introduction to Statistics for Geographers and Earth Scientists.* Macmillan, London

Williams R B G (1986) *Intermediate Statistics for Geographers and Earth Scientists.* Macmillan, London

Wrigley N (1985) *Categorical Data Analysis for Geographers and Environmental Scientists.* Longman, London

DEVELOPING APPROPRIATE SPATIAL ANALYSIS METHODS FOR GIS

S OPENSHAW

The geographical information revolution demands a new style of spatial analysis that is GIS appropriate and GIS proof. The existing spatial analytical toolbox is largely inadequate, consequently there is an urgent need to create more relevant methods and also to educate users not to expect the impossible when analysing geographical data. The real challenge is the need to develop new, largely automated, spatial data exploratory techniques that can cope with the nature of both the geographical data created by GIS and the skill base of typical GIS users. It also needs to emphasize the creative, hypothesis generating, and artistic aspects of geographical analysis, avoid being too dependent on a blinkered and inadequate inferential statistical mentality, and recognize the limitations of working within a geographical domain. A number of useful and applicable techniques are described and optimism is expressed about the opportunities that abound for making good use of spatial analysis within GIS environments.

ON THE NATURE OF SPATIAL ANALYSIS

A good GIS will today probably contain over 1000 commands (or their equivalent) but few, typically none, will be concerned with what might correctly be termed spatial analysis rather than data manipulation. This distinction is critical since spatial data handling procedures such as buffering, overlay, and query are not 'real' analysis operations except in a data descriptive or cartographic sense. It is useful, therefore, to define first what is meant by spatial analysis and then briefly outline the available technology.

The origins of spatial analysis lie in the development of quantitative and statistical geography in the 1950s. Spatial analysis was originally based on the application of the available statistical methods to spatial data (Berry and Marble 1968). Later, it was extended to include mathematical model building and operational research methods (Taylor 1977; Wilson and Bennett 1985). Hagerstrand (1973:69) provided an adequate definition of spatial analysis when he wrote 'to no small degree the recent quantitative analysis in geography represents a study in depth of the patterns of points, lines, areas, and surfaces depicted on maps of some sort or defined by co-ordinates in two- or three-dimensional space'. Most other definitions are similar, for example, Johnston, Gregory and Smith (1986: 446) define spatial analysis as 'quantitative (mainly statistical) procedures and techniques applied in locational analytic work'. Unwin (1981) presents spatial analysis as concerned with the arrangements on maps of four types of data portrayed there: points, lines, areas, and surfaces. The techniques allow both description of the arrangements on individual maps and the comparison of two or more maps so that relationships might be identified. A variety of statistical and geographical analysis procedures have been developed to serve these objectives (Goodchild 1988).

Clearly, spatial analysis is extremely relevant to GIS and the gradual absorption of spatial analysis tools into GIS systems is inevitable. Spatial analysis offers a toolbox that can in principle be applied to all the standard types of geographical information and be performed in one-dimensional space, more commonly in two-, occasionally in three-, and rarely in four-dimensional space. It is important as a means of increasing the functionality of GIS by providing a link between the essentially cartographic domain in which the origins of GIS lie and key areas of applied quantitative, statistical and mathematical analysis, and modelling, of interest to many users of GIS. However, in seeking to meet these objectives the recommended technology has to be capable of coping with the peculiarly complex nature of the spatial data. Several years ago Ripley (1984) talked about the need for a revolution; this need still exists.

This chapter is a critique of existing spatial analysis techniques and their potential for use in GIS. The considerable differences between methods appropriate for environmental and socio-economic applications mean that, apart from some general remarks, it is not possible to consider them both here. Instead, the discussion concentrates on socio-economic applications. Burrough (1991 in this volume) and Bonham-Carter (1991 in this volume) make some relevant comments about environmental applications and useful reviews include Davis (1986), Nielson and Bouma (1985) and Oliver, Webster and Gerrard (1989a, 1989b).

A REVIEW OF THE EXISTING SPATIAL ANALYSIS TOOLBOX

The newcomer to spatial analysis may well require a standard textbook from which to work. This is especially important because of the current lack of spatial analysis procedures in GIS systems and also in statistical packages. A good survey of a wide range of statistical procedures is provided in Upton and Fingleton (1985). Diggle (1983) and Ripley (1981) also provide a useful digest. Simpler introductions are given in Taylor (1977), Unwin (1981) and Wilson (1974) considers modelling applications. In addition, a plethora of quantitative geography and statistical geography textbooks outline most of the standard methods. Unfortunately, there is as yet no globally useful text designed to inform the GIS user specifically about the complete range of spatial analysis methods that might be considered relevant and appropriate to GIS.

It is useful, therefore, to provide a brief summary of the range of available spatial analysis tools by identifying classes of methods appropriate for different geographical data types (Table 25.1). Note that the four basic geographical data types shown in Table 25.1 can often be mapped on to each other. For example, point data can be aggregated to areas, areas can be represented by a point reference, lines can be aggregated to areas, and data for areas converted into a surface and surface values estimated for both points and areas (Gatrell 1991 in this volume). Likewise, levels of measurement can be changed by recoding operations. It should be noted, however, that all spatial data operations involving aggregation and generalization are usually irreversible. This is because they result in the loss of original information and the possible addition of unwanted noise and, sometimes, pattern to the data. It is important that information is held in its most disaggregated form and that it is analysed at that level.

Table 25.1 A simple typology of some spatial analysis methods

Type of geographical data	Methods of analysis
Point	Nearest neighbour
	Quadrat methods
Line	Network analysis and graph theoretic methods
	Fractal dimension
	Edge detection
Area	Shape measures
	Spatial autocorrelation
	Spatial regression
	Regionalization
	Spatial interaction
	Location-allocation modelling
Surface	Image processing
	Bayesian mapping

A common starting point in the analysis sequence is the map generated by GIS. This usually results in the user conjuring up a whole series of questions that involve spatial analysis. Do the map patterns mean anything? Are they 'real' or are they likely to be a chance occurrence? What might be 'causing' a particular pattern? Can the patterns be modelled, predicted, and forecasted? Can the map patterns be manipulated using planning tools? These questions reduce to two key types of spatial analytical activity: (1) spatial pattern description and (2) spatial pattern relationships. These can involve univariate as well as multivariate analysis. It is often statistical in nature but not exclusively so, with mathematical modelling and other forms of *ad hoc* geographical analysis procedures being of interest.

Spatial pattern descriptors

In spatial pattern description, various numerical and statistical descriptions can be obtained to summarize the display. For point data various nearest neighbour and geostatistical methods can be used to summarize patterns; for example, centroid and standard distance for point patterns relating to selected attributes and mean distance to kth nearest neighbours. For area data, the measures of spatial autocorrelation are often employed (Cliff and Ord 1981). Various multivariate statistical methods can be used to summarize complex multi-layered (i.e. multivariable) map data sets. Line data types are generally more difficult to analyse, although various measures such as orientation and intersection frequencies might be useful. Network data can be described using various graph theoretic measures. Finally, surface data are often described by being fitted to various mathematical functions to yield different degrees of pattern; for example, different orders of polynomial trend surface. Sometimes the map patterns relating to data cannot easily be shown in cartographic form; for instance, flow data relating to a complete origin or destination table, although there are exceptions even here.

A few other areas which may cause problems concern the non-ideal nature of spatial data distributions, the lack of linearity of relationships, and the usual problems of interpreting spatially aggregate information (e.g. ecological inference error and the Modifiable Areal Unit Problem (MAUP); see Openshaw 1984). In some areas, specially adapted methods exist which can cope better with the special needs of spatial analysis. For example, the incorporation of a contiguity constraint into cluster analysis, so that regions consist of spatially contiguous areas, is often a useful improvement to a standard cluster analysis procedure.

Spatial pattern relationships

An interest in spatial pattern description soon leads to more sophisticated questions about spatial pattern relationships; indeed, pattern description is seldom an end in itself. For example, if a pattern exists what might be causing it? If there is a particular variable of interest which displays spatial patterning, then what are the principal spatial covariates? The standard approaches involve factor analysis and regression methods to analyse data for spatial associations. However, the use of standard statistical procedures necessitates ignoring the presence of spatial dependencies in the data. If regression is of interest, then it is appropriate to use an explicitly spatial regression model (e.g. see Anselin 1988; Anselin and Griffith 1988; Kennedy 1988).

Problems with spatial pattern description and relationships

It is important to note that both spatial pattern description and relationship analysis methods can be applied in three markedly different contexts: (1) testing *a priori* hypotheses about patterns and relationships present in spatial data; (2) efficient spatial pattern and relationship description; and (3) analysis for purposes of decision support and spatial planning.

One problem with both description and relationship measurement is the need to generalize the results and, perhaps, compare findings in different study regions. This can be handled within an inferential framework. It is usually assumed that the user has a predefined *a priori* hypothesis that was not generated by examining the data on which it is to be tested. Often a general purpose null hypothesis is used; namely, that the map data have been generated by some kind of spatially random process; for example, the kth nearest neighbour distance is similar to what would be expected in spatially random data. If more detail exists then the hypothesis can be more explicit; for example, that cancer incidence does not decline with distance from a nuclear installation or that one region has a higher value on some test statistic than another region. This process is fraught with difficulty. First, it is necessary to have knowledge of the sampling distributions of the test statistic under the null hypothesis; with spatial data standard approximations do not often apply. Second, *any* prior knowledge of the data invalidates the outcome; for instance, if the hypothesis was generated by looking at a map of the data then it could not be properly tested without access to a second, unseen, data set. This *post hoc* hypothesis testing problem is extremely important in a scientific context, yet it runs counter to the long prevailing style of exploratory data analysis used in geography. It also has major implications for spatial model building. One approach is first to run a model, then examine the residuals to define a missing variable, then re-build the model. That is fine provided no tests of significance are used to validate the model but then how is the user supposed to know whether the model is a good one?

Other problems with the use of inferential variants of spatial analysis methods concern: (1) the use of published critical test statistic values will almost certainly be inappropriate because of the spatially autocorrelated nature of geographical data; (2) the power of test statistics used in a spatial analysis context is not usually known; (3) it is not certain as to whether the sampling analogy is meaningful because many geographical data constitute the population and there is no notion of sampling; and (4) problems of multiple testing which often occur in exploratory studies or when mapping probabilities (each zone constitutes a separate hypothesis so critical significance levels need to be corrected downwards).

Some of the difficulties with inferential methods can be overcome. For instance, the use of Monte Carlo significance tests is a neat way of avoiding the need to make asymptotic assumptions about the distribution of test statistics (Besag and Clifford 1989). It is also a good way of dealing with spatially autocorrelated data. Other problems remain less well identified to hamper the unwary in an inferential context. For instance, the use of spatial autocorrelation statistics for ratio variables may invalidate standardized mortality rates. Another avenue which may be used to avoid these problems is to switch to Bayesian methods and leave the frequentist domain altogether. In the long term this may be ideal but at present there are problems in computational tractability. Nevertheless, some GIS-relevant Bayesian mapping procedures exist; (see Clayton and Kaldor 1987, and Alexander, Ricketts and Williams 1989). They have the nice property of seeking to avoid some of the problems in mapping data by taking into account the spatially varying degrees of data reliability, albeit at the expense of low power and a high degree of arbitrariness.

Another way to apply spatial analysis methods is to move away from an inferential approach and regard description as the main purpose in spatial analysis. This involves searching out potentially interesting map patterns without necessarily being in any position to test any hypotheses relating to them. In general, the descriptive use of many statistical methods on spatial data is satisfactory provided no strong reliance is placed on significance testing to validate or test the results. However, this does have implications for comparative study and result generalization. It may also appear to degrade the utility of GIS and spatial analysis, but as is argued in greater detail later, this is quite reasonable given the nature of geographical information. It will be possible with time to develop better statistical procedures for use with spatial data, although this task is proving extremely difficult and in any case it is not necessary for most uses of GIS. There is an argument, therefore, to abandon the traditional geographical applications of statistical inference in favour of a more descriptive approach in which significance tests are used mainly as a results filtering mechanism.

The third view is to focus on the use of spatial analysis as a planning and decision support tool. The conventional concerns of science and statistical inference are now subverted by the need to make decisions based on the results of spatial analyses. Densham (1991 in this volume) provides further details of spatial decision support techniques.

One final aspect concerns the nature of the available spatial analytical procedures in GIS. Most of the methods described in Table 25.1 are not yet available within GIS. This is simultaneously a problem and an advantage. The lack of relevant methods is a problem and it is probably only possible to think of applying spatial analysis tools to problem areas where there is a pre-existing body of expertise in the technology and/or the problems themselves are of sufficient importance to demand special attention. At the same time, the relative absence of unsuitable methods is also an advantage. Unfortunately, it is extremely easy to implement methods that are inherently unsafe and it would be a major error to include methods that exist in the literature, but which are not readily applicable or useful to the GIS era. It is important to try and avoid the worst problems of misuse likely to be generated soon by the availability of a comprehensive menu of spatial analysis tools, through which the user can, without regard to any of the underlying principles, run the same data through everything that exists. That would be fine if the methods were all appropriate to the task in hand.

SOME BASIC PRINCIPLES

The real problem is, therefore, not with the definition of what spatial analysis means or with any associated philosophical limitations, but with identifying the nature of the technology needed to provide basic spatial analytical functionality relevant to GIS. For instance, how is it possible to detect patterns in two-dimensional space, or discover whether some arbitrary map coverages are related in some way, or analyse time-dynamic spatial information? Such questions are common to many different GIS-inspired analyses. Yet it should not be assumed that the existing spatial analysis toolbox that comes from either quantitative geography or spatial statistics is at all useful or appropriate to GIS. It has been argued elsewhere (Openshaw 1989a) that the spatial analytical methods which GIS needs are still mainly absent and await development.

Obvious key functions that are missing from current GIS are basic exploratory geographical analysis tools which can help the user to 'find' and 'describe' patterns and relationships that may exist in spatial databases. This strong emphasis on data exploration, rather than on confirmatory analysis and hypothesis testing, reflects the lack of applicable theory and prior hypotheses in most GIS applications.

The need for exploratory geographical analysis tools has also been stimulated by the vast explosion in geographically referenced information which is creating many new opportunities for spatial analysis in areas where there is little previous research. In many instances, the purpose behind the analysis can only be exploratory and often results from the fact that suddenly some new spatial data exist and because they exist, they need to be analysed. For example, experience has shown that once disease databases are geographically referenced and thus available for spatial analysis, there is only a short time-lag before the data are analysed using the full battery of available methods. The driving force is no longer the academic sector, but a diverse range of applied users. Many of these have little interest in basic research and academic concerns and merely want to use GIS technology to answer pressing practical questions. There is a need, therefore, for simple usable spatial analytical methods that are relevant to GIS.

It is argued that the emerging mountain of real and potentially creatable geographically referenced data challenges the conventional manner by which spatial statistical analysis and modelling are currently performed in an academic context. The challenge can be viewed as involving the need for an automated and more exploratory *modus operandi* in situations which are data rich but theory poor. Some will argue that a mapping capability is all that is required. Indeed maps provide an excellent communications medium for presenting results in a form that most people think they can understand. However, maps provide a very poor form of analysis technology; the human brain is far too easily tricked and misled and the patterns that occur are often far too complex for easy visual recognition and interpretation (Monmonier 1977). There is a clear need for a quantitative exploratory style of spatial analysis that can complement the map-oriented nature of GIS. These analytical tools must be designed to meet such needs without becoming so rigidly statistical that they become: (1) purely tools for researchers; (2) so lacking in creativity that they offer little prospect of new insights; and (3) unable to answer any of the basic questions. Maybe GIS only needs simple technology as the intrinsic limitations of spatial analysis, combined with the absence of process knowledge, argue strongly in favour of a more relaxed, flexible, artistic and less statistical approach than may have been expected. Certainly the new technology has to be creative within limits defined by some statistical analysis process, but without being too constrained by an over-reliance on inappropriate methods. This perception is fundamentally different from the emphasis in spatial analytical research of the last two decades, in which the goal seems to have been greater levels of statistical and theoretical sophistication rather than any strong concern for application. If statisticians and geographical methodologists wish to remain in touch with GIS then they need to develop understandable methods that can answer the questions that typical users are likely to ask.

There is no magic set of spatial statistical tools that can be incorporated into GIS in order to provide an adequate spatial analysis toolbox analogous to what exists for spatial data handling. Instead there is the prospect of a long hard struggle to develop suitable methods that can cope with the very hard problems that characterize this area. There are many practical difficulties that have to be faced. In particular, geographical data are inherently difficult to handle; current GIS seldom contain all the data structures and access paths needed for spatial analysis; spatial data suffer from endemic errors of various kinds and these errors propagate thereby contaminating 'clean' data sets and reducing further the quality of these data. There is probably not much that can be done to eliminate the causes of error and uncertainty in geographical information. What is more important is the development of methods of analysis that can handle data uncertainty rather than simply ignore it.

The research challenge is to build on these principles and assemble a new set of spatial analytical tools. This task is assisted by the recent rapid increases in affordable computer processing power. New computationally intensive numerical- and simulation-based styles of spatial analysis can be developed that may avoid some of the limitations and difficulties of traditional approaches. A computer-intensive route also brings with it a very different perspective that seems more relevant to the needs of GIS. It is possible to 'buy' solutions, which are probably good enough for most users even if they do not necessarily completely satisfy the intellect, merely by throwing computing power at the key problem areas. The improved availability of supercomputers and multiple-processor systems is fundamentally changing the amount of computer power that is available, by two or three orders of magnitude. It is now possible to think about new numerical-based approaches without worrying too much about computer speed restrictions. Development work on today's supercomputers can proceed in the secure knowledge that by the mid-1990s (maybe much earlier), similar levels of performance will characterize the popular workstations on which GIS will be run.

These computer hardware trends also make it feasible to start developing automated spatial analytical methods. This is important as a means of improving the efficiency of exploratory tools and for coping with the thousands of potentially interesting geographical data sets that now exist in the world and which have never been subjected to any form of spatial analysis. It is no longer feasible to think only in terms of hand-crafted manual analysis by experts with one or two years per data set! Nor is it sensible to ignore most of the data. It is not inconceivable that the information locked up in some of these unanalysed data, in the form of spatial patterns and relationships, and not yet identified deducible theories, could be of considerable public, commercial, and academic value. Unless spatial analysis methods relevant to GIS can be developed, many of these data will never be analysed. The real challenge is, therefore, to discover how to trawl through these geographical databases in search of interesting results with a high level of efficiency by devising new forms of spatial analytical methods, rather than castigating this objective as constituting the ultimate in unsound science.

UNDERSTANDING THE LIMITATIONS OF SPATIAL ANALYSIS

In seeking to develop methods of spatial analysis relevant to GIS, it is important to start by being realistic about what spatial analysis can reasonably be expected to deliver. The lessons from the first quantitative revolution in geography suggest that it failed, partly because too many users held wholly unreasonable expectations about what might be obtainable from geographical analysis. In reality, even the most sophisticated spatial analysis procedure will probably not progress the user very far along the path of scientific understanding and in some ways the technology appears to be limited in what it can offer. Some users may find that geographical pattern analysis and description is not particularly useful in their search for process knowledge and causal understanding. Yet in many instances, spatial analysis of the available geographical data is the only available option. The purpose of that analysis would typically be to develop insights and knowledge from any patterns and associations found in the data, which will either be useful in their own right or else provide a basis for further investigation at a later date using different, probably non-spatial and more micro-scale, methods. This function of 'pointing others in the right direction' is an important goal for spatial analysis.

Several problems conspire to restrict what spatial analysis can achieve. They include: (1) the lack of prior theory or hypotheses forcing the user to start by searching for the existence of patterns or relationships without knowing what to look for, or even whether there is anything to find; (2) the difficulties of operating in an exploratory context in which knowledge of the data greatly complicates the testing of *post hoc* hypotheses and models; (3) the available geographical data are usually only surrogates for other information which is missing and often unobtainable (e.g. the use of distance as a proxy for all manner of processes); (4) GIS may be data rich but in most applications few of the key process variables are present; (5) the ecological nature of most analysis is a limiting factor while data aggregation can change the nature of micro-level relationships and sometimes also create spurious new ones; (6) spatial data tend to be characterized by complexity; (7) there are endemic questions about data accuracy and quality; and (8) there are severe difficulties in coping with the time dimension. As a result, spatial analysis in a GIS context is unlikely to result in a greatly improved understanding of causality. This is not so much a deficiency of the methods rather than a recognition of the complexity and limitations under which GIS operate. It is also questionable whether this goal of process understanding based on knowledge of causality is in fact reasonable given the well-known problems of making causal inferences in the non-experimental sciences. At best, all that will be achieved will be some qualitative and descriptive story about how processes may work. A few GIS models may claim to offer process-relevant insights, but at the end of the day they will probably still be incapable of adequately representing the real causal mechanisms.

Spatial analysis in the short term can only be a fairly primitive descriptive science, but maybe for many purposes that is sufficient. The ultimate difficulty is the inherently limited utility of geographical information in studies which attempt to understand process. An example from spatial epidemiology may help to clarify this key statement. Age/sex standardization of incidence rates is a common practice but neither age nor sex covariates are directly causal variables, they are proxies for other unmeasured and unknown process variables; for instance, age cannot cause cancer but other variables related to age might. In geographical analysis also, virtually all the available data are surrogates and proxies for other variables which are either missing from the database or incapable of measurement or not yet identified. It would be sheer folly to go beyond what these sorts of data can sustain. This is not to underestimate the immense potential utility of geographical information, or of the important insights about process that spatial analysis may provide, but merely recognition that there are limits to what can be achieved in a geographical context. Fortunately, many GIS users have only a basic shopping list and often only want to make simple statements about the presence or absence of patterns and relationships. For instance, it is still usually sufficient to identify spatial pattern as a departure from a spatially random process expectation, without having to define precisely what spatial process generating assumption would be appropriate. Despite this apparently simple requirement, current spatial analysis methods are nowhere near meeting these needs and are a long way from attaining their full potential. GIS is revolutionary technology which requires flexible fresh thinking unfettered by the past. In short, it requires a new way of thinking. Table 25.2 offers some guidance for spatial analysts.

DEVELOPING APPROPRIATE SPATIAL ANALYSIS FOR GIS

The problem is where to start. It is apparent that most developers of GIS have in the past seen little need to put much effort into spatial analysis. Also, there is no clear view of what spatial analytical functions are needed. There is very little merit in merely trying to include either a complete statistical package that cannot cope with the special nature of

Table 25.2 Some basic guidelines for spatial analysis in GIS

1. Avoid highly formalized scientific designs.
2. Adopt an exploratory data analysis mentality.
3. Avoid being too statistically blinkered with an over-emphasis on inappropriate inference.
4. Stay within the limitations of geographical analysis.
5. Avoid any technique that either implicitly ignores or explicitly removes the effects of space.
6. Think carefully before using methods left over from the 1960s era of quantitative geography.
7. Avoid the use of asymptotic assumptions, use Monte Carlo simulation instead.
8. Remain aware of the possible effects that data problems can have on the results.

spatial data or even to code-up the complete spatial statistical technology according to Diggle (1983), Ripley (1981) or Upton and Fingleton (1985) for a GIS. This would be pointless because the chosen methods have to be appropriate for typical GIS environments, users, and analysis needs. For example, nearest neighbour methods which assume no positional uncertainty in point coverages are inapplicable, as are spatial regression models which can only function with no more than a few hundred zones and provide no automated predictor search mechanism. Interfacing complex statistical packages, such as GLIM, would be another largely irrelevant diversion of effort, as the methods cannot readily cope with the spatially dependent nature of the data they are meant to process.

One way forward is to define a small set of generic spatial analysis functions, which can be built in as standard GIS operations with their complexity hidden by the use of appropriate interfaces. Another would be to develop a more advanced set of analysis tools, which would seek to provide new analytical functions which are only possible within a GIS environment. One problem involves defining what spatial analysis functions and operations are sufficiently general and generic to justify their inclusion. A related issue concerns the nature of the spatial data handling operations that the spatial analysis methods may require to function and the need to ensure that GIS builders put the necessary hooks into their systems.

In addition, there is the practical necessity of ensuring that the methods can actually work in a GIS environment. A basic set of design objectives for developers of new spatial analysis methods would have to include: an ability to handle large numbers of zones (say 10 000); the need to cope with the nature of geographical data including the presence of uncertainty and errors; a high degree of algorithmic portability; coverage of generic analysis needs; the prospect of an extension into the time domain; a high degree of automation; freedom from critical assumptions and an essentially exploratory *modus operandi*.

A SHORT LIST OF GENERIC SPATIAL ANALYSIS FUNCTIONS

To some extent the importance of spatial analysis to GIS is being recognized, although it is doubtful whether sufficient research resources are being devoted to building practical methods. The US National Center for Geographic Information and Analysis (NCGIA 1989) is clearly aware of the problem and the spatial analysis theme is implicit in several of its initiatives for the first three years. In the United Kingdom, the ESRC's Regional Research Laboratory (RRL) initiative has also identified spatial analysis as one of three major research objectives for the eight RRLs to investigate. Attempts have also been made to develop a research agenda (Openshaw 1990a) and six key areas have been identified (see Table 25.3). It remains to be seen whether any of these procedures migrates into the GIS systems of the 1990s.

Table 25.3 Six key spatial analytical research topics

1. Response modelling for large data sets with mixed scales and measurement levels.
2. Practical methods for cross area estimation.
3. Zone design and spatial configuration engineering.
4. Exploratory geographical analysis technology.
5. Application of Bayesian methods.
6. Application of artificial neural nets to spatial pattern detection.

Underlying all these topics is a concern for exploratory geographical data analysis, restricted to questions that the available geographical information might be capable of answering. This simplifies the technical task as it involves no more than pattern and relationship description. In an applied study, these activities would constitute only the first stage of a more extensive work programme, with the GIS role being limited to providing an indication as to where further research should be performed. However, this is still an extremely important role. Moreover, hypotheses obtained from the analysis of data for one region can be tested (with considerable power) in another. Pattern description and inductive styles of analysis may seem difficult but they can also be extremely creative and may result in new knowledge. Also, the results they produce can often become the basis for action without necessarily risking delaying a response until there is proof of causation (typically involving a 50- to 100-year delay); provided there can be some assurance that the patterns are real and not spurious. This raises another important technical point. The conventional 5 per cent statistical significance level may appear to be both too lax (if the results are likely to cause concern) and too stringent if descriptive power is being lost. It is very easy to confuse descriptive and suggestive results with validatory and confirmatory work. The latter is wholly concerned with Type I errors (finding pattern where none exists) while totally ignoring Type II errors (failing to find pattern when it exists). Quite often the latter may be more critical than the former in exploratory and descriptive GIS based spatial analyses.

The next stage in the argument in favour of exploratory geographical analysis is to define a set of basic generic functions; see Openshaw (1990b). A list is given in Table 25.4 and the key features are expanded here. This is viewed as important because the most difficult task is identifying what functions are required; the subsequent operationalization is often far more easily achieved. It is hoped that by identifying a list of generic methods, which reflect the previous discussion of the need for GIS-relevant spatial analysis technology, that their creation will be encouraged where they do not yet exist, and that they will be more widely used where they do exist.

The idea of a pattern spotter is simply an automated means of identifying evidence of geographical pattern in point data sets without any *a*

Table 25.4 Basic generic spatial analysis procedures.

1. Pattern spotters and testers.
2. Relationship seekers and provers.
3. Data simplifiers.
4. Edge detectors.
5. Automatic spatial response modellers.
6. Fuzzy pattern analysis.
7. Visualization enhancers.
8. Spatial video analysis.

priori hypothesis to test. This problem may occur in a genuine exploratory situation or as a means of avoiding problems of *post hoc* model construction when prior knowledge of a specific geographical database renders suspect any hypothesis testing approach. One realization of this method is the geographical analysis machine discussed in the next section.

A relationship seeker is an attempt to develop a statistical procedure that mirrors the map overlay process. Relationships between a point data coverage and a set of M map overlays can be modelled using Poisson regression. An alternative, more geographical procedure involves a search among 2^{M-1} permutations of map coverages for evidence of spatial pattern being created by the interaction of the overlays with point data of interest. A prototype procedure, termed a Geographical Correlates Exploration Machine (GCEM) has been built (Openshaw, Cross and Charlton 1990). An interesting feature is its use of location as an additional level of surrogate variable. It will allow relationships which occur 'here' but 'not there' to be identified.

Data simplifiers are merely GIS-relevant versions of existing classification methods. They have existed for a few decades but are still absent from most GIS. Regionalization procedures (i.e. classification with contiguity constraints) provide an obvious means of simplifying very large and complex spatial databases to identify patterns. These procedures can deal with extremely large data sets and also handle flow data. Automated zone design procedures provide a solution to a whole range of spatial engineering problems (e.g. redistricting and customized zone design). One reaction to modifiable areal unit effects (Openshaw 1984) is to engineer spatial data aggregations to possess required characteristics. Automatic zoning procedures can effectively achieve this objective providing approximately optimal solutions to various constrained and unconstrained problem formulations. GIS is removing all the historic restrictions on the types of zoning systems available for reporting spatial data and it is important that this new found 'freedom' is properly controlled and used.

Edge detection is a further area of spatial analysis relevant to GIS that is very undeveloped. Zones are usually stored in a vector-based GIS as a set of line segments with topological details. Why not develop spatial analytical tools for analysing the data in a GIS at this level instead of at the zonal scale? Pattern detection now becomes a problem in edge detection.

Spatial response modelling is also of considerable importance. Increasingly, GIS are being used to create multi-scale databases ranging from the micro to the macro. There is a need for automated response models to be developed in which the values of a dependent variable can be predicted by reference to whatever spatial predictor information might be available, and under circumstances where there is minimal prior knowledge of the functional forms that might be most appropriate. One response is a fully automated modelling system (Openshaw 1988). Another is to develop variants of the AID (Automated Interaction Detector: a survey method based on binary segmentation) technique called database modelling (see Openshaw 1989b). No doubt there are other possibilities, but it is important to remember the design objectives that GIS set; for instance, many rather than few possible predictors, no prior knowledge of model specification, non-linearity should be assumed, data errors would not be unusual, mixed measurement scales are not uncommon, and large data sets are standard rather than exceptions.

Fuzzy analysis procedures are clearly relevant to many areas of GIS because they provide a means of dealing with all types of data uncertainty. The question is basically how to incorporate fuzzy analysis into GIS. Currently there are few operational examples, although a fuzzy geodemographic targeting system has been proposed (Openshaw 1989b). The linkages with object-oriented programming should help stimulate academic interest in this area of GIS, but it could be the next century before any practical methods emerge.

Visualization enhancers represent another approach to supplementing the communication power of the basic static map display (see Buttenfield and Mackeness 1991 in this volume). The increasing availability of geographical data with time coordinates revives interest in the use of computer movies as a basic but potentially extremely effective analysis procedure. A time-driven computer movie presentation would enliven an otherwise static display (Tobler 1970; Moellering 1973). The cost of basic computer movie technology based on video recording is now fairly low, although the use of sophisticated animation technology requires access to special video computer hardware. In a GIS application, maybe only simple procedures are needed (for instance, a succession of maps showing data in two or three dimensions). The utility of the visual images might be further enhanced by performing spatial analysis at each time slice. For example, the effects of space–time analysis might be best seen by displaying a movie of N different, but sequential in time, space–time analyses. An additional dimension could be provided by using sound to supply supportive information about the map patterns being viewed. However, this form of spatial analysis delegates the task of spotting patterns and being creative to the human observer. It also puts considerable emphasis on stimulating little understood human cognition systems by supplying selected visual and auditory information.

A final area for investigation concerns the possibility of analysing spatial data at the pixel level. The objective here is to redefine spatial analysis operations at the pixel scale, a form of representation which is common to all spatial data so that a common micro-analytical technology for spatial analysis might be developed. For this application, image processing technology is useful but not adequate and a new set of tools would have to be constructed. Besag (1986) gives one example of how it might be achieved by statistical means; another route could involve cellular automata (a form of computer modelling that creates simple holistic structures out of simple rules applied to microscopic level data). As processing power becomes less of a constraint, entirely different forms of spatial analysis might well emerge in GIS and this may be one of them.

SOME SIMPLE PROCEDURES FOR DETECTING PATTERNS AND RELATIONSHIPS

Finally, a brief case study based on an extension of the author's Geographical Analysis Machine (GAM), for the analysis of point pattern data, might be helpful in illustrating the role of spatial analysis in GIS. The original GAM concept (Openshaw, Charlton and Wymer 1987; Openshaw *et al.* 1988) has been generalized to encompass a wide range of spatial pattern search methods. Openshaw (1989c, 1990c) describes a GAM (g,m,s) procedure where the g parameter relates to the nature of the search geometry (i.e. circles, squares, equal population at risk areas, kth nearest neighbours), m refers to the choice of significance assessment procedure (i.e. descriptive, hypothesis testing, and significance estimation), and s is the type of search strategy employed (i.e. locationally comprehensive, case based, *a priori* site restricted, linear feature, etc.). Variants of this method can be run on a microcomputer and experience in running a GAM identifies many of the key technical issues that occur elsewhere in exploratory spatial analysis.

The original GAM involved the use of a circular pattern detector and a locationally comprehensive search based around intersection points on a lattice. The lattice mesh was set at 0.2 circle radii to ensure that the circles overlapped. This was considered important to allow for positional uncertainty in the point data while a grid search pattern was used to ensure that no locations were excluded. In the original GAM, a range of circle sizes was examined. A Poisson probability was used to screen the results so that only those circles with a relatively small probability of being due to chance were mapped. The map of circles was then used to identify subregions where there appeared to be evidence of departure from a spatially random distribution of points.

This approach can be criticized on the grounds that the significance threshold used to screen the circles needs to be corrected for multiple testing, the overlapping circles re-use some of the data, and no overall measure of Type I map error is computed. All these problems can be overcome by running a GAM on a supercomputer so that a Monte Carlo significance test procedure can be used. However, to some extent these criticisms constitute an irrelevant distraction because they imply that the spatial analysis is concerned not only with pattern detection but also with validation. They also raise severe technical problems. In particular, the large number of implied hypotheses being tested (typically a few million) results in low power and only the most extreme results will tend to survive (Openshaw *et al.* 1989). Additionally, the results also depend on study region boundary and size; the larger the region of interest the greater are the dilution effects. Some of the lost power can be regained by switching from measures of whole map pattern (i.e. total counts of significance circles) to what is termed vicinity analysis. The number of circles can be reduced by defining a series of blobs (or superclusters), each consisting of a set of overlapping circles. The significance testing is based on the frequency with which blobs formed in data generated under a null hypothesis, have more extreme characteristics than the observed data blobs that they overlay (see Openshaw 1990c). There is, however, an argument that the original descriptive GAM is best and that maybe spatial analysis should stop after defining areas where it may be worth performing additional analysis using different data and more precise methods. Certainly fears that the original GAM was prone to large degrees of Type I error proved to be unfounded.

The question now is what variant of the GAM (g,m,s) family can be immediately used in GIS. The need to use a supercomputer is primarily a result of using a locationally comprehensive search strategy. If a less comprehensive analysis is acceptable then the procedure outlined in Appendix A can be run on a microcomputer. This is based on Besag and Newell (1990) who questioned the need for a locationally comprehensive search and recommended a kth nearest neighbour circle method (see the alternatives in Appendix A) as a means of coping with rural–urban differences in population density. It is also computationally far easier to focus only on the observed cases. However, if positional uncertainty in the data is to be simulated then results from the Besag and Newell method and the original GAM would tend to converge. Finally, it is possible to adapt the Appendix A procedure to cope with a search along a buffered linear feature, for instance, an overhead wire. A similar alternative is the Cuzick and Edwards (1990) test.

A different type of spatial analysis problem occurs when it is necessary to test a hypothesis that there is a raised incidence of, say, a disease near a set of *a priori* locations. Appendix B outlines a simple procedure for site-based hypothesis testing. To be scientifically valid, the sites have to be identified prior to any knowledge of the data and if there are multiple sites then an additional correction for multiple testing should be applied. The procedure in Appendix B is a variant of the Poisson maximum method (Stone 1988) which makes no assumption about which distance band is the critical one; it merely examines a wide range and corrects the result for multiple testing using a Monte Carlo method.

A third basic procedure is concerned with measuring the association between a point data coverage and M other coverages. One route is the best coverage permutation search used in GCEM. Another is a Poisson regression model with a focus on analysing the residuals from a well-fitting model for evidence of interesting spatial patterning. Another possibility requires that the dependent coverage is not a point coverage. A random sample of points is generated and an attempt made to identify a relationship using categorical analysis methods (namely, log linear modelling) or a database model of some kind. These types of analyses could be readily performed using standard packages.

CONCLUSIONS

The task of developing appropriate methods of spatial analysis for GIS is extremely important at a time when there is large growth both in the availability of geographical information and in the numbers of users who are potentially interested in spatial analysis. The previous neglect of spatial analysis looks set to become a major impediment to the full exploitation of GIS. There is a danger that the growing imbalance between the availability of geographical data and the limited range of existing analytical technology may slow the growth of GIS and result in widespread failure to make full use of the available information. This discussion has attempted to provide a better understanding of the nature of those spatial analysis methods that seem to be most relevant to GIS. The key features that are considered important are an exploratory function and an emphasis on insight and creativeness. There are dangers in trying to be too statistically pure in situations where the appropriate methods have not been developed and which, in any case, can only really sustain low level description. Perhaps in its GIS guise, spatial analysis can only remain an art and will never aspire to being a science.

APPENDIX A: A SIMPLIFIED GAM FOR A MICROCOMPUTER

Basic Algorithm

Step 1. Create two point data coverages, one of cancer cases or some other rare data to which a Poisson assumption is applicable, the other a measure of the population at risk. The data could refer to points or to small zones which are point referenced. The two point data coverages should be merged so that there is one data set containing both the incidence data and the population at risk counts.

Step 2. For each point with at least one observed case (i), order all other points by distance from it. Apply a selection rule to determine the count of cases and population at risk within a critical distance of (i); see below for alternatives.

Step 3. Compute a Poisson probability of obtaining the observed number of cases given the population at risk under the null hypothesis.

Step 4. If 'significant' at the 5 per cent level then draw the 'circle'.

Step 5. Repeat Steps 2 to 4 for all observed cases

Alternative Selection Procedures

Some alternatives could be: (a) use a fixed radius circle; (b) determine for each case the minimum circle radius sufficient to encompass at least K other cases; and (c) the minimum circle radius to yield a target population at risk or an equal expectation of cases.

Other variations

The search geometry could be changed; the 'circles' could be replaced by 'squares' or 'segments of circles' and so on. The effects of possible covariates could be removed by adjusting the Poisson probability calculation. The effects of positional uncertainty can be handled by repeating the procedure many times (say 99 or 999), each time wobbling (according to some error model) the data coordinates. An approximate measure of robustness can be obtained by computing for each case the amount by which the population at risk could be increased before the result became insignificant. Finally, the effects of multiple testing could be handled by Monte Carlo methods, but these would suffer from study region dependency. Nevertheless, it is important to be aware that if there are M observed cases and with a significance threshold of 5 per cent, then $M*0.05$ significant results would be expected purely by chance. In this spatial context the test is no more than a screening process and, even if a smaller than expected number of significant results occurred in a 'strange' area, then there may well be something interesting occurring. Whether this 'something interesting' is an artefact of the data or is real would be a matter for subsequent investigation.

APPENDIX B: A SITE BASED HYPOTHESIS TESTER

Basic Algorithm

Step 1. Assemble a set of sites to be evaluated and create data as in Appendix A.

Step 2. Select a maximum radial search distance (d).

Step 3. Order the data from an evaluation site by distance. For each different distance band out to distance (d) compute a Poisson probability that the observed cumulative number of cases could have occurred by chance under the null hypothesis.

Step 4. Identify the distance band with the most extreme result.

Step 5. Repeat Steps 3 and 4 for 99 or 999 or 9999 spatial data distributions generated under the null hypothesis and compute the rank of the observed data result. Convert to a measure of probability as a test of the hypothesis.

Observations

It is important that the list of sites to be evaluated is identified prior to obtaining any knowledge of the data. The list should not subsequently be added to in the light of the results. On the other hand, if the purpose is description and not significance testing then a variety of search methods might be employed to 'look' for maximally significant results. This is valid only if the probability of obtaining similarly extreme results in spatially random data was sufficiently small to make any interpretation interesting.

REFERENCES

Alexander F E, Ricketts T J, Williams J (forthcoming) Methods of mapping small clusters of rare diseases with applications to geographical epidemiology. *Geographical Analysis*

Anselin L (1988) *Spatial Econometrics: methods and models*. Kluwer Academic Publishers, Dordrecht

Anselin L, Griffith D (1988) Do spatial effects really matter in regression analysis? *Papers of the Regional Science Association* **65**: 11–34

Berry B J L, Marble D F (eds.) (1968) *Spatial Analysis: A reader in statistical geography*. Prentice-Hall, Englewood Cliffs New Jersey

Besag J E (1986) On the statistical analysis of dirty pictures. *Journal of the Royal Statistical Society B* **48**: 192–236

Besag J E, Clifford P (1989) Generalised Monte Carlo significance tests. *Biometrika* **76**: 633–42

Besag J E, Newell J (forthcoming) The detection of clusters in rare diseases. *Journal of the Royal Statistical Society B*

Bonham-Carter G F (1991) Integration of geoscientific data using GIS. In: Maguire D J, Goodchild M F, Rhind D W (eds.) *Geographical Information Systems: principles and applications*. Longman, London, pp. 171–84, Vol 2

Burrough P A (1991) Soil information systems. In: Maguire D J, Goodchild M F, Rhind D W (eds.) *Geographical Information Systems: principles and applications*. Longman, London, pp. 153–69, Vol 2

Buttenfield B P, Mackaness W A (1991) Visualization. In: Maguire D J, Goodchild M F, Rhind D W (eds.) *Geographical Information Systems: principles and applications*. Longman, London, pp. 427–43, Vol 1

Clayton D, Kaldor J (1987) Empirical Bayes estimates of age-standardised relative risks for use in disease mapping. *Biometrics* **43**: 671–81

Cliff A D, Ord J K (1981) *Spatial Process, Models, and Applications*. Pion, London

Cuzick J, Edwards R (1990) Tests for spatial clustering of events for inhomogeneous populations *Journal of the Royal Statistical Society Series B* **52**: 73–104

Davis J C (1986) *Statistics and Data Analysis in Geology*, 2nd edn. Wiley, New York

Densham P J (1991) Spatial decision support systems. In: Maguire D J, Goodchild M F, Rhind D W (eds.) *Geographical Information Systems: principles and applications*. Longman, London, pp. 403–12, Vol 1

Diggle P H (1983) *Statistical Analysis of Spatial Point Patterns*. Academic Press, London

Gatrell A C (1991) Concepts of space and geographical data. In: Maguire D J, Goodchild M F, Rhind D W (eds.) *Geographical Information Systems: principles and applications*. Longman, London, pp. 119–34, Vol 1

Goodchild M F (1988) A spatial analytical perspective on GIS. *International Journal of Geographical Information Systems* **1**: 327–34

Hagerstrand T (1973) The domain of human geography. In: Chorley R J (ed.) *Directions in Geography*. Methuen, London, pp. 67–87

Kennedy S (1988) A geographical regression model for medical statistics. *Social Science and Medicine* **26**: 119–29

Johnston R J, Gregory D, Smith D M (eds.) (1986) *The Dictionary of Human Geography*, 2nd edn. Blackwell, Oxford

Moellering H (1973) The automatic mapping of traffic crashes. *Surveying and Mapping* **23**: 467–77

Monmonier M S (1977) Maps, distortion and meaning. *Association of American Geographers Resource Paper 75-4*. AAG, Washington

NCGIA (1989) The research plan of the NCGIA. *International Journal of Geographical Information Systems* **3**: 117–36

Nielson D R, Bouma J (1985) *Spatial Analysis of Soil Data*. PUDOC, Wageningen

Oliver M, Webster R, Gerrard J (1989a) Geostatistics in physical geography. Part 1. *Transactions of the Institute of British Geographers* NS **14**: 259–69

Oliver M, Webster R, Gerrard J (1989b) Geostatistics in physical geography. Part 2. *Transactions of the Institute of British Geographers* NS **14**: 270–86

Openshaw S (1984) The modifiable areal unit problem. *CATMOG* **38** Geo Abstracts, Norwich

Openshaw S (1988) Building an automated modelling system to explore a universe of spatial interaction models. *Geographical Analysis* **20**: 31–46

Openshaw S (1989a) Computer modelling in human geography. In: Macmillan W (ed.) *Remodelling Geography*. Blackwell, Oxford, pp. 70–88

Openshaw S (1989b) Making geodemographics more sophisticated. *Journal of the Market Research Society* **31**: 111–31

Openshaw S (1989c) Automating the search for cancer clusters. *The Professional Statistician* **8** (9): 7–8

Openshaw S (1990a) Towards a spatial analysis research strategy for the Regional Research Laboratory initiative. In: Masser J, Blakemore M J (eds.) *Geographical Information Management: methodology and applications*. Longman, London

Openshaw S (1990b) Spatial analysis and GIS: a review of progress and possibilities. In: Scholten H J, Stillwell J C H (eds.) *Geographic Information Systems for urban and regional planning*. Kluwer, Dordrecht, 156–63

Openshaw S (1990c) Automating the search for cancer clusters: a review of problems, progress, and opportunities. In Thomas R W (ed.) *Spatial Epidemiology*. London Papers in Regional Science 21. Pion, London, pp. 48–78

Openshaw S, Charlton M, Wymer C (1987) A Mark 1 Geographical Analysis Machine for the automated analysis of point data. *International Journal of Geographical Information Systems* **1**: 335–43

Openshaw S, Charlton M, Craft A W, Birch J M (1988) An investigation of leukaemia clusters by use of a geographical analysis machine. *The Lancet* **1**: 272–73

Openshaw S, Cross A E, Charlton M E (1990) Building a prototype Geographical Correlates Exploration Machine. *International Journal of Geographical Information Systems* **3**: 297–312

Openshaw S, Wilkie D, Binks K, Wakeford R, Gerrard M H, Croasdale M R (1989) A method for detecting spatial clustering of disease. In: Crosbie W A, Gittus J H (eds.) *Medical Responses to the Effects of Ionising Radiation*. Elsevier Applied Science, London, pp. 295–308

Ripley B D (1981) *Spatial Statistics*. Wiley, New York

Ripley B D (1984) Present position and potential developments: some personal views. *Journal of the Royal Statistical Society* A **147**: 340–48

Stone R A (1988) Investigations of excess environmental risks around putative sources: statistical problems and a proposed test. *Statistics in Medicine* **7**: 649–60

Taylor P J (1977) *Quantitative Methods in Geography*. Houghton Mifflin, Boston

Tobler W R (1970) A computer movie simulating urban growth in the Detroit Region. *Economic Geography* **46**: 234–40

Unwin D J (1981) *Introductory Spatial Analysis*. Methuen, London

Upton G, Fingleton B (1985) *Spatial Data Analysis by Example. Volume 1. Point Pattern and Quantitative Data*. Wiley, New York

Wilson A G (1974) *Urban and Regional Models in Geography and Planning*. Wiley, London

Wilson A G, Bennett R J (1985) *Mathematical Methods in Human Geography and Planning*. Wiley, London

SPATIAL DECISION SUPPORT SYSTEMS

P J DENSHAM

Decision makers increasingly are turning to geographical information systems to assist them with solving complex spatial problems. These systems do not adequately support decision making, however, because they are lacking in analytical modelling capabilities and do not easily accommodate variations in either the context or the process of spatial decision making. One response to these shortcomings is the development of spatial decision support systems which are explicitly designed to address complex spatial problems. The design of such systems, the types of problem to which they can be applied, the decision-making processes they support, and a framework for their implementation and subsequent evolution are examined.

INTRODUCTION

Decision makers faced with a complex spatial problem often have multiple, conflicting objectives for its solution. To be acceptable, a solution must reconcile these conflicting goals. A variety of analytical techniques have been developed to help decision makers solve problems with multiple criteria (for examples in location selection see Starr and Zeleny 1977; Cohon 1978; Nijkamp 1979). Consequently, decision makers have turned to analysts and analytical modelling techniques to enhance their decision making capabilities.

To be effective, these analytical techniques require that a decision maker defines the problem and articulates the objectives for its solution. If the decision maker can do so, the problem can be termed well structured. Many complex spatial problems are ill- or semi-structured (Gorry and Morton 1971; Alter 1980; Hopkins 1984), however, and decision makers cannot define their problem or fully articulate their objectives. The decision making process adopted to solve semi-structured spatial problems has often been perceived as unsatisfactory by decision makers (Densham and Rushton 1988). This perception arises because many mathematical models, including hybrid formulations, fail to capture the important dimensions of spatial problems (Dear 1978). Moreover, analysts, rather than decision makers, have selected the dimensions of the problem that are modelled. This often leads to the selection of variables with inappropriate levels of resolution and geographical extent and, ultimately, results in solutions that are deemed unsatisfactory when evaluated in terms of the quality of the decision-making process that generated them.

To assist decision makers with complex spatial problems, geoprocessing systems must support a decision research process, rather than a more narrowly defined decision-making process, by providing the decision maker with a flexible, problem-solving environment. Such an environment empowers the decision maker in two ways: first, the problem can be explored to increase the level of understanding and to refine the definition; and, second, the generation and evaluation of alternative solutions enables the decision maker to investigate the possible trade-offs between conflicting objectives and to identify unanticipated, and potentially undesirable, characteristics of solutions.

Spatial decision support systems (SDSS) are explicitly designed to support a decision research process for complex spatial problems. SDSS provide a framework for integrating database management systems with analytical models, graphical display and tabular reporting capabilities, and the expert knowledge of decision makers. Such systems can be viewed as spatial analogues of decision support systems (DSS) developed in operational research and management science to address business problems.

This chapter provides an overview of SDSS by differentiating them from geographical information systems (GIS) and examining the types of problem to which they can be applied, the decision-making processes they support, typical system designs, and a framework for their implementation and evolution during the decision research process. It begins with an example of a DSS that illustrates the nature of the problem which SDSS must address. The characteristics of geoprocessing systems in general are then reviewed. Following this, a framework and an architecture for SDSS are presented. Finally, some brief conclusions are offered.

A SEMI-STRUCTURED SPATIAL PROBLEM: BANK BRANCH LOCATION

In recent years the banking industry in the United States has undergone considerable change. Kimball and Gregor (1989) identify three emerging trends in the retail banking sector. First, because non-banks are offering what are traditionally considered to be banking services, banks are facing increasing levels of competition. Secondly, the merger and consolidation of banks, resulting in larger, less-dense branch networks, has been one response to these increased levels of competition.

> 'The best managers will see, however, that the real competitive advantage does not derive from size per se, but from integrating acquisitions quickly, cheaply, and with a minimum of disruption to service delivery.'
> (Kimball and Gregor 1989: 13)

The third trend, therefore, is a shift in management emphasis towards integrating acquisitions with existing branch networks, product lines and operations. Thus, in addition to determining which branches remain in the network and which are closed,

> 'Developing and implementing highly integrated product lines, marketing support functions, and service functions across branch networks and different geographical locations will be the major operations and organizational challenge of the 1990s.'
> (Kimball and Gregor 1989: 13)

Three questions must be addressed in the process of designing branch networks, whether the aim is expansion, reconfiguration, or contraction (Chelst, Schultz and Sanfhvi 1988):

1. How many branches should there be?
2. Where should these branches be located?
3. What services should each branch provide to its customers?

The answers to these questions are interrelated because the network must be considered as a whole rather than as a series of isolated, individual branches. To find answers, bankers must ask other questions, including:

1. How many potential customers are within the market area of each actual or potential branch location?
2. What types of products will customers want to purchase from the bank?
3. What is the accessibility of each site to customers and is it commensurate with the operational needs of the bank (e.g. is it on a main street, does it have a car park, and what other land uses are in the immediate area)?
4. What is the cost of a new site, is there an existing structure, and what are the planning regulations in force?

Some of these questions also are hard to answer because they involve factors which are difficult to evaluate or predict. The problem of designing a network of bank branches must be considered ill-structured because it is impossible to define and to measure precisely the objectives for every possible solution. Often, solutions to ill-structured problems are obtained by generating a set of alternatives and selecting from among those that appear to be viable.

To support bank branch location selection, a geoprocessing system must be flexible enough to enable bank managers to use their chosen decision-making approaches. The managers will want to use the system to identify and employ a variety of measures of performance to evaluate the current branch network; to estimate the current and future levels of market potential and market penetration; to characterize the success of different types of branch when faced with a variety of levels of competition; to generate and evaluate a series of alternative solutions; and, once a network is designed, to monitor performance so that short-term corrective actions are made and commensurate long term strategic plans can be developed.

Thus, to support a decision research process, a geoprocessing system must facilitate the introduction of new factors into analyses. The system also must enable its users to change the relative importance of factors in analyses, both to evaluate the sensitivity of solutions and to reflect different opinions and objectives for the solutions. Finally, the system should be able to display the results of analyses in a variety of ways that help users to understand them.

CHARACTERISTICS OF GEOPROCESSING SYSTEMS

Geographical information systems

The literature on GIS contains many definitions. Often, the functions of capturing, storing, manipulating, analysing and displaying spatial data form the core of these definitions and the idea that GIS are designed to support spatial decision making is implicit (see Maguire 1991 in this volume).

A geoprocessing system, which is to support a decision research process and enable decision makers to use their chosen decision-making processes, must provide geographical information analysis (GIA) capabilities. Current GIS fall short of providing GIA capabilities. First, their support of analytical modelling is lacking as has been argued on several occasions (see Openshaw 1991 in this volume).

A second problem is that many GIS databases, in addition to their query functions, have been designed to support only cartographic display. This design goal handicaps the support of analytical modelling and other functions. For example, many analytical modelling techniques are data intensive. The sets of variables or layers stored in a GIS database often are too sparse to support modelling. Furthermore, the scales and degrees of resolution chosen to support cartographic display may be inappropriate for modelling.

A third problem concerns the graphical and tabular reporting capabilities of GIS. The main metaphor for information exchange between GIS and their users is the map and the database report. A decision maker who is exploring a problem and generating and evaluating alternative solutions will require other forms of graphics and reports, many of them peculiar to the problem domain. Unfortunately, flexible mechanisms for communicating information to the user are not commonly found in GIS.

A final problem concerns the decision making processes supported by GIS. The literature shows that when different people are faced with the same problem, they will adopt a range of decision-making strategies (Davis and Elnicki 1984); they will place different values on variables and relationships; and they will select and use information in a variety of ways. The decision making process applied to ill-structured spatial problems must reflect these inherent difficulties and inter-personal differences. Current GIS designs are not flexible enough to accommodate variations in either the context or the process of spatial decision making. This is reflected in definitions of GIS which largely ignore the role of analytical modelling techniques and the decision-making processes supported.

Spatial decision support systems

Spatial decision support systems are explicitly designed to provide the user with a decision-making environment that enables the analysis of geographical information to be carried out in a flexible manner. These systems have evolved in parallel with decision support systems (DSS) developed for business applications. The development of SDSS has lagged that of DSS by about 10 to 15 years, however. Thus, the DSS literature can be used to guide the design, development, implementation and use of SDSS.

Gorry and Morton's (1971) seminal paper initiated a literature. It documented the development of decision support systems as a response to the perceived shortcomings of management information systems (MIS) in the late 1960s and early 1970s. Despite their advantages, MIS did not adequately support analytical modelling capabilities and did not facilitate the decision maker's interaction with the solution process. The resulting literature on DSS is rich in both theory and applications (see Keen and Morton 1978; Alter 1980; Bonczek, Holsapple and Whinston 1981; Ginzberg and Stohr 1981; Sprague and Carlson 1982; Bennett 1983; House 1983).

DSS, which have been developed for applications including strategic planning, scheduling of operations, and investment appraisal, provide a framework for integrating database management systems, analytical models, and graphics to improve decision-making processes. As with GIS, a variety of definitions of DSS have been developed (e.g. see Alter 1977), but recent definitions have concentrated on the characteristics of systems. Often, these definitions list a series of characteristics that must be present for a system to be considered a DSS. Geoffrion's (1983) definition suggests that a DSS has six distinguishing characteristics:

1. They are explicitly designed to solve ill-structured problems where the objectives of the decision maker and the problem itself cannot be fully or precisely defined.

2. They have a user interface that is both powerful and easy to use.

3. Such systems enable the user to combine analytical models and data in a flexible manner.

4. They help the user explore the solution space (the options available) by using the models in the system to generate a series of feasible alternatives.

5. They support a variety of decision-making styles and are easily adapted to provide new capabilities as the needs of the user evolve.

6. Such systems allow problem solving to be both interactive and recursive – a process in which decision making proceeds by multiple paths, perhaps involving different routes, rather than a single linear path.

Differentiating DSS, SDSS and GIS

The characteristics that Geoffrion uses to define a DSS can also be used to define a SDSS. Because of the nature of complex spatial problems, however, a SDSS will need to provide additional capabilities and functions that:

- provide mechanisms for the input of spatial data;

- allow representation of the complex spatial relations and structures that are common in spatial data;

- include analytical techniques that are unique to both spatial and geographical analysis (including statistics); and

- provide output in a variety of spatial forms including maps and other, more specialized, types.

The characteristics of a SDSS facilitate a decision research process that can be characterized as iterative, integrative and participative. It is iterative because a set of alternative solutions is generated which the decision maker evaluates. Insights gained from this evaluation are input to, and used to define, further analyses. Participation occurs because the decision maker plays an active role in defining the problem, carrying out the analyses and evaluating the outcomes. The benefit of participation is integration: value judgements that materially affect the final outcome are made by decision makers who have expert knowledge that must be integrated with the quantitative data in the models and qualitative information.

A SDSS normally is implemented for a limited problem domain. The database integrates a variety of spatial and non-spatial data and facilitates the use of analytical and statistical modelling techniques. A graphical interface conveys information, including the results of analyses, to decision makers in a variety of forms. Finally, the system both adapts to the decision maker's style of problem solving and is easily modified to include new capabilities (Keen 1980). In sum, the characteristics of a SDSS serve to distinguish it from a GIS.

A FRAMEWORK FOR THE DEVELOPMENT OF SDSS

The DSS literature can both inform and guide the development of SDSS. Of several frameworks used for the development of DSS, Sprague's (Sprague 1980; Sprague and Carlson 1982; Carlson 1983) is readily transferred to the spatial domain. The level of technological development of the system is differentiated from the functional roles of the people who work with the technology.

There are three levels of technology in Sprague's framework (Fig. 26.1). At the lowest level is the SDSS toolbox. This is a set of hardware and software components that can be assembled to build a variety of system modules. At the second level of technology is the DSS generator. A generator is a set of mutually compatible hardware and software modules that can be configured easily to produce a specific SDSS. A specific SDSS is used to address a problem, by combining some or all of the modules in the generator. As the needs of the decision makers change, other modules can be added to the specific SDSS from the generator or, if they do not exist, assembled from the components in the SDSS toolbox.

A SDSS generator represents an intermediate level of technology. By containing a series of mutually compatible modules, it can be rapidly configured to provide a particular set of capabilities. Generators are most likely to be built by system vendors and consultants. They will recoup the cost of developing a generator because the start-up costs of many broadly similar projects will be greatly reduced. Other SDSS users are likely to iterate directly between the top and bottom levels of technology. The SDSS toolbox will be used to develop a specific SDSS to address a problem. Components from the toolbox will be employed directly to supply new capabilities as they are required by decision makers.

Sprague's (1980) framework contains five functional roles, the first three of which correspond

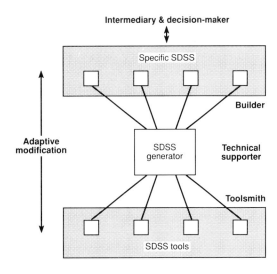

Fig. 26.1 Sprague's three-level framework for developing a SDSS.

to the three levels of technology (Fig. 26.1). Thus, the SDSS toolsmith develops new hardware and software tools for the SDSS toolbox; the technical supporter adds capabilities or components to the SDSS generator; and the SDSS builder configures the specific SDSS from the modules in the SDSS generator. The final pair of roles correspond to users of the specific SDSS. The intermediary sits at a console and interacts physically with the system whereas the decision maker is responsible for developing, implementing and managing the adopted solution. These five roles do not have to be filled by five people; individuals may have more than one function and one person may assume all five roles.

The decision maker specifies the analyses that are to be carried out and uses output from the system to evaluate interim solutions. The result of this evaluation may be a desire to investigate other aspects of the problem which may require new capabilities to be added to the SDSS. The system is updated as required by people filling the technical functional roles using the three levels of technology. Unlike the development path of more traditional geoprocessing systems, this process of system adaptation and evolution occurs rapidly during the decision-making process itself. This process of adaptive modification (Keen 1980) greatly enhances the flexibility and utility of the SDSS to the decision maker.

SDSS ARCHITECTURE

Adopting Sprague's (1980) development strategy for SDSS has implications for the architecture of the system. The addition of new capabilities, in a time frame which will not disrupt unduly the decision research process, is facilitated by a modular design. Working within Sprague's framework, Armstrong, Densham and Rushton (1986) design an architecture for SDSS generators. Their architecture consists of a set of five integrated software modules. Each module provides a group of functionally related capabilities; there are modules for database and model base management systems, display and report generators, and a user interface. To programmers (toolsmiths, technical supporters and builders), the modularity of the system facilitates software engineering; to SDSS users (intermediaries and decision makers), however, the system appears to be a seamless entity.

Figure 26.2 depicts one architecture for a SDSS (Armstrong et al. 1986). The five software modules are represented by boxes. The user interface encompasses the other four modules because all interaction with the user takes place via the interface. The flows of data and information between the modules are represented by the arrows joining them. The decision maker interacts with the system either directly or through the intermediary, employing an iterative solution process. System output – including the solutions to models and database queries in graphical and tabular form – is presented to decision makers who evaluate them. A solution may be accepted by the decision makers or, if unanticipated and unacceptable characteristics are evident, it may be used to help define further analyses.

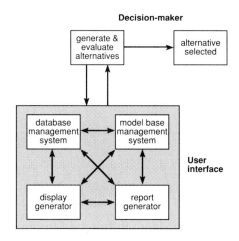

Fig. 26.2 A proposed architecture for a SDSS (after Armstrong, Densham and Rushton 1986).

Database management system

The core of the SDSS is the database management system (DBMS). The DBMS must be able to store and manipulate locational, topological and thematic data types to support cartographic display, spatial query and analytical modelling. Locational data consist of spatial primitives such as coordinates and chains. Topological data are attribute bearing objects including points, nodes and lines (examples include wells, road intersections and railway lines, respectively). Finally, thematic data are the attributes of topological objects (well depth, presence or absence of traffic lights, and the gauge of the track). The DBMS must permit the system user to construct and exploit complex spatial relations between all three types of data at a variety of scales, degrees of resolution and levels of aggregation.

The DBMS found in many GIS use the relational data model. Some fundamental problems occur when this data model is used in spatial applications, however (Calkins and Marble 1987). A study of the DSS literature reveals that alternative data models have proved effective in applications of DSS (Bonczek, Holsapple and Whiston 1984). Armstrong and Densham (1990) examine data models supported by commercially available DBMS. They demonstrate that the extended network model, an enhanced form of the network model, is effective for representing many forms of spatial relationships. A data structure is designed, using the Entity–Category–Relationship model (Chen 1983), to support location selection and is implemented using MDBS Associate's MDBS III.

Model base management system

Three approaches can be used to embed modelling techniques in SDSS. The first, and simplest, is to use the DBMS's macro or script programming language to implement modelling capabilities within the DBMS itself. This approach has several attractions. Capabilities are provided which make it easy to query and manipulate the database; and the only software required for developing models is the DBMS. The disadvantages of this approach are that DBMS macro programming languages tend to be slow because they are interpreted rather than compiled; the programming functions they offer are somewhat restrictive; and, finally, code generally is not portable across platforms and operating systems.

A second approach to incorporating analytical models is to develop libraries of analytical subroutines (Dixon, Openshaw and Wymer 1987). Such a library would be a spatial analogue of the general-purpose modelling and optimization subroutine libraries – including IMSL and NAG – which have been widely adopted. The appeal of this approach is that large numbers of models can be made accessible very easily. A user would invoke these subroutines from their own program via a standard interface. Furthermore, existing codes can be documented and object modules added to the library both easily and rapidly. There are several drawbacks to this approach: unless users are willing to write their own subroutines, they are restricted to using only the algorithms and techniques included in the library; and, second, a library is wasteful in terms of the amount of replicated code it contains. For this reason, a new area of interest in the DSS literature is the development of a model base management system (MBMS).

The development of a MBMS (Applegate, Konsynski and Nunamaker 1986; Konsynski and Sprague 1986) is a third approach to embedding models in SDSS. A MBMS performs a task which is analogous to the function of a DBMS. Instead of storing data, a MBMS stores elements of models. Its purpose, like that of a DBMS, is to use an organizing structure which supports the representation and exploitation of relationships between items and minimizes redundancy of storage. Thus, instead of individual pieces of data, a MBMS contains small pieces of code, each of which solves a step in an algorithm. Because many of these steps are common to several algorithms, this approach saves large amounts of code. The design and implementation of MBMS are attracting attention in the DSS literature. Several approaches are being investigated (Dolk 1986; Orman 1986), including the use of entity–relationship techniques (Blanning 1986).

Algorithmic solution methods are common for analytical models. The algorithms underlying these methods consist of a series of steps. When an algorithm is decomposed into its component parts, these steps are the 'atomic elements' – the smallest fragments of the algorithm. There is a degree of commonality in the steps used in algorithms for solving many types of spatial and non-spatial analytical models. Combining groups of steps in different sequences enables the MBMS to solve a wide range of algorithms. To function, the MBMS needs rules for combining steps. If steps are atomic elements, then combination rules can be thought of as formulae. Thus, when asked to employ a particular algorithm, the MBMS employs the appropriate formula and combines steps in the necessary sequence. This flexibility is achieved with minimal storage because each step cannot be disaggregated further, so redundancy is virtually eliminated.

One advantage of using a MBMS is that the implementation of new algorithms is simplified. In some cases this can occur simply by developing a new formula; in others, new atoms also may be added to the model base. A MBMS provides the researcher with the opportunity to develop and assess new algorithms rapidly. A second advantage is that the model base can be updated easily: individual steps can be replaced by improved versions without changing others. A final advantage concerns the support of modelling strategies. The flexibility of the MBMS permits the designers of the SDSS to support a variety of modelling strategies using new forms of user interfaces (see below).

Graphical and tabular report generators

The graphical and tabular report generators should provide a number of capabilities within the SDSS. The first capability is the generation of high resolution cartographic displays. These displays must be supplemented with other forms of graphics. For example, general-purpose statistical graphics, including two- and three-dimensional scatter plots and graphs, will be useful for exploratory data analysis. More specialized graphics will be necessary for depicting the results from analytical models and sophisticated statistical techniques. These graphics often will be domain specific: the use of strain ellipsoids in analysing geological faults, for example. Finally, tabular reports must augment and support each of these graphical capabilities.

User interface

To support decision making effectively, the user interface of SDSS must be easy to use. Unfortunately, the interfaces of many current geoprocessing systems are modelled on those of general-purpose business systems. These interfaces often are not suited to the graphical display of spatial information. Decision makers wish to receive information in both graphical and tabular forms – they are complementary, not mutually exclusive. Moreover, experience suggests that SDSS users want to interact with the modules of the system using either graphical or tabular representations. For example, the initial solution to a location-allocation model can be selected either by using a mouse to click on locations on a map or by typing in a list of node identifiers; the context in which this is done may determine which medium of interaction is the most appropriate.

The user interface of SDSS needs to represent two spaces: objective space and map space. Objective space depicts the parameters and solution space of an analytical model while map space is a cartographic representation of a study area and the output of the model. While a map space is likely to be displayed as a graphic, an objective space may be represented by either graphics or tables. In a location modelling context, for example, the allocations of fires to fire stations may be depicted by a series of lines between the fires and the fire stations in map space; in objective space, however, a table may simply list each fire and the station to which it is allocated. In contrast, the ranges of individual parameters in the location model may be represented graphically by bars or dials with the current value of the parameter indicated by a line or a needle. The user must be able to view these spaces simultaneously. Moreover, changes made in one space should be reflected automatically in the other space. Thus, changing the values of parameters in the objective space should be reflected by a change, where appropriate, in the allocations of fires to stations. Similarly, moving the location of a fire station in the map space should result in changes in the model in the objective space.

Providing users with this kind of interface will permit them to select data, model parameters, and output both easily and intuitively. Furthermore, such an interface permits the user to visualize the processes which underlie the model and to intervene and manipulate the model during the solution process. SDSS supporting these capabilities is truly providing the user with a problem-solving environment. The user can adopt a variety of decision-making approaches using visual interactive modelling (Hurion 1986) as a key element in the decision research process. Visual interactive modelling will be computationally intensive and the 'responsiveness' (Alter 1980) of the SDSS is important in determining its utility to a decision maker. Decision makers require timely support for their deliberations (Vazsonyi 1978, 1982), so an issue becomes how interactive is visual interactive modelling or how quickly can the results from an analysis be generated and presented to a decision maker? Keen (1983) refers to this as the 'turnaround test'. One approach that may prove fruitful in this area is the use of parallel programming techniques.

One area that is beginning to attract attention in geographical research is how to incorporate expert knowledge about modelling procedures into the SDSS itself. Because the models contained in SDSS often are complex and potentially can be misapplied, the system itself should help the user to select appropriate models, data sets and modelling strategies (Armstrong et al. 1990). To act like an expert analyst, the system must have access to three types of knowledge: a problem is described using environmental knowledge; procedural knowledge is used to help design a solution process and determine the values of parameters in models; and structural knowledge (the steps of algorithms and the data structures on which they operate) is used to solve problems. The elicitation (Waters 1989) and representation of this knowledge are fraught with difficulties.

CONCLUSIONS

SDSS are designed to provide decision makers with a problem solving environment within which they can explore, structure and solve complex spatial problems. The development of these systems requires that geographers increasingly to look to other disciplines for both current and future research findings. These findings must be used to inform and guide the design and implementation of the modules in an SDSS. Despite the increasing frequency with which the terms DSS and SDSS are appearing, the SDSS literature remains small and somewhat fugitive. Perhaps the earliest contributions to this literature stem from an IBM research project (see Carlson et al. 1974; Grace 1975; Holloway and Mantey 1976). More recent contributions have focused on either theoretical developments and implementation issues (Clarke 1989; Densham and Goodchild 1989; Fedra and Reitsma 1989; Jankowski 1989; Waters 1989; Armstrong and Densham 1990) or applications (White 1985; Dobson 1986; Bhatnagar and Jajoo 1987; Davis and Grant 1987; Densham and Armstrong 1987; Gould 1989; van der Vlugt 1989). The increasing interest in SDSS and the growing volume of publications can only be good news for decision makers.

REFERENCES

Alter S L (1977) A taxonomy of decision support systems. *Sloan Management Review* **19**: 39–56

Alter S L (1980) *Decision Support Systems: current practice and continuing challenges*. Addison-Wesley, Reading Massachusetts

Applegate L M, Konsynski B R, Nunamaker J F (1986) Model management systems: design for decision support. *Decision Support Systems* **2**: 81–91

Armstrong M P, Densham P J (1990) Database organization alternatives for spatial decision support systems. *International Journal of Geographical Information Systems* **4**: 3–20

Armstrong M P, Densham P J, Rushton G (1986) Architecture for a microcomputer-based decision support system. *Proceedings of the 2nd International Symposium on Spatial Data Handling*. International Geographical Union, Williamsville New York, pp. 120–31

Armstrong M P, De S, Densham P J, Lolonis P, Rushton G, Tewari V K (1990) A knowledge-based approach for supporting locational decision-making. *Environment and Planning B* **17**: 341–64

Bennett J L (ed.) (1983) *Building Decision Support Systems*. Addison-Wesley, Reading

Bhatnagar S C, Jajoo B H (1987) A DSS generator for district planning. *Information and Management* **13**: 43–9

Blanning R W (1986) An entity–relationship approach to model management. *Decision Support Systems* **2**: 65–72

Bonczek R H, Holsapple C W, Whinston A B (1981) *Foundations of Decision Support Systems*. Academic Press, New York

Bonczek R H, Holsapple C W, Whinston A B (1984) *MicroDatabase Management: practical techniques for application development*. Academic Press, New York

Calkins H W, Marble D F (1987) The transition to automated production cartography: design of the master cartographic database. *The American Cartographer* **14**: 105–21

Carlson E D (1983) An approach for designing decision support systems. In: House W C (ed.) *Decision Support Systems*. Petrocelli, New York, pp. 127–56

Carlson E D, Bennett J L, Giddings G M, Mantey P E (1974) The design and evaluation of an interactive geo-data analysis and display system. In: Rosenfeld J L (ed.) *Information Processing 74, The Proceedings of the IFIP Congress*. North-Holland, New York

Chelst K, Schultz J, Sanfhvi N (1988) Issues and decision aids for designing branch networks. *Journal of Retail Banking* **10**: 5–17

Chen P P (1983) English sentence structure and entity–relationship diagrams. *Information Sciences* **29**: 127–49

Clarke M (1989) Geographical information systems and model based analysis: towards effective decision support systems. *Proceedings of the GIS Summer Institute* Kluwer, Amsterdam

Cohon J L (1978) *Multiobjective Programming and Planning*. Academic Press, New York

Davis D L, Elnicki R A (1984) User cognitive types for decision support systems. *Omega* **12**: 601–14

Davis J R, Grant I W (1987) ADAPT: a knowledge-based decision support system for producing zoning schemes. *Environment and Planning B* **14**: 53–66

Dear M (1978) Planning for mental health care: a reconsideration of public facility location theory. *International Regional Science Review* **3**: 93–111

Densham P J, Armstrong M P (1987) A spatial decision support system for locational planning: design, implementation and operation. *Proceedings of AUTOCARTO 8*. ACSM/ASPRS, Bethesda Maryland, pp. 112–21

Densham P J, Goodchild M F (1989) Spatial decision support systems: a research agenda. *Proceedings of GIS/LIS '89*. ACSM, Bethesda Maryland, pp. 707–16

Densham P J, Rushton G (1988) Decision support systems for locational planning. In: Golledge R, Timmermans H (eds.) *Behavioural Modelling in Geography and Planning*. Croom-Helm, London, pp. 56–90

Dixon J F, Openshaw S, Wymer C (1987) A proposal and specification for a geographical analysis subroutine library. *Northern Regional Research Laboratory Research Report* **3** NRRL, University of Newcastle-upon-Tyne

Dobson M W (1986) Spatial decision support systems for early warning of disaster driven social emergencies. *Proceedings of the 2nd International Symposium on Spatial Data Handling* International Geographical Union, Williamsville New York, pp. 332–48

Dolk D R (1986) Data as models: an approach to implementing model management. *Decision Support Systems* **2**: 73–80

Fedra K, Reitsma R (1989) Decision support and geographical information systems. *Proceedings of the GIS Summer Institute*. Kluwer, Amsterdam

Geoffrion A M (1983) Can OR/MS evolve fast enough? *Interfaces* **13**: 10–25

Ginzberg M J, Stohr E A (1981) Decision support systems: issues and perspectives. In: Ginzberg M J, Reitman W, Stohr E A (eds.) *Decision Support Systems*. North-Holland, New York

Gorry G A, Morton M S (1971) A framework for management information systems. *Sloan Management Review* **13**: 56–70

Gould M D (1989) The value of spatial decision support systems for oil and chemical spill response. *Proceedings of the 12th Applied Geography Conference* Binghampton, pp. 75–83

Grace B F (1975) A case study of man/computer problem solving. *IBM Research Report RJ1483*. International Business Machines, San Jose

Holloway C A, Mantey P E (1976) Implementation of an interactive graphics model for design of school boundaries. *Research Paper 299*. Graduate School of Business, Stanford University

Hopkins L (1984) Evaluation of methods for exploring ill-defined problems. *Environment and Planning B* **11**: 339–48

House W C (ed.) (1983) *Decision Support Systems*. Petrocelli, New York, pp. 167–88

Hurion R D (1986) Visual interactive modelling. *European Journal of Operational Research* **23**: 281–7

Jankowski P (1989) *Knowledge-based Structured Modelling: an application to stream water quality management*. Unpublished PhD dissertation, Department of Geography, University of Washington

Keen P G W (1980) Adaptive design for decision support systems. *Data Base* **12**: 15–25

Keen P G W (1983) Interactive computer systems for managers: a modest proposal. In: House W C (ed.) *Decision Support Systems*. Petrocelli, New York, pp. 167–88

Keen P G W, Morton M S (1978) *Decision Support Systems: an organizational perspective*. Addison-Wesley, New York

Kimball R C, Gregor W T (1989) Emerging distribution strategies in US retail banking. *Journal of Retail Banking* **11**: 4–16

Konsynski B, Sprague R H (1986) Future research directions in model management. *Decision Support Systems* **2**: 103–9

Maguire D J (1991) An overview and definition of GIS. In: Maguire D J, Goodchild M F, Rhind D W (eds.) *Geographical Information Systems: principles and applications*. Longman, London, pp. 9–20, Vol 1

Nijkamp P (1979) *Multidimensional Spatial Data and Decision Analysis*. Wiley, New York

Orman L (1986) Flexible management of computational models. *Decision Support Systems* **2**: 225–34

Openshaw S (1991) Developing appropriate spatial analysis methods for GIS. In: Maguire D J, Goodchild M F, Rhind D W (eds.) *Geographical Information Systems: principles and applications*. Longman, London, pp. 389–402, Vol 1

Sprague R H (1980) A framework for the development of decision support systems. *Management Information Sciences Quarterly* **4**: 1–26

Sprague R H, Carlson E D (1982) *Building Effective Decision Support Systems*. Prentice-Hall, Englewood Cliffs New Jersey

Starr M K, Zeleny M (1977) *Multiple Criteria Decision Making*. North-Holland, Amsterdam

van der Vlugt M (1989) The use of a GIS based decision support system in physical planning. *Proceedings of GIS/LIS '89*. ASPRS, Bethesda Maryland, pp. 459–67

Vazsonyi A (1978) Decision support systems: the new technology of decision making? *Interfaces* **9**: 74–8

Vazsonyi A (1982) Decision support systems, computer literacy, and electronic models. *Interfaces* **12**: 74–8

Waters N M (1989) Expert systems within a GIS: knowledge aquisition for spatial decision support systems. *Proceedings of Challenge for the 1990s* Ottawa, pp. 740–59

White B (1985) Modelling forest pest impacts – aided by a geographic information system in a decision support system framework. *Proceedings of Geographic Information Systems Workshop*. ASPRS, Falls Church Virginia, pp. 238–248

27

KNOWLEDGE-BASED APPROACHES IN GIS

T R SMITH AND YE JIANG

This chapter provides a framework for understanding the application of knowledge-based techniques (KBT) in GIS. It is intended neither as a review of such techniques nor as a survey of their application. It is argued that full first-order logic is a proper theory on which to base such techniques. In terms of understanding the application of KBT, it is contended that expressive and computational power and computational efficiency are far less important than the ease with which applications may be built and with which users may interact with GIS. Current applications of KBT typically involve the use of rules in relation to the main functional components of GIS, with loose coupling between the rule base and the spatial database. The full value of KBT to GIS is likely to be realized only when they are applied in a systematic manner on the basis of formal logic, and when current semantic and optimization issues are settled. Such value will reside in the ability of knowledge-based GIS to model complex spatio-temporal phenomena.

INTRODUCTION

The application of knowledge-based techniques (KBT) in current GIS may appear as little more than the *ad hoc* application of techniques developed initially in the area of artificial intelligence. The goal of the present chapter is to provide a framework in which these applications may be viewed in a more valuable and systematic manner. The significance of a suitable framework for understanding applications of KBT lies in its ability to focus research on important issues.

Throughout the chapter the following view is taken:

1. Database systems (DBS), when implemented in terms of a specific domain of application, provide a model of the domain. A major function of a DBS is to make explicit various properties of the model.
2. GIS are best viewed as DBS that provide models of spatio-temporal domains.

While GIS are increasingly characterized by large volumes of spatial data and while data storage and retrieval are critical issues requiring much research, it may be convincingly argued that analytical and modelling capabilities are a discriminating factor for GIS. In particular, much of the information in a GIS is typically stored in implicit form, especially in the case of raster-based GIS. Hence, it is assumed that a major requirement of GIS is an ability to deduce relatively complex properties of domain models from information that is stored in the data and knowledge bases of the system. This viewpoint is important for understanding the application of KBT in GIS, since a KBT may be viewed as a set of tools that facilitate the construction of computational models of relatively complex domains and provide mechanisms for deriving properties of the domains.

This viewpoint may be refined and a KBT considered as a set of techniques that have been developed for representing 'knowledge' about some domain and for supporting procedures for deriving inferences about the domain from some 'knowledge base' (KB). Logics of various forms are increasingly being chosen as the theoretical basis for such techniques, and a great deal of current research in the highly relevant area of deductive databases (e.g. see Przymusinski 1989) is currently employing both subsets and extensions of full first order logic to provide such a basis. Other techniques that are frequently used, such as those relating to semantic networks, frames and production systems (e.g. see Barr and Feigenbaum 1982a, 1982b) may be usefully viewed as special cases of approaches based on first order logic (Nilsson 1980).

There has been a great deal of recent interest in the application of KBT in the area of DBS, particularly in relation to the use of representational languages involving rules. In particular, concepts such as logic programming, deductive databases, expert DBS and knowledge-based management systems have been developed (Mylopoulos 1986). Several factors must be considered in order to understand the application of KBT to DBS in general and to GIS in particular, including:

- the expressive and computational power of the representational language(s) in the DBS;

- the computational efficiency of the system; and

- the ease with which applications may be written and with which users interact with the system.

It is contended that, while expressive and computational power and computational efficiency are of critical significance, the ease with which applications may be written and the ease with which users may interact with the system are probably the key factors in explaining the application of KBT in DBS in general, and in GIS in particular.

This contention is supported by first arguing that knowledge is not fundamentally different from data, and that any distinction is best viewed in terms of the explicitness of the form of representation. In terms of this viewpoint, data are represented explicitly as the DB extension, while knowledge involves a more implicit and, therefore, a generally more compact, representation as the database intention.

Equivalently, the difference may be expressed in terms of the expressive and computational power of the representational language. This argument is convincing when data and knowledge are modelled in terms of first-order logic. It may be noted that KBT, as interpreted above, add nothing new to conventional techniques in terms of obtaining the full expressive and inferential power of the full first-order logic, while implementations of KBT have yet to be made computationally efficient. It is concluded that KBT are mainly of use in facilitating the building of applications and in facilitating the use of GIS in modelling application domains.

In the sections of the chapter following the presentation of these arguments, several architectures are described for DBS that facilitate the application of KBT. In particular, the discussion focuses on loosely coupled systems (Stonebraker and Hearst 1989) in which rule bases (RBs) are the dominant form of knowledge representation. Examples are then provided of the application of KBT in GIS in terms of various functional components of GIS, including acquisition, storage, access, analysis and interfaces.

THE THREE FACTORS

Before proceeding, it is of value to discuss briefly the three sets of factors listed above, as well as the nature of how change typically occurs in software systems. The function of a GIS is to answer queries. In this context, a query is simply a mapping from the database to some relation defined on the database. Hence the query language of the system is of fundamental significance. This is particularly the case in the context of the present chapter, since full first-order logic is viewed as the appropriate basis for interpreting the applicability of KBT. In relation to logic-based DBS, the query language may be viewed as a single language for expressing queries, data, integrity constraints, views, programs and specifications (Lloyd 1987).

Given this viewpoint, the three factors listed above may be seen as evaluative criteria relating to a single entity, namely the query language of the system. The expressive and computational power of the language relates to the class of functions (and hence queries) that can be expressed and computed in terms of the query language. Although query languages may be devised that are able to express non-computable functions, the only languages of practical interest are those that can compute Turing-computable functions. The essential point is that query languages may vary dramatically in their ability to express (and compute) different classes of queries, ranging from highly restricted languages on relations to languages having the power to express all Turing-computable queries. The efficiency associated with a query language essentially relates to the computational efficiency of the procedures that support the answering of queries expressed in the language. The ease with which applications may be written and the ease of user interaction are clearly related to both cognitive factors and the 'naturalness' with which a given query language matches human representations of some domain of interest. A major goal of the theory of query languages is to provide an understanding of how to design query languages that are natural to use, expressive and efficient in practice.

The current status of KBT in DBS (and in GIS in particular) may be partially understood in terms of how change typically occurs in software systems, since GIS are themselves in part software systems. Ullman (1986a) is followed in listing a typical sequence of events in which:

- a need is perceived;

- *ad hoc* approaches to programming solutions are found;

- the programming tricks are understood; and

- a second generation of researchers automate the programming process with the use of a high level programming language without tricks.

It would appear that the application of KBT in the area of GIS is currently in the stages of need perception and *ad hoc* approaches to programming solutions. This argument, coupled with the idea that the application of KBT is largely concerned with ease of building applications and the ease of system use, appears to explain the currently *ad hoc* nature of their application in GIS.

DATA AND KNOWLEDGE

In order to understand the significance of applications of KBT in GIS, the distinction between data and knowledge must be examined. A variety of such distinctions have been made, including:

1. When dealing with data some automated process can be relied upon to collect the material, while when dealing with knowledge expertise is required to collect the material (Smith and Smith 1977).

2. Data reflect the current state of the world at the level of instances while knowledge deals with abstractions and entity types (Wiederhold 1986).

3. Knowledge is represented in terms of rules.

4. A KB involves a richer semantics for interpretation than does a DB and contains knowledge about something. DBs are more concerned with efficient storage and retrieval (Brodie and Mylopoulos 1986).

5. Knowledge is used chiefly as an attribute of programming systems that support some form of declarative language, which is typically some form of logic (Ullman 1986b).

6. A KB supports recursive queries (Naqvi 1986).

While each of these viewpoints provides some insight, they are ambiguous.

An alternative viewpoint is that there is no essential distinction between data and knowledge. A more refined version of this viewpoint, and one adopted here, argues that: (1) there is a gradation between the expressiveness of representational languages in terms of the classes of statements that can be made concerning some domain; (2) facts are characterized by a restricted class of statements; and (3) knowledge is characterized by a larger class of statements. This view may be exemplified by taking the representational language to be some subset of full first-order logic or an extension of such logic. In order to provide some power to the argument, the adequacy of logic for both representing and making inferences about the data and knowledge in a GIS is briefly discussed.

From a syntactic point of view, a first-order theory consists of an alphabet (namely the constants, variables, function symbols, predicate symbols, connectives, quantifiers and punctuation symbols), a set of axioms and a set of inference rules. The deduction of the theorems of a theory may be characterized in terms of those formulae that are logical consequences of the axioms of the theory using the rules of inference. In relation to this framework, an answer to some query to a DBS may be interpreted in terms of the logical consequences of a set of axioms and a deduction may be viewed in terms of the computation of some function. In applications of first-order logic to database theory (see Lloyd 1987), a standard approach is to use formulae that have the form of rules:

$A \leftarrow A_1,...,A_n$

in which the As are predicates or relations. In particular, facts are special rules having the form:

$A \leftarrow$

and queries take the form:

$\leftarrow A_1,...,A_n$

If it is permitted to use function symbols in the arguments of the predicates and recursion in the rules (i.e. the same predicate symbol can occur on both sides of the implication sign), then any computable function can be expressed in terms of a set of such rules, given a suitable encoding (see Lloyd 1987), which in turn may require the use of negation. It is, therefore, clear that such a representation is conceptually completely adequate for any GIS and any query to a GIS, although there are many semantic and practical issues that currently require resolution before any such implementation is truly feasible. Proper subsets of full first-order logic can be implemented for DB applications with greater ease, but there is a cost in terms of expressive and inferential power. For example, standard (relational) DBs may be viewed as a finite collection of ground atomic sentences ('facts'), each being represented in terms of a single n-place predicate symbol, a set of n individual terms with no variables and a limited inferential capability.

Given the preceding discussion, it is not unreasonable to view 'knowledge' as information that is generally representable in terms of the general formulae of full first-order logic, while facts may be viewed as a proper subset of ground state atomic sentences. This point of view is consistent with the distinctions (2), (3), (5) and (6) above, and is, in fact, the approach that is taken in both logic programming and deductive databases. The significance of the preceding discussion is that it focuses attention on issues relating to expressive power and ease of expression. For example, the use of the (extended Horn-clause) rules described above appears to facilitate greatly the representation of certain classes of knowledge. Hence KBT may be viewed, in general, as techniques that are concerned with the ease with which information that is more than facts, as defined above, may be expressed and used in a deductive manner.

KBT IN NON-SPATIAL DBS

Non-spatial DBS have received far more attention from researchers than have GIS and the application of KBT in such systems has received correspondingly greater attention. Since developments in such systems are strongly influential with respect to current research efforts in GIS, and since GIS may be viewed as a special case of general DBS, there is a need to identify the relative importance of the three factors listed above that are important for the adoption of KBT in non-spatial GIS. It is assumed that the same relative importance applies to GIS, particularly since GIS typically model more complex domains than standard DBS. The discussion is developed by focusing first on standard relational DBS, then on extensions to relational systems and, finally, on logic-based and object-oriented approaches.

It is of interest to note that foundations of the theory of deductive databases may be found in the seminal paper by Codd (1970), in which a formal basis for relational databases was first outlined. A relational database is a collection of individual facts equipped with the capability to manipulate efficiently (update) its contents and to answer queries about it. Typically, relational algebra or relational calculus, which is first-order logic interpreted for relations, is used to implement these functions. Concerning the expressiveness of the representational language in standard relational systems, the tuples ('facts') of relational tables are, as noted above, equivalent to ground atomic sentences. The standard relational query language is not capable of representing recursive queries, such as finding a full set of nested, political regions that contain a given point. The lack of expressive power of the query language is partially related to the fact that the relational calculus is insufficiently powerful to compute transitive closures. In restricted domains of application, however, in which the computational limitations are not a problem, it is relatively easy to write applications, since user interaction in such domains is greatly enhanced by the separation of the 'what' and the 'how' of the querying process in terms of a declarative query language and query optimization techniques. Constraining the expressive and computational power of the query language has led to great computational efficiency, as a result of the use of data independence and optimization techniques.

One solution to the problem of lack of expressive power is to embed the query language in a host language that supports such functionally with iteration. Even with the support of a host language that possesses full computational power, however, standard relational systems are not easy to apply in non-standard domains of application that include, for example, spatial and statistical data (e.g. see Korth and Silberschatz 1986). Applications are hard to build and the systems are difficult to use, since it is difficult to model complex domains involving space and time as well as nested relationships in terms of relational tables. In particular, the expression of queries concerning complex (i.e. nested) objects is difficult, while the number of joins required to answer such queries raises major efficiency issues.

In order to overcome such limitations, extensions have been made to the relational model. Some extensions have involved extending the query language to support some form of iteration or recursion operation. For example, the query language of INGRES (QUEL) has been extended to QUEL* by adding an operation that executes a sequence of QUEL commands until the DB no longer changes. While QUEL* is therefore computationally complete (Varvel and Shapiro 1989), problems remain with respect to the ease with which applications may be written, the ease of user interaction and efficiency. Because it has proven difficult to deal with non-standard applications with such extensions, it may be concluded that linguistic expressive and computational power are not the key elements in explaining the introduction of KBT into non-spatial DBS.

Other extensions to the relational model that have been introduced for coping with non-standard applications have included the use of abstract data types (ADT) and rule-based techniques.

POSTGRES (Stonebraker and Hanson 1988), for example, is an extension to INGRES that has been designed with applications to spatial data in mind, and involves the use of ADT, procedural data types and the use of rules. However, there are still major problems relating to ease of application building, ease of use and efficiency. Major alternatives to extensions of the relational model include (Ullman 1988):

- logic-based approaches;
- object-oriented approaches.

It is noteworthy that these approaches share common threads in their heritage, particularly in terms of KBT developed in artificial intelligence research. Object orientation, for example, traces part of its heritage to the research on semantic networks and frames that was central to many KBT, while predicate calculus was used early as a knowledge representation technique in artificial intelligence research, serving in fact as a unifying language for semantic networks and frames. Furthermore, it is becoming increasingly clear that logic-based approaches essentially include relational DBS as a proper subset.

In relation to the logic-based approach (see Przymusinski 1989), researchers came to realize by the mid-1970s that the capabilities of relational databases were quite limited by their inability to handle deductive and incomplete information. Deductive reasoning is of value in deducing new information from facts and deductive rules which can be included in a database. The need to deal with incomplete information is particularly evident in the case of disjunctive and negative information. Relational databases have no capabilities for storing and handling general deductive rules or for dealing with incomplete information. Deductive databases, however, can store and manipulate deductive rules of reasoning as well as data and are able to answer queries based on logical derivation coupled with some mechanism for handling incomplete information (e.g. Gallaire, Minker and Nicolas 1984; Minker 1988b). Logic programming was based on Kowalski's principle of separating logic and control (Kowalski 1974, 1987). Because of the formal development of logic programming in the late 1970s and early 1980s (Lloyd 1987), it has become clear that logic programming and deductive databases are closely related (Minker 1988a). They are based on the common idea of representing knowledge in terms of logic, and, in particular, of providing computers with a logical specification of the knowledge that is independent of any particular implementation, context free and easy to manipulate.

Logic-based approaches may be viewed in terms of a declarative language involving rules. In terms of limited implementations, such as PROLOG, the use of rules and the uniform representation of 'facts' and rules makes for ease of user application, although the language is not fully declarative in the sense that some rule ordering is required of the user. It is of interest to note that the use of rules has long been thought to be a 'natural' form of representation for human users (Nilsson 1980). The success of this approach depends on assigning precise meaning or semantics to any logic program in order to provide its declarative specification, which can then be compared to the output of some computation. This does not mean that such a computation must be based on some logical proof procedure, but only that logic is the final arbiter of correctness. Finding a suitable declarative semantics of deductive databases and logic programs is a critical research problem, while other major research issues relate to computational efficiency.

Although the object-oriented approach is not yet clearly defined, it may be viewed as a programming system that combines the data manipulation and host languages to support nested objects, encapsulation and object identity. Hence object orientation may be viewed in terms of a language with capabilities for defining ADTs. While object-oriented approaches, in the general sense, have full expressive and computational power, their greatest strength probably lies in the naturalness with which applications may be written and the ease with which users may interact with such systems, since the objects and relations of the object-oriented model may be chosen to reflect the user's model of the domain of application. There is, as yet, no consensus about the definition of an object-oriented DBS (see Kim 1990) and in particular about their relationship to relational and logic-based systems. There are also major concerns about computational efficiency at the present time.

Since questions of expressive and computational power are not fundamentally at issue in any of the approaches, and since computational efficiency is a major issue in all approaches relating to non-standard domains, and in particular for the logic-based approaches that are so highly related to KBT, it is concluded that the ease of building applications and the ease of system use are probably the key factors in explaining the introduction of KBT into such DBS. Hence, the serious use of KBT in GIS is also apparently dictated by similar considerations.

INCORPORATION OF KBT INTO DBS

The introduction of KBT into DB technology has typically taken the form of expert system (ES) shells, production system (PS) languages and logic programming languages (Brodie et al. 1988), although there are other forms, such as the use of constraints (Morgenstern et al. 1988) for describing regularities in an application domain. The basic choice criterion, apart from familiarity, appears to relate to the ease of capture of the semantics of a given domain. These approaches are all characterized by rules, which some researchers regard as facilitating the construction of applications and the ease of user interaction (Nilsson 1980). It is quite possible that such systems represent stages in the evolution of DBS towards full, logic-based systems employing well-formed formulae taking the form of rules. Hence, most of the attention is focused on rule systems.

There are various current architectures that permit the integration of rule-based systems into DBS in general and GIS in particular (Stonebraker and Hearst 1989). The following are possible:

1. To enhance either a rule-based system with limited DBMS capabilities, such as data access, concurrency control or security, or enhance a DBMS with rule-based system capabilities, such as knowledge acquisition and representation techniques and reasoning.

2. To employ 'loose coupling', in which an application is written using an ES shell. This shell typically supports application logic, presentation services and navigation rules and manages the rule base. The shell is then

extended to support calls on an external data manager, and hence is like any other DB user.

3. To employ 'tight coupling' to facilitate communication between the rule-based system and the DBMS by building one system as a shell about the other. Hence, either the rule-based system works as a shell around the DBMS or the DBMS can work as a shell around the rule-based system.

4. To build a fully integrated system, such as a true deductive DBS.

The loose coupling approach is the norm at present in both spatial and non-spatial DB applications, while tight coupling and full integration are difficult to achieve, although POSTGRES is one example of a tightly coupled system. Problems with the loose coupling approach include the following (Naqvi and Tsur 1989; Stonebraker and Hearst 1989):

1. There is semantic mismatch between the language of the front end, which is typically procedural, and the language at the back end, which is typically declarative. This leads to efficiency problems because global optimization is no longer possible.

2. There is a mismatch in the granularity of the data objects between the front end and the back end, since the front end typically deals with a single tuple while the back end deals with a set of tuples.

3. The design of a loosely coupled system can be limited by shortcomings at either end. For example, if the back end cannot handle recursive queries, the front end is limited.

4. The rule base is main-memory resident, hence, for example, the rule base can be lost if the address space of the shell goes away, while rules cannot easily be saved.

5. Dynamic data in which there are changes to values relating to facts create problems. In particular, there is a need to maintain consistency in a cache of DB objects.

6. Non-partitionable applications, in which the whole fact base needs to be accessed before the completion of an inference, lead to poor performance.

Tightly coupled systems are being designed to overcome these problems. In one approach based on logic programming, for example, the objects declared and manipulated by the system are the same as the objects stored and manipulated in the database, while there is no front end/back end distinction (Naqvi and Tsur 1989). In relation to tight coupling, it is noted that a DBMS can be extended to manage an RB; can deal with dynamic data by awakening rules as required by changes in the data; and can handle large spatial DBS.

Attention is now focused on loosely coupled systems, since this architecture has become the standard in spatial DB applications and is of significance in current GIS. The rule processing capabilities of such systems serve several functions, including the following:

1. The provision of the services of a traditional ES.

2. The triggering of external actions in response to changes in the data (including data analysis).

3. The provision of state and transition constraints, including referential and semantic integrity constraints.

The first set of services can be implemented in terms of a standard inference engine, such as a forward or backward chaining, operating on a set of rules. In terms of the second set of services, the predicate of a rule may, for example, contain an analytical procedure that produces output when certain data conditions are mentioned. The third set of services include, for example, the enforcement of semantic integrity constraints which are not generally provided by current DBMS.

A key factor determining the efficiency of DBS, which incorporates the three sets of services, is the mechanism for selecting and firing the appropriate rules. Three mechanisms are currently available, including: (1) indexing the predicates in the LHS of the rules; (2) sequencing over rules and computing logical intersections; and (3) the use of database locks. No completely satisfactory solution has yet been found, and rule selection is an area of active research.

GIS AND KBT

GIS technology is less mature in both conceptional and implementational terms than non-spatial DBS technology. Correspondingly, the introduction of KBT into GIS is at a less advanced stage and, for the most part, may be classified in terms of either system enhancement (a GIS with rule-based capabilities, or an ES with spatial data handling capabilities) or of loose coupling of rule-based applications and GIS. So far, the concepts of tightly coupled systems or knowledge base management systems have not been exploited, while rule-processing capabilities have typically been limited to the provision of the services of a traditional ES.

The most important approaches to the application of KBT in GIS may be discussed and characterized as:

- acquisition;
- storage;
- access;
- analysis and processing;
- interfaces.

Before exemplifying the application of KBT to each of these components, the way the applications relate to the three factors determining the general adoption of KBT is summarized. First, it is clear that KBT, defined in terms of languages supporting knowledge representation and deduction, do not add any new expressive or computational power to languages currently used in GIS. Second, applications of KBT have not been focused on increasing the computational efficiency of GIS. In relation to acquisition, KBT enhance the building of applications in terms of automating procedures for acquiring knowledge. In relation to storage, they have been used to ease the construction of, and access to, very small spatial databases. In relation to access, KBT facilitate the use of GIS by such mechanisms as the use of metadata and query optimization. In relation to analysis, the construction of applications is enhanced by the use of rule-based ES that are loosely coupled to a GIS database. Such systems also provide easy-to-use interfaces to GIS. Finally, in relation to interfaces, KBT facilitate the construction of natural language interfaces, which themselves facilitate the use of GIS.

Acquisition

Automating procedures for data and knowledge acquisition eases the task of system construction. One area of applicability of KBT to this task involves the general concept of 'data dredging' (Naqvi and Tsur 1989), which essentially involves finding and storing regularities in data for various purposes. In particular, inductive learning may be viewed as a special case of data dredging. One goal of data dredging is to reduce the difficulty of constructing knowledge and databases, particularly the acquisition of facts, rules and constraints that increase both the efficiency of the system (in terms of learning DB integrity constraints) and the domain modelling capabilities of the system. In particular, such enhancements make explicit relevant parts of the DB intention; they generate rules for performing inference and constraints for query optimization; and they serve to define new objects and modify data and rules.

Two particular strategies for data dredging of interest in the current context are inductive learning and explanation-based learning. Inductive learning is the derivation of abstractions and generalizations from particular instances. Four basic rules underlie most inductive learning procedures, including the method of agreement, the method of difference, the method of residues and the method of concomitant variation. The procedures also involve criteria for evaluating rules. Major limitations include the number of examples required, the lack of efficient algorithms and the problem of noisy data. Inductive learning has been used, for example, in non-GIS applications to learn rules for ES and DB integrity constraints (Hoff, Michalski and Stepp 1983), while in GIS applications, it has been used in KBGIS-II (Smith et al. 1987) to generate generalized descriptions of complex spatial objects, which are then placed in framelike structures.

In explanation-based learning (Mitchell, Keller and Kedar-Cabelli 1986), the approach is to analyse a single example in terms of a specific application domain and produce and justify a valid generalization of the example. The inputs to such a procedure include a goal concept, a training example, domain theory and operational criteria.

There do not appear to be current applications of this procedure in the field of GIS.

It should be noted the data dredging essentially expands the information base of the system. Key issues for research are the lack of efficient procedures and problems of maintenance.

Storage

KBT currently find little application to issues relating to the storage of large volumes of spatial data, presumably because of efficiency issues. Semantic networks, frames and rule bases have, however, been employed to represent both data instances and data abstractions in GIS. Since these are not particularly efficient storage structures, their use must be predicated upon the ease of construction and the ease of use.

Access

Access to data in GIS, particularly in the case of large DBs, is a major area of application for KBT. There is currently great interest in the use of metadata (which provides a model of a DB in terms of structure and content) as knowledge that can be employed in facilitating content-based search. KBT languages are increasingly being used to represent metadata.

A key application of KBT with respect to access involves query optimization. The use of high-level, declarative query languages generally requires the use of optimization procedures to enhance system efficiency, since users do not supply information for DB navigation. The success of the relational DBS is in large part due to query optimization techniques, while a major bottleneck for the development of logic-based DBS is the lack of good optimization techniques. Query optimization is of potentially great significance for large-scale GIS dealing with complex (i.e. multicomponent and nested) spatial objects with many constraints between the sub-objects and in which the objects are often implicitly represented in a number of data layers.

A major approach to query optimization involves the application of knowledge, typically in the form of rules or integrity constraints, relating to equivalence relations, containment relationships, expected value ranges, sorting orders, functional dependencies (Hammer and Zdonik 1980) and special transformations (Siegel 1989). Such knowledge is typically used to transform a query for more efficient processing. A key requirement in this process is to maintain semantic equivalence between the original and transformed queries.

Static query optimization employs both domain-independent knowledge and domain-dependent (semantic) knowledge to produce a semantically equivalent query and an efficient sequence of operations that provide lower execution costs. Particular transformations are effected through constraint introduction, constraint removal (Siegel 1989) and constraint replacement. These transformations are implemented in terms of a variety of approaches, including theorem proving (Chakravarthy 1985), graph theoretic (Jarke 1984) or heuristic approaches (Siegel 1989). POSTGRES (Stonebraker and Hansen 1988), for example, uses rules to implement such transformations.

Dynamic optimization is an alternative to static optimization and enforces constraints during the search procedure. Such optimization has been employed in KBGIS-II (Smith et al. 1987), for example, where the basic problem is to retrieve complex spatial objects. Forward checking is used dynamically to enforce domain constraints. During the search, the values for any variable are examined sequentially and constraints are explicitly computed in order to check whether the value selected from the domain satisfies the constraints on the variable. Spatial constraint propagation is used to replace the explicit checking of constraints during backtracking by geometrical search within constrained areas of the database. Two forms of dynamic update occur during the search procedure: domain-dependent rules are used to produce semantically equivalent queries about sub-objects, while sub-object search may be reordered according to criteria relating to sub-object existence (as determined by search) and sub-object complexity and frequency (as determined in a knowledge base). Frames, semantic networks and rules are the structures used to represent such knowledge.

Analysis and Processing

Most applications of KBT relating to analysis and processing have involved rule-based approaches and

ES technology. Such applications typically use ES that are, at most, loosely coupled to the spatial DB component of a GIS.

Application of PS and ES techniques in domains involving geographical data has been widespread. Davis and Clark (1989), for example, compiled a bibliography of over 200 articles, written between 1976 and 1989, describing ES applications in the areas of natural resource management that included agriculture, geographical data handling, forestry, environmental law, environmental planning, water resources, and wildlife and vegetation modelling. It is of interest to note that apart from natural language applications, few of the articles describe artificial intelligence techniques other than ES and many of the ES were not coupled to the spatial data-handling capabilities of a GIS.

Robinson, Frank and Karimi (1987) provide a survey of 20 systems involving ES that have been built in order to support various GIS operations in the area of resource management. Many of these systems are loosely coupled to the data handling capabilities of some GIS and many involve the use of ES shell languages. In several applications, the ES may be viewed as an applications-oriented 'interface' to the GIS. For example, ASPENEX (Morse 1987) is an ES providing interface services and interfacing to a GIS (MOSS). The system provides rules on aspen management, while MOSS provides information on the characteristics of aspen stands. Special software provides communication between the ES and the GIS. Among other applications of ES technology are automated interpretation of aerial photography (ACRONYM, Brooks 1983), change-detection in LANDSAT images (FES, Goldberg, Alvo and Karam 1984), automated terrain feature extraction and decision making in economic and urban systems (URBYS, Tanic 1986; GEDDEX, Chandra and Goran 1986).

There have been several applications of ES modules in GIS that have been based upon ES that were originally developed for non-GIS applications. Katz, for example, has essentially emulated the PROSPECTOR system in MAPS, which is a raster-based GIS. In particular, MAPS incorporates Bayesian, fuzzy and certainty factor techniques, which constitute essential elements in PROSPECTOR, in order to process applications such as mineral exploration.

Some ES modules have been constructed using logic programming techniques. For example, Franklin and Wu (1987) have formulated the polygon overlay in PROLOG, while Webster (1989) has shown in detail how point-in-polygon queries may be expressed in the predicate calculus and answered by resolution theorem proving in a PROLOG environment. Yan (1988) has provided a general exposition of some of the elements of the theory of logic programming in the context of GIS. In practical terms, such an approach is of immediate value for systems with little spatial data, but the current lack of development of such a theory in the context of large spatial data sets and complex spatial objects, as well as current problems relating to efficiency, presently inhibit the development of large scale GIS employing such technology.

Interfaces

While some of the ES discussed above may be viewed as providing an interface to a GIS (e.g. ASPENEX), their orientation has related to ease of application building by separating domain modelling and analysis considerations from DB considerations. There are applications of KBT that correspond to more traditional interface concepts. For example, LOBSTER (Frank 1984) is a query language for GIS serving as an interface to an object-oriented, network spatial DBMS (PANDA). The interface is logic based and is implemented in PROLOG syntax. The interface to KBGIS-II (Smith et al. 1987) is a declarative query language based on the predicate calculus.

The most obvious applicability of KBT in this area, however, relates to natural language (NL) interfaces. An NL interface offers users efficient access to a GIS, since details of the system are hidden from the user and the user is not constrained by the disparity between the simplicity of natural language constructs for spatial objects and relations and their complex, low-level representations in GIS (Hendrix et al. 1978).

The success of NL interfaces in non-spatial approaches is in part a result of their limitation to relational databases and SQL (e.g. see Bates, Moser and Stallard 1984). Such interfaces have typically involved the following:

1. Conceptional models of underlying database architecture and contents, and automated

translations of a deep meaning representation of a user's input into SQL.

2. Extensible systems enabling non-language specialists to apply the language system to different application domains within the relational database architecture.

3. Syntactic and semantic modules providing a wide linguistic coverage of natural language.

4. Framelike representation language systems that support a robust model of a user's view of some domain.

5. Automated processes for 'meta-describing' a particular database organization.

Of great importance is the consensus among NL researchers that domain knowledge and its representation is fundamental to the building of a 'working' language system. Success in the area of NL interfaces for GIS, as in most other areas of AI, depends on limiting the domain of application and having a good representation of this domain in the computer. Hence KBT, particularly framelike and semantic network representation schemes, have played an important role in such interfaces because of their ease of use for representing domains of application. An NL interface requires specific domain knowledge of various types including:

1. Generic knowledge about spatial domains, such as the information about spatial relationships analysed by linguists.

2. Knowledge about specific domains of application.

3. Knowledge about the GIS to which the NL interface is connected, such as knowledge about how the data are stored and the operators available in the GIS.

KBT may be used to apply such knowledge in a layered architecture for an NL interface. In such an architecture, the user's query is translated into some meaning representation language. The transformed query is then sent to a mapping module that transforms the query into a GIS-specific set of operators that are sufficient to answer the query. The set of operators is then executed by the relevant GIS. The transformations between NL, meaning language representation and operators is accomplished by the application of knowledge in three language knowledge bases, namely a lexicon, a syntactic rule base and a semantic rule base, as well as knowledge bases relating respectively to general world knowledge, specific GIS system knowledge and specific GIS application domain knowledge. A target representation for the NL input is a network of interrelated domain concepts and relations formally represented in the system spatial domain model employing KBT.

Apart from NL interfaces, there are other applications of KBT that relate to display production. For example, ES have been constructed that automate various cartographic procedures for display, such as name placement (AUTONAP, Freeman and Ahn 1984) and map generalization (MAPEX). These topics are discussed elsewhere in this volume (see Freeman 1991 in this volume; also Muller 1991 in this volume).

CONCLUSIONS

It is concluded that the application of KBT in GIS is largely motivated by issues relating to the ease of constructing applications and the ease of system use, rather than by issues relating to expressive and computational power and efficiency. This viewpoint is of value in understanding current and future applications of KBT. It is to be expected that there will be many more applications in all components of GIS. Also, a more systematic approach to such applications is likely, particularly in terms of object-oriented approaches in the short term and logic-based approaches in the long term. The major force driving such applications will be the desire to construct more powerful DB models of complex spatio-temporal phenomena.

REFERENCES

Barr A, Feigenbaum E A (eds.) (1982a) *The Handbook of Artificial Intelligence*, Vol. I. HeurisTech Press and William Kaufmann, Stanford

Barr A, Feigenbaum E A (eds.) (1982b) *The Handbook of Artificial Intelligence*, Vol. II. HeurisTech Press and William Kaufmann, Stanford

Bates M, Moser M G, Stallard D (1984) The IRUS transportable natural language database interface. *Technical Report*. Bolt, Beranek and Newman

Brodie M, Mylopoulos J (1986) Knowledge bases versus databases. In: Brodie M L, Mylopoulos J (eds.) *On Knowledge Base Management Systems: integrating artificial intelligence and database technologies*. Springer-Verlag, New York, pp. 83–6

Brodie M L, Bobrow D, Lesser V, Madnick S, Tsichritzis D, Hewitt C (1988) Future artificial intelligence requirements for intelligent database systems. In: Kerschberg L (ed.) *Proceedings from the Second International Conference on Expert Database Systems, Tysons Corner, Virginia, 25–27 April 1988*. The Benjamin/Cummings Publishing Company, pp. 45–62

Brooks R A (1983) Model-based three-dimensional interpretations of two-dimensional images. *IEEE Transactions on Pattern Analysis and Machine Intelligence* **PAMI-5**: 140–50

Chakravarthy U S (1985) *Semantic Query Optimization in Deductive Databases*. Unpublished PhD thesis, University of Maryland

Chandra N, Goran W (1986) Steps toward a knowledge-based geographical data analysis system. In: Optiz B (ed.) *Geographic Information Systems in Government*. A Deepak Publishing, Hampton

Codd E F (1970) A relational model of data for large shared data banks. *Communications of the ACM* **13** (6): 377–87

Davis J R, Clark J L (1989) A selective bibliography of expert systems in natural resource management. *AI Applications in Natural Resource Management*. Moscow, Idaho

Frank A U (1984) Extending a network database with PROLOG. *Proceedings of the First International Workshop on Expert Database Systems, Kiawah Island, SC, October*, pp. 665–74

Franklin W R, Wu P Y F (1987) A polygon overlay system in PROLOG. *Proceedings of AUTOCARTO 8*. ASPRS/ACSM, Falls Church Virginia, pp. 97–106

Freeman H (1991) Computer name placement. In: Maguire D J, Goodchild M F, Rhind D W (eds.) *Geographical Information Systems: principles and applications*. Longman, London, pp. 445–56, Vol 1

Freeman H, Ahn J (1984) AUTONAP – an expert system for automatic map name placement. *Proceedings of the 1st International Symposium on Spatial Data Handling*. International Geographical Union, Ohio, pp. 544–71

Gallaire H, Minker J, Nicolas J (1984) Logic and databases: a deductive approach. *ACM Computing Surveys* **16**: 153–85

Goldberg M, Alvo M, Karam G (1984) The analysis of LANDSAT imagery using an expert system: forestry applications. *Proceedings of AUTOCARTO 6*. ACSM/ASPRS, Falls Church Virginia, pp. 493–503

Hammer M, Zdonik S B (1980) Knowledge-based query processing. *Journal of the IEEE* **6**: 137–46

Hendrix G, Sacerdoti E, Sagalowicz D, Slocum J (1978) Developing a natural language interface to complex data. *ACM Transactions on Database Systems* **3** (2)

Hoff W A, Michalski R S, Stepp R E (1983) INDUCE 3: a program for learning structural descriptions from examples. *Final Draft Report*. Chicago, Department of Computer Science, Artificial Intelligence Lab, University of Illinois

Jarke M (1984) Semantic query optimization in expert systems and database systems. *Proceedings of First International Conference on Expert Database Systems*, pp. 467–82

Katz S (1988) Emulating the Prospector Expert System with a raster GIS. In: Thomas H F (ed.) *GIS: Integrating Technology and Geoscience Applications*. National Resource Center, Connecticut, pp. 27–8

Korth H F, Silberschatz A (1986) *Database System Concepts*. McGraw-Hill, New York

Kowalski R (1974) Predicate logic as a programming language. *Proceedings of IFIP-74*, pp. 569–574

Kowalski R (1987) Algorithm = logic + control. *Communications of the ACM* **22**: 424–36

Lloyd J W (1987) *Foundations of Logic Programming*. Springer-Verlag, New York

Minker J (1988a) *Foundations of Deductive Databases and Logic Programming*. Morgan Kaufmann, Los Altos

Minker J (1988b) Perspectives in deductive databases. *Journal of Logic Programming* **5** (1): 33–60

Mitchell T M, Keller R M, Kedar-Cabelli S T (1986) Explanation-based generalization: a unifying view. *Machine Learning* **1**: 47–80

Morgenstern M, Borgida A, Lassez C, Maier D, Wiederhold G (1988) Constraint-based systems: knowledge about data. In: Kerschberg L (ed.) *Proceedings of the Second International Conference on Expert Database Systems, Tysons Corner, Virginia 25–27 April 1988*. Benjamin/Cummings Publishing Company, pp. 23–44

Morse B W (1987) Expert interface to a geographic information system. *Proceedings of AUTOCARTO 8*. ACSM/ASPRS, Falls Church Virginia, pp. 535–41

Muller J-C (1991) Generalization of spatial databases. In: Maguire D J, Goodchild M F, Rhind D W (eds.) *Geographical Information Systems: principles and applications*. Longman, London, pp. 457–75, Vol 1

Mylopoulos J (1986) On knowledge base management systems. In: Brodie M L, Mylopoulos J (eds.) *On Knowledge Base Management Systems: integrating artificial intelligence and database technologies*. Springer-Verlag, New York, pp. 3–8

Naqvi S (1986) Discussion. In: Brodie M L, Mylopoulos J (eds.) *On Knowledge Base Management Systems: integrating artificial intelligence and database technologies*. Springer-Verlag, New York, pp. 93

Naqvi S, Tsur S (1989) *A Logical Language for Data and Knowledge Bases*. Computer Science Press, New York

Nilsson N J (1980) *Principles of Artificial Intelligence*. Tioga Publishing Co., Palo Alto

Przymusinski T C (1989) On the declarative and procedural semantics of logic programs. *Journal of Automated Reasoning* **5**: 167–205

Robinson V B, Frank A U, Karimi H A (1987) Expert systems for geographic information systems in resource management. *AI Applications in Natural Resource Management* **1** (1): 47–57

Siegel M D (1989) Automatic rule derivation for semantic query optimization. In: Kerschberg L (ed.) *Proceedings of Second International Conference on Expert Database Systems, Tysons Corner, 25–27 April 1988*. Benjamin/Cummings Publishing Company, pp. 69–98

Smith J M, Smith D C P (1977) Database abstractions: aggregation and generalization. *Association for Computing Machinery Transactions on Database Systems* **2** (2): 105–33

Smith T R, Peuquet D J, Menon S, Agarwal P (1987) KBGIS-II: a knowledge-based geographical information system. *International Journal of Geographical Information Systems* **1** (2): 149–72

Stonebraker M, Hanson E N (1988) The POSTGRES rule manager. *IEEE Transactions on Software Engineering* **14** (7): 897–907

Stonebraker M, Hearst M (1989) Future trends in expert database systems. In: Kerschberg L (ed.) *Expert Database Systems*. The Benjamin/Cummings Publishing Company, Redwood City, pp. 3–20

Tanic E (1986) Urban planning and artificial intelligence: the URBYS system. *Computers, Environment, and Urban Systems* **10** (3–4): 135–46

Ullman J (1986a) Logic and database systems. In: Brodie M L, Mylopoulos J (eds.) *On Knowledge Base Management Systems: integrating artificial intelligence and database technologies*. Springer-Verlag, New York, pp. 121–24

Ullman J (1986b) An approach to processing queries in a logic-based query language. In: Brodie M L, Mylopoulos J (eds.) *On Knowledge Base Management Systems: integrating artificial intelligence and database technologies*. Springer-Verlag, New York, pp. 147–64

Ullman J D (1988) *Principles of Database and Knowledge-Base Systems*. Computer Science Press, Rockville

Varvel D A, Shapiro L (1989) The computational completeness of extended database query languages. *Journal of the IEEE* **15** (5): 632–8

Webster C J (1989) Point-in-polygon processing in PROLOG. *Technical Reports in Geo-Information Systems* **17**. Wales and the South West RRL, University of Wales College of Cardiff

Wiederhold G (1986) Knowledge versus data. In: Brodie M L, Mylopoulos J (eds.) *On Knowledge Base Management Systems: integrating artificial intelligence and database technologies*. Springer-Verlag, New York, pp. 77–82

Yan S Y (1988) *A Logic Foundation for Expert Geographic Database Systems*. Melbourne, Australia, Department of Computer Science, University of Melbourne.

28

VISUALIZATION

B P BUTTENFIELD AND W A MACKANESS

Visualization is an important component of any effort to understand, analyse or explain the distribution of phenomena on the surface of the earth, and will become increasingly important as volumes of digital spatial data become more unmanageable. Although the principles of designing displays of spatial data have been investigated for centuries, very little use has been made of such principles in GIS. It is argued here that GIS needs to pay much more attention to visualization research and to the principles of good map design. The chapter begins with a history of visualization research in the context of GIS and then presents an overview of the major areas of visualization and cartographic design.

INTRODUCTION

Our awareness of the complexities of the world around us increases our desire to understand the nature of spatial data and spatial pattern. Technological developments increase capabilities to encode, sort, describe and analyse collected information in an efficient way. As technology develops and improves, there is a tendency to ask accordingly more complicated questions. Understanding the nature of spatial data can be extended by technologies that allow us to see the unseen. This may take the form of periodic photography in the infrared spectrum to study vegetative stress in an arid landscape, or magnetic resonance scanning imagery to detect biological tumours, or the generation of statistical surfaces and solids to pursue patterns and trends in *N*-dimensional variable space.

Though the capture of spatial information is accomplished principally by digital means, the encoding strategy and design of the data schema must reflect the visualization task and the nature of spatial information to be studied. Spatial modelling, pattern and trend analysis, inference and guidance in decision making are examples of GIS activities where researchers may benefit from use of visualization. This chapter discusses the impact of the complexity of spatial phenomena and the role of visualization in data access and analysis. The chapter begins with a brief history of visualization and then compares the research scope of visualization as defined in various disciplines. It concludes with a discussion of the impact of visualization in GIS research.

It may be argued that the nature of spatial data and more generally of geographical information mandates the use of visualization for both efficiency and acuity in the analytical process. The volume of data collected by existing and developing technology increases without predictable upper limit, to the point where the 'fire hose' metaphor of data collection has become commonplace. High volume geographical data sources include orbiting satellites and spacecraft, instrumental arrays for oceanic, climatological and geophysical data collection, and archived maps and imagery as well as digital products produced by government mapping agencies (see Fisher 1991 in this volume). High volume sources of spatial data collected beyond the confines of geographical information include medical scanned imagery, supercomputer digital arrays, and architectural and engineering CAD diagrams, among other examples. The common thread for all of this information is its implicit or explicit spatial component, and the frequency with which such information is stored and represented in visual form.

Geographical data and patterns tend to be complex and to change depending on the time, spatial resolution and sampling strategy of collection and analysis. Lewis Richardson's (1961) efforts to determine the length of coastlines and other geographical line features were complicated by the tendency for increasing detail in continuous spatial phenomena to be resolved with decreasing units of measure. Other complexities of spatial information are also relevant. For example, the appearance of a rural land parcel will vary not only between seasons, as evidenced by 'leaf-on' or 'leaf-off' air photography, but also with the spectral resolution at which it is recorded. The appearance of a statistical 'landscape' may also vary, with sampling resolution: migration patterns may be enumerated at a small scale to discern the effects of economic decline in the American rust belt, or at a larger scale to determine the impact of zoning constraints. In all of these examples, visualization of the data is used to identify and understand spatial, temporal and spectral pattern.

The role of visualization in geographical analysis is not limited to maps and remotely sensed imagery, but extends to numeric and statistical analysis as well. Increasing emphasis has been placed in recent years on the effectiveness of data exploration as a powerful analytical tool. Data exploration relies heavily on data charting and description as a first step to identifying outliers, generating research questions about evident trends, and directing the path of modelling and confirmation in subsequent stages of research on the topic. Graphical display has been a cornerstone in recent developments in statistical description and exploration, attesting to its worth as an efficient tool for understanding statistical trend and structure.

The sensitivity of the human sensory and cognitive systems for visual pattern recognition is very strong. This includes detection of meaningful patterns as well as what Waldo Tobler has referred to as 'spatial nonsense'(errors and outliers). It is estimated that at least half of the brain's neurons are associated with vision (McCormick, Defanti and Brown 1987). Interpretation of a graph or chart is often more efficient than interpretation based on a string of numbers representing the same data, and it makes sense to represent reality in abstract form. Tobler (1961) argues that abstraction forms the core of the research process and as Muehrcke (1990: 9) points out, 'it is abstraction, not realism that give maps their unique power'.

Visual perception appears to proceed from a global analysis to more and more finely grained analysis (Navon 1977), and the information processing system of human beings is particularly sensitive to interpretations and subtleties that can be expressed iconically (Kosslyn 1988). However, the limitations of the human visual processing mechanisms must not be underestimated, especially with increasing reliance upon visual displays for interpretive tasks (Cleveland and McGill 1984; Arnheim 1974). Not only do perceptions change with experience, they are context dependent (Zusne 1970). Thus the design of graphical displays forms an important component in understanding the role of visualization.

An argument may be presented for the rise of visualization as a discipline based on several needs: to access pertinent information from an overwhelming volume of collected data; to communicate complex patterns effectively; to formalize sound principles for presentation of data that optimize visual processing skills; and to steer analytical computations for data modelling and interpretation. The chapter will now proceed to trace development of visualization through several disciplinary threads. After describing the field as it is currently defined and conceived, the impact of visualization on GIS will be covered by citing applications and techniques in various phases of the data collection, analysis and display processes. In a summary section, research topics of particular relevance to progress in GIS will be laid out.

THE HISTORY OF VISUALIZATION IN THE CONTEXT OF GIS

The development of technology has accelerated capabilities to collect huge volumes of information, particularly geographical information. Visualization can readily be justified throughout since as data collection becomes easier, the volume of available information continues to increase, and more sophistication is required to sift through the volumes. Precision and consistency have become increasingly important as well. The efficiency of visual tools (imagery, maps and graphical products) and of the human visual processing system cannot be underestimated in terms of their importance for understanding the complexities of spatial information. Printing, photography, flight, plastics, and electronics have facilitated major advances in our ability to collect, manipulate, interpret and disseminate spatial information.

The development of the printing press allowed more efficient dissemination of maps and pictures, alleviating the need to generate every copy as an original. Photography allowed for more accurate recording and archiving mechanisms, particularly for the representation of landscape and terrain. The development of flight capabilities further enhanced photographic archiving, and provided a less costly approach to earth measurement. Additionally, images of the land could be repeated at regular intervals, making possible the temporal monitoring of spatial information. Plastics have been applied to render photographic film emulsions dimensionally stable, thus facilitating multiple colour printing of maps and imagery with good registration. More recently, the use of plastic media for computer disks and tapes provides efficient methods for storing larger volumes of spatial information, although this application was not fully realized until electronic technology was developed for the collection and display of spatial information.

The search for homogeneous regions and unexplained spatial patterns is central to geographical and statistical investigation. It is important to document the role of visualization in the recording of both tangible and non-tangible landscapes, as visual tools have provided access to spatial patterns that are not readily accommodated by the naked eye. The transition of interest in visualizing the statistical landscape began to take hold in the scientific community in the late sixteenth century, with empiricist interests shifting from the physical to the abstract (statistical) world (Flew 1989). Tufte (1983) comments that the invention of data graphics required replacing latitude–longitude with more abstract coordinates whose measure was not based on geographical analogy. Charts and maps have been used to gain scientific insights for at least two centuries (Robinson 1976). Lambert described the relational graphic in 1765, and Playfair published the *Commercial and Political Atlas* in 1786 in which he used spatial dimensions to represent quantitative data (Wainer and Thissen 1981).

Academic study of map design did not emerge as a scientific discipline until after the Second World War (McMaster and Thrower 1987) when mapping gained global prominence for intelligence and strategic planning. The focus upon visual realism in landscape depiction was recognized before the war (Smith 1935; Raisz 1931; Lobeck 1924) and became highly precise in later years with the efforts of Imhoff (1982). One of Imhoff's most important insights was that the visual impression of atmospheric haze could be introduced into terrain depictions by de-saturating colour tints at higher elevations. Interest in symbol design for statistical and thematic mapping began to develop with the publication of a textbook by Erwin Raisz (1948), which included a chapter 'Statistical mapping', and the treatment of thematic mapping in the first edition of Arthur Robinson's (1953) textbook.

As various authors have argued, the choice of representation strategies for illustration of multidimensional data is extremely varied (Monmonier 1988; Mackinlay 1986; Tufte 1983; Wainer and Thissen 1981; Monkhouse and Wilkinson 1971). Their potential use in geographical research was vastly expanded by the advent of automation and was emphasized in geography during and following the 'quantitative revolution' (MacEachren *et al.* 1992). When maps began to proliferate in the analytical process they were used to compare continuous spatial distributions (Robinson 1962; Robinson and Bryson 1957) and to visualize statistical distributions in the metaphor of geographical landscapes (Robinson 1961; Jenks 1963; Warntz 1964). The visualization of residuals from regression and classification was also determined a useful analytical tool (Thomas 1960; Jenks 1967).

Formalization of principles for graphical design has only recently been introduced. Robinson said in 1942 and reiterated three decades later that 'The designing of maps has received little or no ordered examination, yet I know of no other phase of cartography which is in greater need of study' (Robinson 1975: 9). Efforts to derive formal principles for graphical design can be found in several disciplines. Bachi (1968) developed an iconic system whose meaning might be simultaneously understood metrically or synoptically (for use on statistical charts and thematic maps). That is, precise values could be determined values by counting modules within each icon, or by viewing relative magnitudes in greytone progression from white to black (Fig. 28.1). The intention was to facilitate perception of specific values at specific places, as in a statistical table, and still preserve the synoptic pattern as in a picture, map or photograph. Bertin's (1973) system of 'visual variables' demonstrated their manipulation in graphical display and spatial analysis, and formulated principles for their appropriateness for displaying quantitative and qualitative distinctions (Fig. 28.2). Dent (1990) has formalized principles for map design to direct the Gestalt perceptual tasks in map reading, including symmetry, visual balance, contrast and figure–ground relations. Many of his principles are based on the results of empirical research, but the domain of these tests lies primarily with paper displays.

Cartographic research over the last two decades has been concerned with automating traditional cartographic representations and techniques (Yoeli 1982; Groop and Smith 1982). Some innovative graphical techniques have been implemented that would be tedious or, perhaps, impossible to achieve without computer assistance, for example unclassed choropleth maps (Tobler 1973a; see also Lavin and Archer 1984; Brassel and Utano 1979), cartograms (Tobler 1973b), continuous tone isoplethic maps (Lavin 1986), bivariate interpolation (Tobler 1979) and non-linear bidimensional regression (Tobler 1977). The research interest so prevalent in the 1970s in how paper maps are understood, recalled and perceived was not transferred to the electronic environment (but see Peterson 1979; Jenks 1981; Heyn 1984). With the exception of sporadic interest in map animation (e.g. see Moellering 1980) there was little concern in cartography for design of new methods to extend what is possible through the static, printed map.

Currently, the primary focus in cartography does not lie with perceptual or cognitive testing of the efficacy of visual products, nor of the ways that information is utilized in the assimilation of spatial pattern from electronic display. The lack of attention by GIS vendors to perceptually sound graphic defaults and good principles of graphical design may be one consequence. Weibel and Buttenfield (1988) argue that the reliability of decisions based on poorly designed graphic products is not yet recognized as a problem by users of GIS packages, although documentation of the

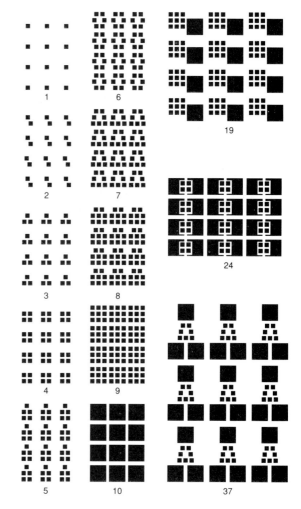

Fig. 28.1 Graphical rational pattern templates for selected values between 1 and 100 (after Bachi 1968).

limitations of perception of colour (Brewer 1989; Olson 1986), size and visual clustering (Gilmartin 1981b; Cox 1976; Slocum 1983; Jenks 1975), greytone value (Leonard and Buttenfield 1989; Kimerling 1985; Williams 1960), type (Shortridge and Welch 1982) and visual complexity (MacEachren 1982; Lavin 1979; Monmonier 1974; Olson 1972) is thorough in the cartographic literature. Cartographers should assert their knowledge of visual perception to improve the quality of visualized information in GIS: the need for reliable graphics is real, even if the demand is not yet recognized.

Visualization

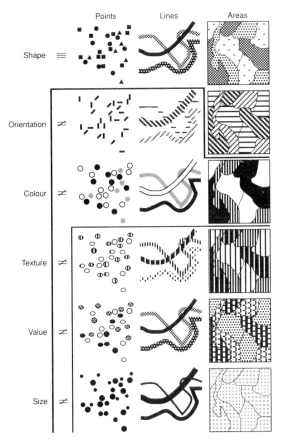

Fig. 28.2 The application of the visual variables to representation of categorical, ordinal and metrical spatial information (after Bertin 1983). The 'equivalence' sign next to Shape indicates that this variable should not be used to distinguish between different categories of points, lines or areas, as it does not by itself provide sufficient contrast. The 'not equivalent' signs next to Orientation and Colour indicate that categorical distinctions are made visually apparent (but notice orientation is excluded from this, for areal symbols). The 'not equivalent' sign for Texture, Value, and Size indicates that ordinal or metric distinctions may be seen for points, lines and areal symbols.

Researchers have become increasingly reliant upon the graphical encoding of information for analysis as well as illustration, although only rudimentary understanding of the relative effectiveness of various symbolizations is evident. The development of *exploratory data analysis* (Cleveland 1985; Chambers *et al.* 1983; Tukey 1977; Mosteller and Tukey 1977) has been driven in part by the creation of innovative graphical tools for data description, hypothesis testing and inference.

More recently GIS has provided a platform for a variety of new graphic and cartographic tools for visualization. With the advent of GIS technology, geographers now have a plethora of graphic and cartographic techniques at their disposal. These include graphic portrayal of temporal data, geographical flows, animated displays, and three-dimensional imaging techniques (Kraak 1988). It is important to realize that these graphical products would be difficult if not impossible to generate without computer assistance. For example, the recent development of graphical human–computer interfaces (HCI) is facilitating GIS researchers' capabilities for pursuing synoptic tasks with iconic command structures. Multiple windows, tear-off windows and point-and-click interface tools originally introduced for Macintosh microcomputers (Apple 1986) are becoming industry standards for most high-level computing platforms. These and other emerging trends will be discussed later in more detail. To understand their impact on GIS fully, it will be helpful to relate visualization research as it is carried out in several related disciplines.

SCOPE AND DOMAIN OF VISUALIZATION

The general aims of visualization techniques have been fairly well established (Robertson 1988; Haber and Wilkinson 1982), Although the scope of visualization research has not been clearly delimited. The links between vision and visualization are also not clearly established. Marr (1982) defined vision as an information-processing task, adding that its study must incorporate the extraction of images from 'the world', and '. . . an inquiry into the nature of the internal representations by which we capture this information and thus make it available as a basis for decisions about our thoughts and actions' (Marr 1982: 3). Visualization may be studied as the products of vision, but this precludes full understanding of the processes underlying their generation, manipulation and comprehension. An alternative is to approach visualization as a subset of the study of vision, and to consider how it is defined in substance and in scope by various scientific disciplines whose research activities relate to GIS.

Definitions of visualization

In October 1986, the US National Science Foundation (NSF) sponsored a panel meeting to advise its Division of Advanced Scientific Computing on priorities for supporting research, particularly in the domain of scientific computing and supercomputing. The panel consensus was that top priority should be placed on the development of visual computing tools, including hardware, software and visual interface tools for graphics and image processing techniques. The panel recommended that NSF establish an interdisciplinary initiative on Visualization in Scientific Computing (ViSC).

In a report of a subsequent NSF workshop held on the ViSC initiative, the domain of visualization incorporates data collection, organization, modelling and representation. It is interesting to note that the human component of visualization is downplayed significantly in both the definition and stated domain of the ViSC report.

> 'Visualization is a method of computing. It transforms the symbolic into the geometric, enabling researchers to observe their simulations and computations.... Visualization embraces both image understanding and image synthesis. That is, visualization is a tool both for interpreting image data fed into a computer, and for generating images from complex multi-dimensional data sets. It studies those mechanisms in humans and computers which allow them in concert to perceive, use and communicate visual information.'
>
> (McCormick *et al.* 1987: 3)

A second definition of visualization is promoted by cartographers and some psychologists. MacEachren *et al.* (1992: 2) define visualization as '... first and foremost, an act of cognition. It is a human ability to develop mental representations that allow us to identify patterns and create or impose order'. This perspective is supported by other authors as well (Miller 1984; Scott 1987). Visualization describes the process of 'creation and manipulation of [mental] images' (Scott 1987: 14). This perspective underlies much of the research in map interpretation (Phillips, DeLucia and Skelton 1975; Gamezo and Rabakhin 1964; McGuigan 1957).

It seems reasonable to incorporate a third aspect of visualization in addition to the cognitively based and computationally based definitions. This aspect incorporates the construction of visual displays and the principles of graphic communication guiding that construction. Visualization extends beyond the confines of hardware and software. It crosses the human/machine divide and includes computer vision/pattern recognition, remote sensing and mechanical data collection, as well as the cognitive processes of visualization, and principles of graphic design. The role of visualization for GIS tasks lies at the interface between these three (computation, cognition and graphic design). All are embraced in the following definition:

> Visualization is the process of representing information synoptically for the purpose of recognizing, communicating and interpreting pattern and structure. Its domain encompasses the computational, cognitive, and mechanical aspects of generating, organizing, manipulating and comprehending such representations. Representations may be rendered symbolically, graphically, or iconically and are most often differentiated from other forms of expression (textual, verbal, or formulaic) by virtue of their synoptic format and with qualities traditionally described by the term 'Gestalt'.

Linking the visualization research domains

To understand the complexity and scope of the topic as applied in various disciplines, it may be helpful to build a conceptual framework linking the domains of visualization research. The diagram in Fig. 28.3 does not represent a model of visualization, as that is beyond the scope of this chapter. Rather the illustration is intended to demonstrate the various research domains associated with a rectangle or other graphic icon) and the computational, cognitive, and mechanical transformations that convert spatial information between domains.

In the framework, arrows represent transformations often studied in the context of computer vision, computational vision, and

Visualization

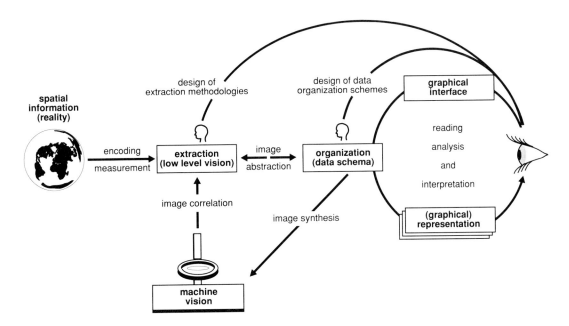

Fig. 28.3 The interrelated disciplines of visualization research (see text for explanation).

mechanical image generation and analysis (Walters 1990). The circular arcs surround arenas of the framework where transformation of information may be modelled as either a cognitive or a machine process. The implication of the eye turned inward towards the circular arcs is that a large part of visualization is internal, and this justifies the relationship of cognitive science and computer science within the scope of the framework. The remainder of this chapter will take the reader through the framework, discussing visualization research in each domain and describing the transformation of spatial information between domains. Examples are cited of published work in GIS that draws upon these research domains.

Encoding and measurement

Spatial information ('reality') can be thought of in similar terms to Marr's reference to 'the world' (discussed in the previous section), that is, passive information to be observed, measured and encoded. The connotation of 'reality' is that the information is continuous, and the connotation of measurement and encoding is that a discrete representation is sampled by photography, survey (geodetic or statistical), scanning, or sensory input. (The discrete nature of sensory input has been empirically demonstrated by several authors: for review and discussion see Bourne, Dominowski and Loftus 1979; Rosinski 1977; Miller 1956.) The information may encode the view outside an office window, a satellite recording multi-spectral images of earth, or it may be someone's remembered representation of a part of reality (e.g. a verbal description of a campus layout). Pinker (1985: 4) defines visual imagery as 'The process of remembering or reasoning about shapes or objects that are not currently before us but must be retrieved from memory or consolidated from a description'.

The purpose of the visualization in a particular situation dictates the internal representation of spatial information (its format, substance and composition), which in turn determines what details need to be filtered out or selected. The nature of the data dictates which sensing device is appropriate for the task. For example scanning in the infrared bandwidth might be used to extract information in $1-10\ \mu m$ wavelengths for a task involving the analysis of crop disease. Information that the sensor is not sensitive to will not be encoded, and thus the extracted scene can be thought of as a discrete sample of the (continuous) information.

Extraction

The extraction process equates to what computer scientists and cognitive scientists term 'early vision' (or low level vision). This domain of visualization research includes '... feature analysis, whereby information about colour, motion, shape, texture, stereo depth and intensity edges are extracted. Another aspect of early vision is image segmentation, whereby the feature information is used to segment the image into regions which have a high probability of having arisen from a single physical cause' (Walters 1990: 4). For example, the scene might include a narrow black band against a coarse textured green area, with a bluish region next to the green. Low level vision would extract and segment the scene based on colour shape and texture to form three regions in the extracted image. Pinker (1985: 3) describes human visual recognition in similar terms, as 'the process that allows us to determine on the basis of retinal input that particular shapes, configurations of shapes, objects and scenes, and their properties are before us'.

In geographical analysis, it may be considered that the sampling frame or sampling design will bias the data collection, and this will impact upon the extraction of enumerated variables (Wrigley 1985; Blalock 1979). Variables (education, income, family structure, ethnic background, etc.) form the extracted spatial information. Visualization of the data (as scatter diagrams, factor loading plots, etc.) provides a statistical equivalent to low level feature analysis. Abstraction and synthesis by regression, clustering or factoring is used to recover higher level descriptions of social structure, quality of life, and other geographical interpretations. The sampling strategy will of course impact upon the nature of the collected data, the form of the descriptive statistical plots, and subsequent interpretation and inference.

Image abstraction and image synthesis

A subsequent transformation referred to in Fig. 28.3 is image abstraction. Together with image synthesis, it is referred to in computer science as scene analysis. Image abstraction uses the feature descriptors extracted in low-level vision to construct higher level image descriptions, by incorporating shape analysis, object recognition and object localization (Walters 1990). These descriptions must be organized in some form of data schema to permit subsequent use in image synthesis (Ballard and Brown 1981). Image synthesis uses the higher level descriptions to attach labels identifying the image regions in more detail. To continue the above example, the scene might represent an asphalt road through a grassy area next to a lake. Identification requires abstracting the low-level descriptors based on knowledge about the nature of roads, vegetation and water bodies.

Organization within a data schema

Knowledge about the nature of spatial information is organized in a data schema and can take many forms. In the case of remote sensing, this form may be multi-spectral reflectance values for a set of pixels previously isolated ('trained') in image classification. In other cases, it may incorporate geometrical definitions about what the feature should look like at certain levels of resolution (Buttenfield 1986; Witkin 1986) or from a particular viewpoint (Walters 1987). Alternatively, knowledge may be based upon a person's expectation of what the image might likely show. The very common visual response to a visual ambiguity or an optical illusion is called a 'double take'; this reassessment of the features in a scene is analogous to the iterations between low-level and high-level machine-based analysis in the framework, although it has not yet been demonstrated that the algorithms for machine-based analysis can mimic the human visual process (Weizenbaum 1976).

The nature of the data dictates the organizing schema, and will bias the image abstraction and synthesis. In the example of the road by the lake, above, rules formalizing the geometry of roads, the visual texture of grassy patches, and the variations in water colour caused by light refraction must be organized in a manner that the feature labels (road, lake, etc.) can be inferred based on input of the low-level descriptions, and rules guiding interpretation of their expected relationships (e.g. roads do not customarily cross water bodies, although bridges and causeways do).

Research on the organizing schema includes data structures work (Samet 1988; Li and Uhr 1987), as the format of storage will facilitate some but not all GIS operations. The organizing schema may be a data structure (a look-up table of feature categories, or a spectral signature histogram, or a numeric data dictionary). Substantive research on the schema is also relevant, for example the set of soils types and associations currently adopted by the US Soil Conservation Service to classify soil parcels, or the hierarchical feature codes used in USGS

Digital Line Graph files. Census categories (county, census division, census tract, block, and block face) provide another data schema that is useful for organizing demographic variables. Each of these schema types will bias the access of information for abstraction or image synthesis, and herein lies the importance of careful schema construction (Lakoff 1987).

Knowledge organization and its relation to visualization may be generalized into several research disciplines. One of the research challenges in cartography relates to the maintenance of multiple materialized views of a landscape, to avoid the time and cost of re-computation (Gunther and Bilmes 1989). In database management, investigation focuses on the multiple representations of a single geographical landscape that are recorded at differing resolutions, and the formation of database links to connect a single feature stored in each digital version (Beard 1989; Bruegger and Frank 1989). The purpose of the links is to render database update more efficient and consistent, that is, to have all versions of a feature 'inherit' the modification applied to any single version. The challenge for visualization is that as geographical features vary structurally with resolution, the update operations may not be uniformly applicable. A city outline may be organized as a coordinate string at one map scale, and at a smaller scale will be represented as a single latitude–longitude location. This will necessitate differing database operations to be applied when incorporating a new subdivision into the urban outline. This has obvious implications for subsequent map representation.

Alternative organizing schemata are applied in other research contexts: the knowledge may be organized in symbolic formulation as a mathematical model. For example, Batty, Longley and Fotheringham (1989) have generated models of urban structure based on fractal and chaotic models. The structural characteristics are influenced by the form and parameters of the model, for example, to introduce self-similarity into the generated images of the urban boundary. The self-similar form of the model will influence a self-similar quality and conversely will necessitate expectations of self-similarity in analysis and inference. It may also be a source of error propagation if applied to the study of phenomena or structures that are scale–dependent, that is, the expectations will bias the visualization process in statistical modelling as well as in image processing. In data modelling terms, the organizational schema must necessarily be both complete and robust to be adequate for more than a single situation (Peuquet 1984).

Machine vision

The research domain of machine vision is also referred to as computer vision, computational vision, image understanding, or robotics, to cite a few variants. Walters (1990) states that machine vision is common to the engineering and to the applications contexts, although in this chapter the role in GIS research is considered an application. The term 'computational vision' is more interdisciplinary and is used in computer science, physics and neuroscience to refer to studies of both computer vision and biological vision. To retain clarity of the conceptual framework in Fig. 28.3, the realm of biological vision and psychophysics will be discussed below in the arena labelled 'reading interpretation and analysis', and computer vision will be discussed first.

Topics of interest in computer vision include the generation of images from identified features (image synthesis). Image correlation research applies the synthetic image descriptions to facilitate subsequent feature extraction for a particular task. In robot vision, for example, the synthesized description of a car door is compared with the vidicon input to determine regions of the door frame where the paint spray should be aimed (Horn 1986). To cite another example, the correlation of a synthesized image with views of terrain below a cruise missile is the determining factor in the navigation route the missile follows. That is, views of terrain are compared with synthetic imagery for common features. When terrain features match the image, the missile either turns to a new heading or altitude, or deposits its payload.

In GIS research the relevance of machine vision is apparent in data input and pattern recognition. Data input is often accomplished by means of semi-automatic or automatic digitization (Clarke 1990). Semi-automatic digitization requires a digitizing tablet and cursor. In this process a human operator uses the cursor to select either critical points ('point-mode digitizing') or else trace map boundaries and other line features ('stream-mode digitizing'). Some disagreement exists among cartographers as to which mode produces a more accurate and recognizable representation of the line features, although this has not been resolved as yet by empirical testing. Automatic digitization, also called scanning, provides very fast encoding but requires subsequent reconstruction of geometry and topology to recover object meanings. Rudiments of geometry (e.g. line continuity) can be reconstructed by line-following algorithms. Topological ambiguities (e.g. line intersections, polygon closures) require subsequent processing. Algorithms for this type of work abound in the computer science literature (for a review see Sedgewick 1984; Pavlidis 1982).

A related type of GIS research involves higher level pattern recognition, that works with (reconstructed) graphic objects and attaches geographical labels to them. This work is particularly important in remote sensing, where line features are classified as roads or rivers (Buttenfield 1987), land use categories are identified from land cover type and texture (Civco 1989), and other geomorphic, geographical or temporal distinctions are rendered (Langran 1989).

Reading, analysis and interpretation

Use of any GIS requires a fluid interaction between human vision and graphical representation, and this is a major distinction between machine and human vision. Access to spatial information stored in a GIS is often most efficiently accomplished by intermediating the process with visual tools, to provide synoptic interaction for synoptic tasks. This in turn requires a data schema that is both complete and robust, and allows for ease of generating graphical displays. These may take the form of map or diagrammatic (graphical) representations, where the research domain of graphic design comes into play. They may take the form of graphical interfaces which relate to user interface research. In the context of GIS research, it is difficult to discuss any one of these research domains (human vision, graphical representation and graphical interfaces) in isolation from one another.

A common thread in all three domains centres on the processes of reading, analysis and interpretation. Map reading is defined as the 'recognition, perceptual organisation and identification of the map elements by the map user, using their knowledge and experience' (Scott 1987: 14). Muehrcke (1986) defines reading to involve identifying items in an image, for example menu bars in a graphical interface, or the title, scale bar and other icons on a map. Determining how many colours (classes of data) are present on a map is part of the reading process. Analysis involves discerning the existence of spatial pattern, and related tasks such as locating the data maxima and minima. To continue the map reading example, this might include discerning which colour represented, say, the highest class and then locating the regions on the map where the highest values occur. Muehrcke continues, by defining interpretation as the process of associating information induced or deduced from analysis with other knowledge to formulate reasons to explain the pattern. (The other knowledge may reside in the data schema, that is, the GIS data structures, or be the user's knowledge.) The entire arena of the design, production and use of graphical materials in GIS may be considered to incorporate these processes. That is to say, reading, analysis and interpretation may be analogous to extraction, modelling and inference.

Graphical representation

Automating the graphical design process has received relatively little attention in computer cartography. Muller (1983:30) supports this idea and highlights the 'growing contradiction in the degree of sophistication in the equipment and programs used and the lack of attention paid to elementary principles of graphic expression'. A number of researchers have undertaken to redress this problem by attempting to encapsulate the art and science of cartography in graphical systems. 'The lack of formal rules for map design is not simply a consequence of cartographic incompetence, or a lack of interest in the map user. It simply reflects the sheer difficulty of deducing a set of rules, capable of universal application. . . The complexity of obtaining information from a map is matched by the complexity of creating it' (Keates 1982: 113).

Some researchers have utilized artificial intelligence techniques to encapsulate the rules and principles governing design (Nickerson and Freeman 1986; Freeman and Ahn 1984; Muller, Johnson and Vanzella 1986; Mackinlay 1986). In cartography, decision making is complex, retrospective and subjective, and the evaluation tasks that take place are complex and ill-defined. Solutions to date have failed to accommodate artistic licence and the agile hand in an integrated fashion (Mackaness and Scott 1988). Research has focused on those aspects of cartography that can be compartmentalized (symbolization, generalization and text placement). The fact that these processes have been studied in isolation from one another has reduced their value for an integrated solution to the automation of map design.

Transformation of information between the GIS system and user is increasingly accomplished by graphical tools, including representations in the form of maps and diagrams, and including graphical interface tools such as mice and tear-off menus. The design of graphical representations on paper maps has been studied intensively in the cartographic literature, as discussed in the previous section on history. Principles for manipulating the visual variables (size, shape, colour, value, texture, orientation and position) have been formalized in cartography by Bertin (1983) and expanded by Dent (1990). Discussion of these principles may be found in other disciplines as well (e.g. see Arnheim 1974; Dondis 1984). Research reporting on the perceptual limitations and their psychophysical compensations has been criticized by some cartographers (Gilmartin 1981a; Shortridge and Welch 1980), although the efficiency of graphics for representing spatial information has remained high on the cartographic research agenda.

Graphical representations may also provide an efficient means to access a GIS data schema and to modify its contents. For example, users can point to a map polygon to assign it attributes, update its boundary, or include it in a map overlay process. The use of a graphic display for this manipulation of the database contents stands in counterpoint to machine vision, wherein direct interaction between the machine and the data schema works efficiently (i.e. generation of a graphical display will not improve efficiency). When analysis and decisions are based upon a graphical representation, it becomes very important that the graphics do not belie the data patterns. This is a complex issue, as it is known that human perception does not work in perfect arithmetic proportions. Compensation for visual estimations of size, value and colour should be incorporated into the graphic defaults of existing GIS software to ensure that bias is minimized in the use of GIS graphics for database manipulation and display.

Graphical interface

The optimal design of both the representation(s) and the method of interaction must reflect the cognitive task, and in particular how the mind assembles and modifies its mental model. For efficient elicitation of salient information, the user must be able to interact with the data and its portrayal in a transparent manner (an interesting visual metaphor), and interaction with the command structure must be designed so as not to distract from the task. The modelling of complex phenomena requires that the data be represented in a variety of media, that we be able to filter, abstract and combine different variables of different type (nominal, ordinal, interval), and formulate complex queries in a flexible manner. This necessitates the use of highly interactive command structures that are transparent in their use. That a spatial language should be developed (with precise syntactic and semantic definitions) for this type of analysis can be in no doubt (Head 1984; Mackinlay 1986).

Design and implementation of visual tools for human–computer interaction (HCI) is an integral component of the GIS process. The elicitation of specific/salient information requires that the user be able to 'interact' with the data and its portrayal transparently, and that interaction with the command structure be designed so as not to distract from the task (Rasmussen 1986). For example, pointing with a mouse and cursor to locate text labels or to make a query about a map polygon is far more transparent than having to remember the polygon identifier and type it on a keyboard. The GIS user locates the items visually, and interacts by visual means to communicate that item to the system. Successful design of a graphical interface requires an understanding of the cognitive process, and, in particular, the organization of the mental model on which decision making is based. In order to make the query mechanics transparent, the interface must be so designed that the user addresses the GIS task in the substantive concepts associated with the problem. For spatial data, this often means allowing the user synoptic access to the data schema. (Further discussion of the design of user interfaces can be found in Frank and Mark 1991 in this volume.)

Human vision

In human vision, the organization of knowledge takes the form of expectations and associations with previous viewed imagery. Ralph Waldo Emerson said 'people only see what they are prepared to see'. Visual expectations will flavour the interpretation of visual imagery. For example, the image of an open box of pencils viewed from directly overhead will appear as three rows of equal cylinders of nearly uniform shape and colour arranged in a rectangular frame (Fig. 28.4). As it is not customary to associate the image of a pencil from the viewpoint of its eraser tip (i.e. pencils are not normally seen from this view), the cylinders in the image may not be identified with the label 'pencils', or at least not make the identification as quickly as with the pencil in side view.

Fig. 28.4 The 'people only see what they are prepared to see' phenomenon. Viewers' expectations may bias their identification of visualized objects (see text for explanation).

The same phenomenon can be important in using a CRT display to identify spatial pattern and trend. For example, very different choropleth maps can result from resetting metric class breaks, or contour intervals, or even the greytones associated with a data set (Fig. 28.5). If a north–south trend is expected in data, it may be difficult to distinguish between meaningful pattern and graphical artefact without knowledge of the underlying analytical and cartographic operations that were used to manipulate the visualized data. *A priori* assumptions about what is expected interact with readiness to accept visualized patterns as accurate and real, and this may hinder spatial decision making and data interpretation.

Efforts by researchers (Cleveland and McGill 1984; Tukey 1977) to develop exploratory graphical techniques have resulted in renewed appreciation for the power of graphical presentations and the need to understand the process of map reading

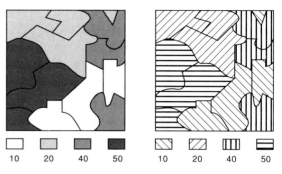

Fig. 28.5 The graphic rendition of spatial information may obscure the pattern of the data, if not bias interpretations based on *a priori* assumptions.

better. If visualization tools are to be designed that facilitate understanding, then as a prerequisite there must be an understanding of the mental processes involved in the cognition of spatial information as well as an understanding of the mental representation of spatial knowledge (for review see Kuipers 1978; McNamara, Ratcliff and McKoon 1984). For example it has been observed that psychological distance in cognitive maps is primarily dependent on route distance rather than Euclidean distance. The design of the London Underground map (and many other subway maps) takes advantage of this fact (see Fig. 9.4).

It is acknowledged that aesthetics encapsulates harmony, composition and clarity and is an integral component of map design (Keates 1982); but perception of these qualities varies between users, as does their importance. The success of a design in communicating spatial pattern depends as much on experience as on social attitudes and desires. Various attempts to elicit cartographic design rules have highlighted the need for a better understanding of cognitive process. This has been manifest, for example, in eye movement studies (Steinke 1987; Castner and Eastman 1985). Though many experiments have been carried out to investigate how people react to visual stimuli, only a small number test map stimuli. Eye fixation patterns during map reading are different from text reading and reflect the comparatively unconstrained nature of the map search process (Taylor and Hopkin 1975). A number of researchers have clearly demonstrated that the eye fixation pattern does depend on the map task (Yarbus 1967). This may be indicative of the formation of different mental map schemata according to the task. It is difficult to design experiments that embody map complexity and can evaluate the effectiveness of the design (Castner and Eastman 1985). Some have challenged the worth of such research, since 'the physical process of making a map... [is] quite different from the mental strategies put to use in processing the map as a stimulus' (Olson 1979: 38).

SUMMARY AND EMERGING TRENDS

Before the advent of computers, the paper on which maps were printed was the database. The portrayal of that information was the exclusive domain of the cartographer. Through the development of GIS and related technologies, demands have been placed on map design for which conventional map making techniques are inadequate. The 'quantitative revolution' coupled with the availability of computers in the 1960s led to a rapid increase in the potential sophistication of graphing techniques and spatial analysis. The fledgling sciences of remote sensing, image analysis and pattern recognition arose, together with computer-aided design and manufacture.

Mapping systems in these disciplines were not developed by geographers or cartographers but by physicists, architectural engineers, mathematicians and those in the medical profession and government agencies. The role of cartography in these systems has been largely ignored. Instead, the graphics packages and the pen plotters have 'replaced' cartographers and their scribing tools. Failure to accommodate sound principles of design into graphical defaults has resulted in the production of some appalling maps, examples of which abound in the literature (e.g. see Tufte 1983). In cartography, 'speed has been analyzed primarily from the production viewpoint. However, speed of consumption is just as important in the presentation of intelligent data' (Robinson 1975: 10).

In this chapter, current definitions of visualization have been drawn from various scientific disciplines in consideration of their relevance to GIS and the analysis of spatial information. Examples of research to demonstrate the role of visualization have been presented from the fields of geography, statistics, cognitive science, robotics, database management, cartography and cybernetics, all of which contribute to visualization of spatial information. Future directions in visualization research will likely address improvements in access and manipulation of larger volumes of spatial data, the development of multidimensional (three-dimensional and higher) data structures such as voxels (McCormick *et al.* 1987) and the implementation of GIS capabilities for temporal analysis and display.

McCormick *et al.* (1987) predict that visualization tools have the potential to restructure fundamentally the way research design in science is carried out. Visualization has ramifications both in terms of database schemata and the perception of what a GIS is and does. GIS is developing into far more than an efficient means to store and manage spatial information (with a single map as an end product). The impediments to further development are not only technological but also conceptual: the lack of complete understanding about the nature of spatial and temporal data continues to obstruct solutions to its manipulation in digital forms. The most important topics in GIS visualization research will relate to human–computer interaction, modelling and sensitivity analysis, and the quality of visualized information.

The sophistication of human–computer interaction will put heavy demands on database design that must also cope with the inherent spatial, spectral and temporal complexity of geographical data. In addition to research on screen format design, use of multiple windows and iconic desktop metaphors, future systems must take advantage of other sensory input such as voice commands, data gloves, voice recognition, and hypertext and hypermapping (Muehrcke 1990; Rhind and Openshaw 1987). Visual tools will be developed to enable browsing large spatial databases at all levels of generality, and without requirements for prior knowledge about the organization and content of the database. The challenge will be to design systems that provide 'not just balance, but an appropriate span of alternative modalities' (Verplank 1988: 372).

The modelling of complex phenomena requires that the data be represented in a variety of media. Facilities must exist to filter, abstract and composite different variables of different type (nominal, ordinal, interval, etc.), and to formulate complex queries in a flexible manner. Handling of massive data sets often takes advantage of supercomputer hardware, making possible dynamic visualization of fields in higher dimensions (including the temporal dimension). For example, interactive steering of numerically intensive calculations may be facilitated by animating model output for selected iterations, to view developing trends and to monitor error propagation.

This necessitates the use of highly interactive command structures that are transparent in their use. A spatial language should be developed for interface/analysis with precise semantic definitions (Mackinlay 1986), and an iconic (non-verbal) command syntax. A purely linguistic approach might generate a computational syntax for specific spatial operations, for example, to link nodes in a network, bind a set of points with an N-dimensional hull, or decompose a complex object or surface into a comprehensive tessellation of simpler objects. Boolean adjectives might be designed for testing contiguity, proximity, equivalent dimensionality and other properties. These operations should be implemented as intrinsic GIS commands, just as MOVE and DRAW were implemented in early graphics libraries.

Research on the quality of visual display extends beyond assessment of positional and attribute errors, and psychophysical testing of symbology. It incorporates research concern for the use of visual tools in GIS simulation and modelling, and for reliability of spatial decision making based on visual displays. At present, the effects of map overlay and other compositing operations on data sets of heterogeneous reliability is not well understood. It must be addressed before graphical designs displaying data reliability can be effectively implemented and evaluated in an empirical manner. Further research is required on spatial cognition, the structure of mental representations and the processing of spatial knowledge, in order to understand what is meant by 'optimal' in terms of the graphic itself, the mix of graphics and the way in which the user interacts with the data and bases decisions upon it.

The study of visualization has arisen from a basic desire to understand the nature of multivariate data. Society appears to be subscribing to an information intensive existence. The firehose metaphor represents a volume and currency of information collection that will force increased reliance upon visual tools for summarizing and interpreting multidimensional patterns.

Visualization will be relied upon increasingly for the efficient interpretation and summary of spatial information. This is true for a number of disciplines, and there is therefore a real need for continued research into the domains of visualization identified in Fig. 28.3 as well as research into the interdependence of those disciplinary domains.

In the firehose metaphor, the use of visualization techniques is analogous to taking multiple discrete slices through a continuous stream of data, in order to build up a picture of its salient qualities. The purpose of visualization in GIS is to enable researchers to do more with the stream of information than simply archive it. The lack of understanding about the nature of the phenomena of interest in geographical research makes it difficult to determine the best means of visualization for specific research tasks. The study of visualization can benefit a wide number of research domains, particularly those whose focus requires dissemination of, and interaction with, multidimensional data.

REFERENCES

Apple Computer Inc. (1986) *Human Interface Guidelines: the Apple desktop interface*. Apple Computer Inc., Cupertino California

Arnheim R (1974) *Art and Visual Perception*. University of California Press, Berkeley

Bachi R (1968) *Graphical Rational Patterns*. Universities Press, Jerusalem, Israel

Ballard D H, Brown C M (1981) *Computer Vision*. Prentice-Hall, Englewood Cliffs New Jersey

Batty M, Longley P, Fotheringham A S (1989) Urban growth and form: scaling, fractal geometry and diffusion-limited aggregation. *Environment and Planning A* 1:1447–72

Beard M K (1989) Design criteria for automated generalization. *Paper presented at International Cartographic Association*, Budapest, August 1989

Bertin J (1973) *Semiologie Graphique*. (Tr. Berg W J). University of Wisconsin Press, Madison Wisconsin

Bertin J (1983) *Semiology of Graphics*. Gauthiers-Villars, Paris

Blalock H M (1979) *Social Statistics*, 2nd edn. McGraw-Hill, New York

Board C (1967) Maps as models. In: Chorley R J, Haggett P (eds.) *Models in Geography*. Methuen, London, pp. 671–725

Bourne L E, Dominowski R L, Loftus E F (1979) *Cognitive Processes*. Prentice-Hall, Englewood Cliffs New Jersey

Brassel K E, Utano J J (1979) Design strategies for continuous tone area mapping. *The American Cartographer* **6** (1): 39–50

Brewer C A (1989) The development of process-printed Munsell charts for selecting map colors. *The American Cartographer* **16** (4): 269–78

Bruegger B P, Frank A U (1989) Hierarchies over topological data structures. *Proceedings of the American Congress on Surveying and Mapping Annual Convention, Baltimore*, Vol. 4. ACSM, Falls Church Virginia, pp. 137–45

Buttenfield B P (1986) Digital definitions of scale-dependent structure. In: Blakemore M J (ed.) *Proceedings of AUTOCARTO London*, Vol. 1. Royal Institution of Chartered Surveyors, pp. 497–506

Buttenfield B P (1987) Automating the identification of cartographic lines. *The American Cartographer* **14** (1): 7–20

Castner H W, Eastman J R (1985) Eye movement parameters and perceived map complexity. *The American Cartographer* **12** (1): 29–40

Chambers J M, Cleveland S, Kleiner B, Tukey P A (1983) *Graphical Methods for Data Analysis*. Duxbury, Boston

Civco D (1989) Knowledge-based land use and land cover mapping. *Proceedings ASPRS/ACSM Annual Convention*, Vol. 3. ASPRS/ACSM, Falls Church Virginia, pp. 276–91

Clarke K C (1990) *Analytical and Computer Cartography*. Prentice-Hall, Englewood Cliffs New Jersey

Cleveland W S (1985) *The Elements of Graphing Data*. Wadsworth, Monterey California

Cleveland W S, McGill R (1984) Graphical perception: theory, experimentation and application to the development of graphical methods. *Journal of the American Statistical Association* **79**: 531–54

Cox C W (1976) Anchor effects and the estimation of graduated circles and squares. *The American Cartographer* **3**: 65–74

Dent B D (1990) *Principles of Thematic Map Design*. Addison-Wesley, Reading Massachusetts

Dondis D A (1984) *A Primer of Visual Literacy*. MIT Press, Cambridge Massachusetts

Fisher P F (1991) Spatial data sources and data problems. In: Maguire D J, Goodchild M F, Rhind D W (eds.) *Geographical Information Systems: principles and applications*. Longman, London, pp. 175–89, Vol 1

Flew A G (1989) *An Introduction to Western Philosophy: ideas and argument from Plato to Popper*. Thames and Hudson, New York

Frank A U, Mark D M (1991) Language issues for GIS. In: Maguire D J, Goodchild M F, Rhind D W (eds.) *Geographical Information Systems: principles and applications*. Longman, London, pp. 147–63, Vol 1

Freeman H, Ahn J (1984) AUTONAP – an expert system for automatic name placement. *Proceedings of the 1st International Symposium on Spatial Data Handling, Zurich*. International Geographical Union, Ohio, pp. 544–69

Gamezo M U, Rubakhin V F (1964) The role of spatial concepts in map reading and the interpretation of aerial photographs. In: Ananyev B G, Lomov B F (eds.) *Problems of Spatial Perception and Spatial Concepts*. (Technical Translation F-164). NASA, Washington, DC

Gilmartin P P (1981a) The interface of cognitive and psychological research in cartography. *Cartographica* **18** (3): 9–20

Gilmartin P P (1981b) Influence of map context on circle perception. *Annals of the Association of American Geographers* **71**: 253–8

Groop R E, Smith R (1982) A dot matrix method of portraying continuous statistical surfaces. *The American Cartographer* **9** (2): 123–30

Gunther O, Bilmes J (1989) The implementation of the cell tree: design alternatives and performance evaluation. *Proceedings BTW '89 – Database Systems for Office Automation, Engineering, and Scientific Applications*. Springer-Verlag, pp. 72–92

Haber R N, Wilkinson L (1982) Perceptual components of computer displays. *IEEE Transactions on Computer Graphics and Applications* **2** (3): 23–35

Head C G (1984) A map as a natural language – new insight into cartographic communication. *Cartographica* **21** (31): 1–32

Heyn B N (1984) *An Evaluation of Map Color Schemes for Use on CRTs*. Unpublished MS thesis, Department of Geography, University of South Carolina

Horn B K P (1986) *Robot Vision*. MIT Press, Cambridge Massachusetts

Imhoff E (1982) *Cartographic Relief Presentation*. de Gruyter, Berlin

Jenks G F (1963) Generalization in statistical maps. *Annals of the Association of American Geographers* **53**: 15–26

Jenks G F (1967) The data model concept in statistical mapping. *International Yearbook of Cartography* **7**: 186–8

Jenks G F (1975) The evaluation and prediction of visual clustering in maps symbolized with proportional circles. In: Davis J C, McCullagh M J (eds.) *Display and Analysis of Spatial Data*. Wiley, London, pp. 311–27

Jenks G F (1981) Lines, computers and human frailties. *Annals of the Association of American Geographers* **71**: 1–10

Keates J S (1982) *Understanding Maps*. Longman, London

Kimerling A J (1985) The comparison of equal value gray scales. *The American Cartographer* **12** (2): 119–27

Kosslyn S M (1988) *Image and Mind*. Harvard University Press, Cambridge Massachusetts

Kraak M J (1988) *Computer Assisted Cartographical Three Dimensional Imaging Techniques*. Delft University Press, Delft

Kuipers B (1978) Modelling spatial knowledge. *Cognitive Science* **2**: 129–53

Lakoff G (1987) *Women, Fire and Dangerous Things: what*

categories reveal about the mind. University of Chicago Press, Chicago
Langran G (1989) *Representing Temporality as a Third GIS Dimension*. Unpublished PhD thesis, Department of Geography, University of Washington
Lavin S J (1979) *Region Perception Variability on Choropleth Maps: pattern complexity effects*. Unpublished PhD dissertation, University of Kansas
Lavin S J (1986) Mapping continuous distributions using dot density shading. *The American Cartographer* **13** (2): 140–50
Lavin S J, Archer J C (1984) Computer-produced unclassed bivariate choropleth maps. *The American Cartographer* **11** (1):49–57
Leonard J J, Buttenfield B P (1989) An equal value gray scale for laser printer mapping. *The American Cartographer* **16** (2): 97–107
Li Z N, Uhr L (1987) Pyramid vision using key features to integrate image-driven bottom-up and model-driven top-down processes. *IEEE Transactions on Systems, Man and Cybernetics*, SMC-17
Lobeck A K (1924) *Block Diagrams*. Wiley, New York

MacEachren A E (1982) Map complexity: comparison and measurement. *The American Cartographer* **9** (1): 31–46
MacEachren A E with **Buttenfield B P, Campbell J C, Monmonier M S** (1992) Visualization. In: Abler R F, Olson J M, Marcus N G (eds.) *Geography's Inner World*. Rutgers University Press, New Jersey
Mackaness W A, Scott D J (1988) The problems of operationally defining the map design process for cartographic expert systems *Proceedings of Austra Carto III, 22–26 Aug, 7th Australian Cartographic Conference, Sydney*. ACA, Sydney, pp. 715–23
Mackinlay J (1986) Automating the design of graphical presentations of relational information. *ACM Transactions on Graphics* **5** (2): 110–41
Marr D (1982) *Vision*. Freeman, San Francisco
McCormick B H, Defanti T A, Brown M D (1987) Visualization in scientific computing. *SIGGRAPH Computer Graphics Newsletter* **21** (6)
McGuigan F J (1957) An investigation of several methods of teaching contour interpretation. *Journal of Applied Psychology* **41**: 53–7
McMaster R B, Thrower N J (1987) University cartographic education in the United States: tracing the routes. *Proceedings International Cartographic Association Conference, Morelia* **2**: 343–59
McNamara T P, Ratcliff R, McKoon G (1984) The mental representation of knowledge acquired from maps. *Journal of Experimental Psychology, Learning, Memory and Cognition* **10** (4): 723–32
Miller A I (1984) *Imagery in Scientific Thought: creating 20th century physics*. Birkhauser, Boston
Miller G A (1956) The magical number seven, plus or minus two: some limits on our capacity for processing information. *Psychological Review* **63**: 81–97
Moellering H (1980) Strategies of real time cartography. *The American Cartographer* **7** (1): 67–75

Monkhouse F J, Wilkinson H R (1971) *Maps and Diagrams: their compilation and construction*. 3rd edn. Methuen, London
Monmonier M S (1974) Measures of pattern complexity for choropleth maps. *The American Cartographer* **1** (2): 159–69
Monmonier M S (1988) Geographical representation in statistical graphics: a conceptual framework. *Proceedings of the American Statistical Association Conference Section on Statistical Graphics*, pp. 1–10
Mosteller F, Tukey J W (1977) *Data Analysis and Regression*. Addison-Wesley, Reading Massachusetts
Muehrcke P C (1986) *Map Use*. JP Publications, Madison Wisconsin
Muehrcke P C (1990) Cartography and geographic information systems. *Cartography and Geographic Information Systems* **17** (1): 7–17
Muller J-C (1983) Ignorance graphique ou cartographie de l'ignorance. *Cartographica* **20**: 17–30
Muller J-C, Johnson R D, Vanzella L R (1986) A knowledge based approach for developing cartographic expertise. *Proceedings of the 2nd International Symposium on Spatial Data Handling, Seattle*. International Geographical Union, Ohio, pp. 557–71

Navon D (1977) Forest before trees: the precedence of global features in visual perception. *Cognitive Psychology* **9**: 353–83
Nickerson B G, Freeman H R (1986) Development of a rule-based system for automatic map generalization. *Proceedings of the 2nd International Symposium on Spatial Data Handling, Seattle*. International Geographical Union, Ohio, pp. 537–56

Olson J M (1972) Autocorrelation as a measure of complexity. *Proceedings American Congress on Surveying and Mapping*. ACSM, Falls Church Virginia, pp. 111–19
Olson J M (1979) Cognitive cartographic experimentation. *The Canadian Cartographer* **16** (1): 34–44
Olson J M (1986) Color and the computer in cartography. In: Durrett H J (ed.) *Color and the Computer*. Academic Press, Boston, pp. 205–21

Pavlidis T (1982) *Algorithms for Graphics and Image Processing*. Computer Science Press, Rockville Maryland
Peterson M (1979) An evaluation of unclassed cross-line choropleth mapping. *The American Cartographer* **6** (1): 21–37
Peuquet D J (1984) Conceptual framework and comparison of spatial data models. *Cartographica* **21** (4): 66–113
Phillips R J, DeLucia A, Skelton N (1975) Some objective tests of the eligibility of relief maps. *Cartographic Journal* **12** (10): 39–46
Pinker S (1985) Visual cognition: an introduction. In: Pinker S (ed.) *Visual Cognition*. MIT Press, Cambridge Massachusetts: pp. 1–96

Raisz E J (1931) The physiographic method of representing scenery on maps. *Geographical Review* **21**

Raisz E J (1948) *General Cartography*. McGraw Hill, New York

Rasmussen J (1986) *Information Processing and Human Machine Interaction: an approach to cognitive engineering*. North Holland, New York

Rhind D W, Openshaw S (1987) The BBC Domesday project: a nationwide GIS for $4448. *Proceedings of AUTOCARTO 8*. ASPRS/ACSM, Falls Church Virginia, pp. 595–603

Richardson L F (1961) The problem of contiguity: an appendix to the statistics of deadly quarrels. *General Systems Yearbook* **6**: 139–87

Robertson P K (1988) Choosing data representations for the effective visualization of spatial data. *Proceedings of the 3rd International Symposium on Spatial Data Handling, Sydney*. International Geographical Union, Ohio, pp. 243–52

Robinson A H (1953) *Elements of Cartography*. Wiley, New York

Robinson A H (1961) The cartographic representation of the statistical surface. *International Yearbook of Cartography* **1**: 53–184

Robinson A H (1962) Mapping the correspondence of isarithmic maps. *Annals of the Association of American Geographers* **52**: 414–25

Robinson A H (1975) Map design. *Proceedings of AUTOCARTO 2*. ASPRS, Falls Church Virginia, pp. 9–14

Robinson A H (1976) Revolutions in cartography. *Proceedings of the American Congress on Surveying and Mapping*. ACSM, Falls Church, pp. 403–08

Robinson A H, Bryson R A (1957) A method for describing quantitatively the correspondence of geographical distributions. *Annals of the Association of American Geographers* **47**: 379–91

Rosinski R R (1977) *The Development of Visual Perception*. Goodyear Publishing, Santa Monica California

Samet H (1988) Recent developments in the use of hierarchical data structures for image databases. *Proceedings Ausgraph 88, Melbourne*, pp. 207–19

Scott D J (1987) *Mental Imagery and Visualization: their role in map use*. Unpublished PhD thesis, Department of Geography, London School of Economics

Sedgewick R (1984) *Algorithms*. Addison-Wesley, Reading Massachusetts

Shortridge B G, Welch R B (1980) Are we asking the right questions? *The American Cartographer* **7** (1): 19–24

Shortridge B G, Welch R B (1982) The effect of stimulus redundancy on the discrimination of town size on maps. *The American Cartographer* **9** (1): 69–80

Slocum T A (1983) Predicting visual clusters on graduated circle maps. *The American Cartographer* **10** (1): 59–72

Smith G H (1935) The relative relief of Ohio. *Geographical Review* **25**: 272–84

Steinke T R (1987) Eye movement studies in cartography and related fields. *Cartographica* **24** (2): 40–73

Taylor R M, Hopkin V D (1975) Ergonomic principles and map design. *Applied Ergonomics* **6** (4): 196–204

Thomas E N (1960) Maps of residuals from regression: their characteristics and use in geographical research. *Geographical Publication No 2*. University of Iowa

Tobler W R (1961) *Map Transformations of Geographical Space*. Unpublished PhD dissertation, Department of Geography, University of Washington

Tobler W R (1973a) Choropleth maps without class intervals? *Geographical Analysis* **3**: 262–65

Tobler W R (1973b) A continuous transformation useful for redistricting. *Annals, New York Academy of Sciences* **219**: 215–20

Tobler W R (1977) *Bidimensional Regression*. Department of Geography, University of California, Santa Barbara

Tobler W R (1979) Smooth pycnophylactic interpolation for geographical regions. *Journal of the American Statistical Association* **74** (357): 519–35

Tufte E R (1983) *The Visual Display of Quantitative Information*. Graphic Press, Cheshire Connecticut

Tukey J W (1977) *Exploratory Data Analysis*. Addison-Wesley, Reading Massachusetts

Verplank W L (1988) Graphic challenges in designing object orientated user interfaces. In: Helender M (ed.) *Handbook of Human Computer Interfaces*. Elsevier, North Holland

Wainer H, Thissen D (1981) Graphical data analysis. *Annual Review of Psychology* **32**: 191–241

Walters D K (1987) Selection of image primitives for general-purpose visual processing. *Computer Vision, Graphics and Image Processing* **37**: 261–98

Walters D K (1990) Computer vision. In: Ralston A, Reilly E (eds.) *Encyclopedia of Computer Science and Engineering*. Van Nostrand Reinhold, New York, forthcoming

Warntz W (1964) A new map of the surface of population potentials for the United States, 1960. *Geographical Review* **54**: 170–84

Weibel R, Buttenfield B P (1988) Map design for geographic information systems. *Proceedings GIS/LIS '88*, Vol. 1. ASPRS/ACSM, Falls Church Virginia pp. 350–9

Weizenbaum J (1976) *Computer Power and Human Reason*. Freeman, San Francisco

Williams R L (1960) Map symbols: the curve of the gray spectrum – an answer. *Annals of the Association of American Geographers* **50**: 487–91

Witkin A P (1986) Scale-space filtering. In: Pentland A P (ed.) *From Pixels to Predicates*. Ablex Publishing, Norwood New Jersey, pp. 5–19

Wrigley N (1985) *Categorical Data Analysis*. Longman, London

Yarbus A L (1967) *Eye Movement and Vision*. (Tr. Haig B). Plenum, New York

Yoeli P (1982) Cartographic drawing with computers. *Computer Applications* **8**

Zusne L (1970) *Visual Perception of Form*. Academic Press, New York

29

COMPUTER NAME PLACEMENT

H FREEMAN

A map is a medium of communication that uses labelled graphics to convey spatial relationships among point, line and area features to its viewer. Generating the graphics – the points and lines that represent the features – has long been managed effectively with well-understood computer techniques. However, the placement of the features' labels or names has proved remarkably resistant to computerization. Positioning the names requires that unambiguous association be achieved between each name and its corresponding feature, that overlap among names be avoided, that cartographic conventions be obeyed and that a high level of aesthetic quality be achieved. The chapter describes the development of a fully automatic, computerized name placement system that approaches the performance of that of an expert cartographer and is applicable to a wide range of map scales and feature densities.

INTRODUCTION

One of the most challenging problems of computerized cartography is that of placing names on a map. This problem, which was first addressed nearly 20 years ago (Yoeli 1972), has only in recent years succumbed to reasonably satisfactory solution. The symbols for which names must be placed – whether they represent area features, line features, or point features – can occur with such a rich diversity and complexity that it is difficult to establish a fixed set of procedures for labelling them. Cartographers have over centuries refined the art of manual name placement and achieved a high level of quality to which the map-reading public has become accustomed. For the performance of an automatic name placement system to be considered satisfactory, it must come close to matching the quality of manual name placement. It simply will not do for a map to be labelled like an engineering drawing!

Some of the subtleties of name placement are illustrated by Fig. 29.1. The (fictitious) island's name spans the entire area feature and conforms to its shape; the association between name and feature is instantaneous and devoid of possible ambiguity. Towns situated on the coast have their name placed 'in the water' to emphasize their coastal location. The placement of names for unbounded area features (e.g. Egabrag Forest) provides an intuitive feeling of the extent and shape of the named feature.

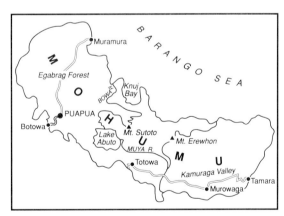

Fig. 29.1 Illustration of map name placement.

As a medium of communication, a map must quickly and effectively communicate spatial relationships to its viewer, whether he or she is an expert skilled in the art of map reading or a layperson. Much progress has been made in the past quarter century towards producing maps with the aid of computers. Map data are stored in large geographical databases from which they can be selectively accessed. Typically, the geographical data are stored separately for large quasi-rectangular geographical regions, bounded by constant-latitude and constant-longitude lines. The data for a particular map region can be 'windowed', or, if the desired region data overlap two or more stored regions, can be extracted by a combination of windowing and region joining.

When maps were produced manually, the process could easily take a year or more and the additional time of a month or so for name placement was not significant. Now that the graphics for a map can be produced in minutes with a computer, the addition of a month's time for name placement is intolerable, and this has placed urgency on the development of an effective automatic name placement procedure.

Except for the pioneering work of Yoeli (1972), automatic name placement did not receive much attention until the early 1980s, when Hirsch (1980) and Kelly (1980) made some noteworthy attempts at automatically placing names for point features. Other efforts that then followed in rapid succession were those of Basoglu (1982), Ahn and Freeman (1983), and Balodis (1983). Most of these early efforts addressed only the placing of point-feature names and their quality was well below that achievable through manual placement.

It was not until 1984 that a software system appeared that could handle the complete map name placement problem (Freeman and Ahn 1984); that is, could place names for area, line and point features. Also about that time, placement quality began to increase significantly, with some automatically labelled maps beginning to exhibit an aesthetic quality approaching that previously associated only with manual placement (Ahn and Freeman 1983). Improvements continued to be made in: (1) being able to place names for a wider range of map scales, from more than 1 : 25 000 to less than 1 : 5 000 000; (2) being able to handle maps with high feature densities; and (3) achieving near-manual aesthetic quality (Doerschler 1985a, 1985b; Doerschler and Freeman 1989).

The techniques developed during this period exhibited considerable diversity, although almost all used some kind of 'rule-based' approach. Some adopted an 'expert system' model in a fairly strict manner (Pfefferkorn *et al.* 1985) whereas others used this model only as a guide and deviated from it for the sake of improved computational performance (Freeman and Ahn 1984; Doerschler and Freeman 1989).

Name placement, especially for high feature density maps, can involve much searching to find an acceptable solution. Some researchers obtained good results by applying linear programming techniques to arrive at optimal spatial allocations of name placements (Cromley 1985, 1986; Zoraster 1986), although there is some question whether such techniques can be effectively applied to large maps, with tens of thousands of features.

Most of the effort in automatic name placement has been concerned with relatively standard topographic maps. However, some investigators have been concerned solely with special-purpose maps, such as those used for displaying census data or in oil exploration (Ebinger and Goulette 1989). Such maps are normally intended for use by personnel trained in a particular technical speciality and, therefore, less subject to demands for high aesthetic quality.

This chapter describes the results of a research programme, started in the early 1980s, to develop a fully automatic map name-placement software system. It begins with a description of the problem, a listing of the objectives to be achieved, and an explanation of why the task was so challenging. Two software systems, somewhat complementary in their underlying approaches, have resulted from the work. Both are rule-based systems, although for both emphasis was placed on computational efficiency rather than on programming orthodoxy. The discussion includes samples of results obtained and, finally, mentions some of the challenges that still remain.

THE NAME-PLACEMENT PROBLEM

The actual data stored in a geographical database can be regarded as being organized in the form of overlays, with each overlay representing a particular kind of geographical information, such as political boundaries, the highway network, the railway system, land use, hydrography, etc. To obtain a map containing specified geographical information for a selected region, the particular overlays that are to be assembled must be indicated.

It would simplify the burden of name placement if the task could be done once for each map overlay and then stored together with the graphics. Unfortunately this is not feasible, as is illustrated by Fig. 29.2, where a new map, represented by the inner rectangle, is to be windowed out of a stored larger geographical region, represented by the outer rectangle. Placing names prior to windowing can create the problems shown: the town Weston will lie in the chosen region, but its name will be cut away. Conversely, for the town Kingston, the name will be retained even though the town will not. Also, the name for Longnameville needs be moved to avoid having it truncated.

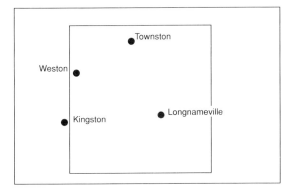

Fig. 29.2 Illustration of why name placement must be delayed until after map boundaries and overlays have been determined.

Moreover, the problem does not just occur along the boundaries of the desired region. In designing a map choices must be made from a large set of available overlays, each corresponding to a different category of features. It is unlikely that a particular map would ever utilize all available overlays. If names were to be placed *a priori*, then a placement configuration would have to be designed that would avoid overlap across all available overlays. This would have an unnecessarily restrictive impact on permissible feature density. Further, for maps using only a small number of overlays, the placement of the feature names would not be optimal. It thus follows that name placement must be deferred until after the following have been established: (1) the boundaries of the desired map; (2) the feature overlays to be included; and (3) the desired map scale. The last named will determine the density of the geographical features that can be accommodated.

General placement guidelines

There are certain broad guidelines that apply to all name placement. These have been well described by Imhof (1962). They are:

G1. There must be an easily perceived, unambiguous association between a feature and its name.

G2. There should be no overlap among names, or among names and point features.

G3. Area feature names should be spaced to conform to the feature's shape and extent.

G4. Line feature names may overlap the feature, although in that case the feature should be interrupted.

G5. Names should be distributed 'naturally'; there should be no regular pattern to the placement, nor should names be excessively clustered.

G6. For small-scale maps using projections such that the parallels (constant-latitude lines) are shown curved, all otherwise horizontally placed names must conform to the curvature of the parallels.

G7. Placement must conform to applicable standards and conventions.

Because the name of an area feature should span the feature and conform to its shape, its placement is the most constrained and most challenging. The placement of point-feature names is much easier, constrained only by the requirement that the name be situated close to the feature. The greatest degree of freedom exists for line features. This suggests that any automatic system for name placement must first address the placement of area-feature names, then point-feature names and, finally, line-feature names. It is helpful if the system can backtrack in case difficult-to-resolve situations are subsequently encountered (e.g. if a point-feature name cannot be satisfactorily placed without moving an area-feature character). Three cases are considered, in decreasing order of degree of placement freedom.

PLACEMENT OF AREA-FEATURE NAMES

The accepted guideline for placing an area-feature name is to have the name span the entire area and conform to its shape, with the size of the font chosen to provide an indication of relative importance. In this way not only is a strong association between the feature and its name established, but also an implicit perception of the size, extent and importance of the feature is conveyed to the reader. In practice this cannot always be achieved because an area feature may have an irregular shape or may consist of disjoint parts (e.g. an archipelago). The problem becomes even more complicated when an area feature does not have an explicit boundary (e.g. the Kamuraga Valley in Fig. 29.1). In such a case, placement of the feature name (together with choice of font size and character spacing) is especially critical as it is the only means by which the extent of the area can be communicated to a reader.

There is the possibility that the boundary of an area feature is more important than the area that it encloses. This is likely to be the case for large areas in a map with which the reader can be presumed to be familiar, but for which he or she may want to know exact boundary locations. The problem then converts to one of linear-feature name placement, with correspondingly increased placement freedom. An illustration of this given in Fig. 29.3. In Fig. 29.3(a), area-feature name placement is used, as would be appropriate if there are many such areas within the map. In Fig. 29.3(b), the boundaries are treated as linear features, as would be more suitable if there are only two or three such areas. In such a situation the reader is likely to be familiar with them and it is the precise boundary locations that are of primary importance.

Bounding of an area feature

The first step in area-feature name placement is explicit identification of the boundary of the area to be labelled, and, preferably, also of the boundaries of the immediately adjacent bounded areas. If an area has no politically or naturally defined boundary, as is likely to be true for a forest, a valley, an ethnic region, or an archipelago, means must be found for developing such a boundary first.

Next the shape of the area must be studied to

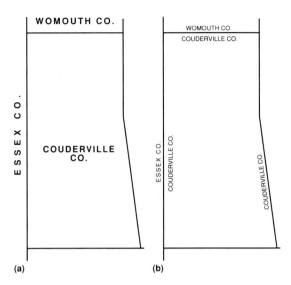

Fig. 29.3 Two alternate schemes for placing area-feature names: (a) normal area-preference name placement; (b) case where the area boundary is deemed more important than the area itself.

decide on the location of the name baseline. The latter is the line (likely to be curved) along which the letters of the name are to be placed with a spacing that causes the name to span as much of the area as possible. The specific rules, which are based on those described by Imhof (1962), are as follows:

A1. Horizontal name placement is acceptable unless such placement would clearly fail to convey the feature's dominant shape. The selection of horizontal placement is influenced by the choice of name placement for neighbouring area features of the same category; that is, horizontal name placement may be selected even if it is only marginally appropriate for the area under consideration but is optimal for the neighbouring area features.

A2. If the scale and projection of the map are such that constant-latitude lines need be shown curved, then all horizontal baselines must be curved to parallel the constant-latitude lines.

A3. The name baseline should closely parallel the dominant centre line of the area. If curved, the curvature must be monotonic (i.e. it may not contain a point of inflection).

A4. The name should be spaced out to extend

from boundary to opposing boundary, with end spacings equal to one-and-a-half times the width of the character spacing.

A5. Non-horizontally placed names must be curved. Such placements should preferably start along the horizontal and then curve away, rather than curve toward the horizontal.

A6. Neighbouring area-feature names of the same category should be curved similarly unless the features' shapes are significantly different.

A7. If an area feature has a severely curving shape, or consists of two or more disjoint parts separated by water, the name may be placed to fall partially outside the confines of the area. However, the name for one area feature should not overlap, even partially, another labelled area feature.

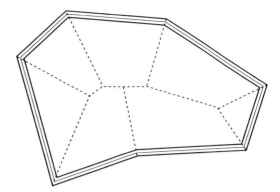

Fig. 29.4 The skeleton of an area feature.

Determination of name baseline

The selection of the name baseline is a challenging task because of the infinite variety of shapes that can be encountered. Initially, a simple test is performed to determine whether horizontal name placement is satisfactory. Such a test would be based on: (1) the out-of-roundness of the area, as determined by the area/perimeter ratio; and (2) the (horizontal) width/height ratio and the placement form, if any, already selected for neighbouring area features of the same category.

If horizontal placement is counterindicated, the 'skeleton' of the feature is computed (Blum 1967). The skeleton can be intuitively described as the locus of points at which uniformly advancing wavefronts from the boundary would meet, as illustrated in Fig. 29.4. Because the skeleton is strongly influenced by minor boundary irregularities, it is necessary to smooth the boundary first. This is accomplished by means of a boundary-approximation algorithm (Ramer 1971).

The skeleton will normally consist of a number of branches and the algorithm requires that the most dominant of these be identified. Typically this will be the longest branch, or the concatenation of two or three long branches that do not differ much in orientation. A smooth curve is next fitted to the selected branch or branches and extended to the boundary at both ends. The actual name-placement baseline will be a line paralleling this but offset by half the height of the selected font's upper-case characters.

The characters can now be placed on the baseline. They should be uniformly spaced along the line, with one-and-one-half times such a space between the boundary and the first and last characters.

Placement evaluation and iteration

Because of the wide variety of possible area-feature shapes, the foregoing method will at times produce totally unacceptable results. This requires that the placement be evaluated *a posteriori*. A special procedure for this has been developed which tests placement quality against a set of quality measures, such as: (1) conformance with dominant shape; (2) excessive baseline curvature; (3) nearness of characters to boundary; (4) possible conflict with the placement of neighbouring similar-category feature names; and (5) inappropriateness of baseline orientation for the particular position on the map. If the evaluation indicates unacceptable placement quality, the process is repeated using one of a number of alternate baseline determination algorithms instead of the skeleton method (Lacroix 1984; Nastelin 1985; Doerschler and Freeman 1989). If none of the algorithms yields acceptable placement, the one yielding the least undesirable one is chosen. Although the objective of the effort is fully automatic placement, it is also recognized that a small amount of subsequent manual editing may at times be called for.

The aesthetic quality of name placement means

the ease and naturalness with which the visual appearance of a name accomplishes its purpose of identifying the feature it is intended to label. A reader should not have to study a name and its surroundings to establish with which feature it is associated, nor to determine the extent of the labelled area feature. In this sense, aesthetics is not mere prettiness, but a key ingredient that enables a map to communicate spatial relationships to its viewers. A map that is of high aesthetic quality is functionally effective.

PLACEMENT OF POINT-FEATURE NAMES

The placement of point-feature names differs significantly from that of area-feature names and is a less demanding task. The primary rules are:

P1. A name must be closely associated with the point feature, preferably by having the initial character of the name in close proximity to the feature.

P2. There is a slight preference for placement somewhat above the feature rather than below it.

P3. There may be no overlap with either names or point features; however, a name may be placed in the inter-character spaces of an area-feature name. Also a name may overlap a line feature, in which case the line feature is normally interrupted.

P4. If a point feature is located near a line feature, or near the boundary of an area feature, the name should be placed on the same side as that of the feature.

P5. For point features located along a large body of water, the name should be placed 'in the water' (this is an exception to the previous rule).

P6. Names should be placed horizontally, to read from left to right. This means that the names will be placed straight for large-scale names and will curve with the curvature of the parallels if the map scale is such that the latter must be shown curved.

P7. There may be no spreading out of characters, nor providing of extra space between words.

P8. In tight situations, a name may be hyphenated, with the two parts placed above each other, or it may be abbreviated. As a last resort, a name may be placed some distance away, with a leader pointing from the name to the feature.

Of the above rules, the only ones that present some difficulty are the avoidance of overlap and the requirement that a name be placed on the same side of a neighbouring line feature as that of the point feature. To avoid overlap, a placement rectangle is defined for each point feature and then overlap with either point features or other names is examined. This is illustrated in Fig. 29.5. Figure 29.5(a) shows the placement rectangle for a point feature. It consists of all the permissible name placements in the area surrounding the feature, with the numbers indicating the relative order of preference (additional but less desirable placements exist, such as centred and directly above or below).

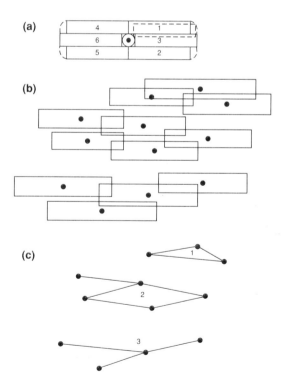

Fig. 29.5 The point-feature placement rectangle.

In Fig. 29.5(b) a number of point features are shown, each with its associated placement rectangle. Considerable overlap exists, although the features clearly separate into three disjoint clusters, as is apparent from the graph in Fig. 29.5(c). For each cluster a search must be conducted to determine the optimum placement for the names in that cluster. Cost values are assigned to the permissible name positions for each feature and a graph search is then conducted to find the minimum-cost solution (Nilsson 1971; Freeman and Ahn 1987).

The reason for Rule P4 is illustrated by Fig. 29.6. The city of Goodtown, to the east of the Tavas River, is properly labelled. However, placement of the name for Poorville is clearly improper. Note how violation of the rule weakens the perceived association between the point feature and the area within which it is located. For the town of Costania, Rule P5 applies and emphasizes the town's coastal location.

Fig. 29.6 Placement of point-feature names relative to linear features.

PLACEMENT OF LINE-FEATURE NAMES

The placement of line-feature names is the least constrained as there is usually no single preferred location and it is, therefore, not taken up until both area-feature and point-feature name placement is complete. The major rules governing line-feature placement are as follows:

L1. Line-feature names must not overlap point features or point-feature names.

L2. The name should reasonably conform to the feature's curvature but should never curve in more than one direction.

L3. Placement should normally be such that the linear feature acts as a base line to the name.

L4. For long linear features, name placement may have to be repeated a number of times.

L5. Names should not have their characters spread out, although extra spacing can be added between words.

L6. Names should not be placed too close to the end points of a linear feature.

L7. Placement of names for vertically oriented features should generally be such as to read upward in the left half of a map and downward in the right half, as such placement presents a preferred aspect angle to the reader.

L8. Abbreviations may be used freely for generic names where the meaning of such abbreviations would be clear from the context (e.g. 'R.' for 'River').

L9. Contour elevation numbers should be placed to break the associated contour lines and to read upward with increasing elevation.

To place a line-feature name, the feature is searched along its extent for permissible locations, taking due note of the above rules. When a satisfactory location is found, the corresponding section of the line feature is extracted and smoothed to serve as the baseline for the name. For multiple-word names, the spacing between words can be adjusted to avoid overlap with other names.

Rule L9, which concerns contour-line labelling, is illustrated by Fig. 29.7. The elevation labels are placed to read upward in the map for increasing elevation, to associate upward reading with the increase in elevation. Just the opposite would be in order for decreasing elevations below sea level.

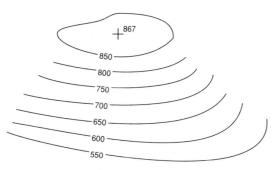

Fig. 29.7 Illustration of elevation contour-line name placement.

RASTER-BASED VERSUS VECTOR-BASED METHODS

For maps of moderate feature density, a vector-based approach can be fast, efficient and yield results of a quality that is barely distinguishable from that which a skilled cartographer might generate with manual placement. However, the vector-based approach starts to run into difficulties for maps of very high feature density, where avoidance of undesirable overlap becomes the dominant consideration. Instead, a raster-based approach, although inherently more complex, is better suited for ferreting out the intricate interleaving needed to squeeze a large number of names and symbols into a small space.

In the research project described here, which extended over a period of nearly six years, both a vector-based and a raster-based system were developed. Both were designed for fully automatic operation and were written in FORTRAN77 for computational efficiency. The vector-based system, AUTONAP (Freeman and Ahn 1984), consisted of about 13 000 lines of code. The raster-based system (Doerschler 1987) is more than 10 times bigger. An example of the results of the vector-based system is shown in Fig. 29.8. The reader should note especially the placement of area-feature names and how these conform to the shape and extent of the associated features.

Maps produced with the raster-based system are shown in Figs. 29.9 and 29.10. The map of Fig. 29.9, of which only a proportion has been redrawn for publication here, was originally generated at a scale of 1 : 1 160 000. It consisted of nearly 4000 features and required the placement of almost 18 000 characters. A large-scale map, a portion of which has been redrawn as Fig. 29.10, was generated to a scale of 1 : 26 000.

CONCLUSION

Automatic name placement, until a decade ago a formidable challenge, appears now well on the way to solution. The remaining tasks involve primarily refinement of the rules, development of more sophisticated procedures for resolving conflicts among rules, and the design of additional rules to cope with specialized thematic and topographic map configurations or with unusual map projections. Such efforts would be aimed mainly at obtaining a level of placement quality that would be indistinguishable from the best that manual placement can offer.

Some good software engineering work would help to reduce computation time, although even with presently existing software this is not excessive. The situation would be different if real-time name placement were required for on-line GIS systems; this particular problem has not been addressed as yet.

REFERENCES

Ahn J, Freeman H (1983) A program for automatic name placement. *Proceedings of AUTOCARTO 6.* ASPRS, Falls Church Virginia, pp. 444–53

Balodis M (1983) Positioning typography on maps. *Proceedings, ACSM Fall Convention, Salt Lake City.* ACSM, Falls Church Virginia, pp. 28–44

Basoglu U (1982) A new approach to automated name placement. *Proceedings of AUTOCARTO 5.* ASPRS, Falls Church Virginia, pp. 103–12

Blum H (1967) A transformation for extracting new descriptors of shape. In: Wathen-Dunn W (ed.) *Models for the Perception of Speech and Visual Form.* MIT Press, Cambridge Massachusetts, pp. 362–80

Cromley R G (1985) An LP relaxation procedure for annotating point features using interactive graphics. *Proceedings of AUTOCARTO 7.* ASPRS, Falls Church Virginia, pp. 127–32

Cromley R G (1986) A spatial allocation analysis of the point annotation problem. *Proceedings of the 2nd International Symposium on Spatial Data Handling.* International Geographical Union, Ohio, pp. 38–49

Fig. 29.8 Part of a small-scale map redrawn for publication. An example of fully automatic name placement using a vector-based system (produced by A. Heard).

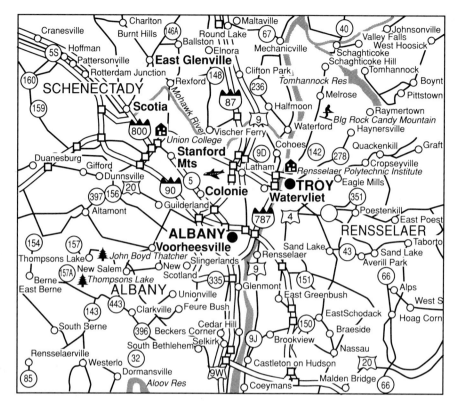

Fig. 29.9 Part of a high-density map redrawn for publication. An example of fully automatic name placement using a raster-based system (produced by J.S. Doerschler).

Doerschler J S (1985a) Map data production for an expert name placement system. *Technical Report IPL-TR-073*. Image Processing Laboratory Rensselaer Polytechnic Institute, Troy

Doerschler J S (1985b) Data structures required for overlap detection in an expert map name placement system. *Technical Report IPL-TR-077*. Image Processing Laboratory Rensselaer Polytechnic Institute, Troy

Doerschler J S (1987) A rule-based system for dense-map name placement. *Technical Report SR-005*. CAIP Centre, Rutgers University 08855–1390

Doerschler J S, Freeman H (1989) An expert system for dense-map name placement. *Proceedings of AUTOCARTO 9*. ACSM/ASPRS, Falls Church Virginia, pp. 215–24

Ebinger L R, Goulette A M (1989) Automated names placement in a non-interactive environment. *Proceedings of AUTOCARTO 9*. ACSM/ASPRS, Falls Church Virginia, 205–14

Freeman H, Ahn J (1984) AUTONAP – an expert system for automatic name placement. *Proceedings of the 1st International Symposium on Spatial Data Handling*. Universitat Zurich-Irchel, Zurich, pp. 544–69

Freeman H, Ahn J (1987) On the problem of placing names in a geographic map. *International Journal of Pattern Recognition and Artificial Intelligence* **1** (1): 121–40

Hirsch S A (1980) *Algorithms for Automatic Name Placement of Point Data*. Unpublished MSc thesis, Department of Geography, State University of New York, Buffalo

Imhof E (1962) Die Anordnung der Namen in der Karte. *Annuaire International de Cartographie II*. Orell Fuessli Verlag, Zurich, pp. 93–129

Kelly P (1980) *Automated Positioning of Feature Names on Maps*. Unpublished MSc thesis, Department of Geography, State University of New York, Buffalo

Lacroix V (1984) An improved area-feature name placement. *Technical Report IPL-TR-064*. Image Processing Laboratory, Rensselaer Polytechnic Institute, Troy

Nastelin J (1985) Optimization of baseline determination for area map annotation. *Technical Report IPL-078*. Image Processing Laboratory, Rensselaer Polytechnic Institute, Troy

Nilsson N J (1971) *Problem Solving Methods in Artificial Intelligence*. McGraw-Hill, New York

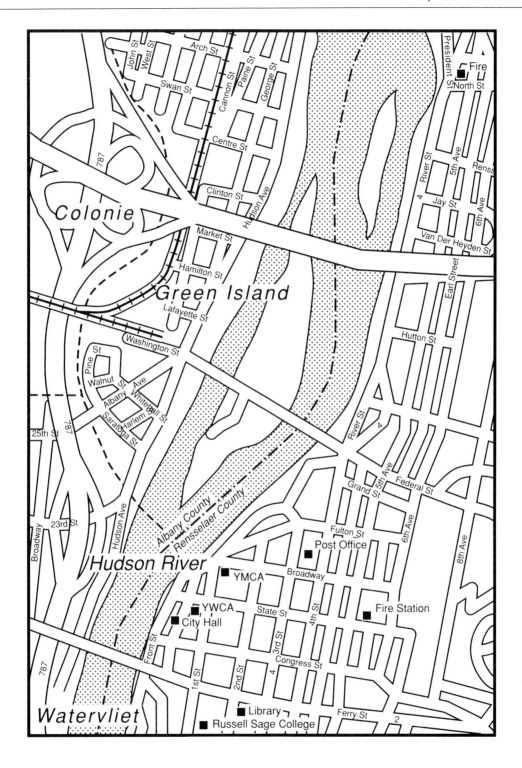

Fig. 29.10 Part of a large-scale map redrawn for publication. An example of fully automatic name placement using a raster-based system (produced by J.S. Doerschler).

Pfefferkorn C, Burr D, Harrison D, Heckman B, Oresky C, Rothermel J (1985) ACES: a cartographic expert system. *Proceedings of AUTOCARTO 7*. ASPRS, Falls Church Virginia, pp. 399–407 and *Cartographic Journal* **15** (2): 72–7

Ramer U (1971) An iterative procedure for the polygonal approximation of plane curves. *Computer Graphics and Image Processing* **1** (3): 244–56

Yoeli P (1972) The logic of automated map lettering. *Cartographic Journal* **9** (2): 99–108

Zoraster S (1986) Integer programming applied to the map label placement problem. *Cartographica* **23** (3): 16–27

30

GENERALIZATION OF SPATIAL DATABASES

J-C MULLER

Generalization procedures to transform and model spatial databases for analytical or display purposes are notably absent within the realm of functions presently available in GIS. The many motivations for generalization include the need for economy, data robustness, multipurpose use, and display and communication. Generalization has an impact on data quality characterized by locational and attribute accuracy, consistency, and completeness. A number of concepts, procedures, and techniques have been developed for generalizing spatial databases and the most important raster and vector approaches are reviewed. A catastrophic approach to generalization is proposed, which shows the way objects undergo sudden rather than smooth changes in the way they are depicted. Finally, the merits of several holistic approaches to generalization are discussed.

INTRODUCTION

Generalization, in its epistemological sense, is a process which attempts to establish the universality of a statement (Hawkins 1983). Such meaning needs to be re-emphasized at a time when there seems to be a confusion between the operational aspects of the procedure and its ultimate goals.
Generalization, of course, is about 'the selection and simplified representation of detail appropriate to the scale and/or purpose of a map' (ICA 1973). But this definition is misleading because it confuses the tools and the objectives. A map, and more generally a spatial database, is a statement about geographical reality and generalization is a process which tends to universalize the content of that statement. Whether generalization is viewed as a transformation operation (Tobler 1966), or as a modelling operation (Hake 1975), its goal is to establish what is universally of interest for the scientist. It is an information-oriented process. These transformation and modelling procedures are subject to a number of constraints, such as maximizing information content while observing specific restrictions (e.g. minimum scale, minimum geometrical dimension and minimum accuracy standards). Generalization is performed for map display and communication purposes, but also, and perhaps more importantly, for analytical purposes. The necessity to understand at which scales or range of scales spatial processes occur is one of the driving forces behind generalization today.

Attempts have been made recently to automate the procedures of generalization. This development, in turn, has led to efforts to formalize a process which had remained highly intuitive and subjective. The identification of rules and their implementation into a system which can simulate the work of a traditional cartographer is one of the most difficult challenges facing the GIS research agenda of the 1990s. Whether those efforts will be successful is still uncertain. Robinson, in the second edition of *Elements of Cartography* (1960: 132) already alluded to these difficulties: 'many cartographers have attempted to analyze the processes of generalization, but so far it has been impossible to set forth a consistent set of rules that will prescribe what should be done in each instance. It seems likely that cartographic generalization will remain forever an essentially creative process, and that it will escape the modern tendency towards standardization....'

This chapter reviews the procedural and technical issues of computer-assisted generalization, against the interlacing background of scale and spatial resolution. The motivations for generalization are considered first. Various concepts of space which correspond to various levels of generalization are envisaged. Database requirements and data models for generalization are then mentioned, with a focus on the vector and the raster models. In the section on procedural tools, a distinction is made between heuristic and rule-based solutions to computer-assisted generalization. The methods of vector and raster generalization are then outlined. This is followed by discussion of independent versus scale dependent databases and the idea of a comprehensive, holistic solution to the generalization of spatial databases. Finally, some brief conclusions are presented.

MOTIVATIONS

Generalization is not only motivated by a reduction of scale representation, as it sometimes appears to be in cartographic manuals (Swiss Society of Cartography 1987). Such a point of view overemphasizes the display and legibility constraints in map production. Generalization consists of the application of a transformation to spatial data and is prompted by four main requirements:

1. *Economic requirements*. Our knowledge of the universe is determined by our data collection procedures which are influenced by financial and technological constraints. The only source for which a database is made available is usually already generalized through discrete sampling procedures. Obvious examples are databases created from existing digitized maps, or data aggregated into census units. Another example is the generalization performed during the acquisition of original topographic information by a topographer or a photogrammetrist. Simplification, selection, geometrical and conceptual combinations are carried out which result in a reduction of information. This process, termed object generalization, produces a primary model of the real world, that is, a topographic basic map referred to as a 'Digital Landscape Model' (DLM) (Grunreich 1985).

2. *Data robustness requirements*. Errors in spatial databases occur at all stages, during data collection, data recording and data manipulation. The sources of error are human, instrumental as well as methodological (i.e. wrong classification procedures). It would be a fallacy to believe that an increased precision in measurement or more extensive data sampling would decrease the chances of error in interpretation. The reverse is probably true, because the true value of a single observation whose measurement is affected by random errors may be hidden through some high-frequency disturbance. Hence, we need generalization in order to filter out the errors and consolidate the trends. A generalized trend is more robust than an individual observation. Smoothing operations to generalize curves and surfaces make this assumption; for instance, there is the notion that if the observations had been more accurate the curve would have been smooth (Whittaker and Robinson 1944).

3. *Multipurpose requirements*. Official surveying and mapping organizations must provide up-to-date topographic–cartographic information for a variety of users (regional planners, geoscientists, ecologists, military, etc.). This information must also be provided at different scales, since natural or human features display scale-dependent properties 'and those levels at which scale-dependence becomes apparent vary from one feature to the next' (Buttenfield 1989: 81). Hence information must be filtered and modelled according to usage and scale significance. In order to adhere to the economic principle of singular acquisition and multiple use, a data flow from the original DLM to a lesser resolution or special purpose DLM must be established through model generalization (Grunreich 1985).

4. *Display and communication requirements*. This is probably the best known motivation for generalization. Decision making in the context of GIS relies heavily on the use of communication maps. These maps represent spatial information collected usually at larger scales through different means, including ground survey, analytical photogrammetry and satellite imagery. Generally, there is a need for data compaction or data compression since the

amount of data collected is much more than can be visually communicated. The notion that there are physical limits to the amount of information that can be displayed on a map is shared by both traditional cartographers and the GIS community. Some thresholds have been suggested (a maximum density of ten graphical marks per square centimetre), beyond which a map becomes illegible (Bertin 1967). The 'heretical alternative: plot everything, allow features to overlap or merge, producing blobs of clutter in high density areas, and then allow the user to zoom in to resolve the ambiguity' (Mark 1989: 69) is intellectually interesting, but requires a computer environment and would not allow the recognition of pattern generating processes at smaller scales. Furthermore, the scale reduction of objects and forms cannot be continued indefinitely. It should terminate when the limit of acuity of the human eye is reached (Swiss Society of Cartography 1987). Therefore, generalization must be used to select, simplify, exaggerate and symbolize information in order to afford communication and understanding. Cartographic symbolization of the digital landscape model leads to the 'Digital Cartographic Model' (DCM) as shown in Fig. 30.1.

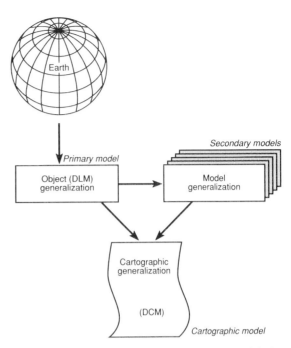

Fig. 30.1 Models derived from the primary Digital Landscape Model (DLM) are special purpose secondary models of reality. They are free of cartographic representational information. Both primary and secondary models may be used to create a cartographic representation of a Digital Cartographic Model (DCM) through the process of cartographic generalization (after Grunreich 1985).

GENERALIZATION IN DATA QUALITY

Data quality is usually characterized by four components:

1. Location accuracy
2. Attribute accuracy
3. Consistency
4. Completeness

Generalization of spatial databases may influence some of these components. Locational accuracy usually decreases through the process of generalization. Lower local accuracy may in turn affect attribute accuracy. As the locations of objects become more uncertain their attributive characterization becomes fuzzier and more complex. Generalization may also affect completeness, since the information is reduced to major trends (e.g. series of parcels may display an anomaly which disappears when looking at them as a community). Consistency could be affected by uneven applications of spatial or temporal abstractions, with inconsistent disappearance or emergence of scale- or time-dependent features. The potentially negative (and positive) effects of generalization on data quality will be considered in the broader framework of relationships between generalization, scale and accuracy, and resolution.

Generalization and scale

A fundamental issue is to decide at which scale the information should be generalized. Ideally, it would be useful to be able to vary the scale according to the level of precision required. Naturally-occurring features often require larger scale for their portrayal than cultural features. This raises intriguing problems of metric representation, but the idea of variable or elastic scaling within a single map is not new (Muller 1982). One might ignore the problem of representation and vary the level of precision (which amounts to a scale variation) at which spatial objects, such as highways and rivers, are encoded in the database. 'Asking the scale of a database is in fact making a query about the lineage of the database' (NCGIA 1989: 13). This lineage is not the same for all objects, some being better documented and requiring more codes of description than others.

Generalization and accuracy

Both statistical and cartographic generalization affect the accuracy of spatial databases. Statistical generalization is a filtering process whose aim is spatial modelling of attributive information attached to locations. Objective constraints, which are imposed during the process of statistical generalization, are the preservation of the spatial mean, variance and form of the distribution. A wrong classification, for instance, may hide the characteristic pattern of a statistical surface. Furthermore, a classification may create crisp boundaries between areas whose boundaries are naturally fuzzy.

Cartographic generalization, the aim of which is visualization, can affect locational accuracy to a great extent. Features may be displaced and their original shape may be distorted. Several criteria have been applied to estimate the accuracy of cartographic generalization, such as minimum vector displacement, minimum change in angularity, preservation of parametric characteristics, and self-similarity. Examples of parametric characteristics are the overall sinuosity of a line, the relationship between x,y coordinate point values and point distance from the origin, as well as the 'structure signatures' proposed by Buttenfield (1986). In contrast to angular deviations and areal displacements, which are derived from a cross-comparison between two lines, a parametric characteristic describes the intrinsic geometry of a single line. A different parameter which could be used is the relationship between line length and resolution of measurement. When the relationship is plotted linear on a log–log graph (power function), the line is said to be statistically self-similar (see Gatrell 1991 in this volume for further discussion). Ideally, the geometrical structure of self-similar objects should not be affected by generalization (Muller 1987). Another criterion is the preservation of relational accuracy. Whereas locational accuracy is partly lost, orientation and connectedness of objects in space must be saved. Quite often spatial databases are created from existing digitized maps. Somehow these digital versions are revered and there is a tendency to believe that they are more accurate than their analogue counterparts. Those databases are only a result of cartographic generalization, however, and are not as reliable as those products referred to earlier as Digital Landscape Models.

Generalization and resolution

Spatial resolution refers to the ability of a recording system in distinguishing closely spaced objects. Clearly, in the case of databases, spatial resolution is determined by the quality of the sampling which was conducted by the data collector (see Fisher 1991 in this volume). A fine sampling will provide better resolutions than a crude one. Furthermore, data may be generalized by resampling at coarser levels of resolution. Hence, generalization will tend to increase the size of the smallest detectable feature.

The way data are sampled is usually not homogeneous, and spatial resolution varies from place to place. The assumption here is that spatial objects and processes vary in size and have different wavelengths. Hence, the data must be reported using different spatial resolutions. For instance, triangulated irregular networks (Weibel and Heller 1991 in this volume) are usually more efficient than uniform sampling grids because they can adapt to the variable conditions of the terrain. Another example is the changing spatial resolution of the county network in the United States. The spatial subdivisions reflect the historic evolution of population settlement and density (Fig. 30.2). Resampling into bigger units, which would reduce or remove (such as through a square lattice) the variance of spatial resolution between east and west, would relatively over-resolve the data in some parts and under-resolve in others. Hence, generalization through coarser sampling must be applied by relative equal amounts taking into account the changing size of the original sampling network. In effect, this means preserving the variance of the original sampling resolution.

As generalization tends to reduce resolution,

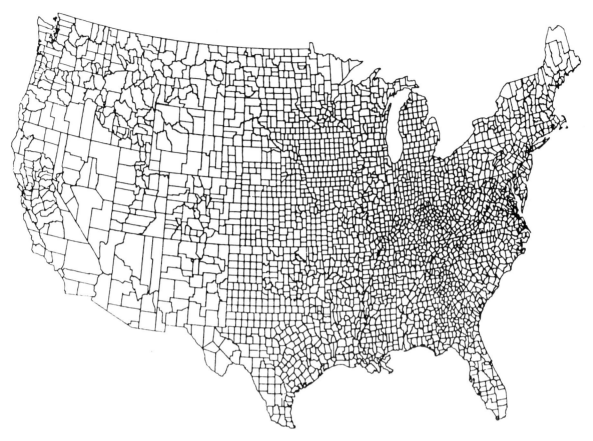

Fig. 30.2 County map of the United States. Uneven sampling reflects uneven population densities as well as historical differences (earlier settlement in the east).

some features which were apparent at larger scale disappear, while others which were previously concealed may emerge. Those are resolution-dependent or scale-dependent features and the purpose of generalization in this case is to uncover those underlying patterns which would otherwise remain hidden. A coarser resolution or a higher level of generalization may provide more explanation over the variance of a spatial variable than finer resolution levels (Tobler and Moellering 1972).

CONCEPTUAL MODELS

Conceptual models are used to provide a framework in which to express spatial relationships. There are basic categories which are recurrent in the GIS literature, such as vector space or raster space, and which reflect the form in which data are basically encoded, organized and manipulated (Egenhofer and Herring 1991 in this volume). We have become so entrenched in those categories that we now have raised the procedures and techniques of handling spatial data to the status of epistemological models. The basic distinction between vector and raster formats also has ramifications in the methods which are used to generalize spatial databases. Those methods will be reviewed in an independent section.

Other categories of space, which are of concern to spatial scientists and which represent different levels of generalization, are the metric, topological and graph-theoretic representations (Gatrell 1991 in this volume; see also Fig. 30.3). The metric space describes the distance relations between spatial objects, and constitutes the lowest level of abstraction. Due to the physical limitations of our tools to measure and represent the position of spatial objects, a discretization takes place which is part of generalization.

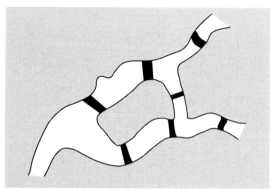

Metric representation

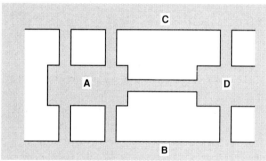

Topological representation

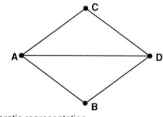

Graph-theoretic representation

Fig. 30.3 Three representations of Königsberg, USSR, corresponding to three different levels of generalization.

The topological space, instead, deals with the existence of connectedness relations between points in space. For instance, connections between areas, across boundaries or between settlements via a set of transport links may be described independently of distance. Hence, spatial databases can be derived which do not include any metric information.

Topological relations may be encoded through tables (Figure 30.4).

A higher level of abstraction is reached through graph-theoretic representations. Here we are only concerned with the conceptual structure of spatial information depicted through graphs in which nodes express concepts and arcs denote relations (Sowa 1984). Neither the metrics nor the topology are preserved. A graph-theoretic mapping of market places (concept) and first-order links (relation) is an example of such representation.

Note that these categories of space illustrate various degrees of generalization at the conceptual level, and do not concern the problems of generalization at the display level. They are meant to provide a theoretical foundation for data structuring. Data structures are determined by requirements in accessibility and manipulation of information whose degree of generality may vary according to the type of GIS analysis which must be performed.

Database requirements

One basic requirement is that 'the database must support a wide variety of products covering various geographical extents across the globe' (Guptill 1989:439). The user must be able to access information at various levels of detail, from local to global scales, and at various levels of abstraction, from individual objects to the 'envelope' of their classes. In other words, geometrical, topological and thematic relationships between 'real world objects' must be stored or be derivable computationally (Rhind 1988) for geometrical description as well as for hierarchical classification and thematic retrieval of spatial entities.

Another requirement is that a database must be based on spatial proximity at both the metric and topological levels. This characteristic is fundamental for accessing local information, identifying neighbours or performing cartographic generalization.

Finally, the database must be object oriented to afford an object-oriented programming approach to generalization. In an object-oriented environment, procedures are bound to the object itself, that is, objects are active and execute their methods (i.e. generalization) directly in response to a received message. Messages usually consist of a destination (i.e. shoreline), an operator name (i.e.

Generalization of Spatial Databases

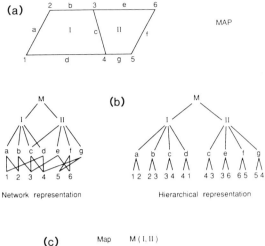

Fig. 30.4 Various ways of representing topological relations: (a) cartographic form; (b) network and hierarchical diagrams; (c) table.

simplification), and a parameter (i.e. bandwidth tolerance). In an object-oriented system, all objects belong to classes. In turn, each class of objects defines instance variables (location, size, colour) which must be instantiated when an individual member of that class (say, a house in the class residential area) is created. Finally, each class is one descendant of a more general class (settlement) that defines the common properties of all its children. Object-oriented programming has gained much popularity in the area of computer graphics. Its main advantage seems to be the ability to support the abstraction of both data and procedures, afford the interaction between objects, and ensure consistency through inheritance trees (Luger and Stubblefield 1989). For instance, the various representations, at different scales, of a single feature may be linked so that they 'inherit' common characteristics. Any update on one of the representations could then appear concurrently across all map-scale layers in the database (Mark 1989). Much work will have to be done, however, in defining what the semantic of a truly object-oriented approach for automated generalization should look like.

Database models

The data models holding the best promises for automated generalization have been based on hierarchical concepts. Strip or binary tree representations (Samet 1984), where a curve is recursively subdivided until a predetermined value of the strip width is reached, lead naturally to the automated generalization of lines.

Hierarchical tessellations of space, whether in the form of triangulation, square or hexagonal tiles, also hold promise. Where space is modelled by quadtrees areas may be visited using an N-shaped path based on the Peano curve (Peano 1890; Morton 1966). Using Peano relations, spatial queries can be resolved elegantly and quickly using Peano tuple algebra according to the rule: a quadrant (--> a tuple) can always be split into four quadrants (tuples). This may be expressed in the form: PR (node#, Peanokey, size). Here, PR denotes a Peano relation; node#, the region name or number; Peanokey, the Peano key of the quadrant; size, the size of the quadrant. This kind of locational relationship may be advantageous for generalization operations, since spatial resolution (determined by the quadrant size), is not a constant but varies according to the density of spatial information. Highly dense information leads to the formation of small quadrants, whereas large quadrants indicate sparse information. Hence, a spatial query of all tuples of small size would yield all areas where more generalization is required. The geodesic hierarchy, referred to as the Quaternary Triangulation Mesh (QTM), is another structure which lends itself to automated generalizations: 'Larger tiles (shorter geocodes) have fuzzier locations than smaller ones (longer codes), and thus have less positional certainty. This property can help one distinguish boulders and fenceposts as monuments' (Dutton 1989:48).

There is a need for comparative research to evaluate the performance of database models for automated generalization.

463

PROCEDURAL TOOLS

GIS which are presently available on the market offer few capabilities for database generalization. Generalization functions are mostly limited to line thinning, dissolving lines and merging attributes, as well as smoothing of digital terrain models. Those functions are usually *ad hoc* and are not supported by a theoretical foundation. For instance, decisions based on spatial autocorrelation are rarely applied in the process of merging polygons. Aggregation to higher administrative units is mainly achieved on the basis of a statistical classification, without considering neighbourliness relationships. Herzog's generalization method based on adaptive filtering processes is a step in the right direction (Herzog 1988). The method assumes spatial autocorrelation and takes into account the value of a polygon weighted by the values of its neighbours as well as the length of their common boundaries in order to reach a decision on aggregation. Generalization has defied GIS designers because contrary to other GIS functions, such as polygon overlay or edge matching, the procedures are not well defined and are difficult to formalize.

Manual versus automated generalization

There is much to be learned from manual methods in the geographical and cartographic disciplines, since statistical and cartographic generalization have been used successfully for many years by human experts. Statistical generalization is spatial modelling for the purposes of spatial analysis, whereas cartographic generalization is performed for the purpose of visual communication (Brassel and Weibel 1988). The first type of activity may also be prompted by the needs of communication, but is usually undertaken for other purposes, such as the extraction of a subset of an original data set for data analysis. The second type of activity, on the other hand, is *always* used for graphic display. There are three kinds of knowledge which are required for generalization:

1. *Geometrical*, where size, form, distance and connectedness are assessed.
2. *Structural*, where the underlying generating processes which gave rise to a phenomenon are analysed.
3. *Procedural*, where appropriate tools (including simplification, selection, classification and symbolization) are identified.

Objective and subjective thinking are both involved in manual generalization. They do not play an equal role, however, and it is obvious that statistical generalization provides a better basis for objective thinking than cartographic generalization. Statistical generalization intervenes mainly in the thematic (attribute) domain and automated solutions based on classification or seriation have already been developed (Muller and Honsaker 1983). One example of techniques applied in the temporal domain is time series analysis. Cartographic generalization, on the other hand, is a conglomerate of many different processes which are difficult to bring into one unified, formalized theory. This is particularly true for those kinds of transformations which are traditionally dependent on visual judgement, such as symbolization. Most efforts towards automation have concentrated on the geometrical aspects of cartographic generalization using various types of procedures. Recent research advocates a rule-based approach to handle the structural and conceptual aspects of the generalization process.

The procedural approach

The procedural approach uses algorithms for the execution of numerical operations. Algorithms have rules expressed in the form of 'IF THEN' statements. They are called conditional statements and are based on string or numeric matching. To arrive at a solution, one must execute those statements in an order which is predetermined by the logic of the program.

The algorithmic or heuristic approach to generalization is typically a very specialized, narrow solution to a specific problem. The thinning of geographical lines through selection and simplification algorithms is a well-known example. Numerous algorithms to perform this task have been published and continue to be published (Zycor 1984; Li 1988; Thapa 1988). Most notable techniques involve the use of epsilon filtering (Perkal 1965) and bandwidth encoding (Peucker 1975). They are based on the view that a digital line is an ordered set of two or more coordinate points. An improvement to this rather simplistic approach is a generalization based on parameterization and self-similarity of the line which attempts to retain its global parametric constituents. The parametric approach was prompted by the idea that the geometrical structure of a geographical line is representative of a physical or human process, and that this structure must be preserved. The Psi–s plot, for instance, has been used by O'Neill and Mark (1987) to differentiate river meanders. The Psi–s plot is a single valued function where the orientation angles at points along the line are plotted against s, the cumulative curvilinear distance along the line. Other types of parameterization were suggested by Buttenfield (1986) who proposed analysis of the 'structure signatures' of a graphic line in terms of its intrinsic geometry. The preservation of the parametric form of a geographical line during the process of generalization is basically a valid argument but is an approach difficult to implement. The possibility, for instance, of adjusting the tolerance parameters of simplification algorithms by using the parametric description of digital lines has not yet been realized.

Fractal geometry provides another powerful method for describing the nature of complex lines. Mandelbrot (1982) identified two properties of irregular forms – self-similarity and fractal dimensionality. A line is self-similar if a part of the line, when isolated and subsequently enlarged, displays similar characteristics to the whole line. Accordingly, fractal dimensionality, a value which is determined by the complexity of the line, remains unchanged whether the line is displayed at a small or large scale. Hence, the preservation of fractal dimensionality is another criterion which could be used to assess the performance of a generalization algorithm (Muller 1987; Kubik and Frederiksen 1983). This criterion may, however, only be applied when a line is statistically self-similar. Efforts based on heuristic solutions have been applied to the generalization of built-up areas, using classification and template matching methods (Meyer 1987). These heuristic methods are being perfected including automated generalization of Digital Landscape Models (Jager 1987).

All the above techniques are based on mathematical procedures and deal with generalization as if it were exclusively a geometrically rooted problem. Cartographic features are not, however, simply geometrical objects. They have geographical meaning and their significance depends on a variety of factors, such as the map's purpose and user's needs. Hence, we need to look at the substantive content of a database as well.

The rule-based approach

Rule-based methods, as the name indicates, are also a collection of 'IF THEN' statements. These statements relate to symbolic matching rather than string matching, where symbols represent facts of reality. Symbols are always related to data, that is, there is no separation between data and program. Non-procedural or data driven language programs are executed by implementing the rules which represent the relationship between the facts. A rule-based approach implies that our knowledge of the generalization process can be formalized into a chain of reasoning paths, each leading to a particular decision or procedure for generalization to take place. Every reasoning path consists of information involving interdependencies and trade-offs which must be made in order to arrive at a solution. The reasoning process can be expressed naturally by IF..., THEN... or THEN..., IF structures (Jankowski and Nyerges 1989). An example of a simple rule may be:

IF BUILDINGS	(OBJECT, SIZE, DISTANCE, SCALE)
AND OBJECTS	(APARTMENT COMPLEX)
AND SIZE	(SMALL)
AND DISTANCE	(THRESHOLD)
AND SCALE	(1 : 20 000)
THEN MERGE	(BUILDINGS)

One could systematize the rules for selection on the basis of user's needs and map functionality. Each single feature in the database could be rated using information requirements identified by user's needs and by examining the relationship of base map elements to thematic features. Necessity factors would be derived for each feature, for each scale, and for each theme (Richardson 1988). Rating matrices could be calculated accordingly, and would function as look-up tables (Fig. 30.5). It is clear that a rule-based approach represents a quantum step beyond the purely algorithmic treatment, including both the tools and the choice of tools to effect generalization.

A catastrophic approach to cartographic generalization

There is a functional relationship between thematic realm, map purpose, scale, and map utility. Cadastral information, for instance, falls within a particular range of scales (say between 1 : 5000 and 1 : 10 000) for which map utility is maximized. For another thematic realm, say land use, the optimum map scale may fall between 1 : 20 000 and 1 : 100 000. The uncertainty about the accuracy of individual observations, and the need to lower random fluctuations and data noise, play an important factor in the determination of scale. Scales which are too large may lead to a representation which is unwarranted by the quality of data sampling or the spatial resolution of the data source. The functional dependence of map utility according to scale, thematic realm, data quality, and map purpose is a topic which requires further study. A simple paradigm may be proposed where utility increases with increasing scales, until a point is reached at which utility starts decreasing (Muehrcke 1969). The curve describing this relationship is probably not a smooth one, as the symbolic representations of cartographic features may change drastically from one scale to another.

That generalization is a phenomenon which involves large variations in the ways nature is abstracted is nothing new. It would be of interest, however, to identify those points where a small variation in scale may cause large variations in the geometrical and substantive content of a map. Those points where a 'catastrophic change' may occur would help us to identify more sharply the range of scales which are suitable for a particular type of map use. The term 'catastrophic' is used here to indicate that the generalization process is discontinuous with respect to scale. It is used as an analogy to catastrophe theory (Thom 1973), although this is concerned with description of the operation of whole systems rather than single elements.

A distinction must be made between geometrical generalization, which involves essentially simplification, enlargement and displacement, and conceptual generalization, which

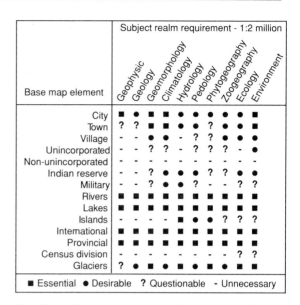

Fig. 30.5 Rating of base map elements according to subject realm for national atlas maps at a scale of 1 : 500 000 (Richardson 1988: 45).

is effected by selection, classification, typification and symbolization.

It is possible to differentiate between the two classes of generalization by using the classical definition of functional mapping. In one-to-one and onto transformation, one-to-one means that distinct elements in map A have distinct images in map B. In mathematical terms, $F: A \to B$, that is if $f(a) = f(a')$, $a = a'$. Further, the function F is said to be onto if every $b \in B$ is the image of some $a \in A$. A function which is both one-to-one and onto is called bijective. It is interesting to note that geometrical generalization (with the subsets simplification, enlargement and displacement), according to the definitions above, is both one-to-one and onto. In contrast, conceptual generalization (with the subsets selection, classification and symbolization) is not a bijective transformation. Depending on the cases, it is either one-to-one or onto. Namely:

	one-to-one mapping	onto mapping
Selection	0	1
Classification	0	1
Symbolization	1	0

A conceptual generalization involving all subsets of conceptual transformations is neither one-to-one, nor onto. Such a transformational view of the process of generalization has already been discussed by Morrison (1974). Reformulated in this context, it is possible to argue that a catastrophic change occurs precisely when the transformation process is no longer bijective. A typical topographic map series in the western hemisphere can be used to illustrate this concept.

1. Below and until 1 : 10 000 scales, an isomorphic mapping is applied. The corresponding maps are like topographic plans for which no generalization or only negligible generalization is necessary (Imhof 1937). The map resolution affords the representation of all natural and man-made features of the visible landscape at true scale.

2. Representations at 1 : 20 000 scale provide the first threshold of an abrupt change. Street and road widths are exaggerated; buildings are simplified, combined and displaced; parcels are regrouped and classified into land use categories. Hence, the crossing from isomorphic mapping to generalized mapping signals the first 'catastrophe'.

3. The representations from 1 : 20 000 until 1 : 200 000 scales show objects which are, for the most part, gradually generalized through the process of geometrical, bijective transformations. Rivers and contours are further simplified; settlements are regrouped and exaggerated; rock outcrops are sketched; slopes and hills are shaded; roads are classified and symbolized. The number of classes of objects which are displayed decreases slowly, but the density of objects per square map unit increases. Until now, the representation of the landscape remains fairly realistic, simulating to a large degree what the landscape looks like from an airplane gaining increasing altitude.

4. The next scale in the topographic/geographical map series is 1 : 500 000. At this point, a second 'catastrophe' may be observed. The geometrical form of many spatial objects vanishes and is merely replaced by an abstract or figurative symbol which has little or no resemblance with the original geographical shape. A town, for instance, is simply shown by a circle; an airport is suggested by the sketch of a plane. It is as if geometrical transformations culminate at a point where qualitative (as opposed to quantitative) changes become suddenly

necessary. The map has evolved from a realistic to a highly symbolized representation with an increasing predominance of communication road networks and place names. Such a map bears little resemblance with the corresponding landscape photographed from the viewing platform of a satellite flying at an altitude of about 50 miles (assuming a camera focal length of about 15 cm). Generalization is mostly conceptual, controlled by a set of transformational tools whose combination leads to a mapping which is neither one-to-one, nor onto. Note that the major challenges for an automated solution to the problem of generalizing topographic databases come from the middle scale range, between 1 : 20 000 and 1 : 200 000, where both geometrical and conceptual transformations must be combined (Fig. 30.6).

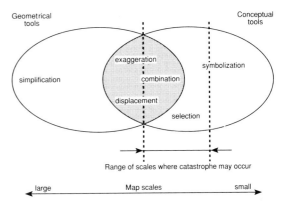

Fig. 30.6 Transformation processes according to map scale. Catastrophe may occur when there is a shift from geometrical to conceptual generalization. Note that some of the procedural tools may be geometrical as well as conceptual. This yields a fuzzy area between the geometrical and conceptual domains.

The threshold point which separates geometrical and conceptual generalization does not occur at the same scale for every cartographic feature and for every thematic realm. Cartographic features of little relevance to the thematic realm, such as a church on a transportation map, may become symbolized sooner than normally expected. In other words, catastrophes occur at different scales for different objects, and are determined by map theme and map function. The relationships between scale, geometrical accuracy, and substantive meaning may be depicted by a manifold of N dimensions (N object classes) describing the behaviour space of map content (Fig. 30.7). This manifold translated into rules may lead the way towards a truly integrated approach to generalization.

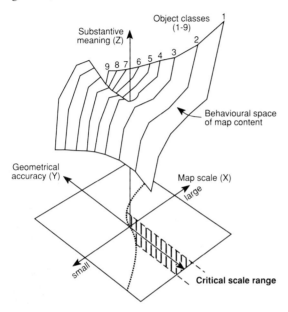

Fig. 30.7 A hypothetical plot describing the relationship between map scale, geometrical accuracy and the substantive meaning of object classes in x,y,z space. The manifold has nine dimensions describing the variation in substantive meaning of each of the nine feature classes. A critical scale range has been identified when a fold catastrophe occurs for geometrical accuracy and substantive meaning for feature classes ranging from 5 to 9.

VECTOR- AND RASTER-MODE GENERALIZATION

Vector and raster models express different perceptions of geographical space. Whereas vectors represent geographical objects qualified by their attribute location, raster cells are spatial 'containers' without regard for any objects, attributes, or properties of space within them (Mark and Csillag 1989). Therefore, it is expected that the underlying principles of vector-mode and raster-mode generalization will be different.

Vector-mode generalization

Vector-mode generalization focuses on the simplification, selection and enhancement of linear objects. The lines may be open or closed depending on the topology of the objects they describe (e.g. rivers versus administrative units).

Eighty per cent of all objects (points, lines, and areas) which are found on a typical medium-scale topographic map consist of lines (United Nations 1989). This, in part, explains the considerable interest raised by the issue of line generalization. Numerous algorithms to perform line generalization have been published in the literature (McMaster 1987). Criteria applied to estimate the quality of generalization usually follow the idea of structure preserving transformation. The structure of the line may be characterized by a number of parameters, such as amplitude and density of high- versus low-frequency details and fractal dimension. In the case of self-similar lines, for instance, a non-modifying structure approach to line generalization would preserve fractal dimension (Fig. 30.8). Applying geometrical criteria to evaluate a geometrical approach to generalization leads to a tautology since both methods and judgement are rooted in the same way of reasoning. Surely, the criteria applied to evaluate the generalizations of a shoreline or a political boundary cannot be the same. Instead, non-geometrical criteria derived from geographical meaning and spatial processes must be applied. A purely geometrical approach to line generalization has been increasingly criticized. More sophisticated methods will be required which take into account the phenomenal aspects of a line (whether it is a 'legislated' line or a mathematically derived contour, for example). Furthermore, rules must be provided which can support 'intelligent' decisions for line selection and elimination.

The amalgamation of smaller polygons into larger polygonal units requires a selective elimination of arcs and represents a special case of vector-mode generalization. The operation is based on the statistical generalization of the associated attributes.

The generalization of buildings and built-up areas has received much attention among German cartographers. Efforts have concentrated on the

Generalization of Spatial Databases

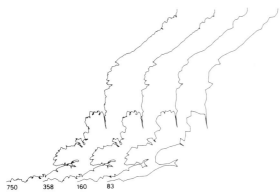

Fig. 30.8 Fractal dimension preserving transformations. The walking generalization algorithm is used to preserve fractal dimension (Muller 1987). Numbers indicate the numbers of points describing the generalized lines.

development of computer-assisted procedures for the generalization of large-scale topographic land survey maps up to about 1 : 5000. The generalization of linear features (e.g. streets) and areal features (e.g. building blocks) can be largely automated (Fig. 30.9). Original attempts were based on geometrically derived algorithmic procedures, such as widening, displacement, simplification and omission (Staufenbiel 1973; Hoffmeister 1978). Recent efforts, however, include structural–conceptual generalization as well as using pattern recognition and expert systems for more complex cartographic generalization models (Grunreich 1985; Powitz and Meyer 1989).

Raster-mode generalization

Whereas vectors lead naturally to an object-oriented approach to generalization, rasters provide the framework for generalization of the attribute component of the data. This is largely a difference of points of view, however, since operationally generalization of objects and their attributes is closely intertwined. One emphasizes data representation while the other is concerned with classification of phenomena. Both affect each other, as has been illustrated in the case of polygon filtering: generalization of the attribute leads to a generalization of the object and vice versa. 'Any treatment of one in isolation from the other will have a high risk of misrepresenting the phenomenon' (Mark and Csillag 1989:68).

McMaster and Monmonier (1989) recognize

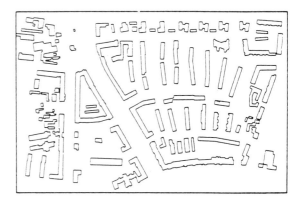

Original map (1/5000)

Generalized map

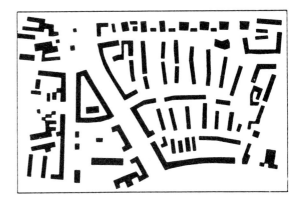

Fig. 30.9 Computer-assisted simplification of building outlines (from Lichtner 1979).

four basic classes of raster-mode generalization operators, including structural, numerical, numerical categorization, and categorical. The following review is a close paraphrase of their article. The logical unit of data in a raster model is a cell (or resel, Tobler 1984), each of which has an associated set of properties. Most of the raster-based generalization techniques were developed in the fields of digital image processing and terrain analysis using some type of moving kernel or window to filter or smooth regions of an image (see Weibel and Heller 1991 in this volume).

Structural generalization involves a reorganization of raster data where the number of cells is modified while the shape of the cell remains unchanged. Usually (but not necessarily) new larger cells are created through resampling of a grid at a lower level of resolution.

Numerical raster generalization, also termed spatial filtering or convolution, reduces the complexity of an image by smoothing the deviations, or reducing the variance of the matrix. The basic operator is a moving kernel or moving-window mask of weighting factors (Fig. 30.10). Each new value of a cell in the output image is computed by multiplying the original neighbouring values by the corresponding coefficients within the kernel. A new image is created by moving the kernel throughout the original matrix. Numerous types of kernels with different weighting factors have been proposed (Jensen 1986). Some of them are dedicated to image smoothing, whereas others (Laplacian filters) are used for image sharpening. In the latter case, one may consider the process of generalization as one of selection where only the edges and boundaries of an image are represented.

$$\begin{pmatrix} 1/9 & 1/9 & 1/9 \\ 1/9 & 1/9 & 1/9 \\ 1/9 & 1/9 & 1/9 \end{pmatrix} \begin{pmatrix} 1/10 & 1/10 & 1/10 \\ 1/10 & 1/5 & 1/10 \\ 1/10 & 1/10 & 1/10 \end{pmatrix} \begin{pmatrix} 1/16 & 1/8 & 1/16 \\ 1/8 & 1/4 & 1/8 \\ 1/16 & 1/8 & 1/16 \end{pmatrix}$$

Fig. 30.10 Typical masks for low pass filtering of an image.

The term numerical categorization, also called image classification in the remote sensing literature, is introduced by McMaster and Monmonier to emphasize the process of classification in the context of numerical generalization. The outcome is a reduction of the data – from ratio level to nominal level – and a change in the visual complexity of the image towards a more interpretable product. Three techniques are commonly used for image classification:

1. Minimum distance to means
2. Parallelepiped
3. Maximum likelihood classification

Categorization involves various operations such as the merging of details into more generic categories (e.g. residential, commercial, and industrial lands are collapsed into 'built-up land'), the aggregation of fine grid cells into coarser ones and various attribute-change operators which alter the attributes for selected isolated cells in order to create a map with a simpler structure. For each of those subcategories, there are many ways of performing categorization. For instance, aggregation may regroup cells on the basis of a non-weighted or neighbourhood-weighted kernel (halo bias, Fig. 30.11), or eroding techniques may alter the attributes of the cells differently depending on the decision rules adopted (Fig. 30.12). Furthermore, the combination of eroding and thickening techniques in raster format may be used to simplify areal forms (Lay and Weber 1983). Here, instead of using a structuring element or kernel to determine whether a pixel must be kept or

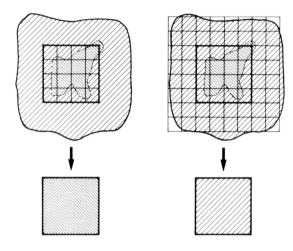

Fig. 30.11 Raster generalization. Finer cells are regrouped into a coarser cell whose attribute is determined by a non-weighted aggregation (left) or a neighbourhood-weighted aggregation (right) (from McMaster and Monmonier 1989).

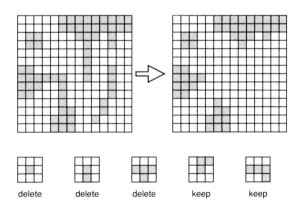

Fig. 30.12 Raster generalization. Erode smoothing (top) based on five decision rules for the moving 3 * 3 kernel (bottom) (from McMaster and Monmonier 1989).

deleted, a blanket of uniform thickness p is added or subtracted at the periphery of a given form. The association between the form A and its characteristic function $K(x)$, may be expressed as:

$k(x) = 1, x \, A$
$k(x) = 0, x \epsilon \, A$

A thickening blanket B is applied to A to yield a new form C:

$C = U(x + y)$ with $x \epsilon \, A, y \epsilon \, B$

An eroding blanket B' of the same thickness p may be subsequently applied to C to yield A':

$A' = U(x - y)$ with $x \epsilon \, A, y \epsilon \, B'$

Generalization occurs when:

$\Sigma k(y) < \Sigma k(y)$
$y \epsilon \, B' \quad y \epsilon \, B$

that is, some pixels of B have been added to A to provide the new generalized form A' (Fig. 30.13 a). It is possible to reverse the operation by using blanket B to erode, and then blanket B' to thicken. Again, generalization occurs if:

$\Sigma k(y) < \Sigma k(y)$
$y \epsilon \, B' \quad y \epsilon \, B$

that is, some pixels of B subtracted from A were not recovered after adding B' (Fig. 30.13b).

Thickening and eroding operations may be repetitively applied in any sequence using different blanket thicknesses in order to arrive at a satisfactory result (Fig. 30.14). These techniques are reminiscent of the epsilon band of Perkal (1965) and could be potentially useful for the generalization of volumetric objects as well.

As mentioned earlier, vectors are boundary oriented, whereas rasters are area oriented. A hybrid approach to generalization would combine those two formats in order to combine their operational powers, possibly at a cost of redundant data storage. The raster strategy is ideally suited for contextual analysis, and would contribute greatly to the vector-based approach to generalization, particularly in the removal of spatial conflicts between vector elements.

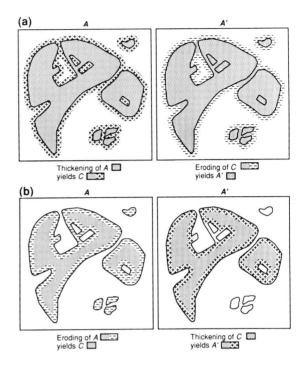

Fig. 30.13 Combinations of thickening/eroding (a) and eroding/thickening (b) techniques for the generalization of areal forms (after Jeworrek 1988). The thickness of the thickening and eroding blankets is held constant. Note that the output A' is very much influenced by the sequence order of the operations.

SCALELESS AND SCALE-DEPENDENT DATABASES

In a scaleless or scale-independent database, the main unit of data collection and revision is set at the level of precision for which the data were captured. Hence, the data are as good as the source. Data collected from ground surveys may be called scale independent, since the notion of scale only appears when those data are being transcribed for analytical or representation purposes, on to a space which is smaller (or larger) than the original surveyed space.

A derived notion for scale-independent databases is the ability to produce cartographic representations at multiple scales from one single source of data, previously referred to as the digital landscape model. Hence, it would be possible to move freely from one level of detail to another appropriate to the scale of display or the precision of data analysis. In order to support multiple

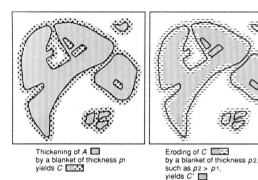

Thickening of C' by a blanket of thickness $p3$, such as $p3 = p2 - p1$, yields A'

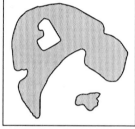
New image A', generalized representation of the original image A

Fig. 30.14 Thickening and eroding blankets used repetitively with blankets of different thicknesses (examples from Jeworrek 1988).

representations from one single source, an object-oriented data structure combined with generalization operators and decision rules must be implemented. Ideally, it should be possible to operate information extraction and generalization in real time by 'zooming in and out' at any place in any sequence and magnitude. This futuristic notion of scale-independent spatial databases has yet to be realized.

A pseudo-version of the scaleless database concept is a hierarchically structured database in which different scale-dependent layers of representation can be accessed without duplication of data. A pyramidal, multilevel data-adaptive structure to handle points, lines, and areas has been proposed by Jones and Abraham (1986). One obvious application is the hierarchical storage of multiple scale-specific versions of a line. Assuming that the points selected for small scale representations are always a subset of those used in larger scale representations, a structure may be provided which 'reduces the overhead of multiple line storage, while avoiding the access overhead of single, large scale storage' (Jones and Abraham 1986). The structure is a 'multiscale line tree'. When the tree is traversed for whichever level is deemed adequate for the scale requirement, only those points required are accessed. Such techniques merely afford the selection and retrieval of information which is considered relevant for a particular level of resolution, however. Other types of transformation for the purpose of generalization, such as amalgamation and transposition of objects, cannot be performed in this framework.

A third option is the multiple purpose, scale-specific storage scheme. Different maps produced at different scales are stored independently yielding scale-dependent databases.

The advantages and disadvantages of scaleless databases

There are at least three arguments for the development of scaleless databases:

1. *To avoid duplication in storage.* There are basic spatial features, such as coastlines, which may usefully be retained throughout all scale layers. In a scale-dependent environment, they will be stored partly or entirely a multiple number of times.

2. *To allow the production of flexible scale-dependent outputs.* Traditionally scales are fixed according to the standard map series (1 : 10 000, 1 : 25 000, 1 : 50 000, etc.). Any scale 'in between' (say, 1 : 33 333) could theoretically be derived from a scaleless environment. The output could be adjusted to a wide variety of modelling and mapping purposes in order to satisfy specific user needs.

3. *To ensure consistency and integrity between the various scale outputs.* With scale-specific databases, updates must be repeated for every version that has been archived. Update operations may become costly when the information is volatile, such as weather, water supply or transportation networks. There is also the increased chance of inconsistency through errors committed during the propagation of change from one digital representation to another. Object definition may vary according to scale and resolution (an industrial plant may

disappear or become part of an industrial zone) and is difficult to maintain consistently in multiple-scale databases.

There are technical as well as theoretical impediments against scale-independent databases. Among the technical obstacles are the very large overheads incurred every time a smaller scale retrieval occurs. These include both the quantity of data to be accessed and the generalization processing costs to bring the data to a suitable level of resolution. Moreover, solutions to generalization are not fully automated and usually require some further interactive editing before they can be used for output. If the same product is to be generated from a single database several times, the same manual edits will have to be repeated. On the other hand, in the multiple, separate, scale-specific database scheme, retrieval for analysis or mapping applications does not require any processing.

Most mapping agencies have adopted the multiple database strategy, although some are already providing, through adequate database design and topology, the potential for an eventual scaleless approach (Guptill 1989). The major impediment to scaleless cartographic databases is theoretical: database systems will remain limited to the option of multiple scale-dependent representations until appropriate algorithms and rule based programs for the generalization of linear and areal features are made available. This step will require a parallel and holistic approach to generalization, based on spatial relationships and geographical phenomena.

TOWARDS HOLISTIC SOLUTIONS?

Features to be generalized are multiple, including waterbodies, landforms, vegetation, railways, highways, roads and streets, boundary lines, settlements, and so on. Factors influencing generalization are many, including scale, user's requirements, source material, legibility constraints, symbol and colour conventions, technical reproduction capabilities, revision requirements, and so on. Procedural tools to perform generalization are multiple, including simplification, enlargement, displacement, combination, selection, symbolization, and exaggeration. But meaning is also multiple, depending on culture and economical goals. A French town is not simply a town. It is characterized by a geographical background which is different from an American city. A road is not simply a winding line. Depending on the user, its generalized representation may express a relationship to connectedness or a slope/distance ratio. A phenomenal approach to generalization away from a purely visual approach has already been advocated elsewhere (Mark 1989). It remains to be seen whether there is an all encompassing model which, like a general-purpose black box, could synoptically relate all features to all factors, tools, and meanings influencing the process of generalization. Would such a universe of formal rules and relationships help us in the practical implementation of programs for batch or semi-batch generalization? Such a model may be intellectually exciting, although it is doubtful whether it is attainable. Practical considerations force us to think in terms of modular processes which are object oriented (one generalization routine to handle names, another to handle lines, etc.) and purpose dependent (settlements will be handled differently whether the map is designed for navigation or tourist purposes). It is doubtful whether generalization programs could even be exported to different countries! (the ratio between lines and built-up areas in the physical/cultural landscape of North America is different from the one in Europe, and would imply a different treatment of the respective objects).

One domain where a holistic view of generalization must be maintained and applied is in the resolution of spatial conflicts. Spatial conflicts arise as a by-product of generalization, as the competition for space increases with a decrease in scale. The resolution of those conflicts requires a simultaneous view of different cartographic features, priorities, and tools. Knowledge-based search and parallel recognition techniques appear to hold the best promises for an automated solution in this field (Mackaness and Fisher 1987). It will be the challenge of future researchers to prove that complex solutions to computer-assisted generalization of spatial databases do not remain an academic issue but can be translated into operational terms.

CONCLUSIONS

This chapter has reviewed the conceptual and technical issues of generalization. It is concluded that generalization is an important issue in the design and operation of GIS. However, the development of robust and widely applicable methods remains as elusive as ever. Potential areas of future research offering most potential are the application of catastrophe theory, the integration of raster and vector approaches and phenomenal generalization.

REFERENCES

Bertin J (1967) *Semiologie Graphique*. Gauthier-Villars and Co., Paris

Brassel K E, Weibel R (1988) A review and conceptual framework of automated map generalization. *International Journal of Geographical Information Systems* 2: 229–44

Buttenfield B P (1986) Digital definitions of scale-dependent line structure. In: Blakemore M J (ed.) *Proceedings of AUTOCARTO London*. Royal Institute of Chartered Surveyors, London, pp. 497–506

Buttenfield B P (1989) Scale-dependence and self-similarity in cartographic lines. *Cartographica* 26: 79–100

Dutton G (1989) The fallacy of coordinates. *Multiple Representations. NCGIA Technical Paper 89–3* National Center for Geographical Information Analysis, Santa Barbara California, pp. 44–8

Egenhofer M J, Herring J R (1991) High-level spatial data structures for GIS. In: Maguire D J, Goodchild M F, Rhind D W (eds.) *Geographical Information Systems: principles and applications*. Longman, London, pp. 227–37, Vol 1

Fisher P F (1991) Spatial data sources and data problems. In: Maguire D J, Goodchild M F, Rhind D W (eds.) *Geographical Information Systems: principles and applications*. Longman, London, pp. 175–89, Vol 1

Gatrell A C (1991) Concepts of space and geographical data. In: Maguire D J, Goodchild M F, Rhind D W (eds.) *Geographical Information Systems: principles and applications*. Longman, London, pp. 119–34, Vol 1

Grunreich D (1985) Computer-assisted generalization. *Papers CERCO-Cartography Course*. Frankfurt a.M

Guptill S C (1989) Speculations on seamless, scaleless cartographic databases. *Proceedings of AUTOCARTO 9*. ASPRS, Falls Church, pp. 436–43

Hake G (1975) Zum Begriffsystem der Generalisierung. *Nachrichten aus dem Karten- und Vermessungswesen*. Sonderheft zum 65 Geburtstag von Prof Knorr: 53–62

Hawkins J M (1983) *Oxford Paperback Dictionary*. Oxford University Press, Oxford

Herzog A (1989) Modeling reliability on statistical surfaces by polygon filtering. In: Goodchild M, Gopal S (eds.) *Accuracy of Spatial Databases*. Taylor & Francis, London, 209–18

Hoffmeister E D (1978) Programmgesteurte Gebandegeneralisierung fur die Topographische Karte 1/25000. *Nachrichten aus dem Karten- und Vermessungswesen* 1 75: 51–62

Imhof E (1937) Das Siedlungsbild in der Karte. *Mitteilungen der Geographisch-Ethnographischen Gesellschaft*. Zurich, Band 37: 17–85

International Cartographic Association (1973) *Multilingual Dictionary of Technical Terms in Cartography*. Franz Steiner Verlag GMBH

Jager E (1987) Computer-assisted symbolization by raster data processing. *Nachrichten aus dem Karten und Vermessungswesen* 1 46: 61–70

Jankowski P, Nyerges T (1989) Design considerations for MaPKBS-Map Projection Knowledge-Based System. *The American Cartographer* 16: 85–95

Jensen J R (1986) *Introductory Digital Image Processing*. Prentice-Hall, Englewood Cliffs New Jersey

Jeworrek J (1988) *Untersuchungen zur automatischen generalisierung von flachen im Rasterdaten format*. Unpublished Master's Thesis, University of Hannover

Jones C B, Abraham I M (1986) Design considerations for a scale-independent cartographic database. *Proceedings 2nd International Symposium on Spatial Data Handling, Seattle*. IGU, Columbus, pp. 384–98

Kubik K, Frederiksen P (1983) Automatic generalization of contour lines. *Paper presented at Eurocarto II, Bolkejo, Norway* 9pp.

Lay H G, Weber W (1983) Waldgeneralisierung durch digitale Rasterdaten verarbeitung. *Nachrichten aus dem Karten und Vermessungswesen* 1 (92): 61–71

Li Z (1988) An algorithm for compressing digital contour data. *The Cartographic Journal* 25: 143–6

Lichtner W (1979) Computer-assisted processes of cartographic generalization in topographic maps *Geo-Processing* 1 183–99

Luger G L, Stubblefield W A (1989) *Artificial Intelligence and the Design of Expert Systems*. The Benjamin/Cummings Publishing Company Inc, New York

Mackaness W A, Fisher P F (1987) Automatic recognition and resolution of spatial conflicts in cartographic symbolization. *Proceedings of AUTOCARTO 8*. ASPRS, Falls Church, pp. 709–18

Mandlebrot B B (1982) *The Fractal Geometry of Nature*. W H Freeman and Co, San Francisco

Mark D M (1989) Multiple views of multiple representations. *Multiple Representations. NCGIA Technical Paper 89–3* National Centre for Geographical Information and Analysis, Santa Barbara California, pp. 68–71

Mark D M, Csillag M (1989) The nature of boundaries on 'area-class' maps. *Cartographica* 26: 65–78

McMaster R B (1987) Automated line generalization. *Cartographica* **24**: 74–111

McMaster R B, Monmonier M (1989) A conceptual framework for quantitative and qualitative raster-mode generalization. *Proceedings of GIS/LIS '89*. ACSM ASPRS, Falls Church Virginia, pp. 390–403

Meyer U (1987) Computer-assisted generalization of buildings for digital landscape models by classification methods. *Nachrichten aus dem Karten- und Vermessungswesen* 2 **46**: 193–200

Morrison J L (1974) A theoretical framework for cartographic generalization with emphasis on the process of symbolization. *International Yearbook of Cartography* **14**: 115–27

Morton G M (1966) A computer oriented geodetic database and a new technique in file sequencing. *IBM Canada-Ontario Report*

Muehrcke P C (1969) *Visual pattern analysis: A look at maps*. Unpublished Doctoral Thesis, University of Michigan

Muller J-C (1982) Non-Euclidean geographical spaces: mapping functional distances. *Geographical Analysis* **14**: 189–203

Muller J-C (1987) Fractal and automated line generalization. *The Cartographic Journal* **24**: 27–34

Muller J C, Honsaker J L (1983) Visual versus computerized seriation: the implications for automated map generalization. *Proceedings of AUTOCARTO 6*. ASPRS, Falls Church, pp. 277–88

NCGIA (1989) Multiple representations. *NCGIA Technical Paper* **89–3**

O'Neill M O, Mark D M (1987) The Psi–s Plot: a useful representation for digital cartographic lines. *Proceedings of AUTOCARTO 8*. ASPRS, Falls Church, pp. 231–40

Peano G (1890) Sur une courbe qui remplit toute une aire plane. *Mathematische Annalen* **36** A:157–60

Perkal J (1965) Translated by Jackowski W. An attempt at objective generalization. *Michigan Inter-University Community of Mathematical Geographers. Discussion Paper* **9**

Peucker T K (1975) A theory of the cartographic line. *Proceedings of AUTOCARTO 2*. ASPRS, Falls Church, pp. 508–18

Powitz B M, Meyer U (1989) Generalization of settlements by pattern recognition methods. *Paper presented at the ICA Conference, Budapest* 7pp

Rhind D W (1988) Geografische Informatiesystemen en Kartografie. *Kartografisch Tijdschrift* **14**: 25–7

Richardson D E (1988) *Rule based generalization for base map production*. Unpublished Master's Thesis, ITC Enschede

Robinson A H (1960) *Elements of Cartography*, 2nd edn. Wiley, New York

Samet H (1984) The quadtree and related hierarchical data structures. *ACM Computing Surveys* **16**: 187–260

Sowa J F (1984) *Conceptual Structures*. Addison-Wesley, Reading Massachusetts

Staufenbiel W (1973) *Zur automation der generalisierung topographischer karten mit besonderer berucksichtigung Grobmabstabiger Gebaudedarstellungen*. Unpublished Doctoral Thesis, University of Hannover

Swiss Society of Cartography (1987) *Cartographic Generalization*, 2nd edn. SGK-Publikationen, Zurich

Thapa K (1988) Automatic line generalization using zero-crossings. *Photogrammetric Engineering and Remote Sensing* **54**: 511–17

Thom R (1973) La theorie des catastrophes: etat present et perspectives. *Manifold* **14**: 16–23

Tobler W R (1966) Numerical map generalization. *Michigan Inter-University Community of Mathematical Geographers Discussion Paper* **8**

Tobler W R (1984) Application of image processing techniques to map processing. *Proceedings of the 1st International Symposium on Spatial Data Handling, Zurich*. Universitat Zurich-Irchel, Zurich (1): 140–44.

Tobler W R, Moellering H (1972) The analysis of scale-variance. *Geographical Analysis* **4**: 34–50

United Nations (1989) Modern mapping techniques. *United Nations Inter-Regional Seminar, Honefoss, Norway*.

Weibel R, Heller M (1991) Digital terrain modelling. In: Maguire D J, Goodchild M F, Rhind D W (eds.) *Geographical Information Systems: principles and applications*. Longman, London, pp. 269–97, Vol 1

Whittaker E, Robinson G (1944) *The Calculus of Observations*, 4th edn. Blackie and Son, London

Zycor N C (1984) Manual and automated line generalization and feature displacement. *Report for the US Army Engineer Topographic Laboratories Fort Belvoir, Virginia 22060 USA, unclassified material*, 2 vols, 204pp.

31

GIS SPECIFICATION, EVALUATION, AND IMPLEMENTATION

A L CLARKE

A general model for GIS acquisition is presented, involving four stages: analysis of requirements, specification of requirements, evaluation of alternatives, and implementation of the selected system. The steps involved in each stage are described. A cost-benefit analysis is used to determine the merits of the proposed acquisition, and a cost-effectiveness analysis is used to evaluate the functionality and performance of alternative systems. The thoroughness of the user requirements analysis and the management of the organizational impacts of GIS acquisition are considered to be critical success factors.

INTRODUCTION

Private or public sector agencies which utilize spatial information may consider, or be advised, that GIS technology would improve the efficiency or effectiveness of their operations. How should such agencies determine whether this is true? Should they develop the system in-house or acquire an existing system? How should they determine which existing system to acquire? What are the critical success factors when GIS technology is implemented for the first time? These are the fundamental questions addressed in this chapter.

Many early GIS were developed by research and development staff within user agencies. Some initial experimental systems developed into operational systems. However, the complexity of current GIS technology and applications is such that this approach is now rarely pursued. The time, costs, and risks involved in development and maintenance of major computer systems, combined with the availability of commercial GIS software, means that most agencies now choose to purchase an existing system, perhaps with some customization, rather than developing their own. This latter approach is assumed in this chapter.

Perusal of this book and other GIS literature (e.g. issues of the periodicals *GIS World* and *Mapping Awareness*) will reveal that there are many vendors of GIS technology and a number of systems are in the public domain. These commercial and public systems exhibit a wide range of functional capabilities, system configurations, data structures, performance characteristics and costs. There is minimal public domain literature comparing the various systems, and their features are changing so rapidly that any such literature is soon out of date. A methodology is therefore required for an agency to determine whether the benefits of acquiring GIS technology are greater than the costs, and if they are, to decide which system to acquire.

The methodology presented here is in the form of a general model for the analysis and specification of GIS requirements, the evaluation of alternative systems, and the implementation of the selected GIS. The 14 steps in the model are described in the next section. In a final section, some management issues and critical success factors associated with the introduction of GIS technology are outlined.

A GENERAL MODEL FOR GIS ACQUISITION

The model presented here is based on current systems development and project management practices, adapted to the GIS environment. It incorporates aspects of the GIS design and evaluation work of Marble *et al.* (1972), Calkins (1983), Dangermond, Freedman and Chambers (1986), Clarke (1988), Guptill (1988) and Bromley and Coulson (1989). The GIS acquisition model comprises four stages, each with a number of steps (Table 31.1).

Table 31.1 The GIS acquisition model.

Stage 1: Analysis of requirements
    1. Definition of objectives
    2. User requirements analysis
    3. Preliminary design
    4. Cost-benefit analysis
    5. Pilot study

Stage 2: Specification of requirements
    6. Final design
    7. Request for proposals

Stage 3: Evaluation of alternatives
    8. Shortlisting
    9. Benchmark testing
    10. Cost-effectiveness evaluation

Stage 4: Implementation of system
    11. Implementation plan
    12. Contract
    13. Acceptance testing
    14. Implementation

The importance of a particular step will vary from project to project and the costs involved must be kept in proportion to the size of the GIS. For small projects, steps such as the pilot study may be omitted and the issues involved in some other steps addressed very quickly.

Stage 1: Analysis of requirements

The first stage is an iterative process for identifying and refining user requirements, and for determining the business case for acquiring a GIS. After each step is completed, the resulting report should be discussed with users and management, and the conclusions from the previous steps should be re-examined and, if necessary, refined.

1. Definition of objectives

The objectives of this step are to define the scope and objectives of the GIS acquisition project, and to obtain management and user support for them. The activities are:

- Review overall agency objectives.
- Develop GIS project objectives.
- Negotiate with management and users.

The acquisition of a GIS must be compatible with the agency mission statement and business plan. Those documents should provide a framework within which specific project objectives can be developed. Objectives should be stated from management's perspective, focus on results and be measurable. Key aspects include cost, time, quality, accuracy and staff impact. Vague statements regarding new technology or improved decision making are not adequate. Users must also be satisfied that the project will result in benefits for them.

The outcome from Step 1 is a document which has management and user endorsement and which commits the agency to proceeding through to a GIS cost-benefit analysis (Step 4). The agreed objectives may, of course, be refined after further analysis.

2. User requirements analysis

The objectives of this step are to determine the user requirements upon which the GIS will be designed and evaluated. The output from a GIS is an information product, obtained by processing geographical data. Three levels of user requirements can therefore be identified: information, processing and data. The analysis activities are:

- Assess existing information, processes and data.
- Identify potential GIS users.
- Define required information products.
- Analyse data requirements.
- Estimate workloads and required performance.

The initial assessment should result in an understanding of what information is being used, who is using it, and how the source data are being collected, processed, stored, and maintained. This is the base against which the alternative of acquiring a GIS will be tested. The required information can be obtained through interviews, documentation reviews and workshops. The report should clearly identify the work flows which relate to spatial data, as well as the characteristics of those data including source, accuracy, format, and volume. The costs of operating those parts of the current system which may be replaced by the proposed GIS must also be identified for use in the cost-benefit analysis.

Potential GIS users include the users of information products (decision makers), people who process data to obtain information (applications specialists) and people who collect and maintain data. For some agencies these functions may be performed by an individual, while for others they will be performed separately by many people. The end-product users may be external clients for whom the agency provides a service. The process and data users will be hands-on users of the proposed GIS and should be relatively easy to identify based on the current systems and processes. However, potential end-product users may include decision makers who do not currently have access to geographical information products due to time, cost or availability constraints. These may be the most difficult and important potential users to identify (Guptill 1988).

The definition of required information products is the key to the user requirements analysis. Products may be in the form of hardcopy and softcopy graphics and reports, and digital data in a range of formats. Applications and data capture staff may require a range of intermediate products for verification purposes. The current geographical information products provide the starting point for determining user needs, but there may well be potential for new and enhanced products. The GIS product definition process should result in a clear statement of the media, format, and content of the required information products.

Data requirements are determined directly from the product definition. The analysis should identify the classifications, accuracy, and update frequency required for each data type.

Workshops and demonstrations may be necessary to explain the options and issues in defining product and data requirements. Structured methods for requirements analysis such as strategic data planning, decision analysis and modelling may also be appropriate (McRae and Cleaves 1986).

The final activity in Step 2 is to estimate the workloads and required performance characteristics of the GIS. These will have a large impact on the proposed hardware configuration and hence on costs. Important aspects include the number of simultaneous users, data volumes, response times, and required production rates. A formal model for GIS workload estimation has been developed by Goodchild and Rizzo (1987). The model uses a library of sub-tasks from which GIS products can be produced, measures of use which represent some demand on the system, and a set of predictors for those measures. The ability of proposed systems to achieve the required performance is evaluated during benchmark testing (Step 9).

The analysis of user requirements may lead to some refinement in the definition of objectives.

3. Preliminary design

The information gathered during Step 2 enables a preliminary design for the GIS to be developed. The design will be used for the cost-benefit analysis of the proposed GIS, and will enable specification of the pilot study. The preliminary design step activities are:

- Develop preliminary database specifications.
- Develop preliminary functional specifications.
- Develop preliminary system models.
- Survey the market for potential systems.

The classifications, accuracy, and update frequency for each data type were identified during the analysis of data requirements. The preliminary database specifications must also identify the sources, volumes, and structures for both spatial and attribute data. Preliminary consideration must be given to the choice of vector or raster (or both) spatial data model and to whether a fully relational or other model is required for attribute data.

Functional specifications are determined directly from the product definition in Step 2 and the database specifications. They define the functions and processes which are required to enable the database to be developed and the information products to be produced. A detailed checklist of generic GIS functions is provided by Guptill (1988) for user interfaces, database management, database creation, data manipulation and analysis, and data display and product generation (see also Maguire and Dangermond 1991 in this volume). The specifications must also identify the requirements for batch, interactive (or both) processing modes for particular functions.

Conceptual models should be developed and documented to describe the logical and physical design of the proposed system. Aspects include hardware, software, communications, processes, people, and organizational arrangements. Alternative models for the hardware and communications architecture may be included. For some agencies, the choice between a distributed and centralized GIS may be a critical design issue. Dangermond (1988) reviews the trends, advantages, and disadvantages of the various GIS architectures.

A market survey should then be conducted to determine the capabilities of systems in relation to the preliminary design. Initially, this may be done through visits to vendors and user sites. The objective is to determine whether the preliminary specifications can be met with current technology. If not, the options are to lower the functionality and performance specifications, or to accept that a major system development component may be included in the acquisition. This informal market survey could be conducted in conjunction with Steps 1 and 2 and the previous activities in Step 3.

A formal market survey involves issuing a call for expressions of interest from GIS vendors, based on the preliminary system specification. The objectives are to identify potential suppliers and the nature of their products, and to advise vendors formally of the agency's GIS plans. This enables the agency to refine the preliminary specifications and system models, and the vendors to prepare for the request for proposals (Step 7).

4. Cost-benefit analysis

The objective of the cost-benefit analysis is to establish the business case for the GIS acquisition proposal. The costs, benefits, impacts, and risks of acquiring a GIS are measured against the alternative of continuing with the current data, processes, and information products. If the preliminary design models include fundamentally different approaches, such as distributed versus centralized systems for an agency with regional offices, it may be necessary to analyse the costs and benefits of the alternatives. The cost-benefit analysis activities are:

- Estimate all costs.
- Identify all benefits.
- Estimate economic value of quantifiable benefits.
- Assess impacts on organization and staff.
- Assess risks.
- Analyse results.

Costs for GIS implementation and operation include those for acquisition and maintenance of hardware and software, data capture and maintenance, training, additional and more highly qualified staff (required for system management, in-house programming, user support and the running of applications), consumables, site preparation and all associated overheads. The cost of the acquisition process may also be included. Recurrent costs should be determined over a nominal system life of at least five years, discounted to present value. Discounting reflects the opportunity cost of capital and enables comparison of costs and benefits which occur at different times during the system life.

Indicative hardware, software, maintenance and training costs should be obtained from two or three appropriate vendors identified during Step 3. If possible, these costs should be validated by discussions with existing user agencies. Data capture costs may range from 10 to 1000 times the hardware and software costs (Guptill 1988). Models of the manual digitizing process developed by Marble, Lauzon and McGranaghan (1984) and Lai (1988) provide a basis for costing this component.

Three categories of GIS benefits may be defined: efficiency, effectiveness and intangible (Prisley and Mead 1987; Maffini and Saxton 1987). Efficiency benefits relate to time and cost savings through faster data processing and a reduction in duplicated effort, while effectiveness benefits relate to improvements in the decision-making process through more timely or new information. Intangible benefits may include an improved public image for the agency, a reduction in confusion caused by contradictory data, improved cooperation between users through data sharing, increased staff professionalism and morale, better ability to cope with unexpected events, new knowledge through improved data analysis and unanticipated applications.

While an economic value can readily be assigned to efficiency benefits, the effectiveness and intangible benefits are harder to quantify. Dickinson and Calkins (1988) and Dickinson (1989) describe methods for estimating the economic value of non-quantifiable GIS benefits. However, Dickinson and Calkins (1988) also recommend that such values be reported separately as they have a larger element of uncertainty. Chorley (1988) argues that rather than quantifying benefits which are inherently intangible, it is more appropriate to provide a clear description and analysis of such benefits to enable judgement by senior decision makers.

The impacts of the proposed GIS on the organization and staff of the agency may be major and so could have a significant bearing on the cost-benefit analysis. The impacts on data collection, data processing, and decision-making staff can be assessed from the user requirements analysis. The impacts on the organization may include changes to the organizational and management structure associated with new technology, new roles and procedures, and new requirements for consultation and cooperation. These institutional issues may have a larger influence on the success of the GIS than technical issues (Foley 1988; Seldon 1987). Early consultation with staff and their representatives regarding these impacts will help to avoid disputes during implementation. There may also be political and legal implications for the agency in terms of responsibility, authority and guarantees associated with the collection and maintenance of data and the dissemination of information products.

The cost-benefit analysis should include an assessment of the risk that the project will not achieve a successful outcome in terms of time, cost, specifications, and benefits. Economic risk may be assessed through a sensitivity analysis by determining the most pessimistic and optimistic values for the quantified costs and benefits. Other risk factors include the complexity of the data and system being considered, the experience and composition of the GIS project team, and the anticipated impact of the system on the organization and staff. Describing risks at this early stage enables senior management either to take action to reduce the risks, or to monitor them closely during the project.

The costs, benefits, impact, and risks may be analysed and presented in a number of ways. Dickinson and Calkins (1988) describe a benefit/cost model based on GIS product values. Griffin and Hickman (1988) describe results of analyses of the present value, savings and investment ratio, discounted payback, breakeven and benefit–cost of an implemented GIS. The minimum requirement is to present the basic economics of the proposal, together with a statement of factors not included in the economic analysis. The basic economic equation is:

operating cost of the system to be replaced
− operating and capital cost of proposed GIS
+ quantified benefits of proposed GIS
= net economic benefit of the proposed GIS
± sensitivity

This net economic benefit must then be assessed against concise statements of intangible benefits and risks, and the impacts on the organization and staff.

Consideration of the cost-benefit analysis is a major milestone in the GIS acquisition project. It may indicate that the proposal should be deferred, that further work must be done on the objectives, requirements and preliminary design, or that the acquisition should proceed to the pilot study step.

5. Pilot study

The primary objective of the pilot study is to test the preliminary GIS design before finalizing the system specifications and committing major resources. Secondary objectives are to develop the understanding and confidence of users in the technology, by demonstrating applications with their data, and to gain some operational experience to assist design of the benchmark test (Step 9). The pilot study activities are:

- Design the pilot study.
- Select a pilot system.
- Acquire pilot data.
- Produce pilot products.
- Analyse results.

The pilot study design document must state the study objectives, address the selection of the pilot system, data and products, and identify the required resources and proposed timetable. It is important for the users to agree the objectives and scope of the pilot study.

A number of potential systems will have been identified during the preliminary design step. The selection of one for the pilot study is based on the apparent match of capabilities to requirements, and the cost of establishing the pilot system. Hardware and software may be leased for the duration of the pilot, or vendors may be prepared to loan systems and provide support. However, it must be emphasized to all parties that the choice of a system for the pilot does not pre-empt the decision on which system will be finally acquired. Users must avoid the pitfall of becoming committed to the system chosen for the pilot through their familiarity with it.

The pilot data should include examples of all data types specified in the preliminary design. A common approach is to select a small but representative geographical area and to acquire all data for that area. The pilot products should also be representative of the final system, and include those considered by the users to be critical for the success of the system. If the choice between raster and vector data models is contentious, the pilot data and products must be selected to enable resolution of that issue.

The pilot study should yield valuable experience and user comments. These results may lead to refinement of the database and system specifications, and to review of the cost and benefit figures and the statements of intangible benefits, impacts, and risks.

Stage 2: Specification of requirements

In the second stage of the GIS acquisition model the results of the analysis of user requirements are developed into a specification against which proposals can be solicited and evaluated.

6. Final design

The objective of this step is to produce design documentation for inclusion in the request for proposals. Activities are:

- Finalize database specifications.
- Finalize functional specifications.
- Finalize performance specifications.
- Specify constraints.
- Specify generic system requirements.

The database functional and performance specifications are finalized by incorporating the results of the pilot study into the preliminary design document. The database specifications are required by vendors for designing their proposed systems. Functional requirements must be specified in detail and classified as either mandatory, desirable or optional. Only those requirements which are essential to the operation of the system should be specified as mandatory, as over-specification will make the evaluation of alternatives difficult and may result in the elimination of innovative proposals. Performance specifications should be stated in terms of the minimum acceptable performance (mandatory workloads), and optimum requirements.

Constraints which must be identified and specified may include existing hardware, software, communication systems, interface requirements and agency policies regarding compatibility and standards. Generic system requirements include maintenance, support, training, user and system documentation, development tools, upgrade paths, security and ergonomics.

7. Request for proposals

The request for proposals (RFP) document combines the final design with the contractual requirements of the agency. The RFP is then released to vendors. The activities are:

- Specify contractual requirements.
- Specify evaluation methodology.
- Release the RFP.

Contractual issues which must be addressed in the RFP include: the acceptability of multiple vendor solutions; the required maturity of proposed systems; provisions for special software development; how constraints must be addressed; general conditions of the proposal; and draft conditions of contract.

The optimum solution to a complex GIS requirement may involve multiple hardware and software vendors. The agency must specify whether it requires a primary contractor to coordinate and accept responsibility for the total project, or whether separate vendors may be contracted to implement parts of the system under the direction of agency staff. The primary contractor may be either the primary vendor or a company which specializes in system integration. Similarly, the RFP must state whether proposals must address the total requirement or whether proposals for discrete parts (such as hardware or data capture systems) will be considered.

The agency must also specify whether proposed solutions must be mature (fully operational), or whether systems currently under development will be considered. There are risks with both positions. Systems under development may appear to promise greater benefits than some operational systems, but there is a significant risk that they will not meet their time or performance specifications. The risk in eliminating such systems is that medium- to long-term potential benefits will be forgone. One intermediate approach is to nominate the benchmark testing date (Step 9) as the cut-off; only those functions which are demonstrable by that date will be considered in the evaluation.

Special software development may include customization of user interfaces, translation software for existing data, unique processing functions, and interfaces to other systems. The processes for developing and reviewing the software specification and design, and for monitoring the implementation, should be specified.

The design constraints identified in Step 6 may be stated in the RFP as mandatory requirements or, preferably, as issues to be addressed by vendors. The latter approach enables vendors to propose alternatives which they consider to be more cost effective than constrained solutions.

General conditions of the proposal will include the closing date, minimum information for a formal tender, conditions for variations to proposals during the evaluation period, and price basis. The RFP document requests vendors to respond to a large number of technical and contractual requirements. Vendors should be required to explain how their proposal complies with each mandatory, desirable and optional functional and performance requirement. They must also respond to every constraint and generic system requirement, and to the draft contractual conditions. The RFP should state that simple responses to complex technical requirements, such as 'complies' or 'understood',

will disqualify the proposal from consideration as a formal tender. A useful approach is to include a questionnaire in the RFP which addresses the issues of most concern to the agency.

Draft conditions of contract (see Step 12) and the evaluation methodology to be employed by the agency should also be outlined in the RFP. The evaluation methodology would be a summary of the shortlisting, benchmark testing and cost-effectiveness evaluation processes (Steps 8–10), and a general description of the evaluation criteria to be used for each step.

Finally, the RFP is released to vendors by letter, advertisement or both. A minimum period of eight weeks should be allowed for vendors to prepare proposals for complex systems. A formal briefing may be provided to interested vendors during the release period.

Stage 3: Evaluation of alternatives

The third stage comprises three successive evaluations designed to identify which one of the proposed systems is the most appropriate for the agency. Boehm (1981) describes a number of performance and cost-effectiveness models which provide decision criteria for choosing between alternative computer systems. The approach described here employs shortlisting based on mandatory functionality and performance criteria, followed by a cost-effectiveness evaluation. Effectiveness is determined by benchmark testing and is quantified by a weighted sum analysis (Boehm's 'figure of merit').

8. Shortlisting

The objective of this step is to determine an initial shortlist of feasible systems by evaluating and scoring the information submitted by vendors. Activities are:

- Perform preliminary evaluation of proposals.
- Score functional requirements.
- Produce initial shortlist.

The preliminary evaluation of detailed proposals should identify any relationships between the proposals, and whether any should be rejected without further evaluation. Reasons for rejection at this early step may include clear failure to meet a mandatory functional requirement, inadequate detail in the response, unacceptable maturity, inability to form part of a total solution, and having costs which greatly exceed the alternatives and the projected budget.

Non-mandatory functional and generic system requirements are then scored from the vendor responses. Each requirement is assigned a weight and each is scored against a numerical scale (Boehm 1981). The weights should be determined in consultation with users, prior to receipt of the proposals. The experience gained during the pilot study should provide a basis for determining the relative importance of functions. Uncertain scores should be highlighted for special attention during benchmark testing. Discussions with other users will greatly assist the scoring of aspects such as the quality of maintenance and support.

The preliminary evaluation and scoring enable an initial shortlist to be produced. A maximum shortlist of five systems is recommended in order to keep the benchmark testing step manageable.

9. Benchmark testing

The objectives of benchmark testing are to confirm the scoring of functional requirements and to determine realistic estimates of performance in terms of workload. This step also enables an informal evaluation of the people behind the proposal. Benchmark testing activities are:

- Design the benchmark.
- Develop the benchmark data and documentation.
- Execute the benchmark.
- Analyse results.

The benchmark design must be based on the functional and performance requirements specified in the RFP. The design must establish the tasks to be performed, the data on which they will be performed and the output required. Guptill (1988) defines a comprehensive set of GIS benchmark tests, and Marble and Sen (1986) present a design for an application-independent benchmark for spatial database systems. Data to be used may include existing digital maps and attribute tables.

Benchmark outputs may include measures of elapsed, CPU and operator times, together with products such as graphics and statistics. Other factors to be evaluated such as the user interface and system documentation should also be noted in the design document. Some vendors may be ambivalent about benchmarks because often the specifications are vague, the cost is out of proportion to the value of the potential contract, and insufficient time is allowed for preparation and completion (Reed 1988). These factors must be considered in the benchmark design.

The benchmark documentation should provide a general description of the tasks to be performed and a copy of the data to be used. Vendors must be able to prepare for the benchmark by loading existing data and ensuring that staff with the appropriate knowledge and expertise are available, but it is neither appropriate nor necessary to provide details of every task to be performed in advance.

Careful records must be kept during execution of the benchmark. The configuration, loading, and software version being used for the benchmark must be noted, in addition to the actual results. Structuring the benchmark design document as a proforma may assist this process. Evaluators must ensure that they understand what is being demonstrated and that all functions are being executed in real time.

The results of the benchmark tests will enable refinement of the functionality scores, and assessment of scores for workload performance. Proposals which prove unable to meet mandatory functional requirements, or which cannot achieve the minimum workload levels, are eliminated at this point.

Goodchild and Rizzo (1987) and Goodchild (1987) distinguish between what they call qualitative and quantitative benchmarks. The purpose of a qualitative benchmark is to determine the degree to which the proposed system can perform the required functions to the satisfaction of the benchmark team. They propose a scale of 'inhibition' to assess the degree to which a given function falls below an ideal performance, and thus inhibits the ability of the system to generate particular products which depend on the function. A quantitative benchmark is used to assess the degree to which the system can indeed perform the required workload within the constraints of personnel working time, available CPU cycles, peripheral devices, and storage capacity.

Each required function is exercised at least once during the benchmark test. Its qualitative performance is assessed by the benchmark team, and its resource utilization is recorded, along with various measures of problem size. These are then used to build predictive models of resource utilization by each function, so that workload can be estimated given the anticipated sizes of production problems. The result is a series of estimates of total resource utilization, which can be compared against the capacities of the proposed system. In one example (Goodchild 1987) the quantitative benchmark showed that the vendor had seriously overestimated the rates of digitizing which could be achieved in production, and also seriously over-configured the system's CPU.

10. Cost-effectiveness evaluation

Proposals which survive the initial shortlisting and benchmark testing steps are finally evaluated for their cost effectiveness. Activities are:

- Form notional configurations.
- Analyse costs for each configuration.
- Compute cost effectiveness ratios.
- Analyse results.

Notional configurations are formed by defining the hardware and software required. Some normalization of hardware, such as the volume of disk storage and number of workstations, may be necessary.

Capital and recurrent operating costs for these configurations over a nominal system life of at least five years are then determined. While only the cost differences are actually required for the purpose of evaluating alternative configurations, the total costs must also be determined to ensure that the original cost-benefit analysis remains valid. Schedules should be prepared showing capital and operating costs in each year, at both constant price and present value.

The cost-effectiveness ratio for each configuration is then computed by dividing the whole-of-life present-value cost by the functional and workload performance score, giving a cost per notional unit of performance. Because those systems which do not meet the required minimum levels of functionality and workload are not on the final shortlist, the ratios are actually a measure of the marginal increase in effectiveness that would be achieved with each surviving configuration.

While the configuration with the best cost-effectiveness ratio (lowest cost per unit of marginal performance) is in theory the optimum choice, it may not be affordable and there may be other factors not included in the evaluation which should also be considered. Other factors may include uncosted differences in the impact each configuration would have on the agency and staff, and concerns regarding the financial viability of vendors. The final report of the evaluation stage must therefore include, for each configuration on the final shortlist: the schedules of total costs (constant prices discounted to present value); the scores for non-mandatory functionality; performance and generic system requirements; a statement of relevant factors which are not included in the costs and scores; and a review of the original cost-benefit analysis.

Stage 4: Implementation of system

The final stage in the GIS acquisition model involves planning the implementation, contracting with the selected vendor or vendors, testing the delivered system, and actual implementation.

11. Implementation plan

The objectives of this step are to ensure smooth implementation and early delivery of benefits by developing a structured implementation plan. Implementation planning activities are:

- Identify priorities.
- Define and schedule tasks.
- Develop a resource budget and management plan.

The priorities for products and data should be reviewed in consultation with the end-product users to identify where early benefits can be achieved. The rationale is that a positive result early in the implementation, even if of modest proportions, will be more beneficial to the success of the GIS than a plan which does not deliver any tangible benefits to end-product users until late in the implementation.

Implementation tasks must then be defined and scheduled. Tasks may include: installation and acceptance testing (Step 13); customization of user interfaces; training of operators and support staff; initial data capture and product development; and medium- to long-term data capture and product development. Staff and cash budgets must then be linked to the schedule and management responsibility assigned.

12. Contract

This step involves integration of the agency's draft conditions of contract with the vendor's response and the implementation plan, to produce a legal contract. Activities are:

- Negotiate general contractual conditions.
- Negotiate special contractual conditions.

General contractual conditions include the contract period, payment schedule, reporting requirements, responsibilities of parties, insurance, warranty, indemnity, arbitration, and provisions for penalties and contract termination.

Special contractual conditions relate to the actual site and implementation plan. Reference must be made to the functionality and performance to be delivered. Other aspects are the processes and schedules for site preparation, delivery, installation, acceptance testing, training, support and maintenance. Procedures for the management of any special software developments must be defined, and the allocation of rights to such software must be stated.

13. Acceptance testing

The objective of this step is to ensure that the delivered GIS meets the contracted performance. Final payment should not be made until all tests have been satisfactorily completed. Activities are:

- Install the system.
- Test functionality.
- Test performance.
- Test reliability.

Installation may involve site preparation, establishment of communications systems, and development of special software and customized interfaces. The functionality and performance tests should be designed to ensure that the contracted specifications can be achieved under normal operating conditions.

Reliability refers to system availability and recovery, under both normal operating conditions and stress. The contract may specify an availability requirement in terms of the maximum down-time allowed per week to accommodate routine and emergency maintenance. Down-time should be closely monitored during acceptance testing. Recovery characteristics should be tested under all combinations of partial and total crash of both hardware and software.

14. Implementation

Activities in this final step are:

- Train users and support staff.
- Perform initial data capture and product development.
- Continue performance monitoring.

Training may be done in phases to build on the experience gained under operating conditions. The effectiveness of the training should be formally evaluated after each phase and the results reviewed in consultation with the vendor. The initial data capture and products should also be evaluated in consultation with the users and, if problems occur, the vendor.

Once the system is in routine operation, continuous performance monitoring should be introduced as a system management task. The performance data collected will help identify bottlenecks in the production process and enable system upgrades or procedure changes to be initiated.

MANAGEMENT OF THE ACQUISITION PROCESS

Organizational alternatives

The general model described above may be performed entirely by agency staff, entirely by external consultants reporting to agency management, or by some combination of agency staff and consultants. Issues which must be considered include the availability, expertise and cost of both in-house staff and consultants, and whether there are political advantages in utilizing consultants for certain steps. Appropriately qualified consultants will have no vested interest in the outcome of their work. This may be an important consideration for some users and for management.

GIS technology encompasses many disciplines and many people in various areas of an agency may be affected by its acquisition. Stakeholders in the acquisition are therefore numerous and diverse. Formation of a multidisciplinary project team, with either representatives from the affected areas or a clear brief to consult with them, is one approach to this diversity. Ideally, the team should contain members with expertise in the applications areas and in computing technology. The project team may undertake certain steps in the process, or be available to assist consultants as required.

Critical success factors

Information System (IS) failure may be defined as the 'inability of an IS to meet a specific stakeholder group's expectations' (Lyytinen and Hirschheim 1987). Expectations may have been explicitly stated in the form of technical specifications and budgets, or they may be unstated and relate to the values and perceptions of the stakeholders, in which case the evidence for failure is low system usage. Why then do some GIS implementations fail to meet expectations?

The Chorley Committee (Department of the Environment 1987) reviewed the UK GIS experience and Tomlinson (1987) reviewed that of North America. The Chorley Committee found that over-ambition, insufficient attention to user needs, conservatism of users, and over-optimistic estimates of data conversion and system development costs were the major causes of difficulties. Tomlinson (1987) considers that failures have been caused by poorly or undefined user needs, poor or no advice, attempts by some agencies to develop their own systems with inadequate resources and exaggerated

goals, and a lack of motivation by users who were not involved in the acquisition process. Tomlinson concludes that the greatest obstacle is the human problem of introducing a new technology which requires not only a new way of doing things, but also has as its main purpose permitting the agency to do many things which it has not done before and often does not understand.

The Chorley Committee identified six factors which make an organizational environment conducive to the successful introduction of GIS: (1) geographical information is essential to operational efficiency; (2) the agency can afford some experimental work and trials; (3) a corporate approach to geographical information and a tradition of sharing and exchanging information; (4) a tradition of a multidisciplinary approach; (5) strong leadership and enthusiasm from management, with a group of enthusiasts at the working level; and (6) some experience of, and commitment to, information technology and the use of existing databases in digital form. The first and last largely reflect the nature of the agency's business, while the other four relate more to its corporate culture. If those cultural characteristics do not already exist, they will need to be developed to ensure that the GIS is a success.

CONCLUSION

The general model for the acquisition of GIS technology provides a framework within which agencies can undertake the analysis and specification of GIS requirements, the evaluation of alternative systems, and the implementation of the selected GIS. The GIS will be a success if the expectations of all stakeholder groups are met. While all of the steps in the model will contribute to this goal, two factors are regarded as critical: the user requirements analysis and the organizational impacts. The user requirements analysis must: (a) be thorough; (b) involve data capture, data processing and end-product users; (c) result in the users being committed to the system; and (d) be the focal point of the evaluation and implementation. The agency's staff must understand the organizational impacts of the acquisition and they must be committed to making the necessary changes.

REFERENCES

Boehm B W (1981) *Software Engineering Economics.* Prentice-Hall, Englewood Cliffs New Jersey

Bromley R D F, Coulson M G (1989) *Geographical Information Systems and the work of a local authority: a case study of Swansea City Council.* Department of Geography, University College Swansea, Swansea

Calkins H W (1983) A pragmatic approach to geographic information system design. In: Peuquet D, O'Callaghan J (eds.) *Design and Implementation of Computer-based Geographic Information Systems.* International Geographical Union, New York, pp.92–101

Chorley R (1988) Some reflections on the handling of geographic information. *International Journal of Geographical Information Systems* 2 (1): 3–9

Clarke A L (1988) Upgrading a digital mapping system. *Proceedings of the Seventh Australian Cartographic Conference.* Australian Institute of Cartographers, Sydney, pp. 238–47

Dangermond J (1988) A technical architecture for GIS. *Proceedings of GIS/LIS '88.* ACSM/ASPRS, Falls Church, pp. 561–70

Dangermond J, Freedman C, Chambers D (1986) Tongass National Forest natural resource management information study – a description of project methodology and recent findings. *Geo-Processing* 3: 51–75

Department of the Environment (DoE) (1987) *Handling Geographic Information.* HMSO, London

Dickinson H J (1989) Techniques for establishing the value of geographic information and geographic information systems. *Proceedings of GIS/LIS '89.* ACSM/ASPRS, Falls Church, pp. 412–20

Dickinson H J, Calkins H W (1988) The economic evaluation of implementing a GIS. *International Journal of Geographical Information Systems* 2 (4): 307–27

Foley M E (1988) Beyond the bits, bytes and black boxes – institutional issues in successful LIS/GIS management. *Proceedings of GIS/LIS '88.* ACSM/ASPRS, Falls Church, pp. 608–17

Goodchild M F (1987) Application of a GIS benchmarking and workload estimation model. *Papers and Proceedings of Applied Geography Conferences* 10: 1–6

Goodchild M F, Rizzo B R (1987) Performance evaluation and work-load estimation for geographic information systems. *International Journal of Geographical Information Systems* 1 (1): 67–76

Griffin J M, Hickman D L (1988) *Cost and Benefit Analysis of Geographic Information System Implementation. Final Report to the Bureau of Indian Affairs.* Battelle, Lakewood Colorado

Guptill S C (ed.) (1988) A process for evaluating geographic information systems. *Federal Interagency Coordinating Committee on Digital Cartography, Technology Exchange Working Group, Technical Report 1.* US Geological Survey, Reston Virginia

Lai P C (1988) Resource use in manual digitization. A case study of the Patuxent Basin geographical information system database. *International Journal of Geographical Information Systems* 2 (4): 329–45

Lyytinen K, Hirschheim R (1987) Information systems failures – a survey and classification of the empirical literature. *Oxford Surveys in Information Technology* 4: 257–309

Maffini G, Saxton W (1987) Deriving value from the modelling and analysis of spatial data. In: Aangeenbrug R T, Schiffman Y M (eds.) *International Geographic Information Systems (IGIS) Symposium, Arlington, Virginia* Vol 3. NASA, Washington DC, pp. 271–90

Maguire D J, Dangermond J (1991) The functionality of GIS. In: Maguire D J, Goodchild M F and Rhind D W (eds.) *Geographical Information Systems: principles and applications.* Longman, London, pp. 319–35, Vol 1

Marble D F, Lauzon J P, McGranaghan M (1984) Development of a conceptual model of the manual digitizing process. *Proceedings of the 1st International Symposium on Spatial Data Handling.* University of Zurich-Irchel, Zurich, pp. 146–71

Marble D F, Sen L (1986) The development of standardised benchmarks for spatial database systems. *Proceedings of the 2nd International Symposium on Spatial Data Handling.* IGU, Columbus Ohio, pp. 488–96

Marble D, Calkins H, Dueker K, Gilliland J, Salmona J (1972) Introduction to the economics of geographical information systems, and geographical information system design: concepts and methods. In: Tomlinson R F (ed.) *Geographical Data Handling. UNESCO/IGU Second Symposium on Geographical Information Systems.* International Geographical Union, Ottawa

McRae S, Cleaves D (1986) Incorporating strategic data-planning and decision analysis techniques in geographic information system design. *Proceedings of Geographic Information Systems Workshop.* ASPRS, Atlanta, pp. 76–86

Prisley S P, Mead R A (1987) Cost-benefit analysis for geographic information systems. *Proceedings of GIS '87.* ASPRS, San Francisco, pp. 29–37

Reed C N (1988) A minimum set of criteria for selecting a turn-key geographic information system: an update. *Proceedings of GIS/LIS '88.* ACSM ASPRS AAG URISA, Falls Church, pp. 867–73

Seldon D D (1987) Success criteria for GIS. In: Aangeenbrug R T and Schiffman Y M (Eds.) *International Geographic Information Systems (IGIS) Symposium, Arlington, Virginia.* Vol 3. NASA, Washington DC, pp. 239–43

Tomlinson R F (1987) Current and potential uses of geographical information systems – the North American experience. *International Journal of Geographical Information Systems* 1 (3): 203–8

32

LEGAL ASPECTS OF GIS

E F EPSTEIN

The legal aspects of geographical information systems are concerned with the relations between people, information and its use. These relations are described and sanctioned in the legal process. Access to, and liability for, data and information are major subjects of attention in the legal regime and ultimately influence the development of systems. Values, procedures and rules in regard to information have developed and evolved over a long period of time. It is likely that these traditional elements will continue to provide the framework for incorporation of changes brought by the computer to the geographical information system institution.

INTRODUCTION

A legal system is about relations between people. Relations exist between people in regard to geographical and land information and its use, and are defined, expressed and sanctioned in the legal process. The set of relations constitutes an institution without a recognized name, but in this chapter it is described as the geographical information institution.

Information use is complex because it is specific to each individual and thus difficult, if not impossible, to generalize. People want something that has important intangible attributes. In particular, users of geographical information systems do not want the tangible elements of the database or tangible products from it, such as the words and numbers and pictures, so much as the intangible and abstract meaning placed on those products – their 'content'. Most users of spatial information systems are primarily interested in the geographical and land data, and information, not in the technology that generates the information products. The technology is but a means to an end; the provision of alternative, efficient means to satisfy a real or perceived demand for information products.

Information influences individual behaviour in ways that are not easily separated from other influences. A legal regime must contend with this complexity, and express relations between people in a reasonable and comprehensible manner. This is typical of any legal regime. However, dealing with people's behaviour in regard to an object is particularly difficult when the object is information. In effect, the legal system sanctions people's behaviour in regard to information. These sanctions include use of technology and other objects, as well as procedures and activities. The forms of expression and sanctions within the legal system ultimately provide incentives and barriers for the development and sustenance of information systems.

The conditions that determine the production and use of geographical information products and services are reflected in the legal regime. Thus, it is appropriate to focus this chapter on the principles, framework and details that constitute the legal regime with respect to data and information. The chapter is, of course, particularly concerned with information about land and the distribution of activities and phenomena over the surface of the earth.

DEFINITIONS

The scope of the legal regime for geographical information is indicated by a set of definitions.

Uses of information

In very broad terms, uses of information fall into three classes, as follows:

- security, especially national security;
- aesthetics, science and education, and satisfaction; and
- management.

National security uses, although undoubtedly significant, are beyond the scope of typical civilian efforts at legal definition. Similarly, the motives that lie behind the use of information in aesthetics, science (in the sense of natural curiosity) and the pursuit of satisfaction are also not readily articulated in a legal regime. Therefore, the primary focus of a geographical and land information legal regime must be land management.

Land management encompasses the activities of land policy formulation, decisions and subsequent implementation actions. The role of data and information, and therefore its use and value, in land management is not well understood. It is a process that requires research and analysis.

Classes of information

Data, information, knowledge and wisdom may be distinguished in an institutional and management context.

- *Data* are observations.
- *Information* is data placed in a particular context. The institutional perspective places data in a context optimally suited for management purposes. A map is an example of an information product – the process of compiling the map, including the interpretation added by the cartographer, transforms data into information.
- *Knowledge* is the contribution of the human mind to the information. Each individual takes from a particular information product an understanding, or knowledge, that is particular both to the product and to the individual.
- *Wisdom* is the knowledge possessed by particular, recognized individuals in a society.

Data and information contribute, along with other important inputs, to a process whose ultimate output is the knowledge, and hopefully wisdom, that determines a policy, decision, or action.

Geographical and land information systems

A GIS is a tool for decision making and an aid for planning and development, consisting of a database containing spatially referenced land-related data, as well as the procedures and techniques for systematically collecting, updating, processing and distributing those data. For the purposes of this chapter, a GIS is comprised of five fundamental elements (see also Maguire 1991 in this volume for further discussion):

- selected data about geographical locations;
- software to manipulate and manage these data;
- hardware upon which the data and software reside;
- people responsible for overseeing GIS operations; and
- procedures for using and maintaining the GIS.

Note the inclusion of the management and use functions, in addition to the more traditional emphasis on data, hardware and software.

A land information system (LIS) is a tool for legal, administrative and economic decision making which consists of two elements. On the one hand, a database containing parcel level (not necessarily parcel based) spatially referenced land-related data for a defined area and, on the other hand, procedures and techniques for the systematic collection, updating, processing and distribution of the data. An LIS emphasizes parcel level data, the level of geographical aggregation where people's rights and interests are defined.

Institutions

An institution is a custom, practice, relationship, or behaviourial pattern of importance in the life of a community or society. The term can also be used narrowly in reference to a specific organization or foundation, such as the assessment institution.

Institutions are very much the focus of a legal regime.

The legal system

The legal system is everywhere. While most people rarely have contact with legislatures and courts, they are constantly in contact with the legal system. The legal system is in the background, for example, when driving down the road to go shopping for products and services: traffic law, workplace rules in automobile manufacturing, product labelling statutes, products liability laws and other examples of law travel are in evidence wherever or whenever even a mundane action takes place. As people's perspective expands in this way, they often find that the legal system is much more than the largely negative set of rules that restrict behaviour or give advantage to others (Friedman 1984).

The legal system includes the three major elements of structure, substance and culture. Structure is represented by the courts, legislatures, agencies and professions that make, interpret or apply rules that influence behaviour and relations with others. Substance is the actual rules, norms and prescribed behaviour patterns. Culture is least obvious, representing people's attitudes towards law in the form of beliefs, values, ideas and expectations. A good example of culture is the distinction between an automobile speed limit (substance) and the expectations among drivers and the police in regard to the actual threshold speed at which police begin to arrest drivers.

The legal system has several functions:

- *Social control and the regulation of behaviour.*

- *Dispute settlement.* This function is particularly important for a discussion of management uses of information. It is useful to note that the dispute or conflict can involve not only individuals and objects but also disagreements between classes, groups, organizations, regions or other distinctions among people.

- *Social engineering.* Because this can have a negative connotation, its meaning is better represented as the achievement of harmony, balance, equity and fairness in government function. Both change and continuity are included, as well as redistribution and definition of property rights. Information can be an important element in this function, providing a means to disclose inequities and to demonstrate fairness.

INFORMATION AS A LEGAL AND ECONOMIC ENTITY

Data and information are distinguishable from all of the other commodities which are the object of appropriation and sanction in a legal system (Mackaay 1982). Information generally, and land-related information particularly, is desired and sought for a variety of reasons. Some derive from what is loosely described as the marketplace, while others derive from a demand for public information whose origin is not the marketplace but a set of statutory mandates which must be met by agencies. These mandates lead to an implicit demand for information. Agencies often assemble data simply because they must do so in order to fulfil their mandates. The use and value of information associated with this statutory demand is not easily related to the so-called marketplace. The result is a set of attributes which distinguish information from other commodities and make it difficult to develop a set of rules that sanction people's behaviour.

Information connotes selection power or choice (Mackaay 1982), and choice among scarce resources is the central question of economics. Lack of information impairs choice, forcing decisions to be made in the presence of uncertainty. As information becomes available, decisions may appear to have been made incorrectly.

Data and information are acquired in connection with a management purpose, and serve as an antidote to uncertainty. If information were costlessly available, then an exhaustive search for information would occur to eliminate uncertainty. Because information acquisition is often expensive, the question becomes how much to acquire. For a management decision, the appropriate action is not a search for the best information, but the best worth searching for. This is determined by the conditions of the particular management activity, under standards that are expressed in the legal process.

Several attributes make information a peculiar commodity from legal and economic perspectives:

- *It is hard to measure quantity of information.* The bit of information in communication and information theory does not correspond to an economically relevant denomination. The system that delivers information messages is not like a transportation system that delivers cars. People are interested in the content that they extract from information (i.e. knowledge), not the messages. It is hard to price information when its quantity cannot easily be measured.

- *It is difficult to define and implement property rights (i.e. appropriability) in information.* Legal sanctions are necessary in order that property rights exist. Specifically, the relations between people in regard to use of information, not just the hardware and software of systems, must be defined. The absence of these property rights, or appropriability, restrains development of an information market. Suppliers will not provide it if there is over-use.

- *Information is not depleted by use.* Its use does not exclude use by others, as occurs with cars, or shoes, or other commodities. Thus, it does not have to be protected from the abuse that would occur if a government car were available for general use.

- *Inspection of the product is characteristic of a commodity market.* However, inspection of information is often tantamount to use. Inspection makes a purchase superfluous.

- *Information can be transmitted and disseminated at low cost.* Physical remoteness of users is now a matter of choice without significant impact on use. Previously, value was generated, in part, by the delivery service process.

- *Information has the character of a public good.* It is generated at public expense to satisfy a demand expressed as a legislative or administrative mandate. Once generated as a public good, its use is not fully understood. It enters a process whose output is a management decision. The ill-defined character of this process has an impact on important aspects of the legal process, such as the application of copyright, disclosure and liability law.

- *Information leaks in the sense that computerization creates more gates than the gatekeepers can patrol.*

The desire to capture and market information increases as automated systems grow to include large databases and complex software. The powerful perception that data and information are valuable and can be captured for sale does not overcome the barriers to achieving these objectives. It remains difficult to define and make effective a legal regime for information that sanctions and enhances the commodity value of information.

LEGAL ASPECTS OF GEOGRAPHICAL AND LAND INFORMATION

There are two elements of the legal regime which are particularly important for the development of geographical and land information systems:

- Access, including questions of ownership, sharing, privacy, political control and cost recovery.

- Liability, including questions of error, misuse of data and information, and compatibility.

Access to data and information

Access is a fundamental issue in GIS development. Data and information are divided and held among various groups, agencies and individuals. Each has a particular interest, opinion, concern, definition, process and use in regard to the material. Each acts in a rational, optimal manner to complete the group's mandate or requirements. Each has a constituency that protects these values.

Access is influenced by the division of data and information among groups, agencies and individuals. This division is according to government level, scientific and professional discipline, and private commercial orientation.

Division of access to data and information

Division by government level At the national and local level, data and information are collected, analysed, assembled and represented by specific agencies, each with its own statutory or administrative mandate. These mandates do not necessarily mention data and information. Instead, the agencies have mandates to administer programmes, develop policies, make decisions, or take actions. Many of these activities require data and information. Each agency acts individually and rationally to design databases that contribute optimally to its activities. The result is databases within agencies, governments and nations, each with its own attributes. These often have incompatible formats, holders who are reluctant to release material to others and other barriers to the flow of data and information. Each agency worries about efforts to establish coordination, fearing that the effort will diminish its ability to fulfil its own statutory mandate.

Transnational information access depends, in part, on willingness of nations to enter into international agreements. These agreements are necessarily a part of national foreign policy. They reflect individual national perceptions of security, political, economic and social interests. Agreements in regard to transnational information flow depend upon a balance of national and international interests. The flow of information can become part of the international flow of commerce, but it can also reflect a concern about confidentiality of personal data, national economy and security. Each nation is likely to attach its values to the integrity of information about its own activities.

Division by scientific and professional discipline Each science has its own language, culture and methods. These appear as carefully delineated definitions and symbols for particular features, as standards for data resolution, as formats and as classifications or other divisions that determine database attributes. These attributes are rationally designed to reflect the needs of the scientists in a discipline. Specific formats and a discipline control over the database impede information flow among disciplines and agencies.

Division by private commercial enterprise The flow of information from privately held databases depends upon the ability of the user to pay for the data. Costs and the desire to protect the often considerable commercial value of the data impede flow.

The set of access laws determine the availability of information, the conditions of availability, and who is able to take advantage of the new and old opportunities provided by the new technology. These matters may be the most important in the development of information systems because they relate directly to the actual availability and use of information rather than the potential provided by the technology. Technology provides new, alternative and efficient means to collect, analyse and disseminate data and information. But if the availability of information products is limited because of access problems, then the potential of geographical information systems will not be fully realized. Every barrier to the flow of information is a barrier to system development. Some barriers may be appropriate, but the issue needs to be examined directly and fully.

The flow of data and information among people and organizations is a significant legal issue. The set of laws that constitute the information access regime are used by the various interests in ways that create barriers and incentives to the flow of information. The set of laws, and the principles behind them, need to be identified, considered and balanced in order to form an access policy.

Fundamental values in access to information

Three fundamental values govern the regime for information access and flow:

1. *Public values*. The fundamental value behind access to data and information laws is the citizen's need to know what governments are up to (White 1973). People view information as having this public value. Data and information are seen as essential to the free market in ideas. There is a concern that a totalitarian society can build information systems overtly designed to enhance government control of its citizens. Ultimately, people seek a legally enforceable right of access to the data and information used by governments to formulate policy, make decisions and take actions (White 1973). There is a long history of access to data and information as the means, not the end, of knowing what governments are doing.

2. *Private values*. Private values reflect a concern about the disclosure of data and information about particular individuals and their property. There are also concerns about disclosures that are seen to be unreasonably detrimental or favourable to individuals or groups and about

the ability to assemble data in ways that were not practical before computers.

3. *Commercial values*. Both site-specific and comprehensive data are perceived to have a commercial value because many people and organizations express a demand for them. Those who hold information and databases seek the flexibility to market this information in a manner not unlike the sales process for other commodities. This includes government agencies as well as private organizations that have data and information. Government as purveyor of information is a complex and controversial concept. Tensions exist between those in government who would market government information products as a commodity and those in the community concerned about limited access to information about what government is up to when public information is closely held and sold at prices restrained only by what a buyer will pay. However, the characteristics that distinguish information from conventional commodities of commerce make it difficult to achieve many of these commercial goals.

Inherently, there is tension between disclosure of information in support of public values, confidentiality, and the desire to sell information. This tension existed long before computers. The legal process is the traditional venue for the achievement of a balance between the several values. Principles have developed over a long period for balancing the elements of this not new problem, principles that remain active and useful.

The legal regime and access to information

The public value in information disclosure is expressed as an enforceable legal right of access to data and information that reveal government activity. The concept that information has long been seen as essential to the free marketplace of ideas is manifested by the 200-year-old First Amendment to the US Constitution. As the historian Henry Steele Commager noted, 'The generation that made the nation thought secrecy in government one of the instruments of Old World tyranny and committed itself to the principle that a democracy cannot function unless a people are permitted to know what their government is up to' (Commager 1973: 106). There can be no unfettered marketplace of ideas without unfettered access to information.

In the United States, public values are made operational in the federal Freedom of Information Act (FOIA) which requires that 'each agency, on request for identifiable records made in accordance with published rules ... shall make the records promptly available to any person' (Freedom of Information Act 1966a). State open records laws apply to state and local government agencies. Although each state has its own law and details, state laws generally reflect the principle of the federal law (Puissegur 1989).

The public value is reflected in the international community by actions such as that of the European Commission which, on 30 December 1988, proposed a freedom of access to information to ensure dissemination of information throughout the community (American Bar Association 1989). The proposal guarantees individuals the right to information about the environment in the possession of public authorities. Information includes all existing data collected or prepared by such authorities contained in completed written documents, data banks, or visual recordings. It also includes certain information supplied by others to the government. An individual is required to make an information request in writing and the government is required to respond within 30 days.

Private values are reflected in concerns and laws about disclosures of information. The United States, in its federal and state legal regimes, requires by statute access to all records, regardless of form, used in government activities but allows specific, narrowly defined exceptions designed to protect personal and proprietary information. The burden is on the agency to show that its data are covered by the exception, rather than on the requester to show that the desired data are accessible.

The US federal Freedom of Information Act is an example of such a law. After provision for disclosure, it specifically excepts data that are:

- specifically required by Executive order to be kept secret in the interest of the national defense or foreign policy;
- related solely to the internal personnel rules and practices of an agency;
- specifically exempted from disclosure by statute;

- trade secrets and commercial or financial information obtained from a person and privileged or confidential;
- inter-agency or intra-agency memoranda or letters which would not be available by law to a party other than the group in litigation with the agency;
- personnel and medical files and similar files the disclosure of which would constitute a clearly unwarranted invasion of personal privacy;
- investigatory files compiled for law enforcement purposes except to the extent available by law to a party other than an agency;
- contained in or related to examination, operating, or condition reports prepared by, on behalf of, or for the use of an agency responsible for the regulation or supervision of financial institutions; or
- geological and geophysical information and data, including maps, concerning wells. (Freedom of Information Act 1966b)

There is a long history of public management of legally protected confidential data and information without substantial controversy. Examples at the national level in the United States include the Census Bureau in the Department of Commerce and the Internal Revenue Service in the Department of Treasury, many of whose records have long been stored in a computer without controversy over unauthorized disclosure. Similarly, the Minerals Management Service (MMS) of the Department of the Interior requires geophysical maps from oil companies when there is an application for an oil lease. The MMS is required to hold this valuable property in confidence for a considerable period and it has done so without controversy (Martin 1983).

A particular concern in the computer age is that geographical data can be aggregated and disaggregated in ways that previously were not possible, with an expanded ability to identify individuals and their property. Some worry that privacy is affected by the ability to glean personal information from geographical data, and that this was previously not possible because paper records were scattered and incompatible, and thus not practically available for analysis. These concerns are addressable directly through continued attention in specific statutes to what is confidential and what is not.

International agreements in regard to the flow of data and information show a concern about personal privacy. For example, in September 1980 the Organization for Economic Cooperation and Development (OECD), consisting of some 19 European countries together with Canada, the United States, Japan, New Zealand and Australia, adopted the Guidelines on the Protection of Privacy and Transborder Flows of Personal Data (hereinafter call the OECD Guidelines). The OECD Guidelines were adopted by 19 member countries on 23 September 1980 and subsequently by the remaining five member countries. A further Declaration on Transborder Data Flows was adopted by the governments of OECD member countries on 11 April 1985. The Council of Europe Convention for the Protection of Individuals with regard to the Automatic Processing of Personal Data (the Council of Europe Convention) came into force on 1 October 1985. The first five states to sign the Convention were Sweden (September 1982), France (May 1983), Spain (January 1984), Norway (February 1984) and West Germany (June 1985). Ratification by any state can take place only when a signatory country has adopted domestic legislation to reflect the Convention (Mann 1987).

The commercial aspect of databases is protected by copyright law, which is designed specifically to protect the commercial value of a work. Ideas are not copyrightable, but specific expressions are. Databases generally fall into the category of compilations which are subject to international and national copyright protections (Karjala 1987).

Copyright and freedom of information Acts are distinct domains of law. Even where public databases are copyrighted, they may still be subject to the disclosure provisions of freedom of information and open records Acts. The relationship between these two legal regimes is not clearly delineated (Kidwell 1990).

Concern about the commercial aspect of information is reflected in international negotiations in regard to transnational information flow. The United States appears to advocate the free flow of information on the premise that information is a commodity in the free flow of commerce. It appears to support the argument that maintenance of controls on access is, in effect, restraint of trade. Transferred to the national and local context, this position suggests that the flow of information from government agency to others, public or private, is undesirably hindered by high levels of fees and charges (Office of Technology Assessment 1981).

Liability for data and information

One of the first questions posed to lawyers is 'What is my liability?' Those who design and operate information systems are not exempted from these concerns (Epstein and Roitman 1987). It is inevitable that there will be errors in data, programs and products of an information system. Managers of these systems want to know what liability they may have and how they can avoid, or at least minimize, their exposure. Those who allege harm from poorly made decisions based, in whole or part, on inappropriate or incorrect data will assert claims that extend to the generators of the information products. Information, once obtained by exercise of various access levers, is used in a process whose final outcome is a management activity involving policy formation, specific decisions and implementation actions. Within and without the data generating agency there are concerns about potential liability for harm that results from use, misuse and unintended use of the data and information.

The ultimate users of maps and other geographical information products are citizens, planners, public officials, lawyers, bankers and similar decision makers, often without expert knowledge or experience with this spatial material or the measurements it may represent. These users want data and information, at reasonable cost, that reduce the uncertainty of their management decisions. Their lack of cartographic knowledge of the products can increase their exposure to liability.

Liability can arise in a variety of contexts. Decisions are made with inaccurate data or misuse of accurate information. The data may be produced by an agency for use by others who are unaware of the data error attributes and may not understand what the information represents, or what computations have been made. Finally, the liability issue has emerged recently as publicly owned geographical information system managers seek to recoup some of their system investment by marketing information products or services to the private sector, which in turn uses the information to make products for others. Having represented that the information is valuable, what is the agency's liability if the data are inaccurate, or, even if accurate, the client misunderstands the information and misuses it? Is the agency liability exposure altered by efforts to market information?

Theories on liability

There are two broad theories of liability most likely to be encountered – breach of contract and negligence (Epstein and Roitman 1987). Other theories, like breach of warranty and strict product liability, may arise. It has been suggested, for example, that strict product liability should be applicable for personal injuries caused by defective medical computer programs. Under strict product liability, it is not necessary to show that the manufacturer of the product was at fault, just that the product was of an inherently dangerous nature and in fact caused the harm. This scenario is unlikely for the case of information system products.

Contracts Contractual liability is the easier of the two broad theories to describe and discuss. This is because the terms of the agreement are a starting point for the allocation of legal duties and responsibilities among the parties and thereby a basis for the determination of liability. Courts will generally uphold contract provisions which clearly describe the products or services to be provided. In the case of a large or complex job for a computer system, the seller is advised to describe carefully the standards which are to be applied to the products or service through warranties or warranty limitations in the contract. On the other hand, the buyer looks for a warranty that the product or service to be provided is suitable for the buyer's intended purpose. Further, the scope of damages can be defined to limit liability by contract. Again, the utility of this type of limitation is different for the buyer and the seller.

The biggest problem with reliance on the negotiation and allocation of duties and responsibilities in the context of the use of information systems in the public sector is that contracts are seldom appropriate or used. This is particularly the case when databases are involved.

For example, the land use regulation and decisions which spawned the use of many computerized systems do not give rise to a contractual relationship between the member of the public and the agency. Even in the context of use of information systems products or services by the private sector, contracts resulting from negotiation between the parties are the exception, if they are used at all. Contracts are important when hardware and software are purchased or where data collection and entry services and products are obtained by organizations from private vendors.

Negligence Negligence arises when a person fails to exercise the standard of reasonable care normally expected of a person in that situation and some damage to another person occurs as a result of that failure. Over considerable time, legislatures and courts have defined the standard of reasonable care in many everyday situations, such as operating an automobile.

Because widespread use of computers is relatively recent, there are not yet many cases concerning liability for computer error. However, in the cases which have addressed the issue, courts generally uphold the basic principle that requires people to take reasonable care when computers are used.

Most cases which deal with the issue of liability for 'computer error' arise where adverse action is taken based on allegedly inaccurate information supplied by a computer. Many of these cases are about loan defaults, utility service terminations and automobile repossessions where the consumer brings errors to the attention of the company, which then persists in its action based on information from its computer system. The lesson of these cases is that reliance on 'computer error' is not a defence to an injury suffered by another person, at least when the error is brought to the attention of those responsible for the data or information. Failure to act when errors are found is the most common problem.

It remains impossible to operate a computer system without some errors in the data and software, many of which may be difficult to detect and correct. Further, the system may operate at an acceptable level of error for the system's regular users, but produce a product which causes damage to an outside user of the system or a person who uses a system product for a purpose different from that for which the system was designed. Whether the system's owners or operators are liable for the error depends largely on the circumstances. However, there are some general rules to consider in assessing the likelihood that a computer system owner will be found liable for damages based on computer error.

It is unreasonable to require no errors from a computer system and it is unlikely that a court would insist on such a standard. Beyond that, the level of care will be developed on a case-by-case basis through application of the broad principles discussed here.

An appropriate level of care must be used in the selection and maintenance of the system (hardware and software) because failure to select and maintain a system which will accurately perform the required tasks may well constitute negligence. There are different levels of care to be considered based on the uses of the system and the likely impact of those uses on outsiders. The more likely a particular system is to have a significant adverse impact on someone, the higher the level of care to which a court may hold the system's developers, owners and operators.

A major concern for system builders is to ensure that the data entry process is designed to achieve an acceptable level of freedom from errors. If somebody claims damage as a result of errors in data entry, a court is likely to examine the process used to determine whether a reasonable standard of care was taken to minimize data entry errors. Achievement of this level of care might require reasonable training procedures, as well as a process for data verification and documentation of procedures and actions.

The broad implication is that the developers and owners of the system must carefully anticipate many of the tasks which a system will perform and how those tasks could adversely affect the product used by people. The term 'system' includes the non-computerized portion of the organization. For example, if the system is responsible for determining tax assessments, sending out notices and initiating adverse action when taxes are not paid, the process should also include an effective mechanism for system operator intervention when an error is brought to his or her attention. It should also include some basic level of competence for the hardware, software and data entry systems. The system must meet a minimal level of competence to protect against such damage. That level is determined by reference to reasonable standards in the community. When the system falls below those standards, liability may well be assessed. Reasonable analysis, procedures and documentation are an effective barrier to liability exposure.

If the system is intended to promote the sale of products and services to outside users, there must be a clear understanding of what the system can and cannot do, and this understanding must be applied to marketing plans. When possible, the types of products and services to be marketed should be assessed during the system development and design. The same analysis, which is used to determine whether the system will meet expected levels of competence for its basic uses, should be applied also to the marketing uses. Uses which can be anticipated should be included in the system design and if minimal levels of competence for these uses cannot be assured, consideration should be given to abandoning them as potential system uses. It is important to note that the degree of public agency liability exposure can increase, in some circumstances, when the agencies act to sell data (Puissegur 1988).

Unanticipated uses for the system will undoubtedly arise after initial design and development. These are probably the most dangerous in terms of potential liability. New and foreseeable uses are within the purview of the original designers and programmers who can determine whether appropriate levels of confidence can be achieved for these uses. Where such an analysis is not possible, or is not reasonable to undertake, the system owner should consider whether any reasonable potential liability is outweighed by the advantages in undertaking the new use and generating the new product.

Liability for misuse of information

Land management activity (policy, decision or action) occurs in an environment of less than complete certainty. The level of uncertainty is determined by the political, social, economic and historical character of the community where the action occurs. The acceptable level of uncertainty ultimately determines the quality of data and information assembled to support land management activity (Epstein and Duchesneau 1984). People are willing to absorb a level of risk, as well as reduce it, when decisions are made (Bedard and Epstein 1984).

Creation of an information package for land management generally requires three actions: data acquisition, analysis and combination. Rapid, specifically designed and creative combination of data represents the great potential of geographical information systems. Thus, the liability implications of making such combinations are worthy of special attention. Data compatibility is a measure of the ability to make appropriate data combinations. If data compatibility is an issue, then several questions arise as an information package is assembled, as indicated in Fig. 32.1 (Epstein and Duchesneau 1984). The import of this process is that if data files exist, if they are of acceptable quality and if they are compatible, then they can be efficiently assembled into an information package for management. But if they are not available, or of poor quality, or incompatible, then supplemental actions should be taken to achieve the desired level of information quality. The computer offers a means to avoid the immediate expense of creating data compatibility. However, this action is fraught with problems that can increase exposure to liability.

Land data and information can be made

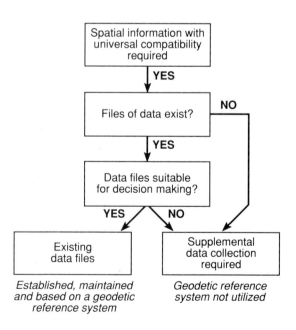

Fig. 32.1 The land-related decision process.

compatible in two ways. In the first, geographical data and information are made compatible when needed by reliance upon facile, computer-based manipulation of the data. Digitized maps and other independent digital files are combined as necessary by sophisticated (or unsophisticated) computer programs designed to generate products which have the requisite pleasing appearance for decision making. Cartographically inexpert users, without sufficient awareness of inherent data quality and compatibility, who rely on this process increase the possibility that inappropriate combinations will be used for management. Errors and problems can be hidden from the unknowing and unwary. Costs appear later in the form of the adverse impacts of poor decisions, including liability actions.

Use of computer programs to create compatibility is the map maker's automated form of 'rubber sheeting'. For example, there are times when the automated combination of files yields a map with several lines where only one is expected and is acceptable, and this makes people nervous. A soothing, smoothing subroutine can be used to eliminate the multiple lines and the nervousness.

Alternatively, compatibility is achieved when it is built into the data as they are collected. This occurs when features are located relative to a common datum, especially a Geodetic Reference Framework (Epstein 1987), which consists of a set of points whose locations are accurately determined with respect to a mathematically defined coordinate system. This system permits spatial referencing of all land data to identifiable positions on the earth's surface. It provides not only an accurate and efficient means for locating features, but also a uniform, effective language for interpreting, relating and disseminating data and information. Use of a Geodetic Reference System for the overlaying and registration process is represented in Fig. 32.2 (National Academy of Sciences 1983).

The ability to determine the locations of features represented on one layer of spatial data relative to those from another is a powerful tool in the analysis and management of land and its resources. Combination of data layers provides a wide range of needs that could not be met before the advent of computers. Combination of data with compatibility built in through reliance on a geodetic reference system avoids many of the problems associated with misuse of data and liability for the resulting harm.

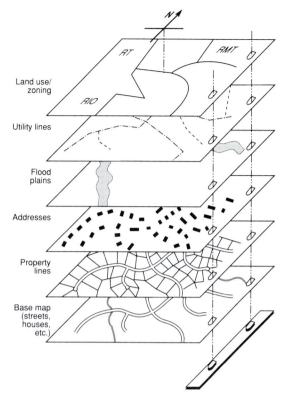

Fig. 32.2 A registered overlay system.

Liability scenarios: the case of maps

Maps may contain errors, may be poorly designed and may be used inappropriately and in ways unintended by their designers. These problems can be categorized as follows:

- Errors and omissions in represented locations.
- Error-free representations that, nevertheless, create foreseeable problems.
- Use of spatial products for unintended purposes, or in unintended ways.

Errors in represented location Errors in locations and in the information about those locations typically result from measurement and data-handling mistakes. National map accuracy standards prescribe a reasonable level of misrepresented locations. In automated map making, data entry occurs when measurement data are transformed into numbers and stored in a computer file or when maps are digitized. A court is likely to consider the process used for data entry and whether or not a reasonable standard of care is established and utilized in the process of design and implementation, including data priority rules and training procedures aimed at minimizing errors.

In a court case (*Indian Towing Co* v. *United States* 1955) the federal government was held to have negligently failed to maintain a lighthouse marked on nautical charts and described in the Light List. In another (*Reminga* v. *United States* 1978) the federal government was held to have inaccurately and negligently depicted the location of a broadcasting tower on an aeronautical chart, contributing to mistakes and resulting fatalities in an airplane accident.

Representations of error-free data These can result in liability when the form of representation is confusing or inappropriate for the user's purposes. In a court action (*Aetna Casualty & Security Co.* v. *Jeppeson & Co.* 1981) it was asserted that a fatal airplane crash resulted from a defective aeronautical chart published by Jeppeson. The chart depicted the instrument approach to an airport from information promulgated by the Federal Aviation Administration (FAA) and described by the FAA in tabular form. The chart graphically displayed two views of the approach, one from above and another as a profile or side view. The court found that the chart had a defect, not in the accuracy of the representation, but in the particulars of the graphic form of representation. The problem was that the profile or side view appeared to be at the same scale as the top view, whereas there was a factor of five between the two. The plane crashed on approach and the cause was determined to be, in part, the pilot's mistaken reliance on a chart feature which appeared to be 15 miles from the airport but which was actually three miles from the airport. The court found that the crew were misled to a degree by the representation and that this contributed to the crash. The court ruled that the chart publishers were at fault because 'The professional must be able to rely on the accuracy of this information if he or she is to benefit from the mechanization or special compilation of the data . . .' (*Aetna Casualty & Security Co.* v. *Jeppeson and Co.* 1981). However, the pilots also shared in the fault: 'The professional . . . will be expected to use his or her professional judgment in evaluating the information and not to rely blindly on what he or she is told by the computer or the charts' (*Aetna Casualty & Security Co.* v. *Jeppeson & Co.* 1981). Here the pilots were found to have been confused by the form of representation.

Unintended and inappropriate uses of maps These occur among public and private users and are most likely where map designers and developers are not available to the user and the user lacks expertise or access to expertise about the map and its represented measurements. Inappropriate combinations of maps and spatial features often occur.

In litigation that reached a state Supreme Court (*Zinn* v. *State* 1983), evidence of the location of the ordinary high water mark (OHWM) for a navigable lake was presented in a regulatory hearing. In a final official report, the hearing examiner sought to indicate that the evidence of the lake level corresponded to an elevation 980 feet above sea level, while evidence of the OHWM corresponded to elevation 990. This evidence was represented by marks and highlights on the contour lines of a USGS 7.5 minute quadrangle map for the area.

Several months after the issuance of the report, the owner of land abutting the lake, a person not a party to the original hearing, brought an action against the state. She asserted harm resulting from a taking of her property without due process of law. She claimed that the map incorrectly represented the boundaries of her property and their relation to the lake and surrounding land, showing incorrectly that most of her land was below the OHWM, and would therefore belong to the state. She asserted that the official report represented a claim by the state to most of her property, created a cloud on the title to her land, and deprived her of her riparian rights to the lake. The state Supreme Court held that it was reasonable for the plaintiff, title attorneys and knowledgeable citizens to conclude, based on the map in the hearing examiner's report, that the state asserted title to the plaintiff's land. The state was liable for the harm imposed on the landowner.

The problem arose because the hearing examiner placed evidence of the OHWM, evidence in the form of observations and measurements by botanists and surveyors, into the context of the

USGS Quadrangle. These data were transformed into information with the characteristics of both the Quadrangle and the data themselves. The final product presents a more complex picture of the land than the observations or the Quadrangle separately. There was justified reliance by the public upon a map-making action that, in this case, was not executed with the proper duty of care. The duty was to make an adequate statement of the location of the OHWM relative to other land features. The map reader 'sees' a combination of the highlighted contour, topography and other features represented in the Quadrangle, and personal experience with the site. The knowledge garnered by this combination is not the same as the combination of OHWM observations with site experience.

An appropriate alternative representation could have been the statement in words and numbers (i.e. without a map) that the OHWM is at a particular elevation. The statement does not place the OHWM observations into the context established by the Quadrangle with its particular attributes of scale and accuracy. The statement requires that the relation between the elevation and other ground features be determined by means other than inspection of the map. The words are not the same as the picture. Another appropriate representation is the use of highlighted contours on a base map of larger, more appropriate scale than that of the USGS Quadrangle (1 : 24 000). This combination presents a different, more reasonable representation of the relationship between an elevation and other land features such as topography, lake surface location and parcel boundaries.

This case illustrates both the use of a base map for a purpose unintended by the professional cartographer and an inappropriate combination of map features for land management. The problems represented here are no less likely, and perhaps more likely, in the age of automated map making.

CONCLUSIONS

This chapter has examined the importance of the legal process to the current and future development and use of GIS. The key elements of the legal regime are access and liability. Access includes questions of ownership, sharing, privacy, political control and cost recovery. Access to information in government, scientific and professional, and private organizations is influenced by public, private and commercial values. Liability includes questions of error, misuse of data and information, and compatibility. Although theories of breach of warranty and strict product liability may arise, the most likely to be encountered in the GIS field are breach of contract and negligence. Already a number of test cases have established precedents in the use of geographical information. The current level of activity, particularly in the applications, suggests that legal aspects of GIS will become significantly more important in the future.

REFERENCES

Aetna Casualty & Security Co. v. Jeppeson & Co. [1981] 642 F. 2nd 339 (9th Circuit)

American Bar Association (1989) The year in review. *Natural Resources, Energy and Environmental Law Review*, American Bar Association, Chicago Illinois

Bedard Y, Epstein E F (1984) Spatial data integration in the information era. *Proceedings of the Federation Internationale des Geometres (FIG) Symposium on the Decisionmaker and Land Information Systems*. Canadian Institute of Surveying and Mapping, Ottawa Ontario, pp. 104–113

Commager H S (1973) Quoted by Justice W O Douglas in EPA v. Mink. 410 US 73: 106

Epstein E F (1987) Litigation over information: the use and misuse of maps. In: Aangeenbrug R T, Schiffman Y M (eds.) *International Geographic Information Systems (IGIS) Symposium, Arlington, Virginia*, Vol. I. NASA, Washington DC, pp. 177–84

Epstein E F, Duchesneau T D (1984) *Use and Value of a Geodetic Reference System.* Federal Geodetic Control Committee National Oceanic and Atmospheric Administration, Rockville Maryland

Epstein E F, Roitman H (1987) Liability for information. *Proceedings of the Urban and Regional Information Systems Association*, Vol 4. URISA, Washington DC, pp. 115–25

Freedom of Information Act (1966a) As amended. *5 USCA §552(a)(3)*

Freedom of Information Act (1966b) As amended. *5 USCA §552(b)(1–9)*

Friedman L M (1984) *American Law*. Norton, New York

Indian Towing Co. v. United States [1955] 350 US 61, 76 S. Ct. 122, 100 L. Ed. 48

Karjala D S (1987) Copyright, computer software, and the new protectionism. *Jurimetrics Journal* **33**: 51–4

Kidwell J (1990) Impact of copyright law. *Workshop on Managing the Risks and Recovering the Costs of Geographic and Facilities Management Systems.* University of Wisconsin-Madison, Madison, Wisconsin

Mackaay E (1982) *Economics of Information and Law.* Kluwer Nijhoff, Boston

Maguire D J (1991) An overview and definition of GIS. In: Maguire D J, Goodchild M F, Rhind D W (eds.) *Geographical Information Systems: principles and applications.* Longman, London, pp. 9–20, Vol 1

Mann J F (1987) *Computer Technology and the Law.* Carswell, Toronto

Martin P H (1983) Disclosure and use of proprietary data: task force report 15. *Natural Resources Lawyer 799.* American Bar Association, Chicago, pp. 802–3

National Academy of Sciences (1983) *Procedures and Standards for a Multipurpose Cadastre.* National Academy Press, Washington DC

Office of Technology Assessment (1981) *Computer-Based National Information Systems.* Congress of the United States, Washington DC, pp. 58–9

Puissegur A (1988) Does charging eradicate the defense of sovereign immunity? *Proceedings of the Urban and Regional Information Systems Association*, Vol. 4. URISA, Washington DC, pp. 358–70

Puissegur A (1989) An overview of state open records laws. *Workshop on Managing the Risks and Recovering the Costs of Geographic and Facilities Management Systems.* Department of Engineering Professional Development, University of Wisconsin-Madison, Madison, Wisconsin

Reminga v. United States [1978] 448 F. Supp. 45 (W. D. Mich.)

White B (1973) Supreme Court opinion in EPA *v.* Mink. 410 US 73

Zinn v. State [1983] 112 Wis. 2nd 417, 334 N.W. 2nd 67

33

MANAGING AN OPERATIONAL GIS: THE UK NATIONAL ON-LINE MANPOWER INFORMATION SYSTEM (NOMIS)

M J BLAKEMORE

This chapter describes the characteristics and management aspects of NOMIS, the UK National On-line Manpower Information System. The system provides geographically-detailed information in a series of domains covering employment, unemployment, job vacancies, demography and socio-economic parameters. It represents a GIS because of the nature of the information and operators that may be applied to the massive (20 Gb) database. The chapter concentrates on management and human resource issues in developing such a system and coping with competition, all within a government policy which demands commercial returns on sales of government-derived data and services.

BACKGROUND

The National On-line Manpower Information System (NOMIS) has been developed for the UK Department of Employment Group by the University of Durham. It was first developed for information covering the northern region in 1978 and, since 1982, the system has been in full operational use. The fundamental attraction of NOMIS to the user base is the immediacy and extent of access to official UK government statistics. Unemployment statistics are released on NOMIS as soon as the official statement has been made in the House of Commons. Employment statistics are distributed primarily via NOMIS and enquiries to official sources are referred to the system as being the fastest and most cost-effective source. NOMIS also integrates a huge variety of data by domain, through time and across space. The management of such a system, based as it is in an academic environment, involves meeting a variety of goals. These include the management of change while maintaining system stability; retaining existing users and attracting new ones; building a cohesive development team, yet allowing for staff changes; developing effective user interfaces and technical documentation; and last, but not least in the academic sector, achieving job satisfaction and rewards for the staff while working in a low pay environment. Thus there is a series of continually evolving management challenges which typify a rapidly evolving system in a highly dynamic geographical and economic environment. These are compounded by the position of NOMIS in the university sector as a fully commercial contract, won by competitive tender. Before considering these management challenges, a description of the complexities of the database is given.

THE DATABASE AND ITS MUTATIONS

As of mid-1990, some 20 gigabytes of local labour market data were held on-line on an Amdahl mainframe at the University of Durham. The

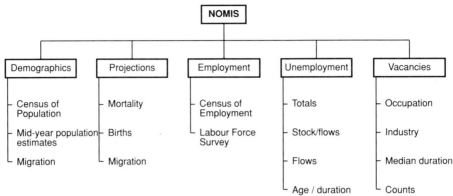

Fig. 33.1 The major data sets available in NOMIS.

information in NOMIS is grouped into five major domains (Fig. 33.1). Demographic data include the decennial Census of Population (some 130 000 Enumeration Districts, each with over 5000 variables), mid-year Estimates of Population, and projections of births and deaths. Migration is estimated quarterly using registrations for National Health Service Family Practitioners Areas, disaggregated by age and sex. Employment statistics are currently biennial (between 1971 and 1977 it was triennial), and is a domain in considerable demand by the commercial sector. The information on unemployment and job vacancies (jobs registered at Job Centres, estimated to be between 30 and 35 per cent of all vacancies) formed the original basis of NOMIS and now exist in several forms, ranging from monthly counts to complex quarterly analyses. Figure 33.2 gives a breakdown of the main data series by area type and periodicity.

The most heavily used data domains have been employment and unemployment; these formed the mainstay of usage in the late 1980s. Into the 1990s, employment remained a dominant domain with use of demographic data increasing very rapidly as users seek to assess the projected 'demographic time-bomb' of declining numbers of youths and growing numbers of the elderly. Data from the decennial 1991 Census, to be released in 1991–93, will be an important new series providing highly detailed and disaggregated lifestyle information.

Primary reasons for using NOMIS are rapid access to the latest information and the comprehensive geographical integration. The system is not oriented to those who want just the occasional table of data – training implications of the support of such casual users are too great and the cost of user support would outweigh the income generated. However, postgraduate research students are seen as important seed-corn and their access to the system is provided as a loss-leader.

Three main methods are used to access NOMIS, the most basic being telephone dial-up at speeds up to 2400 baud. Then there are two high speed networks running at up to 9600 baud. For academic users the Joint Academic Network (JANET) interlinks all universities and polytechnics in the United Kingdom. Commercial users have access to British Telecom's Packet Switching Stream (PSS), which has both direct high speed lines and also a very cost-effective dial-up service, with calls into NOMIS via local nodes and charged at a local rate.

At present, all information in NOMIS comprises official UK government statistics. The sections of the various government departments supplying these statistics are all under the umbrella of the Government Statistical Service (GSS). The data are collected to serve policy requirements of the UK government and, while they are made available to the wider user community, it is policy development that affects the ways in which statistics are collected and reported. Thus, even during the life of NOMIS so far, there have been recalibrations in the definition of 'unemployment' in the United Kingdom, leading to many discontinuities in the time series. This in particular has led some to assert that the figures are being manipulated for political ends – though, in truth, manipulation can only exist if the precise definition is not communicated. A direct effect then is that those wanting to examine trends through time have to cope with breaks in the time series. Since most space–time models assume

Data Sets by Major Geographical Areas

Geographical areas (columns 1–22):

1. Regions
2. Regions and ex Metropolitan Counties
3. Rural Development Areas
4. Training Agency Area Offices
5. Counties (& Scottish Regions)
6. Assisted Areas
7. Local Education Authorities
8. NHS Migration Area
9. District Health Authorities
10. Functional Regions
11. 1984 Travel to Work Areas
12. 1978 Travel to Work Areas
13. Local Authority Districts
14. Parliamentary Constituencies
15. 'Standardised' Employment Offices Areas
16. Employment Office Areas
17. Postcode Sectors
18. 1984, 1987 Wards
19. 1981 Wards
20. 1981 Enumeration Districts

#	Data Files	Periodicity	Start Date	End Date
1.	Census of Employment, Standard Industrial Classification 1980 (by sex, full-time and part-time)	Annual	1981	1984–1987
2.	Census of Employment Standard Industrial Classification 1986 (by sex, full-time and part-time)	Annual	1971	1978
3.			1981	
4.	Labour Force Survey	Annual	1988	
5.	Employees in Employment	Q	1990	
6.	Census of Population, Small Area Statistics		1981	
7.	Occupational Statistics, 10% Sample		1981	
8.	Occupation by Industry 10% Sample		1981	
9.	Population Estimates (England and Wales)	Q	1984	
10.	NHS Migration Data (by age and sex)	Annual	1981	2011
11.	OPCS Projections of Population and Migration	Q	8/1978	
12.	Vacancies and Placings by Industry and Occupation	Q	3/1986	
13.	Vacancies and Placings by Median Duration	M	8/1985	
14.	Unemployment Claimants by 9 published categories	M	6/1983	
15.	Unemployment Claimants by 9 published categories	Q	9/1985	
16.	Unemployment, Claimants by Age and Duration	Q	7/1983	
17.	Unemployment, Claimants by Age and Duration	Q	9/1985	
18.	Unemployment, Inflow and Outflow by Age and Duration	Q	6/1983	
19.	Unemployment, Inflow and Outflow by Age and Duration	M	7/1978	6/1983
20.	Unemployment Register by 7 published categories	Annual	6/1972	6/1978
21.	Unemployment Register by 7 published categories			

NOTE: Additional Series disaggregate the Unemployment Register by Ethnic origin, and by last Industry and Occupation until 1981–1982, when these data ceased to be coded.

Fig. 33.2 NOMIS data sets classified by geographical area.

continuity of definition both through time and of the geographical base, this is highly unrealistic when relying on official statistics.

The 'continuity of geographical base' problem is addressed in many domains by publishing the statistics for a variety of geographies. NOMIS makes data available at all aggregations above a base geography. For example (Fig. 33.3) a simple output list for a set of regions may be requested using acronyms such as 'pca' for parliamentary constituencies. Any set of areas may be aggregated in real time to form a single composite one and the top level of definition enables users to define their own 'non-official' geographical bases by creating 'chain' files which again operate in real time. The geographical bases available include administrative 'wards' (Fig. 33.4) which are 'frozen' in their state at the time of the 1981 Census (so giving spatial consistency for a decade); these build into all the higher level zonal structures. Job Centre areas are the basis for vacancies data but these mutate through time and do not nest with the ward-based geographies. Thus an 'amalgamated' super-set is created for time series and best-fit matches have been made of Job Centres-to-ward bases. Post-code sectors – most popular for commercial sector clients – are also liable to mutate but do nest with Job Centres. Data collected for a range of other geographies and stored in NOMIS, such as unemployment benefit offices (constantly changing), Family Practitioners Areas and Training Enterprise Council structures, further complicate the analysis and comparison of data series. Lastly, the employment data are published in ward structures current at the time of collection, most recently 1984 and 1987. (For a review of data integration problems see Flowerdew 1991 in this volume.)

To give rapid access to this multiplicity of structures, full on-line search facilities exist for all geographical hierarchies, with the option of directing the output list into a file for subsequent input as a command file. The dynamism of the UK geographies is one reason for the very large pre-processing element of NOMIS. A considerable amount of the code is taken up with the sequencing of tape arrivals, initial tape validation, verification of fields and contents, cross-checking of totals against other data series and automatic matches against existing NOMIS geographical structures. In this way, for example, NOMIS automatically checks

---

Some examples of user defined geographies

- Simple list
  pca = 34
  region = 1–12
  1981 opcsward = 1034, 1056–1125, 1127–1200
- Dynamic aggregation to a single area
  User = 'United Kingdom' region = 1–12
- Creating customised user geographies
  A 'chain' file comprising:
  User = 'My area 1' 1984ttwa = 1–12, 15–19
  User = 'My area 2' 1984ttwa = 25–60

Key to geographic units employed:
pca = parliamentary constituency area
opcsward = electoral ward used as an areal unit in the 1981 Census of Population
ttwa = travel to work areas

Fig. 33.3 Some examples of user-defined geographies available in NOMIS.

---

to see if Unemployment Benefit Offices and Job Centres have opened or closed. In such an event, the internal indices are updated, a user message is inserted into system news and documentation is updated and dispatched.

While some may argue that NOMIS is not a GIS in the strict sense (see Maguire 1991 in this volume) – it does not have coverage preparation or an overlay processor – it is widely regarded as such because it delivers cohesive geographically-coded local labour market data, as well as data consistently maintained through time and by thematic classification. Moreover, it copes with typical geographical problems. For example, all NOMIS data refer to UK administrative geographies; while the geographies may be defined through sets of boundaries, their demarcations on the ground are fuzzy and the system has to cope with that characteristic. Furthermore, there are several geographical bases within NOMIS which do not nest yet facilities for matching these exist. But, since the thematic nature of the data is such that within-area homogeneity of density cannot be assumed (while there may be 'x' unemployed in zone 'y' it cannot be inferred that they are equally distributed throughout), use of the 'standard' tool of overlay with such a database would be dangerous.

The way in which the system has developed has been an object lesson in developing management styles. Since 1986, when the system was made available to all user groups, the number of subscribers has increased from 45 to over 300 sites.

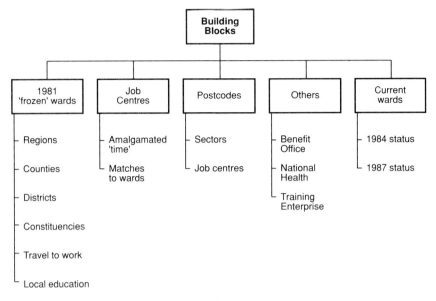

Fig. 33.4 The major geographies available in NOMIS.

The range of information domains also has expanded to include 10 major government suppliers, all of whom have their own internal supply standards, tape formats and geographical labelling; links are maintained with nominated individuals in each data supplying agency to ensure rapid correction of errors. The variety of data suppliers highlights the disaggregated nature of information collection in the United Kingdom. While the US decennial census of population is collected by a single agency (the US Bureau of the Census), the UK census is collected semi-independently by the Office of Population Censuses and Surveys for England and Wales, the General Register Office for Scotland, and the Department of Economic Development in Northern Ireland. Population estimates are collected by the same organizations with the addition of the Welsh Office for Wales. Not only do these different agencies have different technical and other standards but also they have different policies regarding access to data.

CHALLENGES IN MAKING NOMIS A SUCCESS

These challenges will be considered under the following headings:

- Management structures;
- Human resources in the development team;
- Computing resources and service provision;
- User support and financial policy;
- Facilitating new developments while maintaining stability for users.

Management Structures

NOMIS is owned by the Department of Employment Group (ED Group). System development is carried out under contract by the University of Durham, but the equity value of the system resides with the UK Civil (or Public) Service. For the ED Group, the goals are well defined. NOMIS should offer them rapid, timely and comprehensive access to integrated local labour market information; this should facilitate the development of policy, support the briefing of senior management and provide better targeting of resources in the long-term training and development of the UK labour market. It is mandatory that the system must be demonstrably cost beneficial and, increasingly, it must be possible to recover investment from users other than those in the core central government group; both of these objectives reflect UK government policy in general. For the Durham team, the financial objectives are reflected in a goal to reduce dependence on the core central government user group.

The cost benefits of NOMIS can be expressed in both direct and indirect terms. The former are the crucial ones since HM Treasury prefer to see tangible savings in budget as being the main determinant of success. At 1986/87 prices, NOMIS has been saving ED Group £236 000 a year over and above the contract price. This was calculated by the staff savings made directly in the 11 regional Intelligence Units (IUs), where clerical staff formerly had to prepare information manually. This alone justified the existence of the system. The intangible benefits could not easily be directly quantified – a common problem inherent in the benchmarking of complex GIS (see Clarke 1991 in this volume; see also Dickinson and Calkins 1988). Nevertheless, it is clear that they include: the added value of immediacy and enlarged access to detailed national and local information; the cost savings incurred by more effective policy generation; and unspecified direct benefits on staffing experience by the increasing range of other government departments using the system. These now include the Department of Trade and Industry, the Department of the Environment, the Home Office, the Office of Population Censuses and Surveys (the census-taking agency in England and Wales), the Department of Transport, the Welsh Office and the Scottish Development Agency. Further societal benefits accrue to local government, which is now an extensive user of the system, but these are not taken into account in the basic cost-benefit model. Lastly, there is a tangible benefit to the Civil Service in the form of more effective research in the academic community. This forms an important component of advice and briefing material for decision makers.

The position of NOMIS in a higher education institution gives further benefits in the provision of the latest information to the research community at highly advantageous rates. Research students are not charged for the use of NOMIS *per se*, but only for the nominal computer time used on the university mainframe. NOMIS staff have been instrumental in persuading data suppliers that academic researchers should not have to pay for data being accessed, so generating further savings. Moreover, such agreements have long-term benefits to the public service in training individuals who can then work in the various departments using NOMIS data or who can evaluate the data effectively even if in other jobs.

Human resources in the development team

NOMIS is an idiosyncratic system. It has not emerged through either of the commercial or purely academic routes, but has straddled both. In addition, it has never been part of the development strategy to 'break free' of the predominance of the ED Group and other central Civil Service departments who constitute the main user base. The simple rationale is that, since it is owned by ED Group, this 'freedom' can never be on the agenda. However, there has been a firm policy – agreed with ED Group – of diversifying the user base.

The origins of the system were in 1978 with a contract between the then Manpower Services Commission (the forerunner of the Training Commission or TC, thereafter the Training Agency or TA and now re-absorbed back into ED Group as TEED, the Training Education and Enterprise Division) and the Universities of Durham and Newcastle (David Rhind and John Goddard being the principals). Over a period of four years, the code developed into an operational system. The author's personal involvement has been since late 1983. At that time, the system design was the responsibility of a single programmer, Robert Nelson, who now is the NOMIS System Manager. The development team initially comprised him and a mapping assistant (Peter Dodds), both of them were employed on short-term (and hence unsatisfactory) contracts. Thus there was inherent instability at a time when NOMIS was becoming increasingly important as an operational tool for central government. To be fair, blame must be attributed on both sides – the University for allowing strategically important staff to be employed on such unrewarding terms (a situation that exists commonly today in the UK university sector) and the contract sponsors for not evaluating the threat to their investment adequately.

One time-consuming management exercise since 1983 has been to strengthen and professionalize the team. By 1990 there were five main programming and development staff, plus two support staff and a much more effective operational relationship with computer colleagues in the Civil Service. The team still is relatively small for a user base of over 300 sites, but the stress that has been put on team building and skill development has meant that, since 1983, very few staff have left and those few occurrences have been for positive career moves. One final point regarding staffing changes: within the NOMIS team there is a policy of asking staff what they wish to do 'after NOMIS'. This attitude aims to nurture career prospects by encouraging the interchange of information. It means that staff transitions can often be planned with the minimum of disruption. Staff are also encouraged to take on consultancy work for clients and to visit key sites on a regular basis. This allows them to obtain near-market expertise, as well as direct financial reward. Too often in the university sector, research and development staff have been treated as chattels attached to projects – to be discarded when expedient. Conversely, in the Civil Service, the policy of moving staff from job to job every three years or so often means that it is not possible to build the stable base of expertise that is demanded by software and database development.

Computing resources and service provision

At the time of writing (1990), NOMIS is based on an Amdahl mainframe running the Michigan Terminal System (MTS) operating system. In UK terms this is an anachronism, particularly in these days of increasing UNIX orientation. The demise of MTS will occur in 1992, after 25 years of operation in the Universities of Newcastle and Durham. The planned demise offers the opportunity to look at the way in which NOMIS, developed in a FORTRAN-77 context and using the advanced features of a particular operating system, can migrate to more standard systems. This is more than just moving 30 000 lines of code on to another hardware and software platform, although that has been the first 'insurance policy' stage achieved late in 1990. It involves extensive redesign of data and file structures, as well as the user interface. The new system must maintain the highly effective task sharing, facilitated at present by a very tight dynamic overlay design. NOMIS is contracted to enable up to 20 simultaneous 'sign-ons' for central government users alone within the proportion of the university mainframe which is available for the project. The data files are also designed with this in mind. Instead of a relational structure, NOMIS data files are flat files, structured by time–period and directly indexed by the geographical look-up tables.

Data compaction is absolutely crucial. The 20 gigabytes (Gb) of raw data, growing at over 2 Gb a year, are compacted by a two-stage process (Fig. 33.5) into about 13 per cent of the original storage. The file structures allow for arbitrary length direct access files with line lengths of up to 32 767 bytes. This allows all the data for any one area to be stored on the same line, so directly keying them into the geographical indices. Each line is scanned, first to run length encode any zeros (all NOMIS data are non-negative integer) and then to ascertain the maximum value. According to this value, the line is then assembler-compacted into fewer bytes and an extra byte inserted at the beginning to record the compaction level. The impact of this regime is twofold. First, there are massive savings in on-line disk storage – at full commercial contract costs this is a saving of several million pounds a year. Secondly, the fact that some files are compressed to only 1 per cent of original size allows them to be read in a single buffer and rapidly reconstructed in virtual memory. Not only does this mean a faster response time for users, but it is also cheaper since fewer relatively expensive disk-reads are required. This also helps ensure the ease of sharing outlined above. The compaction regime has been replicated on a UNIX host, thus completing another stage in the transition.

**NOMIS
Data Compaction Regime**

- 1. Run-length encode Integer non-negative data
  256 1934 0 0 0 2 0 0 0 231 59 1523 0 0 0
  becomes
  256 1934 −3 2 −3 231 59 1523 −3
  reduces from 15 to 9 32-bit locations (60%)
- 2. Check for maximum values and compress
  <2048 Store as a 12-bit sequence
  <32768 Store as a 16-bit sequence
  <8388608 Store as a 24-bit sequence
  >8388607 Remains as default 32-bit
  Add one extra byte for the compression level (0–3)
  This reduces the example to 25% of original
- 3. The situation in late 1990
  Uncompacted on-line requirement 20.96 gigabytes
  Compacted requirement 2.63 gigabytes (12.55% of original)

Fig. 33.5 The NOMIS data compaction regime.

System security and integrity builds upon the compaction regime. This is fundamental for an on-line system such as NOMIS. It is accepted as fact that once the data are on a user's screen there is no technical way of stopping them from capturing the screen image/contents on a micro (indeed the carefully planned development of effective downloading and data capturing mechanisms is discussed later); thus they must not be available on the system to users before the official release date. But, since NOMIS releases many official statistics on-line at the moment of publication, this means in some cases having them in advance of that date for loading and pre-testing; for users to be able to access them before official release would be a catastrophe. MTS has a multi-layer protection capability which affords protection against such an outcome. All accounts are password protected – normal for any system, of course – although the incentive for NOMIS users to be secure is that they agree to pay all costs on their account. Every use of NOMIS is logged and this forms the basis of the billing system as well as providing a monitoring function if misuse occurs. Misuse has occurred only once and that was an academic user trying to transfer boundary files over JANET. In this instance, the GIMMS mapping package was being used without maps being produced and the file transfer protocol was being accessed; the user formally agreed to destroy all files. Another layer of protection is given by first compacting each NOMIS data file, then encrypting it and finally it is made accessible *only* via NOMIS, and in some cases, only to specified users via a passkey function. Time triggers are set for release of new data. Matching these levels of protection is clearly essential on the UNIX platform and, in a time of increasing threats, needs to provide extra layers of security from file storage to network integrity.

Given all of the above, the three most crucial areas of concern over a period of two years of rapid change are: ensuring a transparent transition to the new system for the user base; retaining and enhancing current data compaction and security regimes; and re-evaluating current storage strategies against reducing real disk costs. The user base will not accept a transition which reduces response times, requires significant re-training or costs more per unit of usage. These all are long-term design issues, involving upward compatibility and long-term testing of systems in parallel.

User support and financial policy

In April 1986, NOMIS was made available to all potential client groups. Until then, its primary remit was to serve the core Civil Service clients and a small number of local authorities and academics. At that time, the user base was around 60 accounts. Since then there has been considerable growth of around six accounts a month. An account normally is used at a single site by staff authorized to have access to NOMIS. The user base has also diversified (Fig. 33.6) with central government now forming only 31 per cent of the total number of sites, although significantly more in terms of income. The commercial agencies now active as clients include business location and geodemographics consultancies, but the largest group by far is the property market consultancy sector. There also has been a significant increase in the number of local government users.

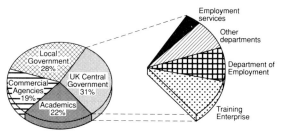

Fig. 33.6 A classification of NOMIS users (percentage number of sites in each category).

The most difficult aspect of this expansion among non-core clients was that of how to charge for an on-line system which delivers such a variety of data and analysis. Most existing on-line databases are 'flat', in that they are mainly free text of the bibliographic or newspaper type. They mostly have fixed charges, based on the amount of time a user is logged on and on the number of transactions made (i.e. abstracts or paragraphs selected). NOMIS charges are based on a collection of items which includes elapsed 'sign-on' time, disk use, processor use, output media and mapping produced. This 'by use' rather than 'flat rate' charging may seem difficult for new users to comprehend so prospective users are offered a number of free runs to help them visualize end costs. Those attending training courses also have access to free-resourced accounts that enable them to experiment without financial penalty.

Charging for use of data is difficult. Since 1986, the UK Department of Trade and Industry's Tradeable Information Initiative has encouraged government departments to generate commercial returns on the sales of their information. The UK attitude to government data is enshrined in a review of the Government Statistical Service (the Rayner Review) carried out in 1981, which formalized the view that information is collected for the purposes of the government and that – unlike the situation in the United States – any other public or private use should be undertaken at a commercial cost. At the time NOMIS was requested to implement charging, there were no other comparable on-line charging regimes in government. The cost structures used by data suppliers assumed outright purchase of data, yet this was unworkable on-line since no user would require all the data; to check an individual account's use of variables would have needed a binary matrix held for each user for every data set. Moreover, the software overheads of checking would have been prohibitive. A regime of bulk discounting over a monthly period was proposed, applicable only to full commercial users; NOMIS successfully persuaded the data suppliers not to charge local authorities or academics for access to their data. This charging regime simply aggregated the number of cells used in each data series and matches the end-month total against a published charge table. All users are advised of the computer time charge and those who are charged for data access are advised of the charges incurred at the end of each run. All those charged for data access can run an audit command to ascertain the running total for the month.

NOMIS pays proper commercial rates for all the software and infrastructure used. But, because it is based in the academic environment, it is university policy only to charge marginal costs to academics using NOMIS for *bona fide* research. Regular management statistics produced include monthly summaries of use by account and charging group, a daily profile of usage peaks, and a day-by-day summary of processor use. Also produced monthly are disk status by data domain, with forward warnings of any capacity problems, and statements of chargeable data use by individual account, plus how that is to be apportioned to data-supplying agencies. 'Sleeping' users, who access NOMIS infrequently, are easily identified using these statistics, although being an 'on-demand' on-line system there has not been a policy of enforcing minimum charges other than the cost of the extensive documentation; this comprised some 2000 pages in 1990, including complete listings of geographical hierarchies and background metadata on the information domains. The documentation itself forms an extensive primer on the UK's local labour market information base.

The actual number of on-line sessions (Fig. 33.7) shows a buoyancy of demand. Central government use is increasing consistently as more departments join. In 1989, for instance, the global amount for all groups increased by some 30 per cent. A matter of considerable concern has been the decline in usage by postgraduate students, a symptom of the decline in both student numbers and their available resources. Such a decline is clearly not in the long-term interest of central government, let alone higher education.

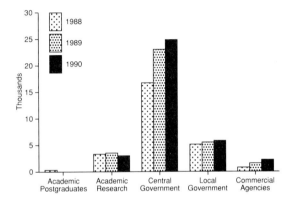

Fig. 33.7 The number of on-line NOMIS session classified by user group.

Facilitating new developments

In the past, NOMIS has been dominantly a centralized on-line system. Users had the ability to route output to line printers, laser printers and plotters but they have relied on the output being posted on to them. In effect, the postal system itself has formed a subset of the NOMIS code, with all user outputs being monitored through the print queues and matched against a daily list to avoid anything being lost or delayed. Optional flags can be used to request fax or courier services. Since 1988, NOMIS has moved more towards being a powerful 'data engine' with an emphasis on downloading outputs into microcomputer packages. Network speeds and reliability now enable this approach to be used operationally, especially when supplemented by more effective error-correcting modems and use of more widely accepted standards and protocols. Structures available include headed files for microcomputer mapping systems, flat data files for statistical analysis, tabular data for word processors and comma-separated value files for spreadsheets. Increasingly, terminal emulator packages are used to customize access, with transparent automatic network dial-up and 'sign-on' and single key functions to upload and download files. While it is supported by NOMIS, the downloading of data is not an unconstrained facility. It is not in the interests either of NOMIS or of the data suppliers to see ever-increasing amounts of data disappearing down the networks. Downloading implies data purchase for subsequent re-use and so is a chargeable facility. The downloading of tabulated outputs, as opposed to raw data, will always automatically include statements on temporal or spatial discontinuities in the selected data, on any important background data and a warning on Crown Copyright. In this way, NOMIS aims to protect the integrity of the data and the rights of data suppliers by making 'best endeavours' to monitor usage. It also aims to make 'best endeavours' to facilitate rapid and effective access to data for the user community. In this way, speed of response does not mean a loss of control over the information base.

Computer mapping is provided by two options: a mainframe interface to GIMMS or a microcomputer route detailed below. On the mainframe, a simple file interface provides a transparent link into a menu-driven interface to the widely used GIMMS package (Carruthers and Waugh 1988). An extensive set of pre-prepared boundary templates are accessible (up to all 9289 wards for England and Wales) and answering a series of questions allows users to produce output ranging from A4 laser to A0 pen plots. Some exploration has been undertaken of the feasibility of providing topographic underlay although it must be admitted that Ordnance Survey pricing policy has been a major constraint in pursuing this. A possible alternative may be the road database developed by the Automobile Association containing roads, settlement outlines and names gazetteer and hydrography. As of mid-1990, discussions on this were still at an early stage.

For microcomputer systems, the main moves are towards the development of customized front ends. This is particularly important for mapping since a supported microcomputer mapping system needs to be able to 'recognize' an arbitrary list of geographical areas requested by a NOMIS user. The PCMAPICS system, developed at University College London, contains full digital mapping facilities and, importantly, has a boundary database facility called GEOBASE. Users can demand a unique group of areas and GEOBASE extracts the relevant boundaries, builds them into a map file, calculates scaling and positioning. This can all be constructed as a menu-driven front end to MAPICS which makes the entire process of extracting information from NOMIS to producing a desktop map into a relatively transparent process. Such developments now increase the amount of consultancy and advice needed by and provided to users, with ever-increasing sophistication of equipment at their sites.

User support and training on a wider scale now takes up a much greater percentage of time than hitherto. Training for use of NOMIS is residential in Durham, using a 'deep immersion' approach over three days with specific training documentation and follow-up opportunities. Video and computer-based tutorial facilities, such as the use of hypertext/ hypercard tutorials have been evaluated and discounted for the present. Such is the need for understanding of the information content on NOMIS (as opposed to the mechanical and technical functions of most GIS) that it may be easier actually to move the command parser down on to micros, together with most of the on-line help documentation, and create a new menu-driven local front end to the system. Like many vendors, the NOMIS team are concerned that, if others take on a training function for NOMIS, then they should be fully trained and legitimated. Most of all, such a policy helps to maintain standards. The success of such a policy is exemplified by the ESRI training policy for ARC/INFO; this has developed from basic courses and primers to a highly structured strategy including training the trainers, extensive workbooks and videos and a comprehensive GIS primer.

Irrespective of its past success, technical sophistication and user growth, the future of NOMIS is very much bound up in the UK government policy regarding the supply and cost of information. For each new data domain, the lead time from first discussion to on-line supply has a mode of around 12–18 months. Some discussions never result in data being added to the system. In terms of management time, some 30 per cent of effort is spent at the acquisition end and another 40 per cent on support for the key users. A goal for the mid-1990s is to be a major host for the 1991 UK Census of Population yet, even in late 1990, there was no indication of cost structures to be charged by the government so that market research could be undertaken to gauge demand. In 1992, the European Community becomes an open market (with the removal of tariffs and trade barriers, and the unconstrained movement of labour) and information dissemination to the 12 member states represents a considerable opportunity. Even here, the opportunities and threats are bewildering. Some multinational corporations are moving rapidly into the on-line information market, supplemented by 'frozen' if frequently redistributed databases in CD-ROM form. Presently, the physical capacity of CD-ROM is a limitation for NOMIS, but a more direct limitation may be the attitude of UK data suppliers who fear the loss of control over their own data when available on distributed media.

UK government policy on a wider scale poses many questions. The 'Next Steps' initiative seeks to move many parts of government into agency status, or even into full privatization. In this, an 'Executive Agency' becomes a separate 'business' or budget centre in its own right, needing to present a balanced budget. This may hasten the development of full cost recovery policies regarding data. The Ordnance Survey and the Employment Service are now two such Executive Agencies. The Health Service is being fundamentally reorganized and the information technology implications of this are considerable. Companies such as British Telecom are starting to market their own employer/ employment database on a national coverage in competition with those from government departments and agencies. Inevitably, therefore, the next five years will see major changes in the structure of the UK information market. The main aim for NOMIS will be to maintain and enhance its reputation of being an efficient and cost-effective broker primarily of government, and eventually European, data relating to the widest definition and requirements of a multinational labour market. Whether such a goal is achievable while remaining based in an academic environment is a debatable point. It may be that significant cash injection will be needed to provide enough resource to compete against other information vendors. The main aim will be to maintain and enhance the reputation of NOMIS as a 'bespoke' information service in a niche market that comprises regular users of local labour market information. Thematically, the information base will expand to embrace domains which strengthen the labour market information (LMI) – but LMI remains the core.

Other systems and resources will address other sectors. The SASPAC system, a self-contained retrieval and analysis package for census data, will again be used widely by those who either wish to analyse only their local area or to concentrate on census data. For academics, it must be admitted, SASPAC also may present an attractive option since its central purchase for the higher education sector will make it a 'free' resource, in sharp contrast to NOMIS. Other users may continue to use the services of the ESRC Data Archive at the University of Essex from where whole data series can be acquired, although not with the immediacy of response possible using NOMIS. Such other services are viewed as complementary to NOMIS and the continuing developments of all three can serve only to strengthen the quality of information handling and use in the United Kingdom. Lastly, there are companies which operate on a global scale, such as Maxwell Communications Group and other on-line hosts. Their strategies are global, highly resourced and potentially highly acquisitive. The only certainty is that the pace of change in the 1990s will make the first ten years of the NOMIS GIS seem like a very leisurely perambulation.

REFERENCES

Carruthers A, Waugh T C (1988) *GIMMS User Manual.* GIMMS Ltd, Edinburgh

Clarke A L (1991) GIS specification, evaluation and implementation. In: Maguire D J, Goodchild M F, Rhind D W (eds.) *Geographical Information Systems: principles and applications.* Longman, London, pp. 477–88, Vol 1

Dickinson H, Calkins H W (1988) The economic evaluation of implementing a GIS. *International Journal of Geographical Information Systems* **2**: 307–27

Flowerdew R (1991) Spatial data integration. In: Maguire D J, Goodchild M F, Rhind D W (eds.) *Geographical Information Systems: principles and applications.* Longman, London, pp. 375–87, Vol 1

Maguire D J (1991) An overview and definition of GIS. In Maguire D J, Goodchild M F and Rhind D W (eds.) *Geographical Information Systems: principles and applications.* Longman, London, pp. 9–20, Vol 1

34

SPATIAL DATA EXCHANGE AND STANDARDIZATION

S C GUPTILL

Spatial data exchange and standardization are important in GIS because they are key elements of the data integration process, that is, bringing together disparate data sets. Standards must be established before spatial data exchange can proceed freely. This chapter introduces the background to the problem of data standardization and exchange, the main methods of exchange are reviewed and the standardization efforts of various groups are discussed. The need for well-defined and agreed standards is emphasized as is information about data quality.

PHILOSOPHY BEHIND DATA EXCHANGE AND STANDARDIZATION

Dictionary definitions of 'exchange' refer to the concept of reciprocal giving and receiving. In the context of GIS, data exchange is a data communication process perhaps better characterized as data import and data export. The data exchange process is not typically reciprocal, rather it involves users importing data that they have purchased from a set of data exporters (providers), typically government agencies or commercial data sources. In addition to these formal data exchanges, numerous informal exchanges of data between researchers also occur. The need to be able to receive data from a number of sources and exchange data between dissimilar GIS presents a number of challenges. From a user perspective the challenge involves integrating a heterogeneous data environment. The various aspects of this heterogeneous environment that affect the import and export operations must be understood for the data exchange or transfer process to be meaningful and successful.

A digital spatial data set represents a certain model of geographical reality. For users to make sense of the data they are receiving, they must understand the conceptual model underlying the data. The process of creating a representation of geographical reality, or more accurately of a given conceptualization of reality, is variously referred to as semantic data modelling, knowledge representation, semantic network description, or, perhaps more broadly, conceptual modelling (see Egenhofer and Herring 1991 in this volume). The various terms have evolved from work in artificial intelligence and database management research and are further discussed in Winston (1984) and Brodie and Mylopoulus (1986).

A conceptual data model is an abstraction device that allows certain aspects of the real world to be captured and represented. The conceptual data model is in the middle of a set of levels of abstraction that run from reality to a physical data model (Teorey and Fry 1982; Peuquet 1984; see also Maguire and Dangermond 1991 in this volume). These levels are shown in Table 34.1.

Every GIS has its own, unique (to varying degrees), conceptual and logical data models that manifest themselves in a unique physical data model. To export a data set, the internal physical data model is converted to a specific file structure on a given type of medium (such as tape or disk). To import a data set, the process in reversed. There are basically two ways to pass data between different GIS (Pascoe and Penny 1990). The first is the direct conversion of data from one system to another (as if translating a book from English to German). The

Table 34.1 Levels of data abstraction.

Level of abstraction	Definition
Reality	The total phenomena as they actually exist.
Conceptual data model	The sets of components and the relationships among the components pertaining to the specific phenomena thought to be relevant to anticipated needs. A data model is independent of specific systems or data structures that organize and manage the data.
Logical data model or data structure	The logical organization of the components of a data model and the manner in which relationships among components are to be explicitly defined.
Physical data model or file structure	A set of rules that specify the machine implementation of a data structure within various computing system environments.

second method is for the parties to agree to use a standardized common (neutral) exchange file structure for exporting and importing data (as if translating a book from English to Esperanto, then Esperanto to German). The creation of such neutral exchange structures (and the supporting conceptual data models, data structures and specifications) is the focus of various standardization efforts that are underway in many countries. Exchange and standardization require an understanding, and in the case of standardization, agreement on, data model and data content constructs. The parties of a data exchange, particularly those on the receiving end, need to understand the conceptual data model and specifications being used to create the data and file structures.

This chapter is organized into four further main sections. The next section provides some background information about data standardization and exchange. It points to the need for a clear understanding of the data model represented by the data. Following this the three main mechanisms for exchange are evaluated, that is, direct translation, the 'switchyard' and the use of neutral exchange file formats. Next the standardization efforts of various countries and groups are reviewed, focusing on the activities in the United States, United Kingdom and the computer graphics arena. Finally, some brief conclusions are presented.

PREREQUISITES FOR DATA EXCHANGE AND STANDARDIZATION

Spatial data sets are collections of locational and non-locational information about selected features, attributes of the features and relationships between the features. In the context of GIS, features are the sum of interpretations of geographical phenomena. Buildings, bridges, roads, streams, grassland and counties are examples of features. Spatial data models that specify the sets of components and relationships among the components must describe both the locational and non-locational aspects of the features of interest.

Spatial data are often used as an all-encompassing term that includes standardized products such as digital cartographic data, remotely sensed imagery and census tract descriptions, as well as more specialized data sets such as seismic profiles, distribution of relics in an archaeological site, or migration statistics. Taken literally, spatial data could refer to any piece of information related to a location. Such a sweeping definition is too unwieldy to deal with in this discussion. The term geographical data, in its broadest sense, does not differ much from spatial data, but is often taken to restrict the subject matter to those features that describe the earth's surface. Digital cartographic data tend to be the encoding of geographical features as they have been represented on a map graphic. This is a simplifying (some might contend restricting) condition applied to the set of geographical data. The cartographic legacy of the data usually causes temporal or three-dimensional aspects of a feature not to be represented. Digital cartographic data are the type of geographical data most often considered when data exchange and standardization of GIS data sets are discussed. Therefore, the remainder of this discussion will focus on this type of information.

The locational aspect of a geographical data set is usually described by one of two types of data models: tessellation models, such as raster models;

Table 34.2 DLG-E feature data specification template.

FEATURE – definition as documented in DLG-E domain of features.

ATTRIBUTE/ATTRIBUTE VALUE LIST:

    Attribute   definitions of attributes and values
    Value   (those common to more than one feature are generic definitions)

DELINEATION – (ground truth) – what the feature looks like on the ground.

DATA EXTRACTION:

Capture Condition – criteria for determining when a feature is to be captured for inclusion in the database. This is independent of source.

Source Interpretation Guidelines – criteria for extracting ground truth, for those situations that are ambiguous, from various sources (image, field, graphic, DLG-3).

Valid Attributes – which attributes are valid for a given scale.

REPRESENTATION RULES:

Composition Rules – under these conditions, feature has these relationships (allowed relationships may not always occur).

Delimiting Rules – definition of the occurrence of a feature instance.

Special Conditions – specific definition rules that are peculiar to a specific feature.

---

or vector models, where graphic elements describe the location and extent of the phenomenon under study. The nature of these spatial models and the ability to convert from one to another are described in Egenhofer and Herring (1991 in this volume) and Peuquet (1981a, 1981b). Suffice it to say that the parties of a data exchange must agree, in specific detail, the characteristics of the spatial model being used to describe the locational aspects of the geographical data set.

The spatial data model must, in addition, handle all of the non-locational information used to describe the features in the database. For users to understand the nature of the data that are being received, there must be a complete specification of the features of interest. A comprehensive specification would include the definition of the features as well as definitions of their attributes and attribute values. Other information required for a complete understanding includes: delineation guidelines, data extraction rules and representation rules. Understanding how the locational component of a feature is represented is of little use unless the user understands what is being described. What is really meant by terms such as 'forest', 'marshlands', 'residential land', or 'bridge'? Do the definitions and specifications of the data producers match the expectations of the user?

To help solve this data definition problem, the US Geological Survey (USGS) has developed the concept of a feature data specification to provide a detailed definition of each feature and how it is modelled (Guptill 1990). Other mapping agencies such as the Institut Géographique National (France) (Salgé and Piquet-Pellorce 1986) and the Landesvermessungamt Nordrhein-Westfalen (West Germany) (Barwinski and Brüggemann 1986) have adopted similar methods. The feature data specifications define the domain of features that may be represented in a spatial database. For each feature in the feature data specification, a domain of attributes is defined. Each attribute is assigned a value, taken from the domain of values specified by the attribute definition authority. In addition to the definitions, guidance is given on how a given feature is delineated, when it is collected, and how it is represented in the spatial data model. This type of information is presented for the US Geological Survey's Digital Line Graph – Enhanced (DLG-E) data (Guptill, 1990) – using the template shown in Table 34.2.

An example of how this template is used is

shown in Table 34.3. In this table, a complete specification of the feature 'road' is provided. The specification includes information that traditionally would be found in topographic map compilation instructions and standards for graphic symbolization and publication.

At first glance this may seem like an excessive amount of information to accompany a data exchange. But as the uses of GIS become more sophisticated this type of information will become imperative. Consider a hypothetical GIS used on recreational watercraft and aircraft to aid navigation. It is reasonable to assume that users would like information on the various types of navigational aids to be in their GIS database. Users of this system get data from both the USGS and the Defense Mapping Agency (DMA). Unfortunately for them, the USGS and DMA have different approaches to providing such data. USGS has one feature 'beacon' that covers an array of signs, lights and electronic facilities that guide mariners and/or airplane pilots (see Table 34.4). DMA has two systems for describing such items resulting in eight different features. One description originates from its hydrographic charts and includes 'electronic beacon', 'light' and 'visual beacon'. The other description is derived from aeronautical charts and includes 'air obstruction light', 'NAVAIDS', 'radar transmitter', 'aircraft facility beacon' and 'approach lighting'. Users will need the type of information shown in the feature specification template in order to determine what information is appropriate for their use and how to derive it from the data provided by two different sources.

The goal of data exchange is the transfer of information to communicate an understanding of the phenomenon being represented. What on the surface may seem to be a straightforward task has many levels of meaning particularly when data content issues are considered. Each of these data content issues needs to be understood for the data exchange process to be completely successful.

MECHANISMS FOR ACHIEVING EXCHANGE

As noted above, data structures specify the logical organization of the components of a data model and its content. File structures specify the implementation of the data structure within a given computing environment. Documentation of these allows computer programs to be written to perform the data exchange. There are three basic design strategies that can be used by data exchange software: direct translation; translation to an internal standard, then retranslation; and translation to a neutral format.

In direct translation the software converts the data in the internal file structure of system A to the internal file structure of system B (see Fig. 34.1). This provides an efficient mechanism for data exchange that requires an understanding of the internal workings of the two systems involved. However, if data exchange between more than two systems is required, the problem becomes more complicated. Add two more systems, C and D, to the data exchange mix. Now instead of two programs being required (translate A to B, translate B to A), 12 would be needed. The number of permutations grows rapidly as more systems participate in the exchange (exchanges between 10 systems would require 90 direct translation routines).

An alternative to direct translation is the concept of a 'switchyard' conversion that avoids the factorial increases as more parties are added to the data exchange. This software translates incoming data to one internal standard, then on output translates the data from the internal standard to that of the desired export format (see Fig. 34.2). For each party added to the exchange, only two translation routines are needed (so data exchange among 10 systems would require only 20 translation routines, rather than the 90 required in the direct translation scenario).

The third method is for the parties to agree to use a standardized common (neutral) exchange file structure. System A translates its internal file structure into the standard structure. System B reads the standard structure and converts it into its own internal file structure (see Fig. 34.3). This method has the significant advantage that, in theory at least, only two software routines are required (one each to read and write the exchange format). The caveat is necessary, however, depending on the amount of flexibility that the neutral file format allows. If the format is highly flexible, with a number of optional fields and records, then one computer program may not be adequate for encoding (or decoding) data to (or from) the neutral

Table 34.3 DLG-E Feature Data Specification for 'Road'

Road – An open way for the passage of vehicles.

ATTRIBUTE/ATTRIBUTE VALUE LIST:

Access restrictions –		The constraints on use.
	Private	Maintained by private funds and not open to the public.
	Restricted	Designated for official use only.
	Toll	Controlled by payment of fee for travel.
	Unknown	
	Unspecified	
Directional status –		The state of movement along the feature.
	Alternating	Movement occurs in both directions, however only one way at a time.
	Bidirectional	Movement occurs in both directions simultaneously.
	Not applicable	
	One way	Movement occurs in only one direction.
	Unknown	
	Unspecified	
Median category –		The existence of a median.
	With median	Curbs or median strips separate opposing traffic lanes.
	Without median	Traffic lanes are not separated by curbs or median strips.
Name –		The proper name, specific term, or expression by which the feature is known.
	(Character identifier)	
	Not applicable	
	Unknown	
Number of lanes or tracks –		
	(Integer value)	
	Unspecified	
	Unknown	
Operational status –		The state or condition.
	Abandoned	Intact but not maintained or intended for use.
	Operational	Usable and intended for use.
	Proposed	Planned in detail, but construction not started.
	Under construction	Construction started, but not complete.
	Unknown	
Road class –		The classification of roads based on design, weatherability, governmental designation, and the Department of Transportation functional classification system.
	1st	Hard-surface highways including Interstate and US numbered highways (including alternates, primary State routes, and all controlled access highways).
	2nd	Hard-surface highways including secondary State routes, primary county routes, and other highways that connect principal cities and towns, and link these places with the primary highway system.
	3rd	Hard-surface highways not included in a higher class and improved, loose-surface roads passable in all kinds of weather. These roads are adjuncts to the primary and secondary highway systems. Also

Table 34.3 *continued*

		included are important private roads such as main logging or industrial roads which serve as connecting links to the regular road network.
	4th	Improved, loose-surface roads passable only in fair weather.
	5th	Unimproved roads passable only with four-wheel-drive vehicles. Included are one-lane roads on levees, and maintenance roads along transmission and other similar features.
	Unknown	
Road type –		The purpose or function.
	General case	Common use.
	Overlook	A pull-off area designated as scenic, having definite entrance and exit points that are separated from the roadway.
	Ramp	An inclined road connecting roads of differing levels.
	Rest area	An access road to service facilities such as service stations, weigh stations, comfort stations, restaurants, and parking areas.
	Runaway truck ramp	A short inclined road constructed of unconsolidated material that exits gradually from and runs adjacent to the right lane of a descending highway, for stopping runaway trucks.
	Traffic circle	A junction of roads that forms a circle around which traffic moves in one direction.
	Unknown	
Route designator –		The official alphanumeric identifier.
	(Alphanumeric identifier)	
	-->Route type	
	Alternate	
	Business	
	Bypass	
	Connector	
	Loop	
	Spur	
	Truck	
	Unspecified	
	Unspecified	
	Unknown	
Width –		The span of the feature perpendicular to traffic flow.
	(Integer value)	
	Unspecified	
	Unknown	

Table 34.3 *continued*

DELINEATION:

    A road is delineated by the edge of all traffic lanes, excluding the shoulders.

DATA EXTRACTION at 1 : 24 000 scale:

    Capture Condition –
    All roads are captured, excluding driveways that are less than 0.25 inch.
    Source Interpretation Guidelines –
    All sources –

    Hard-surface construction is generally concrete, asphaltic concrete, or bituminous macadam. Surfaces are waterproof. Minimum maintenance is required.

    Improved, loose-surface construction is on light foundation and is usually gravel or stone surface, or of some stable material, such as selected sand-clay, treated oil gravel, or light tar-bound macadam. The roads are generally drained and graded, but the surface is not waterproof. Periodic maintenance is required.

    Unimproved-surface construction is usually stabilized soil, sand-clay, or disintegrated rock with poor or no foundation. The road is sometimes drained or graded. If the roads are maintained at all, continual maintenance is required.

    Only class 3 roads are designated to have an access restriction of 'private'.

    Route designators are captured for Interstate highways, US numbered highways, and State highways.

    Names are captured for expressways and turnpikes, historical names required to preserve continuity of a feature, all streets in urban areas, and well-known or posted roads in rural areas.

    Image –

    For dual highways less than or equal to 0.035 inch in overall width, capture the median centerline, with median category value of 'with median' and width with a value for the extent of the road including the median.

    For dual highways greater than 0.035 inch in overall width, capture the centerline of each roadway, with median category value of 'with median' and width with a value for the width of each roadway.

REPRESENTATION RULES at 1 : 24 000 scale:

    Composition Rules –
    If width is less than or equal to 0.05 inch, road is composed of ordered chain(s), vertically related to other feature.

    If width is greater than .05 inch, road is composed of area, connected to junction, with inflow to/outflow from junction, vertically related to other feature.

    Delimiting Rules – Delimit instances using rules for network links.

    Special Conditions – None

Table 34.4 DLG-E feature definition for 'beacon'.

Beacon – A visual, audible, or electronic signal for the guidance of marine or air navigation.

    Name

        (Character Identifier)
        Not Applicable
        Unknown

Navigation Type

    Aeronautical
    Nautical
    Unknown
    Unspecified

Operational Status

    Abandoned
    Operational
    Unknown

Signaling Method

    Daybeacon
    Lighted ------------> Lighthouse Presence
    Radio   With Lighthouse
    Unspecified   Without Lighthouse
    Unknown

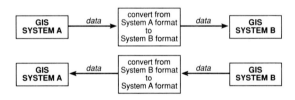

Fig. 34.1 Data exchange between GIS using direct translation.

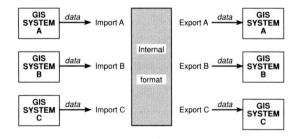

Fig. 34.2 Data exchange between GIS using a data 'switchyard'.

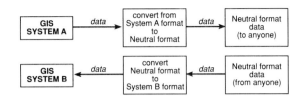

Fig. 34.3 Data exchange between GIS using a neutral format.

format. Separate routines may be needed to handle variations from government agency Y or GIS vendor Z. If this is the case, then the number of routines required for data exchange reverts to the solution given for the data 'switchyard'.

Comparison of methods

The direct conversion scenario provides the most efficient path between two parties exchanging data. A scheme can be devised to translate the set of features, attributes and relationships used in the first system to those used in the second system. The software can be designed to handle the conversion of information that is allowed in one data format but not another. For example, if the first system allows multiple-valued attributes (for example, attribute = building function; attribute value(s) = police station, fire station) and the second does not, then the data exchange software can include routines to alter the data organization to fit the specifications of the second system (attribute value = police and fire station). The major disadvantage is that such routines need to be written for every pairwise permutation of systems involved in the data exchange.

    The data 'switchyard' attempts to retain the advantages of direct conversion, while reducing the number of routines needed to convert the information among the systems involved in the data exchange. The major difficulty is that the hub of the 'switchyard', the internal representation of the data in the central conversion system, must be all-inclusive and be able to accommodate all of the characteristics of the data being imported or exported. The 'switchyard' software, like direct conversion software, can be designed to accommodate differences in data representation in order to place the data into the central internal data set. However, if data sets are transformed on input (e.g. concatenating multiple-valued attributes), then the inverse transformation needs to occur upon output (restoring the multiple-valued attribute from the concatenated representation).

The standardized, neutral file approach reduces the number of routines needed for data exchange. As with the central hub in the data 'switchyard', the neutral file structure must be all-inclusive in order to handle the variety of data structures (and underlying data models) that are used in GIS. Unless the parties of a data exchange agree on a common implementation of the neutral format (each party modelling phenomena in the same fashion and utilizing the same records and fields), varying implementations or dialects of the standard format may emerge. Each of these would require a separate import and export routine, thus defeating the goal of the standardized approach of requiring only two routines. A standardized neutral format that does not allow variations (or dialects) can be written, but typically this reduces the ability of the standard format to handle variations in data sets being exchanged. Trying to achieve a balance between uniformity and flexibility is a constant problem that individuals preparing standards must face. Clearly, however, from the point of view of a user receiving data from a number of sources, the concept of acquiring the information in the same format is very appealing.

To date, the most widely used 'neutral' formats for the exchange of vector data have been fairly rigidly specified data structures, developed by either major data producers (e.g. the DLG format of the US Geological Survey (USGS 1990), or developers of widely used software packages (for example the DXF format of AutoCAD). A similar situation exists with raster data, with the USGS's DEM format (USGS 1987) widely used for elevation data and the computer-compatible tape formats of Landsat (USGS 1984) and SPOT (Centre National d'Etudes Spatiales (CNES) 1989) used for digital image data. These *de facto* standard formats place an emphasis on uniformity and specificity in describing the data rather than providing a flexible envelope capable of holding a wide variety of data descriptions.

STANDARDIZATION EFFORTS

As the sources and amounts of digital spatial data increase, the need to transfer such data between non-communicating systems is becoming increasingly important. The concerns for common data formats and geocoding conventions cut across all topics of spatial data handling. Currently, it is difficult and inefficient for diverse users to use a given set of data. Several forces are causing concern about incompatibility: there is rapid progress and expansion in the area of spatial data processing; increasing amounts of spatial data are being generated and must be stored, catalogued and retrieved; and due to difficulty in sharing information, much of the map automation effort may be duplicative and redundant (Digital Cartographic Data Standards Task Force (DCDSTF) 1988). A spatial data transfer standard offers several potential advantages to users of spatial information: (1) it provides a set of simple cartographic objects from which digital cartographic feature representations can be built; (2) it allows the transfer of digital spatial information between incompatible systems while preserving the meaning of the information; (3) it supplies data quality information to users to permit evaluation of the fitness of data for a particular use; (4) it offers the opportunity to lower project costs by sharing data; and (5) it supports efforts to update data using multiple sources.

A number of efforts are underway to develop standardized data exchange formats for digital cartographic data. These efforts are variations on the 'neutral file structure' theme, with differing degrees of flexibility within the file structure. At a meeting of the International Cartographic Association Working Group on Digital Cartographic Data Exchange Standards representatives of the following countries indicated an active involvement in developing exchange standards: Australia, Canada, China, Federal Republic of Germany, Finland, France, Hungary, Japan, New Zealand, Norway, South Africa, Sweden, Switzerland, United Kingdom, Union of Soviet Socialist Republics, and the United States. The activities of the United Kingdom and the United States will be reviewed here to illustrate two approaches taken on the standardization question. The standardization activities of the computer graphics community are reviewed as an alternative strategy to create a spatial data exchange standard.

United States

In 1980, the US National Bureau of Standards (now the US National Institute of Standards and Technology) signed a memorandum of understanding with the US Geological Survey that resulted in the Survey assuming the leadership in developing, defining and maintaining earth science data elements and their representation standards for use in US Federal Government agencies. With this charter, the Geological Survey began work on several fronts in the area of spatial data exchange standards. One effort began in 1982, when a national committee in the United States, composed of members from private industry, government and academia, began work on a digital cartographic data standard. The national committee was formed under the auspices of the American Congress on Surveying and Mapping and was supported by a grant from the Geological Survey. Professor Harold Moellering of the Ohio State University headed the national committee, which produced nine reports. Report 8 A Draft Proposed Standard for Digital Cartographic Data summarized the committee's activities and work. A separate activity began in 1983, when the Office of Management and Budget issued a memorandum establishing the Federal Interagency Coordinating Committee on Digital Cartography (FICCDC) and naming the Department of the Interior as chair, which was delegated to the US Geological Survey. The purpose of the FICCDC is to coordinate the digital cartographic activities of Federal agencies and through this process avoid duplication in the development of digital cartographic databases. A major duty of the committee is to develop and adopt, for use by all Federal agencies, common standards of content, format and accuracy for digital cartographic data to increase its interchangeability and enhance its potential for multipurpose uses. The standards working group of the FICCDC selected as a priority task the development of a data exchange format and published a report in 1986 entitled 'Federal Geographic Exchange Format'.

In March 1987, the Geological Survey established a task force to combine the proposed cartographic data standard with the geographical exchange format. This combined document was published as the January 1988 issue of *The American Cartographer*.

The responsibility for finalizing the standard rests with the Geological Survey. A maintenance authority within the National Mapping Division was established in 1988 to test the proposed standard, conduct educational workshops, disseminate information and, in general, coordinate activities surrounding the promotion of the standard to the National Institute of Standards and Technology as a Federal Information Processing Standard (FIPS). A Technical Review Board, consisting of technical experts from the Federal Government, the private sector, and the university community who represent a diversity of viewpoints in the collection and use of digital spatial data, was established to oversee the content of the standard as it is being finalized and prepared for submission to the National Institute of Standards and Technology.

Objectives

As stated in the DCDSTF (1988) report, the objectives of the standard are:

1. To provide a mechanism for the transfer of digital spatial information between non-communicating parties using dissimilar computer systems, preserving the meaning of the information, and reducing to a minimum the need for information external to this standard concerning the transfer.

2. To provide, for the purpose of transfer, a set of clearly specified spatial objects and relationships that can represent real-world spatial entities, and to specify the ancillary information that may be necessary to accomplish the transfers required by the cartographic community.

3. To provide a transfer model that will facilitate the conversion of user-oriented objects, relationships and information into the set of objects, relationships and information specified by this standard for the purposes of transfer such that their meaning will be preserved and can be discerned by the recipient of a conforming transfer.

4. To ensure that any implementation of this standard can have the following characteristics:
   (a) the ability to transfer vector, raster, grid, and attribute data, and other ancillary information;
   (b) the implementation methodology can be media independent and extendable to encompass new spatial information as needed;
   (c) an internally contained description of the data types, formats and data structures such that the information items can be identified and processed into the user's native system;
   (d) the data and media formats should be based where practical on existing FIPS, ANSI, ISO, or other accepted standards.

Content

The proposed standard consists of several components. Part I, Definitions and References, includes a conceptual model of spatial data and definitions of fundamental cartographic objects and key terms that serve as conceptual building blocks for the constructs presented in the standard; Part II, Transfer Specification, defines the logical file structure for the transfer of the data; Part III, Data Quality, specifies the form of the quality report and requires the data provider to supply detailed information about the data set being transferred in order for the user to evaluate the fitness of that data for a particular use; and Part IV, Cartographic Features, presents a domain of cartographic entities with standard definitions.

The Definitions and References component defines a set of primitive and simple cartographic objects in zero, one, and two dimensions with which digital cartographic feature representations can be built. Four different data models are supported in the standard. They are a raster (or grid) data model and three variations of vector models: geometry only, topology only, or geometry and topology combined. Definitions are also presented for key conceptual terms that are used throughout the standard.

The Spatial Data Transfer Specification (SDTS) is the method whereby spatial data from one data-handling system can be easily transferred to another data-handling system. The standard provides a modular specification of data types and formats for the full set of digital information to be transferred. Of necessity, the transfer specification is complex because it must handle both vector and raster data. ISO 8211 (1986), 'Specification for a Data Descriptive File for Information Interchange', is a general-purpose interchange standard that is used as the implementation mechanism.

The basic concept underlying the *data quality* component is a 'truth in labelling' concept. The standard requires a report of what is known about the quality of the included data. Five components are available under which to define data quality: lineage, positional accuracy, attribute accuracy, logical consistency, and completeness.

The *cartographic features* component provides a model and definitions for cartographic features. The model consists of entities, attributes and attribute values. A list of topographic and hydrographic entities and attributes is provided with the standard; however, the standard also provides a mechanism for user-supplied definitions to accompany the data transfer.

The transfer specification can be used for the transfer of vector and raster data. Spatial objects represented according to these different data types can be joined into single composite objects, using the same transfer specification representation philosophy. The global and data quality modules specified here are equally applicable to vector and raster data. This consideration has been the primary purpose for including a raster representation of spatial data. It is not the intended scope of this standard to serve as a single basis for the transfer of raster data of all types. Other standards may be used more efficiently for the sole purpose of exchanging specialized raster data.

SDTS specifies a series of transfer modules. Each module contains a collection of module records. Each module record contains data fields that have been grouped together because of the purpose and/or function of that information. Transfer module types are grouped in relation to a certain type of data organization. Groups of actual modules to be transferred are called a transfer. A transfer may consist of a single physical file containing multiple modules, or may consist of multiple physical files each containing one or more modules.

Table 34.5 provides a list of transfer modules grouped according to the following: *global information*, *data quality*, *attributes*, *vector* and *raster*. The content and size of a transfer determine what modules and fields are present and how they are collected into records and the records into files. SDTS allows the user considerable freedom to structure records and files as needed.

Table 34.5 Spatial Data Transfer specification transfer modules.

Transfer modules

GLOBAL INFORMATION

Catalog/Directory
Catalog/Cross-Reference
Catalog/Spatial-Domain
Identification
Security
Internal Spatial Reference
External Spatial Reference
Spatial Domain
Data Dictionary/Definition
Data Dictionary/Domain
Data Dictionary/Schema
Transfer Statistics

DATA QUALITY

Lineage
Positional Accuracy
Attribute Accuracy
Logical Consistency
Completeness

ATTRIBUTES

Attribute Primary
Attribute Secondary

VECTOR

Point-Node
Line
Arc
Ring
Polygon
Composite

RASTER

Raster Definition
Cell
Raster Registration

United Kingdom

In the United Kingdom, the issue of a transfer standard for digital cartographic data has been addressed by the Ordnance Survey (OS), the major supplier of such data. The OS recognized, as early as 1969, that in order to transfer map data from the OS digital production systems to customers, it would be necessary to create a simple transfer format that was readily understood and accepted. Over the years the formats have been modified to allow for the transfer of more complex data. The House of Lords Select Committee on Science and Technology (House of Lords 1984) made a recommendation that a British standard for the exchange of digital map data should be established. Subsequently a Working Party to Produce National Standards for the Transfer of Digital Map Data, under the direction of the OS, was established. Their work resulted in the National Transfer Format (NTF), first released in 1987 (OS 1987) and later updated in 1989.

Objectives

The Working Party established three major objectives for the project:

1. The transfer format must be able to handle all of the data generated by any cartographic system. This rule can be checked by forward and back transfer of data after which no change in information content should have occurred.

2. The techniques used for the transfer format must be capable of being adapted easily for any computer on the market.

3. The structure of the transfer format should be such that development costs are minimized and maintenance is made easy (Sowton and Haywood 1986).

As was the case in the United States, the Working Party was designing a standard to be flexible and versatile within limits imposed by computer hardware and cost. The major reason for national standards is to improve the efficiency of data transfer. The Working Party contends that this can be achieved if three conditions are met: if there is a set of rules for documentation with which every producer and user can become familiar; if there is a common method of presentation of data, accepting that some variation will always be necessary; and if data can be written and read by the same program, irrespective of its detailed specifications (Sowton and Haywood 1986).

Content

NTF is designed for all types of raster and vector map data. To avoid the complications that a transfer format for structured data would impose on other types, five levels of transfer have been developed. These levels are as follows:

Level 0: This is for raster or grid data (e.g. digital elevation data).

Level 1: This is for simple vector data; lines, points, and text are separate entities and each can be given one feature code and one attribute value.

Level 2: Also for simple vector data, but with additional facilities for the addition of multiple, user-defined, attributes to the points, lines and text. Text can be linked to a feature as an attribute.

Level 3: This is for topologically structured data. It will transfer link and node data, polygons and complex objects.

Level 4: This is a user-defined format, intended mainly for topological structures that do not fit easily into Level 3.

All levels require the association of one record with another. At the lower levels this is achieved by adjacency, such that a record containing coordinates will follow immediately after the feature record (line, point) to which it belongs. At Level 3, association is achieved by matching key fields containing unique identifiers. The information to be transferred utilizes three major types of records: volume records, database records, and section records.

The volume records indicate the beginning and end of a transfer of data. Each volume has compulsory header and termination records that are the first and last records of the volume.

The purpose of the database records is to transfer information common to all of the data involved in the transfer. There are four types of database records: the database header record, the data dictionary record, the feature classification record, and the data quality record. The database header record indicates that a new database is starting and gives its name. It also references dictionary, classification and quality reports by name. The data directory records perform two functions. One record type allows the producer to define a transfer format within the rules and constraints of NTF. The second record type allows the producer to define and document attribute fields. The feature classification record allows feature codes used in the data set to be matched with a standard classification scheme, or a user-defined set of definitions. The data quality record is used to transfer information about the data in the database, such as accuracy, copyright information, digitizing scale and map projection.

The section records contain the geographical information that is the subject of the transfer. The specific data record organization depends on the level of the transfer. There are four types of section records. The section header record starts a new section (map) and contains information and parameters essential for interpreting and processing some of the fields in the data records. The section quality record is used in the same manner as the database quality record. The quality record may appear anywhere in a section and it contains quality information specific to particular sets of coordinates. Finally, the data records contain all the descriptive information about the lines, points, names, features and objects that comprise the transfer.

In summary, NTF establishes a set of rules for formatting data on a magnetic tape or other medium, while at the same time offering flexibility. It is possible to transfer simple data sets in an efficient way, or a whole database with multiple relationships. NTF offers a structure and a default option, so that the option can be redefined within the structure to accommodate the unusual. The default option is a pre-defined sequence of data and record formats, with self-identifying records and data fields. Using the data dictionary senders can establish their own classification scheme, record formats and relationships (Sowton and Haywood 1986).

Computer graphics standards

The community of researchers involved with automated cartography and GIS are not the only group interested in establishing exchange standards for graphic data. The scientists and engineers involved in computer graphics, particularly computer-aided design (CAD), have been preparing exchange standards for over two decades. Since by any measure (number of people involved or the annual sales of software systems) the CAD community is far larger than the GIS community, it is imperative that GIS scientists understand the work being done in the CAD community, and are able to judge if that work is applicable to GIS. Information on computer graphics standards is available in a number of references (e.g. Enderle, Grave and Lillehagen 1986; Hopgood and Hubbold 1986; National Computer Graphics Association 1989).

Computer graphics standards can be categorized into several major types. There are device level standards such as the Computer Graphics Interface (CGI). CGI provides a device-level interface that links applications with particular devices. CGI implements the interface between a virtual device defined in a CGI-compatible application program and a particular hardware device, such as a graphics display or plotter. CGI is a draft ISO standard (ISO 2nd DP 9636, 1988). Another device level standard is the Computer Graphics Metafile (CGM). CGM is an ISO standard (ISO 8632, 1987) that defines a standard file content and format for describing pictures (images) in a device independent fashion. This allows images to be exchanged electronically between different types of hardware and applications software.

Two programming interface standards are widely used in computer graphics. One is the Graphical Kernel System (GKS), approved as an ISO standard in both two-dimensional (ISO 7942, 1985) and three-dimensional (ISO 8805, 1988) implementations. The second is the Programmer's Hierarchical Interactive Graphics Standard (PHIGS) also an ISO standard (ISO 9582, 1989). Both GKS and PHIGS provide a uniform programmer's interface for graphics input and output. They consist of subroutine libraries providing graphics subroutines, graphics workstation management and interactive input in a device-independent fashion. The subroutines are callable from high-level languages. These standards provide routines that simplify applications development. Although GKS and PHIGS overlap in their functionality, there are some unique differences. GKS initially was restricted to two-dimensional applications (extensions have been added so now GKS can handle three-dimensional data), while PHIGS was designed from the start for three-dimensional applications. PHIGS also can support hierarchial representation of graphical objects.

The class of computer graphics standards most relevant to the exchange of geographical data files is the graphic data exchange standards. The first of these was the Initial Graphics Exchange Specification, an ANSI standard (ANSI Y14.26M, 1987) first published in 1981. Now in its fifth version, the main application of IGES is the exchange of two-dimensional engineering drawings. In 1984, the French developed an alternative to IGES known as the Système d'Echange et de Transfer (SET), which offers a simplified internal structure when compared to IGES (Aerospatiale Direction Technique 1984).

In the early 1980s, work on a successor to IGES began. This proposed standard is called the Product Data Exchange Specification (PDES). PDES will include capabilities not only for the interchange of 2–D drawing files that IGES handles, but also for the exchange of databases and knowledge bases describing complete 3–D projects. PDES will support dynamic (or active) data exchange, distributed database definition and knowledge-based system definition. In the definition of knowledge-based systems, the PDES scheme will contain both the required data and the rules for using those data. Of particular interest to GIS specialists, is the fact that PDES has capabilities to handle topology and complex features (Warthen 1988).

PDES is also the US contribution to an international project to create a single, internationally accepted data exchange standard. This ISO project is known as the Standard for the Exchange of Product Data (STEP). STEP is planned to be an aggregation or merger of the various related activities, such as IGES, PDES and SET. The goals of STEP mirror the goals of PDES in requiring exchange completeness, archiving completeness, extensibility, efficiency, separation of data content from physical format and the logical classification of data elements. Both PDES and STEP are described in an ISO draft standard (ISO DP 10303, 1988). Three layers are defined in STEP: a physical layer that deals with file format and data structure; a logical layer that contains generic entities and application-specific entities; and the application layer that deals with various applications, such as electrical systems, piping systems, and, potentially, GIS. As a result of joint development, PDES and STEP will probably be identical at least where they share common functionality. However, there will be separate approval processes for PDES and STEP, so the two standards could diverge (Warthen 1988).

Analysis of standards activities

Given the growth in the number of producers and users of geographical information, the drive towards a standard for data exchange is inevitable. The question remaining is what is the best way to achieve such a standard? Mapping agencies in the United States and United Kingdom are leading efforts to establish national spatial data exchange formats. At the same time, the computer graphics industry is leading an international effort to develop a comprehensive data exchange format that might be able to accommodate geographical data as a specific application. The ultimate measure of success of any standard lies in its acceptance in the user community. For this to occur, the computer system vendors must take an active role in developing software tools to encode and decode spatial data between the standard format and their own system format. A concerted effort has been made during the development of the standards mentioned to keep the private sector informed and to use their input to improve the standard. It remains to be seen which is the best path for achieving exchange of spatial data.

Standards are written to accommodate a wide variety of data. This usually means that any given implementation (i.e. the transfer of a specific type of data, such as contours or census tracts) will only utilize a subset of the features (or data elements) available in the standard. As such it is expected that producers and users who regularly exchange the same type of data will quickly establish an appropriate subset of the total transfer package (Sowton and Haywood 1986). The net result is a set of 'standard' or *de facto* implementations of the standard itself.

This concept of a standard within a standard will probably be widely supported by the GIS vendor community. In the case of SDTS, for example, GIS vendors will most likely support the import and export of data utilizing SDTS, but perhaps only the subset of SDTS used by the Geological Survey to provide DLG-E data. If other major sources of data, such as the Census Bureau, employ a different SDTS encoding scheme, the vendors would probably be driven by market forces to support that as well. Agreements by the major providers of data on a common implementation of SDTS would simplify third party data access. Common agreements regarding the use of spatial objects and relationships are probably possible. Agreement on common definitions and representations of various geographical features is a more intractable problem.

CONCLUSIONS

The need to be able to receive data from a number of sources and exchange data between dissimilar GIS presents a number of challenges. From a user perspective the challenge involves integrating a heterogeneous data environment. The various aspects of this heterogeneous environment that affect the import and export operations must be understood for the data exchange or transfer process to be meaningful and successful.

Direct conversion from one system to another is one way to exchange data. However, it is clear that the time for spatial data standards is here. The availability of standards has many advantages to the data collector, processor and user, particularly those who need to utilize data from several sources. A standard transfer specification will facilitate the exchange of spatial data throughout the public and private communities and will enhance the capability for displaying, analysing and integrating spatial data for a growing number of applications. The availability of information about data quality, such as lineage, completeness, accuracy and logical consistency, will help users to evaluate the fitness of the data for a particular use.

Unfortunately there is a multitude of standards from which to choose. At least 16 countries are involved in the process of establishing their own national spatial data exchange standards. Related standards, such as from computer graphics, can be used to exchange spatial data as well. It seems unlikely that an international exchange standard will emerge in the near future. *Inter alia*, data exchanges will rely on the parties mutual understanding of the data model, data content, data structures and file structures employed to represent spatial phenomena.

REFERENCES

Aerospatiale Direction Technique (1984) *Système d'Echange et de Transfer (SET) Specification Rev. 1.1.* IGN, Paris

ANSI Y14.26M (1987) *Initial Graphic Exchange Specification (IGES), Version 3.0.* ANSI, Washington DC

Barwinski K, Brüggemann H (1986) Development of digital cadastral and topographic maps – Requirements, goals, and basic concept. In: Blakemore M J (ed.) *Proceedings of AUTOCARTO London*, Vol. 2. Royal Institution of Chartered Surveyors, London, pp. 76–85

Brodie M J, Mylopoulos J (eds.) (1986) *On Knowledge Base Management Systems.* Springer-Verlag, New York

Centre National d'Études Spatiales (1989) *SPOT Users Handbook*, Volume 2. Centre Spatial de Toulouse, Toulouse, France

DCDSTF (Digital Cartographic Data Standards Task Force) (1988) The proposed standard for digital cartographic data *The American Cartographer* **15**: 1

Egenhofer M J, Herring J R (1991) High-level spatial data structures for GIS. In: Maguire D J, Goodchild M F, Rhind D W (eds.) *Geographical Information Systems: principles and applications.* Longman, London, pp. 227–37, Vol 1

Enderle G, Grave M, Lillehagen F (1986) *Advances in Computer Graphics*, Vol. 1. Springer-Verlag, New York

Guptill S C (ed.) (1990) An enhanced digital line graph design. *US Geological Survey Circular 1048.* USGS, Reston Virginia

Hopgood F R A, Hubbold R J (eds.) (1986) *Advances in Computer Graphics II.* Springer-Verlag, New York

House of Lords (1984) *Remote Sensing and Digital Mapping.* Report 98 of the House of Lords Select Committee on Science and Technology, Her Majesty's Stationery Office, London

ISO 7942 (1985) *Graphical Kernel System (GKS)*; also ANSI X3.124–1985; also FIPS 120. ISO

ISO 8211 (1986) *Specification for a Data Descriptive File for Information Interchange*; also FIPS 123. ISO

ISO 8632 (1987) *Computer Graphics Metafile for the Storage and Transfer of Picture Description Information (CGM)* Parts 1–4; also ANSI X3.122–1986; also FIPS 128. ISO

ISO 8805 (1988) *Graphical Kernel System for Three Dimensions (GKS-3D).* ISO

ISO 2nd DP 9636 (1988) *Computer Graphics Interfacing Techniques for Dialogues with Graphical Devices (CGI)*; also dpANSI X3.161. ISO

ISO DP 10303 (1988) *Product Data Exchange Specification (PDES), STEP Version 1.0; also PDES Working Draft Version 1.0*; also NTIS PB 89–144–794. ISO

ISO 9582 (1989) *Programmer's Hierarchical Interactive Graphics System (PHIGS)*; also ANSI X3.144–1989. ISO

Maguire D J, Dangermond J (1991) The functionality of GIS. In: Maguire D J, Goodchild M F, Rhind D W (eds.) *Geographical Information Systems: principles and applications.* Longman, London, pp. 319–35, Vol 1

National Computer Graphics Association (1989) *Standards in the Computer Graphics Industry.* NCGA, Fairfax Virginia

OS (Ordnance Survey) (1987) *National Transfer Format, Release 1.0.* OS, Southampton UK

OS (Ordnance Survey) (1989) *National Transfer Format, Release 1.1.* OS, Southampton UK

Pascoe R T, Penny J P (1990) Construction of the interfaces for the exchange of geographic data. *International Journal of Geographical Information Systems* **4** (2): 147–56

Peuquet D J (1981a) An examination of the techniques for reformatting digital cartographic data Part 1: the raster-to-vector process. *Cartographica* **18**: (1) 34–48

Peuquet D J (1981b) An examination of the techniques for reformatting digital cartographic data Part 2: the vector-to-raster process. *Cartographica* **18**: (3) 21–33

Peuquet D J (1984) A conceptual framework and comparison of spatial data models. *Cartographica* **21**: (4) 66–113

Salgé F, Piquet-Pellorce D (1986) The IGN small scale geographical database (1 : 100 000 to 1 : 500 000). In: Blakemore M J (ed.) *Proceedings of AUTOCARTO London*, Vol. 1. Royal Institution of Chartered Surveyors, London, pp. 433–46

Sowton M, Haywood P (1986) National Standards for the Transfer of Digital Map Data. In: Blakemore M J (ed.) *Proceedings of AUTOCARTO London*, Vol. 1. Royal Institution of Chartered Surveyors, London, pp. 298–311

Teorey T J, Fry J P (1982) *Design of Database Structures.* Prentice Hall, Englewood Cliffs New Jersey

USGS (1984) *Landsat 4 Data Users Handbook.* Government Printing Office, Reston Virginia

USGS (1987) *Digital Elevation Models, US Geological Survey Data Users Guide 5.* USGS, Reston Virginia

USGS (1990) *Digital Line Graphs from 1:24,000-scale Maps, US Geological Survey Data Users Guide 1.* USGS, Reston Virginia

Warthen B (1988) Move over IGES: Here comes PDES/STEP. *Computer Graphics Review* Nov-Dec, 34–40

Winston P H (1984) *Artificial Intelligence*, 2nd edn. Addison-Wesley, Reading Massachusetts

CONSOLIDATED BIBLIOGRAPHY

Aangeenbrug R T (1982) The future of Geographic Information Systems. *Computer Graphics News* **2** (2): 4

Aangeenbrug R T (1991) A critique of GIS. In: Maguire D J, Goodchild M F and Rhind D W (eds.) *Geographical Information Systems: principles and applications.* Longman, London, pp. 101–7, Vol 1

Aanstoos R, Weitzel L (1988) Tracking oil and gas wells in Texas. *Proceedings of the Ninth Annual IASU Conference. Harnessing the hidden power of your system: maximizing your return-on-investment.* International Association of Synercom Users, Houston

Abel D J (1988) Relational data management facilities for spatial information systems. *Proceedings of the 3rd International Symposium on Spatial Data Handling.* International Geographical Union, Columbus Ohio, pp. 9–18

Abel D J (1989) A model for data set management in large spatial information systems. *International Journal of Geographical Information Systems* **3**: 291–302

Abel D J (1989) SIRO-DBMS: a database tool-kit for geographical information systems. *International Journal of Geographical Information Systems* **3**: 103–16

Abel D J, Smith J L (1986) A relational GIS database accommodating independent partitionings of the region. *Proceedings of the 2nd International Symposium on Spatial Data Handling.* International Geographical Union, Columbus Ohio, pp. 213–24

Abler R F (1987) The National Science Foundation Center for Geographic Information and Analysis. *International Journal of Geographical Information Systems* **1** (4): 303–26

Abler R F, Adams J, Gould P R (1971) *Spatial Organization: the geographer's view of the world.* Prentice-Hall, Englewood Cliffs New Jersey

Acquista C (1986) GENESSIS computer code reference manual. *Photon Research Associates Report R-135–86.* PRA Inc, La Jolla California

ACSM–ASPRS Geographic Information Management Committee (1989) Multi-purpose geographic database guidelines for local governments. *ACSM Bulletin* **121**: 1357–65

Adedeji A (1989) *The African Alternate Framework to Structural Adjustment.* Public Lecture, University of Ottawa, Canada, 23 October 1989

Adlam K H, Clayton A R, Kelk B (1988) A demonstrator for the National Sciences Geodata Index. *International Journal of Geographical Information Systems* **2**: 161–70

Aerospatiale Direction Technique (1984) *Système d'Echange et de Transfer (SET) Specification Rev. 1.1.* IGN, Paris

Aetna Casualty & Security Co. v. Jeppeson & Co. [1981] 642 F. 2nd 339 (9th Circuit)

Aglinfou (1986) *Program för forskning och utveckling inom landskapsinformationsområdet.* LMV-rapport 1986:13 ISSN 0280–5731. Gävle, Sweden

Agterberg F P (1988) Application of recent developments of regression analysis in regional mineral resource evaluation. In: Chung C F, Fabbri A, Sinding-Larsen G R (eds.) *Quantitative Analysis of Mineral and Energy Resources.* D. Reidel Publishing, Dordrecht, pp. 1–28

Agterberg F P (1989) Systematic approach to dealing with uncertainty of geoscience information in mineral exploration. *Proceedings of the 21st APCOM Symposium.* Las Vegas, March 1989, Chapter 18, pp. 165–78

Agterberg F P (1989) Computer programs for mineral exploration. *Science* **245**: 76–81

Agterberg F P, Bonham-Carter G F, Wright D F (1990) Statistical pattern integration for mineral exploration. In: Gaal G (ed.) *Computer Applications in Resource Exploration.* Pergamon Press, Oxford, pp. 1–22

Ahn J, Freeman H (1983) A program for automatic name placement. *Proceedings of AUTOCARTO 6.* ASPRS, Falls Church Virginia, pp. 444–53

Aho A V, Hopcroft J E, Ullman J D (1983) *Data Structures and Algorithms.* Addison-Wesley, Reading Massachusetts

Akima H (1978) A method of bivariate interpolation and smooth surface fitting for irregularly distributed data points. *ACM Transactions on Mathematical Software* **4** (2): 148–59

Aldersey-Williams H (1989) A Bauhaus for the media age. *New Scientist* **1655**: 54–60

Aldus Corporation (1988) *TIFF – Tag Image File Format Specification Revision 5.0 (Final)*

Alegiani J B, Buxton J, Honey S (1989) An in-vehicle navigation and information system utilizing defined

software services. In: Reekie D H M, Case E R, Tsai J (eds.) *Vehicle Navigation & Information Systems Conference, Toronto*, IEEE, Toronto, 156 pp.
Alemi M H, Shariari M R, Nielsen D R (1988) Kriging and co-kriging of soil water properties. *Soil Technology* **1**: 117–32
Alexander F E, Ricketts T J, Williams J (forthcoming) Methods of mapping small clusters of rare diseases with applications to geographical epidemiology. *Geographical Analysis*
Alexandroff P (1961) *Elementary Concepts of Topology*. Dover Publications, New York
ALIC (1987) *National Strategy for Land Information Management*. Australian Land Information Council Secretariat, Canberra
ALIC (1988ff.) *Annual Report*. Australian Land Information Council, Canberra
Allen J H (1988) The World Data Center System, international data exchange and global change. In: Mounsey H M, Tomlinson R F (eds.) *Building Databases for Global Science*. Taylor & Francis, London, pp. 138–53
Alter S L (1977) A taxonomy of decision support systems. *Sloan Management Review* **19**: 39–56
Alter S L (1980) *Decision Support Systems: current practice and continuing challenges*. Addison-Wesley, Reading Massachusetts
Ambron S, Hooper C (1988) *Interactive Multi-media*. Microsoft Press, Redmond, WA
American Bar Association (1989) The year in review. *Natural Resources, Energy and Environmental Law Review*, American Bar Association, Chicago Illinois
American Society for Photogrammetry and Remote Sensing (1989) Interim accuracy standards for large scale line maps. *Photogrammetric Engineering and Remote Sensing* **55**: 1038–40
Amin S (1973) *Neo-Colonialism in West Africa*. Penguin Books, London
Amos L L et al. (1987) *Primary Mapping Economic Analysis, Phase One*, Internal report. US Geological Survey, Reston Virginia
Amos L L et al. (1988) *Primary Mapping Economic Analysis, Phase Two*, Internal report. US Geological Survey, Reston Virginia
Anderson D E, Angel J C, Gurney A J (1978) World Data Bank II. In: Dutton G (ed.) *Harvard Papers on Geographical Information Systems 2*. Laboratory for Computer Graphics and Spatial Analysis, Harvard University, Cambridge Massachusetts
Anderson D R, Thornton J D (1985) *Application of a Geographic Information System (GIS): identification of resources sensitive to acid deposition*. State of Minnesota, St Paul
Anderson J J, Sigmund J M, Cunningham C G, Steven T A, Lanigan J C, Rowley P D (1980) Geologic map of the Delano Peak SW Quadrangle, Beaver County, Utah. *Miscellaneous Field Studies Map, MF-1225*. USGS, Reston
Anderson J R, Hardy E E, Roach J T, Witmer R E (1976) A land use and land cover classification system for use with remote sensor data. *US Geological Survey Professional Paper 964*. USGS, Washington DC
Anderson K E, Callahan G M (1990) The modernization program of the US Geological Survey's National Mapping Division. *Cartography and Geographic Informations Systems* **17** (3): 243–8
Andersson S (1987) The Swedish Land Data Bank. *International Journal of Geographical Information Systems* **1** (3): 253–63
Andersson S (1989) Demand for access to the Swedish Land Data Bank System – a second wave. *Mapping Awareness* **3** (1): 9–12
Angus-Leppan P (1989) The Thailand Land Titling Project: first steps in a parcel-based LIS. *International Journal of Geographical Information Systems* **3** (1): 59–68
Annand K P (1988) A geographic information system for river management. *Proceedings of AM/FM Today. Nottingham Conference*. AM/FM European Division, PO Box 6, CH4005, Basel, Switzerland
Annoni A, Ventura A D, Mozzi E, Schettini R (1990) Towards the integration of remote sensing images within a cartographic system. *Computer Aided Design* **22** (3): 160–6
Anon (1990) The French Revolution of 1989. *Mapping Awareness* **4** (9): 48–9
Anselin L (1988) *Spatial Econometrics: methods and models*. Kluwer Academic Publishers, Dordrecht
Anselin L (1989) What is special about spatial data? Alternative perspectives on spatial data analysis. *Technical Paper 89-4*. National Center for Geographic Information and Analysis, Santa Barbara California
Anselin L, Griffith D (1988) Do spatial effects really matter in regression analysis? *Papers of the Regional Science Association* **65**: 11–34
ANSI Study Group on Database Management Systems (1975) Interim report. *SIGMOD* **7**
ANSI X3H2 (1985) *American National Standard Database Language SQL*. American National Standards Institute, Washington DC
ANSI Y14.26M (1987) *Initial Graphic Exchange Specification (IGES), Version 3.0*. ANSI, Washington DC
Apple Computer Inc. (1986) *Human Interface Guidelines: the Apple desktop interface*. Apple Computer Inc., Cupertino California
Applegate L M, Konsynski B R, Nunamaker J F (1986) Model management systems: design for decision support. *Decision Support Systems* **2**: 81–91
Arbia G (1989) Statistical effect of spatial data transformations: a proposed general framework. In: Goodchild M F, Gopal S (eds.) *Accuracy of Spatial Databases*. Taylor & Francis, London, pp. 249–60
Archer H, Croswell P L (1989) Public access to public information systems: an emerging legal issue. *Photogrammetric Engineering and Remote Sensing* **15** (11): 1575–81
Archibald P D (1987) GIS and remote sensing data integration. *Geocarto International* **3**: 67–73

Ardrey R (1966) *The Territorial Imperative*. Fontana/Collins, London

Armstrong M P, De S, Densham P J, Lolonis P, Rushton G, Tewari V K (1990) A knowledge-based approach for supporting locational decision-making. *Environment and Planning B* **17**: 341–64

Armstrong M P (1988) Distance imprecision and error in spatial decision support systems. In: Aangeenbrug R T, Schiffman Y M (eds.) *International Geographic Information Systems (IGIS) Symposium, Arlington, Virginia*, Vol 2. NASA, Washington DC, pp. 23–34

Armstrong M P, Densham P J (1990) Database organization alternatives for spatial decision support systems. *International Journal of Geographical Information Systems* **4**: 3–20

Armstrong M P, Densham P J, Rushton G (1986) Architecture for a microcomputer-based decision support system. *Proceedings of the 2nd International Symposium on Spatial Data Handling*. International Geographical Union, Williamsville New York, pp. 120–31

Arnheim R (1974) *Art and Visual Perception*. University of California Press, Berkeley

Aronoff S (1989) *Geographic Information Systems: a management perspective*. WDL Publications, Ottawa Canada

Aronson P (1985) Applying software engineering to a general purpose geographic information system. *Proceedings of AUTOCARTO 7*. ASPRS, Falls Church Virginia, pp. 23–31

Aronson P (1987) Attribute handling for geographic information systems. *Proceedings of AUTOCARTO 8*. ASPRS/ACSM, Falls Church Virginia, pp. 346–55

Arthur D W G (1978) Orthogonal transformations. *The American Cartographer* **5**: 72–4

Artin E, Brown H (1969) *Introduction to Algebraic Topology*. Charles E Merrill Publishing Company, Columbus

Arur M G, Narayan L R A, Gopalan N (1989) Challenges of the 90's for Digital Cartography in India. *IX INCA International Seminar on Digital Cartography and Potential Users*. Pre-session Proceedings. Survey of India, Dehra Dun, pp. 7–14

Asrar G (ed.) (1989) *Theory and Applications of Optical Remote Sensing*. Wiley, New York

Association for Geographic Information (1988) *AGI NEWS* **1** (1): 1–8

Association for Promotion of Electronic Industries (1989) *Cartographic database standard*, Tokyo

Atkey R G, Gibson R J (1975) Progress in automated cartography. *Proceedings of the Conference of Commonwealth Survey Officers*. Cambridge, August 1975. Ministry of Overseas Development. Paper J3

AT&T Bell Laboratories (1978) *Bell System Technical Journal* **57** (6)

AT&T Bell Laboratories (1984) *Bell System Technical Journal* **63** (8)

Auerbach S, Schaeben H (1990) Computer-aided geometric design of geologic surfaces and bodies. *Mathematical Geology* **22**: 723–42

AURISA (1976ff.) *URPIS – Proceedings of the Urban and Regional Planning Information Systems Annual Conferences*. Australasian Urban and Regional Information Systems Association Inc., Sydney

AURISA (1985) *Report of the Working Group on Statewide Parcel-based Land Information Systems in Australasia*. Australasian Urban and Regional Information Systems Association Inc., Sydney

AURISA (1989) *Towards the Implementation of a National Strategy for Education and Research in Land and Geographic Information Systems*. Australasian Urban and Regional Information Systems Association Inc., Sydney

AUSLIG (1985) *LANDSEARCH 1: Directory of Commonwealth Land Related Data*. Commonwealth Department of Local Government and Administrative Services, Canberra

Aybet J (1990) Integrated mapping systems – data conversion and integration. *Mapping Awareness* **4** (6): 18–23

Babbage R (1989) Planning the future of defence geographic information systems. In: Ball D, Babbage R (eds.) *Geographical Information Systems: defence applications*. Pergamon Press, Sydney, pp. 232–42

Bachi R (1968) *Graphical Rational Patterns*. Universities Press, Jerusalem, Israel

Baerwald T J (1989) Fostering cooperation among academia, industry, and government – the establishment of the National Center for Geographic Information and Analysis in the USA. In: Grant N G (ed.) *Proceedings of National Conference Challenge for the 1990s GIS*. Canadian Institute of Surveying and Mapping, Ottawa, pp. 4–10

Bak P, Mill A (1989) Three dimensional representation in a Geoscientific Resource Management System for the minerals industry. In: Raper J F (ed.) *Three Dimensional Applications in Geographical Information Systems*. Taylor & Francis, London

Baker H H (1990) Scene structure from a moving camera. In: Blake A, Troscianko T (eds.) *AI and the Eye*. John Wiley, Chichester England, pp. 229–60

Baker K (1989) Using geodemographics in market research surveys. *Journal of the Market Research Society* **31**: 37–44

Ballard D H, Brown C M (1981) *Computer Vision*. Prentice-Hall, Englewood Cliffs New Jersey

Balodis M (1983) Positioning typography on maps. *Proceedings, ACSM Fall Convention, Salt Lake City*. ACSM, Falls Church Virginia, pp. 28–44

Band L E (1986) Topographic partition of watersheds with digital elevation models. *Water Resources Research* **22** (1): 15–24

Band L E (1989) A terrain-based watershed information system. *Hydrological Processes* **3**: 151–62

Band L E, Wood E F (1988) Strategies for large-scale

distributed hydrologic simulation. *Applied Mathematics and Computation* **27**: 23–37

Banting D (1988) Using GFIS for teaching GIS concepts. *Proceedings of GIS/LIS '88*. American Society for Photogrammetry and Remote Sensing, Falls Church, pp. 678–84

Barker G R (1988) Remote sensing: the unheralded component of geographic information systems. *Photogrammetric Engineering and Remote Sensing* **54**: 195–9

Barnard S T, Fischler M A (1982) Computational stereo. *ACM Computing Surveys* **14** (4): 553–72

Barr A, Feigenbaum E A (eds.) (1981) *The Handbook of Artificial Intelligence*, Vol. I. HeurisTech Press and William Kaufmann, Stanford

Barr A, Feigenbaum E A (eds.) (1982) *The Handbook of Artificial Intelligence*, Vol. II. HeurisTech Press and William Kaufmann, Stanford

Barton B A (1976) A note on the transformation of spherical coordinates. *The American Cartographer* **3**: 161–8

Barwinski K, Brüggemann H (1986) Development of digital cadastral and topographic maps – Requirements, goals, and basic concept. In: Blakemore M J (ed.) *Proceedings of AUTOCARTO London*, Vol. 2. Royal Institution of Chartered Surveyors, London, pp. 76–85

Basoglu U (1982) A new approach to automated name placement. *Proceedings of AUTOCARTO 5*. ASPRS, Falls Church Virginia, pp. 103–12

Bates M, Moser M G, Stallard D (1984) The IRUS transportable natural language database interface. *Technical Report*. Bolt, Beranek and Newman

Batjes N H, Bouwman A F (1989) JAMPLES: a computerized land evaluation system for Jamaica. In: Bouma J, Bregt A K (eds.) *Land Qualities in Space and Time. Proceedings of the Symposium organised by the International Society of Soil Science (ISSS), Wageningen, The Netherlands, 22–26 August 1988*. PUDOC, Wageningen, pp. 257–60

Batten L G (1989) National capital urban planning project: development of a 3-D GIS. *Proceedings of GIS/LIS '89*. ACSM/ASPRS, Falls Church Virginia, pp. 781–6

Batty M, Longley P, Fotheringham A S (1989) Urban growth and form: scaling, fractal geometry and diffusion-limited aggregation. *Environment and Planning A* **21**:1447–72

Baumgardner M F (1988) A global soils and terrain digital database. In: Mounsey H M, Tomlinson R F (eds.) *Building Databases for Global Science*. Taylor & Francis, London, pp. 172–80

Baumgardner M F, Oldeman L R (eds.) (1986) *Proceedings of an international workshop on the structure of a digital international soil resources map annex database, held 20–24 January 1986 at the International Soil Reference and Information Centre, Wageningen, The Netherlands*. International Soil Science Society, Wageningen, 138 pp.

Baumgardner M F, Weg R F Van der (1989) Space and time dimensions of a world soils and terrain digital database. In: Bouma J, Bregt A K (eds.) *Land Qualities in Space and Time. Proceedings of a Symposium organised by the International Society of Soil Science (ISSS), Wageningen, The Netherlands, 22–26 August 1988*. PUDOC, Wageningen, 356 pp

Bayard-White C (1985) *An Introduction to Interactive Video*. National Interactive Video Centre, and Council for Educational Technology, London

Beard C, Robbins A M (1990) Scale determination and inset selection within a totally automated map production system. *Cartography and Geographic Information Systems* **17** (1): 57–68

Beard M K (1987) How to survive on a single detailed database. *Proceedings of AUTOCARTO 8*. ASPRS/ACSM, Falls Church, pp. 211–20

Beard M K (1989) Design criteria for automated generalization. *Paper presented at International Cartographic Association*, Budapest, August 1989

Beard M K (1989) Dimensions of use and value of geographic information. In: Onsrud H J, Calkins H W, Obermeyer N J (eds.) *Use and Value of Geographic Information*. Initiative Four Specialist Meeting Report and Proceedings *NCGIA Technical Paper 89-7*. University of California at Santa Barbara, Santa Barbara

Beard M K, Chrisman N R (1986) Zipping: new software for merging map sheets. *Proceedings ACSM (vol 1)* ACSM, Falls Church Virginia **1**: 153

Beard M K, Chrisman N R (1988) Zipping: a localized approach to edgematching. *The American Cartographer* **15** (2): 163–72

Beaumont J R (ed.) (1989) Market analysis. *Environment and Planning A* (Special Edition) **21** (5): 587–653

Beaumont J R (1991) An introduction to market analysis. *CATMOG 53*, Geo-Abstracts, Norwich.

Beaumont J R (1991) GIS and market analysis. In: Maguire D J, Goodchild M F, Rhind D W (eds.) *Geographical Information Systems: principles and applications*. Longman, London, pp. 139–51, Vol 2

Beckett P H T, Burrough P A (1971) The relations between cost and utility in soil survey. IV. Comparisons of the utilities of soil maps produced by different survey procedures and to different scales. *Journal of Soil Science* **22**: 466–80

Beckett P H T, Burrough P A (1971) The relations between cost and utility in soil survey. V. The cost effectiveness of different soil survey procedures. *Journal of Soil Science* **22**: 481–9

Beckett P H T, Webster R (1971) Soil variability – a review. *Soils and Fertilizers* **34**: 1–15

Bedard Y, Epstein E F (1984) Spatial data integration in the information era. *Proceedings of the Federation Internationale des Geometres (FIG) Symposium on the Decisionmaker and Land Information Systems*. Canadian Institute of Surveying and Mapping, Ottawa Ontario, pp. 104–113

Bedell R (1988) *WARP: a program to warp computer drawings, maps and plans*. Terra Investigations and Imaging Ltd, Guildford Surrey

Beek K-J, Burrough P A, McCormack D E (1987) Quantified land evaluation procedures. *Proceedings of a Joint Meeting of ISSS Working Groups on Land Evaluation and Soil Information Systems, Washington 25 April–2 May 1986*. ITC Publication No 6, Enschede, 165 pp

Bell S B M, Diaz B M, Holroyd F, Jackson M J (1983) Spatially referenced methods of processing raster and vector data. *Image and Vision Computing* 1: 211–20

Bennett J L (ed.) (1983) *Building Decision Support Systems*. Addison-Wesley, Reading

Bennett, R J, Wrigley N (eds.) (1981) *Quantitative Geography: retrospect and prospect*. Routledge and Kegan Paul, London

Bentley J L, Ottmann T A (1979) Algorithms for reporting and counting geometric intersections. *IEEE Transactions on Computing* **C-28** (9): 643–7

Bentley T J (1981) *Making Information Systems Work*. The Macmillan Press, London

Benyon D (1990) *Information and Data Modelling*. Blackwell Scientific Publications, Oxford

Berry B J L (1964) Approaches to regional analysis: a synthesis. *Annals of the Association of American Geographers* 54: 2–11

Berry B J L, Baker A M (1968) Geographic sampling. In: Berry B J L, Marble D F (eds.) *Spatial Analysis*. Prentice Hall, Englewood Cliffs New Jersey, pp. 91–100

Berry B J L, Marble D F (eds.) (1968) *Spatial Analysis: A reader in statistical geography*. Prentice-Hall, Englewood Cliffs New Jersey

Berry J K (1985) Computer-assisted map analysis: fundamental techniques. *Proceedings of the 6th Annual NCGA Conference*, Volume 2, pp. 369–86

Berry J K (1987) Fundamental operations in computer-assisted map analysis. *International Journal of Geographical Information Systems* 1 (2): 119–36

Berry J K (1987) The use of a Geographic Information System for storm runoff prediction from small urban watersheds. *Environmental Management Journal* 11 (1): 21–7

Berry J K (1987) Computer-assisted map analysis: potential and pitfalls. *Photogrammetric Engineering and Remote Sensing Journal* 53 (10): 1405–10

Berry J K (1987) A spatial analysis of timber analysis. In: Ripple W J (ed.) *Geographical Information Systems: a compendium*. Falls Church Virginia, pp. 206–11

Berry J K (1988) Computer-based map analysis: characterizing proximity and connectivity. In: Aangeenbrug R T, Schiffman Y M (eds.) *International Geographic Information Systems (IGIS) Symposium, Arlington, Virginia*, Vol 2. NASA, Washington DC, pp. 11–22

Berry J K (1991) GIS in island resource planning: a case study in map analysis. In: Maguire D J, Goodchild M F, Rhind D W (eds.) *Geographical Information Systems: principles and applications*. Longman, London, pp. 285–95, Vol 2

Berry J K, Berry J K (1988) Assessing spatial impacts of land use plans. *International Journal of Environmental Management* 27: 1–9

Berry J K et al. (1989) Development and analysis of a spatial database for the Botany Bay vicinity, Volume 2, final report entitled *Natural and Cultural Resources in the United States Virgin Islands: research, education and management needs*. Tropical Resources Institute, Yale University, New Haven Connecticut

Bertin J (1967) *Semiologie Graphique*. Gauthier-Villars and Co., Paris

Bertin J (1973) *Semiologie Graphique*. (Tr. Berg W J). University of Wisconsin Press, Madison Wisconsin

Besag J E (1986) On the statistical analysis of dirty pictures. *Journal of the Royal Statistical Society B* **48**: 192–236

Besag J E, Clifford P (1989) Generalised Monte Carlo significance tests. *Biometrika* 76: 633–42

Besag J E, Newell J (forthcoming) The detection of clusters in rare diseases. *Journal of the Royal Statistical Society B*

Best R G, Westin F C (1984) GIS for soils and rangeland management. *IEEE Pecora 9 Proceedings Spatial Information Technologies for Remote Sensing Today and Tomorrow, 2–4 October 1984, Sioux Falls*. IEEE, Sioux Falls, pp. 70–4

Beurden S A H A van, Riezebos H Th. (1988) The application of geostatistics in erosion hazard mapping. *Soil Technology* 1: 349–64

Bhatnagar S C, Jajoo B H (1987) A DSS generator for district planning. *Information and Management* 13: 43–9

Bickmore D P (1971) Experimental maps of the Bideford area. *Proceedings of the Conference of Commonwealth Survey Officers*. Cambridge, August 1971. Foreign and Commonwealth Office. Paper E1, pp. 217–23

Bickmore D P (1987) *World Digital Database for Environmental Science – An ICA/IGU Project*. ICA/IGU Joint Working Group on Atlases and Maps, Oxford

Bickmore D P, Shaw M A (1963) *Atlas of Great Britain and Northern Ireland*. Clarendon Press, Oxford

Bie S W (1975) Soil information systems. *Proceedings of the meeting of the ISSS Working Group on Soil Information Systems, Wageningen, The Netherlands, 1–4 Sept. 1975*, PUDOC, Wageningen, 87 pp

Billingsley F C, Anuta P E, Carr J L, McGillem C D, Smith D M, Strand T C (1983) Data processing and reprocessing. In: Colwell R N (ed.) *Manual of Remote Sensing*. American Society of Photogrammetry, Falls Church Virginia, pp. 719–88

Billingsley F C, Urena J L (1984) Concepts for a global resources information system. *Proceedings of the Ninth Pecora Symposium: spatial information technologies for remote sensing today and tomorrow*. IEEE Computer Society Press, Silver Spring, pp. 123–31

Bird D (1989) *Commonsense Direct Marketing*. Kogan Page, London

Birkhoff G, Mansfield L (1974) Compatible triangular finite elements. *Journal of Mathematical Analysis and Applications* 47 (3): 531–53

Birugawa S, Yamamoto S, Okuno T, Kinto Y, Asano Y (1964) Distribution patterns of agricultural land use intensity and crop types. *Tokyo Geography Papers* **8**: 153–86

Bishop M M, Fienberg S E, Holland P W (1975) *Discrete Multi-variate Analysis: theory and analysis*. MIT Press, Cambridge Massachusetts

Bishton A (1990) Mapping from a cartographic extract. *Cartography and Geographic Information Systems* **17** (1): 49–56

Bittlestone R (1990) Financial control in the 1990s. *International Journal of Information Resource Management* **1** (1): 12–18

Black J, Sambura A, Salijevic R (1986) The conceptual and technological framework for the New South Wales Land Information System. *URPIS – Proceedings of the Urban and Regional Planning Information Systems Annual Conferences*, Volume 14. Australasian Urban and Regional Information Systems Association Inc., Sydney, pp. 356–67

Black Report (1984) *Investigation of the Possible Incidence of Cancer in West Cumbria. Report of the Independent Advisory Group*. HMSO, London

Blais, J A R, Chapman M A, Lam W K (1986) Optimal interval sampling in theory and practice. *Proceedings of the 2nd International Symposium on Spatial Data Handling*. International Geographical Union, Columbus Ohio, pp. 185–92

Blakemore M J (1984) Generalization and error in spatial databases. *Cartographica* **21**: 131–9

Blakemore M J (1991) Managing an operational GIS: the UK National On-line Manpower Information System (NOMIS). In: Maguire D J, Goodchild M F, Rhind D W (eds.) *Geographical Information Systems: principles and applications*. Longman, London, pp. 503–13, Vol 1

Blalock H M (1979) *Social Statistics*, 2nd edn. McGraw-Hill, New York

Blanning R W (1986) An entity–relationship approach to model management. *Decision Support Systems* **2**: 65–72

Blatchford R P, Rhind D W (1989) The ideal mapping system. In: Rhind D W, Taylor D R F (eds.) *Cartography Past, Present and Future*. Elsevier, London, pp. 157–68

Blum H (1967) A transformation for extracting new descriptors of shape. In: Wathen-Dunn W (ed.) *Models for the Perception of Speech and Visual Form*. MIT Press, Cambridge Massachusetts, pp. 362–80

Board C (1967) Maps as models. In: Chorley R J, Haggett P (eds.) *Models in Geography*. Methuen, London, pp. 671–725

Boehm B W (1981) *Software Engineering Economics*. Prentice-Hall, Englewood Cliffs New Jersey

Boehm B W (1987) Improving software productivity. *Computer (IEEE)* **20** (9): 43–57

Bolland J D (1986) Digital mapping and facilities management in a UK Water Authority. In: Blakemore M J (ed.) *Proceedings of AUTOCARTO London*, Volume 2. Royal Institution of Chartered Surveyors, London, pp. 162–70

Bonczek R H, Holsapple C W, Whinston A B (1981) *Foundations of Decision Support Systems*. Academic Press, New York

Bonczek R H, Holsapple C W, Whinston A B (1984) *MicroDatabase Management: practical techniques for application development*. Academic Press, New York

Bonham-Carter G F (1991) Integration of geoscientific data using GIS. In: Maguire D J, Goodchild M F, Rhind D W (eds.) *Geographical Information Systems: principles and applications*. Longman, London, pp. 171–84, Vol 2

Bonham-Carter G F, Agterberg F P (1990) Application of a micro-computer based geographic information system to mineral potential mapping. In: Hanley T, Merriam D F (eds.) *Microcomputers in Geology*, Volume 2. Pergamon Press, Oxford, pp. 49–74

Bonham-Carter G F, Agterberg F P, Wright D F (1988) Integration of geological data sets for gold exploration in Nova Scotia. *Photogrammetric Engineering and Remote Sensing* **54** (11): 1585–92

Bonham-Carter G F, Agterberg F P, Wright D F (1990) Weights of evidence modelling: a new approach to mapping mineral potential. *Geological Survey of Canada Paper* **89–9**, pp. 171–83

Bonham-Carter G F, Rogers P J, Ellwood D J (1987) Catchment basin analysis applied to surficial geochemical data, Cobequid Highlands, Nova Scotia. *Journal of Geochemical Exploration* **29**: 259–78

Bonoma T V (1985) *The Marketing Edge*. Free Press, New York

Boots B, Getis A (1988) Point pattern analysis. *Sage Scientific Geography Series, Number 8*. Sage Publications, London

Bouma J (1989) Land qualities in space and time. In: Bouma J, Bregt A K (eds.) *Land Qualities in Space and Time. Proceedings of a Symposium organised by the International Society of Soil Science (ISSS), Wageningen, The Netherlands, 22–26 August 1988*. PUDOC, Wageningen, pp. 3–14

Bouma J (1989) Using soil survey data for quantitative land evaluation. *Advances in Soil Science*. Volume 9. Springer-Verlag, New York, pp. 177–213

Bouma J, Bregt A K (eds.) (1989) *Land Qualities in Space and Time. Proceedings of a Symposium organised by the International Society of Soil Science (ISSS), Wageningen, The Netherlands, 22–26 August 1988*. PUDOC, Wageningen, 356 pp.

Bouma J, Laat P J M de, Awater R H C M, Heesen H C van, Holst A F van, Nes Th. J van de (1980) Use of soil survey data in a model for simulating regional soil moisture regimes. *Soil Science Society of America Journal* **44**: 808–14

Bouma J, Lanen H A J van (1987) Transfer functions and threshold values: from soil characteristics to land qualities. In: Beek K J, Burrough P A, McCormack D E (eds.) *Quantified Land Evaluation Procedures*. ITC Publication No 6, Enschede, pp. 106–10

Bouma J, Lanen H A J van, Breeuwsma A, Wösten H J M, Kooistra M J (1986) Soil survey data needs when studying modern land use problems. *Soil Use and Management* **2**: 125–29

Bourne L E, Dominowski R L, Loftus E F (1979) *Cognitive Processes*. Prentice-Hall, Englewood Cliffs New Jersey

Box E O, Holben B N, Kalb V (1989) Accuracy of the AVHRR Vegetation Index as a predictor of biomass, primary productivity and net CO_2 flux. *Vegetatio* **80**: 71–89

Bracken I, Higgs G, Martin D, Webster C (1989) A classification of geographical information systems literature and applications. *Concepts and Techniques in Modern Geography* **52**: Environmental Publications, Norwich

Bracken I, Higgs G (1990) The role of GIS in data integration for rural environments. *Mapping Awareness* **4** (8): 51–6

Bracken I, Webster C (1989) Towards a typology of geographical information systems. *International Journal of Geographical Information Systems* **3** (2): 137–52

Bracken I, Webster C (1990) *Information Technology in Geography and Planning: including principles of GIS*. Routledge, London

Brand M J D (1986) The foundation of a geographical information system for Northern Ireland. In: Blakemore M J (ed.) *Proceedings of AUTOCARTO London*. Royal Institution of Chartered Surveyors, London, pp. 4–9

Brand M J D, Gray S (1989) From concept to reality. *Proceedings of AGI '89* 5.2.1–5.2.7

Brandenberger A J, Ghosh S K (1985) The world's topographic and cadastral mapping operation. *Photogrammetric Engineering and Remote Sensing* **51** (4): 437–44

Brassel K E (1974) A model for automatic hill-shading. *The American Cartographer* **1** (1): 15–27

Brassel K E, Utano J J (1979) Design strategies for continuous tone area mapping. *The American Cartographer* **6** (1): 39–50

Brassel K E, Weibel R (1988) A review and conceptual framework of automated map generalization. *International Journal of Geographical Information Systems* **2** (3): 229–44

Brauer A (1985) Introduction to the Australian Standard Geographical Classification. *URPIS – Proceedings of the Urban and Regional Planning Information Systems Annual Conferences*, Volume 13. Australasian Urban and Regional Information Systems Association Inc., Sydney, pp. 365–97

Breeusma A, Reijerink J G A, Schoumans O F, Brus D J H van het Loo (1989) *Fosfaatbelasting van bodem, grond- en oppervlaktewater in het stroomgebied van de Schuitenbeek. Rapport 10*. Instituut voor Onderzoek van het Landelijk Gebied, Wageningen, The Netherlands, 95 pp.

Bregt A K (1989) Quality of representative profile descriptions for predicting the land quality moisture deficit at different scales. In: Bouma J, Bregt A K (eds.) *Land Qualities in Space and Time. Proceedings of a Symposium organised by the International Society of Soil Science (ISSS), Wageningen, The Netherlands, 22–26 August 1988*. PUDOC, Wageningen, pp. 169–72

Bregt A K, Beemster J G R (1989) Accuracy in predicting moisture deficits and changes in yield from soil maps. *Geoderma* **43**: 301–10

Brewer C A (1989) The development of process-printed Munsell charts for selecting map colors. *The American Cartographer* **16** (4): 269–78

Bridge J S, Leeder M R (1979) A simulation model of alluvial stratigraphy. *Sedimentology* **26**: 617–44

Briggs D, Mounsey H M (1989) Integrating land resource data into a European geographical information system: practicalities and problems. *Applied Geography* **9** (1): 5–20

Brodie M L, Bobrow D, Lesser V, Madnick S, Tsichritzis D, Hewitt C (1988) Future artificial intelligence requirements for intelligent database systems. In: Kerschberg L (ed.) *Proceedings from the Second International Conference on Expert Database Systems, Tysons Corner, Virginia, 25–27 April 1988*. The Benjamin/Cummings Publishing Company, pp. 45–62

Brodie M L, Mylopoulos J (1986) Knowledge bases versus databases. In: Brodie M L, Mylopoulos J (eds.) *On Knowledge Base Management Systems: integrating artificial intelligence and database technologies*. Springer-Verlag, New York, pp. 83–6

Bromley R D F, Coulson M G (1989) *Geographical Information Systems and the work of a local authority: a case study of Swansea City Council*. Department of Geography, University College Swansea, Swansea

Bromley R D F, Coulson M G (1989) The value of corporate GIS to local authorities. *Mapping Awareness* **3** (5): 32–5

Brooks F P (1987) Grasping reality through illusion: interactive graphics serving science. CHI '90. *SIGCHI Bulletin* (special issue): 1–11

Brooks F P (1987) No silver bullet – essence and accidents of software engineering. *Computer (IEEE)* **20** (4): 10–19

Brooks R A (1983) Model-based three-dimensional interpretations of two-dimensional images. *IEEE Transactions on Pattern Analysis and Machine Intelligence* **PAMI-5**: 140–50

Broome F R (1986) Mapping from a topologically encoded database: the US Bureau of the Census example. In: Blakemore M J (ed.) *Proceedings of AUTOCARTO London*. Royal Institution of Chartered Surveyors, London, pp. 402–11

Broome F R, Godwin L (1990) The Census Bureau's publication map system. *Cartography and Geographic Information Systems* **17** (1): 79–88

Broome F R, Meixler D B (1990) The TIGER database structure. *Cartography and Geographic Information Systems* **17** (1): 39–47

Brotchie J F, Dickey J W, Sharpe R (1980) *TOPAZ – General Planning Model and its Applications at the Urban and Facility Planning Levels*. Springer-Verlag, Heidelburg

Brown C W, Landgraf H F, Uzes F D (1969) *Boundary Control and Legal Principles*, 2nd edn. Wiley, London

Brown G, Atkins M (1988) *Effective Teaching in Higher Education*. Methuen, London

Brown M J, Norris D A (1988) Early applications of geographical information systems at the Institute of Terrestrial Ecology. *International Journal of Geographical Information Systems* **2** (2): 153–60

Bruegger B P, Frank A U (1989) Hierarchies over topological data structures. *Proceedings of the American Congress on Surveying and Mapping Annual Convention, Baltimore*, Vol. 4. ACSM, Falls Church Virginia, pp. 137–45

Bryant J (1990) AMOEBA clustering revisited. *Photogrammetric Engineering and Remote Sensing* **56**: 41–7

Bryden R (1989) GIS: an industry perspective. *Workshop on Strategic Directions for Canada's Surveying, Mapping, Remote Sensing and GIS Activities.* November 1989. Ottawa

Buchmann A, Günther O, Smith T R, Wang Y-F (1989) *Design and Implementation of Large Spatial Databases. Lecture Notes in Computer Science 409.* Springer-Verlag, New York

Bull G A (1960) Comparison of rain-gauges. *Nature* **185**: 437–38

Bunce R G H, Barr C J, Whittaker H A (1982) A stratification system for ecological sampling. In: Fuller R M (ed.) *Ecological Mapping from, Ground, Air and Space.* Institute of Terrestrial Ecology Symposium No. 10. Monk's Wood, Cambridgeshire, pp. 39–46

Bundock M (1987) An integrated DBMS approach for geographic information systems. *Proceedings of AUTOCARTO 8.* ASRPS, Falls Church Virginia, pp. 292–301

Bunge W (1966) *Theoretical Geography.* Gleerup, Lund Sweden

Bureau of the Budget (1947) *National Map Accuracy Standards.* US Government Printing Office, Washington DC

Bureau of the Census (1982) *Guide to the 1980 Census of Population and Housing.* US Department of Commerce, Washington DC

Bureau of the Census (1984) *Guide to the 1982 Economic Census and Related Statistics.* US Department of Commerce, Washington DC

Bureau of the Census (1984) *Guide to the 1982 Census of Agriculture and Related Statistics.* US Department of Commerce, Washington DC

Burgess T M, Webster R, McBratney A B (1981) Optimal interpolation and isarithmic mapping of soil properties: 4. Sampling strategy. *Journal of Soil Science* **32**: 643–59

Burgess T M, Webster R (1980) Optimal interpolation and isarithmic mapping of soil properties: 1. The semi-variogram and punctual kriging. *Journal of Soil Science* **31**: 315–31

Burgess T M, Webster R (1980) Optimal interpolation and isarithmic mapping of soil properties: 2. Block kriging. *Journal of Soil Science* **31**: 333–41

Burke K C, Dixon T M (eds.) (1988) *Topographic Science Working Group, Final Report.* National Aeronautics and Space Administration, Washington DC

Burns K L (1988) Lithologic topology and structural vector fields applied to subsurface prediction in geology. *Proceedings of GIS/LIS '88.* ACSM/ASPRS, Falls Church Virginia, pp. 26–34

Burns K L (1990) Three dimensional modelling and geothermal process simulation. *Proceedings of Symposium on Three Dimensional Computer Graphics in Modelling Geologic Structures and Simulating Processes.* Freiburger Geowissenschaftliche Beitrage **2**: 10–12

Burrough P A (1980) The development of a landscape information system in the Netherlands, based on a turn-key graphics system. *GeoProcessing* **1** (3): 257–74

Burrough P A (1982) Computer assistance for soil survey and land evaluation. *Soil Survey and Land Evaluation* **2**: 25–36

Burrough P A (1983) Multi-scale sources of spatial variation in soil. I. The application of Fractal concepts to nested levels of soil variation. *Journal of Soil Science* **34**: 577–97

Burrough P A (1983) Multi-scale sources of spatial variation in soil II. A non-Brownian Fractal model and its application to soil survey. *Journal of Soil Science* **34**: 599–620

Burrough P A (1986) *Principles of Geographical Information Systems for Land Resources Assessment.* Clarendon Press, Oxford, 194 pp.

Burrough P A (1986) Five reasons why geographical information systems are not being used efficiently for land resources assessment. In: Blakemore M J (ed.) *Proceedings of AUTOCARTO London*, Vol. 2. Royal Institution of Chartered Surveyors, London, pp. 139–48

Burrough P A (1987) Natural resources databases: conceptual units, data structures and natural variation. In Beek K J, Burrough P A, McCormack D (eds.) *Quantified Land Evaluation. Proceedings of a Joint Meeting of ISSS Working Groups on Land Evaluation and Soil Information Systems, Washington 25 April–2 May 1986.* ITC, Enschede, pp. 60–5

Burrough P A (1989) Fuzzy mathematical methods for soil survey and land evaluation. *Journal of Soil Science* **40**: 477–92

Burrough P A (1989) Matching spatial databases and quantitative models in land resource assessment. *Soil Use and Management* **5**: 3–8

Burrough P A (1989) Fractals and geochemistry. In: Avnir D (ed.) *The Fractal Approach to Heterogeneous Chemistry.* Wiley, Chichester, pp. 383–406

Burrough P A (1990) Sampling designs for quantifying map unit composition. In: Mausbach M J, Wilding L (eds.) *Spatial Variability and Map Units for Soil Surveys.* International Soil Science Society Working Group of Soil and Moisture Variability in Time and Space/ American Society of Agronomy, the Crop Science Society of America and the Soil Science Society of America (in press)

Burrough P A (1991) Soil information systems. In: Maguire D J, Goodchild M F, Rhind D W (eds.)

Geographical Information Systems: principles and applications. Longman, London, pp. 153–69, Vol 2

Burrough P A, Beckett P H T (1971) The relations between cost and utility in soil survey. I. The design of the experiment. *Journal of Soil Science* **22**: 359–68

Burrough P A, Beckett P H T (1971) The relations between cost and utility in soil survey. III. The costs of soil survey. *Journal of Soil Science* **22**: 382–94

Burrough P A, Beckett P H T, Jarvis M (1971) The relations between cost and utility in soil survey. II. Conventional or free survey. *Journal of Soil Science* **22**: 369–81

Burrough P A, Bie S W (eds.) (1984) *Soil Information Systems Technology.* PUDOC, Wageningen, 178 pp.

Burrough P A, Veer A A de (1980) Cartographic processes. In: Machover C, Blauth R E (ed.) *The CAD/CAM Handbook.* Computervision Corporation, Massachusetts, pp. 97–120

Burrough P A, Veer A A de (1984) Automated production of landscape maps for physical planning in the Netherlands. *Landscape Planning* **11**: 205–26

Burton I (1963) The quantitative revolution and theoretical geography. *Canadian Geographer* **7**: 151–62

Burton W (1979) Logical and physical data types in geographic information systems. *Geo-Processing* **1** (4): 167–81

Bush V (1945) As we may think. *Atlantic Monthly* **176**: 101–8

Busoni E, Sanesi G, Torri D (1986) Soil moisture regimes and erodibility in the assessment of soil suitability for crops in Tuscany. *Soil Use and Management* **2**: 130–3

Buttenfield B P (1986) Digital definitions of scale-dependent line structure. In: Blakemore M J (ed.) *Proceedings of AUTOCARTO London.* Royal Institute of Chartered Surveyors, London, pp. 497–506

Buttenfield B P (1987) Automating the identification of cartographic lines. *The American Cartographer* **14** (1): 7–20

Buttenfield B P (1989) Scale-dependence and self-similarity in cartographic lines. *Cartographica* **26**: 79–100

Buttenfield B P, Mackaness W A (1991) Visualization. In: Maguire D J, Goodchild M F, Rhind D W (eds.) *Geographical Information Systems: principles and applications.* Longman, London, pp. 427–43, Vol 1

Buxton R (1989) Integrated spatial information systems in local government – is there a financial justification? *Mapping Awareness* **2** (6) 14–16

Buzzell R D (1985) *Marketing in an Electronic Age.* Harvard Business School Press, Boston

Buzzell R D, Gale B T (1987) *The PIMS Principles: linking strategy to performance.* Free Press, New York

CACI (1983) *1981 ACORN Classification.* CACI Market Analysis, 59/62 High Holborn, London.

CADalyst (1989) When reality is not enough. *CADalyst* December: 40–53

Calkins H W (1979) The planning monitor: an accountability theory of plan evaluation. *Environment and Planning* **A 11**: 745–58

Calkins H W (1983) A pragmatic approach to geographic information system design. In: Peuquet D, O'Callaghan J (eds.) *Design and Implementation of Computer-based Geographic Information Systems.* International Geographical Union, New York, pp. 92–101

Calkins H W (1991) GIS and public policy. In: Maguire D J, Goodchild M F, Rhind D W (eds.) *Geographical Information Systems: principles and applications.* Longman, London, pp. 233–45, Vol 2

Calkins H W, Marble D F (1987) The transition to automated production cartography: design of the master cartographic database. *The American Cartographer* **14**: 105–21

Callahan M, Broome F R (1984) The joint development of a national 1 : 100 000 scale digital cartographic database. *Proceedings of the Annual Conference of the American Congress on Surveying and Mapping,* Washington DC, pp. 246–53

Campbell J B (1981) Spatial correlation effects upon accuracy of supervised classification of land cover. *Photogrammetric Engineering and Remote Sensing* **47**: 355–63

Campbell J B (1987) *Introduction to Remote Sensing.* Guildford Press, New York

Campbell W G, Church M R, Bishop G D, Mortenson D C, Pierson S M (1989) The role for a geographical information system in a large environmental project. *International Journal of Geographical Information Systems* **3** (4): 349–62

Canada Department of Forestry and Rural Development (1965) *The Canada Land Inventory: objectives, scope and organisation.* Report No. 1. Ottawa, Canada Land Inventory

Card D H (1982) Using known map category marginal frequencies to improve estimates of thematic map accuracy. *Photogrammetric Engineering and Remote Sensing* **48**: 431–9

Carlbom I (1987) An algorithm for geometric set operations using cellular subdivision techniques. *IEEE Computer Graphics and Applications.* May: 45–55

Carlson E D (1983) An approach for designing decision support systems. In: House W C (ed.) *Decision Support Systems.* Petrocelli, New York, pp. 127–56

Carlson E D (1987) Three dimensional conceptual modelling of subsurface structures. *Proceedings of AUTOCARTO 8.* ACSM/ASPRS, Falls Church Virginia, pp. 336–45

Carlson E D, Bennett J L, Giddings G M, Mantey P E (1974) The design and evaluation of an interactive geo-data analysis and display system. In: Rosenfeld J L (ed.) *Information Processing 74, The Proceedings of the IFIP Congress.* North-Holland, New York

Carruthers A, Waugh T C (1988) *GIMMS User Manual.* GIMMS Ltd, Edinburgh

Carter J R (1985) Curricula standards, certification, and other possibilities in cartographic education. *Technical*

Papers of the 45th Annual Meeting of the American Congress on Surveying and Mapping. ACSM, Falls Church, pp. 2–7

Carter J R (1987) Defining cartography as a profession. *ACSM Bulletin* August, 23–6

Carter J R (1989) On defining the geographic information system. In: Ripple W J (ed.) *Fundamentals of Geographic Information Systems: a compendium.* ASPRS/ACSM, Falls Church Virginia, pp. 3–7

Casley D J, Lury D A (1981) *Data Collection in Developing Countries.* Clarendon Press, Oxford

Cass R (1989) Digital databases for vehicle navigation: review of the state of the art. *Proceedings of the 20th International Symposium on Automotive Technology and Automation, Florence,* IEEE, Toronto, pp. 1241–54

Castner H W, Eastman J R (1985) Eye movement parameters and perceived map complexity. *The American Cartographer* 12 (1): 29–40

Catling I, Belcher P (1989) Autoguide – Route Guidance in the United Kingdom. In: Reekie D H M, Case E R, Tsai J (eds.) *Vehicle Navigation & Information Systems Conference, Toronto,* pp. 1127–44

Caulfield I (1989) The role of GISG and LAMSAC in local government. *Proceedings of the National Mapping Awareness Conference.* Miles Arnold, London

Cavill M V, Greener S (1988) Introducing Geographic Information Systems Technology: concepts, approval and implementation. *URPIS – Proceedings of the Urban and Regional Planning Information Systems Annual Conferences,* Volume 16. Australasian Urban and Regional Information Systems Association Inc., Sydney, pp. 323–30

CCITT, The International Telegraph and Telephone Consultative Committee of the International Telecommunications Union (1985) *CCITT-3 and CCITT-4 – Terminal Equipment and Protocols for Telematic Services. Series T Recommendations Geneva.* CCITT Volume VII, Fascicle VII.3

CEC (1990) CORINE: *Examples of the Use of the Results of the Programme 1985–90.* Directorate General of the Environment, Nuclear Safety and Civil Protection, Commission of the European Communities, Brussels

Cederholm T (ed.) (1989) *Utvecklingsradet for Landskapsinformation Geografiska Informationssystem.* Landmateriverket, Gävle Sweden

Central Office of Information (1988) *Britain 1988.* HMSO, London

Centre National d'Études Spatiales (1989) *SPOT Users Handbook,* Volume 2. Centre Spatial de Toulouse, Toulouse, France

Chadha S M (1989) Presidential Address. *IX INCA International Seminar on Digital Cartography and Potential Users.* Pre-Session Proceedings. Survey of India, Dehra Dun, p. 7

Chakravarthy U S (1985) *Semantic Query Optimization in Deductive Databases.* Unpublished PhD thesis, University of Maryland

Chamberlin D D, Astrahan M M, Eswaran K P, Lorie R A,

Mehl J W, Reisner P, Wade B W (1976) SEQUEL 2: a unified approach to data definition, manipulation, and control. *IBM Journal of Research and Development* 20: 560–75

Chamberlin D D, Boyce R F (1974) Sequel: a structured English query language. In: Rustin R (ed.) *Workshop on Data Description, Access and Control.* ACM SIGMOD, Ann Arbor, Michigan, 249–64

Chambers J M, Cleveland S, Kleiner B, Tukey P A (1983) *Graphical Methods for Data Analysis.* Duxbury, Boston

Chan K (1988) *Evaluating Descriptive Models for Prescriptive Inference.* Unpublished PhD thesis, Harvard University

Chandra N, Goran W (1986) Steps toward a knowledge-based geographical data analysis system. In: Optiz B (ed.) *Geographic Information Systems in Government.* A Deepak Publishing, Hampton

Chappuis A, Golbéry L (1984) Un atlas regional, outil d'aide a la décision en Inde. *Paper read to the 12th International Cartographic Conference, Perth, Australia*

Charlwood G, Moon G, Tulip J (1987) Developing a DBMS for geographic information: a review. *Proceedings of AUTOCARTO 8.* ASPRS, Falls Church Virginia, pp. 302–15

Chavez P S (1984) *US Geological Survey Mini Image Processing System.* USGS Open File Report 84–880

Chazelle B, Edelsbrunner H (1988) An optimal algorithm for intersecting line segments in the plane. *Proceedings, 29th Annual Symposium on Foundations of Computer Science, White Plains*

Chelst K, Schultz J, Sanfhvi N (1988) Issues and decision aids for designing branch networks. *Journal of Retail Banking* 10: 5–17

Chen P P (1976) The Entity–Relationship Model – towards a unified view of data. *Association for Computing Machinery Transactions on Database Systems* 1 (1): 9–36

Chen P P (1983) English sentence structure and entity-relationship diagrams. *Information Sciences* 29: 127–49

Chen S (1987) Geographical data handling and GIS in China. *International Journal of Geographical Information Systems* 1 (3): 219–28

Chen Z-T (1987) *Quadtree and Quadtree Spatial Spectra in Large Geographic Information Systems: the hierarchical handling of spatial data.* Unpublished PhD dissertation, University of California, Santa Barbara California

Chen Z-T, Guevara J A (1987) Systematic selection of very important points (VIP) from digital terrain models for constructing triangular irregular networks. *Proceedings of AUTOCARTO 8.* ASPRS, Falls Church Virginia, pp. 50–6

Chinese Academy of Sciences, Institute of Geography (1987) *Population Atlas of China.* Oxford University Press, Oxford

Chorley R (1988) Some reflections on the handling of geographic information. *International Journal of Geographical Information Systems* 2 (1): 3–9

Chorley R, Buxton R (1991) The government setting of GIS in the United Kingdom. In: Maguire D J, Goodchild

M F, Rhind D W (eds.) *Geographical Information Systems: principles and applications*. Longman, London, pp. 67–79, Vol 1

Chrisman N R (1982) A theory of cartographic error and its measurement in digital databases. *Proceedings of AUTOCARTO 5*. ASPRS, Falls Church, pp. 159–68

Chrisman N R (1982) Beyond accuracy assessment: correction of misclassification. *Proceedings International Society of Photogrammetry and Remote Sensing Commission IV*, 24-IV, pp. 123–32

Chrisman N R (1983) The role of quality information in the long-term functioning of a GIS. *Proceedings of AUTOCARTO 6*, Vol. 2. ASPRS, Falls Church, pp. 303–21

Chrisman N R (1984) The role of quality information in the long-term functioning of a geographical information system. *Cartographica* **21**: 79–87

Chrisman N R (1986) Quality report for Dane County soil survey digital files. In: Moellering H (ed.) *Report 7, National Committee for Digital Cartographic Data Standards*, pp. 78–88

Chrisman N R (1987) Design of geographic information systems based on social and cultural goals. *Photogrammetric Engineering and Remote Sensing* **53** (10): 1367–70

Chrisman N R (1987) Efficient digitizing through the combination of appropriate hardware and software for error detection and editing. *International Journal of Geographical Information Systems* **1** (3): 265–77

Chrisman N R (1988) The risks of software innovation: a case study of the Harvard Lab. *The American Cartographer* **15** (3): 291–300

Chrisman N R (1989) Modeling error in overlaid categorical maps. In: Goodchild M F, Gopal S (eds.) *Accuracy of Spatial Databases*. Taylor & Francis, London, pp. 21–34

Chrisman N R (1991) The error component in spatial data. In: Maguire D J, Goodchild M F, Rhind D W (eds.) *Geographical Information Systems: principles and applications*. Longman, London, pp. 165–74, Vol 1

Chrisman N R, Yandell B (1988) Effects of point error on area calculations. *Surveying and Mapping* **48**: 241–6

Christensen A H J (1987) Fitting a triangulation to contour lines. *Proceedings of AUTOCARTO 8*. ASPRS, Falls Church Virginia, pp. 57–67

Christiansen H N, Sederberg T W (1978) Conversion of complex contour line definitions into polygonal element mosaics. *ACM Computer Graphics* **12** (3): 187–92

Christianson C J (1986) Geoprocessing activities in the Fish and Wildlife Survey. *Proceedings of a Geographical Information Systems Workshop*, American Society of Photogrammetry and Remote Sensing, Falls Church Virginia, pp. 43–6

Churchman C W (1968) *The Systems Approach*. Dell Publishing Co. Inc., New York

Cibula W G, Nyquist M O (1987) Use of topographic and climatological models in a geographic database to improve Landsat MSS classification for Olympic National Park. *Photogrammetric Engineering and Remote Sensing* **53**: 67–75

Civco D (1989) Knowledge-based land use and land cover mapping. *Proceedings ASPRS/ACSM Annual Convention*, Vol. 3. ASPRS/ACSM, Falls Church Virginia, pp. 276–91

Claire R W (1982) Algorithm development for spatial operators. *Proceedings of PECORA 9*, pp. 213–21

Clark D M, Hastings D A, Kineman J J (1991) Global databases and their implications for GIS. In: Maguire D J, Goodchild M F, Rhind D W (eds.) *Geographical Information Systems: principles and applications*. Longman, London, pp. 217–31, Vol 2

Clark D M, Kineman J J (1988) Global databases: a NOAA experience. In: Mounsey H M, Tomlinson R F (eds.) *Building Databases for Global Science*. Taylor & Francis, London, pp. 216–33

Clark I, Houlding S, Stoakes M (1990) Direct geostatistical estimation of irregular 3-D volumes. *Proceedings of Symposium on Three Dimensional Computer Graphics in Modelling Geologic Structures and Simulating Processes*. Freiburger Geowissenschafliche Beitrage **2**: 13–15

Clark J W (1977) Time–distance transformations of transportation networks. *Geographical Analysis* **9**: 195–205

Clark W F (1990) *North Carolina's Estuaries: a pilot study for managing multiple use in the State's public trust waters*. Albemarle-Pamlico Study Report 90–10. Albemarle-Pamlico Study Program, Raleigh North Carolina

Clarke A L (1988) Upgrading a digital mapping system. *Proceedings of the Seventh Australian Cartographic Conference*. Australian Institute of Cartographers, Sydney, pp. 238–47

Clarke A L (1991) GIS specification, evaluation and implementation. In: Maguire D J, Goodchild M F, Rhind D W (eds.) *Geographical Information Systems: principles and applications*. Longman, London, pp. 477–88, Vol 1

Clarke A L, Grün A, Loon J C (1982) The application of contour data for generating high fidelity grid digital elevation models. *Proceedings of AUTOCARTO 5*. ASPRS, Falls Church Virginia, pp. 213–22

Clarke K C (1986) Recent trends in geographic information systems. *Geo-Processing* **3**: 1–15

Clarke K C (1986) Advances in Geographic Information Systems. *Computers, Environment and Urban Systems* **10**: 175–84

Clarke K C (1988) Scale-based simulation of topographic relief. *The American Cartographer* **15** (2): 171–81

Clarke K C (1990) *Analytical and Computer Cartography*. Prentice-Hall, Englewood Cliffs New Jersey

Clarke M (1989) Geographical information systems and model based analysis: towards effective decision support systems. *Proceedings of the GIS Summer Institute* Kluwer, Amsterdam

Claussen H, Lichtner W, Siebold J, Heres L, Lahaije P (1989) GDF, a proposed standard for digital road maps to be used in car navigation system. In: Reekie D H M, Case E R, Tsai J (eds.) *Vehicle Navigation & Information Systems Conference, Toronto*, pp. 324–30

Clayton C, Estes J E (1980) Image analysis as a check on census enumeration accuracy. *Photogrammetric Engineering and Remote Sensing* **46**: 757–64

Clayton D, Kaldor J (1987) Empirical Bayes estimates of age-standardised relative risks for use in disease mapping. *Biometrics* **43**: 671–81

Cleveland W S (1985) *The Elements of Graphing Data*. Wadsworth, Monterey California

Cleveland W S, McGill R (1984) Graphical perception: theory, experimentation and application to the development of graphical methods. *Journal of the American Statistical Association* **79**: 531–54

Cliff A D, Ord J K (1981) *Spatial Processes: models and applications*. Pion, London

Cobb M C (1970) Changing map scales by automation. *Geographical Magazine* **4** (3): 786–8

Cocks K D, Walker P A, Parvey C A (1988) Evolution of a continental-scale geographical information system. *International Journal of Geographical Information Systems* **2** (3): 263–80

Cocks K D, Walker P A (1987) Edging towards a nation-wide resources information system for Australia. *Proceedings of the 21st Conference of the Institute of Australian Geographers, Perth*, pp. 319–25

Codd E F (1970) A relational model of data for large shared data banks. *Communications of the ACM* **13** (6): 377–87

Codd E F (1979) Extending the database relational model to capture more meaning. *Association for Computing Machinery Transactions on Database Systems* **4** (4): 397–434

Codd E F (1982) Relational database: a practical foundation for productivity. *Communications of the ACM* **25** (2): 109–17

Cohen J (1988) A view of the origins and development of Prolog. *Communications ACM* **31** (1): 26–36

Cohen P R (1985) *Heuristic Reasoning About Uncertainty: an artificial intelligence approach*. Pitman, London

Cohon J L (1978) *Multiobjective Programming and Planning*. Academic Press, New York

Cole G, Voller J (1988) Introduction of FM into British Telecom. *Proceedings of AM/FM Today. Nottingham Conference*. AM/FM European Division, PO Box 6, CH4005, Basel, Switzerland

Collins J (1982) *Review of Competitive Database Software*. Savant, Carnforth

Collins W G, El-Beik A H A (1971) Population census with the aid of aerial photographs: an experiment in the city of Leeds. *Photogrammetric Record* **7**: 16–26

Colwell R N (1983) *Manual of Remote Sensing*. American Society of Photogrammetry, Falls Church Virginia

Commager H S (1973) Quoted by Justice W O Douglas in EPA v. Mink. 410 US 73: 106

Commission on Geographical Data Sensing and Processing (1976) *Second interim report on digital spatial data handling in the US Geological Survey*. International Geographical Union, Ottawa

Committee on Earth Sciences (1989) *Our Changing planet: the FY90 research plan – the US global change research program*. Office of Science and Technology Policy, Washington DC

Committee on Global Change (1988) *Toward an Understanding of Global Change: Initial priorities for US contributions to the International Geosphere-Biosphere Program*. National Academy Press, Washington DC

Computer Graphics World (1989) Daratech survey. *Computer Graphics World* November, p. 22

Congalton R G (1986) Geographic information systems specialists. *Proceedings of Geographic Information Systems Workshop*. ASPRS, Falls Church, pp. 37–42

Congalton R G (1988) A comparison of sampling schemes used in generating error matrices for assessing the accuracy of maps generated from remotely sensed data. *Photogrammetric Engineering and Remote Sensing* **54**: 593–600

Congalton R G (1988) Using spatial autocorrelation analysis to explore the errors in maps generated from remotely sensed data. *Photogrammetric Engineering and Remote Sensing* **54**: 587–92

Congalton R G, Odervwald R, Mead R (1983) Assessing Landsat classification accuracy using discrete multivariate analysis statistical techniques. *Photogrammetric Engineering and Remote Sensing* **6**: 169–73

Conklin J (1987) Hypertext: an introduction and survey. *IEEE Computer* **20**: 17–41

Cook R N (1966) The CULDATA system. In: Cook R N, Kennedy J L (eds.) *Proceedings of a Tri-State Conference on a Comprehensive Unified Land Data System (CULDATA)*. College of Law, University of Cincinnati, pp. 53–7

Cook R N, Kennedy J L (1966) (eds.) *Proceedings of a Tri-State Conference on a Comprehensive Unified Land Data System (CULDATA)*. College of Law, University of Cincinnatti

Cooke D F (1980) A review of geoprocessing systems and a look at their future. In: Krammer K, King J (eds.) *Computers in Local Government Urban and Regional Planning*. Auerbach Publishers Inc., Pennsauken, pp. (2.4.1) 1–16

Cooper M A R (1974) *Fundamentals of Survey Measurement and Analysis*. Crosby Lockwood Staples, London

Coote A M (1988) Current developments in field-based digital mapping systems at Ordnance Survey. *Proceedings of Mapping Awareness Conference*. Miles Arnold, Oxford

Copeland B J (1989) *Albemarle-Pamlico Esturine System: Preliminary Technical Analysis of Status and Trends*. Albemarle-Pamlico Study Report 89–13A. Albemarle-Pamlico Study Program, Raleigh North Carolina

Coppock J T (1988) The analogue to digital revolution: a view from an unreconstructed geographer. *The American Cartographer* **15** (3): 263–75

Coppock J T, Barritt M (1978) *Application of digital techniques to information systems for planning*. Consultants' report to the Scottish Development Department, Edinburgh

Coppock J T, Rhind D W (1991) The history of GIS. In: Maguire D J, Goodchild M F, Rhind D W (eds.) *Geographical Information Systems: principles and applications.* Longman, London, pp. 21–43, Vol 1

Corbett J P (1975) Topological principles in cartography. *Proceedings, International Symposium on Computer-Assisted Cartography, AUTOCARTO 2.* Reston, Virginia, US Department of Commerce, pp. 22–33

Corbett J P (1979) Topological principles in cartography. *Technical Paper* 48, US Bureau of the Census, Suitland (also published in *Proceedings of AUTOCARTO 4* 1975, pp. 22–33. American Congress on Survey and Mapping/ American Society for Photogrammetry, Washington DC)

Costanza R, Sklar F H, White M L (1990) Modeling coastal landscape dynamics. *Bioscience* **40**: 91–107

Couclelis H (1989) Geographically informed planning: requirements for a planning-relevant GIS. Presented to the North American meeting of the Regional Science Association, Santa Barbara, November

Coulson M R, Waters N (1990) Teaching the NCGIA curriculum in practice. In: Unwin D J (ed.) *GIS Education and Training, Collected Papers of a Conference, University of Leicester 20–21 March 1990.* Midlands Regional Research Laboratory, Leicester

Cowen D J (1983) Rethinking DIDS: the next generation of interactive colour mapping systems *Cartographica* **21**: 89–92

Cowen D J (1986) PC-CAD manages geographical data. *Computer Graphics World* **9** (7): 38–41

Cowen D J (1988) GIS versus CAD versus DBMS: what are the differences? *Photogrammetric Engineering and Remote Sensing* **54**: 1551–4

Cowen D J, Hodgson M, Santure L, White T (1986) Adding topological structure to PC-based CAD databases. *Proceedings of the 2nd International Symposium on Spatial Data Handling.* International Geographical Union, Columbus Ohio, pp. 132–41

Cowen D J, Mitchell L, Meyer W (1990) Industrial modeling using a Geographic Information System: the first step in developing an expert system for industrial site selection. *Proceedings of GIS/LIS '90*, Volume 1. ASPRS/ ACSM/AAG/URISA/AM-FM, Bethesda Maryland, pp. 1–10

Cowen D J, Shinar W (1989) A GIS-based support system for economic development. *URISA Proceedings* **2**: 138–48

Cowen D J, Shirley W L (1991) Integrated planning information systems. In: Maguire D J, Goodchild M F, Rhind D W (eds.) *Geographical Information Systems: principles and applications.* Longman, London, pp. 297– 310, Vol 2

Cowen D J, White T (1989) A versatile mapping system for the USGS 1 : 100 000 DLGs. *Proceedings of AUTOCARTO 9.* ACSM/ASPRS, Falls Church Virginia, pp. 705–14

Cox B J (1986) *Object-Oriented Programming: An evolutionary approach.* Addison-Wesley, Reading. Massachusetts. 274pp.

Cox C W (1976) Anchor effects and the estimation of graduated circles and squares. *The American Cartographer* **3**: 65–74

Cox N J, Aldred B K, Rhind D W (1980) A relational database system and a proposal for a geographical data type. *Geo-Processing* **1**: 217–29

Craig W J (1989) URISA's research agenda and the NCGIA. *Journal of the Urban and Regional Information Systems Association* **1** (1): 7–16

Crain I K (1990) Extremely large spatial information systems: a quantitative perspective. *Proceedings of the 4th International Symposium on Spatial Data Handling*, Volume 2. International Geographical Union, Columbus Ohio, pp. 632–41

Crain I K, MacDonald C L (1984) From land inventory to land management. *Cartographica* **21**: 40–6

Crapper P F (1980) Errors incurred in estimating an area of uniform land cover using Landsat. *Photogrammetric Engineering and Remote Sensing* **10**: 1295–301

Crapper P F, Walker P A, Nanninga P M (1986) Theoretical prediction of the effect of aggregation on grid cell data sets. *Geo-processing* **3**: 155–66

Crawley K J, Nitze R T (1989) One Hundred Million Connections. GIS/LIS for Public Utilities. *Proceedings of Surveying and Mapping '89*, Royal Institution of Chartered Surveyors, London, Paper F3

Cromley R G (1985) An LP relaxation procedure for annotating point features using interactive graphics. *Proceedings of AUTOCARTO 7.* ASPRS, Falls Church Virginia, pp. 127–32

Cromley R G (1986) A spatial allocation analysis of the point annotation problem. *Proceedings of the 2nd International Symposium on Spatial Data Handling.* International Geographical Union, Ohio, pp. 38–49

Croom F (1989) *Principles of Topology.* Saunders College Publishing, Philadelphia

Crossilla F (1986) Improving the outlier separability in geodetic networks according to the generalized orthomax criterion. *Manuscripta Geodaetica* **11**: 38–47

Croswell P L, Clark S R (1988) Trends in automated mapping and geographic information systems. *Photogrammetric Engineering and Remote Sensing* **54**: 1571–6

Cuddy S M, Laut P, Davis J R, Whigham P A, Goodspeed J, Duell T (1989) Modelling the environmental effects of training on a major Australian army base. *Proceedings SSA IMACS Biennial Conference on Modelling and Simulation, Canberra*

Curran P J, Hay A M (1986) The importance of measurement error for certain procedures in remote sensing at optical wavelengths. *Photogrammetric Engineering and Remote Sensing* **52**: 229–41

Curran P J, Williamson H D (1986) Sample size for ground and remotely sensed data. *Remote Sensing of Environment* **20**: 31–41

Cutter S L (1985) Rating places: a geographer's view on quality of life. *Resource Publications in Geography.* Association of American Geographers, Washington DC

Cuzick J, Edwards R (1990) Tests for spatial clustering of events for inhomogeneous populations *Journal of the Royal Statistical Society Series B* **52**: 73–104

Dacey M F (1970) Linguistic aspects of maps and geographic information. *Ontario Geography* **5**: 71–80
Dale M B, McBratney A B, Russell J S (1989) On the role of expert systems and numerical taxonomy in soil classification. *Journal of Soil Science* **40**: 223–34
Dale P F (1976) *Cadastral Surveys within the Commonwealth*. Her Majesty's Stationery Office, London
Dale P F (1988) Economic considerations in the development of land information systems. *Proceedings from the FIG Land Information Systems Workshop, Bali, Indonesia*, pp. 75–83
Dale P F (1990) All the world's a stage – but where are all the players? *Proceedings of National Mapping Awareness Conference*. Miles Arnold, Oxford, pp. 12.1–12.3
Dale P F (1990) Education in land information management. In: Unwin D J (ed.) *GIS Education and Training, Collected Papers of a Conference, University of Leicester 20–21 March 1990*. Midlands Regional Research Laboratory, Leicester, 6 pp.
Dale P F (1991) Land information systems. In: Maguire D J, Goodchild M F, Rhind D W (eds.) *Geographical Information Systems: principles and applications*. Longman, London, pp. 85–99, Vol 2
Dale P F, McLaughlin J D (1988) *Land Information Management – an introduction with special reference to cadastral problems in Third World countries*. Oxford University Press, Oxford
Dangermond J (1983) A classification of software components commonly used in geographic information systems. In: Peuquet D J, O'Callaghan J (eds.) *Design and Implementation of Computer Based Geographic Information Systems*. IGU Commission on Geographical Data Sensing and Data Processing, Amherst New York
Dangermond J (1986) The software toolbox approach to meeting the user's needs for GIS analysis. *Proceedings of the GIS Workshop, Atlanta, Georgia, 1–4 April 1986*, pp. 66–75
Dangermond J (1987) The maturing of GIS and a new age for geographic information modeling (GIMS). In: Aangeenbrug R T, Schiffman Y M (eds.) *International Geographic Information Systems (IGIS) Symposium, Arlington, Virginia*, Volume 2. ASPRS, Falls Church, pp. 55–67
Dangermond J (1988) A review of digital data commonly available and some of the practical problems of entering them into a GIS. *Proceedings of ACSM–ASPRS St Louis*. ACSM/ASPRS, Falls Church Virginia
Dangermond J (1988) A technical architecture for GIS. *Proceedings of GIS/LIS '88*. ACSM/ASPRS, Falls Church, pp. 561–70
Dangermond J (1989) The organizational impact of GIS technology. *ARC News* Summer: 25–6
Dangermond J (1991) The commercial setting of GIS. In: Maguire D J, Goodchild M F, Rhind D W (eds.) *Geographical Information Systems: principles and applications*. Longman, London, pp. 55–65, Vol 1
Dangermond J, Freedman C (1986) Findings regarding a conceptual model of a municipal database and implications for software design. *Geo-Processing* **3**: 31–49
Dangermond J, Freedman C, Chambers D (1986) Tongass National Forest natural resource management information study – a description of project methodology and recent findings. *Geo-Processing* **3**: 51–75
Dangermond J, Harnden E (1990) *Map Data Standardization*. Environmental Systems Research Institute, Redlands California
Dangermond J, Morehouse S (1987) Trends in computer hardware for geographic information systems. *Proceedings of AUTOCARTO 8*. ASPRS/ACSM, Falls Church: pp. 380–5
Dangermond J, Smith K L (1988) Geographic Information Systems and the revolution in cartography: the nature of the role played by a commercial organization. *The American Cartographer* **15** (3): 301–10
Danziger J N, Dulton W H, Kraemer K L (1982) *Computers and Politics: high technology in American local government*. Columbia University Press, New York
Dartington Institute (1986) *The Potential for Forestry on the Culm Measures Farms of south west England*. Dartington Institute, Dartington Devon
Date C J (1986) *An Introduction to Database Systems*. 2nd edn. Addison-Wesley, Reading Massachusetts
Davenport T H, Hammer M (1989) How executives can shape their company's information systems. *Harvard Business Review* **67** (2): 130–4
Davis D L, Elnicki R A (1984) User cognitive types for decision support systems. *Omega* **12**: 601–14
Davis F W, Dozier J (1990) Information analysis of a spatial database for ecological land classification. *Photogrammetric Engineering and Remote Sensing* **56** (5): 605–13
Davis F W, Dubayah R, Dozier J (1989) Covariance of greenness and terrain variables over the Konza Prairie. *Proceedings of IGARRS 89*, pp. 1322–5
Davis F W, Michaelsen J, Dubayah R, Dozier J (1990). Optimal terrain stratification for integrating ground data from FIFE. *Proceedings of the AMS Symposium on the First ISLSCP Field Experiment (FIFE)*. American Meteorological Society, Boston Massachusetts, pp. 11–15
Davis F W, Simonett D S (1991) GIS and remote sensing. In: Maguire D J, Goodchild M F, Rhind D W (eds.) *Geographical Information Systems: principles and applications*. Longman, London, pp. 191–213, Vol 1
Davis J C (1986) *Statistics and Data Analysis in Geology*, 2nd edn. Wiley, New York
Davis J R (1986) Giving directions: a voice interface to a direction giving program. *Proceedings, 1986 Conference, American Voice I/O Society*. September, pp. 77–84
Davis J R, Clark J L (1989) A selective bibliography of expert systems in natural resource management. *AI Applications in Natural Resource Management*. Moscow, Idaho

Davis J R, Grant I W (1987) ADAPT: a knowledge-based decision support system for producing zoning schemes. *Environment and Planning B* **14**: 53–66

Davis J R, Laut P (1989) An expert system to estimate trafficability in a remote region of Australia. *AI Applications in Natural Resource Management* **3** (1): 17–26

Davis J R, Nanninga P M, Clark R D S (1989) A decision support system for evaluating catchment policies. *Proceedings of the Conference on Computing in the Water Industry, Melbourne*, pp. 205–9

Davis J R, Schmandt C M (1989) The back seat driver: real time spoken driving directions. *Proceedings, First Vehicle Navigation & Information Systems Conference (VNIS '89)*. IEEE, New York, pp. 146–50

Davis J R, Whigham P A, Grant I W (1988) Representing and applying knowledge about spatial processes in environmental management. *AI Applications in Natural Resource Management* **2** (4): 17–25

Davis J S, Deter R S (1990) Hypermedia application: Whole Earth Decision Support System. *Information and Software Technology* **32** (7): 491–6

Dawson M (1989) Developing a sedimentological database on an Apple Macintosh II. *BP International Information Systems Services paper*

Day T, Muller J-P (1988) Quality assessment of digital elevation models produced by automatic stereo matchers from SPOT image pairs. *International Archives of Photogrammetry and Remote Sensing* **27** (B3): 148–59

DCDSTF (Digital Cartographic Data Standards Task Force) (1988) The proposed standard for digital cartographic data. *The American Cartographer* **15** (1): 9–140

De Floriani L, Falcidieno B, Pienovi C, Allen D, Nagy G (1986) A visibility-based model for terrain features. *Proceedings of the 2nd International Symposium on Spatial Data Handling*. International Geographical Union, Columbus Ohio, pp. 600–10

de Man E (1988) Establishing a geographical information system in relation to its use: a process of strategic choice. *International Journal of Geographical Information Systems* **2**: 245–61

Dear M (1978) Planning for mental health care: a reconsideration of public facility location theory. *International Regional Science Review* **3**: 93–111

Deering D (1989) Field measurements of bidirectional reflectance. In: Asrar G (ed.) *Theory and Applications of Optical Remote Sensing*. Wiley, New York, pp. 14–65

Demko G J, Hezlep W (1989) USSR: mapping the blank spots. *Focus* **39** (1): 20–1

Denham C, Rhind D W (1983) The 1981 Census and its results. In: Rhind D W (ed.) *A Census User's Handbook*. Methuen, London, pp. 17–88

Densham P J (1991) Spatial decision support systems. In: Maguire D J, Goodchild M F, Rhind D W (eds.) *Geographical Information Systems: principles and applications*. Longman, London, pp. 403–12, Vol 1

Densham P J, Armstrong M P (1987) A spatial decision support system for locational planning: design, implementation and operation. *Proceedings of AUTOCARTO 8*. ACSM/ASPRS, Bethesda Maryland, pp. 112–21

Densham P J, Goodchild M F (1989) Spatial decision support systems: a research agenda. *Proceedings of GIS/LIS '89*, Vol. 2. ACSM/ASPRS, Falls Church Virginia, pp. 707–16

Densham P J, Rushton G (1988) Decision support systems for locational planning. In: Golledge R, Timmermans H (eds.) *Behavioural Modelling in Geography and Planning*. Croom-Helm, London, pp. 56–90

Dent B D (1990) *Principles of Thematic Map Design*. Addison-Wesley, Reading Massachusetts

Denver L E, Phillips D C (1990) Stratigraphic geocellular modelling. *Geobyte* February: 45–7

Department of Health and Social Security (1989) *Working for Patients*. HMSO, London

Department of the Environment (DoE) (1971) Inter-departmental Committee, chaired by J. D. W. Janes. *Report of the Committee on the Ordnance Survey 1970–71*. Unpublished

Department of the Environment (DoE) (1972) *General Information Systems for Planning*, Department of the Environment, London

Department of the Environment (DoE) (1987) *Handling Geographic Information*. Report of the Committee of Enquiry chaired by Lord Chorley. HMSO, London

Department of the Environment (DoE) (1988) *Handling Geographic Information. The Government's response to the report of the Committee of Enquiry*. HMSO, London

Department of Trade and Industry (1990) *Profiting from Electronic Trading: the case study package*. HMSO, London

Devereux B J (1986) The integration of cartographic data stored in raster and vector formats. In: Blakemore M J (ed.) *Proceedings of AUTOCARTO London 1*. Royal Institution of Chartered Surveyors, London pp. 257–66

Devine H A, Field R C (1986) The gist of GIS. *Journal of Forestry* August, 17–22

Dewdney J C (1983) Censuses past and present. In: Rhind D W (Ed.) *A Census User's Handbook*. Methuen, London, pp. 1–15

Dewdney J C, Rhind D W (1986) The British and United States Censuses of Population. In: Pacione M (ed.) *Population Geography: progress and prospects*. Croom Helm, London, pp. 35–57

Dias H D (1987) Varying information needs for local and regional planning and their implications for planning. *Regional Development Dialogue* **8** (1): 24–8

Dias H D (1989) Initiatives in GIS applications at the Asian Institute of Technology. *Paper given to the International Conference on Geographical Information Systems: approaches for urban and regional planning*. Ciloto, Puncak, Indonesia

Diaz B M, Bell S B M (eds.) (1986) *Spatial Data Processing using Tesseral Methods (collected papers from Tesseral Workshops 1 and 2)*. NERC Unit for Thematic

Information Systems, Natural Environment Research Council, Swindon

Dickinson H J (1989) Techniques for establishing the value of geographic information and geographic information systems. *Proceedings of GIS/LIS '89*. ACSM/ASPRS, Falls Church, pp. 412–20

Dickinson H J, Calkins H W (1988) The economic evaluation of implementing a GIS. *International Journal of Geographical Information Systems* **2** (4): 307–27

Didier M (1990) *Utilité et valeur de l'Information Géographique*. CNIG Economica, Paris

Diello J, Kirk K, Callander J (1969) The development of an automated cartographic system. *Cartographic Journal* **6**: 9–17

Diepen C van, Wolf J, Keulen H van, Rappolt C (1989) WOFOST: a simulation model of crop production. *Soil Use and Management* **5**: 16–24

Diggle P J (1983) *Statistical Analysis of Spatial Point Patterns*. Academic Press, London

Dikau R (1989) The application of a digital relief model to landform analysis in geomorphology. In: Raper J F (ed.) *Three Dimensional Applications in Geographical Information Systems*. Taylor & Francis, London, pp. 51–77

Dimmick S (1985) *Pro-Fortran User Guide*. Oracle Corporation, Menlo Park California

Dixon J F, Openshaw S, Wymer C (1987) A proposal and specification for a geographical analysis sub-routine library. *Research Report 3 Northern Regional Research Laboratory*. NRRL, Department of Geography University of Newcastle, Newcastle-upon-Tyne

Dobkin D, Silver D (1988) Recipes for geometry and numerical analysis, part 1: an empirical study. *Proceedings of Fourth ACM Symposium on Computer Geometry*, pp. 93–105

Dobson M W (1986) Spatial decision support systems for early warning of disaster driven social emergencies. *Proceedings of the 2nd International Symposium on Spatial Data Handling* International Geographical Union, Williamsville New York, pp. 332–48

Dobson M W (1988) Digital cartography in the world of commercial publishing. *Proceedings of the 3rd International Symposium on Spatial Data Handling*. International Geographical Union, Columbus, Ohio, pp. 1–8

Doerschler J S (1985) Map data production for an expert name placement system. *Technical Report IPL-TR-073*. Image Processing Laboratory Rensselaer Polytechnic Institute, Troy

Doerschler J S (1985) Data structures required for overlap detection in an expert map name placement system. *Technical Report IPL-TR-077*. Image Processing Laboratory Rensselaer Polytechnic Institute, Troy

Doerschler J S (1987) A rule-based system for dense-map name placement. *Technical Report SR-005*. CAIP Centre, Rutgers University 08855–1390

Doerschler J S, Freeman H (1989) An expert system for dense-map name placement. *Proceedings of AUTOCARTO 9*. ACSM/ASPRS, Falls Church Virginia, pp. 215–24

DOI (1989) *Managing Our Land Information Resources*. Bureau of Land Management, US Department of the Interior, Washington DC

Dolk D R (1986) Data as models: an approach to implementing model management. *Decision Support Systems* **2**: 73–80

Dondis D A (1984) *A Primer of Visual Literacy*. MIT Press, Cambridge Massachusetts

Dougenik J A, Chrisman N R, Niemeyer D R (1985) An algorithm to construct continuous area cartograms. *Professional Geographer* **37**: 75–81

Douglas D H (1986) Experiments to locate ridges and channels to create a new type of digital elevation model. *Cartographica* **23** (4): 29–61

Douglas D H, Peucker T K (1973) Algorithms for the reduction of the number of points required to represent a digitized line or its caricature. *The Canadian Cartographer* **10**: 112–22

Dowers S, Gittings B M, Sloan T M, Waugh T C, Healey R G (1990) Analysis of GIS performance on parallel architectures and workstation-server systems. *Proceedings of GIS/LIS '90*. ASPRS/ACSM/AAG/URISA/AM-FM, Bethesda, pp. 555–61

Dowman I, Muller J P (1986) Real-time photogrammetric input versus digitized maps: accuracy, timeliness and cost. In: Blakemore M J (ed.) *Proceedings of AUTOCARTO LONDON*, Vol. 1. Royal Institution of Chartered Surveyors, London, pp. 538–43

Downs A (1967) A realistic look at the final payoffs from urban data systems. *Public Administrations Review* **27** (3): 204–10

Dowson E, Sheppard V L O (1952) *Land Registration*. Her Majesty's Stationery Office, London

Doytsher Y, Shmutter B (1981) Transformation of conformal projections for graphical purposes. *Canadian Surveyor* **35**: 395–404

Dozier J (1989) Spectral signature of alpine snow cover from the Landsat Thematic Mapper. *Remote Sensing of Environment* **28**: 9–22

Dozier J, Strahler A H (1983) Ground investigations in support of remote sensing. In: Colwell R N (ed.) *Manual of Remote Sensing*. American Society of Photogrammetry, Falls Church Virginia, pp. 959–86

Driessen P M (1989) Quantified land evaluation: consistency in time and space. In: Bouma J, Bregt A K (eds.) *Land Qualities in Space and Time. Proceedings of a Symposium organised by the International Society of Soil Science (ISSS), Wageningen, The Netherlands, 22–26 August 1988*. PUDOC, Wageningen, pp. 3–14

Drummond J, Bosma M (1989) A review of low-cost scanners. *International Journal of Geographical Information Systems* **3** (1): 83–95

Drysdale R L (1979) *Generalized Voronoi Diagrams and Geometric Searching*. Unpublished PhD dissertation, Department of Computer Science, Stanford University

Dubayah R, Dozier J, Davis F W (1990) Topographic

distribution of clear-sky radiation over the Konza Prairie, Kansas. *Water Resources Research* **26** (4): 679–90

Dueker K J (1974) Urban geocoding. *Annals of the Association of American Geographers* **64**: 318–25

Dueker K J (1979) Land resource information systems: a review of fifteen years experience. *Geo-Processing* **1**: 105–28

Dueker K J (1979) Land resource information systems: spatial and attribute resolution issues. *Proceedings of AUTOCARTO 4* Vol. 2. ASPRS, Falls Church, pp. 328–36

Dueker K J (1980) An approach to integrated information systems for planning. In: Krammer K, King J (eds.) *Computers in Local Government Urban and Regional Planning.* Auerbach Publishers Inc., Pennsauken, pp.(2.1.2) 1–12

Dueker K J (1985) Geographic information systems: towards a georelational structure. *Proceedings of AUTOCARTO 7.* ASPRS/ACSM, Falls Church, Virginia, 172–75

Dueker K J (1988) Urban applications of geographical information systems: a grouping into three levels of resolution. *URISA Proceedings*, Volume 2, pp. 104–9

Duffield B S, Coppock J T (1975) The delineation of recreational landscapes: the role of computer-based information systems. *Transactions of the Institute of British Geographers* **66**: 141–8

Duggin M J (1985) Factors limiting the discrimination and quantification of terrestrial features using remotely sensed radiance. *International Journal of Remote Sensing* **6**: 3–27

Duke J (1983) Interactive video: implications for education and training. *CET Working Paper 22.* Council for Educational Technology, London

Dumanski J B, Kloosterman B, Brandon S E (1975) Concepts, objectives and structure of the Canadian Soil Information System. *Canadian Journal of Soil Science* **55**: 181–7

Dumanski J B, Onofrei C (1989) Crop yield models for agricultural land evaluation. *Soil Use and Management* **5**: 9–15

Dunn C, Newton D (1989) Notes on shortest path algorithms for GIS. *North West Regional Research Laboratory Research Report 3.* North West Regional Research Laboratory, Lancaster

Dutton G (ed.) (1979) *First International Study Symposium on Topological Data Structures for Geographic Information Systems.* Addison-Wesley, Reading, Massachusetts

Dutton G (1989) The fallacy of coordinates. *Multiple Representations. NCGIA Technical Paper* **89–3** National Center for Geographical Information Analysis, Santa Barbara California, pp. 44–8

Earth System Sciences Committee (1988) *Earth System Science, a closer view.* NASA, Washington DC

Eastman J R (1988) *IDRISI: a grid-based geographic analysis system.* Graduate School of Geography Clark University, Massachusetts

Eather P T (1986) The HUB – the Queensland approach to land information system development. *URPIS – Proceedings of the Urban and Regional Planning Information Systems Annual Conferences*, Volume 16. Australasian Urban and Regional Information Systems Association Inc., Sydney, pp. 198–208

Ebdon D (1985) *Statistics in Geography: a practical approach*, 2nd edn. Basil Blackwell, Oxford

Ebinger L R, Goulette A M (1989) Automated names placement in a non-interactive environment. *Proceedings of AUTOCARTO 9.* ACSM/ASPRS, Falls Church Virginia, 205–14

Ebinger L R, Goulette A M (1990) Noninteractive automated names placement for the 1990 decennial census. *Cartography and Geographic Information Systems* **17** (1): 69–78

Ebner H, Reinhardt W, Hössler R (1988) Generation, management and utilization of high fidelity digital terrain models. *International Archives of Photogrammetry and Remote Sensing* **27** (B11): III556–65

Edelsbrunner H (1987) *Algorithms for Computational Geometry.* Springer-Verlag, Heidelberg

Edney P, Cavill M (1989) The Melbourne Knowledge Precinct GIS pilot project. *URPIS – Proceedings of the Urban and Regional Planning Information Systems Annual Conferences.* Volume 17. Australasian Urban and Regional Information Systems Association Inc., Sydney, pp. 325–31

Edralin J (1990) Conference Report. *International Conference on Geographical Information Systems: Application for Urban Regional Planning.* Nagoya, UNCRD

Egenhofer M J (1984) Implementation of MAPQUERY, a query language for land information systems (in German). *Report 79.* Institute for Geodesy and Photogrammetry, Swiss Federal Institute of Technology (ETH), Zurich

Egenhofer M J (1989) A formal definition of binary topological relationships. In: Litwin W, Schek H-J (eds.) *Third International Conference on Foundations of Data Organization and Algorithms (FODO)*, Paris (Lecture Notes in Computer Science, Volume 367). Springer-Verlag, New York, pp. 457–72

Egenhofer M J (1989) Spatial query languages. Unpublished PhD Thesis, University of Maine, Orono

Egenhofer M J (1989) Spatial SQL: a spatial query language. *Report 103.* Department of Surveying Engineering, Orono Maine

Egenhofer M J, Frank A U (1987) Object oriented databases: database requirements for GIS. In: Aangeenbrug R T, Schiffman Y M (eds.) *International Geographic Information Systems (IGIS) Symposium, Arlington, Virginia II.* ASPRS, Falls Church Virginia, pp. 189–211

Egenhofer M J, Frank A U (1988) Designing object-oriented query languages for GIS: human interface aspects. *Proceedings of the 3rd International Symposium on Spatial Data Handling.* International Geographical Union, Columbus Ohio, pp. 79–96

Egenhofer M J, Frank A U (1988) Towards a spatial query language: user interface considerations. *Proceedings, 14th International Conference on Very Large Data Bases, Los Angeles*. Morgan Kaufmann, Los Altos, California, pp. 124–33

Egenhofer M J, Frank A U (1990) Lobster: combining AI and database techniques for GIS. *Photogrammetric Engineering and Remote Sensing* **56** (6): 919–26

Egenhofer M J, Frank A U, Jackson J (1989) A topological data model for spatial databases. In: Buchmann A, Gunther O, Smith T, Wang Y (eds.) *Symposium on the Design and Implementation of Large Spatial Databases* (Lecture Notes in Computer Science, Volume 409). Springer-Verlag, New York, pp. 271–86

Egenhofer M J, Herring J R (1991) High-level spatial data structures for GIS. In: Maguire D J, Goodchild M F, Rhind D W (eds.) *Geographical Information Systems: principles and applications*. Longman, London, pp. 227–37, Vol 1

Egger G (1990) Cost-effective automated data conversion using SysScan's (A)DC and GEOREC. *Proceedings of FIG 90*

Ehlers M (1989) Remote sensing and geographic information systems: towards integrated spatial information processing. *Proceedings of IGARRS 89*, pp. 63–6

Ehlers M, Edwards G, Bedard Y (1989) Integration of remote sensing with geographic information systems: a necessary evolution. *Photogrammetric Engineering and Remote Sensing* **55** (11): 1619–27

Eichhorn G (1981) Das FIG-Symposium in Darmstadt – Eine Zusammenfassung. *Proceedings of FIG XVI Congress, Montreux*, pp. 304.1/1–9

Elachi C (1987) *Introduction to the Physics and Techniques of Remote Sensing*. Wiley, New York

Ellis H (1985) Twenty years of data analysis. In: Holloway S (ed.) *Data Analysis in Practice*. Database Specialist Group, The British Computer Society, London, pp. 99–120

Ellis M Y (1978) *Coastal Mapping Handbook*. United States Government Printing Office, Washington DC

Enderle G, Grave M, Lillehagen F (1986) *Advances in Computer Graphics*, Vol. 1. Springer-Verlag, New York

Englund E, Sparks A (1988) *GEO-EAS User's Guide*. Environmental Monitoring Systems Laboratory, Office of Research and Development, Environmental Protection Agency, Las Vegas, Nevada

Eos Science Steering Committee (1987) *Earth Observing System Volume II. From pattern to process: the strategy of the Earth Observing System*. National Aeronautics and Space Administration, Washington DC

EPA (1987) *Sharing Data for Environmental Results*. State/EPA Data Management Program Project Report 1987. United States Environmental Protection Agency, Washington

Epstein E F (1987) Litigation over information: the use and misuse of maps. In: Aangeenbrug R T, Schiffman Y M (eds.) *International Geographic Information Systems (IGIS) Symposium, Arlington, Virginia*, Vol. I. NASA, Washington DC, pp. 177–84

Epstein E F (1988) Legal and institutional aspects of global databases. In: Mounsey H M, Tomlinson R F (eds.) *Building Databases for Global Science*. Taylor & Francis, London, pp. 10–30

Epstein E F (1991) Legal aspects of GIS. In: Maguire D J, Goodchild M F, Rhind D W (eds.) *Geographical Information Systems: principles and applications*. Longman, London, pp. 489–502, Vol 1

Epstein E F, Duchesneau T D (1984) *Use and Value of a Geodetic Reference System*. Federal Geodetic Control Committee National Oceanic and Atmospheric Administration, Rockville Maryland

Epstein E F, Roitman H (1987) Liability for information. *Proceedings of the Urban and Regional Information Systems Association*, Vol 4. URISA, Washington DC, pp. 115–25

ESRI (1989) *ARC/INFO V5.0 Users Guide*, Volumes I and II. ESRI Inc., Redlands California

ESRI (1989) Integration of geographic information technologies. *ARC News* Winter: 24–5

ESRI (1989) *Network Users Guide*. Environmental Systems Research Institute, Redlands California

ESRI (1990) *ARC News* Spring. ESRI, Redlands California

ESRI (1990) *Understanding GIS – the ARC/INFO Method*. Environmental Systems Research Institute, Redlands California

ESRI (1990) ESRI, IBM, and HTE develop interactive link between ARC/INFO and IBM AS/400 Parcel Management System. *ARC News* Winter: 30

ESSC (1988) *Earth System Science : a program for global change*. Report prepared by the Earth System Sciences Committee for the National Aeronautics and Space Administration, Washington DC.

Estes J E, Bredekamp J H (1988) Activities associated with global databases in the National Aeronautics and Space Administration. In: Mounsey H M (ed.) *Building Databases for Global Science*. Taylor & Francis, London, pp. 251–69

Estes J E, Hajic E J, Tinney L R (1983) Manual and digital analysis in the visible and infrared regions. In: Simonett D S, Ulaby F T (eds.) *Manual of Remote Sensing*, 2nd edn. Vol. 1. American Society of Photogrammetry, Falls Church Virginia, 987–1123

Estes J E, McGwire K E, Fletcher G E, Foresman T W (1987) Coordinating hazardous waste management activities using GIS *International Journal of Geographical Information Systems* **1**: 359–77

Estes J E, Sailer C, Tinney L R (1986) Applications of artificial intelligence techniques to remote sensing. *Professional Geographer* **38**: 133–41

ETAK (1988) *ETAK MapEngine, Programmers Guide*. ETAK, Menlo Park California

Evans I S (1972) General geomorphometry, derivatives of altitude, and descriptive statistics. In: Chorley R J (ed.)

Spatial Analysis in Geomorphology. Methuen, London, pp. 17–90

Evans I S (1979) *An integrated system of terrain analysis and slope mapping. Final report on DA-ERO-591-73-G0040: Statistical characterisation of altitude matrices by computer*. Department of Geography, University of Durham

Evans I S (1980) An integrated system of terrain analysis and slope mapping. *Zeitschrift fur Geomorphologie (supplements)* **36**: 274–95

Everett J, Simonett D S (1976) Principles, concepts and philosophical problems. In: Lintz J L, Simonett D S (eds.) *Remote Sensing of Environment*. Addison-Wesley, Reading Massachusetts, pp. 85–127

Experimental Cartography Unit (1971) *Automatic Cartography and Planning*. Architectural Press, London

Eyre L A (1989) JAMGIS, the first Jamaican Government comprehensive multi-data geographical information system: achievements and problems. *International Journal of Geographical Information Systems* **3** (4): 363–71

Eyton J R (1984) Raster contouring. *Geo-Processing* **2**: 221–42

Fagin R (1979) Normal forms and relational database operations. *Proceedings of the ACM SIG-MOD International Conference on Management of Data*, pp. 153–60

Fandrei G (1989) *Descriptive Characteristics of the Seven Eco-regions in Minnesota*. Minnesota Pollution Control Agency. Draft Report, State of Minnesota, St Paul

Fanon F (1963) *The Wretched of the Earth*. New York, Grove Press

Fanshawe J (1985) *Global Resource Information Database*. UNEP Global Environment Monitoring System, Nairobi

FAO (1976) *A Framework for Land Evaluation*. FAO Soils Bulletin 32, Rome

Federal Interagency Coordinating Committee on Digital Cartography (1989) *Co-ordination of Digital Cartographic Activities in the Federal Government*. FICCDC

Fedra K, Reitsma R (1989) Decision support and geographical information systems. *Proceedings of the GIS Summer Institute*. Kluwer, Amsterdam

Feuchtwanger M (1989) Geographic logical database model requirements. *Proceedings of AUTOCARTO 9*. ACSM/ASPRS, Falls Church Virginia, pp. 599–609.

Finch S, Rhind D W (1986) Cartographic and remote sensing digital databases in the UK. *British Library Information Guide 6*. British Library, London

Finch S (1987) *Towards a national digital topographic data base*. Unpublished PhD thesis, University of London.

Fisher P F (1987) The nature of soil data in GIS: error or uncertainty. In: Aangeenbrug R T, Schiffman Y M (eds.) *Proceedings of International Geographic Information Systems (IGIS) Symposium: the research agenda*, Vol. 3. NASA, Washington DC, pp. 307–18.

Fisher P F (1989) Geographical information system software for university education and research. *Journal of Geography in Higher Education* **13**: 69–78

Fisher P F (1989) Knowledge-based approaches to determining and correcting areas of unreliability in geographic databases. In: Goodchild M F, Gopal S (eds.) *Accuracy of Spatial Databases*. Taylor & Francis, London, pp. 45–54

Fisher P F (1991) Spatial data sources and data problems. In: Maguire D J, Goodchild M F, Rhind D W (eds.) *Geographical Information Systems: principles and applications*. Longman, London, pp. 175–89, Vol 1

Fisher P F, Pathirana S (1989) Evaluation of fuzzy membership of land cover classes in suburban areas of north-east Ohio. *ASPRS Technical Papers, 1989 ASPRS/ACSM Fall Convention*. ASPRS, Falls Church VA, pp. 125–32

Fisher P F, Pearson M P, Clarke S R, Ragg J M (1987) Computer program to assist the automation of soil description. *Soil Use and Management* **3**: 26–31

Fisher T, Wales R Q (1991) 3-D solid modelling of geo-objects using non-uniform rational B-splines (NURBS). In: Turner A K (ed.) *Three Dimensional Modelling with Geoscientific Information Systems*. Kluwer, Dordrecht

Fitzpatrick-Lins K (1978) Accuracy and consistency comparisons of land use and land cover maps from high-altitude photographs and Landsat multispectral imagery. *Journal of Research, US Geological Survey* **6** (1): 23–40

Fitzpatrick-Lins K (1981) Comparison of sampling procedures and data analysis for a land use and land cover map. *Photogrammetric Engineering and Remote Sensing* **47**: 343–51

Flew A G (1989) *An Introduction to Western Philosophy: ideas and argument from Plato to Popper*. Thames and Hudson, New York

Flowerdew R (1991) Spatial data integration In: Maguire D J, Goodchild M F, Rhind D W (eds.) *Geographical Information Systems: principles and applications*. Longman, London, pp. 375–87, Vol 1

Flowerdew R, Banting D (1989) Evaluating the potential role of GIS for a market analysis company. *North West Regional Research Laboratory, Research Report 2*. NWRRL, Lancaster

Flowerdew R, Green M (1989) Statistical methods for inference between incompatible zonal systems. In: Goodchild M F, Gopal S (eds.) *Accuracy of Spatial Databases*. Taylor & Francis, London, pp. 239–47

Flowerdew R, Openshaw S (1987) A review of the problems of transferring data from one set of areal units to another incompatible set. *Northern Regional Research Laboratory, Research Report 4*. NRRL, Lancaster and Newcastle-upon-Tyne

Flynn J J (1990) 3-D computing geosciences update. *Geobyte* February: 33–5

Foley J D (1987) Interfaces for advanced computing. *Scientific American* **257** (4): 83–90

Foley J D, van Dam A, Feiner S K, Hughes J F (1990) *Computer Graphics: Principles and Practice*, 2nd edn. Addison-Wesley, Reading Massachusetts

Foley M E (1988) Beyond the bits, bytes and black boxes – institutional issues in successful LIS/GIS management.

Proceedings of GIS/LIS '88. ACSM/ASPRS, Falls Church, pp. 608–17

Forshaw M R B, Haskell A, Miller P F, Stanley D J, Townshend J R G (1983) Spatial resolution of remotely sensed imagery: a review paper. *International Journal of Remote Sensing* **4**: 497–520

Foster M J, Shand P J (eds.) (1990) *The Association for Geographic Information Yearbook 1990*. Taylor & Francis and Miles Arnold, London

Fournier A, Fussel D, Carpenter L (1982) Computer rendering of stochastic models. *Communications of the ACM* **25** (6): 371–84

Frank A U (1981) Applications of DBMS to land information systems. In: Zaniolo C, Delobel C (eds.) *Proceedings of Seventh International Conference on Very Large Data Bases, Cannes, France*. Morgan Kaufmann Publishers, Los Altos, pp. 448–53

Frank A U (1982) MAPQUERY – database query language for retrieval of geometric data and its graphical representation. *ACM SIGGRAPH* **16** (3): 199–207

Frank A U (1984) Computer assisted cartography – graphics or geometry. *Journal of Surveying Engineering* **110** (2): 159–68

Frank A U (1984) Extending a network database with PROLOG. *Proceedings of the First International Workshop on Expert Database Systems, Kiawah Island, SC, October*, pp. 665–74

Frank A U (1984) Requirements for database systems suitable to manage large spatial databases. *Proceedings of the 1st International Symposium on Spatial Data Handling*, Volume 1. International Geographical Union, Zurich Irchel, pp. 38–60

Frank A U (1986) Integrating mechanisms for storage and retrieval of land data. *Surveying and Mapping* **46**: 107–21

Frank A U (1988) Requirements for a database management system for a GIS. *Photogrammetric Engineering and Remote Sensing* **54** (11): 1557–64

Frank A U, Barrera R (1990) The fieldtree: a data structure for geographic information systems. In: Buchmann A, Gunther O, Smith T R, Wang Y-F (eds.) *Design and Implementation of Large Spatial Databases*. Springer-Verlag, New York, pp. 29–44

Frank A U, Buyong T B (1991) Geometry for 3D GIS in geoscientific applications. In: Turner A K (ed.) *Three Dimensional Modelling with Geoscientific Information Systems*. Kluwer, Dordrecht

Frank A U, Kuhn W (1986) Cell graph: a provable correct method for the storage of geometry. *Proceedings of the 2nd International Symposium on Spatial Data Handling, Seattle*. International Geographical Union, Williamsville New York, pp. 411–36

Frank A U, Mark D M (1991) Language issues for GIS. In: Maguire D J, Goodchild M F, Rhind D W (eds.) *Geographical Information Systems: principles and applications*. Longman, London, pp. 147–63, Vol 1

Frank A U, Palmer B, Robinson V (1986) Formal methods for the accurate definition of some fundamental terms in physical geography. In: Marble D (ed.) *Proceedings of Second International Symposium on Spatial Data Handling, Seattle*. International Geographical Union, Ohio, pp. 583–99

Franklin J, Logan T L, Woodcock C E, Strahler A H (1986) Coniferous forest classification and inventory using Landsat and digital terrain data. *IEEE Transactions on Geoscience and Remote Sensing* **GE-24**: 139–46

Franklin S E, Peddle D R, Moulton J R (1989) Spectral/geomorphometric discrimination and mapping of terrain: a study in Gros Morne National Park. *Canadian Journal of Remote Sensing* **15**: 28–42

Franklin W R (1984) Cartographic errors symptomatic of underlying algebra problems. In: *Proceedings of the first International Symposium on Spatial Data Handling, Zurich*. International Geographical Union, Zurich Irchel, pp. 190–208

Franklin W R (1990) Calculating map overlay polygon areas without explicitly calculating the polygons – implementation. *Proceedings of the 4th International Symposium on Spatial Data Handling*. Zurich International Geographical Union, Columbus Ohio, pp. 151–60

Franklin Wm R (1991) Computer systems and low-level data structures for GIS. In: Maguire D J, Goodchild M F, Rhind D W (eds.) *Geographical Information Systems: principles and applications*. Longman, London, pp. 215–25, Vol 1

Franklin W R, Chandrasekhar N, Kankanhalli M, Akman V, Wu P Y F (1990) Efficient geometric operations for CAD. In Wozny M J, Turner J U, Preiss K (eds.) *Geometric Modeling for Product Engineering*. Elsevier, Amsterdam, pp. 485–98

Franklin W R, Chandrasekhar N, Kankanhalli M, Seshan M, Akman V (1988) Efficiency of uniform grids for intersection detection on serial and parallel machines. In: Magnenat-Thalmann N, Thalmann D (eds.) *New Trends in Computer Graphics (Proceedings, Computer Graphics International '88)*. Springer-Verlag, New York

Franklin W R, Chandrasekhar N, Kankanhalli M, Sun D, Zhou M-C, Wu P Y F (1989) Uniform grids: a technique for intersection detection on serial and parallel machines. *Proceedings of AUTOCARTO 9*. ASPRS/ACSM, Bethesda Maryland, pp. 100–9

Franklin W R, Wu P Y F, Samaddar S, Nichols M (1986) Geometry in prolog. In: Kunii T (ed.) *Advanced Computer Graphics, Proceedings of Computer Graphics Tokyo '86*, pp. 71–8

Franklin W R, Wu P Y F (1987) A polygon overlay system in PROLOG. *Proceedings of AUTOCARTO 8*. ASPRS/ACSM, Falls Church Virginia, pp. 97–106

Fraser-Robinson J (1989) *The Secrets of Effective Direct Mail*. McGraw-Hill, New York

Freedom of Information Act (1966) As amended. *5 USCA §552(a)(3)*

Freedom of Information Act (1966) As amended. *5 USCA §552(b)(1–9)*

Freeman H (1991) Computer name placement. In: Maguire D J, Goodchild M F, Rhind D W (eds.)

Geographical Information Systems: principles and applications. Longman, London, pp. 445–56, Vol 1

Freeman H, Ahn J (1984) AUTONAP – an expert system for automatic name placement. *Proceedings of the 1st International Symposium on Spatial Data Handling.* Universitat Zurich-Irchel, Zurich, pp. 544–69

Freeman H, Ahn J (1987) On the problem of placing names in a geographic map. *International Journal of Pattern Recognition and Artificial Intelligence* **1** (1): 121–40

Freeman J (1975) The modelling of spatial relations. *Computer Graphics and Image Processing* **4**: 156–71

French J R (1989) Hydrodynamics and sedimentation in a macrotidal salt marsh, north Norfolk, England. Unpublished PhD Thesis, University of Cambridge, England

French R (1986) Automobile navigation: where is it going? *IEEE Position Location and Navigation Symposium, Las Vegas*

Friedman L M (1984) *American Law*. Norton, New York

Fritsch D (1990) Towards three dimensional data structures in geographic information systems. *Proceedings of the EGIS '90*, pp. 335–45

Frost & Sullivan, Inc. (1989) *The U.S. Non-Entertainment Automotive Electronics Market*. Frost & Sullivan, New York

Fulton P N, Ingold J H (1989) Highlights of geographic coverage and content for the 1990 census data products program. In: Frazier J W, Epstein B J, Schoolmaster F A (eds.) *Papers and Proceedings of Applied Geography Conferences*, Vol. 12. pp. 215–17

Gaal G (1988) Exploration target selection by integration of geodata using statistical and image processing techniques: an example from Central Finland. *Geological Survey of Finland, Report of Investigation* **80**: 156 pp.

Gahegan M N, Hogg J (1986) A pilot geographical information system based on linear quadtrees and a relational database for regional analysis. In: Diaz B M, Bell S B M (eds.) *Spatial Data Processing Using Tesseral Methods*. Natural Environment Research Council, Swindon, p. 213–32

Gahegan M N, Roberts S A (1988) An intelligent, object-oriented geographical information system. *International Journal of Geographical Information Systems* **2**: 101–10

Gaits G M (1969) Thematic mapping by computer. *Cartographic Journal* **6**: 50–68

Gallaire H, Minker J, Nicolas J (1984) Logic and databases: a deductive approach. *ACM Computing Surveys* **16**: 153–85

Gamezo M U, Rubakhin V F (1964) The role of spatial concepts in map reading and the interpretation of aerial photographs. In: Ananyev B G, Lomov B F (eds.) *Problems of Spatial Perception and Spatial Concepts.* (Technical Translation F-164). NASA, Washington, DC

Gardiner V (1982) Stream networks and digital cartography. *Cartographica* **19** (2): 38–44

Gardiner-Hill R C (1971) Automated cartography in the Ordnance Survey. *Proceedings of the Conference of Commonwealth Survey Officers*. Cambridge, August 1971. Foreign and Commonwealth Office. Paper E3, pp. 235–41

Gardiner-Hill R C (1972) *Professional Paper New Series No. 23*. Ordnance Survey, Southampton

Gardiner-Hill R C (1974) The cosmetics of computer cartography. *Proceedings of the 7th International Conference on Cartography*. International Cartographic Association, Madrid

Garey M R, Johnson D S (1979) *Computers and Intractibility: a guide to the theory of incompleteness*. Freeman, San Francisco

Gargantini I (1982) An effective way to represent quadtrees. *Communications of the ACM* **25** (12): 905–10

Gargantini I (1991) Modelling natural objects via octrees. In: Turner A K (ed.) *Three Dimensional Modelling with Geoscientific Information Systems*. Kluwer, Dortrecht

Garner B J (1986) Geographical information systems technology at the University of New South Wales. *AURISA News* March/June: 3–5

Garnsworthy J (1990) The Tradeable Information Initiative. In: Foster M J, Shand P J (eds.) *The Association for Geographic Information Yearbook 1990*. Taylor & Francis, London, pp. 106–8

Gateaud J (1988) The use of cartography databases in multi-purpose utility applications – an experience report. *Proceedings of AM/FM International – European Division Conference Montreux*. AM/FM European Division, PO Box 6, CH4005, Basel, Switzerland, pp. 15–18

Gatrell A C (1983) *Distance and Space: a geographical perspective*. Oxford University Press, Oxford

Gatrell A C (1991) Concepts of space and geographical data. In: Maguire D J, Goodchild M F, Rhind D W (eds.) *Geographical Information Systems: principles and applications*. Longman, London, pp. 119–34, Vol 1

Gatrell A C, Vincent P (1990) Managing natural and technological hazards: the role of GIS. *Regional Research Laboratory Initiative Discussion Paper 7*. RRL Initiative, Sheffield University

Gault I, Peutherer D (1990) Developing geographical information systems in local government in the UK: case studies from Birmingham City Council and Strathclyde Regional Council. In: Worrell L (ed.) *Geographic Information Systems: developments and applications*. Belhaven, London, pp. 109–32

Gaydos L, Newland W L (1978) Inventory of land use and land cover of the Puget Sound region using Landsat digital data. *US Geological Survey Journal of Research* **6**: 807–14

Geoffrion A M (1983) Can OR/MS evolve fast enough? *Interfaces* **13**: 10–25

Geographical Survey Institute (ed.) (1989) *Digital Mapping*. Kashima Shuppankai, Tokyo

Getis A, Boots B (1978) *Models of Spatial Processes* University Press, Cambridge

Giblin P (1977) *Graphs, Surfaces and Homology*. Chapman and Hall, London

Gibson R J (1974) The production of 1:10,000 scale mapping from large scale database. In: Wilford-Brickwood, Bertrand and van Zuylen (eds.) *Working*

Group Oceanic Cartography Commission III. International Cartographic Association, Enschede, pp. 121–32

Gibson W (1984) *Neuromancer* Ace Science Fiction.

Giles R H (1987) The creation, uses and demise of a Virginia USA Geographical Information System. *Proceedings of the International Geographical Union GIS Workshop Beijing, China.* IGU, pp. 507–24

Gill A (1976) *Applied Algebra for the Computer Sciences.* Prentice-Hall, Englewood Cliffs New Jersey

Gilmartin P P (1981) The interface of cognitive and psychological research in cartography. *Cartographica* **18** (3): 9–20

Gilmartin P P (1981) Influence of map context on circle perception. *Annals of the Association of American Geographers* **71**: 253–8

Giltrap D J (1984) MIDGE – a microcomputer soil information system. In: Burrough P A, Bie S W (eds.) *Soil Information Systems Technology.* PUDOC, Wageningen, pp. 112–19

Ginzberg M J, Stohr E A (1981) Decision support systems: issues and perspectives. In: Ginzberg M J, Reitman W, Stohr E A (eds.) *Decision Support Systems.* North-Holland, New York

Girard M-C (ed.) (1981) *Proceedings of the International Society of Soil Science Working Group on Soil Information Systems Colloquium, 14–17 Sept. 1981, Paris.* Institut National Agronomique, Paris, Grignon (3 volumes). Departement des Sols Nos 4, 5, 6

GISWorld (1990) *GIS Software Survey 1990.* GISWorld Inc., Fort Collins Colorado

GISWorld (1990) *GIS Technology '90: results of the 1990 GISWorld geographic information systems survey.* GISWorld, Fort Collins Colorado, 16 pp.

Gittings B (1989) Education and training – the missing link. In: Shand P, Moore R (eds.) *The Association for Geographic Information Yearbook.* Taylor & Francis and Miles Arnold, London, pp. 323–4

Gittings B, Mounsey H M (1989) GIS and LIS training in Britain: the present situation. *Proceedings of the First National Conference of the Association for Geographic Information, 'GIS as a Corporate Resource'.* AGI, Birmingham England, pp. 4.4.1–4.4.4

Goddard Space Flight Center (1984) Earth Observing System: Science and Mission Requirements, Working Group Report, Volume H 1. *NASA Goddard Space Flight Center Technical Memorandum 86129.* National Aeronautics and Space Administration, Greenbelt Maryland

Goel N S (1989) Inversion of canopy reflectance models for estimation of biophysical parameters from reflectance data. In: Asrar G (ed.) *Theory and Applications of Optical Remote Sensing.* Wiley, New York, pp. 205–51

Goetz A F H (1989) Spectral remote sensing in geology. In: Asrar G (ed.) *Theory and Applications of Optical Remote Sensing.* Wiley, New York, pp. 491–526

Gold C, Cormack S (1987) Spatially ordered networks and topographic reconstructions. *International Journal of Geographical Information Systems* **1** (2): 137–48

Goldberg A (1984) *Smalltalk-80: the interactive programming environment.* Addison-Wesley, Reading Massachusetts

Goldberg M, Alvo M, Karam G (1984) The analysis of LANDSAT imagery using an expert system: forestry applications. *Proceedings of AUTOCARTO 6.* ACSM/ASPRS, Falls Church Virginia, pp. 493–503

Goldstein H, Wertz J, Sweet D (1969) *Computer Mapping: a tool for urban planners.* Battelle Memorial Institute, Cleveland

Golledge R G (1982) Fundamental conflicts and the search for geographical knowledge. In: Gould P R, Olssen G (ed.) *A Search for Common Ground.* Pios, London: 11–21

Golledge R G et al. (1982) Commentary on 'The highest form of the geographer's art'. *Annals of the Association of American Geographers* **72**: 557–8

Gonzalez R C, Wintz P A (1987) *Digital Image Processing* 2nd edn. Addison-Wesley, Reading Massachusetts

Goodchild M F (1978) Statistical aspects of the polygon overlay problem. In: Dutton G (ed.) *Harvard Papers on Geographic Information Systems,* Vol 6. Addison-Wesley, Reading Massachusetts, pp. 1–22

Goodchild M F (1980) The effects of generalization in geographical data encoding. In: Freeman H, Pieroni G (eds.) *Map Data Processing.* Academic Press, New York, pp. 191–205

Goodchild M F (1985) Geographical information systems in undergraduate geography: a contemporary dilemma. *The Operational Geographer* **8**: 34–8

Goodchild M F (1986) Spatial autocorrelation. *CATMOG* 47 GeoAbstracts, Norwich

Goodchild M F (1987) A spatial analytical perspective on geographical information systems. *International Journal of Geographical Information Systems* **1** (4): 327–34

Goodchild M F (1987) Application of a GIS benchmarking and workload estimation model. *Papers and Proceedings of Applied Geography Conferences* **10**: 1–6

Goodchild M F (1988) A spatial analytical perspective on GIS. *International Journal of Geographical Information Systems* **1**: 327–34

Goodchild M F (1988) *Spatial Autocorrelation.* CATMOG (Concepts and Techniques in Modern Geography), Vol. 47. GeoBooks, Norwich

Goodchild M F (1988) Stepping over the line: technological constraints and the new cartography. *The American Cartographer* **15** (3): 311–19

Goodchild M F (1988) Towards an enumeration and classification of GIS functions. In: Aangeenbrug R T, Schiffman Y M (eds.) *International Geographic Information Systems (IGIS) Symposium: The research agenda,* Vol II. AAG, Falls Church Virginia: pp. 67–77

Goodchild M F (1989) Geographic information systems and market research. *Papers and Proceedings of Applied Geography Conferences,* Volume 12. 1–8

Goodchild M F (1990) Keynote address: spatial information science. *Proceedings of the 4th International*

Symposium on Spatial Data Handling, Vol 1. International Geographical Union, Columbus Ohio, pp. 3–14

Goodchild M F (1990) Spatial information science. *Proceedings of 4th International Symposium on Spatial Data Handling*, Vol. 1. International Geographical Union, Columbus Ohio, pp. 3–12

Goodchild M F (1991) Geographical data modelling. *Computers and Geosciences* **17**

Goodchild M F (1991) The technological setting of GIS. In: Maguire D J, Goodchild M F, Rhind D W (eds.) *Geographical Information Systems: principles and applications*. Longman, London, pp. 45–54, Vol 1

Goodchild M F, Anselin L, Deichmann U (1989) A general framework for the spatial interpolation of socio-economic data. Paper presented at the Regional Science Association meeting, Santa Barbara California

Goodchild M F, Dubuc O (1987) A model of error for choropleth maps with applications to geographic information systems. *Proceedings of AUTOCARTO 8*. ASPRS/ACSM, Falls Church, pp. 165–74

Goodchild M F, Gopal S (eds.) (1989) *Accuracy of Spatial Databases*. Taylor & Francis, London

Goodchild M F, Grandfield A W (1983) Optimizing raster storage: an evaluation of four alternatives. In: *Proceedings of AUTOCARTO 6 (2)*. ASPRS, Falls Church, pp. 400–7

Goodchild M F, Kemp K K (eds.) (1990) *Core Curriculum in GIS*. National Center for Geographic Information and Analysis, Santa Barbara

Goodchild M F, Kemp K K (1990) Developing a curriculum in GIS: the NCGIA Core Curriculum Project. In: Unwin D J (ed.) *GIS Education and Training, Collected Papers of a Conference, University of Leicester 20–21 March 1990*. Midlands Regional Research Laboratory, Leicester

Goodchild M F, Lam N S-N (1980) Areal interpolation: a variant of the traditional spatial problem. *Geo-Processing* **1**: 297–312

Goodchild M F, Mark D M (1987) The fractal nature of geographic phenomena. *Annals of the Association of American Geographers* **77**: 265–78

Goodchild M F, Rhind D W (1990) The US National Center for Geographic Information and Analysis: some comparisons with the Regional Research Laboratories. In: Foster M J, Shand P J (eds.) *The Association for Geographic Information Yearbook 1990* Taylor & Francis, London, pp. 226–32

Goodchild M F, Rizzo B R (1987) Performance evaluation and work-load estimation for geographic information systems. *International Journal of Geographical Information Systems* **1** (1): 67–76

Goodchild M F, Wang, Min-Hua (1988) Modeling error in raster based spatial data. *Proceedings of the 3rd International Symposium on Spatial Data Handling*. International Geographical Union, Columbus, Ohio, pp. 97–106

Goodenough D G (1988) The integration of remote sensing and geographic information systems. In: Damen M C J, Smit, G S, Verstappen (eds.) *Symposium on Remote Sensing for Resource Development and Environmental Management, Balkema, Rotterdam*, pp. 1015–28

Goodenough D G (1988) Thematic Mapper and SPOT integration with a geographic information system. *Photogrammetric Engineering and Remote Sensing* **54**: 167–76

Goodenough D G, Goldberg M, Plunkett G, Zelek J (1987) An expert system for remote sensing. *IEEE Transactions on Geoscience and Remote Sensing* **GE-25**: 349–59

Gorry G A, Morton M S (1971) A framework for management information systems. *Sloan Management Review* **13**: 56–70

Gorry G A, Morton M S (1989) A framework for management information systems. *Sloan Management Review* **30** (3): 49–61

Gorte B, Liem R, Wind J (1988) The ILWIS software kernel. *ITC Journal* **19**: 15–22

Gottschalk H-J (1972) Die Generalisierung von Isolinien als Ergebnis der Generalisierung von Flèchen. *Zeitschrift für Vermessungswesen* **97** (11): 489–94

Gould M D (1989) The value of spatial decision support systems for oil and chemical spill response. *Proceedings of the 12th Applied Geography Conference* Binghampton, pp. 75–83

Goward S N, Markham B, Dye D G, Dulaney W, Yang J (1991) Normalized difference vegetation index measurements from the Advanced Very High Resolution Radiometer. *Remote Sensing of Environment* **35**: 257–78

Grace B F (1975) A case study of man/computer problem solving. *IBM Research Report RJ1483*. International Business Machines, San Jose

Grant N G (ed.) (1989) *Proceedings of National Conference Challenge for the 1990s GIS*. Canadian Institute of Surveying and Mapping, Ottawa

Gray P, King W R, McLean E R, Watson E J (eds.) (1989) *Management of Information Systems*. Dryden Press, Chicago

Greasley I (1988) Data structures to organize spatial subdivisions. *Proceedings of ACSM-ASPRS Annual Convention, St. Louis*, pp. 139–48

Green D, McEwen L J (1989) GIS as a component of information technology courses in higher education. Meeting the requirements of employers. In: *Proceedings of the First National Conference of the Association for Geographic Information, 'GIS as a Corporate Resource'*. AGI, Birmingham England, pp. c1.1–c1.6

Green N P A (1987) Teach yourself geographical information systems: the design, creation and use of demonstrators and tutors. *International Journal of Geographical Information Systems* **1** (3): 279–90

Green N P A (1990) Towards truly distributed GIS. *Proceedings of the GIS Design Models and Functionality Conference*. Midlands Regional Research Laboratory, University of Leicester, 8pp.

Griffin J M, Hickman D L (1988) *Cost and Benefit Analysis of Geographic Information System Implementation. Final Report to the Bureau of Indian Affairs*. Battelle, Lakewood Colorado

Griffin M W (1987) A rapid method for simulating three dimensional fluvial terrain. *Earth Surface Processes and Landforms* **12**: 31–8

Griffith D A (1987) Spatial autocorrelation: a primer. *Association of American Geographers, Resource Publications in Geography*. Association of American Geographers, Washington

Grimshaw D J (1988) Land and property information systems. *International Journal of Geographical Information Systems* **2** (1): 67–79

Groop R E, Smith R (1982) A dot matrix method of portraying continuous statistical surfaces. *The American Cartographer* **9** (2): 123–30

Gruijter J J de (1977) *Numerical Classification of Soils and its Application in Survey*. PUDOC, Wageningen, 117 pp.

Grunreich D (1985) Computer-assisted generalization. *Papers CERCO-Cartography Course*. Frankfurt a.M

Guevera J A (1989) Latin America: geo-information for development. *ARC News* **11** (3): 16

Guibas L, Stolfi J (1985) Primitives for the manipulation of general subdivisions and the computation of Voronoi diagrams. *ACM Transactions on Graphics* **4** (2): 74–123

Guinn R (1990) The NJUG Perspective. In: Foster M J, Shand P J (eds.) *The Association for Geographic Information Yearbook 1990*. Taylor & Francis, London

Gulati A K (1989) Digital cartography or GIS for resource management and mapping. IX *INCA International Seminar on Digital Cartography and Potential Users*. Pre-Session Proceedings. Survey of India, Dehra Dun, pp. 128–37

Gunther O, Bilmes J (1989) The implementation of the cell tree: design alternatives and performance evaluation. *Proceedings BTW '89 – Database Systems for Office Automation, Engineering, and Scientific Applications*. Springer-Verlag, pp. 72–92

Guptill S C (ed.) (1988) A process for evaluating geographic information systems. *Federal Interagency Coordinating Committee on Digital Cartography, Technology Exchange Working Group, Technical Report 1*. US Geological Survey, Reston Virginia

Guptill S C (ed.) (1990) An enhanced digital line graph design. *US Geological Survey Circular 1048*. USGS, Reston Virginia

Guptill S C (1986) A new design for the US Geological Survey's National Digital Cartographic Database. In: Blakemore M J (ed.) *Proceedings of AUTOCARTO LONDON*, Volume 2. Royal Institution of Chartered Surveyors, London, pp. 10–18

Guptill S C (1987) Desirable characteristics of a spatial database management system. *Proceedings of AUTOCARTO 8*. ASPRS, Falls Church Virginia, pp. 278–281

Guptill S C (1988) A process for evaluating geographic information systems. Technology Exchange Working Group – Technical Report 1. Federal Interagency Coordinating Committee on Digital Cartography. *US Geological Survey Open-File Report 88–105*. USGS, Reston

Guptill S C (1989) Evaluating geographic information systems technology. *Photogrammetric Engineering and Remote Sensing* **55** (11): 1583–7

Guptill S C (1989) Speculations on seamless, scaleless cartographic databases. *Proceedings of AUTOCARTO 9*. ASPRS, Falls Church, pp. 436–43

Guptill S C (1991) Spatial data exchange and standardization. In: Maguire D J, Goodchild M F, Rhind D W (eds.) *Geographical Information Systems: principles and applications*. Longman, London, pp. 515–30, Vol 1

Guptill S C, Boyko K J, Domaratz M A, Fegeas R G, Rossmeissl H J, Usery E L (1990) *An enhanced Digital Line Graph Design*. US Geological Survey Professional Paper 1048, Washington DC

Gurd F B (1990) Requirements of Geographic Information Systems used for supply/demand analysis of real estate markets. *Proceedings of GIS/LIS '90* **1**: ASPRS/ACSM/AAG/URISA/AM-FM, Bethesda Maryland, pp. 21–5

Guttag J, Horowitz E, Musser D (1978) Abstract data types and software validation. *Communications of the ACM* **21** (12): 1048–64

Guttman A (1984) R-trees: a dynamic index structure for spatial searching. *Proceedings of the Annual Meeting ACM SIGMOD, Boston*, pp. 47–57

Haber R N, Wilkinson L (1982) Perceptual components of computer displays. *IEEE Transactions on Computer Graphics and Applications* **2** (3): 23–35

Hägerstrand T (1955) *Statistiska primäruppgifter, flygkartering och 'dataprocessing'-maskiner. Ett kombineringsprojekt. Svensk Geografisk Årsbok 1955*. Lund, Sweden

Hägerstrand T (1967) The computer and the geographer. *Transactions of the Institute of British Geographers* **42**: 1–20

Hägerstrand T (1973) The domain of human geography. In: Chorley R J (ed.) *Directions in Geography*. Methuen, London, pp. 67–87

Haggett P (1965) *Lotational Analysis in Human Geology*. Edward Arnold, London

Hake G (1975) Zum Begriffsystem der Generalisierung. *Nachrichten aus dem Karten- und Vermessungswesen*. Sonderheft zum 65 Geburtstag von Prof Knorr: 53–62

Hall F G, Badhwar G D (1987) Signature-extendable technology: global space-based crop recognition. *IEEE Transactions on Geoscience and Remote Sensing* **GE-25**: 93–103

Hall F G, Strebel D E, Sellers P J (1988) Linking knowledge among spatial and temporal scales: vegetation, atmosphere, climate and remote sensing. *Landscape Ecology* **2**: 3–22

Hall P A V, Papadopoulos S (1990) Hypertext systems and applications. *Information and Software Technology* **32** (7): 477–90

Hamilton A C, Williamson I P (1984) A critique of the FIG definition of a Land Information System. In: *The Decision Maker and Land Information Systems. Papers and*

Proceedings from the FIG International Symposium, Edmonton, Alberta, pp. 28–34

Hamilton W L (1989) Concurrent development of academic geo-computing facilities and curricula for undergraduate education: a case study. *Proceedings of GIS/LIS '89*. ASPRS/ACSM, Bethesda Maryland, pp. 495–505

Hammer M, Zdonik S B (1980) Knowledge-based query processing. *Journal of the IEEE* **6**: 137–46

Hammond N (1989) Hypermedia and learning: who guides whom? In: Maurer H (ed.) *Computer Assisted Learning*. Springer-Verlag, Berlin

Hammond N, Allinson L (1987) The travel metaphor as design principle and training aid for navigating around complex systems. In: Diaper D, Winder R (eds.) *People and Computers III*. Cambridge University Press, Cambridge, pp. 75–90

Hammond N, Allinson L (1989) Extending hypertext for learning: an investigation of access and guidance tools. In: Sutcliffe A, Macaulay L (eds.) *People and Computers V*. Cambridge University Press, Cambridge, pp. 293–304

Han K H (1985) *Estimation of Major City Population in Korea Using Landsat Imagery*. Unpublished PhD thesis, University of Utah

Hannah M J (1981) Error detection and correction in digital terrain models. *Photogrammetric Engineering and Remote Sensing* **47** (1): 63–9

Haralick R M (1980) Edge and region analysis for digital image data. *Computer Graphics and Image Processing* **12**: 60–73

Haralick R M, Fu K (1983) Pattern recognition and classification. In: Colwell R N (ed.) *Manual of Remote Sensing*, 2nd edn. American Society of Photogrammetry, Falls Church Virginia, pp. 793–805

Haralick R M, Shanmugam K, Dinstein I (1973) Textural features for image classification. *IEEE Transactions on Systems, Man, and Cybernetics* **SMC-3** (6): 610–21

Harding A E, Forrest M D (1989) Analysis of multiple geological data sets from the English Lake District. *IEEE Transactions on Geoscience and Remote Sensing* **27**: 732–9

Harig J (1990) Visualisation of 3-D finite element solutions of Navier–Stokes equations. *Proceedings of Symposium on Three Dimensional Computer Graphics in Modelling Geologic Structures and Simulating Processes*. Freiburger Geowissenschaftliche Beitrage **2**: 36–8

Harper E A, Manheim M L (1989) Geographic information systems in transportation planning. *Paper given to the International Conference on Geographical Information Systems: approaches for urban and regional planning*. Ciloto, Puncak, Indonesia

Harris B (1965) New tools for planning. *Journal of the American Institute of Planners* **31** (2): 90–5

Harris D P (1984) *Mineral Resource Appraisal*. Clarendon Press, Oxford

Harris N (1989) Aid and urbanization – an overview. *Cities* **6** (3): 174–85

Hart A (1988) The New South Wales Land Information System in action. *URPIS – Proceedings of the Urban and Regional Planning Information Systems Annual Conferences*, Volume 16. Australasian Urban and Regional Information Systems Association Inc., Sydney, pp. 25–39

Hart J F (1982) The highest form of the geographer's art. *Annals of the Association of American Geographers* **72**: 1–29

Hart J F (1983) More gnashing of false teeth. *Annals of the Association of American Geographers* **73**: 441–3

Hart J F (1988) Keynote Address. *Proceedings of The International Symposium on the Challenge of Rural Poverty: How to Meet It*. Feldafing, FRG, FAO and DSE, pp. 21–4

Harvey D R (1986) *Countryside Implications for England and Wales of Possible Changes in the Common Agricultural Policy*. Centre for Agricultural Strategy, University of Reading UK

Hastings D A (1986) *Stereo-pair World Map*. NOAA National Geophysical Data Center, Boulder Colorado

Hastings D A (1986) *Global MAGSAT Scalar Anomaly Maps*. NOAA National Geophysical Data Center, Boulder Colorado

Hastings D A (1987) AVHRR Stereography. *Proceedings of the North American NOAA Polar Orbiter Users Group First Meeting*. NOAA National Geophysical Data Center, Boulder Colorado (USA), pp. 121–4. Reprinted in *Photogrammetric Engineering and Remote Sensing* **54**: cover and p. 105

Hastings D A, Moll S H (1986) Using Geographic Information Systems as an initial approach to Artificial Intelligence in the geological sciences. *Proceedings of the 1st Annual Rocky Mountain Conference on Artificial Intelligence*. BREIT International Inc, Boulder, pp. 191–200

Haugen E (1957) The semantics of Icelandic orientation. *Word* **13**: 447–60

Hawkins J M (1983) *Oxford Paperback Dictionary*. Oxford University Press, Oxford

Hayes G E, Romig H G (1977) *Modern Quality Control*. Bruce, Encino California

Haywood P E (ed.) (1986) *Final Draft Papers of the Working Party to Produce National Standards for the Transfer of Digital Map Data*. Ordnance Survey, Southampton

Haywood P E (1986) National transfer standards for Great Britain. *Land and Minerals Surveying* **4** (11): 569–78

Haywood P E (1987) The OS Topographic Database Study – the first stage report. In: Haywood P E (ed.) *Proceedings of Spatially-Oriented Referencing Systems Association (SORSA) Symposium, Durham*. Ordnance Survey

Haywood P E (1988) Structured digital data at OS. *Land and Minerals Surveying* **6** (3): 151–6

Haywood P E (1989) Structured topographic data – the key to GIS. *Proceedings of Association for Geographic Information Conference*, Birmingham, October 1989. AGI, London, pp. B1.1–1.4

Hazelton N W J, Leahy F J, Williamson I P (1990) On the design of a temporally-referenced, 3-D Geographical

Information System: development of a four dimensional GIS. *Proceedings of GIS/LIS '90*. AAG/ACSM/AMFM/ASPRS/URISA, Bethesda Maryland, pp. 357–372

Head C G (1984) A map as a natural language – new insight into cartographic communication. *Cartographica* **21** (31): 1–32

Healey R G (1983) Regional geography in the computer age: a further commentary on 'The highest form of the geographer's art'. *Annals of the Association of American Geographers* **73**: 439–41

Healey R G (1991) Database management systems. In: Maguire D J, Goodchild M F, Rhind D W (eds.) *Geographical Information Systems: principles and applications*. Longman, London, pp. 251–67, Vol 1

Hearnshaw H M, Maguire D J, Worboys M F (1989) An introduction to area-based spatial units: a case study of Leicestershire. *Midlands Regional Research Laboratory Research Report 1*. MRRL, Leicester

Helldén U (1987) An assessment of woody biomass, community forests, land use and soil erosion in Ethiopia. *Lund Studies in Geography, Ser C General, Mathematical and Regional Geography No. 14*. Lund University Press, Lund, 75 pp.

Heller M (1986) Triangulation and interpolation of surfaces. In: Sieber R, Brassel K E (eds.) *A Selected Bibliography on Spatial Data Handling: data structures, generalization and three-dimensional mapping. Geoprocessing Series 6*. Department of Geography, University of Zurich, Zurich, pp. 36–45

Heller M (1990) Triangulation algorithms for adaptive terrain modeling. *Proceedings of the 4th International Symposium on Spatial Data Handling*. International Geographical Union, Columbus Ohio, pp. 163–74

Hendrix G, Sacerdoti E, Sagalowicz D, Slocum J (1978) Developing a natural language interface to complex data. *ACM Transactions on Database Systems* **3** (2)

Her Majesty's Land Registry (1990) *Report on the work of HM Land Registry 1989–90*. Her Majesty's Stationery Office, London

Herndon L, Schertz D L (1989) The Water Erosion Prediction Project (WEPP) – SCS Implementation. *Poster Paper in 1989 ASA-CSSA-SSSA Annual Meetings, Las Vegas, Nevada, 16 October 1989*

Herring J R (1987) TIGRIS: topologically integrated geographic information system. *Proceedings of AUTOCARTO 8*. ASPRS/ACSM, Falls Church Virginia, pp. 282–91

Herring J R (1989) The category model of spatial paradigms. In: Mark D M, Frank A U, Egenhofer M J, Freundschuh S, McGranaghan M, White R M (eds.) *Languages of Spatial Relations: Report on the Specialist Meeting for NCGIA Research Initiative 2*. National Center for Geographic Information and Analysis, Santa Barbara, pp. 47–51

Herring J R (1989) A fully integrated geographic information system. *Proceedings of AUTOCARTO9*. ASPRS, Falls Church, pp. 828–37

Herring J R, Egenhofer M J, Frank A U (1990) Using category theory to model GIS applications. *Proceedings of the 4th International Symposium on Spatial Data Handling, Zurich*. International Geographical Union, Columbus Ohio, pp. 820–9

Herring J R, Larsen R C, Shivakumar J (1988) Extensions to the SQL query language to support spatial analysis in a topological database. *Proceedings of GIS/LIS '88*, Volume 2, ASPRS/ACSM, Falls Church Virginia, pp. 741–50

Herskovits A (1985) Semantics and pragmatics of locative expressions. *Cognitive Science* **9**: 341–78

Herskovits A (1986) *Language and Spatial Cognition: an interdisciplinary study of the prepositions in English*. Cambridge University Press, Cambridge

Herskovits A (1987) *Spatial Prepositions in English*. Cambridge University Press, Cambridge Massachusetts

Herzog A (1989) Modeling reliability on statistical surfaces by polygon filtering. In: Goodchild M F, Gopal S (eds.) *Accuracy of Spatial Databases*. Taylor & Francis, London, 209–18

Herzog A, L'Eplattenier R, Weibel R, Brassel K (1987) Experimental spatial data displays. *Proceedings of the 13th Conference of the International Cartographic Association*, Volume IV. ICA, Morelia, pp. 375–89

Heuvelink G B M, Burrough P A, Stein A (1989) Propagation of error in spatial modelling with GIS. *International Journal of Geographical Information Systems* **3** (4): 303–22

Heyn B N (1984) *An Evaluation of Map Color Schemes for Use on CRTs*. Unpublished MS thesis, Department of Geography, University of South Carolina

Heywood D I, Petch J R (1990) GIS education: a business perspective. In: Unwin D J (ed.) *GIS Education and Training, Collected Papers of a Conference, University of Leicester 20–21 March 1990*. Midlands Regional Research Laboratory, Leicester, 11 pp.

Hibbard W, Santek D (1989) Visualizing large data sets in the earth sciences. *IEEE Computer* **22** (8): 53–7

Hill G J E, Kelly G D (1987) A comparison of existing map products and Landsat for land cover mapping. *Cartography* **16**: 51–7

Hirsch S A (1980) *Algorithms for Automatic Name Placement of Point Data*. Unpublished MSc thesis, Department of Geography, State University of New York, Buffalo

Hittelman A M, Metzger D R (1983) Marine geophysics: database management and supportive graphics. *Computers and Geosciences* **9** (1): 27–33

HMSO (Her Majesty's Stationery Office) (1979) *Report of the Ordnance Survey Review Committee*. Chaired by Sir David Serpell. HMSO, London

HMSO (Her Majesty's Stationery Office) (1983) *Report of the Select Committee on Science and Technology – Remote Sensing and Digital Mapping*. Chaired by Lord Shackleton. HMSO, London

HMSO (1980) *People in Britain – a census atlas*. HMSO, London

Hoare C A R (1987) An overview of some formal methods for program design. *Computer (IEEE)* **20** (9): 85–91

Hodgson J M (1978) *Soil Sampling and Description.* Oxford University Press, Oxford

Hoff W A, Michalski R S, Stepp R E (1983) INDUCE 3: a program for learning structural descriptions from examples. *Final Draft Report.* Chicago, Department of Computer Science, Artificial Intelligence Lab, University of Illinois

Hoffer R M (1978) Biological and physical considerations in applying computer-aided analysis techniques to remote-sensor data. In: Swain P H, Davis S M (eds.) *Remote Sensing: the quantitative approach.* McGraw-Hill, New York, pp. 227–87

Hoffer R M (1989) President's Inaugural Address. *Photogrammetric Engineering and Remote Sensing* **55** (7): 1031–2

Hoffer R M, Fleming M D, Bartolucci L A, Davis S M, Nelson R F (1979) Digital processing of Landsat MSS and topographic data to improve capabilities for computerized mapping of forest cover types. *LARS Technical Report 011579,* p. 159

Hoffmann C (1989) The problems of accuracy and robustness in geometric computation. *IEEE Computer* **22** (3): 31–42

Hoffmeister E D (1978) Programmgesteurte Gebandegeneralisierung fur die Topographische Karte 1/25000. *Nachrichten aus dem Karten- und Vermessungswesen* 1 **75**: 51–62

Holben B N, Fraser R S (1984) Red and near-infrared sensor response to off-nadir viewing. *International Journal of Remote Sensing* **5**: 145–60

Holloway C A, Mantey P E (1976) Implementation of an interactive graphics model for design of school boundaries. *Research Paper 299.* Graduate School of Business, Stanford University

Holstein L (1988) LIS problems and issues in urban areas. *Proceedings from the FIG Land Information Systems Workshop, Bali, Indonesia,* pp. 53–9

Honey S, Milnes K, Zavoli W (1988) *Apparatus for generating a heading signal for a land vehicle.* US Patent 4,734,863.

Honey S, White M (1986) Cartographic databases. In: Lambert S S, Ropiequet S (ed.) *CD/ROM The New Papyrus.* Microsoft Press, Redmond WA, pp. 563–72

Honey S, Zavoli W, Milnes K, Phillips A, White M, Loughmiller G (1989) *Vehicle navigational system and method.* US Patent 4,796,191.

Hopgood F R A, Hubbold R J (eds.) (1986) *Advances in Computer Graphics II.* Springer-Verlag, New York

Hopkins L (1984) Evaluation of methods for exploring ill-defined problems. *Environment and Planning B* **11**: 339–48

Hopmans J W, Stricker J N M (1989) Applications of scaling techniques at a watershed scale. In: Bouma J, Bregt A K (eds.) *Land Qualities in Space and Time. Proceedings of a Symposium organised by the International Society of Soil Science (ISSS), Wageningen, The Netherlands, 22–26 August 1988.* PUDOC, Wageningen, pp. 181–4

Horn B K P (1986) *Robot Vision.* MIT Press, Cambridge Massachusetts

Horn D et al. (1989) Spatial access paths and physical clustering in a low level geo-database system. *Geologisches Jahrbuch* **A 104** (Construction and display of geoscientific maps derived from databases)

Horn M, O'Callaghan J F, Garner B J (1988) Design of integrated systems for spatial planning tasks. *Proceedings of the 3rd International Symposium on Spatial Data Handling.* International Geographical Union, Columbus, Ohio, pp. 107–16

Horwood E M (1980) Planning information systems: functional approaches, evolution and pitfalls. In: Krammer K, King J (eds.) *Computers in Local Government Urban and Regional Planning.* Auerbach Publishers Inc., Pennsauken, pp. (2.1.1) 1–12

House of Lords (1984) *Remote sensing and digital mapping.* Report 98 of the House of Lords Select Committee on Science and Technology, Her Majesty's Stationery Office, London

House W C (ed.) (1983) *Decision Support Systems.* Petrocelli, New York, pp. 167–88

Howe D R (1985) *Data Analysis for Data Base Design.* Edward Arnold, London

Hsu S Y (1971) Population estimation. *Photogrammetric Engineering* **37**: 449–54

Hubert L, Golledge R G, Costanzo C M (1981) Generalized procedures for evaluating spatial autocorrelation. *Geographical Analysis* **13**: 224–33

Hudson J C (1979) (ed.) Seventy-five years of American geography. *Annals of the Association of American Geographers* **69** (1): 185pp.

Hummel J, Reck R (1979) A global surface albedo model. *Journal of Applied Meteorology* **18**: 239–53

Hurion R D (1986) Visual interactive modelling. *European Journal of Operational Research* **23**: 281–7

Hurle G (1989) The status of development of facility management systems within the Australian electricity supply industry. *URPIS – Proceedings of the Urban and Regional Planning Information Systems Annual Conferences,* Volume 17. Australasian Urban and Regional Information Systems Association Inc., Sydney, pp. 350–8

Hutchinson C F (1982) Techniques for combining Landsat and ancillary data for digital classification improvement. *Photogrammetric Engineering and Remote Sensing* **48**: 123–30

Hutchinson M F (1988) Calculation of hydrologically sound digital elevation models. *Proceedings of the 3rd International Symposium on Spatial Data Handling.* International Geographical Union, Columbus Ohio, pp. 117–33

Hutchinson M F (1989) A new procedure for gridding elevation and stream line data with automatic removal of spurious pits. *Journal of Hydrology* **106** (1/2): 211–32

ICA (International Cartographic Association) (1973)

Multilingual Dictionary of Technical Terms in Cartography. ICA, Wiesbaden
ICSU (International Council for Scientific Unions) (1989) *Guide to the World Data Center System: part I(a) Updates, Corrections and Additions to Part 1*. ICSU, Boulder Colorado
ICSU Panel on World Data Centers (1987) *Guide to the World Data Center System*. International Council of Scientific Unions, Boulder Colorado
IGBP Special Committee (1988) *The International Geosphere–Biosphere Programme: a study of global change – a plan for action*. Report No. 4. IGBP Secretariat, Stockholm
IGBP Special Committee (1989) *Pilot Studies for Remote Sensing and Data Management*. Report No. 8. IGBP Secretariat, Stockholm
Imhof E (1937) Das Siedlungsbild in der Karte. *Mitteilungen der Geographisch-Ethnographischen Gesellschaft*. Zurich, Band **37**: 17–85
Imhof E (1962) Die Anordnung der Namen in der Karte. *Annuaire International de Cartographie II*. Orell Fuessli Verlag, Zurich, pp. 93–129
Imhoff E (1982) *Cartographic Relief Presentation*. de Gruyter, Berlin
Inaba K, Aumann G, Ebner H (1988) DTM generation from digital contour data using aspect information. *International Archives of Photogrammetry and Remote Sensing* **27** (B8): III101–10
Indian Towing Co. v. United States [1955] 350 US 61, 76 S. Ct. 122, 100 L. Ed. 48
Ingram I K, Phillips W (1987) Geographic information processing using a SQL-based query language. *Proceedings of AUTOCARTO 8*. ASPRS/ACSM, Falls Church Virginia, pp. 326–35
Intergovernmental Oceanographic Commission (1987) GF3, A general formatting system for geo-referenced data, vol 2, Technical description of the GF3 Format and code tables. *Intergovernmental Oceanographic Commission, Manuals and Guides* **17**: UNESCO, Paris
Intergraph Corporation (1989) *Tigris Imager Reference Manual*. Intergraph Corporation, Huntsville
Intergraph Corporation (1989) *Microstation Analyst (MGA) Reference Manual*. Intergraph Corporation, Huntsville Alabama
Intergraph Corporation (1989) *Relational Interface (RIS) User Reference Manual*. Intergraph Corporation, Huntsville Alabama
International Cartographic Association (1973) *Multilingual Dictionary of Technical Terms in Cartography*. Franz Steiner Verlag GMBH
International Council of Scientific Unions (1989) *Yearbook 1989* ICSU Press, Paris
IOS (International Organisation for Standardisation) (1986) *Office Document Architecture (ODA)*. ISO 8613. ISO, Geneva
Iri M, Okabe A, Koshizuka T, Yomono H (1986) *Computer Geometry and Geoprocessing*, Special publication of *BIT* magazine. Kyoritu Shuppan, Tokyo

Irons J R, Weismuller R A, Petersen G W (1989) Soil reflectance. In: Asrar G (ed.) *Theory and Applications of Optical Remote Sensing*. Wiley, New York, pp. 66–106
ISO DP 10303 (1988) *Product Data Exchange Specification (PDES), STEP Version 1.0; also PDES Working Draft Version 1.0*; also NTIS PB 89–144–794. ISO
ISO 2nd DP 9636 (1988) *Computer Graphics Interfacing Techniques for Dialogues with Graphical Devices (CGI)*; also dpANSI X3.161. ISO
ISO 7942 (1985) *Graphical Kernel System (GKS)*; also ANSI X3.124–1985; also FIPS 120. ISO
ISO 8211 (1986) *Specification for a Data Descriptive File for Information Interchange*; also FIPS 123. ISO
ISO 8632 (1987) *Computer Graphics Metafile for the Storage and Transfer of Picture Description Information (CGM) Parts 1–4*; also ANSI X3.122–1986; also FIPS 128. ISO
ISO 8805 (1988) *Graphical Kernel System for Three Dimensions (GKS-3D)*. ISO
ISO 9582 (1989) *Programmer's Hierarchical Interactive Graphics System (PHIGS)*; also ANSI X3.144–1989. ISO
Ives M J, Lovett R (1986) Exchange of digital records between public utility digital mapping systems. In: Blakemore M J (ed.) *Proceedings of AUTOCARTO London*, Volume 2. Royal Institution of Chartered Surveyors, London, pp. 181–9

Jackson J E (1980) *Sphere, Spheroid and Projections*. Granada, London
Jackson J (1990) Developing an effective human interface for geographical information systems using metaphors. *ACSM/ASPRS Annual Convention* **3** (1): 117–25
Jackson M J (1987) Digital cartography, image analysis, and remote sensing: towards an integrated approach. *Interdisciplinary Science Reviews* **12**: 33–44
Jackson M J, Mason D C (1986) The development of integrated geo-information systems. *International Journal of Remote Sensing* **7**: 723–40
Jackson M J, Woodsford P A (1991) GIS data capture hardware and software. In: Maguire D J, Goodchild M F, Rhind D W (eds.) *Geographical Information Systems: principles and applications*. Longman, London, pp. 239–49, Vol 1
Jager E (1987) Computer-assisted symbolization by raster data processing. *Nachrichten aus dem Karten und Vermessungswesen* 1 **46**: 61–70
James P E, Martin G J (1978) *The Association of American Geographers: the first seventy-five years 1904–1979*. Association of American Geographers, Washington DC
Jankowski P (1989) *Knowledge-based Structured Modelling: an application to stream water quality management*. Unpublished PhD dissertation, Department of Geography, University of Washington
Jankowski P, Nyerges T (1989) Design considerations for MaPKBS-map projection knowledge-based system. *The American Cartographer* **16**: 85–95
Jarke M (1984) Semantic query optimization in expert

systems and database systems. *Proceedings of First International Conference on Expert Database Systems*, pp. 467–82

Jarvis R S (1984) Topology of tree-like networks. In: Gaile G L, Willmott C J (eds.) *Spatial Statistics and Models*. D. Reidel, Dordrecht, pp. 271–91

Jasinski M F, Eagleson P S (1989) The structure of red-infrared scattergrams of semivegetated landscapes. *IEEE Transactions on Geoscience and Remote Sensing* **27**: 441–51

Jenkins G M, Watts D G (1968) *Spectral Analysis and Its Applications*. Holden-Day, Oakland California

Jenks G F (1963) Generalization in statistical maps. *Annals of the Association of American Geographers* **53**: 15–26

Jenks G F (1967) The data model concept in statistical mapping. *International Yearbook of Cartography* **7**: 186–8

Jenks G F (1975) The evaluation and prediction of visual clustering in maps symbolized with proportional circles. In: Davis J C, McCullagh M J (eds.) *Display and Analysis of Spatial Data*. Wiley, London, pp. 311–27

Jenks G F (1981) Lines, computers and human frailties. *Annals of the Association of American Geographers* **71**: 1–10

Jensen J R (1986) *Introductory Digital Image Processing*. Prentice-Hall, Englewood Cliffs New Jersey

Jerie H C, Kure J, Larsen H K (1980) A system approach to Geo-Information Systems. *ITC Journal* 4, International Institute for Aerospace Survey and Earth Science, Enschedé

Jeworrek J (1988) *Untersuchungen zur automatischen generalisierung von flachen im Rasterdaten format*. Unpublished Master's Thesis, University of Hannover

Joffe B A and Wright W (1989) SimCity : Thematic mapping + City management Simulation = an entertaining, interactive gaming tool. *Proceedings of GIS/LIS '89*. ACSM\ASPRS\AAG\URISA\AM/FM, Bethesda Maryland, pp. 591–600

Johnson B D, Mott J J, Robey T (1989) Providing effective access to resources information – progress towards a national directory of Australian resources data. *URPIS – Proceedings of the Urban and Regional Planning Information Systems Annual Conferences*, Volume 17. Australasian Urban and Regional Information Systems Association Inc., Sydney, pp. 260–5

Johnson C G (1975) The role of automated cartography in soil survey. In: Bie S W (Ed.) *Soil Information Systems. Proceedings of the meeting of the ISSS Working Group on Soil Information Systems, Wageningen, The Netherlands, 1–4 Sept 1975*. PUDOC, Wageningen, pp. 48–51

Johnson M (1987) *The Body in the Mind: the bodily basis of meaning, imagination and reason*. University of Chicago Press, Chicago

Johnston R J, Gregory D, Smith D M (eds.) (1986) *The Dictionary of Human Geography*, 2nd edn. Blackwell, Oxford

Jones A R, Settle J J, Wyatt B K (1988) Use of digital terrain data in interpretation of SPOT HRV-1 multispectral imagery. *International Journal of Remote Sensing* **9**: 669–76

Jones C B (1989) Data structures for 3-D spatial information systems. *International Journal of Geographical Information Systems* **3**: 15–32

Jones C B, Abraham I M (1986) Design considerations for a scale-independent cartographic database. *Proceedings 2nd International Symposium on Spatial Data Handling, Seattle*. IGU, Columbus, pp. 384–98

Jones T A (1988) Modeling geology in 3 dimensions. *Geobyte* February: 14–20

Jordan T G, Rowntree L (1982) *The Human Mosaic: a thematic introduction to cultural geography*, 3rd edn. Harper and Row, New York

Journel A G, Huijbregts C J (1978) *Mining Geostatistics*. Academic Press, London

Jupp D L B, Strahler A H, Woodcock C E (1989) Autocorrelation and regularization in digital images: II. Simple image models. *IEEE Transactions on Geoscience and Remote Sensing* **27**: 247–56

Jupp D L B, Walker J, Penridge L K (1986) Interpretation of vegetation structure in Landsat MSS imagery: a case study in disturbed semi-arid Eucalypt woodlands. Part 2. Model-based analysis. *Journal of Environmental Management* **23**: 35–57

Justice C O, Townshend J R G, Holben B N, Tucker C J (1986) Analysis of the phenology of global vegetation using meteorological satellite data. *International Journal of Remote Sensing* **6**: 1271–318

Kainz W (1989) Order, topology, and metric in GIS. *Proceedings of ASPRS-ACSM Annual Convention, Baltimore*. ASPRS/ACSM, Falls Church, pp. 154–60

Kamata et al. (1989) *Introduction to Cartographic Analysis*. Nikkan Kogyo Shinbun, Tokyo

Kamijo S, Okumura K, Kitamura A (1989) Digital road map data base for vehicle navigation and road information systems. In: Reekie D H M, Case E R, Tsai J (ed.) *Vehicle Navigation & Information Systems Conference, Toronto*, pp. 319–23

Kaneda K, Kato F, Nakamae E, Nishita T (1989) Three dimensional terrain modeling and display for environmental assessment. *Computer Graphics (SIGGRAPH '89 Proceedings)* **23** (3): 207–14

Kanemasu E T, Asrar G, Fuchs M (1985) Application of remotely sensed data in wheat growth modeling. In: Day D W, Atkin R K (eds.) *Wheat Growth and Modelling*. Plenum, New York, pp. 407–25

Karjala D S (1987) Copyright, computer software, and the new protectionism. *Jurimetrics Journal* **33**: 51–4

Kates R W (1987) The human environment: the road not taken, the road beckoning. *Annals of the Association of American Geographers* **77** (4): 525–34

Katz S (1988) Emulating the Prospector Expert System with a raster GIS. In: Thomas H F (ed.) *GIS: Integrating Technology and Geoscience Applications*. National Resource Center, Connecticut, pp. 27–8

Kauth R J, Thomas G S (1976) The tasselled cap: a graphic description of the spectral-temporal development of crops as seen by Landsat. *Proceedings of the 3rd Symposium on Machine Processing of Remotely Sensed Data*, Vol. 4B. Purdue University, West Lafayette Indiana, pp. 41–51

Kavouras M, Masry S (1987) An information system for geosciences: design considerations. *Proceedings of AUTOCARTO 8*. ACSM/ASPRS, Falls Church Virginia, pp. 336–45

Kawauchi (ed.) (1988) Recent computer mapping systems. *PIXEL*, Gazou Joho Shori Centre, Tokyo

Keates J S (1982) *Understanding Maps*. Longman, London

Keates J S (1989) *Cartographic Design and Production*, 2nd edn. Longman, London

Keefer B J, Smith J L, Gregoire T G (1988) Simulating manual digitizing error with statistical models. *Proceedings of GIS/LIS '88*. ACSM, Falls Church, pp. 475–83

Keen P G W (1980) Adaptive design for decision support systems. *Data Base* **12**: 15–25

Keen P G W (1983) Interactive computer systems for managers: a modest proposal. In: House W C (ed.) *Decision Support Systems*. Petrocelli, New York, pp. 167–88

Keen P G W, Morton M S (1978) *Decision Support Systems: an organizational perspective*. Addison-Wesley, New York

Kehris E (1989) Interfacing ARC/INFO with GLIM: a progress report. *North West Regional Research Laboratory Research Report 5*. North West Regional Research Laboratory, Lancaster

Kelk B (1991) 3-D GIS for the geosciences. *Computers and Geosciences* **17**

Kelk B, Challen K (1989) Experiments with a CAD package for spatial modelling of geoscientific data. *International Colloquium on 'Digital maps in the Geosciences'*, Würzburg Germany

Kelley A D, Malin M C, Nielson G M (1988) Terrain simulation using a model of stream erosion. *Computer Graphics (SIGGRAPH '88 Proceedings)* **22** (4): 263–8

Kelly P (1980) *Automated Positioning of Feature Names on Maps*. Unpublished MSc thesis, Department of Geography, State University of New York, Buffalo

Kemp Z (1990) An object-oriented data model for spatial data. *Proceedings of the 4th International Symposium on Spatial Data Handling*, Volume 2. International Geographical Union, Columbus Ohio, pp. 659–68

Kennedy S (1988) A geographical regression model for medical statistics. *Social Science and Medicine* **26**: 119–29

Kennedy S (1989) The small number problem and the accuracy of spatial databases. In: Goodchild M F, Gopal S (eds.) *Accuracy of Spatial Databases*. Taylor & Francis, London, pp. 187–96

Kent W (1983) A simple guide to five normal forms in relational database theory. *Communications of the Association for Computing Machinery* **26** (2): 120–25

Kidwell J (1990) Impact of copyright law. *Workshop on Managing the Risks and Recovering the Costs of Geographic and Facilities Management Systems*. University of Wisconsin-Madison, Madison, Wisconsin

Kijima Y (1983) *Urban Image*. Seichosha, Kumamoto

Kimball R C, Gregor W T (1989) Emerging distribution strategies in US retail banking. *Journal of Retail Banking* **11**: 4–16

Kimerling A J (1985) The comparison of equal value gray scales. *The American Cartographer* **12** (2): 119–27

Kimes D S (1981) Remote sensing of temperature profiles in vegetation canopies using multiple view angles and inversion techniques. *IEEE Transactions on Geoscience and Remote Sensing* **GE-19**: 85–90

Kindleberger C (1988) Planning support systems for the 1990s: local government information processing challenges and opportunities. *URISA Proceedings* **3**: 1–21

Kineman J J (1989) *Monthly composites of the NOAA Vegetation Index from April 1985 through December 1988 on a 10' grid*. National Geophysical Data Center, Boulder, Colorado

Kineman J J, Clark D M (1988) Connecting global science through spatial data and information technology. In: Aangeenbrug R T, Schiffman Y E (eds.) *Proceedings of the International GIS Symposium: the research agenda*, Volume 1. American Association of Geographers, Falls Church, pp. 209–27

Kineman J J, Clark D M, Croze H (1990) Data integration and modelling for global change: an international experiment. *Proceedings of the International Conference and Workshop on Global Natural Resource Monitoring and Assessments: preparing for the 21st Century*. Volume 2 American Society of Photogrammetry and Remote Sensing, Falls Church, pp. 660–9

Kineman J J, Hastings D A, Colby J D (1986) Developments in global databases for the environmental sciences: discussion and review. *Proceedings of the 12th International Symposium on Remote Sensing of the Environment*. Volume 2. Environmental Research Institute of Michigan, Ann Arbor, pp. 471–82

King C W B (1988) Computational formulae for the Lambert conformal projection. *Survey Review* **29**: 229, 230, 323–37, 387–93

King D, Daroussin J, Bonneton P, Nicoullaud J (1986) An improved method for combining map data. *Soil Use and Management* **2**: 140–5

King R (1989) Introduction to the special issue on non-English interfaces to databases. *IEEE Transactions on Database Engineering* **12** (4): 1–7

Knuth D E (1973) *The Art of Computer Programming*. Addison-Wesley, Reading Massachusetts

Konecny G (1988) Keynote address: current status of geographic and land information systems. *Proceedings of AM/FM European Conference IV, Montreux*

Konecny G, Lohmann P, Engel H, Kruck E (1987) Evaluation of SPOT imagery on analytical photogrammetric instruments. *Photogrammetric Engineering and Remote Sensing* **53** (9): 1223–30

Konecny G, Pape D (1981) Correlation techniques and devices. *Photogrammetric Engineering and Remote Sensing* **47** (3): 323–33

Konsynski B, Sprague R H (1986) Future research

directions in model management. *Decision Support Systems* **2**: 103–9

Korth H F, Silberschatz A (1986) *Database System Concepts*. McGraw-Hill, New York

Korzybski A (1948) *Science and Sanity: an introduction to non-Aristotelean systems and general semantics*, 3rd edn. The International Non-Aristotelean Library Publishing Co., Lakeville CT

Koshkariov A V, Tikunov V S, Trofimov A M (1989) The current state and the main trends in the development of geographical information systems in the USSR. *International Journal of Geographical Information Systems* **3** (3): 257–72

Kosslyn S M (1988) *Image and Mind*. Harvard University Press, Cambridge Massachusetts

Köstli A, Sigle M (1986) The random access data structure of the DTM program SCOP. *International Archives of Photogrammetry and Remote Sensing* **26** (B4): 128–37

Kotler P (1988) *Marketing Management: analysis, planning implementation and control*. Prentice-Hall, Englewood Cliffs

Kowalski R (1974) Predicate logic as a programming language. *Proceedings of IFIP-74*, pp. 569–574

Kowalski R (1987) Algorithm = logic + control. *Communications of the ACM* **22**: 424–36

Kraak M J (1988) *Computer Assisted Cartographical Three Dimensional Imaging Techniques*. Delft University Press, Delft

Kriegel H-P, Schiwietz M, Schneider R, Seeger B (1989) Performance comparison of point and spatial access methods. In: Buchmann A, Gunther O, Smith T, Wang Y (eds.) *Symposium on the Design and Implementation of Large Spatial Databases* (Lecture Notes in Computer Science, Volume 409). Springer-Verlag, New York, pp. 89–114

Krishnayya J G (1986) *C MAPS (Core System) Specifications*. Research and Systems Institute, Pune, India

Kubik K, Frederiksen P (1983) Automatic generalization of contour lines. Paper presented at Eurocarto II, Bolkejo, Norway 9pp.

Kubik K, Lyons K, Merchant D (1988) Photogrammetric work without blunders. *Photogrammetric Engineering and Remote Sensing* **54**: 51–4

Kubo S (ed.) (1987–89) *Proceedings AUTOCARTO JAPAN 3–5*. Autocarto Japan Organizing Committee, Tokyo

Kubo S (1980) Recent trends in geographic data processing. *Jinbun Chiri* **32** (4): 40–62

Kubo S (1987) The development of geographical information systems in Japan. *International Journal of Geographical Information Systems* **1** (3): 243–52

Kubo S (1990) *GIS and the Population Census*. Bureau of Census, Tokyo

Kubo S (1991) The development of GIS in Japan. In: Maguire D J, Goodchild M F, Rhind D W (eds.) *Geographical Information Systems: principles and applications*. Longman, London, pp. 47–56, Vol 2

Kuennucke B H (1988) Experiments with teaching a GIS course within an undergraduate geography curriculum. *Proceedings of GIS/LIS '88*. ASPRS, Falls Church, pp. 302–07

Kuhn W (1991) Are displays maps or views? *Proceedings of AUTOCARTO 10*. ACSM/ASPRS, Bethesda Maryland

Kuilenburg J van, Bunschoten B, Burrough P A, Schelling J (1981) The digital soil map, scale 1:50 000 of The Netherlands. *Proceedings of the International Society of Soil Science Working Group on Soil Information Systems Colloquium, 14–17 Sept 1981, Paris*. Institut National Agronomique, Paris, Grignon Departement des Sols No. 4 pp. 73–86

Kuilenburg J van, Gruijter J J de, Marsman B A, Bouma J (1982) Accuracy of spatial interpolation between point data on soil moisture capacity, compared with estimates from mapping units. *Geoderma* **27**: 311–25

Kuipers B (1978) Modelling spatial knowledge. *Cognitive Science* **2**: 129–53

Kumar R S (1989) A case for Survey-Net. *IX INCA International Seminar on Digital Cartography and Potential Users*. Pre-Session Proceedings. Survey of India, Dehra Dun, pp. 182

Lacroix V (1984) An improved area-feature name placement. *Technical Report IPL-TR-064*. Image Processing Laboratory, Rensselaer Polytechnic Institute, Troy

Lai P C (1988) Resource use in manual digitization. A case study of the Patuxent Basin geographical information system database. *International Journal of Geographical Information Systems* **2** (4): 329–45

Laing A W, Puniard D J (1989) The Australian Defence Force requirements for land-related information. In: Ball D, Babbage R (eds.) *Geographical Information Systems: defence applications*. Pergamon Press, Sydney, pp. 61–79

Lakoff G (1987) *Women, Fire, and Dangerous Things: what categories reveal about the mind*. University of Chicago Press, Chicago

Lakoff G, Johnson M (1980) *Metaphors We Live By*. University of Chicago Press, Chicago

Lam S-N (1983) Spatial interpolation methods: a review. *The American Cartographer* **10** (2): 129–49

Lamp J (1983) Habilitation thesis. Christian-Albrecht University of Kiel, West Germany

LAMSAC (1989) *An Approach to Evaluating GIS for Local Authorities (Requirements Study)*. LAMSAC, London

Land Agency (ed.) (1986) *Geographic Information System*. The Printing Bureau, The Ministry of Finance, Tokyo

Lanen H A J van, Bregt A K, Bulens J D, van Diepen C A, Hendriks C M A, de Koning G H J, Reinds G J (1989) *Crop Production potential of Rural Areas Within the European Community*. Dutch Scientific Council for Government Policy, The Hague

Langel R A, Phillips J D, Horner R G (1982) Initial scalar anomaly map from MAGSAT. *Geophysical Research Letters* **9**: 269–72

Langford M, Maguire D J, Unwin D J (1989) Modelling population distribution using remote sensing and GIS. *Research Report 3 Midlands Regional Research Laboratory*. MRRL, Leicester UK

Langford M, Maguire D J, Unwin D J (1991) The area transform problem: estimating population using satellite imagery in a GIS framework. In: Masser I, Blakemore M J (eds.) *Geographic Information Management: methodology and applications*. Longman, London

Langran G, Chrisman N R (1988) A framework for temporal geographic information. *Cartographica* **25** (1): 1–14

Langran G (1988) Temporal GIS design tradeoffs. *Proceedings of GIS/LIS '88*, Volume 2. ASPRS/ACSM, Falls Church Virginia, pp. 890–99

Langran G (1989) A review of temporal database research and its use in GIS applications. *International Journal of Geographical Information Systems* **3**: 215–32

Langran G (1989) Accessing spatio-temporal data in a temporal GIS. *Proceedings of AUTOCARTO 9*. ACSM/ASPRS, Falls Church Virginia, pp. 191–98

Langran G (1989) *Representing Temporality as a Third GIS Dimension*. Unpublished PhD thesis, Department of Geography, University of Washington

Lasseter T (1990) An interactive 3-D modelling system for integrated interpretation in hydrocarbon reservoir exploration and production. *Proceedings of Symposium on Three Dimensional Computer Graphics in Modelling Geologic Structures and Simulating Processes*. Freiburger Geowissenschaftliche Beitrage **2**: 45–6

Lauer D (1990) *An Evaluation of National Policies Governing the United States Civilian Satellite Land Remote Sensing Program*. Unpublished PhD dissertation, Department of Geography, University of California, Santa Barbara California

Laurillard D (ed.) (1989) *Interactive Media: working methods and practical applications*. Ellis Horwood, Chichester England

Laurini R, Milleret-Raffort F (1989) Principles of geomatic hypermaps *Ekistics* **56** (338–39): 312–17

Lavin S J, Archer J C (1984) Computer-produced unclassed bivariate choropleth maps. *The American Cartographer* **11** (1):49–57

Lavin S J (1979) *Region Perception Variability on Choropleth Maps: pattern complexity effects*. Unpublished PhD dissertation, University of Kansas

Lavin S J (1986) Mapping continuous distributions using dot density shading. *The American Cartographer* **13** (2): 140–50

Lay H G, Weber W (1983) Waldgeneralisierung durch digitale Rasterdaten verarbeitung. *Nachrichten aus dem Karten und Vermessungswesen* **1** (92): 61–71

Lay J C (1975) Mapping services in Fairfax County, Va. *Proceedings of AUTOCARTO 4*. American Congress on Survey and Mapping/American Society for Photogrammetry, Washington DC, pp. 143–7

Lee T S, Russell J S (1990) Potential applications of Geographic Information Systems to the construction industry. *Proceedings of GIS/LIS '90*, Volume 1. ASPRS/ACSM/AAG/URISA/AM-FM, Bethesda Maryland, pp. 11–20

Leenaers H, Burrough P A, Okx J P (1989) Efficient mapping of heavy metal pollution on floodplains by co-kriging from elevation data. In: Raper J F (ed.) *Three Dimensional Applications in Geographical Information Systems*. Taylor & Francis, London, pp. 37–50

Leenaers H, Okx J P, Burrough P A (1989) Co-kriging: an accurate and inexpensive means of mapping floodplain soil pollution by using elevation data. In: Armstrong M (ed.) *Geostatistics. Proceedings of the third Geostatistics Congress, Avignon, October 1988*. Kluwer, pp. 371–82

Lefschetz S (1975) *Applications of Algebraic Topology*. Springer-Verlag, New York

Leick A (ed.) (1982) Land information at the local level. *Proceedings of the International Symposium, Orono, Maine*

Leick A (1987) GIS point referencing by satellite and gravity. In: Aangeenbrug R T, Schiffman Y M (eds.) *Proceedings of International Geographic Information Systems (IGIS) Symposium: the research agenda*, Vol. 2. NASA, Washington DC, pp. 305–17

Lelewer D A, Hirschberg D S (1987) Data compression. *ACM Computing Surveys* **19** (3): 261–96

Lemmens M J P M (1988) A survey on stereo matching techniques. *International Archives of Photogrammetry and Remote Sensing* **27** (B8): V11–V23

Leonard J J, Buttenfield B P (1989) An equal value gray scale for laser printer mapping. *The American Cartographer* **16** (2): 97–107

L'Eplattenier R (1987) An interactive system for display and analysis of block diagrams. Unpublished MSc Thesis (in German). Department of Geography, University of Zurich, Zurich

Lesslie R G, Mackey B G, Preece K M (1988) A computer-based method of wilderness evaluation. *Environmental Conservation* **15** (3): 225–32

Lewis P (1987) Spatial data handling using relational databases. Unpublished MSc thesis, Department of Geography, University of Edinburgh, Scotland.

Li X, Strahler A H (1985) Geometric-optical modeling of a conifer forest canopy. *IEEE Transactions on Geoscience and Remote Sensing* **GE-23**: 705–21

Li X Z, Sun Y (1986) The research of agricultural information systems at a county level. *Resource and Environment System No 1*. LREIS, Beijing

Li Z N (1988) An algorithm for compressing digital contour data. *The Cartographic Journal* **25**: 143–6

Li Z N, Uhr L (1987) Pyramid vision using key features to integrate image-driven bottom-up and model-driven top-down processes. *IEEE Transactions on Systems, Man and Cybernetics*, SMC-17

Lichtner W (1979) Computer-assisted processes of cartographic generalization in topographic maps *Geo-Processing* **1** 183–99

Lieth H (1975) Primary production of the major vegetation units of the world. In: Lieth H, Whittaker R H (eds.)

Primary productivity of the Biosphere (Ecological Studies 14). Springer-Verlag, New York, pp. 203–15

Liley R (1985) Integration – the big pay-off for geobased municipal systems. *Papers of the Urban and Regional Information Systems Association – URISA '85.* URISA, Ottawa, Canada **2**: 11–27

Lillesand T M, Kiefer R W (1987) *Remote Sensing and Image Interpretation*, 2nd edn. Wiley, New York

Lloyd J W (1987) *Foundations of Logic Programming.* Springer-Verlag, New York

Lo C P, Welch R (1977) Chinese urban population estimates. *Annals of the Association of American Geographers* **67**: 246–53

Lobeck A K (1924) *Block Diagrams.* Wiley, New York

Lodwick W A, Monson W, Svoboda L (1990) Attribute error and sensitivity analysis of map operations in geographical information systems suitability analysis. *International Journal of Geographical Information Systems* **4** (4): 413–28

Lodwick W A (1989) Developing confidence limits on errors of suitability analyses in geographical information systems. In: Goodchild M F, Gopal S (eds.) *Accuracy of Spatial Databases.* Taylor & Francis, London, pp. 69–78

Logan T L, Bryant N A (1988) Spatial data software integration: merging CAD/CAM mapping with GIS and image processing. *Photogrammetric Engineering and Remote Sensing* **53** (10): 1391–5

Loomis R G (1965) Boundary networks. *Communications, Association for Computing Machinery* **8**: 44–8

Lorie R A, Meier A (1984) Using a relational DBMS for geographical databases. *Geo-Processing* **2**: 243

Lovejoy S, Schertzer D (1985) Generalised scale invariance in the atmosphere and fractal models of rain. *Water Resources Research* **21**: 1233–50

Loveland T R, Ramey B (1986) Applications of US Geological Survey Digital Cartographic Products, 1979–1983. *US Geological Survey Bulletin 1583*, United States Government Printing Office, Washington

LREIS (1987) *Proceedings of International Workshop on Geographic Information System, Beijing '87.* Laboratory of Resource and Environmental Information Systems, Academica Sinica, Beijing

Luger G L, Stubblefield W A (1989) *Artificial Intelligence and the Design of Expert Systems.* The Benjamin/Cummings Publishing Company Inc, New York

Lupian A E, Moreland W H, Dangermond J (1987) Network analysis in geographic information systems. *Photogrammetric Engineering and Remote Sensing* **53** (10): 1417–21

Lyall G A (1980) Planning and land assessment in Scotland – the role of the Rural Land Use Information Systems Working Party. In: Thomas M F, Coppock J T (eds.) *Land Assessment in Scotland.* Aberdeen University Press, Aberdeen, pp. 107–17

Lyons H G (1931) Land surveying in early times. *Proceedings of Conference of Empire Survey Officers* pp. 175–180

Lyytinen K, Hirschheim R (1987) Information systems failures – a survey and classification of the empirical literature. *Oxford Surveys in Information Technology* **4**: 257–309

Ma P (1987) An algorithm to generate verbal instructions for vehicle navigation using a geographic database. *East Lakes Geographer* **22**: 44–60

MacEachren A E (1982) Map complexity: comparison and measurement. *The American Cartographer* **9** (1): 31–46

MacEachren A E with **Buttenfield B P, Campbell J C, Monmonier M S** (1992) Visualization. In: Abler R F, Olson J M, Marcus N G (eds.) *Geography's Inner World.* Rutgers University Press, New Jersey

Mackaay E (1982) *Economics of Information and Law.* Kluwer Nijhoff, Boston

Mackaness W A, Fisher P F (1987) Automatic recognition and resolution of spatial conflicts in cartographic symbolization. *Proceedings of AUTOCARTO 8.* ASPRS, Falls Church, pp. 709–18

Mackaness W A, Scott D J (1988) The problems of operationally defining the map design process for cartographic expert systems *Proceedings of Austra Carto III, 22–26 Aug, 7th Australian Cartographic Conference, Sydney.* ACA, Sydney, pp. 715–23

Mackenzie H G, Smith J L (1977) Data storage and retrieval. In: Moore A W and Bie S W (eds.) *Uses of Soil Information Systems. Proceedings of the Australian Meeting of the ISSS Working Group on Soil Information Systems, Canberra, Australia, 2–4 March 1976.* PUDOC, Wageningen, pp. 19–36

Mackinlay J (1986) Automating the design of graphical presentations of relational information. *ACM Transactions on Graphics* **5** (2): 110–41

Maeder S R, Tessar P A (1988) *The Use of Geographic Information Systems for Lake Management in Minnesota.* Minnesota State Planning Agency, Minneapolis

Maes J, Vereecken H, Darius P (1987) Knowledge processing in Land Evaluation. In: Beek K-J, Burrough P A, McCormack D E (eds.) *Quantified Land Evaluation Procedures. Proceedings of the Joint Meeting of the ISSS Working Groups on Land Evaluation and Soil Information Systems, Washington 25 April–2 May 1986; ITC Publication No. 6.* ITC, Enschede, pp. 66–73

Maffini G (1987) Raster versus vector encoding and handling: a commentary. *Photogrammetric Engineering and Remote Sensing* **53**: 1397–8

Maffini G, Arno M, Bitterlich W (1989) Observations and comments on the generation and treatment of error in digital GIS data. In: Goodchild M F, Gopal S (eds.) *Accuracy of Spatial Databases.* Taylor & Francis, London, pp. 55–67

Maffini G, Saxton W (1987) Deriving value from the modelling and analysis of spatial data. In: Aangeenbrug R T, Schiffman Y M (eds.) *International Geographic Information Systems (IGIS) Symposium, Arlington, Virginia* Vol 3. NASA, Washington DC, pp. 271–90

Magnenat-Thalman N, Thalman D (1987) An indexed

bibliography on image synthesis. *IEEE Computer Graphics and Applications* **7** (8): 27–37

Maguire D J (1989) *Computers in Geography*. Longman, London

Maguire D J (1989) The Domesday interactive videodisc system in geography teaching. *Journal of Geography in Higher Education* **13** (1): 55–68

Maguire D J (1989) DEMOGIS Mark 1: an ERDAS based GIS tutor. *Proceedings of AUTOCARTO 9*. ASPRS/ACSM, Falls Church Virginia, pp. 620–30

Maguire D J (1990) A research plan for GIS in the 1990s. In: Foster M J, Shand P J (eds.) *The Association for Geographic Information Yearbook 1990*. Taylor & Francis and Miles Arnold, London, pp. 267–77

Maguire D J (1990) Computer cartography. In: Perkins C R, Parry R B (eds.) *Information Sources in Cartography*. Bowker-Saur, London, pp. 201–13

Maguire D J (1991) An overview and definition of GIS. In: Maguire D J, Goodchild M F, Rhind D W (eds.) *Geographical Information Systems: principles and applications*. Longman, London, pp. 9–20, Vol 1

Maguire D J, Dangermond J (1991) The functionality of GIS. In: Maguire D J, Goodchild M F, Rhind D W (eds.) *Geographical Information Systems: principles and applications*. Longman, London, pp. 319–35, Vol 1

Maguire D J, Goodchild M F, Rhind D W (1991) Section I. Introduction. In: Maguire D J, Goodchild M F, Rhind D W (eds.) *Geographical Information Systems: principles and applications*. Longman, London, pp. 3–7, Vol 1

Maguire D J, Hickin B W, Longley I, Mesev T (1991) Waste disposal site selection using raster and vector GIS. *Mapping Awareness* **5** (1): 24–7

Maguire D J, Raper J F (1990) Design models and functionality in GIS. *Proceedings of the GIS Design Models and Functionality Conference*. Midlands Regional Research Laboratory, Leicester, 10 pp.

Maguire D J, Worboys M F, Hearnshaw H M (1990) An introduction to object-oriented Geographical Information Systems. *Mapping Awareness* **4** (2): 36–9

Maher R V, Wightman J F (1985) A design for geographic information systems training. *The Operational Geographer* **8**: 43–6

Mahoney R P (1985) Digital mapping in SEGAS. *Proceedings of AM/FM International – European Division Conference. Montreux*. AM/FM European Division, PO Box 6, CH4005, Basel, Switzerland, pp. 112–22

Mahoney R P (1986) Digital mapping – an information centre. In: Blakemore M (ed.) *Proceedings of AUTOCARTO London*, Volume 2. Royal Institution of Chartered Surveyors, pp. 190–9

Mahoney R P (1991) GIS and utilities. In: Maguire D J, Goodchild M F, Rhind D W (eds.) *Geographical Information Systems: principles and applications*. Longman, London, pp. 101–14, Vol 2

Makarovic B (1973) Progressive sampling for digital terrain models. *ITC Journal* **1973** (3): 397–416

Makarovic B (1977) Composite sampling for digital terrain models. *ITC Journal* **1977** (3): 406–33.

Makarovic B (1979) From progressive to composite sampling for digital terrain models. *Geo-Processing* **1**: 145–66

Makarovic B (1984) Structures for geo-information and their application in selective sampling for digital terrain models. *ITC Journal* **1984** (4): 285–95

Malin M C, Sheridan M F (1982) Computer-assisted mapping of pyroclastic surges. *Science* **217**: 637

Maling D H (1968) The terminology of map projections. *International Yearbook of Cartography* **8**: 11–65

Maling D H (1973) *Coordinate Systems and Map Projections*. George Philip, London

Maling D H (1989) *Measurements from Maps: principles and methods of cartometry*. Pergamon, Oxford

Maling D H (1991) Coordinate systems and map projections for GIS. In: Maguire D J, Goodchild M F, Rhind D W (eds.) *Geographical Information Systems: principles and applications*. Longman, London, pp. 135–46, Vol 1

Mallet J-L (1991) GOCAD: a computer-aided design program for geological applications. In: Turner A K (ed.) *Three Dimensional Modelling with Geoscientific Information*. Kluwer, Dortrecht

Malone T W, Yates J, Benjamin R I (1989) The logic of electronic markets. *Harvard Business Review* **67** (3): 166–72

Mandelbrot B B (1967) How long is the coast of Britain? Statistical self-similarity and fractional dimension. *Science* **156**: 636–8

Mandelbrot B B (1982) *The Fractal Geometry of Nature*. W H Freeman and Co, San Francisco

Mandelbrot B B (1986) Self-affine fractal sets; parts I, II, and III. In: Pietronero L, Tosati E (eds.) *Fractals in Physics*. Elsevier North-Holland, Amsterdam, pp. 3–28

Mann J F (1987) *Computer Technology and the Law*. Carswell, Toronto

Mapping Science Committee, National Academy of Science (1990) *Spatial Data Needs: the future of the National Mapping Program*. National Academy Press, Washington DC

Marble D F (1979) Integrating Cartographic and Geographic Information Systems education. *Technical Papers of the 39th Annual Meeting of the American Congress on Surveying and Mapping*. ACSM, Falls Church, pp. 493–9

Marble D F (1980) (ed.) *Computer Software for Spatial Data Handling*, 3 volumes. Commission on Geographical Data Sensing and Processing/International Geographical Union, Ottawa Canada

Marble D F (ed.) (1980) *Computer Software for Spatial Data Handling* 3 volumes. IGU Commission on Geographical Data Sensing and Processing for the US Department of the Interior Geological Survey, Ottawa

Marble D F (1989) Letter to PERS. *Photogrammetric Engineering and Remote Sensing* **55** (4): 434–5

Marble D F, Calkins H W, Dueker K, Gilliland J, Salmona J (1972) Introduction to the economics of geographical information systems, and geographical information system design: concepts and methods. In: Tomlinson R F (ed.) *Geographical Data Handling. UNESCO/IGU Second Symposium on Geographical Information Systems.* International Geographical Union, Ottawa

Marble D F, Lauzon J P, McGranaghan M (1984) Development of a conceptual model of the manual digitizing process. *Proceedings of the 1st International Symposium on Spatial Data Handling.* University of Zurich-Irchel, Zurich, pp. 146–71

Marble D F, Peuquet D J (1983) Geographic information systems. In: Colwell R N (ed.) *Manual of Remote Sensing*, 2nd edn. American Society of Photogrammetry, Falls Church, pp. 923–58

Marble D F, Peuquet D J, Boyle A R, Bryant N, Calkins H W, Johnson T (1983) Geographic information systems and remote sensing. In: Colwell R N (ed.) *Manual of Remote Sensing.* American Society of Photogrammetry, Falls Church Virginia, pp. 923–57

Marble D F, Sen L (1986) The development of standardised benchmarks for spatial database systems. *Proceedings of the 2nd International Symposium on Spatial Data Handling.* IGU, Columbus Ohio, pp. 488–96

Marchionini G, Schneiderman B (1988) Finding facts versus browsing knowledge in hypertext systems. *Computer* **3** (1): 70–80

Mark D M (1975) Geomorphometric parameters: a review and evaluation. *Geografiska Annaler* **57A** (3–4): 165–77

Mark D M (1979) Phenomenon-based data structuring and digital terrain modeling. *Geo-Processing* **1**: 27–36

Mark D M (1984) Automated detection of drainage networks from digital elevation models. *Cartographica* **21**: 168–78

Mark D M (1985) Finding simple routes: 'ease of description' as an objective function in automated route selection. *Proceedings, Second Symposium on Artificial Intelligence Applications, Miami Beach*

Mark D M (1987) On giving and receiving directions: cartographic and cognitive issues. *Proceedings of AUTOCARTO 8.* ACSM/ASPRS, Falls Church Virginia, pp. 562–71

Mark D M (1987) Recursive algorithms for the analysis and display of digital elevation data. *Proceedings First Latin American Conference on Computers in Cartography, San José, Costa Rica*, pp. 375–97

Mark D M (1989) Cognitive image-schemata for geographic information: relations to user views and GIS interfaces. *Proceedings of GIS/LIS '89*, Vol. 2. ASPRS/ACSM, Falls Church, pp. 551–60

Mark D M (1989) Multiple views of multiple representations. *Multiple Representations. NCGIA Technical Paper* **89–3** National Centre for Geographic Information and Analysis, Santa Barbara California, pp. 68–71

Mark D M, Aronson P B (1984) Scale-dependent fractal dimensions of topographic surfaces: an empirical investigation, with applications in geomorphology and computer mapping. *Mathematical Geology* **16**: 671–83

Mark D M, Cebrian J A (1986) Octrees: a useful method for the processing of topographic and subsurface data. *Proceedings of ACSM–ASPRS Annual Convention*, Volume 1. ACSM/ASPRS, Falls Church Virginia, pp. 104–113

Mark D M, Csillag F (1989) The nature of boundaries in 'area-class maps'. *Cartographica* **26** (1): 65–78

Mark D M, Frank A U, Egenhofer M J, Freundschuh S, McGranaghan M, White R M (1989) Languages of spatial relations: report on the specialist meeting for NCGIA Research Initiative 2. *Technical Report 89–2*, National Center for Geographic Information and Analysis, Santa Barbara

Mark D M, Gould M D, Nunes J (1989) Spatial language and geographic information systems: cross-linguistic issues. *Proceedings, II Conferencia Latinoamericana sobre el (Technologia de los Sistemas de Informacion Geograficos (SIG).* Universidad de Los Andes, Merida, Venezuela, pp. 105–30

Mark D M, Svorou S, Zubin D (1988) Spatial terms and spatial concepts: geographic, cognitive, and linguistic perspectives. In: Aangeenbrug R T, Schiffman Y M (eds.) *International Geographic Information Systems (IGIS) Symposium, Arlington, Virginia.* NASA, Washington DC, pp. 101–12

Marks D, Dozier J, Frew J (1984) Automated basin delineation from digital elevation data. *Geo-Processing* **2**: 299–311

Marr D (1982) *Vision.* Freeman, San Francisco

Marsman B, Gruijter J J de (1984) Dutch soil survey goes into quality control. In: Burrough P A, Bie S W (eds.) *Soil Information Systems Technology.* PUDOC, Wageningen, pp. 127–34

Marsman B, Gruijter J J de (1986) Quality of soil maps. A comparison of survey methods in a sandy area. *Soil Survey Papers No. 15.* Netherlands Soil Survey Institute, Wageningen, 103 pp

Martin D (1989) Mapping population data from zone centroid locations. *Transactions of the Institute of British Geographers.* NS **14** (1): 90–7

Martin J (1976) *Principles of Database Management.* Prentice-Hall, Englewood Cliffs New Jersey

Martin J (1983) *4th Generation Languages*, Volume 1. Savant, Carnforth Lancashire

Martin P H (1983) Disclosure and use of proprietary data: task force report 15. *Natural Resources Lawyer 799.* American Bar Association, Chicago, pp. 802–3

Marx R W (1986) The TIGER system: automating the geographic structure of the United States census. *Government Publications Review* **13**: 181–201

Marx R W (1990) The TIGER system: yesterday, today and tomorrow. *Cartography and Geographic Information Systems* **17** (1): 89–97

Mason D C, Corr D G, Cross A, Hoggs D C, Lawrence D H, Petrou M, Tailor A M (1988) The use of digital map data in the segmentation and classification of remotely-sensed images. *International Journal of Geographical Information Systems* **2** (3): 195–215

Mason D C, Townshend J R G (1988) Research related to

geographical information systems at the Natural Environment Research Council's Unit for Thematic Information System. *International Journal of Geographical Information Systems* **2**: 121–41

Mason K (1990) Cartographic applications of satellite remote sensing. In: Perkins C R, Parry R B (eds.) *Information Sources in Cartography*. Bowker-Saur, London, pp. 142–67

Masser I (1988) The Regional Research Laboratory Initiative: a progress report. *International Journal of Geographical Information Systems* **2**: 11–22

Masser I (1990) The Regional Research Laboratory initiative: an update. In: Foster M J, Shand P J (eds.) *The Association for Geographic Information Yearbook 1990*. Taylor & Francis and Miles Arnold, London, pp. 259–63

Mateo A, Burrough P A, Comerma J (1987) Analysis espacial de propiedadas de suelo para estudios de modelacion de cultivos en Venezuela. *Proceedings First Latin American GIS Conference, Costa Rica*. Ed. Lyen M, October 1987, Universidad Estatal a Distancia, San José, Costa Rica. pp. 164–78

Mather P M (1987) *Computer Processing of Remotely-sensed Images: an introduction*. Wiley, Chichester

Matheron G (1971) *The Theory of Regionalised Variables and its Applications*. Les Cahiers du Centre de Morphologie Mathématique de Fontainebleau. Ecole Nationale Superieure des Mines de Paris

Matheson G (1986) The implementation of a facilities information system with a major utility organisation. *URPIS – Proceedings of the Urban and Regional Planning Information Systems Annual Conferences*, Volume 14. Australasian Urban and Regional Information Systems Association Inc., Sydney, pp. 203–25

Matsui I (1930) Relations between grade and cultural landscape around Kamimizo. *Geographical Review of Japan* **6**: 1599–627

Matsui I (1931) Statistical observation of scattered village in Tonami Plain. *Geographical Review of Japan* **7**: 459–75

Matsui I (1933) Some problems in spatial distribution, especially in Tama Hill. *Geographical Review of Japan* **8**: 359–1627

Matthews E (1983) Global vegetation and land use: new high resolution databases for climate studies. *Journal of Climatology and Applied Meteorology* **22**: 474–87

Mausbach M J, Reybold W U (1987) In support of GIS in the SCS: SIS. In: Beek K-J, Burrough P A, McCormack D E (eds.) *Quantified Land Evaluation Procedures. Proceeedings of the Joint Meeting of the ISSS Working Groups on Land Evaluation and Soil Information Systems, Washington 25 April–2 May 1986. ITC Publication No. 6*. ITC, Enschede, pp. 77–80

Mausbach M J, Wilding L (eds.) (1990) *Spatial Variability and Map Units for Soil Surveys*. International Soil Science Society Working Group of Soil and Moisture Variability in Time and Space/American Society of Agronomy, the Crop Science Society of America and the Soil Science Society of America

McAleese R (ed.) (1989) *Hypertext: theory into practice*. Intellect Books, Oxford

McBratney A B, Webster R, Burgess T M (1981) The design of optimal sampling schemes for local estimation and mapping of regionalised variables. 1. Theory and method. *Computers & Geosciences* **7**: 331–4

McBratney A B, Webster R (1981) The design of optimal sampling schemes for local estimation and mapping of regionalized variables: 2 Program and examples. *Computers & Geosciences* **7**: 335–65

McBratney A B, Webster R (1983) How many observations are needed for regional estimation of soil properties? *Soil Science* **135**: 177–83

McBratney A B, Webster R (1983) Optimal interpolation and isarithmic mapping of soil properties. V. Co-regionalisation and multiple sampling strategy. *Journal of Soil Science* **34**: 137–62

McConalogue D J (1970) A quasi-intrinsic scheme for passing a smooth curve through a discrete set of points. *Computer Journal* **13** (4): 392–96

McCormick B H, Defanti T A, Brown M D (1987) Visualization in scientific computing. *SIGGRAPH Computer Graphics Newsletter* **21** (6)

McCormick S, Bratt P (1988) Some issues relating to the design and development of an interactive video disc. *Computers in Education* **12** (1): 257–60

McCullagh M J (1981) Creation of smooth contours over irregularly distributed data using local surface patches. *Geographical Analysis* **13** (1): 52–63

McCullagh M J (1982) Mini/micro display of surface mapping and analysis techniques. *Cartographica* **19** (2): 136–44

McCullagh M J (1988) Terrain and surface modelling systems: theory and practice. *Photogrammetric Record* **12** (72): 747–79

McEwen R B (1979) US Geological Survey digital cartographic data aquisition. In: *Mapping Software and Cartographic Data Bases*. Havard Library of Computer Graphics, pp. 136–42

McEwen R B (1980) USGS Digital Cartographic Applications Program. *Journal of Surveying and Mapping Division*. ASCE, **106** (1): 13–22

McEwen R B (1981) *A National Digital Cartographic Data Base*. Computer Graphics in Transportation, The Princeton University Conference

McEwen R B (1982) Observations and Trends in Digital Cartography. *Proceedings ISPRS Commission IV Symposium*. ASP, Falls Church Virginia, pp. 419–31

McEwen R B, Calkins H W (1982) Digital Cartography in the USGS National Mapping Division: a comparison of current and future mapping processes. *Cartographica* **19**: 11–26

McEwen R B, Jacknow H R (1980) USGS Digital Cartographic Data Base. *Proceedings of AUTOCARTO4*. SPRS, Falls Church Virginia, pp. 225–35

McGranaghan M (1989) Context-free recursive-descent parsing of location-description text. *Proceedings, Ninth*

International Symposium on Computer-Assisted Cartography. ACSM/ASPRS, Falls Church, pp. 580–7

McGranaghan M, Mark D M, Gould M D (1987) Automated provision of navigation assistance to drivers. *The American Cartographer* **14**: 121–38

McGranaghan M, Wester L (1988) Prototyping an herbarium collection mapping system. *Proceedings 1988 ACSM-ASPRS Annual Convention*. ACSM/ASPRS, Falls Church, pp. 232–8

McGuigan F J (1957) An investigation of several methods of teaching contour interpretation. *Journal of Applied Psychology* **41**: 53–7

McHarg I L (1969) *Design with Nature*. Doubleday, New York

McHarg I (1987) Keynote speech. *Proceedings of GIS '87*. ACSM/ASPRS, Falls Church Virginia

McKenna R (1988) Marketing in an age of diversity. *Harvard Business Review* **88** (5): 88–95

McKeown D M (1986) The role of artificial intelligence in the integration of remotely sensed data with Geographic Information Systems. *Report CMU-CS-86–174*. Department of Computer Science, Carnegie-Mellon University, Pittsburgh Pennsylvania

McKeown D M, Lai R C T (1987) Integrating multiple data representations for spatial databases. *Proceedings of AUTOCARTO 8*. ACSM/ASPRS, Falls Church Virginia, pp. 754–63

McLaren R A (1989) Choosing GIS/LIS. *FIG Newsletter No.3; Commission 3 Working Group on Land Information Systems in Developing Countries*

McLaren R A (1990) Establishing a corporate GIS from component data sets – the database issues. *Mapping Awareness* **4** (2): 52–8

McLaren R A, Kennie T J M (1989) Visualisation of digital terrain models: techniques and applications. In: Raper J F (ed.) *Three Dimensional Applications in Geographical Information Systems*. Taylor & Francis, London, pp. 79–98

McMaster R B (1987) Automated line generalization. *Cartographica* **24**: 74–111

McMaster R B, Monmonier M (1989) A conceptual framework for quantitative and qualitative raster-mode generalization. *Proceedings of GIS/LIS '89*. ACSM ASPRS, Falls Church Virginia, pp. 390–403

McMaster R B, Thrower N J (1987) University cartographic education in the United States: tracing the routes. *Proceedings International Cartographic Association Conference, Morelia* **2**: 343–59

McNamara T P, Ratcliff R, McKoon G (1984) The mental representation of knowledge acquired from maps. *Journal of Experimental Psychology, Learning, Memory and Cognition* **10** (4): 723–32

McRae S, Cleaves D (1986) Incorporating strategic data-planning and decision analysis techniques in geographic information system design. *Proceedings of Geographic Information Systems Workshop*. ASPRS, Atlanta, pp. 76–86

Meier A (1986) Applying relational database techniques to solid modelling. *Computer Aided Design* **18**: 319–26

Meijerink A M J, Valenzuela C R, Stewart A (1988) ILWIS: the Integrated Land and Watershed Management Information System. *ITC Publication No. 7*. International Institute for Aerospace Survey and Earth Sciences (ITC), Enschede, The Netherlands, 115 pp

Mel B W, Omohundro S M, Robinson A D, Skiena S S, Thearling K H, Young L T, Wolfram S (1988) Tablet: personal computer in the year 2000. *Communications ACM* **31** (6): 639–46

Menon S (1989) *Spatial Search for Multi-component Objects in a Geographic Information System Using Symbolic Models and Hierarchical Data Structures*. Unpublished PhD dissertation, University of California, Santa Barbara California

Merchant D C (1987) Spatial accuracy specification for large scale topographic maps. *Photogrammetric Engineering and Remote Sensing* **53** (7): 958–61

Methley B D F (1986) *Computational Models in Surveying and Photogrammetry*. Blackie, Glasgow

Meyer U (1987) Computer-assisted generalization of buildings for digital landscape models by classification methods. *Nachrichten aus dem Karten- und Vermessungswesen* 2 **46**: 193–200

Meyerson M (1956) Building the middle-range bridge for comprehensive planning. *Journal of the American Institute of Planners* **22** (2): 58–64

Mikhail E M (1976) *Observations and Least Squares*. IEP-Dun-Donnelly Harper & Row, New York

Miller A I (1984) *Imagery in Scientific Thought: creating 20th century physics*. Birkhauser, Boston

Miller C L, Laflamme R A (1958) The digital terrain model – theory and application. *Photogrammetric Engineering* **24** (3): 433–42

Miller E E (1980) Similitude and scaling of soil-water phenomena. In: Hillel D (ed.) *Applications of Soil Physics*. Academic Press, New York

Miller G A (1956) The magical number seven, plus or minus two: some limits on our capacity for processing information. *Psychological Review* **63**: 81–97

Millington A C, Townshend J R G, Kennedy P, Saull R, Prince S, Madams R (1989) *Biomass Assessment in the SADCC Region*. Earthscan Publications, London

Ministry of Construction (1987) *The Urban Information Database*. Keibun Shuppan, Tokyo

Minker J (1988) *Foundations of Deductive Databases and Logic Programming*. Morgan Kaufmann, Los Altos

Minker J (1988) Perspectives in deductive databases. *Journal of Logic Programming* **5** (1): 33–60

Minnesota Department of Natural Resources, Division of Forestry and Office of Planning (1984) *Modelling Direct Economic Returns to Timber Management as a Component of a Comprehensive, Multiple-Use Forest Management Model*. State of Minnesota, St Paul

Minnesota Department of Natural Resources, Division of Minerals (1989) *Glacial Drift Geochemistry for Strategic*

Minerals; Duluth Complex, Lake County, Minnesota. Report 262. State of Minnesota, St Paul

Minnesota Department of Natural Resources, Office of Planning (1986) *DNR-Administered Public Lands: their suitability to meet natural resource management objectives.* State of Minnesota, St Paul

Misra P (1989) Survey of India identification of user needs. *IX INCA International Seminar on Digital Cartography and Potential Users.* Pre-session Proceedings. Survey of India, Dehra Dun, pp. 223–35

Mitchell C P, Brandon O H, Bunce R G H, Barr C J, Tranter R B, Downing P, Pearce M L, Whittaker H A (1983) Land availability for production of wood energy in Great Britain. In: Strub A, Cartier P, Scleser G (eds.) *Energy from Biomass. Proceedings 2nd European Community Conference, Berlin.* Applied Science, London, pp. 159–63

Mitchell C W (1973) *Terrain Evaluation.* Longman, London

Mitchell T M, Keller R M, Kedar-Cabelli S T (1986) Explanation-based generalization: a unifying view. *Machine Learning* **1**: 47–80

Mitchell W B, Guptill S C, Anderson E A, Fegeas R G, Hallam C A (1977) GIRAS – a Geographic Information Retrieval and Analysis System for handling land use and land cover data. *Professional Paper 1059*, USGS Reston Virginia

Moellering H (1973) The automatic mapping of traffic crashes. *Surveying and Mapping* **23**: 467–77

Moellering H (1980) Strategies of real time cartography. *The American Cartographer* **7** (1): 67–75

Moik J G (1980) Digital processing of remotely sensed images. *NASA SP-431.* Scientific and Technical Information Branch National Aeronautics and Space Administration, Washington DC

Molenaar M (1990) A formal data structure for three dimensional vector maps. *Proceedings of EGIS '90*, pp. 770–81

Monkhouse F J, Wilkinson H R (1971) *Maps and Diagrams: their compilation and construction.* 3rd edn. Methuen, London

Monmonier M S (1974) Measures of pattern complexity for choropleth maps. *The American Cartographer* **1** (2): 159–69

Monmonier M S (1977) Maps, distortion and meaning. *Association of American Geographers Resource Paper in Geography*, **75–4**. Association of American Geographers, Washington

Monmonier M S (1982) *Computer-Assisted Cartography: principles and prospects.* Prentice-Hall, Englewood Cliffs New Jersey

Monmonier M S (1985) *Technological Transitions in Cartography.* The University of Wisconsin Press, Madison

Monmonier M S (1988) Geographical representation in statistical graphics: a conceptual framework. *Proceedings of the American Statistical Association Conference Section on Statistical Graphics*, pp. 1–10

Monmonier M S (1990) Geographic Information Systems. In: Perkins C R, Parry R B (eds.) *Information Sources in Cartography.* Bowker-Saur, London, pp. 214–31

Montgomery D, Urban G (1969) *Management Science in Marketing.* Prentice-Hall, Englewood Cliffs

Moon W M (1989) Application of evidential belief theory in geological, geophysical and remote sensing data integration. *Proceedings of IGARRS '89*, pp. 838–41

Mooneyhan D W (1988) Applications of Geographic Information Systems within the United Nations Environmental Programme. In: Mounsey H M, Tomlinson R F (eds.) *Building Databases for Global Science.* Taylor & Francis, London, pp. 315–29

Moore A W, Bie S W (1977) Uses of soil information systems. *Proceedings of the Australian Meeting of the ISSS Working Group on Soil Information Systems, Canberra, Australia, 2–4 March 1976.* PUDOC, Wageningen, 103 pp

Moore A W, Cook B G, Lynch L G (1981) Information systems for soil and related data. *Proceedings of the Second Australian Meeting of the ISSS Working Group on Soil Information Systems, Canberra, Australia, 19–21 February 1980.* PUDOC, Wageningen, 1–10

Morehouse S (1985) ARC/INFO: a geo-relational model for spatial information. *Proceedings of AUTOCARTO 8.* ASPRS, Falls Church Virginia, pp. 388–97

Morehouse S (1989) The architecture of ARC/INFO. *Proceedings of AUTOCARTO 9.* ASPRS/ACSM, Falls Church, pp. 266–77

Morgan J M (1987) Academic geographic information systems education: a commentary. *Photogrammetric Engineering and Remote Sensing* **53**: 1443–5

Morgenstern M, Borgida A, Lassez C, Maier D, Wiederhold G (1988) Constraint-based systems: knowledge about data. In: Kerschberg L (ed.) *Proceedings of the Second International Conference on Expert Database Systems, Tysons Corner, Virginia 25–27 April 1988.* Benjamin/Cummings Publishing Company, pp. 23–44

Morrill R L (1987) A theoretical imperative. *Annals of the Association of American Geographers* **77** (4): 535–41

Morrison J L (1974) A theoretical framework for cartographic generalization with emphasis on the process of symbolization. *International Yearbook of Cartography* **14**: 115–27

Morrison J L (1991) The organizational home for GIS in the scientific professional community. In: Maguire D J, Goodchild M F, Rhind D W (eds.) *Geographical Information Systems: principles and applications.* Longman, London, pp. 91–100, Vol 1

Morse B W (1987) Expert interface to a geographic information system. *Proceedings of AUTOCARTO 8.* ACSM/ASPRS, Falls Church Virginia, pp. 535–41

Morton G M (1966) *A Computer Oriented Geodetic Data Base and New Technique in File Sequencing.* IBN Ltd, Ottawa Canada

Morton Index (1966) In: Tomlinson R F (1972) (ed.) *Geographic Data Handling.* Commission on Geographical Data Sensing and Processing. International Geographical Union, Ottawa Canada

Mosteller F, Tukey J W (1977) *Data Analysis and Regression*. Addison-Wesley, Reading Massachusetts

Mott J (1990) The National Resource Information Centre – data directory, data broker. In: Parvey C, Grainger K (eds.) *A national Geographic Information System – an achievable objective?* AURISA Monograph 4. AURISA, Eastwood New South Wales, pp. 57–60

Mounsey H M (1991) Multisource multinational environmental GIS: lessons learnt from CORINE. In: Maguire D J, Goodchild M F, Rhind D W (eds.) *Geographical Information Systems: principles and applications*. Longman, London, pp. 185–200, Vol 2

Mounsey H M, Tomlinson R F (eds.) (1988) *Building Databases for Global Science*. Taylor & Francis, London

Muehrcke P C (1969) *Visual pattern analysis: A look at maps*. Unpublished Doctoral Thesis, University of Michigan

Muehrcke P C (1978) *Map Use: reading, analysis and interpretation*. J P Publications, Madison Wisconsin

Muehrcke P C (1986) *Map Use*, 2nd edn. JP Publications, Madison Wisconsin

Muehrcke P C (1990) Cartography and geographic information systems. *Cartography and Geographic Information Systems* **17** (1): 7–17

Muessig L F, Robinette A, Rowekamp T (1983) *Application of the USLE to define critical erosion and sedimentation in Minnesota*. Paper given at 38th Annual Meeting of the Soil Conservation Society of America, 31 July–3 August. Hartford, Conneticut.

Mulla D M (1988) Using geostatistics and spectral analysis to study spatial patterns in the topography of southeastern Washington State, USA. *Earth Surface Processes and Landforms* **13**: 389–405

Muller J-C (1977) Map griding and cartographic errors: a recurrent argument. *The Canadian Cartographer* **14**: 152–67

Muller J-C (1978) The mapping of travel time in Edmonton, Alberta. *Canadian Geographer* **22**: 195–210

Muller J-C (1982) Non-Euclidean geographical spaces: mapping functional distances. *Geographical Analysis* **14**: 189–203

Muller J-C (1983) Ignorance graphique ou cartographie de l'ignorance. *Cartographica* **20**: 17–30

Muller J-C (1984) Canada's elastic space: a portrayal of route and cost distances. *Canadian Geographer* **28**: 46–62

Muller J-C (1985) Geographic information systems: a unifying force for geography. *The Operational Geographer* **8**: 41–3

Muller J-C (1987) Fractal and automated line generalization. *The Cartographic Journal* **24**: 27–34

Muller J-C (1991) Generalization of spatial databases. In: Maguire D J, Goodchild M F, Rhind D W (eds.) *Geographical Information Systems: principles and applications*. Longman, London, pp. 457–75, Vol 1

Muller J-C, Honsaker J L (1983) Visual versus computerized seriation: the implications for automated map generalization. *Proceedings of AUTOCARTO 6*. ASPRS, Falls Church, pp. 277–88

Muller J-C, Johnson R D, Vanzella L R (1986) A knowledge based approach for developing cartographic expertise. *Proceedings of the 2nd International Symposium on Spatial Data Handling, Seattle*. International Geographical Union, Ohio, pp. 557–71

Muller J-P (1989) Real-time stereo matching and its role in future mapping systems. *Proceedings of Surveying and Mapping 89*. Royal Institution of Chartered Surveyors, London, Paper C5, 15 pp

Muller J-P, Anthony A, Brown A T, Deacon A T, Kennedy S A, Montgomery P M, Robertson G W, Watson D M (1988) Real-time stereo matching using transputer arrays for close-range applications. *Proceedings of the Joint IAPR Workshop on 'Computer vision – Special Hardware and Industrial Applications'*. Tokyo, Japan. 12–14 October 1988, pp. 45–9

Muller J-P, Day T, Kolbusz J, Dalton M, Richards S, Pearson J C (1988) Visualization of topographic data using video animation. *International Archives of Photogrammetry and Remote Sensing* **27** (B4): 602–14

Muller J-P, Day T, Kolbusz J, Dalton M, Richards S, Pearson J (1988) Visualisation of topographic data using video animation. In: Muller, J-P (ed.) *Digital Image Processing in Remote Sensing*. Taylor & Francis, London, pp. 21–38

Munkres J (1966) *Elementary Differential Topology*. Princeton University Press, Princeton,

Murai S (ed.) (1986) *Proceedings of AUTOCARTO JAPAN 2*. Autocarto Japan Organizing Committee, Tokyo

Murata T (1930) A method for analysing distribution of scattered village. *Geographical Review of Japan* **6**: 1744–53

Murayama Y (1990) *Regional Analysis*. Kokon Shoin, Tokyo

Murphy P A, Zehner R B, Robertson P A, Hirst R (1988) *Computer Use by Local Government Planners: an Australian perspective*. School of Town Planning University of New South Wales, Sydney

Musgrave F K, Kolb C E, Mace R S (1989) The synthesis and rendering of eroded fractal terrains. *Computer Graphics (SIGGRAPH '89 Proceedings)* **23** (3): 41–50

Mylopoulos J (1986) On knowledge base management systems. In: Brodie M L, Mylopoulos J (eds.) *On Knowledge Base Management Systems: integrating artificial intelligence and database technologies*. Springer-Verlag, New York, pp. 3–8

Nag P (1984) *Census Mapping Survey*. International Geographical Union Commission on Population Geography/Concept Publishing Company, New Delhi

Nag P (1987) A proposed base for a Geographical Information System for India. *International Journal of Geographical Information Systems* **1** (2): 181–7

Nagao M, Mukai Y, Sugimura T, Ayabe K, Arai K, Nakazawa T (1988) A study of reducing abnormal elevations in automatic computation of elevations from satellite data. *International Archives of Photogrammetry and Remote Sensing* **27** (B4): 280–8

Nagy G, Wagle S (1979) Geographic data processing. *ACM Computing Surveys* **11** (2)

Nagy Z, Siderelis K C (1990) A GIS model for local water use planning and zoning. *Proceedings of the Tenth Annual ESRI User Conference, Volume 2*. Environmental Systems Research Institute, Redlands California

Naithani K K (1989) The SOI PC/AUTOCAD Photogrammetric Monoplotter System: a tool for rural-urban mapping. *IX INCA International Seminar on Digital Cartography and Potential Users*. Pre-session Proceedings. Survey of India, Dehra Dun, pp. 239–46

Naqvi S (1986) Discussion. In: Brodie M L, Mylopoulos J (eds.) *On Knowledge Base Management Systems: integrating artificial intelligence and database technologies*. Springer-Verlag, New York, p. 93

Naqvi S, Tsur S (1989) *A Logical Language for Data and Knowledge Bases*. Computer Science Press, New York

Nash K (1986) The application of computers to planning tasks in the city of Sydney. *Australian Planner* **24**: 19–23

Nash K (1988) The Sydney City Council Land Information System – a decade on, the dream and the reality. *URPIS – Proceedings of the Urban and Regional Planning Information Systems Annual Conferences*, Volume 16. Australasian Urban and Regional Information Systems Association Inc., Sydney, pp. 1–13

Nastelin J (1985) Optimization of baseline determination for area map annotation. *Technical Report IPL-078*. Image Processing Laboratory, Rensselaer Polytechnic Institute, Troy

Natal/KwaZulu Association for Geographic Information Systems (1989) *NAGIS NEWS* June. Institute of Natural Resources, Pietermaritzburg 3200 Natal South Africa

National Academy of Sciences (1983) *Procedures and Standards for a Multipurpose Cadastre*. National Academy Press, Washington DC

National Computer Graphics Association (1989) *Standards in the Computer Graphics Industry*. NCGA, Fairfax Virginia

National Geophysical Data Center (1985) *Relief of the Surface of the Earth (maps, scale approximately 1 : 39 000 000)*. Report MGG-2. National Geophysical Data Center, Boulder Colorado

National Joint Utilities Group (1986) *NJUG Specification for the Digitisation of Large Scale OS Maps. No. 12.* NJUG, London

National Joint Utilities Group (1988) *The quality control procedure for large scale Ordnance Survey maps digitized to OS 1988. Publication Number 13* NJUG, London

National Research Council (1989) *Numerical Data Advisory Board Annual Report 1988–1989*. National Academy Press, Washington DC

Navon D (1977) Forest before trees: the precedence of global features in visual perception. *Cognitive Psychology* **9**: 353–83

NCGIA (1989) Multiple representations. *NCGIA Technical Paper* **89-3**

NCGIA (1989) The research plan of the National Center for Geographic Information and Analysis. *International Journal of Geographical Information Systems* **3** (2): 117–36

Neal J G, Shapiro S C (1990) Intelligent multi-media interface technology. In: Sullivan J W, Tyler S W (eds.) *Architectures for Intelligent Interfaces: elements and prototypes*. Addison-Wesley, Reading Massachusetts

Neal J G, Thielman C Y, Dobes Z, Haller S M, Shapiro S C (1989) Natural language with integrated deictic and graphic gestures. *Proceedings, DARPA Speech and Natural Language Workshop*. Morgan Kaufmann, Los Altos CA

Needham J (1959) *Science and Civilization in China*, Volume 3. Cambridge University Press, Cambridge

Needham J (1981) *The Shorter Science and Civilization in China* (Abridged C A Ronan), Volume 2. Cambridge University Press, Cambridge

Neiser U (1976) *Cognition and Reality: principles and implications of cognitive psychology*. Freeman, San Francisco

Nelson T (1981) *Literary Machines*. (2nd edn) Theodore Holm Nelson, Swarthmore

Nelson T (1987) *Computer Lib*. Microsoft Press, Redmond, WA

NERC (1988) *Geographical Information in the Environmental Sciences*. (Report of the Working Group on Geographic Information), Natural Environment Research Council, Swindon

Newell R G, Theriault D G (1990) Is GIS just a combination of CAD and DBMS? *Mapping Awareness* **4** (3): 42–45

Newell R G, Theriault D G, Easterfield M (1990) Temporal GIS – modelling the evolution of spatial data in time. *Proceedings of GIS Design Models Conference*. Midlands Regional Research Laboratory, Leicester

Newkirk P (1987) Municipal information systems: challenges and opportunities. *Plan Canada* **27**: 94–100

Newman W M, Sproull R F (1979) *Principles of Interactive Computer Graphics*, 2nd edn. McGraw-Hill, New York

Newton P W, Crawford J R (1988) Microcomputer-based geographic information and mapping systems. In: Newton P.W, Taylor M A P, Sharpe R (eds.) *Desktop Planning: microcomputer applications for infrastructure and services planning and management*. Hargreen, Melbourne, pp. 31–43

Newton P W, Taylor M A P, Sharpe R (eds.) (1988) *Desktop Planning: microcomputer applications for infrastructure and services planning and management*. Hargreen, Melbourne

NEXPRI (1989) *Geographical Information Systems for Landscape Analysis Research Programme*. NEXPRI, University of Utrecht

Nichol D G, Fiebig M J, Whatmough R J, Whitbread P J (1987) Some image processing aspects of a military geographic information system. *Australian Computer Journal* **19** (3): 154–60

Nicholson R (1990) Public access to spatial information:

the use of value added networks in the UK. *Proceedings of EGIS '90*, Volume 2. EGIS Foundation, Utrecht, pp. 782–8

Nickerson B G, Freeman H R (1986) Development of a rule-based system for automatic map generalization. *Proceedings of the 2nd International Symposium on Spatial Data Handling, Seattle*. International Geographical Union, Ohio, pp. 537–56

NICOGRAPH (ed.) (1988) *Computer Mapping*. Nihon Keizai Shinbunsha, Tokyo

Nielsen D R, Bouma J (1985) *Spatial Analysis of Soil Data*. PUDOC, Wageningen

Nielsen J (1990) The art of navigating through hypertext. *Communications of the Association of Computing Machinery* **33** (3): 296–310

Nielsen J (1990) *Hypertext and Hypermedia*. Academic Press, San Diego California

Nievergelt J, Hinterberger H, Sevcik K (1984) The grid file: an adaptable, symmetric multi-key file structure. *ACM Transactions on Database Systems* **9** (1): 38–71

Nievergelt J, Schorn P (1988) Line problems with supra-linear growth (in German). *Informatik Spektrum* **11** (4)

Nijkamp P (1979) *Multidimensional Spatial Data and Decision Analysis*. Wiley, New York

Nijkamp P, De Jong W (1987) Training needs in information systems for local and regional development and planning. *Regional Development Dialogue* **8** (1): 72–119

Nilsson N J (1971) *Problem Solving Methods in Artificial Intelligence*. McGraw-Hill, New York

Nilsson N J (1980) *Principles of Artificial Intelligence*. Tioga Publishing Co., Palo Alto

Nishikawa O, Kubo S (1986) Intensive Utilisation of Geographic Information, In: Hirayama H (ed.) *Perspectives and Tasks Towards an Information Society*. The Science Council of Japan, Tokyo, pp. 131–40

NJUG (1986) *Proposed Data Exchange Format for Utility Map Data*. NJUG 11. National Joint Utilities Group, 30 Millbank, London, SW1P 4RD

NJUG (1986) *NJUG Specification for the Digitisation of Large Scale OS Maps*. NJUG 12. National Joint Utilities Group, 30 Millbank, London, SW1P 4RD

NJUG (1988) *Quality Control Procedures for Large Scale OS Maps Digitised to OS 1988*. NJUG 13. National Joint Utilities Group, 30 Millbank, London, SW1P 4RD

NOAA (1987) *Climate and Global Change: An integrated NOAA program in Earth System Science*. NOAA, Washington DC

Nordbeck S (1962) Location of areal data for computer processing. *Lund Studies in Geography, Series C, General, Mathematical and Regionnal Geography No. 2*, Lund University Sweden

Norrman J (1979) Modeling of complete crop canopy. In: Barfield B G, Gerber J F (eds.) *Modification of the Aerial Environment of Plants*. American Society of Agricultural Engineers, St Joseph Mississippi, pp. 249–77

Norris P (1983) Microdata from the British census. In: Rhind D W (ed.) *A Census User's Handbook*. Methuen, London, pp. 301–19

NRC (1980) *Need for a Multipurpose Cadastre*. National Research Council, Washington DC

NRC (1983) *Procedures and Standards for a Multipurpose Cadastre*. National Research Council, Washington DC

NSSDC (National Space Science Data Center) (1989) *Directory Interchange Format Manual, Version 1.0*. NASA Goddard Space Flight Center, Greenbelt Maryland

Nyerges T L (1980) *Modelling the Structure of Cartographic Information for Query Processing*. Unpublished PhD thesis, Ohio State University

Nyerges T L (1989) Components of model curricula development for GIS in university education. *Proceedings of AUTOCARTO 9*. ASPRS/ACSM, Bethesda Maryland, pp. 199–204

Nyerges T L (1989) Information integration for multipurpose land information systems. *URISA Journal* **1** (1): 27–38

Nyerges T L (1989) Schema integration analysis for the development of GIS databases. *International Journal of Geographical Information Systems* **3** (2): 153–83

Nyerges T L, Chrisman N R (1989) A framework for model curricula development in cartography and geographic information systems. *Professional Geographer* **41** (3): 283–93

Obermeyer N J (1989) A systematic approach to the taxonomy of geographic information use. *Proceedings GIS/LIS '89*, Volume 2. ASPRS/ACSM/AAG/URISA/AM-FM, Bethesda, pp. 421–9

O'Callaghan J F, Garner B J (1991) Land and Geographical Information Systems in Australia. In: Maguire D J, Goodchild M F, Rhind D W (eds.) *Geographical Information Systems: principles and applications*. Longman. London, pp. 57–70, Vol 2

O'Callaghan J F, Mark D M (1984) The extraction of drainage networks from digital elevation data. *Computer Vision, Graphics, and Image Processing* **28**: 323–44

Odland J (1988) Spatial autocorrelation. *Sage Scientific Geography Series Number 9*. Sage Publications, London

OECD (1988) *Activities of the OECD, Report of the Secretary General*. OECD Publications, Paris

Office of Technology Assessment (1981) *Computer-Based National Information Systems*. Congress of the United States, Washington DC, pp. 58–9

Official Journal of the European Community (1985) Council Decision on 27 June 1985 on the adoption of the Commission work programme concerning an experimental project for gathering, coordinating and ensuring the consistency of information on the state of the environment and natural resources in the Community. OJ L 176, 6 July 1985

Ogrosky C E (1975) Population estimates from satellite imagery. *Photogrammetric Engineering and Remote Sensing* **41**: 707–12

Oliver M A, Webster R (1986) Combining nested and linear sampling for determining the scale and form of spatial variation of regionalised variables. *Geographical Analysis* **18**: 227–42

Oliver M A, Webster R (1986) Semi-variograms for modelling the spatial pattern of landform and soil properties. *Earth Surface Processes and Landforms* **11**: 491–504

Oliver M A, Webster R, Gerrard J (1989) Geostatistics in physical geography. Part 1. *Transactions of the Institute of British Geographers* NS **14**: 259–69

Oliver M A, Webster R, Gerrard J (1989) Geostatistics in physical geography. Part 2. *Transactions of the Institute of British Geographers* NS **14**: 270–86

Olle T W (1978) *The Codasyl Approach to Database Management*. Wiley, Chichester. 287pp.

Olson J M (1972) Autocorrelation as a measure of complexity. *Proceedings American Congress on Surveying and Mapping*. ACSM, Falls Church Virginia, pp. 111–19

Olson J M (1979) Cognitive cartographic experimentation. *The Canadian Cartographer* **16** (1): 34–44

Olson J M (1986) Color and the computer in cartography. In: Durrett H J (ed.) *Color and the Computer*. Academic Press, Boston, pp. 205–21

Olson J S (1989) *World Ecosystems* (WE2.0) NOAA/National Geophysical Data Center, Boulder, Colorado

Olson J S, Watts J, Allison L (1983) *Carbon in Live Vegetation of Major World Ecosystems*. US Department of Energy contract No. W-7405–ENG-26. Oak Ridge Laboratory, Oak Ridge Tennessee

Olsson L (1988) Automation of the pipeline register in the City of Stockholm. *Proceedings of AM/FM International – European Division Conference, Montreux*. AM/FM European Division, PO Box 6, CH4005, Basel, Switzerland, pp. 173–7

Olsson L (1989) Integrated resource monitoring by means of remote sensing, GIS and spatial modelling in arid environments. *Soil Use and Management* **5**: 30–7

O'Neill M O, Mark D M (1987) The Psi–s Plot: a useful representation for digital cartographic lines. *Proceedings of AUTOCARTO 8*. ASPRS, Falls Church, pp. 231–40

Openshaw S (1983) Multivariate analysis of census data: the classification of areas. In: Rhind D W (ed.) *A Census User's Handbook*. Methuen, London, pp. 243–64

Openshaw S (1984) The modifiable areal unit problem. *Concepts and Techniques in Modern Geography*. Vol. 38. Geo Abstracts, Norwich

Openshaw S (1988) Building an automated modelling system to explore a universe of spatial interaction models. *Geographical Analysis* **20**: 31–46

Openshaw S (1989) Learning to live with errors in spatial databases. In: Goodchild M F, Gopal S (eds.) *The Accuracy of Spatial Databases*. Taylor & Francis, London, pp. 263–76

Openshaw S (1989) Computer modelling in human geography. In: Macmillan W (ed.) *Remodelling Geography*. Blackwell, Oxford, pp. 70–88

Openshaw S (1989) Making geodemographics more sophisticated. *Journal of the Market Research Society* **31**: 111–31

Openshaw S (1989) Automating the search for cancer clusters. *The Professional Statistician* **8** (9): 7–8

Openshaw S (1990) Spatial referencing for the user in the 1990s *Mapping Awareness* **4** (2): 24–9

Openshaw S (1990) Towards a spatial analysis research strategy for the Regional Research Laboratory initiative. In: Masser J, Blakemore M J (eds.) *Geographical Information Management: methodology and applications*. Longman, London

Openshaw S (1990) Spatial analysis and GIS: a review of progress and possibilities. In: Scholten H J, Stillwell J C H (eds.) *Geographic Information Systems for urban and regional planning*. Kluwer, Dordrecht, 156–63

Openshaw S (1990) Automating the search for cancer clusters: a review of problems, progress, and opportunities. In Thomas R W (ed.) *Spatial Epidemiology. London Papers in Regional Science 21*. Pion, London, pp. 48–78

Openshaw S (1991) Developing appropriate spatial analysis methods for GIS. In: Maguire D J, Goodchild M F, Rhind D W (eds.) *Geographical Information Systems: principles and applications*. Longman, London, pp. 389–402, Vol 1

Openshaw S, Charlton M, Craft A W, Birch J M (1988) An investigation of leukaemia clusters by use of a geographical analysis machine. *The Lancet* **1**: 272–73

Openshaw S, Charlton M, Wymer C (1987) A Mark 1 Geographical Analysis Machine for the automated analysis of point data. *International Journal of Geographical Information Systems* **1**: 335–43

Openshaw S, Cross A E, Charlton M E (1990) Building a prototype Geographical Correlates Exploration Machine. *International Journal of Geographical Information Systems* **3**: 297–312

Openshaw S, Cross A E, Charlton M, Brunsdon C, Lillie J (1990) Lessons learnt from a post-mortem of a failed GIS. *Proceedings of AGI '90*, AGI, London, pp. 2.3.1–2.3.5

Openshaw S, Cullingford D, Gillard A A (1980) A critique of the national census classifications of OPCS and PRAG. *Town Planning Review* **51**: 421–39

Openshaw S, Goddard J (1987) Some implications of the commodification of information and the emerging information economy for applied geographical analysis in the United Kingdom. *Environment and Planning A* **19**: 1423–39

Openshaw S, Mounsey H M (1987) Geographic information systems and the BBC's Domesday interactive videodisk. *International Journal of Geographical Information Systems* **1** (2): 173–9

Openshaw S, Wilkie D, Binks K, Wakeford R, Gerrard M H, Croasdale M R (1989) A method for detecting spatial clustering of disease. In: Crosbie W A, Gittus J H (eds.) *Medical Responses to the Effects of Ionising Radiation*. Elsevier Applied Science, London, pp. 295–308

Openshaw S, Wymer C, Charlton M (1986) A geographical information and mapping system for the

BBC Domesday optical disks. *Transactions of the Institute of British Geographers* NS **11**: 296–304

Ordnance Survey Review Committee (1979) *Report of the Ordnance Survey Review Committee*. HMSO, London

Ordnance Survey (1984) *Report of the Small Scales Digital Map User Needs Study*. OS, Southampton

Ordnance Survey (1985) *Report of the Investigation into Demand for Digital Data from 1:50 000 Mapping*. OS, Southampton

Ordnance Survey (1987) *National Transfer Format, Release 1.0*. OS, Southampton UK

Ordnance Survey (1988) *Annual Report 1987/88*. OS, Southampton

Ordnance Survey (1988) *Ordnance Survey's Contractors' Specification for Digital Mapping*. OS, Southampton

Ordnance Survey (1989) *Annual Report 1988/89*. OS, Southampton

Ordnance Survey (1989) *National Transfer Format, Release 1.1*. OS, Southampton UK

Ordnance Survey (1990) *Annual Report*, HMSO, London

Orenstein J A (1990) An object-oriented approach to spatial data processing. *Proceedings of the 4th International Symposium on Spatial Data Handling*, Volume 2. International Geographical Union, Columbus Ohio, pp. 669–78

Orman L (1986) Flexible management of computational models. *Decision Support Systems* **2**: 225–34

Oswald H, Raetzsch H (1984) A system for generation and display of digital elevation models. *Geo-Processing* **2**: 197–218

Ottoson L (1977) Information systems at the National Land Survey of Sweden. *Cartographica Monograph* 20: 104–14

Ottoson L (1987) *A programme for National Geographic Data Bases in Sweden*. LMV-rapport 1987:8, ISSN 0280-5731. Gävle, Sweden

Ottoson L, Rystedt B (1991) National GIS programmes in Sweden. In: Maguire D J, Goodchild M F, Rhind D W (eds.) *Geographical Information Systems: principles and applications*. Longman, London, pp. 39–46, Vol 2

Ozemoy V M, Smith D R, Sicherman A (1981) Evaluating computerized geographic information systems using decision analysis. *Interfaces* **11**: 92–8

Pandey M K, Dave V S, Kumar S (1989) Relevance of application of digital cartography for development planning process in India. *IX INCA International Seminar on Digital Cartography and Potential Users*. Pre-session Proceedings. Survey of India, Dehra Dun, pp. 304–19

Parent P (1988) Universities and Geographical Information Systems: background, constraints and prospects. *Proceedings of Mapping the Future*. URISA, Washington, pp. 1–12

Parent P, Church R (1987) Evolution of geographic information systems as decision making tools. *Proceedings of GIS '87*. ASPRS/ACSM, Falls Church VA, pp. 63–71

Park S E, Miller K W (1988) Random number generators: good ones are hard to find. *Communications ACM* **31** (10): 1192–201

Parker H D (1988) The unique qualities of a geographic information system: a commentary. *Photogrammetric Engineering and Remote Sensing* **54** (11): 1547–49

Parker H D (1989) GIS software 1989: a survey and commentary. *Photogrammetric Engineering and Remote Sensing* **55**: 1589–91

Parker H D (1989) *The GIS Sourcebook*. GIS World Inc., Fort Collins Colorado

Parrott R, Stutz F P (1991) Urban GIS applications. In: Maguire D J, Goodchild M F, Rhind D W (eds.) *Geographical Information Systems: principles and applications*. Longman, London, pp. 247–60, Vol 2

Parry R B, Perkins C R (1987) *World Mapping Today*. Butterworths, London

Parsloe E (ed.) (1983) *Interactive Video*. John Wiley, Chichester England

Parthasaradhi, E U R, Krishnanunni K (1989) Specifications of a digital topographic base for GIS applications: some experiences from project Vasundharsa. *IX INCA International Seminar on Digital Cartography and Potential Users*. Pre-session Proceedings. Survey of India, Dehra Dun, pp. 320–8

Pascoe R T, Penny J P (1990) Construction of interfaces for the exchange of geographic data. *International Journal of Geographical Information Systems* **4** (2): 147–56

Pavlidis T (1982) *Algorithms for Graphics and Image Processing*. Computer Science Press, Rockville Maryland

Pazner M, Kirby K C, Thies N (1989) *MAP II Map Processor*. Wiley, New York

Peacock D, Rutherford I (1989) Concepts into reality – an account of a GIS implementation in SWEB. *Proceedings of AGI 89 Conference, Birmingham*. AGI, 12 Great George Street, London, SW1P 3AD, pp. 2.3.1–2.3.6

Peano G (1890) Sur une courbe qui remplit toute une aire plane. *Mathematische Annalen* **36** A:157–60

Pearce D, Markandya A, Barbier E B (1989) *Blueprint for a Green Economy*. Earthscan Publications, London

Pech R P, Graetz R D, Davis A W (1986) Reflectance modelling and the derivation of vegetation indices for an Australian semi-arid shrubland. *International Journal of Remote Sensing* **7**: 389–403

Pellew R A, Harrison J D (1988) A global database on the status of biological diversity: the IUCN perspective. In: Mounsey H M, Tomlinson R F (eds.) *Building Databases for Global Science*. Taylor & Francis, London, pp. 330–9

Peplies R W, Keuper H F (1975) Regional analysis. In: Reeves R G, Anson A, Landen D (eds.) *Manual of Remote Sensing*, Vol. 2. American Society of Photogrammetry, Falls Church Virginia, pp. 1947–98

Perkal J (1965) Translated by Jackowski W. An attempt at objective generalization. *Michigan Inter-University Community of Mathematical Geographers. Discussion Paper* **9**

Perkins C R, Parry R B (eds.) (1990) *Information Sources in Cartography*. Bowker-Saur, London

Perl Y, Itai A, Avni H (1978) Interpolation search – a log log n search. *Communications ACM* **21** (7): 550–3

Perrett P, Lyons K J, Moss O F (1989) Overview of GIS activities in Queensland. In: Ball D, Babbage R (eds.) *Geographical Information Systems: defence applications*. Pergamon Press, Sydney, pp. 152–79

Perring F H (1964) Contribution to Session 6, The mapping of vegetation flora and fauna. In: Bickmore D P (ed.) *Experimental Cartography – Report of the Oxford Symposium*. Oxford University Press, Oxford

Perring F H, Walters S M (1962) *Atlas of the British Flora*. Nelson, London

Petach M, Wagenet R J (1989) Integrating and analyzing spatially variable soil properties for land evaluation. In: Bouma J, Bregt A K (eds.) *Land Qualities in Space and Time. Proceedings of a Symposium organised by the International Society of Soil Science (ISSS), Wageningen, The Netherlands, 22–26 August 1988*. PUDOC, Wageningen, pp. 145–54

Petchenik B (1989) The road not taken. *The American Cartographer* **16** (1): 47–50

Peters T (1987) *Thriving on Chaos*. Macmillan, London

Peterson D L, Running S W (1989) Applications in forest science and management. In: Asrar G (ed.) *Theory and Applications of Optical Remote Sensing*. Wiley, New York, pp. 429–73

Peterson M (1979) An evaluation of unclassed cross-line choropleth mapping. *The American Cartographer* **6** (1): 21–37

Petrie G, Kennie T (eds.) (1990) *Terrain Modelling in Surveying and Civil Engineering*. Whittles, Latheronwheel

Peucker T K (1972) Computer cartography. *Commission on College Geography, Resource Paper No.17*. Association of American Geographers, Washington DC

Peucker T K (1975) A theory of the cartographic line. *Proceedings of AUTOCARTO 2*. ASPRS, Falls Church, pp. 508–18

Peucker T K (1978) Data structures for digital terrain models: discussion and comparison. *Harvard Papers on Geographic Information Systems 5 (Proceedings First International Advanced Study Symposium on Topological Data Structures for Geographic Information Systems, held in 1977)*. 1–15

Peucker T K, Chrisman N R (1975) Cartographic data structures. *The American Cartographer* **2** (2): 55–69

Peucker T K, Cochrane D (1974) Die Automation der Reliefdarstellung – Theorie und Praxis. *International Yearbook of Cartography* **XIV**: 128–39

Peucker T K, Douglas D H (1975) Detection of surface specific points by local parallel processing of discrete terrain elevation data. *Computer Graphics and Image Processing* **4**: 375–387

Peucker T K, Fowler R J, Little J J, Mark D M (1978) The triangulated irregular network. *Proceedings of the ASP Digital Terrain Models (DTM) Symposium*. American Society of Photogrammetry, Falls Church Virginia, pp. 516–40

Peuquet D J (1981) An examination of the techniques for reformatting digital cartographic data Part 1: the raster-to-vector process. *Cartographica* **18** (1): 34–48

Peuquet D J (1981) An examination of the techniques for reformatting digital cartographic data Part 2: the vector-to-raster process. *Cartographica* **18** (3): 21–33

Peuquet D J (1984) A conceptual framework and comparison of spatial data models. *Cartographica* **21** (4): 66–113

Peuquet D J (1988) Issues involved in selecting appropriate data models for global databases. In: Mounsey H M, Tomlinson R F (eds.) *Building Databases for Global Science*. Taylor & Francis, London, pp. 66–78

Peuquet D J (1988) Representations of geographic space: toward a conceptual synthesis. *Annals of the Association of American Geographers* **78**: 375–94

Peuquet D J, Zhan C-X (1987) An algorithm to determine the directional relationship between arbitrarily-shaped polygons in a plane. *Pattern Recognition* **20**: 65–74

Pevsner S (1989) Image processing in a GIS environment. In: Barrett E C, Brown K A (eds.) *Remote Sensing for Operational Applications*. The Remote Sensing Society, Nottingham England, pp. 323–30

Pfefferkorn C, Burr D, Harrison D, Heckman B, Oresky C, Rothermel J (1985) ACES: a cartographic expert system. *Proceedings of AUTOCARTO 7*. ASPRS, Falls Church Virginia, pp. 399–407 and *Cartographic Journal* **15** (2): 72–7

Phillips A (1987) *Flux gate sensor with improved sense winding gating*. US Patent 4,646,015.

Phillips M, Blackburn J (1989) The Chrysalis Project: a regional GIS over Jervis Bay. In: Ball D, Babbage R (eds.) *Geographical Information Systems: defence applications*. Pergamon Press, Sydney, pp. 204–31

Phillips R J, DeLucia A, Skelton N (1975) Some objective tests of the eligibility of relief maps. *Cartographic Journal* **12** (10): 39–46

Piercy N, Evans M (1983) *Managing Marketing Information*. Croom Helm, London

Pike R J (1988) The geometric signature: quantifying landslide terrain types from digital elevation models. *Mathematical Geology* **20** (5): 491–510

Pike R J, Rozema W J (1975) Spectral analysis of landforms. *Annals of the Association of American Geographers* **65** (4): 499–516

Pinker S (1985) Visual cognition: an introduction. In: Pinker S (ed.) *Visual Cognition*. MIT Press, Cambridge Massachusetts: pp. 1–96

Piscator I (1987) The Swedish Land Data Bank and its use by local authorities. *Proceedings of Land Use Information in Sweden*. Swedish Council for Building Research, Stockholm Sweden. ISBN 91–540–4665–3, pp. 56–68

Piwowar J M, Le Drew E F, Dudycha D J (1990) Integration of spatial data in vector and raster formats in a geographic information system. *International Journal of Geographical Information Systems* **4** (4): 429–44

Pixar Inc. (1988) *Renderman Interface*. Pixar, San Rafael California

Pleijsier L K (1986) The laboratory methods and data

exchange programme. *Interim Report on the Exchange Round 85–2*. International Soil Reference and Information Centre, Wageningen

Pleijsier L K (1989) Variability in soil data. In: Bouma J, Bregt A K (eds.) *Land Qualities in Space and Time. Proceedings of a Symposium organised by the International Society of Soil Science (ISSS), Wageningen, The Netherlands, 22–26 August 1988*. PUDOC, Wageningen, pp. 3–14

Poiker T K (1985) Geographic information systems in the geographic curriculum. *The Operational Geographer* **8**: 38–41

Porcher E (1989) *Ground Water Contamination Susceptibility in Minnesota*. Minnesota Pollution Control Agency, St Paul

Powitz B M, Meyer U (1989) Generalization of settlements by pattern recognition methods. *Paper presented at the ICA Conference, Budapest* 7pp

Preparata F P, Shamos M I (1985) *Computational Geometry: an introduction*. Springer-Verlag, New York

Press L (1990) Compuvision or teleputer? *Communications of the Association for Computing Machinery* **33** (9): 29–36

Preusser A (1984) Computing contours by successive solution of quintic polynomial equations. *ACM Transactions on Mathematical Software* **10** (4): 463–72

Price S (1989) Modelling the temporal element in land information systems. *International Journal of Geographical Information Systems* **3**: 233–44

Price Waterhouse (1991) Price performance trends. *Computer Weekly* 17 January: 1

Prisley S P, Gregoire T G, Smith J L (1989) The mean and variance of area estimates computed in an arc-node geographic information system. *Photogrammetric Engineering and Remote Sensing* **55** (11): 1601–12

Prisley S P, Mead R A (1987) Cost-benefit analysis for geographic information systems. *Proceedings of GIS '87*. ASPRS, San Francisco, pp. 29–37

Przymusinski T C (1989) On the declarative and procedural semantics of logic programs. *Journal of Automated Reasoning* **5**: 167–205

Puissegur A (1988) Does charging eradicate the defense of sovereign immunity? *Proceedings of the Urban and Regional Information Systems Association*, Vol. 4. URISA, Washington DC, pp. 358–70

Puissegur A (1989) An overview of state open records laws. *Workshop on Managing the Risks and Recovering the Costs of Geographic and Facilities Management Systems*. Department of Engineering Professional Development, University of Wisconsin-Madison, Madison, Wisconsin

Pullar D, Egenhofer M J (1988) Towards formal definitions of topological relations among spatial objects. *Proceedings of the 3rd International Symposium on Spatial Data Handling*. International Geographical Union, Columbus Ohio, pp. 225–42

Pullar D, Egenhofer M J (1988) Towards formal definitions of topological relations amongst spatial objects. *Proceedings of the 3rd International Symposium on Spatial Data Handling*. International Geographical Union, Columbus Ohio, pp. 225–42

Pyle I C (1985) *The Ada Programming Language: a guide for programmers*. Prentice-Hall, Englewood Cliffs New Jersey

Quade E S (1982) *Analysis of Public Decisions*, 2nd edn. North-Holland, New York

Quarmby N A, Saull R J (1990) The use of perspective views in local planning. *International Journal of Remote Sensing* **11**: 1329–30

Quarterman J S, Silberschatz A, Peterson J L (1985) 4.2bsd and 4.3bsd as examples of the Unix system. *ACM Computing Surveys* **17** (4): 379–418

Rada J (1982) The microelectronics revolution: implications for the Third World. *Development Dialogue* **2**: 41–67

Raisz E J (1931) The physiographic method of representing scenery on maps. *Geographical Review* **21**

Raisz E J (1948) *General Cartography*. McGraw Hill, New York

Ramachandran A (1990) The global strategy for shelter: a new challenge for surveys. *Keynote address to the XIX Congress of the International Federation of Surveyors*, Helsinki

Ramer U (1971) An iterative procedure for the polygonal approximation of plane curves. *Computer Graphics and Image Processing* **1** (3): 244–56

Rao M K, Pathan S K, Matieda I Cm, Majumder K L, Yogarajan N, Padmavathy A S (1989) Development of a Geographic Information System around ISROVISION. *IX INCA International Seminar on Digital Cartography and Potential Users*. Pre-session Proceedings. Survey of India, Dehra Dun, pp. 502–3

Raper J F (1988) A methodology for the investigation of landform-sediment relationships in British glaciated valleys. Unpublished PhD Thesis Queen Mary College, University of London

Raper J F (1989) *Three Dimensional Applications in GIS*. Taylor & Francis, London

Raper J F (1989) The geoscientific mapping and modelling system: a conceptual design. In: Raper J F (ed.) *Three Dimensional Applications in Geographical Information Systems*. Taylor & Francis, London, pp. 11–20

Raper J F (1990) An atlas of 3-D functions. *Proceedings of Symposium on Three Dimensional Computer Graphics in Modelling Geologic Structures and Simulating Processes*. Freiburger Geowissenschafliche Beitrage **2**: 74–5

Raper J F (ed.) (1989) *Three Dimensional Applications in Geographical Information Systems*. Taylor & Francis, London

Raper J F, Green N P A (1989) Development of a hypertext based tutor for geographical information systems. *British Journal of Educational Technology* **9**: 3–23

Raper J F, Green N P A (1989) GIST: an object-oriented

approach to a GIS tutor. *Proceedings of AUTOCARTO 9.* ACSM/ASPRS, Falls Church Virginia, pp. 610–19

Raper J F, Kelk B (1991) Three-dimensional GIS. In: Maguire D J, Goodchild M F, Rhind D W (eds.) *Geographical Information Systems: principles and applications.* Longman, London, pp. 299–317, Vol 1

Raper J F, Rhind D W (1990) UGIX (A): the design of a spatial language interface to a topological vector GIS. *Proceedings of the 4th International Conference on Spatial Data Handling.* International Geographical Union, Columbus Ohio, pp. 405–12

Rapp S, Collins T (1987) *Maxi Marketing.* McGraw-Hill, New York

Rasmussen J (1986) *Information Processing and Human Machine Interaction: an approach to cognitive engineering.* North Holland, New York

Rasool S I, Ojima D S (1989) Pilot studies for remote sensing and data management. *International Geosphere Biosphere Program, Global Change Report No. 8.*

Redfern P (1987) *A Study on the Future of the Census of Population: alternative approaches.* EUROSTAT Report 3C, Luxembourg

Redfern P (1989) Population registers: some administrative and statistical pros and cons. *Journal of the Royal Statistical Society A* **152** (1): 1–41

Reed C N (1986) DELTAMAP just another new GIS? *Proceedings of the 3rd International Symposium on Spatial Data Handling.* IGU Commission on Geographical Data Sensing and Processing, Williamsville NY, pp. 375–83

Reed C N (1988) A minimum set of criteria for selecting a turn-key geographic information system: an update. *Proceedings of GIS/LIS '88.* ACSM ASPRS AAG URISA, Falls Church, pp. 867–73

Reeuwijk L P van (1982) *Laboratory methods and data quality. Program for soil characterisation: a report on the pilot round. Part I. CEC and texture. Proceedings of the 5th International Classification Workshop.* Khartoum, Sudan, 58 pp

Reeuwijk L P van (1984) *Laboratory methods and data quality. Program for soil characterisation: a report on the pilot round. Part II. Exchangeable bases, base saturation and pH.* International Soil Reference and Information Centre, Wageningen, 28 pp.

Reeves R, Anding D, Mertz F (1987) First principles deterministic simulation of IR and visible imagery. *Photon Research Associates Report R-024–88.* PRA Inc., La Jolla California

Reisner P, Boyce R F, Chamberlin D D (1975) Human factors evaluation of two database query languages – Square and Sequel. *Proceedings, National Computer Conference (AFIPS)*, pp. 447–52

Reminga v. United States [1978] 448 F. Supp. 45 (W. D. Mich.)

Requicha A A G (1980) Representations for rigid solids: theory, methods, and systems. *ACM Computing Surveys* **12** (4): 437–64

Reybold W, TeSelle G W (1989) Soil geographic databases. *Journal of Soil and Water Conservation* **44** (1): 28–9

Rhind D W (1971) The production of a multi-colour geological map by automated means. *Nachr. aus den Karten und Vermessungswesen* Heft Nr. **52**: 47–51

Rhind D W (1974) An introduction to the digitising and editing of mapped data. In: Dale P F (ed.) *Automation and Cartography.* British Cartographic Society Special Publication, Volume 1, pp. 50–68

Rhind D W (1976) Geographical Information Systems. *Area* **8** (1): 46

Rhind D W (1981) Geographical Information Systems in Britain. In: Bennett R J, Wrigley N (eds.) *Quantitative Geography: retrospect and prospect.* Routledge and Kegan Paul, London, pp. 17–35

Rhind D W (1984) The SASPAC story. *BURISA 60*: 8–10

Rhind D W (1985) Successors to the Census of Population. *Journal of Economic and Social Measurement* **13** (1): 29–38

Rhind D W (1986) Remote sensing, digital mapping and Geographical Information Systems: the creation of government policy in the UK. *Environment and Planning C: Government and Policy* **4**: 91–102

Rhind D W (1987) Recent developments in geographic information systems in the UK. *International Journal of Geographical Information Systems* **1** (3): 229–41

Rhind D W (1988) A GIS research agenda. *International Journal of Geographical Information Systems* **2**: 23–8

Rhind D W (1988) Geografische Informatiesystemen en Kartografie. *Kartografisch Tijdschrift* **14**: 25–7

Rhind D W (1988) Personality as a factor in the development of a new discipline: the case of computer-assisted cartography. *The American Cartographer* **15** (3): 277–89

Rhind D W (1990) Global databases and GIS. In: Foster M J, Shand P J (eds.) *The Association for Geographic Information Yearbook 1990.* Taylor & Francis and Miles Arnold, London, pp. 218–23

Rhind D W (1990) Topographic databases derived from small scale maps and the future of Ordnance Survey. In: Foster M J, Shand P J (eds.) *The Association for Geographic Information Yearbook 1990.* Taylor & Francis, London, pp. 87–96

Rhind D W (1991) Counting the people: the role of GIS. In: Maguire D J, Goodchild M F, Rhind D W (eds.) *Geographical Information Systems: principles and applications.* Longman, London, pp. 127–37, Vol 2

Rhind D W (ed.) (1983) *A Census Users Handbook.* Methuen, London

Rhind D W, Clark P (1988) Cartographic data inputs to global databases. In: Mounsey H M, Tomlinson R F (eds.) *Building Databases for Global Science.* Taylor & Francis, London, pp. 79–104

Rhind D W, Cole K, Armstrong M, Chow L, Openshaw S (1990) An on-line, secure and infinitely flexible database system for the national population census. *Working Report 14 South East Regional Research Laboratory.* SERRL, Birkbeck College, London

Rhind D W, Green N P A (1988) Design of a geographical information system for a heterogeneous scientific community. *International Journal of Geographical Information Systems* **2**: 171–89

Rhind D W, Green N P A, Mounsey H M, Wiggins J C (1984) The integration of geographical data. *Proceedings of Austra Carto Perth*. Australian Cartographic Association, Perth, pp. 273–93

Rhind D W, Green N P A, Mounsey H M, Wiggins J C (1984) The integration of geographical data. *Proceedings of Austra Carto Perth*, Volume 1. Australian Institute of Cartographers, Perth, pp. 237–53

Rhind D W, Hudson R (1980) *Land Use*. Methuen, London

Rhind D W, Mounsey H M (1989) The Chorley Committee and 'Handling Geographic Information'. *Environment and Planning A* **21**: 571–85

Rhind D W, Mounsey H M (1989) GIS/LIS in Britain in 1988. In: Shand P J, Moore R V (eds.) *The Association for Geographic Information Yearbook 1989*. Taylor & Francis, London, pp. 267–71

Rhind D W, Openshaw S (1987) The BBC Domesday system: a nation-wide GIS for $4448. *Proceedings of AUTOCARTO 8*. ACSM/ASPRS, Falls Church Virginia, pp. 595–603

Rhind D W, Tannenbaum E (1983) Linking census and other data. In: Rhind D W (ed.) *A Census User's Handbook*. Methuen, London, pp. 287–300

Rhind D W, Visvalingham M, Evans I S (1980) Making a national atlas of population by computer. *Cartographic Journal* **17** (1) 3–11

Rhind D W, Whitfield R A S (1983) *A Review of the OS Proposals for Digitising the Large Scale Maps of Great Britain*. Consultancy report – unpublished.

Rhind D W, Wyatt B K, Briggs D J, Wiggins J C (1986) The creation of an environmental information system for the European Community. *Nachrichten aus dem Karten und Vermessungswesen Series 2*, **44**: 147–57

Rich C, Waters R C (1988) The programmer's apprentice: a research overview. *Computer (IEEE)* **21** (11): 10–25

Richards J A (1986) *Remote Sensing Digital Image Analysis: an introduction*. Springer-Verlag, New York

Richards J A, Sun G Q, Simonett D S (1987) L-band radar backscatter modeling of forest stands. *IEEE Transactions on Geoscience and Remote Sensing* **GE-25**: 487–98

Richardson D E (1988) *Rule based generalization for base map production*. Unpublished Master's Thesis, ITC Enschede

Richardson L F (1961) The problem of contiguity: an appendix to the statistics of deadly quarrels. *General Systems Yearbook* **6**: 139–87

Richardus P, Adler R K (1972) *Map Projections for Geodesists, Cartographers and Geographers*. North-Holland, Amsterdam

Riezebos H Th. (1989) Application of nested analysis of variance in mapping procedures for land evaluation. *Soil Use and Management* **5**: 25–9

RIN (1990) NAV 90. Land Navigation and Information Systems. *Proceedings of the 1990 Conference of the Royal Institute of Navigation*. Royal Institute of Navigation, London

Ripley B D (1981) *Spatial Statistics*. Wiley, New York

Ripley B D (1984) Present position and potential developments: some personal views. *Journal of the Royal Statistical Society A* **147**: 340–48

Robert P (1989) Land evaluation at farm level using soil survey information systems. In: Bouma J, Bregt A K (eds.) *Land Qualities in Space and Time. Proceedings of a Symposium organised by the International Society of Soil Science (ISSS), Wageningen, The Netherlands, 22–26 August 1988*. PUDOC, Wageningen, pp. 289–98

Robert P, Anderson J (1987) Use of computerised soil survey reports in county extension offices. In: Beek K-J, Burrough P A, McCormack D E (eds.) *Quantified Land Evaluation Procedures. Proceedings of the Joint Meeting ISSS Working Groups on Land Evaluation and Soil Information Systems, Washington 25 April–2 May 1986*. ITC Publication No. 6. ITC, Enschede, 165 pp.

Robertson P K (1988) Choosing data representations for the effective visualization of spatial data. *Proceedings of the 3rd International Symposium on Spatial Data Handling, Sydney*. International Geographical Union, Ohio, pp. 243–52

Robinette A (1991) Land management applications of GIS in the state of Minnesota. In: Maguire D J, Goodchild M F, Rhind D W (eds.) *Geographical Information Systems: principles and applications*. Longman, London, pp. 275–83, Vol 2

Robinove C J (1981) The logic of multispectral classification and mapping of land. *Remote Sensing of Environment* **11**: 231–44

Robinove C J (1986) Principles of logic and the use of digital geographic information systems. *US Geological Survey Circular 977*. USGS, Reston Virginia

Robinson A H (1953) *Elements of Cartography*. Wiley, New York

Robinson A H (1960) *Elements of Cartography*, 2nd edn. Wiley, New York

Robinson A H (1961) The cartographic representation of the statistical surface. *International Yearbook of Cartography* **1**: 53–184

Robinson A H (1962) Mapping the correspondence of isarithmic maps. *Annals of the Association of American Geographers* **52**: 414–25

Robinson A H (1975) Map design. *Proceedings of AUTOCARTO 2*. ASPRS, Falls Church Virginia, pp. 9–14

Robinson A H (1976) Revolutions in cartography. *Proceedings of the American Congress on Surveying and Mapping*. ACSM, Falls Church, pp. 403–08

Robinson A H, Bryson R A (1957) A method for describing quantitatively the correspondence of geographical distributions. *Annals of the Association of American Geographers* **47**: 379–91

Robinson A H, Petchenik B B (1976) *The Nature of Maps: essays toward understanding maps and mapping*. University of Chicago Press, Chicago

Robinson A H, Sale R D, Morrison J L, Muehrcke P C (1984) *Elements of Cartography*, 5th edn. Wiley, New York

Robinson G K (1950) Ecological correlation and the behaviour of individuals. *American Sociological Review* **15**: 351–7

Robinson G M, Gray D A, Healey R G, Furley P A (1989) Developing a geographical information system (GIS) for agricultural development in Belize, Central America. *Applied Geography* **9**: 81–94

Robinson G R (1991) The UK digital Marine Atlas Project: an evolutionary approach towards a Marine Information System. *International Hydrographic Review*, Monaco. **68**: 39–51

Robinson J (1987) The role of fire on earth: a review of the state of knowledge and a systems framework for satellite and ground based observations. *NCAR Cooperative Thesis 112*. National Center for Atmospheric Research, Boulder Colorado

Robinson V B, Frank A U, Karimi H A (1987) Expert systems for geographic information systems in resource management. *AI Applications in Natural Resource Management* **1** (1): 47–57

Robinson V B, Miller R, Klesh L (1988) Issues in the use of expert systems to manage uncertainty in geographic information systems. In: Aangeenbrug R T, Schiffman Y M (eds.) *International Geographic Information Systems (IGIS) Symposium, Arlington, Virginia*, Vol 2. NASA, Washington DC, pp. 89–100

Rodney W (1974) *How Europe Underdeveloped Africa*. Howard University Press, Washington

Roe K (1989) Information overload. *Science* **356** (11): 563

Rogers D F (1985) *Procedural Elements for Computer Graphics*. McGraw-Hill, New York

Roo A de, Hazelhoff L, Burrough P A (1989) Soil erosion modelling using ANSWERS and Geographical Information Systems. *Earth Surface Processes and Landforms* **14**: 517–32

Roo A P J de, Hazelhoff L (1988) Assessing surface runoff and soil erosion in watersheds using GIS technology. *Proceedings EUROCARTO 7, ITC Publication 8*. ITC, Enschede, pp. 172–83

Rosch E (1973) On the internal structure of perceptual and semantic categories. In: Moore T E (ed.) *Cognitive Development and the Acquisition of Language*. Academic Press, New York, pp. 111–44

Rosch E (1978) Principles of categorization. In: Rosch E, Lloyd B B (eds.) *Cognition and Categorization*. Erlbaum, Hillsdale New Jersey, 27–48

Rosenfield G, Melley M (1980) Applications of statistics to thematic mapping. *Photogrammetric Engineering and Remote Sensing* **46**: 1287–94

Rosinski R R (1977) *The Development of Visual Perception*. Goodyear Publishing, Santa Monica California

Rossiter D (1989) ALES: a microcomputer program to assist in land evaluation. In: Bouma J, Bregt A K (eds.) *Land Qualities in Space and Time. Proceedings of a Symposium organised by the International Society of Soil Science (ISSS), Wageningen, The Netherlands, 22–26 August 1988*. PUDOC, Wageningen, pp. 113–16

Rothman J (ed.) (1989) Geodemographics. *Journal of the Market Research Society* (Special Edition) **31** (1): 1–131

Rowe L A (1986) A shared object hierarchy. In: Stonebraker M R, Rowe L A (eds.) *The POSTGRES Papers. Memorandum No. UCB/ERL M86/85*. College of Engineering, University of California, Berkeley

Rowe L A, Stonebraker M R (1987) The progres data model. *Proceedings of the 13th Conference on very large databases*, Brighton, England, pp. 83–96

Rowley J (1990) Land Information Systems. In: Foster M J, Shand P J (eds.) *The Association for Geographic Information Yearbook 1990*. Taylor & Francis, London, pp. 278–84

Rowley J, Gilbert P (1989) The market for land information services, systems and support. In: Shand P J, Moore R V (eds.) *The Association for Geographic Information Yearbook 1989*. Taylor & Francis and Miles Arnold, London, pp. 85–91

Roy A G, Gravel G, Gauthier C (1987) Measuring the dimension of surfaces: a review and appraisal of different methods. *Proceedings of AUTOCARTO 8*. ASPRS, Falls Church Virginia, pp. 68–77

Roy J R, Anderson M (1988) Assessing impacts of retail development and redevelopment. In: Newton P W, Taylor M A P, Sharpe R (eds.) *Desktop Planning: microcomputer applications for infrastructure and services planning and management*. Hargreen, Melbourne, pp. 172–9

Royal Society (1966) *Glossary of Technical Terms in Cartography*. Royal Society, London

RRDN (1986) *Rural Regional Development Newsletter*. AIT, Bangkok

Rüber O (1989) Interactive design of faulted geological surfaces. *Geologisches Jahrbuch* **A 104** (Construction and display of geoscientific maps derived from databases)

Ruggles C L N (1990) An abstract model for the structuring of a spatially indexed set of images. *Proceedings of EGIS '90*, Volume 2. EGIS Foundation, Utrecht, pp. 948–57

Running S W, Nemani R R, Peterson D L, Band L E, Potts D F, Pierce L L, Spanner M A (1989) Mapping regional forest evapotranspiration and photosynthesis by coupling satellite data with ecosystem simulation. *Ecology* **70**: 1090–101

Rushton G (1969) A comprehensive model for the study of agricultural land use patterns. *Computer Assisted Instruction in Geography. Commission on College Geography, Technical Paper No. 2*. Association of American Geographers, Washington DC, pp. 141–50

Rystedt B (1987) *The New National Atlas of Sweden*. LMV-rapport 1987:17, ISSN 0280–5731. Gävle, Sweden

Saalfeld A (1985) Lattice structure in geography. *Proceedings of AUTOCARTO 7*. ASPRS, Falls Church, pp. 482–97

Saalfeld A (1988) Conflation: automated map compilation. *International Journal of Geographical Information Systems* **2** (3): 217–28

Sadovski A, Bie S W (1978) Developments in soil information systems. *Proceedings of the Second Meeting of the ISSS Working Group on Soil Information Systems, Varna/Sofia, Bulgaria, 30 May–June 1977*. PUDOC, Wageningen, 113 pp

Sakashita S, Tanaka Y (1989) Computer-aided drawing conversion (an interactive approach to digitize maps). *Proceedings of GIS/LIS '89, Orlando.* Vol. 2. ASPRS/ACSM, Bethesda Maryland, pp. 578–90

Salgé F, Piquet-Pellorce D (1986) The IGN small scale geographical database (1 : 100 000 to 1 : 500 000). In: Blakemore M J (ed.) *Proceedings of AUTOCARTO London*, Vol. 1. Royal Institution of Chartered Surveyors, London, pp. 433–46

Salgé F, Sclafer M N (1989) A geographic data model based on HBDS concepts: the IGN cartographic database model. *Proceedings of AUTOCARTO 9.* ACSM/ASPRS, Falls Church, pp. 110–17

Salmon R, Slater M (1987) *Computer Graphics.* Addison-Wesley, Reading Massachusetts

Samet H (1984) The quadtree and related hierarchical data structures. *ACM Computing Surveys* **16** (2): 187–260

Samet H (1988) Recent developments in the use of hierarchical data structures for image databases. *Proceedings Ausgraph 88, Melbourne*, pp. 207–19

Samet H (1990) *The Design and Analysis of Spatial Data Structures.* Addison-Wesley, Reading Massachusetts

Satterwhite M, Rice W, Shipman J (1984) Using landform and vegetation factors to improve the interpretation of LANDSAT imagery. *Photogrammetric Engineering and Remote Sensing* **50**: 83–91

Saxena M (1989) Satellite remote sensing for thematic maps. *IX INCA International Seminar on Digital Cartography and Potential Users.* Pre-session Proceedings. Survey of India, Dehra Dun, pp. 400–5

Schacter B J (1983) (ed.) *Computer Image Generation.* John Wiley, New York

Schaeben H (1989) Improving the geological significance of computed surfaces by CADG methods, *Geologisches Jahrbuch* **A 104** (Construction and display of geoscientific maps derived from databases)

Schek H-J, Waterfeld W (1986) A database kernel system for geoscientific applications. *Proceedings of the 2nd International Symposium on Spatial Data Handling.* International Geographical Union, Columbus Ohio, pp. 273–88

Schmidt A H, Zafft W A (1975) Progress of the Harvard University Laboratory for Computer Graphics and Spatial Analysis. In: Davis J C, McCullagh M J (eds.) *Display and analysis of spatial data.* Wiley, London, pp. 231–43

Schönhage S, Strassen V (1971) Schnelle multiplikation grosser zahlen. *Computing* **7**: 281–92

Schott J R, Salvaggio C, Volchok W J (1988) Radiometric scene normalization using pseudoinvariant features. *Remote Sensing of Environment* **26**: 1–16

Schultze C L (1970) Director, Bureau of the Budget, Statement in *Planning, Programming, Budgeting*, 91st Congress, 2nd Session, Subcommittee on National Security and International Operations. US Government Publications Office, Washington DC. pp. 172–3

Schumaker L L (1976) Fitting surfaces to scattered data. In: Lorentz G G et al. (eds.) *Approximation Theory II.* Academic Press, New York, pp. 203–68

Schut G H (1976) Review of interpolation methods for digital terrain models. *The Canadian Surveyor* **30** (5): 389–412

Schweitzer R H (1973) *Mapping Urban America with Automated Cartography.* Bureau of the Census US Department of Commerce, Suitland Maryland

Scott D J (1987) *Mental Imagery and Visualization: their role in map use.* Unpublished PhD thesis, Department of Geography, London School of Economics

SCS (1984) *Soil Survey Manual.* Government Printing Office, Washington DC

SCS (1984) *Technical Specifications for Line Segment Digitizing of Detailed Soil Survey Maps.* Government Printing Office, Washington DC

Seaborn D W (1988) Distributed processing and distributed databases in GIS – separating hype from reality. *Proceedings of GIS/LIS '88*, Volume 1. ASPRS/ACSM, Falls Church Virginia, pp. 141–4

Sedgewick R (1983) *Algorithms.* Addison-Wesley, Reading Massachusetts

Sedunary M E (1988) Land Information Systems – their reasons and rewards. *Proceedings from the FIG Land Information Systems Workshop, Bali, Indonesia*, pp. 66–74

Seldon D D (1987) Success criteria for GIS. In: Aangeenbrug R T and Schiffman Y M (Eds.) *International Geographic Information Systems (IGIS) Symposium, Arlington, Virginia.* Vol 3. NASA, Washington DC, pp. 239–43

Sellers P J (1985) Canopy reflectance, photosynthesis, and transpiration. *International Journal of Remote Sensing* **6**: 1335–72

Sellers P J, Hall F G, Asrar G, Strebel D E, Murphy R E (1988) The first ISLSCP field experiment (FIFE). *Bulletin of the American Meteorological Society* **69**: 22–7

Selvin S, Merrill D W, Sacks S (1988) Transformations of maps to investigate clusters of disease. *Social Science and Medicine* **26**: 215–21

Senior M L (1979) From gravity modelling to entropy maximizing: a pedagogic guide. *Progress in Human Geography* **3**: 179–210

Seymour W A (ed.) (1980) *A History of the Ordnance Survey.* Dawson, Folkestone

Shand P J, Moore R V (eds.) (1989) *The Association for Geographic Information Yearbook 1989.* Taylor & Francis and Miles Arnold, London, pp. 85–91

Shapiro L G, Haralick R M (1980) A spatial data structure. *Geo-Processing* **1**: 313–37

Shepherd I D H (1985) Teaching geography with the

computer: possibilities and problems. *Journal of Geography in Higher Education* **9**: 3–23

Shepherd I D H (1990) Mapping with desktop CAD: a critical review. *Computer Aided Design* **22** (3): 136–50

Shepherd I D H (1990) Computer mapping: 21 roles for AutoCAD. *Bulletin of the Society of University Cartographers* **23** (2): 1–15

Shepherd I D H (1990) Build your own desktop GIS? *Land and Minerals Surveying* **8** (4): 176–83

Shepherd I D H (1991) Information integration and GIS. In: Maguire D J, Goodchild M F, Rhind D W (eds.) *Geographical Information Systems: principles and applications*. Longman, London, pp. 337–60, Vol 1

Shetler T (1990) Birth of the BLOB. *BYTE* **15** (2): 221–6

Shiryaev E E (1987) *Computers and the Representation of Geographical Data*. Wiley, New York

Shmutter B (1981) Transforming conic conformal to TM coordinates. *Survey Review* **26**: 130–6, 201

Shneiderman B (1981) A note on human factors issues of natural language interaction with database systems. *Information Systems* **6** (2): 125–9

Shneiderman B (1983) Direct manipulation: a step beyond programming languages. *Computer* **16**: 57–69

Shneiderman B (1987) *Designing the User Interface: strategies for effective human-computer interaction*. Addison Wesley, Reading Massachusetts

Shortridge B G, Welch R B (1980) Are we asking the right questions? *The American Cartographer* **7** (1): 19–24

Shortridge B G, Welch R B (1982) The effect of stimulus redundancy on the discrimination of town size on maps. *The American Cartographer* **9** (1): 69–80

Shumway C (1986) Summary of the US Forest Service Geographical Information Systems activities. *Proceedings of Geographical Information Systems Workshop*. American Society for Photogrammetry and Remote Sensing, Falls Church, pp. 49–52

Shyue S W (1989) *High Breakdown Point Robust Estimation for Outlier Detection in Photogrammetry*. Unpublished PhD dissertation, University of Washington

Siderelis K C (1991) Land resource information systems. In: Maguire D J, Goodchild M F, Rhind D W (eds.) *Geographical Information Systems: principles and applications*. Longman, London, pp. 261–73, Vol 2

Siderelis K C, Tribble T N (1988) Using a Geographic Information System to prepare a site proposal for the Superconducting Super Collider. *Proceedings of GIS/LIS '88 Volume 1*. ACSM/ASPRS/AAG/URISA, Falls Church Virginia, pp. 459–68

Siegel M D (1989) Automatic rule derivation for semantic query optimization. In: Kerschberg L (ed.) *Proceedings of Second International Conference on Expert Database Systems, Tysons Corner, 25–27 April 1988*. Benjamin/Cummings Publishing Company, pp. 69–98

Sievers J, Bennat H (1989) Reference systems for maps and digital information systems of Antarctica. *Antarctic Science* **1**: 351–62

Silverman B G (ed.) (1987) *Expert Systems for Business*. Addison-Wesley, Reading Massachusetts

Simonett D S (1988) Considerations on integrating remote sensing and Geographic Information Systems. In: Mounsey H, Tomlinson R F (eds.) *Building Databases for Global Science*. Taylor & Francis, London, pp. 105–28

Simonett D S, Reeves R G, Estes J E, Bertke S E, Sailer C T (1983) The development and principles of remote sensing. In: Colwell R N (ed.) *Manual of Remote Sensing*. American Society of Photogrammetry, Falls Church Virginia, pp. 1–32

Simpson S R (1976) *Land Law and Registration*. Cambridge University Press, Cambridge

Singh C B (1989) Indian perspective for automatic cartography – a poser. *IX INCA International Seminar on Digital Cartography and Potential Users*. Pre-session Proceedings. Survey of India, Dehra Dun, pp. 424–6

Singh G (1989) Grid referenced data as a decision support system. *Proceedings of the 2nd National Mapping Awareness Conference*. Miles Arnold, Oxford, pp. 22.1–22.3

Singh S M, Saull R J (1988) The effect of atmospheric correction on the interpretation of multitemporal AVHRR-derived vegetation index dynamics. *International Journal of Remote Sensing* **25**: 37–51

Sinha A K, Waugh T C (1988) Aspects of the implementation of the GEOVIEW design. *International Journal of Geographical Information Systems* **2**: 91–100

Sinton D (1978) The inherent structure of information as a constraint to analysis: mapped thematic data as a case study. In: Dutton G (ed.) *Harvard Papers on Geographic Information Systems*, Volume 6. Addison-Wesley, Reading Massachusetts

SIS (1986) *pMAP User's Guide and Technical Reference, Professional Map Analysis Package (pMAP)*. Spatial Information Systems, Springfield Virginia

Slama C C, Theurer C, Henriksen S W (1980) (eds.) *Manual of Photogrammetry*, 4th edn. American Society of Photogrammetry, Falls Church Virginia

Slingerland R, Keen T R (1990) A numerical study of storm driven circulation and 'event bed' genesis. *Proceedings of Symposium on Three Dimensional Computer Graphics in Modelling Geologic Structures and Simulating Processes*. Freiburger Geowissenschaftliche Beitrage **2**: 97–9

Slocum T A (1983) Predicting visual clusters on graduated circle maps. *The American Cartographer* **10** (1): 59–72

Smallworld Systems (1990) GIS in Europe – summary report. *Geodetical Info Magazine* **4** (4): 28–9

Smith A B (1986) Developments in inertial navigation. *The Journal of Navigation* **39** (3): 401–15

Smith A B (1989) Geographical Information for European Vehicle Navigation Systems. In: Perry (ed.) *Proceedings of Government Computing 1989 (GC 89)*. HMSO, London. pp. 15–17.

Smith A B (1989) Prototyping a navigation database of road network attributes (PANDORA), In: Reekie D H M, Case E R, Tsai J (ed.) *Vehicle Navigation & Information Systems Conference, Toronto*, pp. 331–6

Smith D C, Harslem E, Irby C, Kimball R, Verplank W

(1983) Designing the Star user interface. *Proceedings, European Conference on Integrated Interactive Computing Systems: Stresa, Italy*. North-Holland, Amsterdam

Smith D R, Paradis A R (1989) Three-dimensional GIS for the earth sciences. In: Raper J F (ed.) *Three Dimensional Applications in Geographical Information Systems*. Taylor & Francis, London, pp. 149–54

Smith D R, Paradis A R (1989) Three-dimensional GIS for the Earth Sciences. *Proceedings of AUTOCARTO 9*. ACSM/ASPRS, Falls Church Virginia, pp. 324–35

Smith E A, Crosson W L, Cooper H J, Weng H (1990) Heat and moisture flux modeling of the FIFE grassland canopy aided by satellite derived canopy variables. *Proceedings of the Symposium on FIFE*. American Meteorological Society, Boston Massachusettes, pp. 154–62

Smith E E, Medin D L (1981) *Categories and Concepts*. Harvard University Press, Cambridge Massachusetts

Smith G H (1935) The relative relief of Ohio. *Geographical Review* **25**: 272–84

Smith J L, Mackenzie H G, Stanton R B (1988) A knowledge-based decision support for environmental planning. *Proceedings of the 3rd International Symposium on Spatial Data Handling*. International Geographical Union, Columbus Ohio, pp. 307–20

Smith J M, Smith D C P (1977) Database abstractions: aggregation and generalization. *Association for Computing Machinery Transactions on Database Systems* **2** (2): 105–33

Smith L, Eden R (1989) GIS and natural resource management: the Murray–Darling Basin *URPIS – Proceedings of the Urban and Regional Planning Information Systems Annual Conferences*, Volume 17. Australasian Urban and Regional Information Systems Association Inc., Sydney, pp. 452–60

Smith N S (1987) Data models and data structures for Ordnance Survey. *Proceedings of the Ordnance Survey/SORSA Symposium, Durham, May 1987*.

Smith P (1989) Tomorrow's open land registry and the dawn of a national information system. *Proceedings of National Mapping Awareness Conference*. Miles Arnold, Oxford

Smith T R, Ye Jiang (1991) Knowledge-based approaches in GIS. In: Maguire D J, Goodchild M F, Rhind D W (eds.) *Geographical Information Systems: principles and applications*. Longman, London, pp. 413–25, Vol 1

Smith T R, Menon S, Star J L, Estes J E (1987) Requirements and principles for the implementation and construction of large-scale geographic information systems. *International Journal of Geographical Information Systems* **1** (1): 13–31

Smith T R, Peuquet D J, Menon S, Agarwal P (1987) KBGIS-II: a knowledge-based geographical information system. *International Journal of Geographical Information Systems* **1** (2): 149–72

Snodgrass R (1987) The temporal query language TQUEL. *Association for Computing Machinery Transactions on Database Systems* **12**: 247

Snyder J P (1985) Computer-assisted map projection research. *US Geological Survey Bulletin* **1629**. US Government Printing Office, Washington

Snyder J P (1987) Map projections – a working manual. *US Geological Survey Professional Paper 1395*. Government Printing Office, Washington

Snyder J P (1987) Differences due to projection for the same USGS quadrangle. *Surveying and Mapping* **47**: 199–206

Snyder J P (1987) Labeling projections on published maps. *The American Cartographer* **14**: 21–7

Soil Survey Staff (1976) *Soil Taxonomy*. US Government Printing Office, Washington DC

Somerville I (1989) *Software Engineering*, 3rd edn. Addison-Wesley, Reading Massachusetts, 653pp.

Sommers R (1987) Geographic information systems in local government: a commentary. *Photogrammetric Engineering and Remote Sensing* **53**: 1379–82

South African Society for Photogrammetry, Remote Sensing and Cartography (1987) *Proceedings of Earth Data Information Systems, EDIS 87*. South African Society for Photogrammetry, Remote Sensing and Cartography, Pretoria

Southard R B, Anderson K E (1983) A National Program for Digital Cartography. *AUTOCARTO 5 Proceedings*. ACSM, Falls Church Virginia, pp. 41–9

Sowa J F (1984) *Conceptual Structures*. Addison-Wesley, Reading Massachusetts

Sowton M (1971) Automation in cartography at the Ordnance Survey using digital output from a plotting machine. *Bildmessung und Luftbildwesen* **39** (1): 41–4

Sowton M (1991) Development of GIS-related activities at the Ordnance Survey. In: Maguire D J, Goodchild M F, Rhind D W (eds.) *Geographical Information Systems: principles and applications*. Longman, London pp. 23–38, Vol 2

Sowton M, Green P (1984) Digital map data for computerised land and utility information systems. *Proceedings 10th European Symposium for Urban Data Information Systems – Urban Data Management and the End Users*. Padua, pp. 34–49

Sowton M, Haywood P E (1986) National Standards for the Transfer of Digital Map Data. In: Blakemore M J (ed.) *Proceedings of AUTOCARTO London*, Vol. 1. Royal Institution of Chartered Surveyors, London, pp. 298–311

Spanier E (1966) *Algebraic Topology*. McGraw-Hill, New York

Spiegelhalter D J, Knill-Jones R P (1984) Statistical and knowledge-based approaches to clinical decision-support systems, with an application to gastro-enterology. *Journal of the Royal Statistical Society* **A 147** (1): 35–77

Sprague R H, Carlson E D (1982) *Building Effective Decision Support Systems*. Prentice-Hall, Englewood Cliffs New Jersey

Sprague R H (1980) A framework for the development of decision support systems. *Management Information Sciences Quarterly* **4**: 1–26

Sprinsky W H (1987) Transformation of positional

geographic data from paper-based map products. *The American Cartographer* **14**: 359–66

SSC Central Design Group (1986) *SSC Conceptual Design of the Superconducting Super Collider*. Universities Research Association, SSC-SR-2020C, Washington DC

Star J, Estes J E (1990) *Geographic Information Systems: an introduction*. Prentice Hall, Englewood Cliffs New Jersey

Starr L E (1990) USGS National Mapping Division: preparing for the Twenty-First Century. *Proceedings of GIS/LIS '90*. AAG/ACSM/AM/FM/ASPRS/URISA, Bethesda Maryland, pp. 872–81

Starr L E, Anderson K E (1982) Some Thoughts on Cartographic and Geographic Information Systems for the 1980s. *Pecara VII Symposium Proceedings*. ASP, Falls Church Virginia, pp. 41–55

Starr L E, Anderson K E (1991) A USGS perspective on GIS. In: Maguire D J, Goodchild M F, Rhind D W (eds.) *Geographical Information Systems: principles and applications*. Longman, London, pp. 11–22, Vol 2

Starr L E, Guptill S C (1984) The US Geological Survey and the National Digital Cartographic Data Base. *Proceedings from the FIG International Symposium*. Edmonton Alberta, pp. 166–75

Starr M K, Zeleny M (1977) *Multiple Criteria Decision Making*. North-Holland, Amsterdam

State of North Carolina (1987) *North Carolina Site Proposal for the Superconducting Super Collider (SSC)*, Volumes 1–8. State of North Carolina, Raleigh NC

Staufenbiel W (1973) *Zur automation der generalisierung topographischer karten mit besonderer berucksichtigung Grobmabstabiger Gebaudedarstellungen*. Unpublished Doctoral Thesis, University of Hannover

Stefanovic P, Drummond J, Muller J-C (1989) ITC's response to the need for training in CAC and GIS. *IX INCA International Seminar on Digital Cartography and Potential Users*. Pre-session Proceedings. Survey of India, Dehra Dun, pp. 450–60

Stein A, Hoogerwerf M, Bouma J (1988) Use of soil map delineations to improve (co)kriging of point data on moisture deficits. *Geoderma* **43**: 163–77

Steinitz C F, Parker P, Jordan L (1976) Hand-drawn overlays: their history and prospective uses. *Landscape Architecture* **66** (8): 444–55

Steinke T R (1987) Eye movement studies in cartography and related fields. *Cartographica* **24** (2): 40–73

Steneker M, Bonham-Carter G F (1988) *Computer Program for Converting Arc-Node Vector Data to Raster Format*. Geological Survey of Canada, K1Z 8R7, 300pp.

Stevens S S (1946) On the theory of scales of measurement. *Science* **103**: 677–80

Stewart J C (1987) Geographic criteria for the siting of low level waste disposal sites. *Proceedings of the International Geographic Information Systems (IGIS) Symposium: the research agenda*, Volume 3. AAG, Washington, pp. 87–101

Steyaert L T (1989) Investigating the use of geographic information systems technology in the computer workstation environment for global change research. *Proceedings of the ASPRS/ACSM 1989 annual meeting*, April 1989, Volume 4. American Society of Photogrammetry and Remote Sensing, Falls Church, pp. 46–53

Stiefel M (1987) Mapping out the differences among geographic information systems *The S. Klein Computer Graphics Review*, Fall: 73–87

Stone R A (1988) Investigations of excess environmental risks around putative sources: statistical problems and a proposed test. *Statistics in Medicine* **7**: 649–60

Stonebraker M, Hanson E N (1988) The POSTGRES rule manager. *IEEE Transactions on Software Engineering* **14** (7): 897–907

Stonebraker M, Hearst M (1989) Future trends in expert database systems. In: Kerschberg L (ed.) *Expert Database Systems*. The Benjamin/Cummings Publishing Company, Redwood City, pp. 3–20

Strahler A H (1981) Stratification of natural vegetation for forest and rangeland inventory using Landsat digital imagery and collateral data. *International Journal of Remote Sensing* **2**: 15–41

Strahler A H, Woodcock C E, Smith J A (1986) On the nature of models in remote sensing. *Remote Sensing of Environment* **20**: 121–39

Stroustrup B (1987) *The C++ Programming Language*. Addison-Wesley, Reading Massachusetts

Stroutstrop B (1988) What is object-oriented programming. *IEEE Software* **5** (3): 10–20

Su S (1988) *Database Computers: principles, architectures and techniques*. McGraw-Hill, New York, 497pp.

Suh S, Kim M P, Kim T J (1988) ESMAN: an expert system for manufacturing selection. *Computers, Environment and Urban Systems* **12**: 239–52

Suits G, Malila W, Weller T (1988) Procedures for using signals from one sensor as substitutes for signals of another. *Remote Sensing of Environment* **25**: 395–408

Sullivan J G, Chow A L K (1990) The Wisconsin legislative redistricting project: design interface, training, and policy issues. *Proceedings of GIS/LIS '90*, Volume 1. ASPRS/ACSM/AAG/URISA/AM-FM, Bethesda Maryland, pp. 26–41

Sun Microsystems (1985) *Programming Utilities for the Sun Workstation*. Sun Microsystems

Sun Y, Wang R, Tang Q (1987) Automated cartographic system for population maps. *Proceedings of International Workshop on Geographic Information System, Beijing '87*. LREIS, Beijing, pp. 402–13

Sundaram K V (1987) Integrated approach to training for the establishment and use of information systems for subnational development planning. *Regional Development Dialogue* **8** (1): 54–70

Svorou S (1988) *The Experiential Basis of the Grammar of Space: evidence from the languages of the world*. Unpublished PhD dissertation, Department of Linguistics, State University of New York at Buffalo

Sweet D C (1970) An industrial development screening matrix. *The Professional Geographer* **22**: 124–7

Swiss Society of Cartography (1987) *Cartographic Generalization*, 2nd edn. SGK-Publikationen, Zurich

Switzer P (1975) Estimation of the accuracy of qualitative maps. In: Davis J C, McCullagh M J (eds.) *Display and Analysis of Spatial Data*. Wiley, New York, pp. 1–13

Switzer R (1975) *Algebraic Topology-Homotopy and Homology*. Springer-Verlag, New York

Szegö J (1987) Geocoded real property data in urban and regional planning. *Proceedings of Land Use Information in Sweden*. Swedish Council for Building Research, Stockholm Sweden. ISBN 91-540-4665-3, pp. 87–94.

Szelinski R, Terzopoulos D (1989) From splines to fractals. *Computer Graphics (SIGGRAPH '89 Proceedings)* **23** (3): 51–60

Talmy L (1983) How language structures space. In: Pick H, Acredolo L (eds.) *Spatial Orientation: theory, research, and application*. Plenum, New York, pp. 225–82

Talmy L (1988) How language structures space. In: Mark D M (ed.) *Cognitive and linguistic aspects of geographical space*. National Center for Geographic Information and Analysis Publication. NCGIA, Santa Barbara California

Tanic E (1986) Urban planning and artificial intelligence: the URBYS system. *Computers, Environment, and Urban Systems* **10** (3–4): 135–46

Tarjan R E (1987) Algorithm design. *Communications ACM* **30** (3): 205–12

Tarpley J D (1979) Estimating incident solar radiation at the earth's surface from geostationary satellite data. *Journal of Applied Meteorology* **18**: 1172–81

Tavernier R (1985) *Soil Map of the European Communities. 1 : 1 000 000*. Office for Official Publications of the European Communities, Luxembourg

Taylor D R F (1991) GIS and developing nations. In: Maguire D J, Goodchild M F, Rhind D W (eds.) *Geographical Information Systems: principles and applications*. Longman, London, pp. 71–84, Vol 2

Taylor M A P (1988) Computer models for traffic systems applications. In: Newton P W, Taylor M A P, Sharpe R (eds.) *Desktop Planning: microcomputer applications for infrastructure and services planning and management*. Hargreen, Melbourne, pp. 264–98

Taylor P J (1976) An interpretation of the quantification debate in British geography. *Transactions of the Institute of British Geographers* New Series **1**: 129–42

Taylor P J (1977) *Quantitative Methods in Geography*. Houghton Mifflin, Boston

Taylor P J (1990) Editorial comment: GKS. *Political Geography Quarterly* **9** (3): 211–12

Taylor R M, Hopkin V D (1975) Ergonomic principles and map design. *Applied Ergonomics* **6** (4): 196–204

Teorey T J, Fry J P (1982) *Design of Database Structures*. Prentice Hall, Englewood Cliffs New Jersey

Terada T (1930) Statistical methods on distribution of slopes using maps. *Geographical Review of Japan* **6**: 653–61

Tetzloff D M, Harbaugh J W (1989) *Simulating Plastic Sedimentation*. Van Nostrand Reinhold, New York

Thapa K (1988) Automatic line generalization using zero-crossings. *Photogrammetric Engineering and Remote Sensing* **54**: 511–17

Thatte S (1988) Report on the object-oriented database workshop: implementation aspects. In: Power L, Weiss Z (eds.) *OOPSLA '87 Addendum to the Proceedings. Special Issue of SIGPLAN Notices* **23** (5): 87

Thom R (1973) La theorie des catastrophes: etat present et perspectives. *Manifold* **14**: 16–23

Thomas E N (1960) Maps of residuals from regression: their characteristics and use in geographical research. *Geographical Publication No 2*. University of Iowa

Thomas P J, Baker J C, Simpson T W (1989) Variability of the Cecil map unit in Appomattox County, Virginia. *Soil Science Society of America, Journal* **53** (5): 1470–4

Thompson C N (1978) Digital mapping in the Ordnance Survey 1968–1978. In: Allam (ed.) *Proceedings of the International Society for Photogrammetry Commission IV International Symposium – New Technology for Mapping*. Ottawa, pp. 195–219

Thompson C N (1979) The need for a large scale topographic database. *Proceedings of the Conference of Commonwealth Survey Officers, July 1979*, Foreign and Commonwealth Office. Paper F4

Thompson D (1990) GIS – a view from the other (dark?) side: the perspective of an instructor of introductory geography courses at University level. In: Unwin D J (ed.) *GIS Education and Training, Collected Papers of a Conference, University of Leicester 20–21 March 1990*. Midlands Regional Research Laboratory, Leicester, 16 pp.

Thompson M M (1988) *Maps for America*, 3rd edn. US Government Printing Office, Washington DC

Thoone M (1987) CARIN, a car information and navigation system, *Philips Technical Review* **43** (11/12): 317–29

Tobler W R (1959) Automation and cartography. *Geographical Review* **49**: 526–34

Tobler W R (1961) *Map Transformations of Geographical Space*. Unpublished PhD dissertation, Department of Geography, University of Washington

Tobler W R (1966) Numerical map generalization. *Michigan Inter-University Community of Mathematical Geographers Discussion Paper* **8**

Tobler W R (1969) Satellite confirmation of settlement size coefficients. *Area* **3**: 30–3

Tobler W R (1970) A computer movie simulating urban growth in the Detroit Region. *Economic Geography* **46**: 234–40

Tobler W R (1973) Choropleth maps without class intervals? *Geographical Analysis* **3**: 262–65

Tobler W R (1973) A continuous transformation useful for redistricting. *Annals, New York Academy of Sciences* **219**: 215–20

Tobler W R (1977) *Bidimensional Regression*. Department of Geography, University of California, Santa Barbara

Tobler W R (1979) Cellular geography. In: Gale S, Olsson

G (eds.) *Philosophy in Geography*. D. Reidel Publishing Company, Dordrecht Holland, pp. 379–86

Tobler W R (1979) Smooth pycnophylactic interpolation for geographical regions. *Journal of the American Statistical Association* **74**: 519–30

Tobler W R (1982) Surveying multidimensional measurement. In: Golledge R G, Rayner J N (eds.) *Proximity and Preference: problems in the multidimensional analysis of large data sets*. University of Minnesota Press, Minneapolis, pp. 3–4

Tobler W R (1984) Application of image processing techniques to map processing. *Proceedings of the 1st International Symposium on Spatial Data Handling, Zurich*. Universitat Zurich-Irchel, Zurich (1): 140–44.

Tobler W R (1988) Geographic information systems research agenda: the scientific community perspective. In: Aangeenbrug R T, Schiffman Y M (eds.) *International Geographic Information Systems (IGIS) Symposium, Arlington, Virginia*, Vol 1. NASA, Washington DC, pp. 49–52

Tobler W R (1988) Resolution, resampling and all that. In: Mounsey H M, Tomlinson R F (eds.) *Building Databases for Global Science*. Taylor & Francis, London, pp. 129–37

Tobler W R, Kennedy S (1985) Smooth multidimensional interpolation. *Geographical Analysis* **17** (3): 251–7

Tobler W R, Moellering H (1972) The analysis of scale-variance. *Geographical Analysis* **4**: 34–50

Tomasi S G (1990) Why the nation needs a TIGER system. *Cartography and Geographic Information Systems* **17** (1): 21–6

Tomatsuri Y (1985) Geographic research and data base. *Jinbun Chiri* **37** (3): 270–86

Tomlin C D (1975) *The Tomlin Subsystem of IMGRID*. Unpublished Master's thesis, Harvard University

Tomlin C D (1983) A map algebra. *Harvard Computer Graphics Conference 1983*. Harvard University Graduate School of Design Laboratory for Computer Graphics and Spatial Analysis, Cambridge Massachusetts

Tomlin C D (1983) *Digital Cartographic Modeling Techniques in Environmental Planning*. Unpublished PhD dissertation, Yale University

Tomlin C D (1983) A map algebra. *Proceedings, Harvard Computer Graphics Conference*. Cambridge, Massachusetts

Tomlin C D (1985) The IBM Personal Computer Version of the Map Analysis Package. Laboratory for Computer Graphics and Spatial Analysis, Graduate School of Design, Harvard University

Tomlin C D (1990) *Geographic Information Systems and Cartographic Modelling*. Prentice-Hall, Englewood Cliffs New Jersey

Tomlin C D (1991) Cartographic modelling. In: Maguire D J, Goodchild M F, Rhind D W (eds.) *Geographical Information Systems: principles and applications*. Longman, London, pp. 361–74, Vol 1

Tomlin C D, Berry J K (1979) A mathematical structure for cartographic modelling in environmental analysis. *Proceedings of the 39th Symposium of the American Conference on Surveying and Mapping*, pp. 269–83

Tomlin C D, Tomlin S M (1981) An overlay mapping language. *Regional Landscape Planning: Proceedings of Three Educational Systems*. American Society of Landscape Architects: 155–64

Tomlinson R F (1967) *An Introduction to the Geographic Information System of the Canada Land Inventory*. Department of Forestry and Rural Development, Ottawa Canada

Tomlinson R F (1970) (ed.) *Environment Information Systems*. Commission on Geographical Data Sensing and Processing. International Geographical Union, Ottawa Canada

Tomlinson R F (1972) (ed.) *Geographic Data Handling*. Commission on Geographical Data Sensing and Processing. International Geographical Union, Ottawa Canada

Tomlinson R F (ed.) (1972) *Geographical Data Handling* 2 volumes. IGU Commission on Geographical Data Sensing and Processing for UNESCO/IGU Second Symposium on Geographical Information Systems, Ottawa

Tomlinson R F (1974) *The application of electronic computing methods to the storage, compilation and assessment of mapped data*. Unpublished PhD thesis, University of London

Tomlinson R F (1985) Geographic Information Systems – the new frontier. *The Operational Geographer* **5**: 31–6

Tomlinson R F (1987) Current and potential uses of geographical information systems – the North American experience. *International Journal of Geographical Information Systems* **1** (3): 203–8

Tomlinson R F (1988) The impact of the transition from analogue to digital cartographic representation. *The American Cartographer* **15** (3): 249–62

Tomlinson R F (1989) Letter to PERS. *Photogrammetric Engineering and Remote Sensing* **55** (4): 434–5

Tomlinson R F (1989) Recent trends in GIS technology. *Workshop on Strategic Directions for Canada's Surveying, Mapping, Remote Sensing and GIS Activities*, November 1989, Ottawa

Tomlinson R F (1989) Canadian GIS experience. *CISM Journal* **43** (3): 227–32

Tomlinson R F, Calkins H W, Marble D F (1976) *Computer Handling of Geographical Data*. Natural Resources Research Series XIII, UNESCO Press, Paris

Tomlinson R F, Petchenik B B (1988) (eds.) Reflections on the revolution: the transition from analogue to digital representations of space, 1958–1988. *The American Cartographer* **15** (3): 243–334

Tong L, Richards J A, Swain P H (1987) Probabilistic and evidential approaches for multisource data analysis. *IEEE Transactions on Geoscience and Remote Sensing* **GE-25**: 283–93

Topographic Science Working Group (1988) *Topographic Science Working Group Report to the Land Processes Branch, Earth Science and Applications Division*. NASA Headquarters Lunar and Planetary Institute, Houston

Toppen F (1990) GIS education in the Netherlands: a bit of everything and everything about a bit? In: Unwin D J (ed.) *GIS Education and Training, Collected Papers of a Conference, University of Leicester 20–21 March 1990*. Midlands Regional Research Laboratory, Leicester, 10 pp.

Townshend J R G (1991) Environmental databases and GIS. In: Maguire D J, Goodchild M F, Rhind D W (eds.) *Geographical Information Systems: principles and applications*. Longman, London, pp. 201–16, Vol 2

Townshend J R G, Justice C O (1988) Selecting the spatial resolution of satellite sensors required for global monitoring of land transformations. *International Journal of Remote Sensing* **9**: 187–236

Townshend J R G, Justice C O (1990) The spatial variation of vegetation at very coarse scales. *International Journal of Remote Sensing* **11**: 149–57

Trollegaard S (1985) *Land Information Systems in Denmark*. Ministry of Housing, Copenhagen

Tsichritzis D C, Klug A (eds.) (1975) *The ANSI/X3/SPARC DBMS Framework Report of the Study Group on Database Management Systems*. AFIPS Press, Montvale, New Jersey

Tsichritzis D C, Lochovsky F H (1977) *Data Base Management Systems*. Academic Press, New York

Tsichritzis D C, Lochovsky F H (1982) *Data Models*. Prentice-Hall, New York

Tsichritzis D C, Nierstrasz O M (1988) Fitting round objects into square databases. In: Gjessing S, Nygaard K (eds.) *Proceedings of ECOOP '88, the European Conference on Object-Oriented Programming*. Springer-Verlag, Berlin, pp. 283–99

Tsuzawa M, Okamoto H (1989) Advanced mobile traffic information and communication system (AMTICS). In: *Proceedings of the 20th International Symposium on Automotive Technology and Automation, Florence*, pp. 1145–60

Tucker C J, Townshend J R G, Goff T E (1985) African land-cover classification using satellite data. *Science* **227**: 369–75

Tucker D F, Devine H A (1988) GIS education – eclectic, integrated and evolving *Proceedings GIS/LIS '88*. ASPRS, Falls Church, pp. 528–40

Tufte E R (1983) *The Visual Display of Quantitative Information*. Graphic Press, Cheshire Connecticut

Tukey J W (1977) *Exploratory Data Analysis*. Addison-Wesley, Reading Massachusetts

Tuori M, Moon G C (1984) A topographic map conceptual data model. *Proceedings of the 1st International Symposium on Spatial Data Handling*, Volume 1, International Geographical Union, Columbus Ohio, pp. 28–37

Turnbull M, McAulay I, McLaren R A (1990) The role of terrain modelling in computer aided landscape design. In: Petrie G, Kennie T (eds.) *Terrain Modelling in Surveying and Civil Engineering*. Whittles, Latheronwheel, pp. 262–75

Turner A K (1989) The role of 3-D GIS in subsurface characterisation for hydrogeological applications. In: Raper J F (ed.) *Three Dimensional Applications in Geographical Information Systems*. Taylor & Francis, London, pp. 115–28

Turner A K (1990) *Three-Dimensional Modeling with Geoscientific Information Systems*. NATO Advanced Research Workshop

Turner A K, Kolm K, Downey J (1990) Potential applications of geoscientific information systems (GSIS) for regional ground water flow systems. *Proceedings of Symposium on Three Dimensional Computer Graphics in Modelling Geologic Structures and Simulating Processes*. Freiburger Geowissenschafliche Beiträge **2**: 108–10

Turner M G, Costanza R, Sklar F H (1989) Methods to evaluate the performance of spatial simulation models. *Ecological Modelling* **48**: 1–18

TYDAC (1989) *SPANS User Guide, Version 4.3*. Tydac Technologies Inc., 1600 Carling Ave., Ottawa, Ontario, Canada

Tyrie A (1986) LIS education versus training: a surveying perspective. In: Blakemore M J (ed.) *Proceedings of AUTOCARTO London*, Vol. 2. London, Royal Institution of Chartered Surveyors: 340–50

Ullman J D (1982) *Principles of Database Systems*. Computer Science Press, Rockville Maryland

Ullman J D (1986) Logic and database systems. In: Brodie M L, Mylopoulos J (eds.) *On Knowledge Base Management Systems: integrating artificial intelligence and database technologies*. Springer-Verlag, New York, pp. 121–24

Ullman J D (1986) An approach to processing queries in a logic-based query language. In: Brodie M L, Mylopoulos J (eds.) *On Knowledge Base Management Systems: integrating artificial intelligence and database technologies*. Springer-Verlag, New York, pp. 147–64

UN (1989) *United Nations 1987 Demographic Yearbook*. UN, New York

UNEP Global Resource Information Database (1988) *Report on the meeting of the GRID Scientific and Technical Management Advisory Committee, Jan. 1988*. Report No. 15. UNEP/GEMS/GRID, Nairobi

UNICEF (1988) *The State of the World's Children*. UNICEF Publications, New York

United Nations (1989) Modern mapping techniques. *United Nations Inter-Regional Seminar, Honefoss, Norway*.

United States Congress, Office of Technology Assessment (1990) *Helping America Compete: the role of federal scientific and technical information*. US Government Printing Office, Washington DC

United States Department of Energy, Office of Energy Research, Superconducting Super Collider Site Task Force (1987) *Invitation for Site Proposals for the Superconducting Super Collider (SSC)*. DOE/ER-0315 US Department of Energy, Washington DC

Universities Research Association (1987) *To The Heart of*

Matter – The Superconducting Super Collider. Universities Research Association, Washington DC

Unninayar S (1988) The global system: observing and monitoring change, data problems, data management and databases. In: Mounsey H M, Tomlinson R F (eds.) *Building Databases for Global Science*. Taylor & Francis, London, pp. 357–77

Unwin D J (1980) Make your practicals open-ended. *Journal of Geography in Higher Education* **4**: 37–42

Unwin D J (1981) *Introductory Spatial Analysis*. Methuen, London

Unwin D J (1991) The academic setting of GIS. In: Maguire D J, Goodchild M F, Rhind D W (eds.) *Geographical Information Systems: principles and applications*. Longman, London, pp. 81–90, Vol 1

Unwin D J, Dale P (1990) An educationalist's view of GIS. In: Foster M J, Shand P J (eds.) *The Association for Geographic Information Yearbook*. Taylor & Francis, London, pp. 304–12

Unwin D J et al. (1990) A syllabus for teaching geographical information systems. *International Journal of Geographical Information Systems* **4** (4): 457–65

Upstill S (1990) *The RenderMan Companion: a programmer's guide to realistic computer graphics*. Addison-Wesley, Reading Massachusetts

Upton G, Fingleton B (1985) *Spatial Data Analysis by Example. Volume 1. Point Pattern and Quantitative Data*. Wiley, New York

USBC (1969–73) *Census Use Study Reports 1 to 12*. US Bureau of Census, Washington DC

USGS (1984) *Landsat 4 Data Users Handbook*. Government Printing Office, Reston Virginia

USGS (1986) *Goals of the US Geological Survey*. US Geological Survey Circular 1010

USGS (1986) Digital line graphs from 1:24 000–scale maps. *Data User's Guide*, Vol. 1. US Department of the Interior, Reston

USGS (1986) Land use and land cover digital data from 1:250 000- and 1:100 000-scale maps. *Data User's Guide*, Vol. 4. US Department of the Interior, Reston

USGS (1987) *Digital Elevation Models, US Geological Survey Data Users Guide 5*. USGS, Reston Virginia

USGS (1989) *Digital Line Graphs from 1 : 100 000-Scale Maps*. US Geological Survey Data Users Guide 2. USGS, Reston Virginia

USGS (1990) *Digital Line Graphs from 1 : 24 000-Scale Maps. US Geological Survey Data Users Guide 1*. USGS, Reston Virginia

USGS (1991) *The Spatial Data Transfer Format*. US Geological Survey National Mapping Division, Washington DC

Ustin S L, Adams J B, Elvidge C D, Rejmanek M, Rock B N, Smith M O, Thomas R W, Woodward R A (1986) Thematic Mapper studies of semiarid shrub communities. *Bioscience* **36**: 446–52

van der Vlugt M (1989) The use of a GIS based decision support system in physical planning. *Proceedings of GIS/LIS '89*. ASPRS, Bethesda Maryland, pp. 459–67

van Roessel J W (1987) Design of a spatial data structure using the relational normal form. *International Journal of Geographical Information Systems* **1** (1): 33–50

van Roessel J W, Fosnight E A (1984) A relational approach to vector data structure conversion. *Proceedings of the 1st International Symposium on Spatial Data Handling*, Volume 1. International Geographical Union, Columbus Ohio, pp. 78–95

Varvel D A, Shapiro L (1989) The computational completeness of extended database query languages. *Journal of the IEEE* **15** (5): 632–8

Vazsonyi A (1978) Decision support systems: the new technology of decision making? *Interfaces* **9**: 74–8

Vazsonyi A (1982) Decision support systems, computer literacy, and electronic models. *Interfaces* **12**: 74–8

Ventura S, Sullivan J G, Chrisman N R (1986) Vectorization of Landsat TM land cover classification data. *Proceedings URISA* **1**: 129–40

Veregin H (1989) A taxonomy of error in spatial databases. *Technical Paper 89–12*. National Center for Geographic Information and Analysis University of California, Santa Barbara California

Veregin H (1989) Error modeling for the map overlay operation. In: Goodchild M F, Gopal S (eds.) *Accuracy of Spatial Databases*. Taylor & Francis, London, pp. 3–18

Verhey W H (1986) Principles of land appraisal and land use planning within the European Community. *Soil Use and Management* **2**: 120–4

Verhoef W (1984) Light scattering by leaf layers with application to canopy reflectance modeling: the Sail model. *Remote Sensing of Environment* **16**: 125–41

Verplank W L (1988) Graphic challenges in designing object orientated user interfaces. In: Helender M (ed.) *Handbook of Human Computer Interfaces*. Elsevier, North Holland

Vevany M J (1987) A critical evaluation of the proliferation of automated mapping systems in local governments. In: Aangeenbrug R T, Schiffman Y M (eds.) *International Geographic Information Symposiums: The Research Agenda*, Vol 3. Association of American Geographers, Washington, pp. 165–77

Vincenty T (1971) The meridional distance problem for desk computers. *Survey Review* **21**: 136–40, 161

Vincenty T (1989) The flat earth concept in local surveys. *Surveying and Mapping* **49**: 101–2

von Hohenbalken B and West D S (1984) Manhattan versus Euclid: market areas computed and compared. *Regional Science and Urban Economics* **14**: 19–35

Vonderohe A P, Chrisman N R (1985) Tests to establish the quality of digital cartographic data: some examples from the Dane County Land Records Project. *Proceedings of AUTOCARTO 7*. ASPRS/ACSM, Falls Church, pp. 552–9

Vose M (1990) Hot links to go. *BYTE* **15** (12): 373–7

Wadge G (1988) The potential of GIS modelling of gravity flows and slope instabilities. *International Journal of Geographic Information Systems* **2**: 143–52

Wadge G, Isaacs M C (1988) Mapping the volcanic hazards from Soufriere Hills Volcano, Montserrat, West Indies using an image processor. *Journal of the Geological Society* **145**: 541–52

Wagner G (1990) SICAD: profile of a raster indexed topological vector GIS. *Proceedings of the Conference on GIS Models and Functionality*. Midlands Regional Research Laboratory, University of Leicester

Wainer H, Thissen D (1981) Graphical data analysis. *Annual Review of Psychology* **32**: 191–241

Waldrop M M (1990) Learning to drink from a fire hose. *Science* **248** (11): 674–5

Walker P A, Cocks K D (1984) Computerised choropleth mapping of Australian resources data. *Cartography* **13** (4): 243–52

Walker P A, Hutton P G (1986) Grid cell representation of soil maps: an Australian example. *Australian Geographical Studies* **24** (2): 210–21

Walker P A, Moore D M (1988) SIMPLE – an inductive modelling and mapping tool for spatially-oriented data. *International Journal of Geographical Information Systems* **2** (4): 347–63

Walker T C, Miller R K (1990) *Geographic Information Systems – an assessment of technology, applications, and products*. SEAI Technical Publications, Madison Georgia USA

Wallin E (1990) The map as hypertext: on knowledge support systems for the territorial concern. *Proceedings of EGIS '90*, Volume 2. EGIS Foundation, Utrecht, pp. 1125–34

Walsh S J (1985) Geographic information systems for natural resource management. *Journal of Soil and Water Conservation* **40**: 202–5

Walsh S J, Lightfoot D R, Butler D R (1987) Recognition and assessment of error in geographic information systems. *Photogrammetric Engineering and Remote Sensing* **53**: 1423–30

Walters D K (1987) Selection of image primitives for general-purpose visual processing. *Computer Vision, Graphics and Image Processing* **37**: 261–98

Walters D K (1990) Computer vision. In: Ralston A, Reilly E (eds.) *Encyclopedia of Computer Science and Engineering*. Van Nostrand Reinhold, New York

Wang F, Hall G B, Subaryono (1990) Fuzzy information representation and processing in conventional GIS software: database design and application. *International Journal of Geographical Information Systems* **4** (3): 261–83

Wang S, Elliott D B, Campbell J B, Erich R W, Haralick R M (1983) Spatial reasoning in remotely sensed data. *IEEE Transactions on Geoscience and Remote Sensing* **GE-21**: 94–101

Ware C (1990) Using hand position for virtual object placement. *The Visual Computer* **6** (5): 245–53

Ware C, Osborne S (1990) Exploration and virtual camera control in virtual three dimensional environments. *1990 Symposium on Interactive 3D Graphics: Computer Control* (special issue)

Warntz W (1964) A new map of the surface of population potentials for the United States, 1960. *Geographical Review* **54**: 170–84

Warthen B (1988) Move over IGES: Here comes PDES/STEP. *Computer Graphics Review* Nov-Dec, 34–40

Wasielewski P (1988) Overview of PATHFINDER. *Proceedings of Research and Development Conference, California Department of Transportation, Sacramento*, September 263–4

Waters N M (1989) Expert systems within a GIS: knowledge aquisition for spatial decision support systems. *Proceedings of Challenge for the 1990s* Ottawa, pp. 740–59

Waters R S (1989) Data capture for the Nineties: VTRAK. *Proceedings of AUTOCARTO 9*. ACSM/ASPRS, Bethesda, Maryland, pp. 377–83

Watson G P, Rencz A N, Bonham-Carter G F (1989) Computers assist prospecting. *GEOS* **18** (1): 8–15

Waugh T C (1980) The development of the GIMMS computer mapping system. In: Taylor D R F (ed.) *The Computer in Contemporary Cartography*. Wiley, London, pp. 219–34

Waugh T C, Healey R G (1986) The GEOLINK system, interfacing large systems. In: Blakemore M J (ed.) *Proceedings of AUTOCARTO London*, Volume 1. Royal Institution of Chartered Surveyors, London, 76–85

Waugh T C, Healey R G (1987) The GEOVIEW design. A relational database approach to geographical data handling. *International Journal of Geographical Information Systems* **1**: 101–18

WCED (1987) *Our Common Future*. World Commission on Environment and Development. Oxford University Press, Oxford

Webster C J (1988) Disaggregated GIS architecture: lessons from recent developments in multi-site database management systems. *International Journal of Geographical Information Systems* **2** (1): 67–79

Webster C J (1989) Point-in-polygon processing in PROLOG. *Technical Reports in Geo-Information Systems* **17**. Wales and the South West RRL, University of Wales College of Cardiff

Webster R (1968) Fundamental objections to the 7th Approximation. *Journal of Soil Science* **19**: 354–66

Webster R (1977) *Quantitative and Numerical Methods in Soil Classification and Survey*. Oxford University Press, Oxford

Webster R (1978) Mathematical treatment of soil information. *Proceedings of the 11th International Congress of Soil Science, Edmonton, Canada*, Volume 3. pp. 161–90

Webster R (1985) Quantitative spatial analysis of soil in the field. *Advances in Soil Science* **3**: 2–70

Webster R, Burgess T M (1984) Sampling and bulking strategies for estimating soil properties in small regions. Journal of Soil Science **5**: 127–40

Webster R, Burrough P A (1972) Computer-based soil mapping of small areas from sample data: I. Multivariate classification and ordination. *Journal of Soil Science* **23**: 210–21

Webster R, Burrough P A (1972) Computer-based soil mapping of small areas from sample data: II Classification smoothing. *Journal of Soil Science* **23**: 222–34

Webster R, Burrough P A (1974) Multiple discriminant analysis in soil survey. *Journal of Soil Science* **25**: 120–34

Webster R, Butler B E (1976) Soil classification and survey studies at Ginninderra. *Australian Journal of Soil Science* **14**: 1–24

Webster R, Oliver M (1989) Optimal interpolation and isarithmic mapping of soil properties: VI. Disjunctive Kriging and mapping the conditional probability. *Journal of Soil Science* **40**: 497–512

Webster R, Oliver M (1990) *Statistical Methods in Soil and Land Resource Survey. Spatial Information Series*. Oxford University Press, Oxford

Weibel R (1989) Concepts and experiments for the automation of relief generalisation. Unpublished PhD dissertation (in German). *Geoprocessing Series 15*, Zurich, Department of Geography, University of Zurich.

Weibel R, Buttenfield B P (1988) Map design for geographic information systems. *Proceedings GIS/LIS '88*, Vol. 1. ASPRS/ACSM, Falls Church Virginia pp. 350–9

Weibel R, DeLotto J L (1988) Automated terrain classification for GIS modeling. *Proceedings of GIS/LIS '88*, Volume 2: ASPRS/ACSM, Falls Church Virginia, pp. 618–27

Weibel R, Heller M (1990) A framework for digital terrain modelling. *Proceedings of the 4th International Symposium on Spatial Data Handling*. International Geographical Union, Columbus Ohio, pp. 219–29

Weibel R, Heller M (1991) Digital terrain modelling. In: Maguire D J, Goodchild M F, Rhind D W (eds.) *Geographical Information Systems: principles and applications*. Longman, London, pp. 269–97, Vol 1

Weibel R, Heller M, Herzog A, Brassel K (1987) Approaches to digital surface modeling. *Proceedings First Latin American Conference on Computers in Cartography, San José, Costa Rica*, pp. 143–63

Weibel R, Herzog A (1988) Automatische Konstruktion panoramischer Ansichten aus digitalen Geländemodellen. *Nachrichten aus dem Karten- und Vermessungswesen Series I/100*: 49–84

Weir S (1975) *Getting around town: modifications in a local travel time space caused by expressway construction*. Unpublished MSc thesis. Department of Geography, Pennsylvania State University

Weiser R L, Asrar G, Miller G P, Kanemasu E T (1986) Assessing grassland biophysical characteristics from spectral measurements. *Remote Sensing of Environment* **20**: 141–52

Weizenbaum J (1976) *Computer Power and Human Reason*. Freeman, San Francisco

Welch R A (1990) 3-D terrain modelling for GIS applications. *GIS World*, October/November: 26–30

Welch R A, Usery E L (1984) Cartographic accuracy of Landsat-4 MSS and TM image data. *IEEE Transactions on Geoscience and Remote Sensing* **GE-22**: 281–8

Welch T A (1984) A technique for high performance data compression. *IEEE Computer* **17** (6)

Wellings C (1989) A review of the Association for Geographic Information Yearbook 1989. *Mapping Awareness* **3** (4): 51

Wells D (1988) How object-oriented databases are different from relational databases. In: Power L, Weiss Z (eds.) *OOPSLA '87 Addendum to the Proceedings. Special Issue of SIGPLAN Notices* **23** (5): 81

Werner C (1988) Formal analysis of ridge and channel patterns in maturely eroded terrain. *Annals of the Association of American Geographers* **78** (2): 253–70

Westcott T, Reiman R (1987) Siting the Superconducting Super Collider: a case study of the role of Geographic Information Systems in macro site analysis. *Paper presented at the 42nd Annual Meeting of the Southeast Division of the Association of American Geographers, Charlotte, NC*

Weyer S A, Borning A H (1985) A prototype electronic encyclopedia. *ACM Transactions on Office Information Systems* **31** (1): 63–88

Wharton S W (1989) Knowledge-based spectral classification of remotely sensed image data. In: Asrar G (ed.) *Theory and Applications of Optical Remote Sensing*. Wiley, New York, pp. 548–77

Wheeler P H (1988) *Olmsted County's Farmland Soil Loss Controls*. Rochester–Olmsted Consolidated Planning Department.

Whelan S D (1983) The MIDAS project: considerations for success. *Proceedings of AM/FM International, Keystone, USA*. AM/FM International, 8775 E. Orchard Rd, Suite 820, Englewood, CO80111

Whimbrel Consultants Ltd (1989) *CORINE Database Manual, Version 2.1*. Brussels

White B (1973) Supreme Court opinion in EPA v. Mink. 410 US 73

White B (1985) Modelling forest pest impacts – aided by a geographic information system in a decision support system framework. *Proceedings of Geographic Information Systems Workshop*. ASPRS, Falls Church Virginia, pp. 238–248

White D (1985) A taxonomy of space–time relations. *Proceedings of the Princeton Conference on Computer Graphics and Transportation Planning*. American Society of Landscape Architects

White D (1985) Relief modulated thematic mapping by computer. *The American Cartographer* **12** (1): 62–7

White M S (1984) Technical requirements and standards for a multi-purpose geographic data system. The *American Cartographer* **11**: 15–26

White M (1978) A geometric model for error detection and correction. *Proceedings of AUTOCARTO 3*. ASPRS, Falls Church, pp. 439–56

White M (1991) Car navigation systems. In: Maguire D J, Goodchild M F, Rhind D W (eds.) *Geographical*

Information Systems: principles and applications. Longman, London, pp. 115–25, Vol 2

Whittaker E, Robinson G (1944) *The Calculus of Observations*, 4th edn. Blackie and Son, London

Wiederhold G (1983) *Database Design.* 2nd edn. McGraw-Hill, London, 751pp.

Wiederhold G (1986) Knowledge versus data. In: Brodie M L, Mylopoulos J (eds.) *On Knowledge Base Management Systems: integrating artificial intelligence and database technologies.* Springer-Verlag, New York, pp. 77–82

Wiggins J C (1986) Performance considerations in the design of a map library: a user perspective. *Proceedings of the ARC/INFO Users' Conference.* ESRI, Redlands California

Wiggins J C, Hartley R P, Higgins M J, Whittaker R J (1987) Computing aspects of a large geographic information system for the European Community. *International Journal of Geographical Information Systems* **1** (1): 77–87

Wilding L P, Jones R B, Schafer G M (1965) Variation of soil morphological properties within Miami, Celina and Crosby mapping units in West-Central Ohio. *Proceedings of the Soil Science Society of America* **29**: 711–17

Williams E P J (1971) Digitisation of Large Scale Maps. *Proceedings of ICA Commission III meeting, Paris.* ICA, Paris, Paper II/a

Williams R B G (1984) *Introduction to Statistics for Geographers and Earth Scientists.* Macmillan, London

Williams R B G (1986) *Intermediate Statistics for Geographers and Earth Scientists.* Macmillan, London

Williams R L (1960) Map symbols: the curve of the gray spectrum – an answer. *Annals of the Association of American Geographers* **50**: 487–91

Williams W B P (1982) The Transverse Mercator Projection – simple but accurate formulae for small computers. *Survey Review* **26**: 205, 307–20

Williamson I P (1986) Trends in land information system administration in Australia. In: Blakemore M J (ed.) *Proceedings of AUTOCARTO London 1.* Royal Institution of Chartered Surveyors, London, pp. 71–82

Williamson I P, Blackburn J W (1987) Current developments in Land Information Systems in Australia. *Proceedings of the 21st Conference of the Institute of Australian Geographers, Perth*, pp. 289–97

Willmott C J (1984) On the evaluation of model performance in physical geography. In: Gaile G L, Willmott C J (eds.) *Spatial Statistics and Models.* D. Reidel, Dordrecht, pp. 443–60

Wilson A G (1974) *Urban and Regional Models in Geography and Planning.* Wiley, London

Wilson A G, Bennett R J (1985) *Mathematical Methods in Human Geography and Planning.* Wiley, London

Winograd T, Flores F (1986) *Understanding Computers and Cognition: a new foundation for design.* Addison-Wesley, Reading Massachusetts

Winston P H (1984) *Artificial Intelligence*, 2nd edn. Addison-Wesley, Reading Massachusetts

Wischmeier W H, Smith D D (1978) *Predicting Rainfall Erosion Losses. Agricultural Handbook 537.* USDA, Washington DC

Wise S, Burnhill P (1990) GIS: models of use and implications for service delivery on higher education computing campuses. In: Unwin D J (ed.) *GIS Education and Training, Collected Papers of a Conference, University of Leicester 20–21 March 1990.* Midlands Regional Research Laboratory, Leicester

Witkin A P (1986) Scale-space filtering. In: Pentland A P (ed.) *From Pixels to Predicates.* Ablex Publishing, Norwood New Jersey, pp. 5–19

Woelk D, Kim W (1987) Multimedia information management in an object oriented database system. In: Stocker P M, Kent W (eds.) *Proceedings of the 13th Very Large Databases Conference, Brighton*, pp. 319–29

Woodcock C E, Strahler A H (1987) The factor of scale in remote sensing. *Remote Sensing of Environment* **21**: 311–32

Woodcock C E, Strahler A H, Jupp D L B (1988) The use of variograms in remote sensing: I. Scene models and simulated images. *Remote Sensing of Environment* **25**: 323–48

Woodcock C E, Strahler A H, Jupp D L B (1989) Autocorrelation and regularization in digital images: II. Simple image models. *IEEE Transactions on Geoscience and Remote Sensing* **27**: 247–56

Woodcock J, Loomes M (1989) *Software Engineering Mathematics.* Addison-Wesley, Reading Massachusetts

Worboys M F, Hearnshaw, H M, Maguire D J (1990) Object-oriented data modelling for spatial databases. *International Journal of Geographical Information Systems* **4**: 369–83

Worboys M F, Hearnshaw H, Maguire D J (1990) Object-oriented data and query modelling for geographical information systems. *Proceedings of the 4th International Symposium on Spatial Data Handling.* International Geographical Union, Columbus Ohio, pp. 679–88

World Commission on Environment and Development (1987) *Our Common Future.* Oxford University Press, Oxford

Wösten J H M, Bannink M H, Bouma J (1989) Relation between the questions being asked and the sales and costs at which land evaluation is performed. In: Bouma J, Bregt A K (eds.) *Land Qualities in Space and Time. Proceedings of a Symposium organised by the International Society of Soil Science (ISSS), Wageningen, The Netherlands, 22–26 August 1988.* PUDOC, Wageningen, pp. 213–5

Wray T (1974) The seven aspects of a general map projection. *Cartographica Monograph* **11**, 72 pp.

Wright D F, Bonham-Carter G F, Rogers P J (1988) Spatial data integration of lake-sediment geochemistry, geology and gold occurrences, Meguma Terrane, Nova Scotia. In: MacDonald D R, Mills K A (eds.) *Prospecting in Areas of Glaciated Terrain – 1988.* Canadian Institute of Mining and Metallurgy, pp. 501–15

Wrigley N (ed.) (1988) *Store Choice, Store Location and Market Analysis.* Routledge and Kegan Paul, London

Wrigley N (1985) *Categorical Data Analysis for Geographers and Environmental Scientists.* Longman, London

Wu, Zhong-xing, Yang, Qi-he (1981) A research on the transformation of map projections in computer-aided cartography, *Paper presented at the 10th International Cartographic Conference Tokyo*, 22 pp.

Wyatt B K, Briggs D J, Mounsey H M (1988) CORINE: An information system on the state of the environment in the European Community. In: Mounsey H M, Tomlinson R F (eds.) *Building Databases for Global Science.* Taylor & Francis, London, pp. 378–96

Yan S Y (1988) *A Logic Foundation for Expert Geographic Database Systems.* Melbourne, Australia, Department of Computer Science, University of Melbourne.

Yan S, Zhou M, Shi Z (1987) Chinese Tourism Resource Information System. *Proceedings of International Workshop on Geographic Information System Beijing '87.* LREIS, Beijing, pp. 377–83

Yapa L S (1988) Computer-aided regional planning: a study in rural Sri Lanka. *Environment and Planning B* **15**: 285–304

Yapa L S (1989) Peasants, planners and microcomputers in the Third World. *Earth and Mineral Sciences* **58** (2): 31–3

Yarbus A L (1967) *Eye Movement and Vision.* (Tr. Haig B). Plenum, New York

Yarrow G J (1987) Joint utility mapping. *Proceedings of NJUG 87 First National Conference, Birmingham.* National Joint Utilities Group, 30 Millbank, London, SW1P 4RD

Yarrow G J (1989) Dudley – the lessons. *Proceedings of the National Joint Utilities' Conference*

Yates S R, Yates M V (1988) Disjunctive kriging as an approach to management decision making. *Soil Science Society of America Journal* **62**: 1554–58

Yeh A G (1990) A land information system for the monitoring of land supply in the urban development of Hong Kong. In: Worrell L (ed.) *Geographic information systems: developments and applications.* Belhaven, London, pp. 163–87

Yeorgaroudakis Y (1990) The GIS of the future. *Proceedings of EGIS '90*, Volume 2. EGIS Foundation, Utrecht, pp. 1188–99

Yeung A K W, Lo C P (1985) Cartographic digitizing for geographical application: some hardware and software considerations. *Asian Geographer* **4**: 9–22

Yoeli P (1965) Analytical hill shading. *Surveying and Mapping* **25**: 573–9

Yoeli P (1967) Mechanisation in analytical hill-shading. *Cartographic Journal* **4**: 82–8

Yoeli P (1972) The logic of automated map lettering. *Cartographic Journal* **9** (2): 99–108

Yoeli P (1982) Cartographic drawing with computers. *Computer Applications* **8**

Yoeli P (1983) Shadowed contours with computer and plotter. *The American Cartographer* **10** (2): 101–10

Yoeli P (1985) The making of intervisibility maps with computer and plotter. *Cartographica* **22** (3): 88–103

Yoeli P (1985) Topographic relief depiction by hachures with computer and plotter. *Cartographic Journal* **22** (2): 111–24

Yoshimura S (1930) A method for area measurement and its example. *Geographical Review of Japan* **6**: 1569–84; and 1708–43

Youngman C (1978) A linguistic approach to map description. In Dutton G (ed.) *Spatial Semantics: understanding and interacting with map data.* Laboratory for Computer Graphics and Spatial Analysis, Graduate School of Design, Harvard University

Youngmann C (1989) Spatial data structures for modelling subsurface features. In: Raper J F (ed.) *Three Dimensional Applications in Geographical Information Systems.* Taylor & Francis, London, pp. 129–36

Zadeh L A (1974) *Fuzzy Logic and its Application to Approximate Reasoning, Information Processing.* North-Holland, Amsterdam

Zarzycki J M, Jiwani Z (1986) Canadian standards for exchange of digital topographic data. *Proceedings of the XVIII FIG Congress, Commission V*: 171–181

Zavoli W B (1989) Navigation and digital maps interface for fleet management and driver information systems. *Proceedings, First Vehicle Navigation & Information Systems Conference (VNIS '89)*. IEEE, New York, pp. A9–A14

Zhang Q, Kou Y (1987) A study on the information system for agricultural resources and economy. *Proceedings of International Workshop on Geographic Information System Beijing '87.* LREIS, Beijing, pp. 90–4

Zheng W, Ren F, Cheng Ji-Cheng (1989) Building of micro-GIS tool and its application. *Proceedings of International Conference in Urban Planning and Urban Management.* University of Hong Kong, Hong Kong, pp. 299–314

Zhong S, Zhong E (1987) A preliminary research on Land Resources Information System (LRIS) at Fushui County. *Proceedings of International Workshop on Geographic Information System Beijing '87.* LREIS, Beijing, 433–7

Zhou Q (1989) A method for integrating remote sensing and geographic information systems. *Photogrammetric Engineering and Remote Sensing* **55**: 591–6

Zilles S (1984) Types, algebras, and modelling. In: Brodie M, Mylopoulos J, Schmidt J (eds.) *On Conceptual Modelling.* Springer-Verlag, New York, pp. 441–50

Zinn v. State [1983] 112 Wis. 2nd 417, 334 N.W. 2nd 67

Zobrist A L (1983) Integration of Landsat image data with geographic databases. In: Peuquet D J, O'Callaghan J (eds.) *Proceedings of the United States/Australia Workshop on Design and Implementation of Computer-based Geographic Information Systems.* IGU Commission on Geographical Data Sensing and Processing, Amherst New York, pp. 51–63

Zoraster S (1986) Integer programming applied to the map label placement problem. *Cartographica* **23** (3): 16–27

Zoraster S, Davis D, Hugus M (1984) *Manual and*

Automated Line Generalization and Feature Displacement, ETL-Report ETL-0359 (plus ETL-0359–1). US Army Engineer Topographic Laboratories, Fort Belvoir Virginia

Zuboff S (1988) *In the Age of the Smart Machine*. Heinemann, London

Zusne L (1970) *Visual Perception of Form*. Academic Press, New York

Zycor N C (1984) Manual and automated line generalization and feature displacement. *Report for the US Army Engineer Topographic Laboratories Fort Belvoir, Virginia 22060 USA, unclassified material*, 2 vols, 204pp.

Zyda M J (1988) A decomposable algorithm for contour surface display generation. *ACM Transactions on Graphics* **7** (2): 129–48

LIST OF ACRONYMS

A-P	Albemarle-Pamlico	AURISA	Australasian Urban and Regional Planning Information Systems Association
AAG	Association of American Geographers		
ABS	Australian Bureau of Statistics	AUSLIG	Australian Surveying and Land Information Group
ACORN	A Classification of Residential Neighbourhoods		
ACSM	American Congress on Surveying and Mapping	AVHRR	Advanced Very High Resolution Radiometer
ADMATCH	Address Matching Software		
ADT	Abstract Data Type	BBC	British Broadcasting Corporation
AGI	Association for Geographic Information	BEM	Basic Employment Allocation Model
AGNPS	Agricultural Nonpoint Source Pollution Model	BIOS	Basic Input Output System
		BLOB	Binary Large Object
AID	Automated Interaction Detector	BP	British Petroleum
AIS	Address Information System	BR	Boundary Representation
AIS	Australia Information System	BURISA	British Urban and Regional Information Systems Association
AIT	Asian Institute of Technology		
ALIC	Australian Land Information Council		
AM/FM	Automated Mapping/Facilities Management	CAD	Computer-Aided Design
		CAD	Computer-Aided Drafting
AMEDAS	Automated Meteorological Data Acquisition System	CADD	Computer-Aided Design and Drafting
		CAL	Computer-Assisted Learning
AML	ARC Macro Language	CAM	Computer-Aided Mapping
AMTICS	Advanced Mobile Traffic Information and Communication System	CAMA	Coastal Area Management Act
		CARD	Cartographic Representation of Data
ANSI	American National Standards Institute	CARP	Computer-Assisted Regional Planning
ARDA	Canadian Agricultural Rehabilitation and Development Association	CASS	Crime Analysis Statistical System
		CBRED	Central Bureau for Real Estate Data
ARIS	Australia Resources Information System	CCD	Charge-Coupled Device
		CD-ROM	Compact Disk Read Only Memory
ARJIS	Automated Regional Justice Information System	CFD	Central Board of Real Estate Data
		CGIA	Center for Geographical Information and Analysis
ASCII	American Standard Code for Information Interchange		
		CGIS	Canada Geographic Information System
ASPRS	American Society for Photogrammetry and Remote Sensing	CHEST	Combined Higher Education Software Team
ATM	Adaptive Triangular Mesh		
ATM	Automated Teller Machine	CIA	Central Intelligence Agency

593

List of acronyms

CISM	Canadian Institute of Surveying and Mapping	DR	Dead Reckoning
CLDS	Canada Land Data System	DRIVE	Dedicated Road Infrastructure for Vehicle Safety
CLI	Canada Land Inventory	DSS	Decision Support System
CLISG	Commonwealth Land Information Support Group	DTED	Digital Terrain Elevation Data
CNES	Centre National d'Etudes Spatiales	DTI	Department of Trade and Industry
CODASYL	Conference on Data Systems Languages	DTM	Digital Terrain Model
CODATA	Committee on Data for Science and Technology	EC	European Commission
CORINE	Coordinated Information on the European Environment	ECU	Experimental Cartography Unit
		ED	Enumeration District
		ED Group	Department of Employment Group
CRIES	Comprehensive Resource Inventory and Evaluation System	EDA	Exploratory Data Analysis
		EDI	Electronic Data Interchange
CRISP	Computerized Rural Information Systems Project	EDP	Electronic Data Processing
		EFTPoS	Electronic Funds Transfer at Point of Sales
CRT	Cathode Ray Tube		
CSG	Constructive Solid Geometry	EGA	Extended Graphics Array
CSIRO	Commonwealth Scientific and Industrial Research Organisation	EGIS	European Geographical Information Systems Symposia
CZCS	Coastal Zone Color Scanning	EMR	Department of Energy, Mines and Resources Canada
DBMS	Database Management System	EMS	Emergency Management System
DBS	Database System	EMS	Engineering Modelling Software
DCDSTF	Digital Cartographic Data Standards Task Force	EOS	Earth Observation Satellite
		EPA	Environmental Protection Agency
DCM	Digital Cartographic Model	EPoS	Electronic Point of Sales
DDE	Dynamic Data Exchange	ERDAS	Earth Resources Data Analysis System
DEFM	Demographic and Economic Forecasting Model	ERE	Effective Resolution Element
		ERIN	Environmental Resources Information Network
DEM	Digital Elevation Model		
DFUS	Digital Field Update System	ES	Expert System
DG XI	Directorate General of the Environment	ESA	European Space Agency
		ESRC	Economic and Social Research Council
DGIWG	Digital Geographic Information Working Group	ESRI	Environmental Systems Research Institute
DHA	District Health Authority	ESSC	Earth Systems Science Committee
DID	Digital Image Document		
DIDS	Decision Information Display System	FAA	Federal Aviation Administration
DIDS	Desktop Information and Display System	FGDC	Federal Geographic Data Committee
		FICCDC	Federal Interagency Coordinating Committee on Digital Cartography
DIDS	Domestic Information Display System		
DIME	Dual Independent Map Encoding	FIG	Fédération International de Géomètres
DIP	Document Image Processing	FIPS	Federal Information Processing Standard
DLG	Digital Line Graph		
DLG–E	Digital Line Graph – Enhanced	FOIA	Freedom of Information Act
DLM	Digital Landscape Model	FPC	Family Practitioner Committee
DMA	Defense Mapping Agency		
DMSP	Defense Meteorological Satellite Program	GAM	Geographical Analysis Machine
		Gb	Gigabyte
DOE	Department of Energy	GCDP	Global Change Database Project
DoE	Department of the Environment	GCEM	Geographical Correlates Exploration Machine
DOI	Department of the Interior		
DP	Data Processing		

List of acronyms

GCM	Global Climate Model	ICSU	International Council of Scientific Unions
GD	Geologic Division	IfAG	Institut fur Angewandte Geodasie
GDF	Geographic Data File	IFOV	Instantaneous Field of View
GEBCO	General Bathymetric Chart of the Oceans	IGBP	International Geosphere-Biosphere Programme
GEMS	Global Environmental Monitoring System	IGES	Initial Graphics Exchange Specification
GENESSIS	Generic Scene Simulation Software	IGIS	Integrated Geographical Information System
GEODAS	Geophysical Data System	IGU	International Geographic Union
GF3	General Formatting System for Geo-Referenced Data 3	IJGIS	International Journal of Geographical Information Systems
GIA	Geographical Information Analysis	ILI	Institute for Land Information
GIMMS	Geographic Information Mapping and Management System	ILWIS	Integrated Land and Watershed Management Information System
GIPS	Geographical Information Processing System	IMM	Interactive Multimedia
GIRAS	Geographical Information Retrieval and Analysis System	IMS	Information Management System
		IOC	International Oceanographic Commission
GIS	Geographical Information System	IODE	International Oceanographic Data and Information Exchange
GISG	Geographic Information Steering Group	IS	Information System
GISP	General Information System for Planning	ISD	Information Systems Division
GIST!	Geographical Information Systems Tutor	ISDN	Integrated Services Digital Network
		ISIF	Intermediate Standard Transfer Format
GKS	Graphical Kernel System	ISM	Interactive Surface Modelling
GPS	Global Positioning Satellite	ISO	International Standards Organisation
GPS	Global Positioning System	ISPRS	International Society of Photogrammetry and Remote Sensing
GPV	General Parametric Videoshow		
GRASS	Geographical Resources Analysis Support System	ISSS	International Soil Science Society
GRID	Global Resource Information Database	IT	Information Technology
GSD	Geographical Data of Sweden	ITC	International Institute for Aerospace Survey and Earth Science
GSI	Geographical Survey Institute		
GSM	General Systems Model	ITE	Institute of Terrestrial Ecology
GSS	Government Statistical Service	ITT	Invitation to Tender
GTS	Global Telecommunications System	ITU	Integrated Terrain Unit
GUI	Graphical User Interface	ITU	International Telecommunications Union
HCI	Human-Computer Interaction	IU	Intelligence Unit
HCI	Human-Computer Interface	IV	Interactive Video
HDGCP	Human Dimensions of Global Change Program	IVM	Interactive Volume Modelling
HMLR	Her Majesty's Land Registry	JAMGIS	Jamaica GIS
HMSO	Her Majesty's Stationery Office	JANET	Joint Academic Network
HPGL	Hewlett Packard Graphics Language	JDRMA	Japan Digital Road Map Association
		JIS	Japan Industrial Standard
IAC	Inter-Application Communications		
IBG	Institute of British Geographers	Kb	Kilobyte
IBM	International Business Machines	KB	Knowledge Base
ICA	International Cartographic Association	KBGIS	Knowledge Based Geographical Information System
ICES	International Council for the Exploration of the Sea	KBT	Knowledge Based Technique
ICL	International Computers Limited	KUB	Knoxville Utilities Board

595

LAI	Leaf Area Index	NAGIS	Natal/KwaZulu Association for Geographic Information Systems
LAMIS	Local Authority Management Information System	NASA	National Aeronautics and Space Administration
LAMSAC	Local Authorities Management Services and Computer Committee	NATO	North Atlantic Treaty Organization
LAN	Local Area Network	NCDC	National Climate Data Center
LAS	Land Analysis System	NCGA	National Computer Graphics Association
LCG	Harvard Laboratory for Computer Graphics	NCGIA	National Center for Geographic Information and Analysis
LDBS	Land Data Bank System	NCHS	National Center for Health Statistics
LDC	Less Developed Countries	NCIC	National Cartographic Information Center
LIS	Land Information System		
LMI	Labour Market Information	NDCDB	National Digital Cartographic Data Base
LOTS	Land Ownership and Tenure System		
LR	Land Register	NEC	Nippon Electric Corporation
LREIS	Laboratory for Resource and Environmental Information Systems	NERC	Natural Environmental Research Council
LRIS	Land Resources Information System	NEXPRI	Nederlands Expertise Centruum voor Ruimtelijke Informatiererwerkig
LRU	Least Recently Used		
LTER	Long Term Ecological Research	NGDC	National Geophysical Data Center
LUDA	USGS Land Use Data Analysis	NHS	National Health Service
LZW	Lempel-Zif and Welch	NIC	Newly Industrialized Countries
MAFF	Ministry of Agriculture, Forestry and Fishery	NIMBY	Not In My Back Yard
		NJUG	National Joint Utilities Group
MAGI	Maryland Automatic Geographic Information	NL	Natural Language
		NLA	National Land Agency
MAI	Mean Annual Increment	NLS	National Land Survey
MAP	Map Analysis Package	NMD	National Mapping Division
MAUP	Modifiable Areal Unit Problem	NMP	National Mapping Program
Mb	Megabyte	NNRIS	National Natural Resources Information System
MDS	Multi-Dimensional Scaling		
MFlops	Millions of Floating Point Operations per Second	NOAA	National Oceanographic and Atmospheric Administration
MGRA	Master Geographical Reference Area	NODC	National Oceanographic Data Centres
MIAS	Marine Information Advisory Service	NOMIS	National On-Line Manpower Information System
MIMD	Multiple Instruction Multiple Data		
MIPS	Million Instructions Per Second	NP	Non-Deterministic Polynomial Time
MIS	Management Information System	NRC	National Research Council
MITI	Ministry of International Trade and Industry	NRIC	National Resources Information Centre
		NSF	National Science Foundation
MLMIS	Minnesota Land Management Information System	NSSDC	National Space Science Data Center
		NSW	New South Wales
MMS	Materials Management Service	NTF	National Transfer Format
MOSS	Map Overlay and Statistics System	NTT	Nippon Telephone and Telegram
MS	Metropolitan Map Series	NURBS	Non-Uniform Rational B-Splines
MS-DOS	MicroSoft Disk Operating System		
MSA	Major Statistical Areas	OCR	Optical Character Reader
MSD	Master Survey Drawing	ODA	Office Document Architecture
MSS	Multi-Spectral Scanner	ODA	Official Development Assistance
MTS	Michigan Terminal System	OECD	Organization for Economic Cooperation and Development
NA	Network Analysis	OHWM	Ordinary High Water Mark
NAG	Numerical Algorithm Group	OLWM	Ordinary Low Water Mark

OMB	Office of Management and Budget	RGB	Red, Green and Blue
ONC	Operational Navigation Charts	RGF	Regional Growth Forecast
OODB	Object-Orientated Database	RGS	Royal Geographical Society
OODBMS	Object-Oriented Database Management System	RHA	Regional Health Authority
		RIN	Royal Institute of Navigation
OPCS	Office of Population Census and Surveys	RISC	Reduced Instruction Set Chip
		RLE	Run Length Encoding
OPIS	Oakland Planning Information System	RLUIS	Rural Land Use Information System
OS	Ordnance Survey	RMS	Root Mean Square
OS/2	Operating System/2	RMSE	Root Mean Square Error
OSAC	Oxford System of Automated Cartography	RNODC	Responsible National Oceanographic Data Centres
OSNI	Ordnance Survey of Northern Ireland	ROADIC	Road Administration Information Centre
OSTF	Ordnance Survey Transfer Format		
OSTF+	Ordnance Survey Transfer Format Plus	RPR	Real Property Register
		RRDN	Rural Regional Development Newsletter
PANDORA	Prototyping a Navigation Database of Road Network Attributes		
		RRL	Regional Research Laboratory
PANIC	Potential And Needs, Investments and Capabilities	RSA	Republic of South Africa
		RTPI	Royal Town Planning Institute
PC	Personal Computer		
PCA	Parliamentary Constituency	SA	South Australia
PCB	Polychlorinated Biphenyl	SACS	Small Area Census Studies
PDES	Product Data Exchange Specification	SAE	Society of Automotive Engineers
PDF	Probability Density Function	SAHSU	Small Area Health Statistics Unit
PEX	PHIGS-Extended-to-X	SANDAG	San Diego Association of Governments
PHIGS	Programmers Hierarchical Integrated Graphics System	SASPRSC	South African Society for Photogrammetry, Remote Sensing and Cartography
PI	Primitive Instancing		
PIES	Portable Interactive Editing System	SAV	Submerged Aquatic Vegetation
PIMS	Profit Impact of Market Strategy	SCS	Soil Conservation Service
PIOS	Planning Information Overlay System	SDSS	Spatial Decision Support System
PIOS	Polygon Intersection and Overlay System	SDTS	Spatial Data Transfer Standard
		SET	Système d'Exchange et de Transfer
PLUM	Projective Land Use Model	SIC	Standard Industrial Classification
pMAP	Professional Map Analysis Package	SIF	Standard Interchange Format
PR	Peano Relation	SIM	Survey Information on Microfilm
PS	Production System	SIMD	Simple Instruction Multiple Data
PSF	Point Spread Function	SIMPLE	Spatial and Inductive Modelling Package for Land Evaluation
PSS	Packet Switching Stream		
PUSWA	Public Utilities Street Works Act	SIS	Spatial Information System
		SLDS	Swedish Land Databank System
QA	Quality Assurance	SMHI	Swedish Meteorological and Hydrological Institute
QC	Quality Control		
QLD	Queensland	SOAP	Sophisticated Allocation Process
QMSG	Quantitative Methods Study Group	SOE	Spatial Occupancy Enumeration
QTM	Quaternary Triangulation Mesh	SOI	Survey of India
		SORSA	Spatially Orientated Referencing Systems Association
RAM	Random Access Memory		
RAWP	Resource Allocation Working Party	SOTER	Soil and Terrain Database
RB	Rule Base	SQL	Structured Query Language
REGIS	Regional Geographical Information Systems Project	SR	Sweep Representation
		SRA	Sub-Regional Areas
RFP	Request for Proposal	SSC	Superconducting Super Collider

STEP	Standard for the Exchange of Product Data
STI	Scientific and Technical Information
SUSI	Sale of Unpublished Survey Information
SWEB	South-Western Electricity Board
TA	Training Agency
TAS	Tasmania
TAZ	Traffic Analysis Zones
Tb	Terabyte
TC	Training Commission
TEED	Training Education and Enterprise Division
TIFF	Tag Image File Format
TIGER	Topologically Integrated Geographic Encoding Referencing
TIIWG	Inter-Departmental Working Group on the Tradeable Information Initiative
TIN	Triangulated Irregular Network
TJUG	Taunton Joint Utilities Group
TM	Thematic Mapper
TRIP	Tourism and Recreation Information Package
UIS	Urban Information System
ULI	Council for Research and Development in Land Information Technology
ULI	Utvecklingsradet for Landskapsinformation
UN/ECLAC	United Nations Economic Commission for Latin America and the Caribbean
UNEP	United Nations Environmental Programme
UNITAR	United Nations Institute for Training and Research
URA	User Requirement Analysis
URISA	American Urban and Regional Information Systems Association
URPIS	Urban and Regional Planning Information Systems
USBC	United States Bureau of the Census
USDA	United States Department of Agriculture
USGS	United States Geological Survey
USLE	Universal Soil Loss Equation
UTM	Universal Transverse Mercator
VADS	Value Added and Data Services
VIC	Victoria
ViSC	Visualization in Scientific Computing
VNIS	Vehicle Navigation and Information Systems Conference
WA	Western Australia
WAN	Wide Area Network
WCED	World Commission on Environment and Development
WDDES	World Digital Data for the Environmental Sciences
WEDSS	Whole Earth Decision Support System
WEE	Wind Erosion Equation
WEGS	Western European Geological Surveys
WMO	World Meteorological Organization
WOCE	World Ocean Climate Experiment
WORM	Write Once Read Many
WRD	Water Resources Division
WYSIWYG	What You See Is What You Get
ZUM	Zones for Urban Modelling

AUTHOR INDEX

Numbers in roman refer to volume 1, numbers in italic refer to volume 2.

Aangeenbrug R T 4, 104, *314*
Aanstoos R 377
Abel D J 262, *67, 214*
Abler R F 33, 84, 101, 122, 154, 348
Abraham I M 472
Acquista C 207
Adams J B 122, 203
Adedeji A *71, 72*
Adlam K H *214*
Adler R K 135, 137, 143
Aerospatiale Direction Technique 528
Aetna Casualty & Security Co. v. Jeppeson & Co. 500
Agarwai P 199, 420, 421, 422
AGI News 96
Aglinfou *43*
Agterberg F P *172, 173, 174, 177, 178, 183, 184*
Ahn J 423, 436, 446, 451, 452
Aho A V 217, 220
Akima H 277
Akman V 219
Aldersey-Williams H 315
Aldred B K 151, 372
Aldus Corporation 245
Alegiani J B *124*
Alemi M H *163*
Alexander F E 392
Alexandroff P 150, 231, 233, 235
ALIC *58, 61*
Allen D 286
Allen J H *204*
Allinson L 355, *208*
Alter S L 403, 406, 410

Alvo M *422*
Ambron S 352
American Bar Association 494
American Cartographer, The 181, 186
American National Standards Institute 156, 228, 528
Amin S *73*
Amos L L *17*
Amrhein C 185
Anderson D E 30
Anderson D R 277
Anderson E A 31, 262, *13, 131, 133*
Anderson J *165*
Anderson J E 202
Anderson J J 181
Anderson J R 179, 180, 186, *264, 276*
Anderson K E 31, *3, 12, 13, 16, 23, 304, 305*
Anderson M 66
Andersson S 38, *92, 93*
Anding D 207
Andresson S 186
Angel J C 30
Angus Leppan P 39, *92, 94*
Annand K P *109*
Annoni A *344, 345*
Anselin L 13, 102, 203, 205, 385, 391
Anthony A *223*
Anuta P E 193
Apple Computer Incorporated 278, 431
Applegate L M 409
Arai K 285
Arbia G 170

Archer H *298*
Archer J C *430*
Archibald P D 198, 201
Ardrey R 88
Armstrong M P 122, 257, 407, 410, 411, *133*
Arnheim R 428, 437
Arno M 185, 381, 384
Aronoff S 5, 10, 15, 83, 87, 301, 320, 325, *317*
Aronson P B 193, 260, 263, 339
Arthur D W G 140
Artin E 233
Arur M G *78*
Asano Y *47*
ASPRS 169
Asrar G 192, 205, 206
Astrahan M M 156
AT&T Bell Laboratories 215
Atkey R G *26*
Atkins M 86
Auerbach S 305
Aumann G 278
AURISA *58, 62, 65, 67*
AUSLIG *60*
Avni H 222
Awater R H C M *155*
Ayabe K 285
Aybet J 338, 345

Babbage R *64*
Bachi R 429, 430
Badhwar G D 195, 202
Baerwald T J 95
Bak P 299, 308, 310

599

Baker A M 171
Baker H H 351
Baker J C 180
Baker K *144*
Ballard D H 434
Balodis M 446
Band L E 206, 283, 284, 285
Bannink M H *156*
Banting D 84, 383
Barbier E B *10*
Barker G R 198
Barnard S T 272
Barr A 414, *229*
Barr C J *213*
Barrera R 197, 199
Barritt M 36
Bartolucci L A 191, 203
Barton B A 140
Barwinski K 517
Basoglu U 446
Bates M 422
Batjes N H *165*
Batten L G 299
Batty M 435
Baumgardner M F *155, 156, 224*
Bayard-White C 352
Beard C *134*
Beard M K 171, 182, 344, 435, *302*
Beaumont J R 33, 37, *4, 6, 109, 128, 140, 144*
Beckett P H T *154*
Bedard Y 47, 191, 192, 198, 200, 201, 206, 498, *304*
Bedell R 344
Beek K-J *155*
Beemster J G R *155, 156*
Belcher P *117, 120*
Bell S B M 149, 199, 232
Benjamin R I *148*
Bennett J L 406, 411
Bennett R J 389, *140*
Bentley J L 219
Bentley T J 82
Benyon D 10, *186*
Berry B J L 171, 389
Berry J K 13, 124, 130, 323, 329, 339, 361, 372, *9, 247, 286, 287, 298*
Berry J L 27
Bertin J 155, 430, 431, 437, 458
Bertke S E 193
Besag J E 392, 398, 399
Best R G *164*
van Beurden S A H A *164*
Bhatnagar S C 411

Bickmore D P 23, 34, *25, 223*
Bie S W *153, 154*
Billingsley F C 193, *227*
Bilmes J 435
Binks K 399
Birch J M 399
Bird D *148*
Birkoff G 277
Birugawa S *47*
Bishop M M *184*
Bishton A *134*
Bitterlich W 185, 381, 384
Bittlestone R *149*
Black J *59*
Blackburn J W *58, 59, 60*
Blais J A R 271
Blakemore M J 116, 185, 245, 382, *8, 244*
Blalock H M 434
Blanning R W 409
Blatchford R P *192*
Blum H 449
Bobrow D 418
Boehm B W 217, 483, 484
Bolland J D *111*
Bonczek R H 406, 407
Bonham-Carter G F 344, 390, *7, 173, 174, 176, 177, 178, 179, 183, 184*
Bonneton P *155*
Bonoma T V *140*
Boots B 126, 193
Borgida A 418
Borning A H 355
Bosma M 244
Bouma J 390, *154, 155, 156, 160, 163, 164*
Bourne L E 433
Bouwman A F *165*
Box E O 205
Boyce R F 156
Boyko K J *15, 16*
Boyle A R 191
Bracken I 5, 15, 260, 338, 339, 347, 378, 385
Brand M J D 35, 73
Brandenberger A J 179
Brandon O H *213*
Brandon S E *154*
Brassel K E 274, 288, 290, 292, 430, 464
Bratt P 353
Bredekamp J H 201
Breeuwsma A *155, 164*

Bregt A K *155, 156, 164*
Brewer C A 430
Bridge J S 313
Briggs D J 137, 342, 343, 344, 385, *187, 193, 198, 199*
Brodie M 415
Brodie M J 515
Brodie M L 418
Bromley R D F 478, *89, 297*
Brooks F P 217, 354
Broome F R 30, 122, *134*
Brotchie J F 66
Brown A T *223*
Brown C M 434
Brown G 86
Brown H 233
Brown M D 428, 432, 439
Brown M J 36
Bruegger B P 435
Brüggermann H 517
Brunsdon C *9*
van het Loo Brus D J H *164*
Bryant J 202
Bryant N A 191, 192, 198, 200, 344
Bryden R *74*
Bryson R A 429
Buchanan A 49
Bulens J D *164*
Bull G A 208
Bunce R G H *213*
Bundock M 261, 262
Bunge W 168
Bunschoten B *154, 160*
Burgess T M 170, *155, 159, 160*
Burke K C *223*
Burnhill P 86
Burns K L 308
Burr D 446
Burrough P A 5, 11, 83, 122, 168, 170, 185, 193, 198, 199, 200, 206, 227, 230, 269, 301, 305, 320, 330, 339, 341, 381, 390, *7, 153, 154, 155, 156, 158, 159, 160, 163, 164, 165, 177, 194, 195, 209, 224, 261, 317*
Burton I 88
Burton W 151
Bush V 352
Busoni E *155*
Butler B E *209*
Butler D R 203, 204
Buttenfield B P 102, 115, 287, 398, 429, 430, 432, 434, 436, 458, 460, 465
Buxton J *124*

Buxton R 4, 36, 37, 96, *28, 29, 30, 89, 94, 132*
Buzzell R D *143*

CACI *144*
CADalyst 354
Calkins H W 6, 10, 11, 17, 30, 45, 46, 106, 191, 407, 478, 481, 508, *8, 13, 139, 185, 192, 237, 239, 242, 244, 276, 297, 298, 301, 314*
Callaghan M 30
Callahan G M *13, 16*
Callander J 23, 27
Campbell J B 183, 185, 186, 202
Campbell J C 429, 432
Campbell J R 203
Canada Department of Forestry and Rural Development 185
Card D H 203
Carlbom I 308
Carlson E D 309, 406, 407, 411
Carpenter L 271
Carr J L 193
Carruthers A 512
Carter J R 10, 11, 102, 104
Casley D J 342
Cass R *121*
Castner H W 438, 439
Catling I *117, 120*
Caulfield I 76
Cavill M V 67
CCITT 245
Cebrian J A 308
Cederholm T 98
Centre National d'Etudes Spatiales 523
Chadha S M *76*
Chakravarthy U S 421
Challen K 300, 305
Chamberlin D D 156
Chambers D 478
Chambers R J M 431
Chan K 373
Chandra N 422
Chandrasekhar N 219
Chapman M A 271
Chappuis A *77*
Charlton M E 385, 397, 399, *9*
Charlwood G 261, 263
Chavez P S *13*
Chazelle B 219
Chelst K 404
Chen P P 253, 407
Chen S 79, *80*

Chen Z 199
Chen Z-T 280
Chen Shupeng 39, *5*
Cheng Ji-Cheng *80*
Chinese Academy of Sciences *79*
Chorley R 4, 36, 37, 96, 481, *28, 29, 30, 94, 132*
Chow A L K 247
Chow L *133*
Chrisman N R 22, 28, 30, 33, 84, 112, 122, 132, 165, 168, 169, 171, 172, 178, 180, 182, 185, 200, 204, 227, 235, 285, 323, 324, 341, 344, 381, 383, 384, *89, 194, 196, 298, 318, 319*
Christensen A H J 277, 278
Christiansen H N 304
Christianson C J 30
Church R 11
Churchman C W 235
Cibula W G 203
Civco D 436
Claire R W 373
Clark D M 16, 39, 64, 178, 325, *3, 7, 8, 12, 63, 185, 186, 196, 201, 203, 220, 223, 227, 228*
Clark I 309
Clark J L 422
Clark J W 129
Clark P 175, 178, 182, 204, *223*
Clark P K *188, 194*
Clark R D S 67
Clark S R 15, *300*
Clark W F 263
Clarke A L 61, 116, 278, 478, 508, *94, 191, 192*
Clarke D M *9, 74*
Clarke K C 10, 12, 103, 271, 435
Clarke M 411
Claussem H *124*
Clayton A R *214*
Clayton C *128*
Clayton D 392
Cleaves D 479
Cleveland W S 428, 431, 438
Cliff A D 170, 193, 391
Clifford P 392
Cobb M C *32*
Cochrane D 288
Cocks K D 38, 135, 136, 139, *63, 66, 225*
Codd E F 149, 228, 229, 257, 258, 416
Cohen J 217

Cohen P R *183*
Cohon J L 403
Colby J D *218, 223*
Cole G *111*
Cole K *133*
Collins J 252
Collins T *143*
Collins W G *128*
Colwell R N 192
Comerma J *160*
Commanger H S 494
Commission of the European Communities *186, 188, 193*
Committee on Earth Sciences 220
Committee on Global Change 220
Congalton R G 101, 203
Conklin J 352
Cook B G *153*
Cook R N 23, 26
Cooke D F *297*
Cooper H J 206
Cooper M A R 144
Coote A M *32*
Copeland B J 263
Coppock J T 3, 4, 9, 34, 35, 36, 45, 111, *73, 87, 305, 313, 321*
Corbett J P 31, 151, 327, *134*
Cormack S 288
Corr D G 185, 186, 191, 203, *210*
Costanza R 206, 207, 208
Costanzo C M 128
Couclelis H 112, *316*
Coulson M G 478, *89, 297*
Coulson M R 84, 86
Cowen D J 11, 12, 13, 261, 338, 341, *3, 9, 247, 250, 302, 303, 305, 307*
Cox B J 264
Cox C W 430
Cox N J 151, 372
Craft A W 399
Craig W J *301, 315*
Crain I K 16, 17, 48
Crapper P F 199
Crawford J R 66
Crawley K J 88
Croasdale M R 399
Cromley R G 446
Croom F 231
Cross A E 185, 186, 191, 203, 397, *9, 210*
Crosilla F 171
Crosson W L 206
Croswell P L 15, *298, 300*
Croze H *220, 223*

601

Author index

Csillag F 168
Csillag M 468, 469
Cuddy S M 67
Cullingford D *144*
Cunningham C G 181
Curran P J 204, 205
Cutter S L 376
Cuzick J 399

Dacey M F 372
Dale P F 6, 38, 82, 87, 88, 138, 181, 331, *4, 6, 58, 86, 91, 92, 93, 94, 97, 156, 304, 319*
Dalton M 292, 354
Dangermond J 3, 10, 13, 15, 23, 32, 51, 59, 114, 124, 319, 323, 330, 338, 344, 348, 478, 479, 480, 515, *9, 80, 94, 191, 297, 300, 303, 304, 322*
Danziger J N 105
Darius P *156*
Daroussin J *155*
Dartington Institute *214*
Date C J 254, 255, 256, 258, 261
Dave V S 78
Davenport T H *149*
David S M 191
Davis A W 207
Davis D L 278, 405
Davis F W 13, 47, 112, 186, 193, 199, 205, 206, 240, 325, 339, 385, *171, 207*
Davis J C 390
Davis J R 159, 411, 422, *66, 67*
Davis J S 353
Davis S M 203
Dawson M 315
Day T 272, 285, 292, 354
De S 410
De Floriani L 286
De Jong W 75
de Man E 10
Deacon A T *223*
Dear M 403
Deering D 195, 204, 205
Defanti T A 428, 432, 439
Deichmann U 385
DeLotto J L 283
DeLucia A 432
Demko G J 384
Denham C 183
Densham P J 11, 115, 257, 392, 403, 407, 410, 411, *9, 77, 139, 142, 149, 244, 276, 299, 301*
Dent B D 430, 437

Department of Health and Social Security 75
Department of the Environment 37, 69, 71, 73, 74, 76, 96, 186, 485, *25, 29, 30, 66, 88, 101, 193, 297*
Department of the Interior 88
Department of Trade and Industry *141*
Deter R S 353
Devereux B J 385
Devine H A 11, 82, 84
Dewdney J C 30, 184, *128*
Dias H D 74
Diaz B M 149, 199, 232
Dickey J W 66
Dickinson H J 10, 11, 17, 46, 481, 508, *244*
Didier M *10, 192*
Diello J 23, 27
van Diepen C A *155, 164*
Diggle P 128, 390, 396
Digital Cartographic Data Standards Task Force 125, 165, 166, 169, 180, 322, 346, 523, 524, *318*
Dikau R 283
Dimmick S 262
Dinstein I 283
Dixon J F 409, *142*
Dixon T M *223*
Dobes Z 155, 160
Dobkin D 228
Dobson M W 411, 77
Doerschler J S 446, 449, 452, 454, 455
Dolk D R 409
Domaratz M A *15, 16*
Dondis D A 437
Donimowski R L 433
Dougenik J A 132
Douglas D H 185, 247, 283, 284
Dowers S *321*
Dowman I 185
Downey J 314
Downing P *213*
Downs A 105, 106
Dowson E 85
Doytsher Y 138
Dozier J 193, 199, 203, 204, 205, 206, 284, 285
Driessen P M *155*
Drown C W 181
Drummond J 244, *75, 81*
Drysdale R L 220
Dubayah R 193, 199, 205

Duboc O 166
Duchesneau T D 498
Dudycha D J 343
Dueker K J 11, 26, 166, 341, 478, *247, 299, 300, 304, 305*
Duell T 67
Duffield B S 35
Duggin M J 193, 195
Duke J 352
Dulaney W *209*
Dulton W H 105
Dumanski J B *154, 155, 164*
Dunn C 122
Dutton G 160, 463
Dye D G *209*

Eagleson P S 207
Earth System Sciences Committee 7, *207, 217, 220*
Easterfield M 314, 344
Eastman J R 15, 124, 439
Eather P T 59
Ebdon D 127
Ebinger L R 446, *134*
Ebner H 273, 278
Edelsbrunner H 219, 227, 275
Eden R *64*
Edney P 67
Edralin J *74, 75, 78*
Edwards G 47, 191, 192, 198, 200, 201, 206, *304*
Edwards R 399
Egenhofer M J 92, 103, 113, 124, 154, 155, 156, 157, 160, 198, 227, 229, 230, 231, 233, 235, 236, 245, 264, 310, 320, 323, 325, 330, 339, 461, 515, 517, *122, 134, 172, 174, 314*
Ehlers M 47, 191, 192, 198, 200, 201, 206, 207, *304*
Eichhorn G 87
El-Beik A H A *128*
Elachi C 192, 195
Elliot D B 202
Ellis H 253
Ellis M Y *202*
Ellwood D J *176*
Elnicki R A 405
Elvidge C D 203
Emerson R W 438
Enderle G 528
Engel H 185
Englund E *155*
Environmental Protection Agency *185*

Environmental Systems Research Institute 86, 97, 159, 261, 338, 339, 340, 349
Eos Science Steering Committee 196
Epstein E F 4, 116, 186, 496, 498, 499, *54, 94, 194*
Erich R W 202
Estes J E 5, 6, 10, 11, 83, 103, 120, 191, 193, 194, 198, 199, 201, 202, 203, 320, *128, 218, 227, 250, 317*
Eswaran K P 156
Etak 159
Evans I S 282, *132*
Evans M *143*
Everett J 192, 208
Eyre L A 38, 186
Eyton J R 288

Fagin R 259
Falcidieno B 286
Fandrei G *278*
Fanon F *73*
Fanshawe J *224*
FAO *155*
Fedra K 411
Fegeas R G 31, *13, 15, 16*
Feigenbaum E A 414, *229*
Feuchtwanger M 330
FICCDC *18*
Fiebig M J *67*
Field R C 11
Fienberg S E *184*
Finch S 21, 35, 186
Fingleton B 390, 396
Fischler M A 272
Fisher P F 46, 87, 112, 137, 166, 176, 180, 186, 240, 241, 248, 376, 427, 460, 473, *104, 194*
Fisher T 305, 309
Fitzpatrick-Lins K 171, 180, 186
Flemming M D 191, 203
Fletcher G E *250*
Flew A G 429
Flores F 161
Flowerdew R 114, 124, 184, 323, 328, 340, 342, 343, 383, 384, 385, 506, *189, 262*
Flynn J J 300, 302
Foley J D 288, 290, 354
Foley M E 481
Foresman T W *250*
Forrest M D 203
Forshaw M R B 193
Fosnight E A 254

Foster M J 56
Fotheringham A S 435
Fournier A 271
Fowler R J 273
Frank A U 13, 50, 103, 112, 122, 150, 155, 156, 160, 197, 199, 227, 229, 232, 233, 235, 236, 260, 264, 323, 330, 342, 422, 435, 438, *318*
Franklin S E 203
Franklin W M R 3, 15, 113, 217, 219, 220, 228, 230, 299, 422, *134, 321*
Fraser R S 195
Fraser-Robinson J *148*
Frederiksen P 465
Freedman C 478, *297, 300, 303, 304*
Freedom of Information Act 494, 495
Freeman H R 115, 330, 423, 436, 446, 449, 451, 452
Freeman J 153, 230, 310
French J R 308
French R *118*
Freundschuh S M 160, 229
Frew J 284, 285
Friedman L M 491
Fritsch D 309, 314
Frost and Sullivan Incorporated *115*
Fry J P 515
Fu K 201, 202
Fuchs M 206
Fulton P N 183
Furley P A 342, 385
Fussel D 271

Gaal G *172*
Gahegan M N 261
Gaits G M 35
Gale B T *143*
Gallaire H 417
Gamezo M U 432
Gardiner V 176
Gardiner-Hill R C *26, 31*
Garey M R 222
Gargantini I 230
Garner B J 38, 67, 136, *4, 5, 67, 92, 93*
Garnsworthy J 74
Gateaud J *104*
Gatrell A C 112, 120, 121, 129, 130, 149, 228, 231, 234, 322, 376, 390, 460, 461, *255*
Gault I *260*
Gauthier C 283
Gaydos L 203
Geoffrion A M 406

Gerrard J 390
Gerrard M H 399
Getis A 126, 193
Ghosh S K 179
Giblin P 150
Gibson R J *26, 32*
Gibson W 354
Giddings G M 411
Gilbert P 15
Giles R H 23, *9*
Gill A 230
Gillard A A *144*
Gilliand J 478
Gilmartin P P 430, 437
Giltrap D J *155*
Ginzberg M J 406
Girard M-C *153, 154*
GIS World 299, 319, 324, 477
Gittings B M 82, 84, *321*
Goddard J 10
Goddard Space Flight Center 196, 197, 198
Godwin L *134*
Goel N S 207
Goetz A F H 204
Goff T E *210*
Golbéry L 77
Gold C 288
Goldberg A 217
Goldberg M 202, 203, 422
Golledge R G 83, 102, 128
Golstein H 30
Gonzalez R C 278
Goodchild M F 3, 6, 11, 13, 14, 37, 46, 57, 82, 84, 85, 96, 101, 102, 103, 119, 124, 126, 128, 149, 166, 170, 194, 199, 240, 241, 299, 301, 310, 320, 323, 341, 381, 384, 385, 389, 411, 479, 484, 485, *8, 74, 78, 105, 142, 299, 300, 301, 314, 315, 318, 319, 321*
Goodenough D G 200, 201, 202, 203, 344
Goodspeed J 67
Gopal S 6, 103, 166, 381, 384, *318*
Gopalan N *78*
Goran W 422
Gorry G A 403, 406, *141*
Gorte B 345
Gottschalk H-J 279
Gould M D 159, 160, 411
Gould P R 122
Goulette A M 446, *134*
Goward S N *209*

Grace B F 411
Graetz R D 207
Grandfield A W 124
Grant I W 411, 66, 67
Grant N G 97
Grave M 528
Gravel G 283
Gray D A 342, 385
Gray P *142*
Gray S 73
Greasley I 230
Green D 84
Green M 184, 323, 385
Green N P A 37, 87, 200, 338, 341, 347, 353, 375
Green P *28*
Greener S *67*
Gregoire T G 185, 200
Gregor W C 404
Gregory D 389
Griffin J M 481
Griffin M W 271
Griffith D A 128, 185, 391
Grimshaw D J 35
Groop R E 430
de Gruijter J J *154, 155, 156*
Grun A 278
Grunreich D 458, 469
Guevara J A 280, *81*
Guibas L 275, 280
Guinn R 69
Gulati A K *78*
Günther O 49, 435
Guptill S C 31, 51, 116, 261, 262, 263, 319, 320, 324, 325, 330, 345, 462, 473, 478, 479, 480, 484, 517, *12, 13, 15, 16, 17, 30, 61, 108, 193, 214, 318*
Gurd F B *247*
Gurney A J 30
Guttag J 232
Guttman A 233

Haber R N 431
Hägerstrand T 23, 389, *4, 39, 40*
Haggett P 124
Hajic E J 202
Hake G 457
Hall F G 195, 202, 204, 205
Hall G B 341
Hall P A V 352
Hallam C A 31, *13*
Haller M 277
Haller S M 155, 160

Hamilton A C *87*
Hamilton W L 84
Hammer M 421, *149*
Hammond N 355
Han K H *128*
Hannah M J 285
Hanson E N 417, 421
Haralick R M 200, 201, 202, 283, 372
Harbaugh J W 315
Harding A E 203
Hardy E E 179, 180, 186, 202, *264, 276*
Harig J 301
Harnden E 59
Harper E A 78
Harris B *237*
Harris D P *172*
Harris N *92*
Harrison D 446
Harrison J D *205*
Harslem E 156
Hart A *59*
Hart J F 83, *73*
Hartley R P 39, *188*
Harvey D R *213*
Haskell A 193
Hastings D A 16, 39, 64, 178, 325, *3, 7, 8, 12, 63, 74, 185, 186, 196, 201, 203, 218, 223, 229*
Haugen E 154
Hawkins J M 457
Hay A M 204, 205
Hayes G E 165
Haywood P E 165, 346, 526, 527, 529, *30, 33, 34, 36*
Hazelhoff L 282, *155*
Hazelton N W J 301, 314
Head C G 437
Healey R G 12, 83, 113, 127, 262, 328, 342, 345, 385, *321*
Healey R J 339
Hearnshaw H M 103, 120, 253, 254, 263, 264, 323, 379
Hearst M 414, 418, 419
Heckman B 446
van Heesen H C *155*
Helldén U *155, 165*
Heller M 50, 113, 127, 199, 204, 235, 270, 274, 275, 278, 280, 301, 304, 325, 376, 380, 460, 469, *12, 15, 314*
Hendriks C M A *164*
Hendrix G 422
Henriksen S W 290
Her Majesty's Land Registry *88*

Her Majesty's Stationery Office *28, 132*
Heres L *124*
Herndon L *155*
Herring J R 15, 92, 113, 124, 156, 157, 198, 231, 236, 245, 263, 264, 320, 325, 339, 461, 515, 517, *122, 134, 172, 174, 314*
Herskovits A 154, 229
Herzog A 274, 290, 464
Heuvelink G B M 206, 339, 341, *164*
Hewitt C 418
Heyn B N 430
Heywood D I 82, 83
Hezlep W 384
Hibbard W 290
Hickin B W *250*
Hickman D L 481
Higgins M J 39, *188*
Higgs G 5, 338, 347, 385
Hill G J E 191
Hinterberger H 233
Hirsch S A 446
Hirschberg D S 223
Hirschheim R 485
Hirst R *67*
Hittelman A M *225*
Hoare C A R 217
Hodgson J M *157*
Hodgson M 261
Hoff W A 420
Hoffer R M 94, 191, 202, 203
Hoffmann C 228
Hoffmeister E D 469
von Hohenbalken B 121
Hogg D C 185, 186, *210*
Hogg J 261
Hoggs D C 191, 203
Holben B N 195, 205, *209, 210*
Holland P W *184*
Holloway C A 411
Holroyd F 199
Holsapple C W 406, 407
van Holst A F *155*
Holstein L *89*
Honey S *119, 121, 124*
Honsaker J L 464
Hoogerwerf M *156, 160, 163*
Hooper C 352
Hopcroft J E 217, 218, 220
Hopgood F R A 528
Hopkin V D 438
Hopkins L 403
Hopmans J W *156*

Horn B K P 435
Horn D 314
Horn M 67
Horowitz E 233
Horwood E M *297, 299, 302*
Hössler R 273
Houlding S 309
House W C 406
House of Lords 36, 68, 526
Howe D R 253
Hsu S Y *128*
Hubbold R J 528
Hubert L 128
Hudson J C 27
Hudson R 36
Hugus M 278
Huijbregts C J *159, 160*
Hummel J *208*
Hurion R D 410
Hurle G *64*
Hutchinson C F 203
Hutchinson M F 48, 278, 283
Hutton P G 341

ICSU Panel on World Data Centres *224*
IGBP Special Committee *217, 218, 219*
Imhoff E 47, 429, 447, 448, 467
Inaba K 278
Indian Towing Co v. United States 500
Ingold J H 183
Ingram I K 15
Ingram K J 156, 263
Intergovernmental Oceanographic Commission *208*
Intergraph Corporation 156, 261
International Cartographic Association 135, 457
International Council of Scientific Unions 93, *204*
International Organisation for Standardisation 355
International Standards Organization 525, 528
Irby C 156
Iri M *52*
Irons J R 204
Isaacs M C *212*
Itai A 222
Ives M J *111*

Jacknow H R *13*
Jackson J E 137, 235

Jackson M J 46, 47, 48, 63, 113, 185, 191, 199, 324, 338, 344, 345, *90, 96, 104, 276*
Jager E 465
Jajoo B H 411
James P 27
Jankowski P 145, 146, 411, 465
Janks G F 429
Jarke M 421
Jarvis M *154*
Jarvis R S *285*
Jasinski M F 207
Jenkins G M 195
Jenks G F 430
Jensen J R 470
Jerie H C 75
Jeworrek J 471, 472
Jiwani Z 346
Joffe B A 82, *8*
Johnson B D *63*
Johnson C G *154*
Johnson C R 308
Johnson D S 222
Johnson M 152, 153, 154, 229, 310
Johnson R D 436
Johnson T 191
Johnston R J 389
Jones A R 203
Jones C B 308, 472
Jones R B *154*
Jones T A 308
Jordan L 339, 372
Jordan T G 103
Journel A G *159, 160*
Jupp D L B 194, 207
Justice C O 193, 195, 196, *209, 210*

Kainz W 230
Kalb V 205
Kaldor J 392
Kamijo S *124*
Kaneda K 292
Kanemasu E T 205, 206
Kankanhalli M 219
Karam G 422
Karimi H A 422
Karjala D S 495
Kata F 292
Kates R W 102
Kauth R J 202
Kavouras M 308
Kawauchi *53*

Keates J S 176, 177, 178, 181, 436, 438
Kedar-Cabelli S T 420
Keefer B J 185
Keen P G W 406, 407, 410
Keen T R 299
Kehris E 127, 385
Kelk B 50, 114, 149, 269, 300, 305, 313, *201, 207, 214*
Keller R M 420
Kelley A D 271
Kelly G D 191
Kelly P 446
Kemp K K 84, *319*
Kemp Z 264
Kennedy J L 26
Kennedy P *210, 211*
Kennedy S A 184, 380, 391, *223*
Kennie T J M 271, 299, 300
Kent W 259
van Keulen H *155, 164*
Keuper H F 191
Kidwell J 495
Kiefer R W 185
Kijima Y *49*
Kim M P *302*
Kim T J *302*
Kim W 350, 355, 418
Kimball R C 156, 404
Kimerling A J 430
Kimes D S 207
Kindleberger C *298, 299, 302, 303*
Kineman J J 16, 64, 178, 325, *3, 7, 8, 12, 63, 74, 185, 186, 196, 201, 203, 218, 220, 223, 227, 228*
King C W B 138
King D *155*
King R 160
King W R *142*
Kinneman D 39
Kinto Y *47*
Kirby K C 156
Kirk K 23, 27
Kitamura A *124*
Kleiner B 431
Klesh L 122, 324
Kloosterman B *154*
Klug A 148
Knill-Jones R P *183*
Knuth D E 218, 220, 229
Kolb C E 271, 292
Kolbusz J 292, 354
Kolm K 314
Konecny G 185, 239, 272

de Koning G H J *164*
Konsynski B R 409
Kooistra M J *155*
Korth H F 417
Korzybski A 167
Koshizuka T *52*
Koskkariov A V 11, 38
Kosslyn S M 428
Kostli A 273
Kotler P *140*
Kou Y *79, 81*
Kowalski R 417
Kraak M J 431
Kraemer K L 105
Kriegel H-P 233
Krishnanunni K 77
Krishnayya J G 77
Kruck E 185
Krum G L 308
Kubik K 171, 465
Kubo S 38, 67, 97, *5, 6, 14, 49, 81*
Kuennucke B H 84
Kuhn W 150, 235
van Kuilenburg J *154, 160*
Kuipers B 438
Kumar R S 77
Kumar S *78*
Kure J 75

L'Eplattenier R 290
de Laat P J M *155*
Lacroix V 449
Laflamme R A 269
Lahaije P *124*
Lai P C 480
Lai R C T 356
Laing A W *64*
Lakoff G 152, 153, 229, 435
Lam W K 271
Lam N S-N 274, 275, 380, 385
Lamp J *154*
LAMSAC *89, 90*
Landgraf H F 181
van Lanen H A J *155, 163, 164*
Langford M 385, *128*
Langran G 168, 178, 264, 436, 207, 323
Lanigan J C 181
Larsen H K 75
Larsen R C 156, 263
Lasseter T 309
Lassez C 418
Lauer D 196
Laurillard D 352

Laut P 67
Lauzon J P 245, 324
Lavin S J 430
Lawrence D H 185, 186, 191, 203, *210*
Lay H G 470
Lay J C 30
Le Drew E F 343
Leahy F J 301, 314
Leanoard J J 430
Lee T S *247*
Leeder M R 313
Leenaers H 305, *163, 164, 165*
Lefschetz S 233
Leick A 186, *87*
Lelewer D A 223
Lemmens M J P M 272
Lesser V 418
Lesslie R G *63*
Lewis P 262
Li X Z 207, *79*
Li Z N 434, 464
Lichtner W *124*
Liem R 345
Lieth H *208*
Lightfoot D R 203, 204
Liley R 347
Lille J *9*
Lillehagen F 528
Lillesand T M 185
Little J J 273
Lloyd J W 414, 416, 417
Lo C P 245, *128*
Lobeck A K 429
Lochovsky F H 46, 51, *186*
Lochovsky L C 253
Lodwick W A 341, 384
Loftus E F 433
Logan T L 192, 198, 200, 344
Lohmann P 185
Lolonis P 410
Longley I *250*
Longley P 435
Loomes M 148
Loon J C 278
Lorie R A 156, 261
Loughmiller G *119*
Lovejoy S 195
Loveland T R *154*
Lovett R *111*
LREIS *79*
Luger G L 463
Lupian A E *300*
Lury D A 342
Lyall G A 35

Lynch L G *153*
Lyons H G *85*
Lyons K J 171, *65*
Lyytinen K 485

MacDonald C L 16, 17
Mace R S 271, 292
MacEachren A E 429, 430, 432
Mackaay E 491
Mackaness W A 102, 115, 287, 398, 437, 473
Mackenzie H G *154, 198*
Mackey B G *63*
Mackinlay J 429, 436, 437, 440
Madams R *210, 211*
Madnick S 418
Maeder S R *278*
Maes J *156*
Maffini G 185, 200, 381, 384, 480
Magnenat-Thalman N 354
Maguire D J 3, 5, 6, 10, 13, 16, 21, 22, 45, 49, 51, 56, 82, 87, 101, 103, 104, 111, 114, 120, 124, 227, 253, 254, 263, 264, 319, 322, 323, 324, 325, 328, 329, 333, 337, 351, 379, 385, 405, 479, 490, 506, 515, *5, 8, 88, 128, 191, 226, 250, 302, 314, 315, 316, 317, 322*
Maher R V 84
Mahoney H M *304*
Mahoney R P 33, 121, *6, 28, 29, 88, 92, 104, 113, 247*
Maier D 418
Majumder K L 77
Makarovic B 271, 272
Malila W 195
Malin M C 271, *212*
Maling D H 50, 68, 112, 120, 124, 135, 137, 138, 140, 144, 145, 183, 248, 329, 376, 378
Malone T W *148*
Mandelbrot B B 125, 283, 465, *156*
Manheim M L *78*
Mann J F 495
Mansfield L 277
Mantey P E 411
Mapping Awareness 477
Mapping Science Committee, National Academy of Sciences 19
Marble D F 5, 6, 13, 22, 27, 30, 45, 93, 102, 111, 191, 245, 324, 389, 407, 478, 480, 484, *185, 314*
Marchionini G 353
Mark D M 50, 112, 122, 124, 126,

152, 153, 154, 159, 160, 168, 193,
  229, 272, 273, 274, 282, 284, 286,
  308, 310, 355, 438, 458, 463, 465,
  468, 469, 473, *318*
Markandya A *10*
Markham B *209*
Marks D 284, 285
Marr D 431, 433
Marsman B *155*, *156*
Martin D 5, 385
Martin G J 27
Martin J 251, 252, 253, 257
Martin P H 495
Marx R W 338, *134*, *135*, *305*
Mason D C 185, 186, 191, 199, 203,
  338, 345, *210*, *214*
Mason K 5
Masry S 308
Masser I 77, 84, 96, *315*
Mateo A *160*
Mather P M 12, 139, *173*
Matheron G *159*, *59*
Matieda I Cm 77
Matsui I *47*
Matthews E *208*
Mausbach M J *154*, *155*, *165*
Mauzon J P 480
McAleese R 352
McAulay I 301
McBratney A B *154*, *155*, *156*, *160*,
  163
McConalogue D J *29*
McCormack D E *155*
McCormick B H 428, 432, 430
McCormick S 353
McCullagh M J 269, 274, 277, 288
McEwen L J 84
McEwen R B *12*, *13*
McGill R 428, 438
McGillem C D 193
McGranaghan M 158, 159, 160, 229,
  245, 324, 480
McGuigan F J 432
McGwire K E *250*
McHarg I L 13, 102, 330, 372, *300*
McKenna R *143*
McKeown D M 203, 356
McKoon G 438
McLaren R A 261, 271, 300, 301, 347,
  94
McLaughlin J D 6, 181, *4*, *86*, *92*, *97*
McLean E R *142*
McMaster R B 429, 468, 469, 470
McNamara T P 438

McRae S 479
Mead R A 203, 480.
Medin D L 152
Mehl J W 156
Meier A 261, 307
Meijerink A M J *165*
Meixler D B *134*
Mel B W 216
Melley M 171
Menon S 11, 120, 198, 199, 201, 420,
  421, 422, *218*, *227*
Merchant D C 171, 179
Merrill D W 132
Mertz F 207
Mesev T *250*
Methley B D F 144
Metzger D R *225*
Meyer U 465, 469
Meyer W *247*, *302*, *305*, *307*
Meyerson M *234*, *298*
Michaelsen J 205
Michalski R S 420
Mikhail E H 172
Mikhail E M 142, 144
Mill A 299, 308, 310
Miller A I 432
Miller C L 269
Miller E E *156*
Miller G A 433
Miller G P 205
Miller K W 222
Miller P F 193
Miller R K 56, 122, 324
Millington A C *210*, *211*
Milnes K *119*
Minker J 417, 418
Minnesota Dept of Natural
  Resources, Division of Forestry
  280
Minnesota Dept of Natural
  Resources, Division of Minerals
  281
Minnesota Dept of Natural
  Resources, Office of Planning 280
Misra P 77, *78*
Mitchell C P *209*, *213*
Mitchell L *247*, *302*, *305*, *307*
Mitchell T M 420
Mitchell W B 31, *13*
Moellering H 398, 430, 461, 524
Moik J G 194, 201
Molenaar M 309, 314
Moll S H *229*
Monkhouse F J 429

Monmonier M S 5, 103, 126, 132,
  393, 429, 430, 432, 469, 470
Monson W 341
Montgomery D *142*
Montgomery P M *223*
Moon G C 254, 261, 263
Moon W M *183*
Mooneyhan D W *205*
Moore A W *153*
Moore D M 66, *180*
Moore R 56, 96
Moran L 161
Morehouse S 15, 260, 261, 341
Moreland W H *300*
Morgan J M 83
Morgenstern M 418
Morrill R L 102
Morrison J L 4, 33, 67, 82, 111, 124,
  165, 175, 176, 323, 467, *30*, *317*
Morse B W 422
Morton G M 463
Morton M S 403, 406
Moser M G 422
Moss O F 65
Mosteller F 431
Mott J J *63*, *185*, *193*
Moulton J R 203
Mounsey H M 6, 16, 22, 37, 39, 70,
  84, 137, 177, 338, 341, 342, 343,
  344, 348, 351, 375, 385, *3*, *7*, *29*,
  193, *198*, *199*, *201*, *208*, *225*, *302*,
  305
Mozzi E 344, 345
Muehrcke P 124, 129, 132, 165, 168,
  175, 176, 323, 428, 436, 439, 466
Muessig L F *277*
Mukai Y 285
Mulla D M 193
Muller J-C 116, 126, 129, 130, 176,
  199, 278, 292, 329, 423, 436, 460,
  464, 465, 469, *33*, *75*, *81*, *105*, *189*,
  300
Muller J-P 185, 272, 285, 292, 354,
  223
Munkres J 233
Murphy P A 67
Murphy R E 205
Musgrave F K 271, 292
Musser D 233
Mylopoulos J 414, 415, 515

Nag P 77, *129*
Nagao M 285
NAGIS 98

Author index

Nagy G 227, 286
Nagy Z *264*
Naithani K K 77
Nakamae E 292
Nakazawa T 285
Nanninga P M 199, *67*
Naqvi S 415, 419, 420
Narayan L R A *78*
Nash K *66*
Nastelin J 449
National Academy of Sciences 499
National Center for Geographic Information and Analysis 95, 396, 460, *315*
National Computer Graphics Association 528
National Geophysical Data Center 227
National Joint Utilities Group 37, 70, 248, *29*, *30*, *31*, *111*
National Oceanographic and Atmospheric Administration *222*
National Research Council 93
National Space Science Data Center 214
Natural Environmental Research Council *202*, *203*, *206*, *209*
Navon D 428
NCDCDS 227
Neal J G 155, 158, 160
Needham J *76*
Neiser N 152
Nelson R F 191, 203
Nelson T 352
Nemani R R 206
van de Nes Th. J *155*
Newell J 399
Newell R G 12, 314, 344
Newkirk P *247*
Newland W L 203
Newman W M 290
Newton D 122
Newton P W *66*
NEXPRI 97
Nichol D G *67*
Nichols M 217
Nicholson R 347
Nickerson B G 436
Nicolas J 417
Nicoullaud J *155*
Nielsen D R 390, *154*, *155*, *163*
Nielsen J 352, 355
Nielson G M 271
Niemeyer D R 132

Nierstrasz O M 264
Nievergelt J 228, 233
Nijkamp P 403, *75*
Nilsson N J 414, 418, 451
Nishita T 292
Nitze R T *88*
Nordbeck S 23, 27, *39*
Norman J 207
Norris D A 36
Norris P 184
NRC *87*
Nunamaker J F 409
Nunes J 160
Nyerges T L 84, 145, 146, 342, 343, 347, 372, 465, *319*
Nyquist M O 203

O'Callaghan J F 38, 67, 136, 284, *4*, *5*, *67*, *92*, *93*
O'Neill M O 465
Obermeyer N J *302*
Odervwald R 203
Odland J 128
OECD *73*
Office of Technology Assessment 496
Official Journal of the European Community *187*
Ogrosky C E *128*
Ojima D S *205*
Okabe A *52*
Okamoto H *120*
Okumura K *124*
Okuno T *47*
Okx J P 305, *163*, *164*, *165*
Oldeman L R *155*, *156*
Oliver M A 193, 390, *159*, *163*, *164*
Olle T W 256
Olson J M 430, 439
Olson J S *208*
Olsson L *101*, *155*, *165*
Omohundro S M 216
Onofrei C *155*, *164*
Openshaw S 10, 14, 17, 72, 73, 115, 119, 127, 184, 323, 333, 351, 384, 385, 391, 393, 396, 397, 398, 399, 405, 409, 439, *9*, *130*, *132*, *133*, *140*, *142*, *144*, *145*, *299*, *314*, *325*
Ord J K 170, 193, 391
Ordnance Survey 241, 526, *25*, *27*, *30*, *36*
Ordnance Survey Review Committee 68
Orenstein J A 264
Oresky C 446

Orman L 409
Osborne S 354
Oswald H 278
Ottmann T A 219
Ottoson L 38, 67, 98, *4*, *5*, *40*, *41*, *92*, *93*, *128*, *133*
Ozemoy V M 11

Padmavathy A S 77
Palmer B 235
Pandey M K *78*
Papadopoulos S 352
Pape D 272
Paradis A R 299, 309, *201*
Parent P 11, 101
Park S E 222
Parker H D 11, 94, 191, 200
Parker P 339, 372
Parrott R *8*, *297*, *303*, *314*
Parry R B 5, 179, 325
Parsloe E 352
Parthasaradhi E U R 77
Parvey C A 38, 135, 136, 139, *66*, *225*
Pascoe R T 345, 515
Paterson D L 202
Pathan S K 77
Pathirana S 186
Pavlidis T 436
Pazner M 156
Peacock D *111*
Peano G 463
Pearce D *10*
Pearce M L *213*
Pearson J C 292
Pech R P 207
Peddle D R 203
Pellew R A *205*
Penny J P 345, 515
Penridge L K 194, 207
Peplies R W 191
Perkal J 464, 471
Perkins C R 5, 179, 325
Perl Y 222
Perrett P *65*
Perring F H 23
Petach M *164*
Petch J R 82, 83
Petchenik B B 23, 92, *116*
Peters T *140*
Petersen G W 204
Peterson D L 206
Peterson J L 215
Peterson M 430
Petrie G 299

Petrou M 185, 186, 191, 203, *210*
Peucker T K 33, 166, 185, 200, 227, 235, 247, 272, 273, 274, 284, 288, 464
Peuquet D J 5, 6, 13, 51, 120, 154, 191, 198, 199, 200, 227, 320, 321, 325, 328, 329, 330, 339, 343, 420, 421, 422, 435, 515, 517
Peuther D *260*
Pevsner S 345
Pfefferkorn C 446
Philips W 263
Phillips A *118, 119*
Phillips M *60*
Phillips R J 432
Phillips W W 15, 156
Pienovi C 286
Piercy N *143*
Pierece L L 206
Pike R J 282, 283
Pinker S 433, 434
Piquet-Pellorce D 517
Piscator I *43*
Piwowar J M 343
Pixar Incorporated 299, 300
Pleijsier L K *155*
Plunkett G 202, 203
Poiker T K 84
Porcher E *280*
Potts D F 206
Powitz B M 469
Preece K M *63*
Preparata F P 220, 227, 275, 278, 280
Press L 349
Preusser A 288
Price S 264
Price Waterhouse *321*
Prince S *210, 211*
Prisley S P 185, 200, 480
Przymusinski T C 414, 417
Puissegur A 494, 498
Pullar D 156, 230, 231, 310
Puniard D J *64*
Pyle I C 217

Quade E S *233, 238*
Quarmby N A *212*
Quarterman J S 215

Rada J *76*
Raetzsch H 278
Raisz E J 429
Ramachandran A *78*

Ramer U 449
Ramey B *154*
Rao M K 77
Raper J F 10, 37, 50, 82, 87, 104, 114, 149, 269, 301, 310, 312, 314, 319, 324, 325, 353, *201, 207, 323*
Raper K B *88*
Rappolt C *155, 164*
Rapp S *143*
Rasmussen J 437
Rasool S I *205*
Ratcliff R 438
Reck R *208*
Redfern P *128, 129, 130, 136*
Reed C N 15, 484
van Reeuwijk L P *155*
Reeves R G 193, 207
Reijerlink J G A *164*
Reiman R *270*
Reinds G J *164*
Reinhardt W 273
Reisner P 156
Reitsma R 411
Rejmanek M 203
Reminga v. United States 500
Ren F *80*
Rencz A N *178, 179*
Requicha A A G 299, 307
Reybold W U 177, *154, 165*
Rhind D W 3, 4, 9, 11, 13, 16, 22, 23, 29, 30, 31, 34, 35, 36, 37, 45, 70, 72, 81, 82, 96, 104, 111, 116, 151, 175, 178, 182, 183, 186, 200, 204, 245, 324, 332, 338, 341, 343, 351, 372, 375, 439, 462, *6, 8, 16, 23, 28, 29, 39, 73, 87, 123, 128, 129, 132, 133, 136, 139, 187, 188, 192, 194, 223, 255, 256, 304, 305, 313, 315, 321, 323*
Rice W 203
Rich C 217
Richards J A 192, 201, 202, 203, 207
Richards S 292, 354
Richardson D E 465, 466
Richardson L F 125, 428
Richardus P 135, 137, 143
Ricketts T J 392
Riezebos H Th. *164*
Ripley B D 390, 396
Rizzo B R 46, 479, 484
Roach J T 179, 180, 186, 202, *264, 276*
Robbins A M *134*
Robert P *165*

Roberts S A 261
Robertson A H 431
Robertson G W *223*
Robertson P A 67
Robey T *63*
Robinette A *3, 8, 261, 262, 272, 277, 297, 303, 314*
Robinove C J 202, 330
Robinson A 175, 176
Robinson A D 216
Robinson A H 47, 92, 124, 165, 167, 323, 429, 439, 457
Robinson G 458
Robinson G K 184
Robinson G M 342, 385
Robinson G R *214*
Robinson J 196
Robinson V 235
Robinson V B 122, 324, 422
Rock B N 203
Rodney W *73*
Roe K 103
van Roessel J W 254, 261, 372
Rogers D F 286, 288, 290
Rogers P J 176, *177*
Roitman H 496
Romig H G 165
de Roo A P J 282, *155*
Rosch E 152
Rosenfield G 171
Rosinski R R 433
Rossiter D *156*
Rossmeissel H J *15, 16*
Rothermel J 446
Rothman J *140*
Rowe L A 263, 264
Rowekamp T 277
Rowley J 15, 78
Rowley P D 181
Rowntree L 103
Roy A G 283
Roy J R *66*
Royal Institute of Navigation *124*
Royal Society 135
Rozema W J 282
Rubakhin V F 432
Rüber O 306
Ruggles C L N 351
Running S W 202, 206
Rural Regional Development Newsletter *75*
Rushton G 27, 257, 403, 407, 410, *299*
Russell J S *156, 247*
Rutherford I *111*

Rystedt B 38, 67, 98, *4*, *5*, *43*, *92*, *93*, *128*, *133*

Saalfeld A 230, 343, 344
Sacerdoti E 422
Sacks S 132
Sadovski A *153*
Sagalowicz D 422
Sailer C T 193, 203
Sakashita S 246
Sale R D 124, 165, 175, 176, 323
Salgé F 165, 517
Salijevic R *59*
Salmon R 299, 300
Salmona J 478
Salvaggio C 195
Samaddar S 217
Sambura A *59*
Samet H 5, 6, 49, 124, 149, 199, 227, 230, 233, 234, 325, 434, 463, *174*
Sanesi G *155*
Sanfhvi N 404
Santek D 290
Santure L 261
SASPRSC 98
Satterwhite M 203
Saull R J 195, *210*, *211*, *212*
Saxena M *77*
Saxton W 480
Schacter B J 354
Schaeben H 305
Schafer G M *154*
Schek H-J 314
Schelling J *154*, *160*
Schertz D L *155*
Schertzer D 195
Schettini R 344, 345
Schiwietz M 233
Schmandt C M 159
Schmidt A H 287
Schneider R 233
Schneiderman B 160, 353, 354
Schonhage S 221
Schorn P 228
Schott J R 195
Schoumans O F *164*
Schultz J 404
Schultze C L *238*
Schumaker L L 274, 275
Schut G H 274, 380
Schweitzer R H 30
Sclafer M N 165
Scott D J 432, 436, 437
Scott Morton M S *141*

Seaborn D W 261
Sederberg T W 304
Sedgewick R 220, 436
Sedunary M E *89*, *93*
Seeger B 233
Seldon D D 481
Sellers P J 204, 205
Selvin S 132
Sen L 484
Senior M L 130
Seshan M 219
Settle J J 203
Sevcik K 233
Seymour W A *23*
Shamos M I 220, 227, 275, 278, 280
Shand P J 56, 96
Shanmugam K 283
Shapiro L G 372, 417
Shapiro S C 155, 158, 160
Shariari M R *163*
Sharpe R *66*
Shaw M A 23, 34
Shepherd I D H 49, 87, 114, 323, 341, *74*
Sheppard V L O *85*
Sheridan M F *212*
Shetler T 349
Shi Z *79*
Shinar W *305*
Shipman J 203
Shirley W L *3*, *9*, *247*, *250*
Shiryaev E E 47, 242
Shivakumar J 156, 263
Shmutter B 137, 138
Shneiderman B 156
Shortridge B G 430, 437
Shumway C 30
Shyue S W 171
Sicherman A 11
Siderelis K C *3*, *8*, *247*, *250*, *264*, *270*, *275*, *297*, *303*
Siebold J *124*
Siegel M D 421
Sigle M 273
Sigmund J M 181
Silberschatz A 215, 417
Silver D 228
Silverman B G *143*
Simonett D S 13, 23, 47, 112, 186, 192, 193, 200, 206, 207, 208, 240, 325, 339, 385, *171*, *207*
Simpson S R *85*
Simpson T W 180
Singh C B *79*

Singh G *93*
Singh S M 195
Sinha A K 262
Sinton D 167, 168, 169, 171, 323
Skelton N 432
Skiena S S 216
Sklar F H 206, 207, 208
Slama C C 290
Slater M 299, 300
Slingerland R 299
Sloan T M *321*
Slocum J 422
Slocum T A 430
Smith A B *35*, *118*, *124*
Smith D C P 156, 415
Smith D D *164*
Smith D M 193, 389
Smith D R 11, 299, 309, *201*
Smith E A 206
Smith E E 152
Smith G H 429
Smith J A 193, 194, 201
Smith J L 185, 200, 262, *154*, *198*
Smith J M 415
Smith K L 23, 32
Smith L *64*
Smith M O 203
Smith N S 262
Smith P 73
Smith R 430
Smith T R 11, 49, 64, 115, 120, 198, 199, 201, 264, 420, 421, 422, *143*, *198*, *218*, *227*, *229*
Snodgrass R 264
Snyder J P 137, 138, 139, 141, 143, 144, 248
Soaw J F 462
Soil Conservation Service 177, 180, 186
Soil Survey Staff *153*, *157*
Somerville I 263
Sommers R *247*, *307*
Southard R B *12*
Sowton M 4, 35, 68, 70, 127, 178, 241, 262, 526, 527, 529, *3*, *13*, *14*, *25*, *28*, *30*, *108*, *111*, *123*, *131*, *132*, *133*, *304*
Spanier E 150, 233
Spanner M A 206
Sparks A *155*
Spatial Information Systems 287
Spiegelhalter D J *183*
Sprague R H 406, 407, 409
Sprinsky W H 142

Sproull R F 290
SSC Central Design Group *270*
Stallard D 422
Stanley D J 193
Stanton R B *198*
Star J L 5, 6, 10, 11, 83, 103, 120, 191, 193, 198, 199, 201, 320, *218*, *227*, *317*
Starr L E 31, 67, 127, 262, *3*, *12*, *13*, *20*, *23*, *131*, *133*, *304*, *305*
Starr M K 403
State of North Carolina *270*
Staufenbiel W 469
Stefanovic P 75, *81*
Stein A 339, 341, *156*, *160*, *163*, *164*
Steinitz C F 339, 372
Steinke T R 438
Steneker M 344
Stepp R E 420
Steven T A 181
Stevens S S 322
Stewart A *165*
Stewart J C *250*
Steyaert L T *227*
Stiefel M *297*
Stoakes M 309
Stohr E A 406
Stolfi J 275, 280
Stone R A 400
Stonebraker M R 263, 414, 417, 418, 419, 421
Strahler A H 191, 193, 194, 201, 203, 207
Strand T C 193
Strassen V 221
Strebel D E 204, 205
Stricker J N M *156*
Stroustrup B 217, 264
Stubblefield W A 463
Stutz F P *8*, *297*, *303*, *314*
Su S 262
Subaryono 341
Sugimura T 285
Suh S *302*
Suits G 195
Sukaviriya P 161
Sullivan J G 171, *247*
Sun D 219
Sun G Q 207
Sun Y *79*
Sun Microsystems 224
Sundaram K V *76*, *77*
Svoboda L 341
Svorou S 122, 154

Swain P H 203
Sweet D C 30, *299*
Swiss Society of Cartography 458
Switzer P 199
Switzer R 233
Szegö J *45*
Szelinski R 271

Tailor A M 185, 186, 191, 203, *210*
Talmy L 153, 229
Tanaka Y 246
Tang Q *79*
Tanic E 422
Tannenbaum E 343
Tarjan R E 220
Tarpley J D 204
Tavernier R *194*
Taylor D R F 26, 38, 63, 67, *5*, *92*, *314*
Taylor M A P *66*
Taylor P J 88, 389, 390, *319*, *323*
Taylor R M 438
Teorey T J 515
Terada T *47*
Terzopoulos D 271
TeSelle G W 177
Tessar P A *278*
Tetzloff D M 315
Tewari V K 410
Thalman D 354
Thapa K 464
Thatte S 264
Thearling K H 216
Theriault D G 12, 314, 344
Theurer C 290
Thielman C Y 155, 160
Thies N 156
Thissen D 429
Thom R 466
Thomas E N 429
Thomas G S 202
Thomas P J 180
Thomas R W 203
Thompson C N 28, 33
Thompson D 82
Thompson M M 179, 186, *12*
Thoone M *117*
Thornton J D *277*
Thrower N J 429
Tikunov V S 11, 38
Tinney L R 202, 203
Tobler W R 23, 27, 124, 129, 132, 166, 176, 183, 373, 380, 385, 398, 428, 430, 457, 461, 469, *128*, *321*

Tomasi S G *133*, *305*
Tomatsuri Y *50*
Tomlin C D 5, 6, 13, 15, 51, 102, 114, 149, 232, 233, 329, 330, 339, 341, 361, 372, *285*
Tomlin S M 372
Tomlinson R F 5, 22, 23, 26, 27, 28, 30, 33, 39, 45, 93, 111, 485, *73*, *185*, *314*
Tong L 203
Topographic Science Working Group 209
Toppen F 82, 84
Torri D *155*
Townshend J R G 39, 193, 195, 196, *3*, *7*, *12*, *171*, *185*, *186*, *196*, *209*, *210*, *211*, *214*, *218*, *224*
Tranter R B *213*
Tribble T N *270*
Trofimov A M 11, 38
Trollegaard S *85*
Tsichritzis D C 46, 51, 148, 253, 264, 418, *186*
Tsur S 419, 420
Tsuzawa M *120*
Tucker C J *209*, *210*
Tucker D F 82, 84
Tufte E R 429, 439
Tukey J W 431, 438
Tukey P A 431
Tulip J 261, 263
Tuori M 254
Turnbull M 301
Turner A K 149, 299, 308, 313, 314
Turner M G 208
TYDAC *172*
Tyrie A 82, 84

Uhr L 434
Ullman J D 217, 218, 220, 257, 415, 417
UNEP Global Resources Information Database *224*
UNICEF *72*, *73*
United Nations 468, *127*
United States Bureau of the Budget 169
United States Bureau of the Census 183
United States Geological Survey 177, 186, 523, *11*, *12*, *13*, *16*, *17*
Universities Research Association *270*
Unninayar S *218*, *221*

Unwin D J 4, 16, 62, 77, 82, 84, 85, 86, 88, 111, 124, 125, 128, 322, 323, 376, 385, 389, 390, *128*, *319*
Upstill S 292
Upton G 390, 396
Urban G *142*
Urena J L *227*
URISA *315*
US Congress, Office of Technology Assessment *19*
US Department of Energy, Office of Energy Research *270*
Usery E L 204, *15*, *16*
Ustin S L 203
Utano J J 430
Uzes F D 181

Valenzuela C R *165*
Van Dam A 288, 290
Varvel D A 417
Vazsonyi A 410
Ventura A D 344, 345
Ventura S 171
Vereecken H *156*
Veregin H 168, 200, 203, 381, 384
Verhey W H *164*
Verhoef W 207
Verplank W L 156, 439
de Verr A A *154*
Vevany M J 105
Vincent P *255*
Vincenty T 138
Visvalingham M *132*
van der Vlugt M 411
Volchok W J 195
Voller J *111*
Vonderohe A P 169, 180
Vose M 346

Wade B W 156
Wadge G *212*, *213*
Wagenet R J *164*
Wagle S 227
Wagner G 341
Wainer H 429
Wakeford R 399
Waldrop M M 103
Wales R Q 305, 309
Walker J 194, 207
Walker P A 38, 135, 136, 139, 199, 341, *63*, *66*, *180*, *225*
Walker T C 56
Wallin E 353
Walsh S J 203, 204, *164*

Walters D K 433, 434, 435
Walters S M 23
Wang F 341
Wang Min-Hua *78*
Wang R *79*
Wang S 202
Wang Y-F 49
Wanzell L R 436
Ware C 354
Warntz W 429
Warthen B 528, 529
Wasielewski P *120*
Wastman J R 438
Waterfeld W 314
Waters N M 84, 86, 410, 411
Waters R C 217
Waters R S 246
Watson D M *223*
Watson E J *142*
Watson G P *178*, *179*
Watts D G 195
Watts J 208
Waugh T C 36, 262, 345, 512, *321*
Weber W 470
Webster C 5, 15, 260, 261, 339, 347, 378, 385, 422
Webster R 170, 193, 390, *154*, *155*, *156*, *159*, *160*, *163*, *164*, 209
Van der Weg R F *155*, *156*, *164*
Weibel R 50, 113, 127, 199, 204, 235, 270, 274, 278, 279, 283, 290, 292, 301, 304, 325, 376, 380, 430, 460, 464, 469, *12*, *15*, *314*
Weir S 130
Weiser R L 205
Weismuller R A 204
Weitzel L 377
Weizenbaum J 434
Welch R 204, *128*
Welch R A 302
Welch R B 430, 437
Welch T A 245
Weller T 195
Wellings C 96
Wells D 264
Weng H 206
Werner C 285
Wertz J 30
West D S 121
Westcott T *270*
Wester L 158
Westin F C *164*
Weyer S 355
Wharton S W 194, 202

Whatmough R J 67
Wheeler P H *277*
Whelan S D *112*
Whigham P A 67
Whimbrel Consultants Limited *188*
Whinston A B 406, 407
Whitbread P J 67
White B 411, 493
White D 290, 373
White M 122, 166, *6*, *14*, *54*, *314*, *321*
White M L 206, 207
White M S *119*, *121*, *300*
White R M 160, 229
White T 261, *305*
Whitfield R A S *28*, *29*
Whittaker E 458
Whittaker H A *213*
Whittaker R J 39, *188*
Wiederhold G 255, 415, 418
Wiggins J C 39, 375, *187*, *188*, *196*
Wiggins J S 338, 341
Wilding J P *154*
Wilding L *155*
Wilkie D 399
Wilkinson H R 429
Wilkinson L 431
Williams E P J 27
Williams J 392
Williams R B G 380
Williams R L 430
Williams W B P 138
Williamson H D 205
Williamson I P 301, 314, *58*, *59*, *87*
Willmott C J 285
Wilson A G 389, 390
Wind J 345
Winograd T 161
Winston P H 515
Wintz P A 278
Wischmeier W H *164*
Wise S M 86
Witkin A P 434
Witmer R E 179, 180, 186, *264*, *276*
Woelk D 350, 355
Wolf J *155*, *164*
Wolfram S 216
Wood E F 206, 283
Woodcock C E 193, 194, 201, 207
Woodcock J 148
Woodsford P A 46, 47, 48, 63, 113, 185, 324, *90*, *96*, *104*, *276*
Woodward R A 203
Worboys M F 103, 120, 253, 254, 263, 264, 323, 379

World Commission on Environment and Development 7, 72
Wösten H J M *155, 156*
Wray T 140
Wright D F *173, 174, 176, 177, 178, 183, 184*
Wright W 82, *8*
Wrightman J F 84
Wrigley N 380, 434, *140, 145*
Wu P Y F 217, 219, 422
Wu Zhong-xing 144
Wyatt B K 203, *187, 198, 199*
Wymer C 385, 399, 409, *142*

Yamamoto S *47*
Yan S Y 422, *79*
Yandell B S 169, 185
Yang J *209*
Yang Qi-he 144
Yapa L S *74*
Yarbus A L 438
Yarrow G J *92, 111*
Yates J *148*
Yates M V *163*
Yates S R *163*
Ye Jiang 64, 264, 413, *143, 198, 229*
Yeh A G *260*
Yeorgaroudakis Y 355
Yeung A K W 245
Yoeli P 286, 288, 430, 445, 446
Yogarajan N 77
Yomono H *52*
Yoshimura S *47*
Young L T 216
Youngman C 372
Youngmann C 299

Zadeh L A 148, 152
Zafft W A 28
Zarzycki J M 346
Zavoli W B 159, *119*
Zdonik S B 421
Zehner R B 67
Zelek J 202, 203
Zeleny M 403
Zhan C-X 154
Zhang Q 79, *81*
Zheng W *80*
Zhong E 79
Zhong S 79
Zhou M 79
Zhou Q 192, 198, 200, 201
Zhou M-C 219
Zilles S 233
Zinn v. State 500
Zobrist A L 344
Zoraster S 278, 446
Zubin D 122, 154
Zuboff S *149*
Zusne L 428
Zycor N C 464
Zyda M J 288

SUBJECT INDEX

Numbers in roman refer to volume 1, numbers in italic refer to volume 2, numbers in bold refer to main entry.

0-Cell *134*
1-Cell *134*
2-Cell *134*
2.5D 269, *272*
    Visualization 302, 304
2D 24, 50, 124, 135, 153, 280, 290, 292, 293, 299, 302, 325, *203*, *206*, *272*, *319*
    Cartographic Form 369
    Coordinate Information 262
    Isoline Map 305
    Matrices 234
    Projections 225
    Spatial Data *201*
    Visualization 302
3D 50, 53, 114, 124, 135, 149, 153, 167, 170, 269, 290, 302, 325, 516, 527, *201*, *202*, *203*, *206*, *209*, *319*, *320*
    Applications *317*
    Cartographic Form 369
    Clipping 290
    Coordinates 141
    Data 7, *88*
        Display 280
        Structures 439
    Digital Terrain Model *113*
    GIS **299–317**
    Imaging 431
    Modelling 373, *15*
        Systems 299
    Representation Techniques 307
    Run Encoding 308
    Spatial Data Structuring 299
    Surface *289*

    Technology *319*
    Topography *104*
    Transformation 290
    Triangulated Irregular Network 309
    Vectors Per Second *319*
    Visualization 302–4, *320*
4D 7, *201*, *202*, *207*

A Classification of Residential Neighbourhoods *144*
A/E/C Systems 93
Abstract Data
    Structure 215
    Types 417, 418
Abstraction 242
Access to Data and Information 492
Accuracy 242, *315*
    of Plant Recording *106*
    of Spatial Databases 95
Ada 217, 252
ADABAS 255
ADAMS *49*
ADAPT *66*
Adaptive
    Filtering 464
    Modification 407
    Triangular Mesh Filtering 279, 280
Address
    Coding Guide 25
    Geocoding *300*
    Information System 24
    Matching 343, *304*
        Software 27

Admatch 25
Administrative
    Boundaries 71, 322
    District *131*
    Management Agency 48
ADR 255
Advanced
    Mobile Traffic Information and Communication System *120*
    Visualization Techniques 290–2
Aerial
    Photograph 29, 271, *55*, *288*, *298*, *304*
    Photography 141, 192, 239, *92*, *123*, *128*
    Photointerpretation 192
Aeronautical
    Charting and Information Center, St. Louis 27
    Information Services and Central Photographic Establishment *64*
Affine Transformation 141, **142–3**, 329
AFI3G 98
Agency for International Development 38
Aggregation 103, 343, 390
AGI
    NEWS 96
    Yearbook 51, 56
Agricultural
    Nonpoint Source Pollution Model *278*, *279*
    Research Service *278*
Agriculture 59, 197, 293, 422

Subject index

Air Photography 49, 201, 202
Aircraft Simulator 75
Airfield Design 293
Airport Noise Zones 105
Albemarle-Pamlico 8
    Estuarine Study 262, *263–7*
Alberta LRIS 260
ALES *156*
Algebraic Topology 150, 231
Algorithm Analysis 215
Algorithmic
    Probability 396
    Solution Methods 409
Algorithms 84, **220–3**
ALI/SCOUT *120*
ALIS *49, 50*
Allocation Model *239*
ALSCAL 130
Alternative Reality 354
Ambient Light Transparency 288
Amdahl 503, 509, *133*
American
    Association for Geodetic Surveying 94
    Cartographer, The 23, 94, 524
    Cartographic Association 94
    Congress on Surveying and Mapping 7, 93, 94, 524
    National Standards Institute 252, 525, 527
    Society for Photogrammetry and Remote Sensing 7, 93, 94, 169, 170, 179
    Urban and Regional Information Systems Association 6
AMTECS *54*
Analogue 47
    Attribute Data 175
    Data 175, 272
        Sources **175–83**
    Scanning 244
    Spatial Data 175
Analytical
    Computation 428
    Geometry 228
    Model *281*
    Modelling 405, 408
        Techniques 371
    Photogrammetry 458, *42*
    Stereoplotter 271
    Transformation **139–41**
Angular Field of View 192
Animated Graphics 53
Animation 87, 115

Antarctica 137
Anthropology 152
Anti-Aliasing 290, 300
AOS/VS 58
Apple
    Computer Incorporated 50
    Macintosh 49, 156, 352
Application
    Logic 418
    -Independent Benchmark 484
Applications of GIS *3*, **5–10**
    in the Environmental Sciences *210–14*
    in the Utilities *106*
Appropriate
    Spatial Analysis for GIS **395–6**
    Technology *81*
Arc 47
ARC 341
    Macro Language 341, *257*
ARC/INFO 15, 24, 32, 51, 52, 96, 113, 159, 168, 235, 241, 261, 325, 328, 341, 345, 512, *14, 15, 52, 53, 55, 67, 74, 75, 77, 189, 196, 250, 257, 258, 262, 316, 319, 321*
    Allocate *256, 257*
Arc/Node *153, 157*
    Spatial Data Model 341
    Topological Model 339
ARCDEMO 87
Archaeological Site Recording and Monitoring *90*
Architectural
    CAD Diagram 427
    Planning 301
Architecture 59
    of Very Large GIS Databases 95
Archival Data *201*
Archives 48
ARCNEWS 32, *75*
Arctic *225*
ARCView *324*
Area 85, 102
    Attribute 383
    Cartogram 132
    Class Map 168
    Measurement 114
    Quadtree *172*
Areal
    Interpolation 385
    Weighting 385
Argentina *123, 227*
ARISTOWN *51*

ARITHMICON 24, 31
Array 149, 218, 320
    Fetch 262
Artifacting 208
Artificial
    Intelligence 64, 95, 185, 417, 515, *143, 228, 229, 293, 301, 325*
    Neural Nets 396
ARX *67*
ASCII 224, 325, 346, *174, 176, 180, 228*
Asian Institute of Technology *74*
Aspatial 12, 27
    Object 301
Aspect Vector 278
ASPENEX 422
Assessment of Risk *192*
Association 103
    for Geographic Information 4, 7, 37, 51, 71, **77–8**, 96, 99, *9, 30, 317*
    of American Geographers 7, 33, 93, 94, 97
    of Computer Machinery 33
    of Local Authorities *42*
Asymptotic Assumptions 392
Atlantic Institute 96
Atlas
    of Great Britain and Northern Ireland 23
    of the British Flora 23
ATLAS*GIS 53, *317, 320, 322*
Atlases 92
Atmospheric
    Attenuation 204
    Correction 203
    Model 207
    Path Radiance 204
    Science 114
    Sciences Data *205–6*
Atomic Fragment *135*
Attribute 12, 46, 114, 120, 127, 166
    Accuracy **170–1**, 181, 459
        Test 172
    Association 349
    Attachment *33*
    Change 470
    Conceptual Error 383
    Consistency Checking 344
    Data **183–5**, 324, 338, 339, 340, 341, 343, 347, 479, 525, *205*
        Resolution 342
        Table 350
    Definition 170

Error 440
Information 340, 341
Similarity 128
Audio Tape 349
AUSNOMA *60*
AUSSAT *66*
Australia 38, 67, 93, *4, 5, 92, 93, 94, 95, 225*
　Information System 135
　Resources Information System 38
Australian
　Bureau of Statistics *65*
　Centre for Remote Sensing *60*
　Defence Force *61*
　Federal Resources Database *185*
　Heritage Commission *63*
　International Development Assistance Bureau 39
　Key Centre in Land Information Studies *67*
　Land Information Council *58, 60, 61, 62, 67*
　National
　　Parks and Wildlife Service *63*
　　University *67*
　Natural Resources Information Centre *193*
　Resources
　　Data Bank *66*
　　Information System *66*
　Standard Geographical Classification *65*
　Survey
　　and Land Information Group *5, 60*
　　Office and Division of National Mapping *60*
Authoritative Map 165
AUTOCAD 261, 325, 523, *74*
AUTOCARTO 5, 6, 22, 33, 84, 85, 86
Autocorrelation *195*
　and Regularization in Satellite Imagery **193–5**
Autocovariance 194
Autofact 93
Autoguide *117, 120, 121, 123*
Automap II 24
Automated 23
　Address Matching 26–7
　Cartographic
　　Production *52*
　　Systems *11*

Cartography 27, 30, *144, 262, 321*
Classification *210*
Digital Terrain Model Extraction 285
Generalization 463, *26*
Geographical Databases 56
Graphic Indexing *214*
Intelligence 115
Interaction Detector 398
Interpretation of Aerial Photography 422
Land Titles System *60*
Map
　Making 499
　Production *33*
Mapping/Facilities Management 97, 104, 292, *5, 6, 49, 51, 92*
　International 94, 95
　TODAY Conference 77
Meteorological Data Acquisition System *52*
Regional Justice Information System *257*
Spatial Analysis 394
Teller Machine *145, 150*
Terrain
　Feature Extraction 422
　Analysis 280
Thematic Mapping *155*
Zone Design 397
Automatic
　Digitizing 435, 436
　Image Enhancement *31*
　Line Following *31*
　Name Placement 454, 455
　System 445
　One-pass Generalization 329
　Snapping 344
　Spatial Response Modeller 397
　Text Annotation 344
　Zoning 398
Automobile Association 512
AUTONAP 423, 452
Autoregressive Model 185
Autoroute *35*
Availability of Digital Data *206–7*
Average Variogram *162*
AVHRR 193, 195, 196, *202, 209, 222, 223, 228*
AVL Tree 220
Awareness of GIS *3*
Azimuthal Equal-Area Projection 145

B-reps 309
Backface Elimination 290
Backward Chaining 419
Baghdad *260*
Band Location 195
Bandwidth Encoding 464
Bangladesh *127*
Bartholomews *6*
Baseline Determination Algorithm 449
BASIC 74
Basic
　Employment Allocation Model *248, 249*
　Guidelines for SSSpatial Analysis in GIS 396
　Input Output System *124*
　Terms of Error **166**
Basin Area 285
Batch 45
　Processing 480, *13*
Bathometric Charts *64*
Baud 504
Bayes Rule *171*
Bayesian
　Estimator 202
　Mapping 390
　Methods 392, 396, *172*
　Principles *173*
BBC 83
Beijing Astronomical Observatory *204*
Benchmark 116, 484–5, *96, 189, 322*
Benefits
　of a Land Registration Scheme *92*
　of GIS **14–15**
　of Information Integration 337–8
Benetton Company *143*
Bessell Function *159, 160*
Bias 166, 169, 203, 204
Bideford Experiment *25, 26, 32*
Bijective 231
　Transformation 467
BILDED 306
Binary
　Conversion *176*
　Large Object 349
　Representation *29*
　Segmentation 398
　Signature Map *174*
　Tree 219, 220, 463
Bioclimatology 197

617

Subject index

Biological Conservation 32
Biophysical Resources 57
Birkbeck College, University of
    London 86, 87, *188*, *189*
Birmingham *28*
Bitmap 325
Bivariate
    Interpolation 430
    Quadratic Simplicial B-Spline
        306
Black
    Inquiry 74
    Report (1984) 74
Blind Digitizing *26*
Block
    Encoding 199
    Kriging *164*
Boehm's Figure of Merit 483
Bonne Projection 145
Boolean Operation 308, 321, 330
Borehole 308
    Log *203*
    Records 270
Bosch *115*
    Travelpilot *115*, *116*, *117*, *119*,
        120, *121*
Botswana *211*
Boundary
    Representation 307
    Approximation Algorithm 449
Bounding Nodes 227
Boyce-Codd 259
BP 315
Branch Location Analysis *139*, *140*,
    143, **145–8**
British
    Cartographic Society 96
    Census 380, *131–3*
    Gas *111*
    Geological Survey 186, *203*, *204*
    Library 186
    Military Board of Ordnance *23*
    Oxygen Company *26*
    Telecom 504, 513, *111*
Britton Lee *33*
    IDM Database Computer 262
Brundtland Report 7, *72*
Buffer Zone *191*, *307*
Buffering 322, 329, 389
Building
    Asset Management *90*
    Permit Control *90*
    Walk-Through 354
Bulgaria *153*

Bureau
    of Mineral Resources *63*
    of Rural Resources *63*
Business (Development) Planning
    140, *141*
Byte-Oriented Run-Length Encoding
    245

C 215, 219, 224, 252
C++ 216
Cable
    Television *51*
    Utilities *102–3*
CAD-Based Systems 261
CAD/CAM 32
Cadastral 38, 138
    Data *261*
    Information 466
        System 12, 332, *58*
    Mapping 137, 292, *76*
    Plan *91*
    Records 97
    Station *106*
    Survey *86*
    Surveying *85*
    System *4*
Cadastre 12, 181, *58*, *85*
Calcomp 31, *26*
CALFORM 24, *28*
Calibration 191
    Models **204–6**
Calliper 53
Canada
    Geographic Information System
        17, 22, 23, **28–9**, 45, *314*
    Land
        Data System 17
        Inventory 23, 29, 111, *185*
    Agricultural Rehabilitation and
        Development Administration 29
    Hydrographic Survey 27
    Institute of Surveying and
        Mapping 97
Cancer Screening *130*
Capability Model *300*
Car
    Guidance System *6*
    Navigation *34*, *318*, *321*
    Systems *54*, **115–24**
CARIN *121*
Cartesian
    Axes 143
    Coordinates 124, 135, 136, 139,
        140, 141, 299, 364, *271*

Cartogram 119, **132**, 430
Cartographic
    Acceptability of Data 242
    and Spatial Analytical Concepts
        of GIS 85
    Comparison 385
    Conceptual Error 383
    Data 221, 344, *224*
        Exchange Standard 227
        Interpretation 367
        Sources 272
    Database 385
    Design 427
        Rules 438
    Display 405, 408
    Error 206, 381
    Form 371, 391
    Generalization 247, 292, 457,
        460, 462, 464, *17*
        of Digital Terrain Models 278,
            279, 283
    Image 361
    Information 191, 200
    Measurement Error 381
    Modelling 102, 103, **361–73**, *291*
        Capabilities **367–71**
        Conventions **364–7**
        System 340
        Techniques **371–2**
    Projection 365, *218*, *228*
    Rectification 191
    Representation 125, 471
        of Data 77
    Reprojection 365
    Symbolization *17*
    Symbols 50
Cartography 22, 55, 57, 59, 88, 91,
    92, 101, 115, 139, 141, 167, 168,
    169, 172, 221, 430, 435, 436, 437,
    439, *15*, *102*, *116*, *317*
    and Geographic Information
        Systems 6, 94, **102–3**, *134*
Cartometry 345
Catastrophe Theory 466, 474
Catastrophic Approach to
    Cartographic Generalization
        466–8
Categorical
    Attribute 383
    Coverage 168, 383
    Data 376
        Analysis 380
Cathode Ray Tube 302, 438
CD-ROM 5, 48, 55, 183, 215, 343,

618

349, 352, 513, *15, 53, 54, 65, 74,*
121, 122, 149, 197, 220, 324
CDA 346
CDATA-86 65
CDF 346
Cell 150, 233
Cellular
    Automata 398
    Decomposition 235
    Topology 235
Census 6, *128*, 263, 298, *303, 304, 324*
    Data 183, *261*
    District 253
    Map Production 331, 332
    of Population 71, 504, 513
        and Housing *307*
    Statistics *128*
    Tract *239, 240, 249, 250, 256,*
    257, 305
        Descriptor 516
Center for Urban and Regional
    Analysis 31
Central
    Board of Real Estate Data 38, *43*
    Government 67
        Reporting 90
    Intelligence Agency 27, 30
    Office of Information 67
    Population Register *129*
Centralized GIS 480
Centre
    for Recent Crustal Movements
    203
    for Renewable Resources and
    Environment *205*
    for Resource and Environmental
    Studies 67
    for Soil Geography and
    Classification *205*
    for Spatial Information Systems
    67
Centroid 126, 150
CGIS-CLI 260
CGM 346
Chain Code *314*
Change-Detection in LANDSAT
    Images 422
Channel Pixel 284
Chaotic Model 435
Character Representation *29*
Characteristics
    of an Education System 84
    of Environmental Data Sets
    202–7

of Environmental Databases
206–7
of Geographical Data 103
of Geoprocessing Systems **405–7**
Characterization 312
Characterizing Neighbourhoods *213*
Charge-Coupled Device 243
Chemistry 92, 93
Chernobyl *186, 193*
China 39, 98, *5, 9, 75, 224, 324*
    Tourism Resource Information
    System *79*
Chinese Academy
    of Geological Sciences *204*
    of Sciences *205*
Chorley
    Committee 68, 69, 96, 487, *29,*
    30, 35
    Report 22, *88, 94, 132*
Chorochromatic Map *156*
    Model *158*
Choropleth 28
    Map 168, 438, *120, 156, 158,*
    257
Cinematic Animation 300
City
    Block Distance 231
    Growth *78*
    of Knoxville *112*
    Planning *54*
Civil
    Engineering 59, 286, 287, 293,
    299
    Service 72, 507, 508, 509, 510
Clarion NAVI *117*
Classification 168, **201–4**, 383
    Accuracy 204
    Bias 203
    Errors 202–3, 285
    of Landslide Hazards 283
    of Systems **215–17**
    of Water Tracts *265–7*
Classifying Geographical Data 323
Climatology 92, 197, 293, *205*
Cluster Analysis 201, 391
Clustering 434
Co-Kriging 305, *153, 163, 164*
Co-Regionalized Variable 305
Co-Registered Data Sets *208–9*
Co-Registration 343
Co-Variogram *163*
Coarsening
    of a Digital Terrain Model 280
    of Rectangular Grids 274

Coastal
    Area Management Act *264, 265*
    Planning 59
    Zone Color Scanning System
    202
COBOL 256
CODATA Task Group 93
Codd Normal Forms 261
Code
    Management 217
    of Federal Regulations *267*
Cognitive Science **151–4**, 439
COGO 345
Collection of Spatial Information 429
Colliding Record 218
Colombia *75*
Colour 434
Combined Higher Education
    Software Team 96
Combining Data Sets 280
Commercial
    GIS **56–60**
    Values 494
Commission for Integrated Survey of
    Natural Resources *205*
Committee
    of Enquiry into the Handling of
    Geographic Information 67, 68,
    69–78, *29, 66*
    of Geographical Names in
    Australia *60*
    on Data for Science and
    Technology 93
Commodity Market 492
Common Agricultural Policy *213*
Commonwealth
    Land Information Support
    Group *60*
    Scientific and Industrial
    Research Organization 38, *66*
    Surveyor General *61*
Communications 59
    Planning 75
    Map 458
Community Charge 76
Comparative
    Analysis *262*
    Study 392
Compass *119*
Competitive Tendering *90*
Completeness 242
Composite
    Map Model 339–40, 356
    Sampling 271, 272

Subject index

Comprehensive Resource Inventory and Evaluation System 38, *75*
Compulsory Purchase Order *90*
Computational
  Geometry 227, 275
  Vision 435
Computer
  -Aided
    Design 12, 101, 299, 326, 329, 341, 439, 527
      and Drafting 64
    Drafting 56, *24*
    Mapping *24*
  Analysis of Spatial Data *48*
  -Assisted
    Cartography 84, *45, 75, 80*
    Generalization 458, 473
    Learning 87
    Map Analysis 287, *294*
    Regional Planning *74*
  Cartography 12, 83, 86, 329, 330, 436
  Display of Spatial Data *48*
  Error 497
  Graphics 290, 463
    Interface 527
    Metafile 527
    Standards 527–9
  Mapping 385, 512
  Matching *253*
  Name Placement **445–55**
  Photomontage 354
  Science 22, 57, 113, 149, 152, 215, *15, 102, 156, 314*
Computerized
  Data Analysis *218*
  Rural Information Systems Project *77*
Conceptual
  Data Model 515, 516
  Error 381
  Fuzziness 384
  Generalization 466, 467
  Model 112–13, 113, 320
  Modelling 515
Conceptualization of Reality 51
Concurrency Control 418
Concurrent Processors *15*
Conditional
  Execution 366
  Independence *171, 174, 183, 184*
    Assumption *174, 180*
Conflict Resolution Model **292–3**
Confusion Matrix 203

Connectivity 330, *213*
Conquest 25
Conservation
  Model *290*
  Monitoring Centre *205*
Constraint
  Introduction 421
  Removal 421
  Replacement 421
Constructive Solid Geometry 307
Consulting 60
Containment 330
  Relationship 421
Contiguity 440
  Constraint 391
Continental Environmental Database *186*
Contingency Table 203
Continuous 231
  Coordinate Space 200
  Data 376
    Collection *207*
  Feed Scanner 243, 244
  Spectral Change 195
  Tone Isoplethic Map 430
Contour 287
  Data Model 113
  Digitizing *13*
  Interpolation 288
  Polygon 278
  -to-Grid
    Conversion 280
    Interpolation 278
  -to-TIN Conversion 280
Contouring 287
Conversion Algorithm 378
Convex Hull 275
Convolution 470
Coordinate
  Conversion *13*
  Density Equalization 343
  Geometry 322
  Registration 343
  System 85, 112, 135
  Transformation 85, 248
Coordinating Committee on Locational References 69
Copyright 72, 99
  Law 495
  Design and Patents Act *94*
Core GIS Theory 319
CORINE 137, 260, 342, 344, 385, *7, 164,* **185–99**, *225, 305*
Cost of Data Collection 77

Cost-Effectiveness
  Analysis 477
  Estimate *244*
  Evaluation 485
Cost/Benefit 85, *95, 192*
  Analysis 61, 85, 477, 478, 479, 480–1, *9, 43, 150, 244*
  of GIS *315*
  of Land Information Systems **88–9**
  Ratio *244, 314*
Costs of GIS 46, *3*
Council
  for Research and Development in Land Information Technology *43*
  of Europe Convention 495
Count Data 376
Countryside Commission for Scotland 35
County *131*
  Administration Board *43*
  Council 76
Course Development Project 84
Covariance Matrix 202
Coverage 48, 52, 168
  Database 168
CPU 219, 252, 257, 484, 485, *49, 123, 133*
Creation of a Spatial Decision Support System *301–2*
Credit
  Referencing Agency *143*
  Scoring *140, 143, 149*
Crime
  Analysis
    Mapping System 257
    Statistical System 257
  Control 8, *247, 250*
  Pattern Analysis 90
  Prevention Planning 257
  Reporting 257
    and Interactive Mapping Environment 257, 258
Critical Erosion Targeting 277–8
Crop
  Disease 433
  Modelling *157, 164*
  Suitability Study 293
  -Specific Phenology 202
Cross
  Area Estimation 396
  Linguistic Transfer 160
  -Hairs 243

620

-Indexing 351
-Selling *144*
Crown Copyright 512
CRT *54*
Cubic Interpolation 278
CUBRICON 155
Cultural Landscape *47*
Curriculum
    Content 87
    Requirements *319*
Curvilinear Transformation 329
Customer
    Billing *90*
    Database *149*
    Origin Survey *145*
Customized Zone Design 397
Cut-and-Fill 287
Cybernetics 439
Cyberspace 354

Dangling Chain 382
Danish Meteorological Institute *204*
Daratech Incorporated 14, 56
Data
    Absorption 347
    Access 93, 418, *193*
    Accuracy 112, 395, *17*, *194*
    Acquisition 85, 338, 498, *87*
    Analysis 253–4, 324, 419, 498, *127*, *189–91*, *315*
    and Knowledge **415–16**
    Availability *193*
    Capture 60, 239, 319, 324, 480, *201*, *206*, *207*, *208*, *210*, *315*
        and Processing Algorithms 247–8
        for Digital Terrain Models 270
        Technology 276
    Cataloguing *207*
    Classification 78
    Collection 239, 432, 481, *4*, *6*, *12*, *195*, *318*
        Technology 191
    Combination 498
    Communications *43*
    Compaction 458, 509
    Compilation *127*
    Compression 458, *174*
    Confidentiality *325*
    Conversion 349, *96*
    Definition *197*
    Descriptive File for Information Interchange 78
    Differences 380
    Directory Project *219*

Display 111, *127*
Dissemination *127*
Dredging 420, 421
Editing 319, 324
Entry 113, *276*
Environment 529
Error 398, 496
Exchange 515, 518
    Standards *111*
Exploration 115
Export 515
Format 112, *209*, *319*
Gathering Agencies 116
General *263*
Generalization 324
Glove 315, 354, 439
Import 515
Inconsistency 342
Indexing 29, *207*
Input 252, *189*
Integration 112, 324, 328, 340, 384, 385, *7*, *96*, *189*, *262*
    Modelling *172–4*, 180
    Tools *300*
Integrity 262, *61*
Interpolation 114, 428, 438
Key 348
Layer Intersection 263
Logger 325, 349
Management 93, *5*, *20*, *222*, *242*, *300*
    Support *263*
Manipulation 260, 389, 499
Measurement Scale 375
Media 342
Model *51*, 85, 228, 254, 269, 320, 342, 347, *96*, *318*
Modelling 113, 251, 253, 428, *315*, *318*
    Techniques 251
Models for Soil Survey *156*
Normalization *79*
Observation 375
Oriented Raster Structure 200
Output *191–2*
Presentation 324, 366
Privacy Legislation *149*
Processing 55, 93, 113, 154, 361, 481, *87*, *194*
    System *142*
Quality 78, 93, 395, 459, 523, 525, 526, 529, **89–91**, *155*, *193–6*, *197*, *220*, *319*
    Assessment 293

Query 324
Redundancy 256, 258, 279
Reliability 93
Restructuring 324
Retrieval 113
Robustness 457
Sales *4*
Security 262, *106*
Segregation 232
Sharing *59*
Signposting *193*
Simplifier 397
Sources *318*
    for Digital Terrain Models 270
Standards 116–17, *79*
Storage 85, 113, 252, 324
Structure 85, 112, 113, 114, 228, 324, 342, 434
    Conversion 192, 280
    for Digital Terrain Models 272
    Examples of **218–20**
Switchyard 518, 522, 523
Transfer 112, 319, 324, 515
Transformation 324, 365, 367
Type *209*
Uncertainty 85
Unit 379
Validation 324, *12*
Verification 497
Visualization 115, 354
Volume *315*
    of Digital Terrain Models 279
Database 22, 57, 59, 85, 111, 187, 218, 223, 227, 251, 405, 415, 492, 495, *32*, *55*, *77*, *262*
    Analysis 111
    Computer 262
    Construction *43*
    Creation 479
    Design 111, 251, **252–4**, *17*
    Development 287
    Generalization 464
    Interfaces **154–6**
    Linkages 232
    Locks 419
    Management 12, 83, 84, 329, 435, 439, 479, 515, *33*, *144*, *291*
        System 12, 13, 46, 56, 57, 172, 228, 251, 325, 330, 349, 385, 408, 419, *33*, *142*, *228*, *229*
        Interfacing 347, 349
        Software Components 252
    Manager 217
    Modelling 398

Subject index

Database – cont.
    Models 463
    Representation *107*
    Structures 95
    Systems 413
    Tables 257
    Task Group of the Conference on Data Systems Language 256
    Theory 416
    Tools 216, 251
    Update *196*
    View of GIS 13–14
    Volume *196*
DATACOM/DB 255
Dataquest Incorporated 56
DB2 259
DBASE 346, *74*, *322*
DBF 346
Dbmap 25
DCA 346
DDBMS 347
DDIF 346
Dead Reckoning *116*, *117*
Debugging 223
Decision
    Analysis 479
    Declaration on Transborder Data Flows 495
    Declarative Query Language 421, 422
    Dedicated Road Infrastructure for Vehicle Safety *124*
    Deductive
        Database 414, 416, 417
        Estimation 181
    Information Display System *300*, *302*
    Making *60*, *61*, *74*, *301*, *302*
        in a GIS Context 85
        Model *286*
        Tools *300*
    Model *142*
    Modelling 479
    Research 403
    Resources 24
    Space *236*, *237*
    Support 391
        System 10, 11, 17, 404, *67*, *77*, *142*, *145*, *149*, *276*, *299*, *300*, *301*
            Generator 407
    Tree Analysis *180*
Defence 59, 67, 71
    GIS **75–6**

Scientific and Technology Organization 67
Defence
    Mapping Agency 48, 518
    Meteorological Satellite Program 202
Defining
    Areas for Development *289–92*
    Conservation Areas *288*
    Ecological Research Areas *288–9*
Definition
    Limited 313
    of GIS **10–12**
    of a Land Information System 87
Definitions of Visualization 432
Delaunay Triangulation 220, 275, 276, 278, 305
Delivery Scheduling *35*
Deltamap/Genamap 15
DEMOGIS 87
Demographic
    Analysis 90
    and Economic Forecasting Model *248*
    Data *261*
    Profile *250*
Demography 197, 503
Dempster-Scafer Theory *183*
Denmark *129*
Densification
    of a Digital Terrain Model 280
    of Gridded Digital Terrain Models 280
    of Rectangular Grids 274
Department
    of Administrative Services *60*
    of Agriculture 177, 179, 180, 182, *75*, *154*, *163*, *278*
    of Commerce 495
    of Economic Development 507
    of Employment 503
        Group 507, 508
    of Energy *17*, *213*, *270*, *271*
        Mines and Resources Canada 97
    of Environment, Health and Natural Resources *262*
    of Health 279
    of Housing and Urban Development 30
    of Natural Resources, Division of Forestry 280

of Primary Industries and Energy *63*
of Roads 53
of Science Programming and Earthquake Monitoring *205*
of the Environment 35, 69, 72, 74, 508, *23*, *27*, *132*, *209*
of the Interior 495, 524, *12*, *13*, *15*, *19*
of Trade and Industry 74, 508, 510
of Transport 72, 508
of Treasury 495
Depth Cuing 300
Derived
    Map *26*, *27*, *289*, *290*
Descriptive
    Cartographic
        Model 371
        Modelling Techniques 371
    Mapping *285*
Desktop
    Information Display System 24
    Publishing 348, *314*
Destination
    Finding *115*, *121*, *124*
Determination of Name Baseline 449
Deterministic
    Model **206–7**
    Solution *292*
Developing Countries 67
Development 59
    Areas Model *289*, *291*
    Control 76, 90
    Planning *298*
Device Control 366
DFAULT 306
DG XI *189*
Diagnostic Signature *171*
Dialogue Understanding 158
Dichotomous Data 376
DIF 346
Differential Rectification 290
DIGEST 346, *318*
Digital
    Array 427
    Atlas *304*
    Camera 243
    Cartographic
        Data 251, 254, 260, 516, *11*, *12*, *13*
        Base 76, 77
        Standard *17*

Standards Task Force 165, 523
Feature Representation 523
Model 459
Cartography *11, 12, 78, 154*
Data 175, *298*
　Donor Programme *20*
　Sources **185–6**
Database 324, *317*
Elevation
　Data 203, 527
　Matrices 168
　Model 37, 177, 269, 279, 345, 523, *12, 18, 36, 212, 213, 223, 315, 319*
Equipment Company 52, *33, 321, 324*
Field Update System *31, 32*
Flow Line *28*
Geographic Information Working Group 75
Image Document 343
Landscape Model 458, 459, 460, 465, 471
Line Graph 177, 219, 221, 235, 325, 345, 346, 435, 523, *9, 13, 16, 17, 228, 305, 306*
　-Enhanced 517, 519, 522, 529, *17*
Mapping 73, 127, 299, *28*
Orthophotograph 192, *14*
Photogrammetry 26
Processing 361
Representation 85, **112–14**
　of Information 113
Road Map Association *54*
Simulation 271
Soil Information *155*
Sound Sampler 349
Spatial Data 427, 515, *19*
　Quality *20*
Stereo
　Correlation 271, 272
Street Network *123*
Technology 111
Terrain
　Elevation Data 75, *17, 228*
　Model 126, 170, 345, 349, 464, *47*
　　Application 270, 292–3
　　Editing 278
　　Filtering 278
　　Generation **270–8**
　　Interpolation from

Topographic Samples 274
Interpretation 270, **280–7**
Joining 280
Manipulation 270, **278–80**
Merging 280
Quality Control 285
Visualization 270, **287–92**
Modelling **269–97**
Thematic Global Database *219*
Topographic Mapping 69
　in Australia *64*
Digitizer 15, 57, 242, 243, *80, 250, 287*
Digitizing 46, 49, 59, 70, 113, 124, 137, 175, 185, 272, 328, 379, *43, 90, 110, 188, 203, 207, 222, 250, 324*
　Error 200, 381
　Model 185
　Spatial Data 232
　Station *317*
　Table 377, *30*
　Tablet 56, *74*
DIME 25, 27, **30**, 327, 345, *65, 256, 257, 305*
Dimensionality of Spatial Data **301–4**
Dip Angle *118*
Direct
　Data
　　Conversion 515
　　Retranslation 518
　　Translation 518
　Mail *139, 140, 143*, **148–9**
　Manipulation Interface 354
　Marketing *148*
　Surveying 240
　Transformation 139, **141–3**
Director General of the Military Survey 75
Directorate General of the Environment *187*
Dirichlet
　Polygon *132*
　Tessellation 28, 275, 276
Disaster Management *316*
Disclosure of Information 494
Discrete
　Feature 168
　Sampling 458
　Speech 158
Discretization 312
Disease Database 393
Disjunctive Kriging *153, 163*
Disk
　Drive 253
　Storage 485

Disparate
　Geographical Data 192
　Information 68
Dispersion 365
Display 85
　Issues **115–16**
　of Spatial Information 429
Dispute Settlement 491
Distance
　Learning 87
　Queue 280
Distortion
　Isogram 145
　Pattern 144
Distributed
　Database 45
　GIS 480
　Spatial Database *67*
District
　Council 76
　Health Authority 68, 74
　of Columbia 26
Division of Advanced Scientific Computing 432
DMV *30*
Document
　Digitizing 325
　Image Processing 343
　Scanning 325
Domain
　Consistency Rules *210*
　Modelling 420
　Partition 313
　-Dependent Knowledge 421
　-Independent Knowledge 421
Domains of Visualization Research 432
Domesday
　Community Disk 351
　System 83, 353
　Videodisc 385
Domestic Information Display System 24
Donnelley Marketing Information Service 25
Dot
　Map *45*
　Matrix Printer *287*
　Per Inch 244
Douglas-Peucker Algorithm 246, 247
DPMAP 25
Draft Proposed Standard for Digital Cartographic Data 524

Subject index

Drainage
    Area Transform 284
    Basin Monitoring 293
    Density 283
    Enforcement Algorithm 278
DRASTIC *279*, *280*
Drum Scanner 29, 244
Dual Data Storage 340
Dudley Project 27–8, 34, 111
Dutch
    National Science Foundation 97
    Soil Survey *154*, *164*
        Institute 163
DXF 325, 345, 346, 523
Dynamatch 25
Dynamic
    Data 419
        Exchange 346
    Graphics *263*
        Incorporated 309
    Optimization 421
    Simulation *291*
    Stormwater Simulation Program 278
    Thresholding 244
    Vehicle Routing *247*
    Visualization 440

Earth
    Data Information Systems Conference 98
    Observation
        Satellite 47, 53, 198, 216
        System 196, *229*
    Science 293, *217*
        Data *202–3*
            Directory 15
            Information Network *15*
    Surface Process 191
Earthwork Calculation in Site Planning 293
Easements *109*
East Africa 23, 29
Eastern Europe 98
Ecodisk 353
Ecological
    Characterization *213*
    Fallacy 184
    Interference Error 391
Ecology 59, 197
Economic
    and Social Research Council 37, 77, 81, 84, 96, 396, *66*
        Data Archive 513

Atlas of China 79
    Development *57*
    Geography 275
    Implications of GIS in Australia **64–6**
    Map Series *41*, *42*
Edge
    Based Database 218
    Detection 390, 398
    Detector 397
    Matching 248, 343, 378, *194*, *305*
Edifact 346
EDIS87 98
Education 45, 60, 62, 71, 76, 81, 85, 86, 87, 88, 319, 318
    and Training *325*
Effective Resolution
    Element 193
    of Sensors 193
Egypt 85
Einstein 222
ELAS *13*
Elastic Scaling 460
Electoral Ward *131*
Electricity 69
Electromagnetic
    Flux *6*
    Properties 1193
    Response *176*
    Signal 202
Electronic
    Data
        Interchange *141*, *143*
        Processing *142*
    Drafting *300*
    Funds Transfer at the Point of Sales 145
    Mail 5, *317*
    Market *148*
    Messaging 355
    Point of Sales *144*, *150*
Electrostatic Plotter 50, 56, *305*
Elements of a GIS **15–16**
Elevation 168
    Database 48
    Matrix 273
    Zonation 203
EM Algorithm 385
Emergency
    Management 49, *53*
    System *53*
    Planning *8*, *90*, *110*, *247*, *250*, *255*

Response 47, 104
    Services *113*
    Management *90*
Employment Service 513
EMPRESS DBMS 15
Enclosure 373
End-to-End Systems Study on Surface Temperature Data *219*
Energy Assessment *75*
Engineering *102*, *317*
    CAD Diagram 427
    Modelling Software 305
Enhancement
    of Digital Terrain Models 278
    of the National Digital Cartographic Database *20*
Entity
    -Categorical-Relationship 408
    Construction 313
    Relationship 255
    Model 253
    Modelling 257
    Sets 253
Enumeration District 126, 385, 504, *131*, *132*, *133*
Environmental
    Applications of GIS *3*, *201*
    Change 105, *209*
    Classification System 202
    Constraints *289*
        to Development *291*
    Control and Enforcement *90*
    Crisis 55
    Data 191, *192*, *201*, *202*
        Holdings *202*
    Database *3*, *7*, *59*, *185*, *186*, *187*, *188*, *189*, *192*, *193*, *196*, *197*, *198*
        and GIS **201–15**
    Dimension of GIS *6–8*
    Fly-Over 354
    Geochemistry *208*
    Impact
        Analysis 350
        Assessment *90*
        Study 282, 293
    Knowledge 410
    Law 422
    Management 356, *9*, *185*, *261*
    Modelling 191, 299, 356, *188*, *229–30*
    Monitoring *81*, *222*
    Observation 222
    Overlay *303*
    Planning 59, 293, 422, *53*, *185*

Protection 22, *53*
   Agency 186, *185, 263, 278, 279, 280*
   Department *52*
   Regulation 59
   Resources Information Network *63*
   Science 84
   Survey 192
   Systems Research Institute 3, 21, 23, 24, **31–3**, 51, 52, 96, 113, 168, 328, 349, 512, *74, 75, 250, 257, 262, 314, 316, 319, 322*
Epidemiology 132
EPPL7 53
EPS 346
Epsilon
   Band 471
   Distance 382
   Filtering 464
Equal-Area Projection 377
Equivalence Relations 421
Equivalent Dimensionality 440
ERDAS 241, 344, 345, 372, *15, 263*
Erode Smoothing 470
Eroding 470
   Blanket 471, 472
   Technique 470
Erosion 197
Error 85, 165, 217, 242, 396
   and Accuracy **381–4**
   Correcting Modem 511
   Correction 278, 285
   Detection 285
   Handling 366
   Location 376
   Measurement 376
   Modelling 85, 112
   Propagation 435, *164, 229*
   Tracking 373
Errors 114
   in Representing Location 499
   in Spatial Databases 166, 167, 458
ERS-1 198
ESMAN *302*
Estimate of Population 504
Estimated Point Density Map *173*
Etak 24, *6, 115, 122, 124*
   Map Engine 24
   Navigator *116, 117, 119, 120, 121*
Euclidean 121, 301
   Dimensionality 322
   Distance 119, 120, 129, 130, 132, 438

Geometry 149, 228, 229, 232
   Representation 122
   Space 126, 231
EUROCARTO 6
European
   Commission 39, *7, 185, 187*
   Community 137, 342, 494, 513, *7, 186, 187, 188, 196, 199, 213, 225, 323, 324*
   Division of AM/FM 77
   Environment Agency *185*
   Space Agency *7*
EVA *121*
Evaluating GIS Functions 114
Evaluation of Alternative Fire Station Locations *257*
Evolution **23–6**
Exact Matching 340
Examples
   of Low-Level Spatial Data Structures **233–5**
   of Spatial Data Models **232–3**
Exchange
   Format *205*
   of Data 69
Executive
   Agency 71, 72, 513
   Information System *149*
   Office of the President *303*
Experimental
   Cartography Unit 3, 21, 23, **34–5**, 37, *24, 25*
   Variogram *160*
   Realism 152
Expert System 64, 95, 202, 419, 420, 422, 423, 446, 469, *33, 142, 143, 155, 156, 198, 228, 229, 302, 307, 318*
   Shell 418
Explanation-Based Learning 420
Exploratory
   Data Analysis 431, *228, 229, 299*
   Geographical Analysis 397
   Spatial Analysis 399
Extendible Array 215, 219
External Attribute Database 232
Exxon 308
Eye Fixation Pattern 438

Facility
   Management *298, 304, 316*
   Mapping Systems *317*
   Siting *298*
Factor Loading Plot 434

Factoring 434
Failed GIS *9*
False 3D Image *281*
Family Practitioner
   Committee 74
   Area 506
Far Eastern Research Centre 38
Fault Location *109*
FAX 346, *317*
Feasibility Analysis 61
Feature
   Association 349
   Code *29*
      Specification *29*
   Coded Vector Data *30, 35*
   Database 168
   Density 447
   Extraction 373, 435, *15*
   Generalization 343
   Overlay *15*
   Programming 373
   Recognition *324*
Features of the Variogram *159*
Federal
   Aviation Administration 500
   Geographic
      Data Committee *19*
      Exchange Format 524
   Geographical Data Committee *20*
   Information Processing Standard 524, 525
   Interagency
      Committee on Digital Cartography *19*
      Coordinating Committee on Digital Cartography 524, *18*
   Republic of Germany *4*
Fédération Internationale de Géomètres 93, *87*
   Symposium on Land Information Systems *87*
Ferranti *26*
FES 422
Field
   Survey 324, 338
   Tree 199
FIFE 205
Figure-Ground Relation 430
File
   Management *33*
   Reformatting 365
   Structure 518
   Transfer Protocol 510

Subject index

Filter Mapping 339
Financial
    Analysis *139, 149*
    Control *90*
    Information System *57*
Finite Computer 228, 229
Finland *129*
Fire
    Service 76
    Services Management *90*
First Order Logic 414, 416
Fish and Wildlife
    Management *261*
    Service 30
Fisheries 197
Flatbed Scanner 244
FLINT 306
Floating
    Horizon Algorithm 290
    Point Performance 215
Flood Control 59, *109*
Floodplain Management 32
Floppy Disk 5, *220*
Flow Simulation 373
Flowline 239
FMS/AC *317*
Focal
    Bearing 370
    Combination 370
    Data Transformation 370–1
    Gravitation 370
    Insularity 370
    Majority 370
    Maximum 370
    Mean 370
    Minimum 370
    Minority 370
    Neighbour 370
    Percentage 370
    Percentile 370
    Product 370
    Proximity 370
    Ranking 370
    Rating 370
    Sum 370
    Variety 370
Footpath Maintenance *90*
Footprint 168
Ford Foundation 28
Forest
    Canopy Damage 105
    Management *53, 62*
    Resource Management 331, 332, *280–1, 316*

Forestry 56, 59, 197, 293, 422, *261*
    Commission 35
    Management System 52
Formal Logic 413
Formalization 229
    of Spatial Concepts 230
Formatting System for Geo-referenced Data *206*
Fortran 217, 252, *29, 271*
Fortran77 215, 452, 509
Forward
    Chaining 419
    Solution 139
Fourier Transform 278
Fourth Generation Language 216, 217, 252
Fractal **125–6**, *156*
    Behaviour 194
    Dimension 125, 283, 390, 465, 469
    Geometry 465
    Model 435
France 98, *123, 154, 324*
Free Duct Analysis *109*
Freedom of Information Act 494, *94*
Freight Transport Cost 321
Fujitsu 50, *51, 52, 53*
Functional
    Capabilities of GIS 114
    Classification of GIS 319
    Dependency 421
    Issues **114–15**
Functionality of GIS 324–31
Fuzzy
    Analysis 398
    Classification 170
    Data Attribute 341
    Features *194*
    Geodemographic Targeting System 398
    Logic 324
    Matching 340
    Pattern Analysis 397
    Reasoning 148
    Set 122, 170
    Theory 152, *156*
    Space 122

Gamma Radioactivity *176*
Ganesa Group International 24
Gas 69
Gaussian
    Error 171

Function *159*
    Model *160*
Gazetteer 512, *60, 107*
GCEM 400
GDS/AMS *341*
GEDDEX 422
GEM 346
Genasys 52
General
    Bathymetric Chart of the Oceans *206*
    Format-3 *207, 208*
    Geomorphometry 282
    Information Systems for Planning 34, 69
    Reference Map of Australia *60*
    Register Office 507
    Systems Model *235*
Generalization 111, 115, 292, 329, 390, 437, 457, *33, 189, 194, 209*
    and Accuracy 460
    and Resolution 460–1
    and Scale 459–60
    Decision Rules 472
    in Data Quality **459–61**
    of Spatial Databases **457–74**
    of Volumetric Objects 471
    Operators 472
    Definition of **115–16**
Generalized Mapping System *305*
Generating Binary Predictor Maps **174–6**
Generic
    Scene Simulation Software 207
    Spatial Analysis Functions **396–8**
Geo-Object 308, 309
Geo-Relational Model 339, 340–1, 356
Geo/SQL 53
GEOBASE 512
Geochemical Anomaly *171*
Geochemistry 197
Geocoding 85, 384, *49, 121, 135, 304, 305*
GEODAS *49, 50, 226*
Geodemographic Discriminator *144, 149*
Geodemographics *139*
Geodesic Hierarchy 463
Geodesist 92
Geodesy 137, 138, 169, 171, 172, *60*
Geodetic Control *3*
    Coordinates 227
    Data *11*

Subject index

Position 365
Reference 169, 499
Survey 433
Geographic
 Data
  Technology Incorporated 25
 Information 167
  Steering Group 72, 76
  Systems Speciality Group 94
Geographical 12
 Analysis 103, 191, 395, 406, *144*
  Machine 399
 Concepts 152
 Correlates Exploration Machine 397
 Data 15–16, 45, 81, 196, *124*
  Handling 422, *318*
  Matrix 323
  Models **320–2**
  of Sweden *40, 41–2*
  Structures **320–2**
 Database 175, 324, 328, 342, 394, 397, 446
  Design 319, 320
 Information 68, 69, 70, 71, 73, 77, 78, 96, 167, 191, 489, 490, 529
  Analysis 405
  for Vehicle Navigation *35*
  Institution 489
  Management System Committee *303*
  Processing 269, *13*
  Retrieval and Analysis System 31, *13*
  Science *313*
  Systems in Australia **57–68**
 Intelligence 9
 Names Information *11*
 Partitions 48
 Reality 113
 Reference 14
  System 12, *249, 314*
 Relationships 113
 Sensitivity Analysis 341
 Space 113, 153, 157
 Survey Institute 38, *14, 48, 55*
Geography 22, 57, 92, 439
Geoid 137
Geoidal Reference *203*
Geoinformation *81*
Geokernal 314
Geologic Division *15*
Geological
 Interpretation 293

Map *272*
Mapping 293
Survey of Canada *172*
Geology 50, 92, 114, 126, 139, 168, 178, 197, 293, *15*
Geomatic Hypermap 353
Geometric
 Classes 229
 Concepts 233
 Data Model 157, 230
 Error 285
 Model 207
 Object 230
 Phenomena 102
 Registration 195
 Resolution 195
 Transformation 135, 467
Geometrical
 Encoding *122*
 Generalization 466, 467, 468
 Knowledge 464
 Search 421
Geometry 84, 157
Geomorphological
 Classification 293
 Modelling 283
 Simulation 293
Geomorphology 84, 293
Geomorphometric
 Analysis 282, 286
 Mapping 203
GEONET *15*
Geophysical Data System *225*
Geophysics *15*
Geoprocessing 6, 22, 292
Georeferencing 85
Geoscience 93
 Database 314
Geosciences Data Index *214*
Geoscientific
 Analysis 301
 Spatial Data 301
GEOSET 308
Geosight 24
Geostatistics 170, *154, 164*
GeoVision 52, 261, 328, *316*
Gerber 29
 Plotter 27
Germany *124, 127, 324*
Gestalt
 Approach 103
 Perceptual Task 430
 PhotoMapper *13*
GFIS 52, *314, 316, 319*

GIF 346
Gigabyte 215, 241, 509
GIMMS 36, 510, 512
GIRAS 31, 345
GIS 111, 112, 119, 121, 126, 127, 130, 139, 167, 172, 191, 217, 227, 230, 240, 248, 251, 269
 2000 **320–2**
 Acquisition 116, 477
 and Developing Nations **71–82**
 and Infrastructure **5–6**
 and Knowledge Based Techniques **420–3**
 and Land **5–6**
 and Management 85
 and Market Analysis **139–50**
 and Organizations **105–6**
 and People **5–6**
 and Public Policy **233–44**
 and Utilities **101–13**
 Applications for Urban and Regional Planning Conference 75
 as a Discipline *316–17*
 Database 239, 241, 247
 Design *244*
 Education *319*
 Evaluation **477–87**
 for Policy Analysis and Monitoring **239–41**
 for Public Policy Analysis **237–8**
 Framework **137–9**
 Functionality 85, 114
 Implementation **477–87**
 in China **76–80**
 in India **76–80**
 in Island Resource Planning **285–94**
 in Japan **47–55**
 in the Utilities in the United States *112*
 in Urban Planning in San Diego County **250–9**
 in Utilities in the United Kingdom *110–12*
 Modelling 280, *294*
 News 94
 Plus 53
 Primitives 114
 Programmes in Sweden **39–46**
 Query Language 158
 Research and Education **76–7**
 Society *313*
 Sourcebook 51
 Specification **477–87**

Subject index

GIS – *cont.*
  Support for Public Policy
    Analysis *241–3*
  Terminology 86
GIS/LIS 7, 93, 94, *317*, *320*
GIST! 353
GISTutor 87
GISWorld 6, 15, 51, 56, *316*
Glasgow *260*
GLIM 127, 329, 385, 396
Global
  Analysis 428
  Area Coverage *228*
  Atmospheric Research
    Programme *219*
  Change 92, 93, *217*, *219*
    Database Project *219*
    Diskette Project *219*
    Studies *220*
  Climate Model *208*
  Databases 177, *205*, **217–30**
    in GIS **225–8**
    Systems *225–8*
  Environmental
    Change Project *5*, *47*
    Database *186*
    Monitoring System *74*, *205*, *224*
  Forcing Functions *219*
  Information System for Land
    Cover *205*
  Interdisciplinary Studies *227*
  Interpolation *279*
  Modelling *223*
  Monitoring *8*
    Data Sets *218*
  Optimization 419
  Positioning
    Satellite *54*, *105*, *124*, *324*
    System 47, 169, 186, 240, 318, 324, *6*, *118*, *123*, *317*, *319*, *320*, *321*
  Programmes **218–24**
  Reference Data Sets *218*
  Resource Information Database *74*, *205*, *224*, *225*
  Scale Use 85
  Science 112
  Systems 104
  Telecommunications System *206*
  Thematic Data *217*
  Topological Database *223–4*
  Vegetation Index *209*
  Warming *127*
Goal Planning *292*

GOCAD 306
GOES 198
Goodness-of-Fit *174*, *184*
Gouraud Shading 288
Government Statistical Service 511
GPL 247
GPS World 47
GPV 346
Grained Analysis 428
Graph
  Theory 390, 421
  Theoretic Mapping 462
  Theoretic Representation 462
Graphic 46
  Communication 432
  Fudging 344
  Overlay *300*
  Survey *102*
Graphical
  Encoding of Information 431
  Interfaces 437–9
  Kernel System 300, 527
  Presentation 438
  Report Generator 409–10
Graphics
  Accelerator Chip 300
  Package 46
  Processor 300
GRASS 53, 345, 372, *15*, *314*
Graticule 136, 139
Great
  Barrier Reef Marine Park
    Authority *63*
  Lakes *278*
Greece *188*, *193*
Greenhouse Effect *186*
Greyscale
  Normalization 343
  Thinning 285
GRID 28, 32, 345, 372
  Analysis *49*
  Cell *153*
  Cell Database 168
  Cell GIS 341
  Cell Tessellation 339
  Data 525
    Model 113
  Map *45*
  -on-Grid Transformation 139, **141–3**
  -to-Contour Conversion 280
  Resolution 280
  Smoothing 329
  TOPO 32

Gridded
  Database *5*
  Digital Terrain Model 278, 280
Grids 25
Ground
  Landscape Photography *55*
  Survey 270, 271, 458
Groundwater Modelling *15*
Group Decision Support System *150*
Growth Rates by Sector *56*
GUI 50, 52
Gyro *115*
Gyroscope *118*

H-Resolution Model 194
Halobias 470
Hard Disk 48, *50*
Hardware 85, **243–5**
  Environment for GIS 113
Harvard
  Computer Graphics Weeks 28, 33
  Laboratory for Computer
    Graphics 21, 23, 25, **27–8**, 31, 34
    and Spatial Analysis 3, 328
  Mapping Collection 7
  University 160, *48*
Hash Table 215, 218, 219, 224
Hashing 218, 222
Hazardous
  Vehicle Routing 331
  Waste Management *261*, **267–70**
Health and Safety
  at Work Act *111*
  Control 90
  Board 74
Heathrow Airport *123*
Helmert Transformation **141–2**
Her Majesty's
  Land Registry 67, 68, 71, **73–4**, 78, 181, *93*
  Treasury 508, *25*, *28*
Heuristic Search Procedure 201
Hextree 199
Hidden
  Element Removal 290
  Surface Removal 300
Hierarchical
  Classification 462
  Data Structure 199, 200
  Database
    Models 113
    Structure 251
    System 254, **255–6**

628

Dominance *292*
Land Classification 206
Matching 340
Model Structure 255
Raster Data Structures **199–200**
Sampling Pattern 272
Tessellation 463
Hierarchically Structured Database 472
High-Level
 Programming Languages 234
 Spatial Data Structure 228
Higher
 Education 86, 87
 Level Image Description 434
Highpass Filter 278
Highway
 Maintenance *90*
 Network 72
Hillshading 288
History of Visualization in GIS **428–31**
Hitachi *49, 50, 53*
 CAD-Core Tracer 246
Hitosubashi University *47*
Hokkaido Gas *51*
Holistic Approach to GIS 324
Home Office 508
Honda *14*
 Gyrocator *116*
Hong Kong *75, 76, 123*
Horn Clause Rule 416
House of
 Commons 503
 Lords Select Committee on Science and Technology 67, 68, 526, *29*
HPGL 49, 345, 346
Huffman Run-Length Encoding 245
Human
 Computer
  Interaction 115, 437, 439
  Interface 431
 Dimensions
  of Global Change Programme 55
  of Global Environmental Change Programme *63*
 Error 382
 Information Processing System 428
 Settlements Development Group *74*
 System 112

Visual Processing 428
 System 429
Hybrid
 Data
  Model **260–1**, 341
  Storage 340
 Model 207
Hydrogeological Runoff Modelling 293
Hydrogeology 299
Hydrographer of the Navy 75
Hydrographic
 Charts *64*
 Department of the Admiralty *93*
Hydrologic Phenomena 105
Hydrological Runoff Simulation 282, 283
Hydrology 48, 50, 197, 204, 293, *15*
HyperCard 87, 352
 Tutorial 512
Hypercube 216, 219
Hyperdocument 353
Hypermapping 439
Hypermedia 355
 GIS 356
Hypertext 352, 355, 439
 Tutorial 512
Hypothesis Testing 389
Hypsometric
 Intergral 282
 Tint Display 288

I/O 215, 222
Iberian Peninsula 378
IBM 26, 29, 52, 55, 300, 328, 411, *50, 51, 53, 74, 224, 314, 316, 319, 322, 324*
 PC 223, *9, 287, 291*
 PS/2 223
 RS/6000 *319*
 -PC-MAP 372
Iceland 154
ICL 36, *28, 30*
Identification Error 171
IDMS 256
IDRISI 15, 52, 53, 124, 372, *314*
IGES 345, 346
IGU 33
IIS-MAP *54*
Illumination
 Geometry 195
 Model 288
 Vector 288
ILWIS 341

Image
 Abstraction 434
 Analysis 433, 439
 Based Information System 12
 Brightness 194
 Classification 191, 192, 470
 Correlation 435
 Description 435
 Enhancement 193
 Generation 433
 Local Variance 194
 Overlay 349
 Processing 47, 56, 59, 60, 64, 86, 240, 278, 283, 339, 340, 344, 390, 398, 435, 469, *67, 171, 172, 229, 262*
 Pyramid 194, 199
 Rectification 193
 Resolution 194
 Schema Model of Cognition 152
 Schemata 153, 310
 Segmentation 202, 204
 Sharpening 470
 Smoothing 470
 Space Algorithm 290
 Synthesis 434, 435
 Texture 194
 -to-Image Registration 343
 Understanding 435
Imaging Frequency 195
IMG 346
IMGRID 372
Implementation
 of Irregular Tessellation **234–5**
 of Regular Tessellation 233
IMSL 409
Inclined Contour 288
Inclinometer *118*
Incompatible Areal Units **384–5**
Incremental
 Data Transformation 369
 Triangulation 280
IncrementalArea 369
IncrementalAspect 369
IncrementalDrainage 369
IncrementalFrontage 369
IncrementalLength 369
IncrementalLinkage 369
IncrementalPartition 369
IncrementalVolume 369
Indeterminacy 208
Indexes 49
Indexing 87
India *74, 75, 92, 127*

Indian Ocean *64*
Indicators of Accuracy *112*
Indonesia *75*, *92*
Inductive Learning *420*
Industrial
    Location Modelling *247*
    Screening Matrices *299*
    Site Location *293*
Inertial
    Device *115*
    Navigation Sensor *118*
Inference Net *180*
INFO *260*, *341*
INFO-MAP *24*
Information *10*
    Acquisition *491*
    Based Planning Strategy *247*
    Consistency *338*
    Exchange *28*, *230*
    Handling *41*, *207*
    Infrastructure *299*
    Integration **337–56**
    Interchange *338*
    Linkage *338*
    Management *255*, *314*
    Overload *103–4*
    Processing *431*
    System *148*, *191*
        Failure *487*
        Division *15*
    Technology *70*, *96*, *142*, *150*, *186*, *189*, *192*, *324*
Informix *260*, *349*
    On-Line *349*
Infrared *427*
INGRES *259*, *260*, *263*
INGRES(QUEL) *417*
Inheritance Tree *463*
Initial Graphics Exchange Specification *527*
INS SPACER *54*
INSECT *307*
Installation *57*
Instance
    Method *263*
    Variable *263*
Instantaneous Field of View *192*
Institut fur Angewandte Geodasie *4*, *188*, *195*
Institut Géographique National *517*
Institute
    for Geophysics *204*
    for Land Information *95*, *96*
    of British Geographers *81*, *96*

    of Geography of the Chinese Academy of Sciences *79*
    of Physical and Chemical Research *204*
    of Space and Aeronautical Research *204*
    of Terrestrial Ecology *36*, *186*, *213*
Institutional
    Change *267*
    Issues *85*
Instrumental Survey *32*
Intangible Benefits *244*
Integrated
    Data Model **261–2**
    Database Management System *406*
    Geographical
        Analysis *192*, *197*
        Information System *191*, *200*
    Geometry *150*
    Land and Watershed Management Information System *75*
    Planning Information Systems **297–308**
    Rural Development *74*
    Services Digital Network *216*
    Software *81*
    Spatial Database *11*
    Terrain Unit *344*
    Topology *52*
    Use of Data Sets *212*
Integrating
    Data *201*
    Remote Sensing and GIS **196–201**
Integration
    Model *348*
    of Disparate Data Structures *200*
    of Geoscientific Data ***171–81***
    of Remote Sensing and GIS *191*
Integrity of Data Sets *209*
Intel *223*
    /386 *74*
    /8088 *123*
Intelligence Unit *508*
Intelligent
    Filtering *47*
    Raster *37*
Intensity Edge *434*
Inter-
    Application Communications *346*
    Departmental Working Group

        on the Tradeable Information Initiative *74*
Interactive *45*
    Automatic Systems *246–7*
    Computer Graphics *73*
    Editing *32*
    Generalization *36*
    Hypermedia Systems **352–3**
    Processing *480*
    Spatial Display *105*
    Surface Modelling *263*
    Transformation *300*
    Visualization *287*
    Volume Modelling *309*, *313*
Intercellular Relationship *233*
Interface Translation *160*
Interfaces to GIS *104*
Intergraph *24*, *32*, *52*, *300*, *305*, *325*
    IGDS/DMRS *261*
    Microstation GIS *261*
    Microstation-32 *261*
    TIGRIS *264*
Intermediate Standard Transfer Format *108*
Internal Revenue Service *495*
International
    Cartographic Association *39*, *93*, *523*
    Centre for Recent Crustal Movements *204*
    Council
        for the Exploration of the Sea *206*, *208*
        of Scientific Unions *92*, *55*, *219*
    Data Handling Symposia *7*
    Date Line *226*
    Developments in GIS *3*
    Geographical
        Union *93*, *223*
            Commission *84*
                on Geographical Data Sensing and Processing *29–30*
    Geophysical Year *219*, *224*
    Geosphere-Biosphere Programme *92*, *55*, *63*, *205*, **219–20**
    Gravity Bureau *206*
    Institute for Aerospace Survey and Earth Science *97*
    Journal
        of Geographical Information Systems *6*, *33*, *58*
        of Imaging *6*

Oceanographic
  Commission *206, 206, 208*
  Data and Information
  Exchange *206*
Organisations **92–3**
Policy 104
Society
  of Photogrammetry and
  Remote Sensing 93
  of Soil Science *153*
Soil
  Reference and Information
  Center *204*
  Science Society *155*
Standards Organisation 525,
  527
Symposium on Computer-
  Assisted Cartography 33
Telecommunications Union 245
Union for Conservation of
  Nature and Natural Resources
  205
Interpolation 195, 373, 376, *4, 158,
  175, 176, 177*
  Algorithm 275
  from Contour Data 277–8
  Methods 380
  of Digital Terrain Models 274–5
Interpretation 115
  of Digital Terrain Model Quality
    Assessment 285
  of Digital Terrain Models 269
    for Engineering 286
    for Planning 286
Interpreted Map *289, 290*
Intersection 16
  Frequencies 391
Interspersion 373
Interval Data 322, 437, 439
Intervisibility 114
  Problem 286
Inverse Solution 139
Inverted List Database
  Structure 251
  System **254–5**
Invertible Model 201
Investment Appraisal 406, *9, 139,
  149, 192*
Invitation to Tender 96
Iran *127*
Iraq *323*
Ireland 377
Irish Grid 70
IREX 309, 312

Irregular Tessellation 151, 198, 227,
  233
  Models **150–1**
Irrigation
  Studies *154*
  Water Rights *15*
IRS IA 77
Isarithm 287
Isarithmic Map 45
ISLAND *50, 51*
ISM 345
ISO-8211 78
Iso-Surface 309
Isochrone Map 129
Isogram 145
Isoline 28, 302, 304
Isomorphic Mapping 467
Isotrophic Variogram 194
Israel *128*
ISROVISION 77
ISSCO 32
ITA 67
Italy *130, 324*

Jamaica 186
  GIS 38
Janes Committee 25
Japan 67, *5, 14, 123, 124, 224, 324*
  Digital Road Map Association
    14, 123
  Industrial Standard *48*
  Meteorological Agency *204*
  Standard Grid System *48*
  Surveyors Association 97
Job Centre 504, 506
Joint Academic Network 87, 504, 510
Journal of the Urban and Regional
  Information Systems Association 6
Juridical Cadastre *85*

Kantian Viewpoint 148
Kauth-Thomas Tassled Cap
  Transformation 202
Kawasaki *51*
KBGIS-II 420, 421, 422
KDB-Tree 325
Keiyo Gas *51*
Kenya *75, 224*
Key to Bucket Transformation 222
Kingston Polytechnic 77, *317*
Knowledge
  Acquisition 418
  Base 413, 415

Based
  Approach *210*
  Geographical Information
    System 201
  Management Systems 414
  Search 473
  System 264, 527, *318*
  Techniques **413–23**
    in Non-Spatial Databases
      416–18
  Organization 435
  Representation 414, 515
Knox County *112*
Knoxville Utilities Board *112, 113*
Kokusai 52
Kriging 170, 206, *159, 164, 177*
KUMAP 49
Kuwait *323*
Kyoto University *204*

L-Resolution Model 194
Label 115
Labor Market Information 513
Laboratory
  of Resource and Environment
    Information Systems *5, 79*
Lagrange Multiplier *161*
LAIRD 66
Lambert Conformal Conical
  Projection 137, 139, 377
Lambertian Shading 288
LAMIS 28
LAMM 66
Land
  Administration System 58
  Analysis System *14*
  Characterization *213*
  Classes 111
  Classification Scheme *213*
  Cover
    Change Pilot Project 219
    Classification *212*
    Data Set 177
    Map 180, 186
  Data System 12
  Development 365
  Evaluation *164*
    in Developed Countries *165*
    Model *164*
  Gazetteer 27
  Information 489, 490
    Management 57
    Products and Services 97

631

Land – cont.
  Steering Advisory Committee 58
  System 12, 73, 94, 191, 192, 201, 239, 347, 490, *4*, *5*, *11*, *43*, *86*
    Hub *59*
  Systems 94, 95, **85–97**
    in Australia **57–68**
  Management 22, 59, 121, 205, 490, 498, *3*, *11*, *262*, *278*
    Applications of GIS **275–83**
    Information Center 277, *280*, *281*
  Market Monitoring 90
  Ownership 71, *6*
    Information System 332
    Modelling 331
    Records 86, *90*
  Parcel *91*
    -Based Systems 85, **91–3**
    Referencing *93*
  Policy Formulation 490
  Reclamation 32
  Register *45*
  Registration *4*, 85
    Act (1988) 73, 74
    Systems *94*
  Registry Records *93*
  Resource
    Information System *8*, **261–72**
    Management *272*
  Resources Information Service *262*
  Surface
    Analysis 191
    Classification 192, 204
  Survey 83, 88
  System Mapping *209*
  Taxation *45*, *59*, *92*
  Titles Office *59*
  Titling 38, *92*
  Use 105, 126, 168, *9*
    Analysis *47*
    Code *253*
    Conflict *198*
    Data Set 177
    Decision Making *293*
    Management *90*
    Map 178, 180, 186
    Planning *298*
    Regulation 497
    Valuation *58*

Landesvermessungamt Nordrhein-Westfalen 517
Landform Analysis 283
Landmateriet *4*
Landsat 31, 47, 48, 185, 193, 195, 196, 198, 240, 523, *9*, *77*, *228*
  Multi-Spectral Scanner 135, 141, 185, *195*
  Thematic Mapper 141, 185, 194, *178*, *202*, *228*, *264*
Landscape
  Architecture 59, 299
  Depiction 429
  Design 301
  Ecological Planning *75*
  Planning 102, 339
LANDSEARCH *60*
Landtrac 24
Language 147
  Primitives 153
  Representation 423
  Universals 153
Languages of Spatial Relations 95
Lanzhou Institute for Glaciology and Geocryology *204*
Laplacian Filter 470
Large-Scale Databases *33*
Laser
  Altimetry 270, *223*
  Disk 215
  Printer 511
Laser-Scan 345
  VTRAK 246
Latin American Demographic Centre *75*
Latitude 377, *202*, *203*, *225*, *228*
Lattice 320, 345
Laura Ashley *144*, *147*
Layer 48, *104*
  Concept 150
  Orientation 364
  Resolution 364
Leaf Area Index 204
Leakage Survey *109*
Least-Squares
  Estimation 172
  Fitting 248
Lecture Course 87
Legal
  Aspects of GIS **489–501**
  Cadastre 85
  Implications 85
  Liability *106*

Lempel-Zif and Welch Compression 245
Less Developed Countries 89, *92*
Li-Strahler Geometric-Optical Canopy Model 207
Liability
  for Data and Information 496
  for Misuse of Information 498
Licensed Cadastral Surveyor *93*
Light List 500
Limitations of Spatial Analysis 394–5
Line 85, 102, 328
  Attribute 383
  Continuity 436
  Digitizing 365
  Enhancement 126
  Following 272, *31*
    Algorithms 436
  Generalization 126, 200, 272, 468
  Intersection 436
  -of-Sight 75, 365
  Printer 23, 50, 511
  Segment 125
  Smoothing 329
  Snapping 344
  Symbolization 290
Lineament Interpretation *179*
Linear
  Cartogram 129
  Conformal Transformation 141
  Feature Name Placement 448
  Generalization *195*
  Interpolation 271, 277, 278
    within Triangles 275
  Planning 292
  Programming 446
  Quadtree 230, 233, *172*
Linguistics 152
Link
  Length 285
  Magnitude 285
Link/Node 29
Linkages 113
Linking
  Environmental Data Sets *207–9*
  of Data 69, 70
Literature 5
Live-Link 241
Liveware 15
LOBSTER 422
Local
  Authorities Management Services and Computer Committee 89

Authority 72, 73
    Management Information
        System 36
    Data Transformation 367–8
    Government 67, 71, **76**, 104, 116,
        8
LocalArcCosine 367
LocalArcSine 367
LocalArcTangent 367
LocalCombination 367
LocalCosine 368
LocalDifference 368
LocalMajority 368
LocalMaximum 368
LocalMean 368
LocalMinimum 368
LocalMinority 368
LocalProduct 368
LocalRating 368
LocalRatio 368
LocalRoot 368
LocalSine 368
LocalSum 368
LocalTangent 368
LocalVariety 368
Local Area
    Coverage *228*
    Network 216, 244, *228*
Locating Waste Disposal Sites *250*
Location 92
    Allocation Modelling 329, 390
    Code 348
Locational
    Accuracy 459
    Analytic Work 389
    Attribute *286*
    Coordinates 125
    Data 183, 341, 408
    Information 119
    Reference 348
    Referencing 71, 122, *206*
        System 70, *203*
    Specificity *286*
Log Odd *173*
Logic
    Based
        Database 421
        System 418
    Program 418
    Programming 217, 416, 418, 422
Logical
    Consistency **171–2**
    Data Model 516
    Database Design 252–3, 254

Intersection 419
    Programming 417
Logit *173*
London Underground 438
Long Term Ecological Research 205
Longevity of Databases *206*
Longitude *377, 202, 203, 225, 228*
Lookup Table 341, *173*
Loose Coupling 418, 419
LORAN-C *118, 124*
Loss of Information 113
Lotus 1–2–3 *322*
Lotus PIC 346
Low-Level
    Data Structure 215, **217–20**
    Spatial Data Structure 228, 229–
        30, 233
Lowland Flooding 102
Lowpass Filter 278
Lynx Incorporated 309

MacArthur Foundation *294*
MacGIS 372
Machine Vision 435–6, *229*
Macintosh 52, 53, 87, 431, *317*
Macro 59
Magnetic
    Resonance Scanning Imagery
        427
    Susceptibility *176*
    Tape 46, 48, 216, 527, *13, 25, 29,*
        30, 54, 226
        Drive *228*
MAGSAT *222*
    Anomaly Map *222*
Mailing Target Group *149*
Mainframe 49, 50, 52, 57, 58, 63, 215,
    216, 328, 503, *9, 49, 50, 51, 81, 107,*
    113, 314, 317
Major Statistical Area *249, 253*
MAL *49*
Malaysia 75
Management
    Applications of GIS *3*
    Information *101*
        System 11, 36, 406, *142, 324,*
        325
    of Environmental Data *201*
    of GIS Acquisition **486–7**
    of Information *192*
    of Large-scale Databases 96
    Problems 116
    using GIS *8*

Managing Land Information Systems
    94–7
Manchester *34*
Manhattan
    Distance 121, 122, 129, 231
    Metric 121
    Space 126
Manifold 233
Manipulation of Dig[ital]
    Models 269
Manpower Se[...]
Manual
    Da[...]
    Dig[...]
    Map[...]
    Stereoplotter 271
Many-to-Many
    Mapping 253
    Relationship 256, 257
MAP 51, 53, 168, 372
Map
    Accuracy **179–80**
        Assessment 203
    Algebra 149, 330, 361, 365
    Analysis *286*, ***287–92***, *293*
        Package 75
    Animation 430
    Attribute Data 251
    Audience 177
    Conflation 343, 344
    Coverage **178–9**
    Data 527
    Design 427, 437, 439
    Display *115*
    Distortion 144
    Drawing 366
    Function 467
    Generalization 423
    Integration *172*
    Interpretation 432
    Layer Zones 367
    Layers 364
    Matching *116, 119–20, 122*
        Algorithm *119, 122, 123*
    Overlay 111, 217
        and Statistical System *13, 226*
    Processing 13, 330, *285*
        Model *325*
    Projection 85, 88, 112, 135, 137,
        138, 344, 452
        Knowledge-Based System 145
        Standardization 343
    Reproduction 102
    Retrieval *122–3*

Subject index

Map – *cont.*
   Revision Cycle *12*
   Structure *285*
   Theme *467*
   Transformation *119*
   Update *191*
   View of GIS *13*
Map-ematics *286, 293*
Map-Oriented Vector Structure *200*
MAP/INFO *24, 53, 319*
MAP2 *372*
MapBox *373*
MAPEX *423*
MAPICS *512*
MAPII *372*
MAPMASTER *24*
MAPOI *25*
Mapping
   Awareness *6, 316*
   Science *12*
     Committee of the National Academy of Science *19*
   Soil Properties *7*
   Tools *6*
MAPS *114, 372, 422*
   as Data **285–6**
Marine
   Atlas Project *214*
   Data *203*
   Information
     Advisory Centre *208*
     Service *206*
     System *214*
   Navigation *6, 116*
MARK II *16, 17, 18, 20*
Market
   Analysis **140–2**, *143, 145*
     Information System *12*
   Research *53, 59, 316*
   Survey *144*
   Share *56, 145*
Marketing Information System *139, 140,* **143–5**
Markov Techniques *313*
Markovian Model
   of Cycling *313*
   of Succession *313*
Mars *223*
Marsden Square *203*
Maryland *30*
   Automatic Geographic Information *32*

Master
   Geographical Referencing Area *249, 250, 256, 257*
   Survey Drawing *31, 32, 37*
Masters Plotter *26*
Matchmaker *25*
Mathematical
   Analysis *390*
   Primitive *307*
   Spline *29*
Mathematics *22*
Matrix *75, 320*
Max Metric *231*
Maxi Marketing *143, 144*
Maximum Likelihood *202, 470*
Maxwell Communications Group *513*
Mazda *123*
MDBS Associates *408*
MDBS III *256, 408*
Mean Slope *285*
Measurement
   Error *381*
   Topology *323*
Measures of Spatial Proximity **130–2**
Medicine *92*
Megabyte *319*
Megapel *49*
Memory *57*
   Caching *262*
Mensuration *76*
Mental
   Map *438*
   Model *437*
Menu Handler *252*
Mercator *140*
Merchants Association *287*
Merge Rules *210*
Meta-Information *214*
Metadata *420, 421, 226*
Meteorological
   Agency *52*
   Data *105*
   Space-Time Data *290*
Meteorology *92, 275, 293, 299, 202*
Method
   of Agreement *420*
   of Concomitant Variation *420*
   of Difference *420*
   of Residues *420*
Methods for Counting People **128–9**
Metric
   Representation *459*
   Space **120–2**, *231*
Metropolitan Map Series *133, 134*

Mexico *224*
   City *260*
MIADS *345*
Micad *93*
Michigan
   State University *75*
   Terminal System *509, 510*
Micro-Analytical Technology *398*
Microcomputer *399, 15, 49, 74, 75, 149*
Migration *504, 516*
Military
   Application of Digital Terrain Models *293*
   Intelligence *22*
   Tactics *22*
Mineral Exploration *281*
Minerals *59*
   Management *495, 90*
Minicomputer *52, 57, 58, 63, 69, 215, 216, 15, 66, 321*
Minimal Tension Interpolation *309*
Minimum
   Change in Angularity *460*
   Distance to Means *470*
   Interpolation Error *161*
   Variance *161*
   Vector Displacement *460*
Mining *59, 87, 299*
Ministry
   of Agriculture *67*
     Forestry and Fishery *48, 52*
   of Construction *49, 51, 53, 54*
   of Defence *67, 74, 36, 78, 195*
   of Education *49, 52, 55, 204*
   of Home Affairs *53*
   of International Trade and Industry *48, 51*
   of Posts and Telecommunications *204*
   of the Environment *67*
   of the Treasury *48*
   of Transport *67*
   of Transportation *52*
MINITAB *13, 127, 128, 329*
Minnesota *30, 8, 9*
   Department of Natural Resources *282*
   Forest Inventory *281*
   Geological Survey *281*
   GIS *275*
   Land Management Information System *31*
   Pollution Control Agency *277, 280*

Subject index

MIPS 49, 57, 215
Misclassification Matrices 181
Misregistration 203
Missing Data Problem 380
Mississippi River 278
Misuse of Data and Information 501
Model
    204 Database *133*
    Articulation 253
    Base Management System 408–9
    Construction 272
    Curricula 81
    Development in 3D **310–15**
    for GIS Acquisition **477–86**
    Generalization 458
    of Urban Structure 435
Modelling 27, 55, 312, *7*
Models 103
    of Data Interrelationship 253
    of Spatio-Temporal Domains 413
Modifiable Areal Unit Problem 170, 184, 391, *130*
Modified Mercalli Intensity Scale 268
Modula 215
Modular Course 87
MONARCH 308
Monitoring Energy Use *90*
Monotonic Curvature 448
Monte Carlo
    Method 400, 401
    Significance Test 392, 399
    Simulation 384
Morphism 157
Morton
    Order 308, *314*, *325*
MOS/LOS 198
Mosaic Surface 168
MOSS 345, 372, 422
Motion 434
Motivations for Generalization **458–9**
Mount St Helens 105
MS-DOS 49, 52, 53, *314*
MULATM 66
Multi
    -Image Mosaic 343
    -Resolution Imagery 194
    -Scale Database 398
    -Sensor Imagery 240
    -State
        Categorical Map *175*
        Distance Map *175*
        Ordinal-scale Map *176*
    -Surface Modelling *271*
    -Temporal
        Analysis 195
        Imagery 196, 240
    -Thematic Environmental Data 225
    -User Data Access 262
Multidimensional 46
    Data 129, 429, 440
Multidisciplinary Database 217
Multimedia 47, 55, 115, *320*
    Databases **348–52**
    GIS 323, 351, 356, *52*, *317*
Multinational
    Database 196
    GIS Collaboration *3*
Multiple
    Instruction Multiple Data 216
    Representations 95
    Testing 399
    Valued Attribute 522, 523
Multipurpose
    Cadastre 86, *304*
    Geographical Database *303*
Multiscale Line Tree 472
Multisensory
    Feedback 354
    GIS 356
    Simulation 354
Multispectral Scanner 193, *80*, *202*
Multiuser 45
Multivariable Signature *172*
Multivariate 102
    Analysis 391
    Classification of Landforms 283
    Spatial Database 222
    Statistical Analysis *172*, *180*
Munsell *157*
Murray-Darling Basin Commission *63*
MVS 58

Nadir 193
NAG 409
NAGIS News 98
Nagoya *48*
    University *204*
Name Placement 423
    Freedom 447
NAPLPS 346
Narrowness 373
NASA 186, *7*, *204*, *223*, *229*, *303*
    Earth System Science Programme *220*
Natal/KwaZulu Association for Geographic Information Systems 98
National
    Academy of Sciences *204*, *220*
    Agricultural Information System *79*, *81*
    Atlas of Sweden *39*, *41*, *42–3*
    Bureau of Surveying and Mapping, Beijing 98
    Cartographic Information Center 186
    Center
        for Geographic Information and Analysis 4, 7, 33, 55, 81, 84, 95, 96, 99, 111, 381, 396, *66*, *302*, *315*, *319*
            Core Curriculum 84, 86, 111
        for Health Statistics *16*
    Climate Data Center *206*
    Committee on Digital Cartographic Data Standards 94
    Computer Graphics Association 93
    Council of Science and Technology 55
    Court Administration *43*
    Decision Systems 24
    Developments
        in GIS *3*
        in Official Mapping and GIS *3–5*
    Digital Cartographic Database *11*, *12*, *13*, *14*, *16*, *18*, *20*, *21*
    Estuary Program *263*
    Forest Inventory *63*
    Gazetteer Pilot Study 35
    GEO-DATA System *20*
    Geodetic Vertical Datum of the United States *202*
    Geophysical Data Center *204*, *222*, *225*
    Grid 37, 68, 69, 70, *29*, *36*, *104*, *131*, *132*, *213*
        Data *48*
    Health
        Service 67, **74–5**, 513
            Family Practitioners Areas 504
        Statistics Database *16*
        Survey 71
    Informatics Centre 77
    Institute for Polar Research *204*
    Joint Utilities Group 69, 70, 248, *28*, *30*, *31*, *105*, *111*

National – *cont.*
  Land
    Agency *48, 50*
    Survey *4, 39, 40, 41, 42, 43, 46*
  Mapping 59
    Agencies *3*
    Division 524, *12, 15, 16, 18, 20*
    Program *11, 12, 16, 17, 18, 21*
  Meteorological Center *205*
  Museum of Cartography *5, 47, 55*
  Oceanographic
    and Information Centre *205*
    Data Centres *206*
  On-Line Manpower Information System 116, **503–13**
  Organizations **93–8**
  Park Management *62*
  Parks 38
  Partition File *135*
  Police Agency *52, 54*
  Property Line Base *42*
  Resources Information *63*
  Rivers Authority *111*
  Science Foundation 84, 95, 96, 111, 432, *66*
  Society for Professional Surveyors 94
  Strategy for Land Information Management *61, 62*
  Surveys Coordinating Committee *78*
  Tax Board *45*
  Topographic Database *23, 29*
  Transfer
    Format 77, 78, 325, 346, 526, 527, *30, 108, 318*
    Standards 77
  Water
    Summary *15*
    Well Association *279*
  Well Record Collection *209*
  Wetland Inventory 186
  Wilderness Inventory *63*
  Workshop on Natural Resources Data Management *62*
NATMAP *5*
NATO 376, *196*
Natural
  Environment Research Council 34, 37, 77, *206, 214*
    Unit for Thematic Information Systems 34
  Language 112, 264, 420, 422, *229*

Resource
  Data 185
  Management *163*
    Information System 12
Resources
  Advisory Committee 34
  Data Management System 77
  Information System 77
  Management *63, 64*
Nature
  Conservation 62, *198*
  of GIS *3*
  of Planning *297–9*
  of Space 112
  of Spatial Data 85, **112**, 167
Nautical Chart 168
Navigation 75, 112, *6, 117*
Navigator *115*
Navy Hydrographic Service *64*
NCMM 198
Nearest Neighbour 231, 330, 390
NEC *50*
Nederlands Expertise Centruum voor Ruimtelijke Informatiererwerkig *7, 97*
Negligence 497–8
Neighbourhood 232
  Query 227
  Weighted Kernel 470
Netherlands, The *123, 153, 154, 164*
Network 58, 322
  Analysis 329, 390, *108, 304*
  Communication *320*
  Configuration 371
  Data 391, *261*
  Database 113, 251, 254, **256–7**
  Routing 329, *250*
  Topology 285
Neutral Exchange
  File Structure 518
  Structure 516
New
  Brunswick *178*
  Directions in GIS 85
  Haven Census Use Study 25, 27, 30
  York 30
NICNET 77
NIMBUS-7 198
Nippon Telephone and Telegram *51, 52, 53, 54*
Nissan *14, 115*
  Cedric *115, 116, 117, 119, 120*
Nitrate Leaching *155*

NOAA 186, 193, 196, 198, *7, 202, 204, 206, 209, 220, 222, 223, 225, 226, 227, 287*
Node 257, 306, 27
Nominal
  Data 322, 437, 439
  Record Linkage 343
Non
  -Deterministic Polynomial Time 222
  -Geometric Classes 229
  -Linear Bidimensional Regression 430
  -Metric Spaces **122–4**
  -Satellite Remote Sensing 192
  -Spatial
    Analytical Model 409
    Database Application 419
  -Statistical Interpolation *164*
  -Transitional Variogram *159*
    Model *160*
  -Uniform Rational B-Spline 305, 309
  -Weighted Kernel 470
Normal Forms in a Database 258
North
  Carolina *8*
    Administrative Code *267*
    Center for Geographic Information and Analysis *8, 261, 262, 267, 269, 272*
    General Statutes *267*
    Hazardous Waste Management Commission *267, 269*
    Sea Grant College Program *264*
  Central Soil Conservation Research Laboratory *279*
  East London Polytechnic *317*
  WesternTechnical Institute 28
    University 28
Northern Ireland Land Registry 73
Norway 129, *153, 224*
Nottingham *145, 148*
Nuggett Variance *160*
Numerical
  Algorithm Group 216
  Categorization 470
  Raster Generalization 470
  Transformation **143–4**
Nyquist
  Frequency 195
  Limit 193

Oakland Planning Information
  System 30
Object
  Concept 150
  Generalization 458
  Geometry 193
  Localization 434
  Orientation 120, 324, 417
  Recognition 434
  Rendering 290
Object-Oriented 85, 323, 418, 462, 472
  Database 113, 127, 418, 462, *110*
    Design 328
    Management System **263–4**,
    355
  Programming 373, 398, 462, 463
  System **103**, 463
Objective Knowledge 371
Observatoire de Paris *204*
Ocean Surface Monitoring 196
Oceanography 50, 114, 197
Octree 124, 308, 310, 325
ODA 346, *73*
ODYSSEY 24, 28, 32, 328
OECD 495, *73*
Office
  Document Architecture 355
  of Management and Budget 524,
  17, *18*, *19*
  of Population Censuses and
  Surveys 67–8, 507, 508
Official Development Assistance *72*
Ohio State University 524
Oil Exploration 299
Oman *76*
OMB/Whitehouse 24
On-Line
  Grid Control *109*
  Transformation 344
One-to-Many
  Mapping 253
  Relationship 256, 257
ONKA *66*
Open
  -Cast Mining 271, 293
  Data Format *108*
  System 57
Operating
  System 216, *318*
  Considerations 85
Operational
  Data *276*
  Geographer, The 84
  Issues **116–17**

Navigation Chart *188*, *223*
Planning *276*
Optical
  Character Reader 325
  Disk 106, 215, 352, *15*
  Line Following 244
  Speed Sensor *118*
  Storage 245
Optimal
  Interpolation *158–63*
  Location 121
  Spatial Interpolation *7*
Optimization Model *292*
Optimizing Sampling Networks *154*
ORACLE 216, 259, 260
Orbital
  Inclination 195
  Orientation 195
Order 230
  Relation 230
  Data 376
Ordinal Data 322, 437, 439
Ordnance Survey 27, **34–5**, 67, 68,
  69, 70, **72–3**, 77, 78, 124, 127, 138,
  186, 241, 248, 262, 512, 513, 526, *3*,
  4, *13*, *23*, *93*, *105*, *111*, *123*, *131*, *132*
  Data 29–30, *31*
  Database Project *33–4*
  Digital Map Stock 70
  Digitizing Methods *31*
  Feature Coding *30*
  Map Revision *31–2*
  National Grid 377
  of Northern Ireland **73**, *23*
    Topographic Database 73
  of the Republic of Ireland *23*
  Review 36, 67, 68, *28*
  Topographic Database 36
  Transfer Format *29*, *30*
Oregon 30
Origins of Land Information Systems
  85–7
Orthogonal Coordinate Axes 377
Orthographic Display Techniques 287
Orthophoto 182, 183, 288, 290, *12*
  Mapping *41*
  Production 293
Orthophotoquad *18*
OS (1988) 70
OS/2 49, 52
Osaka *48*
  Gas *51*
  Metropolitan University *49*
OSBASE 35

OSCAR 35, *123*
OSLAND 35
OSU-MAP 372
Overground Networks *103*
Overlap 330
Overlay 57, 114, 324, 341, 389, *213*,
  265
  Digitizing 245–6
  Mapping 102
Oversampling of Contours 272
Ownership and Tenure System *89*
Oxford System of Automated
  Cartography 23, 34
Ozone Hole *186*

Pacific Ocean *64*
PackBits 245
Packet Switching Stream 504
Painter's Algorithm 290
Pair-wise Test *174*
PAMAP *316*
PANACEA 372
PANDA 422
Paper Maps *4*
Papua New Guinea *64*
Paradigm 47
Parallel
  Processing 207, 216, 240, *321*
  Programming 410
  Recognition 473
Parameterization 91, 92, 314
Parcel-Based Land Information
  Systems *62*
Parent-Child Linkage 256
Parliamentary Constituency 506
Parochialism 65
ParrallelPiping 470
Partial 230
  Order 230
Pascal 252
PASCO *52*
Passkey 510
PATHFINDER *120*
Pathfinding *115*, *122*
  Algorithm *121*
Pattern
  Detection 399
  Generation 459
  Recognition 45, 435, 439, 469
  Spotter 397
  Tester 397
PC 52, 57, 58, 63, 215, 216, 244, *15*,
  35, *52*, *53*, *74*, *77*, *156*, *172*, *177*,
  180, *220*, *293*, *314*, *317*, *322*

637

Subject index

PC – cont.
    ARC/INFO 24
    GIS 53
PC-Atlas 43
PC-Based GIS 132
PC-DBMS 261
PC-MAP 24
PCMAPICS 512
PCX 346
PDES 346
Peano
    Curve 463
    Relation 463
    Tuple Algebra 463
Peanokey 463
Pedology 197
Pen Plotter 439
Pennsylvania State University 74
Perceived Spatial Variation 195
Perception 428
Performance
    Evaluation 141
    Monitoring 218
Periodicals 6
Perspective 300
    Block Diagram 290
    Display Techniques 290
    Transformation 290
Pesticide Distribution 155
Phantom Line 235
Phenomenon Fluctuation 381
Phenomenal Generalization 473, 474
Phillips CARIN 117
Philosophy 152
Phong Shading 288
Photo-Essays 106
Photo-Journalism 106
Photogrammetric
    Data 275, 278
        Capture 270, 271, 293
    Digitizing 26
    Engineering and Remote Sensing 6, 22, 94
    Sampling Techniques 271
    Survey 308, 312
Photogrammetry 47, 56, 59, 60, 138, 142, 168, 169, 171, 172, 338, 345, 12, 31, 32, 41, 317
Photographic
    Archiving 429
    Imagery 378
    Reduction 32
Photography 433
Photoimage Map 11

Photointerpretation 56, 59
Photomultiplyer Tube 244
Photorealistic Scene Rendering 292
Physical
    Data Model 516
    Database Design 252–3
    Model 206
    Modelling 191, 192
    Realization 217
    System 112
Physics 93, 275
Picture Cells 232
Pilot
    Application 64
    Studies 62, 96
Pinpoint Analysis Limited 37, 124
PIOS 345
Pipe Utilities 102
Pivot Number 221
Pixel 49, 51, 124, 135, 193, 194, 197, 199, 201, 202, 203, 204, 207, 234, 320, 434
    Magazine 53
    Radiance Value 203
    Re-classification 213
Placement 449
    of Line-Feature Names **451–2**
    of Point-Feature Names **450–1**
Plan
    d'Occupation du Sol 297
    Development 234
Planar
    Enforcement 52, 324
    Graph 217
PLANES 28
PLANET 51, 52
Planimetric
    Data 269
    Footprint 362
    Information 41
    Map 113
Planimetrically Rectified Locational Data 185
Planimetry 113
Planner 92, 104
Planning 84, 119, 197, 286, 293, 8, 57
    Commission of the Government of India 77
    Control 76
    Database 303
    Information
        Overlay System 32
        System 12, **299–302**

Models 294
Tools 391
Planogram 145
Plotter 15, 56, 511, 80, 110, 250
pMAP 124, 130, 372, 287, 291
Point 85, 102, 328
    Pollution 104
    Referencing of Areal Data 39
    Spread Function 192
    Variogram 194
Point-Feature Placement Triangle 450
Point-in-Polygon 128, 172, 422, 158
Point-Mode Digitizing 435
Poisson 397, 399, 400, 401
Polar Coordinates 135, 136
Polarization 194
Polarizing Filter 50
Police Management 90
Policy
    Analysis 8, 238
    Evaluation 242
    Formulation 262
Political
    Districting 298
    Geography 84
    Geography Quarterly 314
Politicians 105
Poll Tax 76
Pollution 97, 197, 9, 109
    Control 76, 90
    Dispersion Model 293
Polychlorinated Biphenyl 268
Polygon 111, 115, 124, 125, 138, 169, 172, 199, 200, 217, 218, 219, 233, 247, 263, 269, 308, 328, 377, 382, 383, 468, 7, 30, 32, 34, 35, 36, 48, 153, 157, 158, 172, 202, 209, 210, 222, 250
    Attribute 34
    Based Database 218
    Closure 436
    Creation 378
    Data Layer 269
    Filtering 469
    Intersection and Overlay System 24
    Lumped Average 164
    Merging 464
    Network 164
    Object 264, 34
    Overlay 126, 128, 149, 169, 170, 172, 181, 231, 322, 339, 422, 13, 209, 261, 262
Polygonization 300

638

Polyhedral Rendering *319*
Polyline 305
Polynomial
 Transformation 139
 Trend *159*
  Surface 391
Polytree 308
POLYVRT 327
Population
 Atlas of China *79*
 Cartogram 132
 Characteristics 322
 Density 168
 Forecasting *90*
 Register *128, 129–31, 135*
 Shift 255
Portable
 Field Computer *154*
 Interactive Editing System *32*
Position Determination **117–21**
Positional
 Accuracy **169–70**
 Completeness *195*
 Data 135
 Error 440
Post
 Census Data Processing 133
 Code 69, 70, 506, *132, 133*
 Office 71
Posterior
 Logit *173*
 Probability *173, 174, 181*
POSTGRES 263, 417, 419, 421
Postscript 346
Potential and Needs, Investments and Capabilities Audit *140*
Practical Class 87
Pre-Census
 Data Processing *133*
 Planning *129*
Pre-Journey Route Planning *35*
Predicate Calculus 417, 422
Prediction 119
Preference Weighting Sub Model *291*
Prescriptive
 Cartographic Modelling Techniques *371–2*
 Map *290*
 Mapping 285
Presentation Graphics *324*
Price Waterhouse *321*
Primary
 Data Capture **240–1**

Map *289, 290*
Mapping Economic Analysis Study *18*
Prime 52
 SYSTEM/9 262
Prime/Wild 320
Primitive
 Entities 373
 Instancing 307, 326
Primitives 12
Primos 52
Principles
 of Graphic Design 432
 of Map Design 115
Prior Probability *174*
Private Values 493
Probability
 Density Function 202, *174*
 Map *174*
Problem
 Clarification *234*
 Sensing *234*
 Translation 231
Procedural
 Data Types 417
 Knowledge 464
 Tools for Generalization of Spatial Databases **464–8**
Procedures for Detecting Patterns and Relationships **399–400**
Proceedings of the International Spatial Data Handling Symposia 58
 Workshop on Geographical Information Systems *79*
Process Knowledge 393
Processor 85
Product Data Exchange Specification 527, 529
Production
 GIS 86
 System Language 418
 Systems 86
Profit Impact or Market Strategy *143*
Programmers Hierarchical Integrated Graphics System 300, 527
Programming Language Interface 252
Progressive Sampling 271, 272
Project
 Data 276
 Management 85, 87
 Planning 276
 Vasundharsa 77

Projection
 Conversion *189*
 Error *220*
Projective Land Use Model *248, 249*
PROLOG 418, 422
Properties 103
 of a Polygon 217
Property
 Database 350
 Development 76
 Gazetteer *27*
 Information System 12
 Investment 76
 Management 54
 Ownership 22
 Rights 492
 Tax Database *50*
 Taxation *53*
PROSPECTOR 422
Protectionism 65
Prototyping 152, *185, 189*
Proximal 28
 Polygon *132*
Proximity 330, 440
 Analysis 329
 Beacon Detection *117*
Proxy Data 395
Psi-s Plot 465
Psychologist 104
Psychology 152
Public
 Decision Making *243*
 Facilities
  Model *256*
  Modelling *256–7*
  Planning *248*
 Health 76
 Policy
  Analysis *233, 234, 235, 242*
   Paradigm *234–5*
  Decision Making *233*
  Support System *238*
 Protection 76
 Utilities Street Works Act 88, *111*
 Values 493
Publishing 60
Punch Card 23
PURSIS *80*
Pycnophylactic Interpolation 385
Pyroclastic Surge *212*
Pythagoras 120
Pythagorean Distance 130, 231

Subject index

Q-Net 65
Quadrangle 136
Quadrat Analysis 390
Quadtree 124, 149, 199, 200, 201,
  230, 233, 234, 261, 308, 325, 328,
  463, *174, 175, 314*
  Map *176, 177*
Qualitative
  Benchmark 484
  Uncertainty 181
Quality
  Assurance 85, *320*
  Control 116, *223, 225, 320*
    Procedure *29*
  of Generalization 468
Quantification
  in Human Geography *47*
  of Attributes *238*
  of Goals *238*
  of Objectives *238*
  of Specific Targets *238*
Quantitative
  Analysis 88, 287, 390, *223*
    of Digital Terrain Data *282*
  Benchmark 484, 485
  Geography 81, 88, 173, 389, 390,
    393
  Land Evaluation 97
  Methods 88, 173, *319*
    Study Group 81
  Model *212*
  Revolution 87, 88, 91, 429, 439
  Visualization 287
Quantization 192
Quaternary Triangulation Mesh 463
Quebec *179*
Queensland
  Centre for Surveying and
    Mapping Studies 67
  Department of Geographic
    Information 67
  University 67
QUEL* 417
Query 147, 389
  Function 405
  Language 228, 252, 417, *96*
  Optimization 420, 421
Querying Geographical Variation 112

R-Tree 199, 233
Radar 324
  Altimetry 270
  Interferometry *223*
RADARSAT 198

Radial Distance *250*
Radiance 191
Radiation 193, 197
Radio Location *115, 117*
  Signal *119*
Radiometer 204
Radiometric
  Calibration 195
  Precision 199
  Rectification 202
  Resolution 192
RAM 49, *117, 122, 319*
Rand McNally 24
Rand-Map 24
Random Error 166
Randomization 221
Randomized Algorithm 215, 221
Rangeland Management *164*
Ranked Data 376
RAPID *59*
Rapid Prototyping 215, 223–4
Raster 13, 21, 50, 51, 52, 53, 56, 75,
  85, 92, 111, 114, 124, 130, 135, 136,
  149, 155, 196, 198, 199, 200, 201,
  230, 233, 239, 240, 244, 245, 246,
  247, 248, 269, 290, 293, 299, 302,
  304, 308, 309, 310, 312, 321, 325,
  328, 329, 338, 348, 364, 385, 413,
  422, 452, 457, 479, *15, 30, 37, 42,
  77, 81, 157, 161, 172, 192, 206, 207,
  212, 213, 218, 222, 262, 278, 306,
  314, 315, 318*
  -based GIS 85
  Contouring 288
  Data 525, 527
    Model 343
    Storage 85
    Structures 200
  Database 330
  Generalization 470
  Handling 345
  Model 320, 516
  Overlay *164*
  Remote Sensing System 191,
    324
  Scanning 272, 325, *16, 52, 203*
  Space 461
  Spatial Structuring 310
  -to-Vector Conversion 246, 247,
    228, 314
  -Vector
    Contrasts 85
    Dichotomy 325
    Restructuring 329

Rasters 232, 234
Rating Matrix 465
Ratio Data 322
Rational Planning Model *237–8*
Ray Tracing 288, 292
Rayner Review 511
Re-Triangulation 280
Real
  Estate 59
  Property Register *45*
Reality 433
Realization in a Computing
  Environment 85
Rebotics 439
Recent Ordnance Survey
  Developments *33–6*
Reclassification 343
Recording Utility Plant *105–6*
Recreation 59
Recreational Planning 32
Rectangular Grid 273
Rectification 343
Recursive Query 416
REDATAM 75
Reduced Instruction Chip Set 299
Redundancy *172*
  in Data 253
Reference Systems **376–8**
Referential Integrity Constraints
  419
Reflectance 168
Reflected Radiance of a Surface 194
Refuse Collection 76
Region *131*
  Growing 185
  Re-classification *213*
Regional
  Analysis 192
  Board of Forestry *43*
  Database Systems 225
  Geographical Information
    Systems Project 65
  Growth Forecasting *248, 253*
  Health Authority 68, 74, 75
  Information System *259*
  Land Survey *43*
  Planning 22, 59
  Research Laboratory 7, 77, 81,
    84, 96, 396, *66, 315*
  Urban Information System *257*
Regionalization 314, 390
Regionalized
  Variable Theory *159–63*
  Variables *159*

Register
    of Population 39
    of Property 39
Registered Overlay System 499
Registers of Scotland 93
Registration Error 220
Registry of Deeds 159
Regression 380, 434, *177*
    Analysis 205, *278*
    Score Map *177*
    Tree Analysis 205
Regular
    Sampling 271
    Tessellation **149–50**, 198, 227, 232–3
Regularization 193, 194
Regulation of Behaviour 491
Relational
    Algebra 257
    Base 419
    Based System 418
    Calculus 416
    Data
        Management Techniques 373
        Model 229
    Database 251, 416, *33*, *158*
        Management System 201, *314*
        System 254, **257–9**
    Geographical Information System 200
    Joins in a Database 258
    Matching *300*
Relationship
    Prover 397
    Seeker 397
Relative
    Accuracy 166
    Nonpoint Source Pollution Potential Study *278*
    Sensor *119*
Relief
    Contour 288
    Shading 371
    Shadow Analysis 286
Remote
    Scanning System 191
    Sensing 6, 12, 22, 47, 53, 56, 83, 84, 92, 101, 112, 124, 168, 170, 185, **191–208**, 192, 239, 240, 271, 290, 293, 329, 338, 353, 432, 434, 436, 439, 470, *28*, *43*, *57*, *60*, *63*, *74*, *77*, *78*, *155*, *157*, *171*, *172*, *186*, *196*, *198*, *207*, *218*, *227*, *281*, *306*, *317*

    as a Resource of Geographical Data **192–6**
Data 344
Database 385
Models 201, 204
Principles 192
Systems 192
Remotely Sensed Imagery 516
RenderMan 292, 300
Reorientation of a Digital Terrain Model 280
Report
    Generation 366
    of the House of Lords Select Committee on Science and Technology 36
    Writer 252
Representation 242
Representative Polygon *176*
Request for Proposals 482, 483, 484
Resel 469
Reservoir Design 287
Residual
    Error 341
    From Regression 429
Resolution
    of Scanners 244
    Theorem Proving 422
Resource
    Allocation Working Party 75
    Analysis 197, 201, *21*
    Assessment *280*
    Based Course 87
    Management 22, 47, 53, 76, 119, 293, 339, *3*, *8*, *11*, *21*, *314*, *316*, *317*
    Optimization *90*
    Planning *250*, *285*
    Provision 83
    Shortage 55
Response Modelling 396
Responsibility for Education in GIS 84
Responsible
    Marine Information Advisory Centre *208*
    National Oceanographic Data Centres *206*
Restricted Zone Design 397
Restrictive Covenant 73
RFT 346
RGB 245
Ridge Line 278
River Rhine *193*

Road
    Administration Information Centre *53*
    Design 287, 293
    Network *59*
Roads 271
    Service 73
Robotics 435
Rome Air Development Center 27
Root Mean Square 243, 285
Rosch-Lakoff-Johnson Model of Cognitive Categories 152
Rotation 231
Route
    Finding *314*
    Planning *26*, *90*
Routeplanner Map Series *36*
Royal
    Australian Army Survey Corps *64*
    College of Art *24*, *25*
    Geographical Society 96
    Observatory of Belgium *204*
    Town Planning Institute 36
RTSI 24
Rubber Sheeting 344, 499, *189*, *194*, *324*
Rule
    Base 414
    Set *267*, *268*, *269*
Rule-Based
    Applications 420
    Expert System 420
    System 419, *37*
Run-Length Encoding 124, 199, 230, 233, 234, 245, 325
Runoff 114
Rural Land Use Information System 35

SAC 372
SACS 24
Sage 25
SAGIS 372
SAGIS89 98
SALADIN 75
Sales
    by Sector 56
    Force Automation *141*
    Forecasting *141*
Sammamish Data Systems 24
Sampling 307–8
    Bias *171*
    Limitation 312

Sampling – *cont.*
    Resolution 460
    Strategy 428
    Techniques 270
San Diego
    Association of Governments 8, *247, 248, 249, 250, 256, 257, 259*
    Council of Governments 24
Sanitary Engineering 59
Sapir-Wharf Hypothesis 153
SAS 13
SASPAC 513, *132*
Satellite 191, 223, 427, *80*
    Data 191, *210*
    Image 349, *55*
    Imagery 271, 458, *14, 128, 135, 178, 195*
    Photography 378
    Radiances 195, 204
    Reflectance Measurement 203
Satimage *43*
Saudi Arabia 76, *123*
Scale
    Conversion 343
    Dependency 193, 323
       in Vegetation Patterns 193
    -Dependent Database **471–3**, 472
    -Free *37*
    Data *25*
    Database *33, 35, 189, 192*
    -Independent Database 472, 473
    of Measurement 193
Scaleless Database **471–3**
Scaling 231
Scanner 15, 57, 241, 243–4, 245, 324, 328, 345, 349, *314*
Scanning 46–7, 59, 64, 113, 185, 433, 436, *12, 15, 31, 37, 194, 324*
Scatter Diagram 434
Scene Analysis 434
Schema 152
    Integration Analysis 343, 344
School
    Districting *298*
    Resource Planning *90*
Schönhage-Strassen 221
Science
    and Engineering Research Laboratory *204*
    Council of Japan *55*
Scientific Analysis 191
SCMAP 372
Scope and Domain of Visualization **431–9**

Scott Polar Research Institute *204*
Scottish
    Development Agency 508
    Department 35, 36
    Tourist Board 35
Screen Forms Management System 252
Screening 105
    Matrix 299
SCRIS 25
SCS 345
SDF 346
Seamless Database 182, *116*
Secondary Data Capture **241–3**
Secretary of State for the Environment 69
Security 76, 418, *61, 96, 325*
SEDMAC 315
SEDSIM 315
Segment 27
Seibu Gas *51*
SEISCO 306
Seismic 270, 308, 516, *171*
Selective Sampling 271, 272
Self-Similarity 435, 460, 465
Semantic
    Data Modelling 103, 515
    Equivalence 421
    Frame 417
    Integrity Constraints 419
    Knowledge 421
    Network 414, 417, 421, 515
Semi
    -Automatic Digitization 435
    -Structured Spatial Problems 403
    -Variogram 194
    -variance *159*
Sensitivity Analysis 439
Sensor
    Calibration 191, 192, 204
    Model 207
    Resolution 194, 204
Sensory Bandwidth 354
Sequent 216, 219
Series Mapping *80*
Serpell Committee *28*
Server 58
Service Planning 76
Set 346
Sewage Disposal *109*
SGML 346
Shackelton Committee 68, *28*

Shaded Contour 288
Shaft Encoder *25*
Shape Analysis 434
Sharebase *33*
Shell 308
Shibata Gas *51*
Shortest Path Algorithm 122
Shuttle 198
SICAD 341
SICAD-HYGRIS 345
Sieve Mapping 339
SIF 345, 346
Silicon Graphics 300, *319*
SimCity *8*
Similarity Transformation 141
Simplex 235
Simplicial
    Decomposition 235
    Topology 235
Simulation 75
Single Instruction Multiple Data 216
SIRO-DBMS 67
Site
    Finding *90*
    Planning *297*
Siting a Superconducting Super Collider **270–2**
SLF 345
Sliver Polygon 341, 382, 383, *195*
Slope Analysis 282
Small Area
    Census Studies 25
    Health Statistics Unit 74
Smalltalk 217
Smallworld Systems 14, 15, *320*
Smoothing
    of Digital Terrain Models 278
    Operations 458
Social
    Control 491
    Engineering 491
    Implications of GIS in Australia **64–6**
    Scientists 92
    Services 76, *57*
       Optimization and Management *90*
       Committee on Vehicle Navigation *124*
Socio-Economic
    Applications of GIS *3*
    Attributes **183–4**
    Data 6
    Databases *219*

Subject index

Software 81, **85–6**, 104, **245–8**
   Development Strategy **223–4**
   Engineering 215, 217
   Exploitation 111
   Integration *320*
Soil 168, *7*
   and Terrain Database Project *224*
   and Water Conservation Board *277*
   Classification *156*
   Conservation 177, 179, 180, 182, 186, *62*, *163*
   Data Model *156*
   Database 177, *164*
   Erosion 282, 293, 365
   Information
     Base *155*
     System 12, *153–65*
   Map
     Database *155*
     Quality *156*
   Mapping *154*
     Unit *157*
   Maps 103
   Moisture Regime *155*
   Pollution Studies *164*, *165*
   Polygon *155*, *156*, *158*, *162*, *163*, *164*
   Profile *154*, *155*, *157*
   Science 293
   Survey 179, 186, *153*
Solid
   Modelling 307
   State Compass *115*, *118*
   Voxel 309
Sonar 270
Sophisticated Allocation Process *248*, *249*, *250*, *253*
Sorting Order 421
SOTER 260, *164*
Source
   Document Distortion 248
   Zone 385
South
   African Society for Photogrammetry, Remote Sensing and Cartography 98
   Australia 89
   Carolina *9*
     Infrastructure and Economic Development Project *308*
     Infrastructure and Economic Planning Project *302*, *305*

Wales 305
Western Electricity Board *104*
Soviet
   Geophysical Committee of the Academy of Sciences of the USSR *204*
   Union 38, 98, *224*
Space 119
   Images 112
     -Bounding 309
     -Filling 309
   -Time
     Interaction in Remote Sensing 196
     Model 323
     Relationships *141*
Spaghetti
   Data Structure 232
   Tessellation 227
Spain 130
SPANS 51, 53, 124, 261, 344, *15*, *172*, *174*, *175*, *177*, *178*, *316*, *317*
Spatial 12, 45, 49, 55, 56, 59, 69, 71, 74, 76, 91, 102
   Analysis 13, 27, 55, 83, 84, 95, 97, 101, 103, 104, 111, 114, 115, 119, 124, 128, 185, 200, 231, 260, 329, 345, 391, 392, 406, 439, 464, *36*, *47*, *55*, *145*, *262*, *316*, *317*, *318*
     Methods for GIS **389–401**
     System *316*
     Tools 389, *139*, *300*
     View of GIS 14
   and Inductive Modelling Package for Land Evaluation 66
   Association *171*, *173*, *175*, *176*, *179*, *180*
   Autocorrelation 102, 128, 170, 194, 390, 464
   Autocovariance *164*
   Base *189*
   Characteristics of Remotely Sensed Data **192–3**
   Clustering 314
   Cognition 112, 440
   Complexity *293*
     of a Landscape *286*
   Comprehensive Database *208*
   Concepts 85, 122, 227, **228–9**, 232
   Configuration 304
     Engineering 396
   Conflict 473

Consistency 506, *188*
Constraint Propagation 421
Content *109*
Context 197
Control 168, 170
Covariance *159*
Coverage 375, *193*
Data 83, 85, 96, 98, 119, 128, 165, 166, 170, 207, 228, 233, 261, 338, 339, 341, 343, 347, 385, 391, 417, 421, 437, 439, 458, 461, 479, 516, *5*, *76*, *94*, *143*, *158*, *175*, *228*, *298*, *302*, *314*
   Aggregation 397
   Analysis *37*, *180*
   Display 95
   Exchange **515–30**
     Standard 524
   Exploratory Techniques 389
   Handling 81, 93, 292, 394, 420, *9*, *66*, *77*, *78*, *241*
   Integration **375–85**
   Model 227, 229, 233, 352, 479, 516, 517
   Query *285*
   Representation 302
   Resolution 342
   Retrieval *214*
   Set 222
   Source 186
   Standard *11*
   Structure **197–200**, 227, 228, 229, *7*, *172*
   Technology *19*
   Transfer 94, 523, 525, *17*
Database 98, 114, 167, 251, 299, 420, 439, 457, 460, 462, 473, 484, *171*, *172*, *174*, **302–4**
   Application 419
   Design *11*, *15*
   Management *285*
   Models 113
   System *134*
   Toolkit 67
Decision 115
   Making 114, 116, 438, 440, *308*
   Support
     System 12, 115, **403–11**, *9*, *139*, *308*, *314*, *318*
        Architecture **408–10**
        Toolbox 407
        in Planning *301*
     Techniques 392
Deduction 122

Subject index

Spatial – *cont.*
    Dependency 391
    Detail *220*, *304*
    Disaggregation 203
    Distribution 168, 429
        of Error 203
    Domain 105, 301, *162*
    Engineering 397
    Entity 340, 373, 375, 462
    Environmental Variation 195
    Error Budget 208
    Evidence 166
    Feature 183, 340
    Filtering 470
    Form 299
    Frame 304
    Framework *3*
    Function 310
    Heterogeneity 206
    Impact *293*
    Incompatibility 344
    Index Structure 233
    Indexing 113, 301, 308
    Information 111, 113, 166, 338, 428, 429, 432, 433, 434, 437, 458, 477, *104*, *261*, *285*, *293*, *294*, *298*, *299*, *300*, *302*, *307*, *323*
        Handling *214*
        Management *94*
        Paradigm *316*
        Processing 166, *285*
        Science 14
        Systems 12, *287*
        Technology 64, *57*
    Integration 207
    Interaction 130, 206, 390, *145*
    Interpolation 380, *157*
    Key 340, 348, *262*
    Knowledge 175, 438, 440, 437
    Language 440
    Location 120, 227, 356, *297*
    Measurements 168
    Model 104, 341, 409, 517, *262*
    Modelling 203, 392, 460, 464, *222*, **286–9**
    Nonsense 428
    Object 85, 113, 119, 120, 124, 125, 126, 127, 128, 227, 228, 229, 230, 232, 304, 421, 460, 525
    Occupancy Enumeration 307
    Optimization *67*
    Overlay 338, 339
    Paradigm 236
    Partitioning *196*
    Pattern 301, 391, 429, 438, *210*, *291*
    Description 391
    Detection 396
    Relationships 391–3
    Planning 391, *75*
    Position 194
    Primitive 408
    Problem 403, 405, 406
    Process 193, 299, 305, 457, 468
    Properties 229
    Proximity 119, 121, 462
    Query 122, 197, 227, 314, 329, 408, 463, 463
        Languages **154–6**, **262–3**
    Reference *36*, *59*
    Referenced Data 299
    Referencing 72, 74, 350, 352, 499, *39*, *202*, *208*
    Regression 390, 391
    Relation 373, 406
    Relationship 92, 95, 132, 200, 373, 445, 461, 473, *195*, *286*, *291*, *293*
    Representation 165, 310
    Resolution 192, 193, 196, 199, 428, 460, 463, *49*, *164*, *172*, *196*, *238*
    Response Modelling 398
    Sampling 171
    Search 329, 338, 339, *154*
    Separation 122, 129
    Similarity 128
    Simulation Modelling 206
    Situations 158
    Specificity *287*
    Statistics 95, 200, 373, 393, 394
    Structure 406
    Template *188*, *189*, *194*
    Theory 301, *302*
    Thesaurus *49*
    Trend 438
    Unit 341, *85*, *241*, *249*
    Variation 170, 192, 193, 380, *156*
        in a Satellite Image 193
        of Soil Properties *154*
    Video Analysis 397
Spatially
    Autocorrelated Data 392
    Orientated Referencing Systems Association 27
    Referenced Data 191, *202*
    Registered Information *303*
    Related Data 68

Spatio-Temporal Statistical Analysis 206
Special
    Purpose GIS *5*
    Transformation 421
Specific Geomorphometry 283–5
Specification Error 205
Spectral
    Analysis 271
    Band Width 192
    Contrast 193
    Coverage Spectral Band Location 192
    Dimensionality 192
    Mapping 203
    Resolution 192, 428
    Response Properties 195
    Separation 203
Specular Reflection 288
Speed of Processing 46
Spherical Variogram *161*
Spheroid 137
Spit Tape 25
Splay Tree 220
Spline
    Curve 233
    Generation Software *29*
Split
    Rules *210*
    System *209*
SPOT 141, 185, 194, 198, 271, 523, *9*, *77*, *202*, *223*, *228*, *306*
Spottiness 373
Spreadsheet *142*, *291*
SPSS 127, 130, 329
Spurious Precision 382
SQL 114, 349, 422
Square
    Lattice 460
    Misclassification Index 171
    Tessellation 199
Sri Lanka *74*, *75*
St Lucia *93*
Standard
    for Digital Cartographic Data Quality 165
    for Exchange of Spatial Data 165
    for the Exchange of Product Data 527, 529
    Industrial Classification *251*
    Interchange Format 325
    Meridian 377
    Query Language 155

Standards
    Australia *61*
    Manual 78
Standing Committee on Rural Land Use 35
Staring Institute for Integrated Land, Water and Rural Survey *163*
State
    Database 272
    Land Information Council 59, *94*
    Plane System 377
    Planning Commission 79
Static
    Query Optimization 421
    Visualization 287
Statistical 22
    Analysis 88, 390, *191*, *300*, *304*
    Correlation *277*
    Data 417
    Description 428
    Generalization 460, 464, 468
    Geography 389, 390
    Graphics 409
    Mapping 429
    Methods 88
    Modelling 435, *7*
    Pattern Recognition 203
    Self Similarity 460, 465
    Survey 433
Statistics 439
    Bureau 52
    Graphics System *228*
    Sweden *45*
Statmap 24
Status of Biological Diversity *205*
Step 346
Stereo
    Aerial Photograph *157*
    Depth 434
    Digitizing *113*
    Visualization System 302
Stereoplotter 325, *13*
STIBOKA *154*
Stochastic
    Analysis in Human Geography *47*
    Uncertainty 206
Stockholm *260*
Storage **48–9**, 409
Storm Surge 102
Straight-Line Graticule 377
Strain Ellipsoid 409
Stratamodel 309

Strategic
    Data *276*
    Planning 479
    Information System 53
    Mapping 53, *317*, *320*
    Planning 406, *276*
Stream
    Line 278
    -Mode Digitizing 435
Street
    Address Matching System 25
    Cleaning 76
    Gazetteer 72
    Light Maintenance *90*
    Map 377
    Network
        Database *318*
        Topology *121*, *124*
Striation 373
Strict-Order Relations 230
Strings 341
Strip Tree 463
Structural
    Generalization 469
    Knowledge 464
Structural-Conceptual Generalization 469
Structure 92
    Preserving Transformation 468
    Signature 460, 465
Structured
    Data 242, *32*
    Query Language **156**, 252, 263, *156*
    Topographic Data *34*
    Vector Data *32*
Student Learning 81
Sub-Regional
    Area 249
    Forecast 249, *250*
Sub-Surface Hydrology 114
Subdivision 330
Subjective Judgement 371
Submerged Aquatic Vegetation *265*, *266*
Subregion 330
Subsetting Mechanism 253
Suitability
    Model *300*
    Ranking *291*
Sumitomo Forestry 52
Sun
    Microsystems 219, 220, *263*
    -Earth-Satellite Geometry 193

Super
    cluster 399
    computer 215, 394, 399, 427, 439, *15*, *218*, *219*
    computing 432
    conducting Super Collider *8*, *9*, *261*, *262*, *271*
    fund *280*
    plan *35*
    position 330
Supervised Classification 202, 203
Supply and Demand Forecasting *247*
Surface 85
    Classification 191
    Flow Modelling 329
    Inflection 371
    Modelling in 3D **304-7**
    Variation 194, 283
Surface-Sensor Geometry 193
Surrogate
    Data 395
    Walk 354
Survey
    Data Capture 293
    Information on Microfilm *34*
    of India *76*, *78*
Surveying 22, 59, 121, 137, 169, 172, *12*, *102*, *317*
    and Mapping 94
    and Photogrammetry 292–3
Surveyor 92
Swansea *145*
Sweden 38, 67, 98, 186, *4*, *93*, *129*
Swedish
    Central Board for Real Estate *92*
    Land Data Bank 38, *39*, *40*, *41*, *42*, **43-6**
    Meteorological and Hydrological Institute *42*
    National Road Administration *42*
    Water Archive *42*
Sweep Representation 307
Switzerland *224*
SYLK 346
SYMAP 24, 28, 33, 34, 36, 372, *48*
Symbolic
    Logic 330
    Manipulation 231
Symbolization 437, 464, *26*
Symbology 232, 440, *17*
Symmetry 430
Symposia 6, 60
Synercom 24, 32

Subject index

Syntactic Pattern Recognition 202
Synthesising Cartographic Data 371
Synthetic
    Aperture Side-Scan Radar *80*
    Imagery 435
    Modelling Techniques 371
SysScan GEOREC 247
System
    Cycle Support **60–1**
    Evaluation 483–5
    Implementation 85
    Planning 85
    Security 509
    Software 85
System/9 15, 52, *320*
Systematic
    Error 166
    Survey 308
Système d'Exchange et de Transfer 527
Systems Analysis 101, *234, 235*

Tables 113
Tabular Report Generator 409–10
Tachymetry 345
Tactical
    Data *276*
    Planning *276*
Tag Image File Format 245, 345
Tagging *16*
Tangible Benefits *244*
Tape 183
    Drive 15
    Triangulation *102*
Target
    Group Index *144, 147*
    Zone 385
Taunton Joint Utilities Group 69, *111*
Taxation 22, *91*
Taxicab
    Distance 121
    Metric 231
Taxonomy of Error in GIS Data **168–72**
Teaching 33, 81, 85
Technical Institute of Darmstadt 87
Technological Imperialism *5*
Tektronix 50, 87
    4010 49
TeleAtlas *123*
Telecom 67
Telecommunications 69
Telescoping *276*
Teleshopping *148*

Television 222, 349
Template Matching 465
Templating 344
Temporal
    Attributes in Spatial Databases 264
    Characteristics of Remotely Sensed Data **195–6**
    Data 101, 251, 342, 431, 439
    Dynamics 373
    Resolution 192
    Variation 195
Terminal 49
    Emulator 512
Terrain
    Analysis 75, 469, *67*
    Data Editing 293
    Intervisibility Calculation 329
    Modelling 113, 114, 235
    Related Information 75
    Representation 114
TerraSoft 341
Terrestrial
    Ecological Data *203–5*
    System 136
Tessellation 329, 440, *225*
    Model 320, 321, 322, 324, 516
Terabyte 216, 229
Text
    Placement 437
    Processor 217
Textbooks **5–6**
Textual Database 341
Textural Analysis 283
Texture 434
TGA 346
Thailand 38, *75, 76, 92, 224*
    Land Titling Project *94*
The Times *127*
Thematic
    Attribute 168, *286*
    Cartography 166, 167
    Data 341, 408, *189, 224*
    Error 381, 383, 384
    Map 92, 176, 429
        Accuracy 203
    Mapper 135, 205, 207, *209*
    Specificity *286, 287*
Themes 48
Theorem Proving 421
Theoretical
    Analysis **220–1**
    Modelling Systems *218*
Theories on Liability 496–8

Theory
    of Error 168
    of Normal Forms 258
Thickening 470
    Blanket 471, 472
Thiessen Polygon 28, 121, 126, 275, 276, *132, 176*
Thinking Machine Corporation 216
Third Generation Language 252
Thresholding 285
TIGER 24, 29, 31, 33, 122, 186, 325, 345, *6, 9, 16, 65, 123, 133, 136, 256, 305, 306, 307*
    Database 48
    Line Files 24
    Spatial Data Structure *135*
    Spatial Database *134*
    System *134–5*
TIGER/Line *134, 135*
Tight Coupling 419
TIGRIS 15, 52, 235
Tile 48, 277, *196*
Time
    Distance 119
    in GIS 323
    Projections 105
    Series Analysis 170, 464
Time-Dynamic Spatial Information 393
TIN-to-Contour Conversion 280
Title Registration *58*
Tokyo *48, 49*
    Astronomical Laboratory *204*
    Gas *6, 49, 51, 54*
    Metropolitan Government *48*
Tolerance 383
TOPAZ *66*
Topographic
    Archive 72
    Base Map *103–5*
    Data *4*
    Database *59, 188*
    Elevation 113
    Features 71
    Incline 363
    Information 25
    Map 92, 168, 169, 176, 182, *41, 42*
    Mapping 139, 287, 293, *3, 4, 23*
    Slope 363
    Surface 269
Topographical Mapping 138, *6*
Topography 113, 193, *113*
Topological
    Attribute 285

Subject index

Data 408
　Structure 231, *11, 27, 30, 32, 33, 36*
　Dimension 125
　Encoding *115, 116*
　Genus 371
　Invariant 231
　Linking 200
　Order 285
　Overlay *300*
　Relation 151, 312
　Relationship 382, *34*
　Space 122
　Spatial Data Model 341
　Transformation 231
　Validation *13, 16*
Topology 31, 58, 122, **124–5, 128–32**, 230–1, *32*
Torrens Systems of Land Registration 58
Toshiba 53
Total Transfer Package 529
Tourism and Recreation 35
Town and Country Planning Act 69, *297*
Toyota *14, 54, 116*
Tracking Vehicle 47
Tradeable Information Initiative 70, 71, **74**, 78, 510, *94*
Traffic 105, *35, 90*
　Accident Analysis *90*
　Analysis 115, 276, *249, 250, 255, 256, 298*
Trafficability Analysis 283
Training 57, 59, 60, 83, 85, 319, 506, 508, *319*
Transaction
　Loggers 14
　Processing System 10, 17
Transfer
　Function *163*
　Model *163*
Transformation 52, 112, 138, **139–44**, 231, 312
Transforming Objects **126–7**
Transitional Variogram *159, 160*
Translation 231
Transnational Information Access 493
Transport
　Planning *90, 110*
　Survey Coding Guide 25
Transportability 69
Transportation 26, 59, 76, 472, *248*

Transverse Mercator 138
　Graticule 377
　Projection 68, 139, 141
　Travel *145, 148, 265*
Trend
　Analysis *264*
　Surface *159*
Tri-state Transport 25
Triangle
　Data Model 113
　Inequality 121
　Nodes 277
Triangulated Irregular Network 125, 126, 235, 273, 274, 306, 325, 376, 460, *314*
　Based Interpolation 275
Triangulation 275
　Based Interpolation 278
Tribal Designated Statistical Area *133*
Trigonometrical Survey 68
Trilateration 129
TRINITY 52
Tropical Resources Institute *294*
TRW Incorporated *143*
TUMSY *54*
Tuple 113, 257, 463
Turbid Medium Model 207
Turing
　Test 157
　-Computable 414, 415
Turnaround Test 410
TYDAC 51, 52, 53, *316*
Types of Database Management Systems Structure **254–63**

UMTA 24
Uncertainty *175, 184*
Unclassed Choropleth Map 430
Underground Networks *103*
Undersampling of Contours 272
UNESCO Natural Resources Research Series 30
UNICEF *72, 73*
Uniform Grid 215, **219–20**, 460
Unimatch 25
Unintended Use of Maps 500
Uniqueness Property 258
United
　Nations
　　Centre for Regional Development 75
　　Economic Commission for

Latin America and the Caribbean 75
　Environmental Programme *74, 187, 205*
　Food and Agriculture Organization *187*
　Institute for Training and Research *224*
States 67
　Bureau
　　of the Budget 26, 179
　　of the Census 3, 21, 25, 26, 30, 33–34, 48, 122, 183, 186, 325, 327, 495, 507, 529, *6, 9, 16, 65, 129, 131, 134, 135, 136, 256, 303, 304, 305, 318*
　Census *6, 133*
　Defense Mapping Agency 182, *17, 223*
　Fish and Wildlife Service 186
　Forest Survey 30
　Forestry Service *281*
　Geological Survey 3, 21, 25, 27, 30, 33, 48, 127, 136, 177, 179, 180, 186, 219, 221, 223, 262, 325, 377, 434, 500, 501, 517, 523, 524, 529, *3, 4, 9, 11, 12–13, 21, 133, 134, 136, 154, 203, 204, 209, 263, 276, 287, 304, 305, 306, 318*
　Global Change Research Programme *220*
　National
　　Bureau of Standards 524
　　Committee for Digital Cartographic Data Standards 166
　　Institute of Standards and Technology 524
　　Map Accuracy Standard 169, 172, 179, 180
　　Ocean Survey 27
　　Naval Observatory *204*
　　Postal Service 24, *131*
　　Soil Conservation Service 434
　　Standard for Digital Cartographic Data 180
　　Standards for Map Accuracy *194*
Univariate Analysis 391
Universal
　Soil Loss Equation *164, 277*
　Transverse Mercator 137, 377, *202, 203*

647

University
 College London 512
 of Amsterdam 97
 of California 32, 33, 95, 223
 of Chicago 28
 of Cincinnati 26
 of Delft 97
 of Durham 36, 81, 503, 507, 508, 509
 of Edinburgh 36, 77
 of Essex 513
 of Leicester 77, 84
 of London 36, 88, *188*, *189*
 of Lund *39*
 of Maine 33, 95, 96
 of Melbourne *67*
 of Michigan 38
 of Minnesota 31
 of Nanjing 98
 of New South Wales *67*
 of New York at Buffalo 33, 95
 of Newcastle 508, 509
 of Ohio State 84
 of Oregon 24
 of Reading 34
 of Saskatchewan 53
 of Tokyo *47*, *49*, *52*
 of Utrecht 97
 of Wageningen 97
 of Washington 24, 26
Unix 15, 49, 50, 52, 58, 215, 217, 224, 300, 509, 510, *263*, *323*
Unlinking Data Sets 209
Unstructured Tessellation Model 321
Unsupervised Classification 201, 202, 203
Urban 104
 and Regional
  Information Systems
   Association 7, 26, 33, 36, 93, 94, 97, *65*, *301*, *315*
   Planning *58*, *68*
 Atlas 24, 30–1
 Data 25, 105
 GIS Applications **247–60**
 Growth Management **236–7**, *238*, *239*
 Information System 12, *49*, *248*
 Infrastructure 92, *314*
 Management 89, *243*
 Planning 22, 59, 104, 293, *218*
 Transportation Studies 111
URBYS 422
USAID *75*

Use and Value of Geographic Information 95
USEMAP *75*
User
 Interface 483, *315*
 Requirement Analysis *95*, *96*
Uses of Information 490
USI II *51*
USSR
 Academy of Sciences 38
 State Committee for Hydrometeorology and Control of the Environment *204*, *206*
Utilities Mapping 292
Utility
 Management 22
 Network *59*
Utvecklingsradet for Landskapsinformation 98

Validation 99, 399
Valuation and Property Assessment *90*
Value
 Added Services *142*, *143*, *325*
 of GIS 106, 116
Valuer General's Department *58*
Variable
 Resolution Display *280*
 Scaling 460
Variogram 194, 271, *159*
Vaster 328
VAX *33*, *51*, *321*
Vector 28, 32, 50, 51, 52, 53, 56, 75, 85, 111, 124, 130, 135, 149, 197, 198, 199, 201, 202, 233, 235, 239, 245, 246, 247, 248, 299, 304, 306, 308, 309, 310, 312, 314, 324, 325, 328, 329, 330, 338, 342, 345, 348, 364, 378, 381, 385, 452, 457, 479, *13*, *15*, *37*, *75*, *104*, *157*, *192*, *206*, *207*, *218*, *223*, *306*, *315*, *318*
 Algorithms 85
 Boundary *175*
 Data 200, 242, 343, 525, 527, *49*
 GIS 191, 340, *172*, *222*, *226*, *262*
 Interchange Format *175*
 Model 320, 322, 324, 517
 Overlay 341
 Polygon *175*, *224*
 Representation System 376
 Space 461
 Spatial Structuring 310
Vector-Mode Generalization **468–9**

Vector-Raster 85, 329, 344, *228*
Vector-Topological System 261
Vectorization 247, 272, *324*
Vegetation 103, 168, 176, 178, 422
Vehicle
 Location Tracking 240
 Navigation 59, 159, *124*
 Routing *298*
Venezuela *161*
Vertex Extraction Algorithm 247
Vibrating Rod Sensor *118*
Video 5, 47, 55, 115, 349, 365, 512
Videodisc 349
Videotape 59
Virgin Islands 9, *287*, *294*
Virtual
 Memory 46, 216, 314
 Reality 315, **353–5**
Visibility Analysis 286
Vision/Pattern Recognition 432
Visual
 Balance 430
 Feedback 278
 Interactive Modelling 410
 Interpretation 287
 Perception 47, 428, 430
 Realism 429
 Simulation 366
 Variable 430
Visualization 75, 85, 91, 92, 102, 115, 132, 240, 280, 299, 312, 315, **427–40**, *67*, *202*
 Enhancer 397, 398
 in Scientific Computing 432
 of Digital Terrain Models 269
 of Geoscientific Data 290
 of Spatial Information 439
 of Terrain *212*
VM/CMS 52, 58, *314*
VMS 52, 58, 87
Voice Recognition 325, 439
Volume of Data 46
Volumetric
 Computation *13*
 Spatial Function 299
Volygon 308
Voronoi
 Diagram 215, 220, 275, 276
 Polygon 126, *175*
Voxel 308, 309, 439
VPT 346

Walking Generalization Algorithm 469

Subject index

Waseda University *49*
Wastewater Management 32
Water 69
    Area Use Classification System
    264, *266*
    Quality *109*, *278*
    Resources 59, 422, *15*, *109*, *209*,
    278–280
    Service 73
Waterfall Model 215, 223
Wayleaves *109*
WDDES 260
Weapons Sighting 75
Weather Balloon 308
Weights of Evidence *180*
    Modelling *172*, *173–4*, *183–4*
Welsh Office 507, 508
West
    Germany *123*
    Indies *212*
Western European Geological Survey
    203
WGS84 Ellipsoid *123*
What You See Is What You Get 217
Wheel Rotation Sensors *115*
Whole Earth Decision Support
    System 353
Wide Area Network 216
Wild A8 Autograph *25*
Wildlife Modelling 422
Wind 293, *277*
Window Retrieval *122*
Windows Metafile 346
WING *50*

Wisdom 490
WK1 346
WKS 346
Word 346, *322*
    Processing *314*
    Processor *291*
WordPerfect 346, *322*
Wordstar 346
Working
    Committee on International
    Oceanographic Data Exchange
    206
    Group
        on Data and Information
        Systems *219*
        on Quantitative Land
        Evaluation *156*
        on Soil Information Systems
        153, *155*
Workstation 46, 49, 50, 52, 53, 57, 58,
    215, 216, 241, 244, 260, 262, 290,
    300, 485, *9*, *15*, *31*, *32*, *34*, *52*, *53*,
    110, *305*, *306*, *307*, *313*, *317*, *319*,
    321
    and Data Compaction 244–5
World
    Data Center System *203*, **204–5**,
    224
    Database II 39
    Digital Database for
    Environmental Science 39, *223*
    Meteorological Organization
    206, *208*
    Ocean Climate Experiment *206*

WORM 48, 343, 352, *74*
Wuhan Technical University 98

X-OS 58
X-Windows 217, 300, *323*
Xerox 50

Yale University *294*

Z-Buffer Algorithm 290
Z-MAP *53*
Zenrin *123*
Zero Dimension 137
Zipping 280, 344
Zonal
    Data Transformation 368–9
    System Overlap 385
ZonalCombination 368
ZonalMajority 369
ZonalMaximum 369
ZonalMean 369
ZonalMinimum 369
ZonalMinority 369
ZonalPercentage 369
ZonalPercentile 369
ZonalProduct 369
ZonalRanking 369
ZonalSum 369
ZonalVariety 369
Zone Design 396
Zone Reclassification 365
Zones for Urban Modelling *248*, *249*
Zoning Maps *298*
Zoology 92

1 307539